EU Law for
Today's Lawyers

Dr Alina Kaczorowska

OLD BAILEY PRESS

OLD BAILEY PRESS
200 Greyhound Road, London W14 9RY

First published 2000

© The HLT Group Ltd 2000

ISBN 1 85836 356 X

British Library Cataloguing-in-Publication.

A CIP Catalogue record for this book is available from the British Library.

Printed and bound in Great Britain.

Contents

Preface *vii*

Table of Cases *ix*

Table of Treaties, Conventions, Statutes and Other Materials *xxxiii*

1 The History of European Unity: from the Roman Empire to the
Treaty of Rome *1*

The Roman Empire – The Roman Catholic Church in the Middle Ages –
Economic integration in Europe in the Middle Ages – The twentieth century –
The United States' vision of the post-war world – The United States and
European reconstruction – The Marshall Plan (the European Recovery
Programme April 1948 – December 1951) – Western European integration –
The United Kingdom and European integration – The French refusal of British
accession

2 The Evolution of the European Communities *29*

The membership of the European Union – Territorial expansion of the
Communities – Consolidation of the European Communities

3 The Treaty of Amsterdam *65*

Pillar 1: the European Community – Pillar 2: common foreign and security
policy (CFSP) – Pillar 3: police co-operation in criminal matters

4 The Institutions of the European Communities and the European Union, Their
Participation in Decision-making and the Principle of Transparency *106*

The European Council – The Council of the European Union – The European
Commission – The European Parliament – The Court of Justice of the European
Communities (ECJ) – The Court of First Instance (CFI) – The Court of Auditors
– Other Community bodies – Legislative procedures – The principle of
transparency

5 Sources of Community Law *161*

Primary sources of Community law – Secondary sources of Community law –
Other Community acts not expressly mentioned in art 249 EC – External
sources which derive from international commitments of the Communities –
Complementary sources of Community law – General principles of Community
law and the case law of the ECJ

6   Fundamental Principles of Community Law: Direct Applicability, Direct Effect, Supremacy of Community Law and a Member State's Liability in Tort   *191*

Direct applicability of Community law – Direct effect of Community law – Supremacy of Community law – The principle of State liability

7   Enforcement of Community Law   *230*

Action under art 226 EC – Action under art 227 EC against a Member State by another Member State – Effect of a ruling confirming a failure of a Member State to fulfil its obligation under the Treaty – Simplified procedures

8   Actions against Community Institutions   *257*

Direct actions for annulment – Indirect action: plea of illegality under art 241 EC – Direct action for failure to act – Action for damages: non-contractual liability of the Community

9   Preliminary Rulings: art 234 EC   *300*

General jurisdiction of the ECJ under art 234 EC – Interpretation of Community law by the ECJ under art 234 EC – Validity of Community law

10   Free Movement of Goods   *329*

Creation of the internal market

11   Customs Union   *332*

External aspect of the customs union between the Member States of the EU – Internal aspect of the customs union between the Member States of the EU

12   The Prohibition of Customs Duties and All Charges Having Equivalent Effect   *336*

Articles 23 and 25 EC – Charges imposed on both domestic and imported products – Exceptions to the prohibition

13   Discriminatory Internal Taxation   *344*

Direct, indirect and reverse discrimination – Article 90(1) EC: similar products – Article 90(2) EC: products in competition – The relationship between art 90 EC and other provisions of the EC Treaty relating to the free movement of goods – Harmonisation of taxation within the European Union

14   Quantitative Restrictions and Measures Having Equivalent Effect on Imports and Exports   *357*

'Measures taken by the Member States' – The definition of quantitative restrictions and measures having equivalent effect – The *Dassonville* formula – National measures indistinctly applicable to domestic and imported goods:

Cassis de Dijon – Measures distinctly and indistinctly applicable to exports: art 29 EC – National measures relating to selling arrangements indistinctly applicable to domestic and imported goods

15   Article 30 EC   *386*

Public morality – Public policy and public security – Protection of the health and life of humans, animals and plants – Protection of national treasures possessing artistic, historic or archaeological value

16   Citizenship of the EU   *393*

Right of free movement and residence within the territory of the Member States – Participation in municipal elections and in elections to the European Parliament – Diplomatic and consular protection – Right to petition the European Parliament and to submit applications to the Ombudsman – Assessment of Union citizenship

17   Free Movement of Workers   *406*

Worker and his family – Right of entry and residence – The principle of non-discrimination – Right to remain in the territory of a Member State after having been employed in that State

18   The Right of Establishment and the Right to Supply and Receive Services (arts 43–55 EC)   *424*

The right of establishment – Freedom to supply and receive services

19   Exceptions to the Free Movement of Workers, Self-Employed Persons, Providers and Recipients of Services   *450*

The concepts of 'employment in the public service' and 'the exercise of official authority' – Derogations justified on the grounds of public policy, public security and public health

20   Competition Law   *459*

Federal nature of EC competition law – Extra-territorial application of competition law – Definition of an undertaking – The concept of activity which 'may affect trade between Member States'

21   Article 81 EC   *469*

Vertical and horizontal agreements – Agreements, decisions and concerted practices – Which have as their object or effect' – Prevention, restriction or distortion of competition – Attenuation of the effect of the art 81(1) EC prohibition – Exemptions – Civil consequences of breaches of art 81(1) EC

22   Article 82 EC   *504*

The concept of joint dominant position – Dominance – The relevant market – The concept of abuse

23   Merger Control   *526*

The scope of application of Merger Regulation 4064/89, as amended – The concept of collective dominance – The procedure under the Merger Regulation – Future reform of merger control

24   Enforcement of Competition Law   *536*

Measures which may be adopted under Regulation 17/62 – Complaints to the Commission in respect of infringements of EC competition law – The Commission's powers of investigation – Hearings – Access to documents – Fines – Judicial review of decisions adopted by the Commission in competition matters – Enforcement of EC competition law before national courts

25   Intellectual Property Rights   *555*

Intellectual property rights and the free movement of goods – Parallel imports from outside the EC and EEA – Intellectual property rights and arts 81 and 82 EC – Harmonisation of intellectual property rights

26   The State and the Common Market   *581*

State Aid – Aid compatible with the common market – Discretionary exemptions: aid which the Commission may consider to be compatible with the common market – Institutional supervision under arts 88 EC – State monopolies and public undertakings

Index   *607*

Preface

In approaching the writing of this work I have sought to make it novel in two ways. First, I have tried very hard to make the content easily readable and comprehensible – whether the reader is an experienced practitioner or a first-year student. At the same time I have not shied away from dealing with the complex and difficult areas of EU law, although I have occasionally minimised those which I consider to be relatively unimportant. Second, I have tried not only to provide a clear and expert exposition of the law but also to make it more interesting and indeed easier to assimilate by setting it in the context of a developing Europe of the last 50 years and, on occasion, of the last two millennia! In short, the style of this work is certainly unique. Therefore, as any author, I hope this book will be your friend in understanding the ever changing but always interesting landscape of EU law.

There are some minor, but useful, points to make. First, the numbering of the articles of the Treaty establishing the European Community (the EC Treaty) and of the Treaty on European Union (the EU Treaty) was changed by the Treaty of Amsterdam which entered into force on 1 May 1999. In order to ensure clarity and consistency the Court of Justice of the European Communities (ECJ) and the Court of First Instance (CFI) introduced a uniform system of citation of the provisions of the four Treaties (ECSC, Euratom, EC, EU). This book follows the said uniform system of citation.

Where reference is made to an article of a Treaty with its post **1 May 1999** numbering, the number of the article is immediately followed by two letters indicating the Treaty concerned:

EU for the Treaty on European Union
EC for EC Treaty
CS for ECSC Treaty
EA for the Euratom Treaty

Therefore, 'art 81 **EC**' refers to art 81 of that Treaty as numbered **after 1 May 1999**. Where reference is made to an article of a Treaty as it stood **before 1 May 1999**, the number of the article is followed by the words 'of the Treaty on European Union', 'of the EC/EEC Treaty', 'of the ECSC Treaty' or 'of the Euratom Treaty' as the case may be. Thus 'art 81 **of the EC Treaty**' refers to art 81 of that Treaty **before 1 May 1999**.

In relation to the EC Treaty and the Treaty on European Union, where reference is made to an article of a Treaty as it stood before 1 May 1999, the initial citation of the article in a text is followed by a reference in brackets to the corresponding provision of the same Treaty as it stands **after 1 May 1999**, as follows:

'Article 85 of the EC Treaty (now art 81 EC)' means that the article has not been amended by the Treaty of Amsterdam.

'Article 51 of the EC Treaty (now, after amendment, art 42 EC)' means that the article has been amended by the Treaty of Amsterdam.

'Article 53 of the EC Treaty (repealed by the Treaty of Amsterdam)' means that the article has been repealed by the Treaty of Amsterdam.

There is an exception to this rule concerning provisions which have been replaced en bloc by the Treaty of Amsterdam and whenever referred to are always referred to as follows:

'Articles 117–120 of the EC Treaty have been replaced by arts 136–143 EC.'

The same rule applies to arts J–J.11 and K–K.9 of the Treaty on European Union:

'Articles J–J.11 of the Treaty on European Union have been replaced by arts 11–28 EU.'

'Articles K–K.9 of the Treaty on European Union have been replaced by arts 29–42 EU.'

Second, it should be noted that recent cases although unreported can be found at the following website: Court of Justice of the European Communities: http://europa.eu.int/cj/en/index.htm. This website contains a weekly bulletin summarising recent judgments and opinions of the ECJ and CFI – and case law – from June 1996.

I would like to thank my wonderful friends from the Old Bailey Press who have provided a remarkable amount of able assistance in the preparation of this book. I particularly thank Professor Cedric Bell for his unflagging courtesy, competence and initiative, and my editor, Vanessa Osborne, for her exemplary co-operation, professionalism and expertise. I also wish to express my gratitude to Linda Clifford for the painstaking manner in which she prepared the final copy of the manuscript. I am deeply indebted to Christopher Ireland, of Irelands Commercial Lawyers in north Hampshire, who saved my work from foolish misstatements and who has given me lots of help.

My mother would have loved to receive a signed copy. Sadly this is not to be. I dedicate this book to her.

Table of Cases

ABI (OJ L143 (1988))   *501*

Accrington Beef Case C–241/95 [1996] ECR 6699 *323*

ACEC–Berliet [1968] CMLR D35   *500*

ACF Chemiefarma *v* Commission Case 41/69 [1970] ECR 661   *126, 152, 159, 184, 274, 472*

Adams Case 145/83 [1985] ECR 3539   *287, 290, 298*

Adalat (OJ L201 (1996))   *482*

AEG Telefunken Case 107/82 [1983] ECR 3151 *472, 491, 499*

Aer Lingus (OJ L54 (1994))   *593*

Agegate Case 3/87 [1989] ECR 4459   *408*

Agreement between Kabel-und Metallwerke Neumeyer AG and Etablissement Luchaine SA, Re [1975] 2 CMLR D40   *573*

Agreements between Gebruder Junghans GmbH, Re [1977] 1 CMLR D82   *573*

Ahlström and Others *v* Commission (Re Wood Pulp Cartel) Joined Cases 89, 104, 114, 116, 117 and 125–129/85 [1988] ECR 5193; [1988] 4 CMLR 901   *276, 462*

Ahlström and Others *v* Commission (Re Wood Pulp Cartel) Joined Cases 89, 104, 114, 116, 117 and 125–129/85 [1993] 4 CMLR 407 *462, 476, 550, 551*

Ahlström Osakeyhtiö Case 89/85 [1993] ECR I–1307   *544*

Air France Case T–3/93 [1994] ECR II–121 *263*

Airtours/First Choice, Commission Press Release, 22 September 1999   *532*

AKZO *v* Commission Case 53/85 [1986] ECR 1985; [1987] 1 CMLR 231   *184, 185, 263, 545*

AKZO Chemie BV *v* Commission Case C–62/86 [1991] ECR I–3359; [1993] 5 CMLR 197 *507, 515, 520, 522, 523*

Alaimo Case 68/74 [1975] ECR 109   *411*

Albany Case C–67/96 [1999] ECR I–5751   *313*

Albatros Case 20/64 [1965] ECR 41   *313*

Alcatel Espace and ANT Nachrichtentechnik [1991] 4 CMLR 208   *573*

Algera Joined Cases 7/56 and 7/57 [1957] ECR 39 *183*

Allied Corporation Cases 239 and 275/82 [1984] ECR 1005   *266, 269*

Allué Case 33/88 [1989] ECR 1591   *415, 417*

Almelo Case C–393/92 [1994] ECR I–1477 *305, 306*

Alpha Steel Case 14/81 [1982] ECR 749   *171*

Alpharma Inc *v* Council of the European Union Case T–70/99R [1999] 3 CMLR 79   *326*

Alpine Investments Case C–384/93 [1995] ECR I–1141   *443, 446*

Alsatel Case 247/86 [1988] ECR 5987   *320*

Alsthom Atlantique Case C–339/89 [1991] ECR I–107   *203*

AM and S Europe *v* Commission Case 155/79 [1982] ECR 1575   *184, 185*

Amelo Case C–393/92 [1994] ECR I–1477   *603*

Amersham Buchler (OJ L314 (1982))   *498*

Amministrazione delle Finanze dello Stato *v* Denkavit Italiana Case 61/79 [1980] ECR 1205   *322, 583*

Amministrazione delle Finanze dello Stato *v* Essevi and Salongo Cases 142 and 143/80 [1981] ECR 1413   *238*

Amministrazione delle Finanze dello Stato *v* San Giorgio Case 199/82 [1983] ECR 3595   *552*

Amministrazione delle Finanze dello Stato *v* Simmenthal SpA Case 106/77 [1978] ECR 629   *191, 220, 221*

Amylum (G R) NV and Tunnel Refineries Limited *v* Council and Commission Cases 116 and 124/77 [1979] ECR 3497   *293, 294*

Andoui and Cornuaille *v* Belgian State Joined Cases 115 and 116/81 [1982] ECR 1665 *454*

Angelopharm GmbH Case C–212/91 [1994] ECR I—171   *275*

Antillean Rice Mills Cases T–480 and 483/93 [1995] ECR II–2305   *270*

Apple and Pear Development Council *v* K J Lewis Case 222/82 [1983] ECR 4083   *339, 358*

Aranitis Case C–164/94 [1996] ECR I–135   *439*

Arblade (Jean-Claude), Arblade & Fils Sarl; Bernard Leloupe, Serge Leloupe, Solfrage Sarl Cases C–369 and 376/96 Judgment of 23 November 1999 (nyr)   *443*

Arthur Bell (OJ L235 (1978))   *479*

ASBL Case 311/85 [1987] ECR 987   *465*

Asia Motor France Case T–28/90 [1992] ECR II–2285   *283, 284*

Asia Motor France Case T–387/94 [1996] ECR II–961   *465*

Asocarne (P) Case C–10/95 [1995] ECR I–4149 *323*

Table of Cases

Assider Case 3/54 [1955] ECR 123   *275*

Assider *v* High Authority Case 5/55 [1954–56] ECR 125   *144*

Association des Centres Distributeurs E Leclerc and Others *v* Sarl 'Au Ble Vert' Case 229/83 [1985] ECR 1   *386*

Associazione Agricoltori della Provincia de Rivigo Case C–142/95P [1996] ECR I–6669   *263*

Assurance Incendie (OJ L35 (1985))   *481*

ASTI Case 213/90 [1991] ECR I–3507   *421*

Atlanta Fruchthandelsgesellschaft *v* BEF Case C–465/93 [1995] ECR I–3761   *326*

Aubertin Cases C–29–35/94 [1995] ECR I–311   *429*

Auditel and AGB Italia SpA (OJ L306 (1993))   *472*

Auer (No 1) Case C–136/78 [1979] ECR 437   *429*

Auer (No 2) Case 271/82 [1983] ECR 2727   *430*

Automec (No 2) Case T–24/90 [1992] 5 CMLR 431   *538*

Automobile Peugeot SA Case T–90 and 136/96 [1997] ECR II–663   *264*

Awoyemi (Ibiyinka) Case C–230/97 [1998] ECR I–6781   *421, 422*

Azienda Nationale Autonoma della Steade Case C–192/98, order of 26 November 1999 (nyr)   *305*

B & I Line *v* Sealink Harbours [1992] 5 CMLR 255   *517, 523*

Bachmann (Hans-Martin) *v* Belgian State Case C–204/90 [1992] ECR I–249   *433, 443*

Balochi Case C–10/92 [1993] ECR I–5105   *320*

Bakkers Hillegom Case C–111/89 [1990] ECR I–1735   *336*

Banco Exterior de España Case C–387/92 [1984] ECR I–877   *584*

Banks Case C–128/92 [1994] ECR I–1209   *47*

Barber *v* Guardian Royal Exchange Case 262/88 [1990] ECR I–1889   *200, 322*

Barr Case C–355/89 [1991] ECR I–3479   *306*

Barra *v* Belgium Case 309/85 [1988] ECR 355   *322*

BASF Cases T–79, 84–86, 91–92, 94, 96 and 98/89 [1992] ECR II–315   *122, 171*

BASF Case C–44/98 [1999] ECR I–6269   *416*

BASF AG *v* Präsident Des Deutschen Patentamts Case C–44/99 (1999) The Times 12 October   *576*

BAT and RJ Reynolds *v* Commission and Philip Morris Cases 142 and 156/84 [1987] ECR 4487   *526*

Battaglia Case 1253/79 [1982] ECR 297   *152*

Bauhuis *v* Netherlands Case 46/76 [1977] ECR 5   *336, 342, 352*

Baustahlgewebe GmbH *v* Commission of the European Communities Case C–185/95P [1999] 4 CMLR 1203   *546, 548, 549*

Bavarian Lager Company *v* Commission Case T–309/97 [1999] 3 CMLR 544   *159*

Bayer Case C–195/91 [1994] ECR I–5619   *259*

Bayer AG *v* Commission Case T–12/90 [1991] ECR II–219   *259*

Bayer Gist-Brocades [1976] 1 CMLR D98   *499*

Bayerische HNL *v* Council and Commission Cases 83 and 94/76 and 4, 15 and 40/77 [1978] ECR 1209   *185, 290, 292, 293, 294, 297*

Bayerische Motorenwerke AG (BMW) and BMW Netherlands BV *v* Ronald Karel Deenik Case C–63/97 [1999] 1 CMLR 1099   *562, 571*

BBC Brown Boveri (OJ L301 (1988))   *500*

Beate Weber Case C–314/91[1993] ECR I–1093   *230*

Becher Case 13/67 [1968] ECR 289 ord   *302*

Becker (Ursula) *v* Finanzamt Munster-Innenstadt Case 8/81 [1982] ECR 53   *200, 212, 219*

Beele Case 6/81 [1982] ECR 707   *369*

Beguelin Import *v* GL Import Export Case 22/71 [1971] ECR 949   *465, 502*

Bela-Mühler Case 114/76 [1977] ECR 1211   *293*

Belasco Case 246/86 [1989] ECR 2117   *467*

Belfiore Case 108/79 [1980] ECR 1769   *259*

Belgapom *v* ITM Belgium SA and Vocarex SA Case C–63/95 [1995] ECR I–2467   *380*

Belgische Radio en Télévisie (BRT) *v* SABAM Case 127/73 [1974] ECR 313   *575*

Belgium Case 1/60 [1962] ECR 331   *144*

Belgium *v* Commission (Re Boch) Case C–234/84 [1986] ECR 2263   *585*

Belgium *v* Commission Case C–142/87 [1990] ECR I–959   *598*

Benedetti *v* Munari Case 152/76 [1977] ECR 163   *321*

Bentjes Case 31/87 [1988] ECR 4635   *205*

Bergandi Case 252/86 [1988] ECR 1343   *344*

Bernardi (Giorgio) *v* Commission Cases T–479 and 559/93 [1994] ECR II–1115   *264*

Berner Allemeine Case C–328/89 [1991] ECR I–3431   *188*

Bernini Case 3/90 [1992] ECR I–1071   *419*

Berrehab, Judgment of 21 June 1988, Series A, No 138, pp155–16   *411*

Bertini Case 98/85 [1986] ECR 1885   *312*

Bethell (Lord) Case 246/81 [1982] ECR 2277
   282
Bettray Case 344/87 [1989] ECR 1621   *408*
BEUC Case C–170/89 [1991] ECR I–5709
   263
BEUC and National Consumer Council Case
   T–37/92 [1994] ECR II–285   *263, 466*
Beus Case 5/67 [1968] ECR 125   *186*
Bickel (Horst Otto), Ulrich Franz Case C–274/96
   [1998] ECR I–7637   *397*
Biehl Case C–175/88 [1990] ECR I–1779   *415*
Birra Wuhrer Case 256/80 [1982] ECR 85   *287*
Blaizot *v* University of Liège Case 24/86 [1988]
   ECR 379; [1989]1 CMLR 57   *322, 449*
Bleis Case C–4/91 [1991] ECR I–5627   *451*
Bluhme (D) (Brown Bees of Læsø) Case C–67/97
   [1998] ECR I–8033   *391*
BMW Belgium SA *v* Commission Cases 32 and
   36–82/78 [1980] ECR 2435   *473*
BNIC (OJ L379 (1982))   *474*
Bobie Getränkevertreieb *v* Haupzollamt Aachen-
   Nord Case 127/75 [1976] ECR 1079   *345*
Bock *v* Commission Case 62/70 [1971] ECR 897
   269, 273, 275
Boehringer Ingelheim Vetmedica GmbH Case
   T–125/96 [2000] 1 CMLR 97   *269*
Boehringer Mannheim *v* Commission Case 45/69
   [1970] ECR 769   *484*
Bollman Case 40/69 [1970] ECR 69   *172*
Bollman Case 62/72 [1973] ECR 269   *320*
Bond Van Adverteerders Case 352/85 [1988] ECR
   2085   *453*
Bonsignore *v* Oberstadtdirector of the City of
   Cologne Case 67/74 [1975] ECR 297   *454*
Bordessa Case C–358 and 416/93 [1995] ECR
   I–361   *422*
Borker Case 138/80 [1980] ECR 1975   *304*
Bosch Case 13/61 [1962] ECR 97, 321   *202,
   321*
Bosch Case 135/77 [1978] ECR 855   *302*
Boscher Case C–239/90 [1991] ECR I–2023
   384
Bosman Case C–415/93 [1995] ECR I–4921
   189, 312, 407, 409, 416
Bouhelier Case 53/76 [1977] ECR 197   *378*
BP Case 77/77 [1978] ECR 1513   *266*
BP-Kemi-DDSF [1979] 3 CMLR 684   *472*
Branco (E) Case T–271/94 [1996] ECR II–3761
   260
Brandsma Case C–293/94 [1996] ECR I–3159
   387
Brasserie de Haecht *v* Wilkin-Janssens (No 1)
   Case 23/67 [1967] ECR 407   *467, 485*

Brasserie du Pêcheur SA *v* Federal Republic of
   Germany; R *v* Secretary of State for
   Transport, ex parte Factortame and Others
   (No 4) Joined Cases C–46 and 48/93 [1996] 1
   CMLR 889   *224, 225, 227*
Bremer-Vulkan Werft (OJ L250 (1997))   *593*
Brentjevis Handelsonderneming BV Joined Cases
   115–117/97 [1999] ECR I–6025   *313*
Bresciani *v* Amministrazione Italiana delle
   Finanze Case 87/75 [1976] ECR 129   *177,
   216, 341*
Brinkmann Tabakfabriken GmbH Case C–319/96
   [1998] 3 CMLR 673   *226*
Bristol Cases C–427, 429 and 436/93 [1996] ECR
   I–3514, 3457   *561, 568*
British Aerospace and Rover Group *v*
   Commission Case C–294/90 [1992] ECR
   I–493   *597, 598*
British Aerospace/VSEL [1995] 4 CMLR 323
   584
British American Tobacco Cases 142 and 156/84
   [1987] ECR 4487   *269*
British Brass Band Instruments *v* Boosey &
   Hawkes [1988] 4 CMLR 67   *515–516*
British Plasterboard (BPB) Industries and British
   Gypsum Ltd *v* Commission Case C–310/93
   [1995] ECR I–865   *522*
Broekmeulen *v* Huisarts Registratie Commissie
   Case 246/80 [1981] ECR 2311   *304, 430*
Brown Case 197/86 [1988] ECR 3205   *408, 449*
Brown *v* Secretary of State for Scotland Case
   125/87 [1988] ECR 1619   *420*
BRT *v* Sabam Case 127/73 [1974] ECR 51   *202*
Bruce of Donington (Lord) *v* Aspden Case 208/80
   [1981] ECR 2205   *302*
BUG-Alutechnik Case C–5/89 [1990] ECR I–3437
   598
Buralux Case C–309/94P [1996] ECR I–677
   270
Burgoa Case 812/79 [1980] ECR 2787   *163,
   302*
Busseni Case C–221/88 [1990] ECR I–495   *173,
   300*

Cadski *v* ICE Case 63/74 [1975] ECR 281   *341*
Camera Care Ltd *v* Commission Case 792/79R
   [1980] ECR 119   *538*
Campus Oil *v* Minister for Industry and Energy
   Case 72/83 [1984] ECR 2727; [1984] 1 CMLR
   479   *310, 319, 363, 390*
Canon Case C–39/97 [1998] ECR I–5507   *566*
Capolongo *v* Azienda Agricola Mayo Case 77/72
   [1973] ECR 611   *338, 582, 599*

Cargill Cases C–248 and 365/89 [1992] ECR I–2987   *171*

Casagrande Case 9/74 [1974] ECR 773   *411*

Casati Case 203/75 [1981] ECR 2595   *200*

Case Concerning Competences of the Courts of Danzig, Advisory Opinion of 3 February 1928, Series B, no 15   *198*

Cassis de Dion *see* Rewe Zentral AG *v* Bundomonopolverwaltung für Branntwein

Castelli Case 261/83 [1984] ECR 3199   *419*

Cato Case C–55/90 [1992] ECR I–2533   *289*

Cayrol Case 52/77 [1977] ECR 2261   *302*

CBEN *v* CLT & IPB (Re Telemarketing) Case 311/84 [1985] ECR 3261   *523*

Celbi Case C–266/91 [1993] ECR I–4337   *353*

Centre Public de l'Aide Sociale de Courcelles *v* Lebon Case 316/85 [1987] ECR 2811   *410, 419*

Centrafarm *v* American Home Products Case 3/78 [1978] ECR 1823   *568*

Centrafarm *v* Sterling Drug Inc Case 15/74 [1974] ECR 1147   *465, 557, 558*

Centrafarm *v* Winthrop Case 16/74 [1974] ECR 1183   *558, 560*

Centros Ltd *v* Erhvervs-og Selskabsstyrelsen Case C–212/97 [1999] 2 CMLR 551   *434*

Century Oil Hellas Case T–13/94 [1994] ECR II–431   *189*

Chambre Syndicale Sidérurgique de la France Cases 24 and 34/58 [1960] ECR 609   *284*

Chanel Case 31/68 [1969] ECR 403   *320*

Charles Jourdan (OJ L35 (1989))   *493*

Chatillon Commentry Neuves Maisins Case 54/65 [1966] ECR 265   *295*

Chevalley Case 15/70 [1970] ECR 975   *281*

Chiron Corporation *v* Murex Diagnostic [1995] All ER (EC)   *88*

Chiron Corporation *v* Organon Teknika (No 2) [1968] FSR 393   *574*

CIA Security International SA *v* Signalson SA et Securitel SA Case C–194/94 [1996] ECR I–2201   *320*

CICCE Case 298/83 [1985] ECR 1105   *461*

CILFIT *v* Ministro della Sanita Case 283/81 [1982] ECR 3415   *182, 316, 317, 318*

Cimbel [1973] CMLR D167   *483*

Cimenteries CBR Cases 8–11/66 [1967] ECR 93   *168*

Cimenteries CBR Cases 10–12 and 15/92 [1992] ECR II–2667   *546*

Cinéthèque SA *v* Fédération Nationale des Cinémas Français Cases 60 and 61/84 [1985] ECR 2605   *371*

CIRFS Case C–313/90 [1993] ECR I–2557   *264, 269, 598*

Clima Chappé/Buderus [1970] CMLR D7   *499*

Clinique Case C–315/92 [1994] ECR I–317   *313*

CMC Motorradcenter GmbH *v* Pelin Baskiciogullari Case C–93/92 [1993] ECR I–5009   *233, 368, 379*

CNL Sucal Hag (No 2) Case C–10/89 [1990] ECR I–3711   *566, 567*

CNTA *v* Commission Case 74/74 [1975] ECR 533   *171, 292, 293, 295*

COAPI (OJ L122 (1995))   *473*

Cobrecaf Case T–514/93 [1995] ECR II–621   *286*

Coditel *v* Ciné Vog Films Case 62/79 [1980] ECR 881   *446, 569*

Coditel (No 2) Case 262/81 [1982] ECR 3381   *446*

Codorniu Case C–309/89 [1994] ECR I–1853   *267, 270, 271, 272*

Coenen Case 39/75 [1975] ECR 1547   *321*

Cofaz Case 169/84 [1986] ECR 391   *269*

Cohn-Bendit [1979] CDE 265   *318*

Colim NV *v* Bigg's Continent Noord NV Case C–33/97 [2000] 2 CMLR 135   *373*

Collins (Phil) *v* Imtrat Handeslgesellschaft mbH; Patricia Im-und Export Verwaltungsgesellschaft mbH and Lief E Kraul v EMI Electrola GmbH Joined Cases C–92 and 362/92 [1993] ECR I–5145   *556*

Comet Case 45/76 [1976] ECR 2043   *552*

Comitato di Coordinamento per la Difesa della Cava *v* Regione Lombardia Case C–236/92 [1994] ECR I–483   *200*

Commercial Solvents Corporation *v* Commission Cases 6 and 7/73 [1974] ECR 223   *467, 523, 525*

Commerzbank Case C–330/91 [1993] ECR I–4017   *432*

Commission *v* BASF (PVC) Case C–137/92P [1994] ECR I–2555   *122, 274*

Commission *v* Belgium Case 77/69 [1970] ECR 244   *232, 246*

Commission *v* Belgium Case 156/77 [1978] ECR 1881   *279, 280*

Commission *v* Belgium Case 102/79 [1980] ECR 1473   *173, 174*

Commission *v* Belgium (No 1) Case 149/79 [1980] ECR 3881   *241, 450, 451*

Commission *v* Belgium (No 2) Case 149/79 [1982] ECR 1845   *450, 451*

Commission *v* Belgium Case 301/81 [1983] ECR 467   *232*

Commission v Belgium (Re Storage Charges)
Case 132/82 [1983] ECR 1649   *340*

Commission v Belgium Case 155/82 [1984] ECR
531   *387*

Commission v Belgium Case 52/84 [1986] ECR
89   *599*

Commission v Belgium Case 85/85 [1986]
ECR1149   *239*

Commission v Belgium Cases 227–230/85 [1988]
ECR 1   *232*

Commission v Belgium (Re University Fees) Case
293/85 [1988] ECR 305   *238*

Commission v Belgium Case 5/86 [1987] ECR
1777   *247*

Commission v Belgium (Re Failure to Implement
Directives) Case C–225/86 [1988] ECR 579
246

Commission v Belgium Case 260/86 [1988] ECR
966   *165*

Commission v Belgium Case 42/87 [1988] ECR
5445   *411*

Commission v Belgium Case C–2/90 [1992] ECR
I–4431   *332*

Commission v Belgium Case C–300/90 [1992]
ECR I–305   *443*

Commission v Belgium Case C–80/92 [1994]
ECR I–1019   *251*

Commission v Belgium Case 89/92 [1983] ECR
531   *365*

Commission v Belgium Case C–133/94 [1996]
ECR I–2323   *241, 244*

Commission v Belgium Case C–173/94 [1996]
ECR I–3265   *451*

Commission v Belgium Case C–11/95 [1996]
ECR I–4115   *245*

Commission v Belgium Case C–344/95 [1997]
ECR I–1035   *409, 413*

Commission v Belgium Case C–263/96 [1997]
ECR I–7453   *246*

Commission v Belgium and Luxembourg Cases
90 and 91/63 [1964] ECR 625   *183, 231,
245*

Commission v Council (ERTA) Case 22/70 [1971]
ECR 263   *114, 260, 262*

Commission v Council Case 275/87 [1989] ECR
259   *276*

Commission v Council Case 16/88 [1989] ECR
3457   *127*

Commission v Council Case 300/89 [1991] ECR
I–2897   *170*

Commission v Council Case C–170/96 [1998]
ECR I–2763   *88*

Commission v Denmark Case 106/84 [1986] ECR
833   *350*

Commission v Denmark (Re Returnable
Containers) Case 302/86 [1989] 1 CMLR 619
371

Commission v Denmark Case C–47/88 [1990]
ECR I–4509   *351, 353*

Commission v Denmark Case C–52/90 [1992]
ECR I–2187   *240*

Commission v Federal Republic of Germany Case
C–191/95 [1998] ECR I–5449   *122*

Commission v France Cases 6 and 11/69 [1970]
CMLR 43   *233, 243, 280*

Commission v France Case 26/69 [1970 ECR 565
243–244

Commission v France Case 7/71 [1971] ECR 1003
231, 232, 236, 238, 244

Commission v France Case (Re French Merchant
Seaman) Case 167/73 [1974] ECR 359
248, 249, 407, 417

Commission v France Case 68/76 [1977] ECR 515
365

Commission v France (Re Advertising of
Alcoholic Beverages) Case 152/78 [1980] ECR
2299   *364*

Commission v France Case 168/78 [1980] ECR
347   *350*

Commission v France (Re Restrictions on
Imports of Lamb) Case 232/78 [1979] ECR
2729   *231, 245*

Commission v France (Re Levy on Reprographic
Machines) Case 90/79 [1981] ECR 283
345, 352

Commission v France (Re Italian Table Wine)
Case 42/82 [1983] ECR 1013   *366*

Commission v France Case 220/83 [1986] ECR
3663   *446*

Commission v France Case 270/83 [1986] ECR
273   *432, 435*

Commission v France Case 290/83 [1985] ECR
439   *584, 586*

Commission v France Case 307/84 [1986] ECR
1725   *451*

Commission v France Case 196/85 [1987] ECR
1597   *349*

Commission v France Case 252/85 [1988] ECR
2243   *174*

Commission v France Case 169/87 [1988] ECR
4093   *253*

Commission v France Case C–62/89 [1990] ECR
I–925   *240*

Commission v France Case C–294/89 [1991] ECR
I–3591   *442, 446*

Commission v France Case C–334/94 [1996] ECR
I–1307   *248, 253, 255*

Commission v France Case C–52/95 [1995] ECR I–4443   *172*

Commission v France Case C–144/97 [1998] ECR I–613   *247*

Commission v French Republic Case C–265/95 [1997] ECR I–6959   *232, 358*

Commission v Germany Case 70/72 [1973] ECR 813   *237, 244, 251, 598*

Commission v Germany Case 247/81 [1984] ECR 1111   *365*

Commission v Germany Case 116/82 [1986] ECR 2519   *242*

Commission v Germany (Re Nursing Directive) Case 29/84 [1985] ECR 1661   *249*

Commission v Germany (German Beer Purity Laws) Case 178/84 [1987] ECR 1227   *224, 370*

Commission v Germany (Re Insurance Services) Case 205/84 [1986] ECR 3755   *424, 442, 443, 446*

Commission v Germany Case 149/86 [1989] ECR 1263   *410*

Commission v Germany (Re Animals Inspection Fees) Case 18/87 [1988] ECR 5247; [1990] 1 CMLR 561   *342, 352*

Commission v Germany Case C–131/88 [1991] ECR I–825   *174*

Commission v Germany Case C–360/88 [1991] ECR I–2567   *174*

Commission v Germany Case C–5/89 [1990] ECR I–3437   *598, 599*

Commission v Germany Case C–57/89 [1991] ECR I–924   *232*

Commission v Germany Case C–58/89 [1991] ECR I–5019   *174*

Commission v Germany Case C–62/90 [1992] ECR I–2575   *188*

Commission v Germany Case C–317/92 [1994] ECR I–2039   *238*

Commission v Germany Case C–422/92 [1995] ECR I–1097   *196, 238, 241*

Commission v Germany Case C–131/93 [1994] ECR I–3303   *391*

Commission v Germany Case C–433/93 [1995] ECR I–2303   *249*

Commission v Germany Case C–96/95 [1997] ECR I–1653   *239*

Commission v Germany Case C–191/95 [1998] ECR I–5449   *239*

Commission v Germany Case C–253/95 [1996] ECR I–2423   *249*

Commission v Germany Case C–217/97 Judgment of 9 September 1999 (nyr)   *174*

Commission v Greece Case 68/88 [1989] ECR 2965   *252*

Commission v Greece Case 192/84 [1985] ECR 3967   *363*

Commission v Greece Cases 194 and 241/85 [1988] ECR 1037   *233*

Commission v Greece Case 70/86 [1987] ECR 3558   *248*

Commission v Greece Case 272/86 [1988] ECR 4875   *235*

Commission v Greece Case 226/87 [1988] ECR 3611, 3620   *242, 605*

Commission v Greece Case C–200/88 [1990] ECR I–4299   *238, 241*

Commission v Greece Case C–347/88 [1990] ECR I–4747   *240, 601*

Commission v Greece Case C–198/89 [1991] ECR I–727   *446*

Commission v Greece Case C–29/90 [1992] ECR 1971   *173*

Commission v Greece Case C–45/91 [1992] ECR I–2509   *248*

Commission v Greece Case C–65/91 [1992] ECR I–5245   *235*

Commission v Greece Case C–105/91 [1992] ECR I–5871   *241, 248*

Commission v Greece (Re Electronic Cash Registers) Case C–137/91 [1992] 3 CMLR 117   *234*

Commission v Greece Case C–210/91 [1994] ECR I–6735   *239*

Commission v Greece Case 391/92 [1995] ECR I–621   *381*

Commission v Greece Case C–120/94R [1994] ECR I–3037   *256*

Commission v Greece Case C–290/94 [1996] ECR I–3285   *451*

Commission v Hellenic Republic Case C–375/95 [1997] ECR I–5981   *239, 347, 349*

Commission v Ireland Case 55/79 [1980] ECR 481   *348*

Commission v Ireland (Re Irish Souvenire) Case 113/80 [1981] ECR 1625   *368, 386*

Commission v Ireland (Re Buy Irish Campaign) Case 249/81 [1982] ECR 4005   *233, 358, 362*

Commission v Ireland Case 74/82 [1984] ECR 317   *237, 239*

Commission v Ireland (Re Dundalk Water Supply) Case 45/87 [1988] ECR 4929   *332, 362*

Commission v Ireland Case C–111/91 [1993] ECR I–817   *436*

Commission *v* Ireland Case C–257/94 [1995] ECR
  I–3041   *252*
Commission *v* Italy (Re Pigmeat) Case 7/61
  [1961] ECR 317   *231, 237, 245, 361*
Commission *v* Italy Case 10/61 [1962] ECR 3, 22
  163, 183
Commission *v* Italy Case 13/63 [1963] ECR 360
  429
Commission *v* Italy Case 7/68 [1968] ECR 423,
  617   *247, 337, 392*
Commission *v* Italy Case (Re Statistical Levy)
  Case 24/68 [1969] ECR 193   *336, 337, 340*
Commission *v* Italy Case 7/69 [1970] ECR 117
  184
Commission *v* Italy Case 31/69 [1970] ECR 25
  232
Commission *v* Italy Case 33/69 [1970] ECR 103
  233
Commission *v* Italy Case 8/70 [1970] ECR 967
  232, 233, 247
Commission *v* Italy Case 7/61 [1961] ECR 633
  387
Commission *v* Italy Case 48/71 [1972] ECR 536
  251, 253
Commission *v* Italy Case 30/72 [1973] ECR 171
  247
Commission *v* Italy Case 39/72 [1973] ECR 101
  172, 186, 238
Commission *v* Italy Case 173/73 [1974] ECR 709
  583
Commission *v* Italy Case 52/75 [1979] ECR 277
  245
Commission *v* Italy Case 147/77 [1978] ECR 1037
  236
Commission *v* Italy Case (Re Regenerated Oil)
  Case 21/79 [1980] ECR 1   *346, 349*
Commission *v* Italy Case 73/79 [1980] ECR 1533
  353
Commission *v* Italy Case 28/81 [1981] ECR 2577
  237
Commission *v* Italy Case 29/81 [1981] ECR 2585
  237
Commission *v* Italy Case 95/81 [1982] ECR 2189
  387
Commission *v* Italy Case 169/82 [1984] ECR 1603
  585
Commission *v* Italy Case 50/83 [1984] ECR 1633
  364
Commission *v* Italy Case 51/83 [1984] ECR 2793
  236
Commission *v* Italy Case 281/83 [1985] ECR 3397
  253
Commission *v* Italy Case 274/83 [1985] ECR 1090
  240

Commission *v* Italy (Re Traffic Statistics) Case
  101/84 [1985] ECR 2629   *243*
Commission *v* Italy Case 154/85 [1987] ECR 2256
  389
Commission *v* Italy Case 168/85 [1986] ECR 2945
  248
Commission *v* Italy Case 225/85 [1986] ECR 2625
  451
Commission *v* Italy Case C–263/85 [1991] ECR
  I–2547   *363*
Commission *v* Italy (Re Housing Aid) Case 63/86
  [1988] ECR 29   *428*
Commission *v* Italy Case 69/86 [1987] ECR 733
  253
Commission *v* Italy Case 257/86 [1988] ECR 3249
  183
Commission *v* Italy Case 22/87 [1989] ECR 143
  223
Commission *v* Italy Case 340/87 [1989] ECR 1483
  341, 352
Commission *v* Italy Case C–360/87 [1991] ECR
  I–791   *174*
Commission *v* Italy Case C–3/88 [1989] ECR
  I–4035   *432*
Commission *v* Italy Case C–157/89 [1991] ECR
  I–57   *174, 232*
Commission *v* Italy Case C–180/89 [1991] ECR
  I–709   *446*
Commission *v* Italy Case C–360/89 [1992] ECR
  I–4301   *442*
Commission *v* Italy Case C–235/89 [1991] FSR 1
  557, 559
Commission *v* Italy Case C–33/90 [1991] ECR
  5987   *174, 235*
Commission *v* Italy Case C–228/91 [1993] ECR
  I–2701   *233*
Commission *v* Italy Case C–296/92 [1994] ECR
  I–1   *239*
Commission *v* Italy Case C–365/97 Judgment of 9
  November 1999 (nyr)   *239*
Commission *v* Luxembourg (Re Gingerbread)
  Cases 2 and 3/62 [1962] ECR 813   *337*
Commission *v* Luxembourg (Re Access to the
  Medical Profession) Case C–351/90 [1992] 3
  CMLR 124   *441*
Commission *v* Luxembourg Case C–118/92
  [1994] ECR I–1891   *421*
Commission *v* Luxembourg Case C–274/93
  [1996] ECR I–2019   *252*
Commission *v* Luxembourg Case C–473/93
  [1996] ECR I–3207   *446, 451*
Commission *v* Luxembourg Case C–46/95 [1997]
  ECR I–1279   *252*

Commission *v* Luxembourg Case C–47/99 Judgment of 16 December (nyr)   *232*

Commission *v* Luxembourg and Belgium (Re Import of Powdered Milk Products) Cases 90 and 91/63 [1964] ECR 1964   *244*

Commission *v* Solvay; Commission *v* ICI Joined Cases C–286 and 288/95P Judgment of 6 April 2000 (nyr)   *123*

Commission *v* Spain Case C–258/89 [1991] ECR I–3977   *242*

Commission *v* Spain Case C–375/92 [1994] ECR I–923   *235*

Commission *v* Spain Case C–414/97 Judgment of 16 September 1999 (nyr)   *240*

Commission *v* The Netherlands Case 89/76 [1977] ECR 1355; [1978] 3 CMLR 630   *342*

Commission *v* The Netherlands (Re Protection of Wild Birds) Case 339/87 [1990] ECR I–851   *248*

Commission *v* The Netherlands Case C–190/90 [1992] ECR I–3265   *174*

Commission *v* The Netherlands Case C–157/91 [1994] ECR I–5899   *239*

Commission *v* The Netherlands Case C–359/93 [1995] ECR I–157   *245*

Commission *v* The Netherlands Case C–157/94 [1997] ECR I–5699   *602*

Commission *v* United Kingdom (Re Tachographs) Case 128/78 [1979] ECR 419   *172, 247*

Commission *v* United Kingdom (Re Tax on Beer on Wine) Case 170/78 [1980] ECR 415   *241, 345, 350*

Commission *v* United Kingdom Case 80/79 [1979] ECR 2923   *69*

Commission *v* United Kingdom Case 804/79 [1981] ECR 1045   *69*

Commission *v* United Kingdom (Re UHT Milk) Case 124/81 [1983] ECR 203   *390*

Commission *v* United Kingdom Case 40/82 [1982] ECR 2793   *365, 388*

Commission *v* United Kingdom (Re Origin Marking of Retail Goods) Case 207/83 [1985] ECR 1202   *370*

Commission *v* United Kingdom Case 60/86 [1988] ECR 3921   *68*

Commission *v* United Kingdom Case C–144/89 [1991] ECR I–3533   *163*

Commission *v* United Kingdom Case C–246/89 [1991] ECR I–4585   *224*

Commission *v* United Kingdom (Re Nationality of Fisherman) Case C–246/89R [1989] ECR I–3125   *251*

Commission *v* United Kingdom Case C–30/90 [1992] ECR I–829   *557, 559*

Commission *v* United Kingdom (Re Bathing Water Directive) Case C–56/90 [1994] 1 CMLR 769   *248*

Commission *v* United Kingdom Case C–40/92 [1994] ECR I–989   *235*

Commission *v* United Kingdom Case C–300/95 [1997] ECR I–2649   *240*

Commission of the European Communities *v* Assidomän Kraft Products AB and Others Case C–310/97P [1999] 5 CMLR 1253   *276, 550*

Commission of the European Communities *v* Kingdom of Belgium Case C–172/98 [1999] ECR I–3999   *425*

Commission of the European Communities, supported by the United Kingdom of Great Britain and Nothern Ireland *v* Kingdom of The Netherlands, Italian Republic, French Republic and Kingdom of Spain Joined Cases C–157–160/94 [1997] ECR I–5699   *603*

Commissionaires Reunis et Ramel Joined Cases 80 and 81/77 [1978] ECR 927   *34*

Commissioners of Customs and Excise *v* Schindler Case C–275/92 [1994] ECR I–1039; [1994] QB 610   *332, 446, 447*

Compagnie Commerciale de l'Ouest Cases 78–83/90 [1992] ECR I–1847   *338, 353*

Compagnie Continentale France Case 169/73 [1975] ECR 117   *290, 292*

Compagnie des Forges de Chatillon *v* High Authority Case 54/65 [1966] ECR 185   *175*

Compagnie Industrielle et Agricole Cases 54–60/76 [1977] ECR 645   *295*

Compagnie Maritime Belge and Others *v* Commission Cases T–24–26 and 28/93 [1997] 4 CMLR 273   *505, 507, 518*

Compagnie Maritime Belge Transport Case 300/93 [1996] ECR II–1910   *473*

Compagnie Maritime Belge Transport Case C–395/96P Judgment of 16 March 2000 (nyr)   *505*

Compassion in World Farming Case C–1/96 [1998] ECR I–1251   *391*

Comptoirs de Vente de la Ruhr Cases 40/59 and 13/60 [1960] ECR 165 and 890   *164, 187*

Computerland Europe SA [1989] 4 CMLR 259   *493*

Conegate Limited *v* HM Customs & Excise Case 121/85 [1986] ECR 1007; [1986] 1 CMLR 739   *388*

Confédération Nationale des Producteurs de
    Fruits et Légumes Cases 16–17/62 [1962]
    ECR 901   *164, 168, 266*
Connaughton, Fitzsimons and Griffin; Murray
    Cases T–541 and 554/93 [1997] ECR II–563
    264
Consorzio Cooperative d'Abruzzo Case 15/85
    [1987] ECR 1005   *171*
Consten Sarl and Grundig GmbH *v* Commission
    Cases 56 and 58/64 [1966] ECR 299; [1966]
    CMLR 418   *466, 470, 472, 484, 490, 493,
    494, 498, 503*
Continental Can *v* Commission Case 6/72 [1973]
    ECR 215; [1972] CMLR D11   *513*
Continental Michelin (OJ L305 (1989))   *479,
    502*
Cook (William) Case C–198/91 [1993] ECR
    I–2487   *269, 596*
Cooperativa Co-frutta *v* Amministrazione delle
    Finanze dello Stato Case 193/79 [1987] ECR
    2085   *351*
Corbeau Case C–320/91 [1993] ECR I–2562
    604
Corbiau *v* CEDEFOB Case C–24/92 [1993] ECR I–1277   *304*
Corsica Ferries Case C–1893 [1994] ECR I–1783
    313
Corticeira Amorim-Algarve Ltd Case C–158/99,
    order of 2 July 1999 (nyr)   *314*
Costa *v* ENEL Case 6/64 [1964] ECR 585   *192,
    193, 196, 202, 203, 217, 218, 315, 602*
Cotrim *v* CEDEFOB Case T–180/98 Judgment of
    28 October (nyr)   *147*
Council *v* European Parliament Case 34/86
    [1986] ECR 2155   *261, 275*
Council *v* European Parliament Case C–284/90
    [1992] ECR I–2328   *261, 275*
Court of Auditors *v* Williams Case 9/81 [1983]
    ECR 2859   *144*
Cowan *v* Trésor Public Case 186/87 [1989] ECR
    195; [1990] 2 CMLR 613   *448*
CPM Meeusen *v* Hoofddirectie Van De Informatie
    Beheer Groep Case 337/97 [1999] ECR
    I–3289   *408, 412, 435*
CRAM Joined Cases 29 and 30/83 [1984] ECR
    1679   *464*
Criminal Proceedings against Calfa Case
    C–348/96 [1999] ECR I–11   *454*
Criminal Proceedings against Keck and
    Mithouard Joined Cases C–267 and 268/91
    [1993] ECR I–6097   *374, 379, 380, 381,
    382, 383, 384, 385, 416*
Criminal Proceedings against Matteo Peralta
    Case C–379/92 [1994] ECR I–3453   *446*

Criminal Proceedings against Peter Leifer and
    Others Case C–83/94 [1995] ECR I–3231
    69
Criminal Proceedings against X Joined Cases
    C–74 and 129/95 [1996] ECR I–6609   *211,
    305*
Crotty *v* Taoiseach [1987] 2 CMLR 666   *59*
CSR Pampryl SA *v* Commission Case T–114/99,
    order of 9 November 1999 (nyr)   *272*
Cullet *v* Centre Leclerc Case 231/83 [1985] ECR
    305   *389*
Customs and Excise Commissioners *v* Samex
    SpA [1983] 3 CMLR 194; [1983] 1 All ER
    1042   *182*

Da Costa en Schaake *v* Nederlandse
    Belastingadministratie Joined Cases
    28–30/62 [1963] ECR 31; [1963] CMLR 224
    315, 316, 321
Dansk Denkavit *v* Ministry of Agriculture Case
    29/87 [1988] ECR 2965   *375*
Dansk Supermarked Case 58/80 [1981] ECR 181
    202
Danvin Case 26/67 [1968] ECR 463   *185*
De Agostini Cases C–34 and 36/95 [1997] ECR
    I–3843   *383*
De Bobadilla (Teresa Fernández) *v* Museo
    Nacional del Prado, Comité de Empresa del
    Museo Nacional del Prado, Ministerio Fiscal
    Case C–234/97 [1999] 3 CMLR 151   *438*
De Boer Buizen Case 81/86 [1987] ECR 3677
    288
De Gezamenlijke Steenkolenmijnen in Limburg
    v High Authority Case 30/59 [1961] ECR 1
    583
De Peiper Case 104/75 [1976] ECR 613   *387*
De Sicco Case 19/68 [1968] ECR 699   *320*
Defrenne *v* SABENA Case 43/75 [1976] ECR 455
    162, 167, 200, 201, 322
Defrenne Case 149/77 [1978] ECR 1365   *186,
    188*
Dekker Case 33/65 [1965] ECR 1116   *309*
Delattre Case 369/88 [1991] ECR I–1487   *381*
Deliège *v* Ligue Francophone de Judo et
    Disciplines ASBL Cases C–51/96 and 191/98
    Judgment of 11 April 2000 (nyr)   *408*
Delimitis *v* Henninger Bräu Case C–234/89
    [1992] 5 CMLR 210   *485, 493, 495*
Demirel Case 12/86 [1987] ECR 3719   *177, 216*
Demo-Studio Schmidt Case 210/81 [1983] ECR
    3045   *538*
Demouche Case 152/83 [1987] ECR 3833
    307

Denkavit *v* France Case 132/78 [1979] ECR 1923; [1979] 3 CMLR 605   *338, 352*

Denkavit Nederland Case 18/83 [1984] ECR 2171   *360*

Deufil Case 310/85 [1987] ECR 901   *583*

Deutsche Babcock Case 328/85 [1987] ECR 5119   *164*

Deutsch Grammophon GmbH *v* Metro-SB-Grössmarkte Case 78/70 [1971] ECR 487   *557*

Deutsche Renault AG *v* Audi AG Case C–317/91 [1993] ECR I–6227   *233, 369, 564*

Deutsche Shell Case C–188/91 [1993] ECR I–363; [1993] CMLR 1043   *177, 303*

Deutsche Tradex Case 38/70 [1971] ECR 154   *184*

Deutschmann *v* Federal Republic of Germany Case 10/65 [1965] CMLR 259   *344, 352*

Dias Case C–343/90 [1992] ECR I–4673   *312, 313*

Diatta *v* Land Berlin Case 267/83 [1985] ECR 567   *317, 410*

Diego Cali *v* SEPG Case C–343/95 [1997] ECR I–1547   *465*

Dietz Case 126/76 [1977] ECR 2431   *288*

Dillenkofer *v* Germany Cases C–178, 179 and 189/94 [1996] ECR I–4845; [1996] 3 CMLR 469   *225, 229*

Dirección General de Defensa de la Competencia *v* Asociación Española de Banca Privada Case C–67/91 [1992] ECR I–4785   *541*

Directeur Régional de la Securité Sociale de Nancy *v* August Hirardin Case 112/75 [1976] ECR 553   *307*

Distillers Case 30/78 [1980] ECR 2229   *497*

Donà Case 13/76 [1976] ECR 1333   *409*

Donckerwolke Case 41/76 [1976] ECR 1921   *69, 365*

Doughty *v* Rolls Royce [1992] I CMLR 1045   *208*

Drefus (Louis) Case T–485/93 [1996] ECR II–1131   *286*

Drexl Case 199/86 [1988] ECR 1213   *348*

Driessen *v* Zonen Cases C–13–16/92 [1993] ECR I–4751   *152*

Dubois et Fils Case T–113/96 [1998] ECR II–125   *292*

Dubois et Fils Case C–95/98P [1999] ECR I–4385   *292*

Dubois et Fils SA and General Cargo Services *v* Garoner (GA) Exploitation SA Case C–16/94 [1995] ECR I–2421   *336*

Dumortier Frères Cases 64 and 113/76, 167 and 239/78, 27, 28 and 45/79 [1979] ECR 3091   *288, 293, 298*

Dunlop Slazenger International Case T–43/92 [1994] ECR II–441   *472*

Duphar BV Case 238/82 [1984] ECR 523   *387, 390*

Dutch Book Association *v* Eldi Records Case 106/79 [1980] ECR 1137   *497*

Dzodzi Cases C–297/88 and 197/89 [1991] ECR I–3783   *308, 409*

Eau de Cologne *v* Provide Case C–150/88 [1989] ECR 3891   *312*

Echternach and Moritz Joined Cases 389 and 390/87 [1989] ECR 723   *412*

Eco System (OJ L66 (1992))   *482*

ED Srl *v* Italo Fenocchio Case C–412/97 [1999] ECR I–3845   *378*

Elliniki Case C–200/89 [1991] ECR I–2925   *188*

Embassy Limousines & Services *v* European Parliament Case T–203/96 [1998] ECR II–4239   *290, 298*

Emesa Sugar (Free Zone) NV *v* European Commission Cases C–363 and 364/98P(R) [1998] ECR I–8815   *326*

EMI Electrola GmbH *v* Patricia Im-und Export Verwaltungsgesellschaft mbH Case 341/87 [1989] ECR 79   *559*

EMI Electrola, Warner Brothers Inc *v* Christiansen Case 158/86 [1988] ECR 2605   *569*

EMI Records Ltd *v* CBS United Kingdom Ltd Cases 51, 86 and 96/75 [1976] ECR 811   *472, 569*

Emrich Case C–247/90 [1990] ECR I–3914   *264*

ENI–Lanerossi Case C–303/88 [1991] ECR I–1433   *586*

Enichem Anic *v* Commission Case C–49/92P [1999] ECR I–4125   *471, 477*

Enka Case 38/77 [1977] ECR 2203   *197, 206*

ENU Case C–107/91 [1993] ECR I–599   *283, 294*

Erauw-Jacquéry *v* La Hesbignonne Case 27/87 [1988] 4 CMLR 576   *482*

Eridanea Cases 10 and 18/68 [1969] ECR 459   *268, 281*

Eridanea Case 230/78 [1979] ECR 2749   *126, 159*

Eridania/ISI (OJ C204 (1991))   *514*

ERT Case 260/89 [1991] ECR I–2925   *234*

Erzberbau Cases 3–18 and 25–26/58 [1960] ECR
    367   *274*
Eurico Italia Cases C–332, 333 and 335/92 [1994]
    ECR I–711   *313*
Euripharm Case C–347/89 [1991] ECR I–1717
    307
Eurocontrol Case C–364/92 [1994] ECR I–43
    465
Europair International and Durodyne-Europair
    Corporation [1975] 1 CMLR D62   *500*
European Parliament *v* Council Case 13/83
    [1985] ECR 1513   *282, 285*
European Parliament *v* Council (Re Comitology)
    Case 302/87 [1988] ECR 5615   *265, 282,
    285*
European Parliament *v* Council (Re Chernobyl)
    Case C–70/88 [1990] ECR I–2041   *265*
European Parliament *v* Council Case C–65/90
    [1992] ECR I–4593   *152, 276*
European Parliament *v* Council (Re Student
    Directive) Case C–295/90 [1992] ECR I–4193;
    [1992] 3 CMLR 281   *266, 276, 395*
European Parliament *v* Council Case C–316/91
    [1994] ECR I–625   *181*
European Parliament *v* Council Case C–388/92
    [1994] ECR I–2067   *274*
European Parliament *v* Council Case C–65/93
    [1995] ECR I–643   *152*
European Parliament *v* Council Case C–21/94
    [1995] ECR I–1827   *276*
European Parliament *v* Council Case C–360/96
    [1966] ECR I–1195   *170*
European Parliament *v* Council and Commission
    Cases C–181 and 248/91 [1993] ECR I–3685
    181, 230, 260
European Parliament *v* Council of the European
    Union Joined Cases C–164 and 165/97 [1999]
    ECR I–1139   *169*
European Parliament *v* Council of the European
    Union Case C–189/97 [1999] ECR I–4741
    136
Eurotunnel SA and Others *v* SeaFrance Case
    C–408/95 [1997] ECR I–6315   *152, 280,
    323*
Evans Medical Case C–324/93 [1995] ECR I–563
    387
Even Case 207/78 [1979] ECR 2019   *418*
Exécutif Régional Wallon *v* Commission (Re
    Glaverbel) Cases 62 and 72/87 [1988] ECR
    1573   *591*
Express Dairy Foods *v* Intervention Board for
    Agriculture Produce Case 130/79 [1981] ECR
    1887   *324*

Extramet Case C–358/89 [1991] ECR I–2501
    270
Faccini Dori Case C–91/92 [1994] ECR I–3325
    175, 206, 240
Federación de Distributares Cinematográficas
    Case C–17/92 [1993] ECR I–2239   *446*
Fédération Français des Sociétés d'Assurance
    Case 244/94 [1995] ECR I–4013   *464*
Fédération Nationale du Commerce Extérieur
    des Produits Alimentaires and Syndicat
    National des Négociants et Transformeurs de
    Saumon *v* French Republic Case C–354/90
    [1991] ECR I–5505   *598*
Fedesa Case C–331/88 [1990] ECR I–4023
    171, 275
Fedetab Case 209/78 [1980] ECR 3125   *474*
Fediol Case 70/87 [1989] ECR 1781   *177*
Felicitas Case 270/81 [1982] ECR 2771   *174,
    205*
Fenacomex Case C–354/90 [1991] ECR I–5505
    202
FERAM Case 23/59 [1959] ECR 501   *290*
Ferriere Acciaierie Sarde *v* Commission Case
    C–102/92 [1993] ECR I–801   *598*
Fiat-Itachi (OJ L21 (1993))   *467*
Fietje Case 27/80 [1980] ECR 3839   *370*
Fink Frucht Case 26/67 [1968] ECR 327   *200*
Fink Frucht Case 27/68 [1968] ECR 341   *202*
Fiorini (Christini) Case 32/75 [1975] ECR 1085
    419
Firma Eggers Sohn & Co *v* Freie Hansestadt
    Bremen Case 13/78 [1978] ECR 1935   *386*
Firma Foto-Frost Case 314/85 [1987] ECR 4199
    165
Firma Leon Van Parys NV *v* Commission Case
    T–11/99 Judgment of 15 September 1999
    (nyr)   *268*
Firma Molkerei Case 28/67 [1968] ECR 211
    191
Firma Sloman Neptun Cases C–72 and 73/91
    [1993] ECR I–887   *203*
Firma Steinike und Weinlig *v* Bundesamt für
    Ernährung und Forstwirtschaft Case 78/76
    [1977] ECR 595   *203, 337, 352, 586, 599*
Fiscano Case C–135/92 [1994] ECR I–2885
    267
FMC Case C–212/94 [1996] ECR I–389   *353*
Foglia *v* Novello Case 194/79 [1980] ECR 745
    311, 312
Foglia *v* Novello (No 2) Case 244/80 [1981] ECR
    3045   *312, 321*
Forcheri Case 152/82 [1983] ECR 2323   *448*

Ford (OJ L327 (1983))   *498*

Ford España *v* Spain Case 170/88 [1989] ECR 2305   *342*

Ford/Volkswagen (OJ C257 (1991))   *587*

Foster and Others *v* British Gas plc Case C–188/89 [1990] ECR I–3313   *208, 586*

Foto-Frost *v* Hauptzollamt Lübeck-Ost Case 314/85 [1987] ECR 4199   *322–323*

Fragd [1989] RDI 103   *324*

France *v* Commission Case 102/87 [1988] ECR 4067   *169, 587, 588*

France *v* Commission (Re Boussac) Case 301/87 [1990] ECR 307   *596*

France *v* Commission Case C–325/91 [1993] ECR I–3283   *263*

France *v* Commission Case C–327/91 [1994] ECR I–3641   *129, 163, 262*

France *v* Commission Cases C–68/94 and 30/95 [1998] ECR I–1375   *532*

France *v* Commission Case C–241/94 [1996] ECR I–4551   *583*

France *v* European Parliament Cases 358/85 and 51/86 [1988] ECR 4821   *108*

France *v* European Parliament Case C–345/95 [1997] ECR I–5215   *109*

France *v* High Authority Case 1/54 [1954 ECR 7   *274*

France *v* United Kingdom (Re Fishing Mesh) Case 141/78 [1979] ECR 2923   *233, 250*

France and Belgium *v* Commission Case C–303/90 [1991] ECR I–5315   *263*

France and Ireland *v* Commission Case C–296/93 [1996] ECR I–795   *126, 159*

France and Others *v* Commission Cases C–68 and 30/95 [1998] ECR I–1375   *505*

France, Italy and the United Kingdom *v* Commission Cases 188–190/80 [1982] ECR 2545   *602, 605*

Francovich and Bonifaci *v* Italian State Cases C–6 and 9/90 [1991] ECR I–5357   *175, 192, 223, 224, 225, 252*

Franz Grad *v* Finanzampt Traunstein Case 9/70 [1970] ECR 825   *204, 207, 215, 302*

Frascogna Case 157/84 [1985] ECR 1739   *419*

Fratelli Constanzo Case 103/88 [1989] ECR 1839   *206, 221*

Fratelli Cucchi *v* Avez SpA Case 77/76 [1977] ECR 987   *337, 338, 352*

Fratelli Grassi Case 5/72 [1972] ECR 443   *320*

Frecassetti (Giordano) *v* Amministrazione delle Finanze dello Stato Case 113/75 [1976] ECR 983   *302*

Freight Transport Association and Others *v* London Boroughs Transport Board [1991] ECR I–5403   *318*

Frilli *v* Belgium Case 1/72 [1972] ECR 457   *418*

Frontini Judgment of 27 December 1973   *194*

Frubo Case 71/74 [1975] ECR 563   *501*

Futura Participation Case C–250/95 [1997] ECR I–2471   *433*

Gaal Case C–7/94 [1996] ECR I–1031   *412*

Garden Cottage Foods Ltd *v* Milk Marketing Board [1983] 3 CMLR 43   *552*

Gauchard Case 20/87 [1987] ECR 4879   *307*

GB-INNO-BM *v* Confederation du Commerce Luxembourgeois Case 362/88 [1991] 2 CMLR 801   *374*

Gebhard Case 55/94 [1995] ECR I–4165   *424*

GEMA [1971] CMLR D35   *575*

GEMA Case 125/78 [1979] ECR 3117   *283*

Gencor Ltd *v* Commission of the European Communities Case T–106/96 [1999[All ER (EC) 289   *462, 529, 531, 532*

General Motors Continental NV *v* Commission Case 26/75 [1975] ECR 1367   *516, 519*

Generics (UK) Ltd *v* Smith, Kline and French Laboratories Ltd [1990] 1 CMLR 416   *315*

Generics (UK) Ltd *v* Smith, Kline and French Laboratories Ltd Case C–191/90 [1993] 1 CMLR 89   *569*

German Ceramic Tiles Case [1971] CMLR D6   *486*

Germany *v* Commission (Brennwein) Case 24/62 [1963] ECR 63   *169, 274*

Germany *v* Commission Cases 52–55/65 [1966] ECR 159   *336, 340, 342*

Germany *v* Commission Case 248/84 [1987] ECR 4013   *585, 593*

Germany *v* Deutsches Milch-Kontor GmbH Case C–426/92 [1994] ECR I–2757   *366, 372*

Gerofabrik (OJ L16 (1977))   *482*

Gerrit Holdijk Joined Cases 141–143/81 [1982] ECR 1299   *377*

Gervais Case C–17/94 [1995] ECR I–4353   *601*

Gesamthochschule Duisburg Case 234/83 [1985] ECR 333   *184*

Gibraltar Case C–298/89 [1993] ECR I–3605   *323*

Gimenez Zaera Case 126/86 [1987] ECR 3697   *203*

Giry and Guérlin Cases 253/78 and 3/79 [1980] ECR 2327   *461*

Giuffrida Case 105/75 [1976] ECR 1395   *275*

Giuliani Case 32/77 [1977] ECR 1863   *324*

Gmurzynska Case C–231/89 [1990] ECR I–4003 *308, 312*

Government of Gibraltar Case 298/89 [1993] ECR I–3605   *267*

Granaria Case 18/72 [1972] ECR 1172   *172*

Granaria Case 101/78 [1979] ECR 623   *288*

Grandes Distilleries Peureux v Directeur des Services Fiscaux Case 86/78 [1979] ECR 89 *346*

Grau-Hupka Case C–297/93 [1994] ECR I–5535 *313*

Gravier v City of Liège Case 293/83 [1989] ECR 593   *239, 322, 448*

Greece v Commission Case 30/88 [1989] ECR 374 *262*

Greece v Council Case C–353/92 [1994] ECR I–3411   *169, 186*

Greenwich Film Case 22/79 [1979] ECR 3275 *467*

Greis Unterweger Case 318/86 [1986] ECR 955 *305*

Grimaldi Case C–322/88 [1989] ECR 4407 *176, 302*

Groener Case 378/87 [1989] ECR 3967   *417*

Groenveld Case 15/79 [1979] ECR 3409 *377*

Groupe des Droites Européennes Case 78/85 [1986] 1754   *261*

Groupement des Cartes Bancaires CB and Europay International Cases T–39 and 40/92 [1994] ECR II–49   *473*

Groupement des Industries Sidérurgiques Luxembourgeoises Cases 7 and 9/54 [1956] ECR 55   *281*

Groupement des Papiers Peints de Belgique Case 73/74 [1975] ECR 1491   *169*

Guérin Automobiles Case C–282/95P [1997] ECR I–1503   *263, 539*

Guiot Case C–272/94 [1996] ECR I–1905   *443, 444*

Gul Case 131/85 [1986] ECR 1573   *409*

Gullung Case 292/86 [1988] ECR 111   *425*

Gutmann Cases 18 and 35/65 [1966] ECR 149 *275*

H v Court of Auditors Case C–416/92 [1994] ECR I–1741   *262*

Haar Petroleum Case C–90/94 [1997] ECR I–4085   *344, 352*

Haegeman Case 96/71 [1972] ECR 1005   *288*

Haegeman Case 181/73 [1974] ECR 449   *177, 178, 262, 302*

Haim v Kassenzahnartzlich Vereinigung Nordrhein Case C–319/92 [1994] ECR I–425 *430*

Hainaut-Sambre Case 4/65 [1965] ECR 1363 *295*

Halliburton Services Case C–1/93 [1994] ECR I–1137   *432*

Hamborner Bergbau Cases 41 and 50/59 [1960[ECR 1016   *284*

Handels-og Kontorfunktionaerernes Forbund I Danmark v Dansk Arbejdsgiverforening Case 109/88 [1989] ECR 3199   *306*

Hansa Fleisch Case C–156/91 [1992] ECR I–5567 *214, 216*

Hansen Case 91/78 [1979] ECR 935   *202*

Hansen v Hauptzollamt Flensburg Case 148/77 [1978] ECR 1787   *346*

Hansen v Hauptzollamt Flensburg Case 91/78 [1979] ECR 935   *601*

Harz Case 79/83 [1984] ECR 1921   *209*

Hasselblad (OJ L161 (1982))   *481*

Hauer Case 44/79 [1979] ECR 3727   *188*

Hauptzollamt Bielefield Case 185/73 [1974] ECR 607   *170*

Hautala (Heidi) v Council of the European Union Case T–14/98 [1999] 3 CMLR 528   *157*

Hauts Fourneaux de Chasse Case 2/57 [1958] ECR 129   *275*

Hauts Fourneaux de Chasse Case 33/59 [1962] ECR 719, 748   *290, 295*

Hauts Fourneaux de Givors Cases 27–29/58 [1960] ECR 527   *164*

Hauts Fourneaux et Acieries Belges Case 8/57 [1958] ECR 225   *185*

Hennessy/Henkell [1981] 1 CMLR 601   *481*

Hercules Case T–7/89 [1991] ECR II–1711   *545*

Hercules Case C–51/92P [1999] ECR I–4235 *546*

Hessische Knappschaft Case 44/65 [1965] ECR 1192   *303, 309, 321*

Het Vlaamse Gewet v Commission Case T–214/95 [1998] ECR II–717   *587*

Hilti AG v Commission Case T–30/89 [1991] ECR II–1439; [1992] 4 CMLR 16   *508, 512, 516, 520, 544, 575*

Hilti AG v Commission Case C–53/92P [1995] ECR I–667   *520*

Hoechst AG v Commission Case 46/87 and 227/88 [1989] ECR 2859   *184, 542, 544*

Hoecks Case 249/83 [1985] ECR 973   *419*

Hoekstra v BDDA Case 75/63 [1964] ECR 177 *409*

Hoffmann-La Roche v Centrafarm Case 107/76 [1977] ECR 957   *307*

Hoffmann-La Roche v Centrafarm Case 102/77
[1978] ECR 1139   568
Hoffmann-La Roche v Commission Case 85/76
[1978] ECR 461   184, 507, 508, 509, 514,
518, 520, 521, 522, 574
Holdijk Cases 141–143/81 [1982] ECR 1299
314
Holtz and Willemsen Case 134/73 [1974] ECR 1
283, 286
Hoogovens Case 14/61 [1962] ECR 485
Hopkins Case C–18/94 [1996] ECR I–2281
47
Hugin Kassaregister AB v Commission Case
22/78 [1979] ECR 1869   467, 516
Hüls Case C–199/92P [1999] ECR I–4287   478
Humblet Case 6/60 [1960] ECR 1125   182, 252
Humblot v Directeur des Services Fiscaux Case
112/84 [1985] ECR 1367   347
Hünermund v Landesapothekerkammer Baden-
Württemburg Case C–292/92 [1993] ECR
I–6787   380
Hupeden Case C–295/94 [1996] ECR I–3375
314
Hurd Case 44/84 [1986] ECR 29   303

Iannelli and Volpi SpA v Ditta and Paolo Meroni
Case 74/76 [1977] ECR 557   202, 203, 353,
357
IBM v Commission Case 60/81 [1981] ECR 2639
263
IBM Personal Computers (OJ L118 (1984))
493
ICAC Case 22/78 [1979] ECR 1168   309
Ideal-Standard Agreement, Re [1988] 4 CMLR
627   491–492, 499
IFG v Freistaat Bayern Case 1/83 [1984] ECR
349; [1985] 1 CMLR 453   342
IFTRA Rules for Producers of Virgin Aluminium,
Re [1975] 2 CMLR D20   481
IFTRA Rules of European Manufacturers of Glass
Containers [1974] 2 CMLR D50   486
IHT Internationale Heiztztechnik GmbH v Ideal
Standard GmbH Case C–9/93 [1994] ECR
I–2789   567
Imperial Chemical Industries v Colmer
(Inspector of Taxes) Case C–264/96 [1998] 3
CMLR 293   432, 433
Imperial Chemical Industries v Commission
(Dyestuffs) Case 48/69 [1972] ECR 619
261, 460, 475
Independent Television Publications Limited v
EC Commission Case T–76/89 [1991] 4
CMLR 745   523

Inter-Environnement Wallonie ASBL v Région
Wallone Case C–129/96 [1997] ECR I–7411;
[1998] 1 CMLR 1057   195, 207, 212, 214,
241, 242
Interhotel Case C–29/89 [1991] ECR I–2276
274
Intermills Case 323/82 [1984] ECR 3809   596
International Chemical Company Case 66/80
[1981] ECR 1191   324
International Fruit Cases 51–54/71 [1971] ECR
1107   365
International Fruit Co v Commission Cases
41–44/70 [1971] ECR 411   266, 272
International Fruit Company NV and Others v
Produktschap voor Groenten en Fruit Cases
21–24/72 [1972] ECR 1219   216, 275
International Handelsgesellschaft Case 11/70
[1970] ECR 1125   187, 219
Internationale Dentalschau (OJ L293 1987))
500
Inzirillo Case 63/76 [1979] ECR 2057   412, 419
Ireks-Arkady Case 238/78 [1979] ECR 2955
293, 295, 297
Ireland v Commission Case 325/85 [1987] ECR
5041   183
Ireland v Commission Case C–307/93 [1993] ECR
I–4191   126, 159
Irish Creamery Milk Suppliers Association Cases
36 and 71/80 [1981] ECR 735   310, 339
Irish Sugar plc Case T–228/97 [2000] All ER (EC)
198   505, 512, 514, 521
Italia Testa Case C–101/96 [1996] ECR I–3081
314
Italian Flat Glass (OJ L33 (1989))   505, 507
Italian Republic Case 32/65 [1966] ECR 563
279
Italy v Commission Case 1/69 [1969] ECR 277
169
Italy v Commission (Re Italian Textiles) Case
173/73 [1974] ECR 709   584, 587
Italy v Commission Case 118/85 [1987] ECR 1987
465
Italy v Commission (Re Alfa Romeo) Case
C–305/89 [1991] ECR I–1603, 1645   585,
598
Italy v Commission Case 360/90 [1993] ECR
I–2097   597
Italy v Commission Case C–364/90 [1993] ECR
I–2097   589
Italy v Commission Case C–47/91 [1992] ECR
I–4145   264
Italy v Council Case 166/78 [1979] ECR 2575
265

Italy v High Authority Case 20/59 [1960] ECR 665 *168, 242, 243*

Iveco/Ford (OJ L230 (1988)) *501*

Jägerskiöld Case 97/98 [2000] 1 CMLR 235 *332*

Jan Van der Haar Cases 177 and 178/82 [1984] ECR 1797 *362*

Javico Case C–306/96 [1998] ECR I–1983 *571*

Jaz International Belgium Case 96/82 [1983] ECR 3369 *486*

John Deere [1985] 2 CMLR 554 *543*

Johnson and Johnson [1981] 2 CMLR 287 *472*

Johnston v Chief Constable of the Royal Ulster Constabulary Case 222/84 [1986] ECR 1651 *185, 208, 309*

Jongeneel Kass Case 237/82 [1982] ECR 483 *377*

Juan Carlos Grau Gomis Case C–165/94 [1995] ECR I–1023 *314*

Junghans [1977] 1 CMLR D82 *500*

Just Vase 68/79 [1980] ECR 501 *353*

Kabel und Metallwerke Neumeyer/Luchaire [1975] 2 CMLR D40 *501*

Kaefer and Procacci v France Cases C–100 and 101/89 [1990] ECR I–4647 *307*

Kahn Scheepvaart Case T–398/94 [1996] ECR II–477 *273*

Kaï Ottung Case 320/87 [1989] ECR 1177 *572*

Kali und Salz v Commission Joined Cases 19 and 20/74 [1975] ECR 499 *502, 531*

Kampffmeyer Cases 5, 7 and 13–24/66 [1967] ECR 317 *288, 290, 294, 299*

Kaufhof Case 29/75 [1976] ECR 431 *273*

Kawasaki (OJ L16 (1979)) *479*

Kazim Kus Case C–237/91 [1992] ECR I–6781 *216*

Kelderman Case 130/80 [1981] ECR 527 *370*

Keller Case 234/85 [1986] ECR 2897 *188*

Kempf Case 139/85 [1986] ECR 1741 *408, 456*

Kerry Milk Case 80/76 [1977] ECR 425 *110*

Kieffer (René) and Romain Thill Case 114/96 [1997] ECR I–3629 *360*

Kirk (Kent) Case 63/83 [1984] ECR 2689 *171, 188*

Kleinwort Benson Case C–346/93 [1995] ECR I–615 *308*

Klomp Case 23/68 [1969] ECR 43 *302*

Kloppenburg Case 70/83 [1984] ECR 1075 *173*

Kloppenburg [1989] 1 CMLR 873 *318*

Knoors v Secretary of State for Economic Affairs Case 115/78 [1979] ECR 399 *430*

Kodak (OJ L147 (1970)) *493*

Kohler Cases 316/82 and 40/83 [1984] ECR 641 *263*

Kolpinghuis Nijmegen BV Case 80/86 [1987] ECR 3969 *174, 206, 211, 213, 214*

Konecke Case 76/79 [1980] ECR 665 *258*

Koninklijke Scholten Honig v Council and Commission Case 101/76 [1977] ECR 3583 *172*

Koninklijke Scholten Honig NV v Council and Commission Case 43/77 [1979] ECR 3583 *294*

Köster Case 25/70 [1970] ECR 1161 *168, 185, 275*

Krantz Case C–69/88 [1990] ECR I–583 *368, 379*

Krap Cases 275/80 and 24/81 [1981] ECR 2489 *278*

Kremow v Austria Case C–299/95 [1997] ECR I–2629 *399*

Krohn Case 175/84 [1986] ECR 753 *285, 286*

Kruidvat (P) Case C–70/97 [1998] ECR I–7183 *273*

KSH NV v Council and Commission Case 101/76 [1977] ECR 797 *267, 268*

Kupferberg Case 104/81 [1982] ECR 3641 *216, 233*

Kus v Landeshaupt Stadt Wiesbaden Case C–237/91 [1992] ECR I–6781 *411*

La Pyramide SARL Case C–378/93 [1994] ECR I–3999 ord *312, 314*

Läärä and Others v Kihlakunnansyyttäjä (Jyväskylä) and Others Case C–124/97 [1999] ECR I–6067 *446*

Ladbroke Racing Ltd Case T–32/93 [1994] ECR II–1015 *283*

Lahlou Hassa Case C–196/96 [1996] ECR I–3945 *314*

Lair v University of Hanover Case 39/86 [1988] ECR 3161 *420, 449*

Lamaire NV v Nationale Dienst voor Afzet Land-en Tuinbouwprodukten Case C–130/93 [1994] ECR I–3215 *352*

Lancôme v ETOS Case 99/79 [1980] ECR 2511 *497*

Lancry and Others v Direction Générales des Douanes and Others Joined Cases C–363 and 407–411/93 [1994] ECR I–3957 *337*

Lawrie Blum v Land Baden-Wurttemburg Case 66/85 [1986] ECR 2121 *407, 420, 451*

Le Manoir Case C–27/91 [1991] ECR I–5531 *408*

Le Pen Case C–210/89 [1990] ECR I–1183
  261, 286
Leendert van Bennekom Case 227/82 [1983] ECR
  3883   *388*
Leeuwarder Papierwarenfabriek BV Case 318/81
  [1985] ECR 3727   *587*
Lefebre Case 188/86 [1987] ECR 2963   *307*
Legia and Gyselinx Case 87/85 [1986] ECR 1707
  384
Lemmerz-Werke Case 11/63 [1965] ECR 835
  171
Leonesio v Italian Ministry of Agriculture Case
  93/71 [1972] ECR 287   *203*
Leplat case C–260/90 [1992] ECR I–643   *307*
Les Assurances du Credit Case C–63/89 [1991]
  ECR I–1799   *293*
Levin v Staatssecretaris von Justitie Case 53/81
  [1982] ECR 1053   *407, 408*
Lévy Case C–158/91 [1993] ECR I–4287   *163*
Liberal Democrats, The Case C–42 [1993] ECR
  I–3153   *130*
Lightweight Paper (OJ L182 (1972))   *502*
Limburgse Vinyl Maatschappij NV and Others v
  Commission (Re PVC Cartel (No 2)) Joined
  Cases T–305, 307, 313–316, 318, 325,
  328–329 and 225/97 [1999] 5 CMLR 303
  277, 551
Lloyd Schufabrik Meyer & Co GmbH v Klijsen
  Handel BV Case C–342/97 [1997] 2 CMLR
  1343   *566, 567*
Lopes (Orlando) Cases C–174 and 175/96P [1996]
  ECR I–6401   *143*
L'Oréal Case 31/80 [1980] ECR 3775   *492*
Lorenz Case 120/73 [1973] ECR 1471   *202, 596*
Lornoy Case C–17/91 [1992] ECR I–6523   *599*
LSFM (OJ L369 (1985))   *466*
Lucchini Case 1252/79 [1980] ECR 3753   *169*
Lück Case 34/67 [1968] ECR 359   *221*
Luigi Spano and Fiat Geotech Case C–472/93
  [1995] ECR I–4321   *206, 211*
Luisi and Carbone v Ministero del Tesoro Joined
  Cases 286/82 and 26/83 [1984] ECR 377
  447
Lütticke (Alfons) Case 48/65 [1966] ECR 19
  238, 264, 284
Lütticke (Alfons) v Hauptzollamt Saarlouis Case
  57/65 [1966] ECR 205   *200, 201, 202, 238,
  344, 345, 352*
Lütticke Case 4/69 [1971] ECR 325   *286, 289,
  290*
Luxembourg v European Parliament Case 230/81
  [1983] ECR 255   *108, 261*
Luxembourg v European Parliament Case 108/83
  [1984] ECR 1945   *108*

Luxembourg v European Parliament Cases
  C–213/88 and 39/89 [1991] ECR I–5643
  108
McNicoll v Ministry of Agriculture Case 296/86
  [1988] ECR 1491   *243*
Magill v Radio Telefis Eirann Case 241/91 [1995]
  ECR 797   *574*
Magnavision NV v General Optical Council
  [1987] 1 CMLR 716   *317*
Maribel (OJ L95 (1997))   *586, 588*
Marimex SpA v Italian Minister of Finance Case
  29/72 [1972] ECR 1309   *338, 386*
Marleasing Case C–106/89 [1990] ECR I–4135
  210, 211, 212, 214
Mars Case 470/93 [1995] ECR I–317   *383*
Marshall v Southampton and South-West
  Hampshire Area Health Authority (No 1)
  Case 152/84 [1986] ECR 723   *208*
Marshall v Southampton and South-West
  Hampshire Area Health Authority (No 2)
  Case C–271/91 [1993] ECR I–4367   *206*
Matra Case C–225/91 [1993] ECR I–3203   *269*
Matra Hachette Case T–17/93 [1994] ECR II–595
  498, 502
Matteucci Case 237/87 [1988] ECR 5589   *419*
Mattheus (Lothar) v Duego Fruchtimport und
  Tiefkuhlkost Case 93/78 [1978] ECR 2203
  31, 312
Maurissen Cases 193 and 194/87 [1989] ECR
  1045   *262*
Max Mara Case C–307/95 [1995] ECR I–5083
  314
Max Neumann Case 17/67 [1967] ECR 571
  171
Mayer v Commission Case T–106/99, order of the
  CFI of 22 October 1999   *263*
Mazzalai Case 111/75 [1976] ECR 657   *209,
  302*
Mehuy and Schott Case C–51/93 [1994] ECR
  I–3879   *360, 374*
Meilicke v ADV/ORGA FA Meyer Case C–83/91
  [1992] ECR I–4871   *312*
Melkunie Case 97/83 [1984] ECR 2367   *308*
Merck and Beecham Joined Cases C–267 and
  268/95 [1996] ECR I–6285   *559*
Merck and Co Inc v Stephar BV Case 187/80
  [1981] ECR 2063   *559*
Merkur Case 97/76 [1977] ECR 1063   *293*
Meroni Case 9/56 [1958] ECR 11   *278*
Meroni Case 15/57 [1958] ECR 185   *164*
Meroni Cases 14, 16, 17, 20, 24, 26 and 27/60
  [1961] ECR 319   *290*

Messner Case C–265/88 [1989] ECR 4209
   414

Metro *v* Saba (No 1) Case 26/76 [1977] ECR 1875
   269, 486, 491, 493, 499, 500, 540

Metro-SB-Großmärkte GmbH *v* Commission (No
   2) Case 75/80 [1986] ECR 3021   *508*

Métropole Télévision Cases T–528, 542, 543 and
   546/93 [1996] ECR II–649   *270, 473, 498*

Meyer-Buckhardt Case 9/75 [1975] ECR 1171
   233

Mezzogiorno (OJ L86 (1991))   *589*

Michelin *v* Commission Case 322/81 [1983] ECR
   3461; [1985] 1 CMLR 282   *508, 509, 517,*
   521, 522, 543

Michelin *v* Michels, Rechtspraak NJB 1994/2, p14
   214

Michelletti Case C–369/90 [1992] ECR I–4239
   394

Michels *v* Fond National de Reclassement
   Handicapes Case 76/72 [1973] ECR 457
   411

Milchförderungsfonds (OJ L35 (1985))   *466,*
   474, 584

Milchwerke Case 31/62 [1962] ECR 971   *280*

Miller International *v* Commission Case 19/77
   [1978] ECR 131   *479, 482*

Ministère Public *v* Deserbais Case 286/86 [1988]
   ECR 4907   *372*

Ministero delle Finanze *v* IN.CO.GE'90 Srl and
   Others Joined Cases C–10–22/97 [1998] ECR
   I–6307   *220*

Ministeur du budget *v* Cercle militaire de la
   caserne France [1990] AJDA 328   *214*

Miro BV Case 182/84 [1985] ECR 3731   *372*

Modesti (M) Case C–191/96 [1996] ECR I–3937
   314

Molitaria Immolese Case 30/67 [1968] ECR 172
   266, 268

Molkerei-Zentrale Westfalen/Lippe GmbH *v*
   Haupzollampt Paderborn Case 28/67 [1968]
   CMLR 187   *224, 309, 348*

Monin Automobiles Case C–428/93 [1994] ECR
   I–1707 ord   *312*

Monteil and Sammani Case 60/89 [1991] ECR
   1561   *381*

Morson and Jhabjan (Re Surinam Mothers) Cases
   35 and 36/82 [1982] ECR 3723   *411*

Mostafa Saddik Case C–458/93 [1995] ECR I–511
   314

Moulins et Huileries de Point-à-Mousson Joined
   Cases 124/76 and 20/77 [1977] ECR 1795
   186, 325

Mulder Case 120/86 [1988] ECR 2321   *295*

Mulder *v* Council and Commission Cases 104/89
   and 37/90 [1992] ECR I–3061   *264, 288,*
   293, 294, 295, 297

Muller-Hein Case 10/71 [1971] ECR 723   *203*

Murphy Case 157/88 [1988] ECR 686   *209*

Musik-Vertrieb *v* GEMA Case 78/80 [1971] ECR
   147   *569*

Musique Diffusion SA *v* Commission Cases
   100–103/80 [1983] 3 CMLR 221   *547, 549*

Mutsch Case 137/84 [1985] ECR 2681   *398,*
   419

Nakajima Case C–69/89 [1991] ECR I–2069
   169, 177

Namur-Les Assurance du Crédit SA *v* Office
   National du Ducroire Case C–44/93 [1994]
   ECR I–3829   *594*

National Panasonic *v* Commission Case 136/79
   [1980] ECR 2033   *188, 542*

National Sulphuric Acid Association [1980] 3
   CMLR 429   *473*

NBV and NVB Case T–138/89 [1992] ECR II–2181
   266

Nederlandse Spoowegen Case 38/75 [1975] ECR
   1439   *219*

Nederlandse Vereniging voor de Fruit en
   Groeten-Importhandel Case 71/74 [1975]
   [1975] ECR 1063   *293*

Nertsvoederfabriek Nederlandse Case 118/86
   [1987] ECR 3883   *378*

Neu EA Cases C–90 and 91/90 [1991] ECR I–3617
   188

New Europe Consulting Ltd and Michael P
   Brown Commission of the European
   Communities Case T–231/97 [1999] 2 CMLR
   1452   *298*

Nillson (Gunnar), Per Olov Hagelgren, Solweig
   Arrborn Case C–162/97 [1998] ECR 7477
   375

NMB Case C–188/88 [1992] ECR I–1689   *178*

NMH Stahlwerke Cases T–134, 136–138, 141,
   145, 147, 148, 151, 156 and 157/94R [1996]
   ECR II–537   *546*

Nold KG *v* Commission Case 4/73 [1974] ECR
   491   *187, 188, 274*

Nölle Case T–167/94 [1995] ECR II–2589   *288*

Norddeutsches Vieh-und Fleischkontor Case 3/70
   [1971] ECR 491   *172*

Nordsee Deutsche Hochsefischerei GmbH *v*
   Reederei Mond Case 102/81 [1982] ECR 1095
   305

Nungesser *v* Commission Case 258/78 [1982]
   ECR 45   *572*

Nungesser v Commission Case 262/81 [1982] ECR 2105   *490*

Odigitria Case T–572/93 [1995] ECR II–2025 *295, 402*
Odigitria Case C–293/95P [1996] ECR I–6129 *402*
Oebel Case 155/80 [1981] ECR 1993   *186*
O'Flynn Case C–237/94 [1996] ECR I–2617 *419*
Oleifici Italiani and Fratelli Rubino v Commission Case T–54/96 [1998] ECR II–3377   *296*
Oleificio Borelli Case C–97/91 [1992] ECR I–6313 *260*
ONEM v Minne Case C–13/93 [1994] ECR I–371 *163*
ONIC v Société Maïseries de Beauce [1985] AJDA 615   *324*
ONPTS v Damiani Case 53/79 [1980] ECR 273 *310*
Opel Austria GmbH Case T–115/94 [1997] ECR II–39   *170*
Openbaar Ministerie v Van Tiggele Case 82/77 [1978] ECR 25   *363*
Opinion 1/75 (Local Cost Standard Undertaking) [1975] ECR 1355   *69*
Opinion 1/91 [1991] ECR I–6079   *162*
Opinion 1/92 [1992] ECR I–2821   *162*
Opinion 1/94 [1994] ECR I–5267   *69, 164*
Orkem Case 374/87 [1989] ECR 3283   *184*
Ortscheit Case C–320/93 [1994] ECR I–5243 *391*
Oscar Bronner GmbH & Co KG v Mediaprint Zeitungs-und Eitschriftenverlag GmbH & Co KG Case C–7/97 [1998] ECR I–779   *523*
Österreichische Unilever GmbH Case C–77/97 [1999] ECR I–431   *382*
OTO Case C–130/92 [1994] ECR I–3281 *344*

Pabst Case 17/81 [1982] ECR 1331   *216*
Paraschi Case C–349/87 [1991] ECR I–4501 *415*
Parker Pen Case T–77/92 [1994] ECR II–549 *466, 482*
Parodi v Banque H Albert de Bary Case C–222/95 [1997] ECR I–3899   *443, 446*
Partie Ecologiste Les Verts v European Parliament Case 294/83 [1986] ECR 1339 *130, 131, 164, 230, 261, 265*
Pastätter Case C–217/89 [1990] ECR I–4584 *295*

Paul Denuit Case C–14/96 [1997] ECR I–2785 *245*
Peeters Case C–369/89 [1991] ECR I–2971   *374*
Perfumes Christain Dior SA and Perfumes Christian Dior BV v Evora BV Case C–337/95 [1997] ECR I–6013   *306, 318, 560, 562, 563, 571*
Pesqueras Echebaster SA Case C–25/91 [1993] ECR I–1719   *284*
Pesqueria Nasco-Montanesa Ord Cases T–452 and 453/93R [1994] ECR II–229   *259*
Peter Case C–290/91 [1993] ECR I–2981   *172*
Peterbroeck Case C–312/93 [1995] ECR I–4599 *310, 353*
Petra Kirsammer-Hack (OJ C001 (1994))   *585*
Pfizer Case 65/87 [1987] ECR 1691   *283*
Pfizer (P) Animal Health SA/NV v Council of the European Union Case T–13/99 [1999] 3 CMLR 79   *326*
Pharmacia and Upjohn SA v Paranova Case C–379/97 [2000] 1 CMLR 51   *568*
Pharmon BV v Hoechst AG Case 19/84 [1985] ECR 2281   *558*
Phillip Morris Case 730/79 [1980] ECR 2671 *586, 587, 590*
Phoenix Rheinrohr Case 20/58 [1959] ECR 153 *263*
Phytheron International SA Case C–352/95 [1997] ECR I–1729   *314*
Piageme Case 85/94 [1995] ECR I–2955   *374*
Piera Scaramuzza v Commission Case C–76/93P [1994] ECR I–5173   *188*
Pietsch (Bernard) Case 296/94 [1996] ECR I–3409   *314*
Pigs Marketing Board (Northern Ireland) v Redmond Case 83/78 [1978] ECR 2347 *316, 357*
Pinna Case 41/84 [1986] ECR 1   *325, 415*
Pioneer Hi-Fi Equipment (OJ L60 (1980) *549*
Piraïki-Patraïki Case 11/82 [1985] ECR 207 *273*
Plaumann v Commission Case 25/62 [1964] ECR 95   *168, 267, 268, 271, 272, 285*
Pleuger Worthington Joined Cases 324 and 342/90 [1994] ECR I–1173   *597*
Politi v Italian Ministry of Finance of the Italian Republic Case 43/71 [1971] ECR 1039 *203, 219*
Polydor Case 270/89 [1982] ECR 239   *177*
Ponente Carni Cases C–71 and 178/91 [1993] ECR I–1915   *220*
Portelange Case 10/69 [1969] ECR 309   *307*

Practice Direction (Supreme Court: References to the Court of Justice of the European Communities) (1999) The Times 19 January *310, 311*

Prais Case 130/75 [1976] ECR 1589   *188*

Prantl Case 16/83 [1984] ECR 1299   *369, 390*

Pretore di Salo *v* Persons Unknown Case 14/86 [1987] 2545   *305*

Procter & Gamble Company *v* Office for Harmonisation in the Internal Market (Trade Marks and Desighns) Case T–163/98 [1999] 2 CMLR 1442   *578*

Procureur de la Republique *v* Waterkeyn Joined Case 314–316/81 [1982] ECR 4337   *252*

Procureur du Roi *v* Dassonville Case 8/74 [1974] ECR 837; [1974] 2 CMLR 36   *357, 361, 362, 364, 367, 368, 377, 379, 384, 466, 558*

Procureur du Roi *v* Royer Case 48/75 [1976] ECR 497   *197*

Produits Bertrand Case 40/75 [1976] ECR 1 *298*

Produits de Maïs Case 112/83 [1985] ECR 742 *324*

Pronuptia Case 161/84 [1986] ECR 353   *480, 492*

Provide Case C–150/88 [1989] ECR 3891   *173*

Providence Agricole de Champagne Case 4/79 [1980] ECR 2823   *324*

Prym/Beka (OJ L296 (1973))   *499*

Pubblico Ministero *v* Manghera Case 59/75 [1976] ECR 91   *176, 200, 202, 302, 601*

Pubblico Ministero *v* Ratti Case 148/78 [1979] ECR 1629   *175, 196, 200, 206*

Punto Casa SpA *v* Sindaco del Commune di Capena Joined Cases C–69 and 258/93 [1994] ECR I–2355   *381*

R *v* Bouchereau Case 30/77 [1977] ECR 1999 *453, 455*

R *v* Customs and Excise, ex parte Lunn Poly [1998] 2 CMLR 560   *600*

R *v* Henn and Darby Case 34/79 [1979] ECR 3795; [1980] CMLR 246   *387, 388*

R *v* HM Treasury, ex parte British Telecom plc Case 392/93 [1996] ECR I–1631   *226, 309*

R *v* Home Secretary, ex parte Evans Medical and MacFarlane Smith Case C–324/93 [1995] ECR I–563   *391*

R *v* Home Secretary, ex parte Vitale and Do Amaral [1996] All ER (EC) 461   *396*

R *v* Immigration Appeal Tribunal, ex parte Antonissen Case C–292/89 [1991] ECR I–745 *409*

R *v* Immigration Appeal Tribunal and Surinder Singh, ex parte Secretary of State for the Home Department Case C–370/90 [1992] 3 CMLR 335   *410*

R *v* Minister of Agriculture, Fisheries and Food, ex parte Hedley Lomas (Ireland) Ltd Case C–5/94 [1996] ECR I–2553   *226*

R *v* Pieck Case 157/79 [1980] ECR 2171   *414*

R *v* Royal Pharmaceutical Society for Great Britain Case 266/87 [1989] 2 CMLR 751   *358*

R *v* Secretary of State for Foreign and Commonwealth Affairs, ex parte Rees-Mogg [1994] 1 All ER 457   *62*

R *v* Secretary of State for the Environment, ex parte RSPB [1995] JPL 842   *318*

R *v* Secretary of State for the Home Department, ex parte Mann Singh Shingara; R *v* Secretary of State for the Home Department, ex parte Abbas Radiom Joined Cases C–65 and 111/95 [1997] ECR I–3343   *457*

R *v* Secretary of State for the Home Department, ex parte Sandhu [1982] 2 CMLR 553   *317*

R *v* Secretary of State for Transport, ex parte Factortame (No 2) Case 213/89 [1991] ECR I–2433   *221, 309, 325*

R *v* Secretary of State for Transport, ex parte Factortame (No 3) Case 221/89 [1991] ECR I–3905   *222, 224*

R *v* Secretary of State for Transport, ex parte Factortame (No 4) *see* Brasserie du Pêcheur

R *v* Secretary of State for Transport, ex parte Factortame (No 5) [1999] 3 CMLR 597 *226, 227*

R *v* Stock Exchange of the United Kingdom and the Republic of Ireland [1993] 1 All ER 420 *319*

R *v* Thompson Case 7/78 [1978] ECR 2247   *332*

R *v* Thompson, Johnson and Woodiwiss Case 7/78 [1978] ECR 2247   *390*

Racke Case 98/78 [1979] ECR 69   *170, 171, 177*

Radiotelevisione Italiana SpA Case C–440/98, order of 26 November 1999 (nyr)   *305*

RAI/United (OJ L157 (1978))   *464*

Rainbow Warrior Case (1990) 82 ILR 499   *245*

Rauch (G) Case 16/64 [1965] ECR 179   *279*

Raulin Case 357/89 [1992] ECR I–1027   *408*

Razanatsimbo Case 65/77 [1977] ECR 2229 *302, 425*

Recep Tetik Case C–171/95 [1997] ECR I–329 *216*

Rechberger (Walter) and Renate Greindl, Hermann Hofmeister and Others *v* Republic of Austria Case C–140/97 [1999] ECR I–3499 *227*

Reed Case 59/85 [1986] ECR 1283   *410*
Reina Case 65/81 [1982] ECR 33   *320, 419*
Reisdorf (J) Case C–85/95 [1996] ECR I–6257
   310
Reisebüro Broede v Sandker Case C–3/95 [1996]
   ECR I–6511   *443*
Remia BV v Commission Case 42/84 [1985] ECR
   2545   *490, 501*
Renault Case 53/87 [1990] 4 CMLR 265   *516*
Rennet Case 61/80 [1981] ECR 851   *501*
Reti Televisive Italiani Cases C–320 and 328/94
   [1996] ECR I–6471   *310*
Rewe Case 158/80 [1981] ECR 1805   *219*
Rewe-Zentral AG v Bundomonopolverwaltung
   für Branntwein (Cassis De Dijon) Case
   120/78 [1979] ECR 649; [1979] 3 CMLR 494
   357, 364, 367, 368, 371, 375, 376, 379, 381,
   383, 384, 386, 428, 446, 601
Rewe-Zentrale Case 45/75 [1976] ECR 181
   350, 602
Rewe-Zentralfinanz GmbH v Direktor der
   Landswirtschaftskammer Westfalen-Lippe
   Case 39/73 [1973] ECR 1039   *341, 342*
Rewe-Zentralfinanz GmbH v
   Landswirtschaftskammer Case 4/75 [1975]
   ECR 843   *365*
Rewe-Zentralfinanz eG v Landwirtschaftskammer
   für das Saarland Case 33/76 [1976] ECR 1989
   552
Reyners (Jean) v The Belgian State Case 2/74
   [1974] ECR 631; [1974] 2 CMLR 305   *200,*
   424, 426, 428, 451
Rey-Soda Case 23/75 [1975] ECR 1279   *324*
Rheinmühlen Joined Cases 146 and 166/73
   [1974] ECR 33   *301, 310, 319*
Richardt Case 367/89 [1991] ECR I–4621   *390*
Richco Commodities Case T–491/93 [1996] ECR
   II–1101   *286*
Richez-Parise Case 19, 20, 25 and 30/69 [1970]
   ECR 325   *290*
Risetia Luigi Geddo v Ente Nazionale Risi Case
   2/73 [1973] ECR 865   *360*
Robertson Case 220/81 [1982] ECR 2349   *369*
Rockfon Case C–449/93 [1995] ECR I–4291
   211
Roders Joined Cases C–367–377 [1995] ECR
   I–2229   *350*
Roquette Case C–228/92 [1994] ECR I–1445
   325
Roquette Frères Cases 138 and 139/79 [1980]
   ECR 3393   *152, 274*
Rossi Case 100/78 [1979] ECR 831   *184*
Rothmans International BV v Commission Case
   T–188/97 [1999] 3 CMLR 66   *128, 158*

Roujanski Case 253/94P [1995] ECR I–7   *260*
Royal Bank of Scotland v Elliniko Dimosio Case
   C–311/97 [1999] ECR I–2651   *432*
Royscot Leasing Ltd (and three other appellants)
   v Commissioners of Customs and Excise
   [1999] 1 CMLR 903   *311*
RSH and Tunnel Refineries Cases 103 and 145/77
   [1978] ECR 2037   *294*
RSV v Commission Case 223/85 [1987] ECR 4617
   599
Rückdeschel Cases 117/76 and 16/77 [1977] ECR
   1753   *324*
Rush Portuguesa Case C–113/89 [1990] ECR
   I–1417   *444*
Russo v Aima Case 69/75 [1976] ECR 45   *223*
Rutili (Roland) v Minister of the Interior Case
   36/75 [1975] ECR 1219; [1976] 1 CMLR 140
   206, 413, 453

SA Fromagerie Franco-Suisse Le Ski [1971] CDE
   561   *222*
Sabel BV v Puma AG, Rudolph Dassler Sport Case
   C–151/95 [1998] 1 CMLR 445   *563, 564,*
   565, 566
Sacchi Case 155/73 [1974] ECR 409   *364, 602*
SADAM Cases 88–90/75 [1976] ECR 323   *125*
Sager Case C–76/90 [1991] ECR I–4221   *443*
Sail Case 82/71 [1972] ECR 136   *309*
Saint-Gobain (OJ L215 (1991))   *587*
Sala (Maria Martinez) v Freistaat Bayern Case
   C–85/96 [1998] ECR I–2691   *396, 419*
Salemo v Commission and Council Cases 87 and
   130/77 and 9 and 10/84 [1985] ECR 2523
   278
Salmon Case C–354/90 [1991] ECR I–5505
   596
Salonia v Poidamani and Giglio Case 126/80
   [1981] ECR 1563   *310, 313*
Salumi Cases 66, 127 and 128/79 [1980] ECR
   1258   *322*
Salumificio de Cornuda Case 130/78 [1979] ECR
   867   *219*
Samenwerkende Elektriciteits
   Produktiebedrijven (SEP) NV v Commission
   Case C–36/92P [1994] ECR I–1911   *185,*
   540, 541
San Michele Case 5–11 and 13–15/62 [1962] ECR
   449   *284, 543*
San Michele Joined Cases 9 and 58/65 [1967]
   ECR 1   *193, 219*
Sandoz Case 277/87 [1990] ECR I–45   *473*
Sanofi/Sythélabo (OJ L95 (2000))   *534*
Santillo Case 131/79 [1980] ECR 1585   *453*

Sanz de Lera Case C–163/94 [1995] ECR I–4821 *422*

Sarrio SA *v* Commission Cases T–339 and 342/94 [1998] ECR II–1727; [1998] 5 CMLR 195 *476, 481*

SAT Case C–364/92 [1994] ECR I–43 *320*

Sayag Case 9/69 [1969] ECR 336, 3219 *185, 287*

Scharbatke Case C–72/92 [1993] ECR I–5509 *353*

Scheer Case 3/70 [1970] ECR 1197 *209*

Schluter Case 94/71 [1972] ECR 307 *307*

Schlüter Case 9/73 [1973] ECR 1135 *203, 263*

Schneider-Import Case 26/80 [1980] ECR 3469 *346*

Schonenberg Case 88/77 [1978] ECR 473 *221*

Schöttle *v* Finanzamt Freudenstadt Case 20/76 [1977] ECR 247 *349*

Schroeder Case 40/72 [1973] ECR 125 *178*

Schul Case 15/81 [1982] ECR 409 *348*

Schul Case 47/84 [1985] ECR 491 *348*

Schumacher Case 215/87 [1989] ECR 617 *332*

Schumacker Case C–279/93 [1995] ECR I–225 *433*

Schutzverband Gegen Unlauteren Wettbewerb Case 254/98 Judgment of 13 January 2000 (nyr) *383*

Schutzverband Gegen Unwesen in der Wirtschaft *v* Weinvertriebs GmbH Case 59/82 [1983] ECR 1217 *368*

Schwarze Case 16/65 [1965] ECR 1081 *300*

Scottish Football Association Case T–46/92 [1994] ECR II–1039 *263*

Scrivner Case 122/84 [1985] ECR 1027 *419*

Seadler (OJ L295 (1987)) *588*

Sebago Inc *v* GB-Unic SA Case C–173/98 [1999] 2 CMLR 1317 *571*

Segers *v* Bestuur van de Bedrijfsvereniging voor Bank-en Verzekeringswezen Case 79/85 [1986] ECR 2375 *435*

Semeraso Joined Cases 418–421, 460–462 and 464/93 and 9–11, 14–15, 23–24 and 332/94 [1996] ECR I–2975 *381, 387*

Sermide Case 106/83 [1984] ECR 4209 *186*

SES Case 88/76 [1977] ECR 709 *266*

Sevince Case C–192/89 [1990] ECR I–3461 *177, 216, 303*

SFEI Case C–39/94 [1996] ECR I–3547 *583*

SGEEM Case 370/89 [1992] ECR I–6211 *286*

Sheer Case 30/70 [1970] ECR 1197 *275*

Shell-Berre [1964] RDP 134 *318*

SIDE Case T–49/93 [1995] ECR II–2501 *597*

Silhouette Schmied GmbH & Co KG *v* Hartlauer Handelsgesellschaft MbH Case C–355/98 [1998] ECR I–4799 *569, 571*

Simet Cases 25 and 26/65 [1967] ECR 40 *259, 278*

Simmenthal Case 70/77 [1978] ECR 1453 *310*

Simmenthal Case 106/77 [1978] ECR 629 *168, 320*

Simmenthal Case 92/78 [1979] ECR 777 *278*

Simmenthal *v* Italian Minister for Finance Case 35/76 [1976] ECR 1871 *366*

SITPAC Onflhor Case C–27/90 [1991] ECR I–155 *169*

Skanavi Case C–193/94 [1996] ECR I–929 *421*

Sloman Neptun Cases C–72–73 [1993] RCT I–887 *584*

SNUPAT Cases 32 and 33/58 [1959] ECR 275 *261, 263*

SNUPAT Cases 42 and 49/59 [1961] ECR 101 *171, 184, 263, 283*

Sociaal Fonds *v* Brachfeld and Chougol Diamond Co Cases 2 and 3/69 [1969] ECR 211 *337*

Societá Italiana Vetro *v* Commission (Re Italian Flat Glass) Cases T–68/, 77 and 78/89 [1992] 5 CMLR 302 *505*

Société Anonyme Générale Sucrière Case 41/73 [1977] ECR 445 *144*

Société Bautiaa Cases C–197 and 252/94 [1996] ECR I–505 *322*

Société Cooperative d'Amélioration de l'Elevage et d'Insémination Artificielle du Béarn *v* Mialocq Case 271/81 [1983] ECR 2057 *602*

Société d'Importation E Leclerc-SIPLEC *v* TFI Publicité SA and M6 Publicité SA Case C–412/93 [1995] ECR I–179 *312, 380, 383*

Société Nationale des Importateurs de Vêtements [1989] AJDA 95 *318*

Société Technique Minière *v* Maschinenbau Ulm Case 56/65 [1966] ECR 235 *466, 472, 479, 484, 490*

Society for the Protection of Unborn Children (Ireland) *v* Grogan Case 159/90 [1991] ECR I–4685 *312*

Sofrimport SARL *v* Commission Case C–152/88 [1990] ECR I–2477 *270*

Solvay Case 27/88 [1989] ECR 3355 *541*

Solvay (OJ L152 (1991)) *467, 509*

Sonito *v* Commission Case C–87/89 [1990] ECR I–1981 *264*

Sotgiu *v* Deutsche Bundespost Case 152/73 [1974] ECR 153 *415, 419, 450*

Spagl Case C–189/89 [1990] ECR I–4539 *295*

Spain *v* Commission Case C–312/91 [1992] ECR I–4117 *264*

Spain (supported by Greece) v Council
(supported by France and the Commission)
Case C–350/92 [1995] ECR I–1995   *274,
557*

SPI and SAMI Cases 267–269/81 [1983] ECR 801
219

Spices [1978] 2 CMLR 116   *500*

Spijker Kwasten BV v Commission Case 231/82
[1983] ECR 259   *172, 268*

SPO Case T–29/92 [1995]ECR II–289   *72*

Spotti (Maria Chiara) Case 272/92 [1993] ECR
I–5185   *415, 417*

Stahlwerke Peine Salzgitter Case T–120/89
[1991] ECR II–279   *165*

Stahlwerke Peine-Salzgitter Case C–220/91
[1993] ECR I–2393   *165, 294*

Statens Kontrol v Larsen Case 142/77 [1978]
ECR 1543   *346*

Stauder v City of Ulm Case 26/69 [1969] ECR 419
110, 187

Ste Enka Case 38/77 [1977] ECR 2212   *173*

Steinhauser v City of Biarritz Case 197/84 [1985]
ECR 1819   *428*

Steymann Case 196/87 [1988] ECR 6159   *408*

Stichting Greenpeace Council (Greenpeace
International) and Others v Commission
Case C–321/95 [1998] ECR I–1651   *271*

Stoeckel Case C–345/89 [1991] ECR I–4047
163

Stoke-on-Trent City Council v B & Q plc Case
169/71 [1993] 1 CMLR 426; [1993] 1 All ER
481   *371, 381*

Stork v High Authority Case 1/59 [1959] ECR 17
187

Suiker Unie Cases 40, 50, 54–56, 111, 113 and
114/73 [1975] ECR 1663; [1976] 1 CMLR 295
465, 475, 517

Sutton (Eunice) Case C–66/95 [1997] ECR
I–2163   *321*

Svenska Journalistforbunder v Council Case
T–174/95 [1998] 3 CMLR 645   *156*

Syndicat des Hautes Graves de Bordeaux [1974]
RTDE 48   *195*

Syndicat Français de l'Express Interantional v La
Poste Case C–39/94 [1996] ECR I–3547
320, 583, 596

Synthetic Fibres [1985] 1 CMLR 787   *483, 498*

Sytraval and Brink's France Case T–95/94 [1995]
ECR II–2651   *597*

Tankstation 't Heukske and Boermans Joined
Cases 401 and 402/92 [1994] ECR I–2199
381, 382

TAO AFI Case C–322/91 [1992] ECR 6373   *263*

Tasca Case 65/75 [1976] ECR 291   *363*

Tawil-Albertini v Ministre des Affaires Sociales
Case C–154/93 [1994] ECR I–451   *430*

TEAM v Commission Case T–13/96 [1997] FCR
II–983   *297*

Tedeschi Case 5/77 [1977] ECR 1555   *302, 313*

Telemarsicabruzzo Cases C–320–322/90 [1993]
ECR I–393   *313*

Tepea Case 28/77 [1978] ECR 1391   *482*

Terhoeve Case C–18/95 [1999] ECR I–345
416, 444

Terrapin (Overseas) Ltd v Terranova Industrie CA
Kapferer and Co Case 119/75 [1976] ECR
1039   *564*

Terres Rouges Consultant SA v Commission
(supported by the Council, Spain and France)
Case T–47/95 [1997] ECR II–481   *270*

Tete (E) v EIB Case T–460/93 [1993] ECR
II–1257   *262*

Tetra Pak (No 1) (OJ L272 (1988))   *574*

Tetra Pak Rausing SA v Commission (No 1) Case
T–51/89 [1990] ECR II–309   *504, 509, 574*

Tetra Pak Rausing SA v Commission (No 2) Case
C–333/94 [1996] ECR I–5951; [1997] 4 CMLR
662   *520, 523, 525, 575*

Teuling Case 30/85 [1987] ECR 2497   *197*

Tezi Textiel Vase 59/84 [1986] ECR 887   *259*

The Netherlands v Commission Case 59/70
[1971] ECR 639   *283*

The Netherlands v Commission Case 13/72
[1973] ECR 27   *169*

The Netherlands v High Authority Case 6/54
[1956] ECR 201   *265*

The Netherlands v High Authority Case 25/59
[1960] ECR 723   *231*

The State v Jean Noël Royer Case 48/75 [1976]
ECR 497; [1976] 2 CMLR 619   *407, 409,
412, 414, 456*

Tiercé Ladbroke Case T–505/93 [1997] ECR
II–927   *572*

Tierce Ladbroke SA v Commission Case T–471/93
[1995] ECR II–2537   *169*

Timex Corporation v Council Case 264/82 [1985]
ECR 861   *269*

Tipp-Ex (OJ L222 (1987))   *482*

Tissier Case 35/85 [1986] ECR 1207   *313*

Toepfer v Commission Cases 106 and 107/63
[1965] ECR 525   *268, 272, 299*

Tombesi Cases C–304, 330, 342/94 and 224/95
[1997] ECR I–3561   *196*

Transocean Marine Paint Case 17/74 [1974] ECR
1063   *184, 275*

Transocean Marine Paint Association [1967] CMLR D9   *500*

Tremblay Case T–5/93 [1995] ECR II–185   *72*

TV 10 SA Case C–23/93 [1994] ECR I–4795   *188*

TWD Textilwerke Deggendorf GmbH Case C–188/92 [1994] ECR I–833   *280, 323*

Tymen (Regina and Robert) Case 269/80 [1981] ECR 3079   *221*

Tyri Lehtonen v Fédération Royale Belge des Sociétés de Basket-Ball ASBL Case C–176/96 Judgment of 13 April 2000 (nyr)   *408*

Uecker & Jacquet Cases 64 and 65/96 [1996] ECR I–3171   *409*

UIC Case T–14/93 [1995] ECR II–1503   *473*

Unger Case 75/63 [1964] ECR 347   *307*

UNICME Case 123/77 [1978] ECR 845   *272*

UNIDI (OJ L228 (1975))   *466*

Unifrex Case 281/82 [1984] ECR 1969   *288*

Unifruit Hellas Case T–489/93 [1994] ECR II–1201   *270, 286*

Union de Pequeños Agricultores Case T–173/98, order of 23 November 1999 (nyr)   *273*

Union Départmentale des Syndicats CGT de l'Aisne v SIDEF Conforama Case C–312/89 [1991] ECR I–997   *371*

Union Deutsche Lebensmittelwerke Case 97/85 [1987] ECR 2265   *268*

Union Nationale des Co-operative Agricoles de Céréales Cases 95–98/74 and 15 and 100/75 [1975] ECR 1615   *293*

Union Syndicale Case 175/73 [1974] ECR 917   *188*

United Brands v Commission Case 27/76 [1978] ECR 207   *507, 508, 512, 516, 517, 518, 519, 520, 525, 547*

United Kingdom v Council Case 68/86 [1988] ECR 855   *49, 184*

United Kingdom v Council (Re Working Time Directive) Case C–84/94 [1996] ECR I–5758   *72, 274*

Universtät Hamburg Case 216/82 [1983] ECR 2771   *280*

UPS Europe SA v Commission of the European Communities Case T–127/98 [2000] 4 CMLR 94   *539*

US v Addyston Pipe and Steel   *490*

US v El Du Pont de Nemours & Co (1956) 351 US 377   *511*

Usines à tubes de la Sarre Cases 1 and 14/57 [1957] ECR 201   *263, 279*

Usines de la Providence Case 29/83 [1965] ECR 1123   *290*

Vaessen/Morris [1979] 1 CMLR 511   *487*

Valsabbia Case 154/78 [1980] ECR 907   *188*

Valsabbia Case 209/83 [1984] ECR 3089   *259*

Van Binsbergen v Bestuur Van De Bedrijfsvereniging Voor De Mataalnijverheid Case 33/74 [1974] ECR 1299; [1973] 1 CMLR 298   *424, 427, 428, 443, 446*

Van Buynder Case C–152/94 [1995] ECR I–3981   *310*

Van den Burgh Lopik v Commission Case 265/85 [1987] ECR 1155   *291*

Van der Kooy v Commission Case 67/85 [1986] ECR 219   *586*

Van der Veldt Case 17/93 [1994] ECR I–3537   *387*

Van Duyn Case 41/74 [1974] ECR 1337   *183, 204, 453, 454*

Van Gend en Loos v Netherlands Case 26/62 [1963] ECR 1   *164, 191, 196, 198, 310, 316, 336*

Van Lackmuller Case 43/59 [1960] ECR 933   *184*

Van Landewyck Joined Cases 209–215 and 218/78 [1980] ECR 3125   *464*

Van Landshoot Case 300/86 [1988] ECR 3443   *325*

Van Megen Sports Group Case 49/95 [1996] ECR II–1799   *482*

Van Poucke (Guido) Case C–71/93 [1994] ECR I–1101   *407*

Van Schaik Case C–55/93 [1994] ECR I–4837   *332*

Van Tiggele Case 82/77 [1978] ECR 25   *585*

Van Wesemael Cases 110 and 111/78 [1979] ECR 35   *446*

Van Zuylen Frères v Hag (No 1) Case 192/73 [1974] ECR 731   *567*

Vanacker (Jose) Case C–37/92 [1993] ECR I–494   *308*

Vander Elst v Office des Migrations Internationales Case C–43/93 [1994] ECR I–3803   *443*

Vandeweghe Case 130/73 [1973] ECR 1329   *303*

Vaneetveld Case C–316/93 [1994] ECR I–763   *206, 314*

Variola Case 34/73 [1973] ECR 981   *194*

Vassen-Göbbels Case 61/65 [1966] ECR 377   *303, 304*

VAT Directives, Re [1982] 1 CMLR 525   *318*

VBBB/VBVB [1982] 2 CMLR 344   *501*

Verband der Sachversierer Case 45/85 [1987] ECR 405   *466*

Verband Sozialer Wettbewerb Case 315/92 [1994] ECR I–317   *364*

Verbond van Nederlandse Ondernemingen Case 51/76 [1977] ECR 113   *200, 205*

Vereeniging van Cementhandelaren Case 8/72 [1972] ECR 977   *467, 474, 480*

Vereiniging van Exporters Cases T–481 and 483/93 [1995] ECR II–2941   *270*

Vereinigt Familiapress Zeitungsverlags-und Vertriebs GmbH *v* Henrich Bauer Verlag Case C–368/95 [1997] ECR I–3689   *372, 382*

Verli Wallace Case 159/82 [1983] ECR 2711   *184*

Verre Plat (OJ L33 (1989))   *467*

Vichy Case T–19/91 [1992] ECR II–415   *491*

Vico-Toshiba (OJ L287 (1991))   *482*

Victoria Film A/S Case C–134/97 [1999] 1 CMLR 279   *304*

Vifka (OJ L291 (1986))   *500*

Viho Europe Case 73/95P [1996] ECR I–5457   *465*

Villeroy Boch (OJ L376 (1985))   *493*

Vimpoltu (OJ L200 (1983))   *479*

Vlassopoulou Case C–340/89 [1991] ECR I–2357   *439*

Völk *v* Vervaecke Case 5/69 [1969] ECR 295   *467*

Volker Graf and Filzmoser Maschinenbau GmbH Case C–190/98 Judgment of 27 January 2000 (nyr)   *416, 417*

Volker Steen Case C–332/90 [1992] ECR I–341   *429*

Volkswagen *v* Commission Case T–62/98 Judgment of 6 July 2000 (nyr)   *549*

Volkswagen AG and Others [1998] 5 CMLR 33   *549*

Volvo *v* Veng Case 238/87 [1989] Case 238/87 [1989] 4 CMLR 122   *516, 574*

Von Colson and Kamann Case 14/83 [1984] ECR 1891   *205, 209, 240*

Von Deetzen Case 170/86 [1988[ECR 2355   *295*

Voogd Vleesimporten Export BV Case C–151/93 [1994] ECR I–4915   *313*

Vreugdenhil Case C–282/90 [1992] ECR I–1962   *288, 294*

Wachauf Case 5/88 [1989] ECR 2609   *188, 219*

Wagamama Ltd *v* City Centre Restaurants [1995] FSR 713   *565*

Wagner Miret *v* Fondo de Garantia Salarial Case C–334/92 [1995] 2 CMLR 49   *211*

Walker (John) Case 243/84 [1986] ECR 875   *350*

Walrave and Koch *v* Association Union Cycliste Internationale Case 36/74 [1974] ECR 1405   *202, 407, 409*

Walt Wilhelm *v* Bundeskartellamt Case 14/68 [1969] ECR 15   *202, 218, 460, 461*

Walter Rau Lebensmittelwerke *v* De Smedt Case 261/81 [1987] ECR 1069   *372*

Watson and Belmann Case 118/75 [1976] ECR 1185   *414*

Webb Case 279/80 [1981] ECR 3305   *445, 446*

Webb *v* EMO Air Cargo (No 2) [1995] 4 All ER 577   *214*

Werhahn Hansamuhle Cases 63–69/72 [1973] ECR 1229   *184, 286, 293*

Westzuker Case 57/72 [1973] ECR 321   *126, 159*

Wijsenbeek (Florus Ariël) Case C–378/97 [1999] ECR I–6207   *398*

Wiljo Case C–178/95 [1997] ECR I–585   *280*

Windsurfing International Case 193/83 [1986] ECR 611   *467, 482*

Wood Pulp Cartel *see* Ahlström and Others *v* Commission

Worms Case 18/60 [1962] ECR 401   *298*

Wünsche Case 69/85 [1986] ECR 947   *302, 322*

Württembergische Milchverwertung-Sudmilch *v* Ugliola Case 15/69 [1969] ECR 363   *414*

Wybot Case 149/85 [1986] ECR 2403   *165, 262*

X Case 12/68 [1969] ECR 116   *184*

X *v* Commission Case C–404/92P [1994] ECR I–4737   *188*

X/Open Group (OJ L35 (1987))   *501*

Yves Rocher Case 126/91 [1993] ECR 2361   *375*

Yves St Laurent et Givenchy Cases T–19 and 88/92 [1996] ECR II–1851   *561–562*

Zanetti Case C–359/88 [1990] ECRI–1509   *196*

Zinc Cartel [1985] 2 CMLR 108   *480*

Zoulika Krid Case C–103/94 [1995] ECR I–719   *216*

Zuckerfabrik Schoppenstadt *v* Council Case 5/71 [1971] ECR 975   *285, 288, 292*

Zuckerfabrik Suderdithmarschen *v* Hauptzollamt Itzehoe Cases C–143/88 and 92/89 [1991] ECR I–415   *218, 325, 326*

Zuckerfabrik Watenstedt Case 6/88 [1968] ECR 595   *267*

Zuchner (Gerard) *v* Bayerische Vereinsbank Case 172/80 [1981] ECR 2021   *466, 547*

Zwartveld Case C–2/88 [1990] ECR I–3365   *230*

Table of Treaties, Conventions, Statutes and Other Materials

Agreement on Social Policy   *89, 90*

Agreement on the Community Patent 1989
     179

Amsterdam Treaty *see* Treaty of Amsterdam 1997

Association Agreement with Cyprus 1972   *43*

Association Agreement with Malta 1973   *43*

Association Agreement with Turkey 1964   *42*

Asylum and Immigration Appeals Act 1993
     84

Atlantic Charter 1942   *14, 23*

Austrian Law on Employees (Angestelltengesetz)
          art 23(1)   *416*
          art 23(7)   *416*

Brussels Convention on Jurisdiction and the
     Enforcement of Judgments in Civil and
     Commercial Matters 1968   *34, 86, 87, 146,
     179, 303*

Brussels Treaty 1948   *18*

Budgetary Treaty 1970   *55, 134, 167*

Budgetary Treaty 1975   *55, 134, 167*

Carriers Liability Act 1987   *84*

Commission Decisions
          89/515/EEC   *549*
          94/90/CS/EC/EA   *156*
          94/810   *544*
          98/273/EC   *549*
          13 July 1994   *476*

Commission Notice of 24 December 1992
     488

Commission Notice of 29 July 1968   *488*

Commission Notice on Agreements of Minor
     Importance 1997   *467, 468*

Commission Notice on Calculation of Turnover
     under the Merger Regulation   *527*

Commission Notice on Co-operation between the
     National Competition Authorities and the
     Commission in the Application of arts 81 and
     82 EC 1997   *536, 552, 553, 554*

Commission Notice on the Concept of
     Concentration under the Merger Regulation
     527

Commission Notice on the Concept of Full
     Function Joint Ventures under the Merger
     Regulation   *527*

Commission Notice on the Concept of
     Undertakings Concerned under the Merger
     Regulation   *527*

Commission Notice on the Dominance of the
     Relevant Market for the Purposes of
     Community Competition Law 1997   *509,
     510, 511, 512, 517*

Commission Notice on the Internal Rules of
     Procedure for Processing Requests for Access
     to the File in Competition Matters 1997
     545

Commission Notice Regarding Fining Policy
     1998   *548*

Commission Notice Regarding Restrictions
     Ancillary to Concentrations   *527*

Commission Recommendation 91/131   *124*

Commission Regulation
          2195/69   *203*

Common Strategy (1999/414/CFSP)   *96*

Common Strategy (1999/877/CFSP)   *96*

Communication of 5 June 1996   *253*

Communication of 10 December 1996   *507*

Communication of 8 January 1997   *253*

Communication on Taxation in the European
     Union   *354*

Community Charter of the Fundamental Social
     Rights of Workers 1989   *89*

Community Patent Convention 1975   *179, 576*
          art 2   *303*
          art 3   *303*
          art 73   *181*

Company Law Directives
          First Company Law Directive *see* EC
          Directive 68/151
          Fifth Directive on Public Limited
          Company Structure   *431*
          Ninth Directive on Groups Containing
          Public Company Subsidiaries   *431*
          Tenth Directive on Cross-border Mergers
          of Public Companies   *431*
          Thirteenth Directive on Takeovers   *431*

Concordat of Worms 1122   *5*

Convention Determining the State Responsible
     for Examining Applications for Asylum
     Lodged in One of the Member States of the
     European Communities 1990 *see* Dublin
     Convention

Convention on Certain Institutions Common to
     the European Communities 1957   *50, 106,
     137, 166*

Convention on Mutual Assistance and Co-
     operation between Customs Administrations
     334

Convention on Mutual Recognition of Companies and Legal Persons 1968   *179, 303, 432*
Convention on the Legal Implications of the Return of Sarre to the Federal Republic of Germany 1957   *166*
Convention on the Participation of Foreigners in Public Life at Local Level 1992   *399*
Convention Relating to the Procedure of Insolvency 1995   *179*
Council Decisions
    65/271   *215*
    70/243   *56*
    76/787   *55, 129*
      art 1   *55*
    87/373   *127*
    88/591   *146*
    91/341/EEC   *334*
    91/440   *271*
    91/482/EEC   *326*
    93/371   *156, 157, 158*
      art 4(1)   *157*
    93/662/EC   *115*
    94/262   *404*
      art 2(2)   *404*
    95/2   *114*
    95/533/EC   *402*
    97/803/EC   *326*
    99/468/EC   *127, 128, 159*
      art 4   *127*
      art 5   *127, 128*
      art 7   *159*
    99/494/EC/CS/EA   *121*
    2000/44/EC/CS/EA   *122*
    26 November 1974   *140*
    20 September 1976   *167*
    8 June 1993   *147*
    29 October 1993   *109*
    29 March 1994   *40, 117*
    26 April 1999   *147*
Council Directives
    64/221   *205, 406, 435, 452, 453, 455, 456*
      art 2(2)   *456*
      art 3   *454*
      art 3(1)   *205, 453, 454, 455*
      art 3(2)   *455*
      art 4   *456*
      arts 5–9   *456*
      art 5   *457*
      art 6   *457*
      art 7   *457*
      art 8   *457, 458*
      art 9   *457, 458*

Council Directives, 64/221 (*contd.*)
    art 9(1)   *457, 458*
    art 9(2)   *457, 458*
    Annex   *456*
    Part II   *456*
  68/151/EEC   *122*
  76/207   *208, 209, 210, 214, 215*
    art 6   *209, 210*
  78/660/EEC   *122*
  80/987   *223*
  81/389   *342, 343*
  85/337/EEC   *244*
  85/375
    art 7   *240*
  89/104/EEC   *560, 565, 566, 570*
    art 4(1)(b)   *564, 565*
    art 5   *560, 561, 562*
    art 5(1)(b)   *566, 567*
    art 6   *560, 561, 562*
    art 6(1)(c)   *563*
    art 7   *560, 561, 562*
    art 7(1)   *570*
    art 7(2)   *561, 563*
  89/552   *245*
  90/314/EEC   *228, 229*
    art 7   *228, 229*
  90/364   *239*
  90/365   *239*
  90/476/EEC   *40*
  93/104   *72, 73*
    art 5   *72*
    art 6(2)   *72*
    art 7   *72*
  98/48/EC   *329*
Council Regulations
  1975/69   *203*
  1293/79   *152*
  2658/87   *333*
  3954/87   *265*
  2045/89   *271*
  2684/90   *40*
  2913/92   *159, 333*
  404/93   *326*
  40/94
    art 63   *262*
  2100/94
    art 73   *262*
    art 74   *262*
  408/97   *136*
  574/99   *81*
  659/1999   *594, 595, 597, 598, 600*
    art 10   *597*
    art 22   *597*
  994/98   *600*

Council Regulations (*contd.*)
    29 February 1968   *110*
Council Resolution at The Hague 1976   *250, 251*
    Annex VI   *250*
Council Resolution of 7 May 1985   *329, 364*
Customs Consolidation Act 1876   *389*

Decision of the Representatives of the
    Governments of the Member States on the
    Location of Seats of Certain Bodies and
    Departments 1993   *150*
Decisions *see also* Commission Decisions;
    Council Decisions; European Parliament
    Decisions; High Authority Decision
        71/224   *575*
        85/257   *56*
        88/376   *56*
        93/591   *113*
        3632/93   *593*
        3052/95   *329*
        96/409/CFSP   *402*
        2496/96/ECSC   *593*
        2228/97/EC   *593*
        1999/64/EA   *592*
        182/1999/EC   *592*
        20 September 1976   *180*
        12 May 1960   *180*
        14 May 1962   *180*
        8 April 1965   *108*
        18 December 1978   *180*
        12 December 1992   *108, 109*
Declaration Concerning the Action Programme
    in the Field of Environment   *180*
Declaration of Anglo-French Union 1940   *8*
Declaration of Moscow 1943   *14*
Declaration on European Identity 1973   *32*
Declaration on Police Co-operation 1992   *103*
Declaration on the Abolition of the Death Penalty
    1997   89
Denmark law of 11 October 1972
    art 3   *194*
Draft Convention on the Crossing of External
    Borders 1991   *86*
Dublin Convention 1990   *85*
    art 18   *85*

EC Directives *see also* Council Directives
    64/427   *430*
    68/151   *210, 211, 431*
        art 11   *210*
    68/360   *317, 406, 411, 412*
        art 1   *409*

EC Directives, 68/360 (*contd.*)
    art 2   *413*
    art 3(2)   *413*
    art 4   *409*
    art 4(1)   *412*
    art 4(2)   *412*
    art 4(3)(c)   *413*
    art 4(3)(d)   *413*
    art 4(3)(e)   *413*
    70/50   *361*
    art 2(1)   *361*
    art 2(3)   *361*
    art 3   *361*
    70/254   *375*
    73/148   *411, 435*
    art 1(c)   *409*
    art 4   *409*
    73/173   *206*
    75/34   *435*
    75/442   *195, 196*
    76/756/EEC   *68*
    76/768/EEC   *382, 383*
    77/128   *206*
    78/176   *246*
    78/456   *243*
    78/686/EEC   *430*
    78/1026   *429*
    80/723   *605*
    80/777/EEC   *213*
    80/897   *211*
    80/1263   *421, 422*
    82/489/EEC   *429*
    83/189   *329, 373*
    83/643   *341*
    87/328   *376*
    88/301   *605*
    88/361   *330*
    89/48/EEC   *437, 438, 439*
    89/106   *246*
    90/270   *211, 212*
    90/364/EEC   *395, 396*
    art 3   *395*
    90/365/EEC   *395, 396*
    art 3   *395*
    90/366/EEC   *395, 396*
    art 4   *395*
    90/388   *605*
    90/434/EEC   *356*
    90/435/EEC   *356*
    90/436/EEC   *356*
    90/531
    art 8(1)   *226*
    90/619   *442*

EC Directives (*contd.*)
  91/156 *195, 196*
    art 1 *196*
  91/439 *421, 422*
  92/12/EEC *355*
  92/51/EEC *437, 438, 439*
  92/79/EEC *355*
  92/82/EEC *355*
  92/84/EEC *355*
  92/108/EEC *355*
  93/7/EC *392*
  93/96/EC *395*
  93/109/EC *129, 401*
  94/74/EC *355*
  94/80 *399, 400*
    art 2(1) *400*
    art 5(3) *400*
    Annex *400*
  95/51 *605*
  96/92 *603*
  96/71/EC *444*
  96/95/EC *354*
  96/99/EC *355*
  97/26 *422*
  98/5/EC *440*
  98/71 *579, 580*
  99/42/EC *437, 438*
EC Regulations *see also* Council Regulations;
  Commission Regulation
  1/58 *110*
  17/62 *124, 494, 533, 536, 537, 540,*
  543, 598
    art 1 *502*
    art 3 *538, 547*
    art 3(2)(b) *538*
    art 4(2) *537*
    art 8(3) *547*
    art 11 *542*
    art 11(2) *541*
    art 11(3) *547*
    art 11(5) *547*
    art 12 *542, 547*
    art 13 *547*
    art 14 *124, 542, 543, 547*
    art 14(1) *542*
    art 14(3) *543, 547*
    art 14(5) *543*
    art 14(6) *543, 544*
    art 15(2) *547*
    art 19 *544*
    art 19(3) *497*
    art 20 *541*
    art 20(2) *541*
  20/62 *203, 204*

EC Regulations (*contd.*)
  99/63
    art 6 *540*
    art 9(2) *544*
  19/65 *494*
  67/67 *494*
  121/67 *204*
  1612/68 *248, 317, 406, 410, 411, 417,*
  435
    arts 1–6 *417*
    art 3 *417*
    art 3(1) *417*
    art 4 *417*
    art 5 *418*
    art 6 *418*
    art 6(2) *418*
    art 7 *418*
    art 7(1) *415, 418*
    art 7(2) *412, 418, 419, 420*
    art 7(3) *419, 420*
    art 7(4) *421*
    art 8 *421*
    art 8(1) *421*
    art 9 *421*
    art 10 *409*
    art 10(1) *409, 412*
    art 10(1)(a) *409*
    art 10(1)(b) *409*
    art 10(2) *409*
    art 10(3) *409*
    art 11 *412*
    art 12 *411, 412*
    Title II *418, 421*
  459/70 *216*
  565/70 *216*
  686/70 *216*
  1251/70 *406, 422, 435*
    art 2 *423*
    art 2(1) *422*
    art 2(2) *423*
    art 3 *423*
    art 3(2) *423*
    art 4 *423*
    art 5 *423*
  1463/70 *247, 248*
  1408/71 *407*
  907/73 *53*
  101/76
    art 2 *250*
    art 3 *250*
  1172/76 *46*
  1984/83
    art 1 *485*

EC Regulations (*contd.*)
2137/85   *431*
2349/84   *572*
4064/89   *124, 459, 460, 462, 489, 509, 526, 527, 528, 529, 530, 531, 532, 533, 534*
    art 1(2)   *529*
    art 2   *530*
    art 2(4)   *531, 535*
    art 3   *528*
    art 3(2)   *531*
    art 11   *124*
    art 12   *124*
    art 23   *528*
330/91   *360*
82/92   *333*
3911/92   *392*
2187/93   *264*
    art 8   *264*
    art 14   *264*
40/94   *578, 579*
    art 7(1)(c)   *578, 579*
    art 7(3)   *578, 579*
    art 59   *578*
    art 60(1)   *578*
    art 60(2)   *578*
    art 62(1)   *579*
    art 63(3)   *579*
2317/95   *81*
240/96   *272, 573*
    art 1   *272*
    art 2(1)   *272*
    art 3   *272*
307/97   *169, 170*
308/97   *169, 70*
1310/97/EC   *527, 529, 531, 532, 533*
447/98   *527, 533*
994/98   *588, 589, 590*
EC Treaty 1957   *23, 24, 26, 27, 30, 45, 47, 48, 49, 54, 61, 64, 66, 68, 69, 70. 71, 73, 86, 88, 89, 91, 92, 93, 100, 101, 105, 106, 108, 111, 112, 113, 114, 118, 119, 123, 124, 125, 126, 135, 137, 140, 141, 145, 146, 161, 162, 163, 164, 165, 166, 167, 169, 170, 172, 176, 177, 178, 179, 180, 181, 182, 187, 192, 193, 194, 195, 198, 199, 201, 202, 203, 204, 207, 216, 217, 218, 219, 222, 223, 230, 231, 232, 233, 234, 235, 236, 244, 245, 247, 248, 249, 250, 251, 253, 255, 258, 261, 262, 265, 274, 275, 278, 280, 281, 283, 284, 292, 293, 301, 302, 321, 322, 329, 332, 339, 344, 351, 359, 360, 379, 393, 394, 395, 397, 398, 400, 403, 407, 424, 427, 441, 442, 444, 448, 455, 460, 471,*

EC Treaty 1957 (*contd.*)
    475, 504, 526, 527, 555, 557, 579, 581, 582, 583, 589, 593, 594, 598, 599, 602, 603, 604
    art 2   *48, 89, 91, 203, 526*
    art 3   *48, 89, 91*
    art 3   *218*
    art 3(c)   *359*
    art 3(g)   *459, 526*
    art 5   *70, 71, 72, 73, 274*
    art 5(1)   *257*
    art 7   *106, 179, 274*
    art 7(1)   *111, 186*
    art 7(2)   *107*
    art 8   *107*
    art 9   *107*
    art 10   *124, 172, 173, 175, 181, 186, 195, 197, 203, 209, 212, 214, 217, 223, 234, 235, 236, 241, 250, 252, 273, 358, 359*
    art 12   *54, 89, 154, 178, 186, 202, 218, 227, 271, 379, 396, 397, 407, 425, 427, 428, 448, 549, 556*
    art 13   *89*
    art 14   *329, 359, 398*
    art 14(2)   *59*
    art 16(1)   *398*
    arts 17–22   *393*
    art 17   *394, 396, 397*
    art 17(1)   *394*
    art 17(2)   *393*
    art 18   *88, 116, 396, 397, 398, 399*
    art 18(1)   *395*
    art 18(2)   *154, 395, 396*
    art 19   *116, 152, 399*
    art 19(1)   *399*
    art 19(2)   *399, 401*
    art 20   *98, 401, 402, 403*
    art 21   *403*
    art 22   *116, 152, 167, 396, 405*
    art 23   *204, 330, 332, 336*
    art 24   *330*
    art 25   *198, 199, 201, 215, 220, 244, 330, 335, 336, 337, 338, 339, 340, 341, 342, 351, 352, 353, 366*
    art 26   *117, 333*
    art 28   *159, 202, 220, 224, 234, 317, 318, 330, 353, 357, 358, 359, 360, 361, 362, 363, 364, 365, 366, 367, 368, 370, 371, 372, 374, 375, 376, 379, 380, 381, 382, 383, 384, 386, 388, 389, 391, 466, 498, 555, 556, 557, 558, 560, 562, 564, 576, 577, 601, 603*
    art 29   *330, 339, 357, 358, 360, 365, 377, 378, 379, 386, 557, 558, 601, 603*

EC Treaty 1957 (*contd.*)

art 30   *255, 329, 330, 343, 357, 358,*
365, 366, 371, 384, 386, 387, 388, 389,
390, 391, 392, 555, 557, 558, 560, 562,
564, 568
art 31   *318, 459, 601, 602, 603*
art 31(1)   *202, 601, 602*
art 31(2)   *202, 601, 602*
art 34(3)   *186, 219*
art 37   *117, 136, 169, 170, 219*
art 39   *54, 202, 205, 248, 389, 406, 407,*
408, 409, 410, 414, 416, 417, 436, 438,
441, 450, 455
art 39(1)   *406, 407*
art 39)2)   *406, 407, 414, 415*
art 39(3)   *205, 406, 409, 452*
art 39(3)(a)   *406*
art 39(3)(b)   *406*
art 39(3)(c)   *406*
art 39(3)(d)   *406*
art 39(4)   *400, 406, 450, 451*
art 40   *168, 406*
art 42   *54, 90, 154*
arts 43–49   *202*
arts 43–55   *424–429*
art 43   *202, 411, 424, 426, 428, 429,*
431, 432, 433, 434, 435, 441, 450, 455
art 43(2)   *152*
art 44(2)   *426*
art 44(2)(g)   *431*
art 45   *117, 400, 426, 427, 431, 450,*
451
art 46   *433*
art 46(1)   *452*
art 46(2)   *116, 154*
art 47(1)   *426*
art 47(2)   *154*
art 48   *425, 431, 433, 434*
art 48(2)   *178*
art 49   *80, 117, 202, 378, 397, 424, 426,*
427, 428, 443, 444, 455
art 50   *202, 427, 441, 442, 443, 444*
art 56   *378*
art 57   *117*
art 59   *117*
art 60   *117*
art 61(e)   *88*
art 62   *81, 168*
art 63   *83*
art 64   *83*
art 65   *86, 87*
art 68   *80, 302*
art 71   *149, 154*

EC Treaty 1957 (*contd.*)

art 75   *117*
art 79   *150*
art 80   *117, 149, 154*
art 81   *71, 164, 259, 269, 276, 459, 460,*
462, 465, 466, 469–503, 504, 505, 509,
527, 528, 529, 531, 535, 536, 547, 548,
549, 552, 553, 554, 555, 572, 573, 586,
587
art 81(1)   *462, 467, 468, 469, 470, 471,*
472, 473, 474, 475, 476, 477, 480, 481,
482, 483, 484, 485, 486, 487, 488, 489,
490, 491, 492, 493, 494, 495, 496, 497,
502, 503, 504, 505, 507, 526, 531, 537,
538, 541, 549, 550, 552, 554, 571, 572,
573
art 81(1)(a)   *469, 480*
art 81(1)(b)   *469, 483*
art 81(1)(c)   *469, 484*
art 81(1)(d)   *469, 486*
art 81(1)(e)   *469*
art 81(2)   *469, 470, 502, 503, 527*
art 81(3)   *461, 466, 470, 487, 488, 489,*
493, 494, 495, 497, 498, 502, 503, 504,
527, 536, 537, 553, 572
art 82   *71, 269, 282, 459, 460, 465, 466,*
487, 489, 497, 504–525, 526, 528, 529,
531, 536, 537, 538, 539, 541, 547, 548,
549, 552, 553, 554, 555, 572, 573, 574,
575, 584, 586, 587
art 82(a)   *504, 518*
art 82(b)   *504, 518*
art 82(c)   *504, 518*
art 82(d)   *504, 518, 523, 575*
art 83   *168, 536*
art 86   *539, 602*
art 86(1)   *602*
art 86(2)   *203, 264, 466, 602, 603, 604,*
605
art 86(3)   *605*
art 87   *117, 203, 339, 353, 459, 539,*
582, 584, 585, 586, 587, 588, 589, 599,
600
art 87(1)   *582, 584, 585, 588, 600*
art 87(2)   *539, 582, 588*
art 87(2)(a)   *582, 588*
art 87(2)(b)   *582, 589*
art 87(2)(c)   *582, 589*
art 87(3)   *582, 589, 590, 592*
art 87(3)(a)   *582, 590, 591, 592*
art 87(3)(b)   *582, 591*
art 87(3)(c)   *582, 589, 592*
art 87(3)(d)   *582, 593*

EC Treaty 1957 (*contd.*)

art 87(3)(e)   *582, 594*

art 88   *323, 459, 539, 581, 582, 588, 589, 594, 600*

art 88(1)   *203, 594*

art 88(2)   *203, 231, 264, 269, 594, 595, 596, 597*

art 88(3)   *202, 596, 599*

art 89   *117, 152, 459, 582, 600*

art 90   *110, 201, 246, 330, 339, 344, 345. 346, 347, 348, 349, 351, 352, 353*

art 90(1)   *202, 344, 345, 348, 350, 351*

art 90(2)   *202, 344, 345, 350, 351*

art 90(3)   *200, 202*

art 91(1)   *597*

art 92   *117*

art 92(2)   *597*

art 92(3)   *597*

art 93   *116*

art 93(2)   *599*

art 94   *72, 116, 329*

art 95   *89, 265, 329*

art 95(4)   *124, 231*

art 95(9)   *255*

art 96   *117*

art 97   *124, 203*

art 98   *587*

art 99   *117, 587*

art 99(2)   *112*

arts 104–124   *75*

art 104   *75, 76, 117, 125*

art 104(2)   *75*

art 104(11)   *75*

art 105(1)   *78*

art 105(2)   *78*

art 105(5)   *116*

art 105(6)   *155*

art 106(5)   *155*

art 107   *117, 125*

art 107(2)   *78*

art 107(3)   *78*

art 107(5)   *167*

art 108   *203*

art 110   *168*

art 111   *117*

art 111(1)   *116, 152*

art 114   *117, 150*

art 115   *125*

art 117   *117*

art 119   *117, 125*

art 120   *117, 125*

art 121   *113, 117*

art 121(1)–(4)   *153*

EC Treaty 1957 (*contd.*)

art 122   *113, 117*

art 122(1)   *78*

art 122(2)   *153*

art 126(2)   *91*

art 128   *149*

art 129   *149, 154*

art 132   *117*

art 133   *117, 150*

art 135   *154, 334*

arts 136–143   *149*

art 136   *203*

arts 137–140   *90*

art 137   *90, 203*

art 137(2)   *154*

art 138   *90*

art 138(2)   *72*

art 139   *90*

art 141   *54, 89, 90, 149, 154, 186, 201, 202*

art 141(3)   *116*

art 142   *90*

art 145   *118*

art 147   *150*

art 148   *149, 154*

art 150   *149*

art 150(4)   *154*

art 151   *593*

art 151(1)   *593*

art 151(5)   *116, 593*

art 152   *149, 154*

art 152(4)   *116*

art 156   *154*

art 157(3)   *116*

art 159   *116*

art 161(1)   *155*

art 162   *154*

art 166   *117*

art 166(1)   *116*

art 166(2)   *116*

art 171   *592*

art 172   *116, 154*

art 174   *170*

art 174(2)   *170*

art 175   *149, 169, 170*

art 175(1)   *154*

art 179   *154*

art 182   *30*

art 190   *116, 156, 167*

art 190(1)   *129*

art 190(4)   *155*

art 191   *131, 135*

art 192(2)   *125, 151*

EC Treaty 1957 (*contd.*)

art 193   *132*
art 194   *133, 403*
art 195   *404*
art 196   *152*
art 197   *132*
art 199   *109, 131*
art 200   *133*
art 201   *120, 133, 134*
art 202   *118, 126*
art 203   *113, 114*
art 205(1)   *116*
art 205(2)   *117, 151*
art 205(3)   *116*
art 206   *116*
art 207   *116*
art 207(1)   *115*
art 207(2)   *114*
art 208   *116, 118, 125, 151*
art 209   *116, 150*
art 210   *117*
art 211   *123, 124, 126, 158, 168, 230, 236, 265*
art 213   *122*
art 213(1)   *119*
art 213(2)   *119*
art 214   *121, 179, 298*
art 214(2)   *120, 133*
art 214(3)   *133*
art 215(2)   *295*
art 216   *120*
art 217   *120*
art 219   *120, 122*
art 220   *87, 145, 162, 182*
art 221   *140, 167*
art 222   *138*
art 223   *138, 179*
art 225   *92, 107, 147, 156*
art 225(1)   *148*
art 225(3)   *155*
art 226   *122, 124, 145, 175, 181, 197, 199, 223, 230, 231, 232, 233, 234, 235, 236, 237, 238, 239, 240, 241, 242, 243, 244, 245, 246, 248, 249, 250, 251, 252, 253, 255, 264, 265, 284, 315, 318, 603, 605*
art 226(1)   *234*
art 227   *145, 181, 199, 230, 231, 245, 249, 250, 251, 252, 253, 255*
art 227(2)   *92*
art 228   *223, 252, 253, 255*
art 228(1)   *234, 251*
art 228(2)   *253, 254, 255*
art 229   *145*

EC Treaty 1957 (*contd.*)

art 230   *31, 72, 111, 124, 142, 143, 145, 147, 148, 175, 177, 181, 234, 242, 243, 245, 257, 258, 259, 260, 261, 262, 263, 264, 265, 266, 267, 270, 271, 272, 273, 274, 277, 278, 279, 280, 281, 282, 283, 284, 285, 286, 294, 295, 301, 323, 326, 327, 527, 540, 542, 549, 551*
art 230(1)   *257, 258*
art 230(2)   *258, 259, 273*
art 230(3)   *258, 259*
art 230(4)   *258, 266, 271*
art 230(5)   *258, 265, 280, 286*
art 231   *257, 275, 324*
art 231(1)   *275*
art 231(2)   *275*
art 232   *124, 145, 147, 234, 245, 257, 276, 281, 282, 283, 284, 285, 286, 538, 539*
art 232(1)   *281*
art 232(2)   *281*
art 232(3)   *281*
art 232(4)   *281*
art 233   *257, 276, 277, 285, 551*
art 233(1)   *281*
art 234   *32, 72, 74, 104, 107, 142, 146, 148, 181, 199, 200, 201, 203, 204, 205, 206, 208, 210, 214, 215, 216, 217, 219, 220, 223, 233, 238, 245, 251, 273, 280, 288, 300–328*
art 234(1)   *300*
art 234(1)(a)   *300*
art 234(1)(b)   *300*
art 234(1)(c)   *300, 307, 322*
art 234(2)   *300, 310, 315, 317, 319*
art 234(3)   *233, 300, 314, 315, 317, 318*
art 235   *145, 147, 257, 285, 286*
art 236   *145, 147*
art 237   *145, 262*
art 238   *145*
art 239   *145, 557*
art 241   *145, 164, 242, 243, 257, 278, 279, 280, 530*
art 241(4)   *273*
art 243   *145, 326*
art 245   *118, 167*
art 247   *117*
art 249   *34, 161, 168, 172, 173, 174, 175, 176, 192, 194, 195, 197, 198, 204, 205, 212, 215, 217, 218, 241, 247, 262, 302, 318*
art 249(3)   *249*
art 250   *116, 125*

EC Treaty 1957 (*contd.*)

art 251   *59, 72, 92, 127, 128, 135, 136, 153, 170, 260, 286, 334, 592*

art 251(1)   *153*

art 251(2)   *153*

art 251(2)(a)   *153*

art 251(2)(b)   *153*

art 251(2)(c)   *153*

art 251(3)   *153*

art 251(4)   *116, 125, 153*

art 251(5)   *116, 125, 154*

art 251(6)   *154*

art 251(7)   *154*

art 252   *72, 116, 169*

art 253   *109, 169, 274*

art 254   *116, 171, 196*

art 254(3)   *171*

art 255   *154*

art 256   *215*

arts 257–262   *148*

art 258   *117, 118*

arts 263–265   *149*

art 265(1)   *149*

art 268   *134*

art 269   *55, 116, 167*

art 272(9)   *135*

art 273   *117, 135*

art 276   *117, 118*

art 280   *80, 93, 116, 155*

art 284   *116, 124*

art 285   *116, 155*

art 286   *89, 116, 155*

art 288   *147, 285*

art 288(2)   *145, 175, 178, 183, 224, 234, 257, 264, 276, 285, 286, 288, 289, 290, 293, 294, 296, 297, 298, 299, 402*

art 288(3)   *286*

art 289   *108, 109, 179*

art 293   *34, 104, 178, 179, 303, 432*

art 295   *555, 557*

art 296   *124, 256*

art 297   *124, 256*

art 298   *181, 231, 256*

art 299(2)   *116*

art 299(3)   *307*

art 300   *117, 129, 150, 163*

art 300(4)   *129*

art 300(6)   *146*

art 300(7)   *177, 178*

art 301   *117*

art 302   *129*

art 303   *129*

art 303(3)   *136, 137, 155*

EC Treaty 1957 (*contd.*)

art 304   *129*

art 305   *164*

art 306   *163*

art 307   *163, 233*

art 308   *48, 72, 116, 167*

art 310   *30, 155*

art 311   *165*

art 314   *110*

Part Two   *167*

Title IV   *80, 81, 87, 88, 101, 104, 116, 125, 145, 203, 302*

Title VII   *74*

Title XII   *593*

Title XV   *592*

Protocol on the Statute of the ECJ
137, 320. See also Statute of the ECJ

art 15   *140*

art 20   *320*

art 29   *141*

art 40   *144*

Title III   *137*

EEA Agreement   *553*

Equal Treatment Directive *see* Council Directive 76/207

European Atomic Energy Treaty 1957   *23, 30, 45, 48, 106, 110, 124, 137, 161, 162, 163, 164, 165, 166, 167, 168, 193, 194, 195, 207, 217, 218, 235, 253, 258, 283, 284, 302, 321, 322, 591, 593*

art 1   *48*

art 2   *48*

art 3   *106*

art 76   *167*

art 85   *167*

art 90   *167*

art 103   *146*

art 104   *146*

art 107d   *404*

art 115   *118*

art 121   *115*

art 134   *150*

art 141   *124*

art 142   *249*

art 144   *264*

art 146   *257*

art 148   *281*

art 150   *146, 300*

art 156   *278*

art 161   *34, 168*

art 172   *209*

art 189   *108*

art 203   *167*

European Atomic Energy Treaty 1957 (*contd.*)
    art 204   *166*
    art 205   *30*
    art 206   *136*
    Protocol on the Statute of the ECJ
      137, 320. See also Statute of the ECJ
      art 15   *140*
      art 20   *320*
      art 29   *140*
      art 40   *144*
      Title III   *137*
European Coal and Steel Community Treaty
    1951   *21, 30, 46, 47, 48, 54, 106, 110, 118,*
    124, 126, 132, 137, 161, 162, 163, 164, 165,
    166, 167, 172, 173, 183, 193, 194, 195, 207,
    217, 218, 235, 258, 261, 283, 284, 290, 302,
    321, 322, 528, 583, 593, 600
    art 4   *47*
    art 5   *69*
    art 14   *34, 118, 161*
    art 20d   *404*
    art 26   *118*
    art 28   *118*
    art 31   *47*
    art 33   *145, 147, 257, 264*
    art 35   *145, 147, 281*
    art 36   *278*
    art 38   *257, 260, 264*
    art 40   *290*
    art 41   *146, 300*
    art 47   *124*
    art 50   *147*
    arts 57–66   *147*
    art 65   *164*
    art 66   *526*
    art 77   *108*
    art 86   *124, 209*
    art 88   *124, 145, 231, 235*
    art 88(2)   *235*
    art 95(1)   *167*
    art 95(2)   *167*
    art 95(3)   *146, 167*
    art 95(4)   *146*
    art 96   *166*
    art 98   *30*
    art 152   *147*
    art 156   *164*
    Protocol on the Statute of the ECJ
      137, 320. See also Statute of the ECJ
      art 15   *140*
      art 20   *320*
      art 29   *140*
      art 40   *144*
      Title III   *137*

European Communities Act 1972   *28, 37, 174,*
    194, 222, 552
    s2(1)   *194*
    s2(2)   *194*
    s2(4)   *222*
European Convention for the Protection of
    Human Rights and Fundamental Freedoms
    1950   *18, 33, 187, 188, 189, 543*
    art 6   *548, 550*
    art 7   *212*
    art 8   *188*
    art 50   *550*
    Protocol 11   *18*
European Convention on the Grant of European
    Patents 1973   *576, 578*
    art 65   *576, 577*
European Defence Community Treaty 1952
    22
European Parliament Decisions
    97/632/CS/EC/EA   *156*
    15 September 1993   *131*
European Parliament Resolution
    8 May 1969   *167*
European Patent Convention 1973 *see* European
    Convention on the Grant of European
    Patents 1973
European Social Charter 1961   *18*

First Company Law Directive *see* EC Directive
    68/151
French Constitution 1958
    art 11   *36*
    art 55   *244*

General Agreement on Tariffs and Trade (GATT)
    13
    art XI   *216*
German constitution
    art 30GG   *67*
    art 73GG   *67*
    art 74GG   *68*
Greek Accession Act   *273*
Greek Law
    No 363/1976   *347*
      art 3(1)   *347*
    No 1676/1986   *347*
    No 1858/1989
      art 1   *347*
    No 2187/1994
      art 2(7)   *347*
Guidelines for the Protection of Unrepresented
    EC Nationals by EC Missions in Third
    Countries   *402*

Guidelines on National Regional Aid   *592*

Hart-Scott-Rodino Act   *489*
High Authority Decision
    22/60   *171*

Immigration Act 1971
    s13   *458*
    s15(3)   *457*
Income and Corporation Taxes Act 1970   *433*
    ss258–264   *433*
    s258(7)   *433*
Inter-institutional Agreement on Procedures for
    Implementing the Principle of Subsidiarity
    1993   *70, 72*
International Convention on the Harmonised
    Commodity Description and Coding System
    333
International Health Regulation No 2 of the
    World Health Organisation of 25 May 1951
    456
Irish Act
    art 2   *194*

Joint Declaration (Council, Commission and EP)
    of 5 April 1977   *188*

Lomé Convention   *37, 302*
Lugano Convention on the Recognition and
    Enforcement of Judgments in Civil and
    Commercial Matters 1988   *87, 146*
Luxembourg Accord 1966   *49, 50, 117*

Maastricht Treaty *see* Treaty on European Union
    1992
Merchant Shipping Act 1988   *224, 227*
Merger Regulation *see* EC Regulation 4064/89
Merger Treaty 1965   *50, 106, 110, 164, 166*
    art 6   *118*
    art 8   *302*
    art 10   *118*
    Protocol on the Privileges and
        Immunities of the European
        Communities   *165, 302*
        arts 8–10   *130*

Naples Convention on Mutual Assistance between
    Customs Administrations 1967   *179*
North Atlantic Treaty 1949   *19*
    art 5   *19*

Opticians Act 1958
    s21   *318*

Paris Charter   *95*
Paris Convention for the Protection of Industrial
    Property 1983   *566*
Protocol of Turin 1948   *20*
Protocol Concerning the Interpretation of the
    1968 Brussels Convention on Jurisdiction
    and the Enforcement of Judgments in Civil
    and Commercial Matters 1971   *181*
Protocol on Privileges and Immunities *see*
    Merger Treaty
Protocol on the Statute of the EIB
    art 30(6)   *262*

Refugee Convention 1951   *189*
Representation of the People Act 2000   *401*
Resolution of the Council and the Ministers of
    Education Concerning the Action
    Programmes in the Field of Education
    180
Resolution of the Council and the
    Representatives of the Governments of the
    Member States Concerning the Progressive
    Creation of Economic and Monetary Union
    180
Resolution of the European Council on Growth
    and Employmnent   *91*
Resolution on Manifestly Unfounded Applications
    for Asylum 1992   *84*
Rome Convention on the Law Applicable to
    Contractual Obligations 1980   *34, 87, 146,
    179, 303*
    art 20   *181*
Rules of Procedure of the Council of the
    European Union   *115, 116*
Rules of Procedure of the Court of First Instance
    1997   *137, 141, 147, 259, 546*
    art 35(2)   *143*
    art 42(2)   *274*
    arts 80–82   *258*
    art 81   *258*
Rules of Procedure of the European Commission
    art 10   *122*
    art 11   *122*
Rules of Procedure of the European Court of
    Justice   *110, 137, 140, 141, 143, 259, 309,
    310, 319, 320, 321*
    arts 29–31   *110*
    art 29(2)   *143*
    art 42(2)   *274*
    art 51   *403*
    arts 80–82   *258*
    art 81   *258*
    art 92   *312*
    art 104   *320*

Rules of Procedure of the European Parliament
1997   *121, 152*
    art 32   *121*
    art 33   *121*
    arts 156–158   *403*
    art 159   *404*
Rules of Procedure of the European Parliament
1999   *121, 130, 131, 152*
    art 32   *121*
    art 33   *121*
Rules of the Supreme Court
    O.114 r1   *319*
    O.114 r2   *319*

Schengen Convention on the Gradual Abolition
    of Checks at the Common Borders 1985
    (Schengen I)   *81*
Schengen Implementing Convention 1990
    (Schengen II)   *81–83*
    art 134   *82*
Sex Discrimination Act 1975   *208, 215*
    s5(3)   *215*
Sherman Act   *489*
    s1   *489*
    s2   *489*
Shops Act 1950
    s47   *381*
Single European Act 1986   *50, 54, 58, 59, 60,
    62, 68, 107, 108, 116, 127, 129, 135, 150,
    152, 155, 166, 255, 329*
    art 1   *51*
    art 2   *111*
    art 3   *51*
    art 30   *51*
    art 130f   *592*
    Title I   *51*
    Title III   *51, 93*
Smithsonian Agreement 1971   *51*
Social Charter *see* Community Charter of the
    Fundamental Social Rights of Workers
Solemn Declaration on European Union 1983
    51
Statute of the Council of Europe 1949   *17*
Statute of the Court of First Instance
    art 53   *275*
Statute of the European System of Central Banks
    167
Statute of the European Court of Justice   *118,
    137, 167, 546*
    art 20   *301*
    art 22(1)   *287*
    art 37   *251*
    art 40   *302*

Statute of the European Court of Justice (*contd.*)
    art 42   *258*
    art 43   *287*
    art 54(1)   *327*

Trade Marks Act 1994   *560, 578*
Transfer Pricing Arbitration Convention 1990
    179
Treaty of Accession 1972 (UK)   *45, 45–46*
Treaty of Amsterdam 1997   *18, 50, 59, 62,
    65–105, 114, 116, 120, 125, 130, 135, 145,
    149, 150, 151, 153, 154, 155, 166, 189, 203,
    253, 255, 302, 334, 335, 593, 600*
    Declaration 32   *120*
    Protocol on the Application of the
        Principles of Subsidiarity and
        Proportionality   *70, 71*
    Protocol on the Institutions with the
        Prospect of Enlargement of the EU
        art 2   *65*
Treaty of Paris 1951 *see* European Coal and Steel
    Community Treaty
Treaty of Rome 1957 *see* EC Treaty; European
    Atomic Energy Treaty
Treaty of the Benelux Economic Union 1958
    20, 306
Treaty on European Union 1992   *18, 31, 34,
    40, 48, 50, 53, 59, 61, 62, 63, 65, 66, 67, 68,
    69, 70, 71, 75, 78, 82, 83, 86, 88, 95, 98, 99,
    103, 106, 107, 108, 110, 112, 113, 116, 119,
    120, 129, 130, 132, 134, 135, 136, 148, 149,
    152, 153, 154, 155, 166, 186, 189, 223, 230,
    253, 257, 265, 394, 399, 400, 402, 592, 593*
    art 1   *70*
    art 2   *70, 80, 91*
    art 3   *98, 108*
    art 3b   *71*
    art 4   *111, 112*
    art 6   *33, 45, 80, 189*
    art 6(1)   *31, 33*
    art 6(2)   *33, 189, 190*
    art 7   *33, 80, 92, 155, 189*
    arts 11–28   *95*
    art 11(1)   *95*
    art 11(2)   *98*
    art 13   *95*
    art 13(2)   *95*
    art 14   *95*
    art 14(2)   *96*
    art 14(4)   *99*
    art 14(5)   *99*
    art 14(6)   *96*
    art 14(7)   *96*

Treaty on European Union 1992 (*contd.*)
    art 15   *95*
    art 15(4)   *95*
    art 17(2)   *99*
    art 18   *99*
    art 19(1)   *98*
    art 22(2)   *99*
    art 23(1)   *97*
    art 26   *97*
    art 29   *89*
    art 30   *102, 189*
    art 30(2)   *102*
    art 31   *88, 89, 102*
    art 31(2)   *89*
    art 35(5)   *104*
    art 35(7)   *104*
    art 36   *104*
    art 40   *66*
    art 40(2)   *104*
    art 46   *88, 158*
    art 47   *89*
    art 48   *146, 162, 166*
    art 49   *31, 155, 189*
    art 46   *70*
    Pillar 1   *62, 65, 80, 156*
    Pillar 2   *18, 34, 42, 63, 65, 88, 97, 104,*
    108, 123, 125, 203

Treaty on European Union 1992 (*contd.*)
    Pillar 3   *34, 42, 63, 65, 88, 101, 102,*
    103, 104, 105, 108, 119, 121, 123, 125,
    145, 156, 178, 203
    Protocol on Social Policy   *89*
    Title VI   *74, 86, 101, 103*
    Title VIII   *158*

Uniform Benelux Law on Trade Marks
    art 13a   *564*
United Nations Charter 1945   *14, 15, 95*
    art 1   *14*
    art 51   *19*
    art 52   *19*

Vienna Convention on the Law of Treaties 1969
    45
    art 2(2)   *164*
    art 31   *182*
    art 39   *162*
    art 54   *45*
    art 56   *45*
    art 60   *244*

Yaoundé Convention   *37, 216*

1 The History of European Unity: from the Roman Empire to the Treaty of Rome

1.1   The Roman Empire

1.2   The Roman Catholic Church in the Middle Ages

1.3   Economic integration in Europe in the Middle Ages

1.4   The twentieth century

1.5   The United States' vision of the post-war world

1.6   The United States and European reconstruction

1.7   The Marshall Plan (the European Recovery Programme April 1948 – December 1951)

1.8   Western European integration

1.9   The United Kingdom and European integration

1.10 The French refusal of British accession

The idea of a peaceful and united Europe did not come suddenly. European unity achieved by peaceful means has been the dream of many people for many centuries but as with any dream it has rarely come true. Although Europe has only flourished and prospered in peace, its history is one of bloodshed and war. There are many examples of military conquest: from the Frankish King Charles the Great (or Charlemagne) and his successful expansion at the expense of neighbouring nations, which led to the Frankish Empire being almost equal in size to that of the Roman Empire (only Britain and Southern Italy were outside his control), to the attempts of the successive Emperors of the Holy Roman Empire that claimed sovereignty over the Christian world, to Napoleon who was the master of Europe at the beginning of the nineteenth century and to Hitler would have been master in the twentieth. In the nineteenth century the use of force in the name of 'national security' became a vital part of national policy for many European leaders.[1] The aggressive use of force, even though the supporting ideologies varied, was often the only device for unifying Europe. In the long run, however, the military conquest of Europe brought only poverty, hunger and despair to all Europeans. Thus, it is interesting to examine in the historical context the few attempts at the unification of Europe when military dominance and the use of force were not involved. In this respect the contribution of the Roman Empire during the *Pax Romana*, the Roman

---

[1] See M Mandelbaum, *The Fate of Nations: The Search for National Security in the Nineteenth and Twentieth Centuries*, New York: Cambridge University Press, 1988.

1

Catholic Church in the Middle Ages and commercial organisations such as the Hanseatic League in the fourteenth century must be considered.

The idea of European unity should not be divorced from the history and politics of the twentieth century – an unhappy period in the history of Europe. Two wars of unimaginable destruction and two ruthless idealogies – Communism and Nazism – both undermining democratic institutions and the liberal tradition of individual rights, both committed to total victory no matter how high the price, tore apart the very fabric of life in Europe. The darkness which descended on our continent was brightened after World War II by modest attempts by western Europe at shaping a better world through a strong, united, prosperous and democratic Europe.

1.1 The Roman Empire

Augustus proclaimed in January 27 BC before the Roman Senate the restoration of the Roman Republic. In fact, this date marked the commencement of a new era for Rome, that is, the beginning of the Roman Empire. Under the principate of Augustus (27 BC–14 AD) peace in Rome and its Empire was established, social and moral renewal took place, administration was reorganised and in the provinces the development of local autonomy was encouraged.[2] The policy was to strengthen the Empire internally. Indeed, no major military operation took place in the first century apart from the conquest of Britain in 44 AD. After the death of Augustus, in his testament which was read publicly in the Senate, he advised the Romans to keep the Empire within its natural boundaries. At that time, and until the conquest of Trajan (98–117 AD) the Empire spread from the Atlantic Ocean on the west to the Euphrates on the east, from the Rhine and Danube in the north to the deserts of Arabia and Africa in the south. The wise recommendation of Augustus was adopted, for various reasons, by his successors. For the two centuries after Augustus' death, and especially during the period of *Pax Romana* (98 AD–180 AD), all wars of expansion ceased; the Empire prospered and its inhabitants became gradually Romanised. For the first time, European unity was a reality. The 41 provinces of the Roman Empire with their 120 million inhabitants remained attached to Rome on a voluntary basis. The vanquished nations abandoned the idea of independence and preferred to stay an integral part of the Empire for many reasons. The most important was that Rome ensured lasting peace, political stability and general security within its provinces by pursuing a comprehensive policy of religious tolerance, moderation and by conferring extensive autonomy on local governments. Furthermore, the Empire had much to offer to its provinces: its exquisite literature represented by the works of Virgil, Horace, Ovid, Lucretius, Cattallus and Tacitus, and the speeches, philosophical works and letters of Cicero; and a language which at the time of the Empire became a true *lingua franca* and which survived the fall of Rome and finds uses even now due to its flexibility and exactitude in many areas such as law, medicine, liturgy, natural science, etc. However, the greatest intellectual achievement of all is certainly Roman law. By 450 BC the customary law of Rome was codified and written in the Twelve Tables. These

---

[2] E Badian, *Roman Imperialism in the Late Republic,* Ithaca, New York: Cornell University Press, 1985; R Duncan-Jones, *The Economy of the Roman Empire,* 2d ed, New York: Cambridge University Press, 1982.

rules as developed with the increase of wealth and importance of Rome formed the *ius civile,* a very formalistic set of legal rules, applied only to Roman citizens. As Rome expanded, the necessity arose for regulating legal relations between Roman citizens and foreigners. The pragmatic solution to this problem was the appointment of a special magistrate, the *praetor peregrinus* in 242 BC. He created law acceptable to both Roman citizens and foreigners called the *ius gentium.* This law was the first truly international law and was based on the commercial law in use in Mediterranean trade, *ius civile* in its less formalistic version, and on principles of equity and *bone fides.* The distinction between *ius civile* and *ius gentium* was obliterated when Roman citizenship was granted to all inhabitants of the Empire in 212 AD. However, the *ius gentium* did not disappear but become an essential part of Roman law. Under the Emperor Justinian in the sixth century AD Roman law was codified in the *Corpus Juris Civilis* which consists of the *Code* (imperial statutes), the *Digest* (jurisprudence), the *Institutes* (elementary treaties) and the *Novellae,* which were added later and comprised legislation enacted by Justinian and his successors. The definition of law formulated by Celsus and cited by Ulpian in the *Digest* reflects the spirit of Roman law. It states that 'Law is the art of the good and fair' (*ius est ars boni et aequi*) and its main objective is justice which, once again according to the Digest, 'is the constant and perpetual will to give each man his rights'. Roman law was inspired by the idea that moral requirements were more important than strict observance of law. Although law had to be enforced as long as it was in force (*dura lex, sed lex*), its blind and strict application might lead to lawlessness (*summum ius summa inuria*), and thus such principles as equity, fairness and humanism (*bonum, aequitas and humanitas*) were taken into consideration in its application and interpretation.[3] For that reason Roman law is eternal and has greatly influenced all European legal systems, including Community law.

Although the intellectual achievements of the Romans were outstanding, they were essentially very practical people. They built an efficient transportation system based upon 50,000 miles of hard-surfaced highways (hence the words 'all roads lead to Rome'), and founded many towns according to strict plans which not only specified that in each city, however small it was, baths, theatres and amphitheatres were a necessity but also regulated the height of buildings and set rules for traffic. Each town was supplied with water by underground channels or aqueducts and from storage tanks the water was carried by lead pipes into houses. In Rome itself fourteen aqueducts, in length totalling 265 miles, delivered about 50 gallons of water a day per head of population. Also, each town had its sewage disposal system. The practical genius of the Romans resulted in many outstanding innovations, eg central heating, new methods of construction following the invention of concrete, and the building of public baths which were designed not only for cleansing the body but, more importantly, to exercise intellect as they were meeting-places endowed with libraries and art exhibits. The list of benefits that the Roman Empire offered to the provinces is long. One of them is that the Romans did not impose their values and civilisation upon conquered nations but absorbed and integrated foreign culture, particularly that of Greece. Also, they gave conquered nations a wide autonomy and did not interfere in local matters unless Roman interests were endangered. In this respect, it is interesting to mention that when Roman legions stationed in the province of Britain were called to defend Rome against

---

[3] On Roman law see R W Lee, *The Elements of Roman Law,* 4th ed, London; Sweet & Maxwell, 1990.

the barbarians, the leaders of the British sent a letter to the Emperor asking for the return of legions. They pleaded their allegiance to Rome, they wanted to be a part of the civilised world of the Roman Empire. As Gibbon said:

> '... the obedience of the Roman world was uniform, voluntary and permanent. The vanquished nations, blended into one great people resigned the hope, nay even the wish, of resuming their independence, and scarcely considered their own existence as distinct from the existence of Rome.'[4]

Thus, the moderate and wise policy of Rome toward its colonies made the Empire very popular amongst the conquered nations. As a result, the relationship between Rome and its provinces was based on voluntary submission to the Roman Empire.

Another important link unifying the Roman Empire was Roman Citizenship. In 212 AD Roman citizenship was granted to all free adult males living within the border of the Empire. At that time all discrimination between Roman and non-Roman population was abolished. In addition, in the Roman Empire discrimination based on race was unknown. Also, under the Roman Empire, its inhabitants enjoyed the freedom of travel and trade. Thus, for example, a Roman from Britannia could travel to Jerusalem without any passport or visa in only six weeks. In respect of trade, no tariffs were erected between different regions of the Empire and only harbour charges were levied on goods. As the older Pliny said:

> 'The might of the Roman Empire has made the world the possession of all; human life has profited by the exchange of goods and by partnership in the blessing of peace.'[5]

Under the Roman Empire a highly sophisticated civilisation was created. All nations living under the rule of Rome enjoyed peace, stability and prosperity, especially during the *Pax Romana*.

It is interesting to note that throughout the Roman Empire there was a single currency.

1.2 The Roman Catholic Church in the Middle Ages

As the Roman Empire in the West declined and eventually fell, Christianity, one of its principal legacies, superseded the Roman Empire as the bearer of the idea of European unity. Indeed, this idea continued down the centuries in the political ambitions of the Roman Church. By the tenth century Roman Catholicism had become the official religion of all European States. Also, the crusading ideal strengthened the unity of Christendom as the military energy of the Europeans was directed toward the Muslims. The success of the first crusade launched in 1095, which captured the city of Jerusalem from the hands of 'infidels' and resulted in the creation of the Kingdom of Jerusalem, enhanced the spiritual unity of Europe and added to the prestige of the popes.

However, the papal leadership in all spiritual and temporal matters in the Christian Empire was not established overnight. In ninth century German Kings Otto I and Otto III

---

[4] E Gibbon, *Decline and Fall of the Roman Empire,* Abridged version, London: Bison Group, 1993, pp24–25.
[5] R H Barrow, *The Romans,* London: Penguin Books, 1962, p97.

appointed and removed popes as they wished. In 1046, King Henry III came to Rome in order to be crowed emperor of the Holy Roman Empire and found three different claimants to the title of pope. He deposed all of them (Sylvester III, Gregory IV and Benedict IX) and appointed his own candidate, a German bishop he had brought with him, as Pope Clement. Initially the successors to the papal throne were imposed in a similar way, but in the following decades the German-born popes started to introduce reforms in order to purify the Church. Pope Leon IX was the first to impose his authority upon the Church, considering himself as the vicar of Christ and therefore in possession of full powers (*plenitudo potestas*) over the Church. The confrontation between the papacy and German emperors over the ultimate authority in the Christian empire lasted for centuries. The struggle of the popes to get rid of lay control in the Church started with the Investiture Controversy which questioned the emperor's practice of appointing all German bishops and bestowing them with ring and staff, symbols of the episcopal office, but preceded by an act of homage to the king. Although the conflict was officially settled by the Concordat of Worms in 1122, and nominally represented a compromise, in fact the spiritual authority of the Church was reaffirmed.

Gregory VII was the greatest reforming pope in the Middle Ages and laid down the foundations for the future of the papacy in Europe. He fought against simony and nicolaitism (clerical marriage and concubinage), confirmed the moral authority of the Church and established its political power. He was so powerful that he deposed and excommunicated the German King and Emperor of the Holy Roman Empire, Henry IV. The excommunication was so effective that Henry IV was forced to go to Italy in 1077 as a penitent and to wait outside the castle of Canossa for three cold January nights begging Gregory VII for absolution.

In their confrontation, both sides invoked legal arguments based on Roman law and Canon law to bolster their claims. The popes argued that they, as the supreme representatives of God on earth, were entitled to exercise universal sovereignty. Had not Christ said to Peter:

> 'To you I shall give the keys of the kingdom of heaven: and whatsoever you shall bind on earth shall be bound also in heaven, and whatsoever you shall loose upon earth will be lost also in heaven'.

The benefit of the legal battle between popes and emperors, however, was the revival of legal studies in Italian universities.[6]

By the twelfth and thirteenth centuries papal leadership in all matters was accepted throughout Europe and the distinction between Church and 'States' as separate entities had disappeared. European kingdoms voluntarily recognised the feudal suzerainty of the papacy.[7] The supreme spiritual authority of the Church, combined with papal primacy and infallibility in all matters, led to their intervention in political affairs. Although Jesus said that 'My kingship is not of this world', all vital political questions of Europe were of concern to, and subject to the interference of, the Church. At its height in twelfth and thirteenth

[6] H Wierussowski, *The Medieval University*, Princeton: Van Nostrand, 1966.
[7] See G Barraclough, *The Medieval Papacy*, New York: W Norton, 1968; H A Oberman, *The Harvest of Medieval Theology*, Cambridge: Labirynth Press, 1963.

centuries, the medieval Church was omnipresent. Furthermore, the Church had developed a system of ecclesiastical courts all over Europe that touched the lives of virtually every person in Christendom. As well as dealing with sacramental matters and the governance of Church property and heresy, the Church's jurisdiction extended into secular areas, including matrimonial causes and legitimacy, wills, sexual crimes, oaths and promises. Appeals went to bishops and through papal legates to Rome, as the pope was the highest judicial authority. By the end of the twelfth century, the papal court was one of the busiest in Europe. To all cases canon law was applied which consisted of a compilation of various rules and regulations (canons) together with papal laws and decisions called *decretals*. All this legal material was published in 1500 in Paris in *Corpus Juris Canonici* (Corpus of Canon law). At that time, lawyers were trained in canon law schools at Bologna and served later as advisers to virtually all the governments in Europe.

The *Respublicana Christiana* of the Middle Ages had unified Europe morally and spiritually. It influenced social, political and economic life in Europe. Christianity had created a common culture and similar way of life throughout Europe.

1.3 Economic integration in Europe in the Middle Ages

Another interesting attempt at unifying Europe took place in the Middle Ages, although economic objectives were at the foreground. With the revival of trade in the tenth century, merchants started to travel throughout Europe in order to sell, buy and place orders for various goods.[8] These commercial activities required the establishment of a common legal framework. Out of necessity the European merchants created their own rules of conduct and fair dealing which formed the *lex mercatoria*. Furthermore, some merchant organisations became very powerful by monopolising the trade of certain goods in some regions of Europe. The most striking example is provided by the Hanseatic League.

Medieval commercial communities and the lex mercatoria

This pragmatic, universal and uniform law, which developed out of the business activities of the guilds and of the maritime cities, was created by practical men engaged in commerce and was administered promptly and efficiently by courts of merchants. This cosmopolitan law would not be workable without such concepts as 'my word is my bond', 'bethink you of my poor honesty' and 'goodwill'.[9] At the centre was the principle of good faith. External factors reinforced the importance of these principles. First, the business practices of merchants were devoid of all legal sanctions. Particularly, at the first stage of formation of the *lex mercatoria*, the royal courts and feudal courts refused to enforce the newly established rules of conduct invented by merchants. Thus, it was in the interests of merchants, and essential to the development of commerce, to deal with litigation involving members of the merchant community. Special courts were instituted which decided on the

---

[8] R S Lopez, *The Commercial Revolution of the Middle Ages, 950–1350,* New York: Cambridge University Press, 1971.
[9] A Kadar, K Hoyle and G Whitehead, *Business Law,* 2d ed, Oxford: Oxford University Press, 1987, p12.

basis of commercial expediency what was fair, just and reasonable under the circumstances of the case. Relying on business practices, usages of trade, legal principles of canon law such as *pacta sunt servanda* and the notion of *bone fides*, the merchant courts settled cases quickly 'between tides' in ports or in the 'piepowder courts' on the last day of a fair. The merchant courts, due to the practical common sense of the judges, themselves merchants and familiar with mercantile practices, achieved excellent solutions for problems regarding international trade. They created a new, flexible and professional set of rules which was truly universal and uniform.

Second, a merchant was closely connected with the community within which he operated. The same group of merchants moved from fair to fair throughout Europe. Everyone knew everyone else or at least could find out easily about the other party. Thus, the reputation of a merchant, his good name, was an essential part of his business. If he wished to earn his living as a merchant, he had to deal in good faith and conduct his affairs honestly. The pressure that could be exercised by the community of merchants made the enforcement of decisions of commercial courts easy, since an undesirable member of the community could be forced out of business if he refused to comply with a judgment rendered by a commercial court.

Also, fairs in the Middle Ages contributed to the development of the *lex mercatoria* as they constituted a meeting place for merchants. The greatest fairs took place in the region of Champagne as it was situated between Flanders and Italy, the two most commercialised areas in Europe, the largest being the 'Hot Fair' at Troyes.[10] During fairs the local authorities ensured safety and honest dealings by appointing 'Keepers of the Fair' who patrolled the market place, kept the master set of measures against which all the merchants' sets of measures had to be calibrated, and protected merchants from unfair competition and the public from defective or underweight goods. Thieves were prosecuted and dishonest merchants barred from all future fairs. The truly international fairs, such as the six trade fairs organised in Champagne, attracted merchants from all over Europe and 'these great international exchanges connected the financial and marketing centres of the south with the manufacturing and trading communities of the north, tying the northern world to the south more effectively than had any system since the political institutions of the Roman Empire'.[11]

Finally, French became the *lingua franca* of commercial communities in Europe.

The Hanseatic League

In the Middle Ages certain organisations of merchants became very powerful. The Hansaetic League, which to some extent can be considered as a forunner of the European Community, is the best example.[12] The League was formed in the 1280s when northern German towns and merchants which mastered trade in the Baltic sea joined in association with merchants

---

[10] J & F Gies, in *Life in a Medieval City*, New York, 1969, describes medieval urban life in the city of Troyes, amid the Champagne fairs.

[11] M Kishlansky, P Geary, P O'Brien, *Civilisation in the West*, Volume A, New York: Harper Collins Publishers, 1991, p275.

[12] See P Dollinger, *The German Hansa*, Stanford: Stanford University Press, 1970.

from Cologne and Rhineland who operated in Flanders and England. The northern German towns set up a political alliance to control northern trade in the twelfth and early thirteenth centuries. Lübeck became the major town from which merchants from Westphalia and Saxonia expanded their trade northward and eastward. The northern German merchants established themselves in Visby, Novgrad, Riga, Reval (now Tallin), Danzing (now Gdansk) and Dorpat (now Tartu), thus monopolising Baltic trade. Once these two powerful associations of merchants united in the Hanseatic League all trade in the Baltic and North Sea was in one hand. The Hanseatic League had mainly commercial objectives: to protect and develop its trading interests; to ensure peace and order in its towns; to protect its ships from pirates and brigands; to ensure safe navigation by building lighthouses and training pilots; to introduce common legislation in all Hanseatic towns; to defend merchants and their goods; to expand its trade by gaining new privileges and monopolies from foreign political leaders; and to gain access to new markets. Usually, the League was against the use of force and relied heavily on loans, bribes and gifts to local authorities where required. The League did not hesitate to resort to blockades of ports and embargoes if its interests were threatened. On one occasion in 1368 it raised an army and crushed the Danes when the Danish King Valdemar IV wanted to deprive the League of its monopoly in the southwestern Baltic. The defeated Danes signed the Treaty of Stralsund in 1370, recognising the League's supremacy in the Baltic by granting it exclusive rights to export Scandinavian fish throughout Europe. The goods that the League shuttled back and forth across the Baltic and the North sea included grain, timber, furs, tar, honey, flax, fish, salt, wax and spices, as well as cloth and other finished products. The League had both established ports at various cities and set up permanent commercial enclaves in towns such as Bruges in Flanders, Bergen in Norway and the Steel Yard in London. At its heights in the fourteenth century the Hanseatic League had a membership of about 100 towns. The only permanent body of the League was its assembly (diet) which met from time to time. With the rise of the nation-state the Hanseatic League declined, its last diet being held in 1669.

1.4 The twentieth century

In the first decades of the twentieth century the idea of European unity was very popular in intellectual circles but was not supported by European public opinion. According to Ward 'another of many ironies which pervaded European studies is that the most substantive intellectual fuel for European Union in the immediate post-1918 years was British'[13] and he cites the examples of Lord Milner's Round Table Movement, the work of British economist Lionel Robbins and William Beveridge, as well as the impact of the British federalist movement upon Sir Winston Churchill which culminated in his famous Declaration of Anglo-French Union on 16 June 1940. Due to the German invasion of France the proposed union failed.

In other European countries the federalist idea resulted in the creation of the Pan-European Movement by Count Richard Coudenhove-Kalergi in 1923 aimed at reinforcing

---

[13] I Ward, *A Critical Introduction to European Law*, London: Butterworths, 1996, p3.

European autonomy and shielding Europe from Soviet and American domination. Also, Giovanni Angelli and Attillo Cabiati advocated a federal structure for Europe in order to replace the inefficient League of Nations. However, the one and only attempt at formalising the idea of a federal Europe came from Aristide Briand, the French Minister for Foreign Affairs. Briand in his speech before the Assembly of the League of Nations on 5 September 1929, backed by the German Foreign Minister, Gustav Streseman, declared that the moment had come for 'a kind of federal link' among European nations. A French memorandum based on his speech was transmitted to all European States who were members of the League of Nations in 1930 and a special European Committee was set up by the League in order to study governmental comments on the French project.[14] Nothing came out of it, European countries showed a total lack of enthusiasm. Furthermore, the death of Aristide Briand in March 1932 and, most importantly, Hitler's rise to power in 1933 stopped any hope of European unity. Unfortunately, attempts at the unification of Europe by force in the twentieth century have been more popular than peaceful means. Indeed, Europe witnessed and survived two powerful ideologies – Communism and Nazism – trying to unify Europe in their own manner.

Communism

The ideological foundations of Communism emanate from the *Communist Manifesto* of Karl Marx who believed that the class struggle which constituted the result of the dialectical nature of history would culminate in world revolution. As Marx wrote in the *Communist Manifesto* of 1848: 'The bourgeoisie produces its own grave-diggers. The fall of the bourgeoisie and the victory of the proletariat are equally inevitable.'[15] However, Marx was unsure whether the old world would perish by a sudden and violent revolution or a continuous and permanent revolution. When the first Communist revolution occurred in Russia it was Vladimir Ilich Ulyanov, known as Lenin, who adapted the ideas of Marx to the Russian conditions. In practice, Communism instead of creating a paradise for the working class became an oppressive, totalitarian regime ruthlessly eliminating political adversaries and completely disregarding fundamental human rights.[16]

The aggressive expansion of Communism by use of all possible means was experienced for the first time during the Soviet-Polish war in 1920. On 25 April 1920, Polish leader, Marshall Josef Pilsudski frightened by the Soviet regime and the sovietisation of eastern Europe, decided to assist Ukraine to became an independent State, and at the same time he pursued his dream of restoring the Grand Polish-Lithuanian-Ukrainian Empire. At that time civil war in Russia was at full strength and both fighting factions – the White and the Red – were exhausted by the ferocious struggle. The Polish army took Kiev but the Red Army recaptured the capital of Ukraine and continued to advance to Warsaw itself. The battle of Warsaw was decisive as to the destiny of Europe. The Red Army created by Leon Trotsky had no intention of stopping at the gates of Warsaw but was set to conquer the entire continent.

---

[14] F Kirgis, Jr, 'The European Communities', in *International Organisations in Their Legal Setting: Documents, Comments, and Questions,* St Paul: West, 1977, p603.

[15] K Marx, *Manifeste Communiste,* Paris: Editions Costes, 1947, p54.

[16] S Fitzpatrick, *The Russian Revolution, 1917–1932,* Oxford: Oxford University Press, 1982.

Josef Pilsudski, with advice from French attaché, General Maxime Weygard, in what is known as the '18 decisive battles in the history of our civilisation', defeated the Red Army, taking 66,000 prisoners and recapturing vast territories of Bieloruss. Thus, the first attempt at conquering the whole world by the Soviet Russia was a total failure. The Treaty of Riga signed between the Poles and the Soviet Russia on humiliating terms for the latter ended the march of the Red Army 'through the heart of Poland to the conquest of Europe and world conflagration'.[17]

The aggressive policy of the Soviet Union, the centre of world revolution, continued. On 23 August 1939 the Molotov-Ribbentrop Non-aggression Pact between the USSR and Germany was signed. The partition of Poland was decided and Hitler's support for the USSR in overtaking Finland, the Baltic States and Bessarabia was promised to Stalin in return for non-interference in Germany's invasion of Poland.

The next opportunity for the USSR to expand was provided by the end of World War II. The 'liberation' of the eastern part of Europe from German occupation by the Red Army gave the Russians an opportunity for military and political control of these countries. Once the Red Army entered it stayed. As a result, nine countries which before 1939 had been independent became incorporated into the Soviet Union as republics (for example, Latvia, Lithuania and Estonia) or became Soviet satellites. Stalin imposed a police state and terror equal to that of Nazi Germany in the 'liberated territory'. Crimes against humanity, and atrocities and contempt for basic human rights, were common in the USSR and all occupied countries. Stalin built a network of concentration camps (gulags) for his own people where millions were worked to death in inhuman conditions. His suspicious and paranoid mind saw imperialist plots everywhere. Tens of millions of people were tortured by his political police, the NKVD, to confess imaginary crimes and then were condemned to death or forced labour in gulags. Two of his crimes are particularly appalling. When Ukraine resisted Stalin's collectivisation of agriculture, as a punishment he imposed very high quotas of delivery of agricultural products and confiscated all foodstuffs. These measures resulted in a famine in Ukraine in 1932–33 and a loss of at least five million lives. At that time, Stalin continued to export Russian grain abroad without any consideration for the peasantry of Ukraine dying from hunger. Also, Stalin had no qualms in committing one of the worst war crimes in the history of mankind. He ordered the execution of Polish military officers, prisoners of the war of 1939, by the NKVD, who shot and then buried the soldiers in mass graves in the woods of Katyn (only 4,443 bodies were found out of 15,000 missing Polish officers).[18] It was also in the name of Communism that the Hungarian uprising in 1956 was crushed by the Red Army and the Hungarian reformist premier, Imre Nagy, was murdered. Subsequent military interventions in Czechoslovakia in 1968, the invasion of Afghanistan in 1979, etc, were also aimed at achieving the expansion of Communism. Fortunately, the Soviet empire collapsed in 1989 – Michail Gorbachev, the laureate of the Nobel Prize of Peace of 1990, accepted the inevitable and set eastern Europe free that year.

---

[17] Quoted by D Lasok, *Law and Institutions of the European Union*, 6th ed, London: Butterworths, 1994, p3.
[18] A Hall, *War Crimes*, London: Blitz Editions, 1993, pp33–41.

Nazism

As to Nazism, the Third Reich was born on 30 January 1933 when Adolf Hitler was sworn as Chancellor of the German Republic by its President, Field Marshal Paul von Hindenburg. Adolf Hitler was not imposed upon the Germans but was lawfully appointed Chancellor (in accordance with the German constitution) as a result of being leader of the largest party, the National Socialist German Worker's Party. Hitler in *Mein Kampf* (My Struggle), which constituted a blueprint for the Third Reich (he wrote it in prison after his unsuccessful putsch of 1923), put forward his ideas of the New Order he intended to build in the conquered Europe. He abandoned the idea of the Hohenzollern Empire which was to expand Germany into Africa and emphasised that German territorial policy should not be fulfilled in the Cameroons but instead almost exclusively in Europe. He wanted to create *Volksgemeinschaft*, a racial community where only the true Aryan would enjoy privileges, and people of 'inferior blood' would become slaves or would be eliminated. This Aryan master race would need living space – *Lebensraum* – which according to Hitler would be found in the East as this territory was inhabited by Slavs, an inferior race (subhumans). According to him the conquest of the Soviet Russia would not pose a major problem for Germany since Russia was under the government of Jewish-Bolsheviks. Hitler hated the capitalists, the socialists, the pacifists, the liberals – all of them were associated with Jews! Once in power, Hitler established a dictatorship and started to implement his policy of crude Darwinism in both internal and external matters. For the German Aryans, the 'Lords of the Earth' who followed blindly and with great enthusiasm, a new era had commenced. In 1936 Hitler invaded the Rhineland, thus freeing Germany from the shackles of the Versailles Treaty, and started a rearmament programme which created jobs for six million unemployed Germans. He incorporated German workers into his programme of *Volksgemeinschaft* by providing subsidised holidays and leisure within his 'Strength through Joy' scheme, and an 'opportunity' to acquire an automobile, the Volkswagen, a symbol of wealth and luxury for every German worker. They, as everybody else paid dearly for their folly and even their Volkswagen never materialised during the Third Reich.[19] Hitler ruthlessly prosecuted his political adversaries – Jews, the mentally sick, the handicapped, gypsies, Jehovah's Witnesses, homosexuals, etc. Indeed, not every German was welcomed in his *Volkgemeinschaft* or was worthy of propagation as the Law for the Protection of Hereditary Health of 14 July 1933 made clear. This legislation authorised the sterilisation of about two million people. Hitler had an obsessive hatred of Jews, blaming them for everything, even the war that he had started, a war which resulted in the extinction of six million Jews. Hitler's course from the Nuremberg Laws of September 1935, which stripped all Jews of their German citizenship, prohibited mixed marriages and any sexual intercourse between Jews and Germans, through the Kristallnacht (Night of Broken Glass of 9–10 November 1938) when Jews and their property were viciously attacked, to the 'final solution'

---

[19] This scheme was one of the biggest swindles of the Third Reich. Every worker had to pay a weekly instalment of five marks out of his salary toward the total of 999 marks. The design of the new car was claimed by Hitler, although in fact it was executed under the supervision of Dr Ferdinand Porsche. Not a single VW was delivered under this scheme to its owner during the Third Reich. For the history of Volkswagen and the use of slave labour and prisoners of war during the Third Reich by Volkswagen: see H Mommsen and M Grieger, *Das Volkswagenwerk und Seine Arbeiter im Dritten Reich,* Düsseldorf: Econ Verlag, 1996.

to the Jewish problem was pre-planned. Its execution was entrusted to Herman Goring and consisted of the physical extermination of European Jews in the gas chambers of Auschwitz, Treblinka, Sobibor, Bergen-Belsen and other concentration camps.

The next step in the German plan was to conquer the entire European continent. The Germans, who were very successful at the beginning, introduced Hitler's New Order in Europe, a reign of terror, sadism and madness. After twelve years, four months and eight days the Third Reich, which was to have lasted for a thousand years, collapsed. Germany surrendered unconditionally at 2.45 am on 7 May 1945 to the allied forces. General Jodl who signed the act of capitulation for Germany was authorised to submit a final plea for his country. He said:

> 'With this signature the German people and the German armed forces are, for better or worse, delivered into the hands of the victors … In this hour I can only express the hope that the victor will treat them with generosity.'

No answer came from the Allied side.[20]

Indeed, forgiveness and reconciliations were not easy. Some 50 million people lost their lives during World War II, 60 million people covering 55 ethnic groups from 27 countries were displaced, 45 million were left homeless, many million were wounded and only some 670,000 were liberated from Nazi death camps. The psychological devastation of survivors, the physical destruction, the genocide, slave labour, mass killing, mass rape, concentration camps and other horrors perpetrated during World War II exceeded anything ever experienced. Europe was shocked by the atrocities and lay in ruins, its inhabitants were hungry, sick and without a future.

The rebuilding of Europe posed not only a formidable challenge but was also the catalyst that led to European unity. Many factors have contributed to a new perception of post-war Europe; most important was the United States vision of the post-war world and of the reconstruction of Europe.

1.5 The United States' vision of the post-war world

The United States' vision of the post-war world was based on President Woodrow Wilson's Fourteen Point Plan, which was outlined on 8 January 1918 in his speech to the US Congress. He advocated free trade, open negotiations, freedom of the sea to all nations in wartime and in peace, reduction of armaments, self-determination for many European nations that were under foreign domination, a reform of the existing colonial system which would take into account the interests of the native people and, above all, establishment of international law and a collective security system which would ensure lasting peace and would make World War I the 'war to end war', the last war in the history of mankind. According to Wilson, in order to oversee the new system:

> '… a general association of nations must be formed under specific covenants for the purpose of

---

[20] W L Shirer, *The Rise and Fall of the Third Reich,* London: Mandarin, 1991, p1139.

affording mutual guarantees of political independence and territorial integrity to great and small states alike.'[21]

The League of Nations was set up in 1920 on the basis of this proposal.[22]

Wilsonian internationalism, which considered war as an atavism and advocated democracy and freedom, served as an ideological foundation for the United States' new international order after World War II, although some modifications were introduced in order to avoid mistakes that were made after 1918. The first concrete measure in this direction was taken by the US in 1943 with the establishment of the United Nations Relief and Rehabilitation Administration to distribute food and medicine to people suffering in the war-stricken areas. The United States' vision of the post-war world encompassed economic, commercial, financial, and political matters. At the Bretton Wood Conference in summer 1944 the monetary and banking issues were discussed by representatives of 44 countries. As a result, the International Monetary Fund was set up which provided the basis for the international monetary system that prevailed until August 1971. Its main function was to supervise the international exchange market intervention system and supply supplementary international reserves if needed.[23] Also, the International Bank for Reconstruction and Development (the World Bank) was established at the same time which finances governments and private projects that further the economic development of Member States when private loans are not available on reasonable terms. Moreover, it provides technical assistance in respect of these projects when appropriate.

The liberalisation of international trade was to be conducted by the International Trade Organisation but did not materialise as the US Congress decided against US participation in the proposed organisation, despite the fact that the United States drafted the organisation's charter in 1945. Instead, the General Agreement on Tariffs and Trade (GATT, which has recently been renamed the World Trade Organisation (WTO)) has become a device for co-ordination on national policies on international trade.[24] The main purpose of GATT (now WTO) is to remove trade barriers by eliminating or reducing tariffs and non-tariff barriers to trade, and outlawing discriminatory practices in international trade. The round of tariff negotiations conducted under the auspices of GATT, known as the Uruguary Round, began in 1986 and was completed in December 1993. It turned out to be a great success. Indeed, the multilateral negotiations resulted in the agreed cut in subsidies for export of agricultural products by 36 per cent in value and domestic farm supports by 20 per cent over six years, while over 40 per cent of manufactured goods would enter foreign markets without tariffs and the remaining tariffs for such goods would be reduced by over one-third. Much stricter protection for intellectual property and the extension of the GATT powers in

---

[21] See Point XIV in *Selected Literary and Political Papers and Addresses of Woodrow Wilson*, Volume 2, New York: Grosset and Dunlap, 1927.

[22] For a comprehensive study of the League of Nations: F Walters, *A History of the League of Nations*, London: Oxford University Press, 1952.

[23] R M Dunn and J C Ingram, *International Economics*, 4th ed, London: John Willey & Sons, 1996, pp479–536.

[24] J Jackson, *The World Trading System, Law and Policy of International Economic Relations*, Cambridge: the MIT Press, 1992, pp27–57.

the enforcement of dumping, subsidies and other areas were agreed.[25] The Seattle conference convened by the WTO in November 1999 did not lead to a new round of trade talks but, nevertheless, initiated important discussions on services and agriculture.

In political matters, the Atlantic Charter, drafted by Roosevelt and Churchill at a meeting on the USS Augusta off Newfoundland in August 1941, outlined the political future of the post-war world. On 1 January 1942 Soviet Russia, together with 26 other nations, approved the Atlantic Charter by signing the Declaration of the United Nations and thus agreeing to Roosevelt's Four Freedoms – freedom of speech, freedom of worship, freedom from want, freedom from fear everywhere in the world – as necessary requirements of peace, the restoration of independence for all States that had lost it to German invasion, as well the right of all people to determine their own form of government, and the creation of a new international system of general security which would effectively disarm aggressor nations. The idea of creating a successor to the League of Nations was carried out and developed in the 'Declaration of Moscow' and at a conference in Teheran in 1943 where Roosevelt, Churchill and Stalin met. This was followed by the Dumbarton Oaks Conference, where representatives of China, the Soviet Union, the United Kingdom and the United States formulated the main principles of the United Nations. At the meeting of Churchill, Roosevelt and Stalin in Yalta in February 1945 it was decided to call for an international conference in San Francisco in order to draft a charter for the United Nations. Also in Yalta important concessions were made to Stalin concerning the Soviet annexation of large sections of eastern Poland in return for free elections to be held in Poland. Roosevelt was convinced that only co-operation between superpowers and their participation in a new international organisation would bring lasting peace. He considered that the failure of the League of Nations was essentially due to the absence of the United States and the Soviet Union within the organisation. The Conference in San Francisco was attended by 260 representatives of 50 States and on 26 June 1945 the Charter of the United Nations was signed.[26] After the five great powers (the United States, the Soviet Union, China, the United Kingdom and France) and a majority of its signatories ratified the Charter, the United Nations was officially established on 24 October 1945.[27]

---

[25] For the detailed contents of the Uruguay Round Agreement: see *The Economic Report of the President: 1994*, Washington DC: US Governmental Printing Office, 1994, pp205–240; J Schott, *The Uruguay Round: An Assessment,* Washington DC: Institute for International Economics, 1994.

[26] Poland was not represented at the San Francisco Conference but signed the Charter later and thus become one of the 51 original signatories.

[27] The main purposes of the United Nations as described in art 1 of the Charter are:

'1. To maintain international peace and security, and to that end: to take effective measures for the prevention and removal of threats to the peace, and for the suppression of acts of aggression of other breaches of the peace and to bring about by peaceful methods, and in conformity with the principles of justice and international law, adjustment or settlement of international disputes or situation which might lead to a breach of the peace.

2. To develop friendly relations among nations based on respect for the principle of equal rights and self-determination of people, and to take other appropriate measures to strengthen universal peace.

3. To achieve international co-operation in solving international problems of an economic, social, cultural, or humanitarian character, and in promoting and encouraging respect for human rights and for fundamental freedoms for all without distinction as to race, sex, language, or religion.

4. To be a centre for harmonising the actions of nations in the attainment of these common ends.'

For brief history of the UN and its transformation after the end of Cold War: see P R Baehr and L Gordenker, *The United Nations in the 1990s,* 2nd ed, London: Macmillan, 1994.

The United Nations has six principal organs: the General Assembly, the Security Council, the Economic and Social Council, the Trusteeship Council, the International Court of Justice and the Secretariat. The system set up by the Charter can work properly only in an atmosphere of co-operation amongst the major powers since they assigned to themselves the role of an international gendarme which is reflected by their voting rights in the Security Council. Indeed, the big five as permanent members of the Security Council are responsible for the maintenance of international peace and security. However, a veto by any of the permanent members is sufficient to block all but procedural resolutions of the Security Council.[28] The veto was one of the major causes of the failure of the Security Council as the relationship between the Soviet Union and the United States steadily deteriorated once the war ended.[29]

Stalin never intended to keep his promises; free elections did not take place in Poland or any other east European country under Soviet Union control. Instead pro-Soviet puppet regimes were established. The US President Truman responded by terminating the Lend-Lease aid to the Soviet Union. On both sides positions hardened and suspicions mounted. The Cold War had begun which ended the possibility of establishing a new world order based on the American ideals. As Winston Churchill said in his speech in Missouri in 1946:

'From Stettin in the Baltic to Trieste in the Atlantic an iron curtain has descended across the continent'.[30]

1.6 The United States and European reconstruction

Three factors have determined the policy of the United States towards European reconstruction: political, economic and humanitarian.

As to the political factor, the Cold War and consequently the division of Europe into two blocs prompted the United States to prevent the spread of Communism at all costs. On 12 March 1947 President Truman announced his approach towards the USSR before Congress. He said:

'At the present moment in world history nearly every nation must choose between alternative ways of life. The choice is too often not a free one … It must be the policy of the United States to support people who are resisting attempted subjugation by armed minorities or by outside pressure.'[31]

His statement is known as the Truman doctrine. Immediately after his speech Truman asked for financial aid of $400 million for Greece and Turkey in order to contain the expansion of Communism in both countries. As the United Kingdom was no longer able to sustain economic and military aid to Greece, where a civil war provoked by Communists had erupted, and to Turkey, which was under pressure from the Soviet Union to set up bases and allow naval passage through the Dardanelles, the United States felt it necessary to intervene.

---

[28] F L Kirgis, 'The Security Council's First Fifty Years' (1995) 89 Am JIL 506–539.
[29] W Lafeber, *America, Russia and the Cold War, 1945–1966,* New York: John Wiley & Sons, 1978.
[30] H Middleton, *Britain and the World since 1750,* Oxford: Basil Blackwell, 1984, p93.
[31] M Kishlansky, P Geary and P O'Brian, *Civilisation in the West,* Volume C, NY: Harper Collins, 1991, p928.

From that time the containment of Communism played an important role in helping European reconstruction.

It was not the only factor that shaped American policy toward Europe. The United States had emerged from the war richer and more powerful than ever. As a main supplier for the allied forces, its industry and business boomed. In 1945–46 the US accounted for half of the gross world products of goods and services and held two-third of the world's gold. Therefore, for the Americans it was necessary to find new markets. Only a prosperous Europe could became a major market for American goods; thus American self-interest has contributed to European recovery.

Finally, there were also humanitarian considerations which should not be minimised. Indeed, the chaos facing post-war Europe was an obstacle to any significant progress towards political stability and economic prosperity. From 1945 to 1947 Europe did not make any significant progress in this direction

1.7 The Marshall Plan (the European Recovery Programme April 1948 – December 1951)

Against the background outlined in the previous section, Truman's Secretary of State, George C Marshall, at a conference at Harvard University on 5 June 1947, announced the American plan for European reconstruction. In order to eliminate 'hunger, poverty, desperation and chaos', the real enemies of freedom and democracy, and to restore 'the confidence of the European people in the economic future of their own countries', Marshall proposed cash grants to all European nations subject to two conditions: European States were to co-operate in the distribution of American aid and they had to abolish progressively trade barriers.[32] All European nations were invited to participate in the Marshall Plan, even the Soviet Union if it contributed some of its resources to the cause. Stalin called the Plan a capitalist plot and forced all countries under his control which had expressed interest in the Plan, such as Poland and Finland, to withdraw. The British Foreign Secretary at that time, Ernest Bevin, told the UK Parliament that when the Marshall proposals were announced he grabbed them with both hands. So did other European countries. As a result of the Marshall Plan $13.6 billion was transferred to Europe, in addition to $9.5 billion in earlier loans and $500 million in private charity donations. The Marshall Plan was a huge success as it helped to restore western European trade and production while controlling inflation. By 1951 western Europe was booming. However, not only the Plan itself but, most importantly, the manner in which it was administered greatly contributed to the unity of Europe. Sixteen European countries participated in the Plan: Austria, Belgium, Denmark, France, Greece, Iceland, Ireland, Italy, Luxembourg, The Netherlands, Norway, Portugal, Sweden, Switzerland, Turkey and the United Kingdom. West Germany joined the Plan later and thus through economic co-operation West Germany was reconciled with other European countries. Under the leadership of France and the United Kingdom, the Committee of European Economic Co-operation was set up to be later replaced by the permanent

---

[32] S Hoffman and C Maier, *The Marshall Plan: A Retrospective*, Boulder Co: Westview Press, 1984, p6.

Organisation for European Economic Co-operation (OEEC) to plan and distribute American aid. The main features of the administration of the Plan were: co-operation among its participants in order to stabilise their economies; intensified planning at the inter-governmental level and thus development of a global approach toward economic recovery; limited nationalisation in all Member States; and co-operation between private and public sectors in order to free market forces, modernise production and raise productivity. The success of reconstruction through centrally co-ordinated planning and co-operation made clear that the best way for Europe to recover international position and prestige was to act as a single entity in world markets. As a result of economic co-operation within the framework of the Marshall Plan, various European organisations began to emerge in order to strengthen inter-governmental integration in political, military and economic matters.

1.8 Western European integration

In the aftermath of World War II, public opinion in many European countries favoured the adoption of a federal approach towards European integration. Winston Churchill delivered a famous speech in September 1946 at the University of Zurich which urged the formation of a United States of Europe.[33] His vision of a United Europe did not include the United Kingdom as he considered that world peace would be ensured if three powerful democratic groups – the United States of America, the United Kingdom and its Commonwealth and a United States of Europe – acted together in areas such as defence and ceratin aspects of foreign policy. The cornerstone of European unity would be the close co-operation between France and Germany. Winston Churchill as an advocate of European unity was asked to chair a meeting held in The Hague in 1948. This so-called Congress of Europe gathered together representatives of non-governmental federalist movements in Europe. It resulted in the creation of the Council of Europe. Its statute was signed on 5 May 1949 in London and entered into force on 3 August 1949.

Political integration of Europe: the Council of Europe

The Council of Europe which has its headquarters in Strasbourg is one of the most efficient and competent inter-governmental organisations in Europe. At its conception it had only ten members. Since the collapse of the Soviet Union and the admission of new members from central and eastern European States, including Russia, the Council of Europe encompasses almost the entire continent and claims a membership of 42 States. Only democratic countries which ensure the protection of human rights may become members of the Council of Europe.

The main objectives of the Council of Europe are: the promotion of European unity by proposing and encouraging common European action in economic, social, legal, and

---

[33] He declared: 'I am going to say something that will astonish you. The first step in the re-creation of the European family must be a partnership between France and Germany. … We must re-create the European family in a regional structure called, it may be, the United States of Europe' in M Charlton, *The Price of Victory*, London: British Broadcasting Corporation, 1983, pp38–39.

administrative matters; the protection of human rights, fundamental freedoms and pluralist democracy; and the development of a European cultural identity. Since the end of the Soviet regime the Council of Europe within its 'oriental' policy provides assistance to central and eastern European countries with their political, legislative and constitutional reforms. In addition, it supervises the protection of human rights in post-Communist democracies.

The greatest achievement of the Council is undoubtedly the adoption of the European Convention for the Protection of Human Rights and Fundamental Freedoms (the ECHR) based on art 3 of the Statute of the Council of Europe under which a Member State 'must accept the principles of the rule of law and of the enjoyment by all persons within its jurisdiction of human rights and fundamental freedoms'.

The Convention was adopted on 4 November 1950 and entered into force in 1953. At the time of writing 42 European States are Contracting States to the ECHR. The ECHR, together with its protocols and procedures for enforcement, constitutes the first and the most efficient regional arrangement for the protection of human rights. Rights protected under the Convention are both civil and political rights. The originality of the ECHR lies in its unique enforcement machinery which has become even more efficient as a result of the entry into force of the 11th Protocol on 1 November 1998.

Although all important problems relating to Europe are discussed and examined by the Council of Europe, its considerable work towards European unity has been to some extent overshadowed by other European organisations. There is no area which the Council has left unattended. Under the auspices of the Council of Europe over 150 conventions have been established and more than 133 are in force in Member States. These include: the European Social Charter of 1961, in operation since 1965, regarding social, economic and cultural rights; the European Code of Social Security; and the conventions on the prevention of torture, terrorism, spectator violence, etc.

Military integration

The Western European Union

The Western European Union (WEU) was founded on 6 May 1955 on the basis of the Brussels Treaty 1948 which provided for collective defence and co-operation in economic, social and cultural matters. Its initial members were: the United Kingdom, France, Belgium, Luxembourg and The Netherlands. West Germany and Italy were allowed to join later. The WEU was intended to strengthen security co-operation among Contracting States and for that reason other activities envisaged by the 1948 Treaty were transferred to the Council of Europe. The WEU, as a result of the creation of NATO, lost its importance at European level. However, it has been revitalised by the Treaty of Maastricht. Under the Pillar 2 of the Treaty on European Union the WEU was recognised as a potentially important component of a future common defence policy. The Treaty of Amsterdam incorporated the WEU into the EU structure with a view to its carving out such important tasks as might in the future be assigned to it, especially in connection with defence implications.

The North Atlantic Treaty Organisation

The Cold War necessitated the establishment of a common European military defence system to respond to the threat of a Soviet attack on western Europe. However, the initiative in this respect came from the United States. The North Atlantic Treaty Organisation (NATO) was established in order to implement the North Atlantic Treaty, signed on 4 April 1949 and in force from 24 August 1949. NATO is based on art 51 of the United Nations Charter, which provides for the right of collective self-defence, and art 52, which recognises the existence of regional arrangements dealing with international peace and security and consistent with the purposes and principles of the United Nations.[34] Its principle objective is described in art 5 of the North Atlantic Treaty which provides 'that an armed attack against one or more of them in Europe or North America shall be considered an attack against them all', and that in the event of such an attack 'each Member State would take individually and in concert with the other Parties such action as it deems necessary, including the use of armed force'. The news of the production of an atomic bomb by the Soviet Union in September 1949 prompted the American Congress to allocate $1.5 billion to arm NATO. Altogether $25 billion were transferred to Member States in the first 20 years of its existence.

Until the end of the Cold war, the United States' contribution to NATO consisted of the deployment of US tactical nuclear weapons in western Europe and approximately 300 thousand members of conventional forces stationed mostly in Germany but also in other NATO countries. The future of NATO has been under consideration since the end of the Cold War in 1990. Indications are that NATO is proposing to change from a military to a political organisation with the objective of maintaining international stability in Europe.

Economic integration – the Benelux Union and the Schuman Plan

In political and military matters European integration has taken a classical form. Through various international organisations European countries decided to co-operate and no limitations were imposed on their national sovereignty. However, a change of approach was adopted by the Benelux countries and the creation of the European Steel and Coal Community based on the Robert Schuman plan.

Benelux Union
The idea of close co-operation between the Benelux countries (Belgium, The Netherlands and Luxembourg) was not new. In 1851 The Netherlands and Luxembourg were linked by a personal union (a common ruler), and further attempts in this direction took place in 1869, 1886 and 1907. Finally, an economic union between Belgium and Luxembourg was signed on 2 July 1921 and entered into force on 1 May 1922. Thus, it is not surprising that towards the end of World War II the governments in exile of Belgium, The Netherlands and Luxembourg signed, on 5 September 1944 in London, the Customs Convention as a first step toward the creation of total economic integration. The Customs Convention was aimed at ensuring free circulation of goods, persons, capital and services, at establishing a common customs duties tariff vis-à-vis the external world, and a common policy in

---

[34] The following States are Contracting Parties to NATO: Belgium, Canada, Denmark, France, West Germany (from 1955 and from 1990 the unified Germany), Greece, Iceland, Italy, Luxembourg, The Netherlands, Norway, Portugal, Spain, Turkey, the UK, the USA, Poland, the Czech Republic and Hungary. In 1966 France formally withdrew from NATO but is still a party to the Treaty.

economic, financial and social matters. The London Customs Convention came into force in 1948. By 1956 almost all barriers to internal trade were eliminated. The success of the customs union prompted the three countries to extend their integration. On 3 February 1958 they signed the Treaty of the Benelux Economic Union which became operative on 1 November 1960. As a result the three countries became one economy and the free movement of goods, labour, capital and services was completed by co-ordination of welfare policies and standardisation of postal and transport rates. Finally, in 1970, all internal border controls were eliminated.

Common institutions were set up in order to supervise the proper functioning of the Union: the Committee of Ministers as its legislative body; the Inter-parliamentary Consultative Council, which is an emanation of national parliaments; the Council of the Economic Union, which is an executive body; the Consultative Economic and Social Council, which has advisory functions in relation to all social and economic matters of common interest; and the Arbitral College, which is empowered to settle disputes arising out of the Treaty and concerning its application. Awards by the Arbitral College are adopted by a majority of votes and are final.

On 31 March 1965 the Benelux Court of Justice was set up in order to ensure the uniform application and interpretation of Union law. It is made up of nine judges (three from the Supreme Court of each Member State) and three Advocates-General. The Benelux Court of Justice delivers preliminary rulings on matters of interpretation of the Benelux Treaties. When such a question is raised before any court of a Member State, that court may, where it considers it necessary to enable it to give judgment, refer the matter to the Benelux Court of Justice for a preliminary ruling. The Council of Ministers may, at any time, ask the Benelux Court of Justice for an advisory opinion on a point of law and without following any special procedure.

The Benelux Economic Union has been very successful. During its early years internal trade between the Benelux countries increased by 50 per cent and the increase in external trade placed them in fifth position behind the United States, the United Kingdom, West Germany and Canada.

The Benelux experiment encouraged other European countries to seek new forms of economic integration.

The Schuman Plan
After World War II France was interested in achieving regional economic arrangements. The first attempt resulted in the signature of the Protocol of Turin on 20 March 1948, which was a blueprint for a customs union between Italy and France. However, this so-called Francital, conceived by Robert Schuman and Count Sforza, never materialised. The failure of Francital and the refusal of the United Kingdom to form a customs union with France to counteract the growing independence and recovery of Germany prompted Robert Schuman, the French Minister for Foreign Affairs, to seek a different solution.[35] Robert Schuman followed the advice of Winston Churchill, who emphasised in his speeches that France should take Germany back into the community of nations. In addition, Robert Schuman, who fought

---

[35] P Gerbet, La *génése du Plan Schuman, dès origines à la Déclaration du 9 mai 1950*, Revue française de science politique, 1956, p525 et seq. See also P Fontaine, *A New Idea for Europe, The Schuman Declaration: 1950–2000*, Luxembourg: Office for Official Publications of the European Communities, 2000.

during World War I on the German side, studied in Bonn and was fluent in German, was the right person to make the first step in the normalisation of relations with Germany. He believed that Europe was facing three problems: economic dominance by the United States, military dominance by the Soviet Union and a possible war with a rejuvenated Germany. The Americans supported the idea of political and economic integration in Europe since it would, in the long term, reduce the cost of their obligations and commitments in Europe. Robert Schuman considered that the best way to achieve stability in Europe was to place the production of steel and coal (two commodities then essential to conduct a modern conventional war) under the international control of a supranational entity. The creation of a common market for steel and coal meant that interested countries would delegate their powers in those commodities to an independent authority. On 9 May 1950[36] Robert Schuman announced his Plan, based on proposals put forward by Jean Monnet, an eminent French economist and the 'father of European integration'. Although in Schuman's Plan only France and Germany were expressly mentioned, Schuman invited other European States to join and 'in particular, Britain, Italy, and the Benelux countries'.

The Schuman Plan was enthusiastically accepted by Germany, and Konrad Adenauer, the German Chancellor, saw it as a breakthrough towards the beginning of German statehood and independence. Personally, Adenauer was in favour of closer relations with the West and for the abandonment of the traditional German policy which for centuries had concentrated on the East. The Schuman plan was advantageous to both parties as it offered a way to regain international respectability for Germany and in the immediate future to gain access to the Saarland, and for France the opportunity to control the German economy. The Schuman Plan attracted attention in many European countries. As a result an international conference was held in Paris on 20 June 1950 attended by France, Italy, West Germany and the Benelux countries in order to consider the Plan. Under the Presidency of Jean Monnet, the conference extended its work for ten months, a draft Treaty being produced on 19 March 1951. The Treaty that created the European Coal and Steel Community (CS) was signed on 18 April 1951 and entered into force on 25 July 1952. The Contracting Parties were: Belgium, France, Italy, Luxembourg, The Netherlands and West Germany. The CS was very successful, and by 1954 all barriers to trade in coal, coke, steel, pig iron and scrap iron were eliminated between Member States. Trade in those commodities rose spectacularly and the common pricing policy and production limits set up by the High Authority, as well as common rules on competition, merger controls, etc, rationalised the production of steel and coal within a wholly integrated market.

The CS has been described as a first step toward a federal Europe.[37] The European Community of Defence was a next stage.

---

[36] The text of the Schuman Plan was delivered to Ernest Bevin by Réné Massigli, the French ambassador in London, and specified that the French wanted: 'To place the French and German production of coal and steel as a whole under a common "Higher Authority" within the framework of an organisation open to the participation of the other countries of Europe ... by pooling basic production and by instituting a new Higher Authority whose decisions will bind France, Germany and other member countries. This proposal will lead to the realisation of the first concrete foundations of a European federation', supra note 33, p98.

[37] As Robert Schuman said while announcing his plan: 'L'Europe ne se fera pas d'un seul coup ni dans une construction d'ensemble: elle se fera par des réalisation concrétes créant d'abord une solidarité de fait', C A Colliard, *Institutions des relations internationales,* 9ème ed, Paris: Dalloz, 1990, p524.

The European Defence Community

In 1950 the tension between the Soviet Union and the United States mounted as the conflict in Korea escalated, and as a result the US commitments in this region increased. The Cold War between the two blocs forced the re-examination of German participation in rearmament and in European defence. Réné Plevin, the French Defence Minister, a personal assistant to Jean Monnet in wartime London, and inspired by Churchill's motion carried out by the Council of Europe in April 1950 regarding the creation of a European army, had drafted a common defence plan. The plan was presented to the Council of Europe in 1951 by Robert Schuman and called for the formation of a supra-national European army in which German soldiers would 'be Europeans, in European uniforms, under European command'. The plan kept the number of German soldiers to a strict minimum, while the financial contribution of Germany was considerable. The idea behind the plan was to let the Germans defend Europe without conferring upon them too much power. It was a very controversial plan but fully endorsed by the US. The plan was transformed into a Treaty which created the European Defence Community, signed on 27 May 1952 in Paris. However, its fate hinged upon British participation in the plan. The UK response came from two British cabinet ministers supporting diametrically opposed positions in two foreign European cities. Maxwell Fyfe, the Home Secretary, declared in Strasbourg that the UK agreed in principle but a few hours later, Anthony Eden, then Foreign Secretary, at a press conference in Rome where he was attending a NATO meeting, pronounced a definitive 'no'. The President of the Council of Europe, Paul-Henri Spaak, a well known Anglophile and a fervent supporter of European federalism, tendered his resignation in protest against the British 'betrayal'. The Council of Europe was outraged and disappointed by the UK answer. As a result, the Plevin plan failed and was formally terminated when the French parliament refused to ratify the Treaty. However, visionaries like Paul-Henri Spaak learnt a precious lesson from this abortive attempt at closer European integration. Only a supra-national organisation requiring surrender of national sovereignty on the part of Member States could achieve European integration. This idea was examined at the meeting of ministers for foreign affairs of the European Coal and Steel Community (CS) in Messina in 1955.

The Messina Conference

In June 1955 in Messina (Sicily) the foreign ministers of the CS decided to 'pursue the establishment of a united Europe through the development of common institutions, a progressive fusion of national economies, the creation of a common market and harmonisation of social policies'.[38] They asked Paul-Henri Spaak to preside over committees to be set up in Brussels in the forthcoming months which would prepare a blueprint for a common programme.[39] It took several meetings of foreign ministers and, an enormous amount of work by many experts and governmental officials, to prepare a draft Treaty. Finally, on 25 March 1957 in Rome, two Treaties were signed: the first established the

---

[38] *Documents on International Affairs*, 1955, p163.
[39] A summary of Part I of the Spaak Report *The Common Market* was published by Political and Economic Planning in Broadsheet, no 405 of 17 December 1956.

European Economic Community (EEC) and the second the European Atomic Energy Treaty (EA). The Treaties came into force on 1 January 1958.

1.9 The United Kingdom and European integration

After World War II the leadership of the United Kingdom was badly needed in building a new Europe; it was the only country in Europe that had neither surrendered nor been invaded by the Germans. The United Kingdom's prestige as liberator had predisposed it to the great destiny of championing the movement towards European integration. Furthermore, during the war the UK had been a home to many European governments in exile and accordingly at that time enjoyed close links with, and the friendship of, the European political and intellectual elite. France, although on the winning side at the end of the war, had been compromised by the Vichy regime, destroyed by English and American bombing, and, like the rest of the continent, was demoralised by years under Nazi occupation. Winston Churchill as early as 1942 had explained his vision of post-war Europe:

> 'I must admit that my thoughts rest primarily in Europe, in the revival of the glory of Europe, the parent continent of modern nations and of civilisation. It would be a measureless disaster if Russian barbarism overlaid the culture and independence of the ancient states of Europe. Hard as it is to say now, I trust that the European family may act unitedly as one, under a Council of Europe in which the barriers between nations will be greatly minimised and unrestricted travel will be possible. I hope to see the economy of Europe studied as a whole.'[40]

However, in his speech in 1946 in Zurich, Churchill made clear that the United Kingdom had assigned for herself the role of a sponsor and a friend of a United States of Europe and would remain aloof from full participation in plans for European integration. There are three essential reasons for the UK's reluctance. First, at that time, the UK was still centre of a great empire with all her colonies intact. As a great sea power with a large empire her interests were not in Europe. As Churchill emphasised 'If there is a choice for the United Kingdom between Europe and the sea, she will always choose the sea.' Second, the UK based her future on the 'special relationship' with the United States. Already, a common language, culture, law and institutions of parliamentary democracy had built solid foundations for a mutual understanding that was further reinforced by a common vision of the post-war world described in the Atlantic Charter. Moreover, the United States emerged after the war as the greatest economic, commercial and military power in the world. The development of the atomic weapon, in which the British fully participated, was an additional factor in maintaining the 'special relationship'. When on 6 August 1945 the Superfortress Enola Gay dropped an atomic bomb on Hiroshima causing the death of about 78,000 people and injuring around 100,000 more, the entire world recognised the US hegemony in international relations. The United Kingdom, because of the close link with the US, had been a nuclear power from the beginning. Finally, World War II had shown the vulnerability of the concept of a nation State and both the governments in exile and those subjected to Nazi occupation had lost faith in this concept. The UK, to the contrary, was convinced that

---

[40] Supra note 33, p13.

her sovereignty should not be undermined and that Britain's insularity had given to its sovereignty an important additional dimension of security.

When, in April 1949, Jean Monnet, the architect of European integration, travelled to London in order to discuss a possible union between France and the United Kingdom, his proposals were turned down. Ernest Bevin, foreign minister in Attlee's government, was not interested because the British government was convinced that the UK was still a great independent power and saw no reason for surrendering sovereignty. However, when on 9 May 1948 the Schuman Plan was announced, the British government was genuinely surprised at the French initiative, furious at not being consulted and felt cheated when it learnt that the plan was known and approved by the United States. The French invitation to join the Plan was declined, and the UK government also refused to participate in any negotiations regarding the future structure of the steel, iron and coal community, including the issue of competencies of the supra-national entity charged with its functioning. The refusal ran contrary to Winston Churchill's view. As leader of the opposition he accused the Labour government of 'piling their own prejudice upon French pedantry'. According to Harold Wilson, Harold Macmillian (also in opposition) had strongly opposed the Schuman Plan, declaring 'he was not having anyone in Europe telling him which pits to close down [and that] we will not allow any supra-national authority to put large numbers of our people out of work in Durham, in the Midlands, in South Wales and Scotland'.[41]

The Labour government at that time did not realise the significance and the implications of the Schuman Plan; the decision not to negotiate over the Plan was taken by the Cabinet when Prime Minister Attlee was on holiday in France and Bevin, the foreign minister, in hospital.

In 1951 the Conservatives came to power and Winston Churchill became Prime Minister, but the change in government did not bring a change in the British position. At that stage it was not too late to join the Schuman Plan as it had not yet been ratified but, contrary to Churchill's federalist speeches in Zurich and Strasbourg and the expectations of all continental western European countries, no shift in UK European policy took place. Churchill's romantic views on Europe did not translate into actions. He confirmed in 1950 what he wrote in 1930 in his article on 'The United States of Europe' which was published in the *Saturday Evening Post* in the United States, that is, that the UK wanted to be 'with Europe but not of it, linked but not comprised'. The British refusal to participate in the European Defence Community disappointed the Europeans as well as the Americans. The subsequent decision of the British government, under Anthony Eden as Prime Minister, concerning the Messina Conference and the refusal to participate in negotiations leading to the Treaty of Rome, finally closed the door for the UK to become an original member of the EC. More importantly, the UK lost its opportunity to shape European integration. At Messina, Russell Bretherton, an under-secretary at the Board of Trade, and a minor official at that, represented the United Kingdom, while eminent politicians and foreign ministers of the CS attended the Conference. Russell Bretherton was instructed before attending the Messina Conference not to commit the UK government to any European initiatives.

The original six did not give up on the UK, and on 7 June 1955 their foreign ministers prompted by the Benelux countries and supported by France sent an invitation to the

---

[41] Supra note 33, p109.

British government to take part in the preparation of a new agenda for Europe. At this stage even the six were uncertain whether they should form a customs union or a free trade area or a common external tariff, and in what fields the integration should be pursued. For that reason the Benelux memorandum submitted at the Messina Conference which put forward the concept of a common market was accepted as a basis for future discussions. Once again, the UK sent Russell Bretherton to Brussels with the same instructions he had been given for the Messina Conference. His presence, short-lived since he was recalled to the UK in November 1955, confirmed the negative attitude of the UK towards European integration.

As the work of 'Spaak committees' focused on plans for a common market, in the absence of any British representatives Paul-Henri Spaak decided to come to London in order to personally convince the British to join the negotiations. After meetings with the Chancellor of the Exchequer and the Foreign Secretary, the position of the UK was clear. European projects were not taken seriously in London and the official British position was that co-operation with Europe was approved but no commitments should be made. Other attempts by Brussels to encompass and enrol the UK into a common market during the period of gestation of the European Communities were regarded by Anthony Eden, the UK Prime Minister, and Rab Butler, the Chancellor of the Exchequer, the two most influential people in the Cabinet, as 'a bore'.[42] In the meantime, in Brussels the European integration took concrete form. The Spaak Report and its recommendations favouring the creation of a common market in the form of a customs union were adopted by the foreign ministers of the six countries in Venice in May 1956.[43] The biggest surprise was the French adherence to this project. It demonstrated that the French government after suffering humiliating defeats in Indo-China in 1954, growing unrest in North Africa and a very difficult economic situation at home had made necessary changes to its traditional policy. According to Charlton: 'Britain's orderly transition from Empire to Commonwealth, and the dimension and nature of her overseas relationship, offered no strict analogy and no similar sense of urgency'[44] in making new arrangements and reassessing traditional foreign policy.

However, the British as a pragmatic nation decided to submit its own proposal in respect of European integration. It was the 'Plan G' regarding the Industrial European Free Trade Association (IEFTA) and confined exclusively to industrial goods. It is still controversial whether the British Plan G was a genuine British initiative, or a rival to a common market or was designed to sabotage the common market. In any event, the British tried to revive OEEC (see section 1.7) in order to use it as a platform for launching Plan G, and especially in order to associate the concept of IEFTA with the European common market. Plan G was rejected by the six when they decided that no association was possible between the 'outer seven' and the common market. It was also considered of peripheral importance by the United States that had enthusiastically supported European integration within the common market from its conception. Nevertheless, in 1960 Plan G became the foundation of the European Free Trade Association (EFTA) comprising the UK, Norway, Sweden, Denmark, Austria, Switzerland and Portugal.

---

[42] Supra note 33, p195.

[43] It was one of the shortest meeting of the Six, in one-and-a-half hours the Conference confirmed the decision to establish the common market, supra note 33, p197.

[44] Ibid, p205.

During 1960s the attitude of the United Kingdom towards European integration changed dramatically. Many considerations dictated the reappraisal of the UK position, but the two most important were the end of the British Empire and the Suez conflict in 1957, the latter of which demonstrated the fragility of the 'special relationship' with the United States. A common military invasion of Suez by the UK, France and Israel was jointly condemned by the Soviet Union and the US and thus destroyed the illusion that the UK was still a great independent power. This was brought home by: the realisation that the UK was too poor to remain as an important nuclear power as it was unable to finance its own long-range missile 'Blue Streak'; the change of the Prime Minister as Anthony Eden resigned suffering from a nervous breakdown after the Suez conflict; and the growing feeling in UK political circles that the place of the UK was in Europe. Economic considerations were also important – the success of the common market being self-evident. In addition, in the 1960s for the first time the UK exported more to Europe than to the Commonwealth. As a result, on 31 July 1961, a formal announcement was made in the House of Commons of the UK's intention to lodge an application for accession to the Treaty of Rome. However, Harold Macmillan, the Prime Minister of the UK at that time, faced an impossible mission: he had to convince General Charles de Gaulle that the British intentions were genuine.

1.10 The French refusal of British accession

In order to understand the French refusal, it is necessary to examine French policy under de Gaulle. His foreign policy was based on two principles. First, he believed in the concept of a nation State and that national interests, not ideologies, were the driving force in international relations. Supra-nationality, being diametrically opposed to the concept of a nation State, was considered a dangerous illusion. It was an illusion since, in reality, only national interests existed and were pursued even within a supra-national structure although in a disguised form. And it was dangerous since the common consciousness inherent to the concept of a nation State could not command allegiance to a supra-national organisation. As a result, the supra-national structure lacked an essential and vital element, namely the common consciousness upon which all national feelings are based and thus could easily serve as a device of American hegemony. The second principle was the policy of 'greatness' (grandeur) for France, that is, independence from any foreign interference. For that reason de Gaulle decided to develop a French nuclear deterrent and thus end the American nuclear monopoly. France was to play a unique role in world politics as a third force, between the Soviet Union and the United States. De Gaulle's vision of Europe was based upon the 'European Europe' as a neutral third force, free of all domination but led by France. As Cerny said, the objective of France was to 'increase (France's) manoeuvrability and to widen her options ... [to] exploit the structural interstices and the margins of the international system' in order to 'escape from the strait-jacket of bi-polar equilibrium' between the Soviet Union and the United States.[45]

---

[45] P Cerny, *The Politics of Grandeur: Ideological Aspects of de Gaulle's Foreign Policy,* Cambridge: Cambridge University Press, 1980, p131.

To emphasise French independence, in 1959 de Gaulle withdrew her Mediterranean fleet from NATO command. De Gaulle disliked the Treaty of Rome but used its structure to further his ideas.

As to the negotiations between France and the UK, the two leaders, de Gaulle and Macmillan had known each other very well. Macmillian and de Gaulle were closely associated during World War II in Algiers, the Allied HQ in the Mediterranean. In 1943 de Gaulle moved the French Committee of National Liberation to Algiers and became its joint president with General Henri Giraud. Macmillan, appointed by Churchill, represented the allied interests in this area and supported de Gaulle in his political struggle against Giraud, which resulted in de Gaulle achieving full control of the French Committee of National Liberation and his recognition as the sole leader of Free France. However, the relations between the UK and de Gaulle had never been easy. De Gaulle deeply resented the fact that he was not invited to the Yalta Conference in 1945. Although Churchill took a hard line against Roosevelt and achieved the recognition of France as one of the powers to participate in the post-war settlement of Germany, de Gaulle was haunted by his Yalta complex and had never shown any gratitude toward the British for their support and assistance during World War II.

On 2 December 1958 de Gaulle was elected president of the Republic and in December 1962 the Gaullists got a parliamentary majority for the first time. The position of de Gaulle in France had never been stronger; he could now shape French foreign policy on his own.

On 14 January 1963 de Gaulle made two announcements: he blocked the British entry to the common market and rejected the United States' offer regarding the development of Polaris missiles within the framework of NATO. Both issues were interrelated. When the UK cancelled the 'Blue Streak' missile programme as being too expensive, she turned to the US for assistance. In exchange for granting the US a base for nuclear submarines at Holy Loch in Scotland, the US offered the UK the 'Skybolt', a nuclear missile, and in the future the most sophisticated weapon, the Polaris submarine. However, the 'Skybolt' missile was cancelled for technical reasons.

In December 1962, after a meeting between Macmillan and de Gaulle, at which the UK was almost certain that France would reject the British bid for entry into the common market, the British Prime Minister went to Nassau to meet the US President Kennedy. The outcome of the Nassau meeting was a triumph for UK diplomacy; the United States agreed to assign Polaris to NATO but under independent control of the UK in a moment of 'supreme national interest'. In addition, Macmillan negotiated the same deal for France. The generous offer from the US, a result of British initiative, was an additional argument in favour of the UK's accession to the Treaty of Rome as it proved that the UK had still a 'special relationship ' with the United States, and that British-French co-operation in the nuclear field, and especially in Polaris, would be beneficial for both countries once the UK was inside the common market.

In these circumstances, de Gaulle announced his veto of British entry to the common market!

De Gaulle's justifications for blocking the UK accession were that the UK was not ready for membership because of her close links with the Commonwealth, her tradition of free trade and her agriculture which would fit badly into the protectionist Common Agricultural

Policy of the EEC. The main reason, however, was the UK's 'special relationship' with the US and for de Gaulle the Polaris deal was supreme proof of the British dependence on United States. He felt that the UK would be an American Trojan horse that would reinforce the American hegemony in his 'European Europe'. A more convincing, but unstated, reason for rejecting the UK application was de Gaulle's fear of France loosing its dominance within the EEC as he had successfully forced the other Member States to implement an agricultural policy favourable to France and opposed any attempts to increase the powers of the Commission and other European institutions. Furthermore, the common market was based on a partnership between France and Germany dominated by France. De Gaulle did not want to share the leadership of Europe or allow a British challenge to French primacy within the common market.

The reasons for the French refusal were epitomised in somewhat emotional terms by Macmillan:

> 'He [de Gaulle] also had a real hatred of the Americans, and a kind of love-hate complex about the British. The truth is – I may be cynical, but I fear it is true – if Hitler had danced in the streets of London, we'd have had no trouble with de Gaulle. What they could not forgive us is that we held on, and that we saved France. People can forgive an injury, but they can hardly ever forgive a benefit.'[46]

Macmillian's disappointment and bitterness are easy to understand. After two years of extremely complex negotiations encompassing multilateral discussions with each Member State of EEC, reappraising the UK policy towards the Commonwealth (which required new arrangements in order to find ways to accommodate the Commonwealth), and convincing public opinion at home as to the necessity of the British entry into a common market, France vetoed the British application.

The second application for membership of the European Economic Community was submitted in 1967 under the Labour government of Harold Wilson. This time the answer from de Gaulle was immediate; once again he blocked the British entry.[47]

A third attempt was made by Edward Heath in 1970. At that time de Gaulle was no longer the President of France. He had resigned after losing a referendum held in February 1969 concerning the reform of the French Senate and measures regarding regional decentralisation. Although these issues were important they were not vital and the referendum provided de Gaulle an elegant means of leaving power without being forced out. In these circumstances there was no opposition to the United Kingdom membership. After concluding negotiations with the EEC in January 1972, the UK became a Member State. The European Communities Act 1972 came into force on 1 January 1973.

---

[46] Supra note 33, p262.

[47] At the press conference on 27 November 1967 he declared that the Common Market: '... is incompatible with Britain's economy as it stands, in which the chronic balance of payments deficit is proof of its permanent imbalance and which, as concerning, sources of supply\credit practices and working conditions, involves factors which that country could not alter without modifying its own nature'... and thus the UK accession: 'means breaking up a Community that was built and operates according to rules which do not tolerate such a monumental exception', Lord Cockfield, *The European Union, Creating the Single Market,* London: Wiley Chancerey Law, 1994, p10.

2 The Evolution of the European Communities

2.1 The membership of the European Union

2.2 Territorial expansion of the Communities

2.3 Consolidation of the European Communities

The main changes in the development of the European Communities can be divided into two categories: first, the geographical expansion of the Communities from six original Members to 15, and upward to 20 and beyond; and, second, consolidation of their structure accompanied by extended co-operation among Member States, both as to the subject-matter and methods of achievement of common objectives.

This chapter focuses on two major issues. First, the requirements for admission of new Members, together with the unprecedented institutional and political challenges posed by the process of enlargement to include central and eastern European countries, Cyprus, Malta and Turkey within the EU. The practical problems resulting from accessions subsequent to the Communities' original formation will also be examined. Second, fundamental reforms to the structure of the European Communities and their implications upon the process of European integration will be analysed. It is quite clear that the vision of Europe presented by the founding fathers more than 50 years ago, with a view of establishing a more market-oriented structure, conflicts with the 'model' of Europe now required. With the globalisation of economics, the technical innovations of the post-World War II era, and the emergence of worldwide electronic networks, the world has become increasingly interdependent and vulnerable to rapidly changing economic forces. Also, many problems such as the widening gap between the north and the south, the rich and the poor and cross-border issues, such as drug-trafficking, money-laundering, organised crime, control of immigration, etc, which threaten the stability of our society, require regulation at international level. The need for common policies on a European or wider scale implies that the traditional role of a nation State with classical power politics has ended. Some people in the United Kingdom and other Member States have not yet grasped the practical implications of this change. By ignoring the reality, this faction of European public opinion continues to perceive the growing competence of the European Union as a loss of national sovereignty. However, the re-definition of common objectives for mankind on a regional as well as an international level constitutes the only answer to the changes of the twenty-first century. As the Belgian Prime Minister, L Tindemans, emphasised in his *Report on the European Union*:

> '... a return to inter-governmental co-operation would not help to solve European problems. Such co-operation tends to underline the differences of power and interest between our countries and does not meet our collective needs.'[1]

[1] EC Bull Supp 1–76; see also J D B Mitchell, 'The Tindemans Report – Retrospect and Prospect' (1976) 13 CMLR 455.

2.1 The membership of the European Union

All Member States of the EU are equal[2] in that they enjoy the same privileges and have to fulfil the same obligations vis-à-vis each other and the EU. Unlike certain international organisations (eg UNESCO) no special status is granted to any Member State of the EU. It is important to note that:

1. Article 182 EC, which allows a Member State to associate with the Community some non-European countries and territories which have a special relationship with that State (overseas territories which are part of a Member State, etc), provides for the territorial extension of the scope of application of the EC Treaty but does not create a genuine association between these territories and the EU which implies participation in European structures.
2. Even if a State has concluded an association agreement with the EC, for example, on the basis of art 310 EC, it is still outside the EC and therefore cannot be considered as a Member State.

Admission to the European Union

The three Communities have been created by multilateral treaties which were negotiated, signed, ratified and entered into force in accordance with classical rules of the law of treaties by the six original Members: Belgium, France, Germany, Italy, Luxembourg and The Netherlands.

All three Communities were open for future accession by other European countries. Before the creation of the European Union the procedure for admission was expressly provided by the three founding Treaties: art 98 CS, art 237 EEC (now repealed) and art 205 EA. All three Treaties provided that a candidate State had to submit its application for admission to the Council which was then required to ask the Commission for an opinion before taking a final decision. That was, however, the only identical part of the admission procedure. A candidate State had to seek admission separately to each Community. The procedure for admission to the CS was different from that relating to the two remaining Communities. Under art 98 CS the conditions for admission were to be determined by the 'decision' of the Council. It was a purely Community matter, and by a unilateral act of the Council a candidate State became a Member State. It had to deposit its accession instrument to the CS with the French government, the depository of the Treaty of Paris of 1951.

In practice, however, there was only one procedure for admission of a new Member State since it had to accede to all three Communities at the same time.[3] Admission to the CS and EA was accessory and a direct consequence of the admission to the EC, the application for which posed the most difficult and complex political and economic problems.

An unwritten but necessary condition of admission was also imposed upon the candidate State, that is, its participation in co-operation, mainly in the area of foreign policy. The

---

[2] In this respect it is interesting to note what Jean Monnet said: 'I have always realised that equality is absolutely essential in relations between nations, as it is between people': Monnet, *Memoirs*, London: Collins, 1978, p97.
[3] According to the Resolution on the co-ordination of the three European Communities adopted by the European Parliamentary Assembly: OJ no 9 of 1958, p260 et seq.

(second) meeting of the Heads of State or Government at Bad Godesberg on 18 July 1961, which laid down foundations for political co-operation among Members States, expressly mentioned that new Members were required to participate in activities leading to political unification.[4]

The Treaty on European Union modified the procedure for admission which is now incorporated in art 49 EU. This provision states that:

> 'Any European State which respects the principles set out in art 6(1) may apply to become a Member of the Union. It shall address its application to the Council, which shall act unanimously after consulting the Commission and after receiving the assent of the European Parliament, which shall act by an absolute majority of its component members.
>
> The conditions of admission and the adjustments to the Treaties on which the Union is founded which such admission entails shall be the subject of an agreement between the Member States and the applicant State. This agreement shall be submitted for ratification by all the Contracting States in accordance with their respective constitutional requirements.'

By virtue of art 49 EU a candidate State accedes to the European Union which implies its admission to all three Communities.

Requirements for admission

The conditions for admission are both substantial and formal. As to the substance, certain legal and political requirements must be satisfied by a new Member State. The procedure for admission is complex and lengthy.

'Legal' requirements imposed upon a candidate State The legal requirements imposed upon a candidate State are specified in the EU and can be easily verified by the European Court of Justice (ECJ). In this respect an action against a 'decision of admission' issued by the Council can be brought under art 230 EC. However, the ECJ is limited solely to reviewing whether the legal conditions and procedural requirements for admission were fulfilled by the Community institutions. Any decision on the merits of a State's admission remains within the discretion of the Council and escapes the jurisdiction of the ECJ. This was confirmed in *Lothar Mattheus v Duego Fruchtimport und Tiefkuhlkost* Case 93/78 [1978] ECR 2203.

In this case the parties entered into a contract on 1 August 1977. According to their agreement the claimant would set up market survey systems in Spain and Portugal, to be operational by the date of the decision of the accession of those States to the EC. In consideration the defendant was to pay a half-yearly lump sum to cover the plaintiff's expenses. The contract contained the following clause:

> 'This agreement is definitively concluded for a period of five years. If the said accession should not in fact or in law prove to be unpracticable, the principal [Duego] shall have the right to terminate this agreement. The decisive factor in determining whether the said accession is practicable in law shall be a decision of the ECJ. In the event of a justifiable termination the Agent shall lose his right to repayment of expenses.
>
> ... The courts in Essen shall have jurisdiction in matters arising out of this agreement.'

---

[4] EC Bull 1961, points 7, 8.

As a result of long delays in respect of the admission of Spain and Portugal Mattheus wrote to the defendants on 29 January 1978 requesting reimbursement of DM 527.85 expenses, the defendants terminated the contract under the above clause and were sued in the local court, Amtsgericht Essen, which made a reference to the ECJ for a preliminary ruling under art 234 EC asking three questions:

1. whether art 237 EEC (now repealed), standing alone or in conjunction with other articles of the EC Treaty, is to be interpreted as meaning that it imposes substantive legal limits on the accession of third countries over and above the formal conditions laid down in art 237 EEC?;
2. what are those limits?; and
3. is the accession of Spain, Portugal and Greece for reasons of Community law not possible in the future?

The ECJ held that art 234 EC empowers it to give preliminary rulings on the interpretation of the Treaty upon reference from any national court or tribunal. The division of powers within the Community is mandatory and it cannot be impeded by arrangements by private persons tending to compel courts to request a preliminary ruling, thus depriving them of the independent exercise of the discretion they are granted by art 234 EC. Article 237 EEC (now repealed) laid down a precise procedure encompassed within well defined limits for the admission of new Member States, during which the conditions for accession were drawn up by the authorities indicated in the article itself. Thus, the legal conditions for such accession remained to be defined in the context of that procedure without it being possible to determine the content judicially in advance. The ECJ cannot give a ruling on the form or subject-matter of the conditions that may be applied. The ECJ has no jurisdiction to give a ruling on the question referred to it by the national court.

As to the legal requirements themselves, there are four of them. First, a candidate State must be recognised as a State. In this respect, reference to the rules of public international law will clarify the legal status of the applying entity. In practice, since the Council must reach a unanimous decision regarding the admission of a candidate State, if the latter is not recognised by any Member State, its application for admission will be rejected. So far no problem has arisen in this area, although the candidacy of Cyprus poses delicate problems. The Republic of Cyprus came into being on 16 August 1960 but, due to many factors, the most important being the Turkish invasion of the island in 1974, is now divided into two sectors: Greek and Turkish. In May 1983 the Rauf Denktash movement, which represents Turkish Cypriots, proclaimed the creation of the Turkish Republic of Northern Cyprus, which although recognised by Turkey is not recognised as an independent State by the international community. Second, a candidate State must be a European State. This requirement can be explained by the fact that the EU wants to preserve the European identity of the Union. In the Declaration on European Identity of 14 December 1973 the Heads of State or Government described the essential elements of European identity as 'principles of representative democracy, of the rule of law, of social justice – which is the ultimate goal of economic progress – and of respect for human rights'.[5] The Commission in its report on *Europe and the Challenge of Enlargement* stated that:

---

[5] EC Bull 1973–12, point 130.

'The term "European" has not been officially defined. It combines geographical, historical and cultural elements... and is subject to review. It is neither possible nor opportune to establish now the frontiers of the European Union, whose contours will be shaped over many years to come.'[6]

At the time of writing, there are 45 States in Europe. Some of them have had a short existence as States, having become independent as a result of the collapse of the Soviet Union and the Yugoslav Federation and through the division of Czechoslovakia into the Czech Republic and Slovakia. Until now, only one non-European State has submitted an application for admission – Morocco in 1985 – which was rejected in 1987 by the Council as being incompatible with art 237 EEC (now repealed).

The third and fourth conditions are set out in art 6 EU. Article 6(1) EU stipulates that: 'The Union is founded on the principles of lib erty, democracy, respect for human rights and fundamental freedoms, and the rule of law, principles which are common to the Member States'. The liberal-democratic model of government of a candidate State, which ensures the respect for civil, political, economic and social rights of its citizens, is a vital element of membership of the EU.[7] Furthermore, art 6(2) EU adds that the EU respects fundamental human rights as guaranteed by the European Convention for the Protection of Human Rights and Fundamental Freedoms of 1950 and as they 'result from the constitutional traditions common to the Member States, as general principles of Community law'. Therefore, only democratic States which respect human rights can apply for membership. These implicit, but essential, conditions were confirmed in practice in relation to Greece. From 1961 Greece was associated with the European Communities with a view to becoming a Member State in the then near future. However, the military coup led by Colonel G Papadopoulos, and the following rule of a ruthless and brutal military junta (1967–1974), stopped Greek progress towards membership. With the restoration of democracy, relations between Greece and the European Communities were resumed. In 1981 Konstantinos Karamanlis, democratically elected President of the Hellenic Republic, finally accomplished his main political objective, that is, membership of the European Communities for Greece.

With adoption of arts 6 and 7 EU the promotion and protection of human rights has been woven into the structures of the EU. Its concern for the advancement of human rights is vital for obvious reasons. As Andrey Sakharow, a Nobel laureate and Russian dissident, once wrote: 'The defence of human rights is a clear path toward the unification of people in our turbulent world, and a path toward the relief of suffering.'[8]

Economic and political requirements A candidate State may satisfy all legal conditions and still be rejected by the EU. The decision is taken by all Member States after they have assessed all advantages and disadvantages flowing from the proposed enlargement. As a result, political and economic criteria play an important role. The level of economic

---

[6] EC Bull Supp 3–92, point 7.

[7] See Frowein, 'The European Community and the Requirement of a Republican Form of Government' (1984) 82 Michigan Law Review 1311 et seq.

[8] *Encyclopedia Britannica*, 20 Macropaedia, 15th ed, p664.

development was crucial in the 1995 enlargement regarding Sweden, Finland, Austria and Norway, all of them wealthy, relatively small and members of the European Economic Area.

As to political requirements, the most important is the acceptance by a candidate State of the 'acquis communautare',[9] which according to the European Parliament constitutes a 'criterion of global integration'.[10] This term means, in the context of accession,[11] the acceptance by a new Member State, without reservation, and from the commencement of its formal membership, of the body of common rights and obligations which bind all EU Member States together. The 'acquis' are constantly evolving and comprise:

1. The normative 'acquis' such as

    -   the founding Treaties and their amendments,
    -   acts enacted by the institutions such as regulations, directives, decisions, recommendations and opinions (art 249 EC, art 14 CS, art 161 EA);
    -   other acts whose adoption is provided by the Treaties (eg rules of procedures, etc);
    -   measures adopted in the area of the external relations of the Communities, such as agreements entered into by any of Communities with one or more third State, with international organisations, or with a national of a third State, as well as so-called 'mixed agreements', that is, agreements and international conventions between Member States and any of the Community, acting jointly;
    -   other agreements whose conclusion have been necessary to attain the objectives of the Treaties, such as the Agreement of January 1957 establishing European Schools. This category also includes agreements concluded on the basis of art 293 EC, such as the 1968 Brussels Convention on Jurisdiction and the Enforcement of Judgments in Civil and Commercial Matters, the 1980 Rome Convention on the Law Applicable to Contractual Obligations, etc;
    -   the Treaty on European Union (TEU) and measures enacted in relation to Pillars 2 and 3 of the TEU as amended by the Treaty of Amsterdam.

2. The political 'acquis' such as declarations, resolutions, principles and guidelines, etc, adopted by the European Council, the Council of the EU. Also common agreements of the Member States regarding development and strengthening of the Communities and the Union.

3. The judicial 'acquis', that is case law of the Court of Justice of the European Communities (ECJ) which outlines the essential characteristics of the Community legal order (direct effect, supremacy, unification, co-operation between ECJ and national courts). However, in the Acts of Accession there is no reference to specific case law for two reasons: first, the rulings of the ECJ are 'acts' of the European institutions and thus

---

[9] This term is usually used in French, see the English version of the TEU, although it was translated as 'Community patrimony' in *Commissionaires Reunis et Ramel* Joined Cases 80 and 81/77 [1978] ECR 927, para. 36. On the 'acquis communautaire': see P Pescatore, *Aspects judiciares de l'acquis communautaire,* RTDE, pp617-651.

[10] In its Resolution on enlargement adopted on 15 July 1993, the European Parliament emphasised that all candidate States must accept the 'acquis communautaire', including the TEU and the objectives of further integration and that the opt-outs options should be eliminated: OJ C225 (1993).

[11] On different aspects of the acquis communautaire: see C C Gialdino, 'Some Reflections on the Acquis Communautaire' [1995] CMLR 1089–1121.

already part of the 'acquis communautaire' and second, it is unnecessary and even dangerous to 'freeze' the case law of the ECJ for new members and, at the same time, allow its further development for older Member States. Indeed, the ECJ is not bound by its own decisions and it may always change the existing case law in order to promote the new and essential objectives of the EU.

The acceptance of the 'acquis communautaire' is a *sine quoi non* of the accession as it encompasses rights and obligations attached to the Union and its institutional framework. Candidate states must accept the 'acquis' before they join the EU. Only in exceptional circumstances are exemptions and derogations granted. Under the accession partnership agreement each candidate State has drawn up a detailed programme for adoption of the 'acquis', together with a timetable and details of the necessary human and financial resources required for the implementation of the 'acquis'.

Procedure for admission

The first step consists of submitting a formal application for admission in the form of a letter signed by the minister for foreign affairs of a candidate State to the Presidency of the Council of the European Union. At that stage the Member States decide whether to initiate negotiations with an applicant State. This process can take a considerable time. The Commission also becomes involved and, after investigations, presents a 'preliminary opinion' which either recommends the opening of negotiations or advises the Member States to wait until certain requirements are satisfied by a candidate State, or expresses its opposition to the admission. This opinion is not binding but is nevertheless of great influence. This influence is demonstrated by the fact that the Commission convinced the Member States to 'freeze' the enlargement of the EC until the completion of the common market.

The Council may take a position regarding the 'preliminary opinion' of the Commission by adopting the 'conclusion', which in the case of Cyprus and Malta confirmed the favourable opinion of the Commission. However, in relation to Greek accession the Council ignored the negative preliminary opinion of the Commission.[12]

Some negotiations have been lengthy and complex (Spain, Portugal), others swiftly and smoothly concluded (Austria, Finland, Norway and Sweden). Until the conclusion of negotiations admission is uncertain. The negotiations are conducted by the Council acting on proposals submitted by the Commission in which the latter endeavours to establish a common basis for negotiations and then plays the role of a broker between the Members States and a candidate State. If no major problems arise the negotiations end with a draft Treaty of Accession which has to be signed by the representatives of all Member States and the candidate State. The Treaty of Accession is usually very short, in the case of the UK it consists of three articles stating that the UK accedes to the three Communities and accepts all Community law, but the Act of Accession annexed to the Treaty of Accession is a voluminous document often accompanied by protocols, annexes and declarations. All these documents, apart from declarations which have an interpretative function, are legally binding.

---

[12] The Council, solely for political reasons, that is, to support nascent democracy in Greece, decided to accept the Greek application for admission: Opinion on the Greek Application for Membership: EC Bull Supp 2–76.

At the end of accession negotiations the Council has to take a final decision after consultations with the Commission and the European Parliament. The opinion of the Commission is not binding but in practice, as the Commission is fully involved in negotiations, its opinion is always followed. The European Parliament (EP) for the first time adopted the assent procedure in 1994 regarding the admission of Austria, Finland, Norway and Sweden. By four 'legislative resolutions' on 4 May 1994, the EP granted its assent to the accession of four new Members. During the proceedings leading to membership of these States, the EP was kept informed by the Council and by the Commission of their progress in negotiations and expressed its comments in several resolutions.

The last stage concerns the ratification of the Treaty of Accession by the Member States and a candidate State in conformity with their respective national constitutional rules. In this respect, in 1972 France used the referendum by virtue of art 11 of the French Constitution to ratify the Treaties of Accession with the UK, Denmark, Ireland and Norway. Also, a candidate State often submits the final acceptance of its future membership to its people. In the last enlargement, all candidate States held national referenda.[13]

The Treaty of Accession enters into force only if all Member States ratify it. In the case of multiple candidatures, non-ratification by any one of them does not affect the accession of others. In the case of Norway, its government notified the EU that it would not, as a result of a negative referendum, ratify the Treaty of Accession. The Council of the EU, including the three new States, on 1 January 1995 adopted a decision 'adjusting the instruments concerning the accession of new Member States to the European Union'[14] and thus gave legal effect to the withdrawal of Norway.

From the signature of the Treaty of Accession to the actual accession a future Member State is kept informed, and is consulted at all levels and in all areas as well as involved in the Community decision-making procedures, although it still has no right to vote. Its presence ensures that the existing Member States are fully aware of any difficulties and opposition to new measures while permitting the new Member State participation in developments which are taking place within the EU.

2.2 Territorial expansion of the Communities

So far, four enlargements have taken place. As a result, the EU covers almost all western Europe and has 371.9 million inhabitants, that is approximately 8 per cent of the world's population.

First enlargement

On 1 January 1973, the UK, Denmark and the Republic of Ireland joined the EC. Norway, following a negative referendum, was not able to accede. The reasons for accession of these

---

[13] Austria on 12 June 1994 (66.6 per cent in favour); Finland on 16 October 1994 (59.9 per cent in favour); Sweden on 13 November 1994 (52.3 per cent in favour); Norway on 28 November 1994 (52.2 per cent against).

[14] OJ L1 (1995). A similar decision was taken by the Council when Norway, following the negative referendum (53.49 per cent against), failed to join the Communities in 1972.

three new Member States were diverse, although the main consideration for Ireland and Denmark were the economic links with the UK.

In the Irish Republic 83 per cent voted in favour of accession. For Ireland the membership of the EC was very attractive as it provided an opportunity to open up new markets on the continent and thus reduce the traditional dependency upon the UK for Irish exports (70 per cent to the UK). Furthermore, as an agricultural country the Irish could only gain from being a party to the Common Agricultural Policy (CAP).

Denmark, mainly an agricultural country, would also clearly benefit from CAP. Its main commercial partner, Germany, was already a Member State while the UK was about to join the EC. The advantages were carefully weighed by the Danes against the disadvantages, mainly the severance of traditional links with other Nordic countries based on inter-governmental rather than supra-national co-operation. In the national referendum, which took place after a negative vote in Norway, 63 per cent of Danes voted in favour of accession.

The most controversial candidate was the UK.[15] After the departure from power of de Gaulle there was no opposition to the United Kingdom membership. However, the accession negotiations lasted one year and focused on the following issues:

1. The length of the transitional period;
2. The question of agriculture. In the UK food was cheap due to imports from Commonwealth countries. The Heath government had two objectives in this respect: in the short term to slow down the impact of CAP by phasing it in as slowly as possible; and in the long term to obtain compensation for the negative impact of the CAP by a satisfactory budgetary arrangement.
3. The UK contribution to the Community budget. It was agreed that its contribution would be 8.64 per cent of the EC budget in 1973, increasing to 18.92 per cent in 1977 with limits on further increases in 1978 and 1979. There was no agreement regarding 1980.
4. New commercial arrangements with Commonwealth countries. These countries were offered participation in the Yaoundé Convention which was later replaced by the Lomé Convention. In addition, the Community General System of Preferences was extended to those countries. The question of exports of Caribbean sugar and New Zealand dairy products to the UK required special arrangements.
5. Fisheries. The first enlargement offered an opportunity for the EEC to create a Common Fishery Policy (CFP) based on free and equal access of the Member States to each other's waters – as a result UK participation in CFP was examined.

The negotiations were concluded in January 1972 when the Treaty of Accession for the four applying States was signed. The European Communities Act 1972 came into force on 1 January 1973. However, the Labour party opposed the terms of the UK entry and promised in its electoral campaign to 'renegotiate' the Treaty of Accession. Indeed, once in power, the question of the UK membership became a main item on the political agenda of the Labour government.[16] In the end the UK membership was approved by the House of Commons (396 to 170) and by the people of the UK in a national referendum (67.2 per cent in favour).

---

[15] The attitude of the UK towards European integration was examined in Chapter 1.
[16] The question of 'renegotiation' is examined in HMSO, *Membership of the European Community: Report on Renegotiation*, Cmnd. 6003, March 1975.

The terms of membership were not favourable to the UK as it gained almost nothing from the Common Agricultural Policy. Indeed, barely 3 per cent of the population were engaged in agriculture, the lowest per centage in Europe. Furthermore, the competitiveness of British industry in the new markets on the continent was doubtful. From 1 January 1973 to 31 December 1986, the UK's net contribution to the EC Budget was £7,772 million, which represented a net payment of £1.52 million per day of membership.[17] The main question was not that the UK contribution was too high, as it was similar to other Member States, but the imbalance between its contribution to and receipts from the EC budget. The UK reaction was to concentrate all efforts on the renegotiation of the financial contribution, which anyway was marginal compared to the UK budget as a whole, instead of taking advantage of the political role that membership of the Community made possible. This negative attitude contributed to the growing unpopularity of the UK within the Community and, at the same time, to the growing unpopularity of the Community with British people. As an observer noted, the reputation of the UK, and particularly Margaret Thatcher in the 1980s, was appalling. Her strategy was to 'rampage from summit to summit as a sort of fishwife Britannia demanding her money back. Fellow leaders, most notably Chancellor Kohl, adopted the habit of getting up and walking out of Council summits, rather than listen to yet another diatribe on the injustice of financial contributions'. They returned once her speech was finished. The clear and persistent failure of British politicians and British public opinion to objectively analyse British interests and the optimal means of pursuing them is one of the main features of British post-war politics. The single-minded pre-occupation of the British government with its financial contribution, and thus the continuation of negative diplomacy, without seeing the opportunity to play a leading role in world affairs through the EC, is difficult to justify on rational grounds. The anti-European feeling ignores the basic facts that the UK sells more to the Irish Republic than to Canada, Australia, New Zealand and South Africa put together, that France buys more from Britain than do all the Commonwealth countries put together, that Britain earns more from selling to The Netherlands than to Korea, Taiwan, Singapore, Indonesia, China and the Philippines, and that the UK exports more to Sweden than to all of Latin America from Rio Grande to Cape Horn.[18]

The UK's reluctance to participate in the Economic and Monetary Union shows that the emotional approach toward the EU is still a very important factor in the UK decision-making process. Self-exclusion from a single currency undermines vital and essential national interests, *inter alia*, the possibility of the decline of the City of London as Europe's major financial centre (already Frankfurt has gained considerable advantages from the absence of the UK in first stages of EMU).[19]

Second enlargement

The second enlargement concerned the Hellenic Republic. Greece submitted its application on 12 June 1975. The negotiations were opened on 25 June 1975. On 23 May 1979 the

---

[17] I Barnes and J Preston, *The European Community,* London and New York: Longman, 1988, p5.
[18] D MacShane, *Left out of Europe?,* Fabian Society, Discussion Paper No 26, London, 1996, p8.
[19] See 'Should Britain Join or Stay Out' (1995) The European 12–16 June.

Treaty of Accession and the Act of Accession were signed. The Hellenic Republic became a Member State on 1 January 1981.

Greece, was the first Eastern European country to join the EC. Its heritage resulting from centuries of Ottoman Turkish Empire rule, combined with its Orthodox Christianity, a legacy of the Byzantine Empire, set Greece apart from other Member States. For Greece, with its inefficient agriculture based upon mainly smallholdings with poor soil and low rainfall, its limited natural resources, weak industry and a fragile democracy as it emerged from years of dictatorship, the attraction of being a Member State was obvious. A transition period of five years was agreed in all areas except tomatoes and peaches, which became included in the CAP at the end of 1987. It has taken many years for Greece to fully benefit from membership and even today, despite considerable financial aid from the EU (eg ECU 2 billion from the Integrated Mediterranean Programmes introduced in 1985), it is still one of the least developed Member States.

Third enlargement

Spain and Portugal joined the EC on 1 January 1986. Spain applied on 28 July and Portugal on 28 March 1977. Both signed the Treaty of Accession on 12 June 1985. The end of military dictatorship in both countries enabled them to submit their application for accession to the Communities.

The negotiations with Spain were protracted, as its proposed accession posed three major economic problems.

1. Spanish agriculture and its competitiveness, especially against that of France and Italy, made its participation in the CAP very controversial;
2. The Spanish fishing fleet was almost equal in size to that of the entire Community and therefore placed the Common Fisheries Policy under strain.
3. Spanish industry, and especially cotton, woollen textiles, clothing and steel, due to low wages, threatened the position of other Member States and posed a challenge to the EC which already had overcapacity problems in these sectors.

Portugal, a small and relatively poor country, posed no such threats to the economy of existing Member States. Its accession was delayed as a result of applying for membership at the same time as Spain.

Furthermore, the negotiations with Spain and Portugal were halted when France decided that, before a new enlargement, the budgetary matters within the EC should be settled. As a result, it was after the Fontainebleu Summit in 1984, which reached an agreement on contributions to the EC budget, that the accession negotiations with Spain and Portugal were resumed.

Fourth enlargement[20]

On 1 January 1995 Austria, Finland and Sweden joined the European Union. Austria

---

[20] On the fourth enlargement: see D Booss and J Forman, 'Enlargement: Legal and Procedural Aspects' (1995) 32 CMLR 95–130.

submitted a formal application on 17 July 1989, Sweden on 1 July 1991, Finland on 18 March 1992 and Norway on 25 November 1992. Formal negotiations commenced on 1 February 1993.

All candidate States were EFTA countries and Members of the European Economic Area.[21] As such they already had considerable experience in working with the EC institutions and in the interpretation and application of EC law. Also, they had the appropriate 'infrastructure', that is, staff, procedures and material support to deal with the negotiations with the EC. The negotiations went smoothly, although the question of the weighting of votes and the threshold of the qualified majority in the Council of the European Union was subject to much controversy which the 'Ioannina Compromise' settled for a while.[22] It was agreed that once the TEU had entered into force, the membership applications would be in respect of the EU. The candidate States were formally informed in this respect on 9 November 1993. The Treaty of Accession was signed on 24 June 1994. As Members of EFTA, the candidate States had to renounce their EFTA membership and terminate all bilateral agreements between themselves and with the Community and all other international agreements incompatible with membership of the European Union.

De facto *enlargement: the case of the German Democratic Republic (GDR)*

On 3 October 1990, in conformity with the West Germany Constitution, the former German Democratic Republic (GDR) became an integral part of the Federal Republic of Germany (FRG). On that date, by virtue of art 299 EC, the territorial scope of application of all three Community Treaties was extended to the former East Germany.[23] Indeed, it was not necessary to revise the EC Treaties as the FRG, the only legal government of Germany, always considered the GDR as part of its country when signing international treaties. However, Germany, taking into account the importance of the re-unification and its impact on German and EU economy, asked other Member States for approval which was formally given by the Dublin Summit on 28 April 1990. Also, the Dublin Summit laid down the transitional measures allowing temporary derogations in the application of EC law to the territory of the GDR in certain areas such as competition policy, protection of environment, etc. Furthermore, transitional tariffs were introduced for goods coming from other post-Communist countries (COMECON) under agreements previously signed by the GDR government (a period of one year from December 1990 to December 1991 was granted to those countries in order to adjust to the new situation).[24] The Commission was empowered to legislate and apply transitional measures.[25]

---

[21] See S Peers, 'An Even Closer Waiting Room?: The Case for Eastern European Accession to the European Economic Area' (1995) 32 CMLR 187.

[22] Council Decision of 29 March 1994 (OJ C105 (1994)), amendment in OJ C1 (1995).

[23] See C W A Timmermans, 'German Unification and Community Law' (1990) 27 CMLR 437–449; C Tomuschat, 'A United Germany within the European Community' (1990) 27 CMLR 415–436.

[24] EC Bull Supp 4–90, points 5–27.

[25] On the basis of the Council Regulation 2684/90 and Council Directive 90/476/EEC: OJ L263 and L266 (1990).

The challenge of enlargement

At the time of writing there are 13 applicant countries: Bulgaria, Cyprus, the Czech Republic, Estonia, Hungary, Latvia, Lithuania, Malta, Poland, Romania, the Slovak Republic, Slovenia and Turkey. Their accession poses a unique challenge. An enlarged EU would acquire 105 milllion new citizens and would increase by 34 per cent in terms of territory, but its total GDP would grow by no more than 5 per cent. The integration of new Member States requires the adjustment of the existing institutional structures and polices to new circumstances.

The Copenhagen Summit of June 1993 stated that the admission is subject to the fulfilment of economic and political requirements by the candidate countries, and the incorporation of the Community 'acquis' (Copenhagen criteria). The Corfu Summit of 24–25 June 1994 accepted the applications for membership submitted by Poland and Hungary and asked the Commission to prepare a report on strategy concerning the accession of these countries. The Commission submitted its conclusions in the communication – *The Europe Agreements and Beyond: a Strategy to Prepare the Countries of Central and Eastern Europe for Accession* – and a follow-up document in July 1994.[26] The Madrid European Council held in December 1995 asked the Commission to prepare a general document on enlargement, its financial implications for the EU and necessary reform of the EU institutions and policies in view of enlargement. The Commission published its action programme on 16 July 1997 in a document called *Agenda 2000* which was endorsed by the Luxembourg European Council in December 1997. *Agenda 2000* is a three-part document:

1. The first part concerns the reform of the main areas of Community policy, including institutional reform, the Common Agricultural Policy (CAP) and structural funds.
2. The second, outlines the EU's financial perspectives for 2000–2006, proposes a new pre-accession financial strategy for the candidate States consisting of replacing the 'Europe agreements' with the accession partnership agreements, and of extending the participation of candidate States in Community programmes. It also provides for the mechanisms for applying the Community 'acquis'. The accession partnership comprises all forms of pre-accession support for a candidate State by the EU, including the Phare Programme, agricultural support, participation in Community programmes, etc. For each candidate State an accession partnership is prepared separately. It assesses the priority areas in which a candidate State needs to make progress and it links EC financial support to the candidate State's progress in the implementation of those priorities. The accession partnerships are spread over a number of years and will last until accession subject to necessary adjustments.
3. The third part focuses on the impact of the enlargement on the EU as a whole.

Agenda 2000 contained the Commission's assessment of the applicant's State of readiness in view of its accession. It recommended the opening of accession negotiations with only six of the 11 applicants at the beginning of 1998 – Hungary, Poland, the Czech Republic, Slovenia, Estonia and Cyprus. On the basis of the Commission's recommendations the Luxembourg

---

[26] COM(94) 320 final and COM(94) 361 final.

European Council held in December 1997 decided that negotiations should start for the six candidate States approved by the Commission, while other candidate States would have to wait until they achieved necessary progress under the accession partnership agreements. This meant that the EU decided to start an overall enlargement process for all candidate countries. This process involves:

1. Meetings for candidate States within the framework of European conferences. These conferences constitute a forum for discussing important issues such as foreign and security policy, justice and home affairs, regional co-operation, etc. All candidate States are invited to attend. The first conference took place in London on 12 March 1998, followed by others usually every six months.
2. The accession process, which was launched in Brussels on 30 March 1998 for all candidate States except Turkey. During the accession process, irrespective of whether or not a particular applicant State has been invited to start accession negotiations, important matters are discussed, such as the pre-accession strategy in respect of each candidate State. Also the so-called 'screening' process (under which a detailed evaluation of a candidate State's legislation takes place with regard to its compatibility with EC legislation and Pillars 2 and 3) is carried out.
3. The accession negotiations themselves, during which conditions for accession are set for each candidate State.

Accession negotiations began on 31 March 1998 with Hungary, Poland, the Czech Republic, Slovenia, Estonia and Cyprus. They are taking place in six bilateral inter-governmental conferences, with six-monthly ministerial meetings and monthly ambassadorial meetings. The Helsinki European Council held on 10 December 1999 expressed satisfaction in respect of accession negotiations with all six countries. No date for their final admission to the EU was fixed, although the Helsinki European Council declared that the EU would be ready to welcome new Members from the end of 2002. This date seems realistic, taking into account that the Inter-governmental Conference on Institutional Reform was formally convened on 14 February 2000 and should be completed by December 2000.

On 13 October 1999 the Commission submitted its annual report on progress towards accession by each of the candidate countries. The report recommended the opening of accession negotiations with Malta, Latvia, Lithuania, Slovakia and, subject to certain conditions, with Bulgaria and Romania. It also recommended the consideration of Turkey as a candidate country, subject to fulfilment by Turkey of certain political criteria. The Helsinki European Council (December 1999) approved the Commission's recommendation. It decided to convene bilateral inter-governmental conferences in February 2000 with Romania, Slovakia, Latvia, Lithuania, Bulgaria and Malta in order to assess each candidate's situation with a view to the opening of accession negotiations.

Turkey

Turkey applied for membership on 14 April 1987. The Commission issued a negative opinion on 17 December 1989[27] recommending more effective application of the existing association agreement signed in 1964. It also considered that the next step in Turkey's route to Brussels

---

[27] *Twenty-second General Report*, 1989, point 801.

was a customs union with the Communities. In January 1996 the customs union was agreed. The main reason for the Commission's negative opinion was Turkey's poor human rights record. The candidacy of Turkey poses, indeed, a difficult problem for the EU: Turkey – half in Europe, half in Asia, with its mostly Muslim population and poor economy – is not ready for membership but, on the other hand, it is a member of NATO and has been patiently waiting for admission for years. The Commission in its regular report for Turkey (1999) noticed that the change of the government in Turkey in November 1998 brought important changes from the point of view of Turkish accession to the EU. The new government has started the process of democratisation. The human rights situation has improved compared to 1998, although there are serious shortcomings. Torture is still widespread but not systematic, rights of minorities are not respected, the Kurdish problem remains unsolved, and a number of political parties have been dissolved (ie the pro-Kurdish Democratic Party). Economically the public deficit and inflation were reduced as compared with 1998. The Commission did not recommend the opening of accession negotiations with Turkey but the Helsinki European Council welcomed Turkey as a candidate State.

Cyprus
Cyprus formally applied for membership on 3 July 1990. Its application was favourably assessed by the Commission. It has been strongly supported by Greece, which has warned that it will use its veto regarding the accession of central and eastern European countries if Cyprus's admission is unduly delayed. The division of Cyprus constitutes the main obstacle to its membership, although the EU declared that this division would not prejudice Cyprus' application.[28] On 3 December 1999 talks started between the two communities under the auspices of the UN Secretary-General. The Helsinki European Council welcomed this initiative but confirmed that the settlement of the Cyprus problem is not a pre-condition of Cyprus's membership of the EU.

Malta
Malta formally applied on 16 July 1990. As in the case of Cyprus, the Commission is in favour of the admission of Malta.[29] The main hurdle in Malta's path to Brussels is its weak economy necessitating major reforms, although Malta is small enough to be assimilated without posing a particular problem for the EU.[30]

The Corfu European Council of 24–25 June 1994 confirmed progress of Malta and Cyprus within the framework of their respective association agreements (signed with Cyprus in December 1972 and with Malta in 1973). Malta's government, elected in 1996, suspended its application for membership of the EU. However, in October 1998 Malta reactivated the application. The Commission adopted on 17 February 1999 an update of its opinion from 1993 and recommended the opening of accession negotiations with Malta. This was endorsed by the Helsinki European Council in December 1999.

---

[28] J Redmond, 'The European Community and the Mediterranean Applicants', in F R Pfetsch (ed), *International Relations and Pan-Europe*, Hamburg: Lit, 1993, p45, although he added that a 'divided Cyprus is unlikely to be welcomed' by the EU.

[29] The Commission issued its opinions concerning Cyprus and Malta simultaneously in 1993: EC Bull 4 and 5–93.

[30] Commission of the European Communities: EC Bull Supp 4–93.

Central and eastern European countries

Central and eastern European countries do not form a homogeneous group. The four 'Visegrad'[31] countries – Hungary, Poland, the Czech Republic and Slovakia – are the most advanced in terms of economy, although the average per capita income in the EU is 8.4 times higher than that of those countries.

From the perspective of the central and eastern European countries the EU is considered as a main stabilising force in terms of economic and political development. Indeed, the EU is prepared and willing to aid these countries. Apart from association agreements, which have been replaced by the accession partnership agreements, the Phare Programme was set up in July 1989 on the basis of a Commission proposal and with assistance from the G-24 industrialised countries. It provides aid for the reconstruction of the economy of central and eastern European countries and encompasses such areas as agriculture, industry, investment, environmental protection, trade and services mainly in the private sector. Also, the European Bank for Reconstruction and Development (EBRD) was set up under the auspices of the G-24 in May 1990 in order to facilitate:

'... the transition towards open market-orientated economies and to promote private and entrepreneurial initiative in the central and eastern European Countries committed to ... multi-party democracy, pluralism and market economy.'[32]

In the fields of cultural and educational assistance, the EU sponsors several programmes such as Tempus (Trans-European Mobility Programme for University Students), which also includes the exchange of academics, ACE (economics), COSINE (infrastructure), SIGMA (government and management), TACIS (similar to Phare but applicable to countries of the former Soviet Union), etc. However, the assistance and aid of the EU is still not sufficient. The Visegrad countries' transition to a market economy has been quite successful, although foreign indebtedness and the necessity to modernise their industries while restructuring agriculture pose serious problems. In other central and eastern European countries the transition period is very painful and their nascent democracy is still very fragile.

The question of the future enlargement is very important for both the EU and the countries in question. The EU has certainly a moral obligation to accept these countries and ensure a peaceful change to their political and economic systems. An unstable and unpredictable situation in central and eastern Europe would threaten peace and prosperity in Europe. The expansion of the EU to encompass those relatively poor countries means that current Member States will have to make sacrifices and collectively assume the burden of admission. Many authors consider that the EU should not fear enlargement, arguing that the admission of central and eastern European countries would improve those countries' real income by an estimated 1.5 per cent to 18.8 per cent, with an annual cost to the EU between zero and $9 billion per year, that is, 0.1 per cent of the EU's total output.[33] The price to the EU for meeting this historic challenge is relatively low. Indeed, as Winstrich stated, the EU:

---

[31] They are known as Visegrad countries from a co-operation agreement concluded at Visegrad (Hungary) on 15 February 1991 between the Czech Republic, Hungary, Poland and Slovakia.

[32] OJ C241 (1990).

[33] T Naudin, 'EU Should Not Shrink from the Challenge of Enlargement' (1997) The European 17–23 April p20.

'... should offer an assurance to those central and eastern European countries who wish to join that, subject to the necessary economic transformation and the maintenance of political pluralism, they would be admitted to membership of the Community within a specific number of years ... Nothing would contribute more to the confidence of those countries, speed up internal reforms and safeguard their democracies than a clear goal within a defined timescale of full membership of the emerging European Union. If further economic adjustments were necessary, those could form part of transitional arrangements of appropriate length after a country joins.'[34]

It should be noted that the EU fully acknowledges the importance of the enlargement. Apart from measures already examined (*Agenda 2000*, accession partnership agreements, etc), a new Directorate-General in charge of enlargement has been created.

Withdrawal and expulsion from the EU

The EC and the EA Treaties are concluded for an indeterminate period of time; however, the CS is limited to 50 years.

The Treaties are silent as to the possibility of withdrawal from the European Communities and the European Union. This omission is not accidental. The Member States wanted to enhance the very serious nature of membership of the Communities. However, in the absence of any provisions in this respect, the question of withdrawal raises many controversies.

It is submitted that the right to withdraw is implicit. The absence of provisions in this respect in the Community Treaties means that the 1969 Vienna Convention on the Law of Treaties will apply. Its art 54 states that where no specific provisions in the treaty provide for its termination, the consent of all contracting parties after consultation will be sufficient to terminate the treaty. In the event that some Member States refuse to give their consent, art 56 of the 1969 Vienna Convention may be invoked. It provides that if a treaty contains no provision concerning termination, and does not provide specifically for denunciation or withdrawal, a contracting party may only denounce or withdraw from that treaty if the parties intended to admit such a possibility or where the right may be implied by the nature of the treaty. Whichever provision of the 1969 Vienna Convention applies, it is clear that a Member State will not be constrained to stay within the EU against its will. This can be implied from the provisions of the Treaty itself. First, art 6 EU underlines the respect of the EU for the national identity of Member States; in the case of flagrant and irreconcilable conflicts between a Member State's interests and the EU policies, that State should be free to leave. This solution can also be justified on practical grounds; it is undoubtably preferable to permit a Member State to withdraw than to jeopardise the existence of the EU. Second, the right to withdrawal was implicitly accepted by the Member States in 1974 when the UK asked for renegotiation of its Treaty of Accession and threatened to withdraw from the Communities unless her requirements were satisfied. Neither the Member States nor the Community institutions opposed the UK's withdrawal or claimed the impossibility of terminating UK membership. The Dublin Summit in May 1975 reduced the previously agreed level of subsequent UK contributions to the EC budget, but neither the Treaty of

---

[34] E Wistrich, *The United States of Europe*, London: Routledge, 1994, p129.

Accession nor the Act of Accession of the UK were modified.[35] Finally, if the people of a particular Member State were unhappy about the membership of the EU (which would be reflected in the result of their parliamentary elections) it is impossible to imagine that the EU will stand against its fundamental principles and oppose the withdrawal.

Until now no Member State has expressed a serious desire to leave the EU, but the Community has twice dealt with a question of State succession, that is, when a part of an existing territory of a Member State has acquired political sovereignty or autonomy from that State. In the case of Greenland, which is the world's largest island and was an integral part of the Kingdom of Denmark at the time of the latter's accession to the Communities, no opposition was expressed to Greenland's subsequent withdrawal. The circumstances were as follows. In 1979 the government of Denmark granted home rule to Greenland; as a result Greenland remains under the Danish crown and its people are still considered as Danish citizens. The island enjoys autonomy in all matters but constitutional affairs, foreign relations and defence. In 1985 the people of Greenland decided in a referendum to withdraw from the European Communities, and negotiations were conducted between the Kingdom of Denmark and other Member States. As a result, the specific provisions for Greenland are set out in the Protocol on special arrangements for Greenland, annexed to the EC Treaty.

The second case concerns the St Pierre and Miquelon islands. Their transformation from an overseas territory into an overseas department was considered as an internal matter of France. The Communities received a notification in this respect from the French authorities.

As to expulsion from the EU, at present this possibility is not provided by the Community Treaties.

2.3 Consolidation of the European Communities

The Robert Schuman Plan announced on 9 May 1950, which set up the European Coal and Steel Community, was the first step towards European integration. Since then the idea of European integration has been very much alive but its actual application has been beset with difficulties and controversies, the most important being the constant struggle between inter-governmentalism and supra-nationality. Indeed, the vision of Europe and the shape of European integration depends upon the form of co-operation chosen by the Member States. Supra-nationality entails important restrictions on national sovereignty and, if successful, leads to the creation of a federal structure. By contrast, inter-governmentalism implies that the Member States' competencies are intact unless otherwise agreed by them. Its ultimate form is a confederation.

The European Coal and Steel Community (CS)

The CS is based on supra-nationality. The Treaty creating the CS was signed on 18 April 1951 in Paris and entered into force on 23 July 1952 between the six original Members. The

---

[35] Regulation 1172/76 of 17 May 1976: OJ L131 (1976).

Member States unanimously decided to appoint Jean Monnet the first President of the High Authority, but the choice of a seat for the institutions was more controversial. In the end Luxembourg has become the 'provisory' headquarters of the CS. The CS Treaty was concluded for a period of 50 years and is due to expire in July 2002. After that date the provisions of the CS Treaty will be incorporated into the EC Treaty.

The fundamental objective of the CS is to support production, research, development and the needs of the coal and steel sectors. Article 4 CS provides a description of the negative mechanisms leading to a common market for coal and steel. The following are prohibited:

1. import and export duties and measures having equivalent effect;
2. quantitative restrictions;
3. discriminatory practices and measures between producers, purchasers, or consumers;
4. subsidies and aids granted by States;
5. restrictive practices aiming at sharing or exploiting of markets.

The main innovation introduced by the Treaty of Paris was the creation of the High Authority. This is made up of representatives of the Member States acting independently in the interest of the CS. The High Authority is in charge of the production and distribution of coal and steel, and entrusted with supra-national competencies, including the power to make legally binding 'decisions' and 'recommendations' directly applicable in Member States. The originality of the institutional structure is also enhanced by the creation of a Special Council of Ministers (now the Council of the EU) – a partly legislative, partly consultative body representing the interests of the Member States; the Common Assembly (now the European Parliament) which is, however, limited to only supervisory and advisory functions; and the Court of Justice responsible for ensuring 'that in the interpretation and application of this Treaty ... the law is observed.'[36]

There are two important differences between the CS Treaty and the EC Treaty: first, the High Authority/the Commission (under the Merger Treaty a single Commission for all three communities was set up) enjoys greater power under the CS Treaty than under the Treaties of Rome; and, second, some provisions of the CS Treaty do not have direct effect while similar provisions of the EC Treaty are directly effective.[37]

The CS has certainly moved European integration forward. Its main achievements were the establishment of a common market for coal and steel within the Member States and the introduction of a common external tariff on these commodities. However, the first major crisis regarding the overproduction of coal showed its shortcomings. The High Authority which wanted to deal with the crises by applying Community measures was overruled by the Council in 1959. As a result, national rather than Community approaches to overproduction of coal prevailed.[38]

---

[36] Article 31 CS Treaty.
[37] *Banks* Case C–128/92 [1994] ECR I–1209; *Hopkins* Case C–18/94 [1996] ECR I–2281.
[38] On the CS see Merry, 'The European Coal and Steel Community: Operations of the High Authority' (1995) 8 Western Political Quarterly 166.

The European Economic Community (EC) and the European Atomic Energy Community (EA)

On 25 March 1957 in Rome the six original Member States signed two Treaties: one establishing the European Economic Community (EC) and the second creating the European Atomic Energy Community (EA), and both entered into force on 1 January 1958. The main objective of the EA Treaty (by virtue of art 1 EA) was to create 'the conditions necessary for the speedy establishment and growth of nuclear industries'. Its tasks are laid down in art 2 EA and encompass: the promotion of research and dissemination of technical information regarding atomic energy; the establishment of uniform standards for health and safety; the promotion of investment; the equitable supply of ores and nuclear fuels; the security of nuclear materials; the international promotion of peaceful uses of nuclear energy; and, finally, the creation of a common market in this area. The institutional framework set up by the EA Treaty is identical to that of the EC Treaty.

The EA Treaty is another sectorial unification which has not been very successful due mainly to French reluctance to co-operate from May 1958. The EA Treaty has been applied only partially. As a result, both Communities – the EA and the CS – for different reasons have been marginalised. They also demonstrate that a sector-by-sector approach is not the best solution to European integration.

The European Economic Community (now known as the European Community (EC) under the Treaty on European Union) has become the most important Community and the heart of European integration. It mainly concerns economic co-operation between Member States, including the establishment of a common market. Additionally, it create the possibility of further co-operation in any area not covered by the Treaty of Rome but chosen by the Member States by common consent (by art 308 EC). Although the economic objectives are in the forefront, the Treaty of Rome also contains a political agenda. Articles 2 and 3 EC laid down the long terms objectives for the EC, that is, the co-ordination of the economic and monetary policies leading to an economic and monetary union between the Member States.

The EC's uniqueness and originality lies in its institutions:

1. the Commission, a supra-national body, the executive of the Communities and the guardian of the Treaty;
2. the Council, which represents the interests of the Member States and is the main legislative body;
3. the Parliamentary Assembly, which from a purely advisory body has evolved into the directly elected European Parliament endowed with some legislative powers;
4. the Court of Justice of the European Communities (ECJ), which is entrusted with the interpretation of the Treaty, settlement of disputes between Member States or against the Community institutions and the enforcement of Community law;
5. a number of complementary bodies, eg, the European Investment Bank, the Court of Auditors, the Economic and Social Committee (ECOSOC), etc.

The first decade of the EC was exceptional in terms of economic growth, investment and internal integration. Small countries like Belgium, Luxembourg and The Netherlands realised that their membership allowed them to have an influence out of proportion to their size upon international matters and international trade.

The Luxembourg Accord

The first disagreement among the Member States occurred in 1965. It is known as the 'empty chair' crisis as France refused to attend the Council meetings from June 1965 to January 1966. The President of the French Republic, Charles de Gaulle, was in favour of inter-governmentalism and thus against the increasing of powers of the Community. The immediate cause of the crisis was the Commission's package of proposals aimed at increasing the competencies of the Commission and the European Parliament (EP). Only the Commission proposal on the adoption of the financing arrangements for the CAP was accepted by France. The two remaining proposals were rejected. The first concerned new methods of financing the Community aimed at ending national contributions towards the budget and replacing it by a system of 'own resources' of the Community mainly provided by the revenue from the common external tariff. This proposal was considered as essential by the Commission. The second proposal concerned increasing the involvement of the EP in decision-making procedures in general and in budgetary matters in particular. It was supported by the EP and by The Netherlands. The proposals were used by France to express its dissatisfaction in two areas. First was the role of the Commission which, under the Presidency of Walter Hallsten, was accused by France of exceeding its competence by acting more like a supra-national rather than inter-governmental body. Second, France was hostile to the major change in decision-making within the Council which consisted of replacing unanimity with qualified majority voting. The EC Treaty provided that at the beginning of the final stage of the transitional period, which was approaching, the new voting system should apply.

In order to dramatise the situation, France decided not to attend the Council meetings (empty chairs!). Under pressure from French farmers de Gaulle decided to negotiate with other Member States (the Commission was not invited). In January 1966 an informal agreement was reached, known as the Luxembourg Accord, which provided that:

> '... in the case of decision which may be taken by majority vote ... the Council will endeavour... to reach solutions which can be adopted by all the Members of the Council ... the French delegation considers that where very important interests are at stake the discussion must be continued until unanimous agreement is reached.'[39]

This meant that unanimous voting was the main way of adopting EC legislation.

The Luxembourg Accord marked a clear return to inter-governmental co-operation and thus constituted a serious blow to supra-nationality. It was the main reason for years of stagnation of the Community as it paralysed progress towards further integration by giving priority to national interests of the Member States, although the Luxembourg Accord has never been recognised as binding under Community law. In *United Kingdom* v *Council* Case 68/86 [1988] ECR 855 the ECJ made clear that the decision-making procedures set up by

---

[39] J Lambert, 'The Constitutional Crises, 1965-66' (1966) 4 Journal of Common Market Studies 226.

the Treaty 'are not at the disposal of the Member States or the institutions themselves'.[40] The role of the Luxembourg Accord has steadily diminished: the first time a reference to the Luxembourg Accord was ignored by the Council was in 1982 when the UK tried to prevent the adoption of the agricultural price package in order to obtain a reduction of the British contribution to the Community budget. Furthermore, when Germany in 1985 successfully invoked the Luxembourg Accord to block a decision on the reduction of cereal prices, the Commission applied interim measures, and thus, in practice, overrode the opposition of Germany. The Single European Act introduced qualified majority voting within the Council as a principle. This has been reinforced by the TEU and the Treaty of Amsterdam.

The Merger Treaty

The idea of rationalising the institutional structure of the Communities was first introduced by the Convention of 25 March 1957 on Certain Institutions Common to the European Communities. The Convention provided for the establishment of a single Assembly (European Parliament), a single Court of Justice and a single Economic and Social Committee for all three Communities. Further rationalisation took place in April 1965 when the Treaty (known as the Merger Treaty) establishing a Single Council and a Single Commission of the European Communities was signed. The Treaty came into force on 13 July 1967. Under the Merger Treaty the three Communities share the same institutions, although they remain legally independent and the competencies of the institutions are subject to the respective Treaties.

The Hague Summit

An important development in shaping future co-operation between Members States took place on the proposal of George Pompidou, the successor of Charles de Gaulle. A meeting was convened in The Hague in December 1969, and Pompidou, more flexible in his approach toward the development of the Community but as opposed to the construction of supra-national Europe as de Gaulle,[41] invited all Heads of State or Government of the Member States to a meeting. The main decisions taken by The Hague Summit concerned:

1. enlargement of the Communities (admission of the UK, Denmark, Norway and Ireland);
2. establishment of European Political Co-operation;
3. adoption of measures leading to economic and monetary union between Member States;
4. introduction of regular meetings of foreign ministers of the Member States;
5. reform of CAP financing;
6. establishment of technical co-operation, introduction of development aid and the social policy on the Community agenda; and finally
7. creation of a European University.

---

[40] See Teasdale, 'The Life and Death of the Luxembourg Compromise' (1993) 31 Journal of Common Market Studies 567.
[41] H Simonian, *The Privileged Partnership: Franco-German Relations in the European Community, 1968–1984*, Oxford: OUP, 1985, p35.

In the immediate period after The Hague Summit the international oil crisis and the budgetary crisis within the Community stunted its growth for almost two decades. Nevertheless, since The Hague Summit its ambitious agenda has been further developed.

Establishment of European Political Co-operation

The Hague Summit decided to examine the best ways of achieving progress in the establishment of a political union. In October 1970, the Davignon Report, named after its author, the political director of the Belgian Foreign Ministry, was adopted by the foreign ministers of the Member States as a basic strategy in this area. It was further approved by the Copenhagen Summit on 23 July 1973.[42] It proposed the harmonisation of foreign policy outside the Community framework and consisted of regular exchanges of information between foreign ministers aimed at facilitating the harmonisation of their respective views and, when possible, leading to a common position. It therefore recommended traditional inter-governmental co-operation in political matters without any supporting common structures. Some changes to European Political Co-operation (EPC) were introduced in a subsequent report which was adopted by foreign ministers meeting in London on 13 October 1981.[43] The above-mentioned reports and the Solemn Declaration on European Union agreed at the Stuttgard Summit in 1983 constituted the foundation of the EPC.[44] It was incorporated in Title III of the Single European Act.[45]

Economic and Monetary Union (EMU)

The establishment of the Werner Committee was a concrete response to The Hague Summit of 1969 in this area. The Werner Report outlined three stages in economic and monetary union, although only the first stage was comprehensively drafted. Its main objective was to create full monetary union by 1980. The first stage of the EMU is better known as 'the snake in the tunnel'. The Werner Plan was modified as a result of crises within the International Monetary Fund.[46] These modifications put it in line with the Smithsonian Agreement of December 1971. In its final version it consisted of the restriction of exchange rate fluctuation among currencies of the Member States to a band of 2.25 per cent of their central parities – it was the 'snake' which was allowed to move within the wider band of 4.5 per cent maximum against the US dollar, that was 'the tunnel'. The 'snake in the tunnel' was launched on 24 April 1972. The currencies of nine countries (six full Members, the UK,

---

[42] *Seventh General Report on the Activities of the European Communities*, Brussels, Luxembourg, 1973, p502 et seq.

[43] EC Bull Supp 3–81, point 14 et seq.

[44] EC Bull 6–1983, points 18–29.

[45] Article 30 SEA and arts 1 and 3 SEA Title I.

[46] The Breton Woods system, established in 1944, provided for the exchange market intervention. The US dollar was tied to gold at $US 35 per ounce and the US government promised to buy and sell at that price. All other Member States of the IMF accepted to specify a par value for their currencies in terms of the $US. As a result, their currencies were tied together at a stable exchange rate. On 15 August 1971 President Richard Nixon announced the end of the US commitment to buy and sell at $US 35 per ounce: G Milton, *Quest for World Monetary Order*, New York: John Wiley, 1980.

Denmark and the Irish Republic) participated in EMU. The devaluation of sterling in June 1972 forced the UK and Ireland to leave the EMU within eight weeks of its creation. Denmark left in June 1972 but returned in October. When the International Monetary Fund collapsed in October 1972, and speculation against the US dollar caused its second devaluation, EMU fell into disarray. Indeed, the tunnel disappeared but the 'snake' survived. The participating Member States were leaving and joining EMU at their convenience (Italy left in February 1973, France in January 1974 and then again in March 1976, etc). However, the 'snake' remained but had changed its nature. It became a mainly 'German snake', that is, it was mainly composed of the deutschmark and currencies of small countries closely linked with Germany (eg The Netherlands).

The failure of EMU can be explained by the conjunction of internal and external factors. The external factor was the collapse of the IMF. As to the internal factors, the main one was the weak commitment of the Member States to EMU which was treated as an additional option in national policies and not as a priority.

EMU was replaced by the European Monetary System (EMS) adopted at the Bremen and Brussels Summits in 1978. It came into force on 13 March 1979. The EMS was created by Roy Jenkins in 1977[47] and strongly supported by Helmut Schmidt, the Chancellor of Germany. The main elements of the EMS were the European Currency Unit (ECU) and the European Exchange Rate Mechanism (ERM). The ECU constituted the Community's alternative currency. It was a unit of currency against which the values of national currencies were measured. The ECU was a composite currency, a 'weighted basket' of currencies of all Member States. The percentage of each national currency was determined by the size of the country, the relative size of the GNP and the share it commanded of the Community's total trade. The ECU, being a composite currency, had become very popular in international credit deals for both businesses and individuals as it reduced monetary risks inherent to international transactions. Member States were forced to accept the ECU as a part of their foreign exchange reserves. The ECU had many functions: it was used in financial settlement between different States; the EC issued its bonds in ECUs; and, most importantly, the ECU was at the heart of the ERM as it was used for the credit and intervention mechanism of the ERM.

Under the ERM the currency of each member State had a value against the ECU as well as a cross-rate against all of the other EMS currencies – the bilateral central rate. Member States agreed to fix their exchange rate against each other within a band of 4.5 per cent but not allowing the value of their currencies to rise or fall by more than within 2.25 per cent around the central rate (except for Italy which was allowed a 6 per cent range). The ERM currencies floated against all other world currencies. The rates of exchange were not irrevocably fixed and thus could be changed by a decision of Member States, although Italy unilaterally devalued the lira in July 1985. In order to ensure the proper functioning of the ERM some intervention and assistance mechanisms were provided:

1. The intervention of central banks. When the currencies of one Member State reached the upper or lower limit of the permitted band against the currency of another Member State, the central banks of both countries had to co-operate in order to maintain both currencies within their bilateral limits, that is sell or buy the currency of another State.

---

[47] R Jenkins, 'European Monetary Union' (1978) 127 Lloyds Bank Review 1–14.

2. The reserve pooling system. The Basle/Nyborg Agreement of September 1987 opened access to short-term finance for central banks of the ERM States in need. Medium term finance could be provided through the Council. Finally, the European Monetary Co-operation Fund[48] provided long term financial assistance. Its objective was to promote:

> '(a) the proper functioning of the progressive narrowing of the margin of fluctuation of the Community currencies against each other;
> (b) interventions in Community currencies on the exchange markets, and settlements between central banks leading to a concerted policy on reserves.'

3. Subsidised loans for ERM members through the European Investment Bank.

The EMS ensured exchange-rate stability, discouraged speculation, controlled inflation and reinforced co-operation between its members in monetary matters. The EMS was very successful until 1992 when it faced a serous problem created by the German government that decided for political reasons (against the advice of the Bundesbank) to unify the currencies of West and East Germany at a 1:1 ratio for much of the money supply and 2:1 for the rest, although the actual exchange ratio should have been 4:1. This resulted in inflation in Germany, followed by the Bundesbank tightening money supply. At that time the UK was entering a recession. The response of the Bank of England was to reflate the British economy which, taking into account the policy of the Bundesbank, ended up forcing the UK to leave the EMS in September 1992. Italy left a few days later. The EMS had to adapt to a new challenge. As a result, the permitted fluctuation bands were widened from 2.24 per cent to 15 per cent (in fact 30 per cent, 15 per cent on each side of the central rate). This meant that floating exchange rates were re-introduced within Europe. The difficulties did not, however, discourage the Member States from signing the TEU.

Establishment of technical co-operation, the introduction of development aid and social policy on the Community agenda

Technical co-operation

In the area of technical co-operation, the Colonna Report of 1970 was a response to The Hague Summit of 1969. Mostly ignored by Member States, this report nevertheless inspired the Commission to create a common industrial policy, especially in the new 'high technology industries'. The Commission has been very successful in this area. From the first programmes – the European Space Agency and Airbus Industries and Euronet-DIANE (Direct Information Access Network for Europe), it has mobilised and brought together many researchers, industrialists and academics. The major achievements are the creation of such programmes as ESPRIT (the European Strategic Programme for Research and Development and Information Technology), BRITE (the Basic Research in Industrial Technologies for Europe), RACE (Research into Advanced Communications in Europe), etc.[49]

---

[48] Regulation 907/73: OJ L89 (1973).
[49] For details: see S A Budd and A Jones, *The European Community, A Guide to the Maze,* London: Kogan Page, 4th ed, 1992, pp87–109.

Development aid

The introduction of development aid has two aspects: aid for developing countries and aid to the poorest regions of the Community in order to reduce disparities in economic conditions both within its borders and in each Member State. The main institution in charge of promoting economic activities and improving living conditions in the less prosperous regions of the Community is the European Regional Development Fund (ERDF). It was created as a temporary body in 1975 on the initiative of the UK in order to compensate for its small share of agricultural subsidies. The ERDF has become a permanent feature of the Community. The development of regional policy, especially after subsequent enlargements, allowing poor countries, like Greece and Ireland, to join the Community, has become an important matter for the Community. From 1975 to 1986, a time of major reform of the ERDF, it distributed nearly ECU 18 billion to the poorest regions in the Community, 91 per cent of which was allocated to five countries: the UK, France, Greece, Ireland and Italy[50] in the form of non-repayable grants. After 1986, new 'quota ranges' were introduced for each Member State, followed by some structural changes in the allocation of the ERDF funds, that is, 30 per cent to 50 per cent of its spending is to be in the form of grants for infrastructure projects, and more emphasis is put on regional and sectorial programmes and projects. The ERDF applies to two categories of programme: purely Community, long-term programmes aimed at areas with social and economic difficulties, and national programmes of interest to the Community which, in general, are jointly financed by the Community and the applicant Member State.

Social policy

The social policy was in a state of infancy until the adoption of the Single European Act. The CS Treaty contained some social provisions designed to alleviate the effect of the reconstruction of the steel and coal industries for workers employed in these sectors. The preamble to the EC Treaty sets out as main long-term objectives 'the constant improvement of the living and working conditions' of peoples of the Member States and underlines the Community commitment to the economic and social progress of the Member States by common action to eliminate the barriers which divide Europe. In practice the social policy, having been mainly developed by the creative approach of the ECJ based on art 12 EC (non-discrimination based on nationality), art 141 EC (equal pay for men and women), art 39 EC (free movement of workers), art 42 EC (social security), etc, or some occasional intervention of the Community such as the First Social Action Programme of 1974, lacked direction. The Social Fund established by the EC Treaty played an important role from its inception. Its main task, at that time, was to compensate for the difficulties that some social groups might experience resulting from structural changes due to the operation of the common market. During the 1960s, a period of economic boom and low unemployment, the Social Fund was mainly involved in the retraining of workers affected by structural changes, but after the 1973 crises (see below) its priority was to combat unemployment. In 1986, 16 million workers in the Community, that is 16 per cent of its workforce, were out of work. In these circumstances the Single European Act acknowledged the need for reformulating the social policy of the Community and set out a agenda for the Social Fund.

---

[50] E Wistrich, *The United States of Europe*, London, New York: Routledge, 1996, p66.

The Community from 1970 to 1985 – years of stagnation

From 1970 to 1985 the Community was in a state of stagnation. The so-called 'Eurosclerosis' can be explained partially by the difficult international situation but more importantly by lack of commitment from the Member States to further integration. Instead of developing an effective strategy for dealing with common problems created by the oil embargo in 1973, each Member State decided to act on its own. As a result, the UK and France signed bilateral agreements with Iran and Saudi Arabia for oil supplies while The Netherlands was left in the cold with its supplies completely cut off by OPEC. National interests and national policies prevailed over Community objectives. The crisis within the Community was also enhanced by three major issues: budgetary matters; the UK contribution to the Community budget; and the reform of the CAP. However, during that period some positive developments took place, such as the reform of the Community budget, the creation of 'own resources' of the Community aimed at replacing the system of national contributions and, finally, in June 1979, for the first time the European MPs were directly elected by people of the Member States.

Major developments

The European Parliament The Parliamentary Assembly by its own resolution of 30 March 1962 changed the name to 'the Parliament'[51] in order to emphasise the role it wanted to play within the Community. In the struggle to become a 'real Parliament' with legislative powers and members elected directly by universal suffrage in all Member States, the EP won two major victories in the 1970s.

First, the budgetary reform of the Community allocated important new powers to the EP. Based on two Treaties signed on 22 April 1970 and 22 July 1975 known as the Budgetary Treaties, the EP acts in conjunction with the Council in budgetary procedures. The respective competencies of these two institutions are determined by the distinction between 'compulsory expenditure' that automatically arises from or forms the inevitable consequence of the Treaty obligations to third parties (eg mainly expenditure on the Common Agricultural Policy) and 'non-compulsory expenditure' regarding expenditure in respect of the institutions (eg structural funds, research, etc). The EP was granted the right to block non-compulsory expenditure. The 1975 Budgetary Treaty also created a new Community institution – the Court of Auditors – which is in charge of the finances of the Community.

The second victory of the EP concerns the introduction of direct elections to the EP. In this respect, the Council Decision and Act of 20 September 1976 on Direct Elections[52] states in art 1 that the Members of the Parliament should be elected by direct universal suffrage. The first election took place in June 1979 (see Chapter 4, below).

Budgetary matters The Budgetary Treaties were complemented by the introduction of the Community's 'own resources'. Article 269 EC provides for the establishment of 'own

---

[51] OJ 1962 p1045.
[52] Council Decision 76/787 (OJ L278 (1976)) with annexed Act on direct elections.

resources' of the Community and thus replaces the system of national contributions to the Community budget. The Member States agreed on the new system in 1970.[53] Since 1 January 1978 the Community budget has been entirely financed by own resources, which currently consists of:

1. agricultural duties and the sugar and isoglucose levies;
2. customs duties imposed on imports from third countries;
3. the VAT resource: up to 1 per cent of VAT levied on the common assessment base[54] which must not exceed 50 per cent of GNP of a Member State;
4. an additional resource introduced in 1988. This is set according to the other three sources of budget revenue and is based on GNP and the application of a rate, set under the budget procedure, to the total GNP of all the Member States.

Recognition of the European Council Informal meetings of the Heads of State or Government of the Member States initiated by The Hague conference in 1969 within the framework of the Common Political Co-operation were recognised as a Community institution by the Paris Summit in December 1974.[55] It was then decided that the European Council would meet regularly three times a year. The number of meetings was reduced to two in 1985.

Major problems

The three major problems that had arisen during the years of stagnation were interrelated. On one hand, the UK's contribution to the Community budget was the main reason for the UK's dissatisfaction with the Community; on the other hand, two-thirds of the Community budget was spent on financing the Common Agricultural Policy. These difficulties were compounded by the intra-Community struggle between the Council and the European Parliament. The crisis reached a climax in December 1979 when the EP rejected the budget in order to express its dissatisfaction regarding its limited participation in the budgetary procedure, and in 1983 it blocked the UK rebate in an attempt to force budgetary reforms. These problems were solved later when the process of European integration was set on course. As to the UK contributions to the Community budget, the Fontainebleu Summit in June 1984 solved the dispute by introducing a 'correction' to the UK's net contribution based on the rules for the calculation of the 'own resources' of the Community.[56] The revision of the Common Agricultural Policy was even more complex. The Delors I package provided a solution for the financing of the CAP which was approved by a special summit in Brussels in February 1988. The third problem, the budgetary disagreement between the EP and the Council, was settled by the Inter-institutional Agreement between the Commission, the Council and the EP in 1988. The Delors I package has eliminated to a great extent

---

[53] Council Decision 70/243 on the Replacement of Financial Contributions from the Member States by the Communities' Own Resources: OJ L94 (1970).

[54] A common assessment base is 1 per cent of the total value of goods and services on which VAT is levied. This means that if a Member State's VAT rate is 20 per cent, 1 per cent is allocated to the Community.

[55] EC Bull 12–1974, point 7ff.

[56] Decision 85/257 (OJ L128 (1985)) which was replaced by Decision 88/376: OJ L185 (1988). The advantage of the system of periodical revision is that any decision in this area requires a unanimous vote by the Council.

potential disagreements between the Community institutions in budgetary matters. It introduced a five-year (1988–92) 'financial perspective' (that is, a draft budget for each year), put a ceiling for expenditure from 1.15 per cent of Community GNP in 1988 to 1.2 per cent in 1992, introduced a new 'own resource' to the Community budget consisting of a percentage of each Member State's share of the Community's GNP and, finally, reduced substantially the Community spending on the CAP – to a maximum of 74 per cent of the growth rate of the Community's GNP, thus allocating more money to structural funds.

Relaunch of European integration

The early 1980s witnessed a new attitude of Member States towards the Community. The unexpected enthusiasm, optimism and commitment to European integration, and a political will on the part of Member States to further the development of the Community, are difficult to explain. Indeed, the change in mood, although surprising, was essential to the survival of the idea of European unity. Among the factors that contributed to the 'Europhobia' was: the improvement of the international economic situation; the commitment of the new French President, François Mitterrand, to the development of the Community, strongly supported by the German Chancellor Helmut Kohl; and the appointment in 1985 of Jacques Delors as President of the Commission, who decided to accelerate the process of integration by submitting concrete projects. An additional stimulus was the realisation by the Member States that only common action could improve the competitiveness of national economies and increase their share in world trade, especially vis-à-vis the US, Japan and the newly industrialised countries. A greater convergence in all fields within the framework of the Community was the answer to the growing interdependence of international trade. Furthermore, national solutions to international problems proved unrewarding and the economic turmoil of 1973 when Member States retreated to protective measures applied at national level was the best example in this respect. As a result, some of the earlier proposals at reforming the Community were re-examined.

In December 1974 the Commission was asked to prepare a report on European Union which was submitted in 1976 by the Belgian Prime Minister, Leo Tindemans. The Tindemans Report set a bold agenda for economic, monetary and political integration headed by a supra-national executive body accountable to a directly elected, bicameral parliament. The Report was considered very controversial and was never seriously examined. Its only practical result was an invitation to the Council and the Commission to prepare annual reports on progress towards the creation of the European Union. More realistic reforms were proposed in 'The Three Wise Men' report prepared at the request of the European Council of 1978 and submitted to it in October 1979.[57] This report emphasised the role of the European Council as a true contributor to the improvement of the decision-making procedures within the Community. It also examined the reasons for failures of the Community institutions to perform their tasks efficiently. It explained that the failure lay 'rather in political circumstances and attitudes that sometimes produced conflicting

---

[57] A N Duff, 'The Report of the Three Wise Men' (1981) 21 Journal of Common Market Studies 237 et seq.

conceptions of the right way forward, and sometimes produced no clear conceptions at all'. However, it did not produce concrete results.

Another important initiative in this area was the report submitted by Altiero Spinelli, a strong supporter of the reforms of the Community leading to closer integration. He founded the so-called 'Crocodile Club' named after a restaurant in Strasburg, a meeting place of the reformers. Their proposal for institutional reforms was endorsed by the European Parliament. As a result the EP set up an Institutional Committee, with Spinelli as a co-ordinating *rapporteur*, responsible for preparing a comprehensive draft regarding the creation of a European Union. The Spinelli Draft Treaty of European Union was adopted with enthusiasm by the EP on 14 February 1984.[58] The Draft Treaty was strongly supported by President Mitterrand and, indeed, at Fontainebleu in June 1984 under his initiative an *ad hoc* committee made up of representatives of the Member States under the chairmanship of James Dooge, leader of the Irish Senate, was set up in order to examine the Draft. At the same time, the Fontainebleu Summit created the Addonnino Committee and entrusted it with the preparation of proposals concerning the free movement of persons within the Community in view of the establishment of Europe of Citizens.[59] The final report of the Dooge Committee was presented at the Brussels Summit in March 1985[60] and adopted by the majority of its members. The report recommended the introduction of the co-decision procedure designed to give more powers to the EP, the recognition of the European Council as a Community institution and the preparation of a new treaty on the European Union.

On 1 January 1985 Jacques Delors was appointed the new President of the Commission. Lord Cockfield, the Commissioner in charge of the internal market, volunteered to prepare the complete Internal Market Programme. His initiative was not only endorsed by Delors but he extended the initial proposal to cover all industries including steel and coal.[61] The Cockfield White Paper was very detailed. It identified the remaining barriers to trade within the Community and set up a timetable for their elimination by the end of 1992. The White Paper and comments on the Dooge Committee Report from Member States were submitted to the Milan Summit in June 1985 which welcomed the White Paper and instructed the Council to initiate a precise programme based on it. However, the main achievement of this summit was the decision of the Heads of State or Government to convene an Inter-governmental Conference (IG) to revise the Treaty despite opposition from the UK, Denmark and Greece.

The conference met in Luxembourg and in Brussels during the autumn of 1985. The three dissenting Member States decided to participate. The outcome of the IG was the Single European Act.

The Single European Act

The SEA was signed on 17 and 28 February 1986 and came into effect on 1 July 1987. Its ratification encountered some difficulties in four Member States: Italy considered that the SEA was not bold enough; Greece delayed its ratification waiting for Denmark's decision on

---

[58] OJ C77 (1984).
[59] *XVIII General Report on the Activities of the European Communities*, 1984, point 5.
[60] EC Bull 3–85, point 3.5.1 et seq.
[61] Lord Cockfield, The *European Union, Creating the Single Market*, London: Wiley Chancery Law, 1994, pp28–59.

whether to ratify or not; for Denmark it was necessary to hold a national referendum; and in Ireland the Irish government was forced by the ruling of its Supreme Court in *Crotty* v *Taoiseach* [1987] 2 CMLR 666 to hold a referendum as the Court held that the SEA provisions on security were in conflict with the Irish constitution.

The SEA was not very ambitious (which was the main reason for its acceptance by the Member States) but had much potential for expansion. The main features of the SEA are:

1. The completion of the internal market by 31 December 1992. Nearly 300 measures were enacted in order to create a European economic area without frontiers.
2. The introduction of qualified majority voting within the Council which applied to two-thirds of the 300 measures necessary to create a common market.
3. The extension of legislative powers of the European Parliament. A new co-operation procedure enhancing the participation of the EP in the decision-making procedures in ten areas was introduced (art 251 EC). Furthermore, a second procedure, the 'assent procedure', gave the EP an important new role. The approval of the EP (by an absolute majority) is required for the admission of new members to the Community and in respect of association agreements with third countries.
4. The formalisation of the European Council as a Community institution.
5. The creation of the Court of First Instance in order to ease the workload of the ECJ.

Many amendments introduced by the SEA have been further developed by the Treaty of Maastricht and the Treaty of Amsterdam. Consequently, they will be discussed in the next chapter. Among them the following are of great importance:

1. The formalisation by the SEA of the mechanism for European Political Co-operation.
2. The extension of the Community competencies to new areas. In some areas the Community was already active, such as environment, research and regional policy, protection of consumer and social cohesion.

The impact of the SEA on European integration is both practical in that it successfully created a single market, 'an area without internal frontiers in which the free movement of goods, persons, services and capital is ensured' (art 14(2) EC), and psychological as it encouraged the Member States to pursue common objectives within the framework of the Community. It paved the way to the Treaty of Maastricht.

From the Single European Act to the Treaty on European Union

The Commission stated that 'if the programme [the SEA] succeeded, it would fundamentally alter the face of Europe'.[62] This was especially true as the SEA contained a hidden agenda, that is the creation of economic and monetary union, a necessary complement to the single market. This approach confirms the 'spillover' theory according to which integration in one area of activity leads to integration in others. However, in order to achieve the objectives laid down in the SEA it was necessary to deal first with persisting internal conflicts. In this respect, the adoption of the Delors I package, which introduced the budgetary discipline, ended the 'British rebate' saga and reformed the CAP, permitting the Commission to put

---

[62] EC Bull 6–1985, point 18.

forward new initiatives. The Commission under the Presidency of Jacques Delors was committed to further integration with a view to introducing EMU. Its motto was 'one market, one money'.

The Hanover Summit of June 1988 reappointed Jacques Delors as President of the Commission. It also affirmed his vision of the Community by declaring that 'in adopting the Single Act, the Member States of the Community confirmed the objective of progressive realisation of economic and monetary union'.[63] The Hanover Summit, most importantly, set up a Committee, chaired by Jacques Delors, to examine the measures necessary for the establishment of EMU. The task of this Committee was to prepare concrete stages leading towards monetary union for the Madrid Summit in June 1989. Jacques Delors, in his annual speech on 17 January 1989 to the EP, assessed progress in the completion of a single market and set the agenda for the newly appointed Commission, that is, to devolve more power to the EP and to create EMU by successive stages. His vision of the Community was clear: it was a 'frontier free economic and social area on the way to becoming a political union',[64] although at this stage political union was not his priority. The Madrid Summit in June 1989 examined the Delors Report[65] without taking particular notice of the changing situation in Europe.[66]

The dismantling of the barbed wire border between Hungary and Austria on 2 May 1989 was the first tear in the 'iron curtain' and started the sequence of events which paved the way for the Communities to become a political union. Indeed, the 'German question' became the main preoccupation of Member States. The old political division between West and East was abolished, the Soviet Union was in a coma, the old order was shattered. Under the pressure of events and uncertainty the Federal Republic of Germany (FRG) accelerated the reunification process. Helmut Kohl, in his ten-point programme on German reunification submitted to the Bundestag on 28 November 1989, emphasised the fact that German unity was entirely a German matter. Nevertheless, in six of the points he underlined the FRG's commitment to the Community, the necessity to embed inter-German relations in an all-European process, as well as further strengthening the Community, especially in the light of the historical changes occurring in Europe.[67] The official policy of Germany on reunification echoed the famous call of Thomas Mann in 1953 'not a German Europe but for a European Germany'.

The hegemony of Germany within the Community haunted all European leaders.[68]

---

[63] EC Bull 6–1988, point 1.1.14.

[64] EC Bull Suppl–89, point 18.

[65] J Delors, *Report on Economic and Monetary Union in the EC* Luxembourg: Office for Official Publications of the European Communities, 1989.

[66] Only a very brief discussion on the changes in the Soviet bloc: see EC Bull 6–1989, Presidency Conclusion, point 1.1.16.

[67] E Kirchner, 'Genscher and What Lies Behind Genscherism' (1990) 13 West European Politics' 159–177.

[68] British Prime Minister Margaret Thatcher strongly opposed reunification of Germany and tried to convince President Mitterrand that indeed, within the EC, Germany's hegemony would assert itself and that France and the UK should act together, as in the past, to prevent, or at least slow, the process of reunification. Mitterrand agreed with her but considered that the reunification was inevitable, and instead of prevention it was better to strengthen the EC through further political integration. (Thatcher wanted to widen the EC to include central European countries and thus counterbalance the excessive influence of a reunited Germany.) See M Thatcher, *The Downing Street Years*, New York: Harper Collins, 1993, pp688–726.

Jacques Delors considered that German reunification was a matter the Germans had to deal with. In his annual speech on 17 January 1990 to the EP he presented his programme for the Commission's forthcoming year and emphasised that East Germany was a special case, that reunification of Germany, although being left to the German nation, nonetheless must be achieved 'through free self-determination, peacefully and democratically, in accordance with the principles of the Helsinki Final Act, in the context of an East-West dialogue and with an eye to European integration'.[69] Indeed, at that time the Brandenburg Gate in Berlin was opened and the first democratic elections in the former German Democratic Republic (GDR) were announced. It was clear that, at this stage, nothing could really stop the inevitable reunion of the German nation.

The President of France, François Mitterrand, began to put pressure on other Member States to create a political union, to counterbalance the implications of German reunification, by closely linking the largest Member State with the Community in political matters.[70] The extraordinary summit held in Dublin on 28 April 1990 formally welcomed East German integration into the Community and in reply Helmut Kohl agreed on the political union alongside EMU. The Dublin Summit asked foreign ministers to prepare proposals regarding co-operation between Member States in political matters for the Dublin Summit in June 1990, and these were to constitute the basis of a second Inter-governmental Conference.[71]

The second summit in Dublin on 25–26 June 1990 decided to convene two Inter-governmental Conferences (IGC) on 14 December 1990, one on EMU and the other on political union. The two IGCs were intended to be parallel with ratification of both instruments taking place within the same time frame. In the course of negotiations two approaches emerged: one favoured a 'Three Pillars' structure, the so-called Temple, consisting of a main agreement based on the EC Treaty and two separate arrangements outside the main framework covering judicial co-operation and a common foreign and security policy (CFSP). The second proposal was more ambitious and suggested the 'tree' model, a single 'trunk' having several branches and treating integration in all three areas as a common foundation (the tree), with special arrangements in particular fields (the branches). The second project was strongly federalist and as such judged too controversial by the foreign ministers to be submitted for consideration at Maastricht. The deliberations of the Inter-governmental Conference were based on the first project with modifications introduced by a second proposal made by The Netherlands on 8 November 1989 which provided for unanimous voting within CFSP while submitting the implementation of adopted measures to a qualified majority vote. The Inter-governmental Conferences began on 15 December 1990. The Maastricht Summit held on 9 and 10 December 1991 approved the text of the TEU. The final version was signed on 7 February 1992 at Maastricht. It was agreed that the process of ratification should be completed by the end of 1992, and its entry into force was to coincide with the completion of a single market. In practice, the process of

---

[69] EC Bull Supp 1–90, point 6.

[70] United Germany with its 77 million people, that is 25 per cent of the entire population of the Community, would account for 27 per cent of its GDP.

[71] R Corbett, 'The Inter-governmental Conference on Political Union' (1992) 30 Journal of Common Market Studies 274.

ratification was fraught with difficulties, it became even more troublesome than the ratification of the SEA!

Ratification of the Treaty on European Union (TEU)

There were impediments to the ratification of the TEU: its rejection by Denmark in a national referendum held on 2 June 1992 (the European Council held in Edinburgh in December 1992 reassured the Danes, and in the second referendum held on 18 May 1993 56.8 per cent voted in favour of the TEU);[72] and the challenge of the TEU before the German Constitutional Court[73] and before the English High Court in *R* v *Secretary of Foreign and Commonwealth Affairs, ex parte Rees-Mogg* [1994] 1 All ER 457 (QBD). The TEU was ratified in the UK on 2 August 1993.

The TEU entered into force on 1 November 1993. It was revised by the Treaty of Amsterdam.

The Treaty on European Union

To examine the main features of the Treaty on European Union is not an easy task. As McAllister said:

'Maastricht is like Janus. It faces both ways: towards inter-governmentalism, and towards some kind of "federal vocation". It is as ambiguous as the oracle of Delphi; as the Community itself. It reflects the extent to which the States are, and are not, able to agree.'[74]

The Treaty itself is a lengthy document, badly drafted. It consists of seven Titles, 17 legally binding protocols and 33 declarations which have an interpretive function. *The Economist* reported half jokingly that the negative referendum in Denmark and a very narrow majority vote in the French referendum regarding the ratification of the TEU could be explained by the fact that these governments gave their people the original version to read, as opposed to Ireland where the Irish government published a booklet summarising the Maastricht Treaty in plain language and consequently won a two-thirds vote in favour.[75] The only justification for producing such a confusing legal document is that the TEU was a transitional treaty. It established a procedure for its own revision.

An inter-governmental conference (IGC) was convened in 1996 to make necessary modifications to the TEU. It opened in Turin on 29 March 1996 and its work culminated in the Draft Treaty adopted by the Amsterdam European Council held on 17–19 June 1997.

The TEU is based on the so-called 'Temple' structure which consists of three pillars, each representing different competences of the European Union. Pillar 1 embraces all existing policies under the previous Treaties and introduces fundamental amendments to the

---

[72] D Howarth, 'The Compromise on Denmark and the Treaty on European Union: A Legal and Practical Analysis' (1994) 31 CMLR 765–805.

[73] M Herdegen, 'Maastricht and the German Constitutional Court: Constitutional Restraints for an "Ever Closer Union" ' (1994) 31 CMLR 235–249.

[74] R McAlister, *From EC to EU, An Historical and Political Survey,* London: Routledge, 1997, p225.

[75] Quoted by P Demaret, 'The Treaty Framework', in D O'Keeffe and P M Twomey (eds), *Legal Issues of the Maastricht Treaty,* London: Wiley Chancery Law, 1994, p3.

Communities. Pillar 2 concerns inter-governmental co-operation on common foreign and security policy (CFSP), and Pillar 3 covers inter-governmental co-operation in the fields of justice and home affairs (JHA). The roof of the Temple consists of common provisions which lay down the objectives of the TEU. The Temple is based (its 'plinth') on the final provisions. The three pillars are linked by the Council of the European Union, a decision-making body common to all pillars. Pillars 2 and 3 are based on inter-governmentalism, they create obligations only amongst the Member States and as such are not incorporated into UK law and therefore cannot be enforced in British courts. The TEU is like a ghost, its spirit is omnipresent but it has no material existence. The TEU has neither legal personality, nor its own institutions, nor a budget. It acts through the Communities with regard to Pillar 1 and through Member States with regard to Pillars 2 and 3.

The objectives of the EU are set out in the Preamble to the TEU and in the common provisions. The main objective of the TEU is to 'establish the foundations of an ever closer union among the people of Europe'. To attain this objective, concrete actions under the TEU consist of:

1. the promotion of balanced and sustainable economic progress through the establishment of an area without internal frontiers, and the reinforcement of internal cohesion,
2. the establishment of a single currency within the framework of economic and monetary union;
3. the promotion of an international identity for the EU through implementation of a common foreign and security policy (CFSP) which might lead to a common defence policy;
4. the establishment of citizenship of the EU;
5. the development of closer co-operation in the fields of justice and home affairs (JHA);
6. the improvement in the effectiveness of the EU institutions mostly by extending the legislative powers of the EP;
7. the extension of EU competences to new policies while reinforcing the existing ones;
8. the affirmation of its commitment to the protection of human rights;
9. the introduction of the principle of subsidiarity;
10. the introduction of the concept of variable geometry which permits differential integration, that is, while all Member States pursue common activities, in certain projects only some of them will participate. The best example is provided by economic and monetary union, the Schengen Agreements, some aspects of the CFSP and JHA.[76]

The European Economic Community was renamed by the TEU. The term 'European Economic Community' was replaced by 'European Community' in order to underline the fundamental changes in its objectives. The most important changes introduced by the TEU to the EC Treaty were:

1. the recognition of the principle of subsidiarity which operates to restrict the Community's involvement in national matters;

---

[76] For excellent studies: see J A Usher, 'Variable Geometry or Concentric Circles: Patterns for the European Union' (1997) 46 ICLQ 243.

2. the establishment of European citizenship which creates new rights for the nationals of Member States;

3. the redefinition of the objectives of the Community in areas such as health, education, training, industrial policy, telecommunications and energy networks, research and development, consumer protection, trans-European networks, and culture;

4. the extension of EC competences in environmental protection and development aid for poor countries;

5. the deepening the Commission's accountability to the European Parliament whilst extending EP participation in decision-making procedures;

6. the establishment of European Economic and Monetary Union depending on the extent to which Member States' economies converge in terms of inflation, interest rates and other criteria laid down in the EC Treaty;

7. the extension of the ECJ's powers in relation to Member States who refuse to comply with its judgments.

3 The Treaty of Amsterdam

3.1 Pillar 1: the European Community

3.2 Pillar 2: common foreign and security policy (CFSP)

3.3 Pillar 3: police co-operation in criminal matters

At 3 am on 18 June 1997 the draft Treaty intended to revise the Treaty on European Union (TEU) was signed by Heads of State or Government acting within the framework of the European Council in Amsterdam.[1] The Commission President, Jacques Santer, resumed the Amsterdam Summit in the following words: 'We set our sights high but had to make do with something less ambitious.' The biggest disappointment of the Amsterdam Summit was the abandonment of further integration of the EU into a federal structure, which was clearly demonstrated by the disagreement on institutional reform. Such important issues as the size of the Commission and the redistribution of voting weights in the Council were left unsettled. In this respect art 2 of the Protocol on the Institutions with the Prospect of Enlargement of the EU, which Protocol is annexed to the Treaty of Amsterdam, provides: 'At least one year before the membership of the European Union exceeds twenty, a Conference of the governments of Member States shall be convened in order to carry out a comprehensive review of the provisions of the Treaties on the composition and functioning of the Institutions.' That Inter-governmental Conference was opened on 14 February 2000 and should finish its work before the end of December 2000.

At Amsterdam the smaller Member States, which usually strongly support supra-nationality, were neither prepared to renounce their right to national representation in the Commission nor to agree on reform of voting within the Council which would have diminished their importance but made the Council more representative of the interests of the people of the EU as opposed to the Member States. Furthermore, Germany one of the main driving forces of unification at Maastricht, strongly opposed any expansion of the EU competences at the expense of national and regional governments. The Chancellor, Helmut Kohl, blocked the extension of majority voting in the Council in relation to industrial policy, social policy, transfer of pensions, social security rights, recognition of professional diplomas and many other areas. He also opposed majority voting on asylum, visa and immigration policies. As a result, for at least five years (that is until the review is due) unanimity will be required in decisions in those areas. The reversal of the priorities of Germany (which focuses on EMU as the main instrument of the integration of Germany into

---

[1] In is interesting to note that Mr Blair made a constructive contribution at the Amsterdam Summit which was noticed by representatives of other Member States. He himself declared before the British House of Commons that: 'We have proved to the people of Britain that we can get a better deal by being constructive, and we have proved to Europe that Britain can be a leading player, setting a new agenda that faces the real challenges of the new century': (1997) The Guardian 19 June, p10.

the EU instead of on political union) led to confirmation by the Amsterdam European Council of the stability pact and the timetable for the Euro. In order to avoid a French veto on these issues, a resolution on growth and employment to complement the stability pact was adopted by the Amsterdam European Council, although the basic disagreement between France and Germany over macro-economic policy is far from being settled.

The UK, Finland, Sweden and Ireland blocked the merger of the Western European Union with the EU. As a result, NATO remains the main defence force for Europe. The Amsterdam Summit agreed to incorporate the Schengen system into the EU but the UK and Ireland opted-out of common border controls. As a general rule under the common foreign and security policy unanimity is still required for the adoption of measures, although such may be adopted by qualified majority voting subject to the dual safeguards: the 'constructive abstention' and the possibility of referring a decision to the European Council if a Member State resorts to a veto. Other important issues such as the reform of the Common Agricultural Policy, the structural funds and the EU budget were left unresolved until the enlargement negotiations. Furthermore, the Amsterdam European Council accepted a multi-speed Europe. Under art 40 EU some Member States will be able to move forward in a number of areas without waiting for others, provided that the Council agrees by a qualified majority. Lastly, the decision concerning future enlargement was postponed.

The final version of the draft Treaty of Amsterdam was signed by the European Council on 2 October 1997 in Amsterdam. The new Treaty has three parts and it substantially amends both the Treaty on European Union and the EC Treaty. It simplifies the latter, although it will be difficult to get used to the new structure of the Treaty. It deletes obsolete provisions, updates others and renumbers almost all of them. All modifications are set out in an explanatory report prepared by the General Secretariat of the Council of the European Union.[2] The Treaty of Amsterdam is accompanied by thirteen protocols, 51 declarations adopted by the Amsterdam European Council (June 1997), and eight unilateral declarations submitted by individual Member States. The Treaty of Amsterdam entered into force on 1 May 1999 following its ratification by all 15 Member States of the European Union by 30 March 1999.

3.1 Pillar 1: the European Community

The Treaty of Amsterdam extends the objectives of the European Union and the European Community. In relation to the EU the objectives include:

1. the promotion of economic and social progress through the strengthening of economic and social cohesion, especially by creating a single currency;
2. the progressive establishment of an area of justice, security and freedom;
3. the further development of the concept of EU citizenship;
4. the implementation of a common foreign and security policy;
5. the strengthening of existing policies and development of them by considering revision of procedures and policies established under the TEU.

---

[2] OJ C353 (1997).

The objectives of the EC have not been changed, although two new areas have been added: the adoption of measures concerning the entry and movement of persons, and the co-ordination of employment polices. All measures adopted by the EC must be assessed in the light of two considerations: the prohibition of discrimination between men and women and the protection of the environment. Therefore, these two consideration are integrated into all Community policies.

The most important concepts and policy areas will be examined. Some of them were established before the Treaty of Amsterdam but further confirmed and clarified by it; others have been introduced by the Treaty of Amsterdam. One of the most important is the principle of subsidiarity.

Principle of subsidiarity

The principle of subsidiarity was not invented by the TEU. It has a long history, it derives from the Catholic doctrine of Thomas Aquinas and has been mainly used by the Roman Catholic Church – namely by Pope Pius XI in his Encyclical letter *Quadragesimo Anno* (1931) and later by Pope John XXII in his *Pacem in Terris* (1963) – to enhance the role of an individual in society in the context of a corporate State (especially a Communist State). According to Pius XI:

> 'It is an injustice, a grave evil and disturbance of right order for a larger and higher association to arrogate to itself functions which can be performed efficiently by smaller and lower societies'.[3]

In the context of social organisation the principle of subsidiarity means that decisions affecting individuals should always be taken at the lowest practical level, as closely as possible to the individuals concerned, and that their initiatives should not be impeded by any authorities in those areas where individuals are the most competent to decide for themselves.

The principle of subsidiarity has its constitutional and political dimension in federations. It allocates powers between federal and local authorities in order to strike a balance between the needs of the federation and the protection of the interests of members of the federation, and thus decides which function should be performed at the federal level, which should be shared by federal and State levels and which are within the exclusive competence of the latter.

The principle is enshrined in the German constitution. Some authors consider that it was the German model of subsidiarity which was adopted by the EU.[4] In the context of the German federation subsidiarity sets up a presumption in favour of the lower authorities (Länder) in decision-making procedures.[5] The allocation of power is clearly regulated by the German constitution, that is, art 73GG enumerates exclusive competences of federal

---

[3] Cited by J Steiner, 'Subsidiarity under the Maastricht Treaty', in D O'Keefe and P M Twomey (eds), *Legal Issues of the Maastricht Treaty'*, London: Wiley Chancery Law, 1994, p50.

[4] Scharpf, 'The Joint-decision Trap: Lessons from German Federalism and European Integration' (1988) 66 Public Administration 239–278.

[5] Article 30GG (German constitution).

authorities such as foreign policy, citizenship, customs matters, etc, while art 74GG provides a list of 27 areas of concurrent power in which federal and Länder authorities share competencies. However, once federal authorities legislate in a specific area of shared competences, they 'occupy the field' and thus the Länder are prevented from making any further regulations and their existing rules in this area are inoperative. The transfer of powers from a lower political unit to the centre is effected only if the former cannot discharge certain powers adequately and effectively, otherwise central authorities cannot interfere. The main function of subsidiarity under the German constitution is to give adequate weight to the interests of Länder. It also protects individuals' freedom which in the context of the German experience under the Nazi regime constitutes an additional safeguard that decisions are taken as closely as possible to the individuals concerned.

Subsidiarity and the allocation of competences between the Community and the Member States

Unlike the German constitution the allocation of power between the Community and the Member States is neither clearly regulated nor is there any mechanism for the allocation of competences within the Community. For that reason the Commission decided that it has the responsibility to decide which competences are exclusive to the Community and which can be shared between the Community and the Member States.[6] According to the Commission the Community has exclusive powers in all essential areas covered by the original EC Treaty.[7] This is seen as being extended to new policy areas established under the SEA and TEU. As a result, the exclusive competences of the EC cover 'at least, those aspects of health, safety environmental and consumer protection policies which are connected with the internal market'.[8]

Indeed, the exclusive competence of the Community in these areas is a logical consequence of the theory of 'occupied fields' also known as the concept of pre-emption. It means that once the Community has legislated in a particular area, the field is occupied and a Member State is precluded from introducing any legislation. The rule suffers no exception. As a result, a Member State cannot justify its action even though it may improve the existing EC measure. The most spectacular example was provided in *Commission v United Kingdom* Case 60/86 [1988] ECR 3921. In this case Directive 76/756/EEC, which harmonised technical requirements regarding motor vehicles, did not mention the 'dim dip' devices which were, for safety reasons, considered as necessary in all motor vehicles sold on the territory of the UK. The ECJ decided that the Directive provided an exhaustive list of necessary devices, the reason for the UK regulation was irrelevant and the UK was in breach of UK law.

The delegation of certain powers by Member States to EC institutions under the provisions of the EC Treaty ensures that, in order to attain the Treaty's objectives, action is taken at Community level. It results in the creation of uniform rules throughout the

---

[6] EC Bull 10–1992, point 116.

[7] Such as removal of obstacles to the free movements of goods, persons, services and capital, the Common Commercial Policy, competition policy, the CAP, the conservation of fishery resources and the common organisation of the fishery markets, the Common Transport Policy.

[8] A G Toth, 'A Legal Analysis of Subsidiarity', in *Legal Issues of the Maastricht Treaty,* supra note 3, p41.

Community. By the transfer of powers to the institutions the Member States have surrendered their power to act unilaterally in these areas. Consequently, action taken by the Community in a particular field is fully justified. The concept of pre-emption is easy to grasp but its actual application is more complex because in many instances it is difficult to determine to what extent the action of the Community pre-empts national competences (provided the Member States are allowed to share competences in that area).[9] Indeed, if the matter is within the exclusive competences of the Community, Member States have no concurrent power, even though the Community has failed to exercise its competences.[10]

The exclusive competence of the Community in the areas in which it has taken action can be explained without reference to the concept of pre-emption. The principle of supremacy of EC law over national law provides sufficient justification for precluding any unilateral legislation by a Member State in an area already regulated by the Community. The principle provides that any national legislation in conflict with EC law must be set aside.

However, the exclusive competence of the Community by pre-emption should be distinguished from that which has been inferred from the EC Treaty by the ECJ. So far, there are only two areas in which the exclusive competence of the Community has been firmly established by the ECJ. In Opinion 1/75 on the Local Cost Standard Understanding [1975] ECR 1355 (confirmed in *Donckerwolcke* Case 41/76 [1976] ECR 1921) and Opinion 1/94 [1994] ECR I–5267 (also in *Criminal Proceedings against Peter Leifer and Others* Case C–83/94 [1995] ECR I–3231) the ECJ held that the common commercial policy is within the exclusive competence of the Community. The second area of exclusive competence of the Community is conservation of the biological resources of the sea: see *Commission* v *United Kingdom* Case 804/79 [1979] ECR 2923.

Subsidiarity under the Treaty of Maastricht

The allocation of power between the Community and the Member States is one of the most controversial aspects of European integration. If a distinction between a confederation and a federation is based on the degree of sovereignty that the participating units enjoy then the EU is neither a federation nor a confederation. It is true that the EC operates in many areas as a federation, but it has institutions which are typical of a confederation. It is submitted that the EU is a *sui generis* organisation. For that reason, the principle of subsidiarity can play many roles in the context of European integration. In order to determine its precise meaning and the functions that it is supposed to fulfil, it is necessary to examine the provisions of the TEU which make reference to subsidiarity.

The principle of subsidiarity, although in a state of gestation, was mentioned in art 5 CS. It was implicit in art 235 EEC concerning the extension of competences of the Community. The Single European Act introduced it explicitly in relation to the protection of the environment. Article 130r(4) EEC stated that the Community shall intervene in environmental matters 'to the extent to which the objectives referred to in paragraph 1 can not be attained better ... at the level of the individual Member States.'

---

[9] For details: see S Weatherill, 'Beyond Preemption? Shared Competence and Constitutional Change in the European Community', in *Legal Issues of the Maastricht Treaty*, supra note 3, pp13–33.

[10] *Commission* v *United Kingdom* Case 804/79 [1981] ECR 1045 concerning the adoption by the UK of conservation measures, albeit the Community has exclusive competences under the Common Fishery Policy.

In the Treaty of Maastricht the principle of subsidiarity is first mentioned in its Preamble and in arts A and B (arts 1 and 2 EU). Article 1 EU states that decisions should be taken as closely as possible to the citizen of the EU. This is solely a political statement as the jurisdiction of the ECJ is limited to areas enumerated in art 46 EU. As a result, the Preamble and art 1 EU have no legal effect. Article 2 EU is similar: it states that the objectives of the EU should be achieved in conformity with the principle of subsidiarity as defined in art 5 EC.

Article 5 EC applies only to the EC Treaty and defines three legal concepts: the concept of conferred powers ('The Community shall act within the limits of the powers conferred upon it by this Treaty and of objectives assigned to it therein'); the principle of proportionality ('Any action by the Community shall not go beyond what is necessary to achieve the objectives by the Community'); and the principle of subsidiarity. Subsidiarity is defined in art 5 EC in the following terms

> 'In areas which do not fall within its exclusive competence, the Community shall take action, in accordance with the principle of subsidiarity, only if and in so far as the objectives of the proposed action cannot be sufficiently achieved by the Member States and can therefore, by reason of the scale or effects of the proposed action, be better achieved by the Community.'

Implementation of the principle of subsidiarity
The Edinburgh Summit in December 1992 examined the reports of the Commission and the Council on the procedural and practical steps needed to implement subsidiarity, which were prepared at the request of the Lisbon Summit of June 1992.[11] The Edinburgh Summit also took into consideration a draft Inter-Institutional Agreement on the application of art 5 EC presented by the European Parliament[12] and a report from the President of the Commission regarding the Commission's review of existing and proposed legislation in the light of the principle of subsidiarity[13] and established guidelines regarding practical and procedural implications deriving from the principle of subsidiarity for EC institutions. The guidelines, which were later completed by the 1993 Inter-institutional Agreement on Procedures for Implementing the Principle of Subsidiarity[14] created certain obligations for the EC institutions.

The principle of subsidiarity under the Treaty of Amsterdam
A Protocol on the Application of the Principles of Subsidiarity and Proportionality annexed to the Treaty of Amsterdam summarises and explains the procedural and practical steps necessary for implementation of these principles by the Community institutions. It sets out three guidelines for the adoption of Community measures which will satisfy the requirement of subsidiarity at the EC level:

1. the matter under consideration has transnational aspects which cannot be properly regulated by an action taken by a Member State and requires a Community action;

---

[11] EC Bull 6–1992, point 8.
[12] EC Bull 12–1992, point 9.
[13] Ibid, point 16.
[14] Its text in Europe, Documents, No 1857, November 1993, p44.

2. an action taken by a Member State alone, or an absence of a Community action, would conflict with the objectives of the EC Treaty;
3. an action taken by the Community would produce clear benefits by reason of its scale or effects as compared with an action taken by an individual Member State.

The Protocol is based on the Edinburgh Conclusions[15] and confirms the existing Community approach to the application of subsidiarity.

The European Commission The Commission has to take the principle of subsidiarity into account in proposing any new legislation. In the preamble to the legislation it has to justify its action in the light of subsidiarity which becomes part of the measure's legal basis. As a result, it is the function of the Commission to show that it is more appropriate to act at Community level. This is very important as it regulates the burden of proof and sets the direction for future developments of the Community. Thus, the Commission has voluntarily withdrawn some proposals for directives (the packaging of foodstuffs, allocation of radio frequencies) and renounced harmonisation in such matters as vehicle number-plates, the regulation of gambling, structures and equipment for fun-fairs and theme parks, etc.[16]

In secondary legislation, the Commission has to give preference to directives rather than regulations and, in particular, framework directives should prevail over detailed directives as they allow Member States to select the most appropriate methods of implementing EC law. Similarly, and non-binding measures such as recommendations, opinions, non-compulsory codes of conduct should be used when appropriate rather than binding measures. In addition, the techniques of minimum standards or the use of mutual recognition, etc, are recommended. This approach was applied by the Commission, prior to the TEU, in the framework for the completion of a single market. Co-operation between Member States should be encouraged and thus the Commission is required to support, complete or supervise such joint initiatives. As a result, the Commission has decided to revise, in the light of the principle of subsidiarity, existing directives in such areas as technical standards, mutual recognition of qualifications, animal welfare, etc.

In addition to the above, wide consultations are required before the Commission puts forward any proposal for a legislative measure. In the area of competition policy, the Commission decided that national authorities, and especially national courts, should play a more important role in the application of arts 81 and 82 EC.[17]

The Commission has to submit an annual report to the European Council and the European Parliament on the application of art 5 EC.

The Council of the European Union The Council must simultaneously examine each proposal submitted by the Commission as well as its own amendments to such proposals, with regard to its merits and in the light of the principle of subsidiarity.

---

[15] Overall Approach to the Application by the Council of the Subsidiarity Principle and art 3b of the Treaty on European Union, Conclusions of the European Council, Edinburgh, December 1992, Annex 2 to Part A.
[16] Ibid.
[17] OJ C39 (1993).

The European Parliament The application of subsidiarity implies the co-operation of the EP, especially since the EP has important legislative competences in many areas under the co-operation procedure (art 251 EC) and the co-decision procedure (art 252 EC). The Inter-institutional Agreement on Procedures for Implementing the Principle of Subsidiarity provides that the EP must take into account the principle of subsidiarity and justify in the light of art 5 EC any amendment which substantially changes a proposal submitted by the Commission.

The European Court of Justice The principle of subsidiarity is not only a socio-political concept but also a fundamental principle of EC law. No special procedure has been established to bring an issue of subsidiarity before the ECJ, although this idea was supported by the EP.[18] Accordingly, the principle of subsidiarity can arise in two types of action: against EC institutions or under art 234 EC. Article 234 EC enables national courts and tribunals to refer to the ECJ questions of Community law that require to be decided in a case pending before them for a preliminary ruling. As to judicial review of acts of EC institutions (art 230 EC), an applicant challenges the act itself by claiming that it was adopted in violation of the requirements laid down in art 5 EC. For the first time[19] the issue of subsidiarity arose in *United Kingdom v Council (Re Working Time Directive)* Case C–84/94 [1996] ECR I–5758.

Here, the UK brought an action for annulment of Council Directive 93/104 concerning certain aspects of the organisation of working time, or in the alternative annulment of art 4, the first and second sentences of art 5, art 6(2) and art 7 of the Directive. The UK challenged the legal base of the Directive. They argued that the Directive should have been adopted under art 94 EC or art 308 EC which require unanimity within the Council instead of art 138(2) EC which imposes only qualified majority voting within the Council. Furthermore, the UK claimed that the Directive was in breach of the principles of proportionality and subsidiarity since the Council failed to demonstrate that the objective of the Directive could better be achieved at Community level than at national level. Finally, the UK claimed that the Council had infringed essential procedural requirements by not providing sufficient reasons for its adoption in the preamble.

The ECJ held that art 138(2) EC was an appropriate legal base for the Directive since it referred to 'working environment' and 'health and safety' which should be interpreted broadly for two reasons. First, the words 'especially in the working environment' militate in favour of broad interpretation of the Council powers under art 138(2) EC. Second, it is supported by the constitution of the World Health Organisation (WHO) which describes health as a state of complete physical, mental and social well-being and not the absence of illness or infirmity. This definition is recognised by all Member States as they are members of the WHO. Thus, the organisation of working hours must be included in the meaning of working environment since it is capable of affecting the health and safety of a particular worker. Only, the second sentence of art 5 of the Directive was annulled. It referred to Sunday as a weekly rest period. The ECJ held that in the context of the diversity of cultural,

---

[18] A G Toth, 'Is Subsidiarity Justiciable?' (1994) 19 European Law Review 268, especially 273.
[19] The CFI was in two cases seised of questions of subsidiarity but left them unanswered: *Tremblay* Case T–5/93 [1995] ECR II–185; *SPO* Case T–29/92 [1995] ECR II–289.

ethnic and religious factors in Member States it should be left to each Member State to decide which day of the week is the most appropriate for a weekly rest day.

The question of subsidiarity and proportionality is the most interesting part of the judgment in the above case. The ECJ confirmed that the principle of subsidiarity can be relied upon by an applicant, although in this case it was invoked to support the main claim and not as an autonomous ground for annulment. Thus, all disputes as to whether subsidiarity as such can be invoked before the ECJ seem to be settled. A measure will be proportionate only if consistent with the principle of subsidiarity. The ECJ made a clear distinction between the principle of proportionality and the principle of subsidiarity. It held that the argument of the UK that the Council could not adopt measures which were as general and as mandatory as those forming the subject-matter of the Directive must be examined in the light of the principle of proportionality, while the argument that the objective of the Directive would be better served at Community level than at national level concerned the principle of subsidiarity. Also, Advocate-General Leger emphasised that the principle of subsidiarity answers the question at which level, Community or national, the adoption of a legislative measure is more appropriate, while the principle of proportionality governs the intensity of the Community action. In other words, the ECJ, on the grounds of subsidiarity, would examine whether a measure adopted by a Member State would achieve the desired Community objective. Under the principle of proportionality the ECJ examined whether less onerous, less restrictive measures adopted by the Community would achieve the aims pursued. In respect of subsidiarity the ECJ demonstrated the necessity of an action at Community level since the objective of raising the level of health and safety through harmonisation 'presupposes Community-wide action'. As to proportionality, in order to verify whether the measure complies with the principle of proportionality it is necessary to ascertain 'whether the means which it employs are suitable for the purpose of achieving the desired objective and whether they do not go beyond what is necessary to achieve it'. In this respect, the ECJ held that the measures adopted by the Directive were necessary and appropriate as they contributed directly to achieving the objective of improving the health and increasing the safety protection of workers and did not exceed what is necessary to achieve such objective. The third plea of infringement of essential procedural requirements was also dismissed. The ECJ stated that the preamble clearly explained the objectives of the Directive and a specific reference to scientific material justifying its adoption was not necessary.

It is interesting to mention that the Edinburgh European Council (December 1993) in its conclusion declared that art 5 EC has no direct effect. Also, the Council of the European Union in its answer to a written question submitted by Victor Arbeloa regarding the direct effect of art 5 EC emphasised that 'it would be difficult to attribute to this provision the direct effect that the EC has acknowledged, through a quite specific and constant jurisprudence, in respect of certain other provisions of the Treaty' because on the one hand the application of subsidiarity by the EC institutions calls for an essential political appraisal, and on the other hand, it leaves the institutions a wide margin of discretion.[20] It is submitted that the question of direct effect of art 5 EC is of minor importance, taking into account that

---

[20] OJ C102 (1994).

if a question of validity of an act of an EC institution arises before a national court, and it refers the matter to the ECJ under art 234 EC, the ECJ will decide whether the act is valid.

Assessment of the principle of subsidiarity

The concept of subsidiarity is, indeed, an elusive concept. It is submitted that its best definition is the following: 'It is a principle for allocating power upwards as well as downwards, but it incorporates a presumption in favour of allocation downwards in case of doubt.'[21] It is not tantamount to decentralisation and it admits degrees of exercise of powers. This entails that the decision should always be taken at the lowest practical level, thus leaving the Community to concentrate on the essential and vital objectives. The principle of subsidiarity maintains the integrity of the Community while allowing the participation of national authorities in decision-making procedures provided they can exercise their functions satisfactorily. Subsidiarity maintains the balance of power between the Community and the Member States, and by imposing the burden of proof upon the Community institutions it affects the allocation of power not only today but, most importantly, in the future. The principle of subsidiarity has been introduced in order to increase efficiency, accountability and transparency in the decision-making procedures of the EC.

However, the practical implications deriving from the principle of subsidiarity will have to be further clarified by ECJ case law, in itself no easy task taking into account the principle's highly political aspects. So far, it has many different interpretations. For Member States hostile to a federal structure of the EU, such as the UK, the principle of subsidiarity constitutes a guarantee of national sovereignty as it precludes the Community from interference in their affairs. For the Commission it is a necessary component of a federal State. Jacques Delors underlined that subsidiarity is the essence of federalism since 'the federal approach is to define clearly who does what'.[22]

Economic and monetary union (EMU)

The most controversial issue of European integration is certainly the creation of economic and monetary union. The TEU introduced a new Title VI which has become Title VII of the EC Treaty containing provisions on the economic and monetary policy of the Union. A number of Protocols to the TEU were attached introducing detailed provisions including special arrangements, the so-called opt outs for the UK and Denmark regarding their participation in the third stage of EMU (they opted out). The Treaty of Amsterdam does not make any significant changes in respect of EMU.

Economic union

The creation of EMU, on the economic side, entails close co-ordination of economic policies of the Member States which constitutes the basis for building the monetary union. This reflects the so-called 'coronation' or 'economic' theory according to which monetary union is the final result, the 'coronation' of the process of economic convergence. This theory is

---

[21] A CEPR Annual Report, 1993: 'Making Sense of Subsidiarity: How Much Centralisation for Europe' (1993) 4 Monitoring European Integration 4.
[22] (1992) Le Figaro 8 June, p1.

strongly supported by the German government and especially the Bundesbank.[23] Surprisingly, the TEU devoted only a few, broadly formulated provisions to the creation of economic union. The Treaty of Amsterdam clarified the provisions of the TEU and introduced more efficient surveillance procedures. Member States are required to consider their economic policies as a matter of common concern and must co-ordinate them with the Council. Two concrete actions are required from Member States at Community level: the adoption of a common policy of price stability and, in respect of fiscal discipline, the setting and implementing of national budgets aimed at avoiding excessive deficits.

With regard to the first objective, it is the responsibility of the European Central Bank to stabilise internal price levels despite changes in the external exchange rate of the Euro (the Euro was adopted as the single currency by the Madrid Summit in December 1995). The overall price structure must be stabilised in order to ensure ability of the Euro to function as a stable store of value.[24] The control of excessive budget deficits is the second objective of economic union. Under art 104 EC the Member States are required to avoid excessive governmental deficits and maintain budgetary discipline. The Commission, in conformity with the criteria set out in art 104(2) EC, must assess a Member State's compliance with budgetary discipline. If these criteria are satisfied or, notwithstanding their fulfilment, if the Commission considers that there is a risk of an excessive deficit in a Member State, it prepares a report which is submitted to the Council. If the Council, after an overall assessment whether an excessive deficit exists or will occur in the future, decides (acting by QMV) that this is the case, it makes recommendations to the Member State concerned to bring an end to that situation within a specific time limit. If a Member State fails to take appropriate actions in response to the recommendations the Council may make its recommendations public. If a Member State further resists the Council may decide to apply one or more of the measures set out in art 104(11) EC. In particular, it may:

1. require the Member State concerned to publish additional information, to be specified by the Council, before issuing bonds and securities;
2. invite the European Investment Bank to reconsider its lending policy towards the Member State concerned;
3. require the Member State concerned to make a non-interest-bearing deposit of an appropriate size with the Community until the excess deficit has, in the view of the Council, been corrected;
4. impose fines of an appropriate size.

Monetary union

The provisions concerning the creation of monetary union are well developed and detailed. Articles 105–124 EC laid down the institutional and policy requirements necessary to create monetary union and formally sanctioned the three-stage programme towards EMU.

---

[23] D R R Dunnett, 'Economic and Monetary Union', in *Legal Issues of the Maastricht Treaty*, supra note 3, p136.

[24] This means that without the price stability policy the prices change whenever the exchange rate of the Euro changes, that is if the Euro depreciates all prices will rise, etc: see E Tower and T Willet, 'The Theory of Optimum Currency Areas and Exchange Rate Flexibility', *Special Papers in International Economics*, No 11, New York: Princeton University Press, 1976.

1. Stage I (from 1 July 1990 to 31 December 1993). The main objectives of the first stage of EMU were: the completion of the Single European Market; the abolition of the then existing restrictions on the free movement of capital; the participation of all Member States in the Exchange Rate Mechanism (ERM); the reduction of exchange rate fluctuations; and the establishment of a closer co-ordination of economic and monetary policies.

2. Stage II (from 1 January 1994). Its main objectives were: to further develop convergence of national economies of the Member States; to gradually ensure independence for the national central banks; and to establish the European Monetary Institute (EMI).[25]

   The first objective was to be attained by introducing the supervision system described in art 104 EC aimed at eliminating excessive government deficits.

   With regard to independence of national banks from governments, all Member States (bar Sweden) have introduced necessary legislation in this respect and, as a result, all central banks are fully independent.

   The European Monetary Institute (EMI) was officially inaugurated on 1 January 1994. It had its seat in Frankfurt and employed about 200 staff. The European Monetary Institute was a temporary body, a forerunner of the European Central Bank. EMI was in charge of preparing the third stage of monetary union, strengthening co-operation between national central banks, supervising proper functioning of the European Monetary System (EMS), encouraging the use of the EMU and furthering co-operation among Member States in monetary matters. Another task of EMI consisted of preparing Euro banknotes. In this respect, on 13 December 1996 in Dublin, the President of the EMI presented the winning designs for Euro money created by Robert Kalina.[26]

   This stage of EMU was crucial for the Member States' participation in the third stage. Before they can proceed to the third stage, they have to meet the following convergence criteria:

   a) Low inflation, not exceeding that of the three best performing Member States by more than 1.5 per cent.

   b) The currency has to remain within the normal fluctuation margins of ERM for at least two years and without being devalued, by unilateral action of a Member State, against the currency of any other Member State. The objective of this criterion is to maintain stable exchange rates for at least two years.

   c) Government debts must not exceed 60 per cent of GDP and annual government borrowing (budget deficit) has to be less than 3 per cent of GDP.

   d) Long-term interest rates must not exceed the average rate of the three lowest rates by more than 2 per cent.

These criteria are very stringent. In order to further EMU, and to clarify the uncertainties surrounding the single currency, the Dublin Summit of 13 December 1996

---

[25] M Moore and T O'Connell, *Monetary Policy in Stage Two of EMU*, Centre for Economic Policy Research Discussion Paper 616, 1992.

[26] The Euro banknotes got a mixed review. They were praised by the Belgian *Le Soir* ('the European currency at last has a face') and much criticised by the UK (*The Sun*: We hate funny money, the *Daily Telegraph*: 'garish Dutch-style sweet wrappers'), and in Finland (*Helsinginsanomat*: 'They look a bit like old Tsarist notes and will probably wind up being worth about as much'): (1996) The European 19-25 December, p17.

adopted 'The Stability and Growth Pact' which focused on a Member State's budget deficit. It was agreed that the Council of Finance Ministers could impose financial sanctions on a government if its budget deficit exceeds 3 per cent of GDP. The financial sanction is imposed by qualified majority vote excluding the culprit Member State. The government will be required to pay a fine of up to 0.5 per cent of GDP in the form of an interest-free deposit equivalent to 0.2 per cent of GDP, plus 0.1 per cent for every percentage point above the 3 per cent deficit ratio, up to a maximum deposit of 0.5 per cent of GDP. However, the deposit will only be required if the government concerned fails to take remedial action within four months. If the government's deficit results from exceptional circumstances beyond its control, such as natural disasters or severe recession – a decline of 2 per cent in GDP over a single year, or in the case of a 'grey area' when GDP declines between 0.75 per cent and 2 per cent – no sanctions will be imposed. The deposit will be lost if the excessive deficit persists after more than two years.

The stability and growth pact on budget discipline and the timetable for EMU was discussed and formally endorsed by the Amsterdam Summit in June 1997. The UK and Denmark decided not to participate in the launching of a single currency. In summer 1998 the European System of Central Banks was established. The third stage commenced on 1 January 1999.

3. Stage III (from 1 January 1999).[27] Eleven Member States participated in the third stage of EMU. Apart from the UK and Denmark who both opted out, Sweden was not ready to participate for structural reasons and Greece did not meet the convergence criteria.[28] On 1 January 1999 the currencies of participating Member States were replaced by the Euro which also became the unit of account of the European Central Bank and of the central banks of the participating Member States. The Euro is divided into 100 cents.

The conversion rate between the Euro and the national currency of each participating Member State is irrevocably fixed. These rates have been adopted by the Council of the European Union[29] and are as follow:

1 EUR	=	40.3399 BEF (Belgian Franc)
1 EUR	=	1.95583 DEM (German Mark)
1 EUR	=	166.386 ESP (Spanish Peseta)
1 EUR	=	6.55957 FRF (French Franc)
1 EUR	=	0.787564 IEP (Irish Punt)
1 EUR	=	1936.27 ITL (Italian Lira)
1 EUR	=	40.3399 LUF (Luxembourg Franc)
1 EUR	=	2.20371 NLG (Dutch Guilder)
1 EUR	=	13.7603 ATS (Austrian Schilling)
1 EUR	=	200.482 PTE (Portuguese Escudo)
1 EUR	=	5.94573 FIM (Finnish Mark)

---

[27] C Monticelli and J Vinals, *European Monetary Policy in Stage Three, What Are the Issues?*, Centre for Economic Policy Research, Occasional Paper 12, 1993.
[28] Greece will join the Euro area on 1 January 2001 after successfully achieving the convergence criteria.
[29] OJ L359 (1998).

Thus, the third stage of EMU became reality. Special bodies were created in order to conduct economic and monetary policy: the European System of Central Banks (ESCB) which under art 105(1) EC is responsible for maintaining price stability, and an independent European Central Bank in charge of the formulation and implementation of the monetary policy of the EU. Under art 105(2) EC the Governing Council of the ECB, made up of the members of the Executive Board and the governors of the national central banks participating in the third stage,[30] formulates the monetary policy, that is, establishes intermediate objectives of the monetary policy, determines interest rates and the supply of reserves in the ESCB, and sets up necessary guidelines for their implementation. Meanwhile, the Executive Board of the ECB, comprising the President, the Vice-President and four other members, implements monetary policy, including giving necessary instructions to national central banks. The ECB is an independent body although it does not enjoy the status of a Community institution. Its status is set out in a separate Protocol, and it has legal personality by virtue of art 107(2) EC, unlike the ESCB. Only persons from Member States without derogations under art 122(1) EC may be members of the Governing Council and the Executive Board of the ECB. In order to integrate the Member States with derogations from the third stage another body has been set up, the General Council (GC). This is made up of the President and Vice-President of the ECB and all governors of the national central banks, including governors from Member States with derogations. Their participation in the GC ensures that they are fully informed and involved in the work of the ESCB. The GC has been set up under art 45 of the Protocol, albeit without prejudice to art 107(3) EC which provides that the ESCB is to be governed by the decision-making bodies of the ECB, that is, the Governing Council and the Executive Board. The General Council has replaced the EMI in relation to those tasks which, by the reason of derogations, still have to be performed in the third stage of EMU. Furthermore, it is a consultative body providing legal advice in the preparations for abrogation of the derogations, and on the scope and implementation of EC law on the prudential supervision of credit undertakings and the stability of the financial system at the request the Council, the Commission and competent authorities of the Member States.

Although the TEU required that the Euro became a single currency from 1 January 1999, in practice there were insufficient notes and coins for circulation at that date. From 1 January 1999 to the year 2002/2003 national currencies will continue to be used in Member States as means of payment. Dual pricing of products appears with conversion tables displayed wherever necessary. In 2002/2003 the Euro will take over as the national currency, although national notes and coins will be exchanged in banks for a considerable period thereafter. From that point financial transactions, wages, salaries, bank accounts, etc, will be in the Euro.

It is interesting to note that the symbol designed for the Euro is closely modelled on the Greek letter *epsilon*. The Commission considers that it 'points back to the cradle of European civilisation and the first letter of Europe'.[31]

---

[30] See I Harden, 'The European Central Bank and the Role of National Central Banks in Economic and Monetary Union', in K Gretschmann (ed), *Economic and Monetary Union: Implications for National Policy-Makers*, Dordrecht: Kluwer, 1993, p149 et seq.

[31] (1997) The European 24–30 July, p23.

Assessment of EMU

The creation of EMU requires significant convergence of the national economies of Member States which involves their close co-operation in economic matters at Community level. In practice a considerable amount of national economic sovereignty has been transferred to EU institutions. Member States participating in the third stage of EMU are no longer able to control their economic policy, especially to set interest rates or devalue their currency. This is the main disadvantage of EMU. However, this argument must be considered in the light of the growing interdependence and internationalisation of economies Does any country actually have any real economic sovereignty left to exercise? On the one hand, interest rates depend on market forces, and on the other hand devaluation of a national currency is a temporary measure which 'backlashes' in creating inflationary consequences, which in turn leads to pressure for higher wages, thus undermining the competitiveness of national products.

It is submitted that the creation of EMU has resulted in a number of advantages:

1. It is a powerful symbol of European integration.
2. The Euro has become one of the dominant world currencies in competition with the US dollar and the Japanese yen. Also, it may result in the Euro enjoying the *seigniorage* position, that is, the ability to finance balance of trade deficits by having other countries keep the Euro as part of their reserves.
3. It results in considerable savings in transaction costs as the cost of exchanging one currency for others has been eliminated. The Euro will become the major transaction or invoicing currency. According to the Financial Market Group of the London School of Economics, by 2002 the global invoicing share for the Euro will be about 28 per cent, with growing potential in trade with central and eastern European countries.
4. For tourists there are no extra cost for converting one currency into another while travelling in the 'EMU territory'.
5. It has increased the attractiveness of the EU to foreign investors and increased the share of the EMU-participating countries in world exports from 17 to 25 per cent. In this respect Andrew Crockett, general manager of the Bank for International Settlements in Basel, said: 'Monetary union in Europe holds the promise of profound change in international finance. The economies sharing the Euro could face the world as the largest single currency area and the largest single trading bloc.'[32]
6. It results in the same inflation rate throughout the EMU territory which is, and will probably remain, very low taking into account the independence of the ECB. Anti-inflationary discipline has been imposed upon Member States like France, Spain, and Italy, well known for their high inflation rates.
7. Management of the EU has been simplified as all payments are made in the same currency.

The suspension of rights of a Member State which violates basic freedoms

The principles of liberty, democracy, respect for human rights and fundamental freedoms

---

[32] K Engelen, 'Why the US is Beginning to Worry about the Euro' (1997) The European 9-15 January, p18.

and the rule of law on which the EU is founded have been recognised as conditions for admission of a new Member and thus resulted in the amendment of art 49 EC. Amended art 6 EU reaffirms the principle of respect for human rights and fundamental freedoms. More importantly, their violation by a Member State is punishable under art 7 EU. This provision states that the Council, meeting in its composition of Heads of State or Government and acting by unanimity (a defaulting Member State is excluded) on a proposal by at least one-third of the Member States or by the Commission, and after obtaining assent from the EP, may determine the existence of a violation of those fundamental freedoms and then acting by a qualified majority may decide to suspend certain rights of the defaulting Member State, including the suspension of its voting rights in the Council. However, in applying this provision the Council must take into account the possible consequences of such a suspension on the rights and obligations of nationals of that Member State.

The progressive creation of an area of freedom, security and justice for EC citizens within five years of the Treaty's ratification

This objective is expressed in art 2 EU which states:

> 'The Union shall set itself … to maintain and develop the Union as an area of freedom, security and justice, in which the free movement of persons is assured in conjunction with appropriate measures with respect to external border controls, asylum, immigration and the prevention and combating of crime.'

The new arrangements bring asylum, immigration, free movement of persons, judicial co-operation in civil matters, police and judicial co-operation in criminal matters and other policies related to the free movement of persons within the realm of EC law. A new Title IV was added to the EC Treaty embracing 'communitarised' areas. Fraud and other illegal activities affecting the financial interests of the Community are now dealt with by the Pillar 1 (art 280 EC). The area of freedom, security and justice will result from measures taken unanimously by the Council within the five years after the entry into force of the Treaty of Amsterdam. At the end of the five-year period majority voting may be introduced in the Council. The Commission and the Member States share the right of initiative and the European Parliament is not directly involved, although it must be consulted. The ECJ has a greater role to play. Under art 68 EC the ECJ has jurisdiction:

1. to give a preliminary ruling on the interpretation of Title IV and on the validity and interpretation of acts adopted by the Community on the basis of this title at the request of a national court of final appeal;
2. the Commission, the Council or a Member State can ask the ECJ to rule on such questions.

However, the ECJ has no jurisdiction to give a ruling on measures taken to abolish all checks on individuals, both EC nationals and non-EC nationals, when they cross internal borders.

On 3 December 1998 the Council and the Commission adopted an action plan on how to best implement the provisions of the Treaty of Amsterdam on the creation of an area of freedom, security and justice.[33] It defined the priority objectives for the next five years and set a timetable of measures necessary for achieving them in the medium term (two years) and the long term (five years). The Vienna European Council held in December 1998 endorsed the action plan. The European Council, which will be held in December 2001, will assess progress made in the creation of the area of freedom, security and justice.

Each area within Title IV EC requires further examination.

Free movement of persons

The progressive establishment of an area of freedom, security and justice has as a main constituent the abolition of border controls between Member States in order to ensure the free movement of persons. This is a sign of supreme trust of one Member State in other Member States, especially taking into account that some Member States, such as Italy or Greece, have long and open coasts whilst others, such as Austria, only have a small number of external border guards. Under art 62 EC the Council, acting by unanimity, has five years from the entry into force of the Treaty of Amsterdam to eliminate internal border controls and in particular:

1. to introduce measures removing border controls for persons within the EU whether or not EC nationals;
2. to set out common rules for the crossing of external borders by non-EC nationals;
3. to establish conditions for the issue of visas for non-EC nationals to enter and stay up to three months within the territory of a Member State.[34]
4. to prepare a list of countries whose nationals are exempted from the visa requirements.[35]

The free movement of persons is to be mainly achieved by the incorporation of the Schengen *acquis* into the framework of Community law as it covers the principal arrangements concerning the common treatment of non-EC nationals and a system of common control at external borders

Schengen II The agreement between France and Germany in July 1984 in Saarbrucken on elimination of frontier controls between the two countries, which was intended as a way of strengthening Franco-German relations, gave birth to the Schengen system. The Benelux countries had already abolished border checks for their nationals and they decided to join the Franco-German project. It resulted in the adoption of the Schengen Convention on the gradual abolition of checks at common borders. On 14 June 1985 the Schengen I agreement was signed between the Benelux countries and France and Germany. It provided that border controls should be abolished on 1 January 1990 between territories of the Contracting Parties. In order to achieve this objective, working groups were established to draw up necessary measures on the relaxation of border controls – such as the introduction of mixed checks at the borders, visual checks on EC nationals (green sticker in the front window of

---

[33] OJ C19 (1999).

[34] Regulation 2317 of 29 May 1995 set out a list of 101 countries and entities whose nationals must be in possession of a visa when crossing the external border of the EU.

[35] Council Regulation 574/1999 of 12 March 1999 has determined the third countries whose nationals must be in possession of visas when crossing the external borders of the Member States: OJ L72 (1999).

cars) and co-ordination of measures strengthening the control of external borders to keep out undesirables by harmonising visa controls, asylum and deportation policies. Also issues relevant to internal security – such as harmonisation of firearms and ammunition laws, police co-operation in combating illegal trade in drugs and serious international crimes – were addressed. Their work culminated in the adoption of the Schengen Implementing Convention on 19 June 1990 (Schengen II) between the same five Contracting States. This Convention entered into force on 1 September 1993. The Amsterdam Summit of June 1997 decided to incorporate the Schengen system into the revised TEU.

In the relationship between the Schengen group and the EC, the Commission had the status of observer at the Schengen meetings. The Schengen system was subordinated to EC law through the compatibility requirement established in art 134 of Schengen II, which states that the Schengen provisions shall only apply if they are compatible with EC law. For that reason it was quite easy to incorporate the Schengen system into the Treaty of Amsterdam.

The main feature of Schengen II is that it abolishes the internal borders of the signatory states and thus creates a single external border where immigration checks for the Schengen territory are carried out in accordance with a single set of rules. Furthermore, if a non-EC national is considered to be unlawfully in one Schengen country, he is deemed to be illegally in all and will be expelled from the Schengen territory. Also, it introduces tight controls on non-EC nationals entering the Schengen territory, aimed at eliminating illegal immigration, and strengthens the co-operation between the police and immigration authorities. Finally, it sets up a system for the computerised exchange of information (known as the Schengen Information System (SIS)), located in Strasbourg, which contains information on policing, crime and immigration, including arrest warrants, missing persons, stolen documents and goods, etc. At its head is the SIRENE system (Supplementary Information Request at the National Entries), an emergency communication system and the central contact point for each Schengen country. Requests for information through the SIS are verified and legally validated.

Thirteen Member States are Contracting Parties to the Schengen II agreement and since 19 December 1999 Norway and Iceland have been associated with it (they have no voting rights but participate on the Schengen Executive Council). The protocol attached to the Treaty of Amsterdam provided for incorporating the Schengen II agreement into the EU framework. In order to do so the Council of the European Union, which replaced the Executive Committee set up under the Schengen agreement, took a number of decisions. On 1 May 1999 it established a procedure incorporating the Schengen Secretariat into the general secretariat of the Council of the EU.[36] The elements of Schengen II which should be incorporated into the EC Treaty (the Schengen *acquis*) were defined by the Council Decision adopted on 20 May 1999.[37]

Not all Member States of the EU participate in Schengen II. The legal position of dissenting Member States – Ireland, the UK and Denmark – is regulated by protocols annexed to the Treaty of Amsterdam. The UK and Ireland may join Schengen II provided the Council of the EU of the 13 participating Member States decides unanimously to accept

[36] OJ L119 (1999).
[37] OJ L176 (1999).

them, while Denmark is given an option to adopt the Schengen principles. If the UK and Ireland decide to participate in the adoption of measures based on the Schengen *acquis* they may do so by notifying the Presidency within a reasonable time. In March 1999 the UK asked to participate in some aspects of Schengen, namely police and legal co-operation in criminal matters, the fight against drugs and the SIS. The Commission gave a favourable opinion on 21 July 1999. It will be for the Council to take a final decision.

Immigration and asylum

Immigration and asylum is covered by art 63 EC. It concerns:

1. the determination of a Member State responsible for dealing with an application for political asylum;
2. the establishment of a minimum standard in relation to qualification for, and grant of, asylum;
3. the establishment of minimum standards for temporary protection of displaced persons from third countries who are unable to return to their home country;
4. the adoption of common rules on immigration policy, including such issues as the conditions of granting long-term visas and residence permits for non-EC nationals, as well as facilitating non-EC nationals legally residing in one Member State to establish themselves in another Member State.

Under art 64 EC the Council is entitled to adopt measures combating illegal immigration and to introduce temporary measures to deal with emergency situations involving a sudden inflow of non-EC nationals seeking protection from outbreak of violence or persecution in their country of origin.

Immigration and asylum, although separate issues, are nevertheless interrelated. The EU Member States become countries of immigration for people who are using an application for asylum as a gateway for immigration. Until the TEU these issues were mostly left to the Member States. For a few reasons the EC decided not to deal with immigration and asylum: this has already been done by the Schengen group, and the *ad hoc* Group on Immigration (see below). Some governments, the UK in particular, considered that these matters were within their exclusive competences and refused to surrender their sovereign rights in border checks, even for travellers from the EC, not trusting continental immigration authorities to keep illegal immigrants outside the UK.

Co-operation between Member States in asylum and immigration matters has a long history although it has been based mostly on ad hoc arrangements. The removal of internal borders, a necessary condition for the completion of the single market, created a need for even closer co-operation among the Member States. Co-operation on immigration and asylum under the umbrella of the EC started when the Council established a 'Group of Co-ordinators' which was instructed to prepare proposals for measures to be implemented by 1 January 1993. It resulted in the submission of the so called 'Palma Document' which was adopted at the Madrid Summit in June 1989. The essential measures proposed by the Palma Document concerned: the introduction of accelerated procedures and common criteria for 'manifestly unfounded' asylum applications; a procedure for preventing asylum-seekers from applying for asylum in more than one Member State; the determination of a Member State responsible for removing immigrants and asylum seekers from the EC; the establishment of a financing system for expulsion; a common list of countries whose nationals need a visa to enter the EU; a common list of inadmissible persons and wanted persons; the introduction of common measures for checks on external borders, accompanied by exchange of information between police and customs etc. The Commission approved the Palma Document and in October 1991 issued to the Council and the European Parliament its own communication on immigration and asylum in which it recognised the link between both matters.[38]

In respect of immigration control, in October 1986, on a proposal by the UK to curb illegal immigration and especially to 'end abuses of the asylum process', an *ad hoc* Group on Immigration was created, made up of the interior ministers of all Member States. The *ad hoc* Group on Immigration drafted many important proposals in this area:

1. In April 1987 on sanctions on airlines bringing in undocumented asylum-seekers and those with false documents. This proposal was implemented in the UK in the Carriers Liability Act in 1987.[39]
2. In 1990 a draft convention to prevent asylum seekers from making more than one application in the EC. This proposal was transformed into the Dublin Convention.
3. In 1990 a draft convention on harmonisation of controls at external borders.
4. In 1991 a proposal for fingerprinting asylum-seekers.
5. In 1992 a draft resolution on criteria and procedures on 'manifestly unfounded' asylum applications.
6. Proposals on harmonisation of policies on expulsion.
7. Proposals on the admission of non-EC nationals for employment.

The work of the *ad hoc* group was presented at the meetings of immigration ministers within the framework of the European Political Co-operation (EPC). Many initiatives of the *ad hoc* Group on Immigration were approved by the Council of Ministers' meetings within the EPC, one such being the creation at the end of 1991 of the Centre for Information, Discussion and Exchange on Asylum (CIREA) containing information on countries of origin of asylum-seekers and thus making it possible to decide which are 'safe' and in which the risks of persecution for political reasons are serious. Although CIREA was strongly criticised by non-governmental organisations, another Centre for Information, Discussion and Exchange on the Crossing of Borders and Immigration (CIREFI) was set up at the end of November 1992 to supervise the common immigration policy and especially to store information on unlawful immigration methods, forged documents, rejected asylum applications, etc.

At a meeting in London in November 1992 the ministers approved the Resolution on Manifestly Unfounded Applications for Asylum. They expressed the wish to incorporate the principles of the Resolution into a legally binding instrument and many States have already introduced national legislation based upon it.[40] The Resolution sets out criteria and the procedure for handling manifestly unfounded applications for asylum. It also introduces an

---

[38] SEC(91) 1857.
[39] Under its provisions carriers liability doubled to £2,000 per passenger.
[40] In the UK the Asylum and Immigration Appeals Act 1993.

accelerated procedure for processing asylum claims within one month. Another important Resolution on a harmonised approach to questions concerning host third countries approved by the 1992 meeting is contained in the Dublin Convention.

Dublin Convention The Convention Determining the State Responsible for Examining Applications for Asylum Lodged in One of the Member States of the European Communities was signed on 15 June 1990 in Dublin. The Amsterdam Summit of June 1997 welcomed the completion of the ratification procedures of this Convention which entered into force on 1 September 1997. The main objective of the Convention is to prevent an asylum-seeker from making multiple applications and from selecting the country of asylum. As a result, if his application is refused in one country, the application is considered as refused by all other Member States. It also acknowledged the first 'safe' country principle. If an asylum-seeker on his way from a country where he was persecuted went through a host third country, that is a country which is considered safe or where he could have applied for asylum, his application in the EC would be deemed unlawful and he would be returned to the host country.

The Convention determines the Member State which should deal with an asylum application, that is, the one which granted him a visa or allowed him illegal entry into the Community, unless he has a close family – only husband or wife or parents or children – with refugee status in an EC country. In that case the State of residence of his close family will deal with his application. The receiving State notifies the responsible State of the presence of an asylum-seeker and sends the asylum-seeker to that State. Under the Dublin Convention the entire Union is treated as one country for the purposes of an asylum application.

Under art 18 of the Dublin Convention a Committee responsible for its implementation was set up. Its Decision 1/98[41] clarified important issues in respect of the implementation of the Convention, such as the exchange of fingerprint data between Member States, the exchange of information on ways and means by which asylum-seekers enter the European Union, and the establishment of close working relationships between officials of Member States carrying out functions in relation to the Convention.

The Dublin Convention has been strongly criticised, inter alia, for creating 'fortress Europe', that is, asylum-seekers suffer great difficulties and privations in their attempts to obtain sanctuary in EC and EFTA countries.[42] Even if they cross the external frontiers, almost all EU countries have introduced new stringent laws on asylum, accelerated procedures without appeal for 'manifestly unfounded' applications, and enforced detention for those that cannot prove their identity. Additionally, compulsory fingerprinting and detention in prisons and special centres is imposed. Further, measures such as carriers being liable for bringing a person without proper documents into the territory of a Member State, or the examination of asylum requests at the border, mean that border guards and stewardesses decide whether a person is entitled to obtain refugee status.

Finally, while Member States seek to eliminate racial violence they are using their own drastic means to justify more immigration controls and anti-refugee measures. In this respect, in 1994 the Commission issued a Communication on Immigration and Asylum

---

[41] OJ L196 (1998).

[42] D O'Keeffe, 'The Schengen Convention: a Suitable Model for European Integration' (1992) 11 YEL 185–219.

Policy which set out the approach that should be taken in order to tackle immigration problems. First, the Union must help to eradicate the causes of immigration. The economic conditions under which many of the potential immigrants have to live under at their place of origin are so appalling that they will try anything to cross the external borders of the Union. They are forced into the asylum admission procedure since there are no other possibilities for them to improve their living standards. Second, the Commission proposes to control immigration by formulating basic principles on admission, conditions of stay and other aspects of immigration policy.[43]

It is interesting to note that a protocol on asylum for nationals of the Union Member States has been annexed to the EC Treaty. It contains one article which provides that, taking into account the respect for fundamental human rights in the Member States, they should, for all legal and practical purposes regarding asylum applications, consider each other as safe countries of origin. They are permitted, nevertheless, to examine applications for political asylum submitted by nationals of other Member States, although in such an event the application should be dealt with on the basis of the presumption that it is manifestly unfounded. The main objective of the protocol is to ensure that terrorist suspects will not take advantage of asylum procedures in another Member State in order to avoid extradition.

Draft Convention on the Crossing of External Borders This Draft Convention was expected to be signed in 1991. It contains common rules for the crossing of external borders by third countries' nationals, introduces stringent conditions for entry of non-EC nationals and establishes via the European Information System (EIS) a joint computerised list of inadmissible third country nationals. The Convention was drafted in such a way as to allow its ratification by the UK. It does not mention internal borders. Nevertheless, the UK refuses to accede to the Convention because of her dispute with Spain over Gibraltar.

Judicial co-operation in civil matters

Judicial co-operation was treated as a less important component of Title VI of the TEU. Under the TEU this topic was dealt with by two working groups: one on criminal law and the other on civil law. They drafted conventions and agreements in those areas, and submitted amendments concerning existing conventions, for example the Brussels Convention on Jurisdiction and the Enforcement of Judgments in Civil and Commercial Matters, the Convention on Extradition, etc. They also recommended adoption of international conventions prepared by the Council of Europe, The Hague Conference on Private International Law, the Rome Institute, etc, to Member States.

Under the Treaty of Amsterdam the importance for citizens of the EU of judicial co-operation in civil matters has been recognised. Article 65 EC provides for improvement and simplification of:

---

[43] The Tampere European Council (15–16 October 1999) emphasised the need for a comprehensive approach to immigration issues consisting of a greater coherence of internal and external policies of Member States and the EU, within their respective competences, in combating poverty, improving living conditions and job opportunities, ensuring respect for human rights with regard to countries of origin of immigrants and asylum-seekers. The partnership agreements between the EU and those countries are considered to be the main elements of this policy: conclusions, points 11 and 12.

1. the system for cross-border service of judicial and extra-judicial documents;
2. the co-operation in taking evidence in one Member State for use in proceedings in other Member States;
3. the rules on the recognition and enforcement of decisions in civil and commercial matters, including in extra-judicial cases. This refers to the modernisation of the 1968 Brussels Convention and the Lugano Convention on the Recognition and Enforcement of Judgments in Civil and Commercial Matters.

Furthermore, art 65 EC provides for the adoption of rules on civil procedure and private international law, and for the elimination of obstacles to the good functioning of civil proceedings

Under the Vienna Action Plan (December 1998) the proposed medium-term measures included the modernisation of the existing conventions (Brussels, Lugano and Rome). Since the entry into force of the Treaty of Amsterdam all those conventions have been subjected to scrutiny by the Commission in the context of the creation of a European judicial area.

The Commission has decided that those instruments should be adopted as Community acts in view of the fact that their subject-matters are now within the scope of at 65 EC Treaty. Consequently, the Commission has submitted:

1. a proposal for a Council Regulation on Jurisdiction and the Recognition and Enforcement of Judgments in Matrimonial Matters and in Matters of Parental Responsibility for Joint Children;
2. a proposal for a Council Regulation on Jurisdiction and the Enforcement of Judgments in Civil and Commercial Matters[44] which broadly reflects the result of the negotiations regarding the revision of the 1968 Brussels Convention; and
3. a proposal for a Council Directive on the Service in the Member States of Judicial and Extra-judicial Documents in Civil and Commercial Matters.

The consequence of adopting the above-mentioned conventions as Community acts will be that there is no need for protocols on their interpretation. They will be regarded in the same way as any Community act and therefore subject to jurisdiction of the Court of Justice under art 220 EC. Furthermore, if adopted under the form of an EC regulation those conventions will enter into force on the same day in all Member States, and will require no action by the Member States to transpose them into national law.

It is interesting to note that Title IV EC, which applies to matters covered by those proposals, does not apply to the United Kingdom, Ireland and Denmark and will not do so unless they 'opt in'. The UK and Ireland have expressed their wish to be fully associated with EC activities regarding judicial co-operation in civil matters and have opted in. Only Denmark has not yet decided whether to 'opt in' or not.

Other medium-term measures include the preparation of an instrument on the law applicable to non-contractual obligations and the creation of a European judicial network similar to the one already in existence for criminal matters. By the end of December 2000 the Council intends to implement the principle of mutual recognition of decisions taken by the competent national authorities.

---

[44] COM(99) 348 final CNS 990154 (not yet published in the Official Journal).

In the long term there are plans to prepare new legal instruments dealing with, inter alia, the law applicable to divorce, jurisdiction and the law applicable to the matrimonial property regime and to succession, and the compatibility of civil procedures. Another initiative includes the establishment of minimum standards ensuring an adequate level of legal aid, and of common procedural rules for simplified and accelerated cross-border litigation on small claims and uncontested claims.

Police and judicial co-operation in criminal matters
Article 61(e) EC provides for adoption of measures in the field of police and judicial co-operation in criminal matters aimed at a high level of security by preventing and combating crime within the EU.

Assessment of Title IV
The incorporation into the EC Treaty of the above-examined areas should be welcomed. The 'communitarisation' of areas previously covered by Pillar 3 not only ensures the free movement of persons in conformity with art 18 EC but, most importantly, confirms that EU citizens are at the centre of Community concerns. Furthermore, measures adopted under art 61(e) EC and Pillar 3 in respect of police and judicial co-operation provide more efficient means for combating terrorism, international organised crime, money laundering, drug trafficking and illegal immigration. The transfer of matters previously covered by Pillar 3 to the EC Treaty remedies the main criticisms of Pillar 3, such as lack of judicial and democratic control and secrecy in decision-making procedures. Under the Treaty of Amsterdam there is a clear structure put in place in order to create an area of freedom, security and justice, whereas the TEU did not set any specific objectives to be achieved in these areas and merely described them as 'matters of common interest'.

Furthermore, the difficulty created by the Treaty of Maastricht resulting from the division of competences between the Community and the Member States acting within the framework of Pillar 3 in these areas is eliminated. This difficulty is well illustrated in *Commission v Council* Case C–170/96 [1998] ECR I–2763 concerning the adoption of measures relating to entry and stay of nationals of third countries in the territory of the EU.

In this case the Commission supported by the European Parliament brought an action for annulment of the Joint Action of 4 March 1996 adopted by the Council on the basis of art 31 EU (previously art K.3) on airport transit arrangements.[45] The French Republic, the Kingdom of Denmark and the United Kingdom intervened in support of the Council. The Commission argued that the Council should have acted on the basis of art 100c EC Treaty (now repealed) and not that of art 31 EU. In the context of art 31 EU the ECJ had to determine whether or not it had jurisdiction.

Article 46 EU (previously art L) excludes the jurisdiction of the ECJ in areas of common foreign and security policy (Pillar 2 of the TEU) and co-operation in justice and home affairs (Pillar 3 of the TEU). For that reason, the government of the UK argued that the ECJ had no jurisdiction to review a measure adopted on the basis of art 31 EU. The ECJ decided otherwise. The Court upheld the arguments of the Commission. The Commission argued

---

[45] OJ L63 (1996).

that because the contested measures should have been adopted on the basis of art 100c EC Treaty (now repealed), which provision was within the jurisdiction of the Court, and because art 47 EU (previously art M) stipulates that a provision such as art 31(2) EU, which provides for the adoption of joint action in the areas specified in art 29 EU (previously art K.1), must not affect the provisions of EC Treaty, the ECJ should have jurisdiction to review that measure. The ECJ held that it had jurisdiction to examine whether or not a measure based on art 31 EU encroached upon the powers conferred on the ECJ in relation to art 100c EC Treaty (now repealed).

Fortunately, the Treaty of Amsterdam clarifies these matters as it brings the areas of visa policy, the terms of issuing residence permits to immigrants, etc, within the realm of Community rules.

The extension of the scope of the principle of non-discrimination

Article 13 EC prohibits discrimination based on 'sex, racial or ethnic origin, religion or belief, disability, age or sexual orientation'. The Council of the European Union is empowered to take all appropriate measures in order to further implement this provision, although unanimity is required for the adoption of such a measure which in addition must be confined 'within the limits of the powers' conferred upon the Community by the EC Treaty. Article 13 EC is to be applied without prejudice to other provisions of the Treaty and thus does not override such articles as art 12 EC, which prohibits discrimination based on nationality, or art 141 EC on equal pay for equal work for men and women. Article 13 EC has been complemented by a Declaration to the Final Act regarding persons with a disability, which Declaration emphasises that their situation should be taken into account in drafting proposals under art 95 EC. The prohibition of discrimination between men and women is strengthened by amendments to arts 2 and 3 EC requiring the Community to promote equality between men and women. Under art 12 EC the Council is empowered (acting by qualified majority) to adopt legislation which has, as its sole purpose, the elimination of discrimination based on nationality. Also, the Amsterdam Summit issued a Declaration on the Abolition of the Death Penalty (recommending abolition) which penalty has already been abolished in most of the Member States and has not been applied in any of them for many years.

In is interesting to note that the protection of the processing of personal data and on the free movement of such data in respect of both individuals and Community institutions was embodied in art 286 EC.

The incorporation of the Social Charter into the EC Treaty

The opposition of the UK government prevented the Community Charter of the Fundamental Social Rights of Workers (Social Charter) from being incorporated into the TEU. This led the remaining Member States to adopt a Protocol on Social Policy and the Agreement on Social Policy under which the UK was a Contracting Party to the Social Protocol (as it constituted an integral part of the EC Treaty) but was excluded from the application of the Agreement on Social Policy. At the Amsterdam Summit (June 1997) the

UK Labour government signed an agreement ending Britain's opt-out and allowed the incorporation of the Agreement on Social Policy into the EC Treaty provisions on social policy, education, training and youth. It is embodied in arts 137–140 EC. Under art 137 EC the Council, acting by qualified majority, is empowered to adopt directives in the following areas:

1. the working environment, particularly in relation to health and safety;
2. working conditions;
3. information and consultation of workers;
4. the integration of persons excluded from the labour market;
5. equality between men and women.

However, unanimity within the Council is required under art 137 EC in relation to five further areas of social policy:

1. social security and social protection of workers;
2. protection of workers where employment is terminated;
3. representation and the collective defence of the interests of workers and employers;
4. conditions of employment for non-EC nationals residing in the EU;
5. financial contribution for job-creation and related initiatives.

In order to safeguard the interests of the Member States in these highly sensitive areas, some limitations are imposed on the competences of the Community. First, art 137 EC excludes pay from its scope of application and thus prevents the establishment of an EC-wide minimum wage. It also precludes the Community from taking measures in relation to the rights of associations of workers and the right to strike. Second, under arts 138 and 139 EC the Commission, while preparing proposals on employment measures, must consult representatives of management and labour at Community level. This requirement is aimed at achieving a consensus between them. In addition, art 139 EC provides that if management and labour representatives indicate an intention to reach a binding agreement on a particular matter the Commission is to give them up to nine months to reach that agreement.

Article 119 of the EC Treaty becomes art 141 EC and its scope of application has been extended to encompass the prohibition of discrimination based on sexual orientation, the possibility for Member States to adopt measures creating positive discrimination and for the Council to adopt, as an objective of its own, by qualified majority, measures ensuring the application of the principle of non-discrimination between men and women in matters of employment and occupation. Article 142 EC requires that Member States maintain the existing equivalence between paid holiday schemes.

In relation to social security, art 42 EC empowers the Council, by qualified majority, to adopt measures in the field of social security as may be necessary to secure freedom of movement for workers. It is expected that under this provision it will be possible to apply the aggregation principle, that is, workers will be allowed to aggregate all periods of work and other qualifications which have been accrued in any Member State in order to determine the amount of social security benefits.

In April 1998 the Commission adopted a communication containing its Social Action

Programme for 1998–2000 which put emphasis on employment. The communication was based on the conclusions of the Amsterdam European Council (June 1997) and the Luxembourg 'jobs summit' (November 1997). Many of its proposal have already been adopted at Community level, in particular in respect of measures to combat social exclusion.

The inclusion of a chapter on employment in the Treaty of Amsterdam

France threatened to veto the Stability Pact if its proposal for a Europe-wide job-creating scheme was rejected. As a result, a new approach towards policy co-ordination in respect of economic growth and employment as part of the preparation for EMU was adopted by the Amsterdam Summit. First, the European Investment Bank[46] will finance socially useful employment projects and, second, anti-unemployment strategy will be co-ordinated at Community level to ensure that the combined policies of Member States do not result in overall recession. Maximising opportunities for growth could reduce unemployment in the EU to between five and seven per cent. This policy is based on the US model introduced by President Clinton, that is the use of monetary expansion and very low interest rates to boost the economy which resulted in sustainable non-inflationary growth and reduced unemployment to 4.8 per cent. In Europe the figure is considerably higher – more than 10.8 per cent (18.2 million people) of the workforce are out of work at the time of writing. The employment policy has been added to the objectives of the Treaty.[47] In this respect art 3 EC provides for 'the promotion of co-ordination between employment policies of the Member States with a view to enhancing their effectiveness by developing a co-ordinated strategy for employment.'

In the Resolution of the European Council on Growth and Employment it was stressed that employment is at the top of the political agenda of the EU. The new Title on Employment involves the Community institutions in the task of fighting unemployment in the EU and co-ordinating national employment policies of the Member States. A new advisory body, the Employment Committee, has been created by the Council to promote co-ordination between Member States on employment and labour market policies.

It is important to note that art 126(2) EC expressly states that employment is still within the exclusive competence of the Member States. The role of the Community is to co-ordinate strategy in this area by creating common guidelines and incorporate the employment objectives in other EC policies. Each year the Labour and Social Affairs Council adopts a set of guidelines which each Member State must implement under its National Action Plan (NAP).

The extension of powers of the European Parliament (EP)

The clear winner at the Amsterdam Summit was the EP. The co-decision procedure has

---

[46] The European Investment Bank is ready to spend up to EUR one billion by the year 2000 to implement the Amsterdam Summit Resolution on Growth and Employment. On 13 September 1997 the President of the EIB presented an interim report in this respect to the informal Council meeting of EU Economy and Finance Ministers at Mondorf-les-Bains. A comprehensive report on the EIB's three-year Amsterdam special programme was submitted and approved during the special jobs summit on 21 November 1997 in Luxembourg.

[47] Amendments to art 2 EU and arts 2 and 3 EC.

been extended to 15 existing Treaty provisions (including free movement of workers and right of establishment, social security for migrant workers, transport policy, the implementation of decisions concerning the Social and Regional funds and vocational training, trans-European networks, research, environment and development aid) and eight new Treaty areas:

1. employment policy;
2. equal opportunities;
3. public health;
4. measures aimed at combating fraud;
5. transparency;
6. customs co-operation;
7. statistics;
8. the establishment of a new body on data protection.

However, in some areas which were transferred to Pillar 1, for example in asylum and immigration matters, the requirement of unanimity in the Council limits the application of the co-decision procedure. The attempt by the EP to include the freedom of movement of, and social security rights for, immigrant workers was unsuccessful. The co-decision procedure itself has been simplified. It is now contained in art 251 EC. The assent procedure has been extended to only one area, that is concerning sanctions imposed on a Member State which is in breach of fundamental principles under art 7 EU.

The Amsterdam Treaty involves national parliaments in the legislative decision-making procedures. The EU in order to give them an opportunity to express their views on matters which may be of particular interest. It requires the Commission to promptly forward all proposals to national parliaments. Subject to exceptions based on urgency, proposals cannot be placed before the Council for six weeks after they are made available to national parliaments.

The establishment of a general principle of transparency

Under art 225 EC any EU citizen or any natural or legal person residing within the EU is entitled to have access to documents from the Council, the Commission and the EP, subject to public policy and private confidentiality restrictions. Also, a Member State can request that its documents are not consulted without its consent.

Miscellaneous matters

Among miscellaneous matters, the following are noted. Belgium was particularly pleased by a declaration on sports teams which emphasises the social importance of sport 'in particular its role in forging identity and bringing people together'. France and Spain were very satisfied by the amendment of art 227(2) EC which now expressly acknowledges special needs of outermost regions such as the French and Spanish overseas departments, Madeira, the Canary Islands and the Azores. Austria and the UK praised the inclusion of animal rights within Community law. They are contained in a protocol attached to the Amsterdam Treaty which requires that the Community institutions and the Member States take animal welfare into account in the adoption or implementation of measures relating to the common market or the Common Agricultural Policy. However, this is subject to religious rites and cultural or regional heritage.

Also, the Amsterdam Treaty strengthens the powers of the EC in combating fraud. Article 280 EC imposes a duty on Member States to counter fraud against the Community in the same manner as it is countered under national law. The Council is empowered to adopt measures, by qualified majority, to combat fraud.

3.2 Pillar 2: common foreign and security policy (CFSP)

The realistic objective of the common foreign policy for the EU is more to agree on a common position in international policy, that is, to speak with one voice, rather than achieve a unified foreign policy conducted by supra-national bodies, with the EU raised to the status of a superpower.

The EC is often described as an economic giant but a political dwarf. Its economic weight in the international arena has not been counterbalanced by a similar political role, except in trade which is considered as a politically neutral activity. The dichotomy can be explained by historical reasons. From its inception the Community was a 'civilian power', that is, an organisation implicitly rejecting power politics and concentrating on economic aspects of European integration.[48] In reality, it lacked military capacity to conduct a defence policy, and this aspect of European affairs had been developed mainly within the framework of NATO. However, the collapse of Communism, the reunification of Germany and the American policy of burden-shedding in military matters have changed perspectives on Europe's future foreign and defence policy.

The common foreign and security policy are two distinct, although closely related, areas. Co-operation in foreign matters was initiated at The Hague Summit in 1969 and resulted in the establishment of European Political Co-operation (EPC), albeit outside the Treaty. It became recognised and incorporated into the structure of the Community in Title III of the Single European Act (SEA) but was not subject to judicial review of the ECJ. Title III SEA declared that Member States would endeavour jointly to formulate and implement a European foreign policy. The improvements to EPC brought by the SEA were:

1. the distinction between foreign ministers' meeting within EPC and within the Council was abolished;
2. an EPC secretariat was set up in Brussels;
3. a mechanism was provided to convene emergency meetings of the Political Committee or Community foreign ministers within 48 hours upon the request of at least three Member States;
4. the Commission and the EP became associated with EPC; and
5. the Commission and the Presidency became responsible for ensuring consistency

---

[48] P Tsakaloyannis, 'From Civilian Power to Military Integration', in J Lodge (ed), *The EC and the Challenge of the Future*, London: Pinter, 1989, p243.

between the external policies of the Community and policies agreed within the framework of EPC.

EPC resulted in the adoption of common positions on many issues such as the Middle East, eastern Europe and South Africa but, in practice, vague declarations after events had taken place and little direct action undermined its importance. Jacques Delors strongly advocated a new approach to the development of a common foreign policy. He distinguished between a single policy for the Community and a common policy for all its States (which is akin to the distinction between a regulation and a directive) and decided that a common policy was more realistic. In effect, only broad guidelines ensure, as in the case of EC directives, the flexible approach in the implementation of a common foreign policy allowing Member States to take into consideration their national traditions and interests. Furthermore, the necessity of adopting a new approach was highlighted when Member States were faced with the Gulf crisis and the deteriorating situation in the former Yugoslavia.

In the Gulf crisis, no agreement was reached among Member States on the use of force against Iraq. The position of Members States varied from immediate and unconditional support for the US military action (the UK Prime Minister, Margaret Thatcher, was at that time in Colorado with President Bush and promised UK support) to the Irish policy of non-intervention based on neutrality.

In relation to the crisis in the former Yugoslavia, the Rome Summit in October 1990 firmly declared its support for unity and territorial integrity of Yugoslavia.[49] However, sympathy for the breakaway Yugoslav republics in some Member States led to a challenge of the Summit declaration. Germany put pressure on other Member States to recognise immediately Croatia and Slovenia. At the meeting of foreign ministers on 16 December 1991 it was decided that the Community should have a uniform policy on the recognition of new States. A special Commission was set up under the chairmanship of Judge Robert Badinter to assess criteria for recognition of new States by the Community.[50] Germany announced that, regardless of the Badinter Report, it would delay recognition of Croatia and Slovenia only until 15 January 1992. As a result, Germany forced the Community's hand despite the fact that the criteria for recognition laid down in the Badinter Report were not being satisfied in either case. Croatia was recognised without safeguards being obtained for a large Serbian minority living there. As a result, Serbia accused the Community of hypocrisy and its credibility as a neutral force was lost. On 6 April 1992 the Community recognised Bosnia, a gesture which to some extent triggered the Serbian 'cleansing' policy and resulted in widespread atrocities on a scale unknown in Europe since World War II.

Finally, the Lisbon Summit of 1992 refused to recognise Macedonia, with firm opposition mounted by Greece. The Summit even ignored its own criteria for recognition which, in the case of Macedonia, were fulfilled, thus destabilising one of the few peaceful regions in the Balkans and increasing the risk of spreading the conflict outside the territory of former Yugoslavia. The Community management, or rather mismanagement, of the crisis in former Yugoslavia exacerbated rather than alleviated the situation. As Dinan stated: 'Far

---

[49] EC Bull 10–1990, Presidency Conclusions, point 1.8.
[50] EPC Press Release, P129/91, 16 December 1991.

from reflecting well on the Community, the Yugoslav war emphasised deep foreign policy differences between Member States and showed the limits of EC international action. The Community's involvement also sapped popular support for European integration and contributed to the Maastricht Treaty ratification crises.'[51]

Indeed, each international crisis revealed divergencies in opinion between Member States and the impossibility of presenting a common front to the outside world. This has also contributed to the incorporation of common foreign and security policy (CFSP) into the Treaty of Maastricht. However, the further deepening of the Yugoslav crises showed, once again, the weakness of unco-ordinated actions by Member States. The reform of CFSP was one of the main tasks of the Intergovernmental Conference. The Treaty of Amsterdam intends to overcome contradictions between ambitious objectives of CFSP and the means of their implementation at the disposal of the EU.

Main objectives of the CFSP and the mechanisms for pursuing them

Articles 11–28 EU describe the principles of the CFSP. Under art 11(1) EU the CFSP has the following objectives:

1. to safeguard the common values, fundamental interests and independence of the Union;
2. to strengthen the security of the Union and its Member States in all ways;
3. to preserve peace and strengthen international security, in accordance with the principles of the United Nations Charter as well as the principles of the Helsinki Final Act and the objectives of the Paris Charter;
4. to promote international co-operation;
5. to develop and consolidate democracy and the rule of law, and respect for human rights and fundamental freedoms.

The objectives of CFSP are to be pursued through three legal instruments: a common position which is defined in art 15 EU; a joint action which is described in art 14 EU; and common strategies which are referred to in art 13 EU. There are no specific definitions for these legal instruments. However, practice shows that a common position is similar to a declaration and thus sets out general guidelines on important international questions. The decision whether to define a common position is taken by unanimity and must be upheld by Member States in international organisations and international conferences.[52] Joint action entails co-ordinated action by the Member States, whereby resources – such as human resources, know-how and financing – are mobilised to attain specific objectives fixed by the Council following general guidelines laid down by the European Council. The Treaty of Amsterdam has added a new policy instrument: common strategies: art 13(2) EU. The European Council is entitled to define, by consensus, common strategies in areas where the Member States have important interests in common. The Council implements common strategies through joint actions and common positions by qualified majority voting. It also recommends common strategies to the European Council. On 4 June 1999 the European

---

[51] D Dinan, *Ever Closer Union?*, London: Anne Rienner Publishers, 1994, pp489-490.
[52] For the Permanent Members of the UN Security Council: see art 15(4) EU.

Council adopted the first Common Strategy (1999/414/CFSP).[53] It concerned the common strategy in respect of Russia and was designated to develop relations between the EU and Russia on the basis of partnership and co-operation, with a particular emphasis on four areas: consolidating democracy and the rule of law; integrating Russia in the European economic and social structures; strengthening stability and security in Europe and beyond; and meeting common challenges facing the European continent. In order to achieve these objectives the EU proposed the introduction of new initiatives, such as establishing high-level dialogue in political and economic matters, the development of common programmes, etc.

The necessity for adopting a joint action is assessed by the Council on recommendations from the European Council in situations where operational action by the EU is required. The Council decides by unanimity whether to adopt a joint action and, if so, sets out its scope, general and specific objectives and, if necessary, its duration, means, conditions and procedures for implementation. However, implementation measures are decided by a qualified majority. A Member State's binding commitment to implement a joint action in the conduct of its national foreign policy may be set aside under one of the derogations provided for in the EU: art 14(6) EU allows a Member State in case of urgency to conduct national policy provided it takes into account the general objectives of the joint action and informs the Council immediately afterwards; art 14(7) EU provides that a special solution may be adopted for Member States that have major difficulties in implementing a joint action, although this special arrangement should neither undermine the objectives of the action nor impair its effectiveness; and, finally, art 14(2) EU states that the Council can always revise a joint action, taking into consideration the changing circumstances affecting its subject-matter. The number of joint actions is steadily rising. Among them are: humanitarian aid for Bosnia; support for the transition to democracy in South Africa and the peace process in the Middle East; administration of Mostar, a Bosnian town, for two years, at the request of the Bosnian Federation (May 1994); the dispatch of a team of observers to Russian parliamentary elections; control on the export of dual-use goods; participation in the Korean Peninsula Energy Development Organisation; the nomination of a special envoy for the African Great Lakes Region; establishment of a Co-operation Programme for Non-proliferation and Disarmament in Russia; and, the most important, the adoption of a 'Stability Pact' in Europe.

Institutions of the CFSP

The main decision-making body within the CFSP is the Council made up of foreign ministers of the Member States which acts as the General Affairs Council. It defines a common position, decides on foreign and security policy matters and determines whether or not they should be subject to a joint action or a common strategy. It meets monthly but can meet at anytime, if necessary. Decisions are taken by unanimity, apart from procedural questions or in cases when, by mutual consent, a decision is taken by qualified majority. The Treaty of Amsterdam introduced two situations in which a measure may be adopted by a qualified majority:

---

[53] OJ L157 (1999). The second Common Strategy (1999/877/CFSP) was adopted on 10 December 1999 in respect of Ukraine: OJ l331 (1999).

1. In respect of decisions applying a common strategy defined by the European Council. However, qualified majority voting will not apply to decisions having military or defence implications.
2. In respect of decisions implementing a joint action or common position already adopted by the Council.

A Member State may exercise 'constructive abstention', that is an abstention which does not hinder the adoption of the decision. If a Member State qualifies its abstention by a formal declaration it is not obliged to apply the decision but must not act in a manner which will conflict with the EU action taken pursuant to that decision. However, the 'constructive abstention' does not apply if the Member States abstaining in such a manner represent more than one-third of Council votes as weighted. The CFSP Council is assisted (as any Council) by COREPER (Committee of Permanent Representatives), which is often overridden by the Political Committee reporting directly to the CFSP Council and consisting of the political directors of the foreign ministries of the Member States. A Corresponding Group made up of other foreign ministry officials is in charge of preparing work not dealt with by the Political Committee as well as liaison functions. Also various working groups made up of officials from foreign ministries, situated in the capitals of the Member States, are entrusted with specific subjects (horizontal–UN, or vertical–Asia, Eastern Europe, etc).

Article 26 EU has created the post of High Representative for the CFSP. This post has been assigned to the Secretary-General of the Council. He assists the Council in all matters relating to the CFSP and, if requested, acts on behalf of the Council in conducting political dialogue with third parties. The High Representative is supported by a policy planning and early warning unit which has been set up by the Treaty of Amsterdam. It is made up of experts in international law and policy from the General Secretariat, the Member States, the Commission and the Western European Union (WEU). Its main tasks consist of:

1. monitoring and analysing developments in areas covered by the CFSP;
2. assessing the EU's foreign and security policy interests and identifying the areas on which CFSP could concentrate in future;
3. providing timely assistance and early warning of events, political crises and situations which may have important consequences for the CFSP;
4. preparing reasoned policy option papers for the Council at the request of either the Council or the Presidency or on its own initiative.

The newly acquired legal personality of the EU finds its uses under Pillar 2. Article 23(1) EU provides that the CFSP Council may authorise the Presidency, acting unanimously, to open negotiations with a third State or international organisations to conclude an international agreement. If the Presidency recommends the conclusion of such an agreement, the Council, acting unanimously, may conclude the agreement. However, it will not be binding on Member States which declare in the Council that their constitutional law prevents them from becoming parties to it.

Role of Community institutions under the CFSP

The TEU has abolished the distinction between the Council acting in the EPC and EC areas. The Council has become a common institution of all three pillars. The main advantage is that the Council can ensure consistency between actions under the CFSP and under the EC Treaty. In this respect art 3 EU emphasises that the Council and the Commission must ensure 'the unity, consistency and effectiveness of action by the Union'.

The Commission is fully associated with the CFSP. It shares the right of initiative with Member States but it is not involved in the implementation of the CFSP.

The role of the European Parliament has not changed, it is still a consultative body. The Presidency of the Council is required to inform and consult with the EP on the 'main aspects and basic choices' of the CFSP and to take its opinions into account. The EP is entitled to ask the Council questions and to make recommendations. It also holds an annual debate on progress in implementing the CFSP. As a result, democratic control of the CFSP by the European Union is still weak as it consists mainly of consultations with the EP.

Commitments of Member States under the CFSP

The TEU has strengthened the commitment of Member States to a common foreign policy. It reinforced the obligations of the Member States to conform to the common positions. Article 11(2) EU stresses that 'Member States shall support a common foreign and security policy and shall refrain from action impairing its effectiveness.'

The main commitment of the Member States within the CFSP is to implement common positions and any joint action of the EU. Member States have obligations vis-à-vis each other in consulting and exchanging information, especially when only some of them are Members of international organisations or attend international conferences where decisions that potentially affect all of them may be taken.

Member States also have obligations vis-à-vis the Union. In this respect, the Member States must support the CFSP actively and unreservedly in a spirit of loyalty and mutual solidarity': art 11(2) EU. If a State is a member of an international organisation where decisions that potentially affect the Union may be taken, that Member State must defend the interests of the EU: art 19(1) EU. In the case of the Permanent Members of the UN Security Council this must be achieved without compromising their responsibilities deriving from the UN Charter. Also, diplomatic and consular missions of Member States and Commission delegations in third countries and international organisations must co-operate in ensuring that the common positions and joint actions are complied with and implemented. Furthermore, they are required to exchange information, carry out joint assessments and contribute to the implementation of art 20 EC, that is, ensure diplomatic and consular protection of EU citizens in countries where their governments are not represented. The Commission has a mission in more than 100 countries and in many international organisations.

Management of the CFSP

The Presidency of the Council is to represent the EU on CFSP matters in international organisations and international conferences. Article 18 EU defines the functions of the Presidency which consist of implementation of common measures and representation of the EU worldwide. The system of 'troika' (that is, the current Presidency, the preceding and the succeeding Presidencies, accompanied by representative of the Commission, acting together in order to ensure the continuity and consistency of the CFSP) has been replaced. Under the Treaty of Amsterdam the Presidency is assisted by the Secretary-General of the Council acting in his capacity of High Representative of CFSP and a representative of the Member State which is next in line for the Presidency. In cases of emergency the Presidency on its own motion or at the request of the Commission or a Member State must convene an extraordinary meeting within 48 hours or an even shorter period (art 22(2) EU).

Common defence policy

With regard to a common defence policy, the Gulf crisis enhanced the attractiveness of belonging to the Western European Union (WEU) comprising at that time nine countries: UK, France, Germany, Belgium, The Netherlands, Luxembourg, Italy, Spain and Portugal. Unlike NATO, the WEU can operate outside Europe and the USA is not a Member State. France is the most enthusiastic supporter of the WEU and when holding the Presidency of the WEU invited all EC countries to attend a meeting on 21 August 1990 to examine the possibility of a military intervention in the Gulf,[54] and especially to assess the role of the WEU in the context of military action outside the remit of NATO. This meeting was parallel to a meeting of foreign ministers of the Community.

On 18 September 1990 Italy, which held the Presidency of the Council, submitted a proposal aimed at merging the Community and WEU.[55] The proposal was too controversial to be seriously considered by Member States, but the Rome Summit in October 1990 agreed in principle on the development of a common security policy without specifying its content or the procedures of co-operation. The future role of the WEU was not decided but the Summit took the position that the WEU should not undermine NATO. In June 1992, at a meeting in Bonn, the foreign ministers and defence ministers of the WEU countries adopted the 'Petersberg Declaration' which set out the objectives for the WEU's future development, mainly conflict prevention and peace-keeping action under the auspices of the Organisation for Security and Co-operation in Europe (previously CSCE), which now comprises 53 members, and the UN Security Council, and human health and rescue tasks.[56]

At Maastricht the Member States agreed to include 'the eventual framing of a common defence policy, which might in time lead to a common defence' into the scope of the TEU. The crucial question regarding the relationship between NATO and the WEU was solved. The WEU was recognised as a means to strengthen the European pillar of the Atlantic Alliance. In this respect art 14(4) and (5) EU underline that the EU defence policy is without prejudice to the obligations arising out of security arrangements whether bilateral (the Eurocorps) or multilateral (NATO) to which Member States are party, provided they are

---

[54] During the Gulf War the WEU was in charge of the co-ordination of naval units of Member States (Operation Cleansweep).

[55] D Dinan, *Ever Closer Union?*, supra note 51, 1994, p471.

[56] The Treaty of Amsterdam incorporates these 'Petersberg tasks' into the structure of EU: art 17(2) EU.

compatible with the objectives of the Treaty. The WEU has become a defence component of the EU and is entrusted with elaboration and implementation of actions and decisions of the EU which have defence implications.

At Maastricht WEU countries made a declaration stating that they welcomed the development of the European security and defence identity. They emphasised that they were determined, taking into account the role of the WEU as the defence component of the European Union and as the means to strengthen the European pillar of the Atlantic Alliance, to put the relationship between the WEU and the other European States on a new basis for the sake of security and stability in Europe.[57] Also, the WEU granted full membership to Greece at Maastricht and invited the remaining EC members to join, to become associate members or to become observers. Ireland, Denmark, Sweden, Finland and Austria have the status of observer which entitles them to participate in the WEU Council and working group meetings and even take part in deliberations if requested. Apart from observers, the following European countries have become 'associate partners': Bulgaria, Romania, Slovakia, Slovenia and the Baltic States. Their status allows them to fully participate in WEU Council meetings, to associate themselves with the decisions of the WEU and to participate in WEU military operations listed in the Petersberg Declaration. Associate members of the WEU are those members which are members of NATO but not of the EU. There are six such countries: Iceland, Norway, Turkey and, since March 1999, Hungary, Poland and the Czech Republic. Their status entitles them to fully participate in the meetings of the WEU Council and its working parties. They may express their views but cannot veto a decision on which the full members of WEU have reached a consensus. They may also join in WEU military operations under WEU command. All together the WEU comprises 28 countries with four different types of status.

The commitment of the WEU to the building of a common European policy in security and defence was welcomed by the Washington Summit of heads of governments of NATO held on 24 April 1999, which stated that 'a stronger European role will help contribute to the vitality of our alliance for the 21st century, which is the foundation of the collective defence of its members.'[58] The Summit offered to facilitate EU access to the collective assets and capabilities of NATO in respect of operations in which NATO itself is not engaged. Meanwhile, the Helsinki European Council meeting on 11 December 1999 gave a new impetus to the WEU. The Helsinki Council stated that the EU should develop an autonomous capacity to launch and conduct military operations in response to international crises in situations where NATO is not involved. It agreed in particular that by 2003 Member States must be able, co-operating on a voluntary basis in operations directed by the EU, to deploy within 60 days and to sustain for at least a year military forces of up to 50,000–60,000 persons in order to carry out the Petersberg tasks. The Helsinki Council also acknowledged the necessity of setting up political and military bodies and structures to ensure strategic direction and political guidance in such operations, as well as developing systems for full consultation, co-operation and transparency between the EU and NATO. Finally, the Helsinki Council agreed that arrangements for non-EU European NATO members and other interested States to contribute to EU military crisis management should be made.

---

[57] N Foster, *EC Legislation*, 5th ed, London: Blackstones, 1994, pp132–135.
[58] NATO press release: NAC–S(99)64.

The Santa Maria Da Feira European Council held on 19–20 June 2000 acknowledged satisfactory progress in respect of the Helsinki mandate on military crisis management by the EU. The Capabilities Commitment Conference will be held in 2000 when Member States will make initial national commitments. After the Nice European Council (December 2000) the permanent political and military structures should be put in place by the EU in order to fully assume the Petersberg tasks.

Assessment of the CFSP

The CFSP is based on inter-governmental co-operation. As a result it is not subject to judicial review by the ECJ, and the involvement of the Commission and the European Parliament is very limited. Progress in the development of the CFSP has been hindered by the requirement of unanimity within the Council on proposed measures, although the decision of the foreign ministers in March 1997 to impose sanctions on Burma in response to its abuse of human rights, especially in relation to child labour, could be considered as a real breakthrough. In this context it is necessary to mention a very successful initiative of the CFSP. Under its auspices a conference attended by 40 countries on 'Stability in Europe' was organised in May 1994 in Paris which focused on ethnic disputes and maintaining peace and stability in eastern Europe. It resulted in the establishment of the 'Stability Pact' in Europe in March 1995 under the supervision of the OCSE. The Treaty of Amsterdam and its subsequent developments demonstrate that the EU has taken further steps in the construction of the European identity in security and defence matters.

3.3 Pillar 3: police co-operation in criminal matters

Pillar 3 of the TEU devoted to co-operation in justice and home affairs has undergone a fundamental change. The creation of the area of freedom, security and justice within the five years following the entry into force of the Treaty of Amsterdam has reshaped Pillar 3. All matters relating to these areas are now part of the EC Treaty to which a new Title IV on 'Visa, asylum, immigration and other policies related to the free movement of persons' has been added. However, the Pillar 3 provisions still include a 'bridge' allowing Member States to transfer areas of competence from Title VI (Pillar 3) to Title IV (EC Treaty). It seems that gradually all areas covered by Pillar 3 will be brought within the EC Treaty. The only remaining area in Pillar 3 is police and judicial co-operation in criminal matters. The Treaty of Amsterdam added two new tasks consisting of combating racism and xenophobia. As a result, under Pillar 3 the main objective of the EU is to prevent and combat:

1. racism and xenophobia;
2. terrorism;
3. trafficking in persons and offences against children;
4. arms trafficking;
5. corruption and fraud.

These objectives are to be achieved through closer co-operation between police authorities, custom authorities and other competent national authorities, both directly and through Europol (see below).

Article 30 EU provides that common action in the field of police co-operation should include: operational co-operation between police, customs and other specialised law enforcement authorities of the Member States to prevent, detect and investigate criminal offences; exchange of information; joint training of police forces, etc. Article 31 EU states that common action on judicial co-operation in criminal matters should include measures facilitating co-operation between relevant national law enforcement authorities, facilitating extradition, preventing conflict of jurisdiction and the establishment of minimum rules in respect of the constituent elements of criminal acts and penalties in the fields of organised crime, terrorism and drug trafficking.

Under Pillar 3 the role of Europol is emphasised. Under art 30(2) EU the Council is required to enact measures enabling Europol to function efficiently, in particular to co-ordinate police operational co-operation in criminal matters.

Police co-operation between Member States has a long history. The first initiative in this area went back to 1976 when the TREVI group (an acronym for Terrorism, Radicalism, Extremism, Political Violence) of interior ministers was established to co-operate on issues of terrorism. This group expanded in the mid-1980s to cover the following areas: TREVI 1 (terrorism), TREVI 2 (police training, public order, forensic science, fingerprint data bases, football hooliganism), TREVI 3 (organised crime and drug trafficking, law enforcement on environmental offences, art theft). There are also some *ad hoc* groups, for instance on International Organised Crime set up in 1992 and on Yugoslavia (1993). The TREVI working groups prepare recommendations on topics they examine which serve as the basis for TREVI senior officials' reports, which in turn are submitted to TREVI ministers' meetings held twice a year prior to the summit meetings of the European Council. After 1991, one of the main tasks of TREVI was the preparation of the groundwork for the establishment of Europol.

Other examples of co-operation in internal security matters among Member States before the entry into force of the TEU[59] are:

1. On drugs: CELAD (Comité Europénne de Lutte Anti-Drogues) created in 1989 in order to co-ordinate cross-border enquiries and exchange of information. It works with the Pompidou Group which was set up in 1972 under the auspices of the Council of Europe to combat drug abuse and unlawful traffic in drugs, and it comprises almost all European States. CELAD also co-operates with the Dublin Group, which is an international forum as it comprises all EU Members, except Finland, plus the Commission, Australia, Canada, Japan, Norway and the USA, for discussion and co-ordination of police assistance against drug-producing and transit countries.
2. On money laundering of drug profits: GAFI (Groupe d'Action Finacière Internationale).
3. On terrorism: PWGOT (the Police Working Group on Terrorism) which was set up in 1979. It is made up of the special branches of all Member States. There is also the Vienna Group which was established in 1978 to combat terrorism and comprises Germany, Italy, Austria, Switzerland and France.

---

[59] For review see R Clutterbuck, *Terrorism, Drugs and Crime in Europe after 1992*, London: Routledge, 1990.

4. On customs co-operation: GAM'92 (Groupe d'Assistance Mutuelle) comprising representatives of the customs authorities in the Member States and a Commission representative whose main task is to prepare measures hindering the smuggling of drugs, firearms and pornographic material.

Under Title VI of the TEU the work of TREVI groups and other organisations was co-ordinated by the Justice and Home Affairs Council. Among the initiatives taken under the Pillar 3 of the TEU was the creation of Europol (European Police Office), a European criminal investigation body, in order to strengthen police co-operation in preventing and combating terrorism, unlawful drug trafficking and others serious forms of international crime, including, if necessary, certain aspects of customs co-operation. The functions of Europol have been further specified in the Declaration on Police Co-operation annexed to the TEU. The Convention on the Establishment of Europol was signed in October 1995 and came into force on 1 October 1998. Europol was set up on 1 July 1999 and has its headquarters in The Hague.

Under the Treaty of Amsterdam Europol is in charge of co-operation between police forces. Its priority is to co-ordinate Member States' actions against international money laundering, drug smuggling, illegal import of nuclear materials, stolen vehicles, illegal immigration networks, trafficking of human beings and the sexual exploitation of children. Europol has set up three databases facilitating exchanges of information on persons suspected of criminal activities. Terrorism and money counterfeiting are also within the competences of Europol. Furthermore, there is a proposal of setting up a European DNA centre under the auspices of Europol.

Also to simplify the working structure all steering groups have been eliminated. The Amsterdam European Council (June 1997) set up a multi-disciplinary group, the GMD, to co-ordinate works of working groups.[60] Further, the European Council, in order to combat organised crime, adopted a plan of action consisting of 30 recommendations for measures necessary to introduce in this area. The Falcons Programme (1998–2002) implements the plan.

In respect of illegal drugs, the European Monitoring Centre for Drugs and Addiction (EMCDA) was set up in February 1993. It collects, examines and compares the existing data in this area and co-operates with European and international bodies. It has its own computer network, the European Information Network on Drugs and Drug Addiction (REITOX). The Amsterdam European Council (June 1997) set up a Horizontal Drugs Group (HDG) to deal with 'cross-pillar' issues concerning drugs. At the request of the Cardiff European Council (June 1998), on 25 May 1999 the Commission presented the fourth action plan to combat illegal drugs, which covers 1999–2004. The plan emphasised that the main objective in the fight against drugs is to reduce demand and supply.

Organisational structure of Pillar 3

Procedurally, the Council translates the objectives of co-operation in the fields of police and judicial co-operation in criminal matters into action by adopting common positions,

---

[60] S Peers, 'Justice and Home Affairs: Decision-making after Amsterdam' (2000) 25 EL Rev 183–191.

framework decisions, decisions and conventions subject to the principle of subsidiarity and conventions without prejudice to art 293 EC. The Treaty of Amsterdam replaces joint actions by framework decisions and decisions. Both are binding upon the Member States but have no direct effect. Furthermore, all conventions may enter into force once they have been ratified by half of the signatory Member States, but for ratifying States only.

The role of the EP has not changed. The EP must be consulted on all measures except common positions and be kept informed of discussions in the areas covered by Pillar 3. In respect of the Commission, it shares with Member States the right to initiate measures in all areas covered by Pillar 3 and must inform the EP of discussions concerning these areas.

The ECJ has become involved in matters covered by Pillar 3, although its jurisdiction is limited. In respect of preliminary rulings, the ECJ jurisdiction is subject to a declaration of acceptance by each Member State. A Member State may allow the ECJ to give preliminary rulings at the request of its courts of final instance or of all courts and tribunals within the meaning of art 234 EC. The authorised courts are entitled to send a request in respect of framework decisions, decisions, conventions and other implementing measures. However, the ECJ has no jurisdiction to interpret the provisions of Pillar 3. This will make the task of the ECJ very difficult. Assessing the validity of an act without interpreting the Treaty itself will be rather complicated. In addition, there are further limitations in respect of an action for annulment. Only the Commission or a Member State has *locus standi* and only against framework decisions and decisions. No action for failure to act is envisaged under Pillar 3. Article 35(5) EU imposes another limitation on the ECJ jurisdiction. It states that the ECJ has no jurisdiction 'to review the validity or proportionality of operations carried out by the police or other law enforcement services of a Member State or the exercise of the responsibility incumbent upon Member States with regard to the maintenance of law and order and the safeguarding of internal security.' The same safeguard clause is inserted in respect of Pillar 2. Thus, under Pillars 2 and 3 all measures which are particularly important from the point of view of individuals are excluded from the ECJ jurisdiction.

Article 35(7) EU provides for additional grounds of ECJ jurisdiction in the event of a dispute between Member States on the interpretation or application of Pillar 3 measures which the Council is unable to resolve within the period of six months of reference of the dispute to the Council.

The role of the Co-ordinating Committee (the 'art 36 EU Committee') which is defined in art 36 EU has been confirmed by the Treaty of Amsterdam. The 'art 36 Committee' is made up of senior officials from Member States. Its main tasks are to co-ordinate the activities falling under Pillar 3, to submit opinions to the Council on its own initiative or at the request of the Council and to prepare meetings of the Council in all areas covered by Pillar 3. This Committee has been in existence since the Rhodes European Council (December 1988).

Pillar 3 is based on the principle of flexibility. Article 40(2) EU allows closer co-operation between some Member States subject to the authorisation of the Council.

Assessment of Pillar 3

Pillar 3 has shrunk considerably. Even the remaining area is already covered by Title IV of the EC Treaty as it is a vital element in the establishment of the area of security. For the five years after entry into force of the Treaty of Amsterdam, however, there should be no major problem in the determination of Member States' powers in police and judicial co-operation matters as the adoption of measures in this area require unanimity. It seems that Pillar 3 will be used mostly to establish closer police and judicial co-operation with third countries and international organisations in criminal matters

Only measures combating racism and xenophobia are not referred to in other provisions of the Treaty. In this respect, the necessity of combating them was emphasised in March 1996 by the Justice and Home Affairs Council which adopted a joint action concerning measures to fight racism and xenophobia. Each Member State has a duty to ensure effective judicial co-operation to punish racism and xenophobia.[61] The EU proclaimed 1997 the European Year against racism and xenophobia. The Amsterdam Summit of June 1997 welcomed the agreement on the establishment of the European Monitoring Centre on Racism and Xenophobia which is based in Vienna.

Interesting post-Amsterdam developments in respect of Pillar 3 include the adoption by the Justice and Home Affairs Council of a common position on negotiations relating to the Draft Convention on Cyber Crime prepared under the auspices of the Council of Europe.[62]

---

[61] It is worth mentioning that political parties such as Le Front National in France legally exist and have seats in the parliament (only one in the parliamentary elections in 1997, but it is one too many). The leader of Le Front National, Jean Marie Le Pen, publicly calls for an end to the 'Islamification of France', claims that gas chambers were an insignificant detail and that all immigrants who entered France after 1974 should be sent home. He also favours the introduction of racial segregation in schools. The following Member States have racist electoral parties: Austria, Sweden, France, Belgium, Germany and Italy

[62] 1999/364/JHA: OJ L142 (1999).

4 The Institutions of the European Communities and the European Union, Their Participation in Decision-making and the Principle of Transparency

4.1   The European Council

4.2   The Council of the European Union

4.3   The European Commission

4.4   The European Parliament

4.5   The Court of Justice of the European Communities (ECJ)

4.6   The Court of First Instance (CFI)

4.7   The Court of Auditors

4.8   Other Community bodies

4.9   Legislative procedures

4.10   The principle of transparency

The institutional structure of the Communities and the European Union is based on original concepts, new to public international law. The CS, the EC and the EA Treaties were at their inception each endowed with an autonomous institutional framework. However, a set of single institutions serving all three Communities was established in two stages. First, under the Convention on Certain Institutions Common to the European Communities signed on 25 March 1957, Assemblies (European Parliaments), the Court of Justice and the Economic and Social Committees of the three founding Treaties were merged. Second, the Merger Treaty signed on 8 April 1965, which entered into force on 13 July 1967, replaced the High Authority and the Commission of the CS – which until then were independent institutions – by a Single Council and a Single Commission, common to all three Communities. As a result, instead of 12 institutions only four were put in place, each carrying out simultaneously all tasks conferred to it under the three founding Treaties. The Treaty of Maastricht recognised the unitary framework of the Communities while adding, the Court of Auditors, first established in 1975, as a fifth common institution. The Treaty of Amsterdam did not introduce any changes to the main structure. Article 7 EC and art 3 EA enumerate five bodies which are entitled to use the name Community institutions. They are:

1. the European Parliament;
2. the Council;

3. the Commission;
4. the Court of Justice;
5. the Court of Auditors.

They form the basic structure of the institutional system of the Communities, although the Treaties provide for the establishment of a number of additional bodies: art 7(2) EC for the Economic and Social Committee and the Committee of the Regions to assist the Council and the Commission; art 8 EC for institutions necessary to carry out tasks peculiar to the economic and monetary union (the European System of Central Banks and the European Central Bank); art 9 EC for the European Investment Bank;[1] and by virtue of art 225 EC the Court of First Instance (CFI) is 'attached' to the ECJ.

The basic institutional structure is completed by two further categories of body: the European Council and a number of bodies which are within the scope of the Treaties and which assist the Council and the Commission in the accomplishment of their tasks. There are agencies, offices and centres such as the European Environmental Agency, the European Training Foundation, the European Agency for the Evaluation of Medicinal Products, the Office for Veterinary and Plant Health Inspection and Control, the European Monitoring Centre for Drugs and Drug Addiction, Europol, etc,

Each of the five Community institutions has a specific role to play in the functioning of the Community. The Council represents the interests of the Member States; the Commission, the interests of the Community; the European Parliament (EP), the interests of the people of the Member States; the Court of Justice (ECJ) ensures that in the functioning of the institutional system the law is observed; and the Court of Auditors is charged with the supervision of the financial aspects of the Community. However, the division of functions between the five institutions does not reflect the Montesquieu system of the 'separation of powers' under which the Parliament is responsible for the performance of the legislative functions, the government for executive functions and the courts for judicial functions. In the Community system the homologue of legislative powers is the Council, which also exercises executive and governmental functions, the Commission is the 'guardian of the Treaty' and as such supervises and, if necessary, enforces Community law. It also initiates and implements Community legislation. The European Parliament, from being solely an advisory body, has evolved into a directly elected body and now participates in the law-making procedures of the Community. The ECJ and the CFI ensure the observance of law in the implementation of the Treaties by the Community institutions and the Member States. Under art 234 EC the ECJ assists national courts in their difficult task of interpretation of Community law and thus ensures homogeneity and uniformity in its application in all Member States.

Until the entry into force of the TEU, the main events in the evolution of the institutional system of the Communities were:

1. The spontaneous creation of a new inter-governmental body, the European Council, which was first recognised as a Community institution by the SEA. The European Council is a political body which defines the general political objectives of the

---

[1] The European Investment Bank is an international organisation established by art 266 EC. Its Statute is annexed to the Treaty.

Community and the Union, although it neither adopts legislative acts nor participates in the formal decision-making procedures,

2. The gradual acquisition by the European Parliament of legislative powers, first in budgetary matters and then under the SEA through the co-operation and the assent procedure in a number of areas.

3. The establishment of co-operation in political matters outside the framework of the Treaty.

The Treaty of Maastricht modified the Community institutional system by strengthening the legislative powers of the EP and establishing new institutions entrusted with the adoption and the implementation of the monetary policies of the Union. The Treaty of Maastricht created the European Union which, under art 3 EU, 'shall be served by a single institutional framework'. It means that certain Community institutions have different roles to play depending upon whether they act as Community institutions or as a body of the European Union. The roles that the Council, the Commission or the ECJ play within Pillars 2 and 3 are fundamentally different from the exercise of their powers under the EC Treaty. Indeed, the institutional structure of the Union which exists alongside that of the Community mainly uses the Community institutions for the achievement of the Union's objectives. This results in a complex relationship between the Communities and the Union. Furthermore, the democratic accountability of Union institutions is even weaker than under the EC Treaty.

The balance of power between the institutions has changed since the creation of the Communities. The change reflects tension between the two visions of the Community: one as an inter-governmental organisation and the other as a supra-national entity. Therefore, the dominance of either the Member States or the Community in the decision-making procedures shapes their outcome and may be integrative or nationalistic. The predominance of the Council, recognised by the founding Treaties, has been diminished by later amendments which have conferred important powers upon the Commission and the European Parliament. Both institutions promote further integration of the Community.

It is important to note that there are certain common rules applicable to all institutions. First, they concern the seat of the institutions. Under art 289 EC, art 77 CS and art 189 EA the seat of the Community institutions should be determined by common accord of the Member States. In practice, the determination of the permanent seats of the Community institutions has always been subject to fierce competition among the Member States. The Decision of 8 April 1965[2] provided a temporary solution by which the seats of the institutions were assigned to three different places: Luxembourg, Brussels and Strasbourg. This compromise gave rise to many political, financial and legal difficulties, especially with respect to where the sessions of the EP were to be held.[3] In this context, an agreement was reached at the Edinburgh Summit on 12 December 1992[4] and subsequently adjusted by the European Council Decision adopted at the Brussels meeting on 29–30 October 1993.[5] As a

---

[2] OJ 152 (1967).
[3] *Luxembourg v EP* Case 230/81 [1983] ECR 255; *Luxembourg v EP* Case 108/83 [1984] ECR 1945; *France v EP* Cases 358/85 and 51/86 [1988] ECR 4821; *Luxembourg v EP* Cases C–213/88 and 39/89 [1991] ECR I–5643.
[4] The Decision of 12 December 1992: OJ C341 (1992).
[5] OJ C323 (1993).

result, the Council, the Commission and the Economic and Social Committee have their seats in Brussels, although the Council, under this agreement, holds its meetings in Luxembourg in April, June and October, and certain departments of the Commission, namely the administrative services of CS and EA, as well as its Statistical Office and the Office for Official Publications, are located in Luxembourg. The ECJ, the CFI, the Court of Auditors and the European Investment Bank have their seats in Luxembourg. The European Parliament is required to hold 12 periods of monthly plenary sessions in Strasbourg and any additional sessions in Brussels. Its secretariat is still located in Luxembourg. The Member States are very sensitive to any changes regarding the seats of the Community institutions. The action for annulment brought by France against the EP's calendar for 1996 provides a good illustration of this point. In *France v European Parliament* Case C–345/95 [1997] ECR I–5215 the French government supported by Luxembourg brought an action for annulment of the vote of the EP of 20 September 1995 adopting the calendar for its part-sessions for 1996 which reduced the number of plenary part-sessions to be held in Strasbourg in 1996 from 12 to 11. The French government argued that the vote in question was adopted in breach of the Edinburgh Decision, in breach of essential procedural requirement and was also contrary to art 253 EC. The EP did not hesitate to challenge the Edinburgh Decision, arguing that it was adopted in breach of art 289 EC as it encroached upon the power of the EP to determine its own internal organisation conferred by art 199 EC.

The ECJ held that by adopting the Edinburgh Decision the Member States had discharged their obligation consisting of definitely locating the seat of the EP in Strasbourg whilst maintaining several places of work for that institution. The ECJ emphasised that the Member States are not only entitled to determine the seat of the EP but also have implied power to specify the activities of the EP which must take place in various locations. As a result, the EP is obliged to hold its 12 ordinary plenary sessions, including budgetary sessions, in Strasbourg where it has its seat. The EP cannot hold additional sessions in any other place unless it has the 12 ordinary sessions in Strasbourg. Consequently, the EP is precluded from reducing the number of session since the Edinburgh Decision has expressly specified the mandatory number of part-sessions which must be held in Strasbourg.

The ECJ stated that although the EP is empowered to adopt appropriate measures to ensure the proper functioning and conduct of its proceedings, its decisions in this area must respect the competence of the governments of the Member States to determine the seats of the Community institutions. Therefore, the Edinburgh Decision has not encroached upon the power of the EP to determine its own internal organisation even though its has imposed certain constraints on the EP which, as the ECJ emphasised, 'are inherent in the need to determine its seat while maintaining several places of work for the institutions.'

The seat of the European Central Bank is located in Frankfurt. The Brussels European Council in its Decision of 29 October 1993 expressed a preference for the allocation of seats for various bodies and agencies in Member States which did not host any Community institutions. As a result, the European Environmental Agency is located in Copenhagen, the European Agency for Evaluation of Medical Products in London, the Agency for Health and Safety at Work in Bilbao, the Office for Harmonisation in the Internal Market (Trade Marks, Designs and Models) in Alicante, the Office for Veterinary and Plant Health Inspection and Control in Dublin, the European Monitoring Centre for Drugs and Drug Addiction in Lisbon.

Second, rules governing the languages of the institutions are also determined by the Council, acting unanimously, without prejudice to the provisions contained in the Rules of Procedure of the ECJ: art 290 EC.[6] This question was resolved in Regulation 1 of 1958 in which the Council decided that national languages of the Member State are official languages of the Community, all equal in rank and status. This principle applies to the CS and EA Treaties as well as to the EU Treaty. Since 1 January 1995 there are 11 official languages of the European Union: Danish, Dutch, English, Finnish, French, German, Greek, Italian, Portuguese, Spanish and Swedish (Ireland agreed to English). Also, all language versions of the Treaties and of Community measures are equally authentic. The Treaty of Paris was drafted in French and only the French version is considered as being authentic. The Treaties of Rome were drawn up in Dutch, French, German and Italian, all four texts being equally authentic: art 314 EC. However, upon the accession of new Member States it was specified that versions in English, Irish, Danish, Greek, Spanish, Finnish, Portuguese and Swedish are also authentic. If there are any discrepancies between different language versions they should be resolved without giving priority to any particular language.[7]

The 11 official languages of the Community entail all official meetings being conducted in all official languages which are translated from one to another. Also, all official documents are in 11 languages, although French and English are imposed as working languages. Furthermore, all individual acts, that is, those addressed to the Member States or to individuals who are subject to the jurisdiction of a Member State, are written in the language of the relevant State, while Community acts of general scope of application, for example Regulations, are written in the nine languages but published in the Official Journal in all 11 official languages. This use of multiple languages in the everyday running of the Community is very costly, but is necessary to ensure equality between Member States and transparency vis-à-vis the citizens of the European Union. In addition, national authorities and courts which often have to apply the Community acts directly to their nationals must have the relevant text in their own national language. The principles of legal certainty and the protection of individual rights strengthen this requirement. Furthermore, conferring official status on 11 languages permits EC nationals to submit their complaints to a particular institution in their own language.

Third, there is a common status applicable to all staff of the Communities and the European Union. The Protocol on the Privileges and Immunities of the European Communities annexed to the Merger Treaty of 1965, and in force since 13 July 1967, provides that the officials and other servants of the Communities should: be treated as officials of international organisations; be immune from legal proceedings in respect of acts performed in their official capacity; be exempt from national taxes on salaries, wages and emoluments paid by the Community; be entitled to the social security benefits established by the Communities, etc. The status of the officials and other servants of the Communities was completed by Council Regulation of 29 February 1968[8] and has since been amended many times.

---

[6] See the proceedings before the ECJ. The language is chosen by the applicant subject to exceptions laid down in arts 29–31 of its Rule of Procedure.

[7] *Stauder* v *City of Ulm* Case 29/69 [1969] ECR 419; *Kerry Milk* Case 80/76 [1977] ECR 425. In practice, common points of the different version should be sought.

[8] OJ L56 (1968).

In this chapter the role of the four main institutions and the European Council will be examined in the context of the complex relationship between the Communities and the European Union. The powers that each institution exercises will be assessed in the light of art 7(1) EC which states that: 'Each Institution shall act within the limits of the powers conferred upon it by this Treaty.' The participation of Community institutions in the decision-making procedures will be examined, as will the principle of transparency.

4.1 The European Council

The European Council plays a very important role in the institutional system of the Communities and the Union, although *sensu stricto* it is neither an institution nor a Community body. It is common to both the European Communities and the European Union. In Paris in December 1974 the Heads of State or Government of the Member States officially agreed that summit meetings held informally since 1972 should thereafter be held on a regular basis. Article 2 of the SEA brought the European Council within the framework of the Community. Its role is further clarified in art 4 EU which provides that:

> 'The European Council shall provide the Union with the necessary impetus for its development and shall define the general political guidelines thereof.
>
> The European Council shall bring together the Heads of State or of Government of the Member States and the President of the Commission. They shall be assisted by the Ministers for Foreign Affairs of the Member States and by a Member of the Commission. The European Council shall meet at least twice a year, under the chairmanship of the Head of the State or Government of the Member State which holds the Presidency of the Council
>
> The European Council shall submit to the European Parliament a report after each of its meetings and a yearly written report on the progress achieved by the Union.'

The formula 'Heads of State or Government' is used to take into account the special constitutional position of the President of the French Republic.

Main tasks

The importance of the European Council stems from the political role it plays in shaping the future of the Communities and the European Union. It exercises four main functions in the context of the Community: it serves as a platform for the exchange of informal views and for unofficial discussions among the leaders of the Member States; it can examine any matter within the competence of the Community as well as any subject of common interest; it gives the necessary impetus for the development of the Community; and it settles sensitive matters and disputes which the Community institutions are not able to resolve, especially those referred by the Council if the European Union (for example, the question of the determination of the UK contribution to the Community budget was settled by the Fontainebleau Summit). The political decisions adopted by the European Council are not legal acts in the sense of the EC Treaty and as such not reviewable under art 230 EC. Their implementation is usually left to the Council. In the exercise of its supreme political power the European Council can be compared to holding a kind of presidential authority of the Community.

The European Council's role within the framework of the European Union is to define the principles and general guidelines. The European Council acts under two pillars, that is in relation to the common foreign and security policy (CFSP) and in the area of police and judicial co-operation in criminal matters, as an inter-governmental body according to rules and procedures provided by the EU Treaty (see Chapter 3).

The European Council is not a Community institution, even when referred to expressly under the EC Treaty, for example in art 99(2) EC. Article 4 EU has clarified its position in this respect as it eliminates any possibility that the European Council can be considered as a peculiar form of the Council of the European Union.

Thus, the European Council has an important impact on the functioning of other Community institutions. First, the Council of the European Union is no longer the supreme decision-making body. Second, the intervention of the European Council in disputes which the Council of the European Union is not able to resolve may dissuade the latter from making all necessary efforts to achieve settlement of these disputes within the Community framework. Third, the Commission is deprived of political initiatives and thus its contribution to the future shape of the Community is very limited. Fourth, the non-accountability of the European Council vis-à-vis the people of the Member States is emphasised by the lack of control by the EP over its activities.

Functioning

The European Council meets twice a year – usually its meetings coincide with the end of a Council Presidency. Extraordinary meetings may also take place (for example, it happened at the end of October 1993 before the entry into force of the Treaty of Maastricht). The European Council is attended by the Heads of State or Government of the Member States, accompanied by their foreign ministers, and the President and Vice-President of the Commission. The Commission, represented by its President and Vice-President, participates in all deliberations, even the most restricted. All deliberations are confidential. The Declarations of the European Council are adopted by common accord.

Preparation of the European Council meetings is carried out by specialised Councils. However, the ministers of foreign affairs of the Member States supervise the preparations and, usually, a meeting of foreign ministers is organised before the European Council meeting. Nevertheless, certain matters which are within the exclusive competences of the Member States, although formally prepared by the Community, that is the Council and the Committee of Permanent Representatives (COREPER), are outside its powers. In addition, the European Council may set up its own working group (made up of national officials and experts) to prepare the meeting and to report directly to the European Council. For example, the preparation of the second scheme concerning the creation of the European Monetary System during 1978 took place outside the Community institutional structure. As a result, the Community institutions did not contribute to its elaboration and their role was limited to its implementation.

4.2 The Council of the European Union

The Council of Ministers is referred to in the Treaties as the Council. Following the entry into force of the Treaty on European Union the Council of Ministers adopted Decision 93/591 on 8 November 1993[9] in which it renamed itself. Since then its official name is 'the Council of the European Union'. The Council is the principal political and legislative institution of the European Communities and the European Union. The Council of the European Union represents the national interests of each Member State and being a purely inter-governmental body its meetings risk degenerating into diplomatic conferences which on some occasions have been difficult to avoid.

Composition

By virtue of art 203 EC:

> 'The Council shall consists of a representative of each Member State at ministerial level, authorised to commit the Government of that Member State.'

This formula introduced by the TEU allows Member States with a federal structure to be represented when the Council is examining matters which are within the exclusive competence of regional governments, by for example a minister of a Länder in Germany or a region in Belgium, instead of a minister of the federal government. In such a case, the regional minister is authorised to act on behalf of the Member State and thus commits the federal government both legally and politically. However, the EC Treaty ruled out meetings of the Council at the level of the Heads of State or Government unless this possibility is expressly provided for by the Treaty.[10]

The Council has no fixed composition, and its membership varies according to the matters under discussion, but always has the same number of members as the number of Member States. Each minister is accompanied by a civil servant as part of a negotiating team. The Commission is also represented, although its influence depends upon the subject-matter under discussion and the competences of the Commission in the area discussed. There are currently about 20 formations of the Council of the EU. Among the specialised Councils are: the General Affairs Council, comprising foreign ministers of the Member States, which co-ordinates the activities of other Councils, examines external affairs and matters of general Community concern; Ecofin, which is attended by finance ministers; and the Internal Market Council, which is made up of ministers in charge of a particular aspect of the internal market. There are also specialised Council meetings in other subject areas such as agriculture, transport, budget, energy, education, culture, etc.

The nature of the Council meetings poses certain problems as they are, at the same time, Council meetings and meetings of the representatives of the Member States. As a Community institution, the Council must follow the rules and procedures prescribed by the Treaties, but as a diplomatic conference the rules of public international law apply. For that

---

[9] OJ L281 (1993).
[10] For example arts 121 and 122 EC.

reason, it is sometimes difficult to determine the legal nature of the acts adopted by the Council.[11]

Presidency

Council meetings are chaired by the Member State holding the Council Presidency which rotates every six months according to the order established by art 203 EC. Under Council Decision 95/2[12] (which laid down the holders of the Presidency for eight-and-a-half years from the accession of Austria, Finland and Sweden), from January 2000 Portugal holds the Presidency, followed by France (from July 2000), Sweden (from January 2001), Belgium (from July 2001), Spain (from January 2002), Denmark (from July 2002) and Greece (from January 2003).

The Member State which holds the Presidency of the Council presides also, during that period, over other bodies, for example, the European Council, COREPER, committees and organs of political co-operation, etc. In addition, at the meetings of the Council of the European Union, the Member State that holds the Presidency is represented in two capacities – as the Member State and as President of the Council.

In practice, the role of the Presidency is very important since the Member State holding it is responsible for setting the priorities for the Council during its six months in office. Thus, the Presidency determines the agenda and the calender of the Council. It also submits to the European Parliament at the end of the Presidency a detailed report of its achievements which is discussed by the latter. The Member States are more and more ambitious in determining the objectives they want to attain during the Presidency.[13] Each tries to make a lasting contribution to the development of the Communities and the Union. In addition, they may put issues of vital national importance on the agenda which are not considered essential in the context of the Community. Outside its political functions the Presidency also has administrative tasks to fulfil, such as to convene the Council meetings on its own initiative or at the request of a Member State or of the Commission, to determine the agenda, to chair the deliberations of the Council, to assist Member States to reach a compromise, and to decide on the time of voting. In the context of the European Union, in the area of CFSP the Presidency represents the Union in international organisations and international conferences. In order to ensure continuity in the work of the Council, the troika system was developed which associated the previous and the next Member States to hold the Presidency with its current holder. The Treaty of Amsterdam changed that system. Under art 207(2) EC the Council is to be assisted by a General Secretariat, under the responsibility of a Secretary-General in his capacity as High Representative for CFSP, and by the Member State which is to be next in line for the Presidency. As a result, the General Secretariat is given express recognition under the EC Treaty.

---

[11] See *Commission* v *Council* Case 22/70 [1971] ECR 263.

[12] OJ L1 (1995).

[13] For example, The Netherlands decided to finalise the Inter-governmental Conference during its Presidency (from January 1997 to the end of June 1977). This objective was successfully achieved when the draft Treaty of Amsterdam was signed on 17 June 1997.

COREPER

The Council is not a permanent body. Each meeting has to be prepared by civil servants acting within a number of committees, the most important being the Committee of Permanent Representatives (COREPER).[14] This body was initially established on an informal basis to ensure the continuity of the Council's work. It was formally recognised by art 4 of the Merger Treaty and is now defined in arts 207(1) EC and 121 EA. COREPER is made up of permanent representatives of the Member States to the European Union. Each Member State has a permanent delegation in Brussels (similar to an embassy) which comprises national civil servants with ambassadorial rank. Article 207(1) EC sets out the tasks of COREPER. It states that:

> 'A committee consisting of the Permanent Representatives of the Member States shall be responsible for preparing the work for the Council and for carrying out the tasks assigned to it by the Council.'

The main objective of COREPER is to prepare proposals which are negotiated prior to the Council meeting and thus avoid unnecessary discussion at ministerial level. There are two forms of COREPER: COREPER I, made up of deputy permanent representatives, which concentrates on more technical issues; and COREPER II, comprising the permanent representatives themselves, which focuses on more general and political matters. The Council forwards the matter to be discussed to COREPER which may create specialist or *ad hoc* committees, working groups, etc, in order to examine it. They then refer the matter back to COREPER for further study. The Commission and often the European Parliament are also involved as they discuss and negotiate the submitted proposal. If there is unanimous agreement on the proposal it is put in Part A of the Council agenda. Unless the Council opposes the proposal and sends it back to COREPER, it will be adopted by the Council. If there is no agreement in COREPER, the matter is put in Part B of the Council agenda for resolution.

The timetable of the Council meetings is prepared in advance. Regular meetings are usually convened once a month, extraordinary sessions can take place any time, but the agenda must be forwarded by the Presidency to the Member States at least 14 days in advance.

Sessions

The Council sessions are very frequent and often very long,[15] the deliberations are in camera. Only the members of the Commission have access and the right to speak. However, in order to ensure transparency, the Edinburgh Summit of 11–12 December 1992 introduced the possibility of public debates.[16] The Council responded by amending its Rules of Procedure. As a result, certain sessions are open to the public and may be broadcast.[17] Also, the results

---

[14] Its name is the French acronym for this Committee of Permanent Representatives.

[15] For example, in 1986 the Council held 79 sessions for a total of 107 days of meetings.

[16] The first broadcast took place on 1st February 1993.

[17] Council Decision 93/662/EC of 6 December 1993: OJ L304 (1993). Also, the EP demanded that the deliberations of the Council be made public: Report Hansch, Doc EP A3–189/92 and Report Giovanni, Doc EP A3–190/92.

of voting are now made public unless the Council by simple majority decides otherwise. Finally, the Council adopted a Code of Conduct on 2 October 1995 concerning access to its working sessions and any statements that result from them.[18]

Voting

The vote in the Council is personal, although under the Council Rules of Procedure a Member of the Council may arrange to be represented at a meeting which he is not able to attend. Usually, he is replaced by the permanent representative or the deputy permanent representative of that Member State. However, his replacement has no right to vote. For that reason, another member of the Council under art 206 EC usually acts on behalf of the absentee member and thus the non-ministerial representative votes in accordance with the instruction forwarded by his government under 'cover' of one of the ministers present. A present member of the Council cannot act on behalf of more that one other member.

The Treaties provided for three modes of voting: by simple majority, by qualified majority or by unanimity. The choice of mode is not left to the Council but depends upon the legal basis of the act in question. Under art 205(1) EC, in the absence of any specific provision the Council acts by a majority of its members. Paradoxically, simple majority voting – which was foreseen as a norm – is exceptional as the Treaties often require qualified majority voting or unanimity. It is worth mentioning that the decision to revise the Treaties which led to the adoption of the SEA was taken by simple majority against the opposition of three Member States, although they later accepted it. Simple majority voting is used in relation to arts 207, 208, 209 and 284 EC.

Unanimous voting which was assigned a privileged place in the original Treaties has lost its importance due to the revisions introduced by the SEA, the TEU and the Treaty of Amsterdam. It is still applied to constitutional or para-constitutional matters (arts 18, 19, 22, 190, 269, 308 EC), to measures intended to create an area of freedom, security and justice under Title IV of the EC Treaty, to certain aspects of harmonisation of national law in the context of the internal market (arts 93 and 94 EC), and to the adoption of measures concerning the common policies (arts 105(5), 111(1), 151(5), 157(3), 159 EC). Also, in common foreign and security policy and in police and judicial co-operation in criminal matters unanimity is the predominant mode of voting. It is interesting to note that under art 205(3) EC abstentions by a member present or represented at the Council do not prevent the adoption of measures which require unanimity. Also, unanimity constitutes the only means for the Council to reject a proposal originating from the Commission under the procedure of art 250 EC, subject to art 251(4) and (5) EC, and in certain cases the position adopted by the EP under art 252 EC procedure.

The Treaty of Amsterdam has extended qualified majority voting (QMV) to a number of areas formerly subject to unanimity: arts 46(2), 166(1) and (2), and 172 EC. It also applied QMV to new areas of activity: arts 141(3), 152(4), 254, 280, 285, 286 and 299(2). The question of further extension of QMV is closely linked with the review of the system of weighting of votes in the Council. This matter is being considered by the Inter-governmental Conference on Institutional Reform.

---

[18] EU Bull 10–1995, point 1.9.1.

Qualified majority voting has gradually become the most frequently used form within the Council. It is based on a 'weight' given to each Member State designated to ensure equality in the decision-making process. The system of weighted votes reflects the size of a Member State, its demographic, economic and political 'weight' within the Community. It has two objectives: first, to ensure that small Member States are not able themselves to block the measure; and, second, that they have sufficient representation to avoid being systematically outvoted by the larger Member States. Under art 205(2) EC, when the Council is required to vote by a qualified majority, the votes (a total of 87) are weighted as follows:

Austria	–	4
Belgium	–	5
Denmark	–	3
Finland	–	3
France	–	10
Germany	–	10
Greece	–	5
Ireland	–	3
Italy	–	10
Luxembourg	–	2
Netherlands	–	5
Portugal	–	5
Spain	–	8
Sweden	–	4
United Kingdom	–	10

A qualified majority requires 62 of the total of 87 votes. If a measure is based on a Commission proposal it requires only any 62 votes; in other cases, that is if a proposal is submitted by the Council, the 62 votes must be cast by at least ten Member States. This has been introduced to ensure the protection of interests of smaller Member States.

Qualified majority voting is applied to a wide variety of areas of EC Treaty: arts 26, 37, 45, 49, 52, 57, 59, 60, 75, 80, 87, 89, 92, 96, 99, 104, 107, 111, 114, 117, 119, 120, 121, 122, 132, 133, 149, 152, 166, 210, 247, 258, 273, 276, 300 and 301.

A qualified majority vote was foreseen as the norm at the end of the transition period. The opposition of France to its introduction in a wide range of policies from 1966 led to a major crisis which was resolved by the Luxembourg Accord in January 1966. The question of qualified majority voting reappeared at the end of accession negotiations with Austria, Finland, Norway and Sweden. Subsequent to the pressure exercised by the United Kingdom and Spain to maintain the number of votes required to block a proposal at 23 votes,[19] the foreign ministers of the Member States reached a compromise at an informal meeting held on 27–29 March 1994, known as the Ioannina Compromise. Under Council Decision of 29 March 1994[20] if the Members of the Council represent a total of between 23 and 26 votes which indicate their intention to oppose the adoption of a measure taken by QMV, the

[19] The majority of the Member States wanted a proportional increase in the number of the votes necessary to block a proposal, from 23 to 26, which fixed the blocking minority at 30 per cent. The UK considered that this increase would give smaller Member States an unfair advantage.

[20] OJ C105 (1994) as amended: OJ C1 (1995).

Council will do all in its power to reach, within a reasonable time, a satisfactory solution which will lead to its adoption by 65 votes out of 87. During that period the President of the Council with the assistance of the Commission and members of the Council will take all necessary initiatives to facilitate the broadest possible consensus within the Council. The Ioannina Compromise means that if there is a sufficient number of votes to constitute a blocking minority under the rules prior to the accession of Sweden, Austria and Finland but not under the post-accession rules, then the President of the Council will interfere in order to obtain a number of votes which would under the old voting rules prevent the blocking of the proposal. This system is of very little practical importance since under both the old and new rules only a group of Member States can block a measure. It was hoped that the Inter-governmental Conference would reform the voting system within the Council. However, this decision was delayed by the Amsterdam European Council (June 1997) until the number of the Member States reaches at least 20.

Competences

The main powers conferred on the Council are defined in art 202 EC. They are: economic policy co-ordination; decision-making; and the conferment of implementing powers on the Commission.

In the context of the Treaties of Rome the Council is the ultimate legislative body. However, under the CS Treaty it is mainly a consultative body. It is consulted in certain areas by the High Authority/Commission, in others it gives its assent in respect of legislative measures adopted by the High Authority (arts 14 and 28 CS). Under the EC Treaty in certain decision-making procedures the Council shares its legislative powers with the European Parliament.

The Council has some 'governmental' functions which it may exercise directly by implementing powers in respect of its own measures or confer on the Commission powers for the implementation of those measures. Also, in external relations the Council acts in a similar way to a government. It authorises the opening of negotiations, confers on the Commission the power to negotiate international agreements on behalf of the Community, and decides whether or not to conclude them. For some agreements, for example in respect of admission of a new Member, the assent of the EP is required. In international organisations and international conferences the Presidency of the Council represents the Communities and the Union. In budgetary matters the Council drafts the proposed budget and participates it its adoption together with the EP. Under art 208 EC the Council may ask the Commission to undertake any studies that the Council considers desirable for the attainment of the common objectives and to submit to it any appropriate proposals. Furthermore, the Council fixes the remuneration of the Commissioners, Judges, Advocates-General and Registrar of the ECJ (art 6 of the Merger Treaty), appoints the members of the Court of Auditors (art 276 EC) and the Economic and Social Committee (art 258 EC), amends the Statute of the ECJ and approves its Rules of Procedure (art 245 EC), and can increase the number of Commissioners, Judges, or Advocates-General.[21]

Under arts 145 EC, 26 CS and 115 EA the Council must ensure co-ordination of the

---

[21] Commissioners (art 10 of the Merger Treaty), Judges (art 221 EC), Advocates General (art 222 EC).

general policies of the Member States. The task is mainly carried out by means of deliberations, consultations, recommendations and studies, although some binding acts may also be adopted by the Council.

In the context of the common foreign and security policy and police and judicial co-operation in criminal matters, the Council is the ultimate decision-making body. On the basis of guidelines adopted by the European Council, the Council must take necessary decisions to implement them. It may also recommend common strategies to the European Council and implement them by adopting joint actions and common positions. Its role under Pillar 3 has considerably diminished as a result of the transfer of visa, asylum, immigratioon and other policies related to the free movement of persons necessary to the progressive creation of an area of freedom, security and justice from Pillar 3 to the EC Treaty.

4.3 The European Commission

Like the Council of Ministers, the Commission has renamed itself following the entry into force of the Treaty of Maastricht. Instead of the Commission of the European Communities the new name, the European Commission, is to be used. The Commission represents the interests of the Communities. As a 'revolutionary' body within the institutional system of the Community, it is also the most controversial institution. It exercises many functions, the most important being the guardianship of the Treaty and the initiation of Community measures.

Composition

Since the enlargement of the EU in 1995 the Commission is made up of 20 members, at least one and not more than two from each Member State. By convention larger Member States, that is Germany, France, Italy, Spain and the United Kingdom, have two Members. The Commissioners must be chosen on the basis of their general competence. Article 213(1) EC specifies that only nationals of the Member States may be appointed Commissioners. Their independence must be beyond doubt. In this respect they take a solemn oath before the ECJ. Their independence requires that, as art 213(2) provides, they:

> '... shall neither seek nor take instructions from any government or from any other body ...
> Each Member State undertakes to respect this principle and not to seek to influence the
> Members of the Commission in the performance of their tasks.'

In order to reinforce their independence during their term of office, they are prohibited from engaging in any other occupation, whether gainful or not, and from any action incompatible with their duties as Commissioners. This excludes Commissioners from being members of a national parliament or of the European Parliament. However, academic activities, research and teaching are compatible with the status of Commissioner.[22]

By virtue of the founding Treaties the Commissioners are designated by common accord

---

[22] For more on incompatibility: see Question E–2752/94 by F Herman (OJ C88 (1995)).

of the Member States, although in practice each Member State submits its candidates subject to possible veto by other Member States. The Treaty of Maastricht modified the procedure for nomination in order to strengthen the position of the President of the Commission, to ameliorate the cohesion of the Commission and, especially, to ensure effective control by the EP over nominations. The Treaty of Amsterdam further emphasised the legitimacy of the Commission and the role of its President. Article 214(2) EC provides that the Member States must nominate the President of the Commission by common accord and that nomination must be confirmed by the EP. In addition it states that:

> 'The governments of the Member States shall, by common accord with the nominee for President, nominate the other persons whom they intend to appoint as Members of the Commission.'

The President and the other members of the Commission thus nominated shall be subject as a body to a vote of approval by the European Parliament. After approval by the European Parliament, the President and the other members of the Commission shall be appointed by common accord of the governments of the Member States. Consequently, the President of the Commission has his say as to the nomination of members of the Commission. Before the entry into force of the Treaty of Amsterdam he was only consulted. In addition, art 219 EC provides for closer co-operation between the members of the Commission and the President. They should 'work under the political guidance' of the President. Declaration 32 attached to the Treaty of Amsterdam confirms that the President should enjoy broad discretion in the allocation of tasks within the Commission and should be allowed to reorganise the Commission.

Under art 217 EC the Commission appoints either one or two Vice-Presidents from among its members.

Term of office

The term of office for the Commissioners has been extended to five years by the TEU in order to synchronise it with that of the EP. The mandate is renewable. Any vacancy, whether by normal replacement, death, resignation or compulsory retirement, is filled for the remainder of the member's term of office by a new member appointed by common accord of the Member States. However, the Commission may decide by unanimity not to fill such vacancy. The procedure concerning the appointment of the President applies also in the case of any vacancy in that office caused by the circumstances stated above: art 214(2) EC.

If a Commissioner no longer fulfils the conditions required for the performance of his duties or has been guilty of serious misconduct the ECJ may, on application by the Council or the Commission, compulsorily retire him. So far the possibility contained in art 216 EC has been applied only once and that was in a case of the total incapacity of a Commissioner. In the event of any breach of obligations imposed upon Commissioners, including those to behave with integrity and discretion even after they have ceased to hold office, sanctions may be imposed by the ECJ consisting of deprivation of pension rights or other benefits. The European Parliament also exercises some disciplinary power, but only over the entire Commission, by submitting a motion of censure under art 201 EC.

For the first time in the history of the European Communities the President of the

Commission (Jacques Santer), was together with all the Commissioners, forced to resign on 15 March 1998. Under the principle of collegiate responsibility the entire Commission, including its President, was in effect dismissed. Mismanagement, fraud, the awarding of financial contracts and other irregularities committed by some of the Commissioners were confirmed by the 'comité de sages' set up jointly by the European Parliament and the Commission following the EP resolution on 14 January 1999 on improving the financial management of the Commission. This occurred after the EP had tried unsuccessfully, shortly after its motion of censure, to dismiss the Commission (293 votes to 232 with 27 abstentions).

At the summit meeting of the Heads of State or Government of the Member States in Berlin on 24–25 March 1999, Romano Prodi was unanimously nominated as the successor to Jacques Santer. His appointment was confirmed by the EP on 5 May 1999 (392 against 72 with 41 abstentions). His team of Commissioners after being interviewed by the EP in accordance with new Rules of Procedure of the EP[23] was approved as the collegiate body (404 votes to 153 with 37 abstentions) in conformity with art 214 EC.

It is interesting to note that under the new Rules of Procedure 1999 the EP 'elects' (arts 32 and 33) the President of the Commission and its members, whilst under the old Rules of Procedure the EP 'participated in the designation of the President of the Commission' (art 32 Rules of Procedure 1997) and 'approved' the Commission (art 33 Rules of Procedure 1997). This is another small step in transforming the EP into a real Parliament.

The Commission's tenure, as replacement for the dismissed Jacques Santer's Commission, was intended to last until 23 January 2000. The EP decided that a new vote in January 2000 was not necessary and subsequently extended the Commission's term of office to 23 January 2005 in order to synchronise it with the tenure of the EP. Romano Prodi intends to introduce important institutional reforms based on greater efficiency, transparency and full accountability of the Commission.[24] At the first working meeting of the new Commission on 18 September 1999, the 20 Commissioners authorised the creation of two new directorates-general, one in charge of enlargement of the EU, the other responsible for Pillar 3. The 24 directorates-general previously identified only by numbers have been named according to their policy area (that is, competition, trade, external relations, etc). Each Commissioner will work from offices in the directorate of which he is in charge, contrary to the previous practice of grouping them together in a single headquarters building. The Commission has adopted a very strict Code of Conduct under which a Commissioner is required to act in accordance with the highest standards of public life. Also, in order to avoid any conflict of interests, Commissioners will be subject to a one-year 'cooling off period' after leaving office during which their prospective jobs could be vetoed by a special ethics committee. This measure is necessary, taking into account the case of Martin Bangemann, industry and telecommunication Commissioner in the Santer Commission, who accepted a post with Telefónica, the Spanish telecom group which he used to regulate. The Council decided to bring proceedings against him before the ECJ[25]

---

[23] OJ L202 (1999).

[24] The Commission New Rules of Procedure: OJ 1252 (1999). The Reform Strategy Programme was published in February 2000.

[25] Decision 1999/494/EC/CS/EA of 9 July 1999: OJ L192 (1999).

based on art 213 EC, which provides that Commissioners 'shall give a solemn undertaking that, both during and after their term of office, they will respect the obligations therefrom and in particular their duty to behave with integrity and discretion as regards the acceptance, after they have ceased to hold office, of certain appointments or benefits .'[26]

Functioning

The Commission is a collegiate body. This means that no member of the Commission is actually empowered to take any decision on his own and that once he has in effect made a decision, issues a declaration, etc, he expresses the position of the entire Commission. The principle of collegiality is based on the equal participation of the Commissioners in the adoption of decisions. This entails that decisions should be the subject of collective deliberation and that all the members of the college of Commissioners should bear collective responsibility at political level for all decisions adopted. This principle means that each measure must be formally approved by the college; its violation may render a measure invalid.[27] However, this principle, has for practical reasons, been attenuated. Apart from the exceptions provided in arts 10 and 11 of the Commission's Rules of Procedure, the principle of collegiality requires that the Commission seeks a broad consensus among its members, although it may also submit the matter to a formal vote.[28] The President of the Commission is only *primus inter pares*, there is no casting vote.

The principle of collegiality was explained in *Commission* v *Federal Republic of Germany* Case C–191/95 [1998] ECR I–5449. In this case the Commission decided to issue a reasoned opinion against the government of Germany for failure to provide for appropriate penalties in cases where companies limited by shares failed to disclose their annual accounts, as prescribed in particular by the First Council Directive 68/151/EEC of 9 March 1968 and the Fourth Council Directive 78/660/EEC of 25 July 1978. When Germany did not comply with the opinion the Commission decided, in conformity with art 226 EC, to bring proceedings before the ECJ against the German government. Both decisions were challenged by the German government as not being the subject of collective deliberations by the college of Commissioners. Germany argued that the issue of the reasoned opinion and commencement of proceedings were delegated to a particular Commissioner. In addition, Germany maintained that the action was inadmissible because the application for a declaration for failure to fulfil obligations under art 226 EC differed from the letter of formal notice.

The ECJ held that the formal requirement for effective compliance with the principle of collegiality varies according to the nature and legal effect of the act. In the case of acts which have no binding legal effect it is not necessary for the college 'itself formally to decide on the wording of the acts which give effect to those decisions and put them in final form'.

---

[26] Unfortunately, the Council decided to withdraw its decision subject to a number of conditions: M Bangemann would not accept any position in Telefónica until 1 July 2000 and would not represent any third party including Telefónica until 31 December 2001: Council Decision 2000/44/EC/CS/EA (OJ L16 (2000)).

[27] *Commission* v *BASF* Case C–137/92P [1994] ECR I–2555 in which the ECJ confirmed the decisions of the CFI regarding *BASF* Cases T–79, 84–86, 91–92, 94, 96 and 98/89 [1992] ECR II–315.

[28] Under art 219 EC simple majority of its Members is required.

In such circumstances it is sufficient if the information on which those decisions are based is available to the members of the college. In the present case, the measures in question had no binding force and necessary information was available to the members of the college.

In addition to the above the principle of collegiality entails that acts adopted by the college of Commissioners must be authenticated by the signatures of the President of the Commission and the Executive Secretary before being notified in the language or languages which are binding to their addresses or published. The objective of authentication is to ensure that the text adopted by the college of Commissioners becomes fixed so that in the event of a dispute it can be verified that the text adopted corresponds precisely to the text notified or published. In *Commission v Solvay; Commission v ICI* Joined Cases C–286 and 288/95P Judgment of 6 April 2000 (nyr) the ECJ held that if an act adopted by the Commission has not been properly authenticated, the Community courts must of their own motion raise the issue and annul the act vitiated by that defect, irrespective of whether or not the lack of authentication caused any harm to a party to the dispute and of whether or not there is any evidence to cast doubt on the authenticity of the notified text.

Despite the principle of collegiality, the Commission divides its tasks among its members, and each Commissioner is allocated one or more policy. Each Commissioner has personal advisers who form his so-called *Cabinet*, which acts as a liaison between the Commissioner and his Directorate(s)-General. The chief of his *Cabinet* is usually the same nationality as the Commissioner and deputises for him as necessary. He also meets weekly with other *Cabinet* chiefs in order to prepare the agenda for the Commission.

The Commission employs approximately 15,000 officials, and about 12 per cent of its administrative staff are involved in translation.

Competences

The competences of the European Commission are described in art 211 EC which provides that:

> 'In order to ensure the proper functioning and development of the common market, the Commission shall:
> – ensure that the provisions of this Treaty and the measures taken by the Institutions pursuant thereto are applied;
> – formulate recommendations or deliver opinions on matters dealt with in this Treaty, if it expressly so provides or if the Commission considers it necessary;
> – have its own power of decision and participate in the shaping of measures taken by the Council and by the European Parliament in the manner provided for in this Treaty;
> – exercise the powers conferred on it by the Council for the implementation of the rules laid down by the latter.'

In addition, the Commission has important managerial and administrative functions and plays a role under Pillars 2 and 3 of the EU Treaty.

The European Commission as the 'guardian of the Treaty'
The most important function of the Commission is to ensure that the provisions of the Treaty and the acts of the institutions are complied with by the Member States, any natural

or legal person under the jurisdiction of a Member State and all EC institutions. In order to fulfil this task the Commission has at its disposal important powers.

First, the Commission is empowered to obtain any necessary information from Member States, individuals and undertakings. Member States have a duty to forward information required by the Commission, notify measures and drafts of measures they intend to adopt and provide explanations concerning any question of law or fact which the Commission considers important. This obligation derives either from specific provisions of the Treaty,[29] or from measures adopted by the EC institutions,[30] or from art 10 EC which requires Member States to co-operate with the Commission in order to facilitate the achievement of the Community's tasks. Also, the Commission may ask individuals and undertakings to forward information[31] and, under its investigative powers, to verify it. A request for information is often the first step in a Commission's investigation of an alleged infringement of Community law by an undertaking in competition matters.[32]

Second, the Commission may take preventative actions. Usually, as mentioned in art 211 EC, the Commission formulates recommendations and delivers opinions intended to ensure effective application of EC law in the future or to suggest the objectives for the Member States in areas within the exclusive national competences. In this respect an interesting example is provided by Recommendation 91/131 of 27 November 1991 to which is annexed the code of practice aimed at combating sexual harassment in the work place.[33]

Third, the Commission is empowered to enforce Community law. The obligation to observe Community law binds individuals, and the Commission may impose pecuniary and/or administrative sanctions upon them by virtue of specific provisions of the CS Treaty, in matters concerning the control of security under the EA Treaty and in competition issues under the EC Treaty. Also the Commission may bring an action before the ECJ against a Member State in breach of Community law under arts 88 CS, 226 EC and 141 EA. Furthermore, if any Community institution violates Community law the Commission may bring an action under arts 230 or 232 EC; this is mostly applied in respect of the Council.

Fourth, the Commission may authorise, in certain circumstances, derogations from the provisions of the Treaties. The expiry of the transition period initially made those powers redundant, although under the Acts of Accession and in respect of measures adopted by Community institutions in relation to international agreements the Commission is still authorised to grant derogations. Under arts 296 and 297 EC or art 95(4) EC the Commission is empowered to authorise measures incompatible with the common market if a Member State is seeking derogation from the application of the Treaty on the grounds of serious economic difficulties, internal disturbances, serious international tension, or if its essential interest of national security is in jeopardy.

In the context of economic and monetary union the Commission monitors budgetary

---

[29] For example, arts 95(4), 97 EC, etc.

[30] Especially, the final provisions of EC directives which impose upon the Member States the obligation to notify the Commission of the adoption of implementing measures.

[31] For example art 47 and 86 CS, art 284 EC.

[32] See Regulation 17/62, especially its art 14; Regulation 4064/89 on Merger Control, arts 11 and 12.

[33] OJ L49 (1992).

discipline in Member States in order to avoid excessive governmental deficits (art 104 EC) and to supervise their balance of payments: arts 119 and 120 EC.

The European Commission as the initiator of legislative measures

The general interest of the Community requires that the Commission's main objective is to foster European integration. Consequently, its right to initiate legislative measures in order to further develop the Community is well justified. In *SADAM* Cases 88–90/75 [1976] ECR 323 the ECJ emphasised that the Commission is entrusted with a general mission of initiative. Therefore, the Commission may not only proceed by way of drafting proposals for legislative measures but can also adopt non-binding measures such as communications, action programmes, reports, white papers, etc, which define general objectives and the means necessary for their attainment and which often result in formal proposals and ultimately in binding acts. In respect of proposals for legislative measures, many provisions of the Treaties of Rome provide that only the Commission may initiate them. The special position of the Commission is recognised in art 250 EC which provides that:

> '(1) Where, in pursuance of this Treaty, the Council acts on a proposal from the Commission, unanimity shall be required for an act constituting an amendment to that proposal …
> (2) As long as the Council has not acted, the Commission may alter its proposal at any time during the procedures leading to the adoption of a Community act.'

This means that the Council may only amend a Commission proposal by acting unanimously, although for its adoption, without an amendment, a simple majority or QMV is often sufficient.[34] Furthermore, if there is any disagreement among the Member States, and unanimity cannot be achieved, the Commission, which is the only institution entitled to change the proposal in question, acts as a broker between various governments and may negotiate a compromise modifying the original proposal or even withdraw it. This solution emphasises the importance attached to Commission proposals which enhance the interest of the Community as a whole, and which may only be rejected if all Member States agree. Thus, the interest of the Community should prevail over national interests.

Although about 95 per cent of all legislative measures are initiated by the Commission, its exclusivity in this respect has been limited. First, The Council and the European Parliament may request the Commission to submit proposals on matters on which they consider that a Community act is necessary for the purpose of implementing the Treaty.[35] Second, under Pillars 2 and 3 other institutions are empowered to submit proposals. In matters relating to economic and monetary union, the ECB shares the initiative with the Commission.[36] Also in these matters the Council and the Member States may request the Commission to make proposals or recommendations: art 115 EC.

Under the Treaty of Amsterdam the Commission enjoys the exclusive right of initiative in new areas brought within the EC Treaty, eg employment and social policy. Under Pillar 3 the Commission shares a right of initiative with the Member States. Under Title IV of the EC Treaty, in areas transferred from Pillar 3 to the EC Treaty, after a transitional period of five

---

[34] The requirement of unanimity in art 250 is subject to art 251(4) and (5).
[35] The Council under art 208 EC and the EP under art 192(2) EC.
[36] Article 107 EC.

years during which the Commission shares the right of initiative with Member States, the Commission will acquire the sole right of initiative.

Executive powers of the European Commission

Article 211 EC provides that the Commission shall have its own power of decision and shall participate in the shaping of measures taken by the Council and by the European Parliament.

Unlike the wide direct powers conferred upon the High Authority/Commission by the CS, under the Treaty of Rome the Commission is empowered to enact legislative measures of general scope of application only in limited areas, ie within the framework of common policies, the CAP being the best example. However, the Commission is more involved in issuing individual legislative measures addressed to Member States, undertakings and individuals. Under the EC Treaty this is mainly in competition matters.

The administration of Community policies necessitates the adoption of numerous binding measures. The Commission also implements the Community budget and administers four special funds: the European Social Fund, the European Development Fund, the European Agricultural Guidance and Guarantee Fund and the European Regional Development Fund.

By virtue of art 211 EC the Commission exercises the powers conferred on it by the Council for the implementation of measures adopted by the latter. As a result, the Commission possesses delegated implementation powers which in practice means that while the Council adopts a framework act (usually a regulation), for example in relation to the CAP, the Commission is in charge of the details and, for example, must fix the quotas, determine the price, etc, through regulations or decisions. The Commission must act within the limits of the authority delegated by the Council, although the ECJ has given a broad interpretation to such delegated implementation powers. It recognises the wide discretion of the Commission, including the possibility of imposition of sanctions and authorisation of derogations.[37]

The drawback of the delegated implementing powers conferred on the Commission is that a system of procedural mechanisms has been established by the Member States in order to supervise the way the Commission exercises those powers. The 'comitology' system was established as a necessary element in the introduction of the CAP in 1962. At that time it was considered politically unacceptable that the Commission alone should implement delegated legislation. A supervision committee was set up comprising national civil servants and presided over by a non-voting Commission representative. With time, the system flourished and was extended to many areas. This pathological growth of 'comitology', instead of being stifled, which in the author's view should have been the case, was recognised by the Single European Act (art 202 EC). However, the necessity to rationalise the system prompted the Council to establish principles and rules governing comitology.

---

[37] *ACF Chemiefarma v Commission* Case 41/69 [1970] ECR 661; *Westzuker* Case 57/72 [1973] ECR 321; *Eridania* Case 230/78 [1979] ECR 2749; *France and Ireland v Commission* Case C–296/93 [1996] ECR I–795 and *Ireland v Commission* Case C–307/93 [1993] ECR I–4191.

Council Decision 87/373[38] laid down the procedures for the exercise of the delegated implementation powers. It provides for three types of committee procedure:

1. The regulatory committee which must approve the proposal by a qualified majority prior to its implementation. In the absence of such support, the proposed measure is referred back to the Council which takes a decision by qualified majority. However, if the Council does not take a decision, the Commission may adopt proposed implementing measures, provided that the Council does not object by a qualified majority.
2. The management committee whose approval is not required but should it disapprove by a qualified majority then the Council must substitute its own measure for that of the Commission.
3. The advisory committee which must be consulted on the draft measure although its opinion is not binding.

As a result, the Commission acts either alone or by virtue of one of three committee procedures.[39]

Since the SEA the principle is that the Commission implements measures adopted by the Council and the latter may exercise such powers itself only in 'specific cases'and in such event 'must state in detail the grounds for such a Decision': see *Commission* v *Council* Case 16/88 [1989] ECR 3457. In order to rationalise the comitology system the Council adopted Decision 1999/468/EC of 28 June 1999[40] laying down the procedure for the exercise of implementing powers conferred on the Commission, which repealed Council Decision 87/373.

By Decision 1999/468/EC the Council tried to achieve three objectives: first, to simplify the system; second, to make it more coherent; and, third, to ensure that the principle of transparency is applied within the framework of committees. The simplification of the requirements for the exercise of implementing powers takes two forms: the reduction of the number of procedures and the increase of the involvement of the EP when a measure is adopted on the basis of art 251 EC. The simplification has been successful in respect of the management procedure. Under art 4 of the said Decision, when the Commission adopts measures contrary to the opinion of the Committees, these measures are to be submitted to the Council which, acting by qualified majority, may take a different decision within a period not exceeding three months from the date of such submission. During that period the Commission may apply the measure or may defer its application. However, if the time limit of three months has elapsed and the Council has not adopted a different measure, the Commission is entitled to apply the proposed measure. The simplification has not been successful in respect of the regulatory procedure, especially when the proposed implementing measure is contrary to the opinion of the regulatory committee: see art 5 of Decision 1999/468.

Decision 1999/468 reinforces consistency and predictability in the choice of type of committee by providing criteria relating to such a choice. The management procedure should be followed in respect of all management matters, although the Decision does not give any definition of such matters. It enumerates some of those areas in which the

[38] OJ L197 (1987).
[39] See K Bradley, 'Comitology and the Law: Through a Glass, Darkly' (1992) 29 CMLR 693.
[40] OJ L184 (1999).

management procedure should be taken, such as the application of the CAP or the CFP or relating to the implementation of programmes with substantial budgetary implications. The regulatory procedure should be used restrictively in relation both to measures of general scope designed to apply essential provisions of basic instruments, including the protection of the health or safety of humans, animals, plants, etc, and to measures designed to adopt or update some non-essential provisions of a basic instrument. In respect of the advisory procedure, contrary to the proposal of the Commission, which wanted to apply it as a basic procedure (in all cases when the management or regulatory procedures do not apply), the Decision stipulates that the advisory procedure should be followed only in appropriate cases. However, the Decision undermines the criteria relating to the choice of committee procedures by stating that they are of a non-binding nature.

In respect of the principle of transparency, three important innovations have been introduced by Decision 1999/468:

1. Each committee has to adopt its own rules of procedure which should be published in the Official Journal.
2. The principles and conditions on public access to documents applicable to the Commission also apply to the committees. The Commission is to be regarded as an author and holder of such documents: see *Rothmans International BV v Commission* Case T–188/97 [1999] 3 CMLR 66. In addition, the Commission must provide a list of all committees which assist it in the exercise of implementing powers and must prepare and publish an annual report on the working of committees.
3. The EP awareness of the working of committees has been increased. The Commission has to inform the EP on a regular basis of committee proceedings, the Commission has to transmit to the EP documents related to activities of committees, and to inform the EP of measures or proposals for measures to be submitted by it to the Council.

The involvement of the EP in the adoption of measures within the framework of comitology has been improved. Under art 5 of the Decision in cases of proposals submitted by the Commission pursuant to a basic instrument adopted under the co-decision procedure (art 251 EC) the EP, if it considers that the Commission has exceeded its implementing powers, should inform the Council of its position, which may be taken into consideration by the Council.

The Council and the Commission have both made declarations on Council Decision 1999/468/EC.[41] In the Commission declaration, it emphasises that in relation to the management procedure it has always been its policy to secure the widest possible support within the committee and that it will take into consideration the position of the members of the committee and act in such a way as to avoid going against any predominant position which might emerge against the appropriateness of an implementing measure. The Commission will also apply this approach in respect of proposals for implementing measures concerning particularly sensitive sectors.

Decision 1999/468/EC constitutes an improvement, even though it cannot resolve by itself the complex and complicated problems created by comitology which can only be achieved within a framework of fundamental institutional reform.

---

[41] OJ C203 (1999).

International functions

The European Commission has delegations (which enjoy diplomatic status) in more than 100 countries. The Commission also liaises with international organisations such as specialised bodies of the United Nations, the World Trade Organisation (art 302 EC), the Council of Europe (art 303 EC), and the Organisation for Economic Co-operation and Development (art 304 EC). The Commission, under art 300 EC, is entrusted with negotiating international agreements between the Community and third countries. Its powers are strictly defined by the Council, which may issue directives and appoint a special committee to assist the Commission and to ensure that the latter acts within the framework of its directives. The necessity for the Commission to conduct negotiations within the limits determined by the Council was emphasised in *France v Commission* Case C-327/91 [1994] ECR I–3641, in which the ECJ annulled an agreement on competition matters between the Commission and the United States. Under art 300(4) EC the Council may, by way of derogation, authorise the Commission to conclude international agreements adopted according to a simplified procedure introduced by the Treaty of Maastricht.

4.4 The European Parliament

The European Parliament, previously known as the Assembly of the European Communities, renamed itself in 1962 in order to emphasise the role it should play in the Community's policy-making process. This role remains limited but has been dramatically increased by each revision of the original Treaties. The Single European Act recognised the new name. The European Parliament, in comparison with other Community institutions in terms of attributed competences and the way it is constituted, has undergone the greatest change since its inception. Since 1979 it has been the only directly elected body in the Communities and as such its claim to be a real parliament has been, to a certain extent, justified. Nevertheless, the EP is still a body which exercises its influence more through powers of persuasion than through votes, and unlike national parliaments it is still not a real, sovereign parliament as it has no power to initiate legislation or to impose taxes.

Composition

In accordance with Council Decision 76/787 and the annexed Act on direct elections of 20 September 1976[42] adopted by the Council on the ground of art 190(1) EC, the Members of the European Parliament are elected by direct universal suffrage. Article 19(2) EC specifies that every citizen of the EU residing in a Member State of which he is not a national is entitled to vote and stand as a candidate in elections to the EP in the Member State in which he resides, under the same conditions as nationals of that State. Directive 93/109/EC provided for a uniform electoral procedure.[43] The first elections were held in 1979 and now take place every five years. In 1999 around 289 million voters from 15 Member States were entitled to vote in the fifth direct elections to the EP, and for the first time the UK as a

---

[42] OJ L278 (1976).
[43] OJ L329 (1993).

whole used proportional representation to elect its 87 MEPs. The first plenary session of the 626 newly elected members of the European Parliament was held in Strasbourg on 20–23 July 1999.

The number of parliamentary seats is determined on the basis of the size of population in each Member State but, in the light of the wide difference between large and small Member States, this is not a strict mathematical formula. For example, Luxembourg has only 350,000 inhabitants while the UK has 60 million. As a result, a compromise was reached which takes into consideration the size of the population in a Member State, while ensuring that the smallest Member States are adequately represented in the EP and that its overall size does not produce an over-large, unwieldy body.

The Member States allocation of MEPs is the following: Austria (21), Belgium (25), Denmark (16), France (87), Finland (16), Germany (99), Greece (25), Italy (87), Ireland (15), Luxembourg (6), Netherlands (31), Portugal (25), Spain (64), Sweden (22) and the UK (87). The Treaty of Amsterdam limits the size of the EP to 700 members even when the EU is enlarged to include candidate States.

Any national of a Member State who is qualified to vote in national elections may stand as a candidate for the EP. However, certain offices are incompatible with membership of the EP, such as membership of national governments of a Member State, of the European Commission, the ECJ or employment by a Community institution. The dual mandate, that is being an MEP at the same time as being a member of a national parliament, is now permitted.

Members of the EP enjoy certain privileges and immunities, such as: freedom of movement when they travel to or from the place of meeting of the EP; immunity from any form of inquiry, detention or legal proceedings in respect of opinions expressed or votes cast in the performance of their duties; during the session of the EP they are granted the same immunities as members of national parliaments in the territory of their own State; and immunity from any measures of detention and from legal proceedings in the territory of any other Member State.[44] However, the immunity can be waived if an MEP commits a criminal offence. In this respect, it is interesting to mention that the EP has modified its Rules of Procedure following the problem raised by the personal bankruptcy of Bernard Tapie, a member of the EP, in order to regulate this kind of situation in the future. In the absence of a uniform electoral procedure at Community level this matter is governed in each Member State by its national electoral laws.[45]

Unlike national parliaments the EP is not divided into the government and the opposition. MEPs sit in multi-national political groupings and not in national groups. Under the Rules of Procedure of the EP a political group is recognised by the EP if it comprises a minimum of 29 members from one Member State, 23 if they are from two Member States, 18 if they are from three Member States and 14 if they are from four or more Member States.

The Treaty of Maastricht, and subsequently the Treaty of Amsterdam, emphasised the

---

[44] See arts 8–10 of the Protocol on the Privileges and Immunities of the European Communities annexed to the Merger Treaty of 1965.
[45] On the consequences of the absence of uniform electoral procedure: see *Partie Ecologiste Les Verts* Case 294/83 [1986] ECR 1339; *The Liberal Democrats* Case C–4/92 [1993] ECR I–3153.

importance of political parties at European level as a factor for integration, since they 'contribute to forming a European awareness and to expressing the political will of the citizens of the Union' (art 191 EC). There are important incentives to form political groups, such as allocation of an office and staff, appointment to parliamentary committees, speaking time, and various rights of initiative and disbursement of funding which is made on a political group basis. As a result of the 1999 election the largest group in the EP is the European People's Party, which includes British Conservative MEPs (224 seats). Next is the Socialist Party, which includes British Labour MEPs (180 seats), then Liberal, Democrats and Reform (43 seats) and the Greens (38 seats).

Functioning

From its inception, the EP has considered itself as a parliament. The Assembly of the CS adopted rules of procedure similar to any parliament. This was recognised by the Treaties of Rome and enhanced by the universal suffrage to the EP. Under art 199 EC the EP adopts its own Rules of Procedure.[46] However, the power of the EP is limited by the obligation to respect the allocation of competences between the Community institutions as determined by the Treaties.[47] Also, the EP cannot unilaterally decide on the location of its seat. As a result, MEPs travel between three working places: Luxembourg, Brussels and Strasbourg.

The EP elects its President for two-and-a-half years. The President chairs debates and exercises an administrative and disciplinary function similar to that of a leader of any national parliament. Fourteen vice-presidents and five quaestors[48] are elected by the EP. Together with the President they form the Bureau of Parliament which is responsible for the organisation and administration of the EP. Until 1993 the Bureau and the chairmen of the political groups formed the Enlarged Bureau which set the detailed agenda for the parliamentary sessions. Since then it has been replaced by the Conference of Presidents.[49] In addition to the tasks which were carried out by the Enlarged Bureau, it organises meetings and relations with other Community institutions, bodies and organisations. The Secretary-General and Secretariat assist the EP in administrative and organisational matters.

The EP may establish permanent, temporary, specialised and general commissions which examine in detail particular topics, prepare opinions at the request of the Council and resolutions concerning new initiatives of the EP. There are 20 permanent (standing) commissions, each dealing with a specific aspect of Community activities. They are of particular importance as they ensure the continuity of the work of the EP. They prepare reports for debates in the EP and liaise with the Commission and the Council during the interval between parliamentary sessions. They can meet at any time at the request of their chairman or the President of the EP. The members of commissions are elected on the basis of proposals submitted by political groups. Political and geographical factors and representations of the parliamentary political groups within a commission are also taken into consideration. In principle, each MEP is a sitting member of one commission and an

---

[46] OJ L202 (1999).
[47] This was emphasised by the ECJ in *Partie Ecologiste Les Verts* Case 294/83 [1986] ECR 1339.
[48] They are in charge of administrative and financial matters directly concerning the MEPs.
[49] The Decision of the EP of 15 September 1993: OJ C268 (1993).

advisory member-suppliant of another. Article 193 EC permits the EP to set up a temporary committee of inquiry to investigate alleged contravention and maladministration in the implementation of Community law. Two committees of inquiry have been set up so far: on the Community transit procedure in 1996 and on the bovine spongiform encephalopathy (BSE) epidemic in 1997.

Sessions

Article 197 EC provides that:

> 'The European Parliament shall hold an annual session. It shall meet, without requiring to be convened, on the second Tuesday in March
>
>   The European Parliament may meet in extraordinary session at the request of a majority of its Members or at the request of the Council or of the Commission.'

In practice, the annual session is never closed, except in August. There are monthly plenary sessions, including the budget session, when the MEPs meet for one week. Between each annual session two weeks are set aside for meetings of the parliamentary commissions and a third week for meetings of the political groups. The sessions are open to the general public.

In principle, the EP acts by an absolute majority of votes cast, although in many matters a positive vote by a majority of its Members is essential.

Competences

Under the original Treaties the EP was only a supervisory and advisory body. Gradually in its 'fight for power', which was given extra strength by direct election, the EP has achieved, apart from sharing budgetary power, an important role in the decision-making procedures of the Community and in the conduct of external relations. There are four main functions which the EP exercises at present: political control, budgetary powers, participation in decision-making procedures and in the external relations of the Communities and the Union.

Political control

Political control exercised by the EP over the Commission was first provided in the CS Treaty. Its form has changed over the years. Under the TEU the Commission became directly accountable to the EP. Furthermore, the political control of the EP now extends over other institutions such as the Council, the bodies in charge of political co-operation and the European Council.

General and permanent political control is exercised by the EP over the Commission and the Council by various means. The EP has power to ask questions: written, oral without debates, oral with debates, and at questions-times, etc. Written questions and answers to them are published in the Official Journal. Oral questions without a debate, which must be first approved by the Bureau, may be put to the Council and the Commission during the plenary session. Oral questions with a debate may only be put by a parliamentary commission, a political group or at least 29 MEPs. Sometimes they lead to a resolution adopted by the EP. Question-time, which is modelled on the British parliamentary tradition, was introduced in 1973: in each plenary session a period of time is especially set aside for questions regarding current affairs. The questions are brief and precise and so are the answers. After each answer any Member of the EP may ask an additional question and, if necessary, at the request of 29 MEPs the question-time may lead to a debate. The possibility of asking questions ensures a follow-up to the legislative and administrative activities of the Commission and the Council and imposes an obligation to justify them before the EP. Also, the EP is entitled to ask questions concerning the development of political co-operation by the foreign ministers of the Member States.

Another general method of political control involves the EP's right to examine annual and periodical reports, programmes of action, etc, submitted by various bodies. By virtue of art 200 EC the Commission must submit an annual report on the activities of the Communities. To this the Commission has on its own initiative decided to annex its annual work programme. In February each year both are discussed by the EP and resumed under a resolution on the general policy of the Communities. Also, every six months the Presidency of the Council submits its report, and the foreign minister of the Member State which holds the Presidency presents a report after each session of the European Council, a symbolic gesture instituted after a request of the EP in 1981. The UK Prime Minister, Margaret Thatcher, was the first to establish a formal link between the European Council and the EP.[50] Since 1973 the President of the Council of Foreign Ministers issues an annual declaration addressed to the EP on progress achieved in matters relating to political co-operation.

Another means of political control by the EP consists of the establishment, at the request of a quarter of its members, of a temporary Committee of Inquiry which investigates alleged contraventions or maladministration in the implementation of Community law. This body ceases to exists on the submission of its report.

By virtue of art 21 EC every citizen of the EU has the right to petition the EP and may apply to the Ombudsman appointed by the EP. Furthermore, under art 194 EC any citizen of the EU, and any natural or legal person residing or having its registered office in a Member State, has the right to address, individually or in association with other citizens or persons, a petition to the EP on a matter which comes within the Community's field of activity and which affects him, her or it directly.

In relation to the Commission, the EP has the right to approve the nomination of the President of the Commission and its members (art 214(2) and (3) EC). The extensive interviews of the candidates conducted by the EP in relation to the nomination of the members of Commission appointed in 1995 and 1999 demonstrate that the power is far from being theoretical. In addition, the EP may force the entire Commission to resign but not its President or a particular Commissioner. In order to avoid abuse, art 201 EC laid down stringent requirements as to the motion of censure: a time of reflection of at least three days after the motion has been tabled is required; a two-thirds majority of the votes cast, representing a majority of the MEPs is necessary to carry the motion of censure; and the vote must be open. A motion of censure is an exceptional measure which would lead to a serious crisis in the EU without achieving the desired objective, unless the objective is to remove the whole Commission. The Commission is not a decision-making body and

---

[50] Report Antoniozzi, EP Doc, session 1–737/81.

represents the interests of the Communities. Often the actual culprit is the Council, and the EP must try to seek co-operation with the Commission to secure the interest of the Communities rather than fight it. Also, the final result, of a motion of censure, provided it is successfully carried, is doubtful. The Commissioners are nominated by the Member States. Nothing would prevent the Member States from nominating the same persons, although without the approval of the EP it is difficult to envisage how the Commission would operate. Nevertheless, art 201 EC provides a powerful weapon for the EP in the complex political interaction between the three institutions: the EP, the Council and the Commission. The threat to use the motion of censure was one of the factors that led to the resignation of the Commission on 15 March 1999.

Budgetary powers

Before the Budgetary Treaties of 1970 and 1975 the EP was only consulted on the Communities' budget. Since then it has acquired important powers to control the budget of the Communities and the European Union. Under arts 268 EC the budget comprises: 'All items of revenue and expenditure of the Community including those relating to the European Social Fund' as well as 'administrative expenditure occasioned for the institutions by the provisions of the Treaty on European Union relating to the common foreign and security policy and to co-operation in the fields of justice and home affairs.'

The Commission prepares a preliminary draft, based on estimates of expenditure submitted by each institution, which is placed before the Council no later than 1 October for the following financial year (from 1 January to 31 December). The Council is entitled to make amendments and, acting by qualified majority, approves a draft budget which is forwarded to the EP for its first reading, no later than 5 October. The EP has 45 days to accept, reject or amend the budget and inaction amounts to the acceptance of the submitted draft budget. The power of the EP to amend the budget depends on the classification of the expenditure. Compulsory expenditure (CE), which relates to those items resulting from Treaty obligations or secondary legislation, mainly the financing of the Common Agricultural Policy, etc, cannot be amended by the EP. The EP may, acting by simple majority of MEPs present, adopt proposals for their modification. Non-Compulsory Expenditure (NCE) covers other items such as social and regional policy, research and aid, etc. The EP, acting by the majority of all MEPs, may amend NCE. In both cases the budget, if amended, is sent back to the Council which must within 15 days modify the budget in line with the amendments or reject them by QMV, otherwise the amendments are deemed to be accepted. The modifications proposed by the EP are dealt with according to their content. If the modifications increase CE they are deemed to be rejected unless the Council accepts them within 15 days acting by QMV. In the event of reduction of CE the Council has 15 days to reject them, otherwise they are deemed accepted. However, in respect of CE the Council may, instead of rejecting the modifications, fix different amounts from those submitted in the first draft. If the Council disagrees with the amendments and modification, which is usually the case, the budget is forwarded to the EP for a second reading. At this stage the EP cannot change CE but in relation to NCE it has, acting by a majority of its Members by three-fifths of the votes cast, 15 days to reject or amend the changes made by the Council to its original amendments . After 15 days the budget is automatically adopted or the EP, using the same voting majority, may reject the amendments of the Council.

The power of the EP to have the last word in respect of NCE should be assessed in the light of constant increase of NCE in the Community budget, from 3.5 per cent per annum in 1970 to 23 per cent per annum in 1980 and 42 per cent per annum in 1992. However, NCE cannot go on increasing without limits. Article 272(9) EC provides that 'if … the actual rate of increase in the draft budget established by the Council is over half the maximum rate, the European Parliament may, exercising its right of amendment, further increase the total amount of that expenditure to a limit not exceeding half the maximum rate.'

The most important prerogative of the EP in budgetary matters is that, acting by a majority of its members and two-thirds of the votes cast, it may reject the budget as a whole. If the budget is rejected a new draft must be prepared. The inconvenience this creates for the institutions is significant, as the previous year's budget continues to operate on a one-twelfth basis for each month. It means that the institutions cannot exceed the previous year's limits, although art 273 EC permits an increase in expenditure on the approval of the Council and the EP. The EP rejected the 1980 and 1985 budgets. As a result, inter-institutional agreements on budgetary discipline and improvement of the budgetary procedure were concluded in 1988[51] and 1993.[52] Furthermore, in a Joint Declaration of 30 June 1982, the EP, the Commission and the Council agreed on a common classification of compulsory expenditure.[53]

Legislative powers

Unlike national parliaments the EP neither has the right to initiate legislative measures nor to adopt them acting on its own accord. Since the introduction of direct elections to the EP it sought to impose on the Commission the duty to unofficially consult the EP in respect of its proposals prior to their presentation to the Council. Under pressure the Commission agreed to inform the EP of the content and financial implications of its proposals under consideration. The Treaty of Maastricht grants power to the EP, acting by a majority of its Members, to request that the Commission submits appropriate proposals on matters on which the EP considers that a Community act is required for the purpose of implementing the Treaty (art 192 EC).

In relation to the participation of the EP in the decision-making procedures of the Community (see section 4.9), each revision of the original Treaty has increased the EP's powers in the adoption of legislative measures. At the beginning, the participation of the EP in decision-making was limited to the obligation imposed on the Council to ask the EP for its opinion in only limited areas specified by the Treaty. The SEA introduced the co-operation procedure, and the assent procedure. The TEU strengthened the legislative role of the EP by adding the procedure under art 251 EC, generally known as the co-decision procedure, under which the EP may, in specific situations, bloc the adoption of a measure by the Council. The Treaty of Amsterdam extended the scope of the co-decision procedure, this procedure effectively replacing the co-operation procedure.

---

[51] OJ L185 (1988).
[52] OJ C331 (1993). For details: see Zangl, 'The Inter-institutional Agreement of Budgetary Discipline and Improvement of the Budgetary Procedure' (1989) 26 CMLR 675
[53] OJ C194 (1982).

Role of the European Parliament in external relations of the Communities and the Union

Until the Treaty of Maastricht the EP played a limited role in the conduct of external relations of the Community. Under arts 238 EEC and 206 EA the EP was consulted in relation to association agreements prior to their conclusion but after they were signed. The EP's fight for more involvement in external aspects of the Communities was quite successful. Under the 'Luns/Westerterp'[54] procedure the EP is notified of any envisaged agreements, that is not only association agreements but also commercial and economic agreements between the Communities and third countries, and is able to discuss them before the opening of negotiations. During the negotiations the appropriate parliamentary commission is informed of their progress by the Commission. After the agreement is signed, but before its conclusion, the EP is formally consulted and informed of its content and essential features. The amendment of art 238 EEC by the Treaty of Maastricht gave the EP a real veto in relation to association agreements. The procedure used for this purpose, the assent procedure, requires that the EP approves the agreement by an absolute majority of its Members. Under art 300(3) EC, apart from association agreements, the assent of the EP is required in relation to 'agreements establishing a specific institutional framework by organising co-operation procedures, agreements having important budgetary implications for the Community and agreements entailing amendment of an act adopted under the procedure referred to in art 251'.

In this context the notion of 'important budgetary implications for the Community' is very important. The ECJ clarified its meaning in *European Parliament v Council of the European Union* Case C–189/97 [1999] ECR I–4741. In this case the European Parliament brought an action for annulment of Council Regulation 408/97 regarding the conclusion on 24 February 1999 of an agreement on co-operation in the sea fisheries sector between the EC and Mauritania, under which EC vessels are allowed to fish off the cost of Mauritania in exchange for payments from the Community budget. The European Parliament contested the legal basis of the Regulation, arguing that the agreement had important budgetary implications for the Community and therefore should be concluded under art 300(3) EC, which involves the EP's assent instead of art 37 EC, according to which the Council is required to obtain the EP's opinion within the simple consultation procedure.

The case marks an important victory for the EP in its struggle for more power, even though its application was dismissed. The ECJ was asked to define the notion of 'important budgetary implications for the Community' following from which the EP powers would be either greater or lesser depending upon what is included within the definition. In order to assess the budgetary implications of international agreements the EP laid down three criteria: the first based on a comparison between the annual financial cost of an international agreement; the second referring to the relative share of expenditure under the agreement in relation to appropriations of the same kind entered under the budget heading concerned; and the third based on the rate of increase in expenditure under the agreement as compared to the previous agreement. The EP concluded that the application of these criteria to the agreement between the Community and Mauritania showed that it had important budgetary implications for the Community because the payments from the

---

[54] The surnames of the Presidents of the Council who accepted the participation of the EP in external matters on behalf of the Council.

Community budget would represent 20 per cent of the budgetary outlay approved by the Community for its external policy. The Council rejected the assessment made by the EP and referred to the overall budget of the Community under which payments to Mauritania represent only 0.07 per cent of the budget and therefore could not be considered as having important financial implications for the EC.

Thus, the ECJ had to resolve very important political and legal questions: the balance of power between the EP and the Council and the possible judicial revision of the EC Treaty in respect of external powers of the EP. If the ECJ had approved the arguments of the EP the latter would have been entitled to negotiate and conclude agreements having important budgetary implications for the Community, including agreements regarding common commercial policy which are expressly excluded from the participation of the EP by art 303(3) EC.

The ECJ rejected the arguments of the EP but did not follow the reasoning of the Council. It held that relatively modest annual expenditure may, over a number of years, represent a significant budgetary outlay. Although the ECJ did not strengthen the external prerogatives of the EP, it warned the Council that if the Council had taken into consideration the comparison of the expenditure under the agreement with the amount of the appropriations designed to finance the Community's external operations (the criterion favoured by the ECJ) it 'would also have been entitled to take the view that the fisheries agreement with Mauritania did not have important budgetary implications for the Community within the meaning of the second subparagraph of [art 300(3) EC]'. This means that the ECJ will approach each case separately in order to assess whether an agreement in question has important budgetary implications. This will force the Council to increase co-operation with the EP in respect of international agreements having important budgetary implications for the Community. Consequently, the EP has indirectly achieved its objective.

4.5 The Court of Justice of the European Communities (ECJ)

The ECJ is located in Luxembourg. It was created separately under each founding Treaty – CS, EC and EA – although under the 1957 Convention on Certain Institutions Common to the European Communities it is recognised as a common institution for all three Communities. The Protocol on the Statute of the ECJ annexed to each founding Treaty which regulates the organisation and competences of the ECJ is still in each case a formally distinct legal instrument. For that reason the TEU provides that Title III of each Protocol, which concerns the procedure before the ECJ, may be modified by the Council acting by unanimity at the request of the ECJ and after consultation with the Commission and the EP. However, there are the same Rules of Procedure[55] for the three Communities. They are adopted by the ECJ but require the unanimous approval of the Council. The ECJ's main task is to ensure that in the interpretation and application of the Treaties the law is observed.

---

[55] The Rules of Procedure, modified in order to take into consideration the accession of Austria, Finland and Sweden to the Communities, were also designed to make the work of both courts more efficient: Modifications of the Rules of Procedure of the ECJ of 11 March 1997 and the Rules of Procedure of the CFI of 12 March 1997: OJ L103 (1997). On 24 May 2000 the ECJ's Rules of Procedure were further amended: OJ L122 (2000).

Composition

The ECJ consists of 15 judges and 8 Advocates-General,[56] both nominated by the Member States by common accord. The number of judges and Advocates-General may be increased by the Council acting unanimously at the request of the ECJ, especially in order to ease the Court's workload or to accommodate a Member State which considers that it is under-represented in the ECJ. Article 223 EC provides that the judges and the Advocates-General are chosen from persons 'whose independence is beyond doubt and who possess the qualifications required for appointment to the highest judicial offices in their respective countries or who are jurisconsults of recognised competence.' The inclusion of jursiconsults allows academics, civil service lawyers and jurists, that is lawyers without professional qualification, to be appointed even though in their own country they would not be eligible for the highest judicial offices. There is one judge from each Member State, although no provision of the Treaties provides for a national balance. In practice, it facilitates the work of the ECJ to have a judge who is an expert in national law of a Member State and in addition speaks the language of that State. The originality of the composition of the ECJ is emphasised by the presence of Advocates-General, who are also members of the Court. By virtue of art 222 EC the function of the Advocate-General is the following:

> 'It shall be the duty of the Advocate-General, acting with complete impartiality and independence, to make, in open court, reasoned submissions on cases brought before the Court of Justice, in order to assist the Court in the performance of the task assigned to it in art 220.'

Thus, the function of the Advocate-General is similar to that of the *commissaire du gouvernement* in the French *Conseil d'Etat* (the highest administrative court). Initially their existence was justified by the importance of an action for annulment in the CS Treaty.[57] An Advocate-General is required to be neutral as between the applicant and the defendant. He represents the interests of justice. He reviews the factual and legal aspects of the case and must reach a conclusion which constitutes his recommendation of how the ECJ should decide the case. The conclusion is very detailed and often suggests original and new legal approaches to the disputed matter, but is not binding on the ECJ. Even if rejected by the ECJ in a particular case, the opinion of an Advocate-General may be later reconsidered in a similar case since it often indicates the direction in which the Community should evolve. Furthermore, the opinion is very useful to help understand the case as the judgments of the ECJ are very short.

The posts of Advocates-General are allocated according to a non-written agreement between the Member States, that is, one from each of the five largest Member States – Germany, France, Italy, Spain and the UK – and the remaining on a rotating basis.

---

[56] Article 222 EC provides that a ninth A-G shall be appointed from 1 January 1995 to 6 October 2000.

[57] For details see A Barov, *Le Commissaire du Gouvernement Devant le Conseil d'Etat et L'Avocat General Pres de la Court de Justice des Communautes Europeennes*, Revue International de Droit Compare, 1974, p809; N Brown, *The Court of Justice of the European Communities*, 3rd ed, 1989, p53.

Term of office

Judges and Advocates-General are appointed for six years, renewable without any limitation. Usually, they hold the office for two terms. In order to ensure continuity in the work of the ECJ there is a rolling programme of replacement of some of the judges and Advocates-General every three years.

The judges and Advocates-General have privileges and immunities similar to other officials of the Communities and additionally are immune from legal proceedings in respect of acts performed in their official capacity, including words spoken or written, but this may be waived by the ECJ. In criminal proceedings in any of the Member States against a judge or Advocate-General, provided the immunity is waived, he must be tried only by the court competent to judge the members of the highest national judiciary. Each judge or Advocate-General before taking up his post at the ECJ must take a solemn oath that he will perform his duties impartially and conscientiously and preserve the secrecy of the deliberations of the Court. The independence of judges or Advocates-General requires that they cannot, during their term of office, hold any political or administrative post or engage in any occupation incompatible with their mandate unless an exceptional exemption is granted by the ECJ. They must behave with integrity and discretion both during and after their term of office.

A judge or an Advocate-General may resign but should hold his office until his successor is appointed. Usual disciplinary measures apply to both judges and Advocates-general. A unanimous opinion of all judges and Advocates-General (other than the person concerned) is required in order to decide that he no longer fulfils the requisite conditions or meets the obligations arising from his office and thus should be disciplined, dismissed or deprived of his right to pension or other benefits.

Organisation

The ECJ remains permanently in session although hearings do not usually take place during judicial vacations. The duration of judicial vacations is determined by the ECJ in the light of the needs of the Court's business. In cases of urgency, the President may convene the ECJ during vacations.

The President of the ECJ is elected for a period of three years (which is renewable) by the judges of the ECJ from among their own number by an absolute majority vote in a secret ballot. The President directs the judicial business and administration of the Court, chairs hearings and deliberations and exercises its competences in relation to applications for interim measures. The President's administrative functions consist of the supervision of the services of the ECJ.

The Registrar is appointed for six years by the ECJ after consultation with the Advocates-General. He is in charge of the day-to-day administration of the ECJ, financial management and accounts. He assists the ECJ in the acts of procedure, that is the acceptance, transmission and custody of documents, and is present in person or by a substitute at all hearings of the ECJ as a chamber and all meetings of the ECJ apart from the disciplinary proceedings and matters outside its competence. He is also in charge of archives and of the publication of the decisions rendered by the ECJ. Officials and other employees attached to the ECJ are accountable to him under the authority of the President of the ECJ.

Each judge and Advocate-General is assisted by three *référendaires* who usually have the same nationality as their senior and form his *Cabinet*. They are lawyers, usually with a Doctorate in Law. They prepare pre-trial studies on the legal aspects of the case at issue and assist in the drafting of judgments and opinions.

In principle, the ECJ sits in plenary session. However, in order to facilitate and accelerate proceedings, art 221 EC allows the Court to form chambers consisting of three, five or seven judges, either to undertake certain preparatory inquiries or to adjudicate a particular category of cases. The frequent use of chambers was approved by the Council in its Decision of 26 November 1974[58] following a request by the ECJ in order to cope with its increasing workload. As a result, the ECJ may forward to its chambers all preliminary questions and all other cases when the applicant is an individual or an undertaking if it considers that the importance or the complexity of the matter does not require that the ECJ sit in plenary session, and provided there is no opposition from either a Member State or a Community institution.[59] In any event, a chamber may decide to send the case back to the ECJ if necessary. The Treaty has recognised the tendency of the ECJ to work in chambers. By virtue of art 221 EC:

> 'The Court of Justice shall sit in plenary session when a Member State or a Community institution that is a party to the proceedings so requests.'

In all other cases the ECJ decides whether or not to sit in plenary session.

Functioning

The quorum for a plenary session is nine judges, for chambers of three or five judges it is three and for chambers of seven judges it is five. In addition, art 15 of the Protocol on the Statute of the ECJ provides that the decisions of the ECJ will only be valid when an uneven number of judges sit in deliberations. The President has no casting vote.

A party to the proceedings cannot apply for a change in composition of the ECJ or its chamber on the basis that there is a judge who has the nationality of that party or that there is no judge from the Member State of that party. In order to ensure that there is no conflict of interest, a judge or Advocate-General is not permitted to take part in a case in which he has previously participated as agent or adviser or has acted for one of the parties or in any other capacity. Also, the President of the ECJ may, for some special reason, decide that a judge or Advocate-General should not take part in the disposal of a particular case.

Procedure

Initially, this must be considered in three parts as follows:

Traditional procedure
The procedure before the ECJ has been inspired by that of the French *Conseil d'Etat*. There are two stages in the proceedings: written and oral. The written stage begins when the

---

[58] OJ L318 (1974). This resulted in the modification of the Rules of Procedure of the ECJ: OJ L328 (1979).
[59] But not if the case is a staff dispute between the Community and its officials or servants.

application from the claimant is received by the Registrar. The application should contain the name and permanent address of the parties, the subject-matter of the dispute, the legal arguments invoked by the applicant and the form of the order sought by him. It must be lodged within the time limit prescribed for such action by the Treaty. Once it is filed with the Registrar, the President of the ECJ appoints from among the judges a judge-rapporteur who prepares a preliminary report on the case. The defendant is notified and has one month to submit a written defence. Subsequently, each party may submit one further written pleading, that is, the applicant may reply to the defendant's defence, and the defendant may lodge a rejoinder (reply to the applicant's reply to his defence). As a result, there are usually two written pleadings from each party (but see below). After the written part is closed the judge-rapporteur submits his report to the ECJ which may recommend certain procedural steps, such as the ordering of a preparatory inquiry, witnesses to be examined, experts' reports, inspection of a place, etc. The oral procedure commences with the reading of the preliminary report of the judge-rapporteur. This is forwarded to the parties before the opening of the oral stage, and comprises the summary of the case, the legal arguments invoked by the parties, and the factual situation based on the evidence presented during the written stage and preparatory enquiry. The next step is the hearing of the parties through their representatives: the Court may also examine experts and witnesses (art 29 of the Protocol on the Statute of the ECJ). At the conclusion of the oral stage the representatives of the parties make closing speeches to the Court, first the claimant and then the defendant. At the end, the Advocate-General delivers his opinion. Usually, at that stage the oral proceedings are closed (although it is still possible in certain circumstances to reopen the oral procedure) and the ECJ proceeds to deliberate on the case. The deliberations must remain confidential. Neither the Advocate-General nor translators, nor legal secretaries are present. During the deliberations the judges will try to reach consensus on the matter. If not, the decision is reached by a majority vote. There are no dissenting or separate opinions, it is a single collegiate judgment. It must state the reasons on which it is based and must be signed by all judges who took part in the deliberations. It is delivered in open court and binding from that date.

Amendments introduced on 1 July 2000

On 1 July 2000 both the ECJ and the CFI amended their Rules of Procedure after obtaining consent of the Council on 16 May 2000.[60] The amendments do not affect the majority of cases but provide necessary flexibility to render the system more effective. The main changes in respect of the ECJ are:

1. the possibility of answering a preliminary reference by a reasoned order if the answer can easily be inferred from existing case law;
2. the application of an accelerated procedure for urgent preliminary references consisting of prioritising certain cases and avoiding various stages of the written procedure;
3. the reduction of the length of the written procedure in all cases (avoiding the second exchange of pleadings);

---

[60] OJ L122 (2000).

4. the possibility of eliminating the oral hearing unless the parties submit reasoned applications setting out the points on which they wish to be heard;
5. the possibility for the judge-rapporteur or Advocate-General to request information from the parties at an early stage;
6. the possibility for the ECJ to request clarification from national courts in art 234 EC proceedings.

In respect of the CFI the main amendments are:

1. the introduction of an expedited procedure in respect of actions for annulment under art 230 EC brought by non-privileged applicants;
2. the reduction of the length of the written procedure where appropriate by elimination of the second exchange of pleadings;
3. the shortening of the time limit for interventions by Member States and third parties affected by the dispute from three months to one month from the publication of the notice in the Official Journal;
4. the use of modern technology (eg documents may be submitted by fax).

Both courts are empowered to issue practice directions without further authorisation from the Council. The above amendments allow the Community courts to deal with each case according to its peculiarity, dealing speedily with simple cases and accelerating and prioritising urgent cases.

Long-term reforms

The above amendments result from the fact that the ever-increasing number of cases had caused long delays in the delivering of judgments. This adversely affect the protection of rights of individuals as justice delayed is justice denied. Both the ECJ and the CFI acknowledged the need for reforms.[61] At the time of writing long-term reforms are under consideration by the Inter-Governmental Conference (IGC). The IGC seeks to redefine the role of the ECJ and CFI, their relationship and the relationship between the Community courts and national courts. The IGC envisages such radical reforms as amendments to art 234 EC which, on the one hand, would increase the jurisdiction of national courts to determine matters of EU law without reference to the ECJ, and, on the other hand, confer jurisdiction on the CFI in respect of preliminary references. Additionally, the possibility of dispensing with the Advocate-General's Opinion in some cases and the establishment of a mechanism reducing the number of appeals from the CFI to the ECJ are under consideration.

There are a number of specific issues in respect of the procedure before the ECJ which require some comment: the parties to the proceedings, the language of the proceedings, the costs and the intervention of third parties.

---

[61] See paper on the *Future of the Judicial System of the European Union*: published in May 1999 by the ECJ and CFI.

Parties to the proceedings

The parties must be represented even in actions for annulment under art 230 EC. The Community institutions and the Member States must be represented by an agent appointed for the particular case (usually a member of the legal services of the institution concerned) and by a member of the legal services of the foreign ministry of a Member State. Individuals, and undertakings must be represented by a lawyer authorised to practise before a court of a Member State. However, such a person cannot represent himself. In *Orlando Lopes* Cases C–174 and 175/96P [1996] ECR I–6401 the ECJ rejected an application submitted by a Portuguese lawyer, who refused to be represented by another lawyer, on the ground that no one is permitted to represent himself.[62] University law teachers who are nationals of a Member State whose law accords them the right of audience (Germany) may represent clients before the ECJ. They enjoy rights and immunities necessary to the independent exercise of their duties.

Language

The ECJ is multilingual. Any official language may be chosen but there is an important limitation. Only one language may be used as the procedural language in a particular case. In the case of an individual or an undertaking or a Member State it is the language of the defendant. If a Community Institution is a party to the proceedings, the applicant may chose the language of the procedure. All procedure is conducted in that language: written pleadings, examination of witnesses, etc. The Rules of Procedure have introduced some changes in respect of the choice of the procedural language. Any derogation from the rules applicable to the choice of the procedural language is decided by the President of the ECJ or the CFI and not by the courts themselves, unless the other party to the proceedings opposes such derogation: art 29(2) Rules of Procedure of the ECJ 1997 and art 35(2) Rules of Procedure of the CFI 1997. In the case of a preliminary ruling the procedural language is that of the court or of the tribunal which referred the question to the ECJ. At the well justified request of one of the parties to the main proceedings before a national court, and provided the view of the other party and the Advocate-General are duly taken into account, the President of the ECJ may authorise the use of a different language in the oral procedure.

The working language of the ECJ is French and, inter alia, the deliberations are conducted in that language.

Costs

The ECJ does not charge parties for its services although in exceptional circumstances they may pay the fees, for example for translation of certain documents. The ECJ, however, determines which party should pay the cost of the proceedings. Usually it is the losing party, although the ECJ may decide otherwise. It is interesting to note that the Rules of Procedure of the ECJ have adopted the German and Italian system in respect of fees paid to a lawyer of the winning party. Thus, the losing party pays the fees of the experts, witnesses, his own lawyer and the lawyer of the other party. Usually, the ECJ does not fix the costs of the

---

[62] It seems that the applicant was not only stubborn, as his appeal from the decision of the CFI was submitted twice and consequently refused on the same ground, but he was also disbarred from the Portuguese Bar: *Europe*, February, 1997, no 42.

proceedings and leaves this question to the parties, although in the case of a disagreement, the party concerned may apply to the ECJ which will settle the matter by an order

Intervention of a third party

The ECJ permits the intervention of a third party in proceedings which have already commenced. Member States and Community institutions may intervene without establishing an interest in the result of the case. Any other person, that is an individual and an undertaking, is required to justify an interest and cannot intervene in cases between Member States, between Community institutions and between Member States and Community institutions. Individuals and undertakings may obtain the necessary information concerning the case from the Official Journal. The Registrar must publish a notice in Official Journal which specifies the date on which the application was lodged, gives the name and the address of the parties, indicates the subject-matter of the dispute and the form of the order sought by the parties and contains a brief statement of the pleas in law on which the application is based. The application to intervene must be limited to supporting the form of order sought by one of the parties and must be lodged within one month of publication of the notice in the Official Journal. A modification of the Rules of Procedure shortened the time-limit from three months to one month.

Revision and interpretation of judgments

There is no appeal from the judgments rendered by the ECJ. The only possibility is the revision of a particular judgment, although conditions for this are very stringent. An application for revision of a judgment will only be admissible by the ECJ 'on discovery of a fact which is of such a nature as to be a decisive factor, and which, when the judgment was given, was unknown to the Court and to the party claiming the revision'. Furthermore, the application must be lodged within ten years from the date of the judgment and within three months of the discovery of that fact: *Belgium* Case 1/60 [1962] ECR 331.

A party to the proceedings before the ECJ or a Community institution may, provided it demonstrates an interest in the decision, ask the ECJ for the interpretation of a judgment if its meaning or scope gives rise to uncertainty.[63] In *Assider v High Authority* Case 5/55 [1954–56] ECR 125 the ECJ emphasised that 'the only parts of a judgment which can be interpreted are those which express the judgment of the Court in the dispute which has been submitted for its final decision and those parts of the reasoning upon which this decision is based and which are, therefore, essential to it ... the Court does not have to interpret those passages which are incidental and which complete or explain the basic reasoning.' Thus, only the operative part of the judgment, the *ratio decidendi*, will be interpreted by the ECJ. The request for interpretation may concern the effect of the judgment but not its application or the legal implications arising from it: *Court of Auditors v Williams* Case 9/81 [1983] ECR 2859.

---

[63] Article 40 of the Protocol on the Statute of the ECJ; see also *Société Anonyme Générale Sucrière* Case 41/73 [1977] ECR 445.

Jurisdiction of the ECJ

By virtue of art 220 EC:

> 'The Court of Justice shall ensure that in the interpretation and application of this Treaty the law is observed.'

The ECJ exercises its powers under the conditions and for the purposes provided for in the Treaties.

In 1999 the ECJ brought 395 cases to a close, delivered 235 judgments and made 143 orders. The number of new cases increased from 485 in 1998 to 543 in 1999. On 4 July 2000, 3,580 cases were under examination: 480 concerning France, 396 Italy and 210 the UK.[64]

There are three categories of proceedings which can be brought before the ECJ: contentious, non-contentious and consultative. Under the Treaty of Amsterdam the ECJ has acquired limited jurisdiction under Title IV of the EC Treaty and in respect of Pillar 3 (see Chapter 3).

Contentious proceedings

In contentious proceedings the ECJ is seised by the parties themselves and decides the matter in the first and last resort, that is the ECJ decides on the merits and delivers a final judgment. This category of dispute is the most common and comprises:

1. actions for annulment of an act having legal effect adopted by a Community institution (arts 230 EC and 33 CS);
2. actions for failure to act brought against a Community institution which has a positive obligation to act imposed by the Treaties (arts 232 EC and 35 CS);
3. pleas of illegality (art 241 EC);
4. actions brought by any natural or legal person to make good damage caused by the Community institutions or by their servants in the performance of their duties – non-contractual liability of the Community (arts 235 and 288(2) EC);
5. action against sanctions imposed by the Community institutions (art 229 EC);
6. appeals from the Court of First Instance including staff disputes (art 236 EC);
7. actions against a Member State for failure to fulfil a Treaty obligation (arts 226 and 227 EC and 88 CS);
8. actions against a Member State for failure to fulfil its obligation under the Statute of the European Investment Bank and the European Central Bank (art 237 EC);
9. actions based on the arbitration clauses contained in a contract by or on behalf of the Community (art 238 EC);
10. actions brought by one Member State against another in the context of a dispute which relates to the subject-matter of the Treaty on the basis of a special agreement between the parties (art 239 EC);
11. applications for interim measures (art 243 EC);
12. actions brought in relation to disputes arising from the agreement on the setting up of the European Economic Area.

---

[64] http://curia.eu.int/en/cp/info.

Non-contentious proceedings

At the request of a national court, the ECJ rules on questions of Community law which have arisen in the national forum. The judgment on the principal issue is given by a national court, and the ECJ answers only the referred question. Non-contentious proceedings comprise any of the following:

1. preliminary rulings concerning the validity of an act adopted by a Community institution (art 41 CS);
2. preliminary rulings concerning the interpretation of EC law and of acts of the Community institutions and the validity of such acts (arts 234 EC and 150 EA);
3. preliminary rulings concerning the interpretation of certain Conventions concluded among the Member States but outside the Community framework, such as the Brussels Convention 1968, the Lugano Convention on Recognition and the Enforcement of Judgments in Civil and Commercial Matters 1988, the Rome Convention on the Law Applicable to Contractual Obligations 1980, etc.

Consultative jurisdiction

Despite its name, the consultative jurisdiction of the ECJ results in binding decisions, although it is not necessary for a dispute to exist on the matter brought to the attention of the ECJ even though in practice this is often the case. The consultative jurisdiction is provided for all three Communities: art 95(3) and (4) CS, arts 103 and 104 EA and art 300(6) EC. In the case of the EC it arises in the context of international agreements between the Community and a third country or countries or international organisations. The Council, the Commission or a Member State may ask the ECJ for its opinion as to whether the envisaged agreement is compatible with the provisions of the Treaty. If the ECJ considers that the agreement in question is contrary to EC law the only way for that agreement to enter into force, apart from its renegotiation, is to revise the Treaty in accordance with art 48 EU. The consultative jurisdiction of the ECJ has become quite popular in recent years.

4.6 The Court of First Instance (CFI)

The CFI is attached to the ECJ. It was created to ease the workload of the ECJ and to enable the latter to concentrate on its fundamental tasks without affecting the effectiveness and the quality of the Community judicial system. It was established by Council Decision 88/591 of 24 October 1988.[65]

It is made up of 15 judges nominated by common accord of the Member States, one from each Member State, although there is no nationality requirement for their appointment. Judges are appointed for a renewable term of six years and a partial replacement takes place every three years. They are subject to the same rules with regard to nomination, privileges, immunities and disciplinary measures as are judges of the ECJ. However, it is not necessary for judges of the CFI to possess the qualifications required for appointment to the highest judicial offices in their respective countries but only those for

---

[65] OJ L319 (1988).

the exercise of judicial office. There are no Advocates-General appointed to assist the CFI but in some cases the judges are called upon to perform the task of an Advocate-General. The CFI sits in chambers of three judges in cases concerning Community staff and of five judges in all other cases, but if an important and complex legal matter is under consideration the CFI may sit in plenary session.

In order to ease the workload of the CFI, it was, under the Council Decision of 26 April 1999 (which entered into force on 1 July 1999), permitted to sit 'when constituted by a single judge'. A judge of the CFI may sit as a single judge only in cases which do not raise any difficulties in law or in fact, which are of limited importance and which do not involve any special circumstances. This applies to:

1. cases concerning officials of the Communities;
2. actions brought by natural or legal persons against the Community institutions under arts 230 and 288 EC, provided that those actions raise only questions already clarified by established case law or form part of a series of cases in which the same relief is sought and of which one has already been finally decided;
3. cases in which the CFI has jurisdiction to give judgments pursuant to an arbitration clause contained in a contract concluded by or on behalf of the Community.

However, certain matters cannot be delegated to a single judge – for example, concerning the implementation of the rules on competition and merger control, regarding aid granted by States and relating to measures to protect trade.

In conformity with the Rules of Procedure of the Court of First Instance a chamber made up of three judges before which a case is pending may decide unanimously to delegate it to a single judge. The first time a single judge at the Court of First Instance of the European Communities delivered a judgment was in *Cotrim* v *CEDEFOB* Case T–180/98 Judgment of 28 October 1999 (nyr). In this case the judgment was delivered only six weeks after the hearing date and one year from the date on which the case was brought before the CFI, as compared to 18 months for similar cases brought before chambers of the CFI.

The CFI has its own Registrar, appointed by its judges, who is in charge of the judicial and practical organisation of the Court. The procedure before the CFI is the same as before the ECJ.

The transfer of jurisdiction to the CFI is based on art 225 EC. It provides that the Council acting unanimously at the request of the ECJ and after consulting the EP and the Commission shall determine the classes of action or proceedings within the jurisdiction of the CFI. As a result, the CFI has jurisdiction in the following matters:

1. disputes between the Communities and their staff (arts 236 EC and 152 CS);
2. under Council Decision of 8 June 1993[66] all actions under arts 230, 232 and 235 EC brought by any natural or legal person against a Community institution under any of the three Treaties;
3. disputes concerning the application of the competition rules to undertakings;
4. actions against the Commission by virtue of arts 33 and 35 CS brought by undertakings and associations of undertakings concerning the application of arts 50 and 57–66 CS

---

[66] OJ L144 (1993).

(levies, production, prices, restrictive agreements, decisions or practices and concentrations).

The transfer of jurisdiction may be extended to other areas with an exception established in art 225(1) EC which clearly states that only the ECJ has jurisdiction to hear and determine questions referred for a preliminary ruling under art 234 EC.

4.7 The Court of Auditors

The Court of Auditors was established in 1975, constituted in 1977 and recognised as a Community institution by the Treaty of Maastricht. It has no judicial functions, thus it is not really a court but an independent auditing body, the Community's financial watchdog.

The Court of Auditors is composed of 15 members, one from each Member State, although there is no specific requirement as to their nationality. Each member must either have belonged to a national external audit body or be 'especially qualified' to carry out the audit. Their independence must be beyond doubt. They are nominated by Member States and appointed by the Council, acting unanimously after consulting the EP, for a six-year renewable term. The usual limitations aimed at ensuring the independence of the members of the Court of Auditors as well as privileges, immunities, disciplinary measures, etc, apply to them. The main task of the Court of Auditors is to ensure that the financial affairs of the Community are properly managed and, especially, that all revenue has been received and all expenditure incurred in a lawful and regular manner. At the end of a fiscal year the Court of Auditors produces annual accounts which, together with the replies of the institutions, are published in the Official Journal. Furthermore, at the request of the institutions the Court of Auditors may prepare special reports and opinions. It may also on its own initiative draft reports on the financial implications of certain programmes or measures envisaged by the Community. In order to fulfil its tasks the Court has extensive investigative powers. The importance of the Court of Auditors has been recognised by the Treaty of Amsterdam. Further, it has *locus standi* under art 230 EC for the purpose of protecting its prerogatives.

4.8 Other Community bodies

The Treaty of Maastricht established a number of new bodies, such as the Ombudsman, the Economic and Social Committee and the Committee of the Regions. It also provided for the creation of new institutions within the framework of EMU: the European Central Bank, the European Monetary Institute, the European System of Central Banks. Their role has been strengthened by the Treaty of Amsterdam.

The Economic and Social Committee (arts 257–262 EC)

The Economic and Social Committee comprises 222 representatives of various categories of economic and social activity, especially, farmers, producers, workers, dealers, craftsman, professionals, as well as the representatives of the general public from all Member States – 24 from each of the largest Member States, 12 or fewer from others. They are appointed by the Council for a four-year renewable term. The Economic and Social Committee is divided into three groups: 'employers' comprising the representatives of employers' organisations and chambers of commerce; 'workers' comprising trade union representatives; and 'various interests' made up of representatives of small businesses, farmers, the professions, craftsmen, environmental and consumer groups, etc. The members of each group are spread over nine working sections, each in charge of a specific policy area. It is an advisory body entrusted with the task of expressing the opinions of these groups in respect of legislative measures prepared by the Council and the Commission, although its opinions are non-binding. Under the Treaty of Amsterdam the EP may also consult it if it deems such consultation appropriate. The consultation of the Economic and Social Committee is compulsory for the Commission when the latter prepares proposals in a number of areas such as the CAP, the right of establishment, the mobility of labour, transport, approximation of laws, social policy, the European Social Fund and vocational training. The Treaty of Amsterdam added new areas on which consultation of the Economic and Social Committee is mandatory. They are: the guidelines and incentives for employment (arts 128 and 129 EC); the social legislation resulting from agreements between management and labour (arts 136–143 EC); measures implementing art 141 EC; and measures relating to public health (art 152 EC). In other areas consultation is optional. Furthermore, the Committee may issue opinions on its own initiative. The Committee has played a very constructive role within the Community as it represents the citizens of the EU and their interests, and thus constitutes a step towards a people's union.

The Committee of the Regions (arts 263–265 EC)

The Committee of the Regions consists of 222 representatives of regional and local bodies of the Member States. Their terms of appointment, office, privileges, etc, are similar to those of the Economic and Social Committee. However, its organisational structure is, under the Treaty of Amsterdam, separate from that of the Economic and Social Committee. The Protocol attached to the EU Treaty providing for a common organisation has been repealed. The Committee of the Regions was created to allow the regions and local authorities to influence and participate in the Community legislative process. Before the entry into force of the Treaty of Amsterdam the Committee of the Regions had to be consulted in a limited number of areas, fewer than in the case of the Economic and Social Committee, mainly in public health, culture and education. Under the Treaty of Amsterdam the Commission must consult the Committee of the Regions in many areas, including all new areas of compulsory consultation provided for the Economic and Social Committee, matters involving the protection of environment (art 175), the Social Fund (art 148), vocational training (art 150), cross-border co-operation (art 265(1)) and transport (arts 71 and 80).

In others areas the Commission, the EP and the Council may consult the Committee. If the Economic and Social Committee is consulted pursuant to art 262 EC (compulsory consultation) the Committee of the Regions must be informed by the Commission or the Council of the request for an opinion and may, if specific regional interests are involved, issue an opinion on the matter. It may also give an opinion on its own[67] but as in the case of the Economic and Social Committee its opinions are not binding. Also, if the Council or the Commission fixes a time limit for the submission of an opinion by the Committee of the Regions or the Economic and Social Committee this may not be less than one month from the notification of the request. The absence of an opinion will not prevent the Council or the Commission from further action.

Other bodies

Among other Communities bodies it is worth mentioning the specialised advisory committees created on the ground of art 209 EC, such as the Committee of Transport under art 79 EC, the Monetary Committee under art 114 EC, special committees set up on the grounds of arts 133 EC and 300 EC, the Committee on the European Social Fund under art 147 EC, and the Scientific and Technical Committee under art 134 EA. In addition, there are a number of bodies created for the administration of Community affairs. Subsequent to the agreement reached in 1993[68] on the location of their seats, a number of bodies were established such as the European Environmental Agency, the European Training Foundation, Office for Veterinary and Plant Health Inspection, etc. In addition, the Community operates a number of funding programmes which benefit both Member States and countries outside the EU, the most important being its structural funds: the European Social Fund, the European Agricultural Guidance and Guarantee Fund and the European Regional Development Fund. With respect to programmes designated for businesses located outside the EU, two are especially important: PHARE (Aid and Assistance for the Reconstruction of the Economy in Central and Eastern Europe) and TACIS (Technical Assistance to the CIS and Georgia).

4.9 Legislative procedures

The legislative process of the Community is very complex for two reasons: first, the revisions of the decision-making procedures in order to give more powers to the EP have led to compromises of extreme complexity; and, second, the tension between inter-governmentalism and supra-nationality in the context of a democratic deficit which the EP, the only democratically elected body in the Community, claims to be able and entitled to legitimately overcome, is reflected in those procedures. The Treaty of Amsterdam simplified the legislative process in the Community in two ways. First, the Treaty of Amsterdam virtually abandoned the co-operation procedure introduced by the Single European Act. This procedure did not substantially limit powers of the Council as the last word belonged to the Council which enjoyed exclusive legislative competences and could override the EP and adopt the disputed measure. Now, this procedure only applies to certain aspects of economic

---

[67] See Hessel and Mortelmans, 'Decentralised Government and Community Law: Conflicting Institutional Developments (1995) 30 CMLR 905.
[68] Decision of the Representatives of the Governments of the Member States on the Location of Seats of Certain Bodies and Departments: OJ C323 (1993).

and monetary union. Second, the Treaty of Amsterdam simplifies the co-operation procedure by removing the possibility of third readings.

The legislative process in the Community involves the co-operation of different institutions even though their contribution varies.

In principle, the legislative process is commenced by the Commission which initiates legislation, although the Council (under art 208 EC) and the EP (under art 192(2) EC) are entitled to ask the Commission to prepare any proposals considered desirable for the attainment of the objectives of the Treaty. Also, in rare cases the Council may, acting by QMV with at least ten Member States in favour, adopt legislation without a previous proposal from the Commission: art 205(2) EC.

The adoption of a proposal by the Commission starts when an appropriate directorate-general formulates a broad outline of an envisaged measure. The draft proposal is then submitted to the widest possible consultation with all interested parties, including governmental authorities, professional bodies, experts, consumer groups, etc, and the Commission's own legal service. This requirement of consultation has been strengthened by the principle of subsidiarity. The external and internal opinions often lead to redrafting or even abandonment of a proposal. Provided this stage has been successfully completed and results in a firm proposal, it is then forwarded to all directorates-general for assessment and amendments. In the light of comments provided by the directorates-general the proposal may be changed accordingly. In this revised version it is then submitted to the College of Commissioners which decides by a simple majority vote whether or not the Commission should proceed. If in the affirmative, the proposal is then submitted to the Council, translated into all official languages of the Community and published in the Official Journal.

Upon receipt of the proposal the Council sends it to the COREPER for further study. In practice, the Commission also forwards the proposal to the EP. Indeed, the EP has gradually extended its consultation prerogatives to areas in which their consultation is not mandatory or otherwise required by the Treaty. This new 'acquisition' by the EP of powers in respect of the legislative process in the Community was consolidated by the Code of Conduct adopted jointly by the Commission and the EP on 9 March 1995.[69]

The inter-institutional triangle – the Commission, the Council and the EP – in the decision-making process constitutes one element common to all types of procedure, although the degree of the actual involvement of the EP, as well as the detail of the Council's vote (whether by a unanimity, QMV or a simple majority), varies depending on the area of policy concerned.

There are three main decision-making procedures in the Community: the consultation procedure, the co-decision procedure and the assent procedure.

Consultation procedure

The consultation procedure was the only one under the original Treaty involving the EP. It requires the Council to obtain the opinion of the European Parliament. This procedure starts with the submission of a formal proposal by the Commission to the Council. The

---

[69] Its text is in *French in Revue Trimestriel de Droit Européen*, 1995, p338.

latter must, and this is mandatory, ask the EP for its opinion on the proposal. The Council is not obliged to follow the opinion delivered by the EP but it must receive it. In *Roquette Frères* Cases 138 and 139/79 [1980] ECR 3393 the Council adopted Regulation 1293/79 on the basis of art 43(2) EC which required the consultation of the EP, but without receiving the opinion from the latter. The Council argued that it requested the opinion but the EP did not reply and thus by its own conduct, and knowing the urgency of the matter, the EP made it impossible for the Council to comply with the consultation requirement. The ECJ held that when the Treaty provides for the consultation of the EP, this requirement must be strictly complied with since 'due consultation of the Parliament in the cases provided for by the Treaty … constitutes an essential formality disregard of which means that the measure concerned is void.' The arguments of the Council would have been accepted if they had exhausted all existing procedural possibilities provided by Community law[70] to force the EP to deliver its opinion which was not the case in *Roquette*. Indeed, the EP has a duty to loyally co-operate with other Community institutions and especially to deliver its opinion within a reasonable time in order to allow the Council to adopt a measure within a required time frame: *European Parliament v Council* Case C–65/93 [1995] ECR I–643. If the Council or the Commission amends its initial proposal substantially the EP must be consulted a second time, unless the modification embodies the amendments suggested by the EP.[71]

Under the 1995 Code of Conduct the Commission has agreed to give the EP reasons why its amendments have not been taken into account, to withdraw proposals which have been rejected by the EP or, if the Commission decides to proceed with the proposal despite its rejection by the EP, to provide justification for its position. Also the Council, under the procedure known as 'Scheel', has agreed to justify its rejection of the EP's amendments.

The consultation procedure has evolved greatly, especially in the light of the 1995 Code of Conduct, for two reasons: first, to allow the EP to play an active role in the decision-making procedures and, second, to emphasise the democratic character of the Community by taking into account the will of the people of the EU through the intermediary of their representatives, the EP.

Originally, the consultation procedure had to be applied, for example, if a measure concerned custom duties, the CAP, the abolition of existing restrictions on freedom of establishment, the abolition of existing restrictions on freedom to provide services, and the approximation of laws. The SEA extended the consultation procedure to the following areas: art 84 EEC on certain aspects of transport policy; and art 99 EEC on the harmonisation of indirect taxes, etc. Under the TEU the following areas were added: art 19 EC on voting rights for nationals of other Member States in municipal and European elections; art 22 EC on recommendations to Member States to increase the rights granted to EU citizens; art 89 EC on State aids; art 100c (now repealed) on the determination of third countries whose nationals must be in possession of a visa when crossing the external borders of the EU; art 111(1) EC on formal agreements on the exchange rate for the ECU vis-à-vis non-Member

---

[70] For example the Council may request emergency procedures which are envisaged in the EP Rules of Procedure or an extraordinary session of the EP provided for in art 196 EC.

[71] *ACF Chemiefarma v Commission* Case 41/69 [1970] ECR 661; *Battaglia* Case 1253/79 [1982] ECR 297; *European Parliament v Council* Case C–65/90 [1992] ECR I–4593; *Driessen v Zonen* Cases C–13–16/92 [1993] ECR I–4751; *Eurotunnel SA and Others v SeaFrance* Case C–408/95 [1997] ECR I–6315.

States; arts 121(2)–(4) and 122(2) EC on the fulfilment of necessary requirements by a Member State for the adoption of a single currency, etc.

Under the Treaty of Amsterdam the EP must be consulted in such areas as agriculture, the freedom to provide services, competition, elimination of technical barriers to trade, own resources, etc.

Co-decision procedure: art 251 EC

The co-decision procedure was introduced by the TEU in 15 areas. It applied mainly to all internal market legislation, including the free movement of workers, the right of establishment, general action programmes relating to environment, research and development, education, culture, trans-European networks, and the protection of consumers.

It was a very complex and time-consuming legislative procedure. For that reason the Treaty of Amsterdam has simplified the procedure by removing the third reading. If the EP rejects the amended proposal at the second reading, the procedure is terminated and the Commission must submit a new proposal and start the procedure again. The co-decision procedure is defined in art 251 EC. It provides that:

'(1) Where reference is made in this Treaty to this Article for the adoption of an act, the following procedure shall apply.

(2) The Commission shall submit a proposal to the European Parliament and the Council.

The Council acting by a qualified majority after obtaining the opinion of the European Parliament,

– if it approves all the amendments contained in the European Parliament's opinion, may adopt the proposed act thus amended;

– if the European Parliament does not propose any amendments, may adopt the proposed act;

– shall otherwise adopt a common position and communicate it to the European Parliament. The Council shall inform the European Parliament fully of the reasons which led it to adopt its common position. The Commission shall inform the European Parliament fully of its position. If, within three months of such communication, the European Parliament:

(a) approves the common position, or has not taken a decision, the act in question should be deemed to have been adopted in accordance with the common position;

(b) rejects, by an absolute majority of its component members, the common position, the proposed act shall be deemed not to have been adopted;

(c) proposes amendments to the common position by an absolute majority of its component members, the amended text shall be forwarded to the Council and to the Commission, which shall deliver an opinion on amendments.

(3) If, within three months of the matter being referred to it, the Council, acting by a qualified majority, approves all the amendments of the European Parliament, the act in question shall be deemed to have been adopted in the form of the common position thus amended; however, the Council shall act unanimously on the amendments on which the Commission has delivered a negative opinion. If the Council does not approve all the amendments, the President of the Council, in agreement with the President of the European Parliament, shall within six weeks convene a meeting of the Conciliation Committee.

(4) The Conciliation Committee, which shall be composed of the members of the Council or their representatives and an equal number of representatives of the European Parliament,

shall have the task of reaching agreement on a joint text, by a qualified majority of the members of the Council or their representatives and by a majority of the representatives of the European Parliament. The Commission shall take part in the Conciliation Committee's proceedings and shall take all the necessary initiatives with a view to reconciling the positions of the European Parliament and the Council. In fulfilling this task, the Conciliation Committee shall address the common position on the basis of the amendments proposed by the European Parliament.

(5) If, within six weeks of its being convened, the Conciliation Committee approves a joint text, the European Parliament, acting by an absolute majority of the votes cast, and the Council, acting by a qualified majority, shall each have a period of six weeks from that approval in which to adopt the act in question in accordance with the joint text. If either of the two institutions fails to approve the proposed act within that period, it shall be deemed not to have been adopted.

(6) Where the Conciliation Committee does not approve a joint text, the proposed act shall be deemed not to have been adopted.

(7) The periods of three months and six weeks referred to in this Article shall be extended by a maximum of one month and two weeks respectively at the initiative of the European Parliament or the Council.'

The co-decision procedure is still complex but it imposes a time limit on the adoption of an act to which this procedure applies and, most importantly, the EP now stands on an equal footing with the Council as the procedure involves joint decision-making. Under the Treaty of Amsterdam the co-decision procedure is a rule. It has been extended to 23 areas, in addition to 15 areas already covered under the TEU. The new areas to which co-decision applies are:

1. prohibition of any discrimination on grounds of nationality (art 12 EC);
2. right to move and reside freely within the territory of the EU for EU citizens (art 18(2) EC);
3. social security for migrant workers (art 42 EC);
4. right of establishment for foreign nationals (art 46(2) EC);
5. arrangements for the professions (art 47(2) EC);
6. implementation of the Common Transport Policy (arts 71 and 80 EC);
7. employment (art 129 EC);
8. some provisions from the 'Social Agreement' incorporated into the EC Treaty;
9. customs co-operation (art 135 EC);
10. measures to combat social exclusion (art 137(2) EC);
11. equal opportunities and equal treatment for men and women (art 141 EC);
12. implementation of the European Social Fund (art 148 EC);
13. vocational training (art 150(4) EC);
14. public health (art 152 EC);
15. trans-European networks (art 156 EC);
16. implementation of the European Regional Development Fund (art 162 EC);
17. research (art 172 EC);
18. environment (art 175(1) EC);
19. development co-operation (art 179 EC);
20. transparency (art 255 EC);

21. measures to combat fraud (art 280 EC);
22. statistics (art 285 EC);
23. setting up an advisory body on data protection (art 286 EC).

Assent procedure

The assent procedure was introduced by the SEA in respect of two aspects of the external relations of the Community: the admission of a new member under art 237 EEC (now repealed) and in the conclusion of association agreements provided for in art 238 EEC (now art 310 EC). The assent procedure is in fact a pure co-decision procedure in which the Council acts on a proposal of the Commission after obtaining assent from the EP. The Council is required to act by unanimity but QMV is sufficient in the conclusion of international agreements. The EP acts by a majority of the votes cast, except for a decision upon an application for membership of the EU where an absolute majority is required.

The TEU has extended the scope of the assent procedure to a number of areas. Under the Treaty of Amsterdam the assent procedure applies to: art 105(6) EC conferring upon the European Central Bank specific tasks concerning policies relating to the prudential supervision of credit institutions and other financial institutions with the exception of insurance undertakings in the third stage of economic and monetary union; art 106(5) EC concerning the amendments of certain articles of the Statute of the European System of Central Banks; art 161(1) EC defining the task, objectives and functioning of the Structural Funds; art 190(4) EC concerning proposals on a uniform procedure for elections to the EP; art 300(3) EC on certain international agreements; art 49 EU concerning the accession of new members; and art 7 EU concerning sanctions imposed on a Member State for a serious and persistent breach of fundamental human rights.

4.10 The principle of transparency

The principle of transparency has two aspects. The first concerns the production by EU institutions of clear and understandable legislative text. In order to satisfy this aspect of transparency, the Treaty of Amsterdam constitutes a consolidated version of the Treaties and renumbers all articles. Furthermore, the Amsterdam European Council (June 1997) adopted a declaration emphasising that Community legislation must be clearly drafted and calls upon all three institutions to establish guidelines for improving the quality of the texts which they draft, amend or adopt.

The second aspect relates to access to information and documents of EU institutions for EU citizens. From the point of view of public access to EU documents the Treaty of Amsterdam has clarified the principle of transparency. A new art 255 EC has been inserted conferring on any natural or legal person residing or having a registered office in a Member State the right of access to EP, Council and Commission documents. Article 255 EC imposes an obligation on the Council to determine the general principles and limits on grounds of public or private interest governing the right to access to all documents within two years of the entry into force of the Treaty of Amsterdam. Article 225(3) EC requires the Council to grant access to documents relating to its legislative activities. As a minimum requirement, the results of votes, explanations of votes and statements in the minutes must be made public. Article 225 EC applies only to Pillars 1 and 3.

All three institutions have already implemented the principle of transparency. The Council in its Decision 93/731, the Commission in its Decision 94/90/CS/EC/EA and the EP in Decision 97/632/CS/EC/EA. All three institutions adopted similar rules in this area. An application for an item of information must be answered within 45 days. If the application is rejected, the applicant has 45 days to submit a confirmatory application for reconsideration of the refusal. If refused a second time, the decision must be made within 45 days of submission of the confirmatory application and notified in writing. Grounds for refusal must be given and must indicate the means of redress that are available to the applicant, for example judicial proceedings, complaints to the Ombudsman, etc. Access may be refused if the disclosure of the document concerned is contrary to:

1. protection of the public interest, in particular public security, the financial interests of the Community, court proceedings or the institution's inquiry activities;
2. protection of commercial or industrial secrecy;
3. protection of the individual and his privacy;
4. protection of confidentiality requested by an EC institution or legal person supplying information or required by the legislation of a Member State supplying that information.

The institution may also request that the applicant should not reproduce or circulate the released document for commercial or publicity purposes without an authorisation of the institution releasing the document.

The general rules are clearly stated but, in practice, they have given rise to many disputes. As a result, the Community judicature has clarified a number of issues concerning the principle of transparency.

In *Svenska Journalistforbunder* v *Council* Case T–174/95 [1998] 3 CMLR 645 the applicant, the Swedish Journalist's Union, applied to the Council of the European Union for access to 20 documents relating to the setting up of Europol. Initially, the applicant was allowed access to two documents and after a meeting of the information working party of COREPER to two further documents. The Council of the European Union refused access to the remaining documents on the grounds that 'their release could be harmful to the public interest (public security) and ... [that] they relate to the Council's proceedings, including the position taken by the members of the Council, and are therefore covered by the duty of confidentiality.' The applicant published an edited version of the Council's justification for refusal on the Internet and invited the public to send their comments to the Council's agents, whose telephone and fax numbers were given. The applicant challenged the decision of the Council refusing access to these documents.

The CFI annulled the decision of the Council which had refused the applicant access to the remaining documents because the decision did not comply with the requirements for reasoning laid down in art 190 EC. The Court of First Instance held that the applicant was to bear its own costs of the proceedings, taking into account that it had abused the procedure by inviting the public to send their comments to the Council's agents (which action was intended to put pressure on the Council to provoke public criticism of its agents in the performance of their duty) and by allowing third party access to the case file of the procedural documents, without the express authorisation of the President of the Court, which was contrary to the Court's procedural rules.

In *Heidi Hautala* v *Council of the European Union* Case T–14/98 [1999] 3 CMLR 528 the Council of the EU refused Ms Heidi Hautala, a Member of the EP, access to a report on conventional arms' export drawn up by a working group within the framework of the common foreign and security policy under the COREU special European correspondence system. Documents written under the COREU system are for internal use of the Council, and in this case the contested report contained the exchange of views of the Member States on the protection of human rights in the recipient countries of exported conventional arms. Ms Hautala learnt of the existence of the report when on 14 November 1996 she put a written question to the Council seeking clarification of the common criteria for arms' export defined by the European Council in Luxembourg in June 1991 and in Lisbon in June 1992. The Council refused access to the contested report on the ground that it contained sensitive information, the disclosure of which would harm the European Union's relations with non-Member States.

The CFI annulled the Council's Decision which refused the applicant access to the contested report. The most important aspects of the judgment are that, first, it specifies the exceptions to the principle of access to documents and, second, it endorses the principle of partial access to such documents. The Court held that art 4(1) of Decision 93/731, which lists the exceptions to access to the Council's documents, should be interpreted and applied strictly so as not to undermine the principle of access to such documents.

The Council argued that under the exceptions set out in art 4(1) of Decision 93/731, the restriction on access applies to documents as such, not to the information contained in them. Ms Hautala, supported by the Swedish government, argued that partial access should be granted in cases covered by art 4(1) in order to ensure the widest possible access to documents. Consequently, the Council had a duty to examine which passages of the contested report could be communicated to her without endangering international relations of the EU. In her case the Council did not examine the question of granting her partial access to the contested report.

The CFI confirmed the principle of the widest possible access to documents. It examined the exceptions set out in art 4(1) of Decision 93/731 in the light of the principle of proportionality. In this respect, the CFI held that the principle of proportionality requires that derogations should remain within the limits of what is appropriate and necessary for achieving a specific objective. In this case the objective was the protection of the public interest with regards to international relations of the EU. The Court stated that this objective could be ensured if the Council considered the possibility of removing certain passages of the document which may harm international relations. The Court concluded that in the context of the principle of the right to information and the principle of proportionality, the Council should examine whether partial access should be granted or whether the report as a whole was covered by the exceptions to access to Council documents. Taking into account that the Council did not make such examination in respect of the contested report, the CFI annulled the Council decision refusing Ms Hautala access to the contested report.

However, the CFI imposed an important restriction upon the duty of the Council to proceed to such an examination in each individual case based on the principle of proportionality and the necessity to safeguard the interests of good administration. The CFI held that 'in particular cases where the volume of the document or the passages to be removed would give rise to an unreasonable amount of administrative work' the Council is allowed to 'balance the interest in public access to those fragmentary parts against the burden of work so caused'. Therefore, the Council is still entitled to refuse partial access to its documents claiming that this would impose an unreasonable amount of work upon it. It seems that the Council has a duty to examine whether or not partial access should be granted, but it will also decide whether this will impose an unreasonable burden of work upon the Council.

In respect of the other argument submitted by Ms Hautala challenging the Council assessment of the release of the contested report as being harmful to international relations of the EU, the CFI held that the Council did enjoy a discretion to refuse access to the entire report drawn up for internal use of the Council. Indeed, under Title VIII of the TEU the Council is entitled to determine the possible consequences which disclosure of the contested report may have for the international relations of the EU. The CFI can only verify procedural rules, that is whether the decision of the Council was properly reasoned, the facts accurately stated and whether there was a manifest error of assessment of the facts or a misuse of powers.

The Council and the French government challenged the jurisdiction of the CFI on the ground that the contested report was drawn up under Title VIII of the Treaty on European Union and therefore was outside the court's jurisdiction within the meaning of art 46 EU. In this respect the Court held that a distinction must be made between the assessment of legality of a document adopted under Title VIII of EU and the assessment of legality of refusal of the Council based on Decision 93/731 concerning public access to its documents. Whilst the CFI lacks jurisdiction in respect of the first-mentioned it has jurisdiction to verify the legality of the refusal of access to Council documents.

In respect of the Commission's duty to allow access to its documents, two important cases clarified its extent. In *Rothmans International BV v Commission of the European Communities* Case T–188/97 [1999] 3 CMLR 66 the applicant, a company incorporated under Netherlands law, and a branch of the multinational Rothmans group which manufactures, distributes and sells tobacco products, in particular cigarettes, challenged the Commission's decision refusing it access to the minutes of the Customs Code Committee on the ground that the Commission was not its author although the contested minutes were in its possession.

The CFI annulled the contested decision which had denied the applicant access to the minutes of the Customs Code Committee. The CFI clarified two important points: first, the nature of comitology, that is the relationship between the Commission and various executive committees; and, second, defined the concept of an author of a document in the light of the principle of access to documents.

By virtue of art 211 EC the Commission exercises the powers conferred on it by the Council for the implementation of measures adopted by the latter. The Commission must act within the limits of authority delegated by the Council, although the ECJ has given a broad interpretation to such delegated implementation powers as it recognises the wide discretion of the Commission in this respect including the possibility to impose sanctions and to authorise derogations.[72]

The Commission argued that taking into account the nature of comitology, the Custom Code Committee, as one of the executive committees established under the Comitology legislation,[73] is entirely distinct from and independent of the Commission. The Court of First Instance decided otherwise. It held that for the purposes of the Community rules on access to documents, 'comitology' committees come under the Commission itself mainly because they have no separate infrastructure, that it, they have no budget, no offices, no archives and no postal address of their own. Furthermore, they cannot be regarded as Community institutions or Community bodies. They are neither natural nor corporate persons. They are neither Member States, nor other international or national bodies. However, in the context of access to public documents they must belong somewhere. The CFI decided that they belong to the Commission. The decision of the CFI is surprising taking into account the purposes of 'comitology', although under art 7 of Decision 1999/468/EC[74] adopted on 28 June 1999 the Commission is in charge of transmitting documents and preparing annual reports regarding works of committees.

The Commission argued that it could not be considered as an author of the contested document because: first, the Commission only acted in its secretarial capacity; second, the contested minutes were adopted by the Customs Code Committee which is therefore their author; and, third, under the Commission Code of Conduct, adopted on 8 February 1994, when a document is held by the Commission but its author is a natural or a legal person, a Member State or an EC institution or other Community, national or international body, the application regarding access to such a document must be addressed to its author.

Once the CFI decided that for the purposes of the Community rules on access to documents the Customs Code Committee came under the Commission itself, the Commission was regarded as the author of the contested minutes. Therefore, the Commission decision refusing the applicant access to the minutes was in breach of the principle of transparency.

In *The Bavarian Lager Company* v *Commission* Case T–309/97 [1999] 3 CMLR 544 the Bavarian Lager Company lodged a complaint with the Commission concerning the UK legislation relating to the purchase of beer under which a large number of pubs in the UK are bound by exclusive purchasing agreements requiring them to obtain their supplies of beer from particular breweries. The Bavarian Lager Company argued that the UK legislation was contrary to art 28 EC as it constituted a measure having an effect equivalent to a quantitative restriction on imports. The Commission decided, after investigation, to start infringement proceedings and to send a reasoned opinion to the government of the UK. In the meantime, the UK announced a proposal to amend the challenged legislation. As a result, the Commission never sent a reasoned opinion to the UK, and informed the Bavarian

---

[72] *ACF Chemiefarma* v *Commission* Case 41/69 [1970] ECR 661; *Westzuker* Case 57/72 [1973] ECR 321; *Eridania* Case 230/78 [1979] ECR 2749; *France and Ireland* v *Commission* Case C–296/93 [1996] ECR I–795 and *Ireland* v *Commission* Case C–307/93 [1993] ECR I–4191.
[73] Council Regulation 2913/92: OJ L302 (1992).
[74] OJ L184 (1999).

Lager Company that the infringement proceedings had been suspended and would be closed after entry into force of the amended legislation.

The Bavarian Lager Company requested a copy of the 'reasoned opinion'. The Commission refused on the grounds that disclosure of the reasoned opinion could undermine the protection of the public interest and, in particular, Commission inspection and investigation tasks. The Bavarian Lager Company challenged this decision.

The CFI approved the Commission's refusal. The CFI held that the exception to the right of access to Commission documents based on the protection of the public interest does not apply to all documents which deal with the infringement procedure. Only documents relating to inspection and investigations are covered by the exception since their disclosure could undermine the proper conduct of the infringement procedure and the duty of confidentiality imposed upon the Commission. The CFI rightly emphasised that in the present case there was no 'reasoned opinion'. It was in fact a draft reasoned opinion drawn up by the Commission in order to be sent to the UK. This document was never signed by the Commissioner responsible or sent to the UK. As a result, the CFI held, it was a purely preparatory document.

5   Sources of Community Law

5.1   Primary sources of Community law

5.2   Secondary sources of Community law

5.3   Other Community acts not expressly mentioned in art 249 EC

5.4   External sources which derive from international commitments
       of the Communities

5.5   Complementary sources of Community law

5.6   General principles of Community law and the case law of the ECJ

In the Treaties there is no classification of the sources of Community law. In its absence, the classification must be based on other factors, such as indications provided by the Treaties, practices established by the Community institutions and the Member States and judgments rendered by the ECJ. The classification of sources of Community law can be based on various criteria. In this respect, it is possible to identify between:

1. written and unwritten sources;
2. internal and external sources;
3. primary and secondary sources;
4. sources established by the Treaty of Paris and by the Treaty of Rome;
5. sources mentioned by the Treaties and those which have been introduced by practice;
6. *senso stricto* sources of Community law which comprise primary and secondary sources and sources in a broad sense comprising all rules applicable to the Community legal order written and unwritten, external and internal.

In order to simplify the classification of sources of Community law, the following typology is suggested:

1. fundamental or primary sources of Community law which are contained in the founding Treaties as amended;
2. secondary sources of Community law which are unilateral acts adopted by the EC institutions on the basis of Treaties;
3. external sources which derive from international treaties concluded between the Communities and third countries;
4. complementary sources of EC law which encompass international conventions, decisions, accords, declarations, resolutions, etc, adopted by the Member States outside the framework of the Treaties but which apply between them;
5. sources resulting from the interpretation of Community law by the ECJ, such as general principles of Community law, and the decisions of Community judicature.

5.1 Primary sources of Community law

The primary sources of Community law comprise the three founding Treaties as amended, together with Protocols annexed to them, and Acts of Accession of new Member States to the existing Communities.

The three founding Treaties

1. The Treaty of Paris of 18 April 1951 established the European Coal and Steel Community (CS) which entered into force on 23 July 1952 for a period of 50 years. At its expiry on 23 July 2002 it will be incorporated into the EC Treaty.
2. The Treaty of Rome of 25 March 1957 established the European Economic Community (EC) which entered into effect on 1 January 1958. Article 312 EC confirms that EC Treaty was concluded for an unlimited period. Its current version is contained in the Treaty of Amsterdam which entered into force on 1 May 1999.
3. The Treaty of Rome of 25 March 1957 established the European Atomic Energy Community (EA) which entered into force on 1 January 1958 and like the EC Treaty was concluded for an unlimited period.

The primary sources are at the top of the hierarchy of sources of Community law, their supremacy implies that all other sources of EC law are subordinate to them. The superiority of the primary sources over other sources of EC law is strengthened by the prohibition of any revision of the Treaties, either by an act or practice of the Community institutions or the Member States, outside the procedures set out in the Treaties themselves. In *Defrenne* Case 43/75 [1976] ECR 455 the ECJ rejected the possibility of revision of the Treaties based on art 39 of the 1969 Vienna Convention on the Law of Treaties, which provides that a revision of a particular treaty may result from a common accord of all contracting parties. The Court held that a modification of the Treaty can only take place, without prejudice to other specific provisions contained in the Treaty, on the grounds of art 236 EEC (now art 48 EU). Since 1957 it has been well established that the Member States are not permitted to act by a common agreement to revise the Treaties outside the existing procedures and therefore exclude the Community institutions from participating in these procedures.[1] However, in the early days of the Communities two exceptions to this principle occurred (see below). Not only the formal requirements prohibit the revision of the founding Treaties outside the procedures envisaged by the Treaties but there are also some limitations *ratione materiae*. In this respect, the ECJ held that some provisions of the EC Treaty, such as art 220 EC which defines the tasks of the ECJ, are not revisable.[2] As a result, some provisions of the founding Treaties are unchangeable and constitute a *'noyau dur'* of the constitutional identity of the Communities.

Primary sources prevail over international treaties concluded between the Communities

---

[1] The conclusion of agreements with third countries which would alter the provisions of the Treaties is included: Opinion 1/91 [1991] ECR I–6079 and Opinion 1/92 [1992] ECR I–2821, both relating to the agreement on the establishment of the European Economic Area.
[2] Ibid.

and third countries. In order to avoid any conflict between them art 300 EC provides for the advisory jurisdiction of the ECJ in respect of the conclusion of international agreements. In addition, a decision of the Council relating to the conclusion of an international agreement with a third country which is in breach of the provisions of the founding Treaties may be challenged before the ECJ (*France* v *Commission* Case C–327/91 [1994] ECR I–3641).

The relationship between international agreements entered into by the Member States and the primary sources of EC law is more complex. It depends whether a Member State concluded the agreement in question prior to or subsequent to its accession to the Communities. In both cases, the principles of public international law apply. Subsequent international agreements should not affect earlier agreements. As a result, international agreements concluded by Member States after their accession to the Communities will be disregarded if incompatible with Community law. Conversely, international agreements concluded before their accession to the Communities prevail over EC law. Article 307 EC endorses both principles. It provides that:

> 'The rights and obligations arising from agreements concluded before 1 January 1958 or, for acceding States, before the date of their accession, between one or more Member States on the one hand, and one or more third countries on the other, shall not be affected by the provisions of this Treaty.
>
> To the extent that such agreements are not compatible with this Treaty, the Member State or States concerned shall take all appropriate steps to eliminate the incompatibility established. Member States shall, where necessary, assist each other to this end and shall, where appropriate, adopt a common attitude.'

However, a Member State is not allowed to invoke previous international agreements in order to escape its obligations imposed by the Treaties. In *Commission* v *Italy* Case 10/61 [1962] ECR 22 the ECJ held that Italy could not invoke GATT provisions on customs duties to escape obligations of the EC Treaty relating to inter-Community exchanges.[3] Nevertheless, art 307 EC imposes an important limitation on a Member State's obligations arising out of an international agreement concluded prior to its accession: the Community cannot be bound by such an agreement vis-à-vis third countries (*Burgoa* Case 812/79 [1980] ECR 2787). In practice, the principle contained in art 307 EC poses difficult problems for national judges in the case of a conflict between international agreements and Community law. This problem is best illustrated by the contradictions between the Conventions of the International Labour Organisations and the EC Directive relating to the night work of women.[4] Finally, all international agreements between the Member States concluded before their accession to the Communities are subject to the special provisions of the Treaty.[5]

The primary sources of EC law, the founding Treaties and their amendments, are considered as the constitutional Treaties. The idea that the founding Treaties establishing the three Communities are different from classical international treaties was recognised by

---

[3] Also, in *Commission* v *United Kingdom* Case C–144/89 [1991] ECR I–3533 the ECJ held that the provisions on the Common Fisheries Policy could not be replaced by conventional rules emanating from an international convention entered into by the UK prior to the accession to the Communities.

[4] *Stoeckel* Case C–345/89 [1991] ECR I–4047; *Lévy* Case C–158/91 [1993] ECR I–4287; *ONEM* v *Minne* Case C–13/93 [1994] ECR I–371.

[5] For example, art 306 EC concerning the customs union between Belgium and Luxembourg as well as the Benelux Union.

the ECJ in *Van Gend en Loos* Case 26/62 [1963] ECR 1, in which the Court held that 'this Treaty is more than an agreement which merely creates mutual obligations between the Contracting States', and that 'the Community constitutes a new legal order of international law' which creates rights and obligations not only for the Member States but more importantly for their nationals which 'become part of their legal heritage'. The constitutional nature of the founding Treaties, as well as the legal implications deriving from their peculiar status under public international law, has been progressively developed by the ECJ. In *Partie Ecologiste Les Verts* v *European Parliament* Case 294/83 [1986] ECR 1339 the ECJ considered the EC Treaty as the 'basic constitutional Charter' of the Community and in Opinion 1/91 [1991] ECR 6079 refused to interpret international accords in the same manner as the EC Treaty taking into account its peculiar nature.

The three founding Treaties are independent vis-à-vis each other. The Merger Treaty envisaged their fusion but it was decided, at that time, to postpone their merger for an indefinite period. The relationship between all three founding Treaties is governed by art 305 EC which provides that, in conformity with public international law, the EC Treaty as a general Treaty shall neither modify the CS Treaty nor derogate from the provisions of the EA Treaty, both being specific Treaties. As a result, the provisions of the CS Treaty do not apply to the EC Treaty. This was endorsed by the ECJ in *Confédération Nationale des Producteurs de Fruits et Légumes* Cases 16–17/62 [1962] ECR 901, in which the Court rejected the application by analogy of the more liberal provisions of the CS Treaty regarding *locus standi* under art 230 EC. Also, in *Hauts Fourneaux de Givors* Cases 27–29/58 [1960] ECR 527, the ECJ held that each time the CS Treaty regulates a specific subject-matter exhaustively, the application of the EC Treaty is excluded. However, if there is a gap in the specific Treaties, that is in the CS or the EA Treaty, the EC Treaty as a general Treaty, and secondary legislation adopted on the basis of the EC Treaty, will fill that gap without the necessity of adopting any specific measures or any declarations on its interpretation. In *Deutsche Babcock* Case 328/85 [1987] ECR 5119 the ECJ held that the EC Treaty applied to products covered by the CS Treaty when the latter contained a gap on a specific point.[6]

The autonomy of each founding Treaty has been undermined by the ECJ. In order to achieve greater uniformity of EC law the ECJ has interpreted provisions contained in one founding Treaty in the light of analogous provisions of the other Treaties. The obvious similarity between them has allowed the ECJ to clarify, by analogy, an obscure provision of one Treaty on the basis of a clear and precise meaning of a similar provision of the other Treaty. In this respect, in *Comptoirs de Vente de la Ruhr* Case 13/60 [1960] ECR 165, the ECJ held that the exact meaning of art 65 CS can be inferred from art 81 EC as the latter can serve as 'indirect support' in the interpretation of art 65 CS. In *Meroni* Case 15/57 [1958] ECR 185 the ECJ extended the scope of application of art 156 CS concerning the plea of illegality by virtue of an analogous ambit of application of art 241 EC. There are two possible justifications for the approach endorsed by the ECJ. First, the EC Treaty can be considered as a fundamental Treaty. It establishes general principles relating to the creation of a common market in all products and services while the EA and the CS Treaties cover only limited markets. As a result, reference to the EC Treaty as a general and fundamental

---

[6] This approach was confirmed in Opinion 1/94 [1994] ECR I–5267.

Treaty is fully justified. Second, the future incorporation of the provisions of the CS Treaty, that is once it expires in 2002, into the EC Treaty emphasises the fundamental nature of the latter.[7]

Protocols, declarations and conventions annexed to the Treaties

In accordance with art 2(2) of the Vienna Convention of 23 May 1969 on the Law of the Treaties, protocols and conventions annexed to the founding Treaties or to the treaties amending the founding Treaties, have the same legal effect as the Treaties themselves. This is confirmed in art 311 EC which states that:

> 'The protocols annexed to this Treaty by common accord of the Member States shall form an integral part thereof.'

This has been confirmed by the ECJ many times.[8] In *Commission* v *Belgium* Case 260/86 [1988] ECR 966 the ECJ held that the violation of provisions contained in the Protocol on the Privileges and Immunities by Belgium constituted a breach of its obligations deriving from the Treaties. Although the terms of protocols could have been incorporated into the founding Treaties, their existence avoids lengthy texts of the revised Treaties.

The declarations annexed to the Treaties are not legally binding. Most of them express an intention of the Member States on a particular point, although there are some unilateral declarations emanating from a particular Member State in which it clarifies its position vis-à-vis other Member States in relation to a particular matter. However, the specific nature of Community law prevents unilateral declarations from acquiring any legal effect – other Member States merely take cogniscance of them. The theory of acquiescement, which applies in public international law and under which unilateral declarations are legally binding on other contracting States, provided they accept them, is rejected under Community law. The ECJ is empowered to resolve any dispute between Member States and to provide clarifications on a particular point of law. Declarations are, nevertheless, of some importance. The ECJ makes reference to declarations in the interpretation of EC law since they often express the intention of Member States or a particular Member State.

Acts of Accession

Acts of Accession are legally binding. They are similar, from the point of view of the legal effect they produce, to the founding Treaties.

---

[7] Nevertheless, the case law of the ECJ on this point is confusing, even for the judges of the Court of First Instance. In *Stahlwerke Peine-Salzgitter* Case C–220/91 [1993] ECR I–2393 the ECJ rejected the judgment of the Court of First Instance (Case T–120/89 [1991] ECR II–279) in which the latter emphasised that the existence of a 'unique legal order' as well as the necessity of strengthening coherence within that system required that the conditions which give rise to the Community's liability were the same under the CS and EC Treaties, and held that although there were some similarities on this point between the CS and the EC Treaty, these conditions must be construed on the bases of the CS Treaty alone.

[8] *Wybot* Case 149/85 [1986] ECR 2403; *Firma Foto-Frost* Case 314/85 [1987] ECR 4199.

Modifications and amendments of the founding Treaties

Modifications and amendments of the founding Treaties can occur within the framework of the founding Treaties by the adoption of new treaties, or outside the procedure of revision in three situations:

1. when there is a consensus of all Member States;
2. when particular provisions of the founding Treaties permit Member States to avoid the necessity of revising the founding Treaty;
3. when the particular nature of a 'decision' adopted by the Council necessitates its ratification by all Member States.

Revision of the founding Treaties according to the procedure provided by the Treaties themselves: art 48 EU

The most straightforward manner consists of the adoption of new treaties under the procedures provided for in the founding Treaties themselves. In this respect, art 48 EU contains a uniform procedure of revision for all three founding Treaties and replaces arts 96 CS, 236 EEC and 204 EA. Under this provision, a proposal for revision is submitted to the Council either by the government of the Member State or by the Commission. The Council, after consulting the EP and the Commission and, where appropriate, the European Central Bank, may deliver an opinion in favour of calling a diplomatic conference of all representatives of the Member States for the purpose of determining by common accord the amendments to be made to the Treaties. A draft treaty produced by such a conference will enter into effect once ratified by all Member States according to their constitutional laws.

Among the most important Treaties which have revised the founding Treaties are: the Merger Treaty 1965;[9] the Single European Act signed at Luxembourg and The Hague on 17 and 28 February 1986; which became operational on 1 July 1987;[10] the Treaty on European Union signed at Maastricht on 7 February 1992, which entered into force on 1 November 1993; and the Treaty of Amsterdam signed on 2 October 1997, which entered into force on 1 May 1999.

Revision of the founding Treaties outside art 48 EU

There are certain mechanisms permitting the revision of the founding Treaties outside art 48 EU.

Common consent of the Member States Under public international law, the consent of all contracting parties to a particular treaty is required for its revision. The Community applied this approach on two occasions through the adoption of international conventions: the Convention of 27 October 1957 on the Legal Implications of the Return of the Sarre to the Federal Republic of Germany; and the Convention of 25 March 1957 relating to Certain Institutions Common to the European Communities. This manner of revising the founding Treaties should be considered as obsolete for two reasons: first, since 1958 it has never been applied; and, second, all three Community institutions have expressly recognised the

---

[9] OJ L152 (1967).
[10] O J L169 (1987).

revision procedure provided for by the founding Treaties as appropriate and confirmed their commitment to it: the ECJ in *Defrenne* Case 43/75 [1976] ECR 455; the Council in its written answer to question no 398/77;[11] the European Parliament in its Resolution of 8 May 1969 and in the Burger Report.[12]

Simplified procedures provided for in the founding Treaties The simplified procedures involve only the Community institutions. Under art 95(2) and (3) CS obligatory consultation with the ECJ is required and its negative opinion blocks any proposed revision. So far this procedure has been applied three times. In two cases the ECJ issued a negative opinion and thus prevented adoption of the proposed measures. In respect of both Treaties of Rome the Council, when using simplified procedures to revise them, must act unanimously on a proposal from the Commission and after consulting the EP.[13] Examples of simplified procedures are given in art 221 EC (the possibility to increase the number of judges of the ECJ), art 245 EC (amendments to the Statute of the ECJ), and art 107(5) EC (amendments to the Statute of the ESCB).

'Decisions' of the Council The Council may revise the founding Treaties on the basis of certain provisions, mainly art 269 EC relating to the 'proper resources' of the Community, art 190 EC concerning the uniform procedure for election to the EP, and art 22 EC which permits the Council to adopt measures to strengthen or add to the rights of the EU citizens laid down in Part Two of the EC Treaty. The most important decisions modifying the founding Treaties adopted under these procedures are: the Council Decision and Act of 20 September 1976 on Direct Elections to the European Parliament, the Budgetary Treaties of 1970 and 1975, decisions under art 22 EC concerning Union citizenship and decisions based on the former art 100c EEC (now repealed) concerning the completion of the internal market.

Doctrine of implied powers By virtue of arts 95(1) CS, 308 EC and 203 EA the Council may extend Community competences in internal and external matters.

5.2 Secondary sources of Community law

Secondary sources of EC law are, in terms of quantity, the most important source of Community law but in the hierarchy of sources they are classified after primary sources and general principles of EC law. Under the founding Treaties, Member States have conferred important legislative powers on the Community institutions which enable them to implement the provisions of the Treaties and thus give full effect to EC law and policies. The founding Treaties carefully avoid any mention of 'law-making powers' or 'legislation' in relation to EC institutions. However, the ECJ has not hesitated to expressly refer to

---

[11] OJ C270 (1977).

[12] EP Doc Session no 215/1968/69.

[13] For example arts 76, 85 and 90 EA.

'legislative powers of the Community' in Case 106/77 *Simmenthal* [1978] ECR 629, or a 'legal system of the Treaty' in *Köster* Case 25/70 [1970] ECR 1161, at least in relation to the EC Treaty.

Secondary sources of EC law are listed in arts 249 EC, 161 EA and 14 CS. Articles 249 EC and 161 EA are identical. Both provide that:

'In order to carry out their task and in accordance with the provisions of this Treaty, the European Parliament acting jointly with the Council and the Commission shall make regulations and issue directives, take decisions, make recommendations or deliver opinions.'

Article 14 CS enumerates similar sources of Community law but uses a different terminology. General decisions mentioned by this provision are equivalent to regulations under arts 249 EC and 161 EA, CS recommendations are the same as EC/EA directives and CS individual decisions are similar to EC/EA decisions.

The secondary sources of EC law are unilateral acts adopted by the Council, the Commission and the European Parliament in 'accordance with the provisions of' the Treaty. Under art 110 EC the European Central Bank also has power to legislate from the beginning of the third stage of EMU. Unilateral acts of the Community institutions are adopted on the basis of the Treaties, and therefore considered as secondary or derived legislation. Only regulations, directives and decisions are legally binding acts. Article 249 EC expressly states that recommendations and opinions have no binding force and thus they are neither legal acts nor considered as sources of Community law.

The ECJ confirmed that the classification of a particular act, that is whether it should be considered as regulation, directive or decision, depends upon its content, not its nomenclature, and has often reclassified them.[14] The choice of a particular form – regulation, directive or decision – for a specific act is determined by reference to a provision of the founding Treaties which constitutes its legal basis. In *Italy v High Authority* Case 20/59 [1960] ECR 665 the ECJ held that if the form is expressly provided in a provision of the Treaty, the competent authority has no choice but to enact it accordingly. The question whether a less restrictive measure can be adopted, for example instead of adopting a regulation the Council adopts a directive, even though a particular provision provides for the first mentioned, was answered affirmatively in art 14 CS. This solution, however, cannot be transposed to the EC and EA Treaties, although the principle of subsidiarity and art 211 EC may justify the use of non-binding measures such as recommendations and opinions but not the substitution of one binding measure for another. However, if there is no indication on this point, or a particular provision leaves the choice open as, for example, art 83 EC or art 40 EC which provides for regulations or directives, or refers only to 'measures' in general as in art 62 EC, the EC institution invested with power to adopt the necessary measures must decide which one is the most appropriate to achieve the objective prescribed by the provision in question (*Cimenteries CBR* Cases 8–11/66 [1967] ECR 93). This choice is, nevertheless, subject to judicial review by the ECJ.

Some formal and substantive requirements must be satisfied for a measure to be legally binding. Formal requirements refer to the authority in the Treaty permitting their adoption

---

[14] *Confédération Nationale des Producteurs de Fruits et Légumes* Case 16–17/62 [1962] ECR 901; *Plaumann* Case 25/62 [1964] ECR 95.

and the manner in which they should be notified to their addressees. With regard to reasons for their adoption art 253 EC provides that measures must 'state the reasons on which they are based and shall refer to any proposals or opinions which were required to be obtained pursuant to this Treaty.' The objective of this requirement was explained in *Germany v Commission (Brennwein)* Case 24/62 [1963] ECR 63 by the ECJ as permitting:

1. the parties concerned by that measure to defend their rights;
2. the ECJ to exercise its supervisory functions; and
3. all Member States and all EC nationals to ascertain the circumstances in which the EC institutions apply the provisions of the Treaty.

The absence or insufficiency of 'reasons' must be raised *ex officio* by courts (*Tiercé Ladbroke SA v Commission* Case T–471/93 [1995] ECR II–2537) and may result in the annulment of a measure by the ECJ.

The measure must indicate its legal basis and the detailed reasons for its enactment.[15] It must be clear and unequivocal (*Italy v Commission* Case 1/69 [1969] ECR 277), taking into account its context and the other rules applicable to that subject-matter, and especially precise if the adoption of a measure is subject to the assessment of an economic situation by an EC institution (*Germany v Commission* Case 24/62 [1963] ECR 143). A less detailed statement of reasons is accepted if the applicant has contributed or participated in the procedure leading to the adoption of a measure[16] or if it derives from a constant practice of EC institutions,[17] but any change in those practices requires more detailed explanations as to its legal basis and the objectives which the measure aims to achieve.

The choice of a legal basis for a particular measure is not easy, especially in the context of the increasing involvement of the EP in decision-making procedures of the EC. Its complexity was examined in *European Parliament v Council of the European Union* Joined Cases C–164 and 165/97 [1999] ECR I–1139, in which the European Parliament brought proceedings against the Council for annulment of Regulations 307/97 and 308/97 concerning the protection of forests against pollution and fire. The EP argued that both Regulations were adopted on an inappropriate legal basis, art 37 EC instead of art 175 EC. Consequently, the EP's prerogatives in respect of the procedure involving its participation in the drafting of legislation were undermined. Their adoption on the basis of art 37 EC meant that the Parliament was merely consulted, whilst art 175 EC provides for the co-operation procedure as defined by art 252 EC. The ECJ annulled both Regulations.

The ECJ confirmed that the choice of a legal basis for a measure must be based on objective factors which are amenable to judicial review taking into account, in particular, the aim and content of the measure. The ECJ stated that when the aims of contested regulations are partly agricultural and partly of a specifically environmental nature then in order to determine the appropriate legal basis the Council has to apply the theory of the 'principal and accessory' (*European Parliament v Council* Case C–70/88 [1990] ECR I–

---

[15] For example, *SITPAC Onflhor* Case C–27/90 [1991] ECR I–155; *Nakajima* Case C–69/89 [1991] ECR I–2069; *Greece v Council* Case C–353/92 [1994] ECR I–3411.

[16] *The Netherlands v Commission* Case 13/72 [1973] ECR 27; *Lucchini* Case 1252/79 [1980] ECR 3753.

[17] *Groupement des Papiers Peints de Belgique* Case 73/74 [1975] ECR 1491; *France v Commission* Case 102/87 [1988] ECR 4067.

2041) unless the measure is intended to pursue both objectives, in which case the measure must be based on the two legal bases: *European Parliament v Council* Case C–360/96 [1996] ECR I–1195. However, the adoption of measures on two legal bases is precluded if the procedures provided for two legal bases are incompatible: *Commission v Council* Case C–300/89 [1991] ECR I–2867. In this respect the ECJ held that:

> 'With more particular reference to the common agricultural policy and the Community environmental policy, there is nothing in the case law to indicate that, in principle, one should take precedence over the other. It makes clear that a Community measure cannot be part of Community action on environmental matters merely because it takes account of requirements of protection for the environment referred to in art 130r(2) of the EC Treaty [art 174(2) EC]. Articles 130r [art 174 EC] and 130s [art 175 EC] leave intact the powers held by the Community under other provisions of the Treaty and provide a legal basis only for specific action on environmental matters. In contrast, art 130s of the Treaty [art 175 EC] must be the basis for provisions which fall specifically within the environmental policy, even if they have an impact on the functioning of the internal market or if their objective is the improvement of agricultural production.'

The ECJ decided that the main objective of both Regulations was the protection of forests, intended to ensure that the natural heritage represented by forest ecosystems is conserved. Although the measures referred to in the Regulations may have certain positive repercussions on the functioning of agriculture, those indirect consequences were incidental to the primary aim of the Community schemes for the protection of forests. For that reason these Regulations should have been adopted on the basis of art 175 EC instead of art 37 EC. As a result, the ECJ annulled both Regulations and held that the Council had infringed essential procedural requirements and undermined prerogatives of the EP.

Another formal requirement concerns the publication of a measure. In *Racke* Case 98/78 [1979] ECR 69 the ECJ held that the fundamental principle of the Community legal order requires that an act emanating from public authorities cannot produce legal effect unless it comes to the knowledge of its addressees. Notification or publication, depending upon the form of a measure, constitutes a necessary condition of its entry into force but does not affect its legality: *Hauptzollamt Bielefield* Case 185/73 [1974] ECR 607. Article 245 EC requires that only regulations, EC measures adopted under the co-decision procedure defined in art 251 EC and directives addressed to all Member States must be published. In fact all EC directives are published in the Official Journal of the European Communities.

The Official Journal of European Communities (OJ) constitutes an important source of information on many aspects of Community activities, including EC legislation. It is published on most weekdays simultaneously in all official languages of the Community, each version has the same pagination. Under 'L' series legislation, treaties, the budget and all binding acts are published; the 'C' series comprises miscellaneous information and notices such as draft legislation prepared by the Commission, common positions adopted by the Council and minutes of the plenary sessions of the European Parliament; and the 'S' series is devoted to the specialised use of firms competing for public contracts. An annex to the OJ contains the debates of the European Parliament.

In this context it is interesting to mention *Opel Austria GmbH* Case T–115/94 [1997] ECR II–39, in which the CFI held that the Council, by expressly antedating the publication in the Official Journal of the regulation at issue, was in breach of the principle of legal certainty.

Under art 254(3) EC other measures must be notified to their addressees. In respect of natural or legal persons they must be notified by registered letter or delivery with acknowledgment[18] or through diplomatic channels, that is ambassadors accredited to the EU instititions, if they reside outside the territory of the EU. Member States are notified through their permanent representatives in Brussels.

The date of entry into force of a particular measure may be specified in the measure itself. If a measure is notified it will enter into force on the day of its notification, and if published and in the absence of any specification by virtue of art 254 EC it is deemed to become operative 20 days after its publication. The ECJ held in *Racke* Case 98/78 [1979] ECR 69 that the day of publication means not the day on which the Official Journal is available in the territory of each Member State but the day when it is available at the seat of the Office for Official Publications of the Communities at Luxembourg which, unless proved to the contrary, is taken to be for evidential purposes the day the Official Journal containing the text of the act in question is published. In relation to acts which require publication, usually a specific date is fixed for entry into force since its immediate entry into force, without any transition period, risks undermining the principles of legal certainty and legitimate expectation: *CNTA* Case 74/74 [1975] ECR 533. In *Max Neumann* Case 17/67 [1967] ECR 571 the ECJ held that immediate entry into force of an act, that is on the day of its publication in the OJ, may be resorted to only in the case of extreme necessity. The institutions concerned must have serious reasons to believe that the delay between the date of the publication of an act and its entry into force would cause prejudice to the Community and that its immediate entry into force is necessary to prevent speculation or a legal void.

In respect of substantive requirements the ECJ has rejected the retroactive application of secondary legislation, apart from exceptional cases when the objective to be achieved by a measure requires this, and provided that the legitimate expectations of the persons concerned by that measure are respected[19] and that the measure does not apply to penal matters.[20] Also, the ECJ confirmed the right to withdraw or to abrogate a measure but laid down certain conditions: when the measure created individual rights the withdrawal is permitted within a reasonable time (approximately six months); solely for reasons of illegality;[21] and provided public and private interests are duly taken into account.[22] When a measure does not afford rights to individuals it may be withdrawn within a reasonable time (two–three years): *Hoogovens* Case 14/61 [1962] ECR 485.

---

[18] Decision 22/60 of the High Authority of 7 September 1960: OJ (1960).

[19] *Racke* Case 98/78 [1979] ECR 69; *Alpha Steel* Case 14/81 [1982] ECR 749; *Cargill* Cases C–248 and 365/89 [1992] ECR I–2987 and I–3045. See F Lamoureux, 'The Retroactivity of Community Acts in the Case Law of the Court of Justice' (1983) 20 CMLR 269–283.

[20] *Kirk* Case 63/83 [1984] ECR 2689; *Fedesa* Case C–331/88 [1990] ECR I–4023.

[21] *BASF* Cases T–79, 84–86, 91–92, 94, 96 and 98/89 [1992] ECR II–315.

[22] *SNUPAT* Cases 42 and 49/59 [1961] ECR 101; *Lemmerz-Werke* Case 11/63 [1965] ECR 835; *Consorzio Cooperative d'Abruzzo* Case 15/85 [1987] ECR 1005.

Regulations

EC/EA regulations, or their equivalent under the CS Treaty (general decisions), are the most important form of Community acts. Regulations ensure uniformity of solutions throughout the Community. They apply *erga omnes* and simultaneously in all Member States. Article 249 EC defines regulations in the following terms:

> 'A regulation shall have general application. It shall be binding in its entirety and directly applicable in all Member States.'

Thus, a regulation is comparable to statutory law in England.

First, it has general applications. The ECJ, in *Koninklijke Scholten Honing* v *Council and Commission* Case 101/76 [1977] ECR 3583, explained this feature of a regulation by stating that it applies 'to objectively determined situations and produces legal effects with regard to persons described in a generalised and abstract manner'. Regulations are expressed in general, abstract terms and the mere fact that it is possible to determine the number or even identity of the persons affected by a particular measure does not call into question its nature as a regulation, provided that the class of those potentially within its scope of application is not closed at the time of its adoption: *Spijker Kwasten BV* v *Commission* Case 231/82 [1983] ECR 259.

Second, a regulation is binding in its entirety which means that its incomplete (*Commission* v *Italy* Case 39/72 [1973] ECR 101) or selective (*Granaria* Case 18/72 [1972] ECR 1172) implementation is prohibited under EC law. Also, its modification, adjunction (*Norddeutsches Vieh-und Fleischkontor* Case 3/70 [1971] ECR 49) or the introduction of any national legislation capable of affecting its content or scope of application is contrary to EC law: *Bollmann* Case 40/69 [1970] ECR 69. These well established principles acquire a special importance in the case of an incomplete regulation. EC regulations are incomplete if they require Member States to adopt necessary measures to ensure their full application. Sometimes this requirement is expressly stated in a regulation itself, as for example the obligation to adopt penal measures in order to ensure its efficient application. In this respect, the ECJ held in *Commission* v *France* Case C–52/95 [1995] ECR I–4443 and *Commission* v *United Kingdom (Re Tachographs)* Case 128/78 [1979] ECR 419 that a Member State had a duty to create new criminal offences in order to implement certain provisions of challenged regulations. The obligation to complete a regulation may also be based on art 10 EC which provides that Member States shall take all necessary measures to fulfil their obligations arising from the Treaty. Whichever applies, national measures are subordinate to the provisions contained in a regulation and must neither alter them nor hinder their uniform application throughout the Community: *Peter* Case C–290/91 [1993] ECR I–2981.

Third, regulations are directly applicable in all Member States. This means that they become part of the national law of the Member States at the date of their entry into force. Their implementation into national law is not only unnecessary but more importantly prohibited by Community law: *Commission* v *Italy* Case 39/72 [1973] ECR 101.

The direct effect of EC regulations will be examined in Chapter 6.

Directives

EC/EA directives or their equivalent under the CS Treaty (recommendations) are defined in art 249 EC in the following terms:

'A directive shall be binding as to the result to be achieved, upon each Member State to which it is addressed, but shall leave to the national authorities the choice of form and methods.'

The main difference between EC/EA directives and CS recommendations is that the former are addressed solely to the Member States while the latter may be addressed to Member States and undertakings. Apart from this, in *Busseni* Case C–221/88 [1990] ECR I–495, the ECJ held that rules applicable to EC directives also apply to CS recommendations.[23]

Directives are used to harmonise national legislation, regulations and administrative provisions. Unlike regulations they require co-operation between the Community and the Member States. They respect the autonomy of national institutional and procedural systems while imposing upon the Member States the obligation of achieving a necessary result and thus an identical legal solution for a particular question in all Member States. That is why a directive is described as being able to 'intrigue, derange, devise, all this is due to its peculiarity'.[24] There are three main features of EC directives.

First, unlike regulations, directives have no general application. EC/EA directives are binding only on their addressees, that is a particular Member State or some Member States or all of them. Nevertheless, they have general scope of application when they are addressed to all Member States. In such a situation, they require that a certain result must be obtained throughout the Community within a specific time limit. In *Kloppenburg* Case 70/83 [1984] ECR 1075 the ECJ qualified EC directives addressed to all member States as acts having general application.

Second, art 10 EC imposes on an addressee Member State an obligation to achieve the objective of a directive but leaves the choice of measures, procedures, methods, etc, necessary to achieve that result to its discretion. However, in order to achieve the prescribed result EC directives are often very precise and detailed. For that reason, EC directives often leave little or no choice as to their implementation. As a result, in many cases, EC directives must be implemented into national law as they stand. In this respect, in *Ste Enka* Case 38/77 [1977] ECR 2212, the ECJ held that it results from art 249 EC that a discretion left to the Member States as to the choice of forms and methods is subject to the result that the Council or the Commission intended to obtain. Thus, if necessary, an addressee Member State may be left without any margin of appreciation as to the manner of its implementation.[25] In particular, EC directives aimed at creating the common market were very detailed. The drawback of this approach is that the drafting process is very long. A new approach based on the principle of subsidiarity recommends the use of framework directives which leaves a wide margin of discretion to Member States as to the choice of forms and

---

[23] [1991] CMLR 415, note G Bebr.

[24] R Kovar, *Observations sur l'intensité normative des directives*, Mélange P Pescatore, p359. 'La directive intrigue, derange, devise, sa singularité en est la cause.'

[25] This position has been confirmed in other cases: *Commission v Belgium* Case 102/79 [1980] ECR 1473; *Provide* Case C–150/88 [1989] ECR 3891; *Commission v Greece* Case C–29/90 [1992] ECR 1971.

methods of their implementation, but results in an increase in litigation as to whether or not they have been correctly introduced into national law.[26]

The essential objective of directives is to achieve the prescribed result. This means that national law of the Member State must be in conformity with the prescribed results once the time limit for the implementation of a directive elapses. For that reason, sometimes no changes are necessary at national level if under national law the prescribed result has already been achieved. Nevertheless, in the majority of cases, an addressee Member State has to implement an EC directive into national law. The ECJ held that it is not necessary to copy the text of a directive into a national text, although it seems the best way to avoid any disputes.[27] Partial or selective implementation of a directive is contrary to EC law. Also, its implementation cannot be limited to a certain territory of a Member State. In this respect, in *Commission v Italy* Case C–157/89 [1991] ECR I–57 (also *Commission v Italy* Case C–33/90 [1991] ECR I–5987), the ECJ held that a Member State cannot invoke the autonomy of some of its regions in order to avoid implementation of some provisions of a directive.

The choice of methods and forms of their implementation has been restricted by the ECJ. The Court held that they must ensure legal certainty and transparency.[28] The ECJ stated in *Commission v Belgium* Case 102/79 [1980] ECR 1473 (and also in *Commission v Germany* Case C–360/88 [1991] ECR I–2567) that a simple administrative practice or an internal circular are not sufficient to ensure legal certainty (*Commission v Germany* Case C–58/89 [1991] ECR I–5019), since they are easily modified by national administration and lack adequate publicity.

In the United Kingdom EC directives are usually implemented by statutory instruments under the European Communities Act 1972 and sometimes by an Act of Parliament.

Third, it is clear from the wording of art 249 EC that an addressee Member State is responsible for their implementation into national law. Usually directives provide for a specific time limit within which they must be brought into effect in the territory of Member States. It is very important to note that directives enter into force at the date specified by them, or if no date is specified then 20 days after publication, but produce their full legal effect after the expiry of a fixed time limit which varies depending upon the subject-matter of the directive. In most cases the time limit is restricted to two years. Before the expiry of the purported time limit no obligations arise from a directive for individuals as the ECJ held in *Kolpinghuis* Case 80/86 [1987] ECR 3969. However, once the time limit elapses the situation changes dramatically: see Chapter 6. In *Felicitas* Case 270/81 [1982] ECR 2771 the ECJ held that the general principle is that in all cases when a directive is correctly implemented into national law it produces legal effects vis-à-vis individuals through the implementing measures adopted by a Member State concerned. Thus, it becomes a part of national law. An individual is entitled to invoke a directive and base his claim upon it if a directive has been incompletely or incorrectly implemented by a Member State. However,

---

[26] See QE no E–3106/93: OJ C102 (1994).

[27] *Commission v France* Case 252/85 [1988] ECR 2243; *Commission v Italy* Case C–360/87 [1991] ECR I–791; *Commission v The Netherlands* Case C–190/90 [1992] ECR I–3265; *Commission v Germany* Case C–217/97 Judgment of 9 September 1999 (nyr).

[28] *Commission v Germany* Case C–131/88 [1991] ECR I–825; *Commission v Germany* Case C–58/89 [1991] ECR I–5019.

non-implementation of a directive within a prescribed time limit produces the following results:

1. it becomes directly applicable (*Ratti* Case 148/78 [1979] ECR 1629);
2. if its provisions are directly effective an individual may rely on them in proceedings before a national court;
3. the Commission may bring an action under art 226 EC against a Member State concerned for breach of EC law (see Chapter 7);
4. provided certain conditions are satisfied, an individual may sue a defaulting Member State for damages (*Francovich* Case C–6/90 [1991] ECR I–5357; *Faccini Dori* Case C–91/92 [1994] ECR I–3325).

In this context, it is interesting to note that all directives in their final provisions impose upon addressee Member States an obligation to provide a list of measures which have been taken in order to implement them. This facilitates the task of the Commission and provides information on the state of national law in this area. When a Member State does not notify the Commission, or provides an incomplete notification even though it has taken all necessary measures, it is still in breach of art 10 EC and the Commission is empowered to bring an action before the ECJ by virtue of art 226 EC.

Decisions

EC/EA decisions and CS individual decisions have no general scope of application. They may be addressed to a particular Member State or to any legal or natural person. The definition of a decision is provided in art 249 EC which states that:

'A decision shall be binding in its entirety upon those to whom it is addressed.'

And it is explained in *Compagnie des Forges de Chatillon* v *High Authority* Case 54/65 [1966] ECR 185 as:

'A measure emanating from the competent authority, intended to produce legal effects and constituting the culmination of procedure within that authority, whereby the latter gives its final ruling in a form from which its nature can be identified.'

Decisions are similar to administrative acts issued by national authorities. In most cases, decisions are issued by the Commission in competition matters or by the Council if a Member State fails to fulfil Community obligations. Decisions are binding in their entirety, which means that they may prescribe not only a particular result to be achieved but also the forms and methods necessary to achieve it. This distingushes them from directives which are merely binding as to the result to be achieved. A decision may be very detailed. Decisions are directly effective vis-à-vis their addressees but in certain cases, that is if a person (natural or legal) proves that he/she/it is directly and individually concerned by it, such a person may bring annulment proceedings under art 230 EC as well as claim damages under art 288(2) EC: see Chapter 8.

Non-binding acts: recommendations and opinions

Article 249 EC expressly provides that recommendations and opinions have no binding force. Although they are not sources of EC law, their importance should not be underestimated, in particular in respect of recommendations adopted by the Council or the Commission which invite Member States to adopt a specific line of conduct. Recommendations and opinions are adopted in areas in which the Community has no legislative powers or when a transitional period is necessary in order to achieve a certain stage in which the EC institutions would be empowered to adopt binding measures. Indeed, a recommendation is often an instrument of indirect action of EC institutions intended to prepare the next stage of development in a particular area. In this context, the only difference between a recommendation and a directive is that the former has no binding force. In *Grimaldi* Case C–322/88 [1989] ECR 4407 the ECJ held that recommendations are not devoid of all legal effect. National judges are obliged to take them into consideration in the interpretation of EC law.

In opinions EC institutions express their views on a given question.

5.3 Other Community acts not expressly mentioned in art 249 EC

In *Manghera* Case 59/75 [1976] ECR 91 the ECJ held that art 249 EC does not provide an exhaustive list of acts of EC institutions producing legal effect. Other acts not mentioned in that provision are also binding provided they are not contrary to the provisions of the Treaty. Indeed, outside art 249 EC there are other sources of EC law which are not secondary legislation *stricto sensu* but nevertheless constitute an important source of EC law.[29] In this category two kinds of acts can be distinguished:

1. Acts which are recognised by the founding Treaty such as: internal regulations which regulate the composition, functioning and procedures of each EC institution; directives, recommendations and opinions which one EC institution addresses to another; and decisions issued by EC institutions which are known under a German name as 'Beschlusse' – such decisions should not be confused with decisions under art 249 EC which in the German version of the Treaty are called 'Entscheidunsen'.
2. Acts outside the framework of the EC Treaty such as resolutions, deliberations, conclusions, communications, common declarations of two or more EC institutions, etc, adopted by various EC institutions. The European Parliament has expressed its concern as to the increasing number of new acts adopted by EC institutions outside the EC Treaty.[30] In *Pubblico Ministero* v *Manghera* Case 59/75 [1976] ECR 91 the ECJ held that EC institutions are empowered to adopt those acts provided that their provisions are in conformity with the EC Treaty.

---

[29] See European Parliament, Report Kirk, Doc 148/78 of 30.5.1978.
[30] See Report Burger, EP Doc. session no 215/68–69 of 12.03.1969.

5.4 External sources which derive from international commitments of the Communities

By virtue of art 300(7) EC international agreements entered into by the Community with third countries or international organisations are binding upon the EC institutions and the Member States. This provision reiterates the fact that the principle of public international law, according to which only contracting parties to an international agreement are bound by them, does not apply in the context of the Community. Furthermore, the principle of supremacy of Community law strengthens the peculiar position of the Member States vis-à-vis international agreements concluded between the Community and third parties. In *Haegeman* Case 181/73 [1974] ECR 449 the ECJ held that the provisions of international agreements, from their entry into force, form an integral part of the Community legal order. This is also extended to mixed agreements: *Demirel* Case 12/86 [1987] ECR 3719. It means that international agreements acquire *ipso facto*, that is solely because they are international agreements, and from the date of their entry into effect, the force of law in the Community legal order. No express incorporation into Community law is required. The decision of the ECJ in *Haegeman* comfirmed that international agreements do not need to be implemented into EC law by an internal act of the Council. EC law favours the monist approach.[31] As a result international agreements become an integral part of Community law, independently of any internal act adopted by the Council and without any need for their implementation into EC law. As Advocate-General Rozes stated in *Polydor* Case 270/89 [1982] ECR 239, an internal act by which the Council expresses the willingness of the Community to be bound by an international agreement does neither modify its nature nor its legal effects, but has only 'instrumental' character.

The EC Treaty is silent as to the conditions for entry into force of an international agreement. In practice, a decision or a regulation adopted by the Council and reproducing in its annex the text of an international agreement is published in the Official Journal. In *Racke* Case 98/78 [1979] ECR 69 the ECJ held that an international agreement cannot produce its legal effects before its publication in the OJ. As to the date of entry into force, international agreements usually specify that date in their final provisions. For that reason, a decision or a regulation relating to the conclusion of an international agreement contains a provision stating that the date of its entry into force will be published in the OJ.

If an international agreement to which the Community is a contracting party provides for the establishment of a body empowered to supervise or monitor its proper functioning or its uniform application in all contracting States, then any decisions adopted by such a body also form an integral part of the Community legal order.[32] The same solution applies to 'recommendations' of such bodies because of their 'direct link' with an international agreement.[33]

In the hierarchy of sources of EC law, international agreements concluded between the

---

[31] In this respect, in *Fediol* Case 70/87 [1989] ECR 1781, the ECJ made ambiguous statements.

[32] *Bresciani* Case 87/75 [1976] ECR 129; *Sevince* Case C–192/89 [1990] ECR I–3461; *Nakajima* Case C–69/89 [1991] ECR I–2069.

[33] *Deutsche Shell* Case C–188/91 [1993] ECR I–363; [1993] CMLR 1043–1050, note by F Castillo de la Torre.

Communities and third countries or international organisations are situated below primary sources and general principles of EC law but above the secondary sources.

In *Schroeder* Case 40/72 [1973] ECR 125 the ECJ held that international agreements and all unilateral acts of the EC institutions adopted in relation to their conclusion within the meaning of art 300(7) EC prevail over secondary sources of EC law. As a result, all unilateral measures such as regulations, directives and decisions must be interpreted in conformity with international agreements. Any conflicting secondary legislation may be annulled by the ECJ by virtue of art 230 EC: *NMB* Case C–188/88 [1992] ECR I–1689. Also any breach of an international agreement by EC institutions may give rise to liability for damages under art 288(2) EC: *Haegeman* Case 181/73 [1974] ECR 449.

The direct effect of international agreements will be discussed in Chapter 6.

5.5 Complementary sources of Community law

Complementary sources of EC law result from agreements between Member States in areas which are within national competences. These agreements are classic international treaties. They create legal obligations between the contracting parties, although they are not independent vis-à-vis the Community legal order. Indeed, they are considered as complementary sources since the subject-matters of these agreements are within the scope of the Treaty or constitute the extension of the objectives defined in the EC Treaty. The relationship between these agreements and EC law differs depending upon the form they take. In this respect a distinction should be made between: international conventions concluded between the Member States on the basis of the EC Treaty; various decisions and agreements concluded by the representatives of governments of the Member States within the Council; and declarations, resolutions and common positions adopted by common accord of the Member States.

Conventions concluded between the Member States

The EC Treaty itself provides for the conclusion of international agreements between Member States in order to avoid difficulties which may arise due to the intensification of exchanges and the increased mobility of natural and legal persons within the common market. In this respect art 293 EC enumerates areas of private international law which are recommended for harmonisation: the protection of persons and their individual rights in the context of art 12 EC; the elimination of double taxation and mutual recognition of companies or firms within the meaning of art 48(2) EC; the retention of legal personality of companies and firms in the event of transfer of their seats from one Member State to another; mergers between companies and firms registered in different Member States; and the recognition and enforcement of judgments and arbitral awards throughout the Community. In the context of the transfer of many areas relating to co-operation in civil matters from Pillar 3 to the EC Treaty, the importance of art 293 EC has been considerably reduced. For historical reasons, it is interesting to note that a number of conventions have been concluded on the basis of art 293 EC, the most important being

1. the 1968 Brussels Convention on Jurisdiction and the Enforcement of Judgments in Civil and Commercial Matters;
2. the 1968 Convention on Mutual Recognition of Companies and Legal Persons, together with a protocol on its interpretation;
3. the Transfer Pricing Arbitration Convention adopted on 23 July 1990;
4. the Convention Relating to the Procedure of Insolvency of 23 November 1995;
5. the 1980 Rome Convention on the Law Applicable to Contractual Obligations;
6. the convention relating to bankruptcy.

The characteristic features of these conventions, which distinguish them from other international agreements, are: first, they are concluded for an undefined period of time; second, only the Member States may become contracting parties to these conventions; third, with each enlargement new Member States must ratify them as the 'acquis communaitaires'; fourth, their entry into force is conditional upon their ratification by all Member States; fifth, in order to ensure uniformity in their application very often the ECJ has jurisdiction to interpret them; and, finally, the Council and the Commission are involved in their preparation. In connection with the last item, the Council and the Commission initiate work relating to a particular convention; the Commission assists the representatives of the Member States in the drafting of its text; the Council and the Commission formally express their views on the draft convention which are published as their opinions in the OJ; a convention is signed during the session of the Council by the plenipotentiaries of the Member States; and the instruments of ratification are deposited with the General Secretariat of the Council.

The participation of the Council and the Commission in the preparation of conventions under art 293 EC is also common to other conventions concluded between the Member States outside the provisions of the Treaty but which are nevertheless considered as necessary in order to facilitate the application of EC law. In this respect, the following conventions have been concluded: the 1967 Naples Convention on Mutual Assistance between Customs Administrations, the 1975 Community Patent Convention and the 1989 Agreement on the Community Patent.

Decisions and agreements concluded by the representatives of the governments of the Member States meeting within the Council

These kinds of decisions and agreements are concluded by the representatives of the governments of the Member States meeting within the Council as a diplomatic conference, not as the EC Council. The Treaty itself provides for them in certain circumstances, for example under art 214 EC for nomination of members of the Commission, or appointments of judges of the ECJ under art 223 EC, or by virtue of art 289 EC for determination of the seats of EC institutions. From the early days, the representatives of the governments of the Member States decided to take the opportunity of these meetings to adopt measures necessary to ensure the proper functioning of the Community even outside the framework of the Treaty. These measures, although necessary, cannot be adopted by the EC institutions since the latter can only act within the limit of their competences: art 7 EC.

There are three areas in which this type of decision or agreement have been adopted by representatives of the governments of the Member States meeting within the Council:

1. In matters which the Treaty itself reserves for the Member States. For example, under arts 15 and 24 EEC (now repealed) concerning the acceleration of elimination of customs duties and the establishment of common customs tariffs, a number of decisions relating to the acceleration were adopted: on 12 May 1960[34] and on 15 May 1962.[35]
2. In matters outside the Treaty. For example, a Decision of 18 December 1978 concerning the suppression of certain postal taxes on presentation to the customs.[36]
3. In matters partially within the scope of the Treaty. For example, a Decision of 20 September 1976 concerning Economic Co-operation within the Mixte Committee EEC/Canada.[37]

The decisions and agreements of the representatives of the governments of the Member States are usually adopted on a proposal submitted by the Commission and after consulting the EP. They are published in the OJ and often their implementation is left to the EC institutions. Another feature of this type of act is that they are adopted by unanimity and signed by all representatives of the governments of the Member States, unlike acts of the Council which are signed only by the President of the Council.

From a legal point of view these decisions and agreements are considered as international treaties concluded in a simplified form. As a result, Member States are bound by these decisions and agreements and they constitute a complementary source of Community law.

Declarations, resolutions and common positions adopted by common accord of the Member States

These are basically political statements of the Member States. They have no legal effect and are non-binding. In most cases they are adopted jointly by the Council and the Member States and contain guidelines as to the future policy of the Community in areas of shared competences. There are many examples of these kinds of non-binding acts such as the Resolution of the Council and the Representatives of the Government of the Member States Concerning the Progressive Creation of Economic and Monetary Union,[38] the Declaration Concerning the Action Programme in the Field of Environment,[39] the Resolution of the Council and the Ministers of Education Concerning the Action Programme in the Field of Education,[40] etc.

---

[34] OJ 1215 (1960).
[35] OJ 1284 (1962).
[36] OJ L6 (1979).
[37] OJ 1260 (1976).
[38] OJ C28 (1971).
[39] OJ C112 (1973).
[40] OJ C38 (1976).

Assessment of complementary sources

The complementary sources of Community law are in a position of inferiority vis-à-vis primary sources and general principles of EC law. They originate outside the framework of the Treaty. Complementary sources of EC law cannot derogate from the provisions of the EC Treaty. The relationship between complementary sources and secondary sources is more complex. In the areas in which the Community has exclusive competences the complementary sources are excluded and the Member States, unless expressly authorised, have no powers to adopt legislative acts. In the areas of concurrent competences, and especially on the grounds of art 298 EC, the secondary sources prevail over complementary sources. This situation has a double justification. First, it results from art 10 EC which requires that Member States facilitate the accomplishment of the Community's tasks by the EC institutions and imposes a duty upon the Member States to abstain from adopting any act capable of jeopardising the objectives of the Treaty. Second, complementary sources often expressly acknowledge their subordination to EC law. In this respect, art 20 of the Rome Convention on the Law Applicable to Contractual Obligations expressly states that:

> 'This Convention shall not affect the application of provisions which, in relation to particular matters, lay down choice of law rules relating to contractual obligations and which are or will be contained in acts of the institutions of the European Communities or in national laws harmonised in implementation of such acts.'

In the area of exclusive competences of the Member States, the Community institutions may only adopt secondary legislation when authorised by complementary sources. As a result, complementary sources prevail over secondary legislation.

Complementary sources occupy a special place in the legal system of the Community. They cannot derogate from the provisions of the EC Treaty. Article 10 EC ensures that any violation of the EC Treaty by complementary law may give rise to proceedings under arts 226 and 227 EC. Nevertheless, proceedings under arts 230[41] or 234 EC are excluded in relation to complementary law (*European Parliament* v *Council* Case C–248/91 [1993] ECR I–3685), although the ECJ may have jurisdiction to interpret some complementary law on the basis of specific provisions contained in a particular convention, such as art 73 of the Convention on the Community Patent, or a special protocol, such as the 1971 Protocol Concerning the Interpretation of the 1968 Brussels Convention on Jurisdiction and the Enforcement of Judgments in Civil and Commercial Matters.

5.6 General principles of Community law and the case law of the ECJ

This category of sources of EC law results from the activities of the ECJ (including the Court of First Instance). The special position of the ECJ as a law-maker requires some explanation.

---

[41] However, an action against measures adopted on the basis of complementary law is permitted: *European Parliament* v *Council* Case C–316/91 [1994] ECR I–625.

Case law of Community judicature

The ECJ as an EC institution enjoys a special status for a number of reasons. First, until the establishment of the Court of First Instance, the ECJ was the one and only judicial institution in the Community. Its authority is similar to that of national supreme courts such as the House of Lords in the United Kingdom or the Cour de Cassation in France. There is no control over and no appeal against its decisions. The creation of the Court of First Instance has not changed the position of the ECJ. The latter constitutes an appellate court on points of law from the decisions of the Court of First Instance.

Second, under art 220 EC the ECJ must 'ensure that in the interpretation and application of this Treaty the law is observed.' Thus, its mission is not only to apply the law expressly laid down by or under the Treaty but, more importantly, to promote its continuous development, to supplement its provisions as well as to fill gaps in the Treaty. Bingham J in *Customs and Excise Commissioners* v *Samex SpA* [1983] 3 CMLR 194; [1983] 1 All ER 1042 (Commercial Court) described this as 'a creative process of supplying flesh to a spare and loosely constructed skeleton'.

Third, the ECJ in order to carry out its tasks, relies on a variety of methods of interpretation and a number of interpretive devices. Even though the interpretation of EC law is based on art 31 of the 1969 Vienna Convention on the Law of Treaties which provides that interpretation should be based on the ordinary meaning of the terms of a treaty in the context and in the light of its object and purpose, the ECJ has given priority to the interpretation 'in the general context' (systematic method) and 'in the light of its object and purpose' (teleological method) over the literal interpretation of the Treaty: *Humblet* Case 6/60 [1960] ECR 1125. In *CILFIT* Case 283/81 [1982] ECR 3415 the ECJ emphasised the particular difficulties in the interpretation and application of EC law. The Community legislation is drafted in several languages and each version is authentic. Thus, the comparison of different versions is sometimes necessary. Furthermore, the Community law uses terminology and refers to legal concepts which are peculiar to it. Autonomous and Community meanings of legal concepts differ from those known under national laws of the Member States. In *CILFIT* the ECJ resuméd the complexity in the interpretation of the EC law in the following terms:

> ' ... every provision of the Community law must be placed in its context and interpreted in the light of the provisions of Community law as a whole, regard being had to the objectives thereof and to its state of evolution at the date on which the provision in question is to be applied.'

Also, the ECJ relies on other methods of interpretation depending upon the case and the degree to which the provision to be interpreted is ambiguous, obscure and imprecise. This is the most characteristic feature of the ECJ: the wide eclectism of the methods used to interpret EC law combines with a willingness to draw from each of them the maximum effectiveness. The originality and autonomy of EC law vis-à-vis international law and national laws of the Member States, the need to maintain the coherence of the Community system and to ensure its unity and homogeneity require and, at the same time, allow the ECJ to became a law-maker. Whether this 'judicial legislation' should be criticised or on the contrary be considered as an asset, is a different matter.[42] There is no doubt that the ECJ has

---

[42] See R Lecourt, *L'Europe des juges*, Bruxelles: Bruylant, 1976.

considerably contributed to European integration and to the creation of dynamic and evaluative Community law.

General principles of Community law

In the 'judicial legislation' a special place is given to the general principles. These are unwritten rules of law which a judge has to apply (but not to create), although the preliminary stage to their application is necessarily creative. The reference to the general principles has the objectives of avoiding denial of justice and strengthening the coherence of Community law.

There is no reference to general principles in the CS Treaty. However, in *Algera* Joined Cases 7/56 and 7/57 [1957] ECR 39 the ECJ confirmed the existence of general principles applicable to the Community legal order on the basis that these principles are recognised by all legal systems of the Member States. The EC Treaty in art 288(2) expressly refers to 'general principles common to the laws of the Member States' according to which non-contractual liability of the Community is to be determined. However, the ECJ has not limited the reference to the general principles to this area. To the contrary, it has applied them to all aspects of EC law.

In formulating general principles the ECJ draws inspiration from many sources:

1. public international law and its general principles inherent to all organised legal systems;
2. national laws of the Member States by identifying the general principles common to the laws of the Member States;
3. EC law by inferring the general principles from the nature of the Communities; and
4. fundamental human rights.

Public international law and general principles inherent to all organised legal systems

The creation of a new international legal order by the Community did not preclude the ECJ from making reference to the general principles of public international law. The ECJ has endorsed some of them, that is the principle of compatibility of the successive conventional obligations (*Commission v Italy* Case 10/61 [1962] ECR 3) or the right of a national to enter and remain in the territory of his own country (*Van Duyn* Case 41/74 [1974] ECR 1337), and rejected others as contrary to this new legal order. For example, the principle of reciprocity especially under its form of the *exeptio non adimpleti contactus* was considered by the ECJ as incompatible with the Community legal order: *Commission v Belgium and Luxembourg* Cases 90 and 91/63 [1964] ECR 625.

The most important principle of public international law recognised by the ECJ is the principle of legal certainty which is in itself vague. In the context of EC legislation it means that the law must be certain and its legal implications foreseeable, especially in its application to financial matters: *Ireland v Commission* Case 325/85 [1987] ECR 5041. At national level, it means that national legislation implementing EC law must be worded in such a way as to be clearly understandable to those concerned as to their rights and obligations: *Commission v Italy* Case 257/86 [1988] ECR 3249. The ECJ has given a concrete scope of application to the principle of legal certainty in order to escape its tautological nature and to clarify its content. As a result, under the principle of legal certainty, the following rules have been established by the ECJ:

1. the principle of non-retroactivity of administrative acts (*Gesamthochschule Duisburg* Case 234/83 [1985] ECR 333);
2. the principle of good faith which requires that EC institutions in administrative and contractual matters act in conformity with that principle (*Van Lackmuller* Case 43/59 [1960[ECR 933);
3. the principle of *patere legem* (*Deutsche Tradex* Case 38/70 [1971] ECR 154; *United Kingdom* v *Council* Case 68/86 [1988] ECR 855);
4. the principle of vested or acquired rights (*Rossi* Case 100/78 [1979] ECR 831; *Verli Wallace* Case 159/82 [1983] ECR 2711);
5. the principle of legitimate expectations which means that 'those who act in good faith on the basis of law as it is or seems to be should not be frustrated in their expectations'.[43] This has given rise to many cases in the context of commercial activities of individuals and undertakings.[44]

Another category of general principles taken from public international law concerns the procedural rights necessary to safeguard the protection of substantive rights, such as the right to defence and especially to a fair hearing in administrative proceedings[45] and before courts,[46] including respect for the latter in the preliminary enquiry of the Commission in competition cases.[47] In addition, certain principles relating to the proper and sound administration of justice,[48] such as the refusal to recognise the possibility of an extraordinary appeal without any written text[49] or the continuity of the composition of an administrative body in a procedure capable of resulting in the imposition of pecuniary sanctions,[50] are also inspired by general principles of law.

General principles common to the laws of the Member States

It is not necessary that a general principle is recognised by legal systems of all Member States. It is sufficient if a given principle is common to a certain number of national legal systems, although 'non negligible divergences' constitute an obstacle to its recognition: *Hoechst* Case 46/87 [1989] ECR 2859. Advocate-General Slynn in *AM and S Europe* v *Commission* Case 155/79 [1982] ECR 1575 explained the manner in which the ECJ discovers unwritten principles of EC law by citing H Kutscher, a former judge at the ECJ. He explains:

'… when the Court interprets or supplements Community law on a comparative law basis it is not obliged to take the minimum which the national solutions have in common, or their

---

[43] Wyatt and Dashwood, *European Community Law,* section on The general Principles of Community Law, chapter 4.
[44] See Sharpston, 'Legitimate Expectations and Economic Reality' (1990) 15 European Law Review 103.
[45] *Commission* v *Italy* Case 7/69 [1970] ECR 117; *Transocean Marine Paint* Case 17/74 [1974] ECR 1063; *Hoffmann-La Roche* Case 85/76 [1978] ECR 461; *AKZO* Case 53/85 [1986] ECR 1985.
[46] *SNUPAT* Case 42/59 [1961] ECR 101.
[47] *Orkem* Case 374/87 [1989] ECR 3283.
[48] *Werhahn Hansamuhle* Cases 63–69/72 [1973] ECR 1229.
[49] *X* Case 12/68 [1969] ECR 116.
[50] *ACF Chemiefarma* Case 41/69 [1970] ECR 661.

arithmetic mean or the solution produced by a majority of the legal systems as the basis of its decision. The Court has to weigh up and evaluate the particular problem and search for the "best" and "most appropriate" solution. The best possible solution is the one which meets the specific objectives and basic principles of the Community ... in the most satisfactory way' (p1649).

Therefore, the discovery of general principles common to the Member States is based on a comparative study of national laws of the Member States but avoids any mechanical or mathematical approach leading to the lowest common denominator. To the contrary, the spirit of national laws, their evolution and general features are taken into consideration by the ECJ. A general tendency, or sometimes lack of it, may also inspire the judges. For example, the principle of proportionality was known only to German law but has become a general principle of Community law since it responds to the need of the Community legal order. In the process of discovery of general principles, the ECJ is entitled to choose the most appropriate from the point of view of the objectives of the Community law. It has, for example, recognised a principle which is rejected by all Member States but one (that is, the concept of exercise of public functions by an agent which has a broad meaning in five Member States but the ECJ favoured its narrow meaning which is recognised in one Member State only),[51] and rejected a principle common to national laws of all Member States but incompatible with the requirements of Community law.[52] Once the ECJ incorporates a national principle into EC law, it becomes an independent, autonomous principle which may have different meaning from the one known to national laws. Among the principles common to the national laws of the Member States the ECJ has discovered the following:

1. the principle of equality in respect of economic regulation (*Hauts Fourneaux et Acieries Belges* Case 8/57 [1958] ECR 225);
2. the principle of the hierarchy of legal measures which allows legislative acts to be distinguished from measures necessary for their implementation (Case 25/70 *Köster* [1970] ECR 1161);
3. the principle of unjust enrichment (*Danvin* Case 26/67 [1968] ECR 463);
4. the principles concerning tortious liability of the EC institutions (*Bayerische HNL* Case 83/76 [1978] ECR 1209);
5. the principle of confidentiality of written communications between lawyer and client (*AM and S Europe* v *Commission* Case 155/79 [1982] ECR 1575);
6. the principle of access to the legal process (*Johnston* v *Chief Constable of the Royal Ulster Constabulary* Case 222/84 [1986] ECR 1651);
7. the principle of the protection of business secrets of an undertaking (*AKZO* Case 53/85 [1985] ECR 1985; *SEP* Case C–36/92P [1994] ECR I–1911).

General principles inferred from the nature of the Communities

The ECJ has inferred from the specific nature of the Communities and from the objectives and the context of the Treaties a certain number of principles. Some of them concern institutional law of the Communities, other are inherent to the creation of the internal

---

[51] *Sayag* Case 9/69 [1969] ECR 3219.
[52] *Danvin* Case 26/67 [1968] ECR 463.

market. The first category of general principles reflects the political and economic structure of the Community. These principles are:

1. The principle of solidarity which is based on mutual trust between the Member States: *Commission v Italy* Case 39/72 [1973] ECR 101. Solidarity is required in internal and external relations of the Member States. The Treaty of Maastricht has further developed the principle of solidarity and recognised it as a binding objective of the Treaty. This principle has two aspects: within the Community it applies to all Member States, and in the context of the European Union it extends to the people of the Member States. In practice it means that all Member States should contribute to the harmonious development of the Union and thus the principle of solidarity strengthens the economic and social cohesion within the EU.

2. The principle of loyal co-operation between EC institutions and Member States, and between Member States themselves based on art 10 EC.

3. The principle of subsidiarity, and equality between Member States which has already been examined in Chapter 3.

4. The principle of limited powers which is implicit in art 7(1) EC and according to which EC institutions must act within the limits of the powers conferred upon them by the Treaty.

5. The principle of occupied fields and attributed powers which concerns the division of competences between the Community and the Member States.

6. The principle of proportionality which has already been discussed.[53]

As to the second category, these principles strengthen the objectives of the Community and the neo-liberal philosophy of the internal market. The principle of equality prohibits all forms of discrimination (direct and indirect) based on nationality[54] as recognised by art 12 EC, on gender[55] which is embodied in art 141 EC, and on distinction between producers and consumers within the framework of the common agricultural market under art 34(3) EC. It also applies to similar situations unless the differentiation is objectively justified,[56] and vice versa to the same treatment of different situations.[57]

Some principles are well rooted in Community law, others are more dubious. In this respect the ECJ in *Greece v Council* Case C–353/92 [1994] ECR 1–3411 followed Advocate-General Jacobs' opinion and rejected the principle of Community preference which was acknowledged as a general principle of EC law in previous decisions: *Beus* Case 5/67 [1968] ECR 125, especially 147. This rejection demonstrates that the list of general principles is not exhaustive or definitive.

Also related to the proper functioning of the common market are the principles of the free movement of goods, people, services and capital, the principle of the homogeneity of the common market, the principles relating to competition, etc.

---

[53] See also De Burca, 'The Principle of Proportionality and Its Application in EC Law' (1993) 13 Yearbook of European Law 105.

[54] *Oebel* Case 155/80 [1981] ECR 1993.

[55] *Defrenne* Case 149/77 [1978] ECR 1365.

[56] *Moulins et Huileries de Point-à-Mousson* Joined Cases 124/76 and 20/77 [1977] ECR 1795.

[57] *Sermide* Case 106/83 [1984] ECR 4209.

The most important principles which derive from the objectives of the Treaty, and have been developed by the ECJ in order to promote effective enforcement of EC law within the national legal systems of the Member States, are the principles of direct effect, direct applicability, supremacy of EC law, *effet utile* and the principle of the liability of Member States in damages for breaches of EC law vis-à-vis individuals. These principles will be examined in Chapter 6.

Fundamental human rights

At their inception the Communities focused on economic objectives. This consideration and the existence of the European Convention on Human Rights explain why the question of human rights has been relatively neglected. Nevertheless, the ECJ was confronted with fundamental human rights issues quite early on. The question of the fundamental rights which arose before the ECJ concerned the alleged contradictions between obligations imposed by the High Authority of the CS and the rights which were granted to undertakings under their national constitutional law. On the one hand, these rights and freedoms contained in national constitutions were superior to any other sources of law and their observance was imposed on any public authorities of Member States in their dealings with the public. Thus, it was impossible to permit national constitutional laws to prevail over Community law without compromising its uniform application throughout the Community. On the other hand, the founding Treaties neither contained any reference to fundamental human rights nor imposed on EC institutions any requirement to observe these rights. It was the task of the ECJ to find a solution to this legal impasse. For the first time, in *Stork v High Authority* Case 1/59 [1959] ECR 17,[58] the ECJ when determining the relationship between fundamental human rights and Community law refused to allow the examination of Community law in terms of its compliance with fundamental human rights and freedoms contained in national constitutions, as this approach would challenge the supremacy of Community law. The criticism expressed by Member States, and especially the German Constitutional Court, led the ECJ to alter its position in an *obiter* statement in *Stauder v City of Ulm* Case 29/69 [1969] ECR 419, in which it held that fundamental human rights constituted general principles of Community law and as such were protected by the ECJ. This position was further elaborated in *Internationale Handelsgesellschaft* Case 11/70 [1970] ECR 1125 when the Court emphasised that:

> 'The protection of such rights, whilst inspired by the constitutional traditions common to the Member States, must be ensured within the framework of the structure and objectives of the Community.'

This solution was considered as insufficient. In order to increase the protection of fundamental human rights, the ECJ decided to make reference to international conventions in this area, especially to the European Convention on Human Rights and Fundamental Freedoms signed in Rome on 4 November 1950 to which all Member States are contracting parties. In *Nold KG v Commission* Case 4/73 [1974] ECR 491 the ECJ held that 'international treaties for the protection of human rights on which the Member States have

---

[58] See also *Comptoirs de Vente de la Ruhr* Case 40/59 [1960] ECR 890 when the ECJ refused to invalidate Community law on the grounds of national law, even contained in the constitution.

collaborated or of which they are signatories, can supply guidelines which should be followed within the framework of Community law.'

Nevertheless, the ECJ highlightened that these rights are not absolute and 'far from constituting unfettered prerogatives, [they] must be viewed in the light of the social function.' Thus it is legitimate that 'these rights should, if necessary, be subject to certain limits justified by the overall objectives pursued by the Community, on condition that the substance of these rights is left untouched.'

Subsequently the ECJ has recognised, *inter alia*, the following rights:

1. the right to equal treatment including non-discrimination based on gender (*Defrenne* Case 149/77 [1978] ECR 1365);
2. the right to exercise economic and professional activities, although this may be legitimately restricted in the light of the social function of the protected activity;[59]
3. the right to private and family life, domicile and correspondence as set out in art 8 of the ECHR, but this does not exclude the interference of public authorities under the conditions defined by law and necessary to ensure public security and economic welfare of a country, or actions exercising the enforcement powers of the Commission in competition matters;[60]
4. the right to property (*Hauer* Case 44/79 [1979] ECR 3727), but commercial interests in which the risk factor is inherent to their substance are not protected (*Valsabbia* Case 154/78 [1980] ECR 907);
5. the right to medical secrecy (*Commission v Germany* Case C–62/90 [1992] ECR I–2575);
6. the right to association (*Union Syndicale* Case 175/73 [1974] ECR 917);
7. the right to free speech (*Elliniki* Case C–200/89 [1991] ECR I–2925; *TV 10 SA* Case C–23/93 [1994] ECR I– 4795);
8. the right to religious freedom (*Prais* Case 130/75 [1976] ECR 1589);
9. the principle of non-retroactivity of penal measures (*Kent Kirk* Case 63/83 [1984] ECR 2689).
10. the principle *'nulla poena sine lege'* (*Berner Allemeine* Case C–328/89 [1991] ECR I–3431).

Procedural rights – such as the right to defence, access to the court's fair hearing, etc – protected under the ECHR have also been recognised by the ECJ. In addition, in *Wachauf* Case 5/88 [1989] ECR 2609 the ECJ held that the protection of fundamental human rights is not only imposed on EC institutions, especially when they adopt binding measures, but also on the Member States in their application of such measures. Thus, national authorities in applying EC law must ensure 'as far as possible' that human rights are protected.

The importance of fundamental human rights prompted the Council, the Commission and the European Parliament to sign a Joint Declaration on 5 April 1977 which expressed their attachment to the protection of human rights. Although the Declaration was solely a political statement, it has initiated a new approach, that is the need for the Community to

---

[59] *Nold* Case 4/73 [1974] ECR 491; *Hauer* Case 44/79 [1979] ECR 3727; *Keller* Case 234/85 [1986] ECR 2897; *Neu EA* Cases C–90 and 91/90 [1991] ECR I–3617.

[60] *National Panasonic* Case 136/79 [1980] ECR 2033; *X v Commission* Case C–404/92P [1994] ECR I–4737; *Piera Scaramuzza v Commission* Case C–76/93P [1994] ECR I–5173.

incorporate the European Convention on Human Rights into Community law. This initiative was blocked by the Member States at the Maastricht Conference and, finally, in Opinion 2/94 the ECJ held that the EC had no competence to accede to the ECHR without revising the Treaty.

The Treaty of Maastricht incorporated two provisions relating to human rights, the first being art F(2) (now art 6(2) EU) which provides that:

'The Union shall respect fundamental rights, as guaranteed by the European Convention on Human Rights and Fundamental Freedoms signed in Rome on 4 November 1950 and as they result from the constitutional traditions of the Member States, as general principles of Community law.'

Although art F(2) envisaged fundamental human rights in the context of the EU and, in particular, as general principles of Community law, the Community judges have explicitly referred to this provision in a number of cases.[61] The second provision was art K.2 TEU (now art 30 EU) which provided that matters of common interest in co-operation in the fields of justice and home affairs shall be dealt with in accordance with the requirements of the ECHR and the 1951 Refugee Convention.

The Treaty of Amsterdam reinforces the EU commitment to the protection of human rights. The principles of liberty, democracy, respect for human rights and fundamental freedoms and the rule of law on which the EU is founded have been recognised as conditions for admission of a new Member and thus resulted in the amendment of art 49 EU. Article 6 EU reaffirms the principle of respect for human rights and fundamental freedoms. Furthermore, art 6 EU states that the EU 'shall provide itself with the means necessary to attain its objectives and carry through its policies'. In respect of human rights the concrete action of the EU has already been initiated. The Cologne European Council held in June 1999 decided to draw up a charter of the basic human rights of EU citizens by December 2000. The Tampere European Council held in October 1999 reached an agreement on the composition, method of work and practical arrangements for the body entrusted with this task.

Under art 7 EU 'serious and persistent violation' of human rights by a Member State is punishable under art 7 EU. This provision states that the Council meeting in the composition of the Heads of State or Government and acting by unanimity (a defaulting Member State is excluded) on a proposal by one-third of the Member States or by the Commission, and after obtaining the assent from the EP, may determine the existence of a violation of those fundamental freedoms, and then acting by a qualified majority may decide to suspend certain rights of the defaulting Member State, including the suspension of its voting rights in the Council. However, in applying this provision the Council must take into account the possible consequences of such a suspension on the rights and obligations of natural and legal persons.

---

[61] Article F(2) (now art 6(2) EU) is not enforceable before the ECJ. For that reason, Community judges can only make reference to this provision: see *Century Oil Hellas* Case T–13/94 [1994] ECR II–431; *Bosman* Case C–415/93 [1995] ECR I–4921.

Assessment of general principles of Community law

In the hierarchy of sources, general principles are as important as founding Treaties,[62] especially fundamental principles which are expressly acknowledged by art 6(2) EU which imposes the respect of them upon the European Union and all its institutions. The ECJ recognises other general principles in so far as they are compatible with the founding Treaties and fundamental human rights.

The general principles of EC law are, nevertheless, superior to secondary legislation.

---

[62] J A Usher, *General Principles of EC Law*: Longman, 1998.

6 Fundamental Principles of Community Law: Direct Applicability, Direct Effect, Supremacy of Community Law and a Member State's Liability in Tort

6.1 Direct applicability of Community law

6.2 Direct effect of Community law

6.3 Supremacy of Community law

6.4 The principle of State liability

Community law is neither foreign nor external to the legal systems of the Member States. To the contrary, it forms an integral part of national laws. Its peculiar position is due to the manner it which it penetrates the national legal order of the Member States. The three long-established fundamental principles developed by the ECJ – that is, direct applicability, direct effect and supremacy of Community law – strengthen its autonomy and determine the degree of its integration into the national laws of the Member States, as does the fourth which goes side by side with those three and establishes a Member State's liability for damage to individuals caused by a breach of Community law for which that Member State is responsible.

The definition of direct applicability of Community law was given in *Amministrazione delle Finanze dello Stato v Simmenthal SpA* Case 106/77 [1978] ECR 629 by the ECJ in the following terms:

> 'Direct applicability ... means that rules of Community law must be fully and uniformly applied in all Member States from the date of their entry into force and for so long as they continue in force.'

It was further explained in *Firma Molkerei* Case 28/67 [1968] ECR 211 in which the ECJ held that direct applicability ensures that the provisions of Community law penetrate into the national legal order of the Member States without the need for their implementation. Furthermore, direct applicability depends on the source of Community law, for some it is automatic and general in scope, for others it is conditional and limited.

The principle of direct effect is the most complex and difficult part of Community law. In *Van Gend en Loos v Netherlands* Case 26/62 [1963] ECR 1 the ECJ distinguished Community law from recognised principles of public international law relating to the law of the treaties and held that 'Community law ... not only imposes obligations on individuals but it is also intended to confer upon them rights' which national courts must protect.

These provisions are not only entirely independent from national law but in most cases an individual can rely on them where national rules preclude enforcement of Community law. The ECJ has established the general criteria of direct effect which requires that a provision, in order to produce direct effect, must be clear and precise, unconditional and must be incorporated into the internal legal order of the Member States without any national or Community implementing measures.

The supremacy of Community law means that primacy must be accorded to Community law over national laws of the Member States. This fundamental principle was established by the ECJ in *Costa* v *ENEL* Case 6/64 [1964] ECR 585 in which the ECJ held:

'... the law stemming from the Treaty, an independent source of law, could not, because of its special and original nature, be overridden by domestic provisions, however framed, without being deprived of its character as Community law and without the legal basis of the Community itself being called into question.'

The principle of a Member State's liability was established in *Francovich* v *Italian State* Cases C–6 and 9/90 [1991] ECR I–5357, in which the ECJ stated that 'a principle of State liability for damage to individuals caused by a breach of Community law for which it is responsible is inherent in the scheme of the Treaty.'

This chapter focuses on these fundamental principles and examines the complex relationship between Community law and national law of the Member States.

6.1 Direct applicability of Community law

Direct applicability is a matter well known to public international law. It concerns the manner of introduction of international law into municipal law. Public international law does not regulate the conditions on which provisions of international treaties become incorporated into municipal law in order to be applied by national courts. It is left to each country to decide on the relationship between international and municipal law. In this respect, there are two theories: dualist and monist. Under the dualist theory international law and municipal law are independent and separate systems. As a result, an international treaty duly ratified produces legal effect only at international level, that is, it is only binding on the contracting States. In order to be applied by national courts it is necessary to incorporate an international treaty into the State's legal system to enable it to take effect at the national level. The integration of international law into municipal law constitutes the most important feature of the dualist doctrine. However, once an international provision is implemented into national law, it is applied by national courts as any other municipal provision not as an international one.

In the monist system the unity between international and municipal law means that international law automatically becomes law within a contracting State. It is directly applicable. There is no need for reception of an international treaty as it becomes an integral part of national law of a contracting State once the procedure for its ratification is completed. An international provision is applied by municipal courts as such and not as a provision of domestic law.

Community law, due to its specificity, gives preference to the monist theory. In this respect, art 249 EC provides that regulations are directly applicable in all Member States. More importantly, the preference for the monist theory derives from the nature of the

Community. Only a monist system is compatible with the idea of European integration. In *Costa v ENEL* Case 6/64 [1964] ECR 585 the ECJ emphasised the peculiar nature of EC law by stating that the Member States have created:

'... a Community of unlimited duration, having its own institutions, its own personality, its own legal capacity and capacity of representation on the international plain and, more particularly, real powers stemming from a limitation of sovereignty or a transfer of powers from the States to the Community, the Member States have limited their sovereign rights, albeit within limited fields, and have thus created a body of law which binds their nationals and themselves.'

This confirmation is even more evident in the following passage extracted from the same decision in which the ECJ held that:

'By contrast with ordinary international treaties, the Treaty has created its own legal system which, on the entry into force of the Treaty, became an integral part of the legal systems of the Member States and which their courts are bound to apply.'

As a result, Community law cannot tolerate national divergencies as to their relations vis-à-vis international law since the dualist system jeopardises the attainment of the objectives of the Treaty and is contrary to the spirit and objectives of Community law. Member States may preserve the dualist system in relation to international law but it is excluded in relations between Community law and national law. As a result, Community law becomes an integral part of national law without any need for its formal implementation, and national judges are bound to apply it. Furthermore, it occupies a special place in the domestic legal systems of the Members States as it is applied as Community law and not as municipal law.

Direct applicability of the founding Treaties

The original signatories of the three founding Treaties have ratified them according to national constitutional procedures. In monist countries, such as France, the Treaties were incorporated into municipal law on the basis of their ratification.[1] In dualist countries, such as Belgium, Germany and Italy, it was necessary for national parliaments to intervene in order to supply the national legal basis for the Treaties and thus recognise their binding effect in municipal law, first by authorising their governments to ratify them and, second, to incorporate them into domestic law in a legislative form similar to the British Act of Parliament. To neutralise the effects of the dualist approach, in *San Michele* Joined Cases 9 and 58/65 [1967] ECR 1 the ECJ refused to acknowledge any conditions for implementation of the Community Treaties into the municipal law of the Member State and held that the Treaties are binding and should be applied by national judges not as internal law but as Community law.

For Member States which have joined the Communities subsequent to their creation the principle of direct applicability of the Treaties was obvious and case law of the ECJ clarified this point beyond any doubt. Since membership is conditional upon the acceptance of the 'acquis communautaire', the various accession acts have expressly recognised direct

---

[1] JORF of 22.2.1958.

applicability, direct effect and supremacy of EC law. In the United Kingdom s2(1) of the European Communities Act 1972 recognises direct applicability of Community law. It provides that:

> 'All such rights, powers, liabilities, obligations and restrictions from time to time created or arising by or under the Treaties, as in accordance with the Treaties *are without further enactment to be given legal effect* or used in the United Kingdom shall be recognised and available in law, and enforced, allowed and followed accordingly; and the expression "enforceable Community right" and similar expressions, shall be read as referring to one to which this subsection applies.'

Section 2(2) of the Act further confirms that Community law forms an integral part of the law of the United Kingdom.

Although Community law is incorporated into the law of the UK by means of implementing legislation, more specifically by the European Communities Act 1972, it does not emanate from the British Parliament and cannot be applied by British courts as municipal law. Upon their ratification, the Treaties automatically became law in the UK. Implementing legislation was not necessary but the UK as a dualist country decided that upon accession, from a purely national perspective, it was necessary to make Community law applicable within the national legal system by means of an Act of Parliament. In Ireland the Treaties were implemented by an Act of Parliament very similar to the 1972 British European Communities Act. Article 2 of the Irish Act provides expressly that from 1 January 1973 the Treaties as well as measures adopted by EC institutions shall be binding and form an integral part of Irish law. In Denmark art 3 of the law of 11 October 1972 relating to the Accession of Denmark to the European Communities introduced the Treaties directly into national law without any implementing measures, although Denmark is also a dualist country.

Regulations

The direct applicability of regulations is expressly recognised in art 249 EC. Their direct applicability is recognised by s2(1) of the European Communities Act 1972 in the United Kingdom. Not only are any implementing measures unnecessary, they are prohibited by Community law. In *Variola* Case 34/73 [1973] ECR 981 the ECJ was asked whether provisions of a regulation can be implemented into Italian law by internal measures reproducing the contents of that regulation in such a way as not to affect its substance. The ECJ held that:

> 'By virtue of the obligations arising from the Treaty and assumed on ratification, Member States are under a duty not to obstruct the direct applicability inherent in regulations and other rules of Community law.'

As a result, implementing measures are considered as a hindrance to their direct applicability and as such prohibited under Community law. The Constitutional Court of Italy recognised the arguments of the ECJ in the *Frontini* case,[2] in which it held that it

---

[2] Judgment of 27 December 1973, Frontini Foro it. 1974, I, 314.

derived from the logic of the Community system that EC regulations should not, as directly applicable legislative acts, be subject to national implementing measures capable of modifying, imposing conditions as to their entry into force, substituting, derogating or abrogating them, even partially.[3] In monist countries direct applicability of EC regulations is self-evident. In France, in *Syndicat des Hautes Graves de Bordeaux*,[4] the French Conseil d'Etat (highest administrative court) in its Decision of 22 December 1978 held that EC regulations by virtue of art 249 EC become, from their publication, an integral part of national law of the Member States. The French Constitutional Council also confirmed this.[5]

Directives and decisions

Directives are addressed to the Member States under the Treaties of Rome and to undertakings under the CS Treaty. Article 249 EC provides that Member States are under an obligation to achieve the objectives set out in EC directives but forms, procedure and methods necessary to attain these objectives are left at the discretion of the addressee Member States. Whether EC directives are directly applicable is a matter of controversy. For English scholars EC directives are not directly applicable since they require implementing measures.[6] For others, especially from monist Member States, States have only powers to implement directives, which is quite different from the reception of international treaties into the municipal system.[7] They make a distinction between the competence *d'execution* and the competence of *reception* and argue that Member States exercise the former in relation to EC directives but not the latter. They refuse to accept that until the transposition of EC directives into municipal law they do not exist from a legal point of view. In this respect, Judge P Pescatore said that a directive cannot be considered as 'a judicial non-entity from an internal viewpoint'.[8]

The question of direct applicability of EC directives was considerably clarified by the ECJ in *Inter-Environnement Wallonie ASBL v Région Wallonne* Case C–129/96 [1998] 1 CMLR 1057. Inter-Environnement Wallonie ASBL, a non-profit-making organisation, applied to the Belgian Conseil d'Etat for the annulment of a Walloon Regional Council Decree which expressly purported to implement Directive 75/442 on hazardous waste, as amended by Directive 91/156, and which was issued during the period prescribed for the transposition of Directive 91/156. The applicant argued that the Decree was contrary to the Directive as it did not include within its definition of waste a substance or object which directly or indirectly forms an integral part of an industrial production process. The Belgian Conseil d'Etat referred two questions to the ECJ for a preliminary ruling:

1. concerning the interpretation of arts 10 and 249 EC Treaty and, in particular, whether

---

[3] [1974] RTDE 48.

[4] [1979] RTDE R.526, 717, concl. Genevois.

[5] Decisions of 30 December 1977 [1979] RTDE 142, note G Isaac and J Molinier.

[6] See, for example, J Tillotson, *European Community Law*, 2nd ed, London: Cavendish, 1996, p69.

[7] For example, R Kovar, 'La contribution de la Cour de justice à l'édification de l'ordre juridique communautaire', in *Collected Courses of the Academy of European Law*, IV–I, especially p57.

[8] 'A non-être juridique du point de vue interne', in *L'effet des directives communautaires, Essay de démythification*, Paris: Dalloz, 1980, p171.

those provisions preclude Member States from adopting national legislation contrary to a non-implemented EC directive before the period for its transposition has expired, and

2. concerning the interpretation of art 1(a) of Council Directive 75/442 as amended by Council Directive 91/156 in order to determine the meaning of 'waste'.

The second question was answered first by the ECJ and may be dealt with briefly. The ECJ, following earlier case law,[9] held that a substance is not excluded from the Community definition of 'waste' merely because it directly or indirectly forms an integral part of an industrial production process. The interpretation of 'waste' provided by the ECJ demonstrated that the Decree of the Walloon Regional Council conflicted with the definition of 'waste' contained in art 1 of Directive 91/156. However, the Decree was adopted almost one year before the end of the transposition period prescribed by Directive 91/156. For that reason, it was necessary for the ECJ to clarify the obligations imposed on Member States by Community law in respect of non-implemented EC directives during their transposition period.

In the above case the ECJ has confirmed two important points. First, that EC directives are directly applicable from the moment of their notification to Member States to which they are addressed. The ECJ has dispelled all doubts in this respect, although art 254 EC states that EC directives adopted in accordance with the co-decision procedure and directives addressed to all Member States must be published in the Official Journal of the European Communities and enter into operation on the date specified in them or, in the absence of any specification, on the twentieth day following their publication. The ECJ confirmed that all EC directives whether published in the Official Journal of the European Communities, or those which do not require publication (all other directives), enter into force at the date of their notification to their addressees and not at the end of the transposition period laid down in the directive itself.

Second, the decision of the ECJ confirmed that a directive is directly applicable from the time of its notification to a Member State concerned, although it only becomes legally effective from the expiry of the implementation period. It has been well established that before the expiry of the prescribed time limit no obligations or rights arise from a directive for a Member State or for individuals: *Ratti* Case 148/78 [1979] ECR 1629. For that reason, it has been widely accepted that until the transposition of directives into national law, or the expiry of the time limit prescribed for their implementation, they do not exist from a legal point of view. They are not considered directly applicable.

The above view has been challenged by the author.[10] In this respect, it is submitted that the conditions for implementation of EC directives differ from those required for incorporation of international law into domestic law, and that Community law does not fit into the classic international law system but creates a new legal order considered as *sui generis* by the ECJ.[11] It is also submitted that Community law rejects the dualist theory in relation to the incorporation of Community law into the national law of Member States.

---

[9] *Tombesi* Cases C–304, 330 and 342/94 and 224/95 [1997] ECR I–3561; *Commission v Germany* Case C–42/92 [1995] ECR I–1097; *Zanetti* Case C–359/88 [1990] ECR I–1509.

[10] See her article: 'A New "Right" Available to Individuals under Community Law' (1999) 5 European Public Law 79–90.

[11] For example, *Van Gend en Loos* Case 26/62 [1963] ECR 1; *Costa v ENEL* Case 6/64 [1964] ECR 585. See: D Wyatt, 'New Legal Order, or Old' (1982) 7 EL Rev 147–66.

There are further justifications for the direct applicability of EC directives from the date of their notification to a Member State concerned. Indeed, a Member State does not enjoy an unlimited discretion in relation to the choice of form and method of national implementing measures. Such measures are subject to two requirements. The first relates to time limits imposed for their implementation, enforceable either under art 226 proceedings or at the suit of individuals. Failure of a Member State to implement an EC directive within the prescribed time limits does not severely affect individual litigants, in that:

1. They may rely on directly effective provisions of the directive in national proceedings.
2. Even if direct effect cannot be invoked, national courts are bound to interpret national law in the light of the wording and purposes of the relevant directive so as to achieve the result intended by its provisions.
3. Where neither direct effect nor indirect effect can be pleaded, they may bring an action in damages against the defaulting Member State and thus be compensated for losses resulting from the Member State's failure.

Second, Member States enjoy a degree of flexibility in relation to the form and methods to be used to attain the objectives of the directive. However, the validity of national implementing measures is assessed on the basis of criteria set up by Community law. These criteria require that national authorities choose the most appropriate form and methods in order to ensure the 'effet utile' of EC law (*Royer* Case 48/75 [1976] ECR 497) and to achieve the result that the Council or the Commission wish to obtain at Community level by adopting a particular directive: *Enka* Case 38/77 [1977] ECR 2203.

In addition to the above points in favour of direct applicability of EC directives, the decision of the ECJ in the case under discussion can now be invoked. The ECJ held (in response to the first question) that by virtue of arts 10 and 249 EC Member States have the obligation to refrain from adopting and bringing measures into force during a directive's transposition period if such measures are likely to seriously compromise the result required by the directive.

The limitation imposed upon legislative freedom of a Member State during the prescribed transposition period can only be explained if EC directives are directly applicable. In this respect the Commission stated that on the basis of arts 10 and 249 EC a Member State has a kind of standstill obligation which means that during the implementation period no national measures should be adopted (whether or not they intend to implement the directive) which 'increase the disparity between the national and Community rules' and result in jeopardising the achievement of one or more of the objectives of the directive. Furthermore, the adoption of such a measure would create legal uncertainty for individuals. The existence of the standstill obligation demonstrates, the author submits, that EC directives are directly applicable from the time of their notification to a Member State concerned. Otherwise, there is no justification for the imposition of the standstill obligation if EC directives have no legal existence during the transposition period. The idea of restricting legislative powers of a Member State in relation to measures purporting to implement a directive during its transposition period is not new. It was suggested by Advocate-General Mancini in *Teuling* Case 30/85 [1987] ECR 2497 that the freedom of action of a Member State before the end of the implementation period 'does not include the power to aggravate the defect which the directive is intended to remedy. Indeed, it may be that measures adopted during the prescribed period must of necessity be measures intended to transpose the Community provisions. Such measures must at least not conflict with the requirements laid down in those provisions' (para 7 of the Opinion).

The decision of the ECJ in this case demonstrates that the role played by EC directives in the framework of the Community legal system is more important than, at first glance, art 249 EC may suggest. They are directly applicable from the moment of their notification to a Member State concerned and as such form an integral part of national law long before the expiry of the time limit prescribed for their implementation.

In respect of EC decisions, they are directly applicable, irrespective of whether they are addressed to a Member State or to a natural or legal person.

6.2 Direct effect of Community law

Under public international law, some provisions of international treaties may confer rights on individuals or impose some obligations upon them. This possibility was recognised for the first time by the Permanent Court of International Justice (PCIJ) in the *Case Concerning Competences of the Courts of Danzing*[12] in which it was held that an exception to the principle of individuals not being subject to public international law arises if the intention of the contracting parties was to adopt a treaty which creates rights and obligations for them capable of being enforced by national courts. The PCIJ emphasised that this intention must be expressed and not inferred from the treaty, since this kind of international treaty constitutes an exception to a general principle. These treaties are qualified under public international law as 'self-executing'. They become automatically part of the national law of the contracting parties and are directly applicable by their national courts.

This exception has become a principle under Community law. In *Van Gend en Loos* Case 26/62 [1963] ECR 1 the ECJ delivered one of the most important decisions from a point of view of development of Community law: it held Community law directly effective and thus creating rights and obligations for EC nationals enforceable before national courts. The Court rejected the solution of public international law and without any justification based on the provisions of the Treaty, since there is neither an express provision in the Treaty nor a clear intention of the Member States in this respect, decided that Community law is directly effective.

In 1960 Van Gend imported unreaformaldehyde, a chemical product, into The Netherlands from Germany. In December 1959 The Netherlands enacted legislation which modified the Benelux tariff system and which brought into effect the Brussels Convention on Nomenclature unifying the classification of goods for customs purposes. Under the new nomenclature Van Gend's product was reclassified. This resulted in an increase in the duty payable on unreaformaldehyde to 8 per cent on an *ad valorem* basis as compared to 3 per cent payable previously under Dutch law. On the 14 January 1958 the EC Treaty came into force. Its art 12 (now substantially amended as art 25 EC) provided that:

---

[12] Advisory Opinion of 3 February 1928, Series B, no 15, esp 17.

'Member States shall refrain from introducing between themselves any new custom duties on imports or exports or any charge having equivalent effect, and from increasing those which they already apply in their trade with each other.'

Van Gend challenged the increase as contrary to art 12 EEC. When his claim was rejected by the customs inspector, he appealed to the Dutch Tariecommissie (Customs Court) in Amsterdam. Under art 234 EC the Custom Court submitted two questions to the ECJ: first, whether art 12 EEC (now art 25 EC) could create rights for individuals as claimed by Van Gend and, second, provided the answer to the first question was affirmative, whether the modification in customs duties was prohibited by art 12 EEC.

The governments of Belgium, West Germany and The Netherlands submitted additional memoranda to the ECJ claiming that art 12 EEC created obligations for Member States and not rights for individuals. As a result, if a breach of EC law occurred the proceedings should solely be based on arts 226 and 227 EC.

The ECJ based its decision on a systematic and teleological interpretation of art 12 EEC, and held that 'art 12 [now art 25 EC] of the Treaty establishing the European Economic Community produces direct effect and created rights which national courts must protect.' The Court invoked a number of arguments in support of its decision. It stated that direct effect confirms the peculiar nature of Community law. First, the objectives of the Treaty imply that the Treaty itself is 'more than an agreement which created mutual obligations between the contracting states'. Indeed, the Community 'constitutes a new legal order of international law … the subjects of which comprise not only Member States but also their nationals.' Second, it stems from the Treaty's preamble, which refers not only to the Member States but also to its people, that Community law affects both the Member States and their citizens. It also requires the co-operation of the latter in the functioning of the Community through its institutions such as the EP and the Economic and Social Committee. Third, the Court invoked an argument drawn from art 234 EC that the Member States 'have acknowledged that Community law has an authority which can be invoked by their nationals before those courts and tribunals'. From all these arguments the ECJ inferred that Community law 'independently of the legislation of Member States … not only imposes obligations on individuals but is also intended to confer upon them rights which become part of their legal heritage.' The rejection of public international law is clear cut when the ECJ states that 'Those rights arise not only where they are expressly granted by the Treaty, but also by reason of obligations which the Treaty imposes in a clearly defined way upon individuals as well as upon the Member States and upon the institutions of the Community.' Therefore, the fact that the addressees of a provision of the EC Treaty are the Member States 'does not imply that their nationals cannot benefit from this obligation'. To the contrary, the Treaty confers rights upon EC nationals not only when its provisions expressly provide so but also when they impose clearly defined obligations upon the Member States. In addition, direct effect of Community law ensures its effectiveness since 'The vigilance of individuals concerned to protect their rights amounts to an effective supervision in addition to the supervision entrusted by arts [226 and 227 EC] to the diligence of the Commission and of the Member States.'

Criteria of direct effect

It was left to the ECJ to determine the conditions under which a provision of EC law becomes directly effective. The criteria that emerged from decisions of the ECJ rendered mostly under art 234 EC are simple. A provision of Community law in order to produce direct effect must be:

1. sufficiently clear and precise;[13]
2. unconditional (*Casati* Case 203/75 [1981] ECR 2595, also *Ursula Becker* Case 8/81 [1982] ECR 53); and
3. self-executing, that is, must not require implementation by the Member States or EC institutions (*Defrenne* Case 43/75 [1976] ECR 455).

However, the ECJ has subsequently clarified these requirements. First, it held that lack of clarity or precision did not hinder a provision from producing direct effect if that provision may be clarified or defined in more precise terms by means of interpretation by a Community or national judge: *Fink Frucht* Case 26/67 [1968] ECR 327, *Defrenne* Case 43/75 (above) and *Barber* Case C–262/88 [1990] ECR I–1889. Second, a condition attached to a provision which suspends its application does not nullify its direct effect but merely delays it until the realisation of the condition or the expiry of the time limit: *Reyners* Case 2/74 [1974] ECR 631 and *Pubblico Ministero v Manghera* Case 59/75 [1976] ECR 91. A provision is still considered as unconditional, although it requires the adoption of some implementing measures on the part of a Member State or an EC institution, if neither a Member State nor an EC institution has a discretion to adopt those measures. In this respect, under art 90(3) EC Member States are required to eliminate or to 'correct' provisions of national fiscal laws which discriminate against imports from other Member States. In *Alfons Lütticke v Hauptzollamt Saarlouis* Case 57/65 [1966] ECR 205 the ECJ held that the Member States in order to implement art 90(3) EC had no discretionary powers and thus decided this provision was directly effective. In *Ursula Becker v Finanzamt Munster-Innenstadt* Case 8/81 [1982] ECR 53 the ECJ held that if implementation measures concerned solely procedural matters, a provision in question is still considered as unconditional and as such may be enforced before national courts.

It is submitted that the criteria of direct effect are not set in stone but depend upon the context in which Community law is applied by a national court. If a national judge has to apply EC law in the absence or in place of national law then a provision of Community law must, from all points of view, be unconditional, clear and sufficiently precise to take the place of national law. However, if a national judge has to verify whether national law is compatible with a provision of Community law, the provision produces direct effect if the 'limits of appreciation' which it contains are unconditional, clear and sufficiently precise: *Verbond van Nederlandse Ondernemingen* Case 51/76 [1977] ECR 113. Finally, if a national judge has to interpret national law in the light of Community law, or determine the liability of national authorities in breach of Community law, the criteria of direct effect are further attenuated.

---

[13] *Pubblico Ministero v Ratti* Case 148/78 [1979] ECR 1629; *Ursula Becker* Case 8/81 [1982] ECR 53. The formula 'clear and precise' was examined in *Comitato di Coordinamento per la Difesa della Cava v Regione Lombardia* Case C–236/92 [1994] ECR I–483.

Vertical and horizontal direct effect

Vertical direct effect means that an individual may enforce Community law in national courts against the State. Horizontal direct effect means that he may rely on Community law in proceedings before a national court against another individual, that is any natural or legal person. In practice, this distinction is very important since it considerably limits the scope and the effectiveness of EC law in the case of a provision which may only produce vertical direct effect.

Direct effect of the Treaties

The ECJ in *Van Gend en Loos* (see above) held that direct effect of the provisions of the EC Treaty is not automatic since they must be clear and precise, but it established that art 12 (now substantially amended as art 25 EC) was vertically directly effective. The question whether other provisions of EC Treaty can produce vertical direct effect was decided by the ECJ in *Alfons Lütticke v Hauptzollampt Saarlouis* Case 57/65 [1966] ECR 205.

In this case Lütticke imported whole milk powder from Luxembourg on which German customs levied duty and a turnover tax. Lütticke claimed that the imported product should be exempt from turnover tax as domestic natural milk and wholemilk powder were exempt under the Turnover Tax Law. The Finangericht des Saarlands referred to the ECJ under art 234 EC to ascertain whether art 90 EC, which prohibits the imposition of such taxes, has direct effect and if so whether it confers rights upon individuals which national courts must protect. The ECJ held that art 90 EC does produce such individual rights which must be enforced by national courts. Therefore, all doubts as to vertical direct effect of the EC Treaty provisions were dispelled.

The question of horizontal direct effect of Treaty provisions was decided by the ECJ in *Defrenne v SABENA* Case 43/75 [1976] ECR 455. In this case Miss Defrenne, who was employed as an air hostess by a Belgian airline company, SABENA, claimed for losses she sustained in terms of pay she received as compared with male cabin stewards doing the same work. The Court de Travail referred to the ECJ under art 234 EC to ascertain whether she could rely on art 141 EC which prohibits all discrimination between men and women workers and thus requires that they receive equal pay for performing the same tasks in the same establishment or service. However, art 141 EC required further implementation measures.

The ECJ held that in her case it was not difficult to apply art 141 EC as the facts clearly showed that she was discriminated against. It stated that:

> '... the prohibition on discrimination between men and women applies not only to the action of public authorities, but also extends to all agreements which are intended to regulate paid labour collectively, as contracts between individuals.'

However, in cases of discrimination which could not be easily identified implementation measures adopted by the Community or the Member States may be necessary. This case has established that some provisions of the Treaty may produce horizontal direct effect.

The case law of the ECJ has gradually elucidated which provisions of the Treaty have direct vertical and horizontal effect.

Provisions of the Treaty which produce both vertical and horizontal direct effect

1. The provisions relating to competition policy are particularly apt to produce vertical and horizontal direct effect and thus can be invoked by one undertaking against another undertaking before national courts: *BRT v Sabam* Case 127/73 [1974] ECR 51; *Bosch* Case 13/61 [1962] ECR 97. They are: arts 81 and 82 EC, 65–66 CS, 78, 81 and 83 EA concerning security control.

2. The provisions concerning the free movement of workers and of self-employed persons, that is arts 39, 43, 49, 50 EC and art 12 EC which prohibits discrimination based on nationality.[14] In this respect *Walrave and Koch v Association Union Cycliste Internationale* Case 36/74 [1974] ECR 1405 is particularly interesting. Here, the plaintiffs were prohibited by their sports association from competing in professional events on the grounds of their nationality. The ECJ held that discrimination as prohibited under art 12 EC applies not only to the action of local authorities but extends to rules emanating from private bodies which aim at collectively regulating gainful employment as an employee under art 39 EC or as a self-employed person under arts 43–49 EC.

3. As already examined, art 141 EC produces vertical and horizontal direct effect. Also, art 28 EC which provides for the free movement of goods could be relied upon by an individual against another individual in proceedings before national courts as stated in *Dansk Supermarked* Case 58/80 [1981] ECR 181.[15]

Provisions of the Treaty which have only direct vertical effect These provisions create rights for individuals which can only be enforced against the Member States. The first group of provisions concerns those which impose upon the Member States a prohibition. For example:

1. art 31(2) EC which prohibits the introduction of new discriminatory measures relating to State monopolies of a commercial nature (*Costa* Case 6/64 [1964] ECR 585; *Hansen* Case 91/78 [1979] ECR 935);

2. art 88(3) which prohibits the granting by a Member State of new aid without notifying the Commission (*Lorenz* Case 120/73 [1973] ECR 1471; *Fenacomex* Case C–354/90 [1991] ECR I–5505);

3. art 90(1) and (2) EC which prohibits discriminatory taxation of imports (*Lütticke* Case 57/65 [1966] ECR 205; *Fink Frucht* Case 27/68 [1968] ECR 341).

The second group concerns provisions of the Treaty which impose on a Member State an obligation to adopt necessary measures in specific areas. For example:

1. art 31(1) EC concerning State monopolies (*Manghera* Case 59/75 [1976] ECR 91);

2. art 90(3) EC concerning the elimination of discriminatory taxation on imports (*Lütticke* Case 57/65 [1966] ECR 205).

---

[14] For vertical direct effect: see *Walt Wilhelm* Case 14/68 [1969] ECR 15.
[15] For vertical direct effect: see *Iannelli* Case 74/76 [1977] ECR 557.

Provisions of the Treaty which have no direct effect[16]

1. art 2 EC which enumerates objectives of the EC Treaty (*Alsthom Atlantique* Case C–339/89 [1991] ECR I–107);
2. art 10 EC which requires that Member States must take all necessary measures to fulfil their obligations arising out of the Treaty (*Schlüter* Case 9/73 [1973] ECR 1161);
3. art 86(2) EC (*Politi* Case 43/71 [1971] ECR 1039; *Muller-Hein* Case 10/71 [1971] ECR 723);
4. arts 87 and 88(1), (2) EC which prohibits State aid (*Iannelli* Case 74/76 [1977] ECR 557; *Steinicke and Weinlig* Case 78/76 [1977] ECR 595);
5. art 97 EC relating to the obligatory consultation of the Commission by the Council on some legislative measures (*Costa* v *ENEL* Case 6/64 [1964] ECR 585);
6. art 108 EC (*Schlüter* Case 9/73 [1973] ECR 1135);
7. arts 136 and 137 EC relating to social policy (*Gimenez Zaera* Case 126/86 [1987] ECR 3697; *Firma Sloman Neptun* Cases C–72 and 73/91 [1993] ECR I–887).

To this list certain provisions of the Treaty of Amsterdam must be added, in particular provisions of Title IV of the EC Treaty and those relating to Pillars 2 and 3.

Regulations

Regulations are directly applicable and may produce both vertical and horizontal direct effect. The vertical direct effect of EC regulations was recognised in *Leonesio* v *Italian Ministry of Agriculture* Case 93/71 [1972] ECR 287. In this case under Council Regulation 1975/69 and Commission Regulation 2195/69 relating to a scheme to reduce dairy herds and over-production of dairy products, payments to farmers who slaughtered their dairy cows should be made within two months. The Italian government delayed implementation of the scheme until the introduction of necessary budgetary provisions (part of the cost was paid by national authorities). Leonesio slaughtered her dairy cows but did not receive payment within the two-month period. Leonesio brought an action before a national court against the Italian Ministry of Agriculture for payment.

Under art 234 proceedings the ECJ held that:

'Regulations were of direct effect, creating a right in the applicant Leonesio to a payment which could not be conditional or altered by national authorities, and which was immediately enforceable in the national courts.'

Politi v *Ministry of Finance of the Italian Republic* Case 43/71 [1971] ECR 1039 is the leading case concerning horizontal direct effect. The Politi organisation imported meat, and under Italian Law, no 330 of 15 June 1950, they were required to pay a duty of 0.5 per cent of the consignment value and a statistical levy which was imposed under art 42 of the Decree of the Italian President, no 1339 of 21 December 1961 and no 723 of 26 June 1965. Politi considered that the statistical levy should not have been imposed and sought judicial review before the court of the President of the Tribunale di Torino on the grounds that under art 14(1) EEC (now repealed) and EC Regulation 20/62 of 4 April 1962 'charging of any customs

---

[16] On this subject see R Kovar, *Note sur les critères du droit communautaires non directement applicable*, Mélange Dehousse, Nathan, Paris, Labor, Bruxelles, volume II, 1979, p227.

duty or charge having equivalent effect' on imports from Member States was incompatible with the intra-Community levy system. Further art 18(1) EEC (now repealed) provided that all levies equivalent to customs duties or charges having equivalent effect on imports from third countries should be abolished. The Italian court sought advice from the ECJ under art 234 EC to determine whether Regulation 20/62 which was by then replaced by Regulation 121/67 conferred individual rights which the national courts must protect.

The ECJ held that charges having equivalent effect are prohibited under art 23 EC and as a result Regulation 20/62 was unlawful and individuals were permitted to challenge it before the national courts.

Directives – the recognition of vertical direct effect of EC directives by the ECJ

There are three main arguments invoked against direct effect of EC directives. First, art 249 EC provides that only EC regulations are directly applicable. *A contrario*, EC directives are neither directly applicable nor directly effective. Second, EC directives have no general application. They are addressed only to the Member States and it is left to them to determine the form, methods and procedures necessary to attain the objectives being pursued. Therefore, EC directives cannot create rights for individuals since the latter are not addressees of EC directives and individual rights can only be conferred by national measures implementing EC directives. Third, the difference between EC regulations and EC directives disappears if the latter produce direct effect. This equality between them from a legal point of view would be incompatible with the EC Treaty since its provisions expressly provide that only EC directives are appropriate to harmonise specific areas of Community law.

The ECJ answered those arguments by emphasising the necessity to confer direct effect to EC directives. First, the binding force of EC directives is incompatible with the refusal to confer on them direct effect. Individuals should invoke them in appropriate circumstances. Second, the principle of *effet utile*, which has been applied by the ECJ in order to promote effective enforcement of Community law within the legal systems of the Member States,[17] requires the recognition of the direct effect of EC directives which entails their application by national courts. The third argument is inferred from art 234 EC which provides a procedure for national courts to consult the ECJ on interpretation and validity of EC law, without making any distinction among various legislative acts adopted by EC institutions. The ECJ considered that art 234 EC implies that EC directives can also be invoked by individuals in proceedings before national courts. As a result, EC directives should be directly effective.

The ECJ first invoked the possibility that EC Directives may produce direct effect in *Franz Grad v Finanzampt Traunstein* Case 9/70 [1970] ECR 825. In this case the question concerned direct effect of a Council Decision, and the ECJ stated that other measures mentioned in art 249 EC may produce direct effect, *inter alia*, EC directives. In *SACE* Case 33/70 [1970] ECR 1213 the ECJ was asked to give its ruling on the combined effect of directly effective provisions of the EC Treaty and the EC directive implementing them. The first decision of the ECJ in which direct effect of an EC directive was expressly recognised was *Van Duyn* Case 41/74 [1974] ECR 1337.

---

[17] See R Ward, 'National Sanctions in EC law: A Moving Boundary in the Division of Competence' (1995) 1 European Law Journal 205.

Miss Van Duyn, a Dutch national, arrived at Gatwick Airport on 9 May 1973. She intended to work as a secretary at the British headquarters of the Church of Scientology of California. British immigration authorities refused her leave to enter on the grounds of public policy. Although it was not unlawful to work for the Church of Scientology, the government of the United Kingdom warned foreigners that the effects of the Church's activities were harmful to the mental health of those involved. Miss Van Duyn challenged the decision of the immigration authorities on two grounds: art 39 EC which grants workers the rights to free movement between Member States, subject to its paragraph 3 which imposes limitations on grounds of public policy, public security or public health; and art 3(1) of Directive 64/221 which further implements art 39(3) EC and which provides that measures taken by Member States regarding public policy must be 'based exclusively on the personal conduct of the individual concerned'. She claimed that art 3(1) of Directive 64/221 was directly effective and that the refusal to allow her to enter the UK was not based on her conduct but on the general policy of the British government towards the Church of Scientology.

For the first time an English court referred to the ECJ under art 234 EC. The High Court asked whether both art 39 EC and the Directive were directly effective. The ECJ held that both produced direct effect. In particular, the ECJ held that 'given the nature, general scheme and wording [of art 3(1) of Directive 64/221] its effectiveness would be greater if individuals were entitled to invoke it in national courts.' Therefore, based on the principle of *effet utile*, the ECJ decided that art 3(1) of Directive 64/221 was directly effective.

The case law of the ECJ regarding EC directives has further elucidated the concept of direct effect. Three main tendencies have appeared. The general rule is that EC directives must be correctly implemented into national law, which means that individuals can rely on their provisions in national courts through the national implementing measures: *Felicitas* Case 270/81 [1982] ECR 2771. As a result, there should be no need to verify whether a provision of an EC directive satisfies the three criteria for direct effect, that is, it must be clear and precise, unconditional and self-executing. In this way, an individual may secure rights conferred by EC directives in the manner envisaged by art 249 EC. Therefore, the question of direct effect does not arise since the correct transposition of provisions of EC directives means that they are part of national law. The question whether an EC directive has been correctly implemented into national law concerns, in reality, the conformity of national law with EC law and not the question of direct effect: *Verbond van Nederlandse Ondernemingen* Case 51/76 [1977] ECR 113. Thus, any provision of an EC directive implemented into national law may be invoked in any dispute (including a dispute between individuals) in order to verify whether national authorities have implemented it in accordance with requirements specified in the directive: *Verbond van Nederlandse Ondernemingen* Case 51/76 [1977] ECR 113 at 127. Furthermore, implementing measures may be called into question in the process of interpretation of national law in conformity with Community law. In this respect in *Von Colson and Kamann* Case 14/83 [1984] ECR 1891 the ECJ held that national courts in applying national law, and especially its provisions implementing EC directives, have a duty to interpret national law in the light of the text and objectives of that directive in order to achieve the results envisaged in art 249 EC: see also *Bentjes* Case 31/87 [1988] ECR 4635.

Second, in order to curtail non-implementation of EC directives by the Member States within a specific time limit, usually laid down in the measures themselves, the ECJ held in *Pubblico Ministero v Ratti* Case 148/78 [1979] ECR 1629 that, provided the provisions of an EC directive are sufficiently precise and unconditional, its non-implementation in the prescribed period does not affect its direct effect.

Ratti was selling solvents and varnishes. He fixed labels to certain dangerous substances in conformity with Directives 73/173 and 77/128 but contrary to Italian legislation of 1963. He was prosecuted by the Italian authorities for breach of Italian legislation. Directive 73/173 had not been implemented in Italy, although the time limit prescribed for its implementation elapsed on 8 December 1974. Also Directive 77/128 was not transposed into Italian law but the time limit for its implementation had not yet expired. The Milan Court asked the ECJ under art 234 EC which set of rules should be applied, national law or Directives 73/173 and 77/128.

The ECJ held that if the provisions of an EC directive are sufficiently precise and unconditional, although not implemented within the prescribed period, an individual may rely upon them. However, if the time limit for implementation into national law had not been reached at the relevant time, the obligation was not directly effective.

A logical corollary of *Ratti* is that a Member State which has failed to transpose an EC directive within the prescribed time limit cannot rely on an unimplemented directive in proceedings against individuals: *Kolpinghuis Nijmegen* Case 80/86 [1987] ECR 3969.

Direct effect of an EC directive becomes an issue only if the implementation measures adopted by a Member State are incompatible with its provisions (*Enka* Case 38/77 [1977] ECR 2203; *Fratelli Constanzo* Case 103/88 [1989] ECR 1839), or insufficient (*Rutili* Case 36/75 [1975] ECR 1219), or as in *Ratti* when a Member State failed to implement a directive within the prescribed time limit.

Finally, EC directives can only produce vertical direct effect. This has been confirmed many times by the ECJ despite contrary opinions of Advocates-General[18] and was expressly confirmed in *Faccini Dori* Case C–91/92 [1994] ECR I–3325 in the following terms:

> 'The effect of extending that case law [horizontal direct effect] to the sphere of relations between individuals would be to recognise a power in the Community to enact obligations for individuals with immediate effect, whereas it has competence to do so only where it is empowered to adopt regulations.'[19]

Indirect horizontal direct effect of EC directives

The refusal of horizontal direct effect for EC directives means that even if conditions for direct effect are satisfied by provisions of EC directives, an individual cannot rely on them in proceedings brought against another individual. As a result, an individual cannot enforce his rights because the other party involved is an individual.[20] This is obviously an unjust and unfair situation since, for example, if an individual is employed in the public sector he may

---

[18] Conclusions of Van Gerven in *Marshall* Case C–271/91 [1993] ECR I–4367 at 4381; Jacobs in *Vaneetveld* Case C–316/93 [1994] ECR I–763 at 765; Lenz in *Faccini Dori* Case C–91/92 [1994] ECR I–3325.

[19] Confirmed in *Luigi Spano and Fiat Geotech* Case C–472/93 [1995] ECR I–4321.

[20] On this question: see V Prechal, 'Remedies after *Marshall*' [1990] CMLR 451.

bring proceedings against his employer based on the direct effect of an EC directive, but if he works in the private sector he has no remedy against an employer in breach of an EC directive. In order to overcome the practical implications deriving from its refusal to confer horizontal direct effect on EC directives, the ECJ has developed two approaches: first, extending the meaning of a State or a body emanating from the State and, second, imposing a duty on national courts to interpret national law in conformity with Community law. In *Inter-Environnement Wallonie ASBL* v *Région Wallonne* Case C–129/96 [1998] 1 CMLR 1057 the ECJ extended the above-mentioned obligation of interpretation to unimplemented directives before the expiry of the time limit prescribed for their implementation.

The main reason why the ECJ opted for such complex legal devices is that many Member States have resisted the recognition of vertical direct effect of EC directives. *A fortiori*, the imposition of horizontal direct effect of EC directives by the ECJ risks causing more harm than good to European integration. Indeed, the ECJ is much criticised for its revolutionary approach towards the application and interpretation of Community law. Its use of the concept of *effet utile* provides a good example. In public international law the concept of *effet utile* is applied by an international judge when he is confronted with two possible interpretations of a legal provision, one which confers some meaning on it and the other which devoids it of any significance. He gives priority to the former. The ECJ not only sets aside the interpretation which devoids a provision of its *effet utile* but, more importantly, rejects any interpretation which results in limitations or weakening of the *effet utile* of that provision. In *Franz Grad* Case 9/70 [1970] ECR 825 the ECJ held that:

> '... it would be incompatible with the binding effect attributed to decisions by art [249 EC] to exclude in principle the possibility that persons affected might invoke the obligation imposed by a decision.'

Furthermore, the ECJ in interpreting Community law takes into consideration the evolving nature of the Community and thus interprets Community law in the light of new needs which did not exist at the time of ratification of the founding Treaties. The development of the Common Commercial Policy provides the best illustration in this respect. Also the ECJ has inferred from Community law concepts such as supremacy of Community law, direct applicability, direct effect, the existence of external competences based on parallel internal competence and the doctrine of 'acquis communautaire'. The Court is the guardian of unity and of the very existence of the Communities. On the one hand, the ECJ, if possible, introduces concepts which are necessary for the survival of the law of the Community as a special species of international law but, on the other hand, it is sometimes more diplomatic in its approach towards Member States. Instead of antagonising them the ECJ achieves its objectives by more subtle means. The indirect horizontal affect of EC directives is the best example in this respect.

Extension of the concept of a State On the basis of vertical direct effect of EC directives an individual has directly enforceable rights on which he may rely in an action against a Member State in proceedings before the national courts. The obvious question is what bodies are considered as belonging to the State. In general, the answer is rather simple. The dichotomy of public/private bodies is known in all Member States. Nevertheless, the ECJ in order to maximise the effect of EC directives has introduced an autonomous meaning of a public body. In *Marshall v Southampton and South-West Hampshire Area Health Authority (Teaching) (No 1)* Case 152/84 [1986] ECR 723 Miss Marshall, an employee of the area health authority, was required to retire at the age of 60 while for her male colleagues the retirement age was 65. She was dismissed at the age of 62. Miss Marshall, who wished to remain in employment, argued that the British Sex Discrimination Act 1975, which excluded from its scope of application provisions in relation to death and retirement, was contrary to Council Directive 76/207 on Equal Treatment. The UK had adopted this Directive but had not amended the 1975 Act believing that discrimination in retirement ages was allowed. The Court of Appeal asked the ECJ under art 234 EC whether the dismissal of Miss Marshall was unlawful and whether she was entitled to rely upon Directive 76/207 in national courts.

The ECJ answered in the affirmative to both questions. It held that the area health authority was a public body regardless of the capacity in which it was acting, that is public authority or employer. It added that:

> 'The argument submitted by the United Kingdom that the possibility of relying on provisions of the directive against the respondent qua organ of the State would give rise to an arbitrary and unfair distinction between the rights of State employees and those of private employees does not justify any other conclusion. Such a distinction may easily be avoided if the Member State concerned has correctly implemented the directive into national law.'

Subsequently, the ECJ has elucidated the concept of a State and given to it a wide interpretation.[21] In *Foster and Others v British Gas plc* Case C–188/89 [1990] ECR I–3313 the ECJ provided a definition of a body which is an emanation of a State. It is a body

> '... whatever its legal form, which has been made responsible pursuant to a measure adopted by a public authority, for providing a public service under the control of that authority and had for that purpose special powers beyond those which resulted from the normal rules applicable in relations between individuals.'

It results from that definition that three criteria should be satisfied in order to consider an entity as an emanation of the State. First, it must be made responsible for providing a public service; second, it must provide that service under the control of the State; and, third, it must have special powers to provide that service beyond those normally applicable in relations between individuals. This test has been applied by national courts, including the British courts, to determine whether an organisation can be considered an emanation of the State. In *Doughty v Rolls Royce* [1992] 1 CMLR 1045 the Court of Appeal decided that although Rolls Royce was 100 per cent owned by the State, as the latter was its sole shareholder and thus any services it provided were under control of the State, it did not fulfil the remaining criteria established in *Foster*. As a result, Doughty in a very similar situation to Miss Marshall could not invoke Directive 76/207 and was barred from commencing proceedings against Rolls Royce.

Interpretation of national law in conformity with Community law by national courts

National judges are required to interpret national law in conformity with Community law.

---

[21] *Johnston v Chief Constable of the Royal Ulster Constabulary* Case 222/84 [1986] ECR 1651. The latter was considered as an emanation of a State.

This principle constitutes a logical consequence of the supremacy of EC law and applies in relation to all Community law[22] irrespective of whether or not a provision of EC law is directly effective. National law, whether posterior or subsequent, must conform to Community law. Furthermore, in *Von Colson and Kamann* Case 14/83 [1984] ECR 1891 the ECJ emphasised that national judges are obliged to interpret national law in the light of the text and objectives of Community law, which in this particular case was an EC directive. This solution is based on two premises. First, on arts 10 EC, 86 CS and 172 EA which impose upon the Member States a duty of loyal and active co-operation. Article 10 EC provides that Member States must take all appropriate measures, whether general or particular, to fulfil their obligations arising out of the Treaty and resulting from measures adopted by EC institutions. They must facilitate accomplishment of the tasks of EC institutions. This means that the Member States must adopt implementing measures vis-à-vis the Treaties and acts of EC institutions. Second, in *Scheer* Case 30/70 [1970] ECR 1197 the ECJ held that under art 10 EC the Member States have a duty to do whatever possible to ensure *effet utile* of the provisions of Community law. According to the ECJ art 10 EC applies to all national bodies, including national courts, which have a duty to ensure that national law conforms with Community law and thus the requirement of the principle of *effet utile* is satisfied, that is, rights vested in individuals by Community law are protected by national courts. This device is especially useful to ensure the indirect horizontal effect of EC directives as the combined effect of art 249 EC, art 10 EC and the principle of *effet utile* secures adequate enforcement of any obligations imposed on individuals.

The possibility of obliging national courts to interpret national law in conformity with Community law was for the first time mentioned in *Mazzalai* Case 111/75 [1976] ECR 657, para 10, when the ECJ approved the conclusion of Advocate-General Darmon who said that the interpretation of an EC directive may be useful for national judges in order to ensure that their interpretation and application conforms to the requirements of Community law. However, it was two decisions of the ECJ rendered the same day, *Von Colson and Kamann* Case 14/83 (see above) and *Harz* Case 79/83 [1984] ECR 1921, that provided a new solution to the problem of lessening the effect of the vertical/horizontal public/private dichotomy regarding EC directives.

Both Von Colson and Harz were females discriminated against on grounds of gender when applying for a job: Von Colson, in the public service as she applied for the post of prison social worker, and Harz in the private sector when she applied to join a training programme with a commercial company. Under German law implementing Council Directive 76/207 they were entitled to receive only nominal damages, that is, reimbursement of their travel expenses. They claimed that such implementation was contrary to art 6 of Directive 76/207 which provides that:

> 'Member States shall introduce into their national legal systems such measures as are necessary to enable all persons who consider themselves wronged by failure to apply to them the principle of equal treatment ... to pursue their claims by judicial process after possible recourse to other competent authorities.'

Both applicants argued that they should be offered the post or receive substantial damages.

---

[22] In relation to a provision of the Treaty: see *Murphy* Case 157/86 [1988] ECR 686.

The German labour court referred under art 234 EC to the ECJ the following questions: whether art 6 of Directive 76/207 was directly effective and whether under that Directive Member States were required to provide for particular sanctions or other legal consequences in cases of discrimination on grounds of sex against a person seeking employment.

The ECJ avoided the question of direct effect of art 6 of Directive 76/207 and instead concentrated on the interpretation of national law in conformity with EC law. It held that national law must be interpreted in such a way as to achieve the result required by the Directive regardless of whether the defendant was the State or a private party. It stated that sanctions for discrimination were left to national law and, on the one hand, that the employer is not obliged to offer a contract of employment to an applicant being discriminated against on the ground of gender but, on the other hand, decided that *effet utile* requires that

> '... when a Member State chooses to penalise breaches of prohibition by the award of compensation, then in order to ensure that it is effective and that it has a deterrent effect, that compensation must in any event be adequate in relation to the damage sustained and must therefore amount to more than purely nominal compensation such as, for example, the reimbursement only of the expenses incurred in connection with the application. It is for a national court to interpret and apply the legislation adopted for the implementation of the Directive in conformity with the requirements of Community law, in so far as it is given discretion to do so under national law.'

The German labour court found that it had power to award damages to both plaintiffs not exceeding six months gross salary.

In both cases the interpretation of national law in conformity with the Directive resulted in providing an efficient remedy to the applicants tantamount to conferring on art 6 of Directive 76/207 horizontal direct effect. The question arose whether the interpretation in conformity with Community law was restricted to national law implementing EC measures or extended to all law. The answer was provided by the ECJ in *Marleasing* Case C–106/89 [1990] ECR I–4135. In this case under the Spanish Civil Code a company could be nullified on the grounds of 'lack of cause'. Marleasing claimed that the defendant company was established in order to defraud its creditors, that the founders' contract was a sham and since the contract of association was void for 'lack of cause', he as one of the lenders could recover his debt personally from those behind the scheme. The defendants argued that under art 11 of the EC First Company Directive 68/151, which provided an exhaustive list of the grounds on which the nullity of company may be declared, lack of cause was not mentioned. Directive 68/151 was not implemented in Spain, although the prescribed time limit for its implementation had elapsed. The Spanish court asked the ECJ under art 234 proceedings whether art 11 of Directive 68/151 was directly effective and whether it prevented a declaration of nullity on grounds other than those enumerated in that provision.

The ECJ confirmed that EC directives could not produce horizontal direct effect, thus the defendant could not rely on art 11 in proceedings against another individual. Also art 11 of Directive 68/151 exhaustively listed the grounds of nullity and did not include the grounds on which Marleasing relied. Nevertheless, the ECJ held that based on its judgment in *Von Colson* a Spanish court was obliged 'so far as was possible' to interpret national law, whether it pre-dated or post-dated the Directive, in the light of its terms. This meant that a

Spanish court had to interpret Spanish law in such a way as to disregard provisions of the Spanish Civil Code which pre-dated Directive 68/151.

Marleasing is a very controversial case. On the one hand, it states that the obligation to interpret national law in conformity with EC law is demanded only 'as far as possible', on the other hand it does not require a national judge to interpret a national provision in the light of the Directive. It simply strikes down a conflicting national provision which was never intended to implement the Directive.[23] The ECJ has, to a certain extent, elucidated the meaning of *Marleasing* in *Wagner Miret v Fondo de Garantia Salarial* Case C–334/92 [1995] 2 CMLR 49.

Wagner Miret was employed as a senior manager in a Spanish company that became insolvent. Under Directive 80/897 Member States were required to set up a fund compensating employees in the case of insolvency of their employer. Spain established such a fund but it did not apply to senior management staff. The ECJ held that Directive 80/897 was not precise enough to produce direct effect and that Spanish law clearly limited access to the fund. Spanish law could not be interpreted in such a way as to include senior management staff within a group of people to be compensated from that fund. As a result, the duty to interpret national law in conformity with Community law is not absolute so as to interpret national law *contra legem* but only 'so far as possible'. However, Wagner Miret was not left without remedy as he could bring proceedings against Spain for incorrect implementation of Directive 80/897 which caused him damage (the so-called '*Francovich* remedy' which will be discussed in section 6.4).

It seems that the ECJ has limited the scope of *Marleasing*. National courts are under a duty to take into consideration all national law, whether adopted before or after the directive, concerning the matter in question in order to determine whether national legislation can be interpreted in the light of the wording and the purpose of the directive. The interpretation *contra legem* is required 'as far as possible'. A question arises as to the meaning of the formula 'as far as possible', ie what is the limit of national courts' obligation regarding the interpretation of national law in the light of the wording and the purpose of the directive?

In this respect the ECJ established that the uniform interpretation of Community law must be qualified in criminal proceedings where the effect of interpreting national legislation in the light of the directive would be to impose criminal liability in circumstances where such liability would not arise under the national legislation taken alone. In *Kolpinghuis Nijmegen BV* Case 80/86 [1987] ECR 3969 the ECJ held that the obligation for a national judge to make reference to the terms of the Directive, when he interprets relevant provisions of national law, is limited by the general principles of Community law and especially by the principle of legal certainty and non-retroactivity. This was further explained in *Criminal Proceedings against X* Joined Cases C–74 and 129/95 [1996] ECR I–6609, in which an Italian judge within the preliminary ruling proceedings under art 234 EC asked the ECJ to interpret some provisions of Directive 90/270 on the minimum safety and health requirements for work with display screens.[24] The Italian court did not exclude that the interpretation provided by the ECJ would have determined or

---

[23] See also *Luigi Spano and Fiat Geotech* Case C–472/93 and *Rockfon* Case C–449/93 [1995] ECR I–4291.
[24] OJ L156, L216 (1990).

aggravated liability of individuals in breach of that Directive, although Italian law which implemented its provisions did not provide for any penal sanctions. The ECJ held that:

'... the obligation on the national court to refer to the content of the Directive when interpreting the relevant rules of its national law is not unlimited, particularly where such interpretation would have the effect, on the basis of the Directive and independently of legislation adopted for its interpretation, of determining or aggravating the liability in criminal law of persons who act in contravention of its provisions.'

The ECJ explained that the principle of legality in relation to crime and punishment and especially the principle of legal certainty, its corollary, precludes bringing criminal proceedings in respect of conduct not clearly defined as culpable by law. In support of its decision the ECJ referred to the general principles of law which result from the common constitutional tradition of the Member States and art 7 of the ECHR.

The 'as far as possible' caveat, which attenuates the requirement of the principle of uniform interpretation, will certainly allow national courts to avoid *contra legem* interpretation of national law, but the circumstances in which this possibility may be invoked will have to be determined by the ECJ.

The obligation imposed on national courts to interpret national law in conformity with EC law has been further extended in *Inter-Environnement Wallonie ASBL* v *Région Wallonne ASBL* Case C–129/96 [1998] 1 CMLR 1057. Until this decision an individual had no remedy under Community law or national law in relation to both national rules not intended to implement an EC directive which were enacted in breach of that directive's underlying objectives during its transposition period and national provisions which pre-dated the directive. Under national law these rules were valid.[25] It has been well established that these national rules can only be interpreted in conformity with the directive from the expiry of the time limit prescribed by the directive.[26] This restriction on the duty of a national court to construe national provisions in a manner consistent with EC law can be explained by the peculiar nature of EC directives, that is that the transposition period is necessary in order to give time to a Member State to adopt law, regulations and administrative provisions necessary to ensure implementation of the directive. In written observations submitted by the governments of Belgium, France and the UK in *Inter-Environnement Wallonie* the three governments emphasised that, pending the final date for implementation of a directive, a Member State is allowed to enact measures contrary to it. However, only the UK government pointed out that although a Member State remains free to do so it flows from the combined effect of arts 10 and 249 EC Treaty that a Member State is precluded from adopting measures 'which would have the effect of making it impossible or excessively difficult for the State to give proper effect to the directive when it subsequently introduces measures to transpose the directive into national law': [1998] 1 CMLR 1064 (para 25). This preclusion has been maintained by the ECJ.

A consequence flowing from the above is that during the directive's implementation period a national court is entitled to review the legality of both national implementing measures and national measures enacted during that period which are not intended to transpose an EC directive. However, in relation to measures which purport to implement an

---

[25] See *Becker* Case 8/81 [1982] ECR 53.
[26] For example in *Marleasing* Case C–106/89 [1990] ECR I–4135 at 4147, Advocate-General Van Gerven, Opinion.

EC directive a distinction must be made between national provisions intended to constitute full and definitive transposition of the directive and national provisions which introduce transitional measures or measures designed to implement the directive in stages. The ECJ addressed this question and held that in the case of the first-mentioned measures their incompatibility might indicate that the result prescribed by the directive would not be achieved within the prescribed time limit as it would be impossible for a Member State to amend them in time and thus they should be struck down by a national court. In the case of the second-mentioned measures their incompatibility may only be temporary and therefore a national court should not declare them invalid before the end of the directive's transposition period.

The question whether or not an individual is allowed to challenge national implementing measures adopted before the end of a directive's transposition period, on the basis of the principle of the interpretation of national law in conformity with Community law, has not been unequivocally answered by the ECJ. In *Kolpinghuis Nijmengen BV* Case 80/86 [1987] ECR 3969 the Dutch District Court referred to the ECJ a hypothetical question in this respect. It asked whether a national court is required to interpret a national rule in the light of an applicable directive if at the material date (that is the time the proceedings were commenced before a national court) the period for the Member State to adopt national law had not yet expired. The ECJ declined to answer the question and stated that in the light of the circumstances of this case it was irrelevant whether or not the implementation period had expired.

In this case the circumstances were that Directive 80/777/EEC, on the approximation of the laws of the Member States relating to the exploitation and marketing of natural waters, had not been implemented in The Netherlands within the prescribed time limit. After its implementation period had elapsed, but before the entry into force of national implementing measures, criminal proceedings were brought against Kolpinghuis for non-compliance of its beverage (called 'mineral water' but which consisted of tap water and carbon dioxide) with art 2 of the Dutch Inspection Regulations of the Municipality of Nijmengen which prohibited the marketing of waters of 'unsound composition' as mineral waters. The problem with the Dutch Regulation was that it did not define the expression 'unsound composition', although Directive 80/777/EEC contained specific provisions as to the composition of mineral water. The Dutch public prosecutor argued that the Directive in question should guide the national court in the interpretation of a national law which pre-dated the Directive, since from the end of the transposition period the Directive had the force of law in The Netherlands. The situation in this case was that a national rule not intended to implement Directive 80/777/EEC was not clear and precise, The Netherlands failed to take had necessary implementing measures in relation to that Directive within the prescribed time limit, its transposition period expired after the proceedings were commenced against Kolpinghuis and the latter faced criminal charges. In those circumstances the ECJ held that a Member State in order to impose criminal liability on individuals could not rely on its own failure to fulfil an obligation arising out of the Treaty. Furthermore, this decision was based on the well established principle that EC directives can never impose direct obligations on individuals since they are addressed to Member States and therefore individuals may only be bound by the implementing legislation or regulations which a Member State to which the directive is addressed is obliged to enact.

However, in *Kolpinghuis* the Commission in its written observation stated that:

'A national court may, in interpreting a provision of national law, be guided by provisions of a directive which do not have direct effect in the relevant area, but there is no rule of Community law requiring it to do so.'[27]

As a result, there has been no uniform Community approach in respect of the interpretation of national law in conformity with an EC directive before the time limit for its implementation. The French Conseil d'Etat accepts that an individual may invoke provisions of an EC directive, as a point of reference in interpretation of national law, and especially national implementing measures even before the end of the implementation period prescribed by that directive, regardless of whether or not they are directly applicable.[28] Also Advocate-General Jacobs stated in *Hansa Fleisch* Case C–156/91 [1992] ECR I–5567 as well as in *Inter-Environnement Wallonie* that national courts were bound to interpret national implementing legislation in the light of the wording and the objectives of the directive. He used particularly strong terms to support this statement in *Inter-Environnement Wallonie* when he said that:

'... the duty to interpret implementing provisions consistently with the directive arises, not from the expiry of that [transposition] period, but from the duty of the national court under [art 10] to co-operate with other national authorities in their endeavour to implement the Directive. It would plainly be absurd if a national court were permitted to frustrate the intention of the national legislature by refusing to interpret implementing provisions in conformity with the Directive where they were capable of being so interpreted.'[29]

However, the practical importance of the duty imposed on a national court to interpret national law in conformity with Community law should not be overestimated. Even if such an obligation exists in relation to national implementing measures during a directive's transposition period, it is limited by two considerations: the obligation arises only when the national provision is open to interpretation and thus national courts will refuse to interpret national provisions *contra legem* (that is, if the provisions in question are clear and unambiguous they cannot be disregarded); and the principle of legal certainty, in the sense of legal predictability of law, often prevents national judges from construing national rules in conformity with Community law.[30]

The Marleasing *principle in the United Kingdom* In *Webb* v *EMO Air Cargo (No 2)* [1995] 4 All ER 577, the first British case after *Marleasing*, the House of Lords asked the ECJ under art 234 EC for some clarifications on the question of interpretation of national law in conformity with EC law and especially on its application to pre-dated national legislation.

Mrs Webb was offered a temporary job to replace her colleague who was on maternity leave. Before the commencement of Mrs Webb's employment she discovered that she was pregnant and as a result was in effect dismissed. She argued that this was unlawful under Directive 76/207 which prohibits discrimination based on sex. The House of Lords called to

---

[27] Case 80/86 [1987] ECR 3969 at 3975.
[28] *Ministeur du budget* v *Cercle militaire de la caserne France* [1990] AJDA 328.
[29] *Inter-Environnement Wallonie* Case C–129/96 [1998] 1 CMLR 1037 at 1071.
[30] Eg The Hoge Raad in *Michelin* v *Michels*, Rechtspraak NJB 1994/2, p14.

interpret the Sex Discrimination Act 1975 which implemented Directive 76/207 asked the ECJ under art 234 EC proceedings whether Mrs Webb's dismissal was contrary to Directive 76/207.

The ECJ held that Mrs Webb's dismissal was in breach of Directive 76/207. As a result the House of Lords had to interpret the Sex Discrimination Act 1975 as required by Directive 76/207. The House of Lords interpreted s5(3) of the Act, which provided that in order to determine discrimination a comparison between the treatment of women and men must be based on similar 'relevant circumstances', as meaning that 'relevant circumstances' meant, in the case of Mrs Webb, her unavailability for work due to pregnancy and not as previously stated by the House of Lords as simply her unavailability for work. The House of Lords held that a male employee could not be dismissed on those grounds and thus Mrs Webb's dismissal was discriminatory.

The House of Lords in *Webb* clearly accepted the decision of the ECJ in *Marleasing*, that is, that national legislation pre-dating Community law must be interpreted in conformity with the latter.

Decisions

A decision adopted under art 249 EC addressed to a legal or natural person is directly vertically effective. It creates rights and obligations vis-à-vis its addressee. A decision is directly effective and may be enforced by a Member State under art 256 EC. Also, a decision may confer rights on a third party which may be invoked in proceedings before a national court. For example, a decision adopted by the Commission vis-à-vis an undertaking in breach of competition law may be relied on by another undertaking which is a victim of the anti-competitive practice of the former.

The direct effect of a decision addressed to a Member State was a matter of controversy. Similar arguments as in the case of EC directives were advanced. The main difference between EC decisions and EC directives is that usually no implementation measures are required as the obligations are imposed only on a Member State, although this is not always the case. In *Franz Grad v Finanzampt Traunstein* Case 9/70 [1970] ECR 825 the ECJ recognised that the combined effect of a Treaty provision, a directive and a decision may have direct effect and therefore create rights for individuals enforceable before national courts. In this case Council Decision 65/271 of 13 May 1965 placed the German government under an obligation to introduce a common VAT system for road haulage, to abolish specific taxes in existence and not to introduce new ones thereafter. A harmonising directive laid down the deadline for the implementation of the Decision. In addition, art 25 EC prohibits introduction of any new custom duties or charges having equivalent effect. However, the German government levied a tax on the carriage of goods, in this case a consignment of preserved fruit from Hamburg to Austria. The claimants, a haulage contractor, challenged the transport tax as contrary to Decision 65/271. The court, Finanzgericht Munchen, made reference under art 234 to the ECJ to determine whether the Decision produced direct effect.

The ECJ held that the Decision did have direct effect and thus conferred individual rights which must be protected in national courts. The ECJ emphasised that 'it would be incompatible with the binding effect attributed to decisions by art [249 EC] to exclude in principle the possibility that persons affected might invoke the obligation imposed by a decision.' The ECJ decided that the obligation in question was sufficiently clear and unconditional to produce direct effect.

The ECJ based its reasoning exclusively on *effet utile*. This approach was confirmed in relation to a decision standing alone in *Hansa Fleisch* Case C–156/91 [1992] ECR I–5567. Also decisions adopted by a body created by an international treaty concluded between the Community and third countries may produce direct effect.[31] There are not many cases on the direct effect of decisions.

Decisions can only produce vertical direct effect. The justification for the rejection of horizontal direct effect being the same as for EC directives.

International agreements concluded between the Community and third countries

The ECJ has the same approach towards international agreements concluded between the Community and third countries as monist countries. An individual may rely on the provisions of an international agreement in proceedings before national courts provided they are capable of conferring rights upon individuals and satisfy the criteria for direct effect, that is they are clear and precise, unconditional and self-executing. This principle was established in *International Fruit Company NV and Others* v *Produktschap voor Groenten en Fruit* Cases 21–24/72 [1972] ECR 1219.

The claimants challenged import licensing and quota-setting regulations imposed upon importers as being contrary to art XI GATT. Under art 234 EC the ECJ was asked whether measures adopted by Community institutions are valid under international law in that Regulations 459/70, 565/70 and 686/70 are contrary to art XI GATT. The ECJ held that the provisions of international law must be capable of conferring rights on individuals before they can be invoked. Article XI did not create rights for individuals. As a result, EC regulations cannot be affected by art XI GATT.

In *Bresciani* Case 87/75 [1976] ECR 129 the ECJ allowed individuals to rely on the provisions of an international agreement concluded between the Community and third countries. In *Kupferberg* Case 104/81 [1982] ECR 3641 the ECJ held that neither the nature nor the economy of an international agreement can prevent an individual from relying on its provisions in proceedings before national courts. The best summary of the case law of ECJ in this respect is given in the conclusion of Advocate-General M Darmon in *Demirel* Case 12/86 [1987] ECR 3719. He emphasised that a provision of an agreement concluded between the Community and third countries may be considered as producing direct effect when, in relation to its terms, object and nature, it contains a clear and precise obligation which is not subordinated to the intervention of any subsequent act. This means that a provision of an international agreement, which may be drafted in terms identical to those of the EC Treaty (which was recognised as capable of producing direct effect), may not be regarded as directly effective since the object and nature of that agreement constitutes a *sine quoi non* of direct effect. Direct effect of provisions in free trade (*Kupferberg* Case 104/81 [1982] ECR 3641), co-operation (*Zoulika Krid* Case C–103/94 [1995] ECR I–719) and association[32] agreements has been recognised by the ECJ.

---

[31] For example a decision adopted by the Association Council EEC-Turkey: *Sevince* Case C–192/89 [1990] ECR I–3461; *Kazim Kus* Case C–237/91 [1992] ECR I–6781; *Recep Tetik* Case C–171/95 [1997] ECR I–329.

[32] *Bresciani* Case 87/75 [1976] ECR 129 (Yaoundé Convention); *Pabst* Case 17/81 [1982] ECR 1331 (Association agreement between the EEC and Greece).

The form in which an international agreement was introduced into Community law, that is by a decision or a regulation adopted by the Council, is not taken into consideration by the ECJ in determining whether or not a provision produces direct effect.

6.3 Supremacy of Community law

There is no mention of supremacy of Community law in the founding Treaties. The absence of any express provision is not, however, a gap in Community law but a result of diplomacy and caution. Indeed, an express provision would have confirmed the federal nature of the Community and thus prevented some Member States from acceding to the Communities. For that reason less controversial formulas were used, such as art 249 EC which conferred binding effect upon measures adopted by the EC institutions and art 10 EC which required that Member States abstain from taking measures capable of compromising the attainment of the objectives of the Treaty.

In practice, however, the issue of supremacy arose before national courts which referred to the ECJ for clarification under the procedure laid down in art 234 EC. It was the task of the ECJ to firmly establish the principle of supremacy of Community law as the *sine qua non* of the existence of the Community itself and its peculiar nature in the international legal order. In *Costa v ENEL* Case 6/64 [1964] ECR 585 the ECJ recognised the supremacy of Community law over the national law of the Member States. Costa was a shareholder of a private undertaking nationalised by the Italian government on 6 September 1962. When assets of many private undertakings were transferred to ENEL, Costa, who was also a lawyer, refused to pay an electricity bill for £1 sent by ENEL and was sued by the latter. He argued, *inter alia*, that the nationalisation legislation was contrary to various provisions of the EC Treaty. The Milanese Giudice Conciliatore referred this question to the ECJ under art 234 EC. The Italian government claimed that the referral was 'absolutely inadmissible' since a national court which is obliged to apply national law cannot avail itself of art 234 EC. In the meantime the Italian Constitutional Council decided in favour of national legislation on 7 March 1964 by applying the dualist theory.

In the above case the ECJ established one of the most important principles of Community law: the supremacy of EC Law. The ECJ based its reasoning on three arguments:

1. Direct applicability and direct effect of Community law would be meaningless if a Member State was permitted by subsequent legislation to unilaterally nullify its effects by means of a legislative measure which could prevail over Community law. The Court held that:

   'The Treaty has created its own legal system which on the entry into force of the Treaty, became an integral part of the legal systems of the Member States and which their courts are bound to apply ... The integration into the laws of each Member State of provisions, which derive from the Community and more generally the terms and the spirit of the Treaty, make it impossible for the State, as a corollary, to accord precedence to a unilateral and subsequent measure over a legal system accepted by them on a basis of reciprocity.'

217

Furthermore the ECJ stated that:

> 'The precedence of Community law is confirmed by art 249, whereby a regulation "shall be binding" and "directly applicable in all member States". This provision, which is subject to no reservation, would be quite meaningless if a State can unilaterally nullify its effects by means of a legislative measure which could prevail over Community law.'

2. By transferring certain competences to the Community institutions the Member States have limited their sovereignty. The ECJ held that:

> 'By creating the Community of unlimited duration ... and more particularly real powers stemming from a limitation of sovereignty or a transfer of powers from the States to the Community, the Member States have limited their sovereign rights, albeit within limited fields, and have thus created a body of law which binds both their nationals and themselves.'

3. Uniformity of application of Community law which ensures homogeneity of the Community legal order. In this respect the ECJ held that:

> 'The executive force of Community law cannot vary from one State to another in deference to subsequent domestic laws, without jeopardising the attainment of the objectives of the Treaty set out in art 3 EC and giving rise to the discrimination prohibited by art [12 EC].'

The ECJ summarised its reasoning in the following terms:

> '... the law stemming from the Treaty, an independent source of law, could not, because of its special and original nature, be overridden by domestic legal provisions, however framed, without being deprived of its character as Community law and without the legal basis of the Community itself being called into question.'

This statement constitutes the essence of supremacy of Community law. The position of the ECJ has not changed since its decision in *Costa*. If anything, the ECJ has become more radical in confirming the obvious implications of supremacy of Community law vis-à-vis the Member States. Indeed, whatever the reaction of the Member States and no matter how long it takes to gain full recognition of this principle by the Member States, for the Community supremacy is a necessary requirement of its existence. In order to achieve the objectives of the founding Treaties, which are to uniformly apply EC law throughout the Community,[33] to ensure the proper functioning of an internal market, and to become a fully integrated structure, the supremacy of Community law must be respected by the Member States. Otherwise, the Community will cease to exist.[34]

Supremacy of Community law is based on the fact that contrary to ordinary international treaties the founding Treaties have created their own legal system. Its supremacy results from the peculiar nature of the Community and not from concessions made by constitutional laws of the Member States. For that reason, primacy of Community law does not depend on which theory each Member State applies in order to determine the

---

[33] In *Zuckerfabrik Suderdithmarschen* Cases C–143/88 and 92/89 the ECJ held that uniformity of application of EC law constitutes a fundamental requirement of the Community legal order: [1991] ECR I–415 at para 26.

[34] As the ECJ explained in *Walt Wilhelm* Case 14/68 [1969] ECR 15.

relationship between national and international law and which, in any event, varies from one Member State to another.

The supremacy of Community law is unconditional and absolute, all Community law prevails over all national law. It means that all sources of Community law, the provisions of the Treaties, secondary legislation – regulations,[35] directives,[36] decisions[37] – general principle of Community law,[38] and international agreements concluded between the Community and third countries,[39] irrespective of whether or not they are directly effective, prevail over all national law. Also Community law is superior to all provisions of national law: legislative, administrative, jurisdictional and constitutional. In relation to the constitutional laws of the Member States, in *San Michele* Joined Cases 9 and 58/65 [1967] ECR 1[40] the ECJ confirmed that a provision of national constitutional law cannot be invoked in order to nullify the application of Community law since such is contrary to the Community legal order.

As resumed in the two following paragraphs In *International Handelsgesellschaft* Case 11/70 [1970] ECR 1125 the ECJ held that Community law prevails over national constitutional law, including fundamental human rights enshrined in the constitution of a Member State. In this case EC regulations set up a system of export licences, guaranteed by a deposit, for certain agricultural products. The system required that products be exported during the validity of a licence, otherwise the deposit would forfeited. The plaintiffs lost a deposit of DM 17,000 and argued that the system introduced by EC regulations and run by the West Germany National Cereals Intervention Agency was in breach of the fundamental human rights provisions contained in the German constitution, in particular the principle of proportionality. The Frankfurt Administrative Court referred to the ECJ under art 234 EC to determine the validity of one of the two regulations in question.

The ECJ confirmed the supremacy of Community law over national constitutional law in the following terms:

> '... the law stemming from the Treaty, an independent source of law, cannot because of its very nature be overridden by rules of national law, however framed, without being deprived of its character as Community law and without the legal basis of the Community itself being called in question. Therefore, the validity of a Community measure or its effect within a Member State cannot be affected by allegations that it runs counter to either fundamental rights as formulated by the constitution of that State or the principles of a national constitutional structure.'

Nevertheless, the ECJ held that fundamental human rights, taking into account their importance, cannot be disregarded by the Community. Respect for them forms an integral part of the general principles of EC law and the protection of such rights must be ensured within the framework of the structure and objectives of the EC. In this case, the ECJ declared the regulation in question as valid and the system of deposits as an appropriate method of attaining the objectives of arts 34(3) and 37 EC concerning the common organisation of the agricultural markets.

---

[35] *Politi* Case 43/71 [1971] ECR 1039; *Marimex* Case 84/71 [1972] ECR 89.
[36] *Rewe* Case 158/80 [1981] ECR 1805; *Becker* Case 8/81 [1982] ECR 53.
[37] *Salumificio de Cornuda* Case 130/78 [1979] ECR 867.
[38] *Wachauf* Case 5/88 [1989] ECR 2609.
[39] *Nederlandse Spoowegen* Case 38/75 [1975] ECR 1439; *SPI and SAMI* Cases 267–269/81 [1983] ECR 801.
[40] The decision was rendered in relation to CS.

The conflict between national law enacted prior to the entry into force of the Treaties and EC law has been resolved in favour of Community law. All pre-dating national law is deemed to be abrogated or at least devoid of its legal effect inasmuch as it is contrary to Community law. This has been confirmed in the case examined above. Similarly, in a conflict between Community law and national law post-dating the entry into effect of the Treaties the former prevails. One of the most important cases is this respect is *Amministrazione delle Finanze* v *Simmenthal* Case 106/77 [1978] ECR 629 in which the ECJ defined the task of national judges faced with conflicting provisions of national law and Community law. Simmenthal imported a consignment of beef from France to Italy. He was asked to pay for veterinary and public health inspections carried out at the frontier. He paid but sued in the Italian court for reimbursement of money, arguing that the fees were contrary to Community law. After reference to the ECJ, which held that the inspections were contrary to art 28 EC as being equivalent in effect to quantitative restriction and that the fees were consequently unlawful under art 25 EC being charges equivalent to customs duties, the Italian court ordered the Italian ministry to repay the fees. The ministry refused to pay, claiming that a national statute of 1970 under which Simmenthal was liable to pay fees still prevented any reimbursement and could only be set aside by the Italian Constitutional Court. The question was referred once again to the ECJ under art 234 EC.

The ECJ confirmed that in the event of incompatibility of a subsequent legislative measure of the Member State with Community law every national judge must apply Community law in its entirety and must set aside any provision of national law, prior or subsequent, which conflicts with Community law. The ECJ held that:

> '... any provisions of a national legal system and any legislative, administrative, or judicial practice which might impair the effectiveness of Community law by withholding from the national court having jurisdiction to apply such law the power to do everything necessary at the moment of its application to set aside national legislative provisions which might prevent Community rules from having full force and effect are incompatible with those requirements which are the very essence of the Community law.'

As a result, national courts should not request or await the prior setting aside of an incompatible national provision by legislation or other constitutional means but of its own motion, if necessary, refuse the application of conflicting national law and instead apply Community law. In *Ministero delle Finanze* v *IN.CO.GE.'90 Srl and Others* Joined Cases C–10–22/97 [1998] ECR I–6307 the ECJ clarified its judgment in *Simmenthal*. In this case IN.CO.GE.'90 and 12 other Italian limited liability companies paid a special annual administrative charge for entering them on the register of companies (tassa do concessione governativa). This charge was declared unlawful by the ECJ in *Ponente Carni* Cases C–71 and 178/91 [1993] ECR I–1915. The companies subject to the charge sought to recover their payments. The Italian authorities refused the reimbursement. They argued that the Italian courts had no jurisdiction over fiscal matters and that the claims were time-barred. The Italian district magistarates' court in Rome referred a question to the ECJ relating to the consequences arising under Italian law from the incompatibility of the domestic charge with EC law. Questions of classification of the charge and of procedural law were at issue. If a national judge had to disapply national law which implemented EC law, including its provisions on the classification of the charge in question, as contrary to EC law, and classified the charge on the basis of Italian law, the charge in question would cease to be of a fiscal nature and would fall within the general rules for recovery of amounts paid but not due with the consequence of depriving the charge of any existence in law.

The Commission argued that a national provision incompatible with EC law should be treated as non-existent and void. The ECJ disagreed. It stated that:

> 'It cannot [...], contrary to the Commission's contention, be inferred from the judgment in *Simmenthal* that the incompatibility with Community law of a subsequently adopted rule of national law has the effect of rendering that rule of national law non-existent. Faced with such a situation, the national court is, however, obliged to disapply that rule, provided always that this obligation does not restrict the power of the competent national courts to apply, from among the various procedures available under national law, those which are appropriate for protecting the individual rights conferred by Community law.'

As a result, inconsistent domestic law should be disregarded but any rights conferred by EC law have to be enforced under domestic procedure.[41]

However, the classification or reclassification of a charge is a matter for national law. The ECJ emphasised that in the absence of Community rules governing the matter the principle of procedural autonomy applies, that is, a Member State is entitled to establish 'alongside a limitation period applicable under the ordinary law to actions between private individuals for the recovery of sums paid but not due, special detailed rules governing claims and legal proceedings to challenge the imposition of charges and other levies.' However, the national rules cannot deprive Community law of its effect and therefore national provisions must not be less favourable than those governing similar domestic actions and must not render virtually impossible or excessively difficult the exercise of rights conferred by Community law. Whatever the classification of a charge a Member State is required to repay charges levied in breach of Community law.

The obligation to give full effectiveness to Community law, and thus to protect rights which it confers upon individuals, empowers a national judge to suspend, as an interim measure, the application of national law which he suspects to be in conflict with Community law,[42] although it might be contrary to national law to do so.

As a result, based on the supremacy of Community law, national judges are able to resolve any difficulties which they may encounter while facing a conflict between national law and Community law. Similarly, administrative authorities are required to set aside any national provision incompatible with Community law: *Fratelli Constanzo* Case 103/88 [1989] ECR 1839. In relation to sanctions, especially of a penal nature, ordered by virtue of national law incompatible with Community law, those sanctions are considered as devoid of legal basis: *Schonenberg* Case 88/77 [1978] ECR 473 and *Regina and Robert Tymen* Case 269/80 [1981] ECR 3079.

---

[41] See also *Lück* Case 34/67 [1968] ECR 359.
[42] *R v Secretary of State for Transport, ex parte Factortame (No 2)* Case C–213/89 [1991] ECR I–2433; see the principle of supremacy in the United Kingdom.

The principle of supremacy of Community law in the UK

Two of the original Member States (Italy and Germany) had difficulties in accepting the principle of supremacy of Community law as such, and most of them experienced difficulty in recognising it in relation to their constitutions. This principle was not expressly mentioned in the founding Treaties but the necessity to ensure the uniform application of EC law in all Member States, as well as the requirements of the evolving Community, resulted in its slow recognition although for reasons other than stated by the ECJ in *Costa* (see above). It seems that only two original Member States, that is Belgium and Luxembourg, accepted the reasoning of the ECJ without demurring and recognised the supremacy of Community law based on the peculiar nature of the Community legal order.[43]

In principle, there should be no difficulties in the United Kingdom with recognition of the supremacy of Community law since when a State accedes to the Communities it must accept the 'acquis communautaire'. At the time of the accession of the United Kingdom, the principle of supremacy was already well rooted in Community law. Furthermore, s2(4) of the European Communities Act 1972 provides that 'any enactment passed or to be passed ... shall be construed and have effect subject to the foregoing provisions of this section.' As a result, all legislative acts enacted subsequent to the European Communities Act 1972 are subject to Community law and thus any conflict between Community law and subsequent national legislation should be resolved in favour of the former on the grounds of supremacy of EC law. For many years, however, the British judiciary tried to reconcile the irreconcilable: the principle of supremacy of EC law with Dicey's model of parliamentary sovereignty according to which there are no limits to the legislative power of Parliament subject to the exception that Parliament cannot limit its own powers for the future. This means that no legislation enacted by Parliament is irreversible. The breakthrough came in *R v Secretary of State for Transport, ex parte Factortame (No 3)* Case C–221/89 [1991] ECR I–3905.

Their Lordships accepted the decision of the ECJ gracefully. Lord Bridge said:

> 'If the supremacy within the European Community of Community law over national law of Member States was not always inherent in the EEC Treaty it was certainly well-established in the jurisprudence of the European Court of Justice long before the United Kingdom joined the Community. Thus, whatever limitation of its sovereignty Parliament accepted when it enacted the European Communities Act 1972 it was entirely voluntary. Under the terms of the Act of 1972 it has always been clear that it was the duty of a United Kingdom court, when delivering final judgment, to override any rule of national law found to be in conflict with any directly enforceable rule of Community law.'

6.4 The principle of State liability

The principle that a Member State should be liable in damages to individuals who have

---

[43] The Cour de Cassation of Belgium in the decision of 27 May 1971, *SA Fromagerie Franco-Suisse Le Ski* [1971] CDE 561, note Pescatore; V K Lenaerts, 'The Application of Community Law in Belgium' [1986] CMLR 253; and the Supreme Court of Justice of Luxembourg in its decision rendered on 14 July 1954, although Luxembourg is a dualist country: M Thill, 'La primauté et l'effect direct du droit communautaire dans la jurisdrudence luxembourgeoise' [1990] RFDA 978.

suffered loss as a result of that State's infringement of Community law is today one of the cornerstones of Community law. Its origin can be found in *Russo v Aima* Case 69/75 [1976] ECR 45, in which the ECJ held that a Member State should pay compensation for damage caused by its own breach of Community law but refer to national law to lay down the necessary conditions applicable to tortious liability.

There are many justifications for the introduction of this principle into Community law. The less obvious and not mentioned in *Francovich and Bonifaci v Italian State* Joined Cases C–6 and 9/90 [1991] ECR I–5357, which established Member States' liability in tort, is that many Member States in the late 1980s delayed the implementation of EC directives which were mainly used to complete the internal market. There was no effective remedy since penalties against defaulting Member States were introduced in the amended art 228 EC by the TEU. The best way to ensure implementation of an EC directive was to allow individuals to enforce their rights before national courts, that is to permit them to sue a defaulting Member State for loss that they had suffered, especially in cases where the EC directives were not directly effective or when individuals had no remedy based on indirect horizontal effect. The leading case in this area is *Francovich*.

Francovich, as a result of the bankruptcy of his employer, lost 6,000,000 lira. He sued his former employer but could not enforce the judgment against him (the latter was insolvent). He decided to commence proceedings against the Italian State for sums due or for compensation in lieu under Council Directive 80/987, which was not implemented in Italy although the prescribed time limit had already elapsed. Directive 80/987 on protection of employees in the event of the insolvency of their employers required that the Member State set up a scheme under which employees of insolvent companies would receive at least some of their outstanding wages.[44] In *Commission v Italy* Case 22/87 [1989] ECR 143 the ECJ under art 226 EC held Italy in breach of EC law for non-implementation of Directive 80/987. The Italian court made reference to the ECJ under art 234 EC to determine whether the provision of the Directive in relation to payment of wages was directly effective and whether the Italian State was liable for damages arising from its failure to implement the Directive.

The ECJ held that the provision in question was not sufficiently clear to be directly effective, but made the following statement in relation to the second question: 'It is a general principle inherent in the scheme of the Treaty [that] a Member State is liable to make good damage to individuals caused by a breach of Community law for which it is responsible.' The ECJ justified the new principle on the basis of supremacy of Community law, *effet utile* and art 10 EC, which requires Member States to take all appropriate measures to ensure the fulfilment of their obligations arising out of the Treaty.

In *Francovich* the ECJ, in upholding a claim against the Italian government for non-implementation of a directive held that a Member State may be liable for losses that could be directly attributed to its failure to implement a directive provided that the date for such implementation has expired; that the provisions of that directive are unconditional and sufficiently precise to confer rights upon individuals; and that the action is brought against the State. This judgment firmly recognised that a plaintiff may rely upon the vertical effect

---

[44] Council Directive 80/987 was implemented in the United Kingdom in the Employment Protection (Consolidation) Act 1978 as amended. It set up the Redundancy Fund which provides payments for employees of insolvent companies.

of directives and rejected reliance upon horizontal effect to the dismay of some who consider that 'the distinction between public and private [law] is unjustified'.[45]

In this case the ECJ has established three conditions necessary to give rise to liability in the case of total failure of a Member State to implement a directive:

1. the result required by the directive must include the conferring of rights for the benefit of individuals;
2. the content of those rights must be clearly identifiable by reference to the directive;
3. there must be a causal link between the breach of the State's obligation and the damage suffered by the individual.

Under Community law it has been established that any provision is unconditional where neither a Member State nor a Community institution is required to take any measures to implement it or to give it effect: *Molkerei-Zentrale Westfalen/Lippe GmbH v Haupzollampt Paderborn* Case 28/67 [1968] CMLR 187. To be sufficiently precise in the above context requires that the terms relied upon by the plaintiff define with sufficient clarity to enable a national court to decide the identity of the persons entitled to the benefit from that right and to ascertain whether the plaintiff is such a beneficiary, the extent and content of that right and the identity of the legal body charged with providing that right: *Francovich* Case C–6/90.

However, in *Francovich* the ECJ left many questions unanswered. They were clarified in *Brasserie du Pêcheur SA v Federal Republic of Germany; R v Secretary of State for Transport, ex parte Factortame and Others (No 4)* Joined Cases C–46 and 48/93 [1996] 1 CMLR 889. The facts of these cases are as follows:

1. Case C–46/93 *Brasserie du Pêcheur SA v Federal Republic of Germany*
   Brasserie, a French brewer, was forced to cease exports to Germany as its beer did not comply with the purity standards imposed by the Biersteuergesets (Law on Beer Duty, BGBI.I p144). In *Commission v Germany* Case 178/84 [1987] ECR 1227 the ECJ had already ruled that such a ban was incompatible with art 28 EC.
2. Case C–48/93 *R v Secretary of State for Transport, ex parte Factortame and Others*
   The United Kingdom government enacted the Merchant Shipping Act 1988 which made the registration of fishing vessels dependent upon conditions as to the nationality, residence and domicile of their owners. Factortame, being a Spanish owned company, was deprived of its right to fish. In *Factortame (No 3)* Case C–221/89 [1991] ECR I–3905 the ECJ held such legislation to be contrary to EC law. This was confirmed in *Commission v United Kingdom* Case C–246/89 [1991] ECR I–4585.

The ECJ held that Member States could be liable under Community law for breaches of the EC Treaty and of Community measures in certain defined circumstances.

First, the Court abolished the disparity between the conditions governing liability of the Community institutions based on art 288(2) EC and the conditions under which the Member States may incur liability for damage caused to individuals in like circumstances. In this respect the ECJ stated:

---

[45] Lord Slynn of Hadley, 'A Judgement on the European Court' (1993) 30 International Corporate Law 32.

'... the conditions under which the State may incur liability for damage caused to individuals cannot, in the absence of particular justification, differ from those governing the liability of the Community in like circumstances. The protection of the rights of individuals derived from Community law cannot vary on whether a national authority or a Community institution is responsible for the damage': *Brasserie du Pêcheur* Case C–46/93.

Second, the ECJ clarified the conditions of liability. They are as follows:

1. The rule of law which has been infringed must be one which is intended to confer rights on individuals.
2. The breach must be sufficiently serious to merit an award of damages. To be held liable a Member State must have 'manifestly and gravely' disregarded its obligation. In order to assess whether this condition is satisfied national courts should take into consideration a number of factors such as: the clarity and precision of the EC rule breached, the element of discretion in the adoption of legislative acts by national authorities, whether or not the infringement was intentional or accidental, whether any error of law was excusable, whether any action or advice on the part of the Commission had contributed to the breach, etc.
3. There must be a direct causal link between the Member State's default and the loss suffered by the applicant.

The apparent disparity between the original criteria laid down in *Francovich* and those adopted above was explained by the ECJ as being 'in substance ... the same since the condition that there should be a sufficiently serious breach, although not expressed in *Francovich*, was nevertheless evident from the circumstances of the case': *Dillenkofer* v *Germany* Cases 178, 179 and 189/94 [1996] 3 CMLR 469.

These conditions for State liability apply to all breaches of Community law, whether legislative, executive or administrative. A State is liable regardless of the organ of State whose act or omission infringed Community law. Also, it is irrelevant whether the provision in question is directly effective or not. Whichever is breached, a Member State may be liable. The ECJ emphasised that direct effect constitutes a minimum guarantee and thus *Francovich* liability is a necessary corollary of the *effet utile* of Community law.

Third, an applicant suing a Member State need not prove that the authorities were at fault. The ECJ stated in *Dillenkofer* that 'reparation for loss or damage cannot be made conditional upon fault (whether intentional or negligent) going beyond that of a sufficiently serious breach of Community law.'

Fourth, the ECJ has placed the onus upon national courts to uphold such rights under national rules for public tortious liability by imposing upon them the duty to 'verify whether or not the conditions governing state liability for a breach of Community law are fulfilled'. The Court laid down the criteria which might be used by national courts in order to determine the measure of damages. National courts are charged with ensuring that the protection of Community law rights is given equal status and may not be less favourable than the protection afforded to similar rights arising under domestic law. National courts may not impose any procedure that makes it more difficult or even impossible for an individual to rely upon those rights. The UK's rule on the award of exemplary damages against a public official for oppressive, arbitrary or unconstitutional behaviour should be carried over to claims for breaches of EC law.

In respect of what is to be considered as a sufficiently serious breach, the ECJ held that 'where a Member State was not called upon to make any legislative choices and possessed only considerably reduced, or even no discretion, the mere infringement of Community law may be sufficient to establish a sufficiently serious breach'.[46] This approach was confirmed in *R v HM Treasury, ex parte British Telecom plc* Case 392/93 [1996] ECR I–1631 which concerned the failure to properly implement art 8(1) of Directive 90/531. In this case the ECJ found that the Member State concerned had a wide discretion of power in the field in which it was acting; that the wording of the provisions of the original Directive was imprecise and as a result was capable of being interpreted in the manner implemented; that implementation had been carried out after taking legal advice as to the Directive's meaning; and that there was no ECJ case law on the subject nor any objection from the Commission as to the interpretation applied. In the light of the above there was not a sufficiently serious breach of Community law. Conversely, in *R v Minister of Agriculture, Fisheries and Food, ex parte Hedley Lomas (Ireland) Ltd* Case C–5/94 [1996] ECR I–2553 which concerned the United Kingdom authorities' refusal to grant an export licence in breach of a directive, the ECJ stated that 'where the Member State was not called upon to make any legislative choices and possessed only considerably reduced, or even no discretion, the mere infringement of Community law may be sufficient to establish a sufficiently serious breach'. In the *Factortame* saga, after the preliminary ruling delivered by the ECJ, the question for the domestic courts was to determine whether the UK's breaches of EC law were sufficiently serious as to entitle the respondents to compensation. The Divisional Court held that the UK's breach of EC law was sufficiently serious to give rise to liability in damages to individuals who suffered loss as a consequence of that breach. The Court of Appeal upheld the decision of the Divisional Court. The Secretary of State appealed to the House of Lords. He argued that:

1. The UK had a wide measure of discretion in dealing with a serious economic problem. Therefore it cannot be said that when exercising its discretion the UK manifestly and gravely disregarded its powers.

2. No liability could be imposed on the UK, even if there was a breach of EC law, since the breach was excusable for a number of reasons: first, the law in this area was unclear until the ECJ had given judgments; and second, the conduct of the UK could be objectively justified on substantive grounds, taking into account that, on the one hand, under the common fisheries policy quotas allocated to Member States were to be protected by them and, on the other hand, under international law it was a State's prerogative to decide who should be entitled to register a vessel and fly its flag.

The House of Lords held in *R v Secretary of State for Transport, ex parte Factortame and Others (No 5)* [1999] 3 CMLR 597 that the adoption of legislation which was discriminatory on the ground of nationality in respect of the registration of British vessels

---

[46] *R v Minister of Agriculture, Fisheries and Food, ex parte Hedley Lomas (Ireland) Ltd* Case C–5/94 [1996] ECR I–2553. See also *Brinkmann Tabakfabriken GmbH* Case C–319/96 [1998] 3 CMLR 673.

was sufficiently serious to give rise to liability in damages to individuals who suffered loss as a consequence.

The judgment of the House of Lords is not surprising. In *R v Secretary of State for Transport, ex parte Factortame and Others (No 4)* Case C–48/93 [1996] 1 CMLR 889 the ECJ had already dealt with arguments invoked by the Secretary of State. In this respect Lord Slynn (in *Factortame (No 5)*) said:

'It was obvious that what was done by the government was not done inadvertently. It was done after anxious consideration and after taking legal advice ... The shortness of the transitional period, the fact that there was no way in domestic law of challenging the statute, and that the respondents were obliged not merely to avoid being removed from the old register but to apply to be put on the new register, all emphasised the determination of the government to press ahead with the scheme despite the strong opposition of the Commission and the doubts of its officials. Therefore, it seems clear that the deliberate adoption of legislation which was clearly discriminatory on the ground of nationality was a manifest breach of fundamental Treaty obligations.'

Lord Hope emphasised that if in the present case damages were not to be held recoverable, it would be hard to envisage any case, short of one involving bad faith, where damages would be recoverable.

All Law Lords agreed that the breach of Community law by the UK was sufficiently serious to entitle the respondents to compensation for damage directly caused by that breach.

Another interesting aspect of the present case is that under the Merchant Shipping Act 1988 a vessel could be registered as British if it was British owned, and it was British owned if its legal owners and not less than 75 per cent of the beneficial owners were qualified persons or qualified companies. In order to be regarded as a 'qualified person' it was necessary to be a British citizen resident and domiciled in the UK, and a 'qualified company' had to be incorporated in the UK and have the relevant percentage of its shareholders and the relevant percentage of its directors as qualified persons. The House of Lords examined the conditions regarding residence and domicile as it was clear that a condition concerning nationality was laid down in art 12 EC. In respect of domicile the House of Lords agreed that it should be treated in the same way as nationality. Thus, that condition was also considered breached and the breach as being sufficiently serious. In relation to residence Lord Slynn held that, on the one hand, the condition was excusable taking into account the aim of the legislation which was to protect the livelihood of British fishing communities, but, on the other hand, it was not, taking into account that this condition was applied not only to fishermen but also to shareholders and directors of companies owning fishing vessels. Consequently, the condition of residence could not be justified where the discrimination was so obvious. Furthermore, the British government all along took the view that the residence condition in itself was not sufficient to achieve its objective and so taken separately could not be justified.

A number of interesting questions regarding a Member State's liability in tort were raised in *Walter Rechberger and Renate Greindl, Hermann Hofmeister and Others v Republic of Austria* Case C–140/97 [1999] ECR I–3499. In this case the claimants were subscribers to the Austrian daily newspaper, *Neue Kronenzeitung*, which wanted to reward their loyalty to its newspaper by offering them, by a way of gift, a four- or seven-day trip to one of four European destinations. The offer was generally free of charges for the subscribers (save for airport taxes) but there was a charge of ATS 500 if they travelled alone. A person travelling with a subscriber was required to pay the price set out in the brochure. Subscribers who accepted the offer were required to pay the organiser a deposit of 10 per cent of the relevant charges, the balance being payable no later than ten days before the scheduled departure date. The offer was so successful that the travel organiser Arena-Club-Reisen could not cope with the demand and went bankrupt. In the meantime the advertising campaign organised by the newspaper was held by the Austrian Supreme Court to be in breach of Austrian competition law.

Under the Act of Accession the Republic of Austria had to implement Council Directive 90/314/EEC by 1 January 1995. Article 7 of that Directive provides that the organiser of a package tour or holiday is to provide 'sufficient evidence of security for the refund of money paid over and for the repatriation of the consumer in the event of insolvency'.

When the subscribers asked to be reimbursed they faced two problems. The first was that the bank guarantee issued by the travel organiser in conformity with national law implementing Directive 90/314 was insufficient to reimburse the travel costs they had paid. The second was that some subscribers had made bookings in 1994 but legislation implementing Directive 90/314 applied only to packages booked after 1 January 1995 with a departure date of 1 May 1995 or later. Even the 'lucky' subscribers who were covered by the legislation could only recover from the bank guarantee 25.38 per cent of the amount paid.

In these circumstances the plaintiffs brought an action against the Republic of Austria, before an Austrian court, for failure to implement art 7 of Directive 90/314 correctly and in good time. The referring court asked the ECJ a number of questions: first, whether art 7 of Directive 90/314 applied to public relations trips being a part of an advertising campaign that infringed national competition law; second, the time limit for providing the security set out in art 7 of Directive 90/314; third, whether defective transposition of art 7 constituted a sufficiently serious breach of Community law giving rise to a right to compensation; and, finally, for some clarifications as to the causal link between the failure of a Member State to implement a directive correctly and the damage sustained by the individuals, in particular whether a State's liability in tort can be precluded by imprudent conduct on the part of the travel organiser or by force majeure.

First, the ECJ held, that Directive 90/314 applied to public relations trips. In this case the trip was offered by a daily newspaper as a gift exclusively to its subscribers and constituted a part of an advertising campaign which was in breach of national competition law. The ECJ decided that the plaintiffs were exposed to risks arising from the insolvency of the organiser of the package travel, the risks against which art 7 of Directive 90/314 is intended to protect consumers. Therefore, taking into account the objective of art 7 it applied to them since it applies even if the consideration the purchaser is required to pay does not correspond to the total value of the package or relates only to a single component of it. The fact that the advertising campaign was unlawful was irrelevant as to the classification of the trip as package travel within the meaning of the Directive.

Second, the ECJ dealt with the conditions under which State liability gives rise to a right to compensation, in particular whether the Austrian authorities committed a sufficiently serious breach. In *Dillenkofer* Cases C–178, 179 and 189/94 [1996] ECR I–4845 the ECJ held that non-implementation of a directive within the prescribed time limit constitutes, *per se,* a serious breach of Community law and consequently gives rise to a right of reparation for individuals suffering injury. In that case the ECJ clarified the conditions for non-contractual liability of a Member State. In the case of non-implementation of a directive within the prescribed time limit, a Member State 'manifestly and gravely' disregards the limits of its discretion and therefore will be held liable. However, in the present case, only art 7 of Directive 90/314 was incorrectly implemented. In this respect, the ECJ held that art 7 of the Directive leaves no discretion to a Member State and thus Austria could not limit its application to package travel booked after 1 January 1995 with a departure date of 1 May 1995 or later since art 7 applies to all contracts for package travel entered into from 1995 onwards and relating to trips to be taken after that date. The ECJ clearly stated that: 'The limitation of the protection prescribed by art 7 to trips with a departure date of 1 May 1995 or later is manifestly incompatible with the obligations under the Directive and thus constitutes a sufficiently serious breach of Community law.'

Also, the reimbursement of 25.38 per cent of the amount paid by the plaintiffs was in breach of the Directive since art 7 clearly states that there should be 'refund of money paid over'.

Third, the referring court asked the ECJ a question regarding the causal link between the breach of the State's obligation and the harm suffered by the injured parties, in particular whether this link can be interrupted by imprudent conduct on the part of the travel organiser or the occurrence of exceptional or unforeseeable events. The ECJ rejected the possibility of exoneration or attenuation of a State's liability on the grounds of force majeure or the imprudent conduct of the travel organiser. In this respect the ECJ held:

> 'Article 7 of the Directive imposes an obligation of result, namely to guarantee package travellers the refund of money paid over and their repatriation in the event of the travel organiser's bankruptcy. Such a guarantee is specifically aimed at arming consumers against the consequences of the bankruptcy, whatever the causes of it may be.'

This solution is fully justified taking into account that a State's liability is based on its failure to fulfil an obligation arising from EC law and thus different and separate from liability of the parties to a contract made between them.

In the present case the referring court had already established the existence of such a link.

7 Enforcement of Community Law

7.1   Action under art 226 EC

7.2   Action under art 227 EC against a Member State by another Member State

7.3   Effect of a ruling confirming a failure of a Member State to fulfil its obligation
       under the Treaty

7.4   Simplified procedures

This chapter, together with Chapter 8, is concerned with the enforcement of Community law. The European Union is based on law and has, as one its ultimate objectives, the creation of what is referred to as 'the Union of Law'. The Union of Law, an expression first employed by the one time President of the Commission, Walter Hallsten, has since been referred to in many decisions of the ECJ.[1] The preamble to the Treaty of Maastricht emphasises this feature of the Union. It confirms the Member States' commitment to 'the principle of liberty, democracy and respect for human rights and fundamental freedoms and the rule of law'.

Consequently, a Member State, a Community institution, an undertaking established in the EU, a citizen of the Union and any natural or legal person within the jurisdiction of a Member State has to observe Community law. The control of the legality of acts of Community institutions and the enforcement of Community law vis-à-vis Member States ensures that the expression of the 'Union of Law' is not an empty one.

The availability of an action for failure to fulfil an obligation arising from the Treaty, which may be brought against a defaulting Member State, enhances the originality of the Community legal order. The fact that the Community can enforce compliance with its rules through effective sanctions against a Member State which is in breach of its obligations confers a unique status on Community law. Its peculiarity is further emphasised by the Commission's powers to initiate proceedings against a defaulting Member State in its role as the 'guardian of the Treaties' within the meaning of art 211 EC. Thus, contrary to the rules of public international law, an EC institution and not the other Member States,[2] is responsible for ensuring that the Member States comply with Community law. Furthermore, the ECJ has exclusive, mandatory and unreserved jurisdiction in all types of actions for failure by a Member State to fulfil an obligation. The system of sanctions which may be imposed upon a defaulting Member State which refuses to comply with a judgment

---

1 *Partie Ecologiste Les Verts* Case 294/83 [1986] ECR 1339; *Zwartveld* Case C–2/88 [1990] ECR I–3365; *Beate Weber* Case C–314/91 [1993] ECR I–1093; *European Parliament v Council and Commission* Cases C–181 and 248/91 [1993] ECR I–3685.
2 Under art 227 EC Member States are also empowered to bring an action against another Member State for an alleged breach of Community law but only after the matter has been laid before the Commission.

of the ECJ constitutes a forceful means to bring about a change in that Member State's conduct.

The comparison between public international law and Community law in respect of a State's responsibility for the infringement of its international obligation demonstrates that there are a number of features which enhance the originality of Community law.

First, in *Commission v France* Case 7/71 [1971] ECR 1003 the ECJ held that the liability of a Member State is not, for the purposes of the enforcement procedures, conditional upon the existence of loss suffered by another Member State

Second, the principle of public international law under which no liability is placed upon the State unless it is at fault is rejected by Community law. Indeed, as the ECJ held in *The Netherlands v High Authority* Case 25/59 [1960] ECR 723 an action under art 226 EC aims at ensuring that the interests of the Community prevail over the inertia and resistance of the Member States. Also, some defences which a State may plead under public international law in order to exonerate itself from liability have been rejected by the ECJ as incompatible with the Community legal order.[3]

Third, an action for failure to fulfil a Treaty obligation also has a broader context: the judgment of the ECJ is not only rendered against the defaulting State but often it determines the exact scope of an obligation imposed upon a Member State: *Commission v France* Case 7/71 [1971] ECR 1003. This accords with the fact that uniformity in the application of Community law constitutes one of the main objectives of the enforcement action under art 226 EC.

The EC Treaty provides for administrative and judicial procedures aimed at ensuring the observance of Community law. They are contained in arts 226, 227, 88(2), 95(4) and 298 EC. This chapter focuses on the most important and most often used procedure provided for in art 226 EC.[4] Also, art 227 EC and the procedures which derogate from arts 226 and 227, and which apply in special circumstances, will be examined. They are provided for in art 95(4) which concerns the harmonisation of national laws and art 298 EC which concerns the adoption of national measures dealing with matters of public security in times of war, international tension and internal disturbance.

7.1 Action under art 226 EC

Article 226 EC states:

'If the Commission considers that a Member State has failed to fulfil an obligation under this Treaty, it shall deliver a reasoned opinion on the matter after giving the State concerned the opportunity to submit its observation.

    If the State concerned does not comply with the opinion within the period laid down by the Commission, the latter may bring the matter before the Court of Justice [ECJ].'

---

[3] For example, the defence based on necessity in *Commission v Italy* Case 7/61 [1961] ECR 317 or reciprocity in *Commission v Belgium and Luxembourg* Joined Cases 90 and 91/63 [1964] ECR 625; *Commission v France* Case 232/78 [1979] ECR 2729.

[4] There are important differences between arts 226 EC and 88 CS which concern actions against Member States for failure to fulfil their obligations under the Treaty, although they share some common features.

Under art 226 the following will be examined:

1. the definition of the failure of a Member State to fulfil an obligation under the Treaty;
2. the determination of the kind of obligation which is likely to give rise to an action under art 226 EC;
3. the procedure which the Commission must observe in the pursuance of its tasks under art 226 EC;
4. the procedure before the ECJ, including the legal effect of its judgment;
5. sanctions which the Commission is empowered to impose on a Member State which refuses to comply with a judgment of the ECJ rendered in proceedings under art 226 EC.

Definition of a failure of a Member State to fulfil its obligation under the Treaty

The failure to fulfil an obligation under the Treaty entails that there is an obligation imposed by the Treaty. The obligation must be well determined, that is, art 226 EC requires that a Member State must be in breach of a specific and precise obligation (*Commission* v *France* Case 7/71 [1971] ECR 1003). The failure under art 226 EC may consist of some action taken by a Member State, such as the application of national law incompatible with Community law, the adoption of a legislative act contrary to EC law (*Commission* v *Italy* Case C–157/89 [1991] ECR I–57), an express refusal to fulfil an obligation imposed by EC law, or it may arise from its failure to act. In many cases under art 226 EC the Commission initiates proceedings against a Member State for non-implementation of EC directives within the prescribed time limit.

When a Member State does not take all necessary measures required under Community law it is also liable under art 226 EC. Therefore, failure by a Member State to fulfil an obligation is assessed in the light of the nature and scope of that obligation (*Commission* v *Italy* Case 31/69 [1970] ECR 25) and may result from an action or from an omission or a failure to act: see *Commission* v *French Republic* Case C–265/95 [1997] ECR I–6959 in Chapter 14, section 14.1. In *Commission* v *Belgium* Case 301/81 [1983] ECR 467 the ECJ held that in order to constitute a failure to fulfil an obligation it is not necessary to prove opposition or inertia on the part of a Member State.

The failure within the meaning of art 226 EC arises regardless of the national body which is at the origin of the action or inaction. In *Commission* v *Belgium* Case 77/69 [1970] ECR 244 (also *Commission* v *Italy* Case 8/70 [1970] ECR 967) the ECJ held that this principle applies even to a constitutional, independent body. In this case, the Belgian government tried to plead in its defence the independence of the Belgian Parliament, which could not be forced by the government to adopt a required legislative act. The ECJ answered that:

> '... the liability of a Member State under art [226] arises whatever the agency of the State whose action or inaction is the cause of the failure to fulfil its obligations, even in the case of a constitutional independent institution.'

In *Commission* v *Belgium* Cases 227–230/85 [1988] ECR 1 (see also *Commission* v *Germany* Case C–57/89 [1991] ECR I–924; *Commission* v *Luxembourg* Case C–47/99 Judgment of 16 December 1999 (nyr)) the ECJ emphasised that the national division of competences between central and regional authorities which, especially in the context of a federal State, may result in a large measure of autonomy being conferred on the local or regional authorities would not constitute a sufficient defence for a Member State even if the local authorities are solely empowered to implement necessary local legislation and failed to do so. Also, the failure by any private or semi-public body which is controlled by a Member State to fulfil the obligations under the Treaty is imputable to that Member State. In *Commission v Ireland (Re Buy Irish Campaign)* Case 249/81 [1982] ECR 4005 Ireland was held liable under art 226 EC for financing through the Irish Goods Council, a government-sponsored body, a campaign to 'Buy Irish' which promoted Irish products to the disadvantage of imports, even though the Irish Goods Council could not adopt binding measures and the campaign was a failure.

It results from the case law of the ECJ that a Member State is liable under art 226 EC if the failure is imputable to a national government, or a national parliament or even a court or a tribunal. In this respect, the Commission initiated proceedings against the French Cour de Cassation and the German Bundesfinanhof (the highest court in financial matters)[5] although both cases were settled. This is not surprising in the context of the traditional independence of the judiciary. In *Meyer-Buckhardt* Case 9/75 [1975] ECR 1171 Advocate-General Werner suggested that an action under art 226 EC should be taken if a national court of last resort wrongly fails to refer a question on the interpretation of Community law to the ECJ for a preliminary ruling under art 234(3) EC. Once again, this is a very delicate matter and the Commission would certainly prefer to settle such cases if possible. The ECJ itself, in the context of the procedure under art 234 EC, especially in *Motorradcenter* Case C–93/92 [1993] ECR I–5009 (also *Deutsche Renault* Case C–317/91 [1993] ECR I–6227) recognised the possibility that judgments of national courts may infringe Community law.

It is important to note that whichever body is at the origin of the failure to fulfil an obligation under the Treaty the action under art 226 EC is always taken against the Member State.

Determination of an obligation which is likely to give rise to an action under art 226 EC

The term 'an obligation under this Treaty' is widely interpreted. It comprises not only obligations imposed by the Treaties, protocols, annexes and all other primary sources, but also the Community secondary legislation – regulations (*Commission v Italy* Case 33/69 [1970] ECR 103; *Commission v Italy* Case 8/70 [1970] ECR 967), decisions (*Commission v France* Cases 6 and 11/69 [1970] CMLR 43) and directives.[6] Also included are binding acts, not expressly mentioned in art 249 EC (*France v United Kingdom* Case 141/78 [1979] ECR 2923), adopted by Community institutions and obligations arising from international agreements concluded between the Community and third countries which by virtue of art 300(7) EC are 'binding on the institutions of the Community and on Member States'.[7] It is

---

[5] See question no 1907/85: OJ C137 (1986).

[6] The majority of proceedings under art 226 EC concern EC directives.

[7] *Kupferberg* Case 104/81 [1982] ECR 3641; *Commission v Greece* Cases 194 and 241/85 [1988] ECR 1037; *Commission v Italy* Case C–228/91 [1993] ECR I–2701.

still uncertain whether the infringement of complementary sources will give rise to an action under art 226 EC. In respect of rulings of the ECJ, under art 226 EC the non-compliance of the Member State concerned constitutes a breach of Community law by that Member State which is dealt with under art 228(1) EC.

It is submitted that the failure of a Member State to fulfil its obligations arising from the general principles of Community law may also give rise to liability of a Member State under art 226 EC. First, the ECJ has underlined in many cases that general principles of Community law form an integral part of Community law. Second, they may be invoked in proceedings against Community institutions under arts 230, 232 and 288(2) EC, *a fortiori* this solution should also be applied to Member States in breach of Community law. Third, in *ERT* Case C–260/89 [1991] ECR I–2925, the ECJ held that the general principles of Community law are binding on the Community institutions and on the Member States when they act within the scope of Community law.

In the context of obligations likely to give rise to the liability of a Member State under art 226 EC, it is interesting to examine art 10 EC which provides that:

'Member States shall take all appropriate measures, whether general or particular, to ensure fulfilment of the obligations arising out of this Treaty or resulting from action taken by the institutions of the Community. They shall facilitate the achievement of the Community's tasks. They shall abstain from any measure which could jeopardise the attainment of the objectives of this Treaty.'

This provision was considered for a long time as an interpretive device requiring Member States to act in good faith. Gradually, its scope of application has been extended. First, art 10 EC has served to strengthen the binding effect of the Community obligations imposed upon the Member States. Second, the ECJ has imposed, by virtue of art 10 EC, the obligation on national courts to interpret national law in conformity with Community law. Third, art 10 EC has become an independent and autonomous source of obligation. As a result, a breach of art 10 EC gives rise to liability of the Member States under art 226 EC. In *Commission v Greece (Re Electronic Cash Registers)* Case C–137/91 [1992] 3 CMLR 117 the ECJ explained the autonomous function of art 10 EC.

In this case Greek law enacted in 1988 required the use of electronic cash registers by certain retailers. However, the approval of such registers was conducted by national authorities which refused to certify any register containing less than 35 per cent add-on value from Greece. Other Member States complained to the Commission that this policy was contrary to art 28 EC. During the investigation the Commission sent two faxes to the Greek Permanent Representation in Brussels asking for more information. None came. The Commission considered that the lack of response constituted an infringement of art 10 EC. In those circumstances, the Commission issued a formal notice under art 226 EC against Greece but the latter did not submit its observation on the alleged incompatibility of Greek law with Community law. Finally, the Commission delivered the reasoned opinion which is required as a part of the proceedings under art 226(1) EC prior to its judicial part which takes place before the ECJ. No reply was received by the Commission in response and the Commission decided to bring proceedings before the ECJ.

The government of Greece challenged the Commission proceedings. It claimed that it gave the Commission all necessary information concerning the legislation in question at a meeting in Athens in September 1990 and a year later sent the Commission the text of a new Act. According to the Greek government there was no reason for providing additional information required by the Commission as the latter was fully aware of the situation before the action under art 226 EC was brought. The Commission argued that the Greek government provided the required information two years after it was requested and that at that stage the time limit fixed by the reasoned opinion had elapsed.

The ECJ held that Greece had violated art 10 EC. The ECJ stated that 'the failure to reply to the Commission's questions within a reasonable period made the task which it has to perform more difficult and therefore amounts to a violation of the obligation of co-operation laid down in art [10 EC].'

It results from the case law of the ECJ that art 10 EC imposes a positive duty on Member States to co-operate with the Commission in its investigations into alleged violations of Community law. Failure to do so is in itself sufficient to give rise to liability of a Member State under art 226 EC,[8] regardless of whether a Member State refuses or simply ignores the request of the Commission for information (*Commission* v *Greece* Case 272/86 [1988] ECR 4875; *Commission* v *Spain* Case C–375/92 [1994] ECR I–923) or omits to forward necessary indications allowing the Commission to exercise its role of 'guardian of the Treaty'.[9]

Procedure under art 226 EC

The procedure itself reflects the philosophy of art 226 EC, that is, that the action should not be brought unless there is no other way of enforcing Community law. The use of non-contentious means in the proceedings under art 226 EC constitutes one of its dominant features. Furthermore, the Commission plays a central role in any action against a Member State for failure to fulfil its obligations stemming from the Treaty. Under art 88 of the Treaty of Paris the Commission/High Authority has an exclusive competence in initiating proceedings and the Member States may only invite the High Authority to act. Also, under the CS Treaty the High Authority has jurisdiction to give a binding decision confirming the failure of a Member State to fulfil its obligation under the Treaty and the ECJ intervenes exclusively in its appellate capacity.[10] Under the Treaties of Rome the Commission does not enjoy a monopoly in initiating the proceedings but it plays a predominant role in deciding whether or not proceedings should be brought against a Member State which is believed to be in breach of Community law.

In proceedings under art 226 EC two phases can be distinguished: the informal phase and the formal phase. The latter comprises the administrative and the judicial stage.

Informal phase
In the informal phase the Commission enjoys a double discretion: first, it decides whether or not a Member State is in breach of art 226 EC; and; second, it assesses various aspects of

---

[8] See also *Commission* v *Italy* Case C–33/90 [1991] ECR I–5987; *Commission* v *Greece* Case C–65/91 [1992] ECR I–5245.

[9] For example, *Commission* v *United Kingdom* Case C–40/92 [1994] ECR I–989.

[10] Under art 88(2) CS a Member State has two months to appeal to the ECJ after notification of the decision of the High Authority.

the situation in question, especially by placing it in the political context in order to determine whether to commence proceedings against the defaulting State. Indeed, in many cases the Commission may decide not to act when faced with sensitive political issues. For example, the United Kingdom was in breach of Community law for more than 20 years by not introducing national legislation required by the ECJ subsequent to its ruling in *Van Duyn*.[11] Advocate-General Roemer in *Commission v France* Case 7/71 [1971] ECR 1003 suggested that in certain circumstances the Commission should abstain from initiating proceedings under art 226 EC: when there is a possibility to reach a settlement; when the effect of the breach of Community law is minor; when the proceedings of the Commission would exacerbate a major political crisis in the defaulting Member State, especially in the context of a minor violation of Community law by that Member State; or when there is a possibility that the provision in question would be modified or annulled in the near future.

Usually, a violation of Community law by a Member State is brought to the attention of the Commission by individuals or undertakings affected by the breach.[12]

The number of complaints against the Member States addressed to the Commission by natural or legal persons rises each year: 1995 (955), 1996 (819), 1998 (1,128). Also, the total number of complaints registered by the Commission, resulting from its own inquiries, and all other sources of information, has increased from 171 in 1995 to 2,134 in 1998.

In 1998, France was classified in first place in terms of the number of complaints and the number of proceedings commenced under art 226 EC (of a total number of complaints of 1,228, 18 per cent were addressed against France; of a total number of proceedings commenced of 804, 15.05 per cent were against France).[13]

All complaints are registered by the General Secretariat of the Commission and are the subject of reports concerning the situation of the presumed violations of the Treaties. These reports are periodically examined by the chief of the private office or *Cabinet* of each Commissioner and their observations are forwarded to the Commission. Once there is sufficient evidence that a Member State is in breach of Community law the appropriate Directorate-General initiates proceedings. At this stage the Commission invites the Member State concerned to provide some explanations and that Member State is reminded that it has an obligation to co-operate under arts 10 and 211 EC: *Commission v Italy* Case 147/77 [1978] ECR 1307. The request for information takes the form of a 'letter pre-226' proceedings which fixes a time limit for the reply. Usually, the Commission and representatives of the Member State discuss the matter. Sometimes, the negotiations between them take a considerable amount of time, sometimes both parties will settle the matter immediately. The length of time spent during the informal phase is of some importance, especially when the Commission decides to take formal proceedings against the defaulting Member State. Usually, the longer the period of time spent on the informal proceedings the more easily the ECJ will accept a short deadline for compliance imposed by the Commission in the formal proceedings. The existence of informal proceedings

---

[11] The violation was finally rectified by the Immigration (European Economic Area) Order 1994 (SI 1895/1994).

[12] R Rawlings 'Citizen Action and Institutional Attitudes in Commission Enforcement' (2000) 6 European Law Journal 4.

[13] See the 16th Annual Report on the application of Community law submitted by the Commission to the EP in July 1999. The figures for the UK are as follows: complaints against the UK = 5.23 per cent, proceedings commenced against the UK = 5.47 per cent.

emphasises the non-punitive nature of art 226 EC. The objective of the provision is to terminate the violation of Community law and not to exacerbate the dispute. However, if no settlement is possible, the Commission will start the formal proceedings.

Administrative stage

The administrative stage can be analysed from the point of view of the subsequent acts which the Commission is under a duty to adopt vis-à-vis the defaulting Member State: the letter of formal notice and the reasoned opinion.

Letter of formal notice In *Commission v Italy* Case 51/83 [1984] ECR 2793 the ECJ held that the letter of formal notice constitutes an essential formal requirement under art 226 EC and its omission would result in the inadmissibility of an action under art 226 EC. The letter of formal notice determines the scope of the case and cannot be widened even at the stage of the reasoned opinion. The letter of formal notice invites a defaulting Member State to submit its observation on the disputed matters. It guarantees the right of defence to the Member State concerned, although the latter is not obliged to reply. Usually, the Commission gives a defaulting Member State two months to reply but in urgent matters the time may be shortened. The procedure may be terminated if the Commission is convinced that in the light of the explanations provided by the Member State there is no violation of Community law, or if the latter corrects its failure immediately. Otherwise, after the expiry of the time limit fixed in the letter of formal notice, the Commission will issue a reasoned opinion.

Reasoned opinion The main difference between the letter of formal notice and the reasoned opinion is that the former 'is intended to define the subject-matter of the dispute and to indicate to the Member State ... the factors enabling it to prepare its defence' (see *Commission v Italy* Case 51/83 above), while in the reasoned opinion the Commission must establish the legal arguments in respect of the alleged failure of a Member State to fulfil its obligation under the Treaty.[14] The reasoned opinion invites the defaulting Member State to cease the infringement and indicates the appropriate measures that should be taken to that end: *Commission v Italy* Case 7/61 [1961] ECR 317; *Commission v Germany* Case 70/72 [1973] ECR 813. It also fixes a time limit for the Member State concerned to comply, usually two months, but in urgent cases this period may be shortened. The time limit cannot be changed by the ECJ (*Commission v Italy* Case 28/81 [1981] ECR 2577; *Commission v Italy* Case 29/81 [1981] 2585), although it will be taken into account when the ECJ determines whether the Commission gave a 'reasonable time' to comply with the reasoned opinion. In *Commission v Ireland* Case 74/82 [1984] ECR 317 the ECJ viewed with disapproval the period of five days given in the reasoned opinion to Ireland to amend its legislation which had been in force for more than 40 years. There was no urgency and this period was considered by the ECJ as unreasonable, although the action was not dismissed. The ECJ took into consideration the fact that the Commission issued its reasoned opinion on 9 November 1981 and referred to the ECJ on 19 February 1982.

---

[14] In *Commission v Italy (Re Pigmeat)* Case 7/61 [1961] ECR 317 the ECJ held that 'the opinion referred to in art [226] of the Treaty must ... contain a sufficient statement of reasons to satisfy the law.'

In *Amministrazione delle Finanze dello Stato* v *Essevi and Salongo* Cases 142 and 143/80 [1981] ECR 1413, in proceedings under art 234 EC, the ECJ held that the Commission is not the final arbiter as to the determination of the rights and obligations of the Member States. If a Member State has complied with the reasoned opinion it does not mean that the State may invoke its compliance to prevent future parties from claiming that the Member State is still in violation of Community law. However, if the Member State concerned complies with the reasoned opinion within the prescribed time limit the Commission is barred from bringing proceedings before the ECJ: *Commission* v *Greece* Case C–200/88 [1990] ECR I–4299. Otherwise, the Commission may commence the next step in the proceedings under art 226 EC, that is bring the matter before the ECJ.

The discretion that the Commission enjoys under art 226 EC applies throughout the proceedings. The Commission may decide at any stage to set aside the proceedings, even after the time limit for compliance with the reasoned opinion elapses. The wide discretion of the Commission is justified by the fact that under art 226 EC the Commission has no obligation to act. The ECJ in *Commission* v *France* Case 7/71 [1971] ECR 1003 held that the proceedings under art 226 EC are not contained in the pre-established time limit 'since, by reason of its nature and its purpose, this procedure involves a power on the part of the Commission to consider the most appropriate means and time limits for the purposes of putting an end to any contravention of the Treaty.' The Commission is the master of proceedings under art 226 EC. This aspect of the Commission's discretion is enhanced by the possibility of bringing proceedings against a defaulting Member State even when the latter has complied with the reasoned opinion but after the expiry of the time limit specified in it. The Commission may decide to bring proceedings before the ECJ many years after the expiry of the time limit fixed in the reasoned opinion.[15] In *Commission* v *Italy* Case 7/61 [1961] ECR 633 the ECJ recognised that the Commission may have an interest in determining whether or not a violation of Community law has occurred. Furthermore, in *Commission* v *Italy* Case 39/72 [1973] ECR 101 the ECJ held that its ruling in such a case may be useful, especially in order to establish the basis of the Member State's liability vis-à-vis other Member States, the Community and the individuals concerned.

It is also necessary to note that neither the letter of formal notice nor the reasoned opinion have binding legal effect. For that reason they cannot be challenged under art 230 EC. In *Alfons Lütticke* Case 48/65 [1966] ECR 19 the ECJ stated that the reasoned opinion was merely a step in the proceedings.

Judicial proceedings

The ECJ has gradually developed its own conditions for admission of actions under art 226 EC, in particular to ensure that a defaulting Member State's rights to defence are protected. The ECJ will dismiss an application under art 226 EC in the following circumstances:

1. *If the time limit fixed by the Commission either in the letter of formal notice or in the reasoned opinion is not reasonable.* In *Commission* v *Belgium (Re University Fees)* Case 293/85 [1988] ECR 305, which concerned the compliance of Belgium with the ECJ

---

[15] In *Commission* v *Germany* Case C–422/92 [1995] ECR I–1097 there was a delay of six years; in *Commission* v *Germany* Case C–317/92 [1994] ECR I–2039 the delay was two years.

ruling in *Gravier*, Belgium had only eight days to reply to the letter of formal notice and 15 days to comply with the reasoned opinion. The ECJ held that the prescribed time limits were insufficient for Belgium, taking into account the complexity of the matter.[16] The ECJ will take into account many factors in deciding whether or not the time limit fixed by the Commission may be considered as reasonable. In *Commission v Belgium* Case 85/85 [1986] ECR 1149 (see also *Commission v Ireland* Case 74/82 [1984] ECR 317) the ECJ held that a period of 15 days was reasonable in the light of the considerable length of time taken by the informal proceedings.

2. *If the complaints and legal arguments in the application under art 226 EC are not identical to those invoked in the letter of formal notice and the reasoned opinion.*[17] The case law of the ECJ demonstrates that the Court has rigorously applied this requirement, on the one hand, to protect the defaulting Member State against new complaints and legal arguments of the Commission and, on the other hand, to counterbalance the discretion which the Commission enjoys under art 226 EC: *Commission v Germany* Case C–191/95 [1998] ECR I–5449; *Commission v Italy* Case C–365/97 Judgment of 9 November 1999 (nyr). However, it seems that the ECJ, which used to be excessively strict with regard to this formal requirement, has changed its position: *Commission v Hellenic Republic* Case C–375/95 [1997] ECR I–5981. Indeed, in a number of cases the Member States invoked the argument of discrepancies in order to avoid proceedings. In *Commission v Germany* Case C–96/95 [1997] ECR I–1653 the ECJ declared the application admissible despite the fact that the government of Germany considered that the Commission modified the legal grounds as compared to the previous submission presented in the letter of formal notice and in the reasoned opinion.

In this case, the Commission did not receive any information from Germany concerning implementation measures in relation to Council Directive 90/364 on the right of residence for persons who have sufficient resources to avoid having to rely on the social security system in the host State (the so-called Playboy Directive), and Directive 90/365 on the right of residence for employees and self-employed persons who have ceased their occupational activity. As a result, the Commission decided to issue a letter of formal notice. The German government replied that the Länder authorities had been informed by means of a circular of the obligation to grant a residence permit to the beneficiaries of both Directives. Subsequently the government of Germany informed the Commission that the principle of supremacy of Community law, which is incorporated into the German law on immigration (Auslandergesetz), guaranteed the proper application of both Directives in Germany and that, in addition, EC directives would be incorporated in new legislation which was being prepared (Aufenthaltgesetz/EWG). The Commission considered that Germany did not implement both Directives correctly and delivered a reasoned opinion. The German government repeated its previous arguments. At that stage the Commission brought proceedings before the ECJ. The German

---

[16] In *Gravier v City of Liège* Case 293/83 [1989] ECR 593 the ECJ held that the fees (so called 'minerval') imposed upon EC nationals studying in Belgium were discriminatory and in breach of art 49 EC which ensures the free movement of services throughout the Community.

[17] For example, in *Commission v Greece* Case C–210/91 [1994] ECR I–6735; *Commission v The Netherlands* Case C–157/91 [1994] ECR I–5899; *Commission v Italy* Case C–296/92 [1994] ECR I–1.

authorities argued that the application was inadmissible since the complaints in the administrative stage and in the judicial stage were not identical. The Commission responded that in all proceedings the complaints were identical, that is, they concerned the non-implementation of EC directives. The ECJ confirmed that the Commission had not modified the essence of its complaints.

It seems that the ECJ is now more concerned with the essence of the complaints than with the actual terms used in the letter of formal notice and the reasoned opinion.[18]

The Commission's application must state precisely the grounds on which it is based, as well as provide some legal and factual indications. It cannot simply refer to the letter of formal notice and the reasoned opinion: *Commission v Greece* Case C–347/88 [1990] ECR I–4747; *Commission v Denmark* Case C–52/90 [1992] ECR I–2187.

The burden of proof is placed on the Commission. In *Commission v United Kingdom* Case C–300/95 [1997] ECR I–2649 the ECJ provided clarification in respect of the Commission's obligation to prove its allegation that a Member State is in breach of art 226 EC. In this case the Commission argued that the United Kingdom was in violation of art 7 of Council Directive 85/375 on product liability, as it was implemented without transposing its text verbatim. However, the form and methods of implementation of directives are left at the discretion of the Member State. What counts is that the objectives of the directive are attained. The Commission considered that this was not the case since the British courts have to interpret art 7 of Directive 85/375 *contra legem* in order to achieve the objectives of that Directive. The ECJ reminded the Commission that in order to establish the failure of a Member State to fulfil its obligations the Commission could not base its application under art 226 EC on a presumption or a simple allegation: *Commission v France* Case C–62/89 [1990] ECR I–925. As a result, the ECJ rejected the application submitted by the Commission. The ECJ held that in order to assess the scope of national legislative or administrative provisions the Commission must take into account the way that national courts interpret those provisions in practice. Thus, the Commission must not only establish that a Member State is in breach of Community law, but also prove that national courts in practice interpret the provision in question contrary to EC law. It seems, therefore, that the ECJ has set out a presumption in favour of interpretation by national courts in conformity with Community law, which is, in any event, required under Community law.[19] It is submitted that this solution, which confers on national courts the role of guardian of Community law, is contrary to the principle of legal certainty, especially when national courts have to interpret the provision of national law which implements Community law *contra legem* in order to attain the objectives required by the directive.

Also, in the judicial stage, the ECJ fully investigates the merits of the case and the Member State may invoke new arguments in its defence.[20] The ECJ decides the matter *ab novo* taking into consideration the situation as it was at the expiry of the time limit fixed in

---

[18] In *Commission v Italy* Case 274/83 [1985] ECR 1090 the ECJ permitted the Commission to make certain modifications in support of its arguments.

[19] See *Von Colson and Kamann* Case 14/83 [1984] ECR 1891; *Faccini Dori* Case C–91/92 [1994] ECR I–3325.

[20] Contrary to the opinion of the Commission the ECJ confirmed in *Commission v Spain* Case C–414/97 Judgment of 16 September 1999 (nyr) that the Member State's right to defence entails that new arguments may be invoked before the ECJ.

the reasoned opinion.[21] However, in certain circumstances, especially in the light of the interests of the Community, the ECJ may take into account any changes occurring after the deadline: *Commission v Greece* Case C–105/91 [1992] ECR I–5871; *Commission v Germany* Case C–422/92 [1995] ECR I–1097. The ECJ may, in the light of the legal arguments submitted by both parties during the proceedings under art 226 EC, give an interlocutory ruling inviting the Commission and the Member State concerned to find a solution ensuring the effective application of Community law but, as with any interlocutory decision, the proceedings can be reopened if necessary: *Commission v United Kingdom* Case 170/78 [1980] ECR 415; *Commission v Belgium* Case 149/79 [1980] ECR 3881. Additionally, the Commission is entitled to request interim measures.

Defence

The ECJ has strictly interpreted the defences available to Member States. The philosophy of art 226 EC requires that the defaulting Member State puts an end to the violation of Community law as soon as possible and thus some traditional defences recognised under public international law are not appropriate to the peculiar nature of the Community legal order.

Successful defences

Josephine Steiner has rightly pointed out that 'Many defences to an action under art [226] have been attempted; few have succeeded.'[22] She added that the best defence for a defaulting Member State it to deny the obligation. The plea of a procedural irregularity in the adoption of a Community measure also constitutes an excellent defence. However, the strict approach to the interpretation of defences offers little hope for a defaulting Member State. Even the fact that the time limit prescribed in the secondary legislation has not yet expired may not be invoked. In this respect in *Inter-Environnement Wallonie ASBL v Région Wallonne* Case C–129/96 [1997] ECR I–7411 the Commission in its written observation stated that infringement proceedings on the basis of art 226 EC should not be brought until the end of the transposition period. However, in the oral proceedings before the ECJ the Commission changed its view. It stated that the standstill obligation imposed by virtue of arts 10 and 249 EC on a Member State during a directive's transposition period justifies such an action on the part of the Commission. Nevertheless, the Commission stated that although it would be possible to bring infringement proceedings against a defaulting State during that period, individuals should be precluded from deriving rights from the breach of the standstill obligation by a Member State.

Advocate-General Jacobs argued that the Commission should not have at its disposal the right to initiate proceedings under art 226 EC against a Member State that has, during a directive's transposition period, enacted measures likely to seriously compromise the result prescribed by that EC directive. He emphasised that arts 10 and 249 EC should not have a general blocking effect on a Member State's freedom of action before the end of the

---

[21] *Commission v Greece* Case C–200/88 [1990] ECR I–4299, especially if the implementation of a directive was not notified to the Commission; *Commission v Belgium* Case C–133/94 [1996] ECR I–2323.
[22] J Steiner, *EC Law*, 4th ed, London: Blackstone, 1994, p347.

transposition period since; in some circumstances, it would be necessary for a Member State to make adjustments to the existing arrangements which may be based on methods and objectives which materially differ from those underlying the directive but which would be necessary to maintain the coherence and effectiveness of the national legal system until national provisions are replaced by Community law. Furthermore, he considered that Member States would be reluctant, or even hostile, to adopt certain directives knowing that pending their implementation into national law Member States might be required to introduce some measures contrary to the objective envisaged by a directive which may, in turn, result in a Member State being subject to infringement proceedings under art 226 EC.

It is submitted that the Commission, for two reasons, should be allowed to bring an action based on art 226 EC against a Member State which is in breach of the standstill obligation. First, the ECJ has implicitly resolved the above-mentioned problems by imposing an obligation on a national court to examine whether the national provisions are intended to constitute full transposition of the directive, as well as to take into consideration their effects and duration. In the following passage from *Inter-Environnement Wallonie ASBL* Case C–129/96 [1997] ECR I–7411 the ECJ advises a national court how to proceed if national provisions are contrary to the objectives set out in the directive. It states that: 'Member States [are] entitled to adopt transitional measures or to implement a directive in stages in which case the incompatibility of transitional national measures or the non-transposition of some provisions of the directive would not necessarily compromise the prescribed result.' Consequently, national rules which are contrary to the objectives of a directive, but necessary in order to attain the results envisaged by it, will be upheld by a national court if a Member State provides a sufficient justification for their temporary existence. Second, the Commission agreed that individuals should not, before the expiry of the period fixed for its implementation, be entitled to derive any rights from a Member State's failure to perform the obligations which the directive entails.

There are a few successful defences recognised as valid under art 226 EC:

Unlawful obligation The best defence for the Member State concerned is to bring an action for annulment under art 230 against the challenged measure. The ECJ has permitted the defaulting Member State to call into question the validity of the Community act in art 226 EC proceedings. It seems quite strange that a defaulting Member State may challenge the validity of Community acts in the proceedings under art 226 EC in view of the fact that Member States have privileged *locus standi* under art 230 EC. Indeed, initially the opposite was the case.[23] There is still no clear justification for the change of attitude of the ECJ, but it seems that the reason is provided by art 241 EC which permits indirect action for annulment of Community measures and thus, at least theoretically, an escape from the strict deadline of art 230 EC. However, the ECJ has limited this possibility to two situations. The first was discussed by the ECJ in *Commission v Greece* Case 226/87 [1988] ECR 3620 in which the ECJ stated that a Member State may call into question the legality of a decision if it is affected by evident and serious vices which render it 'non-existent'. With regard to regulations, in *Commission v Germany* Case 116/82 [1986] ECR 2519 (also *Commission v Spain* Case C–258/89 [1991] ECR I–3977) the ECJ accepted that the illegality of EC

---

[23] For example, *Italy v High Authority* Case 20/59 [1960] ECR 665.

regulations may be invoked as a defence in proceedings under art 226 EC. The second exception was established in *Commission v France* Case 6/69 [1970] CMLR 43 in which the French government successfully proved that the decision in question was adopted in an area in which the Member State had exclusive competence. This solution is in conformity with the requirements laid down in art 241 EC.

Force majeure Another possibility for a Member State is to invoke *force majeure*, although so far this defence has not been successfully pleaded because the ECJ has always strictly interpreted this concept. As a result, what are considered under national law as exonerating circumstances, such as unforeseeable and irresistible political events – namely the dissolution of a national parliament, political difficulties, governmental crises, delays in the legislative procedure, social and economic disorders, etc – were rejected by the ECJ.[24] The only circumstance in which *force majeure* may be successfully pleaded is in the case of a quasi-absolute impossibility to perform the obligation. In *Commission v Italy (Re Traffic Statistics)* Case 101/84 [1985] ECR 2629 the government of Italy was close to succeeding. In that case, it argued that following a bomb attack by the Red Brigade on the Ministry of Transport' data-processing centre, which destroyed its vehicle register, it was impossible to comply with EC Directive 78/546 which required the Member State to forward statistical data in respect of the carriage of goods by road. However, the delay of four-and-a-half years between the terrorist attack and the implementation of the Directive was considered as too long to exonerate Italy. In this respect the ECJ held that:

> '... although it is true that the bomb attack, which took place before 18 January 1979, may have constituted a case of *force majeure* and created insurmountable difficulties, its effect could only have lasted a certain time, namely the time which would in fact be necessary for an administration showing a normal degree of diligence to replace the equipment destroyed and to collect and prepare the data. The Italian government cannot therefore rely on that event to justify its continuing failure to comply with its obligations years later.'

The definition of *force majeure* was provided in *McNicoll v Ministry of Agriculture* Case 296/86 [1988] ECR 1491 in proceedings under art 230 EC, but it can be transposed to proceedings under art 226 EC. The ECJ held that:

> '... whilst the concept of *force majeure* does not presuppose an absolute impossibility of performance, it nevertheless requires that non-performance of the act in question be due to circumstances beyond the control of persons pleading *force majeure*, that the circumstances be abnormal and unforeseeable and that the consequences could not have been avoided through the exercise of all due care.'

Uncertainty as to the exact meaning of the obligation Under art 226 EC the Commission must determine with precision or at least sufficiently from a legal point of view, the obligation which a Member State has violated: *Italy v High Authority* Case 20/59 [1960] ECR 665. This requirement has been used by Member States as a defence under art 226 EC. At first, the ECJ recognised this defence but, in limited circumstances, that is, only if the ambiguity concerned the essential aspect of the obligation: *Commission v France* Case

---

[24] See Magliveras, 'Force Majeure in Community Law' (1990) 15 European Law Review 460.

26/69 [1970] ECR 565; *Commission v Germany* Case 70/72 [1973] ECR 813. Gradually the ECJ has accepted that even in proceedings under art 226 EC the Member States are still entitled to elucidation by the ECJ of the exact scope of the obligations they are supposed to fulfil, especially in the event of divergent interpretations: *Commission v France* Case 7/71 [1971] ECR 1003. However, the extent of the ECJ's acceptance of this defence is still difficult to determine. In this respect, in *Commission v Belgium* Case C–133/94 [1996] ECR I–2323, the government of Belgium pleaded, *inter alia*, the obscurity and ambiguity of a provision concerning the concept of 'chemical installation' under Council Directive 85/337/EEC on environmental impact assessment. The Commission implicitly agreed with Belgium as the Commission subsequently undertook to define later the precise meaning of that concept. The ECJ held Belgium in breach of art 226 EC.

Unsuccessful defences

The ingeniousness of Member States in constructing defences to art 226 EC is astonishing. Over the years, they have attempted to plead every justification imaginable for their failure to fulfil their obligations under the Treaty. One of the most interesting cases concerned a defence which is recognised under public international law but rejected by Community law as contrary to the spirit and objectives of the Community legal order. In *Commission v Luxembourg and Belgium (Re Import of Powdered Milk Products)* Cases 90 and 91/63 [1964] ECR 1964 the ECJ rejected a defence based on reciprocity. In that case Luxembourg and Belgium were in breach of art 25 EC. They argued that their action would have been legal if the Commission had introduced certain measures which it was authorised to enact, and that under public international law if one party fails to perform its obligation the other is entitled to withhold its own performance. The ECJ held that:

> 'In fact the Treaty is not limited to creating reciprocal obligations between the different natural and legal persons to whom it is applicable, but establishes a new legal order which governs the powers, rights and obligations of the said persons, as well as the necessary procedures for taking cognisance of and penalising any breach of it. Therefore, except where otherwise expressly provided, the basic concept of the Treaty requires that the Member State shall not take the law into their own hands. Therefore, the fact that the Council failed to carry out its obligations cannot relieve the defendants from carrying out theirs.'

This is a straightforward rejection of the defence based on reciprocity. It this context it is interesting to note that both art 60 of the 1969 Vienna Convention on the Law of Treaties and the constitutions of some Member States, for example art 55 of the French Constitution, recognise the *exceptio inadempleti contractus*. However, the decision of the ECJ is fully justified taking into account that in the international legal order there is no international court which exercises permanent and mandatory jurisdiction in respect of disputes between sovereign States. The position is otherwise in the Community context: first, the objectives of the Treaty require that unilateral actions on the part of a Member State are prohibited; and, second, under the Treaty the unlawful actions or omissions either of other Member States or the Community institutions are investigated and properly sanctioned. Thus, there is neither the need nor any justification for permitting the Member States to 'take the law into their own hands'. The strict application of this principle by the ECJ entails that any unilateral action of a Member State aimed at correcting the effect of a violation of Community law by another Member State is prohibited. In *Commission* v *France* Case 232/78 [1979] ECR 2729 the ECJ held that:

'A Member State cannot under any circumstances unilaterally adopt, on its own authority, corrective measure or measures to protect trade designed to prevent any failure on the part of another Member State to comply with the rules laid down by the Treaty.'

This statement was repeated almost verbatim by the ECJ in *Paul Denuit* Case C–14/96 [1997] ECR I–2785 in which a Belgian judge, although under art 234 EC proceedings, asked the ECJ whether Belgium was entitled to take unilateral measures against Member States in breach of Council Directive 89/552 which established a single audio-visual area in the Community, especially to oppose the re-transmission to the territory of Belgium of programmes broadcast by national broadcasting bodies of another Member State which did not comply with certain provisions of the Directive.[25] Prohibition of unilateral action means that if a Member State considers that another Member State has failed to fulfil its obligations under the Community law it should bring an action under art 227 EC against the defaulting State or ask the Commission to act under art 226 EC. It is worth noting that:

1. A Member State cannot plead in its defence that another Member State is also in breach of the same obligation even though the Commission has not initiated proceedings against that State: *Commission* v *France (Re Restrictions on Imports of Lamb)* Case 232/78 [1979] ECR 2729.
2. Furthermore, neither a Member State which is an alleged victim of a violation of Community law by another Member State nor any other Member State is allowed to plead that violation in its defence: *Commission* v *Italy* Case 52/75 [1976] ECR 277.
3. A Member State cannot rely in its defence under art 226 EC on the fact that a Community institution has acted unlawfully or failed to act when it was under a duty to act. Articles 230 and 232 EC ensure in such a case an appropriate procedure for the very purpose of rectifying those problems: *Commission* v *Belgium and Luxembourg* Cases 90 and 91/63. In *Commission* v *The Netherlands* Case C–359/93 [1995] ECR I–157 the ECJ held that this solution also applies when a Community institution fails to comply with its own obligations under the Treaty subsequent to a failure by a Member State.

Another defence recognised under public international law, but rejected by the ECJ, is based on necessity. The criteria for such a defence are very stringent: there must be exceptional circumstances of extreme urgency, the *status quo ante* must be re-established as soon as possible and the State concerned must act in good faith.[26] In *Commission* v *Italy (Re Pigmeat)* Case 7/61 [1961] ECR 317 Italy banned all imports of pork into Italy from other Member States in order to avert an economic crisis. The ECJ held that with respect to emergency situations the appropriate remedy was laid down in art 226 (now repealed) and, for reasons similar to those under the principle of reciprocity, declared the unilateral action by Italy to be in breach of Community law.

---

[25] Another case which confirms this principle is *Commission* v *Belgium* Case C–11/95 [1996] ECR I–4115.

[26] The defence of necessity was successfully invoked by the United Kingdom when it bombed the Torrey Canyon, a ship flying the Liberian flag which was grounded outside the British territorial waters, as it represented a threat of an ecological disaster, but this defence failed in the *Rainbow Warrior Case* (1990) 82 ILR 499.

A defence based on the peculiarity of national systems, especially their constitutional and administrative and institutional organisation, was rejected by the ECJ. In *Commission v Belgium* Case 77/69 [1970] ECR 244 the government of Belgium claimed *force majeure* in order to exonerate itself from responsibility for breach of art 90 EC. It argued that its attempts to pass the necessary legislation were fettered by the Belgian Parliament, a body which the government had no power to compel to act. Indeed, draft legislation to amend the discriminatory tax scheme on wood was submitted to the Belgian Parliament but had fallen with the dissolution of Parliament. The ECJ firmly held that the Member State was liable under art 226 EC whenever an agency of the Member State, including a constitutionally independent institution, fails to fulfil its obligation arising from Community law.

Another rejected defence was based on the division of powers between central and regional authorities. In *Commission v Belgium (Re Failure to Implement Directives)* Case C–225/86 [1988] ECR 579 the Belgian government stated that it was constitutionally unable to compel some of its regions to comply with a decision of the ECJ. In this case the ECJ delivered a ruling in February 1982 against Belgium for failure to implement a number of EC directives within the prescribed time limit. In July 1985 Belgium was still in breach of the decision of the ECJ as the directives in question had not been implemented in certain constituent part of its territory, namely in the Walloon and Brussels regions. The Commission brought another action under art 226 EC against Belgium. The Belgian government claimed that its failure resulted from constitutional limitations imposed upon the central government by the Belgian constitution. At national level the Royal Decree on the discharge of waste water into surface water, which implemented Directive 78/176, was adopted in 1986. However, the central government had neither power to compel regional authorities (in this case in the Walloon and Brussels regions) to implement Community legislation where the directives were, despite the efforts of regional governments, not wholly implemented nor to substitute them for local legislation

The ECJ rejected the arguments submitted by the government of Belgium. The ECJ held that:

> '... each Member State is free to delegate powers to its domestic authorities as it considers fit and to implement directives by means of measures adopted by regional or local authorities. That division of powers does not however release it from the obligation to ensure that the provisions of the directive are properly implemented in national law ... a Member State may not plead provisions, practices or circumstances existing in its internal legal system in order to justify failure to comply with its obligations under Community law.'

A defence based on circumstances existing in the Community legal order was rejected in *Commission v Belgium* Case C–263/96 [1997] ECR I–7453. Here, the originality of the defences submitted by Belgium in order to justify its failure to implement Directive 89/106 on construction products within the prescribed time limit merit some comment.

Belgium argued that the Directive required the adoption of further implementing measures at Community level. This point had been confirmed by the Moliter group charged which the task of simplifying legislative and administrative acts adopted by the Community institutions. The government of Belgium stated that the delays in the adoption of further implementing measures by the Community institutions justified non-implementation of the Directive and argued that Belgium's failure did not adversely affect the creation of the internal market in construction products, taking into account the fact that the market, due to the delays on the part of the Community, had not yet been established. The Belgian government also argued that the Directive had been modified by subsequent directives on several occasions and that its final version was in the process of preparation.

The ECJ rejected all defences submitted by Belgium. It held that non-adoption of further implementing measures on the part of the Community institutions could not justify a failure to transpose the Directive and the ECJ rejected the defence based on circumstances existing in the Community legal order. In this respect, the ECJ emphasised that the obligation of implementation which results from art 249 EC cannot be modified according to the circumstances, even though those circumstances have their source in the Community legal order. The ECJ underlined that the obligations arising out of the EC Treaty are assessed objectively, that is they are not conditional upon the existence of loss and therefore a Member State may not rely on the argument that the failure to adopt measures to transpose a directive had no adverse impact on the functioning of the internal market or of that directive. The failure to fulfil an obligation results solely from non-implementation of a directive within a prescribed time limit. This also means that a directive must be transposed regardless of the fact that it may be subject to future modifications and amendments.

It can be seen that the following defences were rejected by the ECJ: the dissolution of the national Parliament (*Commission v Italy* Case 7/68 [1968] ECR 617; *Commission v France* Case C–144/97 [1998] ECR I–613), the mandatory deadline imposed by a national constitution for the accomplishment of necessary formalities (*Commission v Italy* Case 30/72 [1973] ECR 171) and administrative difficulties (*Commission v Belgium* Case 5/86 [1987] ECR 1777).

Political difficulties cannot be pleaded in order to justify a failure to comply with obligations resulting from Community law. In *Commission v Italy* Case 8/70 [1970] ECR 967 a defence based on a ministerial crisis in Italy was rejected. Indeed, in the light of the political turbulence in Italy after World War II, the acceptance of this defence would have paralysed the operation of Community law in that country. Interesting arguments relating to political difficulties were submitted by the United Kingdom in *Commission v United Kingdom (Re Tachographs)* Case 128/78 [1979] ECR 419. In this case the Commission brought an action under art 226 EC against the UK for failure to comply with Regulation 1463/70 relating to the introduction of tachographs in commercial vehicles. By this regulation tachographs were made compulsory and had to replace the use of individual control books. They were strongly opposed by the trade unions in the UK ('the spy in the cab'). The government of the UK suggested that the installation and use of tachographs should be on a voluntary basis. It argued that the resistance from the trade unions would result in strikes in the transport sector and thus seriously damage the whole economy of the UK.

The ECJ held that Regulation 1463/70, as any other regulation, is binding in its entirety in the Member State and thus its incomplete or selective application would breach Community law. In addition, the ECJ stated that it was inadmissible for a Member State to disapply those provisions of the Regulation which it considers contrary to national interests. Practical difficulties in the implementation of a Community measure cannot permit a Member State to unilaterally opt out of fulfilling its obligations, since the Community institutional system ensures that due consideration is given to them in the light of the principles of the common market and the legitimate interests of the other Member States. As a result, the ECJ rejected the possibility of political difficulties as a justification for non compliance with Regulation 1463/70.

Defences based on economic difficulties (*Commission v Greece* Case 70/86 [1987] ECR 3558) or the threat of social troubles or specific local conditions (*Commission v United Kingdom (Re Bathing Water Directive)* Case C–56/90 [1994] 1 CMLR 769; *Commission v The Netherlands (Re Protection of Wild Birds)* Case 339/87 [1990] ECR I–851) were rejected by the ECJ. In *Commission v Greece* Case C–45/91 [1992] ECR I–2509 the Greek government tried to justify its failure to implement the directive on the safe disposal of toxic waste upon the 'opposition by the local population'. This argument was rejected and the ECJ repeated that a Member State cannot rely on an internal situation to justify its failure to fulfil its obligations under the Treaty.

Also, the ECJ rejected a defence based on the minimal effect of the violation of Community law. There is no de *minimis rule* under art 226 EC. The scale or the frequency of the infringement cannot justify the failure of the Member State to fulfil is obligations under the Treaty. In *Commission v Greece* Case C–105/91 [1992] ECR I–5871 the Greek government admitted that its tax scheme on foreign vehicles was unlawful and discriminatory, but argued that the Greek vehicles which were eligible for tax concessions represented no more than 10 per cent of the internal demand and thus there was no manifest discrimination. This argument was rejected.

Another rejected defence was based on the argument that administrative practices ensure that national law in breach of Community law is not applied in fact. In *Commission v France (Re French Merchant Seamen)* Case 167/73 [1974] ECR 359 the French government attempted to justify the existence of national law (the French Code Maritime enacted in 1926) which was in breach of Community law on the basis that it was no longer enforced in practice. The Code required a ratio of three Frenchmen to one foreigner for certain jobs on French merchant ships. This provision was in breach of art 39 EC and EC Regulation 1612/68. The ECJ held that although according to the French government this provision was a secondary hindrance, since it was not applied in practice by the French Administration and that there was in addition a ministerial circular to this effect, the uncertainty resulting from its continued existence constituted itself a hindrance incompatible with the requirements of the free movement of workers. It is interesting to mention that France did not comply with the decision of the ECJ. As a result, the Commission, after more than 20 years, brought further proceedings against France. In *Commission v France* Case C–334/94 [1996] ECR I–1307 the French government repeated the same arguments as 20 years before with the knowledge that since 1973 the ECJ had confirmed in many cases that neither a ministerial circular nor an administrative practice, even long established, are adequate measures to ensure the proper application of Community law.[27] It was probably proof of the famous French sense of humour (which certainly did not amuse the ECJ), when the French government declared that new French legislation aimed at replacing the Maritime Code, which should have been adopted in the then near future, was in preparation.

---

[27] For example, *Commission v Italy* Case 168/85 [1986] ECR 2945.

Another defence which was based on direct effect of Community law was invoked in *Commission v France* Case 167/73 [1974] ECR 359. It failed as the ECJ held that it was likely to confuse EC nationals and create legal uncertainty. This is, indeed, an interesting defence under which, on the one hand, the supremacy of EC law ensures that in the case of a conflict between Community law and national law the former will prevail and, on the other hand, that an individual may rely on directly effective provisions of Community law in proceedings brought before a national court. After some hesitation[28] the ECJ in *Commission v Germany* Case C–433/93 [1995] ECR I–2303 held that under art 249(3) EC the application of a directive must be ensured by implementing measures adopted by a Member State independently of the possible direct effect of its provisions. In *Commission v Germany* Case C–253/95 [1996] ECR I–2423 the ECJ added that the direct effect is invoked only in special circumstances, in particular when a Member State has not taken the necessary implementing measures as required under the directive or if it has adopted implementing measures but they have not conformed with the directive. The ECJ emphasised that direct effect constitutes a minimum guarantee resulting from the binding nature of the obligation imposed upon the Member State by the directive and is insufficient in itself to ensure its full and complete application.

7.2 Action under art 227 EC against a Member State by another Member State

For the Member States an alternative to proceedings under art 226 EC is provided in art 227 EC which states that:

'A Member State which considers that another Member State has failed to fulfil an obligation under this Treaty may bring the matter before the Court of Justice (ECJ).

Before a Member State brings an action against another Member State for alleged infringement of an obligation under this Treaty, it shall bring the matter before the Commission.

The Commission shall deliver a reasoned opinion after each of the States concerned has been given the opportunity to submit its own case and its observations on the other party's case both orally and in writing.

If the Commission has not delivered an opinion within three months of the date on which the matter was brought before it, the absence of such opinion shall not prevent the matter from being brought before the Court of Justice.'

The Treaties of Rome, art 227 EC and art 142 EA, recognise the autonomous right of any Member State to act against another Member State that has failed to fulfil its obligations arising from Community law. A Member State is not required to justify its interest to act and thus may bring an action against the defaulting State if it believes that the general

---

[28] *Commission v Germany (Re Nursing Directive)* Case 29/84 [1985] ECR 1661, in which the ECJ held that a defence based on the direct effect of Community law might be accepted provided that three conditions were satisfied: administrative practice must fully ensure the application of Community law; there must be no legal uncertainty concerning the legal situation which the directive regulates; and individuals concerned must be aware of their rights. In this case those conditions were not satisfied.

interests of the Community necessitate such action, or if it considers that the illegal conduct of another Member State affects its own vital interests. However, the Commission is very much involved in such proceedings: first, before a Member State brings an action against another Member State, the Commission must be seised; second, the Commission must proceed in exactly the same manner as under art 226 EC, that is, it investigates the matter and gives both parties an opportunity to submit their arguments orally and in writing; and, finally, the Commission delivers a reasoned opinion within three months of the date on which the matter was brought.

The involvement of the Commission serves two purposes. On the one hand the Commission acts for a period of three months as an intermediary between the Member States concerned, it attempts to settle the case and find an acceptable solution. The period of three months is essentially a 'cooling off' period during which the Commission endeavours to resolve the matter in the light of the Community interest. On the other hand, the participation of the Commission in proceedings under art 227 EC emphasises its privileged role as the 'guardian' of the Treaty and the exceptional nature of an action against a Member State by another Member State. The case law in respect of art 227 EC confirms this point. Actions under art 227 EC are extremely rare and in general never reach the ECJ. So far the ECJ has delivered only one judgment under art 227 EC, that is, in *France v United Kingdom (Re Fishing Mesh)* Case 141/78 [1979] ECR 2923.

In this case the United Kingdom enacted an Order in Council concerning the size of the mesh of fishing nets. Fishing policy is within the exclusive competence of the Community, but under the Resolution adopted by the Council at The Hague meeting in 1976, and pending the implementation of the appropriate measures by the Community, the Member States were permitted to take unilateral interim measures to ensure the protection of fishery resources. Annex VI to the Council Resolution requires that a Member State which intends to take conservation measures notifies the other Member States. Furthermore, those measures must be approved by the Commission which must be consulted at all stages of the procedure. The United Kingdom failed to do so. The United Kingdom argued that the measures taken to conserve fishing stocks were not unilateral as they were adopted under the North-East Atlantic Fisheries Convention and thus there was no need to consult the Commission and the other Member States. The Commission delivered a reasoned opinion in favour of France. It stated that the United Kingdom failed in its obligation arising from art 10 EC and that in the light of divergences of interest, which made it impossible for the Community to establish a common policy in the area of the conservation of the biological resources of the sea, the consultations with other Member States and the Commission were even more necessary. France decided to bring the matter before the ECJ because the Commission did not assume responsibility for continuing the action.

The ECJ held that the United Kingdom was in breach of art 10 EC, Annex VI to the Hague Resolution and arts 2 and 3 of Regulation 101/76 which set out a common structural policy for the fishing industry which requires Member States to notify any alterations to fishery rules.. The ECJ held that Annex VI to the Hague Resolution, in the words of which 'the Member States will not take any unilateral measures in respect of the conservation of resources except in certain circumstances and with due observance of the requirements set out above', must be understood as referring to any measure of conservation emanating from the Member State and not from the Community authorities. The duty of consultation arising under the Hague Resolution thus also covers measures adopted by a Member State to comply with one of its international obligations in this matter. Such consultation was all the more necessary in this case since it is common ground, as has been emphasised by the French government and the Commission and accepted by the government of the United Kingdom itself, that the UK Order in Council, although carrying out certain recommendations of the North-East Atlantic Fisheries Convention, nevertheless in some respects goes beyond the requirements flowing from those recommendations.

Disputes between Member States concerning the application of the Treaty are, for political reasons, settled under art 226 EC. This solution is advantageous to the Member States for two reasons. The Member State concerned avoids unnecessary confrontations with another Member State while achieving the objectives sought, that is, compelling the defaulting Member State to comply with Community law. The Commission bears the burden of proof and conducts the investigations. Furthermore, under art 37 of the Statute of the ECJ the Member State or the other Community institutions may intervene to support or reject the application of the Commission in the case brought before the ECJ.[29]

In this context it is interesting to note that the 1999 refusal of France to sell British beef was dealt with under art 226 EC, although the UK often threatened to initiate proceedings under art 227 EC.

7.3 Effect of a ruling confirming a failure of a Member State to fulfil its obligation under the Treaty

There is no express provision in the EC Treaty regarding the legal effect of the ECJ rulings under art 226 EC. However, it results from art 228(1) EC that they are declaratory in nature. In this respect art 228(1) EC provides that:

> 'If the Court of Justice finds that a Member State has failed to fulfil an obligation under this Treaty, that State shall be required to take the necessary measures to comply with the judgment of the Court of Justice.'

Thus, the defaulting Member State must take all necessary measures in order to remedy the failure and its consequences both in the past and in the future: *Commission v Germany* Case 70/72 [1973] ECR 813. Furthermore, national courts and national authorities of the defaulting Member State are required to disapply any national law declared incompatible with Community law and to take all appropriate measures to ensure the effective application of the latter: *Commission v Italy* Case 48/71 [1972] ECR 536. If the judgment concerns the interpretation of Community law, its effect under art 226 EC is similar to that of ECJ rulings rendered under art 234 EC (see Chapter 9). For individuals there are two important

---

[29] In such case the ECJ grants or refuses leave to intervene in support of the order sought by the Commission or the Member State concerned. For example, in *Commission v Belgium* Case C–80/92 [1994] ECR I–1019, the ECJ granted the United Kingdom leave to intervene in support of the form of order sought by the Commission. In *Commission v United Kingdom (Re Nationality of Fishermen)* Case C–246/89R [1989] ECR 3125 the ECJ granted leave to Spain to intervene in support of the form of order sought by the Commission and to Ireland to intervene in support of the form of order sought by the United Kingdom. However, private parties are not permitted to intervene.

aspects of a ruling under art 226 EC. In *Procureur de la Republique v Waterkeyn* Joined Cases 314–316/81 and 83/82 [1982] ECR 4337 the ECJ held that:

'... if the Court finds in proceedings under arts [226] to [228] ... that a Member State's legislation is incompatible with the obligations which it has under the Treaty the courts of that State are bound by virtue of art [228] to draw the necessary inferences from the judgment of the Court. However, it should be understood that the rights accruing to individuals derive, not from that judgment, but from the actual provisions of Community law having direct effect in the internal legal order.'

This means that, first, if the provision of Community law is not directly effective, an individual cannot invoke it in proceedings before a national court which will apply a national provision contrary to Community law even though the ECJ has expressly recognised that provision as being in breach of EC law. Second, for individuals who have suffered loss resulting from the infringement of Community law by a Member State, the ruling of the ECJ confirming the failure of the Member State to fulfil that particular obligation provides sufficient evidence for national courts to award them pecuniary compensation: *Francovich* Case C–6/90 [1991] ECR I–5357.

However, the ECJ is not a federal court and thus it is not empowered to annul national law incompatible with Community law[30] or to compel a defaulting Member State to comply with its judgment by granting an injunction or imposing pecuniary penalties.

In the context of judgments rendered by the ECJ under art 226 EC, it is interesting to mention *Commission v Luxembourg* Case C–274/93 [1996] ECR I–2019. In this case the ECJ gave judgment in default of appearance. Indeed, Luxembourg neither replied to the letter of formal notice, nor to the reasoned opinion nor submitted its arguments during the proceedings before the ECJ. Default of appearance is very unusual[31] although this case had many peculiarities: the ECJ accepted the application from the Commission even though the complaint in the judicial stage concerned the incorrect implementation of a directive, while in the administrative stage the Commission submitted that Luxembourg did not implement the directive in question and failed to provide information as to the implementing measure. As already discussed, failure of the Commission to ensure that the complaint remains the same in all stages of the proceedings under art 226 EC results in the rejection by the ECJ of the application. Probably, the attitude of Luxembourg induced the ECJ to accept the application as it stood, although the ECJ could have limited the complaint to the provisions which were incontestably non-implemented[32] or invoked art 10 EC to sanction the failure of Luxembourg to co-operate in the proceedings.[33]

---

[30] For example, *Humblet* Case 6/60 [1960] ECR 1125.

[31] Also *Commission v Greece* Case 68/88 [1989] ECR 2965.

[32] As suggested by Advocate-General Jacobs. This possibility was recognised in *Commission v Ireland* Case C–257/94 [1995] ECR I–3041.

[33] It seems that the government of Luxembourg has a habit of ignoring letters of formal notice and the reasoned opinions delivered by the Commission: see conclusions of Advocate-General Elmer in *Commission v Luxembourg* Case C–46/95 [1997] ECR I–1279 concerning Directive 89/618/ EA.

Failure to comply with a ruling under art 226 EC

The Treaties of Rome do not specify a time limit for compliance with a judgment rendered under art 226 EC. However, the ECJ has imposed strict conditions in this respect. In *Commission v Italy* Case 69/86 [1987] ECR 733[34] the ECJ held that:

'Article [228 EC] does not specify the period within which a judgment must be complied with. However, it is beyond dispute that the action required to give effect to a judgment must be set in motion immediately and be completed in the shortest possible period'.

Non-compliance with judgments rendered under art 226 EC became a serious problem in the late 1980s when the Commission started to pursue defaulting Member States more vigorously than previously and discovered that Member States were more than reluctant to co-operate with the Commission on many matters. Until the entry into force of the Treaty of Maastricht the excessive delays and flagrant refusals on the part of the defaulting Member States to comply with the judgments of the ECJ were not subject to any sanctions. The Commission as the guardian of the Treaty was bound to take the necessary steps to compel a defaulting Member State to remedy the breach: *Commission v Italy* Case 281/83 [1985] ECR 3397. This merely consisted of introducing second proceedings based on art 226 EC for the breach of art 228 EC: *Commission v Italy* Case 48/71 [1972] ECR 536. In such circumstances, where there were no sanctions, a more radical approach was necessary. The Treaty of Maastricht accordingly addressed this situation, as indicated below.

Pecuniary sanctions under art 228(2) EC

The TEU added a new para 2 to art 228 EC, endorsed by the Treaty of Amsterdam. Article 228(2) EC provides that:

'If the Commission considers that the Member State concerned has not taken such measures it shall, after giving that State the opportunity to submit its observations, issue a reasoned opinion specifying the points on which the Member State concerned has not complied with the judgment of the Court of Justice.

If the Member State concerned fails to take the necessary measures to comply with the Court's judgment within the time limit laid down by the Commission, the latter may bring the case before the Court of Justice. In so doing it shall specify the amount of the lump sum or penalty payment to be paid by the Member State concerned which it considers appropriate in the circumstances.

If the Court of Justice finds that the Member State concerned has not complied with its judgment it may impose a lump sum or penalty payment on it.

This procedure shall be without prejudice to art 227.'

In the Communication of 5 June 1996 the Commission adopted a method of calculating the pecuniary sanctions which was further elaborated in the Communication of 8 January 1997. This Communication contained the detailed mode of calculation of penalties applicable to

---

[34] See also *Commission v France* Case 169/87 [1988] ECR 4093 and *Commission v France* Case C–334/94 [1996] ECR I–1307, which has probably set a record – more than 20 years of non-compliance! (that is, between the judgment of the ECJ in the original infringement proceedings given on 4 April 1974 and the subsequent proceedings based on art 228 EC).

all types of non-compliance with the original judgment. The Commission fixed the 'basic uniform lump sum' at EUR 500 per day of delay, as adjusted by two co-efficient multiplicands which take into account the gravity of the infringement and the period of non-compliance. For example, the Commission considers as very serious a breach of the principle of non-discrimination, and as serious an infringement of provisions ensuring the four freedoms.[35] The first multiplicand is within the scale from 1 to 20 and the second from 1 to 2. Furthermore, in order to make the penalty a real deterrent to non-compliance with the judgment, the Commission established an 'invariable factor' for each Member State which takes into consideration the financial capacity of the defaulting State, which is calculated on the basis of the GNP of each Member State, combined with its allocation of votes in the Council. It is within the scale of 1 to 26.4. The invariable factors for each Member State are fixed at the following levels.[36]

Member State	Invariable Factor	Example of penalty with minimum duration and severity	Example of penalty with maximum duration and severity
Belgium	6.2	3,115	186,888
Denmark	3.9	1,935	116,130
Germany	26.4	13,188	791,293
Greece	4.1	2,030	121,786
Spain	11.4	5,682	340,903
France	21.1	10,530	631,771
Eire	2.4	1,180	70,783
Italy	17.7	8,852	531,150
Luxembourg	1.0	500	30,000
The Netherlands	7.6	3,776	226,567
Austria	5.1	2,549	152,961
Portugal	3.9	1,933	115,972
Finland	3.9	1,644	98,652
Sweden	5.2	2,578	154,683
United Kingdom	17.8	8,906	534,344

The Commission favours a daily penaltiy payment based on the above table as being more appropriate than the imposition of a lump sum penalty.

The ECJ is not bound by the figure suggested by the Commission. It may increase or reduce the fine or may decide not to impose any penalty at all. The Commission has, on several occasions, commenced proceedings to lead to a fine as envisaged in art 228(2) EC. It seems, however, that the threat of the imposition of fines constitutes a real deterrent. In 1998 the Commission closed its files in all cases where a fine under art 228(2) EC was about

---

[35] *Agence Europe*, no 6742, 6.6.1996.
[36] The European Commission, IP/97/5: OJ C63 (1997).

to be imposed on Member States. This means that all defaulting Member States decided to comply with the judgments of the ECJ and avoid payment of a fine!

In respect of art 228(2) EC an interesting point was raised by Advocate-General Fenelly in *Commission v France (Re The French Maritime Code II)* Case C–334/94 [1996] ECR I–1307. He argued that if a defaulting Member State failed to comply with the original judgment the Commission should bring the second proceedings under art 228(2) EC instead of art 226 EC. He considered that art 228(2) EC contains a specific procedure which applies only to cases of non-compliance with original judgments. According to him, art 228(2) EC presents an imperative character which implies that an action against a defaulting Member State under art 226 EC would be misconceived, taking into account that the failure was already declared in the original proceedings on the same basis. Although Advocate-General Fenelly submitted his suggestion on 15 of his 22 pages of conclusions, the ECJ declined to reply. Thus, the relationship between art 226 EC and art 228 EC, and especially its para 2, is still unclear.

7.4 Simplified procedures

Under certain provisions of the EC Treaty proceedings against a defaulting Member State for a breach of EC law are simplified. The common point of such procedures is the possibility for the Commission or the Member States to bring the matter directly before the ECJ in a much shorter period of time than under arts 226 or 227 EC. Usually, the administrative stage takes a different, simplified form and the Commission is not bound to deliver a reasoned opinion.

Procedure under art 95(9) EC

The SEA introduced a simplified procedure in arts 100a(4) and 100b EEC which allowed the Member States, on the grounds of major needs defined in art 30 EC, to apply national provisions incompatible with the harmonisation measures adopted by the Council. The grounds are public policy, public morality, public security, the protection of health and life of humans and animals, protection of national treasures possessing artistic, historic or archaeological value and protection of intellectual property, or relating to protection of the environment or of working conditions. The Treaty of Amsterdam modified the procedure in art 100a(4) (now art 95(9) EC) and repealed art 100b. Under the Treaty of Amsterdam these national measures must be based not only on art 30 EC but also on the protection of environment or the working environment. As before, the national measures must be notified to the Commission which decides whether or not to authorise them. Under art 95(9) EC by way of derogation from the procedure of arts 226 and 227 EC, the Commission or any Member State may bring proceedings directly before the ECJ if it considers that a Member State has applied national rules incompatible with the establishment and functioning of the internal market, the protection of environment or the protection of the working environment without prior authorisation from the Commission.

Procedure under art 298 EC

Under art 298 EC in the circumstances described in art 296 EC, that is, in matters relating to national security (in particular connected with the production of or trade in arms, ammunition and war material), or under art 297 EC in the event of war, serious internal disturbances, or international tension, a Member State is not permitted to adopt measures distorting the conditions of competition in the common market. If it does the Commission or any Member State may bring the matter directly before the ECJ without prior authorisation of the Commission.[37]

---

[37] So far this procedure has been used once in *Commission v Greece* Case C–120/94R [1994] ECR I–3037, Ord of the ECJ of 29 June 1994, and concerned the imposition by Greece of restrictions on the movement of goods from the former Yugoslav Republic of Macedonia.

8 Actions against Community Institutions

8.1   Direct actions for annulment

8.2   Indirect action: plea of illegality under art 241 EC

8.3   Direct action for failure to act

8.4   Action for damages: non-contractual liability of the Community

Under art 5(1) EC all Community institutions are required to act within the limits of the powers conferred upon them by the Treaties. Community law provides a number of mechanisms ensuring that EC institutions function properly and do not exceed their powers. The Community judicature – the ECJ and the Court of First Instance – exercises jurisdiction similar to administrative courts in the Member States. The role of the ECJ is very similar to the French Conseil d'Etat (the highest administrative court in France).

Community law recognises three direct actions against Community institutions:

1. action for annulment of Community acts under art 230 EC;
2. action for failure to act against Community institutions under art 232; and
3. action for damages caused by the Community to individuals involving non-contractual liability of the former under arts 235 and 288(2) EC.

In addition, an indirect action, the so-called plea of illegality, defined in art 241 EC, may be brought against Community institutions.

8.1 Direct actions for annulment

Actions for annulment are provided for in arts 33 and 38 CS, 146 EA and 230 EC. Although they were inspired by the French administrative procedure, they reflect the peculiarity of the Community legal order – in particular in respect of the conditions of admissibility of an action for annulment which are very restrictive for certain categories of applicants. These conditions are set out in art 230(1) EC. The grounds for annulment are provided in art 230(2) EC and the effect of annulment is regulated in arts 231 and 233 EC.

The TEU substantially altered art 230 EC. The TEU recognised the right of the European Parliament (EP) and the European Central Bank (ECB) to challenge the legality of Community acts, albeit limited to actions seeking to safeguard their prerogatives. Also, the TEU extended the category of reviewable acts to include acts adopted jointly by the European Parliament and the Council, acts of the European Parliament and acts of the ECB. The Treaty of Amsterdam conferred limited *locus standi* on the Court of Auditors. Like the EP and the ECB the right of challenge is limited to protection of the prerogatives of the Court of Auditors.

Article 230 EC provides:

'(1) The Court of Justice shall review the legality of acts adopted jointly by the European Parliament and the Council, of acts of the Council, of the Commission and the ECB, other than recommendations and opinions, and of acts of the European Parliament intended to produce legal effects vis-à-vis third parties.

(2) It shall for this purpose have jurisdiction in actions brought by a Member State, the Council or the Commission on grounds of lack of competence, infringement of an essential legal requirement, infringement of this Treaty or any rule of law relating to its application, or misuse of powers.

(3) The Court shall have jurisdiction under the same conditions in actions brought by the European Parliament, by the Court of Auditors and by the ECB for the purpose of protecting their prerogatives

(4) Any natural or legal person may, under the same conditions, institute proceedings against a decision addressed to that person or against a decision which, although in the form of a regulation or a decision addressed to another person, is of direct and individual concern to the former.

(5) The proceedings provided for in this Article shall be instituted within two months of the publication of the measure, or of its notification to the plaintiff, or, in the absence thereof, of the day on which it came to the knowledge of the latter, as the case may be.'

An action for annulment is similar to what is known under English law (also recognised in Scottish law) as an application for judicial review.

Conditions for challenging Community acts

The conditions for challenging Community acts relate to: the time limit for bringing an action for annulment; the category of reviewable acts; and the category of applicants permitted to act on the basis of art 230 EC.

Time limit

The time limit is different for each Community: one month under the CS Treaty and two months under the EC and EA Treaties. It is regrettable from the point of view of convenience that the subsequent amendments to the founding Treaties have omitted to provide the same time limit for bringing an action for annulment for each Community.

The time limit begins to run from the date of publication of an act in the Official Journal of the European Communities, or from its notification to the applicant.[1] If the act was published, by virtue of art 81 of the Rules of Procedure of the ECJ and the CFI, the commencement of the time limit is extended by 15 days, and further extension is granted to take into consideration the distance of the applicant from the Community courts.[2] For an applicant from the United Kingdom the extension amounts to an additional ten days. Therefore, the time limit for such an applicant is two months, plus 15 days, plus ten days. In

---

[1] In *Konecke* Case 76/79 [1980] ECR 665 the ECJ held that the time limit starts to run the day after the notification takes place.

[2] Article 42 of the Statute of the ECJ and arts 80–82 of the Rules of Procedure of the ECJ and the CFI.

the absence of publication or notification the time limit starts to run on the day when the act came to the knowledge of the applicant.[3]

The time limit is rigorously enforced by the Community courts. Once it elapses, the application is deemed inadmissible *d'office*,[4] that is the act is immune from annulment. This is justified by the principle of legal certainty and equality in the administration of justice: *Valsabbia* Case 209/83 [1984] ECR 3089.

In *Simet* Cases 25 and 26/65 [1967] ECR 40 the ECJ accepted an exception to the strict observance of the time limit based on *force majeure*. See also *Bayer* Case C–195/91P [1994] ECR I–5619.

Other excuses have been rejected by the Community courts, a number of which were raised in *Bayer AG v Commission* Case T–12/90 [1991] ECR II–219. In this case the Commission sent notification to the applicant company fining it for a number of infringements of art 81 EC. The company brought an action under art 230(2) EC to have Commission's decision judicially reviewed. In response, the Commission argued that the application was inadmissible as time-barred under art 230(3) and the ECJ's Rules of Procedure.

The applicant company argued that the action was not time-barred and relied on three separate contentions to support this argument. First, it was submitted that the Commission was guilty of a number of irregularities in the notification. In particular, the Commission notified the decision to the company's registered office and not to the company's legal department with which it had conducted all previous correspondence. Second, the company claimed that its internal organisational breakdown was an excusable error. Finally, the applicants pleaded unforeseeable circumstances in order to justify the delay in submitting the application under art 230 EC.

The Court of First Instance (CFI) rejected all three arguments. The Court held that in the notification the Commission complied with the necessary formalities contained in its Rules of Procedure as it sent the decision by registered letter with postal acknowledgment of receipt. The letter duly arrived at Bayer's registered office. Both the arguments relating to excusable error and *force majeure* were also rejected. The CFI held that the delay had been caused by fault on the part of the applicants and Bayer could not claim that it committed excusable error. In this respect, the fact that the Commission sent a letter to the applicant's registered office, whereas it had previously addressed all its communications directly to the applicant's legal department, could not constitute an exceptional circumstance since this is a normal procedure. The inadequate functioning of the applicant's internal organisation was the reason why the letter was not forwarded to the legal department. This circumstance could not be considered as unforeseeable and *force majeure* since in order to establish the existence of *force majeure* there must 'be abnormal difficulties, independent of the will of the person concerned and apparently inevitable, even if all due care is taken'.

---

[3] *Tezi Textiel* Case 59/84 [1986] ECR 887. However, in the absence of a formal notification and provided that the applicant knew the content of the final position adopted by an EC institution, the time limit starts to run at the time the definite decision came into his knowledge: *Pesqueria Vasco-Montanesa* Ord Cases T–452 and 453/93R [1994] ECR II–229.

[4] For example, *Belfiore* Case 108/79 [1980] ECR 1769.

Reviewable acts

Under the terms of art 230 EC the following acts adopted by Community institutions are reviewable: acts of the Council and the Commission other than recommendations and opinions; acts adopted jointly by the European Parliament and the Council, that is, acts adopted within the framework of the procedure laid out in art 251 EC; acts of the ECB other than recommendations and opinions; and acts of the European Parliament intended to produce legal effects vis-à-vis a third party. As a result, reviewable acts must be examined from two perspectives: the author of the act and the nature of the act.

Author of the act Only acts adopted by EC institutions are reviewable. As a result, acts adopted by a particular Member State or Member States are excluded from the scope of art 230 EC. This principle is self-evident but in practice it is not always easy to determine whether a particular act should be considered as adopted by a Community institution or a Member State. For example, in *Oleificio Borelli* Case C–97/91 [1992] ECR I–6313 (confirmed in *E Branco* Case T–271/94 [1996] ECR II–3761) the ECJ held as inadmissible an act adopted by a Member State within the framework of a very complex Community procedure concerning the granting of aid from Community structural funds. Therefore, if an act constitutes an element of Community procedure it is not within the scope of art 230 EC. Second, sometimes Member States act within the Council but outside its competence as a Community institution. The question how to determine whether an act, irrespective of its form and name, adopted by the Council is an act of the Council or an act adopted by the Member States meeting within the framework of the Council (that is as an international conference) was resolved in *Commission v Council (ERTA)* Case 22/70 [1971] ECR 263. In this case the ECJ had to decide, *inter alia*, whether deliberations concerning the European Road Transport Agreement were reviewable under art 230 EC. The ECJ held that the qualification of an act depends on the determination of who, at the envisaged time, had competence to negotiate and conclude an agreement. The legal effect of the deliberations varies depending upon whether they are considered as an act within the competence of the Community or as an expression of policy co-ordination between the Member States in a specific area. The ECJ decided that the deliberations belonged to the first category since the Community had competence to negotiate and conclude the ERTA, and as such they were reviewable under art 230 EC. The opposite decision was rendered by the ECJ in *European Parliament v Council and Commission* Cases C–181 and 248/91 [1993] ECR I–3685 in which the ECJ held inadmissible for the purposes of art 230 EC an act adopted on the proposal of the Commission by 'the Member States meeting within the Council' granting emergency aid to Bangladesh, in so far as there is no exclusive competence of the Community in the area of humanitarian aid.

It is submitted that an act adopted by the European Council should not be excluded from being reviewable under art 230 EC if that act was intended to produce legal effects.[5] Nevertheless, the Community courts, so far, seem to be reluctant to accept it: *Roujanski* Case C–253/94P [1995] ECR I–7.

If one EC institution delegates certain powers to another EC institution, the question

---

[5] Answers of the Council to Certain Parliamentary Questions, Q no 193/76 (OJ C269 (1976)) and Q no 294/76 (OJ C294 (1976)).

arises: who is the author of the act? In this respect, the case law of the ECJ is well established – the author of the act is the institution which has delegated its competences: *SNUPAT* Cases 32 and 33/58 [1959] ECR 275. This solution is justified for two reasons: first, the delegate institution may adopt an act which would not be reviewable and thus the applicants would be prevented from challenging it under art 230 EC; and, second, the delegate institution is empowered to implement the measure but on its own has no competence to adopt it. Also, if a certain task is delegated to a particular person, for example if the Commission empowers one of the Commissioners to inform the addressee that an act has been adopted by the Commission, that act is deemed to emanate from the Commission.[6]

Until the entry into force of the TEU, acts adopted by the European Parliament were not formally reviewable. In practice, the ECJ, on a number of decisions, recognised that acts of the EP were reviewable. In *Luxembourg v European Parliament* Case 230/81 [1983] ECR 255 the deliberations of the EP concerning the change of its seat were challenged by Luxembourg. The ECJ held the action admissible on the grounds that these deliberations concerned all three Communities and based its decision on art 38 CS Treaty which permits a challenge to acts of the Parliament. The full recognition of acts of Parliament as reviewable by the ECJ constitutes one of the cases of judicial revision of the Treaty. This was well justified, taking into account the evolution of the EP from an advisory and supervisory body to a body involved in the decision-making procedures. It was also necessary in the light of the doctrine of *effet utile* in relation to the control of the legality of acts of EC institutions, in particular those intended to produce legal effect vis-à-vis a third party. In *Les Verts* Case 294/83 [1986] ECR 1339 the ECJ could not make reference to art 38 CS as in *Luxembourg v European Parliament* Case 230/81 since the applicant was a legal person and as such its action for annulment was ruled out under both the CS and the EC Treaties. As a result, the ECJ recognised reviewability of acts emanating from the Parliament and explained that since the EC is a Community based on the rule of law, neither the Member States nor Community institutions can escape the control of the requirement that their acts conform with the basic constitutional charter, that is the EC Treaty. It further added that:

> 'Measures adopted by the European Parliament in the context of the [EC] Treaty could encroach on the powers of the Member States or of the other institutions, or exceed the limits which have been set to the Parliament's powers, without its being possible to refer them for review by the Court. It must therefore be concluded that an action for annulment may lie against measures adopted by the European Parliament intended to have legal effects vis-à-vis-third parties.'

The case law of the ECJ demonstrates that reviewable acts of the EP comprise not only acts adopted by the EP as an institution but also by its organs, such as its Bureau for the allocation of funds amongst political parties (*Les Verts* Case 294/83) or the Declaration of the President of the European Parliament regarding the adoption of the Community budget: *Council v European Parliament* Case 34/86 [1986] ECR 2155; *Council v European Parliament* Case C–284/90 [1992] ECR I–2328. Acts which are not considered as reviewable under art 230 EC include: the act establishing a Parliamentary Commission of inquiry (*Groupe des Droites Européennes* Case 78/85 [1986] ECR 1754), the waiver of immunity

---

[6] See *ICI* Case 48/69 [1972] ECR 619. The ECJ has accepted the validity of the delegation of signature.

(*Wybot* Case 149/85 [1986] ECR 2403) or acts emanating from the EP's political parties or political groups: *Le Pen* Case C–210/89 [1990] ECR I–1183.

Acts adopted by the Court of Auditors are also reviewable. Although the EC Treaty is silent in this respect, the ECJ in *Maurissen* Cases 193 and 194/87 [1989] ECR 1045 accepted an action for annulment brought by a union against the Court of Auditors. All uncertainty was dispelled by the ECJ in *H v Court of Auditors* Case C–416/92 [1994] ECR I–1741.

On the basis of the EC Treaty, acts adopted by the following EC institutions are reviewable: the European Investment Bank under art 237 EC;[7] the European Investment Fund under art 30(6) of the Protocol on the Statute of the EIB; the Board of Appeal of the Community Trade Mark Office under art 63 of Council Regulation 40/94;[8] and the Community Plant Variety Office and its Board of Appeal under arts 73 and 74 of Council Regulation 2100/94.[9]

International agreements concluded between the Community and third countries cannot be considered as acts emanating from EC institutions. Since a Member State or Member States and third countries participate in their adoption they cannot be classified as Community acts. It is submitted that the ruling of the ECJ in *Haegeman* Case 181/73 [1974] ECR 449 in which the Court decided otherwise should be rejected. Indeed, the reviewability of international agreements between the Community and third countries ignores the distinction between international agreements themselves and acts adopted by EC institutions regarding the conclusion or application of such agreements. In the first case, the ECJ should not exercise jurisdiction under art 230 EC because international agreements are not acts of EC institutions, they are international treaties within the meaning of public international law. However, in the second case, the ECJ should be empowered to annul, for example, a decision of the Commission concerning the conclusion of an agreement with a third country (*France v Commission* Case C–327/91 [1994] ECR I–3641) or a decision regarding the application of an international agreement (*Greece v Commission* Case 30/88 [1989] ECR 374) because those acts emanate from EC institutions and as such are reviewable under art 230 EC.

Nature of the act The ECJ has considerably extended the category of reviewable acts. In *Commission v Council (ERTA)* Case 22/70 [1971] ECR 263 it held that not only acts listed in art 249 EC can be challenged under art 230 EC but also any act which has binding legal effects whatever its nature and form. This means that all acts adopted by EC institutions which produce legal effects vis-à-vis third parties are reviewable. The content and scope of application of an act are determining factors, not the form and name of the act. The case law of the ECJ has clarified this point in relation to borderline cases since, in practice, it is not difficult to determine whether an act produces binding legal effect vis-à-vis the applicant.

The following acts are considered as reviewable under art 230 EC:

1. Deliberations of the Council in ERTA: Case 22/70 *Commission v Council*.

---

[7] In *E Tete v EIB* Case T–460/93 [1993] ECR II–1257 the CFI specified that acts of the EIB are reviewable within the limits defined by art 237 EC.
[8] OJ L11 (1994).
[9] OJ L227 (1994).

2. A communication of the Commission which by means of interpretation of a directive has introduced new obligations: *France* v *Commission* Case C–325/91 [1993] ECR I–3283.
3. A code of conduct adopted with a view to co-ordinating management of structural funds but published in the section 'Communication and information' of the Official Journal: *France and Belgium* v *Commission* Case C–303/90 [1991] ECR I–5315.
4. A letter from the Commission: *Usines à tubes de la Sarre* Case 1/57 [1957] ECR 201.
5. A decision orally communicated to the applicant: *Kohler* Cases 316/82 and 40/83 [1984] ECR 641; *Air France* Case T–3/93 [1994] ECR II–121.
6. An official declaration made by the Commissioner in charge of competition matters declaring the EC Merger rules inapplicable to the acquisition of Dan Air by British Airways: *Air France* Case T–3/93.
7. A letter from the Commission stating reasons for rejecting a complaint under competition law: *BEUC* Case T–37/92 [1994] ECR II–285.

The ECJ held that the following acts are not reviewable under art 230 EC:

1. All acts which only confirm an existing situation since they do not modify the legal position of the applicant: *SNUPAT* Cases 42 and 49/59 [1961] ECR 101.
2. All acts which set up a global policy of the Community in a specific area, that is establishing programmes of the Community, since they envisage future measures and thus do not change the current legal situation of the applicant: *Schlüter* Case 9/73 [1973] ECR 1135; *Associazione Agricoltori della Provincia di Rivigo* Case C–142/95P [1996] ECR I–6669.
3. All internal measures adopted by EC institutions which produce legal effects only vis-à-vis that institution such as instructions, internal rules, circulars, etc: *Phoenix Rheinrohr* Case 20/58 [1959] ECR 153; *TAO AFI* Case C–322/91 [1992] ECR 6373 (Ord). However, they may be challenged indirectly, provided they produce binding legal effect, if an individual decision is based on such internal measures: *SNUPAT* Case 32 and 33/58 [1959] ECR 275.
4. All preparatory acts of EC institutions, since the challengeable act must be a final statement of an institution's position, not merely an interim position. In *IBM* v *Commission* Case 60/81 [1981] ECR 2639 (see also *Guérin Automobiles* Case C–282/95P [1997] ECR I–1506) the Commission's decision to commence proceedings against IBM and a statement of objections to its marketing practices as being incompatible with arts 81 and 82 EC (which was annexed to the decision) was considered as a step in the proceedings. The idea behind this rule is that work of EC institutions would be paralysed if preparatory acts were reviewable. However, an action for annulment of such acts is allowed if they produce binding effects or if they constitute a final position in ancillary proceedings which would result in the adoption of a final decision. This distinction is difficult to determine in practice, especially in cases concerning competition law, State aid and anti-dumping measures. For example, a decision to forward documents to the complaining undertaking[10] was considered as reviewable as well as a decision to deny access to a file in an anti-dumping case (*BEUC* Case C–170/89 [1991] ECR I–5709), and a

---

[10] See *AKZO* Case 53/85 [1986] ECR 1985 and *The Scottish Football Association* Case T–46/92 [1994] ECR II–1039; but see *Mayer* v *Commission* Case T–106/99, order of the CFI of 22 October 1999.

decision to refuse to initiate proceedings under art 86(2) EC (*CIRFS* Case C–313/90 [1993] ECR I–2557) or art 88(2) concerning State aid (*Spain* v *Commission* Case C–312/91 [1992] ECR I–4117; *Italy* v *Commission* Case C–47/91 [1992] ECR I–4145), but not a letter refusing to protect confidentiality of documents forwarded to the Commission by the applicant: *Automobiles Peugeot SA* Cases T–90 and 136/96 [1997] ECR II–663.

5. A decision of the Commission to refuse to initiate proceedings against a Member State which is in breach of Community law under art 226 EC. In *Lütticke* Case 48/65 [1966] ECR 19 the ECJ held that a part of the procedure prior to bringing the Member State before the ECJ constitutes a stage which is designed to invite the Member State to fulfil its obligations arising out of the Treaty, whereupon the Commission states its position by issuing an opinion which at this stage cannot be considered as producing binding legal effects. This position of the ECJ has been confirmed in many cases: *Sonito* v *Commission* Case C–87/89 [1990] ECR I–1981; *Emrich* Case C–247/90 [1990] ECR I–3914; *Giorgio Bernardi* v *Commission* Cases T–479 and 559/93 [1994] ECR II–1115.

6. Regulation 2187/93 which was adopted by the Council in order to comply with ECJ rulings concerning illegality of Council regulations allocating milk quotas.[11] It contained a proposal for compensation for approximately 12,000 farmers who were entitled to damages by virtue of art 288(2). In *Connaughton, Fitzsimons and Griffin; Murray* Cases T–541 and 554/93 [1997] ECR II–563 the applicants brought an action for annulment of arts 8 and 14 of Regulation 2187/93 which provided that the acceptance of compensation by a farmer precluded him from any other action, irrespective of its nature, against any Community institutions. The CFI held that the Regulation in question was only a proposal and as such did not produce legal effects. Consequently, it was not considered as a reviewable act within the meaning of art 230 EC. The CFI emphasised that once the proposal was accepted it would produce legal effects vis-à-vis the applicant, but not before.

Applicants under art 230 EC

Article 230 EC establishes three categories of applicants:

1. privileged applicants which may bring an action for annulment against all reviewable acts and are not required to justify their interest to act;
2. semi-privileged applicants, such as the European Parliament and the ECB, which may only challenge acts in order to defend their prerogatives;
3. non-privileged applicants who have a reduced legal ability to bring an action under art 230 EC, in the sense that they may only challenge certain reviewable acts provided they demonstrate their special position vis-à-vis the act they wish to challenge.

Privileged applicants

Under art 33 and 38 CS the High Authority, the Council and the Member States and, under arts 230 EC and 144 EA, the Council, the Commission and the Member States are privileged

---

[11] For example, *Mulder* Cases 104/89 and 37/90 [1992] ECR I–3061; see section 8.4 of this Chapter.

applicants. They may challenge any reviewable acts and have unrestricted *locus standi*.[12] In relation to the Commission this is justified on the basis that the Commission is the guardian of the Treaty as specifically provided in art 211 EC. The extension of this facility to the Council is a logical consequence of its position within the institutional framework of the Community. The Member States as contracting parties to the Treaty are particularly interested in defending their rights affected by unlawful measures adopted by the Community institutions. A Member State under its unrestricted *locus standi* may challenge an act addressed to another Member State (*The Netherlands v High Authority* Case 6/54 [1956] ECR 201) or even an act which was adopted with its consent (*Italy v Council* Case 166/78 [1979] ECR 2575 that is, it voted in favour of the measure in the Council). The only condition for privileged applicants is that they must challenge an act within the time limit set out in art 230(5) EC.

Semi-privileged applicants

Until the TEU the European Parliament was denied *locus standi*. This was logical in the sense that acts adopted by the EP were not reviewable under art 230 EC. However, once acts of the EP were reviewable (*Partie Ecologiste Les Verts v European Parliament* Case 294/83 [1986] ECR 1339 and *Council v Parliament (Re Commission Budget)* Case 34/86 [1986] ECR 2155), the EP argued that its position as an applicant should also be recognised. In *European Parliament v Council (Re Comitology)* Case 302/87 [1988] ECR 5615 the ECJ refused to confer on the EP even limited *locus standi* under art 230 EC and held, *inter alia*, that the Commission as the guardian of the Treaty could introduce an action for annulment of acts which would endanger the prerogatives of the EP. In this case Advocate-General Darmon suggested that the EP should have limited *locus standi* to maintain the institutional balance of power, especially in cases where its interests or rights were directly affected by acts of the Commission or the Council. In such circumstances the position of the EP was worse than that of a non-privileged applicant. Nevertheless, in took the ECJ two years to reverse its position. In *European Parliament v Council (Re Chernobyl)* Case 70/88 [1990] ECR I–2041 the ECJ conferred on the EP the status of a semi-privileged applicant.

In this case, the EP challenged Council Regulation 3954/87 concerning the permitted levels of radioactive contamination in food and feeding stuffs after the nuclear accident at Chernobyl. The EP argued that the Regulation should be adopted under art 95 EC which required the opening of the co-operation procedure, instead of art 31 EA which imposes upon the Council the obligation to merely consult the EP. The EP claimed that its prerogatives were infringed by Council Regulation 3954/87.

The ECJ held that the mechanisms provided under the Treaties did not always allow censure of acts adopted by the Council or the Commission in violation of competences of the EP. The ECJ referred to the suggestions of Advocate-General Darmon made in the *Comitology* case and decided that the action of the EP was admissible under art 230 EC. However, the ECJ imposed a restriction on the EP: the admissibility of an action for annulment submitted by the EP is limited, it must be intended to protect its prerogatives and must be based solely on violations of its prerogatives.

The ECJ has consolidated this approach by rejecting any supplementary restrictions

---

[12] *Locus standi* means literally recognised position, right to intervene, right to appear in court.

which the Council tried to impose on the EP in subsequent cases: *European Parliament v Council* Case C–295/90 [1992] ECR I–4193.

Non-privileged applicants

Non-privileged applicants under art 230 EC are natural or legal persons. In order to justify *locus standi* they must show that they have an existing interest protected under Community law. It is stressed that the interests must exist 'at present'. Interests regarding a future legal situation, the coming into existence of which is uncertain or subject to possible changes of circumstances in law, or in fact, are excluded from the scope of art 230 EC.[13] Also an applicant cannot challenge a decision which is favourable to his interests, such as a decision of exemption, negative clearance, etc, under competition law. Furthermore, an applicant must prove that the contested measure has affected his personal situation detrimentally.[14]

Reviewable acts
Under art 230(4) EC a non-privileged applicant may challenge:

1. a decision addressed to the applicant (this is a classical case of judicial review);
2. a decision in the form of a regulation which must be, however, of direct and individual concern to the applicant

The difference between a regulation and a decision was explained by the ECJ in *International Fruit Co v Commission* Cases 41–44/70 [1971] ECR 411. The ECJ held that the essential feature of a decision results from the limitation of its addressees, while a regulation has essentially a general scope of application as it is applicable not to a limited number of addressees, named or otherwise individually identified as in the case of a decision, but to a category of persons envisaged *in abstractio* and in their entirety.

The case law of the ECJ as to the determination of circumstances in which a decision is disguised under the form of a regulation has evolved. At first, the ECJ considered that this might happen in the situation in which the entire regulation is in fact a decision which an EC institution has adopted with the exclusive or main purpose of evading a procedure specifically prescribed by the Treaty for dealing with the applicant, in other words misusing its powers: *Confédération Nationale des Producteur de Fruits et Légumes* Cases 16 and 17/62 [1962] ECR 901. In the next stage the ECJ accepted that a true regulation may also be addressed to defined persons: *Molitaria Immolese* Case 30/67 [1968] ECR 172. Finally, the ECJ recognised that a regulation may in fact be a bundle of decisions addressed to each applicant: *International Fruit Co v Commission* Cases 41–44/70. However, the ECJ considered that a provision of a regulation cannot have at the same time general and individual scope of application: *International Fruit Co v Commission* Cases 41–44/70. Under the influence of the so-called theory of 'hybrid regulations' developed by Advocates-General, in particular Advocate-General Verloren Van Themaat in *Allied Corporation* Cases 239 and 275/82 [1984] ECR 1005 and which applied mostly to anti-dumping cases, the ECJ has

---

[13] For example, *NBV and NVB* Case T–138/89 [1992] ECR II–2181.

[14] This is assessed favourably to the applicants: *BP* Case 77/77 [1978] ECR 1513; see *SES* Case 88/76 [1977] ECR 709 in which the challenged measure had no influence on the situation of the applicant.

softened its position. In *Codorniu* Case C–309/89 [1994] ECR I–1853 the ECJ recognised that provisions of a regulation may have at the same time both general and individual scope of application. In this case the ECJ held that the regulation was 'by nature and by virtue of its sphere of application of a legislative nature' which did not prevent it from being of individual concern to some of those who were affected. Thus, it seems that the ECJ accepts that an act of general application may also affect the interests of an individual. However, as the ECJ emphasised in *Zuckerfabrik Watenstedt* Case 6/68 [1968] ECR 595 the fact that a provision of a regulation may, in practice, affect its addressees differently one from another does not call into question its nature as a Regulation when the situation to which it applies is objectively determined. The case law of the ECJ suggests that the criterion which is essential in the determination of the nature of an act is whether the group of the potential addressees of the act is open or closed. If it is open the act has no limitation *ratione tempore*. If the group is closed an act applies retroactively or immediately by creating rights and obligations for a limited and easily identifiable group of persons, unless the membership of that fixed and ascertainable group is determined by an objective situation connected with the objective of that act: *KSH NV v Council and Commission* Case 101/76 [1977] ECR 797.

Very often, the ECJ avoids making a distinction between a decision and a regulation by declaring that the contested act is not of direct and individual concern to the applicant. Article 230 EC requires that the ECJ decides first whether the act is a decision or a regulation before examining the subjective situation of an applicant vis-à-vis that act.

Decision addressed to another person which is of direct and individual concern to the applicant The ECJ has broadly interpreted the notion of a decision addressed to another person. Such a person may be not only an individual ie any natural or legal person, but also a Member State[15] or a third country.[16] As to EC directives, the ECJ seems to accept the possibility that an action for annulment of a directive can be admissible provided a directive contains provisions which could be equated with a decision and that the applicant is directly and individually concerned by them: *Government of Gibraltar* Case C–298/89 [1993] ECR I–3605; *Asocarne* Case C–10/95P [1995] ECR I–4149.

Individual concern

The most confusing and complicated question under art 230 EC is the issue of individual concern, mostly because of inconsistency in the decisions of Community courts in this area. Individual concern was defined by the ECJ in *Plaumann v Commission* Case 25/62 [1963] ECR 95. Plaumann was an importer of clementines. Under the Common Customs Tariff he paid 13 per cent customs duty as did any importer of clementines from outside the Community. The government of Germany asked the Commission for authorisation under art 25(3) EEC (now repealed) to suspend this duty. The Commission refused and issued a decision in this respect. Plaumann challenged this decision.

The ECJ held that Plaumann was not individually and directly concerned by the

---

[15] In most cases an individual applicant challenges a decision addressed to a Member State, for example, *Plaumann* Case 25/62 [1964] ECR 95. See case law on individual and direct concern.

[16] See *Fiscano* Case C–135/92 [1994] ECR I–2885 in which the ECJ considered that a Swedish company was individually and directly concerned by a decision addressed by the Commission to the government of Sweden.

Commission's decision, although he was affected, as any importer of clementines, by the decision. His commercial activities were such that could at any time be practised by any person and thus he did not distinguish himself from others in relation to the challenged decision. The ECJ stated that individual concern may only be invoked if persons other than the addressees of the decision demonstrate that 'that decision affects them by reason of certain attributes which are peculiar to them or by reason of circumstances in which they are differentiated from all other persons by virtue of these factors distinguishing them individually just as in the case of the person addressed'.

The ECJ has restrictively interpreted 'certain peculiar attributes' or 'circumstances which differentiate' a person from others when challenging a decision addressed to another person or a regulation in the form of a decision. As a result, the ECJ refused to recognise that a person was individually concerned in the following situations: in the *Plaumann* case when the decision concerned specific activities, that is importers of clementines; when the number of the affected persons was limited;[17] when an undertaking was the only one concerned by a measure in a particular Member State (*Spijker Kwasten BV v Commission* Case 231/82 [1983] ECR 259; *Union Deutsche Lebensmittelwerke* Case 97/85 [1987] ECR 2265); when an undertaking operated in a determined zone and the regulation expressly applied to that geographically delimited zone (*Molitaria Immolese* Case 30/67 [1968] ECR 172); when an undertaking was a direct competitor of another undertaking to which the decision was addressed (*Eridania* Cases 10 and 18/68 [1969] ECR 459); and when the number of undertakings concerned was limited to three undertakings in a Member State but potential competitors would not be in a position to enter the market for at least two years: *KSH NV v Council and Commission* Case 101/76 [1977] ECR 797.

In the above cases the applicants were considered as being members of an 'open class', that is anyone may at any time practice the commercial activity in question and potentially join the group of producers of particular goods. The case law of the ECJ indicates that in order to be individually concerned a person must prove that at the time the measure was adopted it was possible to identify all potential applicants. This only happens if the membership of that class was fixed at that time which means, in practice, that only in respect of retrospective measures is it possible to invoke individual concern as was confirmed in *Toepfer v Commission* Cases 106 and 107/63 [1965] ECR 525. Toepfer applied for an import licence for maize on 1 October 1962 on which day the German authority mistakenly reduced the levy on imports of maize from France to zero. The German intervention agency realised the mistake and refused to grant licences from the 2 October 1962. Three days later the Commission confirmed the ban and authorised the German authorities to impose the levy. Toepfer challenged the Commission's decision on the grounds that he was individually and directly concerned.

The ECJ held that he was individually concerned because the number and identity of those individually concerned 'had become fixed and ascertainable' before the contested decision was made. They were a 'closed group': the decision affected their interests and position in a way significantly different from other importers who might wish to apply for a licence after the decision but during the remaining period of the ban. Therefore, only those

---

[17] In *Plaumann*, there were 30 importers of clementines. A similar situation arose in *Firma Léon Van Parys NV v Commission* Case T–11/99 Judgment of 15 September 1999 (nyr).

who applied on 1 October were individually concerned, since from 2 to 4 October applications were refused and on the 4 October the Commission issued its decision. As a result, Toepfer was within the closed group who applied on 1 October; the larger group, that is those who applied between 2 and 4 October, was open since they were refused licences and could reapply thereafter without loss to them as the levy would be the same after 2 October.

Similarly, in *Bock v Commission* Case 62/70 [1971] ECR 897 the ECJ held that Bock was individually concerned by a decision adopted by the Commission because when he applied for a licence to import Chinese mushrooms the German authorities refused to grant it and asked the Commission to confirm their decision which the latter did. Not only was the decision issued to deal with his application but Bock belonged to the ascertainable and fixed group of importers at the time of adoption of that decision. However, the ECJ has gradually attenuated the necessary requirements for individual concern.

First, in the various areas characterised by the existence of non-contentious procedures which involve more or less direct participation of undertakings in the adoption of the measures. If an applicant assists the Commission in the preparation of the measure then his association with the adoption of the measure differentiates him from others and his individual concern is self-evident: *Boehringer Ingelheim Vetmedica GmbH* Case T–125/96 [2000] 1 CMLR 97. This is mostly used in competition, anti-dumping and State-aid cases. For example, if a complaint is lodged against a competitor for an alleged breach of arts 81 and 82 EC which leads to a decision of the Commission exempting the latter or confirming that there is no breach of competition rules on its part, then the complaining undertaking is individually concerned by the decision addressed to another undertaking (*Metro* Case 26/76 [1977] ECR 1875; *British American Tobacco* Cases 142 and 156/84 [1987] ECR 4487), not because it is in competition with the other undertaking but because it initiated the proceedings which resulted in the adoption of the measure. Similarly, a decision of the Commission to refuse the opening of proceedings under art 88(2) EC concerning aid granted to an undertaking by a Member State may be challenged by the undertaking which made the original complaint to the Commission: *Cofaz* Case 169/84 [1986] ECR 391; *William Cook* Case C–198/91 [1993] ECR I–2487; *Matra* Case C–225/91 [1993] ECR I–3203.

In the context of the common market, dumping occurs when a non-EC undertaking sells its products below domestic market prices which is at the same time a price below the real cost of the goods. This strategy is used to penetrate the market and to eliminate the existing competitors. An undertaking affected by such dumping conduct of a foreign undertaking complains to the Commission which may adopt a provisional regulation and request the Council to issue a definite regulation imposing an anti-dumping duty to counterbalance the competitive advantage of the foreign undertaking – this is determined in the light of the effect of the dumping on EC undertakings, especially the one that lodged a complaint. In *Timex Corporation v Council* Case 264/82 [1985] ECR 861[18] the applicant challenged a regulation which was adopted because of Timex's complaints concerning cheap mechanical watches coming from the Soviet Union. The regulation imposed an anti-dumping duty, taking into account information forwarded by Timex. However, Timex also

---

[18] There are many similar cases, for example *Allied Corporation* Case 239/82 [1984] ECR 1005; *CIRFS* Case C–313/90 [1993] I–2557.

claimed that the new duty was too low. The ECJ held that because the regulation was based on the situation of Timex, that undertaking was individually concerned. It is interesting to note that in *Métropole Télévision* Cases T–528, 542, 543 and 546/93 [1996] ECR II–649 the Commission argued that the applicant was not individually concerned as it did not participate in the preparation of the measure. The CFI replied that effective participation in the adoption of a measure cannot be required in order to establish an individual concern as it would amount to the introduction of an additional requirement which is not provided for in art 230 EC. Therefore, the CFI has rightly indicated that participation in the adoption of a measure constitutes solely a factor facilitating the recognition of an individual concern, but it is not a necessary requirement.

Second, the restrictive interpretation of requirements relating to individual concern has been relaxed in respect of other areas. In some cases the determination of individual concern has been based on the assessment of the economic situation of the applicant vis-à-vis the measure in question. The unrealistic approach to *locus standi* based on the assumption that as long as any person at any time may practise a particular activity or join a particular class of producers has been not been applied in some cases. In *Sofrimport SARL v Commission* Case C–152/88 [1990] ECR I–2477 the ECJ for the first time assessed the influence of a regulation on the economic interests of the applicant. Sofrimport shipped apples from Chile prior to the regulation suspending import licences for Chilean apples. When the regulation came into force the apples imported by Sofrimport were in transit. The French authorities refused to issue an import licence to Sofrimport and the latter challenged the regulation. The ECJ held that an earlier regulation imposed a duty upon the Community authorities to take into consideration, when adopting a new regulation, the circumstances of goods in transit, thus importers with goods in transit constituted a fixed and ascertainable group and could be considered as individually concerned. The only logical explanation of the ECJ decision was that Sofrimport's economic interests were affected to such a degree that they were successful in their action for annulment. Subsequent case law of the ECJ applies this approach although in a different context.[19]

This approach has been applied to anti-dumping cases. In *Extramet* Case C–358/89 [1991] ECR I–2501 the economic analysis of the situation of an undertaking, and its degree of dependence vis-à-vis the effect that the regulation had on the market, differentiated and individualised the applicant from other undertakings so as to allow him to claim individual concern.[20]

The really intriguing and puzzling judgment was delivered in *Codorniu* Case C–309/89 [1994] ECR I–1853. Codorniu, a Spanish producer of quality sparkling wines, had been the holder of a graphic trade mark since 1924 in relation to one of its wines designed as 'Gran

---

[19] See *Unifruit Hellas* Case T–489/93 [1994] ECR II–1201; *Antillean Rice Mills* Cases T–480 and 483/93 [1995] ECR II–2305; [1995] Europe (November), no 375, comm D Simon; *Vereiniging van Exporters* Cases T–481 and 483/93 [1995] ECR II–2941; *Buralux* Case C–309/94P [1996] ECR I–677. However, it was rejected in *Terres Rouges Consultant SA v Commission (supported by the Council, Spain and France)* Case T–47/95 [1997] ECR II–481, in which the largest importer of bananas from Cote d'Ivoire (70 per cent of the market) was denied an individual concern in respect of a regulation adopted by the Commission in order to comply with the requirement of GATT and international agreements concluded between the Community and certain South American countries.

[20] See A Arnull, 'Challenging EC Anti-dumping Regulations: The Problem of Admissibility' [1992] European Competition Law Review 73.

Cremant de Codorniu'. In certain regions of France and Luxembourg the word 'cremant' was also used for a certain quality of wine. The producers in those countries asked the Community to adopt a regulation which would reserve the word 'cremant' only for their sparkling wine. Council Regulation 2045/89 restricted the use of word 'cremant' to wines originating in France and Luxembourg in order to protect the traditional description used in those areas. Codorniu challenged the Regulation.

The ECJ held that Codorniu was differentiated from other producers of wine since it had registered and used the word 'cremant' since 1924. Although Regulation 2045/89 was a true regulation it did not prevent it from being of individual concern to Codorniu which was badly affected by the Regulation. Also, the restriction of the word 'cremant' to wine originating from a certain region of France and Luxembourg could not be objectively justified and, in addition, was contrary to art 12 EC which prohibits discrimination based on nationality.

Subsequent to the ECJ decision in *Codorniu* there were high expectations that the ECJ would confirm its new approach and that it would extend *locus standi* in respect of non-privileged applicants. However, this did not occur as evidenced by *Stichting Greenpeace Council (Greenpeace International) and Others* v *Commission* Case C–321/95 [1998] ECR I–1651, the first case of the ECJ after *Codorniu*. In this case the CFI had found against Greenpeace, the nature conservancy foundation, who brought an action on behalf of its members. The CFI had, on 9 August 1995, declared inadmissible Greenpeace's action for annulment of the Commission's decisions taken between 7 March 1991 and 29 October 1993 to disburse to the Kingdom of Spain ECU 12,000,000 from the European Regional Development Fund pursuant to Council Decision 91/440 concerning financial assistance for the construction of two power stations in the Canary Islands. Greenpeace appealed, arguing: first, that the CFI had erred in the interpretation and application of art 230(4) EC as it had failed to take into consideration the nature and specific character of the environmental interests underpinning its action; second, that the CFI was wrong to take the view that reference to national laws on *locus standi* was irrelevant for the purposes of art 230 EC; third, that the order of the CFI was contrary to the case law of the ECJ as well as the declaration of EC institutions and Member States on environmental matters; and, fourth, the applicant set up its own criteria for *locus standi* for a non-privileged applicant in environmental matters which criteria, according to the applicants were satisfied in the present case.

The ECJ confirmed the order of the CFI, rejecting the action for annulment brought by Greenpeace International. The ECJ decided to apply the restrictive approach based on the 'closed class' test introduced by *Plaumann* Case 25/62 [1963] ECR 95. The ECJ rejected the opinion of Advocate-General Cosmas suggesting the evolution of conditions of admissibility in respect of actions brought by non-privileged applicants under art 230(4) EC in matters relating to the protection of the environment. Also, the ECJ confirmed its case law in respect of the right of associations, including those active in the field of the protection of the environment, to bring an action for annulment under art 230 EC. The ECJ rejected the possibility for an association to have *locus standi* under art 230 EC. According to the ECJ this possibility would lead to the development of an *actio popularis* contrary to the philosophy of art 230 EC.

It is submitted that the decision of the ECJ in *Codorniu* should be regarded as an exception rather than a rule. Subsequent case law of the Community judicature confirms the restrictive approach to *locus standi* of non-privileged applicants. Nevertheless, in *Codorniu* the ECJ accepted that the provision of an EC regulation can be, at the same time, of both general and individual scope of application. Also, the ECJ recognised that the protection of intellectual property rights may confer on its holder the right of challenge under art 230 EC. In *Codorniu* the fact that the applicant was prevented from using his trade mark caused him, from the point of view of his economic interests, to be in such a disadvantageous position that he was differentiated from other undertakings and thus individually concerned by the regulation in question. In *CSR Pampryl SA v Commission* Case T–114/99 (order of 9 November 1999 (nyr)) the facts were very similar to *Codorniu* but the applicant did not register the use of the name 'cidre Pays d'Auge'. The CFI held that the applicant had not differentiated himself from others and consequently was not individually concerned.

Direct concern

An applicant under art 230 EC must demonstrate both individual and direct concern, and they apply cumulatively. The ECJ stated in *Plaumann* that direct concern alone is of no avail if the applicant is not individually concerned by a decision. Indeed, in the majority of cases the question of individual concern is examined by the Community courts and if the applicant cannot establish this first requirement then the second is not investigated. Direct concern means that a Member State has no discretion in implementing a Community act. The best way to illustrate this point it to examine *UNICME* Case 123/77 [1978] ECR 845 in which the ECJ rejected an application under art 230 EC on the grounds of lack of direct concern because a Member State retained a discretion, that is, there was an imposition of the autonomous will of the Member State between the decision and its effect on the applicant.

In this case, under a Council regulation the importation of Japanese motor-cycles was allowed only by holders of an import licence issued by the Italian government. The applicants, Italian importers of such-motor cycles and their trade association, UNICME, challenged the regulation. The ECJ held that the applicants were not directly concerned since the Italian government had a discretion as to the grant of import licences. As a result, they were concerned not by the regulation but the subsequent refusal of import licences by the Italian authorities.

If a Member State has no discretion as to the application of a Community measure, the applicant can claim that he is directly concerned. For example, in *International Fruit Co v Commission* Cases 41–44 [1971] ECR 411 the granting of import licences for dessert apples, which was based on a Community rule, was modified by a Commission regulation. The Commission imposed specific rules on the Member States for dealing with such applications. As a result, national authorities had no discretion in the matter. Similarly, if a Member State decides first how to deal with a particular issue and then asks the Commission to confirm its decision, as happened in *Toepfer* Cases 106 and 107/63 [1965] ECR 525, the applicant is directly concerned by the Community measure. A Member State must follow a subsequent confirmation of the Commission.

The strict requirements regarding direct concern have been attenuated by the

Community courts. In *Piraïki-Patraïki* Case 11/82 [1985] ECR 207 (see also *Bock* Case 62/70 [1971] ECR 897; *Kaufhof* Case 29/75 [1976] ECR 431) the ECJ held that the possibility for a Member State to take further measures than provided by a Community act itself does not prevent an applicant from invoking direct concern since the link between the applicant and a Community act has not been severed by a mere possibility that a Member State may take authorised measures which in this case was highly unlikely.

In *Piraïki-Patraïki* the Commission permitted the French government to impose quotas on imports of yarn from Greece. Although the French authorities had discretion as to whether or not to impose new quotas, in the light of previous restrictions imposed on such imports and the request to use new quotas submitted to the Commission by the French government, it was highly unlikely, or as the ECJ held 'purely theoretical', that the French authorities would not exercise their discretion. As, in addition, Greek producers of yarn on the basis of an express provision of the Greek Accession Act, had concluded export contracts prior to the decision, they were also individually concerned and thus successfully challenged the decision.

It is submitted that the requirements under art 230 EC regarding both direct and individual concern are too restrictive. The need for the Community courts not to be flooded with applications under art 230 EC should not prevent individuals from exercising their rights, especially the right to due process. Even though they have other means at their disposal to enforce their rights, such as art 241(4) EC or art 234 EC, the basic point is that the case law of the ECJ on individual concern applies regardless of the way they choose to claim their rights. In this respect, in *Union de Pequeños Agricultores* Case T–173/98 (order of 23 November 1999 (nyr)), the applicants had no remedy under national law as they could not challenge the validity of the regulation in question via art 234 EC. The contested regulation annulled State aid granted to the applicants. The government of Spain refused to challenge the regulation under art 230 EC, notwithstanding an express request submitted by the commune of Andalusia. The CFI held that the peculiarities of national legal systems could not modify the requirements of art 230 EC since it would require a Community judge to act beyond his powers: see *Kahn Scheepvaart* Case T–398/94 [1996] ECR II–477. The CFI held that a solution to the problem presented in this case should be found in art 10 EC, that is a Member State is required to take necessary measures to ensure the effective protection of rights conferred on individuals by EC law. As a result, the applicants should bring proceedings before a national court and request the effective protection of their rights under art 234 EC: *P Kruidvat* Case C–70/97 [1998] ECR I–7183.

This solution confirms that the situation of applicants should be assessed realistically in the light of the true effect of a Community measure on their particular situation. Although the ECJ seems to have softened its approach towards the determination of individual concern, it is still not sufficient.

Grounds for annulment

Article 230(2) EC sets out the grounds for annulment which are:

1. lack of competence;
2. infringement of an essential procedural requirement;

3. infringement of the Treaty or any rule of law relating to its application; and

4. misuse of powers.

The Community courts must apply the first two grounds *ex officio* in any event (*France v High Authority* Case 1/54 [1954] ECR 7; *Interhotel* Case C–29/89 [1991] ECR I–2276), and the last two only if invoked by the applicant. It is very important to claim all grounds, since new grounds introduced after the expiry of the time limit are inadmissible under art 42(2) of the Rules of Procedure of the ECJ and art 42(2) of the Rules of Procedure of the CFI. Also, reference to all possible or probable grounds which is permitted under art 230 EC is highly recommended because the Community courts are empowered to specify and further crystallise the grounds invoked by the applicant: *Nold* Case 4/73 [1974] ECR 491.

Lack of competence

This ground is similar to substantive *ultra vires* in British administrative law, which occurs when the administration acts beyond its powers. Under arts 5 and 7 EC the EC institutions have only the powers conferred upon them by the Treaty. It was considered that this ground would be invoked often, especially by the Member States because of the encroachment of the Community law upon national competences of the Member States. This has not materialised. As a result, this ground is rarely used, mostly because the applicants prefer to base their claims on the infringement of the Treaty.[21] This ground is mainly invoked in cases challenging the legal basis of Community measures.[22]

Infringement of an essential procedural requirement

Infringement of an essential procedural requirement is analogous to procedural *ultra vires*. It occurs when an EC institution fails to comply with a mandatory procedural requirement in the adoption of the measure, for example the Council fails to consult the EP when the Treaty requires mandatory consultation of the European Parliament prior to the adoption of a measure. The ECJ has annulled acts which provided for optional consultation of the EP where the Council did not give enough time to the EP to issue its opinion (*Roquette Frères v Council* Cases 138 and 139/79 [1980] ECR 3393) or when the EP was not reconsulted when an act of the Council substantially altered an original proposal submitted to the EP: *ACF Chemiefarma* Case 41/69 [1970] ECR 661; *European Parliament v Council* Case C–388/92 [1994] ECR I–2067. When an EC institution fails to comply with its own internal rules of procedure, the ECJ will annul the act in question: *Commission v BASF (PVC)* Case C–137/92P [1994] ECR I–2555.

The failure to provide reasons for an act required by art 253 EC is most often invoked under this ground: *Germany v Commission (Brennwein)* Case 24/62 [1963] ECR 63.

Infringement of the Treaty or any rule of law relating to its application

This is the most often invoked ground. It comprises not only the provisions of the Treaty

---

[21] For example: see *Erzberbau* Cases 3–18 and 25–26/58 [1960] ECR 367.

[22] Spain (*supported by Greece*) v *Council* (*supported by France and the Commission*) Case C–350/92 [1995] ECR I–1995; *United Kingdom v Council (Re Working Time Directive)* Case C–84/94 [1996] ECR I–5758.

but all sources of Community law, including the general principles of Community law[23] and infringements of an international agreement concluded between the Community and third countries: *International Fruit* Cases 21–24/72 [1972] ECR 1219.

Misuse of powers

The ECJ has adopted the same definition of misuse of powers as under French administrative law (*detournment de pouvoir*): *Hauts Fourneaux de Chasse* Case 2/57 [1958] ECR 129. Misuse of powers takes place when Community institutions have used their powers for objectives other than those provided by the Treaty. Thus, a legitimate power is used for an illegal end or in an illegal way. This ground is often invoked but rarely successfully because of the burden of proof it imposes on the applicant, as well as the fact that in the case of multiplicity of objectives which an EC institution may legitimately pursue the ECJ will annul an act only if it was adopted with the exclusive objective of achieving objectives other than prescribed by the Treaty or evading a procedure specifically provided by the Treaty for dealing with the circumstances of the case: *Fedesa* Case C–331/88 [1990] ECR I–4023. Misuse of powers was successfully invoked in the context of a dispute between the Community and its staff when the Community servants proved that an EC institution acted in bad faith.[24]

Effect of annulment

The effect of annulment of a Community act is described in art 231 EC, which provides:

> (1) If the action is well founded, the Court of Justice shall declare the act concerned to be void.
> (2) In the case of a regulation, however, the Court of Justice shall, if it considers this necessary, state which of the effects of the regulation which it has declared void shall be considered as definitive.'

As a result, the effect of annulment is that an act is void. The decision of the ECJ applies *erga omnes*: *Assider* Case 3/54 [1955] ECR 123. The successfully challenged act is void immediately, from the day on which the ECJ renders its decision. This means that the act in question is devoid of past, present and future legal effects. In respect of decisions rendered by the Court of First Instance, under art 53 of its Statute the act is void from the expiry of the time limit for appeal or from the time the appeal is rejected. In principle, a decision of annulment has a retroactive effect subject to art 231(2) regarding annulment of a regulation. In that case, the ECJ, if it considers necessary, indicates which of the effects of the regulation should be considered as definitive. Therefore, the ECJ may declare some or all of its provision to be operative. Also, acts other than regulations may be declared void *ex nunc*, for example budgetary provisions (*Council v European Parliament* Case 34/86 [1986] ECR 2155; *Council v European Parliament* Case C–284/90 [1992] ECR I–2328) or directives:

---

[23] *Bock* Case 62/70 [1971] ECR 897; *Transocean Marine Paint* Case 17/74 [1974] ECR 1063. For a breach of an EC directive (see *Angelopharm GmbH* Case C–212/91 [1994] ECR I–171) and for a successful challenge of implementing measures based on secondary legislation but in breach of the latter: see *Köster* Case 25/70 [1970] ECR 1161; *Sheer* Case 30/70 [1970] ECR 1197.

[24] In *Gutmann* Cases 18 and 35/65 [1966] ECR 149 a Community official was transferred to Brussels in the interest of the service but in fact it was a disciplinary transfer; *Giuffrida* Case 105/75 [1976] ECR 1395.

European Parliament v *Council (Re Student Directive)* Case C–295/90 [1992] ECR I–4193. Use of the declaratory power of the ECJ may be justified for a number of reasons, such as the need for legal certainty (*European Parliament* v *Council* Case C–21/94 [1995] ECR I–1827), respect for legitimate expectation, or the the need to suspend the effects of annulment until a competent institution adopts an act which will replace the one struck down by the ECJ: *European Parliament* v *Council* Case C–65/90 [1992] ECR 4593; *Commission* v *Council* Case 275/87 [1989] ECR 259.

Under art 233 EC a decision of annulment imposes upon the Community institution whose act has been declared void an obligation 'to take the necessary measures to comply with the judgment of the Court of Justice'. If that institution refuses to comply with the decision of the ECJ the aggravated party may bring an action under art 232 EC, and, if appropriate, commence an action for damages under art 288(2).

In *Commission of the European Communities* v *AssiDomän Kraft Products AB and Others* Case C–310/97P [1999] 5 CMLR 1253 the ECJ provided important clarifications concerning the effect of its own judgment annulling a decision adopted by the Commission. This case closes the saga of the *Wood Pulp Cartel* cases. In *Ahlström and Others* v *Commission (Re Wood Pulp Cartel)* Joined Cases 89, 104, 114, 116, 117 and 125–129/85 [1993] 4 CMLR 901 the Commission found more than 40 suppliers of wood pulp in violation of Community competition law, despite the fact that none of these companies was resident within the European Community. Fines were imposed on 36 of these undertakings for violation of art 81(1) EC. Among those fined were nine Swedish undertakings, who paid their fines. Subsequently, 26 of the undertakings appealed to the ECJ against the decision. They challenged the Commission's finding that they had breached art 81(1) EC through concertation of prices for their products by means of a system of quarterly price announcements. However, the nine Swedish undertakings that had already paid fines, including AssiDomän, decided not to participate in the annulment proceedings.

The Court annulled the decision of the Commission that the undertakings concerned infringed art 81(1) EC through concertation of prices for their products, on the grounds that the Commission had not provided a firm, precise and consistent body of evidence in this respect. As a result the ECJ annulled most of the fines entirely and reduced to EUR 20,000 the other fines imposed on the undertakings which had instituted proceedings.

AssiDomän Kraft Products and other undertakings which did not join in the annulment proceedings asked the Commission to reconsider their legal position in the light of the ECJ's judgment and to refund to each of them the fines which they paid to the extent that they exceeded the sum of EUR 20,000. However, the undertakings in question were not the addressees of the judgment. The Commission refused to refund them on the grounds that it had already complied with the ECJ order by reducing the fines in respect of the undertakings participating in the proceedings, and that the decision of the ECJ had no necessary impact on the fines imposed upon the Swedish undertakings. The latter responded by challenging that decision before the Court of First Instance.

The Court of First Instance held that although the Commission issued one decision in the Wood Pulp cases that decision, in fact, consisted of a bundle of 43 separate decisions, each of which was independent of the others. Consequently, the annulment or modification of 26 fines left the remaining fines unaffected. However, the CFI upheld the appeal of the

Swedish undertakings on the ground of art 233 EC, which provides that when an act adopted by an EC institution has been declared void that institution should take the necessary measures to comply with the judgment of the Court of Justice. The CFI decided that this obligation could extend to persons who were not party to any appeal before the ECJ and thus the Commission should re-examine the legality of the unchallenged decision in the light of the grounds of the annulling judgment and determine whether, following such re-examination, the fines paid must be refunded. The CFI annulled the Commission's decision refusing to refund the fines already paid by Swedish undertakings. At that stage, the Commission challenged the decision of the CFI which was the subject of the current appeal.

The ECJ reversed the decision of the CFI and held that the Swedish undertakings were not entitled to have the fines reduced. The ECJ justified its judgment on two grounds. First, the Community judicature cannot rule *ultra petita*, that is the scope of the annulment which it pronounces may not go further than that sought by the applicant and thus unchallenged aspects concerning other addressees did not form part of the matter to be tried by the Community judicature. Second, although the authority *erga omnes* exerted by an annulling judgment attaches to both the operative part and the *ratio decidendi* of the judgment, it cannot entail annulment of an act not challenged before the Community judicature but alleged to be vitiated by the same illegality. Consequently, art 233 EC cannot be interpreted as requiring the institution concerned to re-examine identical or similar decisions allegedly affected by the same irregularity addressed to addressees other than the applicant. The ECJ also added that the judgment of the CFI was contrary to art 230 EC since it side-stepped the time limit for bringing legal proceedings against acts adopted by EC institutions and thus undermined the principle of legal certainty. Furthermore, this principle also precluded the re-examination of unchallenged decisions.

The judgment of the ECJ is fully justified in so far as the Commission's decision is regarded as a bundle of individual decisions against each participating undertaking and not as a single decision addressed to all of them. This solution has been confirmed in *Limburgse Vinyl Maatschappij NV and Others v Commission (Re PVC Cartel (No 2))* Joined Cases T–305, 307, 313–316, 318, 325, 328–329 and 335/97 [1999] 5 CMLR 303, in which a number of undertakings successfully challenged the Commission's decision on the ground that it had not been signed by the appropriate persons. The ECJ held that the challenged decision was binding on those undertakings who had not appealed, although it was void in respect of undertakings that lodged the appeal.

Although the solution consisting of considering the Commission's decision as a bundle of separate decisions addressed to each participating undertaking penalises undertakings which decide not to appeal it is, at the same time, fair. Undertakings may decide not to challenge a Commission decision in competition matters for a number of reasons, the most important being that the appeal procedure involves considerable investment in terms of time and money. Hindsight is very useful but the fact is that if an undertaking has chosen to economise by not spending time and money on an appeal and the judgment of the court in similar matters arrives after the limitation period has expired it will be too late to jump on the bandwagon. Conversely, if the outcome is against the appellant the decision not to participate will be well justified.

8.2 Indirect action: plea of illegality under art 241 EC

Article 241 EC provides:

> 'Notwithstanding the expiry of the period laid down in the fifth paragraph of art 230, any party may, in proceedings in which a regulation adopted jointly by the European Parliament and the Council, or a regulation of the Council, of the Commission or of the ECB is at issue, plead the grounds specified in the second paragraph of art 230 in order to invoke before the Court of Justice the inapplicability of that regulation.'

The indirect action contained in arts 241 EC, 156 EA and 36 CS originates from French administrative law where it is known as the exception of *illegalité*. Unlike actions under art 230 EC, the plea of illegality is not time-barred but it requires a direct relationship between the challenged act and the allegedly invalid regulation: *Simet* Cases 25 and 26/65 [1967] ECR 40. The grounds for an action under art 241 EC are the same as in an action for annulment under art 230 EC, that is, lack of competence, infringement of an essential procedural requirement, infringement of the Treaty or any rule of law relating to its application and misuse of powers.

The procedure under arts 241 EC, 156 EA and art 36 CS[25] does not provide for an independent form of action. The plea of illegality can only be invoked as an ancillary plea, as a means by which an applicant in support of an action challenging implementing measures addressed to him or to a third person or (in the case of direct and individual concern) to the applicant, pleads the illegality of the general measure upon which the implementing measures are based. In practice, the plea of illegality is mostly used to challenge individual decisions based on EC regulations whose validity is called into question: *Krapp* Cases 275/80 and 24/81 [1981] ECR 2489.

The main feature of the plea of illegality is that it allows, subject to certain conditions, softening of the stringent requirements imposed under art 230 EC as to access to the Community judicature in terms of *locus standi* and the time limit. The ECJ held in *Salemo v Commission and Council* Cases 87 and 130/77 and 9 and 10/84 [1985] ECR 2523 that:

> 'The sole purpose of art [241 EC] is to protect parties against the application of an unlawful regulation where the regulation itself can no longer be challenged owing to the expiry of the period laid down in art [230 EC]. However, in allowing a party to plead the inapplicability of a regulation, art [241 EC] does not create an independent right of action; such a plea may only be raised indirectly in proceedings against an implementing measure, the validity of the regulation being challenged in so far as it constitutes the legal basis of that measure.'

Thus, the plea of illegality constitutes an alternative way of judicially reviewing Community acts, permitting any person to raise indirectly the question of validity of a Community act.

This point is well illustrated by *Simmenthal* Case 92/78 [1979] ECR 777. Simmenthal, an Italian meat importer, claimed that the fees for health and sanitary inspection carried out at the Italian border were unlawful. He challenged under art 230 EC a decision adopted by

---

[25] Article 36 CS is formulated in more restrictive terms under which it is open to undertakings wishing to challenge pecuniary sanctions imposed by the High Authority, but was in *Meroni* Case 9/56 [1958] ECR 11 considered by the ECJ as being of general scope of application due to the fact that the plea of illegality is based on general principles of law ensuring the respect of legality of Community acts.

the Commission and, in support of his action, indirectly under art 241 EC a number of regulations and notices, especially notices of invitation to tender of 13 January 1978, upon which that decision was based and which he could not challenge directly due to the elapse of a two-month time limit.

The ECJ held that notices of invitation to tender are general acts 'which determine in advance and objectively, the rights and obligation of the trader who wishes to participate', and as acts of general application cannot be challenged under art 230 EC. Only the challenged decision, which was adopted in consequence of the tender, could be of direct and individual concern to Simmenthal and thus reviewable under art 230 EC. As a result, Simmenthal was allowed to challenge indirectly under art 241 EC those regulations and the notices of invitation to tender of 13 January 1978, although as the ECJ stated the latter were not *sensu stricto* measures laid down by Regulation.

Article 241 EC is subject to certain conditions regarding acts capable of being subject to the plea of illegality and the applicants

Requirements imposed by art 241 EC

Article 241 EC provides that a regulation adopted jointly by the European Parliament and the Council and a regulation of the Council, the Commission or the ECB may be challenged under art 241 EC. However, the ECJ has widely interpreted this provision. As a result, the plea of illegality may be invoked, not only against regulations adopted by the above-mentioned institutions but also against any act of general application capable of producing legal effects similar to EC regulations.

Applicants

Article 241 EC cannot be used to circumvent the requirements of art 230 EC. For that reason the addressees of individual acts who have not challenged them within the time limit prescribed by art 230(5) EC are not permitted to rely on the plea of illegality (*Commission v Belgium* Case 156/77 [1978] ECR 1881), apart from the case of an individual decision being null and void, that is non-existent (*Usines à Tubes de la Sarre* Cases 1 and 14/57 [1957] ECR 201), or being a part of a 'complex procedure comprising a number of interdependent acts' as for example, in *G Rauch* Case 16/64 [1965] ECR 179 concerning the recruitment of a Community official.

The Commission and some Advocates-General suggested a restrictive interpretation of art 241 EC in relation to Member States in order to compensate the stringent requirements for *locus standi* under art 230 EC in relation to individuals.[26] However, the ECJ reluctantly permits Member States to invoke the plea of illegality for a different reason. The reason for its reluctance is that the exception of illegality may encourage Member States to ignore certain regulations and thus not challenge them within the time limit. This would jeopardise the principle of legal certainty. The ECJ recognised that a Member State may rely on the plea of illegality in order to challenge a regulation which served as a legal foundation for another regulation which implemented the former: *Italian Republic* Case 32/65 [1966]

---

[26] See G Bebr, 'Judicial Remedy of Private Parties against Normative Acts of the EEC, the Role of the Exception of Illegality' [1966–67] CMLR 7, esp 11–13.

ECR 563. It is still uncertain, although in general the ECJ seems rather unenthusiastic, whether a Member State may invoke the plea of illegality within the framework of enforcement proceedings under art 226 EC: *Commission v France* Cases 6 and 11/69 [1970] CMLR 43; *Commission v Belgium* Case 156/77 [1978] ECR 1881.

Community institutions, unlike the Member States and individuals, are not required to prove their interest while invoking plea of illegality.

Exclusive jurisdiction of the Community courts under art 241 EC

The ancillary nature of the plea of illegality requires, as the ECJ emphasised in *Milchwerke* Case 31/62 [1962] ECR 971, that non-application of a regulation may only be invoked in procedures brought before the ECJ itself (now also before the CFI) on the basis of other provisions of the Treaty. This statement needs to be examined more closely. First, the plea of illegality cannot be invoked in proceedings before national courts. There is, however, an indirect possibility based on art 234 EC and not on art 241 for an applicant to rely on the plea of illegality in national proceedings. An applicant who challenges national measures introduced to implement a Community act is allowed to invoke the plea of illegality: *Unversität Hamburg* Case 216/82 [1983] ECR 2771. As national courts have no jurisdiction to declare a Community act void, and provided they have reasons to believe that the Community act is invalid, they will, under art 234 EC, ask the ECJ to determine the validity of such an act. However, its ancillary nature is still preserved under art 234 EC, that is the plea of illegality cannot be invoked on its own. Furthermore, the ECJ has introduced two important limitations in this respect. In *TWD Textilwerke* Case C–188/92 [1994] ECR I–833, as confirmed in *Wiljo* Case C–178/95 [1997] ECR I–585 (see also *Eurotunnel SA v SeaFrance* Case C–408/95 [1997] ECR I–6315), the ECJ established a firm principle that once the time limit for a direct action under art 230 EC elapses, the Community courts would consider as inadmissible proceedings under art 234 EC in relation to an applicant who had *locus standi* to bring a direct action under art 230 EC but neglected to do so within the time limit prescribed under art 230(5) EC. The ECJ justified its decision on the basis of the principle of legal certainty. In this case, TWD Textilwerke was individually and directly concerned by a decision addressed to a third party. *A fortiori*, this solution is even more obvious vis-à-vis the addressees of a decision. It results from the case law of the ECJ that national courts may only refer the question of pleas of illegality under art 230 EC in two situations after the expiry of the time-limit prescribed in art 230(5) EC: when the applicant challenges the validity of a regulation, or in the case of a decision, only if the latter was neither addressed to the applicant nor of direct and individual concern to him.

Effect of a successful action under art 241 EC

If the applicant is successful, the general act, which may be called a parent act, is rendered inapplicable only to his case. The implementing measure is annulled in respect of the applicant. The parent act nevertheless is still in force since it cannot be declared void as it was 'perfected' or rendered immune from direct challenge under art 230 EC by lapse of time, although in practice the institution which adopted the parent act will amend or repeal that act as under art 233(1) EC the institution in question is under a legal obligation to comply which the ECJ's judgment.

8.3 Direct action for failure to act

When a Community institution has a positive obligation to act, that is, it must adopt certain measures required by the Treaty but fails to do so, art 232 EC confers jurisdiction upon the Community courts to compel such an Institution to act. Article 232 EC provides:

> '(1) Should the European Parliament, the Council or the Commission, in infringement of this Treaty, fail to act, the Member States and the other institutions of the Community may bring an action before the Court of Justice to have the infringement established.
> (2) The action shall be admissible only if the institution concerned has first been called upon to act. If, within two months of being so called upon, the institution concerned has not defined its position, the action may be brought within a further period of two months.
> (3) Any natural or legal person may, under the conditions laid down in the preceding paragraphs, complain to the Court of Justice that an institution of the Community has failed to address to that person any act other than a recommendation or an opinion.
> (4) The Court of Justice shall have jurisdiction, under the same conditions, in actions or proceedings brought by the ECB in areas falling within the latter's field of competence and in actions or proceedings brought against the latter.'

The action under art 232 EC is similar to the historic English writ of mandamus or, in Scotland , to the petition for an order requiring the specific performance of a statutory duty.

An action for failure to act is common to the three Communities. The procedure is respectively governed by arts 35 CS, 232 EC and 148 EA. Under art 35 CS an action for failure to act may be brought only against the High Authority when the latter is legally bound to adopt a decision or a recommendation but fails to fulfil this duty. However, in *Groupement des Industries Sidérurgiques Luxembourgeoises* Cases 7 and 9/54 [1956] ECR 55, the ECJ held that this action should be considered akin to an action for annulment. As a result, there are the same requirements as to *locus standi* and the same grounds as in an action for annulment. Under the Treaties of Rome an action for failure to act is separate from an action for annulment and has its own specific requirements even though in *Chevalley* Case 15/70 [1970] ECR 975 the ECJ held that an action under art 232 EC provides an applicant with a method of recourse parallel to that of art 230 EC. The relationship between arts 232 and 230 EC was explained by the ECJ in *Eridania* Case 10 and 18/68 [1969] ECR 459.

In this case the Commission had granted aid to three Italian sugar refineries which was contested by other sugar producers before the Commission. The Commission refused to annul its decision. This resulted in an action both for annulment under art 230 EC and for failure to act under art 232 EC brought by the other producers. The ECJ held that the applicants could not succeed under art 232 EC since the refusal of the Commission to annul its decision was tantamount to an act rather than to a failure to act. Also, the applicants were prevented from bringing an action under art 230 EC as they were not able to prove that they were directly and individually concerned by the decision. The ECJ emphasised that art 232 EC should not be used to circumvent the requirements set out in art 230 EC.

Article 232 EC imposes its own conditions as to the applicant, the defaulting institution and the procedure.

Defaulting institution

Article 232 EC states that the EP, the Council, the Commission and the European Central Bank are the EC institutions against whom an action for failure to act may be brought.

Applicants

There are three categories of applicant – privileged, semi-privileged and non-privileged.

In respect of privileged applicants, art 232 EC provides that Member States and the other institutions of the Community may bring an action before the Court of Justice. This group of applicants is not required to justify their interest in the act. They may bring an action against any failure or any omission and in respect of any act, be they regulations, directives, decision, recommendations, opinions, or even a proposal concerning the Community budget (*European Parliament v Council* Case 302/87 [1988] ECR 5615), provided the Community law imposes a duty to act. The EP, which was initially excluded from bringing an action for annulment under art 230 EC, has always been included in the list of privileged applicants. The ECJ in *European Parliament v Council* Case 13/83 [1985] ECR 1513 formally recognised the right of the EP to bring an action under art 232 EC.

The ECB is considered a semi-privileged applicant, that is, it has *locus standi* to raise an action for failure to act in respect of areas within its fields of competence.

Non-privileged applicants are any natural and legal person complaining that 'an institution of the Community has failed to address to that person any act other than a recommendation or an opinion'. The literal interpretation of this formula implies that an applicant may only challenge the failure of an institution to adopt an act addressed to him, that is an individual decision. This would *a priori* limit his *locus standi* under art 232 EC even more than under art 230 EC. Fortunately, the ECJ has given a liberal interpretation of art 232 EC and assimilated actions for annulment with actions for failure to act in respect of *locus standi* of non-privileged applicants. This was clearly confirmed in *Lord Bethell* Case 246/81 [1982] ECR 2277.

Lord Bethell, a Member of the EP and Chairman of the Freedom of the Skies Committee complained to the Commission about anti-competitive practices of a number of European airlines in relation to passenger fares. He argued that the Commission was under a duty to submit proposals under art 82 EC in order to curtail those practices. Unsatisfied with the answer from the Commission he brought an action for failure to act against the Commission under art 232 EC, claiming that the Commission's reply amounted in fact to a failure to act and, alternatively under art 230 EC, arguing that this answer should be annulled.

The ECJ held that the application of Lord Bethell would be admissible only if the Commission 'having been duly called upon … has failed to adopt in relation to him a measure which he was legally entitled to claim by virtue of the rules of Community law.' Lord Bethell although indirectly concerned by the measure as a user of the airlines and

Chairman of the Freedom of the Skies Committee which represented users, was nevertheless not in the legal position of a potential addressee of a decision which the Commission has a duty to adopt with regard to him. His application under article 230 EC was rejected for the same reason. The analogy between *locus standi* of non-privileged applicants under art 230 EC and art 232 EC was thus confirmed by the ECJ.

The similarity between arts 230 and 232 EC means that an application under art 232 EC is admissible if the applicant is directly and individually concerned by a measure which an EC institution has failed to adopt, including a decision addressed to a third party but of individual and direct concern to the applicant.[27] It is still uncertain whether a non-privileged applicant is entitled to force the Community institutions to adopt a normative measure of general application.[28]

Procedure

The procedure under art 232 EC comprises two stages: an administrative stage and a judicial stage which take place before the Community courts.

Administrative stage

An action for failure to act may be brought before the Community courts only if the institution concerned has been called upon to act by the applicant who notified it of the complaint and indicated what precise measures he wished that institution to take in this respect: *S Maziere* Cases 114–117/79 [1980] ECR 1529. There is no time-limit for the submission of a complaint but in *The Netherlands v Commission* Case 59/70 [1971] ECR 639 the ECJ held that the right to notify the Commission of its omission or failure to act should not be delayed indefinitely and that the complaint should be lodged within a 'reasonable time'. This decision was rendered in relation to the CS Treaty but it seems that this solution can also be transposed to the Treaties of Rome. Once the institution concerned is notified of the complaint it has two months to define its position. The main problem is to determine what is meant by the phrase 'define its position'. The ECJ has gradually elucidated this notion. In the early cases under art 232 EC the Court held that the institution had defined its position if it had adopted any act apart from a reply asking the applicant to wait (which could not be considered as an answer)[29] or referring to the position previously taken. For example, when the Commission sends a letter refusing to start proceedings against a competitor undertaking, it defines its position: *GEMA* Case 125/78 [1979] ECR 3117. However, refusal to take measures which are required under a specific procedure amounts to a failure to act, for example an applicant is entitled to an answer, even stating the refusal of the Commission to act: *Asia Motor France* Case T–28/90 [1992] ECR II–2285; *Ladbroke Racing Ltd* Case T–32/93 [1994] ECR II–1015. Gradually, it has become

---

[27] In *ENU* Case C–107/91 [1993] ECR I–599 the ECJ recognised this possibility within the framework of the EA Treaty and in *Ladbroke Racing Ltd* Case T–32/93 [1994] ECR II–1015 the CFI extended it to the EC Treaty.

[28] In *Holtz and Willemsen* Case 134/73 [1974] ECR 1 the ECJ rejected this possibility but *Pfizer* Case 65/87 [1987] ECR 1691 confirms rather the uncertainty than a firm rejection.

[29] It happens usually when the Commission conducts further investigations concerning that matter: *SNUPAT* Cases 42 and 49/59 [1961] ECR 101.

clear that art 232 EC is aimed at failures caused by abstention to define the position, or the adoption of a measure, but not the adoption of an act different from that which was requested by the applicant: *ENU* Case C–107/91 [1993] ECR I–599; *Pesqueras Echebaster SA* Case C–25/91 [1993] ECR I–1719.

The result is that an institution defines its position by issuing a statement of its views on a particular matter or its proposal for action or, in the case of refusal, the reason for not taking a particular action.

Silence or refusal to act by the institution concerned are not necessarily tantamount to a failure to act. The institution concerned must be legally bound under the Community law to act. Conversely, if it has a discretion in this respect, an action for failure to act is not admissible. This point is illustrated by *Alfons Lütticke* Case 48/65 [1966] ECR 19.

Lütticke argued that a German tax on the import of milk powder was contrary to art 90 EC. He asked the Commission to take an enforcement action against Germany under art 226 EC. The Commission replied that the tax was not contrary to Community law and as a result, it did not intend to take action under art 226 EC. The ECJ held that by refusing to act the Commission defined its position and, second, under art 226 EC the Commission enjoyed a large measure of discretion whether or not to start proceedings

As a result, an applicant cannot force the Commission to act since he is not legally entitled to a particular measure. The Commission has no duty to act with respect to him. For that reason successful actions are rare under art 232 EC.

Once an institution concerned defines its position the proceedings under art 232 EC are *ipso facto* terminated. The applicant, provided he is legally entitled to a specific measure and unhappy about the answer he obtained from a particular institution, may bring proceedings against that institution under art 230 EC to annul the decision adopted in his case. In this context it is interesting to note that unsuccessful applicants under art 232 EC, that is when the ECJ decides that the institution in question did define its position, often ask the ECJ to transform their action under art 232 EC into an action under art 230 EC. The ECJ has always refused. Its refusal may have serious consequences for the applicant if the time limit of two months provided under art 232 EC has already elapsed since it would also mean that the time limit for bringing an action under art 230 has also expired: *Asia Motor France* Case T–28/90 [1992] ECR II–2285.

Judicial stage

If the institution concerned does not define its position within two months the applicant has another two months to bring proceedings before the Community courts under the Treaties of Rome, but only one month under the CS Treaty. The applicant is required to submit an application limited to the points he raised in the original complaint: *Chambre Syndicale Sidérurgique de la France* Cases 24 and 34/58 [1960] ECR 609; *Hamborner Bergbau* Case 41 and 50/59 [1960] ECR 1016. The time limit is strictly enforced by the ECJ: *San Michele* Cases 5–11 and 13–15/62 [1962] ECR 449; *Pesqueras Echebastar* Case C–25/91 [1993] ECR I–1719. If after the commencement of an action under art 232 EC, but before the judgment of the Community courts, the institution in question defines its position, the application is considered as admissible but 'without object'.[30] This solution seems unfair to the applicant, especially if he envisages bringing an action under art 288(2) EC against the institution concerned. The ECJ justified its position by stating that the decision in such circumstances would have no effect in respect to the defaulting institution.

The consequence of a successful action under art 232 EC is that the ECJ declares the failure to act of the institution concerned, which under art 233 EC 'shall ... take the necessary measures to comply with the judgment of the Court of Justice' within a reasonable period of time: *European Parliament v Council* Case 13/83 [1985] ECR 1513.

8.4 Action for damages: non-contractual liability of the Community

Exclusive jurisdiction of Community courts regarding non-contractual liability of the Community is based on art 235 EC which provides:

'The Court of Justice shall have jurisdiction in disputes relating to the compensation for damage provided for in the second paragraph of art 288.'

The CFI has jurisdiction in actions for damages brought by individuals, while the ECJ exercises its jurisdiction in actions commenced by the Member States.

Article 288(2) states:

'In the case of non-contractual liability, the Community shall, in accordance with the general principles common to the laws of the Member States, make good any damage caused by its Institutions or by its servants in the performance of their duties.'

Non-contractual liability of the Community is a corollary to the transfer of certain powers to the Community institutions by Member States which requires that individuals are protected against unlawful conduct of the Community.

Autonomous nature of an action under art 288(2) EC

In the majority of cases an action for damages is based on illegality of Community acts. For that reason, an action under art 288(2) EC may 'reopen' the time limit imposed by arts 230 and 232 EC, and especially allows natural and legal persons to challenge Community acts without needing to satisfy the very strict requirements of arts 230 and 232 EC. In Case 25/62 *Plaumann* [1963] ECR 95 the ECJ seemed to adopt a restrictive approach by refusing to award damages for the reason that the action in damages intended in reality to nullify the decision against which the applicant had also brought an action for annulment but failed. However, in subsequent cases the ECJ has clearly established that an action for damages under art 288(2) EC is independent (*Krohn* Case 175/84 [1986] ECR 753). In *Zuckerfabrik Schöppenstedt* Case 5/71 [1971] ECR 975[31] the ECJ held that an action in damages under

---

[30] In *European Parliament v Council* Case 302/87 [1988] ECR 5615, the Council submitted a draft of the Community budget after the EP submitted its application under art 232 EC.

[31] See also Conclusions of Advocate-General Roemer who analyses the case law of the Community courts in relation to art 288(2) EC: pp992–93.

arts 235 and 288(2) EC is autonomous as it has a special role to play within the system of remedies. The difference between an action for annulment and an action for damages is that the latter is intended not to nullify a particular measure but to make good damage caused by the EC institution in the exercise of its functions. The autonomous nature of an action under art 288(2) EC is subject to one exception. If an action for damages would have the same effects as an action for annulment but the applicant did not institute the latter within the prescribed time limit, the former will be inadmissible. As the ECJ emphasised in *Krohn* Case 175/84 [1986] ECR 753 this happens only in exceptional situations when the action in damages would result in the payment of an amount corresponding to the sum already paid by the applicant in the performance of an individual decision. Therefore, if an application under art 288(2) EC is intended in reality to nullify an individual decision which has become definitive (that is, immune from annulment due to the expiry of the time limit provided for in art 230(5) EC) or is otherwise designed to provide a means of escaping the restrictions imposed by art 230 EC, it will be rejected: *Krohn* Case 175/84 [1986] ECR 753; *Cobrecaf* Case T–514/93 [1995] ECR II–621. The CFI in *Louis Dreyfus* Case T–485/93 [1996] ECR II–1101 and *Richco Commodities* Case T–491/93 [1996] ECR II–1131 confirmed the exception and emphasised that the burden of proof is placed upon the party who alleged that the claim was in essence for the annulment.

In addition, a decision under art 288(2) EC produces binding legal effects solely vis-à-vis the applicant, as opposed to a decision under art 230 EC which is valid *erga omnes*.[32]

An action for damages is also independent from an action for failure to act under art 232 EC: *Lütticke* Case 4/69 [1971] ECR 325; *Holtz and Willemsen* Case 134/73 [1974] ECR 1.

Parties to proceedings under art 288(2) EC

Any natural or legal person, as well as a Member State, may bring an action under art 288(2)EC provided they have suffered loss resulting from unlawful conduct of the Community or its servants in the performance of their duties.

An action may be brought against the Community institution or institutions responsible for causing damage: *Werhahn* Cases 63–69/72 [1973] ECR 1229. In practice, the defendant is either the Commission or the Council or when an act was adopted by the Council acting on a proposal submitted by the Commission then both. An action may also be brought against the European Investment Bank (*SGEEM* Case 370/89 [1992] ECR I–6211) and the European Central Bank (as provided by art 288(3) EC). Subject to the exception mentioned next, the European Parliament, the ECJ and the CFI can only become defendants in actions brought by their staff.[33] The exception is that if the EP and the Council adopt jointly an act within the co-decision procedure set out in art 251 EC the EP may become a defendant. However, the EP cannot be liable for the conduct of its political groups.[34]

---

[32] See also *Unifruit Hellas EPE* Case T–489/93 [1994] ECR II–1201.

[33] Whilst in theory, such is possible, in practice the ECJ cannot be a judge and a party in the same proceedings.

[34] See *Le Pen* Case C–210/89 [1990] ECR I–1183. This was an action for a defamatory statement contained in a brochure.

Time limit

The admissibility of an action for damages is subject to a time limit. Under art 43 of the Statute of the ECJ an applicant may bring such an action within five years from the event giving rise to the claim. However, the ECJ has interpreted this provision broadly. The *dies a quo* is considered to be the time when the damage has materialised, not the time of the occurrence of the event or fact giving rise to damage.[35]

Distinction between liability of the Community and liability of its servants

The Community must make good any damage caused by its institutions and by its servants in the performance of their duties. Vicarious liability principles apply and the Community is liable if a servant acted in the course of his duty. In *Sayag* Case 9/69 [1969] ECR 336 the ECJ held that the Community is liable solely for those acts of its servants which by virtue of internal and direct relationship, constituted the necessary extension of the tasks conferred on the Community institutions. This very restrictive approach requires that if the conduct of a servant which gave rise to damage was performed outside the course of his duties, that is on a 'frolic of his own', the action should be brought against him before a national court which has jurisdiction *ratione loci* and the conditions for liability will be determined under the administrative law of the forum. Conversely, if a wrongful act or omission was committed by a particular employee acting in the course of his duties, the victim should commence proceedings before the Community courts, that is the CFI, and the conditions for liability will be determined according to Community law. By virtue of art 22(1) of the Statute of the ECJ if there is joint liability then the Community, after compensating the victim, may bring an action against a servant in order to recover all or part of damages paid to the victim.

Distinction between liability of the Community and liability of the Member States

Very often the Community institutions confer upon national authorities the task of applying or implementing Community measures. When the conduct of the national authority causes damage to individuals the question arises: who is liable, the Member State or the Community? The best solution for the applicant would be to permit him to claim compensation for his loss at his option: before national courts or before the ECJ. Unfortunately, this option is rejected by Community law for many reasons, the most important being that neither has a Community judge jurisdiction to decide cases against the Member States in tort nor have national judges jurisdiction to decide such cases against the Community institutions. Second, the division of competences between the Community and the Member States in general, and in relation to a disputed matter in particular, prohibits encroachment on each other's sphere of competence. For that reason, three situations can be distinguished.

---

[35] See *Birra Wuhrer* Case 256/80 [1982] ECR 85. However, the *dies a quo* is postponed if the damage come to the knowledge of the applicant after the expiry of the five-year time limit: *Adams* Case 145/83 [1985] ECR 3539. Also this period will be suspended by any other proceedings before the Community courts.

Liability of national authorities for wrongful or negligent implementation or application of lawful Community acts

In this case, an action for damages should be brought against national authorities before national courts according to national procedure, and the conditions for liability should be determined by national administrative law. In *Granaria* Case 101/78 [1979] ECR 623 the ECJ held that the question of compensation for loss incurred by individuals caused by a national body or agents of the Member States, resulting from either their infringement of Community law or an act or omission contrary to national law while applying Community law, is not covered by art 288(2) and has to be assessed by national courts according to the national law of the Member State concerned.

Liability of national authorities in the case of application or implementation of unlawful Community acts

When national authorities have correctly applied or implemented an unlawful Community measure, there is no fault on the part of a Member State concerned. As a result, the Community is liable. National courts have exclusive jurisdiction if the action is for payment of money. The question of validity of a Community act is subject to proceedings under art 234 EC since only the ECJ has jurisdiction to declare a Community act void. Once a measure is declared void by the ECJ a national court may award compensation for the total damages suffered by the applicant: *Haegeman* Case 96/71 [1972] ECR 1005; *Vreugdenhil* Case C–282/90 [1992] ECR I–1962. Exclusive jurisdiction of national courts in actions for payments entails that such actions will be declared inadmissible in the Community courts unless the applicant has exhausted all avenues to obtain a remedy in his national courts and still has not obtained compensation. There are exceptions to exclusive jurisdiction of national courts: first, the applicant may bring an action directly before the Community courts if it is impossible for national courts to order payments in the absence of Community provisions authorising national authorities to pay the claimed amount;[36] and, second, if an action before national courts will for procedural or other reason not result in the payment of the alleged damages: *Unifrex* Case 281/82 [1984] ECR 1969; *De Boer Buizen* Case 81/86 [1987] ECR 3677; *Nölle* Case T–167/94 [1995] ECR II–2589.

In all actions which do not involve payments of money the Community courts have jurisdiction: *Dietz* Case 126/76 [1977] ECR 2431; *Vreugdenhil* Case C–282/90 [1992] ECR I–1962; *Mulder* Cases C–104/89 and 37/90 [1992] ECR I–3061.

Joint liability of the Community and a Member State

In *Kampffmeyer* Cases 5, 7 and 13–24/66 [1967] ECR 317 the ECJ held that if there is a joint liability of the EC and a Member State for an unlawful act the applicant must first bring an action before national courts. As a result, a national court must refer the case under art 234 to the ECJ which will decide whether or not the act in question is lawful. If not, then the measure will be annulled by the ECJ. At that time, the national court will assess solely the liability of the Member State and consequently award damages corresponding to the damage caused by national authorities. The next step for the applicant is to bring an action before the CFI to determine liability of the Community and award appropriate damages.

---

[36] For example, *Dumortier Frères* Case 64/76 [1979] ECR 3091; *Schöppenstedt* Case 5/71 [1971] ECR 975.

It is submitted that the solution adopted in relation to the division of responsibility between the Community and the Member State is too complex, time-consuming and confusing. In some cases where neither national courts nor Community Courts have jurisdiction to decide a particular case a denial of justice may result.[37]

Conditions for Community liability under art 288(2) EC

Article 288(2) EC contains general guidance concerning non-contractual liability of the Community and leaves the ECJ to determine specific rules in this area. Indeed, art 288(2)EC is unique as it requires the ECJ to establish the conditions of liability based on 'general principles of the laws of the Member States'. This means that general principles of laws of Member States regarding liability of public authorities are relevant. Furthermore, it is not necessary that a particular rule is recognised in all Member States since this would lead to a lowest common denominator and thus ensure the minimum protection for victims of wrongful conduct of the Community. The ECJ's approach is selective and based on a comparative study of national legal systems in the context of the specific requirements of Community law. This approach leaves the ECJ a considerable margin of appreciation in the selection of general principles appropriate to the particular needs of the Community. This is necessary taking into account the complexity of actions for damages based on art 288(2) EC. On the one hand, the ECJ exercises its jurisdiction in relation to non-contractual liability in the context of disputes involving economic policies of the Community and thus must take into account its legal implications when awarding damages to the applicant or determining unlawful conduct on the part of the Community institutions. On the other hand, the ECJ must often resolve the delicate question of delimitation of competences between the Community and the Member States.

In *Lütticke* v *Commission* Case 4/69 [1971] ECR 325 the ECJ held that general principles common to certain Member States concerning the conditions of liability are:

1. unlawful conduct on the part of the Community;
2. damage to the applicant; and
3. a causal link between the conduct of the Community institution and the alleged damage.

In relation to liability for legislative acts the ECJ has developed original solutions appropriate to deal with its peculiar nature. At first glance the above three conditions are very generous to the applicants but in practice successful actions under art 288(2) EC are rare.

Unlawful conduct on the part of the Community

The determination of unlawful conduct on the part of the Community and its servants is based on the concept of fault which is explicitly mentioned in arts 34 and 40 CS. The fault of the system or the *'faute de service'* refers to the Community institutions and, in the case of their servants, liability is based on *'faute personnelle'* which is a personal wrongful act or omission of the servant of the Community acting in the course of his duty. Article 40 CS

---

[37] The best illustration is provided by *Cato* Case C–55/90 [1992] ECR I–2533.

refers to the fault of the system and the case law of the ECJ has gradually determined the meaning of this expression. First, liability can only be based on fault. As a result liability without a fault, that is, based on risks or stemming from a duty of guarantee was rejected: *FERAM* Case 23/59 [1959] ECR 501; *Hauts Fourneaux de Chasse* Case 33/59 [1962] ECR 719. Second, art 40 CS has been interpreted restrictively. As a result, the concept of fault was rejected in the conduct of economic policies (Case 33/59, conclusions of M Lagrange). Third, the ECJ has refused to determine different degrees of the gravity of fault and has instead used such formulae as 'inexplicable bad management' or 'inexcusable mistakes' (*Meroni* Case 14/60 [1961] ECR 319) or 'manifest lack of diligence' (*Usines de la Providence* Case 29/63 [1965] ECR 1123) which amount to serious fault. Article 288(2)EC does not mention fault but makes reference to the general principles of the national laws of the Member States. However, the ECJ has interpreted art 288(2) EC in the light of its previous case law regarding the CS Treaty. While this approach ensured homogeneity of the Community legal system, and coherence of its solutions, it lacked originality and required some adjustments – these have been made, for example, in establishing the liability of the EC Community for legislative acts. The concept of the fault of the system was recognised under the EC Treaty (*Kampffmeyer* Case 5/66 [1967] ECR 317) although the ECJ has since preferred to use different formulas such as 'illegality of the conduct of the institutions' (*Lütticke* Case 4/69 [1971] ECR 325) and 'manifest and grave disregard of the limits on the exercise of [the institution's] power': *Bayerische HNL* v *Council and Commission* Case 83/76 [1978] ECR 1209. Under the cover of the above formulae, the ECJ has sought to interpret the meaning of wrongful conduct by a Community institution.

Lasok explained that the fault of the system 'occurs where damage results from the malfunctioning of Community institutions or Community servants'.[38] The Community exercises both administrative and legislative function, and its system may occasionally fall below the standard of sound and efficient administration.

The fault of the system comprises all defects in the organisation and the functioning of the service, such as defaulting organisations of the service (*FERAM* Case 23/59 [1959] ECR 501), negligence in the management (*Meroni* Cases 14, 16, 17, 20, 24, 26 and 27/60 [1961] ECR 319), inappropriate supervision (*Fives Lille Cail* Cases 2 and 3 /61 [1961] ECR 501), breach of the principle of confidentiality of information obtained by the Commission (*Adams* Case 145/83 [1985] ECR 3539), forwarding of erroneous information by the Community institutions (*Richez-Parise* Cases 19, 20, 25 and 30/69 [1970] ECR 325; *Compagnie Continentale France* Case 169/73 [1975] ECR 117), and breach of the provisions relating to hygiene and security at work: *Grifoni* Case 308/87 [1990] ECR I–1203. Unlike French law where there is a difference between simple and serious fault, the case law of the ECJ makes no distinction in the degree of fault. The Community will be liable in damages in cases of inexcusable errors or manifest and grave lack of diligence. This matter was examined by the CFI in *Embassy Limousines & Services* v *European Parliament* Case T–203/96 [1998] ECR II–4239.

In this case, the EP published a tender notice in the Official Journal of the European Communities in respect of a contract for the transport of members of the EP using

---

[38] D Lasok, Lasok & Bridge, *Law and Institutions of the European Union,* 6th ed, London: Butterworths, 1994, p273.

chauffeur-driven vehicles. The applicant, Embassy Limousines & Services SA, submitted its tender and on 4 December 1995 received a favourable opinion of the Advisory Committee on Procurements and Contracts (ACPC) of the EP. On 12 December 1995 the applicant informed the EP of measures it had taken to respond to the urgency of the situation in which the EP found itself, consisting of entering into contracts for leasing cars and renting mobile telephones, engaging drivers and attending to their social security, health insurance and tax situation. However, the opinion of the ACPC was not confirmed by the EP, which decided to renew a contract with a company that had previously provided these services, annulled the invitation to tender and reopened a new invitation to tender. The applicant requested the EP not to annul the contested invitation to tender and to award it the contract or to pay it satisfactory compensation. The EP rejected the requests.

The CFI held that the EP was liable for damages suffered by the applicant. In respect of non-contractual liability when the applicant claims failure of administration he has to prove the wrongful conduct of the institution, the existence of damage and a causative link between the two. Therefore, his task is less onerous than in cases where the applicant is seeking to establish liability of the Community for wrongful acts having legal effect. In respect of the first element, that is the wrongful conduct of the EP, the CFI assessed whether the conduct of the EP was wrongful in two sets of circumstances: the annulling of the contested invitation to tender and during the contested tendering procedure itself. In the first-mentioned situation the CFI held that, on the one hand, the EP had no obligation to award the contract and, on the other hand, it could not be liable for any compensation with respect to tenderers whose tenders have been rejected. Furthermore, there had been no serious and manifest error on the part of the EP, taking into account that it enjoyed a broad discretion in deciding whether or not a contract should be awarded to a particular tenderer. The CFI found that the EP did not exceed the proper bounds of its discretion when annulling the contested invitation to tender. However, in the second situation, that is in respect of its conduct during the contested tendering procedure, the EP was in breach of the principle of the protection of legitimate expectations since it let the applicant believe that the contract would be awarded to it. The CFI emphasised that the right to rely on the principle of the protection of legitimate expectations 'extends to any individual who is in a situation in which it is apparent that the Community administration has led him to entertain justified expectations'.[39] In the present case, it was reasonable and realistic for the applicant to make the necessary investments in order to have an infrastructure capable of providing the service required by the EP. Although the applicant was not expressly invited by the EP to do so, the EP induced a legitimate expectation on the part of the applicant to make such investments by encouraging him to take a risk which went beyond that normally run by tenderers in a tendering procedure. Furthermore, the EP was in breach of the principle of transparency: it delayed informing the applicant of the reasons for which it decided not to award the contract to it, and it failed to inform the applicant that it had awarded a contract, on a provisional basis, to a different undertaking.

[39] See *Van den Bergh Lopik* v *Commission* Case 265/85 [1987] ECR 1155.

Liability for legislative acts

In determining liability in tort the ECJ has taken into account the fact that as time passes the activities of the Community institutions gradually involve less classic administration and more and more economic administration with its associated financial decisions involving the exercise of a wide discretion by the Community institutions as they have to make choices of economic policies. Such factors as the complexity inherent in economic choices, difficulties in the application and interpretation of legislative measures in this area, and the wide margin of discretion exercised by the EC institutions have led the ECJ to accept the liability of EC institutions only in exceptional cases. In *Bayerische HNL* Case 83/76 [1978] ECR 1209 the ECJ emphasised that 'exercise of the legislative function must not be hindered by the prospect of action for damages whenever the general interest of the Community requires legislative measures to be adopted which may adversely affect individual interests', and that 'in a legislative context ... the Community cannot incur liability unless the institution concerned has manifestly and gravely disregarded the limits on the exercise of its powers.'

The case law of the ECJ has dissociated the concepts of illegality and fault one from the other. In *CNTA* Case 74/74 [1975] ECR 533 the ECJ held that violation of the principle of legitimate expectation caused damage to the applicants since the adoption of an act which withdrew compensatory payments was valid but nevertheless entered into force immediately without transitional measures. As a result, the Community was liable for a lawful act which had been adopted in such circumstances as to cause damage to the applicant. Conversely, an illegal act may not give rise to liability. This was expressed in *Zuckerfabrik Schöppenstedt v Council* Case 5/71 [1971] ECR 975 in the following terms:

> 'When legislative action involving measures of economic policy is concerned, the Community does not incur non-contractual liability for damage suffered by individuals as a consequence of that action, by virtue of the provisions contained in art [288], second paragraph, of the Treaty, unless a sufficiently flagrant violation of a superior rule of law for the protection of the individual has occurred.'

This formula is based on the German concept of Schutznortheorie. It is referred to under EC law as the 'Schöppenstedt formula'. It requires proof of the three conditions relating to non-contractual liability in general, that is: unlawful conduct on the part of the Community, damage to the applicant and a causal link between the conduct of the Community institution and the alleged damage. In addition, in respect of legislative acts adopted by the Community, another three conditions must also be satisfied, that is: there must be a breach of a superior rule of law, the breach must be sufficiently serious and the superior rule must be one for the protection of the individual.

The *Schöppenstedt* formula requires some comments. First, it is important to highlight that in *Compagnie Continentale France* Case 169/73 [1975] ECR 117 the ECJ held that non-contractual liability of the Community institutions is excluded in cases where a provision of the Treaty causes damages to the applicant.[40] Thus, the Community institutions are liable in damages resulting from the adoption of a legislative measure. Second, this formula

---

[40] See *Dubois et Fils* Case T–113/96 [1998] ECR II–125, confirmed by the ECJ in *Dubois et Fils* Case C–95/98P [1999] ECR I–4385.

enhances the fact that EC institutions are particularly protected against actions in damages under art 288(2) EC for the very simple reason that all legislative acts imply that their authors enjoy a large margin of discretion. Indeed, it is not important whether a legislative act concerns economic policies *sensu stricto*, or other areas such as transport, social policy etc, what is important is that an institution has a wide discretion and must exercise it in the interests of the Community. It must make choices in conducting the Community policies in the areas of competences of the Community in order to attain the objectives which are essential for integration of national policies and especially to harmonise national laws in specific areas (*Les Assurances du Credit* Case C–63/89 [1991] ECR I–1799), regardless of the fact that those legislative measures may adversely affect individual interests. The threat of numerous applications for damages must not hinder the Community in its policy-making. For that reason the requirements contained in the Schöppenstedt formula are very restrictive and rigorous. The applicant has to demonstrate the following three facets:

Breach of a superior rule of law

This requirement has as its objective the exclusion of claims founded upon minor illegality. The rule in question must occupy a fundamental place in the Community legal order. It comprises, *inter alia*, provisions of the Treaty and general principles of Community law. In *CNTA v Commission* Case 74/74 [1975] ECR 533[41] a regulation which entered into force immediately after its publication, and which did not provide for a transitional period and abolished compensation for the effect of exchange rate fluctuations in trade in colza and rape seeds, was held legal but contrary to the principle of legitimate expectation in relation to undertakings which had already obtained export licences fixing the amount of compensation in advance and concluded contracts prior to the abolition of the compensation scheme. In the *Second Skimmed Milk Powder* case (*Bayerische HNL* Cases 83 and 94/76 and 4, 15 and 40/77 [1978] ECR 1209) the ECJ held that the regulation concerning the compulsory purchase of Community stocks of skimmed milk powder was contrary to the principle of non-discrimination.[42] In *Bela-Mühler* Case 114/76 [1977] ECR 1211, which concerned the same regulation, the ECJ held that it was also disproportionate to the objective to be achieved. Among others principles recognised by the ECJ are: the principle of the protection of acquired rights (*Union Nationale des Co-operative Agricoles de Céréales* Cases 95–98/74 and 15 and 100/75 [1975] ECR 1615), the principle of proportionality (*Werhahn* Cases 63–69/72 [1973] ECR 1229) and the principle of non-retroactivity: *Nederlandse Vereniging voor de Fruit en Groenten-Importhandel* Case 71/74 [1975] ECR 1063.

The superior rule must be one for the protection of the individual

Not only must the rule have the protection of rights of individuals as an object, but it must have the *effect* of providing such protection. This excludes reliance by the applicant upon such rules as those regarding the decision-making procedure, for example, non-consultation

---

[41] See also *Merkur* Case 97/76 [1977] ECR 1063; *Mulder* Case C–104/89 [1992] ECR I–3061.

[42] There are many cases concerning the principle of non-discrimination and equality: *Ireks-Arkady* Case 238/78 [1979] ECR 2955; *Amylum* Cases 116 and 124/77 [1979] ECR 3497; *Dumortier Frères* Cases 64 and 113/76, 167 and 239/78, 27, 28 and 45/79 [1979] ECR 3091.

of the EP in the adoption of a measure which was required by that procedure or absence of a proposal from the Commission or non-respect of the division of competences between the Community institutions: *Vreugdenhil* Case C–282/90 [1992] ECR I–1962. However, it is not necessary that the relevant rule has exclusively as its object the protection of individuals. It is sufficient that it also has an effect on the protection of individuals, in general. In *Kampffmeyer* Case 5, 7 and 13–24/66 [1967] ECR 317, in which the facts were similar to the case of Alfred Toepfel, the ECJ held that the failure of the Commission to investigate fully the protective measures concerning the imposition of the levy on maize had infringed a rule of law which was of a general nature as it referred to the free trade in maize, and the support of this market was, nevertheless, for the protection of individuals.

Breach must be sufficiently serious

The ECJ has interpreted this requirement in a very restrictive way. A bad or wrong manner of exercising a discretion by an EC institution will only give a right to reparation if the institution 'manifestly and gravely disregarded the limits on the exercise of it powers': *Bayerische HNL* Cases 83 and 94/76 and 4, 15 and 40/77 [1978] ECR 1209. In the particular case of *Bayerische HNL* the ECJ explained that manifest and grave disregard has to have an obvious (manifest) and serious (grave) effect on the applicant undertaking. It held that this was not fulfilled since the measure affected a wide range of undertakings, had a small effect on the price of feed as compared to other factors and thus was within the inherent economic risks of that particular trade. As a result, the Community did not manifestly and gravely disregard the limits of its powers. This restrictive interpretation reached its highest point in *G R Amylum NV and Tunnel Refineries Limited v Council and Commission* Cases 116 and 124/77 [1979] ECR 3497 and *Koninklijke Scholten Honig NV v Council and Commission* Case 43/77 [1979] ECR 3583, the so-called *Isoglucose* cases, in which a regulation imposing levies on the production of isoglose was successfully challenged under art 230 EC (*RSH and Tunnel Refineries* Cases 103 and 145/77 [1978] ECR 2037) prior to the application for damages. The regulation had such an effect on the remaining three or four isoglucose undertakings in the Community that, for example, Koninklijke had to close its business. The ECJ held that only if the conduct of an EC institution was 'verging on the arbitrary', which was not the case here, would it be considered as a sufficiently serious breach. The ECJ refused to award damages. The interests of the Community prevailed, it was entitled to limit the production of isoglucose and stabilise the market, although some mistakes were made which resulted in the annulment of the regulation. This much criticised approach led to the rejection of most applications under art 288(2) EC but it seems that the ECJ has softened its approach subsequent to its decision in the *Isoglucose* cases. In *Stahlwerke Peine-Salzgitter* Case C–220/91P [1993] ECR I–2393, which concerned liability of the CS, the ECJ held that conduct 'verging on the arbitrary' is not a necessary requirement. Also, in *Mulder* Cases C–104/89 and 37/90 [1992] ECR I–3126 the Court held that in the absence of 'the peremptory public interest' the Community cannot justify a measure which is gravely illegal and thus the Community would incur liability in such circumstances.

In this case Mulder and other farmers submitted an application under art 288(2) claiming that they suffered loss as a result of various Community regulations dealing with over-production of dairy products. Under the regulations they were paid a premium for five years for not selling milk and milk products. At the end of this five-year period they applied for 'special reference quantities' which would have allowed them to come back on the market. They failed but successfully challenged this regulation under art 230 EC: *Mulder* Cases 120/86 [1988] ECR 2321 and *Von Deetzen* Case 170/86 [1988] ECR 2355. Later they were allocated quantities equivalent to 60 per cent of their marketing capacities prior to the five-year period. This regulation was also successfully challenged in *Spagl* Case C–189/89 [1990] ECR I–4539 and *Pastätter* Case C–217/89 [1990] ECR I–4584).This 40 per cent reduction for dairy farmers not participating in the five-year scheme was more than double the highest reduction.

The ECJ confirmed the Schöppenstedt formula and returned to its old statement that in relation to legislative acts involving choices in economic policy the Community institutions enjoyed a wide discretion and thus they were liable only if they had manifestly and gravely disregarded the limits of the exercise of their powers. Also, as previously stated, the ECJ held that in order to incur non-contractual liability the damage must go beyond the bounds of normal economic risks inherent in the activities relevant to a particular sector. As result, the ECJ decided that the Community incurred liability in relation to the regulation allocating 'special reference quantites', but not the one which imposed the 60 per cent rule. However, in the case of the regulation concerning the allocation of 'special reference quantities', although the ECJ held that the group of people affected was clearly defined, it comprised more than 12,000 farmers who were entitled to claim approximately of EUR 250 million.

Nevertheless, the change of approach of the Community courts in application of the Schöppenstedt formula has not eliminated the requirement that only grave illegality in the absence of the peremptory public interest of the Community would permit the applicants to successfully claim damages under art 215(2) EC: *Odigitria* Case T–572/93 [1995] ECR II–2025; [1995] Europe (August/September), no 290, comm D Simon and F Gazin.

Damage

The damage suffered must be real and certain regardless of whether it is present or future: *Hauts Fourneaux de Chasse* Case 33/59 [1962] ECR 748. It must not be purely hypothetical (*Chatillon Commentry Neuves Maisins* Case 54/65 [1966] ECR 265; *Hainaut-Sambre* Case 4/65 [1965] ECR 1363) or speculative: *Compagnie Industrielle et Agricole* Cases 54–60/76 [1977] ECR 645; *CNTA* Case 74/74 [1975] ECR 533. The compensation may be obtained for all damage suffered which comprises *damnum emergens* (the actual loss) and *lucrum cessans* (the income which would have been earned). Advocate-General Capatori said in *Ireks-Arkady* Case 238/78 [1979] ECR 2955 that damage 'covers both a material loss ... a reduction in a person's assets and also the loss of an increase in those assets which would have occurred if the harmful act had not taken place'.

As to the actual amount of damages, it is generally negotiated between the parties. In the case of a large number of applicants, the Commission and the Council submit a collective offer of indemnification as happened in *Mulder* but if rejected by the applicants the ECJ determines the amount of damages.[43]

---

[43] The Council and the Commission adopted a regulation regarding the modality of indemnification (OJ C/198 (1992)) which was rejected by the applicants. At the end the ECJ determined the amount of compensation: Cases C–104/89 and 37/90 *Mulder and Others*.

In respect of damages a distinction must be made between damage caused by legislative acts and all other situations. In the latter a number of conditions must be met: there must be unlawful conduct of the Community institution, there must be real and certain damage and there must be a direct causal link between the unlawful conduct of the institution concerned and the alleged damage: *Oleifici Italiani and Fratelli Rubino v Commission* Case T–54/96 [1998] ECR II–3377. In *Embassy Limousines & Services v European Parliament* Case T–203/96 (see above) the applicant could not claim any compensation in respect of its participation in a tendering procedure as its expenses would have been incurred by any tenderer whose tender was not accepted. As a result the compensable damage included 'expenses and charges incurred by reason of [the applicant's] certainty of winning the contract', 'expenses of recruitment, medical examinations, training and familiarisation expenses for the drivers' and 'preparation, negotiation for fleet of vehicles, telephone contract, parking'. Also, the CFI compensated the applicant for moral damage it had suffered caused by the uncertainty in which it had found itself, as well as for its efforts made in order to respond to the urgency of the situation in which the EP found itself.

This approach was also applied in *New Europe Consulting Ltd and Michael P Brown v Commission of the European Communities* Case T–231/97 [1999] 2 CMLR 1452.

Since 1991 New Europe Consulting Ltd (NEC) had been involved in carrying out a number of management advice projects within the PHARE programme. During one of these projects in Hungary, NEC encountered several problems concerning the general financial implementation of that programme. The government of Hungary sent a report to the Commission in this respect. The Commission official in charge of that programme sent a fax to the programme co-ordinators in Poland, Hungary, the Czech Republic and Romania informing them that NEC did not satisfy its financial commitments in Hungary, and therefore should not be considered as a reliable partner, and asking them to pass his message on to any person concerned. Also, he strongly recommended not to consider any proposal from NEC in order to avoid problems which might damage the PHARE programme. As a result, NEC was never again chosen for any projects within the framework of PHARE. Almost a year later, Mr Brown, a manager of NEC who in the meantime had learnt of the fax, met with officials from the Commission. As a result, a second fax was sent to all the European Union delegations 'rectifying' the previous fax and recommending that any exclusion from shortlists be removed. However, NEC was still convinced that it had been unjustly excluded from projects carried out within the framework of PHARE. NEC contacted the Commission again. The Commission sent a fax ensuring NEC that it was not on a black list.

However, NEC were still dissatisfied and brought an action against the Commission under art 288(2) EC. The Court of First Instance ordered the Commission to pay damages in the amount of EUR 100,000 to NEC and damages in the amount of EUR 25,000 to its manager, Michael P Brown.

The CFI rejected the argument that the Commission was guilty of a manifest lack of care in respect of the rectification of its mistake. The CFI held that although the rectification was made one year after the original fax was sent it was done as soon as the Commission realised the mistake had occurred. The CFI also stated that the principle of the protection of legitimate expectations was not breached, taking into account that the desired 'effect' of the rectification could not be the securing of a contract within the PHARE programme since contracts are not awarded automatically but are made after a comparative assessment of tenders by the recipient State.

The most interesting aspect of the present case is the assessment of the damages suffered by NEC and its manager Michael Brown. The CFI rejected the claim regarding the damage resulting from the loss of profit on the ground that it was neither real nor certain. The CFI emphasised that the public tendering system set up under the PHARE system, under which the contracting authority has a large margin of discretion in deciding to award a contract, means that the tenderer cannot be certain of securing the contract even if he is proposed by the evaluation committee: *TEAM* v *Commission* Case T–13/96 [1997] FCR II–983. Therefore, the fact that the tenderer submitted his tender did not presuppose that he would be awarded the PHARE project contract. However, the CFI agreed that the conduct of the Commission seriously harmed NEC's image as well as the reputation of its manager, who tried many times to salvage the company's reputation in the eyes of the PHARE programme co-ordinators and of the Commission. He was kept in a state of uncertainty by the Commission and forced to make fruitless efforts to change the situation created by the Commission itself. Furthermore, there was no doubt that there was a causal link between the conduct of the Commission and the damage suffered by NEC and its manager. As a result, the applicants were awarded damages.

In relation to damages caused by legislative acts the requirements are more stringent, that is, in addition to conditions relating to damage which apply to all cases under art 288(2) EC in this area, the damage must be abnormal and special: *Bayerische HNL* Cases 83 and 94/76 and 4, 15 and 40/77 [1978] ECR 1209. The first requirement that damage must be special means that the measure must affect a limited and clearly defined group, which was not the case in *Bayerische* since the measure applied to a large number of people, producers of cattle, poultry and pork. In *Ireks-Akady* Case 238/78 [1979] ECR 2955 the measure concerned a limited and clearly defined group, the producers of quellmehl. Also, in this case the ECJ held that the second requirement relating to abnormal or grave damage was satisfied since 'the damage alleged by the applicants goes beyond the bounds of the economic risks inherent in the activities in the sector concerned', unlike the situation in *Bayerische* where an increase of 2 per cent in the price of animal feedstuffs was deemed within the inherent economic risks of that sector of business.

The requirement that damage must be special and abnormal contributed to the limitation of successful applications under art 288(2) EC. So far, the ECJ has awarded damages for the effects of regulations in two series of cases: *Ireks-Arkady* and three other decisions rendered the same day, and *Mulder* in which the economic operators were considered as a clearly defined group of economic agents (producers who had marketed no milk in the reference year upon which 'reference quantities' were based), although it comprised a large number of people.

There is also a duty to mitigate loss. In *Mulder* the ECJ reduced the damages awarded by the amount of profit which the producers could have reasonably earned from alternative activities, although the ECJ made no suggestion as to alternative activities. However, the term 'reasonable' implies that fundamentally different activities from their previous business were not considered as alternatives.

The Community law also recognises contributory negligence. If the applicant has contributed through his own negligence to the resulting damage, the amount of damages will be reduced proportionately to the loss he has brought upon himself. In *Adams* Case 145/83 [1985] ECR 3539 the ECJ held that Adams contributed through his negligence to the resulting damage and reduced by half the awarded amount.

Adams was employed by the Swiss-based multinational Hoffman-La Roche. He forwarded confidential information to the Commission concerning breaches of art 86 by his employer, for which the latter was heavily fined. During the proceedings Hoffman-La Roche asked the Commission to disclose the name of the informant. The Commission refused but forwarded to Hoffman-La Roche certain documents which enabled them to identify Adams as the source of leaked information which was contrary to the duty of confidentiality contained in art 214 EC. In the meantime Adams moved to Italy where he set up his own business. Hoffman-La Roche, due to its international connections, destroyed the business established by Adams in Italy. The Commission failed to inform Adams that his former employer was planning to persecute him. On his return to Switzerland Adams was arrested by the Swiss police for economic espionage and held in solitary confinement. His wife committed suicide. Adams brought proceedings before the ECJ against the Commission for loss of earnings and loss of reputation as a result of his conviction and imprisonment.

The ECJ held that the Commission was liable for the breach of duty of confidentiality as it allowed Adams to be identified as an informer, and awarded Adams £200,000 in damages for his mental anguish and lost earnings and £176,000 for costs, half the amount he had demanded. The reason for the reduction was Adams' contributory negligence. The ECJ held that Adams contributed to the resulting damage by failing to warn the Commission that he could be identified from the confidential documents, and by failing to inquire about progress of proceedings, especially before returning to Switzerland.

Causation

A direct causal link must be established between the damage suffered and the unlawful conduct: *Worms* Case 18/60 [1962] ECR 401. The burden of proof is on the applicant: *Produits Bertrand* Case 40/75 [1976] ECR 1. In *Dumortier Frères* Cases 64/76 and 113/76, 167 and 239/78 and 27, 28 and 45/79 [1979] ECR 3091 the ECJ held that there is no obligation to compensate all prejudicial consequences, however remote, resulting from the unlawful legislative act. In this case a regulation which abolished production refunds for maize grits but not for maize starch, both used in brewing and baking and thus in direct competition, was successfully challenged by the producers of maize grits. The ECJ held that the regulation was contrary to the principle of non-discrimination and equality, affected a limited and clearly defined group, that is, the producers of maize grits, and the damage exceeded the bounds of the inherent economic risks in this sector of business. In addition, when adopting the regulation, the Council disregarded the advice of the Commission to re-introduce the refunds. As a result of the successful action under art 230 EC, the producers of maize grits brought an action under art 288(2) EC. They claimed compensation in relation to loss of refunds prior to this date, lost sales and the closure of factories by two producers and bankruptcy of a third one. The ECJ awarded damages only in relation to the loss of refunds. The reduction in sales was not considered as resulting from the abolition of refunds since the producers decided not to increase prices of maize grits and thus pass the loss to their purchasers. The closing of factories and the bankruptcy were not a sufficiently direct result of the withdrawal of refunds. Therefore, too remote a damage will not give rise to the right of reparation. This matter was also examined by the ECJ in *Kampffmeyer* Cases 5, 7 and 13–24/66 [1967] ECR 317 in which the facts were identical to *Toepfer* Cases 106 and 107/63 [1965] ECR 525 already discussed, that is, as a result of a mistake made by German authorities the import levy for maize from France was fixed at zero. When the mistake was discovered, the German authorities refused to grant licences for imports of maize and asked the Commission to raise the levy and confirm the ban which the latter did three days later. The Commission decision was successfully challenged under art 230 EC and the German importers asked for compensation under art 288(2) EC. The ECJ held that only those importers who had concluded contracts to buy French maize before their applications for import licences had been rejected were entitled to claim damages. As a result, those who performed their contracts were awarded damages in respect of the higher levies which they had to pay. The importers who cancelled their contracts were awarded damages in respect of penalties payable for breach of contract. However, they were only entitled to 10 per cent of the profits which might have been made, taking into account that the expected profit was of a purely speculative nature. The importers who did not enter into contracts before applying for import licences had no right to compensation.

9 Preliminary Rulings: art 234 EC

9.1   General jurisdiction of the ECJ under art 234 EC

9.2   Interpretation of Community law by the ECJ under art 234 EC

9.3   Validity of Community law

Article 234 EC provides:

'(1) The Court of Justice shall have jurisdiction to give preliminary rulings concerning:
(a) the interpretation of this Treaty;
(b) the validity and interpretation of acts of the Institutions of the Community and the ECB;
(c) the interpretation of the statutes of bodies established by an act of the Council, where those statutes so provide.
(2) Where such a question is raised before any court or tribunal of a Member State that court or tribunal may, if it considers that a decision on the question is necessary to enable it to give judgment, request the Court of Justice to give a ruling thereon.
(3) Where any such question is raised in a case pending before a court or tribunal of a Member State, against whose decision there is no judicial remedy under national law, the court or tribunal shall bring the matter before the Court of Justice.'

Preliminary rulings are common to all three Communities and respectively defined in arts 41 CS,[1] 150 EA[2] and 234 EC. They constitute the main form of co-operation between national courts and the ECJ. In *Schwarze* Case 16/65 [1965] ECR 1081 the ECJ emphasised this aspect of preliminary rulings by stating that on the basis of the mechanism of co-operation established in art 234 EC, national courts and the ECJ, within their respective competences, are called upon to contribute directly and reciprocally to the rendering of a judgment. Indeed, the ECJ under art 234 EC is not a court of appeal. It assists national courts to reach a correct decision from the point of view of Community law. Article 234 EC allows national courts, when applying Community law, to adjourn the proceedings pending before them and to seek advice from the ECJ on the interpretation or validity of EC law. The contribution of the ECJ to a final judgment is incidental since it only elucidates referred issues, and it is the national court that delivers the judgment. It may be said that there are four stages in the procedure under 234 EC. First, there is a dispute before a national court involving EC law; second, the national court refers the question concerning the interpretation or validity of Community law to the ECJ; third, the ECJ gives its decision on the specific issue which was the subject-matter of the referral; and, fourth, it is the task of a

---

[1] Under art 41 CS the jurisdiction of the ECJ is limited to the validity of Community law but the court, by analogy to art 234 EC, extended its jurisdiction to interpretation of Community law in *Busseni* Case C–221/88 [1990] ECR I–495.
[2] Article 150 EA has never been invoked.

national judge to draw conclusions from the decision of the ECJ in relation to the dispute at hand.

Proceedings under art 234 EC are not adversarial, and the parties to the original proceedings are not involved, although art 20 of the Statute of the ECJ offers them the opportunity to make written and oral observations. Also, the Member States, the Commission and the Council, which must be notified upon receipt of a reference, are invited to make their positions known on a specific issue if they so wish.

The main reason for preliminary rulings lies in the peculiarity of Community law. The principle of supremacy requires that Community law is uniformly applied in all Member States, that is, that EC law has the same meaning and effect throughout the Community. Thus, the main objective of art 234 EC is to ensure that national courts when applying EC law – which they do independently from one another and are always more or less influenced by their own legal system – will reach the same solution on a point concerning EC law. In *Rheinmühlen* Case 166/73 [1974] ECR 33 the ECJ held that:

> 'Article [234] is essential for the preservation of the Community character of the law established by the Treaty and has the object of ensuring that in all circumstances this law is the same in all States of the Community.'

At the same time the mechanism under art 234 EC ensures that national courts are not placed in a position of subordination vis-à-vis the ECJ, since in a certain sense it is a dialogue between a Community judge and a national judge. They must co-operate and not encroach upon one another's jurisdiction, as national law and the Community law are still two separate legal systems.

Article 234 EC greatly contributes to the legal protection of individuals, and it allows them, via national courts, to have access to the ECJ. The stringent requirements concerning *locus standi* for non-privileged applicants under art 230 EC are to a certain extent alleviated by the possibility provided by preliminary rulings. The importance of preliminary rulings to homogeneity and uniformity of Community law is enhanced by the fact that only the ECJ is empowered to give them. The Court of First Instance has no jurisdiction under art 234 EC.

This chapter focuses on the main features of the procedure under art 234 EC.

9.1 General jurisdiction of the ECJ under art 234 EC

The ECJ has jurisdiction both to interpret Community law and to assess the validity of Community acts adopted by its institutions. As a result, the ECJ exercises two different functions under art 234 EC, although both contribute to define the scope of application of Community law. The interpretation of Community law under art 234 EC has become the main activity of the ECJ. In respect of the validity of Community measures, national courts have no jurisdiction to declare a Community act invalid. Only the ECJ can make a declaration of its invalidity; national courts must refer to the ECJ whenever the validity of an act is at issue. There are, however, certain conditions under art 234 EC common to the exercise of both functions which must be satisfied before the ECJ accepts a reference. They concern the provisions of Community law capable of being referred to the ECJ, the status of the body allowed to refer and the territorial jurisdiction of the ECJ under art 234 EC.

Community law capable of being referred to the ECJ

National courts may ask the ECJ to rule on the interpretation of primary sources of Community law: the founding Treaties as amended,[3] protocols and annexes to the Treaties and the acts of accession to the Communities: *Burgoa* Case 812/79 [1980] ECR 2787. Under the Treaty of Amsterdam art 68 EC extends the jurisdiction of the ECJ to give preliminary rulings in respect of Title IV (on Visa, Asylum, Immigration and Other Policies Related to the Free Movement of Persons) and art EU in respect of provisions on police and judicial co-operation in criminal matters. Both articles are subject to important limitations: see Chapter 3.

The validity of primary sources, taking into account their constitutional nature, cannot be determined by the ECJ.

The ECJ has jurisdiction to both interpret and determine the validity of secondary legislation. In *Franz Grad* Case 9/70 [1970] ECR 825 the ECJ held that all acts of the Community institutions, without distinction, are capable of being referred under art 234 EC. This comprises not only acts expressly mentioned in art 249 EC, or in the Treaty, but all other acts adopted outside its framework such as, for example, resolutions of the Council: *Manghera* Case 59/75 [1976] ECR 91. National courts may also refer questions concerning Community law which is not directly effective since the exact meaning of national law which they have to apply, and which implements Community directives or decisions addressed to a Member State, may pose difficult interpretation problems (*Mazzalai* Case 111/75 [1976] ECR 657) or may give rise to doubts as to their validity: *Tedeschi* Case 5/77 [1977] ECR 1555. Furthermore, the ECJ has jurisdiction to interpret non-binding acts such as recommendations (*Giordano Frecassetti* v *Amministrazione delle Finanze dello Stato* Case 113/75 [1976] ECR 983; *Grimaldi* Case C–322/88 [1989] ECR 4407) and opinions. It is obvious that the validity of non-binding acts is decided by national courts.

Under the EC and EA Treaties not only acts emanating from the Council and the Commission but also those emanating from the EP (*Lord Bruce of Donington* v *Aspden* Case 208/80 [1981] ECR 2205) and from the ECJ can be referred for interpretation. This also applies to a decision of the ECJ (*Bosch* Case 135/77 [1978] ECR 855), but art 40 of the Statute of the ECJ precludes the parties to the original proceedings which were subject to a preliminary ruling rendered by the ECJ from requesting an interpretation of that ruling: *Becher* Case 13/67 [1968] ECR 289 ord. However the validity of judgments of the ECJ cannot be challenged: *Wünsche* Case 69/85 [1986] ECR 947.

In respect of international agreements concluded between the Community and third countries in *Haegemann* Case 181/73 [1974] ECR 449[4] the ECJ held that they were to be considered as acts adopted by the Community institutions within the meaning of art 234 EC. The assimilation of international agreements into Community acts is very important since it ensures uniformity in their interpretation and application throughout the Community, although national courts or tribunals of third countries, and contracting

---

[3] Article 8 of the 1965 Merger Treaty provides for its interpretation by the ECJ which includes the Protocol on the Privileges and Immunities of the European Communities annexed to that Treaty: *Klomp* Case 23/68 [1969] ECR 43.

[4] This case concerned an association agreement between EEC and Greece and the position has been confirmed in many cases, for example in *Cayrol* Case 52/77 [1977] ECR 2261 concerning the association agreement between the EEC and Spain and *Razanatsimbo* Case 65/77 [1977] ECR 2229 concerning the Lomé Convention.

parties to those agreements, are neither allowed to refer to the ECJ under art 234 EC nor bound by its judgments. The jurisdiction of the ECJ to give preliminary rulings is also extended to the decisions adopted by bodies created by such international agreements in order to ensure their proper application.[5]

In relation to complementary sources of Community law, they are concluded between the Member States and as such are excluded from the scope of art 234 EC. In *Vandeweghe* Case 130/73 [1973] ECR 1329 (see also *Hurd* Case 44/84 [1986] ECR 29) the ECJ ruled out the possibility that the interpretation or the validity of such agreements may be referred under art 234 EC even if they are concluded under art 293 EC. For that reason, international agreements concluded between Member States often expressly confer upon the ECJ the task of interpreting their provisions and thus ensure their uniform application throughout the Community. In this respect, the agreement itself may contain a provision conferring an interpretative role on the ECJ, such as arts 2 and 3 of the Community Patent Convention.[6] Very often a protocol is annexed to the Convention relating to its interpretation by the ECJ, as in the case of the 1968 Brussels Convention on the Jurisdiction and Enforcement of Judgments in Civil and Commercial Matters, or the 1968 Convention on Mutual Recognition of Companies and Legal Persons, or the 1980 Rome Convention on the Law Applicable to Contractual Obligations.

Courts and tribunals which can refer to the ECJ

Article 234 EC specifies that only courts and tribunals may ask for preliminary rulings. This excludes the parties to a dispute referring directly to the ECJ. If a contract concluded between private parties specifies that any dispute on a point of Community law should be referred to the ECJ, the latter will decline jurisdiction. Private parties cannot impose upon the ECJ jurisdiction under art 234 EC: *Hessische Knappschaft* Case 44/65 [1965] ECR 1192; *Mattheus* Case 93/78 [1978] ECR 2203.

In most cases the question whether or not a particular body is a court or a tribunal is self-evident. However, on a few occasions the ECJ has had to determine the status of a referring body in the context of art 234 EC. Indeed, uniformity in the application of Community law throughout the Community requires that the definition of a court or a tribunal for the purposes of art 234 EC is independent from national concepts, which vary from one Member State to another, and has an autonomous, Community meaning. The case law of the ECJ has gradually determined the criteria permitting identifying a body which is considered as 'a court or a tribunal' under art 234 EC. Apart from all judicial bodies expressly recognised as such under national law of a Member State, the ECJ held that other bodies can refer under art 234 EC provided they meet certain requirements. In *Vassen-Göbbels* Case 61/65 [1966] ECR 377 the ECJ held that technical factors, such as whether the type of procedure is adversarial or not, the involvement of national authorities in the appointment of the members of that body, and the mandatory jurisdiction of that body imposed by national law upon the parties to the dispute, were all relevant for the purpose of

---

[5] See *Sevince* Case C–192/89 [1990] ECR I–3461; it also includes non-binding recommendations of such bodies: *Deutsche Shell* Case C–188/91 [1993] ECR I–363.
[6] OJ L401 (1989).

art 234 EC. In *Vassen-Göbbels* the ECJ confirmed that a Dutch social security arbitration tribunal could refer under art 234 EC since:

1. its members and the chairman were appointed by the Dutch Minister for Social Affairs and Public Health who also laid down the rules of procedure;
2. it was a permanent body which settled disputes under art 89 of the RBFM;[7]
3. the procedure was adversarial;
4. the jurisdiction of the social security arbitration tribunal was compulsory in all disputes involving the social security authority and the insurer;
5. this body was bound to apply rules of law and not equity.

In *Corbiau* Case C–24/92 [1993] ECR I–1277 the ECJ examined the relationship between a body and the person that took the decision being challenged in the proceedings before that body in determining whether the latter is a court or tribunal. In *Corbiau*, the Director of Taxation (Directeur des Contributions) in Luxembourg was not considered as a court or tribunal in the context of art 234 EC and could not refer to the ECJ because there was an institutional link between the Luxembourg tax authorities which made a decision challenged by Corbiau and the Director of those authorities. As a result, he was not a third party to the proceedings. Further indications regarding 'functional' aspects of competences of a national body were provided in *Borker* Case 138/80 [1980] ECR 1975 in which the Paris Conseil de l'Ordre des Avocats à la Cour (Paris Bar Council) was not considered as a court or tribunal within the meaning of art 234 EC because that body was not exercising any judicial function, but in fact 'made a request for a declaration relating to a dispute between a member of the Bar and the courts or tribunals of another Member State'. In *Broekmeulen* Case 246/80 [1981] ECR 2311 the reference from the Appeals Committee for General Medicine, which was established by the Royal Netherlands Society for the Promotion of Medicine and not considered as a court or tribunal under Dutch law, was accepted by the ECJ for the following reasons: the national authorities appointed the chairman and one-third of the members of the Society's body which constituted, according to the ECJ, a significant degree of involvement of The Netherlands public authorities in its composition; the procedure was adversarial; there was no appeal from the Appeals Committee to the courts; and, most importantly, any general practitioner, whether Dutch or from another Member State, intending to establish himself in The Netherlands was compelled to have his status recognised by the Society, and in the case of refusal the Appeals Committee was competent in the last resort to decide the question of his registration as a doctor. The protection of the right of establishment for doctors from other Member States was emphasised by the ECJ. It stated that if a professional body, acting under a certain degree of governmental supervision, was assigned the task of implementing Community law and this body together with the public authorities 'creates appeal procedures which may affect the exercise of rights granted by Community law, it is imperative, in order to ensure the proper functioning of Community law, that the Court should have an opportunity of ruling on issues of interpretation and validity arising out of such proceedings.'

However, in *Victoria Film A/S* Case C–134/97 [1999] 1 CMLR 279 the Skatteratts-

---

[7] Reglement van het Beamtenfonds voor het Mijenbedriff, the Regulation governing the relations between social security and those insured by it.

nämnden (Swedish Revenue Board), which assesses the situation of the applicant from the point of view of internal taxation and delivers only preliminary decisions prior to binding decisions of the Swedish tax authorities, was not considered as a court or a tribunal within the meaning of art 234 EC as its activities were administrative in nature. In this respect the ECJ held that:

> 'Skatterättsnämnden does not [...] have as its task to review the legality of the decisions of the tax authorities but rather to adopt a view, for the first time, on how a specific transaction is to be assessed to tax. Where, upon application by a taxable person, Skatterättsnämnden gives a preliminary decision on a matter of assessment or taxation, it performs a non-judicial function which, moreover, in other Member States is expressly entrusted to the tax authorities.'

If a body exercises only administrative functions it is not regarded as a court or tribunal within the meaning of art 234 EC.[8]

The question whether a body which exercises not only a judicial function but also other tasks may be considered as a court or tribunal within the meaning of art 234 EC was addressed in *Pretore di Salo v Persons Unknown* Case 14/86 [1987] ECR 2545. The referral from an Italian pretore, a magistrate who initially acts as a public prosecutor and then as an examining magistrate, concerning the interpretation of an EC directive was accepted by the ECJ on the ground that the request emanated from a body that acted in the general framework of its task of judging, independently and in accordance with the law, despite the fact that certain functions performed by that body were not *sensu stricto* of a judicial nature.[9] However, a referral from an Italian public prosecutor was rejected by the ECJ in *Criminal Proceedings against X* Cases C–74 and 129/95 [1996] ECR I–6609. Advocate-General Ruiz Jarabo Colomer stressed that the main task of the Procura della Repubblica is to submit evidence during the trial and thus it is a party to the proceedings. Further, it does not exercise judicial functions and as such should not be considered as a court of tribunal under art 234 EC.

Private arbitration

The issue of private arbitration has also been examined by the ECJ. In *Nordsee Deutsche Hochsefischerei GmbH v Reederei Mond* Case 102/81 [1982] ECR 1095 the parties to the disputed contract inserted an arbitration clause in the original contract providing that any disagreement between them on any question arising out of the contract would be resolved by an arbitrator and that all recourse to the ordinary courts was excluded. When a problem concerning the performance of that contract by a number of German shipbuilders arose, an arbitrator was appointed by the Chamber of Commerce of Bremen, in accordance with the contract, but a dispute arose between the parties concerning his appointment. The arbitrator asked the ECJ to give a preliminary ruling but the latter refused to recognise the arbitrator as a court or tribunal within the meaning of art 234 EC for two reasons. First, that the parties to the dispute freely selected arbitration as a way of resolving any dispute

---

[8] See *Azienda Nazionale Autonoma della Steade* Case C–192/98 and *Radiotelevisione Italiana SpA* Case C–440/98, order of 26 November 1999 (nyr), in which referrals from the 'Corte dei Conti' were rejected.
[9] Confirmed in *Greis Unterweger* Case 318/86 [1986] ECR 955; *Almelo* Case C–393/92 [1994] ECR I–1477.

between them; and, second, that neither were German public authorities involved in the choice of arbitration by the parties nor were they 'called to intervene automatically in the proceedings before the arbitrator'. The ECJ emphasised that if private arbitration raises questions concerning Community law, national courts may have jurisdiction to examine them, either in the framework of assistance they provide for arbitral tribunals, especially in the context of certain judicial measures which are not available to the arbitrator, or in the interpretation of the law applicable to that contract, or within the framework of control which they exercise in relation to arbitration awards: *Almelo* Case C–393/92 [1994] ECR I–1477.

It is submitted that the refusal to recognise an arbitrator as a court or tribunal under art 234 EC will be subject to further development since the advantages that arbitration offers to businessmen – choice of their own arbitrators, confidentiality of proceedings, more speedy and less expensive proceedings as compared to those conducted before national courts (although the last two points are subject to a certain degree of scepticism) – will be seriously undermined if arbitrators, who are bound to deal with more and more disputes involving Community law, are not allowed to refer to the ECJ. Furthermore, arbitration as an extra-judicial method of settling disputes is well recognised in all Member States.

If public authorities are involved in arbitration, for example as in *Handels-og Kontorfunktionaerernes Forbund I Danmark* v *Dansk Arbejdsgiverforening* Case 109/88 [1989] ECR 3199, the situation is very different from that set out above. In that case a Danish Industrial Arbitration Board was recognised as a court or tribunal within the scope of art 234 EC, since its jurisdiction was imposed upon the parties if they could not agree on the application of a collective agreement, its composition and procedure was governed by Danish law and its award was final.

Territorial jurisdiction of the ECJ

Article 234 EC provides that only courts and tribunals of the Member States may ask for preliminary rulings. As a result, neither courts located in third countries nor international courts are permitted to refer to the ECJ under art 234 EC.

The position of courts common to a number of Member States which are in fact international courts was examined in *Perfumes Christian Dior SA and Perfumes Christian Dior BV* v *Evora BV* Case C–337/95 [1997] ECR I–6013. The ECJ held that a court like the Benelux Court[10] should be allowed to make referrals to the ECJ since being a court common to a number of Member States it has the task of interpreting Community law.

The ECJ has given a wide interpretation to the territorial scope of application of art 234 EC. It accepted a reference from a court situated in the Isle of Man, which is outside the system of British courts (*Barr* Case C–355/89 [1991] ECR I–3479) on the ground that the United Kingdom under its act of accession is responsible for the Isle of Man external relations. Also, an administrative court of Papeete in Polynesia was allowed to make a referral to the ECJ under art 234 EC. The government of the United Kingdom argued that

---

[10] The Benelux Court was established on 31 March 1965 to ensure that the Benelux Union law (Belgium, Luxembourg and The Netherlands signed the Treaty of the Benelux Economic Union which became operative on 1 November 1960) is interpreted and applied uniformly throughout the Benelux Union.

the court of Papeete was not within the jurisdiction of France as it was situated in a French overseas department and that under art 299(3) EC it was outside the territorial scope of application of Community law. The ECJ held that this court under French law was considered as a French administrative court and that the question referred was within the jurisdiction of the ECJ as it concerned the application of the special conditions on association of overseas territories which includes French Polynesia: *Kaefer and Procacci* v *France* Cases C–100 and 101/89 [1990] ECR I–4647; also *Leplat* Case C–260/90 [1992] ECR I–643.

References in interlocutory proceedings

In *Hoffmnan-La Roche* v *Centrafarm* Case 107/76 [1977] ECR 957 the ECJ held that preliminary references can be made in the course of interlocutory proceedings. It is very unusual for a national court to make such a referral taking into account, on the one hand, the nature of interlocutory proceedings which require prompt resolution of the submitted matters and, on the other hand, that an interlocutory issue can be examined again during the main proceedings.

9.2 Interpretation of Community law by the ECJ under art 234 EC

The ECJ has jurisdiction to interpret Community law. The interpretation comprises:

1. The determination of the exact meaning and scope of application of the provisions of Community law as well as the concepts which those provisions expressly or implicitly describe (*Portelange* Case 10/69 [1969] ECR 309), such as for example the concept of non-discrimination.
2. The determination whether or not EC regulations need to be further completed or specified by national legislation: *Schlüter* Case 94/71 [1972] ECR 307.
3. The determination of the application of the provisions of Community law (*ratione materiae, ratione personae, ratione temporis*), the legal effect they produce and especially whether or not they are directly effective.
4. The determination of the meaning and legal implications of the principle of supremacy of Community law vis-à-vis national laws of the Member States.
5. The interpretation of the statutes of bodies established by an act of the Council, where those statutes so provide by virtue of art 234(1)(c) EC.

The role of the ECJ under art 234 EC is to interpret Community law not national law. Therefore, the question of interpretation of, and the validity of, national law is outside the jurisdiction of the ECJ,[11] although in some cases when national law is at issue national courts formulate the questions in a manner that makes them relevant to Community law or the ECJ, by selecting specific aspects relevant to Community law, interprets, to some extent, national law. In *Directeur Régional de la Securité Sociale de Nancy* v *August Hirardin* Case

---

[11] For example, *Unger* Case 75/63 [1964] ECR 347; *Lefebre* Case 188/86 [1987] ECR 2963; *Gauchard* Case 20/87 [1987] ECR 4879; *Demouche* Case 152/83 [1987] ECR 3833; *Euripharm* Case C–347/89 [1991] ECR I–1717.

112/75 [1976] ECR 553 (and see also *Melkunie* Case 97/83 [1984] ECR 2367) the ECJ justified this interference in the following terms:

> 'Although the Court when giving a ruling under art [234], has no jurisdiction ... to pronounce upon a provision of national law, it may however provide the national court with the factors of interpretation depending on Community law which might be useful to it in evaluating the effects of such provision.'

There is a further exception, which fortunately seems to have declined in use, to the principle that the ECJ has no jurisdiction to give preliminary rulings upon questions relating to national law It occurs when national law expressly refers to Community law. The ECJ accepted a referral in *Dzodzi* Cases C–297/88 and 197/89 [1991] ECR I–3783 and *Gmurzynska* Case C–231/89 [1990] ECR I–4003 and thus, in fact, interpreted national law. This approach of the ECJ, which certainly ensures uniformity in the application of Community law, was rightly criticised by Advocate-General Dermon in his conclusions in the above-mentioned cases, and it seems that the practice has gradually been abandoned by the ECJ. In *Jose Vanacker* Case C–37/92 [1993] ECR I–494[12] the ECJ held that national courts should interpret national law.

Another problem with the interpretation of Community law by the ECJ under art 234 EC is that it is not easy to draw a line between the interpretation and the actual application of EC law. Under art 234 EC the ECJ has jurisdiction to interpret Community law *in abstratio* and objectively. However, the necessity to assist national courts in rendering a judgment in a particular case requires that the Community judges give their decision within the context of the law and facts of that case.

The essential aim of art 234 EC is to create a spirit of co-operation between national courts and the ECJ. For that reason it is important that each court acts within its jurisdiction. The ECJ must only interpret Community law while national courts must apply it in the context of a particular dispute. However, in practice the boundary between interpretation and application is fluid and varies depending upon the degree of precision of the question asked by national courts, the complexity of the factual and legal context of the dispute, etc. For that reason the ECJ is in a difficult position. On the one hand, if its decision is too precise, it pre-determines the outcome of the dispute and a national judge has no discretion at all but must follow the preliminary ruling given by the ECJ. As a result, the ECJ instead of interpreting Community law is applying it, thus encroaching upon the jurisdiction of national courts and undermining the division of competences between national courts and the ECJ which is contrary to the spirit and the terms of art 234 EC. On the other hand, if the preliminary ruling is too general, the interpretation of a provision of Community law is too abstract and the national judge has a large measure of discretion so that the preliminary ruling may instead of clarifying a particular question obscure it even more. This approach calls into question the main objective of art 234 EC, that is the uniformity of application of Community law throughout the Community. Indeed, it is not easy for the ECJ to reach a decision which is neither too precise nor too general,

---

[12] Also confirmed in *Kleinwort Benson* Case C–346/93 [1995] ECR I–615 which concerned the interpretation of the 1968 Brussels Convention on Recognition and the Enforcement of Judgments in Civil and Commercial Matters. This solution is transposable to art 234 EC: Europe [1995] (May) no 192, comm DS and AR.

particularly, in relation to the validity of national law, in the light of the principle of supremacy of Community law. Some decisions of the ECJ under art 234 EC have left no doubts as to the outcome of the case.[13]

In the context of preliminary rulings on the interpretation of Community law it is important to underline that the ECJ refuses to consider its rulings as irrevocable. As a result, the ECJ may modify its interpretation of Community law and thus national courts are entitled to bring the same or a similar matter (although based on different facts or supported by new legal arguments)[14] before the ECJ by way of a subsequent reference for a preliminary ruling under art 234 EC. For that reason a new referral (or a referral concerning the same or a similar question) cannot easily be dismissed by the ECJ. For example, in *Molkerei-Zentrale* Case 28/67 [1968] CMLR 187 the ECJ examined at length new arguments invoked against its previous interpretation. If the referred question is identical to the one already decided the ECJ may accept the preliminary question but refer to its previous ruling: *Hessische Knappschaft* Case 44/65 [1965] ECR 1192. Under the amended Rules of Procedure of the ECJ, in force since 1 July 2000, the ECJ is entitled to dispose of similar references from national courts by means of a reasoned order, where the answer can clearly be deduced from existing case law: see Chapter 4, section 4.5.

Distinction between discretionary and compulsory reference by national courts to the ECJ

There are two possible approaches to attempting to ensure uniformity in the application of Community law. One is compulsory referral to the ECJ each time a national court or tribunal has difficulties with the interpretation or the validity of Community law. This would be inconvenient in terms of the duration of proceedings and the heavy workload imposed upon the ECJ. The second is to grant an unlimited discretion to national courts (whatever their position in the hierarchy of national judicial system) as to whether or not to refer to the ECJ. However, to grant such a discretion to these courts would jeopardise the homogeneity of Community law. Article 234 EC represents a compromise between those two approaches. Thus, national courts or tribunals against whose decisions there is no judicial remedy under national law 'shall bring' a question of interpretation of Community law before the ECJ, while other national courts or tribunals have unfettered discretion in matters of referrals. The idea behind this compromise is that in the case of obviously wrong decisions of lower courts on a point of Community law an appeal to a superior court will rectify that mistake, especially in the light of a mandatory referral to the ECJ by the courts of last resort.

---

[13] See *Dekker* Case 33/65 [1965] ECR 1116; *Sail* Case 82/71 [1972] ECR 136; *R v Secretary of State for Transport, ex parte Factortame (No 2)* Case C–213/89 [1990] ECR I–2433; *Johnston* Case 222/84 [1986] ECR 1651; *British Telecom* Case C–292/93 [1996] ECR I–1631.

[14] In *ICAC* Case 22/78 [1979] ECR 1168 the ECJ upheld its previous ruling on the ground that the new referral did not demonstrate any new factual or legal circumstances which would lead to a different interpretation.

Discretion of national courts and tribunals to refer: art 234(2) EC

The lower courts within the meaning of art 234(2) EC have an unfettered discretion to refer to the ECJ. Article 234 EC recognises the exclusive jurisdiction of national courts to decide whether or not to refer a question to the ECJ. As a result, a national judge has the sole discretion as to whether to refer. Neither the parties to the dispute, nor their legal representatives, nor any other public authorities, which under certain national legal systems may interfere in the proceedings, can force a national court to refer to the ECJ under art 234 EC. To the contrary, a national judge may decide to refer, even if the parties to the dispute have not raised the issue (*Salonia* v *Poidamani and Giglio* Case 126/80 [1981] ECR 1563) or not to refer, even if so requested by one of them (*Van Buynder* Case C–152/94 [1995] ECR I–3981), or both as in *Reti Televisive Italiana* Cases C–320 and 328/94 [1996] ECR I–6471. In *J Reisdorf* Case C–85/95 [1996] ECR I–6257 the ECJ held that parties may not challenge as irrelevant to the dispute a question referred by a national judge to the ECJ. National procedural rules cannot impose restrictions on the court's discretion in this respect. In *Rheinmühlen* Joined Cases 146 and 166/73 [1973] ECR 33 (see also *Peterbroeck* Case C–312/93 [1995] ECR I–4599) the ECJ emphasised that 'a rule of national law whereby a court is bound on points of law by the rulings of a superior court cannot deprive the inferior courts of their power to refer to the ECJ questions of interpretation of Community law involving such rulings'. National courts may refer a question at any stage of proceedings. The ECJ in *Simmenthal* Case 70/77 [1978] ECR 1453 held that the proper administration of justice requires that a question should not be referred prematurely, although it is outside the jurisdiction of the ECJ to specify at which particular point of the proceedings the national courts should ask for preliminary rulings.[15] The ECJ has emphasised many times that national courts have the best knowledge of the case and that, taking into account their responsibility for rendering correct judgments, they alone are competent to assess the relevance of the question of Community law raised in the dispute and the necessity of obtaining a preliminary ruling.[16]

In order to facilitate the tasks of national courts and tribunals the ECJ issued a Note containing recommendations on the technical aspects of the referral under art 234 EC.[17] Indeed, the Note is very useful since the initial liberal approach changed over the years and, although the ECJ maintains a strict policy of non-interference vis-à-vis national courts and tribunals over matters of what to refer, when to refer and how to refer, it has introduced certain requirements, especially concerning the existence of a genuine dispute, the relevance of the referred question to the dispute at issue and the determination of the factual and legal context of the dispute. Under the amended Rules of Procedure in force since 1 July 2000 the ECJ may request clarification of preliminary references from the relevant national court.

In *Practice Direction (Supreme Court: References to the Court of Justice of the European Communities)* (1999) The Times 19 January it was emphasised that courts

---

[15] See *Irish Creamery Milk Suppliers' Association* Cases 36 and 71/80 [1981] ECR 735; *Campus Oil* Case 72/83 [1984] ECR 2727.

[16] For example in *ONPTS* v *Damiani* Case 53/79 [1980] ECR 273; *Van Gend en Loos* Case 26/62 [1963] ECR 1.

[17] Note informative sur l'introduction de procédure préjudicielles par les juridictions nationales: Activités de la Cour de justice et du Tribunal de première instance, no 31/96: Europe [1997] (January) no 8, comm DR.

referring issues to the Court of Justice of the European Communities under art 234 EC[18] should ensure that the reference is in the form most helpful to the court at Luxembourg which has to answer the questions posed.

This *Practice Direction* should be examined in the light of the decision of the Court of Appeal in *Royscot Leasing Ltd (and three other appellants)* v *Commissioners of Customs and Excise* [1999] 1 CMLR 903 in which the Commissioners of Customs and Excise asked the Court of Appeal to withdraw a referral for a preliminary ruling to the ECJ on value added tax appeals against the four above-mentioned applicants. The Court of Appeal held that, although it was entitled to order the withdrawal of a reference to the ECJ on its own initiative, it should do so only when it was manifest that the reference would not fulfil any useful purpose. Consequently, the court should exercise its power of withdrawal only in exceptional cases. The Court of Appeal refused to withdraw the referral for the following reasons. First, the fact that the ECJ did not invite the referring court to withdraw its reference showed that the question could not be regarded as *acte clair*. Second, the Court of Appeal emphasised that the greater the progress that the case had made in the ECJ since the referral, the greater was the significance of any absence of a suggestion by the ECJ that the referral should be withdrawn. In this case, the oral hearing on the referral was due shortly in Luxembourg and it was clear that a considerable amount of work had been done on the case.

Existence of a genuine dispute

In *Foglia* v *Novello* Case 104/79 [1980] ECR 745 the ECJ refused to give a preliminary ruling on the ground that there was no genuine dispute between the parties to national proceedings. In this case Foglia, an Italian wine merchant, entered into a contract with Novello, an Italian national, for the delivery of liqueur wine to a person residing in France. They inserted an express clause providing that Novello would not pay any unlawfully levied taxes. The French authorities imposed a tax on the importation of the wine to France which Foglia paid, although his contract with a shipper also provided that he should not be liable for any charges imposed in breach of the law of free movement of goods. Foglia brought proceedings against Novello who refused to reimburse the French tax levied on Foglia.

The ECJ declined to exercise jurisdiction under art 234 EC on the ground that there was no real dispute in the case. It held that:

> 'It … appears that the parties to the main action are concerned to obtain a ruling that the French tax system is invalid for liqueur wine by the expedient of proceedings before an Italian court between two private individuals who are in agreement as to the result to be obtained and who have inserted a clause in their contract in order to induce the Italian court to give a ruling on the point. The artificial nature of this expedient is underlined by the fact that Foglia did not exercise its rights under French law to institute proceedings over the consumption tax although it undoubtedly has an interest in doing so in view of the clause in the contract by which it was bound and moreover by the fact that Foglia paid the duty without protest.'

Both parties had the same interest in the outcome of the dispute which was to obtain a ruling on the invalidity of the French legislation since under their contracts they were not

---

[18] OJ C224 (1992).

liable to pay for any unlawful charges imposed by France; their action was a collusive and artificial device aimed at obtaining a ruling and not a genuine dispute which the ECJ could settle.

When the Italian court later asked the ECJ to provide clarification of its preliminary judgment in *Foglia v Novello* Case 104/ 79, the ECJ accepted the second reference but once again declined, on the same grounds (*Foglia v Novello (No 2)* Case 244/80 [1981] ECR 3045), its jurisdiction to give a preliminary ruling. The existence of a real dispute in proceedings before a national court is determined from the point of view of art 234 EC. Thus, neither the fact that the parties challenge national legislation of one Member State before a court of another Member State, nor their agreement to 'organise' proceedings before a national court leading to the preliminary ruling, is sufficient to prevent a real dispute from being dealt with by the ECJ: *Société d'Importation E Leclerc-SIPLEC v TF1 Publicité SA and M6 Publicité SA* Case C–412/93 [1995] ECR I–179; *Bosman* Case C–415/93 [1995] ECR I–4921. In *Eau de Cologne v Provide* Case C–150/88 [1989] ECR 3891 a German manufacturer of eau de cologne brought an action against an Italian company, Provide, when the latter refused to accept the products and make payments on the ground that the packaging of the products was incompatible with Italian law so that they could not be marketed in Italy even though the packaging was in conformity with Community law. The ECJ accepted the referral from a German court, although the compatibility of Italian law with Community law was at issue.

The decision of the ECJ in *Foglia v Novello* has been much criticised[19] but the ECJ has affirmed its position in a number of cases: *Bertini* Case 98/85 [1986] ECR 1885; *Gmurzynska* Case C–231/89 [1990] ECR I–4003. In addition the ECJ has provided further specifications as to the existence of a genuine dispute. In *Mattheus* Case 93/78 [1978] ECR 2203 the ECJ declined to exercise its jurisdiction under art 234 EC because the referred question concerned not the interpretation of Community law in force but the opinion of the Court on the enactment of future law. The ECJ also refuses to answer general or hypothetical questions: *Dias* Case C–343/90 [1992] ECR I–4673. In *Meilicke v ADV/ORGA FA Meyer* Case C–83/91 [1992] ECR I–4871 the question of compatibility of the German legal theory of disguised non-cash subscription of capital with the Second Company Law Directive was considered hypothetical as it was irrelevant to the dispute in question.

In this context it is interesting to note that when the referred questions do not concern a genuine dispute, and have no real connection with Community law, the ECJ has developed a new manner to deal with them. Instead of declaring them inadmissible under art 234 EC, the ECJ under art 92 of its Rules of Procedure issues an order which declares them manifestly inadmissible.[20]

Another aspect concerning the existence of an actual dispute was examined by the ECJ in *Society for the Protection of Unborn Children (Ireland) v Grogan* Case 159/90 [1991] ECR I–4685. In this case the plaintiff asked the Irish High Court for an injunction prohibiting Irish student organisations distributing information concerning abortion clinics in the United Kingdom as contrary to the Irish Constitution. The High Court, in the context

---

[19] See E Bebr, 'The Possible Implications of *Foglia v Novello (No 2)*' (1982) 19 CMLR 421.
[20] *Monin Automobiles* Case C–428/93 [1994] ECR I–1707 ord; *La Pyramide SARL* Case C–378/93 [1994] ECR I–3999 ord.

of interlocutory proceedings, referred the question whether the prohibition of the distribution of information on abortion was in breach of EC law (provision of services) to the ECJ. In the meantime the decision to refer was appealed to the Irish Supreme Court, which granted the injunction but did not quash the part of the High Court referral regarding the issue of whether the defendants were entitled under the Community provision on the freedom to provide services to distribute the information on abortion clinics in the United Kingdom.

The ECJ found a very diplomatic solution to the highly sensitive issue. The ECJ refused to give a preliminary ruling on the ground that it had no jurisdiction to hear a referral when the proceedings before the referring court were already terminated.

Relevance of a referred question to the main dispute

The relevance of a referred question to the actual dispute was for the first time clearly assessed in *Salonia* v *Poidamani and Giglio* Case 126/80 [1981] ECR 1563, in which the ECJ held that it could reject a reference since the national court was seeking to obtain a preliminary ruling on the interpretation of Community law quite clearly not relevant to the actual case. As a result, the ECJ declined its jurisdiction under art 234 EC to answer a question which had no connection with the subject-matter of the main action (*Dias* Case C–343/90 [1992] ECR I–4673; *Eurico Italia* Cases C–332, 333 and 335/92 [1994] ECR I–711), or as the ECJ held in *Corsica Ferries* Case C–18/93 [1994] ECR I–1783 which 'does not respond to the objective need to resolve the main action' or to assess the validity of Community acts which do not apply to a particular dispute: *Grau-Hupka* Case C–297/93 [1994] ECR I–5535. However, this new approach is attenuated by the ability of the ECJ to reformulate the question referred by a national court (*Tissier* Case 35/85 [1986] ECR 1207; *Clinique* Case C–315/92 [1994] ECR I–317), or to take into consideration a provision of Community law which the national court did not mention in its referral: *Voogd Vleesimport en Export BV* Case C–151/93 [1994] ECR I–4915. Furthermore, in *Albany* Case C–67/96 [1999] ECR I–5751 and *Brentjevis Handelsonderneming BV* Joined Cases 115–117/97 [1999] ECR I–6025 the ECJ stated that there is a presumption that a referred question is relevant to the main dispute.

Determination of the factual and legal context of the dispute

In the Note containing recommendations on the technical aspects of the referral under art 234 EC (see above) the ECJ emphasised that the request for a preliminary ruling should state all the relevant facts with clarity and precision, the legal context of the dispute, the reasons which compelled the judge to ask for a referral and the arguments submitted by the parties to the dispute. The ECJ has underlined that a well drafted referral contributes to a better comprehension of the factual and legal context of the dispute and thus permits the Member States and the Community institutions to submit their observations and the ECJ to give a useful reply. Stringent formal requirements have been gradually introduced by the ECJ. In the early cases the ECJ held that it was not a task of the ECJ to verify the facts and the qualification of the legal nature of the referred question: *Albatros* Case 20/64 [1965] ECR 41; *Tedeschi* Case 5/77 [1977] ECR 1555. In later cases the ECJ declined to exercise its jurisdiction under art 234 EC for lack of relevant information (*Telemarsicabruzzo* Cases

C–320–322/90 [1993] ECR I–393), while recent cases demonstrate that the insufficient contextualisation of a dispute will lead to the ECJ rejecting the referral as manifestly inadmissible.[21] However, the strict requirement of contextualisation of a dispute is of lesser importance in areas in which the facts are not that essential, for example, if the referred question concerns the validity of acts of the Community. In *Hupeden* Case C–295/94 [1996] ECR I–3375 and *Bernard Pietsch* Case C–296/94 [1996] ECR I–3409 a national court formulated the referred question in very lucid terms – Is the provision X of Regulation Y valid? – and the ECJ accepted the referral. In *Vaneetveld* Case C–316/93 [1994] ECR I–763 the ECJ held that despite insufficient information submitted by the national court on the legal and factual context of the dispute (which was less imperative in this case as the subject-matter concerned technical points) the ECJ was able to formulate a useful reply.

In this context it is interesting to note that the factual situation as described by a national court is accepted by the ECJ although it may be inexact or even erroneous! In *Phytheron International SA* Case C–352/95 [1997] ECR I–1729 the national Court submitted not only insufficient information, as it did not mention the holder of the disputed trade mark in France and in Germany, but also provided the ECJ with erroneous factual and legal information as it stated that the place where the product was manufactured was in Turkey when in fact it was Germany. The ECJ gave a preliminary ruling which in the light of new facts was irrelevant to the main dispute. The ECJ justified its decision on the ground of legal certainty and the right to defence, in particular it took into account that the holder of the disputed trade mark was not a party to the main dispute and therefore could not submit his arguments to the ECJ. Consequently, by taking into account new facts the ECJ would deprive the Member States and the Community institutions of their right to present their observations within the framework of the preliminary ruling: *Holdijk* Cases 141–143/81 [1982] ECR 1299. This approach was confirmed in *A Moksel* Case C–223/95 [1997] ECR I–2379 in which a German court erroneously described the factual situation of the dispute. The ECJ held that the separation of functions between national courts and the ECJ within the framework of art 234 EC means that it is the task of a national court to determine the particular factual circumstances of each case, and the ECJ has jurisdiction solely to give a ruling on the interpretation and the validity of Community law on the basis of the facts submitted by the national court.

Mandatory referral of national courts of last resort: art 234(3) EC

The exact meaning of art 234(3) EC, which states that if a question of interpretation of Community law 'is raised in a case pending before a court or tribunal of a Member State, against whose decision there is no judicial remedy under national law, the court or tribunal shall bring the matter before the Court of Justice', has been clarified by the ECJ.

The first point elucidated by the ECJ was the definition of 'courts or tribunal' within the

---

[21] The ECJ issued an order of manifest inadmissibility of referrals for lack of information in *La Pyramide SARL* Case C–378/93 [1994] ECR I–3999; *Mostafa Saddik* Case C–458/93 [1995] ECR I–511; *Juan Carlos Grau Gomis* Case C–165/94 [1995] ECR I–1023, *Max Mara* Case C–307/95 [1995] ECR I–5083; and in four cases: *Italia Testa* Case C–101/96 [1996] ECR I–3081; *M Modesti* Case C–191/96 [1996] ECR I–3937; *Lahlou Hassa* Case C–196/96 [1996] ECR I–3945 and *Corticeira Amorim-Algarve Ltd* Case C–158/99, order of 2 July 1999 (nyr).

scope of art 234(3) EC. In this respect the ECJ decided that courts against whose decision there is no judicial remedy under national law (ie under national law there is no right of appeal against their decisions) are within the scope of art 234(3) EC. This formula, however, comprises not only final appellate courts in each Member State but also all courts which decide a case in the last instance. In *Costa v ENEL* Case 6/64 [1964] ECR 585 the Giudice Conciliatore in Milan was the court of last instance because of the small sum of money involved in the dispute, that is £1, which Costa refused to pay. As a result, any court or tribunal against whose decision, in a given case, there is no judicial remedy falls within art 234(3) EC, although in other cases an appeal would be possible against decisions of that court and tribunal. In the United Kingdom there is still uncertainty whether the Court of Appeal should be considered as a final appellate court in cases where leave to appeal to the House of Lords is unobtainable.[22] In *Generics (UK) Ltd v Smith, Kline and French Laboratories Ltd* [1990] 1 CMLR 416 the Court of Appeal held that:

> 'We are not ... the final appellate court for the purposes of art [234] of the Treaty even though an appeal to the House of Lords lies only with leave ... So we are not obliged to refer the question to the EEC Court of Justice. But we have discretion.'

It is submitted that the best solution in cases where the right of appeal or judicial review is conditional upon the granting of leave consists of imposing upon the lower courts the obligation of either granting such leave or referring to the ECJ. Once the proceedings are no longer pending before that court the principle of legal certainty requires that the proceedings will not be reopened before that court. If leave to appeal to the House of Lords is denied it seems that the parties still have the possibility of complaining to the Commission under art 226 EC. According to Weatherill and Beaumont, on one occasion the Commission brought proceedings against France under art 169 EC 'for an allegedly manifest error of application of Community law by the Cour de Cassation in failing to overturn the decision of a lower court in favour of the French prosecuting authorities'.[23]

The second point which the ECJ has clarified in respect of art 234(3) EC concerns conditions relating to mandatory references by national courts of last resort. Indeed, at the first glance it seems that the terms of art 234(3) EC are imperative and that they impose an obligation upon the courts of last instance to ask for a preliminary ruling each time the interpretation of Community law is at issue. This impression is reinforced by the formula used in art 234(2) EC, which provides that national courts or tribunals may refer to the ECJ if they consider that a preliminary ruling is necessary to enable them to give judgments, is absent in art 234(3) EC. The above impressions are, however, not correct. In *Da Costa en Schaake v Nederlandse Belastingadministratie* Joined Cases 28–30/62 [1963] ECR 31 the ECJ held that art 234(3) EC 'unreservedly' requires the courts of last resort to refer, but it recognised one exception. It is not necessary to refer if the ECJ has already interpreted the same question in an earlier case since 'the authority of an interpretation under art 234 already given by the Court may deprive the obligation [to refer] from its purpose and thus empty it of its substance'. Such is the case especially when the question raised is identical

---

[22] The question was addressed in *Chiron Corporation v Murex Diagnostic* [1995] All ER (EC) 88 (CA) but not settled.

[23] *EC Law,* 2nd ed, London: Penguin Books, 1995, p202.

with a question which has already been the subject of a preliminary ruling in a similar case. In *Da Costa* the question asked was identical to that raised in *Van Gend en Loos* Case 26/62 [1963] ECR 1. In *Pigs Marketing Board* Case 83/78 [1978] ECR 2347 the ECJ held that the court should assess the relevance of the question raised before it in the light of the necessity to obtain the preliminary ruling. These two exceptions were restated and further developed in *CILFIT v Ministro della Sanita* Case 283/81 [1982] ECR 3415 in which the extent of the discretion of courts of last resort was fully explained. Here, the Italian Ministry of Health imposed an inspection levy on imports of wool coming from other Member States. An Italian importer of wool challenged the levy. The Italian court considered that the case law on this matter was reasonably clear but, as a court of final instance, it was uncertain whether or not it should refer the question of the legality of this fixed health inspection levy to the ECJ. The Italian court asked the ECJ whether it was obliged to refer under art 234(3) EC when Community law was sufficiently clear and precise and there were no doubts as to its interpretation.

The ECJ held that the courts of last resort like any other courts or tribunals have the discretion to assess whether a referral is necessary to enable them to give judgment They are not obliged to refer if a question concerning the interpretation of Community law raised before them is not relevant to the dispute, that is, if it can in no way affect the outcome of the case. The ECJ confirmed the principle of *Da Costa* by stating that if the ECJ had already dealt with the point of law in question, even though the questions were not strictly identical, the court of last resort is not obliged to refer. Finally, the ECJ held that there is no obligation to refer if 'the correct application of Community law may be so obvious as to leave no scope for any reasonable doubt as to the manner in which the question raised is to be resolved. Before it comes to the conclusion that such is the case, the national court or tribunal must be convinced that the matter is equally obvious to the Courts of the other Member States and to the Court of Justice (ECJ).'

In *CILFIT* the ECJ endorsed the French doctrine of *acte clair*, according to which the court before which the *exception prejudicielle* is raised concerning the interpretation or validity of a particular provision must refer it to a competent court in order to resolve that question, but only if there is real difficulty concerning the interpretation of its validity or if there is a serious doubt in this respect. However, if the provision is clear and if its validity is obvious, the court may apply it immediately. It stems from *CILFIT* that it is not necessary for a court of last resort to refer if:

1. The question of Community law is irrelevant to the dispute.
2. The question of Community law has already been interpreted by the ECJ, even though it may not be identical. However, this does not mean that national courts, whatever their position in the hierarchy of national courts, are prevented from referring an identical or a similar question to the ECJ. In *CILFIT* the ECJ clearly stated that all courts remain entirely at liberty to refer a matter before them if they consider it appropriate to do so.
3. The correct application of Community law is so obvious as to leave no scope for reasonable doubt. This follows from the French theory of *acte clair*. However, the ECJ added that before a national court concludes that such is the case it must be convinced that the question is equally obvious to courts in other Member States and to the ECJ itself. Furthermore, the ECJ added three requirements which a national court must take

into consideration when deciding that the matter is clear and free of doubts. First, it must assess such possibility in the light of the characteristic features of Community law and especially the difficulties that its interpretation raise, that is that it is drafted in several languages and all version are equally authentic. Second, it must be aware that Community law uses peculiar terminology and has legal concepts which have different meaning in different Member States. Finally, a national court must bear in mind that every provision of Community law must be placed in its context and interpreted in the light of the provisions of Community law as a whole, its objectives and the state of its evolution at the date on which that provision is to be applied.

The ruling in *CILFIT* has also explained the circumstances in which any court or tribunal as mentioned under art 234(2) should refer to the ECJ for a preliminary ruling. As a result it applies to any courts or tribunals of a Member State if they consider that a preliminary ruling on the question of interpretation of Community law is necessary in order to enable them to give judgment (art 234(2) EC), and to a court or tribunal of a Member State against whose decision there is no judicial remedy under national law (art 234(3)EC). In the case of courts within the scope of art 234(2) EC, the ruling in *CILFIT* assists them in deciding whether or not to refer, while under art 234(3) EC it should be interpreted more strictly, that is, the court of last resort must refer to the ECJ if there are any reasonable doubts as to the meaning of a provision of Community law. However, in practice the endorsement by the ECJ of the doctrine of *acte clair* has sensibly extended the discretion of the courts of last resort. It has also increased the risk of conflicting decisions being rendered by the highest courts in each Member State. On many occasions national courts have decided not to refer to the ECJ on the basis of this doctrine and imposed their own interpretation of Community law, and thus prevented the ECJ from expressing its views. In the United Kingdom in *R* v *Secretary of State for the Home Department, ex parte Sandhu* [1982] 2 CMLR 553 the House of Lords refused to refer to the ECJ, even though the question whether a divorced Indian husband of an EC national who was threatened with deportation from the UK was entitled to stay on the basis of Directive 68/360 was far from being clear and free of doubts. The House of Lords decided that certain statements delivered *obiter* by the ECJ in *Diatta* v *Land Berlin* Case 267/83 [1985] ECR 567 were applicable to this case. However, in *Diatta* the spouses were separated and the matter was examined in the light of Regulation 1612/68 regarding rights of residence of members of the family of a worker, while in *Sandhu* they were divorced and the divorced husband based his claim on Directive 68/360.[24] Mr Sandhu was deported despite the fact that he was previously married to a German national, he and his wife had established their domicile in the UK, his son whom he often visited in Germany, where his former wife returned after their divorce, was born in the UK and Mr Sandhu had permanent employment in the UK which allowed him to financially support his son. Also in *Magnavision NV* v *General Optical Council* [1987] 1 CMLR 716 the Divisional Court on the basis of the ruling in *CILFIT* refused to certify that certain points of law should be examined by the House of Lords, without which no appeal could be made to the ECJ. In this case the defendant raised the question of Community law, more precisely the application of art 28 EC concerning the free movement of goods, in

---

[24] For detailed examination of this case: see P Beaumont and Campbell, 'Preliminary Rulings' (1985) 53 SLG 62–64.

relation to his conviction for breach of s21 of the Opticians Act 1958 which prohibited the sale of optical appliances without the supervision of a registered medical practitioner or optician. The Divisional Court decided that there was no infringement of art 28 EC by s21 of the Opticians Act 1958 (although this point was very controversial) and thus refused to refer to the ECJ. The defendant was left without a remedy.

Sometimes the Court of Appeal and the House of Lords disagree on the interpretation of Community law as in *Freight Transport Association and Others v London Boroughs Transport Board* [1991] ECR I–5403. In this case the Court of Appeal held that the local regulations restricting vehicle noise emissions were in breach of Community law, while the House of Lords, based on the ruling in *CILFIT*, decided the contrary and refused to refer the matter to the ECJ.[25]

Also, in other Member States national courts of last resort abuse the doctrine of *acte clair*. For example, in France the Conseil d'Etat refused to refer to the ECJ the question of interpretation of art 31 EC despite the fact that its exact meaning was uncertain.[26] Probably the best example of the abuse of the doctrine of *acte clair* is provided by the case of *Cohn-Bendit* [1979] CDE 265) in which the French Conseil d'Etat imposed its own interpretation of art 249 EC upon all administrative courts in France, contrary to the case law of the ECJ. However, the French Conseil d'Etat is not the only superior court in this position.[27]

This kind of infringement of art 234(3) EC threatens the very existence of Community law and for the individual concerned results in a denial of justice. For that reason the Commission consider that proceedings under art 226 EC may be brought against national courts in the case of blatant abuse of art 234(3) EC.[28]

The third point deals with circumstances where a group of Member States (eg Benelux) has created a supreme court but each individual Member State retains its own supreme court (eg the Hoge Raad in The Netherlands). The question being: which is obliged to refer to the ECJ? Both courts are courts of last resort. In *Perfumes Dior SA and Perfumes Christian Dior BV v Evora BV* Case C–337/95 [1997] ECR I–6013 the ECJ held that subject to the *CILFIT* guidelines, if the Hoge Raad prior to making a reference to the Benelux Court on matters of interpretation of the Benelux Treaty refers to the ECJ, the Benelux Court has to accept a preliminary ruling of the ECJ and is not obliged to submit to the ECJ a question

[25] In *R v Secretary of State for Environment, ex parte RSPB* [1995] JPL 842 the House of Lords referred to the ECJ. It was faced with conflicting views on the interpretation of the EC Birds Directive which was clear and obvious for all concerned, but the Divisional Court and the majority of the Court of Appeal held that under this Directive the Secretary of State could take into consideration economic factors in determining whether a particular area should be excluded from a Special Protection Area for Birds, while the dissenting judge in the Court of Appeal argued that economic factors should not be taken into account by the Secretary of State.
[26] Judgment of 19 June 1964, *Shell-Berre* [1964] RDP 134, concl. N Questiaux [1964] AJDA, note Laubadere; see also the decision of the Conseil d'Etat of 12 October 1979, *Société Nationale des Importateurs de Vêtements* [1989] AJDA 95.
[27] In the Netherlands the Hoge Raad, Judgment of 22 December 1965 [1967] CDE 84; in Germany the Bundesfinanzhof, Judgment of 23 July 1968 [1969] AWD 203; also the rejection by that court (the German Federal Fiscal Court) of the direct effect of directives in *Re VAT Directives* [1982] 1 CMLR 525 and in a decision of 25 April 1985 in *Kloppenbburg* [1989] 1 CMLR 873. See G Bebr, 'Article 177 of the EEC Treaty in the Practice of National Courts' [1977] ICLQ 264.
[28] See the answers of the Commission to the Parliamentary questions: OJ C71 (1968); OJ C161 (1975); OJ C137 (1986).

in substantially the same terms before deciding the matter. However, the Benelux Court is obliged to refer to the ECJ if the Hoge Raad decides not to ask for a preliminary ruling.

Procedure before the ECJ under art 234 EC

On 1 July 2000 procedural changes to the ECJ's Rules of Procedure were introduced in order to make the system more efficient and flexible. In respect of preliminary rulings, the most important change is that the ECJ may apply accelerated procedure for urgent preliminary references and may derogate from various stages of the prescribed written procedure. It may also dispense with the oral hearing if it serves little or no purpose (see Chapter 4, section 4.5).

The procedure under art 234 EC is not adversarial and in reality constitutes a dialogue between national courts or tribunals and the ECJ. In this respect in the Note[29] to national courts the ECJ emphasised that until its preliminary ruling is given the ECJ would stay in touch with the referring court to which it would send copies of relevant documents, such as observations, conclusions of the Advocate-General, etc. Also, the ECJ expressed a wish to be informed by the sending court of the actual application of the preliminary ruling to the main action and to obtain a copy of the final decision rendered by that court.

The reference can only be made by national courts or tribunals within the meaning of art 234 EC. The procedure for reference by English courts is provided in the ordinary rules of proceedings for those courts.[30] The information that a referring court must provide is very similar to that specified in the ECJ Note, that is the name of the parties, the factual and legal context of the dispute, including the domestic law and relevant provisions of the Community law, and the contentions of the parties. The ECJ held in *Bosch* Case 13/61 [1962] ECR 89 that no particular form is required for reference, but emphasised in *Wagner* Case 101/63 [1964] ECR 383 that the referring court is free to formulate it in direct and simple form.

As to an appeal against a decision to refer, in *Rheinmühlen* Joined Cases 146 and 166/73 [1974] ECR 33 the ECJ held that an order for reference is subject to the remedies normally available under national law. In England RSC O.114 r1 provides that a reference to the ECJ is a final order and thus an appeal lies to the Court of Appeal without leave. An appeal against an order for reference made by the Court of Appeal is subject to the leave of the House of Lords. Usually the order is not sent to Luxembourg before the expiry of the time for appealing, but discretion lies with the referring court. In *R v Stock Exchange of the United Kingdom and the Republic of Ireland* [1993] 1 All ER 420 the Court of Appeal overturned the decision of a lower court to refer to the ECJ and held that when the criteria of the ruling in *CILFIT* are satisfied and the referring court could have resolved the matter itself with complete confidence there was no need for reference. In *Campus Oil* v *Minister for Industry and Energy* Case 72/83 [1984] 1 CMLR 479 it was recognised that national rules of procedure in this area should not inhibit lower courts which have unfettered discretion under art 234(2) EC to refer. However, it is outside the jurisdiction of the ECJ to

---

[29] OJ C224 (1992).
[30] Reference for the High Court is contained in RSC O.114 rl, the form is governed by O.114 r2 which is Form 109 in the Supreme Court Practice.

verify whether the decision to refer was taken in conformity with national procedural rules: *Reina* Case 65/81 [1982] ECR 33; *Balocchi* Case C–10/92 [1993] ECR I–5105, confirmed in *Syndicat Français de l'Express International* Case C–39/94 [1996] ECR I–3547.

The procedure for the ECJ is set out in the Protocol on the Statute of the ECJ annexed to each founding Treaty and in the Rules of Procedure of the ECJ. Article 234 proceedings are very similar to proceedings before French courts. The emphasis is on written pleadings more than on the oral procedure. Once the Registry of the ECJ has formally acknowledged the referral it is translated into the other official languages of the Community. The Registrar notifies the Community institutions, especially the Commission, which as guardian of the Treaties is almost always involved in the proceedings, the Council if the disputed act was adopted by the latter, the Member States and the parties to the original proceedings, all of whom have two months to submit their written observations. Under art 20 of the Statute of the ECJ only notified parties are entitled to submit observations. The text of the referral is published in the 'C' series of the Official Journal. At this stage the ECJ designates one of its judges as the 'judge rapporteur'. He prepares a preliminary assessment of the referral for the exclusive use of the ECJ and decides whether some procedural measures are necessary, such as reports from expert witnesses, etc. At this stage an Advocate-General is appointed. Under the amended ECJ's Rules of Procedure both the judge rapporteur and Advocate-General are entitled to request information from the parties at this early stage of proceedings. It is interesting to note that once the ECJ is seised by the referring court it has jurisdiction to give a preliminary ruling until the withdrawal of the reference by the sending court: *Simmenthal* Case 106/77 [1978] ECR 629. In *CIA Security International SA, Signalson SA et Securitel SA* Case C–194/94 [1996] ECR I–2201 the ECJ rejected the argument of the original parties that modification of the national law applicable to the dispute, subsequent to the referral, rendered the preliminary ruling unnecessary. The ECJ held that this question should be assessed by the referring court which was solely competent to decide whether or not the preliminary ruling was still required in order to enable it to give judgment. In *Chanel* Case 31/68 [1969] ECR 403 the ECJ held that when, in a matter of which it is seised, it is informed by the referring court, or the superior court, that an appeal has been lodged in the national court against the relevant national decision the ECJ proceedings should be postponed until the decision of the referring court is confirmed by the superior court and, if it is overturned, the ECJ will set aside the art 234 EC proceedings.

The next stage is the oral procedure which commences with a report submitted by the judge rapporteur stating the facts of the referral and the contentions of the parties, followed by a very short hearing, lasting approximately 30 minutes, for each party to present their arguments as well as the Commission or the Council or any other EC institution or a Member State which has submitted written pleadings. The oral and written pleadings of the parties must be limited to the legal context as determined by the referring court: *Bollman* Case 62/72 [1973] ECR 269. The parties are neither allowed to change the content of the question formulated by a national judge nor to add their own questions (*Alsatel* Case 247/86 [1988] ECR 5987), nor declare the referral without object: *Fratelli Grassi* Case 5/72 [1972] ECR 443. Furthermore, the original parties are not entitled to challenge the jurisdiction of the ECJ (*SAT* Case C–364/92 [1994] ECR I–43) or to involve in the proceedings persons other than those specified in art 20 of the Protocol of the ECJ: *De Sicco* Case 19/68 [1968]

ECR 699. This rule also applies to the Community institutions and the Member States participating in the proceedings: *Coenen* Case 39/75 [1975] ECR 1547. In the context of the original parties' involvement in the proceedings under art 234 EC it is interesting to note that their role seems to have increased. In this respect *Eunice Sutton* Case C–66/95 [1997] ECR I–2163 is especially instructive. In this case the ECJ instead of answering the question asked by the referring court actually replied to questions submitted by the original party to the proceedings, Mrs Sutton. As a result, the referring court obtained an answer to a question it did not ask. This action of the ECJ was contrary to the position held since 1965 and often expressed in the formula used in *Hessische Knappschaft* Case 44/65 [1965] ECR 1192, according to which it is solely for national courts to determine the questions to be referred to the ECJ and the parties to a main action are neither entitled to change their content nor to declare them without object. The oral part of proceedings is terminated when the Advocate-General has given his opinion on the case.

The reference procedure is still time-consuming as it takes at least 18 months. For that reason in some cases preliminary rulings have been used as tactical devices. The best example is provided by the Sunday trading cases[31] in which referral to the ECJ permitted the defendant companies to trade on Sundays while awaiting the preliminary rulings. Over a number of years the defendants who were in breach of the Shops Act argued that the latter was contrary to the Community provisions on the free movement of goods. In order to speed up the proceedings the ECJ's amended Rules of Procedure (in force since 1 July 2000) allow the ECJ to dispense with the oral hearing unless the parties submit reasoned applications setting out the points on which they wish to be heard.

The costs of the proceedings under art 234 EC are incidental to the national proceedings and as such the referring court decides this question: *Bosch* Case 13/61 [1962] ECR 107. Nevertheless, in some cases under art 104 of the ECJ's Rules of Procedure the ECJ may itself grant legal aid to the original parties.

Effect of preliminary rulings concerning the interpretation of Community law

The Treaties are silent on the legal effect of preliminary rulings concerning the interpretation of Community law. In *Da Costa* Cases 28–30/62 [1963] ECR 31 the ECJ defined the legal effects of preliminary rulings: the referring court is bound by the interpretation given by the ECJ either in reply to the question or when it decides an identical question. The ratio legis of the proceedings under art 234 EC requires that the preliminary ruling rendered by the ECJ is taken into consideration by the referring court. However, the obligation to take into account the reply from the ECJ is limited. Only if the latter permits the referring court to resolve the dispute at issue is such a ruling binding on it. Otherwise, the referring court may seise the ECJ with the same question in a second referral as happened in *Foglia* v *Novello (No 2)*. The situation is different if the ECJ not only replies to the referred question but also defines the temporal effects of the preliminary ruling. In *Benedetti* v *Munari* Case 52/76 [1977] ECR 163 the ECJ held that 'the rule as …

---

[31] Case 145/88 [1989] ECR 765; comm by Gormley (1990) 27 CMLR 141; also A Arnull, 'What Shall We Do on Sunday' 16 ELR 112.

interpreted may, and must, be applied by the courts even to legal relationship arising and established before the judgment ruling on the request for interpretation.'

This retroactive effect of the preliminary ruling, that is from the entry into force of the provision in question, has many drawbacks. On one hand, national rules on the limitation period differ from one Member State to another and, on the other hand, the *ex tunc* effect of the preliminary ruling is contrary to the principle of legal certainty. For these reasons in some cases the ECJ decided to take into consideration the fact that the *ex tunc* effect may cause serious problems in respect of *bona fide* legal relationships established before the preliminary ruling[32] and restricted its temporal effects. Only the ECJ may limit it *ex nunc* and only in the case in which the ruling was given, not in any subsequent case. For example, in *Barra v Belgium* Case 309/85 [1988] ECR 355 the ECJ refused to restrict the temporal effect of its ruling. Similarly, in *Gravier v City of Liège* Case 293/83 [1985] ECR 593 it did not impose any temporal restrictions. As a result, illegal fees charged by the Belgian authorities for vocational training courses for nationals from other Member States were reimbursed to those who claimed them before the ruling in *Gravier* was given. However, in *Blaizot* Case 24/86 [1988] ECR 379 and *Defrenne* Case 43/75 [1976] ECR 455 the ECJ decided to limit *ex nunc* the temporal effect of the rulings. This meant that the rulings applied only to those who started proceedings before the ruling was made and those who in future may have similar claims. In *Blaizot* the ECJ held that university education was within the scope of the Treaty as it constituted vocational training. As a result the illegal fees charged for those courses by Belgium were only reimbursed to students who had already brought proceedings before Belgian courts and could not be charged to future students. In *Defrenne* claims for backdated pay could only be made by those who had already started legal proceedings or submitted an equivalent claim prior to the date of the ruling. The difference in salary between male stewards and female air hostesses were to be abolished *ex nunc*.

9.3 Validity of Community law

The question of validity of acts adopted by EC institutions may also be referred to the ECJ under art 234 EC. However, as already noted, the ECJ can neither rule on the validity of the founding Treaties (taking into account their constitutional nature) nor on the statutes of bodies established by an act of the Council mentioned in art 234(1)(c) EC. Further, the ECJ will refuse to give preliminary references concerning the validity of its own decisions: *Wünsche* Case 69/85 [1986] ECR 947.

Requirements in referrals on validity of Community acts

There is no distinction between the various courts within a hierarchy of national courts in matters relating to validity. Lower courts and the courts of final resort must refer to the ECJ if there are doubts as to the validity of a Community measure. In *Foto-Frost v Hauptzollamt*

---

[32] For example, *Defrenne* Case 43/75 [1976] 455; *Salumi* Cases 66, 127 and 128/79 [1980] ECR 1258; *Denkavit Italiana* Case 61/79 [1980] ECR 1205; *Blaizot* Case 24/86 [1988] ECR 379; *Barber* Case C–262/88 [1990] ECR I–1889; *Société Bautiaa* Cases C–197 and 252/94 [1996] ECR I–505.

Lübeck-Ost Case 314/85 [1987] ECR 4199 the ECJ provided guidance to national courts as to preliminary rulings on the validity of Community acts. In this case Frost applied to a German municipal court to declare a decision issued by the Commission invalid on the grounds that it was in breach of requirements set out in a Council regulation which delegated authority to the Commission to adopt decisions. The German court requested a preliminary ruling as to whether it could review the validity of the decision in question.

The ECJ held that for the uniformity of Community law it is especially important that there are no divergences between Member States as to the validity of Community acts since this would jeopardise the very unity of the Community legal order as well as detract from the fundamental requirement of legal certainty. The ECJ drew a comparison between its exclusive jurisdiction under art 230 EC and its jurisdiction to give preliminary rulings on the validity of Community acts. It stated that the coherence of the system requires that where the validity of Community measures is challenged before national courts the jurisdiction to declare an act invalid must be reserved to the ECJ. As a result the ECJ held that 'national courts have no jurisdiction themselves to declare the acts of Community institutions invalid'.

This case confirmed that the ECJ has exclusive jurisdiction to declare an act of a Community institution invalid. Accordingly, whilst national courts may consider the validity of Community acts and may declare them valid, they must if they have doubts as to their validity make reference to the ECJ under art 230 EC.

In *TWD Textilwerke Deggendorf GmbH* Case C–188/92 [1994] ECR I–833 the ECJ excluded, in certain circumstances, the possibility of referring a question of validity. The ECJ precluded the beneficiary of aid (which was the subject of a decision adopted on the ground of art 88 EC and who could have challenged its validity but let the prescribed time limit under art 230 EC elapse) from challenging the validity of measures implementing a decision adopted by national authorities in proceedings before a national court. This means that when an applicant does not bring an action in annulment under art 230 EC within the prescribed time limit national courts are precluded from making a reference to the ECJ under art 234 EC in respect of the validity of such an act.

In *Eurotunnel SA and Others* v *SeaFrance* Case C–408/95 [1997] ECR I–6315 the ECJ clarified its decision in *TWD Textilwerke*: if a Community act is addressed to natural or legal persons and thus they are directly and individually concerned, they will be precluded from challenging the validity of that act in the context of a preliminary ruling if they have not brought an action for annulment pursuant to art 230 EC within the prescribed time limit. In this respect the ECJ transposed its solution regarding EC regulations to EC directives: *Accrington Beef* Case C–241/95 [1996] ECR 6699. In *Eurotunnel* the challenged Community directives were addressed in general terms to Member States. They offered an option to them which *a priori* precluded the applicants from being directly concerned by the directives. In addition, the challenged provisions were not directly applicable to the applicants. As a result, it would have been extremely difficult for Eurotunnel to establish *locus standi* under art 230 EC even though in some cases the ECJ has accepted an action for annulment challenging EC directives addressed to the Member States provided the applicants were directly and individually concerned: *Gibraltar* Case C–298/89 [1993] ECR I–3605; *P Asocarne* Case C–10/95 [1995] ECR I–4149.

Effect of a preliminary ruling on validity

The peculiarity of the legal effects of preliminary rulings on the validity of Community acts derives from their close connection with actions for annulment under art 231, as well as the distinction between a preliminary ruling confirming the validity of the act concerned and a ruling declaring that act invalid. In the first case, the referring court, as well as all other courts and tribunals within the meaning of art 234 EC, may apply the act or if they believe, based on other considerations, that it is invalid refer again to the ECJ under art 234 EC.

However, if the ECJ declares the challenged act invalid the situation is different. In *International Chemical Company* Case 66/80 [1981] ECR 1191 the ECJ held that although the preliminary ruling declaring a Community act invalid is addressed to the referring national court, it constitutes at the same time sufficient justification for all other national judges to consider the act in question invalid in respect of judgments they may render. However, the ECJ added that its declaration in respect of invalidity of a Community act should not prevent national courts from referring again a question already decided by the ECJ if there are problems regarding the scope or possible legal implications of the act previously declared invalid. The extent of the ECJ's liberal approach in this area is illustrated in *Giuliani* Case 32/77 [1977] ECR 1863 in which the ECJ agreed to answer a question as to whether it still maintained its position in respect of an act previously declared invalid. This approach is justified by the fact that a Community act declared invalid under art 234 EC is still in force. Only the Community institution which adopted the act in question is empowered to annul or modify it, as well as to compensate the damage it caused. In addition, only national authorities are entitled to nullify a national provision which was adopted in order to implement or to apply an invalid act: *Rey-Soda* Case 23/75 [1975] ECR 1279. In this context it is important to note that the ECJ may declare only a part of the act invalid: *Express Dairy Foods* Case 130/79 [1981] ECR 1887. The analogy with the effects of a successful action for annulment is obvious. For that reason, the ECJ decided that it is in each case empowered to specify the particular consequences deriving from the invalidity of an act.

First, the ECJ held that it had jurisdiction to limit the temporal effect of preliminary rulings. In principle, all preliminary rulings have retroactive effect, including those confirming or denying the validity of Community acts: *Rückdeschel* Cases 117/76 and 16/77 [1977] ECR 1753. The ECJ has applied by analogy art 231(2) EC in the context of article 234 EC. In *Produits de Maïs* Case 112/83 [1985] ECR 742 the ECJ held that the coherence of the Community legal order provides sufficient justification for the application of art 231 EC in the context of art 234 EC. When the ECJ decides that a regulation is invalid *ex nunc* (ie with effect from the date of the decision but only as to the future) under art 234 EC the referring court is barred from drawing any consequences from the ECJ declaration on invalidity of the act, even for the parties to the main action in which the question of validity arose: *Providence Agricole de Champagne* Case 4/79 [1980] ECR 2823. This solution has been strongly criticised by national courts which consider that the ECJ has encroached upon their jurisdiction, since under art 234 EC national courts have to apply Community law to the main dispute.[33] The justification provided by the ECJ was based on the principle of legal

---

[33] For example, the judgment of 26 June 1985 of the French Conseil d'Etat in *ONIC v Société Maïseries de Beauce* [1985] AJDA 615, concl Genevois; or the judgment of 21 April 1989 of the Italian Constitutional Court in *Fragd* [1989] RDI 103.

certainty. The strong opposition of national courts was taken into account by the ECJ in *Roquette* Case C–228/92 [1994] ECR I–1445 in which it held that the exceptional effect *ex nunc* should not deprive those who had already commenced proceedings or made an equivalent claim of the rights stemming from the recognition of invalidity of Community acts. *Inter alia*, for that reason in many cases the ECJ applies the solution in *Defrenne*, that is, the temporal limitations are not imposed upon either the parties to the main action or those who had already brought legal proceedings or made an equivalent claim prior to the date of the judgment: *Pinna* Case 41/84 [1986] ECR 1.

Second, the ECJ has authorised itself to replace the invalidated provisions by appropriate alternatives while the adoption of required measures by the institution concerned is awaited: *Van Landshoot* Case 300/86 [1988] ECR 3443.

Third, the ECJ has reserved to the Community institution concerned the exclusive right to draw conclusions from the invalidity of its act and to take the necessary measures to remedy the situation: *Moulins et Huileries de Point-à-Mousson* Case 124/76 [1977] ECR 1795.

Interim relief

In the context of the validity of Community acts the question of interim measures arises with a particular intensity, although it may also have some importance in relation to the interpretation of Community law. Indeed, sometimes for a party to the proceedings the question of interim relief is vital if his rights under Community law are to have any substance. The ECJ in *Zuckerfabrik Suderdithmarschen* v *Hauptzollamt Itzehoe* Cases C–143/88 and 92/89 [1991] ECR I–415 established the conditions for obtaining interim relief. The referring court asked the ECJ to assess the validity of a regulation and to determine whether that court had jurisdiction to suspend a national administrative act based on that regulation. The ECJ replied that a national court could suspend the application of a national measure implementing a Community act until the ruling of the ECJ, provided that a ruling had been sought from the ECJ. The suspension is conditional upon the making of a reference to the ECJ by a national court. The suspension of the operation of a national measure is permitted only if certain stringent conditions are satisfied:

1. there must be a serious doubt as to the validity of the Community act;
2. the matter must be urgent;
3. there must be a risk to the applicant of serious and irreparable harm, that is, damages would not be an adequate remedy;
4. the interests of the Community must have been duly taken into account by the national court concerned.

The conditions for the suspension of national legislation which implements a Community act are the same as in an application for interim relief under art 230 EC. In *R* v *Secretary of State for Transport, ex parte Factortame (No 2)* Case C–213/89 [1990] ECR I–2433 the ECJ held that if national law prevented the court from granting interim relief such rule of national law should be set aside. In that case this led to the interim suspension of the operation of a statute.

In *Atlanta Fruchthandelsgesellschaft* v *BEF* Case C–465/93 [1995] ECR I–3761 the ECJ held that a national court may in certain circumstances grant interim relief from the application of a Community act. In this case Council Regulation 404/93 provided for a revised system of import quotas for bananas from non-ACP countries. The German Federal Food Office (BEF) granted Atlanta such reduced quotas. Atlanta challenged the Regulation and asked for interim relief. The German court asked the ECJ whether it could, while awaiting a preliminary ruling, by an interim order temporarily resolve the disputed legal positions and, if so, under what conditions and whether a distinction should be made between an interim order designated to preserve an existing legal position and one which was intended to create a new legal position.

The ECJ confirmed its reasoning in *Zuckerfabrik*, as well as its jurisdiction under art 243 EC, to order any necessary interim measure. In relation to the first question the ECJ held that:

> 'The interim legal protection which the national courts must afford to individuals under Community law must be the same, whether they seek suspension of enforcement of a national administrative measure adopted on the basis of a Community Regulation or the grant of interim measures settling or regulating the disputed legal positions or relationships for their benefit.'

As a result, a Community act may be suspended by a national court provided the latter has made reference to the ECJ under art 230 EC. As to the conditions they are very stringent. Indeed, to those laid down in *Zuckerfabrik* the ECJ added the following:

1. the national court must justify why it considers that the ECJ should find the Community measure invalid;
2. the national court must take into consideration the extent of the discretion allowed to the Community institutions resulting from the ECJ's case law;
3. the national court must assess the Community interest in the light of the impact of suspension on the Community legal regime and the appropriateness of financial guarantees or security;
4. the national court must take into account any previous art 230 judgments concerning the disputed legislation.

In the context of *Atlanta* it is interesting to note that under the ECJ's strict conditions for an interim order set out in this case Atlanta would never have obtained interim relief from a national court, taking into account that Regulation 404/93 was previously and unsuccessfully challenged in two actions under art 230, once by Atlanta, which could not satisfy the requirements for *locus standi*, and once by Germany.

The stringent requirements affecting interim measures were applied in *Emesa Sugar (Free Zone) NV* v *European Commission* Cases C–363 and 364/98P(R) [1998] ECR I–8815. The company Emesa, recognised as taking part in the Lomé agreement between the EU and the ACP countries, located on the island of Aruba, transformed sugar intended for export to the EU. The Council Decision 97/803/EC of 25 July 1997 provided for a revised system of import quotas for sugar from ACP/PTOM limiting them to 30,000 tonnes per annum and thus modified its Decision 91/482/EEC regarding the terms of association of French overseas territories with the Community. Emesa challenged that decision under art 230 EC and in separate proceedings asked for its suspension on the ground of urgency and the irreparable harm that its continuous application would cause to Emesa, namely bankruptcy. The Court of First Instance rejected the application for this interim measure on the basis that damage would be purely financial and therefore could not be considered as irreparable, and that Emesa had not submitted any evidence as to the threat of bankruptcy even though one of its factories had already been closed and another had temporarily ceased activity as a result of the challenged decision. Emesa contested the decision of the CFI before the ECJ, arguing that the CFI should have first examined the matter of urgency and then the question of harm and that the CFI erroneously assessed both conditions for granting an interim measure, that is that damage would be an adequate remedy and that the matter of urgency must be incontestably proved by Emesa.

The ECJ instead of itself delivering a decision regarding interim measures by virtue of art 54(1) of its Statute referred the case back to the Court of First Instance. This meant that the question of interim measures was further delayed which might have resulted in the bankruptcy of Emesa. For Emesa the question of interim relief was vital if its rights under Community law were to have any substance. It seems that one has to take time in matters of urgency in order to be granted interim relief!

The ECJ annulled the order of the Court of First Instance, although it referred the matter back to the CFI. The Court confirmed that in the context of interim measures the CFI enjoyed a large measure of discretion and that it may examine the conditions for granting such measures in the order it prefers, that is, urgency before the question of *fumus bonu juris*. The ECJ confirmed that the burden of proof is on the applicant.

In general, it is very difficult for the applicant to obtain interim relief, in particular in the context of Community measures adopted to protect public health. This is well illustrated in *R Pfizer Animal Health SA/NV* v *Council of the European Union* Case T–13/99 and *Alpharma Inc* v *Council of the European Union* Case T–70/99R [1999] 3 CMLR 79.

Under a Council regulation adopted on 17 December 1998 four antibiotics, including virginiamycin and bacitracin zinc, were withdrawn from the list of additives authorised for use in animal feed and banned from sale in all Member States with effect from 1 July 1999. Both named antibiotics, when administered regularly, boost animals' growth. Both are also used in human medicine. Pfizer Animal Health SA/NV, a company incorporated under Belgian law, the sole producer of virginiamycin, and Alpharma Inc, a company established in the USA, which was a producer of bacitracin zinc, challenged the Council regulation under art 230 EC and at the same time applied for the immediate suspension of its operation.

The President of the Court of First Instance dismissed the application on the ground that the protection of public health must prevail over economic considerations. 'Mad cow disease' and the 'dioxin' scandal have made the Community institutions, including the Community judicature, very sensitive to the requirement of the protection of public health.

The application of the principle of precaution was at the centre of the discussion. The applicant claimed that for the ban to be justified the risk to human health must be unacceptable. The applicant argued that there was no evidence that bacteria which had become resistant due to the feeding to livestock of antibiotic additives such as virginiamycin and bacitracin zinc may be transmissible from animals to human. The Council did not agree. It considered that the principle of precaution requires that the Council takes necessary measures in order to protect human health, unless there is scientific evidence proving that there is no risk to human health. The President of the Court of First Instance shared the Council's vision of protecting human health. The President of the CFI observed that since it was impossible to rule out that the use of the antibiotics in the raising of animals increases the risk of anti-microbial resistance in human medicine the contested regulation should be upheld. It is interesting to note that the President of the CFI, by weighing up the various interests and deciding that the protection of public health must take precedence over economic considerations, gave, at an early stage, a decision as to the substance of the matter and thus prejudged the final judgment of the CFI in this case. This is not his role in the context of proceedings for interim relief, although consumers should welcome his manner of assessing the circumstances in which the competent authorities should, as a precautionary step, adopt harsh measures in order to protect human health.

10 Free Movement of Goods

10.1 Creation of the internal market

10.1 Creation of the internal market

The creation of a common market where goods, people, services and capital move freely was one of the main objectives of the EC Treaty. The Single European Act (SEA) gave a new impetus to the achievement of this objective. The SEA replaced the term 'common market' by 'an internal market' and defined it as:

> '... an area without internal frontiers in which the free movement of goods, persons, services and capital in ensured in accordance with the provisions of the Treaty' (art 14 EC).

Based on a White Paper prepared by Lord Cockfield, more than 300 measures were introduced to bring the national markets of all Member States into one economic area without internal frontiers. The internal market was completed on 31 December 1992.

Whilst the Community has competence to take all appropriate measures with the aim of establishing the internal market, those measures are difficult to determine a *priori*. During the period leading up to the completion of the internal market the Community harmonised the laws in the Member States which directly affected its establishment and proper functioning. In this respect arts 100 and 100a EC Treaty (arts 94 and 95 EC) were most frequently used. However, the approach under art 100 EC Treaty (art 94 EC), consisting of legislative harmonisation of national technical standards across the Community, was too slow to achieve the objective of a single market. For that reason a new approach to technical harmonisation and standards was adopted by Council Resolution of 7 May 1985. Directives adopted under the new approach set out 'essential requirements', such as safety requirements or other requirements in the general interests, and attestation procedures on the basis of which it is determined whether the product in question meets these requirements. If it does, it carries a CE mark. A Member State cannot, on technical grounds, refuse access to a national market for such a product.

The new strategy focuses on two issues:

1. The prevention of new technical barriers to intra-Community trade. The Community tries to tackle this problem by exchanging information on national measures allowed under art 30 EC within a procedure established under Decision 3052/95[1] and Directive 83/189[2] as amended many times.[3] The Directive requires the Member States to notify

---

[1] OJ L321 (1995).

[2] OJ L109 (1983).

[3] Repealed and amended by Council Directive 98/48/EC of the European Parliament and of the Council laying down a Procedure for the Provision of Information in the Field of Technical Standards and Regulations and of Rules on Information Society Services: OJ L217 (1998).

their draft technical regulations to the Commission and other Member States, thus providing the Commission with an opportunity to verify their conformity with EC law and, if necessary, to exercise its right to impose a standstill.

2. The harmonisation of European standards by European standardisation bodies. There are three standardisation bodies (the European Committee for Standardisation, the European Committee for Electrotechnical Standardisation and the European Telecommunications Standards Institute) which draft proposals for European standards for a wide range of products

The free movement of goods is the foundation of the Single European Market (SEM). It involves the elimination of all obstacles to trade, such as customs duties and charges having an equivalent effect (arts 23–25 EC), quantitative restrictions and all measures having equivalent effect (arts 28 and 29 EC), although art 30 EC provides for exceptions to arts 28 and 29 EC. It also prohibits discriminatory internal taxation upon goods of other Member States: art 90 EC. The topic of the free movement of goods within the framework of the internal market encompasses such areas as State aid and subsidies (arts 87–89 EC) *per se* in breach of art 28 EC, but which are still considered as necessary elements of national economic policy. Because Member States often favour national contractors in major public contracts for the supply of goods, work and services to public authorities and utilities the matter of public procurement of both goods and services is included when considering the internal market. The EC has adopted a number of measures to combat domestic bias.

The free movement of people and services allows EC nationals to work as employees or self-employed persons anywhere in the EU, and be treated without discrimination based on nationality in the host Member State. There are still some obstacles to the exercise of the right to free movement of workers, the right of establishment and the provision of services, especially in relation to the recognition of professional qualifications.

Under the freedom of establishment and the freedom to provide services the self-employed enjoy rights similar to those of workers. The right of establishment means that any EC national is entitled to set himself up in whichever Member State he wishes and to conduct business under the conditions laid down for the nationals of that State. The exercise of the rights of establishment and to provide services are also granted to companies and firms established in Member States of the EU. The free movement of services is hindered by the fact that the service sector is difficult to deregulate.

The ability for capital to move freely has been successfully accomplished. Directive 88/361[4] eliminated all restrictions on movement of capital and ensured access to the financial systems and products of all Member States.

The European Union is the biggest internal market in the world. It is 40 per cent larger than that of the United States. In general, Member States have successfully implemented almost all legislation necessary to the proper functioning of the internal market. By November 1997 26.7 per cent of internal market legislation had not been implemented as compared with 12.6 per cent in November 1999, by which time ten of the 15 Member Staters had an implementation deficit below 4 per cent.

As a result of abolition of internal borders the need for 70 million documents was

---

[4] OJ L178 (1988).

obviated. Between 1997 and 1998 alone the value of intra-EU foreign investment doubled. Mergers and acquisitions within the EU trebled between 1986 and 1992 and reached a new record level in 1998. Service providers account for more than half of merger activity (53 per cent of all deals in 1998 against 42 per cent in 1992). Price dispersion for private consumption between the EU countries has fallen from 23 per cent in 1990 to an estimated 14.7 per cent in 1998. Since 1993 growth in intra-Community manufacturing trade has outpaced GPD growth.

The internal market has reached a stage of maturity which requires not only the enforcement of existing Community legislation but essentially the improvement of the market's efficiency, internally and internationally. These objectives have been addressed by the Community. In the international context the EU is involved in multilateral trade negotiations within the framework of the World Trade Organisation (WTO). In respect of the internal dimension, on 24 November 1999 the Commission adopted a Communication setting out its strategy for the internal market for the next five years. The strategy focuses on four main objectives, namely: improving the quality of life of citizens of the EU; enhancing the efficiency of the Community product and capital markets; improving the business environment; and exploiting the achievements of the internal market in a changing world. Within each of these objectives, the strategy includes specific target actions whose implementation and level of priority will be assessed periodically.

The European Council meeting held in Lisbon on 23–24 March 2000 addressed the issues of European competitiveness with a view to transforming the EU into the most competitive and dynamic knowledge-based economy in the world. The Summit provided the EU's response to the change in the world economy driven by globalisation and rapid technological development. The Summit approved a far-reaching integrated strategy combining a wide range of different policies, at the centre of which is the internal market. For each policy specific targets were set out with deadlines for action.[5] In respect of the internal market, the Summit expressed its commitment to accelerate the pace of structural reforms and, in particular, emphasised that low cost utilities are a pre-condition of competitiveness. For that reason, the Summit called for greater liberalisation in areas such as gas, electricity, postal services and transport (a deadline was set for the end of 2000). Also public procurement, especially its opening up to EU-wide competition, was recommended (by 2003 all necessary steps must be taken for EC and governmental procurement to take place on-line).

---

[5] See 'The Lisbon Summit: Concrete Action to Stimulate European Competitiveness', 21 Single Market News, May 2000, pI–II.

11 Customs Union

11.1   External aspect of the customs union between the Member States of the EU

11.2   Internal aspect of the customs union between the Member States of the EU

Article 23 EC provides that the customs union between the Member States covers all trade in goods. The ECJ defined 'goods' as all products which have a monetary value and may be the object of commercial transactions: *Jägerskiöld* Case 97/98 [2000] 1 CMLR 235. This definition was extended in *Commission v Belgium* Case C–2/90 [1992] ECR I–4431 to include waste. In this case the ECJ refused to make a distinction between recyclable waste which has commercial value and non-recyclable waste which has no intrinsic value. Accordingly, there are now in free circulation between Member States not only goods which have commercial value but also goods which are capable of generating costs for undertakings.

The Treaty applies to consumer goods including medical products (*Schumacher* Case 215/87 [1989] ECR 617) and goods originating in non-Member States which have completed customs formalities at the external frontier of the EU and are in free circulation between Member States.

In *R v Thompson* Case 7/78 [1978] ECR 2247 the ECJ held that gold and silver collectors' coins should, provided they were not in circulation as legal tender, be regarded as goods within the meaning of the Treaty. In *Commission v Ireland (Re Dundalk Water Supply)* Case 45/87 [1988] ECR 4929 the ECJ held that goods and materials supplied in the context of the provision of services are also included. However, advertisement materials, lottery tickets which are sold in one Member State for a lottery organised in another Member State (*Schindler* Case C–275/92 [1994] ECR I–1039) and the supply of goods such as car body parts, oils, etc, for the repair of vehicles (*Van Schaik* Case C–55/93 [1994] ECR I–4837) in another Member State are outside the scope of art 23 EC but covered by the provisions of the EC Treaty relating to the free movement of services. Therefore, not necessarily anything that can be valued in money and may be the subject of market transactions is considered as 'goods' within the meaning of art 23 EC. Other provisions of the EC Treaty may be concerned, for example, shares, bonds and other securities which can be valued in money and form the subject of commercial transactions concern the free movement of capital; the organisation of lotteries (*Schindler*) is not related to goods but to the provision of services.

Any customs union has two dimensions: internal, which involves the creation of a single customs territory between the participating States in which all customs duties and other restrictions on trade between the participating States are abolished; and external, which requires that the same customs duties and trade regulations apply to trade with all non-participating States. Article 23 EC regulates both external and internal aspects of the customs union. It states that:

'The Community shall be based upon a customs union which shall cover all trade in goods and which shall involve the prohibition between Member States of customs duties on imports and exports and of all charges having equivalent effect, and the adoption of a common customs tariff in their relations with third countries.'

The transformation of the EU customs union into the EU single market has brought substantial changes to the functioning of the EU. This has resulted in a number of provisions of the Treaty of Amsterdam being amended or repealed. In addition, the creation of a single market has brought new challenges for customs officials in all 15 Member States as it requires efficient, high-quality controls at the external borders.

Although the achievements of the EU in respect of customs integration are spectacular, taking into account that all internal customs duties have been eliminated and the internal market put in place, the road ahead will not be easy because of challenges posed by an increasingly globalised economy and the future enlargement of the EU involving the integration of new Member States into the existing structure.

11.1 External aspect of the customs union between the Member States of the EU

The external dimension of the customs union is based on the Common Customs Tariff and the Common Commercial Policy. The first important step in shaping the external dimension of the customs union took place on 1 July 1968 with the establishment of a Common Customs Tariff (CCT) for industrial products coming from outside the Community. The CCT sets a specific rate of customs duty for each of the various products identified in a special nomenclature.[1] Under the Common Commercial Policy the Member States fix the tariff rates for customs charges due on goods imported into the Community. The system was substantially reformed in 1988 when the Combined Nomenclature (CN) was introduced by virtue of Council Regulation 2658/87. The CN is based on the International Convention on the Harmonised Commodity Description and Coding System and thus it uses the same nomenclature as the main commercial partners of the Community. The CN includes both the requirements of the CCT and the external trade statistics of the Community. Under Regulation 2658/87 each year a new regulation is adopted which applies from 1 January and which updates the CN and the rates of duty of the CCT. Alongside the CN, the Community applies the integrated Community tariff (TARIC, known as a 'working tariff') which is a data bank for use by national customs authorities.

In order to unify the Community rules and procedures in respect of trade with non-Member States the Council adopted Regulation 2913/92 on 12 October 1992. This established the Community Customs Code[2] which consolidated all of the Community customs legislation into a single text and set up a framework for the Community's import and export procedures. The most important provisions of the Community Customs Code

---

[1] Under art 26 EC the CCT must be fixed by the Council acting by a qualified majority on a proposal from the Commission.

[2] OJ L 302 (1992). It entered into force on 1 January 1994 and was subsequently amended by Regulation 82/92 which incorporated the results of the Uruguay Round and which entered into force on 1 January 1997.

relate to the Common Customs Tariff, the tariff classification of goods, the value of goods for customs purposes, the origin of goods, customs debts and their recovery, the appeal procedure against decisions of the customs authorities, etc.

Community customs law is administrated by national customs authorities. There are 130,000 customs officials in 15 Member States, and they are gatekeepers of the European Union. They collect customs duties and transfer them to the Community (minus 10 per cent which covers the administration expenses of national customs authorities). These customs duties represent the own resources of the Community. The Customs Code Committee, consisting of representatives of Member States and chaired by a representative of the Commission, supervises the functioning of the entire system.

The completion of the common market on 31 December 1992 necessitated substantial changes in respect of the external dimension of the Community customs union. The abolition of internal customs borders enhanced the importance of controls at the external borders and the need for the 15 different customs administrations to act as one entity. Article 135 EC, which was added by the Treaty of Amsterdam, reflects the new approach. It provides that the Council should take measures, acting in accordance with the procedure in art 251 EC, to strengthen customs co-operation between Member States and between the Commission and the Member States. Taking into account that customs intervention is no longer possible between the external border and the place of the final destination of goods, the EC introduced a number of initiatives in order to strengthen customs co-operation between the Member States. One of them is the Matthaeus programme, designed to prepare customs officials of Member States for the implications of the internal market, in particular the uniform application of Community legislation at the external borders. It consists of the exchange of customs officials and of vocational training for them.[3] However, the most interesting initiative was a comprehensive action programme for customs in the Community. Called Customs 2000, this was a five year programme (from 1 January 1996 to 31 December 2000). This aimed at modernising the national customs administrations and at increasing co-operation between them and the Commission in order to ensure that EC customs are applied uniformly at the external borders and that the single market works to the best effect. This programme, being very successful, has been extended and updated as 'Customs 2002'.[4] It provides, inter alia, for visits to customs posts by teams from the Commission and Member States in order to see customs procedures in action and to identify the best and the worst practices. It also provides for the support of the Commission for any action aimed, in particular, at strengthening the combating of fraud by improving customs administration methods, by using sophisticated new technology and by the exchange, analysis and exploitation of information,

The adoption by the Council on 18 December 1997 of an Act drawing up the Convention on Mutual Assistance and Co-operation between Customs Administrations was of vital importance.[5]

---

[3] Council Decision 91/341/EEC: OJ L187 (1991). In the first year of its existence about 1,800 customs officials participated in exchanges. It is considered by the Commission as a very successful programme. Each year a report is published by the Commission on the implementation of the Matthaeus programme.

[4] OJ C317 (1999).

[5] OJ C24 (1988).

11.2 Internal aspect of the customs union between the Member States of the EU

The customs union constitutes the foundation of the European Union's internal market. On 1 January 1993 the single market became a reality and all customs borders between Member States were abolished. Spot checks may take place for drugs and immigration purposes but routine border checks were abolished. Since 1 January 1993 customs officials in all 15 Member States have worked more for the Community than for national governments.

The Treaty of Amsterdam reflects the changes which have taken place. It repealed arts 13–17 EC Treaty which laid down a timetable for the abolition of customs duties and charges having equivalent effect. The completion of the Common market 'an area without internal frontiers' made them redundant. However, the main provision which prohibits 'customs duties on imports and exports or any charges having equivalent effect' between Member States still remains: art 25 EC. The main reason for its existence is that despite the fact customs duties on imports and exports have disappeared, it is always possible for a Member State to unilaterally impose charges which, although at first glance are not customs duties, are in fact equivalent to them.

12 The Prohibition of Customs Duties and All Charges Having Equivalent Effect

12.1 Articles 23 and 25 EC

12.2 Charges imposed on both domestic and imported products

12.3 Exceptions to the prohibition

12.1 Articles 23 and 25 EC

In *Van Gend en Loos* Case 26/62 [1963] ECR 1 the ECJ ruled that art 25 EC was directly effective. Article 25 EC has been strictly interpreted by the ECJ. In *Germany v Commission* Cases 52–55/65 [1966] ECR 159 the ECJ held that the prohibition of customs duties and charges having equivalent effect constituted the 'logical and necessary complement' to the creation of a customs union between Member States and *a fortiori* the common market, and should be considered as 'a basic norm, and any exceptions must be clearly and unambiguously provided for'.

There is no definition of 'charges having equivalent effect to customs duties' in the Treaty. The ECJ in *Commission v Italy (Re Statistical Levy)* Case 24/68 [1969] ECR 193 defined charges having equivalent effect to a customs duty as:

'... any pecuniary charge, however small and whatever its designation and mode of application, which is imposed unilaterally on goods by reason of the fact that they cross a frontier and which is not a custom duty in the strict sense ... even if it is not imposed for the benefit of the State, is not discriminatory or protective in effect and if the product on which the charge is imposed is not in competition with any domestic product.'

The Community judicature has clearly defined not only this concept but also the scope of application of art 25 EC. Its case law shows that to be classified as such, a charge having equivalent effect to a customs duty has the following characteristics:

1. It must be a pecuniary charge. Other obstacles are within the scope of the provisions relating to the free movement of goods: *Bauhuis* Case 46/76 [1977] ECR 5.
2. Its amount is irrelevant. Even a small charge or a charge below the direct and indirect costs of services provided by the customs authorities[1] is prohibited by art 25 EC.
3. It may result not only from a unilateral measure imposed by a Member State or other public authorities but also from an agreement concluded between individuals. In *Dubois et Fils SA and General Cargo Services v Garoner (GA) Exploitation SA* Case C–16/94 [1995] ECR I–2421 Dubois and General Cargo, forwarding agents, refused to pay a

---

[1] See *Bakkers Hillegom* Case C–111/89 [1990] ECR I–1735.

'transit charge' imposed on them by GE, the owner of an international road station near Paris where the customs authorities had offices. GE imposed the charge for vehicles completing customs clearance at their station in order to offset the costs of having the customs authorities on their premises. Dubois and General Cargo argued that a 'transit charge' was in breach of art 25 EC. The ECJ held that a 'transit charge' was within the scope of art 25 EC, although it was not imposed by a Member State but resulted from an agreement concluded between a private undertaking (GE) and its customers (Dubois and General Cargo)

4. Its designation and mode of application is irrelevant for the application of art 25 EC. Thus, it is considered as a charge having equivalent effect whether it is called a special charge,[2] or a 'price supplement',[3] or a fee levied in order to defray the costs of compiling statistical data.[4]

5. Its beneficiaries or its destination are irrelevant. In *Sociaal Fonds v Brachfeld and Chougol Diamond Co* Cases 2 and 3/69 [1969] ECR 211 a levy imposed under Belgian law on imported diamonds which was not protectionist (Belgium is not a producer of diamonds), but was designated to provide social security benefits for workers in the diamond industry, was regarded as contrary to art 25 EC. Similarly, a charge the purpose of which was to protect the historical and artistic heritage of a Member State was considered as unlawful: *Commission v Italy* Case 7/68 [1968] ECR 617.

6. It must be imposed by the reason of, or on the occasion of, the crossing of a frontier by goods, but the time and the place of imposition is not relevant. In *Firma Steinike und Weinlig v Bundesamt für Ernährung und Forstwirtschaft* Case 78/76 [1977] ECR 595 the ECJ held that a charge need not be levied at a border. Even a regional frontier is included. In *Lancry and Others v Direction Générale des Douanes and Others* Joined Cases C–363 and 407–411/93 [1994] ECR I–3957 the charge called 'dock dues' was imposed on all goods imported, irrespective of their country of origin, and including France itself, into French overseas territories. The purpose of 'dock dues' was to raise revenue in order to encourage the local economy. Lancry, who imported flour from France to Martinique, challenged 'dock dues' as contrary to art 25 EC. The ECJ held that a charge levied at a regional frontier is within the scope of art 25 EC. This provision expressly refers to intra-State trade because it is presumed that there are no internal obstacles to trade within Member States. The abolition of internal taxes is a pre-condition of the creation of the customs union between Member States. The charge imposed at a regional frontier constituted 'at least as serious' an obstacle to the free movement of goods as a charge levied at national frontiers. Indeed, regional customs frontiers undermine the unity of the Community customs territory. Charges may be imposed prior to import, at the time of import or subsequently. Article 25 EC encompasses charges imposed at any stage of production or marketing if levied by reason of importation: *Firma Steinike und Weinlig* Case 78/76 [1977] ECR 595.

7. Compensatory taxes are also charges having equivalent effect. In *Commission v Luxembourg (Re Gingerbread)* Cases 2 and 3/62 [1962] ECR 813 the governments of

---

[2] See *Commission v Luxembourg* Cases 2 and 3/62 [1962] ECR 813.
[3] See *Fratelli Cucchi v Avez SpA* Case 77/76 [1977] ECR 987.
[4] See *Commission v Italy (Re Statistical Levy)* Case 24/68 [1969] ECR 193.

Luxembourg and Belgium imposed a special import duty on imported gingerbread in order to compensate for the price difference between domestic gingerbread and imported gingerbread, the domestic gingerbread being more expensive as the result of high internal rate of taxation on rye. The ECJ held that a special import duty levied on imported gingerbread was a charge having effect equivalent to a customs duty. The objective of the tax was not to equalise the taxes on gingerbread but to equalise the very price of it!

12.2 Charges imposed on both domestic and imported products

There are three categories of charge: charges imposed solely on imported goods, charges imposed on both domestic and imported goods and charges imposed exclusively on domestic goods. Each category must be examined in the light of art 25 EC.

Charges imposed solely on imported goods

If a charge is imposed only on imported products, and provided it does not constitute one of the exceptions to the prohibition laid down in art 25 EC, it is clearly in breach of that provision. There are no possible justifications for it.

Charges imposed on both domestic and imported goods

In this respect it is important to distinguish whether a charge is imposed in the same way on domestic products and on imported products and assess its purpose.

In *Marimex SpA v Italian Minister of Finance* Case 29/72 [1972] ECR 1309 (see also *Denkavit v France* Case 132/78 [1979] 3 CMLR 605) a charge imposed on both domestic and imported meat in respect of a veterinary inspection carried out in order to verify whether meat satisfied health standards required by Italian legislation was held unlawful by the ECJ. This was on the ground that the inspections of imported meat were conducted by a body different from that inspecting domestic meat and which applied criteria different from those applied by the domestic meat inspection body.

Even if charges imposed on both domestic and imported products are applied in the same way and according to the same criteria they may be in breach of art 25 EC if the proceeds of the charge are to exclusively benefit domestic products. In *Capolongo v Azienda Agricola Maya* Case 77/72 [1973] ECR 611 (see also *Compagnie Commerciale de l'Ouest* Cases C–78–83/90 [1992] ECR I–1847) Italy imposed a charge on all egg boxes, domestic and imported, in order to finance the production of paper and cardboard in Italy. The charge constituted a part of an overall charge on cellulose products. The ECJ held that although the charge applied without discrimination both to domestically produced and imported egg boxes it was to benefit domestic manufacturers alone and as such was discriminatory and constituted a charge having equivalent effect to a customs duty. The strict approach adopted by the ECJ in this case was relaxed in subsequent cases. In *Fratelli Cucchi v Avez SpA* Case 77/76 [1977] ECR 987 the ECJ set out criteria which should be applied in order to assess whether a particular charge which is applied indiscriminately on both domestic and imported products is contrary to art 25 EC. In this case the same charge was levied on domestic and imported sugar but its proceeds were designated to finance the sugar industry, in particular to benefit two groups, the beet producers and the sugar-processing industry. The ECJ held that such a charge would be considered as being of equivalent effect to a customs duty if the following criteria were met:

1. if it has the sole purpose of financing activities for the specific advantage of domestic products;
2. if the domestic products on which a charge is imposed and the domestic products which are to benefit from it are the same; and
3. if the charge imposed on the domestic products was made in full.

When applying the above-mentioned criteria due regard must be had to other provisions of the EC Treaty, in particular art 90 EC prohibiting direct and indirect discriminatory taxation and art 87 EC on State aid. If domestic products only partially benefit from the proceeds of the charge, that charge may constitute a discriminatory tax in breach of art 90 EC. Also a charge may, in fact, be a form of state aid prohibited under the EC Treaty.

Charges imposed exclusively on domestic goods

The approach of the ECJ to charges which are imposed exclusively on domestic goods is different from that concerning imported products. It is, indeed, unusual for a Member State to discriminate against goods produced domestically and thus afford preferential treatment to imported goods. Such reverse discrimination was examined by the ECJ in *Apple and Pear Development Council v K J Lewis* Case 222/82 [1983] ECR 4083. The Apple and Pear Development Council, a semi-public body, was set up to conduct research, to provide information, to collect statistics and to promote the consumption of apples and pears in England and Wales. A domestic levy was imposed on apples and pears grown in England and Wales to finance the Council's activities. Lewis, a grower of apples and pears, refused to pay the compulsory levy as being contrary to EC law. The ECJ found that the levy did not apply to imported products and thus was compatible with art 25 EC. However, such a levy may be unlawful if it infringes art 29 EC. In *Irish Creamery Milk Suppliers' Association v Ireland* Cases 13 and 71/80 [1981] ECR 735 a charge solely applied to some Irish agricultural products at the time of delivery for processing, storage and export was at issue. The ECJ held that, if it had been possible to demonstrate that the charge fell more heavily on sales for export than on domestic products, the duty would have been be in breach of art 25 EC. However, that was not so in this case!

12.3 Exceptions to the prohibition

A pecuniary charge is deemed to escape the prohibition embodied in art 25 EC if it is levied for services rendered to the trader or a service required under Community law. Both exceptions, as with any exceptions to a general rule, have been strictly interpreted by the Community judicature.

A service rendered to the trader

Member States have tried to justify the imposition of charges on a number of grounds, the most popular being that a charge is in fact a fee paid for a service rendered to the trader. The first time this 'justification' was invoked was in *Germany v Commission* Joined Cases 52–55/65 [1966] ECR 159. The ECJ defined fees levied by Germany on importers for the provision of an import licence as a charge having equivalent effect to a customs duty on the ground that it did not bring any benefit to the importer.

The ECJ has gradually specified strict conditions which, when they apply cumulatively, allow a charge to escape the prohibition of art 25 EC. A charge levied on goods by reason of the fact that they cross a frontier is not a charge having equivalent effect to a customs duty if it constitutes consideration, for a specific service actually and individually rendered to the trader, proportionate to that service. Therefore a charge will be lawful if it satisfies three criteria:

The service must be of genuine benefit to the trader

The condition that a service must provide a genuine benefit to the trader is very difficult to satisfy taking into account the strict interpretation by the ECJ of a 'genuine benefit'. In *Commission v Italy (Re Statistical Levy)* Case 24/68 [1969] ECR 193 the Italian government imposed a levy on all imports and exports designed to finance the gathering of statistics. It argued that the statistical service was for the benefit of both importers and exporters. The ECJ held that the advantage provided to importers was too general and uncertain to be considered as a service rendered to the trader.

The assessment of a service which provides genuine benefit to the trader was further explained in *Commission v Belgium (Re Storage Charges)* Case 132/82 [1983] ECR 1649; [1983] 3 CMLR 600. In this case the Belgian authorities introduced a system whereby goods in Community transit could undergo customs clearance either at the border or in assigned warehouses within Belgium. If customs clearance in a warehouse was selected by the trader, the customs authorities imposed charges on the goods in respect of storage costs. The Commission took exception to the levying of these costs, alleging that they were charges having an equivalent effect to customs duties and as such were prohibited under arts 9, 12, 13 and 16 of the EC Treaty [art 25 EC]. The Commission brought proceedings against Belgium before the ECJ.

The ECJ held that charges which are assessed as part of the process of customs clearance on Community goods or goods in free circulation within the Community, constitute charges having equivalent effect if they are imposed solely in connection with the completion of customs formalities. The ECJ admitted that the use of a public warehouse in the interior of the country offered certain advantages to importers. Nevertheless, taking into account that such advantages were linked solely with the completion of customs formalities (which, whatever the place, were always compulsory) and that the storage charges were payable in any event when the goods were presented at the public warehouse solely for the purposes of completion of customs formalities, even though they had been exempted from storage and the importer had not requested that they be put in temporary storage, the charges were in breach of art 25 EC.

Member States have often tried to justify charges in respect of health inspections, arguing that they provide a benefit to the trader consisting of recognising the quality of imported goods. This justification was rejected by the ECJ. In *Rewe-Zentralfinanz GmbH* v *Direktor der Landwirtschaftskammer Westfalen-Lippe* Case 39/73 [1973] ECR 1039 charges imposed in relation to health inspections on apples were considered as charges having equivalent effect on the grounds that the inspections were not carried out for the specific benefit of the trader but for the public benefit as a whole. Similarly, in *Bresciani* v *Amministrazione Italiana delle Finanze* Case 87/75 [1976] ECR 129 the ECJ held that charges in respect of veterinary inspections carried out on imported raw cowhides were of equivalent effect to customs duties since the inspection was mandatory under Italian law, and thus did not provide a specific service to the importer as all importers were obliged to submit to the inspection. In addition, they were conducted in the general interest and thus the inspection fees should have been paid by the beneficiaries, that is the general public which benefits from the free movement of goods within the Community.

The service must provide a specific benefit to the trader

The service must be specific. This means that the trader must obtain a definite specific benefit, enhancing his personal interest, not the general interest of all traders operating in the particular sector of the economy. This condition was applied, for the first time, in *Cadsky* v *ICE* Case 63/74 [1975] ECR 281. Cadsky exported vegetables from Italy to Germany. The Italian government imposed a mandatory quality control on products crossing the Italian frontier for which it charged exporters. Cadsky refused to pay. The Italian government argued that the challenged fees represented payment for a service rendered to the trader since quality control constituted a recognition of quality of his products abroad and, in addition, contributed to the improvement of the reputation of Italian vegetables on external markets and thus enhanced the competitiveness of Italian products. The ECJ held that the charge did not constitute payment for a service rendered to the operator, because this condition is satisfied only if the operator in question obtains a definite specific benefit. In this case all Italian vegetables exporters benefited from the service.

The individualisation of the benefit as a condition justifying a charge was also evident in *Commission* v *Italy Case* 340/87 [1989] ECR 1483 in which Italian customs authorities offered traders, at their request, an opportunity to complete customs formalities outside business hours, for which a charge was levied. Working hours of the Italian customs officials were only six hours a day. The ECJ pointed out that Directive 83/643 (then in force) required customs posts to be open for at least ten hours a day, without interruption, from Mondays to Saturdays, and for at least six hours, without interruption, on Sundays. In addition, for a charge to escape the prohibition of art 25 EC it is necessary for the service provided to be genuine and individualised. In this case, the last condition was not satisfied. The ECJ held that Italy was in breach of EC law as it imposed fees on traders for administrative and customs formalities which were, partially, carried out during normal opening hours of customs posts. The opening hours for customs posts, being harmonised under an EC Directive, could not be considered as a specific service rendered to the trader.

341

The sum charged must be proportionate to the cost of the service

The third condition is that the sum charged for the service must be proportionate to the cost of that service. This condition was explained by the ECJ in *Ford España v Spain* Case 170/88 [1989] ECR 2305 in which a charge based on the value of goods was declared unlawful on the ground that it did not represent the actual costs of service. Ford España received a bill based on 1.65 per cent of their cars' value for clearance through customs and for other goods imported to Spain. The Spanish government argued that the sum represented fees for services rendered to Ford España. The ECJ accepted that in this case the service was genuine and the benefit was of the required specific nature. Nevertheless, the charge was in breach of art 25 EC as it was based not on the costs of the service but on the value of the goods and as such was not commensurate with the service.[5]

A mandatory service

If a service is required under Community law or under international law a Member State is allowed to charge for that service provided the amount charged does not exceed the real cost of providing the service.[6] This exception was examined by the ECJ in *Commission v Germany (Re Animals Inspection Fees)* Case 18/87 [1990] 1 CMLR 561.

In this case measures were brought into effect throughout the European Community by Council Directive 81/389 which permitted Member States to carry out veterinary inspections on live animals transported into or through their national territories. Certain German provinces, known as 'Länder', charged fees for the cost of conducting those inspections. The charges imposed were justified, according to the German government, to cover the actual costs incurred in maintaining the inspection facilities. The Commission argued that these charges amounted to charges having an equivalent effect to customs duties and could not be justified under the Directive. Accordingly, the Commission brought an action against Germany before the ECJ.

The ECJ held that charges imposed in relation to health inspections required by Community law are not to be regarded as having equivalent effect to custom duties if the following conditions are satisfied:

1. They do not exceed the actual costs of the inspections in connection with which they are charged.
2. The inspections in question are obligatory and uniform for all the products concerned in the Community. It should be noted that Directive 81/389 imposed on all Member States of transit and destination of live animals an obligation to carry out veterinary inspections and therefore the inspections were mandatory and uniform for all the animals concerned in the Community.
3. The inspections are prescribed by Community law in the general interests of the Community. Such inspections were prescribed by Directive 81/389 and the objective of the Directive was the protection of live animals during international transport. As a

---

[5] See also *Germany v Commission* Cases 52–55/65 [1966] ECR 159; *Rewe-Zentralfinanz v Landwirtschaftskammer Westfalen-Lippe* Case 39/73 [1973] ECR 1039.

[6] *Bauhuis v Netherlands* Case 4/76 [1977] ECR 5; *Commission v Netherlands* Case 89/76 [1977] ECR 1355; [1978] 3 CMLR 630; *IFG v Freistaat Bayern* Case 1/83 [1984] ECR 349; [1985] 1 CMLR 453.

result, inspections were carried out in the general interest of the Community and not a specific interest of individual States.

4. The inspections promote the free movement of goods, in particular by neutralising obstacles which could arise from unilateral measures of inspection adopted in accordance with art 30 EC.

The above-mentioned Directive harmonised the laws of the Member States regarding the protection of animals in international transport. The standardisation of the inspections promoted the free movement of goods, taking into account that it eliminated the possibility for a Member State to adopt measures restricting trade on grounds of the protection of the health and life of animals by virtue of art 30 EC.

The ECJ held that charges imposed in relation to health inspections were not charges having equivalent effect to a custom duty as they satisfied the above mentioned criteria. The fees represented charges genuinely incurred for such services did not amount to charges having equivalent effect to customs duties. The ECJ specified that the negative effect that such a fee may have on intra-Community trade could be eliminated only by virtue of Community provisions providing for the harmonisation of fees, or imposing the obligation on the Member States to bear the costs entailed in the inspections or, finally, establishing that the costs are to be paid out of the Community budget.

13 Discriminatory Internal Taxation

13.1 Direct, indirect and reverse discrimination

13.2 Article 90(1) EC: similar products

13.3 Article 90(2) EC: products in competition

13.4 The relationship between art 90 EC and other provisions of the EC Treaty relating to the free movement of goods

13.5 Harmonisation of taxation within the European Union

Article 90 EC provides:

> 'No Member State shall impose, directly or indirectly, on the products of other Member States any internal taxation of any kind in excess of that imposed directly or indirectly on similar domestic products.
>
> Furthermore, no Member State shall impose on the products of other Member States any internal taxation of such a nature as to afford indirect protection to other products.'

Fiscal barriers to trade may result not only from customs duties and charges having equivalent effect to them but also from the imposition on imported products of national taxes with which domestic products are not burdened. Article 90 EC guarantees that this will not happen. Its main objective is to ensure that the internal taxation system of a Member State makes no distinction between domestic and imported products. This was clearly stated by the ECJ in *Bergandi* Case 252/86 [1988] ECR 1343 in which it held that art 90 EC 'must guarantee the complete neutrality of internal taxation as regards competition between domestic products and imported products'.

However, art 90 EC applies only to products from the Member States and to products originating in non-Member States which are in free circulation in the Member States. It does not apply to products imported directly from non-Member States: *OTO* Case C–130/92 [1994] ECR I–3281.

In order to reduce the risk of the application of discriminatory internal taxation in respect of products from other Member States the ECJ, in one of its earliest judgments, recognised that art 90 EC is directly effective. In *Lütticke GmbH v Hauptzollamt Saarlouis* Case 57/65 [1966] ECR 205[1] the ECJ held that art 90 is clear, unconditional and not qualified by any condition, or subject to the requirement of legislative intervention on the part of the Community institutions. Consequently, it is of direct effect in the relationship between a Member State and an individual.

Article 90(1) EC deals with imported products which are so similar to domestic products

---

[1] See *Deutschmann v Federal Republic of Germany* Case 10/65 [1965] CMLR 259; *Haahr Petrolium* Case C–90/94 [1997] ECR I–4085.

that they require the same tax treatment. Article 90(2) EC refers to products which although not similar, are nevertheless in competition with domestic products, and thus domestic products should not be protected from competitive pressures by an internal system of taxation. Even partial, indirect and potential competition is taken into account.

If a Member State breaches art 90(1) EC the remedy consists of equalising taxes between similar domestic and imported products. However, if a Member State infringes art 90(2) EC it must remove the protectionist taxes which implies that often there will be a different rate of taxation in respect of competing products. In *Commission v United Kingdom (Re Tax on Beer and Wine)* Case 170/78 [1980] ECR 415 following the decision of the ECJ the UK removed the unlawful element of protection by adjusting tax rates for beer upwards and for wine downwards, but there were still different rates applied to both products.

13.1 Direct, indirect and reverse discrimination

Article 90 EC does not prohibit internal taxation. A Member State is free to set up a system of taxation which it considers as the most appropriate in respect of each product. The ECJ held in *Commission v France (Re Levy on Reprographic Machines)* Case 90/79 [1981] ECR 283 that a genuine tax is a measure relating to a system of internal dues applied systematically to categories of products in accordance with objective criteria irrespective of the origin of the products.

Direct discrimination

Direct discrimination against imported products is easy to spot. For that reason, there are only a limited number of cases in which the Community judicature has identified direct discrimination against imported products. It happened in *Lütticke GmbH v Hauptzollamt Saarlouis* Case 57/65 [1966] ECR 205. Lütticke imported wholemilk powder from Luxembourg on which the German customs levied duty and a turnover tax. Lütticke challenged a claim for payment of turnover tax on the ground that domestic natural milk and wholemilk powder were exempt from it.

The ECJ insists on equal treatment of domestic and imported products, even though in some instances an internal tax may be beneficial to most importers and disadvantageous only to a few of them. In *Bobie Getränkevertreieb v Hauptzollamt Aachen-Nord* Case 127/75 [1976] ECR 1079 German legislation on beer provided for one rate of taxation for domestic beer, which rate increased in proportion to the output of the brewery (from DM 12 to 15 per hectolitre), and a different rate for imported beer which was taxed at a flat rate (DM 14.40 per hectolitre). The objective of the variable domestic rate was to ensure the survival of small German breweries. An importer of large quantities of beer from another Member State was better off as compared to a large German brewer as the former paid DM 0.60 less per hectolitre of beer. However, an importer of small quantities of beer from another Member State was at a disadvantage as compared to a German brewer of a similar size. He was taxed at DM 14.40 rather than DM 12 per hectolitre. The ECJ held that the German legislation on the taxation of beer was in breach of art 90 EC. The Court rejected the argument of

Germany that the overall effect of a national taxation system should be taken into consideration. The ECJ emphasised that any discrimination is incompatible with art 90 EC and thus two different systems of taxation, one which applies to domestic products and another which deals with similar imported products, cannot be justified. Despite the fact that the tax system which applied to imported products ensured broad equivalence, it nevertheless, in some cases, placed importers at a comparative disadvantage. A Member State must choose a system, whichever it considers the most appropriate, in respect of all the similar taxed products. In this case the German Bundesfinanzhof rejected the argument of the claimant that all imported beer should be taxed at a flat rate of DM 12 per hectolitre. It stated that the variable rate should be upheld but applied indiscriminately to all domestic and imported beer.

Article 90 EC also ensures that if treatment which would otherwise be preferential is given to domestic products it must be extended to similar imported products. In *Commission v Italy (Re Regenerated Oil)* Case 21/79 [1980] ECR 1[2] Italy levied lower charges on regenerated oil than on ordinary oil on the grounds of protection of the environment, but refused to extend this advantage to imported regenerated oil. Italy justified its refusal on the basis that it was impossible to distinguish, by means of the then experimental testing methods, whether imported oil was of primary distillation, or regenerated. Italy argued that taking into account the very high production costs of regenerated oils as compared to oils of primary distillation, and the impossibility of distinguishing them, many importers would claim the benefit of the lower tax rates and thus avoid paying the higher rates of tax imposed on ordinary oils. This would lead to tax evasion in respect of imported products. The ECJ disagreed. It held that imported products should not, in any way, be prevented from obtaining the same tax advantages as products produced in Italy. It was for the importers, who wished to enjoy the lower tax rate, to prove that the oils imported were regenerated. Although the Italian authorities were entitled to require some evidence that removed the risk of tax evasion, they could not set standards of proof higher than necessary. The ECJ held that, for example, certificates issued by appropriate authorities of the exporting Member State should provide sufficient evidence.

Reverse discrimination

It is extremely rare that a Member State imposes higher taxes on domestic goods than on identical or similar imported goods. It may, for example, occur if a Member State intends to discourage export of a valuable scarce commodity (*Statens Kontrol v Larsen* Case 142/77 [1978] ECR 1543) and, indeed, there are other possible circumstances. In *Grandes Distilleries Peureux v Directeur des Services Fiscaux* Case 86/78 [1979] ECR 89 France imposed higher taxes on domestic alcohol than on imported alcohol which resulted in domestic products suffering a comparative disadvantage. The ECJ held that discriminatory treatment against domestic goods as compared with imports was outside the scope of art 90 EC. The main consideration of art 90 EC is to ensure neutrality of the system of internal

---

[2] See also *Hansen v Hauptzollamt Flensburg* Case 148/77 [1978] ECR 1787; *Schneider-Import* Case 26/80 [1980] ECR 3469.

taxation in respect of imported products. However, the principle of tax neutrality also entails that goods for export on which a higher tax is imposed than on other domestic goods is within the scope of art 90 EC, as a higher tax imposed on such products may affect the pattern of trade between Member States. The neutrality of the internal taxation is not challenged when lower taxes are imposed on goods for export than on other domestic goods since this does not create an obstacle to the free movement of goods. Only domestic goods destined for the home market are affected.

Indirect discrimination

Direct discriminatory taxation is easy to detect in the light of the strict prohibition embodied in art 90 EC. As a result, Member States have tended to try to conceal by subtle means discriminatory internal charges imposed on imported products. This was examined in *Humblot v Directeur des Services Fiscaux* Case 112/84 [1985] ECR 1367. Under French law the annual tax on cars in France differentiated between cars below 16 hp (the tax rate was progressively increased up to a maximum of FF 1,100) and above 16 hp (a flat rate tax of FF 5,000 was applied). France did not manufacture cars above 16 hp. Consequently, all French-made cars were subject to a maximum tax of FF 1,100, but all imported cars more powerful than 16 hp were subject to a higher tax. Humblot, who bought a Mercedes in France, challenged the French law. The ECJ held that the French law was in breach of art 90 EC as it was protectionist and discriminatory in respect of cars imported from other Member States. It did indirectly discriminate against imported cars, although there was no formal distinction between imported and domestic cars.

As can be seen, not only the rate of direct and indirect internal taxation on domestic and imported products but also the basis of assessment and rules regarding the imposition of the tax are important in determining whether there is a breach of art 90 EC.

Commission v Hellenic Republic Case C–375/95 [1997] ECR I–5981 provides an interesting example. In this case the Commission brought proceedings against the Hellenic Republic for introducing and maintaining in force the following national rules contrary to art 90 EC Treaty:

1. Article 1 of Greek Law No 363/1976, as amended by Law No 1676/1986, relating to a special consumer tax applicable to imported used cars under which in the assessment of their taxable value only a 5 per cent reduction of the selling price of equivalent new cars was permitted for each year of age of the used cars and the maximum reduction was fixed at 20 per cent of the value of equivalent new cars.
2. Article 3(1) of Law No 363/1976, which was replaced by art 2(7) of Law No 2187/1994, concerning the determination of the taxable value of cars in order to levy the flat-rate added special duty which contained no reduction for used cars.
3. Article 1 of Law No 1858/1989, as amended many times, regarding the reduction of a special consumer tax for anti-pollution technology cars applied only to new cars and not to imported used cars with the same technology.

The Commission stated that the Greek government was in breach of art 90 EC since the above-mentioned legislation created a system of internal taxation which indirectly discriminated against used cars imported from the other Member States in comparison with cars bought in Greece. The Greek government rejected the arguments of the Commission.

The ECJ held that national rules for calculating special consumer tax and flat-rate added duty in order to determine the taxable value of imported used cars were in breach of art 90 EC. In respect of the special consumer tax applicable only to imported used cars, the ECJ rejected the argument submitted by Greece that the special consumer tax was also applied to domestic used cars when they were first purchased within the country, and that part of it remained incorporated in the value of those cars. The ECJ emphasised that the special consumer tax on imported used cars was usually higher than the proportion of the tax still incorporated in the value of used cars already registered and purchased on the Greek market, taking into account that the annual depreciation in the value of cars is considerably more than 5 per cent, that depreciation is not linear, especially in the first years when it is much more marked than subsequently, and, finally, that vehicles continue to depreciate more than four years after being put into circulation.

Also the ECJ condemned a special consumer tax for anti-pollution technology cars, which was applied only to new cars and not to imported used cars with the same technology, as being in breach of art 90 EC. Thus, the ECJ held that the Hellenic Republic failed to fulfil its obligations under art 90 EC.

Assessment of taxation

The ECJ has interpreted the term 'directly or indirectly' broadly. Article 90 EC applies not only to national taxation systems that discriminate according to the origin of goods but also to any tax which on its face discriminates on the basis of other factors and results in placing imported products at a disadvantage as compared with domestic products. In *Molkerei-Zentrale v Hauptzollamt Paderborn* Case 28/67 [1968] CMLR 187 the ECJ held that tax must be imposed at the same stage in the marketing chain. Thus, a Member State when calculating the rate of taxation in respect of an imported product must take into consideration all taxes levied on domestic products at earlier stages of their production, including charges levied on raw materials and semi-finished products. However, the ECJ emphasised that the importance of these charges diminishes in inverse proportion to the number of completed stages of production and distribution. This factor should also be taken into account by a Member State when it is laying down charges for imported and domestic products which are similar within the meaning of art 90(1) EC.

Discriminatory conditions attached to the application of a tax are also in breach of art 90 EC. In *Commission v Ireland* Case 55/79 [1980] ECR 481 the ECJ held that a tax which was applied without distinction to both imported and domestic products according to the same criteria, but which provided for several weeks' grace in paying the amount due for domestic producers while requiring importers to pay it immediately on importation, was in breach of art 90 EC. In *Schul* Case 15/81 [1982] ECR 409[3] the ECJ condemned a Member State for imposing its VAT without taking into consideration the residual part of VAT which was incorporated in the value of the product at the time of importation and already paid in the exporting Member State. In *Drexl* Case 299/86 [1988] ECR 1213 the ECJ condemned

---

[3] See also *Schul* Case 47/84[1985] ECR 1491. For comments on both cases: see OJ C13 (1986).

national law which imposed more severe penalties on undertakings in breach of VAT on imported products than on undertakings in breach of VAT on domestic products. In *Schöttle v Finanzamt Freudenstadt* Case 20/76 [1977] ECR 247 a charge imposed on the transport of goods according to the weight of the goods was condemned as it discriminated against imported products, taking into account the immediate effect on their costs.

Objective justification

Differential taxation of products which may serve the same economic ends is not prohibited under art 90 in so far as it is justified on the basis of objective criteria. However, direct discrimination based on nationality of the product can never be objectively justified. In *Commission v Hellenic Republic* Case C–375/95 [1997] ECR I–5981, examined above, the ECJ held that national rules granting tax advantages, that is, reducing the special consumer tax which applied only to new anti-pollution technology cars and not to imported second-hand cars with the same technology, could not be objectively justified under art 90 EC. A Member State cannot, without offending against the prohibition on discrimination laid down in art 90 EC, confer tax advantages on low emission cars while refusing those advantages to cars satisfying the same criteria imported from other Member States. Therefore, the imported used cars were discriminated against on the ground of nationality. This is always unlawful. Differential taxation, where the criterion for charging a higher rate is the importation itself and where domestic goods are by definition excluded from the heaviest taxation, is always in breach of art 90 EC.

Indirect discrimination, even if it results in discrimination against imported products, may, nevertheless, be justified, if it is based on objective criteria. The ECJ has taken a liberal approach in respect of these criteria. They may be based on the nature of the use of the raw materials, the processes employed in the production or manufacturing of goods, or may refer to general objectives of economic policy of a Member State, such as the protection of the environment or the development of regional policy so far as those policies are compatible with EC law. In *Commission v France* Case 196/85 [1987] ECR 1597 France levied lower taxes on sweet wines produced in a traditional and customary fashion in certain regions of France than on imported liqueur wines. The tax differentiation was not directly discriminatory as all similar wines, irrespective of the country of origin, could qualify for a lower rate of taxation. It was for France to justify indirect discrimination. In this respect France showed that natural sweet wines were produced in areas of low rainfall and poor soil, in which regions whose economy depended on wine production. France argued that its regional policy was to encourage production in poor growing areas and thus develop those regions. The ECJ accepted that a lower taxation levy on French sweet wines was objectively justified. Similarly, in *Commission v Italy* Case 21/79 [1980] ECR 1, Italy imposed a tax on imported and domestic cars based on their capacity to pollute which was objectively justified on the ground of the protection of the environment, although in the particular circumstances it imposed a heavier burden on imported cars than on domestic cars.

13.2 Article 90(1) EC: similar products

Article 90(1) EC prohibits the imposition of a higher rate of taxation on imported products than on similar domestic products. In this context it is necessary to define the concept of similarity. The ECJ emphasised in *Commission v France* Case 168/78 [1980] ECR 347 (see also *Roders* Joined Cases C–367–377 [1995] ECR I–2229) that similarity should be assessed widely on the ground of analogy and comparability of their uses rather than on strict identity. Two criteria are used in order to determine similarity within the meaning of art 90(1) EC.

The first criterion refers to the objective characteristics of domestic and imported products. In *John Walker* Case 243/84 [1986] ECR 875 the ECJ had to decide whether whisky and fruit liqueur wines were similar products for the purposes of art 90(1). The ECJ specified the objective characteristics as relating to origin, production and organoleptic qualities, in particular the taste and alcohol content of these products. In both products the same raw material – alcohol – was found but its content in whisky was twice that in liqueur wines. However, the production and organoleptic qualities were very different. For that reason the Court held that they were not similar products within the meaning of art 90(1) EC.

The second criterion is that if it is shown that domestic and imported products share the same objective characteristics, their similarity must be determined from the point of view of consumers. In *Rewe-Zentrale* Case 45/75 [1976] ECR 181 the ECJ held that products are similar from the point of view of consumers if they are considered by them as having similar characteristics and meeting the same needs.

In *Commission v Denmark* Case 106/84 [1986] ECR 833 the ECJ applied both criteria in respect of wine made from the grape and wine made from other fruits. They share the same objective characteristics as both are made from agricultural products, have the same alcohol content and are produced by means of the same process of fermentation. Also, from the point of view of consumers they satisfy the same needs and are highly substitutable. The ECJ held that wines made from the grape and wines made from other fruits were similar products within the meaning of art 90(1) EC.

If products are similar a Member State must equalise the taxes. However, if they are in competition, which is envisaged in art 90(2) EC, a Member State is required to remove any protective element incorporated into the tax – this does not always lead to the imposition of the same tax on competing domestic and imported products.

13.3 Article 90(2) EC: products in competition

The concept of 'products in competition' is wider than the concept of 'similar products'. In *Commission v United Kingdom (Re Tax on Beer and Wine)* Case 170/78 [1980] ECR 415 the ECJ explained the scope of application of art 90(2) EC in respect of 'products in competition'. It was one of many so-called 'spirit cases'. The UK maintained different levels of internal taxation for beer (£0.61 per gallon) and wine (£3.25 per gallon). Wine was mostly imported while beer was predominantly a domestic product. The Commission decided that this tax difference amounted to discrimination against imported wine and that by increasing the tax on wine the British government was encouraging consumers to buy beer. The UK argued that the two products were not interchangeable and therefore there was no breach of art 90 EC. The ECJ held that art 90(2) EC applies when products, without fulfilling the criterion of similarity laid down in art 90(1) EC are, nevertheless, in competition. In order to determine the existence of a competitive relationship it is necessary to take into account not only the present state of the market but also 'possible developments regarding the free movement of goods within the Community and the further potential for substitution of products for one another which might be revealed by intensification of trade'. The ECJ stated that wine and beer were, to a certain extent, substitutable as they were capable of meeting the same needs of consumers. To measure the degree of substitutability consumers' habits in a Member State, or in a particular region, should be taken into account, although these habits should not be regarded as immutable. Indeed, the tax policy of a Member State should not crystallise consumers' habits and thus consolidate an advantage gained by domestic producers. The Italian government submitted that it was appropriate to compare beer with the most popular, lightest and cheapest wine because those products were in real competition. The ECJ agreed and held that the decisive competitive relationship between beer and wine must be established by reference to the lightest and cheapest wine. Those products were in competition. Consequently, the ECJ found the UK in breach of art 90(2) EC.

It should be noted that where there are no similar domestic products, only art 90(2) EC may be invoked by importers. In *Cooperativa Co-frutta v Amministrazione delle Finanze dello Stato* Case 193/79 [1987] ECR 2085 Italy imposed a high tax on bananas. Italy is not a producer of bananas (its production was considered as insignificant and thus was not taken into consideration). On the grounds that consumption taxes were imposed on other exotic products such as coffee, cacao, etc, in order to raise revenue for the State, the ECJ decided that bananas formed part of a broader Italian taxation system which was based on objective criteria unconnected with the origin of the product. The ECJ considered that bananas were, nevertheless, in competition with other table fruits. Taking into account the high tax imposed on bananas as compared to other table fruits the ECJ concluded that Italy, by setting such a high rate of taxation in respect of bananas, indirectly protected domestic table fruits. Consequently, Italy was held in breach of art 90(2) EC. However, where there are no competing national products a tax imposed by a Member State on such a product is outside the scope of art 90 EC but may be caught by art 28 EC: *Commission v Denmark* Case C–47/88 [1990] ECR I–4509.

13.4 The relationship between art 90 EC and other provisions of the EC Treaty relating to the free movement of goods

The relationship between arts 25 and 90 EC

The connection between arts 25 and 90 EC is very close, taking into account that art 90 EC supplements the provisions of the EC Treaty relating to the abolition of customs duties and charges having equivalent effect. However, arts 25 and 90 EC operate at different levels. Article 25 EC aims at ensuring that fiscal impediments are eliminated when the products of Member States are crossing each others national borders, whilst the purpose of art 90 EC is to make sure that, whatever the internal tax system of a Member State, it does not discriminate directly or indirectly against products from other Member States. A fiscal charge is either a customs duty or a charge having equivalent effect to it or it is part of a general system of internal taxation. For that reason arts 25 and 90 are complementary, yet mutually exclusive.[4] The impositions cannot be applied simultaneously as they cannot belong to both categories at the same time. Although in many cases it is difficult to distinguish between charges having equivalent effect and discriminatory internal taxation, there are some helpful clues which may render it less difficult.

First, in principle, if a fiscal charge is imposed exclusively on imported products it is likely to be a charge equivalent to a customs duty. If a fiscal charge is levied on both domestic and imported products it is more likely to be part of internal taxation. In *Firma Steinike und Weinlig v Bundesamt für Ernährung und Forstwirtschaft* Case 78/76 [1977] ECR 595 the ECJ held that 'financial charges within a general system of internal taxation applying systematically to domestic and imported products according to the same criteria are not to be considered charges having equivalent effect'.

Second, a charge within the scope of art 25 EC is *a priori* unlawful, while a tax imposed under art 90 EC is lawful unless it discriminates against imported products on the ground of nationality.

Third, in order to distinguish between a charge and a tax it is helpful to examine the definition provided by the ECJ. The ECJ defined a charge having equivalent effect to a customs duty as encompassing any pecuniary charge, however small and whatever its designation and mode of application, which is imposed unilaterally on domestic or imported goods by reason of the fact that they cross a frontier.[5] In *Commission v France (Re Levy on Reprographic Machines)* Case 90/79 [1981] ECR 283 the ECJ held that a genuine tax is a measure relating to a system of internal dues applied systematically to categories of products in accordance with objective criteria irrespective of the origin of the products. Therefore, if a charge is part of internal taxation, and is based on criteria that are objectively justified by the nature of the product and its quality or function rather than the fact of crossing a national border, it will be considered under art 90 EC.

Fourth, in order to distinguish between arts 25 and 90 EC the ECJ has applied a criterion based on the destination of the proceeds of the charge. In *Fratelli Cucchi v Avez* Case 77/76 [1977] ECR 987 the ECJ stated that if a charge is imposed on both domestic and imported products and

1. has the sole purpose of providing financial support for the specific advantage of the domestic products; and
2. domestic taxed products and the benefiting domestic products are the same; and

---

[4] See *Deutschmann v Germany* Case 10/65 [1965] CMLR 259; *Lütticke* Case 57/65 [1966] ECR 205; *Haahr Petrolium* Case C–90/94 [1997] ECR I–4085.

[5] *Bauhuis v Netherlands* Case 46/76 [1977] ECR 5; *Denkavit v France* Case 132/78 [1979] ECR 1923; *Commission v Germany* Case 18/87 [1988] ECR 5427; *Commission v Italy* Case 340/87 [1989] ECR 1483; *Lamaire NV v Nationale Dienst voor Afzet van Land-en Tuinbouwprodukten* Case C–130/93 [1994] ECR I–3215.

3. the charge imposed on the domestic products is made good in full to domestic producers

that charge is to be considered as a charge having equivalent effect to a customs duty. Also when a charge is applied without discrimination to domestic and imported products, but the revenue from it is appropriated wholly to domestic products and thus fully offsets the burden imposed on them, it may also constitute a State aid in breach of art 87 EC. It is for the Commission to decide whether that is the case. However, if there is a partial compensation, a charge is incompatible with art 90 and as such prohibited so far as it discriminates against the imported products. In *Celbi* Case C–266/91 [1993] ECR I–4337 the ECJ held that if the revenue from such a charge is used only partially to provide advantages to domestic products, the charge will constitute discriminatory taxation contrary to art 90 EC. The ECJ emphasised that 'the criterion of the offsetting of the burden on domestic products is to be construed as requiring financial equivalence, to be verified over a reference period, between the total amount of the charge imposed on domestic products and the advantages exclusively benefiting those products'.

Fifth, if a charge is incompatible with art 90 EC, it is prohibited only to the extent to which it discriminates against imported products,[6] whereas a charge under art 25 EC is unlawful *in toto*. In both cases unlawful charges must be repaid. Under the principle of autonomy of national procedural rules it is for the domestic legal system of each Member State to lay down procedural rules applicable to actions for recovery of sums unduly paid under arts 25 and 90 EC. Such rules, however, may not be less favourable than those governing similar domestic actions and may in no circumstances be framed in such a way as to render it virtually impossible or excessively difficult in practice for individuals to enforce their claims before national courts.[7]

The relationship between arts 87 and 90 EC

Article 87 EC concerns State aid. In *Commission* v *Italy* Case 73/79 [1980] ECR 1533 the ECJ held that arts 87 and 90 EC are complementary and may be applied cumulatively.

The relationship between arts 28 and 90 EC

Articles 28 and 90 EC are mutually exclusive.[8] However, internal taxes, which are outside the scope of art 90 EC because there are no comparable domestic products, may be in breach of art 28 EC if the charges levied on imported products are so excessively high as to constitute an obstacle to the free movement of goods.[9]

---

[6] *Just* Case 68/79 [1980] ECR 501; *Scharbatke* Case C–72/92 [1993] ECR I–5509.
[7] *Peterbroeck* Case C–312/93 [1995] ECR I–4599; *FMC* Case C–212/94 [1996] ECR I–389.
[8] *Ianelli and Volpi* Case 74/76 [1977] ECR 557; *Compagnie Commerciale de l'Ouest* Cases C–78–83/90 [1992] ECR I–1847.
[9] *Commission* v *Denmark* Case C–47/88 [1990] ECR I–4509.

13.5 Harmonisation of taxation within the European Union

There is substantial disagreement between, and fierce resistance by, some Member States, especially the UK, concerning the harmonisation of taxes within the EU. The debate on taxation within the Council has a long and stormy history but has acquired a new dimension in the light of the completion of the common market on 1 January 1993 and the introduction of the Euro on 1 January 2000.

The EU-wide approach to taxation was launched in March 1996 following the Commission Communication on Taxation in the European Union. The Communication took into consideration all forms of taxation, that is, VAT, direct and indirect taxation, and social security contributions, in the context of major challenges facing the EU, namely: the proper functioning of the Common Market, the last stage of development of Economic and Monetary Union and the necessity to combat unemployment. The Communication emphasised the harmful effect of tax competition. Subsequent to the Commission's Communication, the Dublin European Council (December 1996) set up the Taxation Policy Group (TPG) which was in charge of preparing a package of proposals aimed at eliminating harmful tax competition. In October 1997 a package of proposals was published in a Communication from the Commission to the Council entitled 'Towards Tax co-ordination in the European Union – A Package to Tackle Harmful Tax Competition'. The Communication identified the harmful effect of tax competition in respect of employment, the functioning of the common market and EMU. In respect of employment, the Communication stated that since 1980 there had been a shift of tax burden from capital to labour, from more skilled and more mobile employees to less skilled and less mobile. This increasing tax burden on labour produced a negative effect on employment and growth in Europe. In respect of the development of the common market and EMU the differences in national tax systems had become more visible and thus they had encouraged cross-frontier fraud in respect of capital. The Communication proposed a package of measures to tackle harmful tax competition. The package was to be based on the introduction of three components: a code of conduct on company taxation, Community measures in respect of taxation of income from savings and Community measures regarding withholding taxes on interest and royalty payments between companies. Unfortunately, at the Helsinki European Summit (December 1999) the UK opposed all proposed measures to co-ordinate tax policy in the EU and curtail harmful tax competition.

VAT, excise duty and company taxation

In respect of VAT, excise duty and company taxation the EU has achieved considerable progress.

VAT
The harmonisation of VAT within the European Union has not yet been achieved. Under Directive 96/95/EC the Council fixed the level of the standard rate of VAT for the period of two years, from 1 January 1997 to 31 December 1999. Under the Directive each Member State is allowed to fix its standard rate of VAT for the supply of goods and services at not less

than 15 per cent from 1 January to 31 December 1998. In December 1998 a proposal was published for a standard rate of VAT at between 15 per cent and 25 per cent, to be applied from 1 January 1999. Thus, the minimum rate is fixed at 15 per cent and the maximum rate at 25 per cent .

Excise duty

On 17 December 1990 the Council reached an agreement on the principle rules governing the movement and supervision of products subject to excise duties and traded between professional traders in Member States. The Community decided to harmonise excise duty in respect of the key products in intra-Community trade: tobacco, alcoholic beverages and mineral oils. Community measures deal with:

1. The structure of excise duties. Directive 92/12/EEC[10] provides a general framework for the trade, holding and movement of goods prior to payment of excise duties. It applies to mineral oils, alcoholic beverages and manufactured tobacco products. The general rule is that excise duty should be paid in the Member State of consumption of the relevant product. There is no limit on purchase for personal consumption. The excise duties are paid in the Member State of purchase. Indicative allowances at the time of writing are as follows:

   800 cigarettes
   400 cigarillos
   200 cigars
   1 kg tobacco
   10 litres spirits
   20 litres aperitifs
   90 litres of wines, of which no more than 60 litre are sparkling
   110 litres beer

   The onus is upon a person to prove that goods in excess of the above are for personal use. If he fails he will be liable to pay excise duties.
2. The rate of excise duty. The rate on alcohol and alcoholic beverages was harmonised by Directive 92/84/EEC,[11] on cigarettes, and manufactured tobacco other than cigarettes, by Directive 92/79/EEC[12] (for cigarettes the minimum duty is 57 per cent of the retail selling price!), and for mineral oils by Directive 92/82/EEC.[13]

Company taxation

There are three main Community measures dealing with company taxation at Community level:

---

[10] OJ L76 (1992), as amended by Directive 92/108/EEC (OJ L390 (1992)), Directive 94/74/EC (OJ L365 (1994)) and Directive 96/99/EC: OJ L8 (1997)w.
[11] OJ L316 (1992).
[12] OJ L316 (1992).
[13] OJ L365 (1994).

1. Directive 90/434/EEC[14] on the common system of taxation applicable to mergers, divisions, transfers of assets and exchange of shares concerning companies of different Member States. The Directive provides for the imposition of tax on capital gains arising from the above operations once they have been realised.

2. Directive 90/435/EEC[15] on the common system of taxation applicable to parent companies and their subsidiaries in different Member States. It concerns the distribution of profits received by companies in one Member State which come from their subsidiaries in other Member States, and the distribution of profits by companies in one Member State to companies in other Member States of which companies they are subsidiaries. The main objective of the Directive is to avoid double taxation of dividends distributed by a subsidiary located in one Member State to its parent established in another Member State.

3. The third measure is a Convention (Directive 90/436/EEC)[16] on the elimination of double taxation in connection with the adjustment of profits of associated undertakings.

---

[14] OJ L225 (1990).
[15] OJ L225 (1990).
[16] OJ L225 (1990).

14 Quantitative Restrictions and Measures Having Equivalent Effect on Imports and Exports

14.1 'Measures taken by the Member States'

14.2 The definition of quantitative restrictions and measures having equivalent effect

14.3 The *Dassonville* formula

14.4 National measures indistinctly applicable to domestic and imported goods: *Cassis de Dijon*

14.5 Measures distinctly and indistinctly applicable to exports: art 29 EC

14.6 National measures relating to selling arrangements indistinctly applicable to domestic and imported goods

The elimination of non-tariff barriers to the free movement of goods is governed by arts 28–30 EC. The Treaty of Amsterdam repealed arts 31, 32, 33 and 35 EC Treaty as redundant in the light of the completion of the internal market.

Article 28 EC provides that:

'Quantitative restrictions on imports and all measures having equivalent effect shall be prohibited between Member States.'

Article 29 repeats the same obligation in respect of exports. Article 30 contains exceptions to the prohibition laid down in arts 28 and 29 EC.

Article 28 EC has been used by the ECJ as the principal tool for the removal of all barriers to the free movement of goods. Its scope of application has been gradually extended in order to respond to the development of the Community and its changing economic objectives.

Article 30 EC contains derogations from arts 28 and 29 EC. All three provisions are directly effective.[1]

Article 28 EC is very short. However, it covers a number of concepts which will be examined below.

---

[1] In respect of art 28 EC: see *Ianelli and Volpi SpA* v *Ditta and Paolo Meroni* Case 74/76 [1977] ECR 557; for art 29 EC: see *Pigs Marketing Board (Northern Ireland)* v *Redmond* Case 83/78 [1978] ECR 2347.

14.1 'Measures taken by the Member States'

Article 28 EC is addressed to the Member States and concerns measures taken by them. The expression 'measures taken by the Member States' has been broadly interpreted to include measures taken by any public body (whether legislative, executive or judicial) as well as any semi-public body.[2] In *R v Royal Pharmaceutical Society for Great Britain* Case 266/87 [1989] 2 CMLR 751 the ECJ had to decide whether a measure adopted by a professional body, such as the Pharmaceutical Society of Great Britain, may come within the scope of arts 28 and 29 EC.

The Pharmaceutical Society of Great Britain is a professional body established to enforce rules of ethics for pharmacists throughout the United Kingdom. This organisation convenes periodic meetings of a committee which has statutory authority to impose disciplinary measures on pharmacists found to have violated the rules of professional ethics. The Society enacted rules which prohibited a pharmacist from substituting one product for another having the same therapeutic effect, but bearing a different trade mark, when doctors refer to a particular brand of medication. Pharmacists were therefore required to dispense particular brand-name products when these were specified in prescriptions. This rule was challenged as being a measure having an equivalent effect to a quantitative restriction as prohibited by art 28 EC.

The ECJ held that art 28 EC applies not only to rules enacted by the Member States but also encompasses rules adopted by a professional body such as the Royal Pharmaceutical Society for Great Britain which exercises regulatory and disciplinary powers conferred upon it by statutory instrument. The ECJ stated that professional and ethical rules adopted by the society, which required pharmacists to supply, under a prescription, only a particular brand name drug, may constitute measures having equivalent effect to quantitative restrictions in breach of art 28 EC. It should be noted that in this case the measures were justified under art 30 EC.

Private companies supported financially or otherwise by a Member State when carrying out activities contrary to art 28 EC are within the scope of art 28 EC: *Commission v Ireland* Case 249/81 [1982] ECR 4005.

Until 1995 it had always been accepted that the prohibition contained in art 30 EC concerned action taken by the Member State, not passivity or inaction. However, the ECJ decided otherwise in *Commission v French Republic* Case C–265/95 [1997] ECR I–6959. In this case the Commission brought proceedings under art 226 EC Treaty against France for failure to take all necessary and proportionate measures to prevent the free movement of fruit and vegetables from being obstructed by actions of private individuals. France had failed to fulfil its obligations under arts 28 and 10 EC, as well as its obligations flowing from the common organisation of the markets in agricultural products. For a decade the Commission received complaints regarding the passivity of the French government in face of acts of violence and vandalism – such as interception of lorries transporting agricultural products from other Member States and destruction of their loads; threats against French supermarkets, wholesalers and retailers dealing with those products; damaging of such products when on display in shops, etc – committed by French farmers. The Commission

---

[2] See *Apple and Pear Development Council v K J Lewis Ltd* Case 222/82 [1983] ECR 4083.

supported by the government of Spain and the UK stated that on a number of occasions the French authorities showed unjustifiable leniency vis-à-vis the French farmers, for example, by not prosecuting the perpetrators of such acts when their identity was known to the police since often the incidents were filmed by television cameras and the demonstrators' faces were not covered. Furthermore, the French police were often not present on the spot, even though the French authorities had been warned of the imminence of demonstrations, or they did not interfere, as happened in June 1995 when Spanish lorries transporting strawberries were attacked by French farmers at the same place within a period of two weeks and the police who were present took no protective action. The government of France rejected the arguments submitted by the Commission as unjustified.

The ECJ held that France was in breach of its obligations under art 28 EC, in conjunction with art 10 EC, and under the common organisation of the markets in agricultural products for failing to take all necessary and proportionate measures in order to prevent its citizens from interfering with the free movement of fruit and vegetables.

This is one of the landmark decisions of the ECJ. The ECJ inferred from the requirements imposed by arts 3(c) EC and 14 EC, which are implemented in art 28 EC, that art 28 EC is also applicable where a Member State abstains from taking the measures required in order to deal with obstacles to the free movement of goods which are not created by the State.

Abstention thus constitutes a hindrance to the free movement of goods which is just as likely to obstruct intra-Community trade as is a positive act. However, art 28 EC in itself is not sufficient to engage the responsibility of a Member State for acts committed by its citizens but is so when read in the light of art 10 EC, which requires the Member States not merely themselves to abstain from adopting measures or engaging in conduct liable to constitute an obstacle to trade but also to take all necessary and appropriate measures to ensure that fundamental freedom regarding the free movement of goods is respected on their territory.

Notwithstanding the fact that the ECJ recognises that a Member State has exclusive competences in relation to the maintenance of public order and the safeguard of internal security, it assesses the exercise of that competence by a Member State in the light of art 28 EC! As a result, the ECJ stated that the French authorities failed to fulfil their obligations under the Treaty on two counts: first, they did not take necessary preventive and penal measures; and, second, the frequency and seriousness of the incidents, taking into account the passivity of the French authorities, not only made the importation of goods into France more difficult but also created a climate of insecurity which adversely affected the entire inter-Community trade.

The decision of the ECJ has far-reaching implications. It means that a Member State may be liable under art 28 EC linked with art 10 EC if it does not prevent or adequately punish conduct of its economic operators which is capable of hindering the free movement of goods. Therefore, a Member State is forced to intervene in situations where, for example, private individuals decide to promote domestic products to the detriment of those from other Member States or otherwise obstruct intra-Community trade.

The prohibition of quantitative restrictions and of all measures having equivalent effect applies not only to national measures but also to measures adopted by the Community institutions. The ECJ stated in *Denkavit Nederland* Case 18/83 [1984] ECR 2171 (and in *Mehuy and Schott* Case C–51/93 [1994] ECR I–3879) that measures adopted by Community institutions are capable of falling foul of arts 28 and 29 EC. However, in *René Kieffer and Romain Thill* Case C–114/96 [1997] ECR I–3629 the ECJ appeared to place a firmer emphasis on the possibility that Community acts of general application may hinder intra-Community trade. In this case criminal proceedings were brought against René Kieffer and Romain Thill for failing in 1993 and 1994 to provide information regarding statistical declarations required under Regulation 3330/91. The Regulation in question imposes upon Member States the obligation to collect from every undertaking above a certain size detailed declarations of all intra-Community imports and exports. In order that necessary information could be gathered, undertakings concerned were obliged to incur costs and considerable effort since they had to provide complex data for each transaction, whatever its value (in particular, the eight-digit code from the combined nomenclature). The Criminal Court of Luxembourg (Tribunal de Police) referred two questions to the ECJ:

1. whether the obligation to provide detailed declarations imposed upon undertakings under Regulation 3330/91 may constitute a measure having equivalent effect to quantitative restriction contrary to arts 28 and 29 EC; and
2. whether the obligation in question is in breach of the principle of proportionality as it constitutes an unjustified hindrance to the free movement of goods, as well as going beyond what is necessary to achieve the objective of general interest pursuant to Regulation 3330/91.

The ECJ held that Regulation 3330/91 may constitute a quantitative restriction prohibited by arts 28 and 29 EC and as such its validity may only be upheld in circumstances where it can be shown that there are objectively justifiable reasons for the adoption of the rules in question. In the present case the ECJ upheld the validity of Regulation 3330/91 on the ground that the aim it pursued, namely the completion of the internal market by establishing statistics on the trading of goods between Member States, justified the imposition upon undertakings of an obligation to provide complex data in relation to each intra-Community transaction. Although the obligation in question involved costs and inconvenience for the undertaking concerned, it was not disproportionate as it did not go beyond what was necessary to achieve the objective of general interest pursued by Regulation 3330/91.

14.2 The definition of quantitative restrictions and measures having equivalent effect

The EC Treaty neither defines quantitative restrictions nor measures having equivalent effect. There is no problem in defining quantitative restrictions as these have been in use for centuries. They restrict the import or export by amount or by volume. The most common restrictions on the physical quantity of imports or exports are quotas and bans. In *Risetia Luigi Geddo v Ente Nazionale Risi* Case 2/73 [1973] ECR 865 the ECJ defined them as any measures which amount to a total or partial restraint on imports, exports or goods in transit. A total restraint refers to a ban. In *Commission v Italy (Re Pigmeat)* Case 7/61 [1961] ECR 317 the ECJ condemned such a ban as contrary to art 28 EC.

In respect of measures having equivalent effect the first official, but still incomplete, definition was given in 1967 by the Commission in response to a parliamentary question.[3] Under pressure from the Member States and the EP the Commission decided to provide guidance as to the meaning and scope of 'measures having equivalent effect' in Directive 70/50[4] which was adopted on the basis of art 33(7) EEC and therefore applicable only to measures to be abolished during the transitional period. It has, however, provided important clarification of the notion of 'measures having equivalent effect' and is still considered as a non-binding guideline to the interpretation of art 28 EC. Article 2(3) of the Directive gives a generic definition of measures having equivalent effect and divides them into two categories:

1. *'measures, other than those applicable equally to domestic or imported products'*, that is 'distinctly applicable' measures that 'hinder imports which could otherwise take place, including measures which make importation more difficult or costly than the disposal of domestic production' (art 2(1) of the Directive);

2. *'measures which are equally applicable to domestic and imported products'*, that is 'indistinctly applicable' measures (art 3 of the Directive). These measures are in breach of art 28 EC 'where the restrictive effect of such measures on the free movement of goods exceeds the effects intrinsic to trade rules'. This occurs when they are disproportionate to their purpose or where 'the same objective cannot be attained by other measures which are less of a hindrance to trade'.

14.3 The *Dassonville* formula

On the basis of the Commission's Directive 50/70 the ECJ elaborated its own definition of measures having equivalent effect in *Procureur du Roi v Dassonville* Case 8/74 [1974] ECR 837; [1974] 2 CMLR 436. In this case a trader imported Scotch whisky into Belgium. The whisky had been purchased from a French distributor and had been in circulation in France. However, the Belgian authorities required a certificate of origin, which could only be obtained from British customs and which had to be made out in the name of the importers, before the goods could be legally imported into Belgium. As the certificate of origin could not be obtained for the consignment, the defendants went ahead with the transaction. They were charged by the Belgian authorities with the criminal offence of importing goods without the requisite certificate of origin. The defendants claimed that the requirement of a certificate of origin in these circumstances was tantamount to a measure having an effect equivalent to a quantitative restriction and therefore was prohibited by art 28 EC. The Belgian court referred to the ECJ for a preliminary ruling on this question.

The ECJ defined the concept of a measure having an equivalent effect to a quantitative restriction on imports as being all trading rules enacted by Member States which are

---

[3] Written Question, M Delinger (OJ 59 (1967)).
[4] OJ L13 (1970).

capable of hindering directly or indirectly, actually or potentially, intra-Community trade. This is know as the *Dassonville* formula. This formula includes both distinctly applicable measures affecting imports and indistinctly applicable measures affecting imported and domestic products. The formula is very broad, the effect of the measure, including its potential effect (*Commission v Ireland (Re Buy Irish Campaign)* Case 249/81 [1982] ECR 4005), is decisive in determining whether it should be considered as a MEQR and discriminatory intent is not required. Even if a national measure has no significant effect on trade it is still in breach of art 28 EC. In *Jan Van der Haar* Cases 177 and 178/82 [1984] ECR 1797 Dutch excise law regulating the resale of tobacco products, which restricted imports of these products to a very small degree and provided for alternative ways of marketing them, was held to be in breach of art 28 EC. The ECJ emphasised that art 28 EC does not recognise the *de minimus* rule as it

> '... does not distinguish between measures ... according to the degree to which trade between Member States is affected. If a national measure is capable of hindering imports it must be regarded as having an effect equivalent to a quantitative restriction, even though the hindrance is slight and even though it is possible for imported products to be marketed in other ways.'

Discrimination against imported products may be formal or material. Formal discrimination occurs when national measures treat similar situations in different ways which results in the hindering of trade between Member States, that is, imposes certain customs formalities, mandatory inspections or licensing requirements which result in additional costs and delays on imports but do not apply to domestic goods. Material discrimination takes place when a national measure theoretically treats different situations in the same way but in practice imposes additional costs for the importer and thus constitutes an obstacle to the free movement of goods (for example, requirements concerning the packaging or the content of imported products). A national measure based on an apparently neutral criterion will amount to material discrimination if only domestic products can satisfy that criterion. In *Commission v Ireland* Case 45/87 [1988] ECR 4929 the Dundalk District Council laid down certain specifications concerning a tender for the construction of the Dundalk water supply scheme which could only be satisfied by one undertaking established in Ireland. It required the use of asbestos cement pressure pipes 'certified as complying with Irish Standard Specification 188:1975 in accordance with the Irish Standards Mark Licensing Scheme of the Institute for Industrial Research and Standards'. The ECJ held that the specification constituted a measure having equivalent effect to a quantitative restriction and therefore was in breach of art 28 EC.

The *Dassonville* formula has been applied in numerous cases. In order to illustrate its breadth it is worthwhile examining some of them.

National measures encouraging discrimination

Discrimination based on nationality of goods, in this context, is considered to be the worst type of discrimination. In *Commission v Ireland (Re Buy Irish Campaign)* Case 249/81 [1982] ECR 4005 the Irish Goods Council conducted a campaign to promote Irish products, 'Buy Irish'. The objectives of the campaign were set by the Irish Ministry of Industry which also financed the campaign. The ECJ held that the campaign was in breach of art 28 EC as it intended to substitute domestic goods for imported goods in the Irish market and thus check the flow of imports from other Member States. This was so notwithstanding that fact the campaign was a failure and that the Irish government adopted non-binding measures in promoting Irish products. The ECJ stated that the decisions of the Irish Council of Goods were capable of influencing the conduct of traders and consumers in Ireland.

National measures which give preference for domestic products or confer some advantages on domestic products

The ECJ considers that such measures amount to quantitative restrictions. In *Campus Oil* Case 72/83 [1984] ECR 2727 Irish legislation imposed on importers of petroleum products an obligation to acquire a certain percentage of their requirements from a State-owned refinery operating in Ireland at prices fixed by the competent Irish ministry. The Irish legislation gave preference to domestic products and as such was in breach of art 28 EC (although the legislation was justified under art 30 EC). In *Commission* v *Greece* Case 192/84 [1985] ECR 3967 the Greek government imposed on the Agricultural Bank of Greece an obligation not to finance any purchase of imported agricultural machinery unless there was proof that no similar machinery was manufactured in Greece. This measure was considered as a measure having equivalent effect to a quantitative restriction. Similarly, in *Commission* v *Italy* Case C–263/85 [1991] ECR 1–2457 Italian legislation which enabled public bodies to obtain State aid conditional upon the purchase of vehicles made in Italy was held in breach of art 28 EC since it modified the flow of vehicles from other Member States and thus constituted a hindrance to the free movement of goods.

Restrictions relating to the price of goods

In periods of high inflation governments may use a prices policy in order to stabilise the national economy. A Member State may impose a maximum selling price for a particular product in order to artificially limit its price. When inflation is low, a Member State may decide that certain categories of traders should have a minimum income. To achieve this objective a Member State may impose minimum prices for some goods.

In *Tasca* Case 65/75 [1976] ECR 291 the Italian authorities imposed a maximum price on both imported and domestic sugar. Tasca ignored this restrictions and tried to sell sugar above the maximum price. When criminal prosecutions were commenced against him, he argued that the Italian law was contrary to art 28 EC. The ECJ held that while national legislation blocking price increases on sugar did not in itself constitute a measure having equivalent effect, as it applied indistinctly to imported and domestic sugar, it may, in certain circumstances, be in breach of art 28 EC. This happens where a maximum selling price is fixed at such a low level that the sale of imported products becomes, if not impossible, at least more difficult or costly than the disposal of domestic production.

In *Openbaar Ministerie* v *Van Tiggele* Case 82/77 [1978] ECR 25 criminal proceedings were brought against Van Tigelle for selling gin below the national fixed price. The ECJ stated that the fixing of a minimum price to both imported and domestic products was not in breach of art 28 EC provided it did not impede imports. According to the ECJ this may happen 'when a national authority fixes prices or profit margins at such a level that imported products are placed at a disadvantage in relation to identical domestic products, either because they cannot profitably be marketed in the conditions laid down or because the competitive advantage conferred by lower prices is cancelled out'. In this case the ECJ held that the Dutch law was in breach of art 28 EC.

Restrictions relating to the marketing of imported products, in particular their access to certain channels of distribution

In *Sacchi* Case 155/73 [1974] ECR 409 the ECJ emphasised that national measures which 'favour within the Community, particular trade channels or particular commercial operators in relation to others' are prohibited under art 28 EC. The best example was provided in the *Dassonville* case in respect of the requirement imposed on Belgian importers of whisky to provide a British certificate of origin made out in their name, even though they purchased whisky in free circulation in France and it was almost impossible or extremely difficult for them to satisfy such a requirement.

In *Commission* v *France (Re Advertising of Alcoholic Beverages)* Case 152/78 [1980] ECR 2299 France imposed restrictions on the advertising of grain spirits such as whisky, gin and vodka which were almost entirely imported, while no such restriction was placed on the advertising of fruit-based spirits such as brandy almost exclusively produced in France. The ECJ held that such restrictions may amount to a measure having equivalent effect to a quantitative restriction if there is a possibility that they may affect the marketing prospects of imported goods.

Restrictions relating to technical standards

Technical requirements and standards laid down by Member States can constitute one of the most important barriers to the free movement of goods. Until the harmonisation of technical norms and standards resulting from Community measures adopted pursuant to Council Resolution of 7 May 1985, which introduced a new approach in this area, Member States very often, under cover of the protection of consumers, invoked technical rules and standards in order to try to protect national markets.

In *Verband Sozialer Wettbewerb* Case C–315/92 [1994] ECR I–317 the ECJ specified examples of technical measures capable of hindering intra-Community trade as relating to 'designation, form, size, weight, composition, presentation, labelling, packaging'.[5]

An example of the protectionist application of national measures relating to technical rules and standards is provided in *Commission* v *Italy* Case 50/83 [1984] ECR 1633. In this case Italy prohibited importation from other Member States of used buses which had been constructed more than seven years previously. Under Italian ministerial decree such buses were prevented from being tested for roadworthiness, a condition necessary for their registration. Italy argued that such a restriction was necessary in order to ensure road

---

[5] See under *Cassis* principles: section 14.4.

safety. The Commission found out that Italian buses seven years old and more were neither withdrawn from circulation nor subject to a roadworthiness test because the Italian law applied exclusively to imported products and treated domestic products differently. This amounted to a measure having equivalent effect to a quantitative restriction.

Import licences and other similar procedures applicable to imported products

The ECJ held that import licences and other similar procedures, even if they are only formalities, constitute measures having equivalent effect to quantitative restrictions in so far as they intend to limit or delay importations.[6] In *Commission v United Kingdom (Re Imports of Poultry Meat)* Case 40/82 [1982] ECR 2793 the UK introduced a licencing system for poultry imported from all Member States except Denmark and Ireland. This amounted in practice to a ban, in breach of art 28 EC. The UK argument based on the protection of health of animals, in particular the prevention of the spread of a highly contagious disease affecting poultry known as Newcastle disease, was rejected for a number of reasons. These were that: the measure was introduced to respond to pressure by domestic poultry breeders concerned about the increased volume of poultry imported from other Member States (especially from France); it was imposed before Christmas (when consumers traditionally buy poultry, especially turkey); and there had been no outbreak of Newcastle disease in France for five years!

All the above reasons convinced the ECJ that the UK had introduced the licensing system in order to safeguard commercial interests, in particular in the light of massive State aid granted to French poultry breeders by the French government.

National measures which require that only persons established within a national territory may apply for a licence to sell products coming from other Member States are unlawful per se. The ECJ in *Commission v Belgium* Case 89/92 [1983] ECR 531 condemned Belgian law requiring that only persons established in Belgium were allowed to ask for an authorisation to sell pesticides. In *Commission v Germany* Case 247/81 [1984] ECR 1111, the ECJ applied the same solution to a German law imposing similar restrictions in respect of pharmaceutical products.

Phyto-sanitary inspections

Phyto-sanitary inspections constitute an effective way of excluding imported products from national markets, or at least of making imports or exports more difficult or more costly. Nevertheless, phyto-sanitary inspections may be justified under art 30 EC. In *Rewe-Zentralfinanz GmbH v Landwirtschaftskammer* Case 4/75 [1975] ECR 843 apples imported into Germany were subject to systematic sanitary inspections designed to control a pest called San José scale which was not to be found in domestic apples. The ECJ held that such inspections constituted measures having equivalent effect, although in this case they were justified as there was a genuine risk of spreading the disease to domestic apples if no

---

[6] See *International Fruit* Cases 51–54/71 [1971] ECR 1107; *Commission v France* Case 68/76 [1977] ECR 515; *Donckerwolcke* Case 41/76 [1976] ECR 1921.

inspection was carried out on imported apples. Provided there is no discrimination against imported products, and thus inspections are not arbitrary, they will be justified under art 30 EC. However, in most cases systematic inspections are arbitrary and result in making imports more difficult or costly. In *Simmenthal v Italian Minister for Finance* Case 35/76 [1976] ECR 1871 Germany imposed at its frontiers mandatory health inspections on meat for which charges were imposed on importers. The ECJ held that systematic health inspections carried out at frontiers are in breach of art 28 EC, in particular the delays inherent in the inspections and the additional costs which the trader may incur are likely to make imports more difficult and more costly. In *Commission v France (Re Italian Table Wine)* Case 42/82 [1983] ECR 1013 Italian wine imported into France was subject to a double control: first, it was tested by the Italian authorities, then by the French authorities. Inspections conducted at the French frontier were systematic. The Italian wine was delayed at the French frontier for an excessive period of time pending the results of analyses carried out by French authorities. The ECJ condemned these inspections for three reasons: they were carried out on a systematic basis, they caused excessive delay and they were discriminatory, taking into account that domestic wine was not tested in a similar manner.

The position of EC law in respect of inspections was restated by the ECJ in *Germany v Deutsches Milch-Kontor GmbH* Case C–426/92 [1994] ECR I–2757. Deutsches Milch-Kontor GmbH (DMK) purchased skimmed-milk powder in Germany and exported it to Italy for processing into compound feeding-stuffs. At the German frontier German authorities carried out systematic inspections of skimmed-milk powder in order to verify whether it qualified for export refund under Regulation 986/68. A sample was taken from each lorry transporting skimmed-milk powder. DMK was charged for those inspections. DMK argued that the inspections were in breach of arts 29 and 25 EC. DMK contended that the inspections provided no benefit for the exporter (since DMK was not the recipient of the aid, but merely a vehicle for its transmission) and that they imposed considerable financial burdens on DMK as the costs for analysing the samples were unduly high and liable to deter traders from carrying out such transactions. The ECJ held that systematic inspections carried out at the frontier constituted obstacles to the free movement of goods in breach of arts 28 and 29 EC. However, frontier inspections serving the same purpose are permissible if carried out by means of spot checks. The German government argued that inspections were carried out at the frontier for practical and financial reasons, while the Commission considered that only frontier inspections could prevent fraud during the transportation of skimmed-milk powder from the German factory to the Italian processing undertaking. The ECJ rejected both arguments. It held that a Member State could not rely on art 29 EC in order to lighten the administration's burden or reduce public expenditure, especially when the costs of the inspection were passed on to the trader. In respect of the argument concerning the prevention of fraud, the ECJ emphasised that a Member State could not act in breach of art 29 EC, that is apply systematic frontier inspections prohibited under that provision, in order to prevent fraudulent evasion of Community rules. In addition, the ECJ rightly noted that fraud could not be ruled out during transport within Germany or within the Member State of destination of goods (Italy). In respect of the costs of the systematic frontier inspections charged to DMK, the ECJ held that since such inspections were unlawful their costs could not be justified. They constituted charges having equivalent effect to customs duties on exports even though they corresponded to the actual costs of the inspections.

14.4 National measures indistinctly applicable to domestic and imported goods: *Cassis de Dijon*

The ECJ was very aware that in the absence of Community rules in certain sectors it was for Member States to lay down the conditions on access to national markets for imported products. A decision needed to be made as to what extent national legislation was to be tolerated. This matter was decided in *Rewe-Zentral AG v Bundermonopolverwaltung für Branntwein (Cassis De Dijon)* Case 120/78 [1979] ECR 649; [1979] 3 CMLR 494.

German legislation governing the marketing of alcoholic beverages set a minimum alcohol strength of 25 per cent per litre for certain categories of alcoholic products. This regulation prevented an importer from marketing Cassis de Dijon, a French liqueur with an alcohol strength of between 15 and 20 per cent, in Germany. The German government invoked human health and consumer protection concerns as the justification for the prohibition. The importer challenged the German legislation in the German court, which then referred the matter to the ECJ for a preliminary ruling.

The ECJ established two fundamental rules in respect of indistinctly applicable measures:

1. the rule of reason according to which, in the absence of common rules, obstacles to the free movement of goods resulting from disparities between national laws relating to the marketing of the products in question must be accepted in so far as those provisions may be recognised as necessary in order to satisfy mandatory requirements relating in particular to the effectiveness of fiscal supervision, the protection of public health, the fairness of commercial transactions and the defence of the consumer; and

2. the rule of recognition which provides that there is no valid reason why goods which have been produced and marketed in one Member State should not be introduced into any other Member State.

The decision in this case displaced the previous assumption that art 28 EC did not apply to a national measure unless it could be shown that the measure discriminated between imports and domestic products or between different forms of intra-Community trade.

Under the first rule, certain measures which are within the *Dassonville* formula will not infringe art 28 EC provided they are necessary to protect a mandatory requirement enumerated in the first rule. The list of mandatory requirements is not exhaustive. The ECJ may add additional justifications if necessary.

Under the second rule there is a presumption that goods which have been lawfully marketed in one Member State will comply with mandatory requirements of the State into which they are being imported. For that reason a national measure restricting intra-Community trade must not only pursue a legitimate objective but must be necessary and proportionate for the attainment of that objective

The ECJ applied the above-mentioned rules to the case at issue. The justification based on the protection of public health by the German government was rejected. The ECJ held that the argument that alcoholic beverages with a low alcohol content may more easily induce a tolerance towards alcohol than more highly alcoholic beverages could not be accepted, taking into account that the consumers could buy on the German market an extremely wide range of weak or moderately alcoholic products, most of them in a diluted form. The protection of consumers against unfair practices on the part of producers and distributors of alcoholic beverages by means of fixing of minimum alcohol contents was also rejected. In this respect the ECJ emphasised that this objective could be ensured by requiring the importers to display an indication of origin and the alcohol content on the packaging of products. Therefore, the German government did not provide any valid reason why alcoholic beverages lawfully produced and marketed in France should not be introduced into Germany. As a result, the unilateral requirement imposed by Germany of a minimum alcohol content for the purposes of the sale of alcoholic beverages constituted a measure equivalent to a quantitative restriction and as such was incompatible with art 28 EC.

Subsequent case law of the ECJ has clarified both rules laid down in *Cassis de Dijon*. In their application it is important to note that:

1. Equal treatment of imported and domestic products is required under the *Dassonville* formula. If there is discrimination between them the *Dassonville* formula applies and not the principle of *Cassis de Dijon*. This was clearly stated by the ECJ in *Commission v Ireland (Re Irish Souvenirs)* Case 113/80 [1981] ECR 1625 and confirmed in *Schutzverband Gegen Unwesen in der Wirtschaft v Weinvertriebs GmbH* Case 59/82 [1983] ECR 1217. In this case Italian law required that vermouth marketed in Italy had at least 16 per cent of alcohol by volume. Weaker vermouth could be made only for export. Under German law, there was no minimum alcohol requirement for vermouth. Foreign vermouth could be marketed in Germany if it could lawfully be sold in the state of manufacture. As a result, Italian producers of vermouth below 16 per cent of alcohol by volume could neither sell in Italy nor in Germany. The ECJ held that the German legislation applied only to imported products and as such was discriminatory. Italian law was irrelevant since the discriminatory effect should be assessed in the light of the legislation of the Member State of marketing alone.

2. It is not necessary to rely on the 'rule of reason' if the restrictive effects of national measures are too uncertain and too indirect[7] because they would not constitute measures having equivalent effect. The possibility of excluding national measures on this ground was applied by the ECJ in *CMC Motorradcenter GmbH v Pelin Baskiciogullari* Case C–93/92 [1993] ECR I–5009. In this case Motorradcenter, a German dealer in motor-cycles, not an authorised dealer for any particular brand, bought a Yamaha motorcycle from a German importer who had acquired it from an authorised French dealer. The German importer obtained an assurance that purchasers could avail themselves of the guarantee as against any authorised Yamaha dealer. The general conditions of sale of Motorradcenter specified that the purchaser could assert his rights under the guarantee as against either the vendor or undertakings approved by the

---

[7] See *Krantz* Case C–69/88 [1990] ECR I–583.

manufacturers or importers. When Mrs Baskiciogullari bought a Yamaha motor-cycle she was not informed that despite the general conditions of sale authorised German dealers of Yamaha generally refused to repair, under the guarantee, motor-cycles which had been the subjects of parallel import. When Mrs Baskiciogullari learnt about this practice she refused to take delivery of the motor-cycle. Under the German law of contract the seller is obliged to draw the purchaser's attention to the conduct of the authorised German dealers. Mrs Baskiciogullari was sued by Motorradcenter for damages. On appeal, the German court referred to the ECJ the question whether the obligation to inform the purchaser constituted a measure having an effect equivalent to a quantitative restriction. The ECJ held that the obligation to provide information prior to contract imposed by the German law of contract did not itself constitute an obstacle to the free movement of goods, but the fact that certain authorised Yamaha dealers refused to repair motor-cycles under the guarantee constituted an obstacle to the free movement of goods. The ECJ stated that since the German contract law applied indistinctly to all contractual relationships in respect of all products coming from other Member States, the restrictive effects which the obligation to provide information might have on the free movement of goods was too uncertain and too indirect to constitute a measure having equivalent effect.

3. The opportunity offered by the ECJ to Member States to justify national measures on the grounds of the mandatory requirements has been often relied upon. Taking into account the number of cases it is impossible to examine the case law in this areas . However, two defences have been used more often than others by Member States: the protection of public health and the defence of consumers. The ECJ has always strictly interpreted additional justifications available to Member States under the rule of reason. Only exceptionally have Member States been successful in this respect. Among cases in which the ECJ held that national measures may be necessary to protect consumers it is interesting to mention *Beele* Case 6/81 [1982] ECR 707. In this case the ECJ stated that national legislation prohibiting slavish imitations of products of a third party was justified on the ground that such slavish imitations were likely to confuse the consumers as to what products were genuine and what were imitations. However, in *Prantl* Case 16/83 [1984] ECR 1299 the ECJ held that when there was a close resemblance between a German bottle known as a 'bocksbeutel', in which expensive wine from a particular region of Germany was sold, and an Italian bottle, traditional to Italy in which cheap imported Italian wine was sold, Germany could not rely on the protection of consumers to prohibit the sale of the Italian wine in Germany. The ECJ emphasised that as long as the Italian bottle was traditional to Italy, not an imitation of the German bottle, there was no reason to prohibit its sale in Germany.[8]

Another case, *Robertson* Case 220/81 [1982] ECR 2349, concerned Belgian legislation prohibiting the sale in Belgium of silver-plated articles not stamped either with a Belgian hallmark or a hallmark of the Member State of exportation containing information equivalent to that provided by Belgian hallmarks. The ECJ agreed that hallmarks must be intelligible to consumers of the Member State of importation.

---

[8] But see *Deutsche Renault AG v Audi AG* Case C–317/91 [1993] ECR I–6227.

However, in most cases the ECJ held that national measures intended to protect consumers were not necessary, and that the objectives pursued by national measures could be achieved by other means which would be less of a hindrance to intra-Community trade. One of the leading cases in respect of the protection of public health is *Commission v Germany (German Beer Purity Laws)* Case 178/84 [1987] ECR 1227. Under German law the use of additives in beer was banned and the marketing in Germany of beer containing additives was prohibited. In other Member States the use of additives was authorised. The Commission brought proceedings against Germany for breach of art 28 EC. The German government argued that the prohibition was necessary, taking into account that beer was consumed in 'considerable quantities' in Germany. The ECJ held that there was no scientific evidence, in particular from research conducted by FAO (Food and Agriculture Organisation), the WHO (World Health Organisation) and the Community's own Scientific Committee for foods, that additives constituted a danger to public health. Under the rule of reason it was for a Member State to submit convincing evidence based on scientific research. However, the ECJ agreed that the drinking habits of the German population might have justified the prohibition of certain additives, but not all of them. As a result the German Beer Purity Laws were disproportionate as they went far beyond what was necessary to protect public health. This question of permissible ingredients in foods has arisen in a significant number of cases: in respect of 'pain brioché' (*Kelderman* Case 130/80 [1981] ECR 527), alcoholic beverages (*Fietje* Case 27/80 [1980] ECR 3839), pasta, cheese, etc. Since 1985 under the new approach towards technical harmonisation and standards the conditions relating to the use of additives have been unified. Community measures are based on the 'positive lists' of additives which enumerates those which are permitted in food. All other additives are prohibited. In order to be on the positive list an additive must satisfy stringent criteria:

a) from a technical point of view there must be a sufficient need for such an additive;
b) the pursued objective cannot be attained by using other technical or economic methods;
c) the additive presents no danger whatsoever to health; and
d) use of the additive should not confuse consumers.

Another example of an unsuccessful defence based on the protection of consumers is provided by a UK national requirement that the country of origin of products must be indicated. In *Commission v United Kingdom (Re Origin Marking of Retail Goods)* Case 207/83 [1985] ECR 1202 the UK argued that for consumers it was necessary to have a clear indication of the country of origin of goods (for certain goods such as textiles, electrical goods) as it gave an indication as to their quality. The ECJ held that such a requirement merely enabled consumers to assert any prejudice they might have against foreign goods. UK legislation was contrary to art 28 EC as it slowed down the economic interchange between Member States. The ECJ held that manufacturers were free to indicate the country of origin but should not be compelled to do so.

4. In the absence of Community rules in a particular area a national measure which applies without discrimination to both domestic and imported products may escape the art 28 EC prohibition in so far as it is considered as being necessary in order to satisfy mandatory requirements. In *Cassis de Dijon* the ECJ stated that mandatory requirements may relate in particular to the effectiveness of fiscal supervision, the protection of public health, the fairness of commercial transactions and the defence of the consumer. This list is not exhaustive. Therefore, it is always possible for a Member State to justify national legislation on the grounds of mandatory requirements which are not mentioned in *Cassis de Dijon*. Contrary to art 30, which contains an exhaustive list of possible justifications to the prohibition laid down in art 28 EC, under *Cassis de Dijon* Member States are offered a wider choice. Subsequent case law of the ECJ shows that a number of mandatory requirements have been added to those enumerated in *Cassis de Dijon*;

   a) *The protection of the environment*
      In *Commission v Denmark (Re Returnable Containers)* Case 302/86 [1989] 1 CMLR 619 the ECJ held that the protection of the environment is a mandatory requirement which may restrict the scope of application of art 28 EC. Under Danish law beer and soft drinks were required to be marketed only in containers that could be re-used. Distributors of such products had to establish deposit-and-return schemes and recycle them. The containers had to be approved by the Danish National Agency for the Protection of Environment. The Danish government acknowledged that these requirements were unduly onerous to foreign manufacturers and for that reason permitted the use of non-approved containers subject to very strict limits (3,000hl per year for foreign products). The Commission challenged these requirements as contrary to art 28 EC. The ECJ extended the list of mandatory requirements laid down in *Cassis* to include the protection of the environments, although it rejected it in this particular case! The ECJ stated that the requirement that only containers approved by the Danish Agency could be used was disproportionate and the concession for limited quantities was insufficient to remedy the violation of art 28 EC.

   b) *The protection of the socio-cultural identity of a Member State*
      In *Cinéthèque SA v Fédération Nationale des Cinémas Français* Cases 60 and 61/84 [1985] ECR 2605 French legislation prohibited the marketing of videos of films during the first year of the film's release, irrespective of whether the film was made in France or elsewhere, on the ground of the protection of the French film industry. The ECJ held that the protection of cultural activities constitutes a mandatory requirement. And, in *Stoke-on-Trent City Council v B & Q plc* Case 169/91 [1993] 1 CMLR 426, the ECJ recognised the protection of national and regional socio-cultural characteristics as a mandatory requirement covered by the rule of reason.

   c) *The improvement of working conditions*
      In *Union Départmentale des Syndicats CGT de l'Aisne v SIDEF Conforama* Case C–312/89 [1991] ECR I–997 the ECJ held that the protection of workers may constitute a mandatory requirement.

d) *The maintenance of press diversity*

In *Vereinigte Familiapress Zeitungsverlags-und Vertriebs GmbH v Henrich Bauer Verlag* Case C–368/95 [1997] ECR I–3689 the ECJ held that maintenance of press diversity may constitute an overriding requirement justifying a restriction on free movement of goods.

e) *The prevention of fraud*

In *Germany v Deutsches Milch-Kontor GmbH* Case C–426/92 [1994] ECR I–2757 the ECJ recognised that the prevention of fraud constituted a legitimate concern of a Member State and as such may constitute a mandatory requirement.

5. A national measure indistinctively applicable to both domestic and imported products may be justified under the rule of reason in so far as it is proportional to the objective which such a national measure intends to achieve. The principle of proportionality has played an important role in excluding national measures when the objective they sought could be achieved by less stringent means. It has been applied in particular in relation to the use of generic names, presentation of products and the advertising of products.

a) *The use of generic names*

In *Ministère Public v Deserbais* Case 286/86 [1988] ECR 4907 French law stated that only cheese containing a minimum 40 per cent fat could use the name 'Edam'. Deserbais imported Edam cheese from Germany which was lawfully produced there but contained only 35 per cent fat. When criminal proceedings were brought against Deserbais he argued that French law was contrary to art 28 EC. The ECJ held that French law was disproportionate to the objectives it sought to achieve. Consumers would be adequately protected by appropriate labelling informing them about the fat content of German Edam cheese. Similarly, in *Miro BV* Case 182/84 [1985] ECR 3731 the ECJ held that a generic name 'jenever' which was reserved under Dutch law for gin containing a minimum of 35 per cent alcohol could not preclude Belgian jenever which contained only 30 per cent alcohol from being sold in The Netherlands, taking into account that Belgian jenever was lawfully produced and marketed in Belgium and appropriate labelling of Belgian jenever in respect of its alcohol content would be sufficient to protect consumers. The ECJ so decided despite the fact that a higher tax was imposed in The Netherlands on Dutch jenever and thus it would be placed at a comparative disadvantage as compared to Belgian jenever.

b) *Presentation of the products*

The principle of proportionality has been especially useful in curbing national measures which imposed certain requirements concerning the presentation of the products. In *Walter Rau Lebensmittelwerke v De Smedt* Case 261/81 [1987] ECR 1069 under Belgian law margarine could only be sold in cube-shaped boxes in order to distinguish it from butter. The ECJ held that the requirement was disproportionate since consumers would be sufficiently protected by appropriate labelling of the product. The ECJ emphasised that appropriate labelling would achieve the same objective as national measures with less hindrance to intra-Community trade.

c) *Language*

In *Colim NV v Bigg's Continent Noord NV* Case C–33/97 [2000] 2 CMLR 135 the ECJ restated its case law on linguistic requirements. Both parties to the national proceedings operated different department stores in the Dutch-speaking province of Limburg. Colruyt NV, a company of which Colim was a subsidiary, submitted an application to the national court for an order, subject to financial penalties for non-compliance, restricting the defendant Bigg's store from selling 48 products which, in breach of the Law on Trade Practices and Consumer Information and Protection (the WHPC), did not carry, on the packaging or labelling, any particulars in Dutch. Bigg's responded by bringing a counterclaim that Colim was selling various products in its store without labelling in Dutch, and that national provisions contained in the WHPC were inapplicable because they had not been notified to the Commission as required by Directive 83/189. In these circumstances a national court referred to the ECJ two questions: first, whether the obligation to give mandatory labelling particulars, instructions for use and guarantee certificates for products (at least) in the language or languages of the area in which those products are placed on the market constitutes a 'technical regulation' within the meaning of Directive 83/189 and, if so, whether such technical regulations should have been notified to the Commission; and, second, whether, and to what extent, a Member State may require information appearing on imported products to be given in the language of the area in which those products are sold or in another language which may be readily understood by consumers in that area.

The ECJ held that the obligation to give mandatory labelling particulars, instructions for use and guarantee certificates for products at least in the language or languages of the area in which the products are placed on the market does not constitute a 'technical regulation' within the meaning of Directive 83/189/EEC. Therefore, there is no obligation to notify such technical regulations to the Commission.

The ECJ made a distinction between linguistic requirements imposed by Community law and information required by national law to appear on imported products. A Member State cannot impose additional language requirements if a Community measure fully harmonises language requirements. In the absence of full harmonisation of language requirements applicable to information appearing on imported products, a Member State may adopt national measures requiring such information to be provided in the language of the area in which the products are sold or in another language which may be readily understood by consumers in that area. However, national language requirements must apply without distinction to both national and imported products and must be proportionate to the objective of consumer protection. In particular they must be restricted to information which a Member State makes mandatory and which cannot be appropriately conveyed to consumers by means other than translation.

The ECJ emphasised that it is necessary for a national judge to distinguish between the obligation to convey certain information about a product to a consumer and the obligation to give that information in a specific language. The first-mentioned obligation concerns the product directly, whilst the second-mentioned obligation merely specifies the language in which information directly concerning the product must be provided. Consequently, the second-mentioned obligation cannot constitute a 'technical regulation' within the meaning of Directive 83/189 since it is an ancillary rule necessary in order for the information to be effectively communicated.

In respect of language requirements the ECJ distinguished between the situation where there is complete Community harmonisation (and thus a Community measure requires the national language or languages to be used for certain categories of products) and where there is only partial Community harmonisation or none at all. In the first case, any additional national language requirements are prohibited. In the second case, a Member State may impose additional language requirements. However, such requirements may constitute measures having equivalent effect to quantitative restrictions within the meaning of art 28 EC in so far as imported products have to be given different labelling which involves additional costs for the importers.[9] For that reason, the ECJ specified that: first, national language requirements must be restricted to the information made mandatory by the Member State concerned; second, the possible use of such means of communication as designs, symbols or pictograms which can be understood by consumers must not be excluded by national measures requiring the use of a specific language; and, third, national language requirements must be applied without distinction to both national and imported products and must be proportionate to the objective of consumer protection.

In this case, the ECJ confirmed that national language requirements which involve the need to alter the packaging or the labelling of imported products cannot be regarded as selling arrangements.[10]

The decision of the ECJ in this case is in line with its previous case law regarding national language requirements.[11]

d) *Advertising*

Until the judgment of the ECJ in *Criminal Proceedings against Keck and Mithouard* Joined Cases C–267 and 268/91 [1993] ECR I–6097 (see section 14.6) the compatibility of national rules relating to the advertising of products with art 28 EC was assessed under the principle of proportionality. These cases are now only of historical interest, taking into account that since *Keck* advertising is considered as relating to selling arrangements and thus outside the scope of art 28 EC. In a number of cases decided before *Keck* the ECJ emphasised that art 28 EC 'cannot be interpreted as meaning that national legislation which denies the consumer access to certain kinds of information may be justified by mandatory requirements concerning consumer protection': *GB-INNO-BM* v *Confederation du Commerce Luxembourgeois* Case 362/88 [1991] 2 CMLR 801. In *GB-INNO-BM* the ECJ held that

---

[9] See *Mehuy and Schott* Case C–51/93 [1994] ECR I–3879.
[10] See *Keck and Mithouard* Cases C–267 and 268/91 [1993] ECR I–6097.
[11] See *Piageme* Case C–85/94 [1995] ECR I–2955; *Mehuy and Schott* Case C–51/93 [1994] ECR I–3879; *Peeters* Case C–369/89 [1991] ECR I–2971.

Luxembourg law prohibiting the distribution of leaflets in Luxembourg by a supermarket chain established in Belgium (which was in conformity with Belgian law) promoting certain products and stating the duration of special offers, as well as containing a comparison of prices between the previous year and the current year, was disproportionate to the objective of consumer protection. The government of Luxembourg argued that the prohibition concerning the duration of the special offers was to avoid consumer confusion between special and half-yearly clearance sales, the time and duration of which was also restricted under national rules. In respect of the prohibition against stating previous year prices in leaflets, the government of Luxembourg claimed that the consumers could not remember these prices and consequently were not able to decide whether they were genuine. Furthermore, comparison of prices might exercise excessive psychological pressure on the consumers. The ECJ rejected both justifications. The Court stated that: first, advertisers must provide genuine information; second, the consumers must have all necessary information in order to make their choice with full knowledge of the facts; and, third, the objective sought by Luxembourg legislation could be attained by less restrictive means. The same conclusions were reached by the ECJ in *Yves Rocher* Case 126/91 [1993] ECR 2361 in which German legislation prohibiting comparison of prices (between previous prices and current prices for the same products) was held to be in breach of art 28 EC.

6. The principles laid down in *Cassis de Dijon* were established in order to remedy the absence of Community rules in a particular area. Under the doctrine of pre-emption, once the Community legislates in a field it occupies that field and Member States are precluded from taking any legislative measures in it. Consequently, when national laws of the Member States have been harmonised at Community level, the legality of additional requirements imposed by a Member State in the harmonised area depends upon whether or not the Community harmonisation is complete or partial. This question arose in *Dansk Denkavit v Ministry of Agriculture* Case 29/87 [1988] ECR 2965. In this case Directive 70/524 was enacted to harmonise all the national laws of the Member States with regard to both the presence of additives and the labelling requirements for feedstuffs. However, Danish importers of animal feedstuffs were required to obtain approval from the Danish authorities prior to import. In particular, foreign feedstuffs were required to comply with certain procedural and labelling requirements which exceeded those specified in the Community directive harmonising procedures for such imports throughout the Community.

The ECJ held that Directive 70/524 was intended to harmonise all the material conditions for marketing feedstuffs, including the identification of additives and their purity. Consequently, a Member State was prohibited from imposing additional health inspections not provided for by the Directive itself. As a result the justification based on the protection of public health was rejected by the ECJ.

However, sometimes it is difficult to distinguish which aspects have been harmonised and which are still within the competence of a Member State. This is well illustrated in *Gunnar Nilsson, Per Olov Hagelgren, Solweig Arrborn* Case C–162/97 [1998] ECR I–7477. Here the Swedish authorities brought criminal proceedings against a group of individuals who were selling bovine semen taken from Belgian bulls for insemination of Swedish cows. Swedish law prohibited the use of semen from bulls of breeds with specific genetic weaknesses, and Belgian bulls were considered as such a breed. The offenders argued that Swedish law was contrary to art 28 EC and that the product in question was subject to harmonised importation rules under EC law. The Swedish authorities claimed that the national law was justified on the ground of the protection of animal health and in particular the protection of animals from any breeding liable to entail suffering for animals or to affect their behaviour. The Swedish court referred two questions to the ECJ:

a) whether art 28 EC or Directive 87/328 precludes national rules under which authorisation is required for insemination activities concerning bovine animals, in particular the distribution of and insemination with semen; and

b) whether art 28 EC or Directive 87/328 precludes national rules prohibiting or subjecting to certain conditions the insemination and breeding of bovine animals where those activities are liable, in the opinion of the competent national authorities, to entail suffering for animals or affect their natural behaviour, or where the breed in question is regarded by those national authorities as carrying genetic defects.

The ECJ held that the harmonisation of national rules at Community level as to the conditions for acceptance for breeding of pure-bred breeding animals of the bovine species and their semen precluded a Member State from imposing any supplementary requirement in relation to control of imports of bovine semen based on zootechnical or pedigree considerations. The ECJ held that Directive 87/328 constituted a complete harmonisation of rules in this area and as such took into consideration the legitimate interests of Member States. Consequently, a Member State, in order to justify national rules preventing the use of the semen imported from another Member State, could invoke none of the arguments that the breed carried genetic defects, or that the use of semen would entail suffering for animals or that the use of semen would affect their natural behaviour. Such semen being, on the basis of tests carried out in conformity with Community law, accepted by that State for artificial insemination of pure bred cows.

The ECJ held that Swedish law could be justified only if it was intended to regulate the qualifications and operations of inseminators since neither art 28 EC nor Directive 87/328 impose any restrictions on a Member State in respect of the distribution of semen and on insemination activities provided that national rules in this area apply without distinction as to the origin of the product.

7. On 3 October 1990[12] the Commission adopted a Communication concerning the consequences of the *Cassis de Dijon* case which emphasised the importance of the rule of recognition. According to the Communication

'Any product imported from another Member State must in principle be admitted to the territory of the importing State if it has been lawfully produced, that is, conforms to rules

---

[12] OJ C252 (1980).

and processes of manufacture that are customary and traditionally accepted in the exporting country, and is marketed in the territory of the latter.'

14.5 Measures distinctly and indistinctly applicable to exports: art 29 EC

Article 29 prohibits quantitative restrictions and measures having equivalent effect on exports. The ECJ explained in *Groenveld* Case 15/79 [1979] ECR 3409 that national measures are considered as measures having equivalent effect to quantitative restrictions on exports if they

'... have as their specific object or effect the restriction of patterns of exports and thereby the establishment of a difference in treatment between the domestic trade of a Member State and its export trade in such a way as to provide a particular advantage for national production or for the domestic market of the State in question at the expense of the production or of trade of other Member States.'

As a result, in the application of art 29 EC two situations must be distinguished: first, when national measures apply, without distinction, to domestic products for export and domestic products for the national market; and, second, when national measures make a distinction between domestic products for export and for the domestic market and thus domestic products for export are placed at a disadvantage as compared to domestic products intended exclusively for the national market.

National measures which apply, without distinction, to domestic products for export and domestic products for the national market

The *Dassonville* formula does not apply to such a situation. If national measures apply without distinction to the above types of products there is no breach of art 29 EC. In *Gerrit Holdijk* Joined Cases 141–143/81 [1982] ECR 1299 The Netherland's legislation on enclosures for fatting calves required that the dimensions of the enclosure should be such that the animals were able to lie down on their sides unhindered. The companies, prosecuted under Dutch law, argued that the majority of enclosures in The Netherlands did not conform to such requirements and that the measure affected mostly exports as 90 per cent of veal production in The Netherlands was intended for export. The ECJ held that since Dutch legislation did not make any distinction as to whether the animals or their meat were intended for the national market or for export there was no breach of art 29 EC. The same reasoning was applied in respect of Dutch legislation providing an exhaustive list, as well as strict requirements for production, of the types of cheese which may be produced in The Netherlands, including traditional Dutch cheeses such as Gouda and Edam: *Jongeneel Kass* Case 237/82 [1982] ECR 483. All other cheeses were prohibited. The Commission argued that the restriction of types of authorised cheeses was contrary to the principle of an open market and that it was in conflict with the Community policy of widening demand for cheese by increasing the variety of products offered. The ECJ rejected both arguments and stated that a Member State was empowered to enact such legislation provided that, first, it applied indistinctly to all domestic products whether intended for the domestic trade or for export and, second, it did not discriminate against imported products or hinder the importation of products from other Member States. Not only the protection of the consumer or public health but also, as in this case, the promotion of the quality of domestic products was considered by the ECJ as providing sufficient justification for enacting national rules of this type. It seems that provided they do not actually discriminate against export, the ECJ is prepared to tolerate national measures which have an adverse effect on domestic producers, by adding costs and difficulties.

National measures which make a distinction between domestic products for export and for the domestic market

Such measures are, when domestic products for export are placed at a disadvantage as compared to domestic products for the national market, in breach of art 29 EC. In *Bouhelier* Case 53/76 [1977] ECR 197 a quality control imposed only on exports was held to be a measure equivalent to a quantitative restriction on export. Similarly, in *Nertsvoederfabriek Nederlandse* Case 118/86 [1987] ECR 3883 the requirement that producers of poultry for export deliver poultry offal to their local authorities was considered as a ban on exports and thereby in breach of art 29 EC.

It seems that the ECJ is very lenient in respect of national measures even if they make a distinction between goods intended for domestic trade and for exports. In this respect it is interesting to examine *ED Srl v Italo Fenocchio* Case C–412/97 [1999] ECR I–3845.

In this case ED, an Italian company, supplied goods to Mr Fenocchio, a resident of Berlin, to the value of ITL 19,933,700. Mr Fenocchio paid ITL 100,000 by way of down-payment but not the balance. ED applied to the Pretura Circondariale di Bologna (District Magistrates' Court in Bologna) for a summary payment order in respect of the outstanding sum against Mr Fennocchio. Under Italian law the use of the special procedure for a summary payment order is prohibited where the debtor resides abroad. The referring court explained that the original justification for the prohibition was to avoid the debtor's ignorance of an action commenced against him or him not becoming aware of it until after expiry of the period laid down for opposing it, which would prevent the exercise of his right to defend the action. The referring court asked the ECJ to ascertain whether the prohibition was compatible with arts 29, 49 and 56 EC.

The ECJ held that art 29 EC does nor preclude national legislation which excludes recourse to the procedure for obtaining summary payment orders where service on the debtor is to be effected in another Member State. This decision seems very controversial, taking into account that the Italian provision prohibiting recourse to the simplified procedure for debt recovery seems to be in breach of art 29 EC as it establishes a difference in treatment between the domestic and the export trade of a Member State since it applies specifically to exports and creates disadvantage for Italian exporters. The rule is distinctly applicable and it discriminates against export. As such it is subject to the *Dassonville* formula and should have been declared in breach of art 29 EC. The ECJ decided otherwise. The Court held that the effect of the national procedural provision on exports was too uncertain and indirect to hinder trade between Member States. As a result, the Italian procedural provision is not in breach of art 29 EC since it does not discourage Italian sellers from selling goods to purchasers established in other Member States.[13]

It is interesting to note that the ECJ applied, for the first time, in the context of art 29 EC, the concept that the effect of national measures may be too uncertain and indirect to hinder trade between Member State.

The decision of the ECJ in this case is surprising in the sense that the ECJ did not declare as unlawful a national procedural rule which was patently discriminatory. In this respect, Advocate-General G Cosmas in his Opinion held the Italian procedural rule was contrary to the principle of non-discrimination laid down in art 12 EC. The ECJ confined its answer to the question submitted by the referring court.

14.6 National measures relating to selling arrangements indistinctly applicable to domestic and imported goods

In *Criminal Proceedings against Keck and Mithouard* Joined Cases C–267 and 268/91 [1993] ECR I–6097 the ECJ moved away from the wide application of the *Dassonville* formula and thus set new limits on art 28 EC.

In this case the French authorities commenced criminal proceedings against Keck and Mithouard for selling goods at a price lower than their acquisition cost (resale at a loss) which was in breach of a French law of 1963, as amended in 1986, although that law did not ban sales at a loss by manufacturers. Both offenders argued that the law in question was contrary to fundamental freedoms under the EC Treaty – free movement of goods, persons, services and capital – as well as in breach of EC competition law. The French court referred to the ECJ.

The ECJ dismissed all the arguments except one based on the free movement of goods. The Court re-examined its case law on the scope of art 28 EC and, at the same time, departed from its earlier decision in *Dassonville* by stating that the *Dassonville* formula did not apply to selling arrangements if national rules *prima facie* contrary to art 28 EC affect all the traders operating within the national territory and provided they affect in the same manner, in law and fact, the marketing of both domestic and imported products even though they may have some impact on the overall volume of sales. The Court did not provide any definition of selling arrangements. However, it gave some indications concerning the criteria for identifying 'selling arrangements' outside the scope of art 28 EC.

National measures relating to selling arrangements must apply, first, indistinctly to all traders operating within the territory of a Member State and, second, they must affect in the same manner, in law and fact, the marketing of both domestic and imported products even though they may have some impact on the overall volume of sales.

Keck does not modify the principles laid down in *Cassis de Dijon*. It relates to the *Dassonville* formula. In particular, it excludes from the scope of art 28 EC indistinctly applicable measures which relate to selling arrangements. Consequently, the *Dassonville*

---

[13] The ECJ cited a number of cases supporting its conclusions, ie *Krantz* Case C–69/88 [1991] ECR–I–583; *Motorradcenter* Case C–93/92 [1993] ECR I–5009.

formula applies to national indistinctly applicable measures which relate to the goods themselves. In *Keck* the ECJ gave some examples of rules relating to goods themselves. They concern such requirements as designation, form, size, weight, composition, presentation, labelling and packaging of goods.

In respect of selling arrangements, in the absence of any definition, point 16 of the judgment provides some assistance as it states that national rules which apply to domestic and imported products without any distinction (indistinctly applicable measures), and which do not restrict trade between Member States, should not be considered as measures having equivalent effect. Once these two conditions are satisfied 'the application of such rules to the sale of products from another Member State is not by nature such as to prevent their access to the market or to impede access any more than it impedes the access of domestic products. Such rules, therefore, fall outside the scope of art [28 EC].'

The scope of application of Keck

Subsequent case law of the ECJ confirms that *Keck* is not one of a kind, but inaugurated a new approach to the free movement of goods. In *Belgapom v ITM Belgium SA and Vocarex SA* Case C–63/95 [1995] ECR I–2467 the ECJ confirmed its ruling in *Keck*. In this case, the scenario was very similar to *Keck* as it concerned the Belgian law on Commercial Practices and Consumer Protection (1991) which prohibited resale at a loss. The Belgian law defined resale at a loss as taking place when 'the price is not at least equal to the price at which the product was invoiced at the time of supply'. Also under that legislation any sale yielding very low profit margins was considered as being within its scope. When Vocarex, a franchisee of ITM, bought a consignment of potatoes at BF 27 per 25 kg and resold them at BF 29 per 25 kg, it was accused by Belapom of selling at a loss, taking into account that all other Belgian outlets had agreed to sell at BF 89 per 25 kg. Vocarex argued that the Belgian law was in breach of art 28 EC. The ECJ decided otherwise. The Court held that art 28 EC did not apply to this situation as it concerned selling arrangements.

The second area in which *Keck* has been applied is advertising. In *Hünermund v Landesapothekerkammer Baden-Württemburg* Case C–292/92 [1993] ECR I–6787 German rules established by a professional body imposed a partial ban on advertising for pharmacists in order to restrict excessive competition between them. Pharmacists were not allowed to advertise on the radio, on TV or at the cinema. They were allowed to advertise in newspapers and magazines but only to state the address, name and phone number of the practice and the name of the proprietor. Hünermund challenged these rules. The ECJ held that German rules applied to all pharmacists and thus were indistinctly applicable. Furthermore, the ECJ confirmed that advertisement as a method of sales promotion was a selling arrangement and as such was outside the scope of art 28 EC.

The application of Keck to advertising was confirmed in *Société d'Importation E Leclerc-SIPLEC v TFI Publicité SA and M6 Publicité SA* Case C–412/93 [1995] ECR I–179 in which French legislation prohibiting the broadcasting of televised advertisements for the distribution sector was held by the ECJ as relating to selling agreements and thus outside the scope of art 28 EC.

The third area concerns national rules regarding the closing of shops on Sundays and bank holidays.[14]

The fourth area concerns national rules conferring a monopoly right to distribute certain products to a specific group of people. In *Commission v Greece* Case 391/92 [1995] ECR I–621 Greek legislation reserved to pharmacists the distribution of pharmaceutical products. The ECJ, contrary to its previous decision in *Delattre* Case 369/88 [1991] ECR I–1487 (and *Monteil and Sammani* Case 60/89 [1991] ECR 1561), considered that the Greek legislation related to selling arrangements and was therefore outside the scope of art 28 EC.

Keck: *its legal consequences*

The obvious consequence of *Keck* is that a number of previous decisions of the ECJ are now obsolete, in particular in the areas examined above. The absence of discrimination against imported goods as compared to domestic goods excludes *ipso facto* selling arrangements from the scope of application of *Cassis de Dijon*. As a result the principle of proportionality cannot be applied. This means that the Community judicature has no jurisdiction to control whether a national measure which applies to selling arrangements, without making any distinction between domestic and imported goods, is necessary and appropriate to the objective pursued by a Member State. In pre-*Keck* decisions the principle of proportionality was strictly applied by the ECJ. It is particularly well illustrated in *Stoke-on-Trent City Council v B & Q plc* Case 169/91 [1993] 1 CMLR 426; [1993] 1 All ER 481 concerning the long running saga of the compatibility of the Sunday trading laws of the United Kingdom with art 28 EC.

Section 47 of the Shops Act 1950 prohibited the opening of shops in England and Wales on Sundays except for the sale of certain items. The defendants were prosecuted by their local authority for opening their shop on Sundays contrary to this statute. In their defence, the defendants claimed that the prohibition of Sunday opening was contrary to art 28 EC because this entailed a restriction on trade which had a discriminatory effect on the sale of goods from other Member States. The matter was finally appealed to the House of Lords, which referred to the ECJ for a preliminary ruling along with a number of other cases pending before the lower courts concerning similar points of Community law.

The ECJ held that the appraisal of the proportionality of the contested national rules involved weighing the national interest in attaining the aim pursued by them against the Community interest in ensuring the free movement of goods. In order to verify that the restrictive effects on intra-Community trade of the rules at issue did not exceed what was necessary to achieve the aim in view, the ECJ had to consider whether those effects were direct, indirect or purely speculative, and whether those effects did not impede the marketing of imported products more than the marketing of national products. The ECJ held that the statute was compatible with art 28 EC. These restrictions had a legitimate socio-economic function which was recognised under Community law. In contrast in *Punto Casa SpA v Sindaco del Commune di Capena* Joined Cases C–69 and 258/93 [1994] ECR

---

[14] See *Tankstation 't Heukske and Boermans* Joined Cases 401–402/92 [1994] ECR I–2199; *Punto Case* Joined Cases C–69 and 258/93 [1994] ECR I–2355; *Semeraso* Joined Cases 418–421, 460–462 and 464/93 and 9–11, 14–15, 23–24 and 332/94 [1996] ECR I–2975.

I–2355 (decided after *Keck*) the ECJ held that Italian legislation on the closure of retail outlets on Sundays related to selling arrangements and as such was outside the ambit of art 28 EC. As a result, no justification is necessary for national measures relating to selling arrangements provided they are applied equally to domestic and imported products, that is, affecting them in the same manner in law and fact.

Taking into account the lack of definition of selling arrangements Member States have, to a considerable extent, regained their competence in regulating trade in respect of goods coming from another Member State. It seems that the ECJ is widely interpreting the concept of selling arrangements and that any hesitation as to the qualification of a national measure, that is whether or not it relates to the product itself or concerns a selling arrangement, is resolved in favour of the latter. In *Tankstation 't Heukske Vof and Boermans* Cases C–401 and 402/92 [1994] ECR I–2199 the ECJ held that Dutch legislation which regulated compulsory closing of petrol retail outlets was outside the scope of art 28 EC.

The main question is how to determine whether a particular national rule concerns the nature of the product itself or the selling arrangements. In this respect *Keck* has introduced a false dichotomy between the rules relating to selling arrangements and rules relating to the characteristics of the product. Post-*Keck* cases show that nobody is really certain what should be considered as selling arrangements! In *Vereinigte Familiapress Zeitungsverlags- und Vertriebs GmbH* v *Henrich Bauer Verlag* Case C–368/95 [1997] ECR I–3689 Austrian legislation concerning the prohibition of the sale of periodicals containing games or competitions for prizes was at issue. The Austrian government argued that the prohibition concerned a method of promoting sales and as such was a selling arrangement outside the scope of art 28 EC. Henrich Bauer Verlag, the German publisher of the weekly magazine *Laura*, which was distributed in Austria and which contained a crossword puzzle offering readers sending the correct solution the opportunity to enter a draw for prizes of DM 500, claimed that the Austrian law was a quantitative restriction contrary to art 28 EC. The ECJ held that:

> 'Even though such legislation is directed against a method of sales promotion, it bears on the actual content of the products, in so far as the competitions in question form an integral part of the magazine in which they appear, and cannot be concerned with a selling arrangement. As a result, the national legislation in question, as applied to the facts of the case, is not concerned with a selling arrangement within the meaning of the judgment in *Keck and Mithouard*.'

The simplicity and uniformity in the application of art 28 EC has gone.

Another example of the perversity of *Keck* is provided in *Österreichische Unilever GmbH* Case C–77/97 [1999] ECR I–431. In this case Austrian legislation, which was enacted in order to implement Directive 76/768/EEC, prohibited the incorrect or misleading advertising of cosmetic products. Directive 76/768/EEC exhaustively harmonised national rules relating to packaging and labelling of cosmetic products. Under that Directive Member States were required to take all necessary measures to ensure that labelling, presentation and advertising of cosmetic products were not used in such a manner as to attribute to those products certain characteristics which they did not have. The ECJ held that Austrian legislation prohibiting improper and misleading advertisement of cosmetic products was disproportionate to the objective sought by the Directive. The interesting aspect of this case is that the ECJ confined its reasoning to the application of the Directive, although the referring court expressly asked for some clarifications in respect of the scope of art 28 EC. However, the ECJ escaped any embarrassment because the Directive in question exhaustively regulated the matter. Indeed, if the Directive had not done this the ECJ would have had to consider separately from each other the advertising on the label of the product concerned and the advertising of it on TV. Advertising on the label is considered to be incorporated into the product and thus concerns the nature of the product itself and as such is within the scope of art 28 EC: see *Mars* Case C–470/93 [1995] ECR I–317. The prohibition of misleading and incorrect advertisement on the label might be justified under imperative requirements of the rule of reason set out in *Cassis de Dijon* subject to the principle of proportionality. Taking into account the facts of the above case the Austrian law in question would have been regarded as disproportionate and declared unlawful by the ECJ. However, the advertising on TV of cosmetic products in the light of previous decisions of the ECJ, in particular *Leclerc-SIPLEC* Case C–412/93 [1995] ECR I–179 and *De Agostini* Cases C–34 and 36/95 [1997] ECR I–3843, would have escaped the application of art 28 EC as being selling arrangements. Consequently, because of Directive 76/768 national rules on advertisement on TV were held disproportionate, although under the *Keck* approach alone they would be lawful as being outside the scope of art 28 EC.

The perversity of the above case, and its interest, lay in the fat that in the absence of harmonising Community measures the rules set by *Keck* would have led to the situation where art 28 EC would have to be applied in two different and opposing ways to the same form of advertising (Austrian law made no distinction between them). The different ways being:

1. the application of art 28 EC to the advertisement on the label under which national rules in this area would be considered disproportionate and therefore unlawful; and
2. the application of *Keck* under which national rules concerning the advertisement of the same product on TV would be outside the scope of art 28 EC and therefore lawful.

On this occasion the ECJ found a way to escape its potential embarrassment, but the case only serves to highlight the perversity of *Keck*.

It may be considered that in the above case the undertakings advertising cosmetic products in Austria on TV were lucky to have the Austrian legislation in question declared unlawful on the ground of the principle of proportionality, so allowing their advertising to continue if desired. Whereas, in the absence of Directive 76/768/EEC they would have been prosecuted for misleading and improper advertisement on the basis of *Keck*.

When considering the outcome of the above case it is difficult to comprehend why the exhaustive harmonisation of national rules justifies a hindrance to the free movement of goods. If national measures constitute an obstacle they should be removed, whether or not there are Community rules.

Each new judgment is more and more confusing. In *Schutzverband Gegen Unlauteren Wettbewerb* Case C–254/98 Judgment of 13 January 2000 (nyr), under Austrian law bakers, butchers and grocers were permitted to offer for sale, on rounds from locality to locality, goods they had been authorised to sell under their trading licences, provided they operated within a specific area of Austria (Verwaltungsbezirk) in which they were permanently established. TK-Heimdienst, a retail trader, offered his groceries for sale on rounds in a district in which he was not established. The Schutzverband, an association for the protection of the economic interests of undertakings, brought an action for an order restraining TK-Heimdienst from selling his goods in a district in which he was not established. The referring court asked whether Austrian legislation was in conformity with art 28 EC. The referring court stated that although Austrian legislation regulated a particular mode of selling which should be classified as a selling arrangement, nevertheless it could be capable of amounting to a disguised restriction as defined in *Legia and Gyselinx* Case 87/85 [1986] ECR 1707 and *Boscher* Case C–239/90 [1991] ECR I–2023 (both pre-*Keck* decisions). The above would apply in particular to a trader from another Member State wishing to sell goods on rounds in Austria, taking into account that such a trader would have to set up and operate a permanent establishment in Austria in addition to his business in the Member State where he had his principal establishment.

The Advocate-General followed the reasoning in *Keck* and concluded that art 28 EC did not apply to Austrian legislation as it concerned selling arrangements. The ECJ held that although Austrian legislation related to selling arrangements it did not affect in the same manner the marketing of domestic products and the marketing of products from other Member States, as traders from other Member States would necessarily bear additional costs which would make that mode of selling unprofitable to them. This is par excellence the reasoning which was applied by the ECJ before *Keck*! The next step of the ECJ is even more surprising. The ECJ examined whether Austrian legislation was capable of being justified under art 30 EC! In this respect the ECJ stated that 'whilst it is true that the protection of public health is one of the grounds capable of justifying derogations from art [28 EC], that objective can be attained by measures that have effects less restrictive of intra-Community trade' (that is, rules on provisions of refrigerating equipment in the vehicles used). Indeed, the answer is obvious – Austrian legislation was in blatant breach of art 28 EC. The ECJ concluded that Austrian legislation was within the scope of art 28 EC and, although it concerned selling arrangements, it was in breach of that provision. As Rigaux stated, this decision raises a number of questions.[15] Should it be regarded as a return to the pre-*Keck* approach? Does it provide new clarifications in respect of the post-*Keck* case law? Or does it give rise to new uncertainties regarding the application of *Keck*?

It is submitted that the explanation given by the ECJ in *Keck* for its change of approach to the scope of application of art 28 EC is less than convincing. The *Dassonville* formula, although much criticised, was one of the main driving forces towards the creation of the internal market which, as the ECJ emphasised, has always been founded on the principle of a free market economy. This entails that any obstacle to the free movement of goods, whether it concerns the product itself or its modality of sale, should be abolished. Furthermore, under the rule of reason introduced by *Cassis de Dijon*, national peculiarities which may obstruct free movement of goods are duly taken into consideration and assessed in the light of the principle of proportionality. *Keck* creates a risk of impeding the free movement of goods. It focuses on the factual and legal equality between traders but ignores the fact that national rules, which may not discriminate in law or in fact, may, nevertheless,

---

[15] *Europe*, March 2000, 74.

inhibit access to the market as evidenced by national rules on advertising, sale at a loss, etc. Indeed, commercial strategies concerning a product (advertising, or a method of sales promotion such as resale at a loss or below a minimum price imposed by national law) from the point of view of commercialisation are as important as the product itself and those things considered to be incorporated into it, for example, its packaging, quality etc. *Keck* focuses on the objective of national rules, that is whether or not they discriminate, in law or in fact, against products imported from other Member States and not on the effect of such rules, that is whether or not they affect access to markets in any of the Member States in terms of the volume of sales, and whether or not they are proportionate to the objective intended by national rules. This approach calls into question the foundations of the common market which requires unfettered access to national markets for goods coming from other Member States.

It seems that although the ECJ introduced *Keck* in order to clarify its case law, *Keck* is surrounded by ambiguity and inconsistency and has, in fact, introduced unnecessary complexity and confusion.

15 Article 30 EC

15.1 Public morality

15.2 Public policy and public security

15.3 Protection of the health and life of humans, animals and plants

15.4 Protection of national treasures possessing artistic, historic
or archaeological value

Article 30 EC provides:

'The provisions of arts 28 and 29 shall not preclude prohibitions or restrictions on imports, exports or goods in transit justified on grounds of public morality, public policy or public security; the protection of health and life of humans, animals or plants; the protection of national treasures possessing artistic, historic or archaeological value; or the protection of industrial and commercial property.[1] Such prohibitions or restrictions shall not, however, constitute a means of arbitrary discrimination or a disguised restriction on trade between Member States.'

The list provided in art 30 EC is exhaustive. All exceptions must be interpreted strictly, otherwise they will undermine the general rule set out in arts 28 and 29 EC.[2] Article 30 applies only to distinctly applicable measures. Indistinctly applicable measures restricting imports are subject to the rule of reason under *Cassis de Dijon*. Only exceptionally may indistinctly applicable measures be considered under art 30 EC. This occurs when national measures are clearly discriminatory in their effect on imports or fall within one of the exceptions laid down in art 30 EC. It emerges from the examination of case law regarding the application of art 30 EC that:

1. Distinctly applicable measures can never be justified under the rule of reason.[3] This was clearly stated by the ECJ in *Commission* v *Ireland (Re Irish Souvenirs)* Case 113/80 [1981] ECR 1625. Under Irish law souvenirs which were considered as typically Irish (eg, Irish round towels and shamrocks) but imported from other Member States should be stamped either with the indication of their place of origin or with the word 'foreign'. As a result, importers of Irish souvenirs were discriminated against as compared to Irish producers of Irish souvenirs as they were burdened with an additional requirement imposed by Irish legislation and suffered a reduction in sales, taking into account that tourists wanted to buy 'original' souvenirs. Irish law was clearly discriminatory. The

---

[1] See Chapter 25 on intellectual property.
[2] See for example *Marimex* Case 29/72 [1972] ECR 1309; *Firma Eggers Sohn & Co* v *Freie Hansestadt Bremen* Case 13/78 [1978] ECR 1935.
[3] See also *Association des Centres Distributeurs E Leclerc and Others* v *'Au Ble Vert' Sarl* Case 229/83 [1985] ECR 1.

Irish government argued that national measures were necessary to protect consumers and to ensure the fairness of commercial transactions. The ECJ held that as those grounds were not mentioned in art 30 they could not be relied on pursuant to that Article.

2. Purely economic objectives, such as the necessity of ensuring the balance of payments, the reduction of public spending, or the survival of an undertaking, cannot be justified under art 30 EC.[4]

3. The pursuit of the objectives enumerated in art 30 EC is not in itself sufficient to justify national measures restricting intra-Community trade. They must also be necessary and proportionate to these objectives. In this respect the ECJ held in *Commission v Belgium* Case 155/82 [1984] ECR 531 that:

> '... [public health] measures are justified only if it is established that they are necessary in order to attain the objective of protection referred to in art [30 EC] and that such protection cannot be achieved by means which place less of a restriction on the free movement of goods within the Community.'

In order to determine whether national measures are necessary the ECJ will examine their restrictive effects – direct, indirect, actual and potential – on trade between Member States and whether these result in impeding access to a national market for imported products any more than they impede access of domestic products.[5] For example, in *Brandsma* Case C– 293/94 [1996] ECR I–3159 the ECJ held that it would not be 'necessary' to carry out technical analyses or laboratory tests on imported goods if they had already been conducted in another Member State.

In respect of the principle of proportionality, the ECJ has emphasised that if a Member State has a choice between different measures capable of attaining the same objective, it must chose the one which least hinders the free movement of goods.[6] In *De Peiper* Case 104/75 [1976] ECR 613 the ECJ held that national measures intended to facilitate the task of the public authorities, or to reduce public expenditure, could only be justified if alternative arrangements would impose unreasonable burdens on the administration.

4. Article 30 EC provides that national measures permitted under art 30 EC must not constitute a means of arbitrary discrimination or a disguised restriction on trade between Member States. In *R v Henn and Darby* Case 34/79 [1979] ECR 3795 the ECJ emphasised that the purpose of the prohibition is it to:

> '... prevent restrictions on trade based on the grounds mentioned in the first sentence of art [30 EC] from being diverted from their proper purpose and used in such a way as either to create discrimination in respect of goods originating in other Member States or indirectly to protect certain national products.'

In order to determine whether a national measure which discriminates against imported

---

[4] *Commission v Italy* Case 7/61 [1961] ECR 633; *De Peiper* Case 104/75 [1976] ECR 613; *Commission v Italy* Case 95/81 [1982] ECR 2189; *Duphar BV* Case 238/82 [1984] ECR 523; *Evans Medical* Case C–324/93 [1995] ECR I–563.

[5] See *Semeraso* Joined Cases 418–421, 460–462 and 464/93 and 9–11, 14–15, 23–24 and 332/94 [1996] ECR I–2975.

[6] For example, *Van der Veldt* Case 17/93 [1994] ECR I–3537.

goods is arbitrary, or constitutes a disguised restriction aimed at protecting domestic goods, a comparison between the treatment of domestic goods and imported goods is necessary. The differentiation must be justified on objective grounds, that is it must be genuine.[7]

5. It is incumbent on national authorities to prove that a national measure which restricts trade between Member States is justified under art 30 EC. The ECJ in *Leendert van Bennekom* Case 227/82 [1983] ECR 3883 held that 'it is for the national authorities to demonstrate in each case that their rules are necessary to give effective protection to the interests referred to in art [30 EC]'.

15.1 Public morality

In principle, it is for each Member State to determine, in accordance with its own scale of values and in the form selected by it, the requirements of public morality in its territory. Thus, art 30 EC permits a Member State to establish it own concept of 'public morality'. The qualification of the word 'in principle' is important as it allows the Community to interfere, in particular in order to prevent a Member State from imposing double standards of morality, one applicable to domestic goods and another to imported goods, thus discriminating against the latter on the ground of public morality.

In this respect it is interesting to contrast *R v Henn and Darby* Case 34/79 [1979] ECR 3795; [1980] CMLR 246 with *Conegate Limited v HM Customs & Excise* Case 121/85 [1986] ECR 1007; [1986] 1 CMLR 739.

In *Henn and Darby* the defendants imported a number of consignments of obscene films and publications into the UK from The Netherlands. They were caught by customs officials and charged with the criminal offence of being 'knowingly concerned in the fraudulent evasion of the prohibition of the importation of indecent or obscene articles'. In their defence, the defendants claimed that the prohibition on the importation of pornographic material was contrary to art 28 EC, as it constituted a measure having an equivalent effect to a quantitative restriction. The ECJ held that art 28 EC is subject to a number of exceptions, one of which is contained in art 30 EC and relates to restrictions intended to protect public morality. The British legislation fell within the scope of this exception and consequently the criminal charges were consistent with Community law. The ECJ upheld the arguments of the UK government, even though the UK applied double standards in that in the UK only pornographic materials likely to 'deprave or corrupt' were prohibited, whilst it was lawful to trade in 'indecent or obscene' literature. This meant that the UK imposed more stringent conditions on imported goods than on domestic goods, which was contrary to the principle of non-discrimination based on nationality.

The above situation was rectified in *Conegate*. In this case a British company set up businesses importing inflatable dolls from Germany into the United Kingdom. A number of consignments of the products were seized by customs officials on the ground that the dolls were 'indecent and obscene', and accordingly subject to the prohibition on imports

---

[7] The concept of 'disguised restrictions' was examined in *Commission v UK* Case 40/82 [1982] ECR 2793.

contained in the Customs Consolidation Act 1876. Although national rules prohibited the importation of these dolls, no regulation prevented their manufacture in the United Kingdom. The company brought an action for recovery of the dolls. In particular, it was alleged that the prohibition order contravened art 28 EC and was accordingly a measure having an effect equivalent to a quantitative restriction. In reply, the British authorities claimed that the measures were justified under art 30 EC in order to protect public morality.

The ECJ held that the United Kingdom could not rely on art 30 EC to prohibit the importation of products, when no internal provisions had been enacted to prevent the manufacture and distribution of the offending products within the United Kingdom. To allow a Member State to prevent the importation of particular goods, while simultaneously allowing nationals to manufacture such products, would amount to discrimination on the ground of nationality. The argument of the UK based on the fact that no articles comparable to those imported by Conegate were manufactured in the United Kingdom was rejected. The ECJ stressed that as long as UK law did not exclude the possibility of manufacturing such articles importation from another Member State could not be prevented.

It seems that in the light of the objective of completion of the internal market, the ECJ decided that double morality standards should be abolished.

15.2 Public policy and public security

Member States have rarely invoked derogations based on public policy and public security. The assessment of national measures necessary to ensure public security and public order is left to the Member States which have to find the right balance between the extent of rights conferred on individuals and the requirements of public policy or public security. Public policy refers to the fundamental interests of society. Public security concerns the safeguarding of the institutions of a Member State, its essential public services and the survival of its inhabitants. Public security and public policy exceptions laid down in art 30 EC apply only to the free movement of goods and not to other provisions of the Treaty. Therefore derogations, based on public policy and public order, relating to the free movement of persons embodied in art 39 EC have been construed more broadly than derogations under art 30 EC. Consequently, the ECJ has often decided that the requirements of the free movement of goods override considerations based on public policy and public security. Both derogations have been treated by the ECJ as exceptions of last resort. In *Cullet v Centre Leclerc* Case 231/83 [1985] ECR 305 the French government imposed maximum prices for fuel, arguing that the maintenance of these prices limits was necessary to avoid civil disorder, including violence. The ECJ rejected this argument on the ground that the French government did not show that 'it would be unable, using means at its disposal, to deal with the consequences which an amendment of the rules in question … would have upon public order and security'. Therefore, national measures may be justified on the ground of public policy if a Member State shows that in their absence civil unrest would be more than the national authorities could be expected to cope with. Similarly, in *Commission v Italy* Case 154/85 [1987] ECR 2256 an Italian Ministerial Decree concerning the registration of vehicles, which set out more stringent requirements in respect of registration of used imported vehicles which had already been registered in the country of exportation than in respect of new cars, was considered as a measure having equivalent effect to a quantitative restriction. The Italian government tried to justify the decree on the ground of public order, in particular the necessity to combat the trafficking of stolen vehicles. The ECJ stated that under the decree the registration of imported used cars took longer, was more complex and was more expensive than that of new cars. This could not be justified on the ground of public order, taking into account that the multiplication of requirements relating to registration did not constitute an efficient manner of detecting and preventing the trafficking of stolen vehicles.

One of the first cases in which public security was successfully invoked concerned the UK legislation prohibiting, on the one hand, import of coins, and on the other hand, destruction and melting of UK coins even if they were no longer legal tender: *R v Thompson, Johnson and Woodiwiss* Case 7/78 [1978] ECR 2247. Criminal proceedings were commenced against a number of British citizens who, despite the ban, imported coins into the UK. The ECJ held that the ban was a measure equivalent to a quantitative restriction but was justified on the ground of public policy because the need to protect the right to mint coinage was one of the fundamental interests of society.

The public security exception has been successfully relied upon by Member States in respect of national legislation regulating transport of dangerous substances. In *Richardt* Case 367/89 [1991] ECR I–4621 the introduction of special authorisation in respect of transit of strategic material was justified on the ground of public security.

In *Campus Oil Ltd v Minister for Industry and Energy* Case 72/83 [1984] ECR 2727 Irish law required that importers of petroleum products purchase up to 35 per cent of their requirements from the State-owned refinery at a fixed price. The measure was clearly discriminatory and protective. The Irish government argued that this measure was necessary to maintain viability of the only petroleum refinery in Ireland, especially in the event of a national crisis. The ECJ accepted that an interruption of supplies of petroleum products was a matter of public security and public policy.

It is not necessary for national legislation to provide for penal sanctions in order to be considered as being concerned with public policy within the meaning of art 30 EC: *Prantl* Case 16/83 [1984] ECR 1299.

15.3 Protection of the health and life of humans, animals and plants

The basic principle under this heading is that a Member State must, in order to justify national measures on these grounds, demonstrate that there is a genuine risk to health and life: *Duphar BV* Case 238/82 [1984] ECR 523. Therefore, national measures must not serve as a pretext for introducing disguised discrimination against imported products. This happened in *Commission v United Kingdom (Re UHT Milk)* Case 124/81 [1983] ECR 203 in which the UK imposed a requirement that UHT milk should be marketed only by approved dairies or distributors. This involved re-packaging and re-treatment of all imported milk. The UK government argued that the measure was necessary to ensure that the milk was free from bacterial or viral infections. The ECJ held that there was evidence that milk in all Member States was of similar quality and subject to equivalent controls. For that reason the requirement, although it applied to both domestic and imported goods, was considered as disguised discrimination and therefore examined under art 30 EC.

The derogation based on the protection of the health and life of humans, animals and plants has been successfully relied on in a number of cases. For example, in *R v Home Secretary, ex parte Evans Medical and MacFarlane Smith* Case C–324/93 [1995] ECR I–563 in which the refusal to grant an importation licence for diamorphine, a heroin substitute for medical purposes, was justified in order to ensure the reliability of supply of diamorphine in the UK and to avoid risk of unlawful traffic in diamorphine. In *Ortscheit* Case C–320/93 [1994] ECR I–5243 German law prohibiting the advertising of medical products which had not yet been authorised in Germany was justified on the ground of public heath. However, these products which were lawfully on sale in other Member States could be imported by individual consumers.

The protection of health and life of animals was successfully pleaded in *D Bluhme (Brown Bees of Læsø)* Case C–67/97 [1998] ECR I–8033. In this case criminal proceedings were instituted against Ditlev Bluhme for breach of Danish law prohibiting the keeping on the island of Læsø of bees other than those of the subspecies *apis mellifera mellifera* (brown bees of Læsø). Mr Bluhme argued that the prohibition constituted a measure having equivalent effect to a quantitative restriction and as such was contrary to art 28 EC, whilst the Danish authorities claimed that such legislation, even if in breach of art 28 EC, was justified on the ground of the protection of the health and life of animals.

The ECJ held that Danish legislation prohibiting the keeping on the island of Læsø of any species of bee other than the subspecies *apis mellifera mellifera* constituted a measure having an equivalent effect to a quantitative restriction within the meaning of art 28 EC, but it was justified under art 30 EC on the ground of the protection of the health and life of animals. The ECJ recognised that the threat of the disappearance of the Læsø brown bee was, by reason of the recessive nature of the genes of the brown bee, undoubtedly genuine in the event of mating with golden bees. The establishment by the national legislation of a protection area within which the keeping of bees other than Læsø brown bees was prohibited, for the purpose of ensuring the survival of Læsø brown bees, therefore constituted an appropriate measure in relation to the aim pursued.

However, the ECJ failed to fully explain the relationship between national measures and the protection of the health and life of animals within the meaning of art 30 EC. Such an explanation would be welcomed taking into account that in previous cases in this area the justifications based on the protection of the health and life of animals were made in the context of the prevention of propagation of animal diseases (*Commission v Germany* Case C–131/93 [1994] ECR I–3303) or the prevention of unnecessary suffering by animals: *Compassion in World Farming* Case C–1/96 [1998] ECR I–1251. In *Bluhme* the ECJ stated that such national measures 'contribute to the maintenance of biodiversity' and 'by so doing, they are aimed at protecting the life of those animals and are capable of being justified under art 30 of the Treaty'. The relationship between the maintenance of biodiversity and the protection of the environment, which is outside the scope of art 30 EC, should have been more clearly explained by the ECJ, taking into account that the ECJ has always emphasised that exceptions to art 28 EC must be strictly interpreted.

15.4 Protection of national treasures possessing artistic, historic or archaeological value

Member States are free to determine their national treasures possesssing artistic, historic or archaelogical value. By virtue of art 30 EC they may also impose restrictions on exports of such national treasures. The scope of this derogation is uncertain as there is no case law in this respect. In *Commission v Italy (Re Export Tax on Art Treasures)* Case 7/68 [1968] ECR 423 the ECJ held that the desire to protect national treasures could not justify charges. Therefore, the imposition of quantitative restrictions and charges having equivalent effect seems to be the only way to protect national treasures. This was recognised by the French Conseil d'Etat (highest administrative court in France) which held that French legislation prohibiting export of objects of art or objects of historic value was justified on the ground of art 30 EC.[8]

The completion of the internal market prompted the Community to adopt certain measures ensuring that the free movement of goods would not increase illegal exports of national treasures of a Member State. These measures are: Directive 93/7/EC on the Return of Cultural Objects Unlawfully Removed from the Territory of a Member State[9] and Regulation 3911/92 on the Control of the Export of Cultural Goods.[10]

---

[8] CE 25 March 1994, Syndicat National de la Librairie Ancienne et Moderne.
[9] OJ L74 (1993).
[10] OJ L395 (1992).

16 Citizenship of the EU

16.1 Right of free movement and residence within the territory of the Member States

16.2 Participation in municipal elections and in elections to the European Parliament

16.3 Diplomatic and consular protection

16.4 Right to petition the European Parliament and to submit applications to the Ombudsman

16.5 Assessment of Union citizenship

The concept of European citizenship highlights a new dimension of European integration and especially underlines that the Community has extended its competences beyond economic and social domains.[1] Indeed, it seems unrealistic to build a political Union without granting special rights to, and imposing some obligations upon, its citizens. The EC Treaty provides that one objective of the Union is to 'strengthen the protection of the rights and interests of the nationals of its Member States through the introduction of a citizenship of the Union'. In order to give substance to these rights, and thus to go beyond a mere declaration, Part Two was inserted into the EC Treaty: arts 17–22 EC. Article 17(2) states that 'Citizens of the Union shall enjoy the rights conferred by this Treaty and shall be subject to the duties imposed thereby', albeit no specific duties are mentioned in the EC Treaty. It seems that apart from an implied civic duty to vote there are no duties imposed on EU citizens.

Union citizenship as it stands now is little more than a symbol of European identity, as is the European flag adopted in 1986 (the 12 stars will remain no matter how many new States join the EU as they are said to represent a 'symbol of perfection').The European anthem adopted in 1972 (the prelude to the 'Ode of Joy' from Beethoven's Ninth Symphony) and the existence of the European Day on 9 May to commemorate the Schuman Declaration are also part of the 'paraphernalia' of citizenship. The main objective is to bring the concept of European integration closer to ordinary people, rather than to confer important rights and benefits.

EU citizenship rights are limited as compared with the citizenship rights attached to a national of a Member State. There are, however, seven identifiable rights, some of which are of little practical importance for two reasons: some have already been granted to EC nationals residing in other Member States and thus the EC Treaty only confirms the existing

---

[1] For the historical background: see D O'Keeffe, 'Union Citizenship', in *Legal Issues of the Maastricht Treaty*, London: Wiley Chancery, 1994, pp87–107..

situations; others need to be further developed in order to grant real benefits to EU citizens. The rights conferred by the EC Treaty are:

1. the right of free movement;
2. the right to residence within the territory of the Member States;
3. the right to vote and stand for municipal elections in the State of residence, under the same conditions as nationals of that State;
4. passive and active voting rights for elections to the European Parliament;
5. the right to diplomatic and consular protection in a third State in which the Member State of the national of that State is not represented;
6. the right to petition the European Parliament; and
7. the right to submit complaints to the Ombudsman.

These rights may be added to, or strengthened by, the Council and a mechanism for their review is provided.

EU citizenship is based on nationality of a Member State. Article 17(1) states that 'Every person holding the nationality of a Member State shall be a citizen of the Union. Citizenship of the Union shall complement and not replace national citizenship.' This point is enhanced in the Declaration on Nationality of a Member State attached to the TEU which provides that:

> '... wherever in the Treaty establishing the European Community reference is made to nationals of the Member State, the question whether an individual possesses the nationality of a Member State shall be settled solely by reference to the national law of the Member State concerned.'

Consequently, matters relating to nationality are within the exclusive prerogative of a Member State. This was confirmed by the ECJ in *Michelletti* Case C–369/90 [1992] ECR I–4239 where the ECJ held that the determination of conditions governing the acquisition and loss of nationality were, according to international law, matters which fell within the competence of each Member State, whose decision must be respected by other Member States. As a result, a Member State has to accept as an EC national anyone who has nationality of another Member State regardless of the conditions of acquisition of that nationality. Furthermore, the EU cannot interfere in the nationality laws of the Member States as they are outside the scope of the Treaty.

The requirement of nationality of a Member State as a prerequisite of EU citizenship means that nationals of third countries, refugees and stateless persons legally residing in a Member State do not acquire any rights under art 17 EC. In practice, about 8–9 million people residing legally in the EU are excluded from benefiting from EU citizenship, even though they contribute to the prosperity of the EU and are treated in Member States on an equal footing with nationals.

16.1 Right of free movement and residence within the territory of the Member States

Article 18(1) EC recognises the right of free movement and provides for freedom of residence within the territory of the Member States. However, it specifies that those rights are subject to limitations and conditions laid down in the Treaty and in measures adopted to give them effect. Under art 18(2) EC the Council may adopt measures facilitating the exercise of those rights. Such measures must be proposed by the Commission and require the unanimous vote of the Council and the assent of the European Parliament.

In practice, art 18(2) is of real importance for EC nationals who are not economically active since the right of free movement and residence of persons economically active has already been recognised under the EC Treaty.[2] Workers, the self-employed, providers of services and their families, as defined in secondary legislation, are entitled to move freely and to reside in any Member State unless their presence is contrary to public policy, public security or public health of the host State. Therefore, the right of the economically inactive to move freely and to reside in another Member State is within the ambit of art 18(2). On 28 June 1990 the Council adopted three directives:

1. Directive 90/365/EEC[3] granting the right of free movement to employees and self-employed persons and their family members who have ceased their occupational activity;
2. Directive 90/364/EEC (the so-called 'Playboy Directive')[4] governing the right of residence of nationals of Member States and their families who are not covered by other provisions of the EC Treaty but have sufficient resources to avoid being a burden on the social security system of the host Member State and who are covered by sickness insurance in respect of all risks in the host Member State; and
3. Directive 90/366/EEC concerning the right of residence for students[5] and their family members. Directive 90/366/EEC was challenged by the EP in *European Parliament* v *Council* Case 295/90 [1992] 3 CMLR 281 in which the ECJ annulled the Directive on the ground that it was adopted on an improper legal basis but preserved its effects pending adoption of a new Directive. On 29 October 1993 the Council adopted Directive 93/96/EC on the right of residence for students.[6]

An important limitation on the right of residence provided by all three Directives is that persons covered by them must not become a burden on the social security system of the State of residence. As a result they must have health insurance and adequate means of support. Their right expires if they default on any of the conditions of their residence as prescribed by the Directives,[7] or they may be precluded on the grounds of public policy, public security and public health. The definition of family members is more restrictive than

---

[2] B Wilkinson, 'Towards European Citizenship? Nationality, Discrimination and Free Movement of Workers in the European Union' (1995) 3 European Public Law 417–529. He examines the right of free movement for workers in the light of art 18 EC.

[3] OJ L180 (1990).

[4] OJ L180 (1990).

[5] OJ L180 (1990).

[6] OJ L317 (1993).

[7] Article 3 of Directives 90/364 and 90/365 and art 4 of Directive 90/366.

that regarding economically active persons. It seems that the three Directives mentioned above may well be substantially changed in the future.[8]

Article 18 EC was invoked in *R v Home Secretary, ex parte Vitale and Do Amaral* [1996] All ER (EC) 461. In this case the applicants, both EC nationals, challenged a deportation order. They had been receiving income support for a number of months and according to the Department of Employment were not actively seeking employment. Both applicants disagreed with the Department of Employment and argued that regardless of its allegations they were, as EU citizens, allowed to reside in the UK. The Divisional Court rejected their argument and held that neither the right to free movement nor the right to reside freely were free-standing or absolute and that, taking into account the limitations imposed in arts 18(2) and 22 EC, art 18 did not provide every citizen of the Union with an open-ended right to reside freely within every Member State.

Subsequently, the ECJ further clarified the scope of art 18 EC when, for the first time, it invoked the concept of citizenship of the European Union embodied in arts 17 and 18 EC in *Maria Martinez Sala v Freistaat Bayern* Case C–85/96 [1998] ECR I–2691. In this case the German authorities of the Freistaat Bayern (State of Bavaria) refused to grant a child-raising allowance for a child of Mrs Martinez Sala, a Spanish national who had resided in Germany for many years. The basis of residence was: first, a residence permit (until May 1984); second, documents specifying that she had applied for an extension of her residence permit; third, a residence permit issued on 19 April 1994 and expiring on 18 April 1995; and, fourth, a one-year extension (to 18 April 1996) of the residence permit which expired on 18 April 1995. Mrs Martinez Sala was born in 1956 and came to Germany in 1968. Between 1976 and 1986 she had various jobs and was in employment again from 12 September to 24 October 1989. After that she received social assistance from the German authorities. When she applied for child-raising allowance in January 1993 she did not have a residence permit. Her application was refused on the grounds that she was neither a German national nor in possession of a residence entitlement/residence permit. She challenged that decision before a German court which referred to the ECJ for a preliminary ruling, inter alia, the question whether a national of one Member State who resides in another Member State, where he is employed and receives social assistance, has the status of worker

The ECJ stated that a national of a Member State lawfully residing in the territory of another Member State may rely on art 18 EC in all situations within the scope of application *ratione materiae* of Community law. The ECJ stated that art 18 EC attaches to the status of citizen of the Union the rights and duties laid down by the Treaty, including the right, in art 12 EC, not to suffer discrimination on grounds of nationality within the scope of application *ratione materiae* of the Treaty.

The ECJ made reference to art 18 EC in response to the argument submitted by the German authorities that Mrs Marinez Sala was not a worker within the meaning of art 39 EC and therefore outside the scope of application of art 12 EC. The ECJ replied that even if she was not a worker (and that was to be determined by the German court) she was a citizen of the European Union and as such entitled to move and to reside freely within the

---

[8] The Commission emphasised in its report on the implementation of the three Directives that there is a further need to inform citizens of their rights and that substantive changes to the existing legislation are under discussion. COM (1999) 127; Bull 3–1999, point 1.1.2.

territories of the Member States as well as not to be subject to discrimination based on nationality prohibited by art 12 EC. There are two important implications relating to this decision: first, art 18 EC is directly effective; and, second, the scope of application of the principle of non-discrimination on the grounds of nationality embodied in art 12 EC has been considerably extended via the application of art 18 EC.

Also, in *Horst Otto Bickel, Ulrich Franz* Case C–274/96 [1998] ECR I–7637 the ECJ invoked the concept of citizenship of the EU. In this case the Italian authorities commenced criminal proceedings against Mr Bickel, an Austrian national, who drove his lorry at Castelbello in the Trentino-Aldo Adige region of Italy under the influence of alcohol and Mr Franz, a German national, who, while visiting the same region of Italy, was found by a customs inspection in possession of a type of knife that is prohibited in Italy. Both offenders made a declaration before the District Magistrate of Bolzano that they had no knowledge of Italian and requested that the proceedings were conducted in German on the basis that the German-speaking citizens of the province of Bolzano were permitted to use German in relations with the judicial and administrative authorities located in that province or entrusted with responsibility at regional level. The referring court asked the ECJ whether the situation of both offenders was within the scope of EC Treaty and, if so, whether the right conferred on the German-speaking minority living in the province of Bolzano should be extended to nationals from other German-speaking Member States travelling or staying in that area.

The ECJ based its reasoning on the freedom to provide services, which includes the freedom for the recipients of services to go to another Member State in order to receive a service there. Article 49 EC, therefore, covers all nationals of Member States who, independently of other freedoms guaranteed by the Treaty, visit another Member State where they intend, or are likely to, receive services. Such persons (and they included both Mr Bickel and Mr Franz) are free to visit and move around within the host State.

In that regard, the exercise of the right to move and reside freely in another Member State is enhanced if the citizens of the Union are able to use a given language to communicate with the administrative and judicial authorities of a State on the same footing as its nationals. Consequently, persons such as Mr Bickel and Mr Franz, in exercising that right in another Member State, are in principle entitled, pursuant to art 12 EC, to treatment no less favourable than that accorded to nationals of the host State so far as concerns the use of languages which are spoken there.

The ECJ confirmed that although the rules of criminal law and criminal procedure are within the competence of a Member State, that competence cannot be exercised contrary to the fundamental principles of Community law, in particular the principle of equality of treatment as stated in art 12 EC. The ECJ based its reasoning on arts 17 and 18 EC rather than on the principle of non-discrimination on the ground of nationality, as the Court wished to emphasise the equality of treatment among the citizens of the EU. From this perspective, the reference to the citizenship of the EU permitted the ECJ to compare German-speaking nationals of the province of Bolzano with German-speaking nationals from other Member States. The ECJ considered that the latter when travelling or staying in that province were disadvantaged in comparison with the former. Therefore, the requirement of residence in the province of Bolzano as a condition for benefiting from a special linguistic regime was neither justified on the ground of objective criteria nor related to nationality nor proportional to the aim of Italian rules intended to protect the ethno-cultural German-speaking minority residing in the province of Bolzano. The decision of the ECJ in this case confirms that the ECJ pays special attention to the protection of rights and facilities of individuals in linguistic matters: see *Mutsch* Case 137/84 [1985] ECR 2681.

However, Member States are entitled to carry out passport controls at internal Community borders in order to establish the nationality of the person concerned. This was confirmed by the ECJ in *Florus Ariël Wijsenbeek* Case C–378/97 [1999] ECR I–6207. In this case Mr Wijsenbeek, a Dutch national, refused to present and hand over his passport to the national police officer in charge of border controls at Rotterdam Airport when he was entering The Netherlands on 17 December 1993. He was ordered by the Kantonrechter to pay a fine of HFL 65 and to serve one day's imprisonment for breach of The Netherlands' legislation requiring Dutch nationals, when entering The Netherlands, to present travel and identity papers in their possession to officials responsible for border controls and to establish by any other means their Dutch nationality. Mr Wijsenbeek appealed from the decision of the Kantonrechter and the appellate court referred a question regarding the compatibility of the Dutch legislation with Community law to the ECJ.

The ECJ examined art 14 EC, regarding the establishment of the common market on 1 January 1993, an area without internal frontiers in which, inter alia, the free movement of persons is ensured in accordance with the EC Treaty, and art 18 EC, under which citizens of the EU have the right to move and reside freely within the EU territory subject to limitations and conditions laid down in the EC Treaty and to measures adopted to give it effect. The ECJ held that art 14 could not be construed as meaning that the obligation to ensure the free movement of persons automatically arose on 1 January 1993, since such an obligation presupposed harmonisation of the Member States' laws governing the crossing of the external borders of the EC, immigration, the grant of visas, etc. Furthermore, as long as Community provisions concerning these issues have not been adopted the exercise of the rights in art 16(1) EC presupposes that a person concerned is required to establish that he has the nationality of a Member State. At the time of the events in the present case there were no such common rules. Consequently, even if citizens of the EU had an unconditional right under arts 14 and 18 EC, the Member States retained the right to carry out identity checks at the internal frontiers of the EU in order to establish whether the person concerned was a national of a Member State.

In the absence of Community rules in this area, the Member States are entitled to impose penalties for refusal to hand over a passport by an EU citizen provided that the penalties are comparable to those applicable to similar infringements of national law and proportionate. In this case, a term of imprisonment was disproportionate and as such constituted an obstacle to the free movement of persons.

It is interesting to note that the Commission submitted a proposal for a directive on the elimination of controls on persons crossing internal borders.[9] The proposal defines the concept of 'internal frontiers' and 'frontier control or formality'. In its opinion on the proposal the EP stressed the importance of unconditional free movement for both citizens and legal residents of the EU.

---

[9] OJ C289 (1995) which is still under consideration before the Council for a common position.

The ECJ confirmed that art 18 EC does not apply to wholly internal situations. In *Kremzow v Austria* Case C–299/95 [1997] ECR I–2629 an Austrian national who was imprisoned in Austria tried to rely on art 18 EC. The ECJ held that there was no connection between his situation and EC law. The ECJ emphasised that 'Whilst any deprivation of liberty may impede the person concerned from exercising his right to free movement, a purely hypothetical prospect of exercising that right does not establish a sufficient connection with Community law to justify the application of Community provisions.'

16.2 Participation in municipal elections and in elections to the European Parliament

Article 19 EC confers both active (right to stand as a candidate) and passive (right to vote) rights in respect of municipal (art 19(1) EC) and EP (art 19(2) EC) elections on an EC national residing in a Member State of which he is not a national under the same conditions as nationals of that State. Further measures (mentioned below) were necessary in order to implement those rights.

Participation in municipal elections

Participation in municipal elections for EC nationals residing in a Member State of which they are not nationals is important as it contributes to their integration into the society of a host member State. It is also in line which the Council of Europe Convention of 5 February 1992 on the Participation of Foreigners in Public Life at Local Level, provided they fulfil the requirement of residence. The situation in Member States before the TEU was disparate: some of them – like Ireland, Denmark and The Netherlands – granted generous access to all foreign residents to participate in local elections. In the UK, Irish and Commonwealth citizens were given local voting rights, in Spain these rights were based on reciprocity, and in France, Germany and Luxembourg only nationals had electoral rights at the municipal level.

The Council adopted Directive 94/80[10] on 19 December 1994 conferring on citizens of the Union the right to vote and stand as candidates in local elections in their Member State of residence under the same conditions as nationals of that State. The Directive allows multiple voting. For example, a French national residing in England and Belgium is entitled to exercise his voting rights in both countries. Furthermore, the Directive gives no definition of residence. It only provides that the owners of holiday homes are not considered as residents in the Member State where their holiday homes are situated unless they are allowed to participate in municipal elections on the basis of reciprocity (art 4(2) of Directive 94/80). To illustrate reciprocity, an Englishman who owns a holiday home in Barcelona will be allowed to vote and stand at municipal elections in Spain only if a Spanish national who owns a holiday home in Southampton has the same rights in England.

---

[10] OJ L368 (1994).

Some derogations are permitted in order to accommodate Member States with a very high percentage of resident nationals from other Member States. If more than 20 per cent of foreign residents are nationals of the EU without being nationals of that State, the exercise of their electoral rights may be subject to the requirement of a certain period of residence in that State. This derogation concerns mostly Luxembourg where 26.3 per cent of the population are foreign residents and 92.7 per cent of them are EC nationals.[11]

The adoption of Directive 94/80 posed three problems: first, in some Member States the granting of local election rights to EC residents was contrary to their Constitution; second, the matter of the determination of the local government unit; and, third, the question of the determination of the public offices which nationals of other Member States may hold.

As to the first problem, at the time of ratification of the TEU the necessary amendments to the constitutions of the following Member States were introduced: France,[12] Germany, Spain and Portugal.

The second matter was partially solved by Directive 94/80, which in art 2(1) provides a definition of the basic local government unit, and partially by the Member States which in the Annex to the Directive listed the types of administrative entity. Article 2(1) defines the basic local governmental unit as 'certain bodies elected by direct universal suffrage and ... empowered to administer, at the basic level of political and administrative organisation, certain local affairs on their own responsibility'. However, the reference to national law in determination of those bodies resulted in wide diversity in the levels of government accessible to EC citizens. In the UK, Ireland and Denmark, EU nationals residing in these countries are entitled to passive and active voting rights in respect of all levels of government below a national government, while in France, Belgium and The Netherlands they are limited to the lowest level.[13] The list of administrative entities provided by the UK encompasses 'counties in England, counties, county boroughs and communities in Wales, regions and islands in Scotland, districts in England, Scotland and Northern Ireland, London boroughs, parishes in England, the City of London in relation to ward elections for common councilmen': Annex to Directive 94/80.

Finally, the question of access to certain offices elected by direct universal suffrage, such as the post of mayor or alderman (a member of the local executive), is regulated in art 5(3) of Directive 94/80 which states that 'the office of elected head, deputy or member of the governing college of the executive of a basic local government unit if elected to hold office for the duration of his mandate' may be reserved to nationals of a Member State. This solution is contrary to European integration but in line with arts 39(4) and 45 EC which exclude nationals of Member States resident in other Member States from access to employment in the public service and from activities which involve the exercise of official authority. As a result Directive 94/80 strengthens the limitations already existing under the EC Treaty instead of abolishing any difference in treatment between nationals and non-nationals of the EU! In general Directive 94/80 is very modest. It confers passive and active voting rights in municipal elections which are of little importance in the political life of any

---

[11] Commission Report on Voting Rights in Local Elections for Community Nationals: EC Bull Suppl 2/96.
[12] P Oliver, 'The French Constitution and the Treaty of Maastricht' [1994] ICLQ 1.
[13] For details see P Oliver, 'Electoral Rights under Article 8B of the Treaty of Rome' (1996) 33 CMLR 473–498.

Member State.[14] The grant of electoral rights in national parliamentary elections, in direct presidential elections or in referenda would give real meaning to citizenship of the EU.

Participation in elections to the European Parliament

Article 19(2) EC confers on citizens of the EU the right to vote and to stand in elections to the European Parliament in the Member State of their residence, under the same conditions as nationals of that State. The Council wanted to adopt a measure in this respect before the elections to the EP which were to be held in June 1994. As a result, Directive 93/109[15] was adopted on 6 December 1993 and successfully implemented in all 12 Member States before the elections to the EP.[16] The main feature of Directive 93/109 is its minimal interference in the national electoral laws of the Member States. The Directive does not harmonise national legislation of the Member States.

There are two obstacles regarding the establishment of a uniform procedure for elections to the European Parliament:

1. The regionalisation of voting lists which should take place in 2004 at the latest in the five largest Member States in terms of population (Germany, France, the UK, Italy and Spain). Regionalisation may engender regional tensions in Spain and it is likely to further divide the French political classes which have tried for several years to settle this question in relation to the envisaged reform of the French electoral system.
2. The principle of preference which permits electors to select a candidate outside the order established by the political parties in each Member State. It will certainly prove difficult to obtain unanimous approval of the Council of the European Union of the principle of preference which is contrary to the interests of national political parties since it restricts their choice of eligible candidates.

It is expected that the Council will adopt a decision regarding a system of uniform elections to the EP by 2004.

16.3 Diplomatic and consular protection

Article 20 EC states that an EC national is, in the territory of a third country in which the Member State of which he is a national is not represented, entitled to the diplomatic and consular protection of any Member State, under the same conditions as nationals of that State. In international practice when a State has no representation in the territory of another State it often conducts diplomatic relations, including protection of its nationals, indirectly with the assistance of other States which have permanent diplomatic offices there. Many countries cannot afford embassies, even in the most strategic places from a point of

---

[14] In the UK the Representation of the People Act 2000 enacted on 9 March 2000 governs the right to vote or to stand in both municipal and European Parliamentary elections.
[15] OJ L329 (1993).
[16] The deadline for its implementation was very tight, 1 February 1994.

view of international politics.[17] Also, diplomatic relations between two countries can be suspended or terminated which often requires third countries to act on their behalf.[18] The innovation introduced in art 20 EC is that any EC national in a third country where his Member State is not represented may ask any Member State for assistance and that State is obliged to offer him diplomatic and consular protection on the same conditions as its own nationals. However, it is uncertain whether a Member State can actually endorse a claim on behalf of an EC national, although this is more an academic question than a real problem for an EC national since as an EC national he possesses nationality of one Member State which under international law can act on his behalf.

The scope of art 20 EC is limited by the procedure provided for enactment of further measures in this area which is based on inter-governmental co-operation. Article 20 EC states that Member States 'shall establish the necessary rules among themselves and start the international negotiations required to secure this protection'. The TEU provided for the establishment of such rules before 31 December 1993. On 1 July 1993 the Guidelines for the Protection of Unrepresented EC Nationals by EC Missions in Third Countries were introduced. Although the Guidelines were severely criticised as being incomplete and non-binding[19] they provided an important basis for further developments of art 20 EC. They ensured that nationals of a Member State not represented in a third country were entitled to ask the Mission of any other Member State for assistance and possible repatriation in the event of death, accidents, violent attacks, severe illnesses or arrest. This possibility is very important taking into account that all of the Member States have representations in only four countries: China, Japan, Russia and the USA. In 17 countries only two Member States have representation. In order to make the Guidelines legally binding the Council adopted on 19 December 1995 Decision 95/553/EC[20] on the protection of EU citizens in territories where their own Member State or the State which permanently represents their Member State maintains no accessible permanent mission or relevant consulate. This was complemented by Decision 96/409/CFSP[21] on Emergency Travel Documents which provides for the issue by Member States of a common format emergency travel document to citizens of the EU in places where their Member State has no permanent diplomatic or consular representation or in other specific circumstances.

In the context of diplomatic protection it is interesting to mention *Odigitria* Case T–572/93 [1995] ECR II–2025 in which the CFI seemed to recognise that the Community has a duty to offer diplomatic protection to EC citizens and EC firms. In this case the applicant brought an action under art 288(2) against the Commission for failure to take appropriate measures for the protection of his rights and interests in a third State. The application was rejected on the ground that the applicant did not submit evidence of the Commission's failure to act. The ECJ rejected the appeal from the decision of the CFI on the basis that the applicant did not submit new elements in law: *Odigitria* Case C–293/95P

---

[17] For example, Gambia closed its embassy in Washington in 1985 for financial reasons.

[18] For example, when Fidel Castro came to power the USA cut off all diplomatic relations with Cuba. The Swiss and Czechoslovakian embassies in Havana acted on behalf of the USA and Cuban governments for many years.

[19] See the Report on the Operation of the Treaty on European Union: Sec (95) 731 final, p9.

[20] OJ L314 (1995).

[21] OJ L168 (1996).

[1996] ECR I–6129[22]. Both decisions suggest that the Commission is under an obligation to provide diplomatic protection to EC citizens. Unfortunately, the ECJ did not explain whether it rejected the appeal because, under art 51 of its Rules of Procedure, no new legal arguments were invoked by the applicant or whether it agreed with the decision of the CFI. It is submitted that the obligation of the Community to provide diplomatic protection to EC citizens is doubtful. First, the one and only provision of the Treaty which refers to diplomatic protection is art 20 EC. It expressly imposes this duty on Member States and not on the Community. Second, this area is within the competence of the Council and implicitly within the scope of inter-governmental co-operation of the Member States.

16.4 Right to petition the European Parliament and to submit applications to the Ombudsman

Article 21 EC states that a citizen of the Union may petition the European Parliament and apply to the Ombudsman in accordance with the procedure provided in art 194 EC.

The right to petition the EP

The right to petition the EP existed before the adoption of art 21 EC under arts 156–158 of the Rules of Procedure of the European Parliament.[23] The innovation is that not only citizens of the EU are entitled to petition but also any natural or legal person residing or having its registered office in a Member State. There are certain limitations under art 194 EC: first, the matter must come within the fields of activity of the Community; and, second, the matter must affect the petitioner directly.[24] The Committee on Petitions, a special committee which was set up to deal with petitions, decides on the admissibility of petitions. If a petition is admissible the Committee may ask the Commission or other body to provide information. Once there is enough information the petition is put on the agenda of the Committee. At its meeting a representative from the Commission is invited to make an oral statement and comment on the Committee's written reply in respect of the matter raised in the petition. Depending on the case further action may be taken by the Committee.

If the petition is a special case requiring individual treatment, the Commission will get in touch with the relevant authorities or submit the case to the permanent representative of the Member State concerned. In some cases the Committee may ask the President of the EP to make representations to the national authorities in person.

If the petition is of general interest, that is, a Member State is in breach of EC law, the Commission may start proceedings against the offending Member State.

If the petition concerns a political matter, the EP or the Commission may use it as the basis for a political initiative. The individual case is not taken up but the petition may result in initiating or prompting an action at Community level.

---

[22] *Europe*, January 1997, No 6, comm FL.
[23] In 1977 the EP adopted a resolution demanding that the right to petition be attributed to EC nationals.
[24] On the subject see E Marias, 'The Right to Petition the European Parliament after Maastricht' (1994) 19 European Law Review 169–185.

In each case an applicant is informed of the result of the action taken on the basis of his petition. From mid-1997 to mid-1998, 582 petitions were declared admissible and 529 inadmissible.

The right to apply to the Ombudsman

The right to apply to the Ombudsman is defined in arts 195 EC, 20d CS and 107d EA. Article 195 EC provides that 'The European Parliament shall appoint an Ombudsman empowered to receive complaints.' This Article was completed by Council Decision 94/262 of 9 March 1994[25] which laid down the regulations and general conditions governing the performance of the Ombudsman's duties.

The Ombudsman is nominated by the European Parliament after its elections and holds office for the duration of its term and may be reappointed. The procedure for his appointment is provided in art 159 of the Rules of Procedure of the European Parliament. According to art 2(2) of Decision 94/262 the Ombudsman must be a citizen of the EU, chosen from persons whose independence is beyond doubt and must possess the qualifications required for appointment to the highest judicial offices in his Member State or have experience and the competences recognised as necessary for exercise of the functions of Ombudsman. He may be removed from office by the ECJ at the request of the European Parliament if he no longer satisfies the conditions required for the performance of his duties or no longer meets the obligations resulting from his office or is guilty of serious misconduct. He may not hold any office of an administrative or political nature nor engage in any occupation or profession paid or unpaid during his term of office. His role is to act independently, in the general interests of the Community, and thus he must neither seek nor take instructions from anybody. The Ombudsman provides a guarantee of independence and impartiality.

He is empowered to receive complaints from citizens of the EU as well as any natural and legal person residing or having its registered office in a Member State. The Ombudsman's competences *ratione materie* are limited to maladministration in the activities of EC institutions or bodies.[26] Such limitation is very disappointing since complaints regarding maladministration by national bodies in pursuance, or in violation, of EC law are the most important and vital to ordinary people. This limitation has been recognised by the European Ombudsman. According to him two-thirds of the complaints received are outside the mandate of the European Ombudsman because they concern the activities of national authorities. In order to assist EU citizens, the European Ombudsman called for a closer co-operation between the European Ombudsman and national ombudsman.[27] The remedies for maladministration by Community institutions are already provided by Community Treaties, and it should be noted that they are more adequate and more efficient than those resulting from the successful intervention of the Ombudsman.

---

[25] OJ L113, 114 and 115 (1994).

[26] Apart from the ECJ and the Court of First Instance acting in their judicial role.

[27] In this respect in 1998 five queries from national ombudsman were dealt with by the European Ombudsman and the latter advised 259 complainants to consult his national colleagues: The European Ombudsman press release No 7/99.

The Ombudsman may make investigations on his own initiative as well as from complaints coming from individuals, or submitted to him through members of the European Parliament, except if the alleged facts are, or have been, the subject of legal proceedings. If the Ombudsman decides that the complaint is well founded, he refers the matter to the institution concerned which has three months to express its views. After the expiry of that period, if the institution in question has not taken appropriate measures to resolve the matter, the Ombudsman must draft a report which may include recommendations and forward it to the EP and the institution concerned. However, he may then only inform the complainant of this process – no legal remedy is provided. In this context, the existence of the Ombudsman seems superficial.[28] This is emphasised by his subordination to the ECJ in that he cannot investigate complaints against maladministration in the activities of the ECJ or the Court of First Instance.

16.5 Assessment of Union citizenship

The introduction of Union citizenship responds to the EU's concern that the EU should be of direct relevance to the individual citizen. It is of great importance to EC nationals who live and work in another Member State. In this respect, it is interesting to mention that of 420,000 UK citizens living in other Member States, nearly a quarter live in Germany. Also, UK citizens are the largest EU minority group in six of the 15 Member States: Denmark, Greece, Spain, Ireland, Portugal and Sweden. They are the second largest group in Italy and The Netherlands. Furthermore, in the UK there are 768.000 non-national EU residents, 1.3 per cent of the entire population. About 140.000 EU students study in an EU country other than their Member State and their favourite destinations are Germany, the UK and France.[29]

The most important aspect of Union citizenship is its dynamic character, it must evolve to follow progress achieved by the EU. In this respect art 22 EC provides that:

> '... the Council, acting unanimously on a proposal from the Commission and after consulting the European Parliament, may adopt provisions to strengthen or to add to the rights laid down in this Part, which it shall recommend to the Member States for adoption in accordance with their respective constitutional requirements.'

As a result, the Council may only increase the list of rights granted to EU citizens and not reduce them. Also art 22 EC provides that the Commission is obliged to prepare every three years a report on the application of the provisions concerning citizenship of the EU and to forward such a report to the EP, the Council and the Economic and Social Committee.

---

[28] Because the competences of the Committee on Petitions and the Ombudsman overlap, the EP stated that they should complement each other rather than compete: EP 200.788/fin, p23.
[29] *The European*, EP News, December 1996, p2.

17 Free Movement of Workers

17.1 Worker and his family

17.2 Right of entry and residence

17.3 The principle of non-discrimination

17.4 Right to remain in the territory of a Member State after having been employed in that State

Article 39 EC provides:

'(1) Freedom of movement for workers shall be secured within the Community.

(2) Such freedom of movement shall entail the abolition of any discrimination based on nationality between workers of the Member States as regards employment, remuneration and other condition of work and employment.

(3) It shall entail the right, subject to limitations justified on grounds of public policy, public security or public health:

(a) to accept offers of employment actually made;

(b) to move freely within the territory of Member States for this purpose;

(c) to stay in a Member State for the purpose of employment in accordance with the provisions governing the employment of nationals of that State laid down by law, regulation or administrative action;

(d) to remain in the territory of a Member State after having been employed in that State, subject to conditions which shall be embodied in implementing regulations to be drawn up by the Commission.

(4) The provisions of this Article shall not apply to employment in the public service.'

Secondary legislation adopted on the basis of arts 39(3)(d) and 40 EC gives effect to the principle of the free movement of workers. The most important secondary legislation is:

1. Directive 68/360 on the right of entry and residence;
2. Regulation 1612/68 on access to, and conditions of, employment;
3. Regulation 1251/70 on rights to remain in the territory of a host Member State after having been employed there;
4. Directive 64/221 concerning Member States' right to derogate from the provisions of the EC Treaty on the free movement of persons on the grounds of public policy, public security and public health.

The right to free movement of workers is not absolute. It suffers two exceptions: first, employment in the public service may be reserved to nationals of a host Member State; and, second, restrictions may be justified on the grounds of public policy, public security and public health.

Article 39 EC is directly effective since the entry into force of Regulation 1612/68 on 15

October 1968.[1] In *Walrave and Koch* Case 36/74 [1974] ECR 1405 the ECJ held that art 39 EC is also horizontally directly effective. In this case the rules of the International Union of Cyclists Association, an international sporting association which was neither a public body nor part of the State, imposed nationality requirements in respect of 'pacemakers' and 'stayers' in the world cycling championships. The ECJ ruled that a nationality requirement was contrary to art 39 since the prohibition of discrimination 'does not only apply to the action of public authorities but extends likewise to rules of any nature aimed at regulating in a collective manner gainful employment and the provision of services'.[2]

17.1 Worker and his family

The concept of a worker

There is no definition of a worker in the EC Treaty, although Regulation 1408/71 defines a worker as a person insured under a social security scheme.[3] The ECJ has broadly interpreted the concept of a worker (*Levin v Staatssecretaris von Justitie* Case 53/81 [1982] ECR 1053) and given it an autonomous Community meaning. In *Lawrie-Blum v Land Baden-Wurttemberg* Case 66/85 [1986] ECR 2121 the ECJ held that a 'worker' within the meaning of art 39 EC is a person who performs services of some economic value for and under the direction of another person, in return for which she/he receives remuneration.

There are two aspects of the definition provided by the ECJ. First, the concept of a worker must be defined in accordance with objective criteria relating to an employment relationship. The essential feature of an employment relationship is that for a certain period of time a person performs services for, and under the direction of, another person in return for which he receives remuneration. In Case 66/85 Deborah Lawrie-Blum, a British national was, after successfully passing her examination for the profession of teacher, refused admission to the period of probationary service which had to be completed in order to become a teacher in Germany. During the probationary period a trainee teacher is considered as a civil servant and receives remuneration for conducting classes. Under the German law of länder Baden-Württemberg only German nationals were admitted to probationary service. Deborah Lawrie-Blum challenged the decision of the German authorities on the basis of arts 12 EC and 39(2) EC. The länder contended, inter alia, that a trainee teacher was not a 'worker' within the meaning of art 39(2) EC.

The ECJ held that a trainee teacher who, under the direction and supervision of the school authorities, is undergoing a period of service in preparation for the teaching profession, during which he provides services by conducting classes and receives remuneration, must be considered as a 'worker' under art 39(1) EC irrespective of the legal nature of the employment relationship (public/private sector): *Guido Van Poucke* Case C–71/93 [1994] ECR I–1101. Also, the personal and property relations between spouses

---

[1] *The State v Jean Noël Royer* Case 48/75 [1976] ECR 497; *Commission v France (Re French Merchant Seamen)* Case 167/73 [1974] ECR 359.

[2] This was confirmed in Case C–415/93 *Bosman* [1995] ECR I–4921.

[3] OJ L149 (1971).

resulting from marriage do not exclude, in the context of the organisation of an undertaking, the existence of a relationship of subordination which is characteristic of an employment relationship. The ECJ held in *CPM Meeusen v Hoofddirectie Van De Informatie Beheer Groep* Case C–337/97 [1999] ECR I–3289 that a person who is related by marriage to the director and sole shareholder of the company for which she or he pursues an effective and genuine activity is classified as a 'worker' within the meaning of art 39 EC.

The ECJ stressed in a number of cases that provided the activities performed are effective and genuine, a person should be considered as a worker even though such a person is not employed full time or receives pay lower than that for full-time employment. In *Kempf* Case 139/85 [1986] ECR 1741 a German part-time music teacher working in The Netherlands from 1981–1982, whose income was below a national minimum salary, received supplementary benefit in the form of sickness benefit and general assistance. When he applied for a residence permit in The Netherlands his application was refused on the ground that his income was insufficient to meet his needs. The ECJ held that Kempf should be considered as a worker, irrespective of the fact that he was employed on a part-time basis. The ECJ held that if the activity performed is effective and genuine a person should be considered as a worker even though his salary is insufficient to support him and he has to rely on some other means to bring his income to subsistence level: *Levin* Case 53/81 [1982] ECR 1035. It is also irrelevant whether the money used to supplement the income is obtained from the individual's private means or from public funds. Also, a person who works occasionally, according to the needs of the employer (*Raulin* Case 357/89 [1992] ECR I–1027) or within the framework of an apprenticeship contract (*Le Manoir* Case C–27/91 [1991] ECR I–5531), should be considered as a worker for the purposes of art 39 EC.

In *Agegate* Case 3/87 [1989] ECR 4459 the ECJ held that fishermen paid only when caught fish were sold were considered as workers as they performed activities which were effective and genuine. However, if a person's work is so limited as to be marginal or ancillary (*Brown* Case 197/86 [1988] ECR 3205) he will not be regarded as a worker. In order to distinguish between genuine and effective and marginal or ancillary employment a national court should take into account the duration and the regularity of the activity concerned: *Raulin* Case C–357/89.

Second, in order to be considered a worker a person must perform some economic activities. In *Bettray* Case 344/87 [1989] ECR 1621 the ECJ held that participation in a drug rehabilitation scheme for which its participants were paid did not involve performance of economic activities and therefore was outside the scope of art 39 EC. However, a plumber working for a religious community who did not receive any remuneration but worked for his keep and some pocket money qualified as a worker since he performed effective and genuine activity of an economic nature: *Steymann* Case 196/87 [1988] ECR 6159.

In respect of activities involving sport[4] only those which are of an economic nature are

---

[4] See new developments in this area. In *Tyri Lehtonen v Fédération Royal Belge des Sociétés de Basket-Ball ASBL* Case C–176/96 Judgment of 13 April 2000 (nyr) the ECJ held that rules of a professional organisation preventing professional sportsmen from taking part in competitions if they have been transferred after a specific date may constitute an obstacle to freedom of movement of workers. In *Deliège v Ligue Francophone de Judo et Disciplines ASBL* Cases C–51/96 and 191/97 Judgment of 11 April 2000 (nyr) the ECJ held that the selection rules for international tournaments laid down by sport federations are not in themselves contrary to EC law.

within the scope of art 39 EC. As a result, a professional football player (*Bosman* Case C–415/93 [1995] ECR I–4921) or a cyclist or a coach (*Walrave* Case 36/74 [1974] ECR 1405) are regarded as workers, whilst the selecting of national representatives did not involve any economic activities: *Donà* Case 13/76 [1976] ECR 1333; *Walrave* Case 36/74.

In respect of persons who are unemployed, in *The State* v *Jean Noël Royer* Case 48/75 [1976] ECR 497 the ECJ held that art 39(3) EC included the right to enter a host Member State in search of work, although it did not fix any time-limit for such a search.[5] It seems that a six-month period can be considered as a reasonable time for the purpose of seeking employment. This was implied from the ECJ decision in *R* v *Immigration Appeal Tribunal, ex parte Antonissen* Case C–292/89 [1991] ECR I–745 in which the ECJ accepted that if after a six-month stay in a host Member State for the purpose of seeking employment an EC migrant had failed to find employment, a deportation order could be issued, unless the migrant provided evidence that he was actively seeking employment and had a genuine chance of being employed.

Also, temporary unemployment does not change the status of 'worker' of a migrant EC national who lost his job due to illness or accident. In *Hoekstra* v *BBDA* Case 75/63 [1964] ECR 177 a Dutch worker who became ill during her visit to Germany sought to recover the costs of her medical treatment in Germany from a Dutch voluntary insurance scheme to which she had contributed while in employment. The ECJ ruled that she was still a worker, despite the fact that she had lost her job, as she was capable of taking another.

Family of a worker

Article 10(1)(a) and (b) of Regulation 1612/68 provides that the members of a worker's family are: his/her spouse, their children who are under the age of 21 or dependent and dependent ascendants of a worker and his/her spouse. The right to the free movement of a member of an EC worker's family is not independent but derives from the right conferred upon the worker. As a result, a member of a worker's family cannot rely on EC law unless an EC national exercises his right to work in another Member State.[6]

Article 10 of Regulation 1612/68, arts 1 and 4 of Directive 68/360 and arts 1(c) and 4 of Directive 73/148, provide that the Member States must grant the spouse and children of a worker rights of residence equivalent to that granted to the person himself.

A member of an EC worker's family is entitled to reside with a worker in a host Member State and to have access to employment, irrespective of her/his nationality and profession. If the profession is regulated within the meaning of Community secondary legislation, and a member of a family of an EC worker satisfies the conditions for taking up or pursuing a professional activity in a regulated profession, a host Member State must recognise the professional qualification of such a person: *Gül* Case 131/85 [1986] ECR 1573.

Both art 10(1) and (2) of Regulation 1612/68 are subject to art 10(3) which requires a worker to provide his family with accommodation considered normal for national workers

---

[5] However, in *Commission* v *Belgium* Case C–344/95 [1997] ECR I–1035 deportation of an unemployed person who had been seeking a job for only three months was regarded as contrary to art 39 EC.

[6] See *Dzodzi* Cases C–297/88 and 197/89 [1990] ECR I–3783; *Uecker & Jacquet* Cases 64 and 65/96 [1996] ECR I–3171.

in the area where the worker is employed. This requirement applies only when the worker first arrives: *Commission* v *Germany* Case 249/86 [1989] ECR 1263.

The right to reside with a worker is conferred on dependent descendants aged 21 and more and dependent ascendants of a worker and her/his spouse. In *Lebon* Case 316/85 [1987] ECR 2811 the ECJ held that the concept of a dependent member of a worker's family results from the factual situation and should not be assessed in the light of national legislation of a host Member State.

Spouses

Regulation 1612/68 expressly mentions only a spouse of an EC worker. In *Diatta* Case 267/83 [1985] ECR 567 the ECJ held that it is not necessary for spouses to live under the same roof. This decision was delivered in the context of spouses living separately and intending to obtain a divorce (the wife was of Senegalese nationality, her husband was a French national working in Germany). In *Reed* Case 59/85 [1986] ECR 1283 the ECJ held that by virtue of the principle of non-discrimination a Member State cannot refuse a cohabitee of a worker who is an EC national the right to reside with the worker in so far as national law provides this possibility for its own nationals. As a result, Miss Reed, a British national was allowed in The Netherlands to stay with her English cohabitee of five years.

So far the ECJ has not decided on the right of residence of a divorced spouse who is a non-EC national and who was married to an EC national. In *R* v *Immigration Appeal Tribunal and Surinder Singh, ex parte Secretary of State for Home Department* Case C–370/90 [1992] 3 CMLR 335 Mr Singh, an Indian national, married a British citizen in the United Kingdom in 1982. The couple then left the UK to work in Germany for three years where both obtained employment. They subsequently returned to the UK to start a private business. However, at no time during this period did Mr Singh acquire British nationality. A decree nisi of divorce was pronounced against Mr Singh in July 1987 and the date of expiry of his temporary leave to stay in the UK, which had been periodically extended during his marriage, was brought forward to September of that year. After the expiry of his temporary leave, Mr Singh remained in the UK without permission and, in December 1988, the Secretary of State for the Home Department issued a deportation order against him. In February 1989, after the deportation proceedings had commenced, the decree absolute of divorce was pronounced.

Before the decree absolute had been granted the issue of deportation came before the Immigration Appeal Tribunal, which held that Mr Singh was entitled to remain in the UK on the ground that he, as a spouse of a British citizen, had Community rights under the principles of the free movement of persons and the right of establishment. The Secretary of State applied to the High Court for judicial review of this decision and that court referred the question of Mr Singh's right to remain in the UK under Community law to the ECJ for a preliminary ruling.

The ECJ did not rule whether Mr Singh was entitled to remain in the UK after final decree was granted but confined its decision to the interpretation of the rights of Mr Singh during the period before decree absolute, since proceedings were commenced against Mr Singh before that event. The Court held that a national of a Member State who has gone to another Member State in order to work there as an employed person pursuant to art 39 EC and returns to establish himself in order to pursue an activity as a self-employed person in the territory of the Member State of which he is a national has the right, under art 43 EC, to be accompanied in the territory of the latter State by his spouse, a national of a non-Member country, under the same conditions as are laid down by Regulation 1612/68, Directive 68/360 or Directive 73/148.

This decision in the above case should be assessed in particular in the light of the principle set up in *Morson and Jhabjan (Re Surinam Mothers)* Cases 35 and 36/82 [1982] ECR 3723 under which Community law does not apply to 'wholly internal situations'. In these cases two Dutch nationals working and residing in The Netherlands wanted to bring their mothers of Surinamese nationality to reside with them in The Netherlands. Under Dutch law they were not permitted to do so and the ECJ held that Community law did not apply to their situation as there was no link connecting it with EC law.

It is submitted that both the above situations should be resolved on the basis of art 8 of the European Convention of Human Rights, taking into account that fundamental principles of human rights are part of Community law. In this respect the European Court of Human Rights in *Berrehab*[7] held that the expulsion of a divorced husband whose child remained in Belgium was contrary to art 8 the ECHR. The European Court of Human Rights did not grant an automatic right of residence to a divorced spouse but took into consideration the degree of contact between the divorced parent and the child. This solution is also in line with the ECJ judgment in *Kus v Landeshaupt Stadt Wiesbaden* Case C–237/91 [1992] ECR I–6781 in which it was decided that a Turkish national who married an EC national (and on that basis was granted a right of residence in a Member State) was allowed to reside after his divorce on two grounds. First, he was lawfully working in that Member State and, second, on the basis of certain provisions of the EEC-Turkey Association Agreement. In this case the ECJ held that the divorce did not affect the legality of his continuing residence.

Children

Under art 12 of Regulation 1612/68 children of a worker are entitled to admission to general education, apprenticeship and vocational training courses under the same conditions as nationals of a host Member State. In *Michels v Fonds National de Reclassement Handicapes* Case 76/72 [1973] ECR 457 the ECJ ruled that the list of educational arrangements for such children was not exhaustive. In this case a mentally handicapped son of an Italian worker, who was employed in Belgium before his death, was entitled to rehabilitation benefits from a fund set up to assist people whose employment prospects were seriously affected by handicap.

Children of workers are also entitled to general measures of support, such as grants and loans: *Casagrande* Case 9/74 [1974] ECR 773; *Alaimo* Case 68/74 [1975] ECR 109. In *Di Leo v Land of Berlin* Case C–308/89 [1990] ECR I–4185 a daughter of an Italian worker employed in Germany was entitled to financial support provided under German law even though she studied in Italy. The principle of non-discrimination required that she was placed in the same position as children of nationals of a host Member State. In *Commission v Belgium* Case 42/87 [1988] ECR 5445 the ECJ held that children of migrant workers

---

[7] 21 June 1988, Series A, No 138, pp15 and 16.

(including workers who have retired or died) are to be treated in respect of access to all forms of State education on an equal footing with children of national workers. In respect of the right of a dependant child of a national of one Member State who pursues an activity as an employed person in another Member State while maintaining his residence in the State of which he is a national, the child can rely on the principle of equal treatment in order to claim, under the same conditions as are applicable to children of nationals of the State of employment, social benefit under art 7(2) of Regulation 1612/68 regarding study finance, and in particular without any further requirement as to the child's place of residence: *CPM Meeusen v Hoofddirectie Van De Informatie Beheer Groep* Case C–337/97 [1999] ECR I–3289.

A child of a worker is entitled to continue his education in a host Member State after the worker has returned to a home Member State. This is so even where a child has interrupted his study in a host Member State and subsequently returns because it is impossible for him to continue his study in his home Member State: *Echternach and Moritz* Joined Cases 389 and 390/87 [1989] ECR 723. See also *Inzirillo* Case 63/76 [1976] ECR 2057.

In *Gaal* Case C–7/94 [1996] ECR I–1031 the ECJ held that art 12 of Regulation 1216/68 applies also to children who are over 21 years old and independent. In this case Gaal was a Belgian national born in 1967 in Belgium but brought up in Germany and he received an 'orphan's allowance' in Germany after his father's death in 1987. He was studying biology at university in Germany and in 1989 applied for funds to study for a year at university in the UK. He was not financially dependent on his mother. His application was refused by the German authorities on the grounds that he was over 21 years old and financially independent. The ECJ ruled that art 12 of Regulation 1612/68 should not be subject to the same conditions of age or dependency as are the rights governed by arts 10(1) and 11 of that Regulation. Consequently, art 12 encompasses children who are over 21 years of age and independent. The ECJ emphasised that it would be contrary to the letter and to the spirit of art 12 to construe it in such a manner as to render students already at an advanced stage in their education ineligible for the financial assistance available in a host Member State as soon as they reach 21 years or are no longer dependent on their parents.

17.2 Right of entry and residence

The right of nationals of a Member State to enter the territory of another Member State and reside there for the purposes of employment – whether to look for work or pursue activities as employed or self-employed persons, or to rejoin their spouse or family – is conferred directly by the EC Treaty. This was decided by the ECJ in *The State v Jean Noël Royer* Case 48/75 [1976] ECR 497; [1976] 2 CMLR 619. Secondary legislation only determines the scope of, and provides detailed rules for the exercise of, the rights conferred directly by the EC Treaty. In respect of workers art 4(1) and (2) of Directive 68/360 provides that Member States shall 'grant' the right of residence in their territory to persons who are able to produce the documents listed in the directive and that 'proof' of the right of residence is constituted by issue of a special residence permit by a host Member State. Under Directive 68/360, which is directly effective, the rights of entry and residence encompass:

1. The right for EU citizens to leave their home Member State with a view to pursuing activities as an employed person in another Member State: art 2.
2. The right to enter the territory of another Member State on production of a valid identity card or passport. No other documents are required. However, a host Member State may require an entry visa for family members who are not EU nationals: art 3(2).
3. The right to obtain a residence permit, on production of the document with which an EC migrant entered the territory of a host Member State, and a confirmation of engagement from the employer or a certificate of employment. In order to obtain a residence permit family members of a worker must produce their documents of entry and a document issued by the competent authorities of their home Member State or the Member State of their previous residence proving their relationship with the worker. If they are dependent on the worker they are required to submit a document issued by the same authorities certifying that they are dependent on the worker or that they lived under his roof in that country: art 4(3)(c), (d) and (e).

The question whether a host Member State may restrict residence of a migrant worker to part of the national territory was examined by the ECJ in *Roland Rutili v Minister of the Interior* Case 36/75 [1975] ECR 1219; [1976] 1 CMLR 140. Rutili was an Italian national who resided in France and, between 1967 and 1968, actively participated in political and trade union activities. The French authorities grew increasingly concerned with his activities, and issued a deportation order. This was subsequently altered to a restriction order requiring him to remain in certain provinces of France. In particular, the order prohibited him from residing in the province in which he was habitually resident and in which his family resided. Rutilli challenged the legality of these measures on the ground that they interfered with his right of freedom of movement. The question was referred to the ECJ for a preliminary ruling.

The ECJ interpreted the right of a Member State to limit the free movement of workers on the ground of public policy and concluded that this right must be construed strictly. In particular, a Member State cannot, in the case of a national of another Member State, impose prohibitions on residence which are territorially limited except in circumstances where such prohibitions may be imposed on its own nationals. Consequently, if a Member State has no power to restrict the residence of its own nationals to a specific area then it has only two options in relation to an EC migrant worker, either to refuse his entry or to permit him to reside in the whole of the national territory.

A residence permit should either be issued free of charge or the fee charged should not exceed the costs of issuing identity documents to nationals: *Commission v Belgium* Case C–344/95 [1997] ECR I–1035. It is issued for at least five years and is renewable automatically for five years. However, when in the case of a worker who has been involuntarily unemployed for more than 12 consecutive months it is renewed for the first time the period of residence may be restricted to not less than 12 months.

A residence permit cannot be withdrawn on the ground that, as a result of temporary incapacity to work due to illness or accident or involuntary unemployment, a worker is no longer employed.

A residence permit

In *The State v Jean Noël Royer* Case 48/75 [1976] ECR 497; [1976] 2 CMLR 619 the ECJ held that the right of entry and residence is granted directly by art 39 EC and therefore is independent from the question of a residence permit. Royer was a French national who had been convicted of minor offences, and prosecuted for a number of armed robberies but never convicted. His wife was also a French national, but worked in Liège in Belgium. He visited his wife in Belgium, but omitted to comply with the administrative formalities upon entry into the country. He was subsequently convicted of illegal entry and residence in Belgium and left the country. Some time later, Royer returned to Belgium, but again failed to comply with the necessary administrative formalities. He was served with a ministerial decree of expulsion which alleged that his presence was a danger to public policy in Belgium. As a defence, Royer invoked art 39 EC, and the related Community directives, to establish that he was entitled to enter and remain in Belgium as a worker.

The ECJ gave direct effect to art 39 EC and relied on the directives implementing the right of workers and their families to reside in other Member States to reject the need for a permit in order to acquire residence in other Member States. A residence permit has only declaratory and probatory force. Consequently, a failure to comply with formalities regarding entry and residence cannot justify a decision ordering expulsion from the territory of a host Member State[8] or temporary imprisonment. In respect of sanctions that a Member State may impose on nationals from other Member States for failure to comply with administrative requirements regarding entry and residence, such sanctions are subject to the principle of proportionality. In *Messner* Case C–265/88 [1989] ECR 4209 a requirement under Italian law imposing on all immigrants the obligation, sanctioned by criminal penalties, to register with the police within three days of their arrival was considered as disproportionate. Any national measures which are disproportionate to the objectives of the Treaty in the area of free movement of persons will be struck down by the ECJ as contrary to Community law.

17.3 The principle of non-discrimination

The legal situation of EC nationals working in a host Member State results not only from art 39 EC and secondary legislation implementing this provision, but also from a broad interpretation by the ECJ of the principle of non-discrimination which is expressly mentioned in art 39(2) EC. The main role of the principle of non-discrimination is to ensure equality in treatment between a national worker and a migrant worker as regards employment, remuneration and other conditions of work and employment. Not only direct discrimination but also indirect discrimination based on nationality is prohibited. In *Württembergische Milchverwertung-Sudmilch v Ugliola* Case 15/69 [1969] ECR 363 an Italian national employed in Germany challenged German legislation which provided that military service in the Bundeswehr should be taken into account in calculating his seniority in employment. Ugliola performed his military service in Italy. He argued that German

---

[8] See *Watson and Belmann* Case 118/75 [1976] ECR 1185; *R v Pieck* Case 157/79 [1980] ECR 2171.

legislation, by not including similar provision for services in other armies of other Member States, was in breach of the principle of non-discrimination. The German government submitted that its legislation was not discriminatory since it applied to any national of any Member State who served in the Bundeswehr and did not apply to any German national who performed his military service in other Member States. The ECJ held that the likelihood of a national of other Member States serving in the Bundeswehr was more hypothetical than real. Consequently, German legislation indirectly discriminated against nationals from other Member States who work in Germany.

The principle of non-discrimination requires not only that the same rules are applicable to similar situations but also that different situations are treated differently. The case law of the ECJ shows that art 39(2) prohibits all form of indirect discrimination which, by applying distinguishing criteria other than nationality (for example, such as residence), achieve in practice the same discriminatory result. However, in certain circumstances indirect discrimination may be justified.

Indirect discrimination in respect of a separation allowance was invoked in *Sotgiu* v *Deutsche Bundespost* Case 152/73 [1974] ECR 153 by an Italian worker whose family lived in Italy and who was employed by the German postal service in Germany. Under German law a separation allowance at DM 10 per day was paid to workers residing within Germany at the time of their recruitment, while workers of German nationality as well as workers from other Member States received the allowance at DM 7.50 per day if at the time of their recruitment they resided abroad. Sotgiu relied on art 7(1) of Regulation 1216/68 and the principle of non-discrimination. During the proceedings it became clear that workers residing in Germany at the time of their recruitment received a larger allowance under two conditions: the payment was conditional upon their willingness to move to their place of work and it was limited to the first two years of employment. Neither condition applied to workers who resided abroad at the time of their recruitment. The ECJ held that the application of criteria other than nationality, in this case the the place of residence at the relevant time, could in certain circumstances have a discriminatory result in practice. This would not be the case when the payment of a separation allowance was made on conditions which took into consideration objective differences in the situations of workers, for example the place of residence of workers at the time of their recruitment. The difference in the amount paid to both groups of workers could be objectively justified taking into account that one group of workers received an allowance temporarily while for the other group it was of unlimited duration.

Rules of national law which although indistinctly applicable to both national workers and migrant EC workers (that is they make no distinction based on nationality) but essentially affect only migrant workers (*Pinna* Case 41/84 [1986] ECR 1; *Allué* Case 33/88 [1989] ECR 1591), or the majority of them (*Spotti* Case 272/92 [1993] ECR I–5185), are considered as indirectly discriminatory. Also national rules indistinctly applicable to both national workers and migrant workers which establish conditions which can be more easily satisfied by national workers than migrant workers (*Paraschi* Case C–349/87 [1991] ECR I–4501) or which create a risk that migrant workers would be treated less favourably than national workers (*Biehl* Case C–175/88 [1990] ECR I–1779) are contrary to the principle of non-discrimination.

It emerges from the case law of the ECJ that a national rule, unless objectively justified and proportionate to the objective it intends to achieve, will be considered as indirectly discriminatory if it affects migrant workers to a greater extent than national workers and thus might place migrant workers at a disadvantage as compared with national workers.

In the context of indirect discrimination the decision of the ECJ in *Volker Graf and Filzmoser Maschinenbau GmbH* Case C–190/98. Judgment of 27 January 2000 (nyr) clarified a number of matters. In this case Mr Graf, an Austrian national who had been employed by Filzmoser since 1992, terminated his contract of employment in 1996 in order to move to Germany to take up new employment. Filzmoser refused to pay Mr Graf compensation equal to two months' salary on termination of employment. Filzmoser relied on art 23(7) of Austrian Law on Employees (Angestelltengesetz) under which an employee is not entitled to compensation if he gives notice, leaves prematurely for no important reason or bears responsibility for premature dismissal. Mr Graf challenged this provision as contrary to art 39(2) EC which prohibits national rules precluding or deterring a worker from ending his contract of employment in order to take a job in another Member State (see *Terhoeve* Case C–18/95 [1999] ECR I–345) and invoked art 23(1) of the above-mentioned Austrian law which provides that 'If the employment relationship has continued uninterruptedly for three years, the employee shall be entitled to a compensation payment on termination of that relationship.' The referring court was uncertain as to the application of the decision of the ECJ in *Bosman* Case C–415/93 [1995] ECR I–4921 to the above situation.

The ECJ confirmed its decision in *Bosman*. Article 39 EC applies to national rules which impede the free movement of persons and are indistinctly applicable to both national workers and migrant EC workers. In this respect, the Austrian court clearly established that art 23(7) of the Austrian Law on Employees was not discriminatory as it did not restrict cross-border mobility to a greater extent than mobility within Austria. Further, the loss of compensation equal to two months' salary on termination of employment was not such as to be a perceptible restriction on the freedom of movement for workers (as stated in *Bosman*).

However, the conclusion of the ECJ concerning the scope of application of art 39 EC to such situations is of great importance. It is necessary to impose limitations on the application of art 39 EC in order to avoid the ECJ's previous experiences regarding the provisions on the free movement of goods. Article 39 EC cannot become a 'catch all' provision. In this respect the ECJ had two options: first, consisting of applying *Keck and Mithouard* Cases C–267–268/91 [1993] ECR I–6097 to such situations and thus referring to the criterion based on the objective of national rules; or, second, to focus on the effect of national rules: see *BASF* Case C–44/98 [1999] ECR I–6269. The ECJ decided to combine both approaches. At first it seemed to favour the solution in *Keck* by stating that national rules indistinctly applicable, which preclude or deter a national of a Member State from leaving his Member State of origin to enter the territory of another Member State in order to take up employment there, constituted an obstacle to the free movement of workers. However, the ECJ emphasised that 'in order to be capable of constituting such an obstacle, they must affect access of workers to the labour market'. At this stage the ECJ applied the second approach consisting of the assessment of the effect of the contested Austrian legislation on access to the labour market. In *Bosman* the impact of rules set up by the

Belgian Football Association on access to the labour market was considerable, taking into account the amount of the penalty payment. In the *Graf* case the situation was different. As the ECJ pointed out, not only the small amount of compensation but also the fact that the entitlement to compensation was not dependent on the worker's choosing whether or not to continue his employment, but on a future and hypothetical event, namely the subsequent termination of his contract without such termination being at his own initiative or attributable to him, led the ECJ to conclude that

> '... such an event is too uncertain and indirect a possibility for legislation to be capable of being regarded as liable to hinder freedom of movement of workers where it does not attach to termination of a contract of employment by the worker himself the same consequences as it attaches to termination which was not at his initiative or is not attributable to him.'

This solution avoids all inconveniences deriving from the application of the approach based on *Keck* in the area of free movement of workers.

The rule of equal treatment laid down in art 39 EC applies to all aspects of employment including eligibility for employment, conditions of work, remuneration and other conditions of work and employment. Regulation 1612/68 gives substance to the requirements of art 39 EC.

Eligibility for employment

Articles 1 to 6 of Regulation 1612/68 guarantee to migrant workers the right to take up available employment in the territory of a host Member State with the same priority as nationals of that State. Article 3 provides that national provisions and practices which limit the right to seek or to pursue employment or which impose conditions not applicable to nationals on migrant EC workers are inapplicable. However, art 3(1) allows a Member State to impose conditions 'relating to linguistic knowledge required by reason of the nature of the post to be filled'. In *Groener* Case 378/87 [1989] ECR 3967 the ECJ held that national rules, which required that appointment to a permanent full-time post as a lecturer in public vocational schools in Ireland was conditional upon proficiency in Gaelic, were justified. Although knowledge of Gaelic was not required for the performance of the duties of teaching art in Ireland, the requirement was not in breach of art 3(1) of Regulation 1612/68 as it was a part of a national policy for the promotion of the national language and therefore constituted a means of expressing national identity and language in the Irish Republic. It was also non-discriminatory, and not disproportionate to the objective pursued. However, in *Maria Chiara Spotti* Case C–272/92 [1993] ECR I–5185 and *Allué* Case 33/88 [1989] ECR 1591, in the context of German law which provided for contracts of limited duration for foreign language teaching assistants, the ECJ held that such contracts were in breach of art 39 EC and rejected the argument submitted by the German government that the requirement was intended to ensure up-to-date tuition.

Under art 4 of Regulation 1612/68 Member States must not restrict by number or percentage the number of foreign nationals to be employed in a particular area of activity. In *Commission* v *France* Case 167/73 [1974] ECR 359 the 1926 French Maritime Code set a ratio of three French to one non-French for the employment of French merchant seamen in the crew of merchant ships. The justification submitted by the French government that the requirement was not used in practice, as oral instructions were given to appropriate national authorities not to apply it, was rejected. The ECJ ruled that non-application of the requirement was a matter of grace, not of law, and thereby created uncertainty for all parties concerned.

Under art 5 of Regulation 1612/68 Member States must offer EC migrant workers the same assistance in seeking employment as is available to nationals. Article 6 of the Regulation provides that the engagement or recruitment of a national of one Member State for a post in another Member State should not depend on medical, vocational or other criteria which are discriminatory as compared with those applied to national workers. However, when an employer actually offers a job to a national of another Member State he may expressly condition this offer on the candidate undergoing a vocational test: art 6(2).

Equality in employment

Article 7(1) of Regulation 1612/68 provides that:

> 'A worker who is a national of a Member State may not, in the territory of another Member State, be treated differently from national workers by reason of his nationality in respect of any conditions of employment and work, in particular as regards remuneration, dismissal, and, should he become unemployed, reinstatement or re-employment.'

This provision confirmed the prohibition of all discrimination direct and indirect against EC migrant workers and should be read in the light of the relevant case law of the ECJ.

The most controversial provision of Title II of the Regulation is its art 7(2) under which EC migrant workers are entitled to 'the same social and tax advantages as national workers'.

The ECJ defined social advantages in *Even* Case 207/78 [1979] ECR 2019 as including all advantages 'which, whether or not linked to a contract of employment, are generally granted to national workers primarily because of their objective status as workers or by virtue of the mere fact of their residence in the national territory'. Consequently, such advantages are granted to national workers because they are workers or because they reside within the territory of a Member State. They are extended to EC migrant workers in order to facilitate the free movement of workers in the EU.

In this case Even, a French national living in Belgium, challenged a reduction of his pension, which was applied to persons who received early retirement, on the ground that the reduction was not applied to Belgian nationals who received a World War II service invalidity pensions granted by the allied nations. Even was a recipient of a similar pension granted under French legislation. The ECJ held that Even was not subject to the reduction as a World War II service invalidity pension granted to Belgian nationals, being a pension, was not a social advantage within the meaning of art 7 of Regulation 1612/68.

Social advantages are different from social security benefits: *Frilli* v *Belgium* Case 1/72 [1972] ECR 457. Migrant EC workers are entitled to social security benefits only if they pay contribution to a social security scheme in a host Member State.

In the context of the principle of equality in employment, the following persons are entitled to social and tax advantages:

1. EC migrant workers but not EC nationals who are seeking employment in a host

Member State. In *Centre Public de l'Aide Sociale de Courcelles* v *Lebon* Case 316/85 [1987] ECR 2811 a French national who was living in Belgium applied for the Belgian minimex (a minimum income allowance). She was not a worker within the meaning of art 39 EC but she was seeking a job. The ECJ made a distinction between workers already in employment and those who are in search of work. Only the former are entitled to social advantages. By virtue of art 7(2) EC migrant workers are entitled to a vast range of benefits. In *Reina* Case 65/81 [1982] ECR 33 an Italian couple residing in Germany obtained an interest-free discretionary loan on the birth of their child payable only to German nationals living in Germany, such being intended to increase the birth rate in Germany and granted by a credit institution set up under public law. In *Hoecks* Case 249/83 [1985] ECR 973 an unemployed worker was entitled to a minimum subsistence allowance, and in *Mutsch* Case 137/84 [1985] ECR 2681 the use of one's own language in judicial proceedings was considered as being a social benefit. Also included within the definition of social advantages are: an old-age pension falling outside the scope of the national social security rules (*Frascogna* Case 157/84 [1985] ECR 1739), a state payment to cover funeral expenses (*O'Flynn* Case C–237/94 [1996] ECR I–2617) and a child-raising allowance: *Maria Martinez Sala* Case C–85/96 [1998] ECR I–2691.

Contrary to rules governing access to employment, EC migrant workers once employed in the public sector are also entitled to social advantages: *Sotgiu* Case 152/73 [1974] ECR 153.

2. Members of a worker' family, provided they are dependent. They are indirect beneficiaries of social benefits. In *Fiorini (Christini)* Case 32/75 [1975] ECR 1085 an Italian widow living in France claimed the special fare reduction card issued by the French Railways to the parents of large families. The ECJ held that since the family was entitled to remain in France after the worker's death and that the card was available to the families of deceased French workers, it should not be denied to the families of deceased workers from other Member States. In subsequent cases the following were considered as social advantages: a disability allowance claimed by an Italian worker in France for his adult son (*Inzirillo* Case 63/76 [1976] ECR 2057), a guaranteed income paid to old people in Belgium claimed by an Italian widow living with her retired son in Belgium (*Castelli* Case 261/83 [1984] ECR 3199) and a minimum income allowance claimed by members of the family of an unemployed worker: *Scrivner* Case 122/84 [1985] ECR 1027.

In *Bernini* Case 3/90 [1992] ECR I–1071 the ECJ held that a study grant should be categorised as a social advantage within the meaning of art 7(2) of Regulation 1612/68. As a result, a dependent child of a migrant EC worker is entitled to obtain study finance under the same conditions as are applicable to children of national workers. In *Matteucci* Case 237/87 [1988] ECR 5589 the ECJ ruled that a scholarship to study abroad, which was a part of a reciprocal agreement between Belgium and Germany, should be granted to a son of an Italian worker employed in Belgium who wanted to study in Germany.

Education

By virtue of art 7(3) of Regulation 1612/68 EC migrant workers are entitled to access to training in vocational schools and retraining centres under the same conditions as national workers. The ECJ has restrictively interpreted this provision. In *Lair v University of Hanover* Case 39/86 [1988] ECR 3161 the ECJ held that 'the concept of vocational training is a more limited one and refers exclusively to institutions which provide only instruction either alternating with or closely linked to an occupational activity, particularly during apprenticeship. That is not true of universities.' Luckily for Lair the narrow construction of art 7(3) was compensated for by the ECJ's generous approach to art 7(2), which in the same case ruled that entitlement to study finance is to be regarded as a social advantage under art 7(2) of the Regulation. Consequently, a person who has kept his status as a worker can rely on art 7(2) to obtain means of financial support from a host Member State to take courses to improve his professional qualifications and social advancement.

The above rule is subject to limitations imposed by the ECJ in respect of workers who voluntarily become unemployed in order to undertake a course of study and workers who enter a host Member State and take up employment for a short period of time with a view to subsequently undertaking studies.

The first situation occurred in *Lair*. Lair was a French national who had worked in Germany as a bank clerk for two-and-a-half years and was then made redundant, and for the next two-and-a-half years was working but had spells of involuntary unemployment. She was considered as a worker and therefore entitled to retain that status when she decided to study languages and literature at the University of Hanover. However, when she applied for a maintenance grant her application was refused. She challenged the refusal. The ECJ ruled that although she was a worker 'some continuity between the previous occupation and the course of study' was required in order to obtain a grant for university education. In her case, there was no link between her previous job and her subsequent studies. Consequently, she was entitled to the payment of registration and tuition fees but not to assistance given in the form of maintenance grants. However, if a worker becomes involuntarily unemployed and is 'obliged by conditions of the job market to undertake occupational training in another field of activity' he will be entitled to general measures of support such as grants and loans.

The second situation was examined by the ECJ in *Brown v Secretary of State for Scotland* Case 125/87 [1988] ECR 1619. Brown was a holder of dual nationality, French and British. He was employed as a trainee engineer with Ferranti plc in Edinburgh for nine months with a view to studying in engineering at Cambridge. His work was a form of pre-university industrial training as it was a prerequisite for his admission to university. Conversely, he would not have been employed by his employer if he had not already been accepted by the university. When he applied for a grant his application was refused on the ground that he was not a resident of the UK during the previous three years as required by UK legislation. He challenged this decision.The ECJ held that Brown was a worker as he fulfilled the three criteria laid down in *Lawrie-Blum* (see section 17.1), that is he was engaged in genuine and effective economic activity. However, the ECJ decided that Brown was not entitled to a grant despite his status of a worker because he 'acquired that status exclusively as a result of his being accepted for admission to undertake the studies in question'. Therefore, if employment is merely ancillary to studies a migrant worker is not entitled to financial assistance.

Trade union rights

Title II of Part I of Regulation 1612/68 regarding equality of treatment also covers equal trade union rights: art 8. An EC migrant worker is entitled to equal treatment in respect of the exercise of trade union rights, including the right to vote and to be eligible for the administration and management posts of a trade union. The ECJ ruled that art 8 of the Regulation applies to organisations similar to trade unions, that is their objective is the protection of workers. Consequently, in a situation where EC migrant workers are mandatory members of professional associations, and have to pay compulsory contributions, national legislation cannot deny them the right to vote in elections to choose members of their professional associations: *ASTI* Case C–213/90 [1991] ECR I–3507; *Commission* v *Luxembourg* Case C–118/92 [1994] ECR I–1891.

Also, an EC migrant worker has the right of eligibility for workers' representative bodies within the undertaking. However, he may be excluded from the management of bodies under public law and from the exercise of an office under public law.

Article 7(4) of the Regulation provides that clauses in collective and individual employment contracts are void in so far as they authorise or provide for discriminatory conditions in respect of EC migrant workers.

Equal treatment in matters of housing and house ownership

Article 9 of the Regulation ensures equal treatment of EC migrant workers in matters of housing and house ownership. In *Commission* v *Greece* Case 305/87 [1989] ECR 1461 the ECJ condemned Greek legislation prohibiting foreign nationals from owning immovable property located in certain regions of Greece (namely, in areas close to Greek external borders), since this applied to approximately 55 per cent of the Greek territory.

Derogations from national rules

Article 8(1) of Regulation 1612/68 provides that its provisions in no way derogate from national rules which are more favourable to EC migrant workers. The ECJ has always encouraged Member States to apply more favourable national rules, not only in respect of EC migrant workers, but also to nationals of third countries lawfully residing within the EC. This approach is well illustrated in *Ibiyinka Awoyemi* Case C–230/97 [1998] ECR I–6781. In this case criminal proceedings were commenced against Ibiyinka Awoyemi, a Turkish national, for not exchanging his Community driving licence issued by one Member State for a driving licence of the Member State of his current residence, Belgium, within the prescribed time-limit as required under Directive 80/1263. Although Directive 80/1263 did not impose any criminal penalties in the event of failure to exchange a driving licence within the prescribed time limit, Belgian implementing legislation specified such a failure as subject to criminal penalties. The obligation to exchange was abolished by Directive 91/439 which, at the time of the alleged offence, was not in force. The Belgian court asked the ECJ whether it was allowed to apply retroactively the more favourable provisions of Directive 91/439, even though the alleged offence took place before the expiry of the time limit prescribed for the implementation of Directive 91/439 and in the absence of national implementing legislation.

The ECJ held that Directive 80/1263 made no provision for the penalties to be imposed in the event of breach of the obligation to exchange driving licences. As a result, in the absence of Community rules governing the matter, the Member States remained competent in principle to impose penalties for breach of such an obligation. However, the offender was a national of a third country and as such could not invoke the principle of free movement of persons in order to challenge penal sanctions imposed under Belgian law. In *Skanavi* Case C–193/94 [1996] ECR I–929, where a national of a Member-State was prosecuted for a similar offence in Belgium, the ECJ held that a Member State was precluded from imposing a criminal penalty in this area so disproportionate to the gravity of the infringement as to become an obstacle to the free movement of persons.

The retroactive application of Community law in order to attenuate the application of penal law has already been permitted by the ECJ in relation to the free movement of capital.[9] Its application in the *Awoyemi* case is not surprising, especially in that the relevant Member State had a well established principle of retroactive effect of more favourable provisions of criminal law.

It is interesting to note that by virtue of Directive 97/26[10] a driving licence issued by one Member State must be recognised in all other Member States. In the event of change of residence, an EC national is not obliged to exchange a driving licence issued in his Member State for a driving licence of a host Member State.

17.4 Right to remain in the territory of a Member State after having been employed in that State

Regulation 1251/70 deals with the right of an EC migrant worker to remain in the territory of a host Member State after having been employed there. The preamble to the Regulation emphasised that the right to remain is a corollary of the right to reside in a host Member State. The right to remain is extended to the family of a worker. Further 'in the case of the death of the worker during his working life, maintenance of the right of residence of the members of his family must also be recognised' (seventh recital).

Under art 2(1) of Regulation the right to remain permanently in the territory of a host Member State is granted to retired workers, workers suffering incapacity and frontier workers, provided they satisfy the following conditions:

1. Retired workers. A worker who reaches the statutory age for entitlement to an old-age pension must have been employed in that State for at least the previous 12 months and have been continuously resident there for more than three years.
2. Incapacitated workers. Such a worker must have resided continuously in the territory of a host Member State for more than two years, and have ceased work there as an employed person as a result of permanent incapacity to work. However, if such

---

[9] See *Bordessa* Case C–358 and 416/93 [1995] ECR I–361; *Sanz de Lera* Case C–163/94 [1995] ECR I–4821.
[10] OJ L150 (1997).

incapacity is the result of an accident at work, or an occupational disease entitling him to a pension for which an institution of that State is entirely or partially responsible, no condition as to the length of residence is imposed.

3. Frontier workers. A worker who is employed in the territory of a host Member State while retaining his residence in the territory of a home Member State must have been continuously employed for three years and must have returned to his home Member State daily or at least once a week.

The period of time spent working in a host Member State counts as working in a home Member State for the purposes of retirement and incapacity. Retired or incapacitated workers are not subject to the residence and employment requirements if they are married to a national of a host Member State or if having been a national of a host Member State they lost that nationality by marriage to a national of another Member State working in the host Member State: art 2(2).

The beneficiaries of the right to remain in a host Member State have two consecutive years, from the time when they first become entitled, to decide whether or not to exercise it. During that time they may leave the territory of a host Member State without forfeiting their right which can be exercised without any formality: art 5.

Under art 3 of Regulation 1251/70 members of the family of a retired or incapacitated worker are entitled to reside permanently in the territory of a host Member State after the death of that worker. However, if a worker dies during his working life, before having acquired the right to remain, his family is only entitled to remain permanently if one of the following conditions is satisfied:

1. the worker has resided continuously in that State for at least two years;
2. his death resulted from an accident at work or an occupational disease;
3. the surviving spouse is a national of that State or has lost the nationality of that State by marriage to the worker: art 3(2).

Article 4 provides that temporary absences not exceeding three months per year, longer absences due to compliance with obligations of military service, periods of involuntarily unemployment duly recorded by the competent employment authorities, and absences due to illness or accident should be considered as periods of employment for the purposes of art 2 of the Regulation.

Under art 5 the beneficiaries of the right to remain permanently in the territory of a host Member State are entitled to a residence permit, valid for a least five years throughout the territory of that State and automatically renewable.

18 The Right of Establishment and the Right to Supply and Receive Services (arts 43–55 EC)

18.1 The right of establishment

18.2 Freedom to supply and receive services

Article 43 confers the right of establishment whilst art 49 EC grants the right to supply and receive services. These rights attach to both natural persons who are nationals of Member States and legal persons established in Member States. Article 43 EC (*Jean Reyners v The Belgian State* Case 2/74 [1974] ECR 631; [1974] 2 CMLR 305) and art 49 EC (see *Van Binsbergen* Case 33/74 [1974] ECR 1299) are directly effective.

The right of establishment and the right to provide services are not identical. The provisions of the EC Treaty relating to the right to supply services are applicable only if the provisions on the right of establishment are not applicable: *Gebhard* Case 55/94 [1995] ECR I–4165. The distinction between the above rights is based on the period of time during which natural or legal persons exercise the economic activities in question in the territory of a host Member State. In *Gebhard* the ECJ emphasised that the regularity, periodicity and continuity of the service should be taken into consideration. The ECJ defined the concept of establishment broadly. Consequently, the right of establishment involves a permanent and continuous presence in the host Member State which allows 'a Community national to participate on a stable and continuous basis in the economic life of a Member State other than his own'. In respect of legal persons the ECJ held in *Commission v Germany (Re Insurance Services)* Case 205/84 [1986] ECR 3755 that an enterprise (in this case an insurance company) was established in a host Member State 'even if its presence is not in the form of a branch or agency but consists merely of an office managed by the enterprise's own staff or by a person who is independent but is authorised to act on a permanent basis for the enterprise'.

The provision of services involves temporary and occasional pursuit of economic activities in a host Member State and therefore does not require, as a matter of principle, a person to reside, even for the duration of the service, in the host Member State.[1] Article 50 EC refers to services being as 'normally provided for remuneration, in so far as they are not governed by the provisions relating to freedom of movement for goods, capital and persons'. Services can be provided in all sectors of economy.

Natural persons

Nationals of a Member State are entitled to exercise the right of establishment irrespective

---

[1] However, in ceratin circumstances this may be required: see *Van Binsbergen* Case 33/74 [1974] ECR 1299.

of whether or not they reside within the territory of the EU or in a third country. However, nationals of a third country lawfully residing in a Member State cannot rely on art 43 EC in order to establish themselves in another Member State: *Razanatsimba* Case 65/77 [1977] ECR 2229. The right to provide services is restricted to EU citizens who are established in a Member State

If a national of a Member State has double nationality, the most favourable to the exercise of his right of establishment/provision of services will be taken into account. In *Gullung* Case 292/86 [1988] ECR 111 a lawyer, who was a holder of both French and German nationality, was allowed in France to rely on his German nationality .

Legal persons

The right of establishment and the right to provide services are granted to companies and firms. Article 48 EC contains a definition of 'companies and firms'. It covers companies or firms constituted under civil or commercial law, including co-operative societies, and other legal persons governed by public or private law. Only companies and firms fulfilling the following conditions are entitled to exercise the right to freedom of establishment:

1. They must be formed in accordance with the law of a Member State.
2. They must have their registered office, central administration or principal place of business within the Community. In the context of the provision of services, if a company's central administration or principal place of business is located outside the EU the company's activities must have an 'effective and continuous link with the economy of a Member State, excluding the possibility that this link might depend on nationality, particularly the nationality of the partners or the members of the managing or supervising bodies, or of persons holding the capital stock'.[2]
3. Legal persons must pursue economic activities for remuneration. Non-profit-making undertakings are excluded from the scope of art 48 EC. However, this does not mean that other provisions of the EC Treaty are not applicable to non-profit-making entities. In *Commission of the European Communities* v *Kingdom of Belgium* Case C–172/98 [1999] ECR I–3999 Belgian law required that in order for the legal personality of a non-profit-making association to be recognised, there must be a member of Belgian nationality on the governing body of that association or three-fifths of the members must be of Belgian nationality. The Commission considered this requirement as contrary to Community law as it discriminated on grounds of nationality. The Commission invoked art 48 EC, even though non-profit-making associations are outside its scope of application. The ECJ, however, relied solely on the principle of non-discrimination laid down in art 12 EC. The ECJ held that the Kingdom of Belgium was in breach of art 12 EC and confirmed that non-profit-making associations are within the scope of Community law. Consequently, national legislation concerning non-profit-making organisations should be reviewed in the light of the principle of non-discrimination.

---

[2] *Common Market Reporter*, para 1546, OJ 1962, 32.

The general programme for the abolition of restrictions from 1961 to the ECJ decisions in Reyners and Van Bisbergen

Articles 52 and 59 EC Treaty (amended arts 43 and 49 EC) provided for abolition of restrictions on the freedom of establishment and on the freedom to provide services by progressive stages. In the course of the transitional period (it ended on 31 December 1969) the Council was required to draw up a general programme for the abolition of existing restrictions in these areas. On 18 December 1961[3] the Council adopted two general programmes for the abolition of restrictions, the first concerning the freedom of establishment and the second relating to the provision of services. Both programmes set out the general conditions necessary to achieve the freedom of establishment and freedom to provide services in respect of each type of activity by progressive stages. A major consequence of the programmes was the adoption by the Council of a number of directives covering various sectors of the economy, such as mining and quarrying, forestry, energy, coal, the film industry, food manufacturing and beverage industries, etc. However, the task assigned to the Council by virtue of arts 52 and 59 EC Treaty was far from being completed at the end of the transitional period. In these circumstances two decisions delivered by the ECJ dramatically changed the approach of the Community towards the removal of the restrictions.

The right of establishment: *Reyners v The Belgian State*

In *Reyners v The Belgian State* Case 2/74 [1974] ECR 631 Jean Reyners, a Dutch national born and bred in Belgium, a holder a Belgian doctorate in Law (docteur en droit), sat the necessary examinations to become an advocate in Belgium. The Belgian legislation provided that only Belgian nationals could be called to the Belgian Bar. Reyners challenged the compatibility of this legislation with art 43 EC. The Belgian Conseil d'Etat referred the matter to the ECJ under the preliminary ruling procedure. During these proceedings, the Belgian Bar and the government of Luxembourg submitted that the profession of advocate was excluded from art 43 EC as its activities were connected with the exercise of official authority within the meaning of art 45 EC. In Belgium an advocate may be called upon to sit as a judge in certain cases, and a judge exercises official authority.

In this case the ECJ established three principles.

First, the ECJ held that the fact that art 43 EC stated that the restrictions on the freedom of establishment 'shall be abolished by progressive stages in the course of the transitional period' did not affect the right of nationals of one Member State wishing to establish themselves in another Member State to enjoy immediate protection. The ECJ held that art 43 EC imposed an obligations to attain a precise result which was not conditional upon the implementation of a programme of progressive measures. Such a programme would only facilitate the attainment of the prescribed result. As a result, after the expiry of the transitional period art 43 EC has become directly applicable despite the absence, in a particular sphere, of directives prescribed by arts 44(2) and 47(1) EC.

Second, the ECJ held that art 43 EC had to be interpreted in the light of the whole

---

[3] OJ 2 (1962).

scheme of the EC Treaty, including art 12 EC which prohibits any discrimination on the grounds of nationality. Third, the ECJ stated that the exception to freedom of establishment contained in art 45 EC did not apply to the profession of advocate as it was restricted to activities which involved a direct and specific connection with the exercise of official authority.

The provision of services: *Van Binsbergen*

In *Van Binsbergen* v *Bestuur Van De Bedrijfsvereniging Voor De Mataalnijverheid* Case 33/74 [1974] ECR 1299; [1973] 1 CMLR 298 Van Binsbergen was represented before the Dutch social security court by Kortmann, a Dutch national. During the proceedings Kortmann, a legal adviser and representative in social security matters, moved from The Netherlands to Belgium and from there he corresponded with the Dutch court. He was informed by the court registrar that only persons established in The Netherlands were permitted to represent their clients before the Dutch social security court and as a permanent resident of Belgium he could no longer act for Van Binsbergen. Kortmann challenged this provision of the relevant Dutch statute on procedure in social security matters as incompatible with art 49 EC.

The ECJ established four principles in this case. First, the ECJ held that arts 49 and 50 EC are directly effective. Second, the ECJ emphasised that both provisions are subject to the principle of non-discrimination based on the ground of nationality. Third, the ECJ decided that national rules may impose restrictions on the provision of services provided these rules are not discriminatory. In this respect the ECJ held that:

> '... taking into account the particular nature of the services to be provided, specific requirements imposed on the person providing the service cannot be considered incompatible with the Treaty where they have as their purpose the application of professional rules justified by the general good – in particular rules relating to organisation, qualifications, professional ethics, supervision and liability – which are binding upon any person established in the State in which the service is provided, where the person providing the service would escape from the ambit of those rules by being established in another Member State.'

Fourth, national rules imposing restrictions on the provision of services will be compatible with arts 49 and 50 EC if they are objectively justified by the need to ensure observance of professional rules of conduct, provided such rules are non-discriminatory, objectively justified and proportionate.

To summarise, national restrictions should be assessed in the light of these four criteria, that is non-discrimination based on the grounds of nationality, their suitability for securing the attainment of the objective they pursue, the necessity of the objective justification for such restrictions and their proportionality as to the objectives which they intend to achieve.

In this case, the requirement of permanent residence applied without discrimination to nationals and non-nationals, and it was objectively justified by the general good, that is, by the need to ensure observance of professional rules of conduct especially those connected with the administration of justice and those relating to professional ethics. As to the third criterion the ECJ held that the requirement of permanent residence was disproportionate as the objective of the proper administration of justice could be achieved by less restrictive measures, such as the choosing of an address in the Member State in which the service is provided. This test has clear parallels with the *Cassis de Dijon* case although, the ECJ has refused to adopt a *Keck* case limitation to the freedom to provide services: *Alpine Investments* Case C–384/93 [1995] ECR I–1141.

It is also interesting to note that *Van Binsbergen* concerned a Dutch national, who provided services in The Netherlands, acting for a Dutch client before a Dutch court. The fact that he was established in Belgium brought the case within the scope of Community law. Therefore, in some cases EC law protects nationals of a Member State against their own State!

The decisions of the ECJ in *Reyners* and *Van Binsbergen* have important implications with regard to the application of the provisions of the EC Treaty relating to the freedom of establishment and the provision of services. From the end of the transitional period art 43 and art 49 EC became directly effective and therefore they can be relied upon by individuals in proceedings before national courts. Furthermore, art 12 EC may be invoked to challenge a national rule, whether in the form of a nationality or a residence requirement, which is discriminatory. The principle of non-discrimination has been broadly interpreted in the context of the right of establishment and the right to provide services. Both direct and indirect discrimination is prohibited. The principle of non-discrimination covers both the taking up and pursuit of a particular activity. This was decided by the ECJ in *Steinhauser* v *City of Biarritz* Case 197/84 [1985] ECR 1819. In this case a German national, who was a professional artist and who resided in Biarritz, applied to the local authorities to rent a 'crampotte' (a kind of a fisherman's hut used locally for the exhibition and sale of works of art). His application was refused on the grounds that only French nationals were allowed to rent a 'crampotte'. Steinhauser challenged this decision. The ECJ held that the principle of non-discrimination applies not only to the taking up of activity as a self-employed person but also the pursuit of that activity in the broadest sense. In *Commission* v *Italy (Re Housing Aid)* Case 63/86 [1988] ECR 29 the ECJ held that a cheap mortgage facility available only to Italian nationals should also have been available to all EC providers of services in Italy so long as the nature of the service provided was such as to require a permanent dwelling in Italy.

In the application of provisions relating to the right of establishment and the freedom to supply services the principle of non-discrimination on the grounds of nationality plays a very important role for two reasons: first, there is no secondary legislation in these areas comparable to Regulation 1612/68 and, second, the principle of non-discrimination provides the only legal basis of challenging national rules which are discriminatory in areas where recognition and harmonisation at Community level have not yet been achieved in a particular profession.

However, a distinction must be made between the application of the principle of non-discrimination in respect of the exercise of the right of establishment and the exercise of the right to provide services. With respect to the right of establishment the principle of non-discrimination based on the ground of nationality requires that nationals of other Member States are treated in a host Member State in the same manner as nationals of that State. Nationals of a host Member State and nationals of other Member States established in the territory of a host Member State are in exactly the same situation. However, the application of 'national treatment' to the providers of services from other Member States is inappropriate. The principle of non-discrimination requires that different situations are treated differently: *Italy* v *Commission* Case 13/63 [1963] ECR 360. Consequently, any restriction, even if indistinctly applicable to national providers of services and providers of services from other Member States, which is liable to prohibit, impede or render less advantageous the activities of a provider of services established in another Member State where he provides similar services, must be abolished.

Reverse discrimination

It is interesting to note that reverse discrimination is permitted under EC law relating to the freedom of establishment and the provision of services. In this respect two situations should be distinguished: wholly internal situations to which national law is applicable[4] and situations in which a national of a Member State is denied the benefit of more favourable provisions of EC law than national law because he is a national of that State even though his circumstances are ones to which EC law applies.

In the first situation, a national of a Member State is placed in a less advantageous position than a national of another Member State who has established himself in that State. For example, under Directive 82/489/EEC which lays down measures to facilitate the effective exercise of the right of establishment and freedom to provide services in hairdressing, six years' professional experience as a hairdresser is sufficient to exercise that profession in a host Member State. However, in France in order to work as a hairdresser a French diploma in hairdressing is required. A French hairdresser who fails an examination to become a hairdresser cannot rely on his six years' experience in France in order to practice the profession. The explanation is that Directive 82/489/EEC does not harmonise the conditions of access to the profession of hairdresser in Member States. It established the conditions for the exercise of the right of establishment in a host Member State for that profession.

In the second situation, there is some connection between the situation at issue and EC law. For example, in *Auer (No 1)* Case C–136/78 [1979] ECR 437 a national of Austria obtained in Italy a diploma as a veterinary surgeon. Subsequently, he moved to France where he acquired French nationality. In France when he applied to the professional body for veterinary surgeons to be allowed to practice in France, his application was refused. At that time, the implementation period for Directive 78/1026/EEC concerning the mutual recognition of diplomas, certificates and other evidence of formal qualifications in veterinary medicine, including measures to facilitate the effective exercise of the right of establishment and freedom to provide services, had not yet expired. As a result, on the grounds of art 43 EC his qualification was not recognised in France. However, once the transitional period expired, Mr Auer reapplied. The French court refused to recognise his qualification, considering it 'inconceivable' that Mr Auer, a French national by naturalisation, should be treated more favourably than French nationals by birth who were holders of French diplomas. The ECJ held that although the Directive was not implemented into French law, once the transitional period expired Mr Auer was entitled to rely on the

---

[4] See, for example, *Volker Steen* Case C–332/90 [1992] ECR I–341; *Aubertin* Cases C–29–35/94 [1995] ECR I–311.

unimplemented Directive taking into account that the terms of the Directive were clear, precise and unconditional: *Auer (No 2)* Case 271/82 [1983] ECR 2727. The same conclusions were reached by the ECJ in *Knoors v Secretary of State for Economic Affairs* Case 115/78 [1979] ECR 399 in which a Dutch national, who practised as a plumber, in Belgium was refused permission to work as a plumber in The Netherlands even though Directive 64/427 governing certain trade skills was applicable to him as it covered the training and experience he had acquired. The Dutch authorities argued that Knoors was trying to evade the application of national rules and that Directive 64/427 did not apply to nationals seeking to establish themselves in their own State. The ECJ decided otherwise.[5]

The situation when EC nationals obtain their qualification in a non-Member State, exercise their right of establishment in a host Member State and subsequently seek to practice in their own Member State was examined by the ECJ in *Tawil-Albertini v Ministre des Affaires Sociales* Case C–154/93 [1994] ECR I–451 and in *Haim v Kassenzahnärtzliche Vereinigung Nordrhein* Case C–319/92 [1994] ECR I–425. In *Tawil-Albertini*, a French national obtained a dental qualification in Lebanon which was subsequently recognised in Belgium where he practised as a dentist. When he applied for authorisation to practice in France he was refused on the ground that his qualification was obtained in a non-Member State and therefore Directive 78/686/EEC concerning the mutual recognition of diplomas, certificates and other evidence of the formal qualifications of practising of dentistry did not apply to him. Tawil-Albertini argued that he was covered by the Directive since his qualification was recognised in Belgium. The ECJ ruled that in respect of qualifications obtained in a non-Member States the recognition is based on agreements between the States in question. Any Member State could recognise the equivalence of a qualification obtained in a non-Member State but was not required to do so as Directive 78/686/EEC did not cover such situations. However, professional experience gained in another Member State should be taken into account. This was decided in *Haim*, in which a German national who obtained his qualification in a non-Member State and subsequently practised for eight years in Belgium (he was also admitted to practice in Germany) was refused permission to work on a social security scheme in Germany unless he completed a further two years' preparatory training course. He argued that his professional experience in Belgium should be taken into account by the German authorities. The ECJ held:

> 'The competent national authority, in order to verify whether the training period requirement prescribed by the national rules is met, must take into account the professional experience of the plaintiff in the main proceedings, including that which he has acquired during his appointment as a dental practitioner of a social security scheme in another Member State.'

This approach is in line with Council Recommendation 89/49[6] encouraging the Member States to recognise diplomas and other evidence of formal qualifications obtained in non-Member States by EC nationals

---

[5] Similar decisions were given in *Broekmeulen v Huisarts Registratie Commissie* Case 246/80 [1981] ECR 2311.
[6] OJ L19 (1989).

The right of establishment and the right to provide services are not absolute

The exercise of both rights is subject to important limitations. One is based on art 45 EC which provides that the Chapter on the freedom of establishment does not apply to activities which are connected, even occasionally, with the exercise of official authority. Other limitations may be imposed on the grounds of public policy, public security and public health by a host Member State: see Chapter 15.

18.1 The right of establishment

Article 43 provides:

> 'Within the framework of the provisions set out below, restrictions on the freedom of establishment of nationals of a Member State in the territory of another Member State shall be prohibited. Such prohibition shall also apply to restrictions on the setting up of agencies, branches, subsidiaries by nationals of any Member State established in the territory of any Member State.
>
> Freedom of establishment shall include the right to take up and pursue activities as self employed persons and to set up and manage undertakings, in particular companies or firms within the meaning of the second paragraph of art 48, under the conditions laid down for its own nationals by the law of the country where such establishment is effected, subject to the provisions of the Chapter relating to capital.'

Exercise of the right of establishment by legal persons

Harmonisation of company law within the EC

By virtue of art 44(2)(g) EC the Community has undertaken an extensive programme of harmonisation of company laws of Member States. The First Company Law Directive was adopted in 1968.[7] This programme, although not yet completed, has resulted in the creation of uniform rules on company law at Community level providing reasonable protection for companies, creditors and shareholders. Secondary legislation in this area is too substantial to be discussed in this book. Of 13 directives harmonising company law four still pose difficulties: the Fifth Directive on Public Limited Company Structure, the Ninth Directive on Groups Containing Public Company Subsidiaries, the Tenth Directive on Cross-border Mergers of Public Companies and the Thirteenth Directive on Takeovers.[8]

New forms of business organisation have been created by the Community. Regulation 2137/85 on the European Economic Interest Grouping (EEIG)[9] which entered into force in August 1985 and, because it required to be supplemented by national provisions, has only been applied since 1 July 1989, allows existing companies from more than one Member State to 'enter into a contract to collaborate in a joint venture for a particular purpose and for a particular period of time'. EEIGs encourage co-operation between small and medium-

---

[7] OJ L65 (1968).
[8] The revised version of the Thirteenth Directive was approved by the Council on 21 June 1999.
[9] OJ L199 (1985).

size businesses at European level in all areas where joint action may be useful, while preserving their legal and economic independence.

In order to provide businesses with the opportunity to conduct their activities Europe-wide upon a scale corresponding to the internal market the Community has prepared a draft regulation for a statute for European companies[10] under which companies registered in different Member States will be offered the option to merge and thus to constitute trans-national economic units, the so-called *Societas Europea* (SE).

Other forms of co-operation between companies from different Member States are envisaged by three proposals relating to a European association (EA), a European Co-operative Society (SCE) and a European Mutual Society (ME)

In this context it is interesting to mention the failure of one of the most important initiatives in this area. Article 293 EC requires the Member States to enter into negotiations with a view to concluding certain conventions. One of them concerns 'the mutual recognition of companies or firms within the meaning of the second paragraph of art 48, the retention of legal personality in the event of transfer of their seat from one country to another, and the possibility of mergers between companies or firms governed by the laws of different countries'. The Convention on the Mutual Recognition of Companies and Bodies Corporate was adopted on 29 February 1968. It has been signed but will probably never enter into force due to the refusal of a number of Member States to ratify it.

The principle of non-discrimination

In respect of companies and firms art 43 EC prohibits any discrimination between branches and subsidiaries established in a host Member State and companies and firms which have their principal establishment in the territory of a host Member State. Both direct[11] and indirect (*Commission v Italy* Case C–3/88 [1989] ECR I–4035; *Halliburton Services* Case C–1/93 [1994] ECR I–1137) discrimination is prohibited. The question of indirect discrimination often emerges in respect of a host Member State's taxation system which tends to favour companies and firms having their principal establishment in that Member State. This was examined by the ECJ in *Imperial Chemical Industries v Colmer (Inspector of Taxes)* Case C–264/96 [1998] 3 CMLR 293.

In this case ICI together with another company, both residents in the UK, formed a consortium through which they beneficially owned Coopers Animal Health (Holdings) Ltd. The sole business of the latter was to hold shares in 23 trading companies which were its subsidiaries. Some of the subsidiaries were residents in the UK (4), some in other Member States (6) and some outside the territory of the EU. Within the subsidiary companies residing in the UK was Coopers Animal Health Ltd (CAH). ICI applied for tax relief under

---

[10] The concept dates back to 1910! Within the EC, at the proposal of the French government submitted in March 1965, a draft statute for SEs was prepared in 1966. Due to lack of progress negotiations were suspended in 1982. The Commission Memorandum on the Internal Market, Industrial Co-operation and the Statute for the European Company (COM(88)320 Final) relaunched the project. The main problem with the proposal is the matter of whether SEs should be viewed from a strictly economic perspective or whether labour law and social policy considerations should be taken into account in formulating the rules for their structure. The future of the proposed Regulation is still uncertain.

[11] *Commission v France* Case 270/83 [1986] ECR 273; *Commerzbank* Case C–330/91 [1993] ECR I–4017; *Royal Bank of Scotland v Elliniko Dimosio* Case C–311/97 [1999] ECR I–2651.

ss258–264 of the Income and Corporation Taxes Act 1970 in order to set off losses incurred by CAH. This was refused on the ground that CAH (Holdings) Ltd was not a holding company within the meaning of s258(7) of the Act since the majority of the subsidiaries were not resident in the UK. ICI challenged that decision and argued that the residence requirement under the Act was contrary to arts 43 and 48 EC. The House of Lords referred two questions to the ECJ: first, whether the residency requirement under the Income and Corporation Taxes Act 1970 was in conformity with arts 43 and 48 EC and, second, concerning the scope of application of EC law where the subsidiaries were established in non-Member States.

The ECJ held that although direct taxation was in principle within the competence of each Member State it must nevertheless exercise its powers of direct taxation in conformity with Community law: see *Schumacker* Case C–279/93 [1995] ECR I–225. In the circumstances described in *Colmer*, national legislation hindered the freedom of establishment since it set up differential tax treatment of consortium companies established in the UK as compared with those established in other Member States. The justifications provided by the UK were rejected by the ECJ. In respect of the UK argument concerning tax avoidance the ECJ replied:

'As regards the justification based on the risk of tax avoidance, suffice it to note that the legislation at issue in the main proceedings does not have the specific purpose of preventing wholly artificial arrangements, set up to circumvent United Kingdom tax legislation, from attracting tax benefits, but applies generally to all situations in which the majority of a group's subsidiaries are established, for whatever reason, outside the United Kingdom. However, the establishment of a company outside the United Kingdom does not, of itself, necessarily entail tax avoidance, since that company will in any event be subject to the tax legislation of the State of establishment.

In answer to the argument that revenue lost through the granting of tax relief on losses incurred by resident subsidiaries cannot be offset by taxing the profits of non-resident subsidiaries, it must be pointed out that diminution of tax revenue occurring in this way is not one of the grounds listed in art 56 of the Treaty [art 46 EC] and cannot be regarded as a matter of overriding general interest which may be relied upon in order to justify unequal treatment that is, in principle, incompatible with art 52 of the Treaty [43 EC].

Furthermore, the risk of charges being transferred, which the legislation at issue is designed to prevent, is entirely independent of whether or not the majority of subsidiaries are resident in the United Kingdom. The existence of only one non-resident subsidiary is enough to create the risk invoked by the United Kingdom Government.'

The argument based on the maintenance of cohesion of the national tax system submitted by the government of the UK was rejected[12] as neither satisfying the conditions established in *Hans-Martin Bachmann v Belgian State* Case C–204/90 [1992] ECR I–249 nor fulfilling the criterion of proportionality. The ECJ confirmed that while a particular provision of national law must be disapplied in relation to a situation covered by EC law, the same provision could be applied in a situation falling outside the scope of EC law. The ECJ held that art 10 EC did not require the national court to interpret its legislation in conformity

---

[12] In *Futura Participation* Case C–250/95 [1997] ECR I–2471 the ECJ was more inclined to favour the maintenance of a national tax system.

with EC law or to disapply the legislation to situations falling outside the scope of EC law. However, this may create legal uncertainty which a Member State should avoid in so far as it might affect rights deriving from EC law.

Articles 43 and 48 EC do not require that a company or branch or a subsidiary conduct any economic activity in a host Member State. This was confirmed by the ECJ In *Centros Ltd v Erhvervs-og Selskabsstyrelsen* Case C–212/97 [1999] 2 CMLR 551, in which the ECJ clearly stated that the fact that a company does not conduct any business in the Member State in which it has its registered office but pursues its activities only in the Member State where its branch is established is not sufficient to prove the existence of abuse or fraudulent conduct which would entitle the latter Member State to deny that company the benefit of the provisions of Community law relating to the right of establishment.

In this case Mrs Bryde, a Danish national, in May 1992 registered her company Centros in the UK, taking advantage of the UK law which did not impose any requirement on limited liability companies as to the paying-up of minimum share capital. During the summer of 1992, Mrs Bryde requested the Danish Trade and Companies Board to register a branch of Centros in Denmark. The Board refused on the grounds that Centros had never traded since its formation and that Mrs Bryde was, in fact, seeking to establish in Denmark not a branch but a principal establishment by circumventing Danish rules concerning the paying-up of minimum capital fixed at DKK 200,000. Centros challenged the decision of the Danish Trade and Companies Board.

The ECJ held that it was contrary to arts 43 and 48 EC for a Member State to refuse, on the above-mentioned grounds, to register a branch of a company formed in accordance with the law of another Member State in which it had its registered office but in which the company itself was not engaged in any business activities. The ECJ confirmed its liberal approach towards freedom of establishment by stating that national rules regarding the prevention of fraud cannot justify restrictions which impair the freedom of establishment of companies. In his advisory opinion, Advocate-General La Pergola suggested that in the light of the evolution of the Community the freedom of establishment should be approached in the same manner as the free movement of goods, that is, the principles of *Cassis de Dijon* should apply. The echo of his suggestion can be found in the statement of the ECJ that only 'imperative requirements' in the general interest may justify national measures hindering the exercise of the right to freely set up a branch in other Member States.

The ECJ did not 'look behind the veil' of a company, it applied the provisions relating to the right of establishment. Therefore, the fact that Mrs Bryde was taking advantage of more lenient company law in the UK permitting her to avoid paying the capital required by Danish law for the establishment of a company, and that the main purpose of establishing her company in the UK was to open a branch in Denmark which actually was intended to be a principal establishment, did not constitute an abuse of the right of establishment. In this respect, the ECJ held that:

> '... the fact that a Member State may not refuse to register a branch of a company formed in accordance with the law of another Member State in which it has its registered office does not preclude that first State from adopting any appropriate measure for preventing or penalising fraud, either in relation to the company itself, if need be in co-operation with the Member State in which it was formed, or in relation to its members, where it has been established that

they are in fact attempting, by means of the formation of the company, to evade their obligations towards private or public creditors established on the territory of a Member State concerned. In any event, combatting fraud cannot justify a practice of refusing to register a branch of a company which has its registered office in another Member State.'

The decision in the present case in not surprising taking into account that the ECJ in previous cases applied a restrictive approach to national measures intended to fight fraud which imposed restrictions on the freedom of establishment.[13]

The only danger of this approach is that it might create the so-called 'Delaware' effect within the EU. Under the 'Delaware' effect many states in the USA have introduced very lenient rules in respect of the formation of companies (in particular in relation to the protection of creditors) in order to attract new companies. In the context of the EU it will be necessary to harmonise national laws of the Member States in this area in order to prevent some Member States from introducing new legislation aimed at attracting businesses from other Member States but at the cost of weaker protection for creditors.

National measures adopted by a host Member State which apply different treatment to branches and subsidiaries established in a host Member State from that applied to companies or firms having their principal establishment in that State are permitted under art 43 EC so long as they fulfill four conditions: they must be applied in a non-discriminatory manner; they must be justified by imperative requirements in the general interest; they must be suitable for securing the attainment of the objective which they pursue; and they must not go beyond what is necessary in order to attain the objective pursued.

Exercise of the right of establishment by self-employed persons

Secondary legislation has been adopted with to facilitate the exercise of the right of establishment by the self -employed. This includes:

1. Directive 73/148 on the right of entry and residence which applies to both self-employed persons and providers and recipients of services (it is similar in scope to Directive 68/360 for workers).
2. Directive 64/221/EEC regulating restrictions on entry and residence within a host Member State based on the grounds of public policy, public security and public health.
3. Directive 75/34 granting to the self-employed the right to remain permanently in a host Member State after having been self-employed there (similar in scope to Regulation 1251/70 for workers).

However, in respect of the self-employed there is no secondary legislation similar in scope to Regulation 1612/68. As a result, in many areas self-employed persons established in a host Member State must rely on the principle of non-discrimination. In *CPM Meeusen* v *Hoofddirectie Van De Informatie Beheer Groep* Case C–337/97 [1999] ECR I–3289 a dependent child of a self-employed person, residing in a home Member State but pursuing

---

[13] *Commission* v *France* Case 270/83 [1986] ECR 273 in which the right of establishment was exercised in order to benefit from tax advantages in another Member State and *Segers* v *Bestuur van de Bedrijfsvereniging voor Bank-en Verzekeringswezen* Case 79/85 [1986] ECR 2375 concerning social security benefits.

his activity in another Member State, challenged the requirement of residence which prevented her from obtaining study finance.[14]

Miss Meeusen, a Belgian national and resident at the material time, commenced her study in August 1993 at the provincial Higher Technical Institute for Chemistry in Antwerp, which was for the purposes of the financing of studies regarded as a Dutch institution of higher education. Both her parents were Belgian nationals, resident in Belgium. Her father was the director and sole shareholder of a company established in The Netherlands. Her mother was employed there by that company two days a week. When Miss Meeusen applied to the relevant Dutch authorities for a study grant her application was ultimately rejected on the ground that she did not reside in the State of her parents' employment. Miss Meeusen appealed. She argued that the right to have her study financed could not be subject to the requirement that she live or reside in the territory of the Member State where her parents were employed, any more than it could be related to nationality. The ECJ agreed.

The ECJ emphasised that the concept of a 'worker' could not be extended to include a director of a company of which he is the sole shareholder as that person is not carrying out his activity in the context of a relationship of subordination: *Asscher* Case C–107/94 [1996] ECR I–3089. Therefore, Miss Meeusen's father could not be regarded as a 'worker' within the meaning of art 39 EC. However, her father was a self-employed person and therefore she could invoke the principle of non-discrimination in the context of freedom of establishment.

In the above case the requirement of residence was considered as being unjustified. In the context of the freedom of establishment, the principle of non-discrimination requires that a national of one Member State who pursues activities as a self-employed person in another Member State should benefit from the same treatment as the host State's own nationals. In *Commission* v *Luxembourg* Case C–111/91 [1993] ECR I–817 the ECJ held that the prohibition of discrimination in the context of the freedom of establishment covers not only specific rules on the pursuit of professional activities but also encompasses any measure which, pursuant to any provision laid down by law, regulation or administrative action in a Member State or resulting from their application, hinders nationals of other Member States in their pursuit of activities as self-employed persons by treating nationals of other Member States differently from its own nationals. The imposition of a residence requirement was discriminatory in nature.

Mutual recognition of diplomas and qualifications

The main limitations on the exercise of the right of establishment (as well as the right to provide services or to have access to employment in a host Member State as a worker) concern the conditions relating to admission to a particular profession. Indeed, whether an EC migrant works in his capacity as a worker, as self-employed or as a provider of services the exercise of his professional activities is conditional upon recognition by a host Member State of the fact that he is adequately qualified to carry them out. In order to implement the free movement of economically active persons within the EC the harmonisation of rules on the recognition of diplomas and professional qualifications is of vital importance.

---

[14] See Chapter 17 on the free movement of workers in respect of her entitlement to study finance derived from her mother's status as a worker.

There are two approaches to harmonisation of the rules relating to the mutual recognition of diplomas and professional qualifications. The first consists of the harmonisation of the rules in respect of individual professions or a particular sector of the economy. This approach was applied under the general programme adopted in 1961 during the transitional period. Progress under the sectoral directives was slow and this approach was not appropriate to the requirements of the internal market, although it resulted in a number of directives covering many professions such as architects, dentists, doctors, midwives, nurses, veterinary surgeons, hairdressers, etc, and a variety of economic sectors.

The second approach relates to Directive 89/48/EEC[15] which provides for a general system for the recognition of higher education diplomas awarded on completion of professional education and training of at least three years' duration. The Directive applies to all regulated professions for which university diplomas awarded for a course of at least three years duration are required. Professions already covered by sectoral directives are unaffected by Directive 89/48, which was supplemented by Directive 92/51/EEC on a second general system for the recognition of professional education and training which was considered as 'the final part of a series of measures aiming at ensuring that qualifications obtained by a Community national in another Member State are recognised by the host Member State. Recognition is based on the principle of mutual trust, without any prior coordination of the types of training for the various professions concerned.'[16] Directive 92/51/EEC covers higher or post-secondary education diplomas obtained after a period of less than three years and secondary education diplomas. It also applies to persons who have not obtained diplomas but have acquired professional experience. Both Directive 89/48/EEC and Directive 92/51/EEC were supplemented by Directive 1999/42/EC of the European Parliament and of the Council of 7 June 1999 Establishing a Mechanism for the Recognition of Qualifications in Respect of the Professional Activities Covered by the Directives on Liberalisation and Transitional Measures and Supplementing the General Systems for the Recognition of Qualifications.[17]

Directive 1999/42/EC simplifies and provides important clarifications in respect of the previous directives. It applies to all activities listed in Annex A which nationals of Member States wish to pursue in a host Member State in a self-employed or employed capacity. Some activities listed in Annex A are not covered by the previous Directives. For that reason, Directive 1999/42 establishes a mechanism for the recognition of diplomas awarded by another Member State and for the recognition of professional qualifications on the basis of professional experience acquired in another Member State.

In respect of the recognition of diplomas awarded by another Member State Directive 1999/42/EC combines the case law of the ECJ, in particular its decision in *Vlassoupoulou* Case C–340/89 [1991] ECR I–2357 with provisions of Directives 89/48 and 92/51. A host Member State is required to carry out a comparative examination of diplomas. If there is no substantial difference between them a diploma awarded by another Member State must be recognised as equivalent. If there is a substantial difference between them, a host Member State must give the applicant the opportunity to demonstrate that he has acquired the

---

[15] OJ L19 (1989).
[16] OJ L209 (1992).
[17] OJ L201 (1999).

knowledge and skill which were lacking. He is entitled to choose between an adoption period and an aptitude test. In the case of a manager of an undertaking covered by Part One of Annex A, a host Member State may require an adoption period or an aptitude test, although a host Member State should endeavour to take into consideration the applicant's preference as between those alternatives.

The application should be examined within the shortest possible time and should take no longer than four months from the date on which the application was submitted. The decision given by a competent national authority, or the absence of such decision, is subject to appeal.

In respect of the recognition of professional qualifications on the basis of professional experience acquired in another Member State, Directive 1999/42/EC divides the activities mentioned in Part One of Annex A into six categories (there are six lists). The number of years of professional experience and the capacity in which the applicant was employed, that is as a manager, self-employed or employee, are taken into consideration for each category of activities. The Directive also deals with such requirements as: proof of good character, financial standing, insurance, etc. Directive 1999/42/EC must be implemented before 31 July 2001.

The difference between the recognition of professional qualifications in regulated and non-regulated professions is well illustrated in *Teresa Fernández de Bobadilla v Museo Nacional del Prado, Comité de Empresa del Museo Nacional del Prado, Ministerio Fiscal* Case C–234/97 [1999] 3 CMLR 151. In this case Ms Fernández de Bobadilla, a Spanish national residing in Madrid, after obtaining her Bachelor of Arts degree in History of Art at the University of Boston, USA, completed her Master of Arts degree in fine arts restoration at Newcastle upon Tyne Polytechnic in the United Kingdom in 1989. A grant from the Prado Museum helped her to study in the UK. From 1989 to 1992 she worked for the Prado under a temporary contract as a restorer of works of art on paper.

Under the terms of the collective agreement concluded in 1988 by the Prado and staff representatives, the post of restorer was reserved to persons possessing the qualifications awarded by the restoration department of the Faculty of Fine Arts or by the School of Arts in Spain or any other foreign qualification recognised by the competent authorities. In October 1992 Ms de Bobadilla applied to the relevant department of the Ministry of Education to have the degree obtained in the UK officially recognised as equivalent to the Spanish degree in the conservation and restoration of cultural assets. She was informed that in order to recognise her English diploma she would have to demonstrate, through examinations arranged in two parts, sufficient knowledge of the 24 subjects listed in the notice.

On 17 November 1992, the Prado organised a competition for a permanent post of a restorer of works of art on paper. The application of Ms de Bobadilla was rejected on the ground that she did not satisfy the requirements laid down in the collective agreement. Ms de Bobadilla brought an action for annulment of such requirements as contrary to the Spanish constitution and art 39 EC.

The ECJ made a distinction between a situation where a profession is regulated within the meaning of Directives 89/48 and 92/51 and where a profession is not regulated for the purposes of these Directives. In the first-mentioned situation a Member State cannot require that a candidate's qualifications are officially recognised by its competent national authorities. The recognition is automatic. Therefore, it is necessary to determine whether the profession of restorer of works of art is regarded as regulated. In this respect, the ECJ emphasised that the definition of a regulated profession for the purposes of the above-mentioned Directives is a matter of Community law and therefore where the conditions for taking up or pursuing a professional activity are directly or indirectly governed by legal provisions, whether laws, regulations or administrative provisions, that activity constitutes a regulated profession. In this context the question arises whether the collective agreement concluded between the Prado and staff representatives could constitute 'laws, regulations or administrative provisions' for the purposes of the EC Directives in question (*Aranitis* Case C–164/94 [1996] ECR I–135), or in other words whether the profession of art restorer is regulated by the collective agreement. In order to answer this question it is necessary to determine whether the collective agreement has a general scope of application, that is in a general way governs the right to take up or pursue a profession, or whether it governs relations only between the employer and the employees within a single public body. It is for the national court to determine the scope of the collective agreement.

If the collective agreement has a general scope of application then it may be classified as rules regulating a professional activity for the purposes of Directives 89/48 and 92/51 and therefore one or other of Directives 89/48 and 92/51 will apply to the proceedings commenced by Ms Fernández de Bobadilla. Consequently, if either of these two Directives applies, the national court must, in order to establish whether she may apply for a permanent post as restorer of cultural assets, examine whether the applicant satisfies the conditions laid down in the Directive concerned. Also, if one or other of Directives 89/48 or 92/51 is applicable, a public body cannot require that a candidate's qualifications be granted official recognition by the competent national authorities. However, if the collective agreement has a limited scope of application and therefore governs relations only between the employer and the employees within a single body, the profession of restorer of cultural assets is not regulated within the meaning of Directives 89/48 and 92/51, Community law does not, in principle, preclude a public body in a Member State from restricting access to a post to candidates holding qualifications awarded by educational institutions of that Member State or any other foreign qualification officially recognised by the competent authorities of that Member State. Nevertheless, where the qualifications are awarded in another Member State, the procedure for granting official recognition must comply with the requirements set out by the ECJ in *Vlassopoulou* Case C–340/89 [1991] ECR I–2357. Consequently, the competent authorities of the Member State in which the recognition is sought must take into account the diplomas, certificates and other evidence of the qualifications of the applicant acquired in order to practise that profession in another Member State and compare them with the qualifications required by the host Member State. If the comparison reveals that the knowledge and qualifications certified by the foreign diploma correspond to those required by the national provisions, the diploma should be recognised by the host Member State. If there is a partial equivalence, the host State is entitled to require the person concerned to demonstrate that he or she has acquired the additional knowledge and qualification needed. However, where there is no general procedure for official recognition laid down by the Member State, or where that procedure does not comply with the requirements of Community law, it is for the public body advertising a particular post to investigate whether the diploma awarded in another Member State, together, where appropriate, with practical experience, is to be considered as equivalent to the qualification required. In the present case, the Museum of Prado was particularly well placed to assess the candidate's actual knowledge and abilities for two reasons: it had already employed the candidate and it made a grant to the candidate to help her to obtain a diploma in the UK.

Lawyers' right to establishment

In 1998 the European Parliament and the Council adopted Directive 98/5/EC on the right of establishment for lawyers who have obtained professional qualifications in the home Member State and wish to practise their profession on a permanent basis in any other Member State. The Directive required implementation by 14 March 2000. The Directive applies to employed and self-employed lawyers and in the UK encompasses solicitors, barristers and advocates. The main features of Directive 98/5/EC are that:

1. A lawyer establishing himself in another Member State must use the professional title which he has obtained in his home Member State. This restriction was deemed necessary in order to avoid confusion between the lawyer's home State qualification and the qualification required by the host Member State. The professional title must be expressed in the official language of the home Member State.
2. A lawyer who wishes to establish himself in another Member State must register with the competent authorities of the host Member State.
3. There are no restrictions as to the areas of law in which a lawyer is permitted to practise in the host Member State. This means that such a lawyer can give legal advice on both the law of the host and home Member States, as well as EC law and international law. This is subject to two exceptions. First if a host Member State reserves some activities – such as the preparation of deeds, the administration of estates or the creation and transfer of interests in land – for certain categories of lawyers, and in other Member States those activities are performed by non-lawyers, a host Member State is permitted to exclude lawyers from other Member States from carrying out those activities. Second, the requirement for a lawyer from another Member State to act in conjunction with a lawyer from a host Member State while representing a client in the courts of a host Member State has been maintained.
4. The rules of personal conduct and etiquette of both a home and a host Member State apply to a lawyer wishing to practise in a host Member State.
5. The competent authorities of a host Member State are entitled to bring disciplinary proceedings against a lawyer from another Member State registered in the host State who fails to meet the professional standards required by that State under the same conditions as applied to lawyers qualified in the host Member State.
6. The Directive has substantially revised the conditions under which a lawyer from another Member State may qualify as a lawyer in a host Member State: first, if he effectively and regularly pursues his practice in the host Member State in the law of that State for three years; and, second, even if he practises the law of his home Member State or EC law or international law he may obtain the host Member State's qualification

provided he carries out his professional activities in a host Member State for three years and satisfies the host Member State's authorities as to his competence with regard to that State's law.

Rules established by professional bodies

Professional bodies in a host Member State may impose various formalities necessary to become a member of the profession as well as rules of professional conduct. The ECJ's position on the subject is that national rules imposing restrictions on the right of establishment must fulfil four criteria in order to be justified. They must apply without distinction to nationals and non-nationals; they must be justified by imperative requirements in the general interest; they must be suitable for the attainment of the objective which they pursue; and they must not go beyond what is necessary to attain that objective. These criteria were not fulfilled in *Commission* v *Luxembourg (Re Access to the Medical Profession)* Case C–351/90 [1992] 3 CMLR 124.

In this case under Luxembourg law doctors, dentists and veterinary surgeons with practices in other Member States were prohibited from practising in Luxembourg without the express permission of the Luxembourg authorities. However, this prohibition did not apply to members of these professions from Luxembourg. The Commission brought proceedings against Luxembourg on the grounds that the requirement to obtain express permission was in breach of arts 39 and 43 EC as it discriminated between nationals and non-nationals.

The ECJ held that Luxembourg was in breach of its obligations under arts 39 and 43 EC by requiring nationals of Member States to obtain a special permission before practising in Luxembourg. Any derogations from the terms of these articles must be justified on objective grounds and must not be unduly harsh or restrictive. In the circumstances of the present case, the restrictions were considered to be too restrictive and therefore unjustified.

18.2 Freedom to supply and receive services

Article 49 EC provides:

> 'Within the framework of the provisions set out below, restrictions on freedom to provide services within the Community shall be prohibited in respect of nationals of Member States who are established in a State of the Community other than that of the person for whom the services are intended.'

Services are defined in art 50 EC as being normally provided for remuneration and not covered by the provisions of the EC Treaty relating to the free movement of persons, capital and goods. Also art 50 EC defines services, in a non-exhaustive list, as including the following activities: of an industrial character, of a commercial character, of craftsmen and, of the professions.

The freedom to provide services differs from the freedom of establishment in that it involves legislation of two Member States, the Member State of the establishment of the provider of services and the Member State where the service is provided. For that reason only some and not all rules relating to the right of establishment apply to the provision of services.

In addition, providers of services can be divided into two groups:[18] active providers of services, when a provider is established in one Member State and actively seeks customers in another Member State where a particular service in supplied; and passive providers of services, when a provider of services is passive in his relationship with a customer and it is a customer who must travel to a Member State where the provider of services is established in order to receive a particular service. The first category will be examined under the freedom to supply services; the second category under the freedom to receive services, taking into account the different rules applicable to them.

Freedom to supply services

Article 50 EC provides that, without prejudice to the provisions on establishment, a person providing a service may, in order to do so, temporarily pursue his activity in the State where the service is provided, under the same conditions as are imposed by the State on its own nationals. However, national legislation is normally applicable to providers of services established in that State and not to providers of services established in another State. Therefore, it would be unfair to providers of services established in another Member State to be treated in the same manner as providers of services established in a Member State where the service is to be provided. The ECJ emphasised that the principle of non-discrimination also applies when different situations are subject to the same rules. In *Commission v France* Case C–294/89 [1991] ECR I–3591 the ECJ held that national rules which are normally applicable to nationals of that State in respect of a permanent activity pursued by persons employed in that State cannot be applicable in their entirety and in the same way to activities in that State of a temporary nature pursued by persons established in another Member State.

There are three key principles that ensure the proper application of the EC Treaty provisions in respect of the free movement of services.

The principle of non-discrimination
EC law prohibits all discrimination based on nationality or on the residence of a provider of services. All discrimination whether direct or indirect (*Commission v Italy* Case C–360/89 [1992] ECR I–4301) on the ground of nationality is prohibited. *A priori* a requirement of residence is also prohibited taking into account that such a requirement would deprive the provisions guaranteeing the freedom to provide services of all practical effectiveness: *Commission v Germany* Case 205/84 [1986] ECR 3755. However, the prohibition of requirements relating to residence is less absolute than that relating to nationality. Theoretically, the residence requirement can be justified if it is essential to the attainment

---

[18] This distinction is based on Directive 90/619: OL L330 (1990).

of a legitimate objective (*Van Binsbergen*) although so far the ECJ has never regarded it as objectively justified.[19]

The prohibition of indistinctly applicable measures which are liable to prohibit or otherwise impede the activities of a provider of services and their justifications

The principles applied in the area of the free movement of goods and the freedom to provide services are similar. The free movement of goods and services goes beyond mere prohibition of discrimination based on nationality as it covers disproportionate and unjustified restrictions. In *Säger* Case C–76/90 [1991] ECR I–4221[20] the ECJ held that restrictions on the free movement of services, even if they are indistinctly applicable, are in breach of EC law if they are of a nature to prohibit or render more difficult the exercise of activities of a provider of services in a host Member State as compared to a person established in that State. This means that for a provider of services in a host Member State it should not be more difficult to reach potential customers than for a person established in that Member State providing similar services. Also restrictions imposed by a Member State of establishment on a provider of services are included. In this respect, in *Alpine Investments* Case C–384/93 [1995] ECR I–1141,[21] a Dutch prohibition on 'cold calling' by providers of financial services established in The Netherlands was considered as an obstacle to the free movement of services. Obstacles take various forms, eg the requirement of authorisations, more favourable rules on taxation in respect of providers of services established in a host Member State, or requirements of a host Member State relating to social protection of temporarily deployed workers for the purpose of providing services in a host Member State. This matter was examined by the ECJ in *Jean-Claude Arblade, Arblade & Fils Sarl* and *Bernard Leloup, Serge Leloup, Solfrage Sarl* Cases C–369 and 376/96 Judgment of 23 November 1999 (nyr). Under Belgian legislation construction undertakings, irrespective of their place of establishment, carrying out work in Belgium are required to pay their workers the minimum remuneration, to pay 'timbres-intermpéries' and 'timbre-fidelité' contributions to each worker, to draw up and keep various social documents and to produce these documents at the request of the competent Belgian authorities.

Arblade and Leloup, two French construction undertakings, carried out construction works in Belgium. During the period between 1991 and 1993 they deployed workers on Belgian sites. When checks were carried out on the sites in 1993 the competent Belgian authorities requested the production of various social documents from these French undertakings. Both undertakings refused on the grounds that they had complied with all the French legislation and that the obligations imposed by the Belgian legislation were in breach of arts 49 and 50 EC. Criminal prosecutions were commenced against the French undertakings. The Huy Criminal Court (the Tribunal Correctionnel de Huy) referred to the

---

[19] See *Commission v Germany* Case 205/84 [1986] ECR 3755. However in *Commission v Belgium* Case C–300/90 [1992] ECR I–305 and *Bachmann v Belgium* Case C–204/90 [1992] ECR I–249 the ECJ accepted that some advantages could be given only to companies established in a Member State.

[20] As confirmed in subsequent cases: *Vander Elst v Office des Migrations Internationales* Case C–43/93 [1994] ECR I–3803; *Guiot* Case C–272/94 [1996] ECR I–1905; *Reisebüro Broede v Sandker* Case C–3/95 [1996] ECR I–6511; *Parodi v Banque H Albert de Bary* Case C–222/95 [1997] ECR I–3899.

[21] However, restrictions other than those relating to access to the market or to modalities of the exercise of activities are outside the scope of art 49 EC.

ECJ for a preliminary ruling regarding the compatibility of various social obligations provided by the Belgian legislation with arts 49 and 50 EC.

The ECJ examined a number of issues concerning social protection of workers temporarily deployed in a host Member State in the light of EC provisions regarding the freedom to provide services. The ECJ made a number of preliminary points, the first concerning the argument of the Belgian government that arts 49 and 50 EC should be construed in the light of Directive 96/71/EC laying down Community rules aimed at ensuring minimum social protection for such workers, although at the material time the time limit for its implementation had not elapsed.[22] The ECJ confirmed that national courts may apply more favourable provisions of Directive 96/71 in accordance with its earlier case law (*Awoyemi* Case C–320/97 [1998] ECR I–6781), although Community law does not impose such an obligation.

Second, the ECJ held that the fact that national provisions are classified as being of public order does not exempt them from compliance with the EC Treaty. This is a direct consequence of the principle of supremacy of Community law over national law. Therefore, the Belgian legislation should be examined in the light of requirements imposed by EC law, in particular deriving from the fundamental principle of freedom to provide services.

In respect of the protection of workers, especially those who work in the construction industry, the ECJ held in *Guiot* Case C–272/94 [1996] ECR I–1905 that this consideration could be viewed as being of an overriding nature and therefore justified national restrictions imposed on the free movement of services. By contrast, national administrative provisions, in principle, cannot be justified (*Terhoeve* Case C–18/95 [1999] ECR I–345), apart from the situation where they are necessary to ensure compliance with substantive national provisions relating to the overriding reasons of public interest: *Rush Portuguesa* Case C–113/89 [1990] ECR I–1417. In this context the ECJ examined the restrictions to the free movement of services imposed by the Belgian legislation.

The important aspect of the present case is that the most favourable social legislation should be applied to workers temporarily carrying out work in another Member State. In respect of the requirement imposed on an employer providing services to pay his workers the minimum remuneration in the Member State where they provide services, the ECJ held that a Member State is entitled under EC law to impose the payment of the minimum remuneration to any person who provides services within its territory, irrespective of the place of establishment of his employer, as well as to enforce those rules by appropriate means: *Rush Portuguesa* Case C–113/89 and *Guiot* Case C–272/94. The application of that obligation is subject to review by the national courts. However, criminal prosecutions against an employer may only be commenced in so far as the national rules imposing this obligation are sufficiently precise and accessible and thus it would not be impossible or excessively difficult in practice for such an employer to comply with it.

In respect of other social contributions which a host Member State may impose on an employer, as a provider of services, to pay to that Member State's fund, in addition to those

---

[22] The Directive entered into force on 16 December 1999. Its main objective is to remove uncertainties and obstacles which may hinder the freedom to provide services, by increasing legal certainty and allowing identification of the terms and conditions of employment applicable to workers who carry out temporary work in a host Member State.It also intends to avoid risks of abuse and exploitation of posted workers.

which he has already paid to the fund of the Member State of his establishment, the ECJ held that the employer's contributions are justified only if they afford workers a real social advantage, additional to that which they already enjoy in the home Member State and that the contributions are payable by all providers of services operating within the territory of the host Member State in the industry concerned.

In relation to the obligations of an administrative nature regarding drawing up and keeping of social and labour documents, the ECJ stated that a similar obligation had been imposed on French undertakings in respect of the same workers and the same periods of activity. Consequently, such an obligation imposed by the Belgian legislation constituted an additional expense and an additional administrative and economic burden and as such hindered the free movement of services. However, the effective protection of workers, as well as the fact that national substantive provisions can only be enforced by means of the production of certain documents, may justify the keeping of these documents on site or in other places within the territory of a host Member State in order to make them available to the authorities of that Member State responsible for carrying out checks. Thus, it is for a host Member State to verify whether and to what extent social or labour documents kept in accordance with rules of the Member State of establishment comply with rules laid down by the host Member State. If they are similar, as they were in the present case, the employer is not required to keep two sets of documents since the objective pursued by a host Member State can be achieved by less restrictive means, that is, production, within a reasonable time, of similar documents kept in the Member State of establishment or of copies kept on site or in an accessible place. However, a host Member State cannot require the keeping of certain documents in order to make it easier for its authorities to perform their supervisory task. Consequently, in the present case the ECJ held that the requirement that an employer retains social documents within the territory of a host Member State for a period of five years at the address of a natural person was unjustified.

The principal of mutual recognition

The concept of mutual recognition requires a host Member State to take into consideration rules of a home Member State of a provider of services in order to determine whether the public interest which a host Member State wants to protect is not already protected by rules applying to the service provider in a Member State where he is established.

In *Webb* Case 279/80 [1981] ECR 3305 the ECJ held that when a host Member State applies its rules it must take into consideration national professional rules applicable to the provider of services in his home Member State. In this case criminal proceedings were brought against Webb for running a manpower agency which was established in the UK but recruited workers to work temporarily in The Netherlands. Webb was licensed in the UK to supply workers but not in The Netherlands where he only provided services. He was already subject to similar rules to those of The Netherlands in his home Member State. Such a duplication of rules was unjustified.

Justification for national restrictions

Any restriction imposed by national law which is liable to prohibit, impede or render less advantageous the activities of a provider of services as compared to a person established in a host Member State may only be justified by imperative requirements in the general interest applicable to all persons and undertakings operating in the territory of a Member State where the service is provided, in so far as that interest is not safeguarded by the rules to which the provider of such a service is subject in the Member State of his establishment: *Webb* Case 279/80 [1981] ECR 3305; *Commission v Italy* Case C–180/89 [1991] ECR I–709; *Commission v Greece* Case C–198/89 [1991] ECR I–727. Consequently, a Member State may justify national measures restricting the freedom to provide services in the following circumstances where:

1. there is no harmonising EC legislation in the area concerned;
2. national restricting measures are adopted in the general interest;
3. those measures must be applied indistinctly, thus not discriminating against providers who are established in another Member State but providing services in a host Member State;
4. national restricting measures must be objectively necessary, proportionate and must respect the principle of mutual recognition which in the context of the provision of services means that a host Member State must take into consideration whether the interest in question is not safeguarded by the rules to which the provider of such a service is subject in the Member State of his establishment.

As in the rule of reason laid down in the *Cassis* case there is no exhaustive list of imperative requirements in the general interest. The case law of the ECJ indicates that the following imperative requirements in the general interest have been accepted: reputation of national markets (*Alpine Investments* Case C–384/93 [1995] ECR I–1141), rules of professional conduct and the good administration of justice (*Van Binsbergen* Case 33/74 [1974] ECR 1299; *Commission v France* Case C–294/89 [1991] ECR I–3591), and the protection of the following: consumers (*France v Commission* Case 220/83 [1986] ECR 3663),[23] persons proposing for life assurance policies (*Commission v Germany* Case 205/84 [1986] ECR 3755), workers (*Webb* Case 279/80 [1981] ECR 3305), receivers of certain services (*Van Wesemael* Cases 110 and 111/78 [1979] ECR 35), holders of intellectual property rights (*Coditel v Ciné Vog Films* Case 62/79 [1980] ECR 881; *Coditel (No 2)* Case 262/81 [1982] ECR 3381), the environment (*Matteo Peralta* Case C–379/92 [1994] ECR I–3453) and of a particular language or culture (*Federación de Distributares Cinematográficas* Case C–17/92 [1993] ECR I–2239; *Commission v Luxembourg* Case C–473/93 [1996] ECR I–3207), etc.

The reasoning of the ECJ is well illustrated in *Läärä and Others v Kihlakunnansyyttäjä (Jyväskylä) and Others* Case C–124/97 [1999] ECR I–6067. In this case under Finnish legislation, a single public body was granted rights to organise lotteries and betting, to manage casinos and to operate slot machines. Funds collected by that body were used to finance non-profit-making causes. The public body consisted of 96 organisations operating in the areas of health and social activities. It was called RAY. In 1996 the English company, CMS, entered into a contract with a Finnish company, TAS, under which TAS was given the

---

[23] See also tourists (*Commission v Italy* Case C–180/89 [1991] ECR I–709); gamblers (*Schindler* Case C–275/92 [1994] ECR I–1039); customers of a bank (*Parodi v Bangue Albert de Bary* Case C–222/95 [1997] ECR I–3899).

exclusive right to instal and operate in Finland slot machines for a commission representing a percentage of the profit made from their use. CMS had manufactured the slot machines, delivered them to Finland and remained their owner. Criminal proceedings were brought against Markku Läärä, the chairman of TAS, for operating slot machines in Finland without licence and contrary to the above-mentioned Finnish gaming legislation. He argued that the Finnish legislation was contrary to Community law, in particular in breach of EC rules on freedom to provide services. The Finnish Court of Appeal (Vaasan Hovioikeus) referred to the ECJ a preliminary question on the compatibility of the Finnish gaming legislation with Community law.

The ECJ held that the Finnish gambling legislation was not discriminatory on the ground of nationality as it applied without distinction to all economic operators irrespective of the Member State of their establishment. However, it constituted an obstacle to freedom to provide services, taking into account that it directly and indirectly prevented operators from other Member States from making slot machines available to the public with a view to their use in return for payment.

The reasoning of the ECJ followed the established pattern. National rules imposing restrictions on the freedom to provide services must fulfil four criteria in order to be justified. They must apply without distinction to nationals and non-nationals, they must be justified by imperative requirements in the general interest, they must be suitable for the attainment of the objective being pursued, and they must not go beyond what is necessary to attain that objective. In this respect, the ECJ held that:

'The objectives of the Finnish legislation, to limit exploitation of the human passion for gambling, to avoid the risk of crime and fraud, and to authorise gaming activities only in order to collect funds for charitable purposes, concerned the protection of consumers and the maintenance of order in society, and were to be regarded as overriding reasons relating to public interest.'

The judgment in this case confirmed that of the ECJ in *Commissioners of Customs and Excise* v *Schindler* Case C–275/92 [1994] QB 610; [1994] ECR I–1039 involving the operation of lotteries in which it was held that Member States enjoyed a large measure of discretion in matters relating to such activities. Thus, it was for Member States to assess whether it was necessary to restrict or even prohibit the activities concerned, taking into consideration their social and cultural characteristics, with a view to maintaining order in society. In this context, it is not surprising that the ECJ held that the solution adopted by Finland, that is to grant to a single public body exclusive rights to operate slot machines and to use funds collected by RAY for charitable purposes, was not disproportionate to the objective pursued.

Freedom to receive services

In *Luisi and Carbone* v *Ministero del Tesoro* Joined Cases 286/82 and 26/83 [1984] ECR 377 the ECJ held that the freedom to provide services includes the freedom for the recipient of the services to go to another Member State in order to receive a service there without being obstructed by restrictions. However, in such a situation a national of a Member State should be treated in the same manner as nationals of the host Member State. For the recipients of services the principle of non-discrimination on the ground of nationality determines their legal protection in a host Member State. This was established by the ECJ in *Cowan v Trésor Public* Case 186/87 [1989] ECR 195; [1990] 2 CMLR 613.

In this case a British national, Ian Cowan, was violently assaulted outside a Metro station in Paris. The perpetrators of the offence were never apprehended. Mr Cowan applied to the Commission d'Indemnisation des Victims d'Infraction, the French equivalent of the Criminal Injuries Compensation Board, for compensation for his injuries. The French Code of Criminal Procedure allows compensation to be paid to victims of assaults if physical injury has been sustained and compensation cannot be sought from another source. However, the same Code of Criminal Procedure restricted the payment of compensation to French nationals and holders of French residence permits. On this grounds Mr Cowan's application for compensation was refused by the French Treasury. Mr Cowen challenged this decision relying on art 12 EC. He argued that art 12 prohibited discrimination based on nationality and that such discrimination prevented tourists from going freely to other Member States to receive services.

The ECJ held that since the right to receive services was embodied in the EC Treaty, it was subject to the prohibition of discrimination on the grounds of nationality as prescribed by art 12 EC. Laws and regulations which prevent the exercise of this right were declared to be incompatible with Community law and, in the circumstances of this case, the requirement of French nationality or a French residence permit in order to claim compensation for criminal injuries constituted unjustifiable discrimination. The ECJ held that tourists, among others, must be regarded as recipients of services.

In the context of the freedom to receive services the most controversial matter is whether a national of another member State is entitled to be treated in a host Member State in respect of such services as education and medicine in the same way as nationals of that State taking into that they are not commercial activities but are public services.

The matter of education was considered by the ECJ in *Gravier v City of Liège* Case 293/83 [1985] ECR 593. In this case Gravier, a French national, was accepted by the Liège Académie des Baux-Arts for a four-year course in the art of strip cartoons. She was considered as a foreign student and charged a special fee, known as 'minerval', which Belgian nationals, irrespective of their place of residence and EC nationals and their families working in Belgium, were not required to pay. She challenged the fee as discriminatory. She argued that the minerval constituted an obstacle to her freedom to receive services and that vocational education was within the scope of the EC Treaty as the ECJ recognised in *Forcheri* Case 152/82 [1983] ECR 2323. The ECJ decided in favour of Gravier. It held that art 12 EC prohibited any discrimination based on nationality and applied to all areas covered by the EC Treaty. The minerval was discriminatory and as such was in breach of art 12 EC.

This decision raised many controversies in Member States. One of them was the definition of vocational training which the ECJ defined very broadly in *Gravier* as including all forms of teaching which prepares for and leads directly to a particular profession, trade or employment. Furthermore, contrary to the Opinion of Advocate-General Sir Gordon Slynn in *Gravier*, the ECJ refused to discuss the organisation and financing of such courses. Member States which financed university courses from public funds (in Belgium the minerval covered only 50 per cent of the cost of the course, the remaining 50 per cent came from public funds) were deeply concerned.

In *Blaizot* Case 24/86 [1989] 1 CMLR 57 the ECJ clarified the definition of vocational training. In this case Blaizot, following the decision of the ECJ in *Gravier*, sought reimbursement of the minerval charged for his university course in veterinary science. The ECJ held that university education constituted vocational training:

> '... not only where the final exam directly provides the required qualification but also insofar as the studies provide specific training (ie where the student needs the knowledge so acquired for the pursuit of his trade or profession), even if no legislative or administrative provisions make the acquisition of such knowledge a prerequisite.'

Therefore all courses, other than those which are intended to improve the general knowledge of the students rather then prepare him for an occupation, are considered as vocational courses. However, the entitlement to general measures of support, such as loans and grants, is available only to workers and their families under the conditions laid down by the ECJ in *Lair* Case 39/86 [1988] ECR 3161 and *Brown* Case 197/86 [1988] ECR 3205.

19 Exceptions to the Free Movement of Workers, Self-Employed Persons, Providers and Recipients of Services

19.1 The concepts of 'employment in the public service' and 'the exercise of official authority'

19.2 Derogations justified on the grounds of public policy, public security and public health

There are two exceptions to the free movement of persons. Under arts 39(4) and 45 EC a host Member State may reserve access to employment in the public service to its own nationals. The second exception is based on the protection of public order, public security and public health.

19.1 The concepts of 'employment in the public service' and 'the exercise of official authority'

Under art 39(4) EC the provisions of art 39 EC 'shall not apply to employment in the public service' and by virtue of art 45 EC the provisions relating to the freedom of establishment and the freedom to provide services 'shall not apply, so far as any given Member State is concerned, to activities which in that State are connected, even occasionally, with the exercise of official authority'. Under art 39(4) EC access to certain posts may be limited by reason of the fact that in a Member State persons appointed to such posts have the status of civil servants.

Different terms used in these provisions led some Member States to interpret the derogation from the free movement of persons differently from that applicable to the freedom of establishment and the provision of services. The ECJ rejected this approach: *Sotgiu* Case 152/73 [1974] ECR 153 at 156 and *Commission v Belgium (No 1)* Case 149/79 [1980] ECR 3881; *Commission v Belgium (No 2)* Case 149/79 [1982] ECR 1845.

The ECJ has interpreted both derogations restrictively. In *Commission v Belgium (No 1)* the ECJ ruled that employment in the public service concerned

'... posts which involve direct or indirect participation in the exercise of powers conferred by public law and duties designed to safeguard the general interests of the State or other public authorities. Such posts in fact presume on the part of those occupying them the existence of a special relationship of allegiance to the State and reciprocity of rights and duties which form the foundation of the bond of nationality.'

In this case the ECJ made a distinction between the tasks 'belonging to the public service properly so called' and activities of 'an economic and social nature which are typical of the public service yet which by their nature still come under the sphere of application of the Treaty'. Only the first are within the scope of the derogation. Therefore, two elements are necessary in order to invoke the exception embodied in art 39(4) EC: the post in question must involve both the exercise of power conferred by public law and the safeguarding of the general interest of the State.

In respect of the exercise of power conferred by public law, the ECJ held in *Reyners* Case 2/74 [1974] ECR 631 that art 45(1) EC must be restricted to those activities which in themselves involve a direct and specific connection with the exercise of official authority. This refers to authority emanating from the sovereignty of the State and involves the exercise of powers granted by the State to require compliance, by coercion, if necessary.

The concept of the safeguarding of the general interest of the State is more difficult to define. In this respect the Commission Notice[1] published in 1988 is particularly helpful. The Notice reviewed certain sectors of employment which are for the most part considered to be 'sufficiently remote from the specific activities of the public sphere as defined by the European Court that they would only in rare cases be covered by the exception of art [39(4) EC]'. This concerns: public health care services, teaching in State educational establishments, research for non-military purposes in public establishments and public bodies responsible for administering commercial services.

It emerges from the case law of the ECJ that arts 39(4) and 45 EC cover only high level posts, the holders of which owe a special allegiance to the State based on the bond of nationality (for example, members of the armed forces, police, judiciary, etc).

In a number of cases (*Commission v Italy* Case 225/85 [1986] ECR 2625; *Commission v Belgium (No 1) and (No 2)* Case 149/79 the Member States have tried unsuccessfully to challenge the restrictive approach of the ECJ. In *Commission v France* Case 307/84 [1986] ECR 1725 the ECJ held that the post of a nurse in French public hospitals is not within the scope of art 39(4) EC. Similarly, neither a researcher employed by the Italian National Council of Research (*Commission v Italy* Case 225/85 [1987] ECR 2625) nor a teacher in a secondary school (*Bleis* Case C–4/91 [1991] ECR I–5627), nor a trainee teacher during probationary service (*Lawrie-Blum* Case 66/85 [1986] ECR 2121) should be regarded as employed in the public sector. Furthermore, the ECJ has, in a number of cases, condemned some Member States for reserving employment in the following sectors to their nationals: distribution of gas; electricity; health; education; all modes of transport, including municipal and regional transport; civil research; telecommunications and postal services; radio and television; opera and municipal orchestras (*Commission v Luxembourg* Case C–473/93 [1996] ECR I–3207; *Commission v Belgium* Case C–173/94 [1996] ECR I–3265; *Commission v Greece* Case C–290/94 [1996] ECR I–3285).

---

[1] OJ C72 (1988).

19.2 Derogations justified on the grounds of public policy, public security and public health

The right to freedom of movement is subject to limitations based on the grounds of public policy, public security and public health. The derogation in respect of workers is expressly provided for in art 39(3) and in respect of self-employed persons and providers and receivers of services in art 46(1) EC. The derogation also applies to members of their families who have acquired free movement rights under the EC Treaty. Council Directive 64/221/EEC of 25 February 1972[2] on the Co-ordination of Special Measures Concerning the Movement and Residence of Foreign Nationals which are Justified on Grounds of Public Policy, Public Security or Public Health regulates the application of the three derogations from the right to freedom of movement conferred on EC nationals by Community law. These derogations being exceptions to the provisions of the EC Treaty, must be interpreted restrictively. No Community definition is provided in respect of these derogations. The Directive only describes the situations in which a Member State may prevent an EC national from exercising his right to enter its territory on the grounds of public policy, public security and public order. It also covers the matter of issue or renewal of residence permits and expulsion from the territory of a host Member State. The Directive permits a Member State a certain discretion in the application of these derogations, provided its exercise is within the limits of the EC Treaty. Furthermore, Directive 64/221/EEC provides procedural safeguards for EC nationals from other Member States seeking to enforce their rights of entry and residence in a Member State. However, an increasing number of complaints lodged by EU citizens with the Commission regarding restrictions imposed by Member States when applying Directive 64/221, prompted the Commission to clarify how EC law should be applied to Member States' restrictions on citizen's fundamental rights of residence and free movement.

In 1999 the Commission issued a Communication[3] clarifying the right of EU citizens to reside and to move freely within the territory of the European Union. In order to improve implementation of citizens' rights by reducing differences between Member States' interpretation of Community law, the Commission has taken into consideration the case law of the ECJ in this area and the legal implications of the concept of EU citizenship introduced by the Treaty of Maastricht and confirmed by the Treaty of Amsterdam. The Communication restates the fundamental principles set out by Directive 64/221 as follows:

First, under Directive 64/221, a Member State may take measures to restrict or refuse entry into its territory, issue or renewal of residence permits or to order expulsion solely on the basis of the personal conduct of the individual concerned. Previous criminal convictions are not in themselves sufficient grounds for taking such measures. The Member States must demonstrate that the individual concerned represents a 'genuine and sufficiently serious threat' affecting one of the fundamental interests of society in order to justify such restrictions. Second, EU citizens should be informed of the grounds of any measure taken and offered access to the remedies specified in Directive 64/221. Third, a measure taken cannot remain in force indefinitely. An individual concerned has a right to re-examination

---

[2] OJ L121 (1972).
[3] (1999) 18 *Single Market News* 13.

after a reasonable time has elapsed. Fourth, a failure by an EU citizen to comply with entry and residence formalities is not sufficient to justify his expulsion.

The Communication also specifies that when Member States adopt measures on grounds of public policy, public security and public health, they are bound to respect the fundamental principles of Community law, in particular, the principle of free movement of persons and the principle of proportionality. The Communication is intended to deal with a number of specific problems:

1. Excessive delays in dealing with applications for a residence permit. The Commission stated that Member States should examine such applications without unnecessary delays and respect a six months' deadline as a maximum, which maximum should only ever be approached in cases where specific reasons of public order justify the need for examination in depth.
2. When expulsion or other measures are taken a Member State must assess all relevant circumstances and proceed on a case-by-case basis rather than apply them as general preventive measures.
3. The safeguards, guarantees and remedies set out in Directive 64/221 must be strictly respected, including the right to re-examination of a decision and the right to be informed of the grounds for any measure as well as for legal consequences.
4. Special attention must be attached to the protection of family life, the rights of EU citizens residing on a long-term basis in another Member State of the EU, and the rights of EU minors and third country nationals who are family members of EU citizens.

Public policy and public security

The ECJ has developed the following principles in respect of public policy and public security exceptions:

1. All derogations to the free movement of persons must be interpreted strictly: *Van Dyun* Case 41/74 [1974] ECR 1337; *Rutili* Case 36/75 [1975] ECR 1219; *R v Bouchereau* Case 30/77 [1977] ECR 1999.
2. All measures taken on the basis of Directive 64/221 must be proportional to the objective pursued by them: *Bond Van Adverteerders* Case 352/85 [1988] ECR 2085.
3. The concept of public policy, public security and public health cannot be determined unilaterally by Member States. Although a Member State is free to determine the requirements of public policy and public security in the light of its national needs, the ECJ has jurisdiction to ensure, from the perspective of EC law, that a Member State exercises its discretion within the limits of the Treaty: *Van Duyn*; *Rutili*; *Bouchereau*.
4. The majority of the provisions of Directive 64/221 are directly effective: *Van Duyn*; *Santillo* Case 131/79 [1980] ECR 1585.

Directive 64/221 imposes four limitations on a Member State in respect of the application of the public policy and public security exceptions. There are:

Personal conduct of the individual concerned
Article 3(1) of Directive 64/221 provides that 'measures taken on grounds of public policy or

of public security must be based exclusively on the personal conduct of the individual concerned'. The ECJ emphasised that measures adopted on grounds of public policy and for the maintenance of public security against the nationals of Member States of the Community cannot be justified on grounds extraneous to the individual case. Only the 'personal conduct' of those affected by the measures is to be regarded as determinative. This was explained by the ECJ in *Bonsignore v Oberstadtdirector of the City of Cologne* Case 67/74 [1975] ECR 297. In this case an Italian national permanently residing in Germany, Carmelo Bonsignore, shot his brother by accident. The weapon he used was a pistol he had illegally acquired. He was fined for this offence but no punishment was imposed for the accidental killing of his brother. The German authorities ordered his deportation for 'reasons of a general preventive nature' based on 'the deterrent effect which the deportation of an alien found in illegal possession of a firearm would have in immigration circles having regard to the resurgence of violence in the large urban cities'. The German court referred to the ECJ a question whether art 3 of Directive 64/221/EEC prohibits deportation for reasons of a general preventive nature when it is clear that the individual concerned would not commit further offences.

The ECJ held that a Member State should base the decision on deportation solely on the requirements embodied in art 3(1) of Directive 64/221, that is taking into account exclusively the personal conduct of the individual concerned. Future behaviour is only relevant in so far as there are clear indications that the individual would commit further offences. Article 3(1) of Directive 64/221 prevents the deportation of a national of a Member State if such deportation is ordered for the purpose of deterring other aliens, that is, if it is based on reasons of a 'general preventive nature'.

The concept of personal conduct was further clarified in *Van Duyn*. Miss Van Duyn was a member of the Church of Scientology. The referring court asked two question: whether membership of organisations should be considered as 'personal conduct' within the meaning of art 3(1) and, if so, whether such conduct must be illegal in order to justify the application of the public policy exception. The ECJ answered that past association cannot count as personal conduct but present membership of an organisation, being a voluntary act of the person concerned, counts as 'personal conduct'. The activities of the Church of Scientology were not illegal in the UK. However, the UK government considered them as socially harmful. The ECJ held that it is not necessary that the conduct in question is illegal in order to justify exclusion of EC nationals from other Member States as long as a Member State makes is clear that such activities are 'socially harmful' and has taken some administrative measures to counteract the activities. However, the ECJ reversed its position in *Andoui and Cornuaille v Belgian State* Joined Cases 115 and 116/81 [1982] ECR 1665. Andoui and Cornuaille were French women who were refused a residence permit in Belgium on the grounds that they were 'waitresses in a bar which was suspect from the point of view of morals'. The ECJ held that a Member State may only justify restrictions on the admission to, or residence within, its territory on nationals of another Member State if it adopted, with respect to the same conduct on the part of its own nationals, repressive measures or other genuine and effective measure intended to combat such conduct.

The matter of personal conduct in the light of art 3(1) of Directive 64/221 was examined in *Criminal Proceedings against Calfa* Case C–348/96 [1999] ECR I–11. In this case

Donatella Calfa, an Italian national, went on holiday to Crete where she was convicted of the possession and use of prohibited drugs. She was sentenced by a Greek court to three months' imprisonment and expulsion for life from Greek territory. Under Greek penal law foreign nationals convicted of certain drug offences were automatically subject to an expulsion order for life unless for some compelling reason, particularly related to family matters, their continued residence in Greece was allowed. Donatella Calfa challenged the expulsion order as contrary to a number of provisions of the EC Treaty, especially arts 39, 43 and 49 EC and Directive 64/221/EEC

The ECJ held that Donatella Calfa, as a tourist, was a recipient of services in another Member State and as such within the scope of application of art 49 EC. The ECJ emphasised that although national legislation in criminal matters is within the competence of a Member State, the requirements of EC law set limitations on Member States' powers. Such legislation should not limit the fundamental freedoms guaranteed by Community law. The ECJ held that expulsion for life from a territory of a Member State was an obstacle to the freedom to receive services under art 49 EC, as well as the freedom of establishment under art 43 EC and the free movement of workers contained in art 39 EC. In those circumstances it was necessary to examine whether the expulsion order could be justified under art 46 EC and art 3(1) of Directive 64/221 on the ground of public policy. The ECJ emphasised that the exception to the free movement of persons should be interpreted restrictively and decided that the expulsion order could not be justified on the ground of public policy since the Greek legislation provided for an automatic expulsion for life following a criminal conviction without taking into account the personal conduct of the offender or whether that conduct created a genuine and sufficiently serious threat affecting one of the fundamental interests of society. In this respect the ECJ held that:

> '... the legislation at issue in the main proceedings requires nationals of other Member States found guilty, on the national territory in which that legislation applies, of an offence under the drugs laws, to be expelled for life from that territory, unless compelling reasons, in particular family reasons, justify their continued residence in the country. The penalty can be revoked only by a decision taken at the discretion of the Minister for Justice after a period of three years. Therefore, expulsion for life automatically follows a criminal conviction, without any account being taken of the personal conduct of the offender or of the danger which that person represents for the requirements of public policy.'

The ECJ held that arts 39, 43 and 49 EC and art 3(1) of Directive 64/21/EEC precluded legislation which required a Member State's courts to order expulsion for life from its territory of nationals of other Member States found guilty on that territory of the offences of obtaining and being in possession of drugs for their personal use.

Previous criminal convictions

Article 3(2) of Directive 64/221 provides that 'previous criminal convictions shall not in themselves constitute grounds for the taking of such measures'.

The matter of previous conviction was examined by the ECJ In *R v Bouchereau* Case 30/77 [1977] ECR 1999. In this case Bouchereau a French national, was convicted in the UK of possession of illegal drugs in January 1976 and again in June 1976. He challenged a deportation order made against him on the grounds of art 39 EC and art 3(2) of Directive

64/221. The ECJ held that a likelihood of re-offending may be found in the past conduct, although previous criminal convictions do not in themselves constitute grounds for taking measures on the basis of public policy or public security. The Court stated that it is possible that past conduct alone may constitute a threat to the requirements of public policy when the individual concerned has a 'propensity to act in the same way in the future' as he did in the past. The ECJ emphasised that a measure taken on the ground of public policy is justified if the conduct of the individual concerned constitutes 'a genuine and serious threat to requirements of public policy affecting one of the fundamental interests of society'.

Non-compliance with formalities regarding entry and residence in a host Member State
Non-compliance with administrative formalities imposed on EC migrant workers and their families in respect of entry and residence never justifies an expulsion from the territory of a host Member State: *Royer* Case 48/75 [1976] ECR 497.

Economic considerations
Article 2(2) of Directive 64/221 provides that Member States are not allowed to invoke public policy derogations for economic purposes. The judgment of the ECJ in *Kempf* Case 139/85 [1986] ECR 1741 implies that a Member State cannot refuse a residence permit on economic grounds. When an EC migrant exercises effective and genuine activity in the territory of a host Member State the fact that his remuneration is not sufficient to satisfy his needs, and that he receives social security benefits or social assistance from a host Member State, are not sufficient to deny him his right to reside in the territory of that State.

Public health

Article 4 of Directive 64/221provides that only diseases and disabilities enumerated in an Annex to the Directive may justify restrictions on entry or the issue of a first residence permit. The Annex divides diseases and disabilities into two group: Group A concerns diseases and disabilities which may threaten public health (infectious and contagious diseases) and Group B the diseases and disabilities which might endanger public policy or public security (such as drug addiction or mental illnesses). Listed diseases are those which are subject to quarantine in accordance with the International Health Regulation No 2 of the World Health Organisation of 25 May 1951 (such as tuberculosis, syphilis and other infectious diseases). Diseases and disabilities occurring after a first residence permit has been issued do not justify refusal to renew the residence permit or expulsion from the territory of a host Member State.

Procedural safeguards under Directive 64/221/EEC

Directive 64/221/EEC also provides procedural safeguards for EC nationals from other Member States seeking to enforce their rights of entry and residence in a host Member State. Part II of Directive 64/221 (arts 5–9) sets out important procedural rights for individuals who are refused the rights of entry and residence granted by the Treaty and by secondary legislation.

By virtue of art 5 an EC migrant is entitled to remain in the host Member State pending a decision either to grant or to refuse him a residence permit. As the Communication of the Commission emphasised such a decision should be taken as soon as possible and, in any event, not later than six months from the date of application for the residence permit. Article 6 provides that an applicant must be informed of the grounds on which the decision has been taken except where this is contrary to the interests of State security. Official notification is required for any decision to refuse the issue or renewal of a residence permit or to expel an applicant from the territory of a host Member State: art 7. Save in cases of urgency, the period allowed for leaving the host Member State, which must be expressly stated in the notification, must be not less than 15 days when no residence permit has yet been granted and one month in all other circumstances.

Articles 8 and 9 of Directive 64/221/EEC establish requirements for remedies against decisions of immigration authorities excluding EC nationals from the territory of a host Member State. Article 8 requires that a Member State provides the same remedies for nationals of other Member States as those available to its own nationals in respect of decisions concerning entry, renewal of residence permit or expulsion. Under art 9(1) of the Directive a decision refusing renewal of a residence permit or ordering the expulsion of the holder of a residence permit from the territory of a host State should be suspended (save in cases of urgency) until an opinion has been obtained from a competent authority of the host State different from that which has taken the challenged decision. Before that competent authority the applicant must have a right of defence and of assistance and representation in three situations: 'where there is no right of appeal to a court of law, where such an appeal may be only in respect of validity of the decision, or where the appeal cannot have suspensory effect'. Article 9(2) of the Directive concerns a decision in respect of a refusal to issue a first residence permit or a decision ordering expulsion before the issue of such a permit but does not indicate the conditions precedent to the exercise of that right. Both provisions were explained by the ECJ in *R* v *Secretary of State for the Home Department, ex parte Mann Singh Shingara; R* v *Secretary of State for the Home Department, ex parte Abbas Radiom* Joined Cases C–65 and 111/95 [1997] ECR I–3343. In separate proceedings for judicial review each applicant was refused leave to enter the United Kingdom. Mr Shingara, a holder of French citizenship, was refused entry to the UK in 1991 on the grounds of public policy and public security. The notice refusing him entry specified that the Secretary of State had personally decided that it would be contrary to the interests of public policy and public security to admit him to the UK, and that under s15(3) of the Immigration Act 1971 he was not entitled to appeal against this decision. In 1993, Mr Shingara was admitted to the UK on the basis of his French identity card but seven days later was arrested in Birmingham and detained as an illegal entrant and duly returned to France. The Secretary of State indicated that the deportation decision was based on the fact that Mr Shingara was promoting Sikh terrorism. On that occasion he was granted leave to apply for judicial review, but in fact did not apply.

Mr Radiom, a holder of Iranian and Irish nationality who by some legal means obtained an indefinite residence permit for the UK in 1983, worked in the UK for the Iranian consular services from 1983 to 1989. Following the severing of diplomatic relations between the UK and the Islamic Republic of Iran in 1989 Mr Radiom was asked by the Home Office to leave the UK within seven days, after which time, if he stayed within the country, he would be detained and deported on the grounds of public security. He decided to voluntarily leave the UK but subsequently submitted an application to the Home Office for a residence permit claiming that as an EC national he was entitled to work in the UK. The application was refused and Mr Radiom was informed by the Secretary of State that it was considered that his presence in the UK would still pose a threat to public security since he was a supporter of violence against dissidents as advocated by the Iranian government. He was also refused a right of appeal against this decision notwithstanding the fact that he was an EC national.

Both applicants argued that the United Kingdom law refusing them the opportunity of an appeal against the decision of the Secretary of State to deny them entry to the UK on the grounds of public policy and public security was contrary to Community law, in particular arts 8 and 9 of Directive 64/221/EEC. They both applied for judicial review of the Home Office decisions.

The main issue under art 8 of the Directive was that a decision made by the Secretary of State under s13 of the Immigration Act 1970, which excluded an EC national from that State's territory on the grounds of 'public good', was not subject to appeal, although it remained subject to judicial review as does any act of administration. The ECJ emphasised that the requirements of art 8 of the Directive are satisfied if EC nationals from other Member States have the same legal remedies as are available to nationals of a host State, in the present cases consisting of general judicial review provisions.

Article 9 of Directive 64/221/EEC posed a problem of interpretation. The ECJ held that the right of appeal against decisions enumerated in art 9(2) applies in the three situations mentioned in art 9(1). This interpretation is consistent with the objective of art 9 of the Directive which is intended to mitigate the effect of deficiencies in the remedies referred to in art 8 of the Directive.

The ECJ held that where an EC national is refused entry into the territory of another Member State on the grounds of public security, and does not challenge this decision, and later applies for a residence permit, and a new decision confirming the previous one is issued against him, he has a right of appeal within a reasonable time against the second decision, notwithstanding the fact that he did not appeal against the first.

20 Competition Law

20.1   Federal nature of EC competition law

20.2   Extra-territorial application of competition law

20.3   Definition of an undertaking

20.4   The concept of activity which 'may affect trade between Member States'

Only a perfect market tilting toward low prices which are consistent with the cost of manufacture and supply, in which undertakings compete with each other for customers, and which is good for both buyers and sellers alike as it promotes innovation and choice whilst keeping the economy efficient, does not need any correction by the rule of law since it constitutes a self-balancing system. However, the ideal market does not exist. Therefore, the considerations as to what constitutes anti-competitive conduct and what kind of conduct on the part of undertakings requires control by competition policy are subject to wider political, social and economic objectives. The main objectives of EC competition policy are to further internal market integration, to ensure its uniformity, to maintain its overall efficiency, to protect small and medium-sized undertakings whilst ensuring equal treatment for all undertakings and to protect consumers.

The principal objective of competition law is set out in art 3(g) EC which provides that 'the activities of the Community shall include ... the institution of a system ensuring that competition in the common market is not distorted'. The IX Commission Annual Report on competition law emphasised that the first objective of competition law is to maintain open and unify the common market.[1] In order to transform a number of heterogeneous, isolated national markets into a single market it is necessary to take a dynamic approach consisting of adjusting competition law to the continuously changing objectives of the Community against the background of a global economy, of preventing Member States from taking protectionist measures (especially in periods of economic difficulties) by the grant of State aids (art 87–89 EC), of subjecting State monopolies to competition rules (art 31 EC) and, the most important, of preventing and abolishing restrictive practices and anti-competitive behaviour of undertakings which seek to partition the common market in order to apply artificial prices and unfair conditions to their customers: arts 81 and 82 EC and Merger Regulation 4064/89.

Economic efficiency, as a fundamental objective of competition policy, was emphasised by the XXIII Annual Report on competition policy.[2] It stated that stimulation of sustained economic growth, competitiveness and employment had always been the *raison d'être* of competition policy. Therefore, EC competition policy encourages the optimal allocation of

---

[1] The European Commission, Brussels, 1979.
[2] The European Commission, Brussels, 1994, pp24–25.

resources and stimulates research and development, innovation and investment. Through this mechanism resources and employment are moved from one sector to another.

Another objective of EC competition policy is to ensure the conditions of effective competition under which undertakings have equal opportunities to compete. The IX Annual Report on competition policy emphasised that the principle of loyalty in the market requires: first, that all undertakings, public and private, EC and those established outside the EC but operating within the common market directly or through their subsidiaries, should be treated equally; and, second, that special attention should be given to small and medium-sized undertakings which, in the context of the common market (no longer protected by customs and duties), may find it difficult to compete with larger undertakings from other Member States. In this respect, the Commission encourages collaboration between them and adopts competition rules with a view to ensuring that they have a chance to enter the market and to expand. The Commission and the EP consider small and medium-sized undertakings as the main potential providers of new employment.

Finally, EC competition policy seeks to ensure that consumer demand is met at the lowest possible cost and that consumers benefit from the competition.[3]

This chapter focuses on the competition rules set out in arts 81 and 82 EC and Merger Regulation 4064/89. Article 81 EC prohibits and renders null and void, subject to some exceptions, any agreements between undertakings, decisions by associations of undertakings and concerted practices which may affect intra-Community trade and which has as its object, or effects, the prevention, restriction or distortion of competition within the Community. Article 82 EC prohibits any abuse, by one or more undertakings, of a dominant position within the common market or any substantial part of it in so far as it may affect intra-Community trade. Merger Regulation 4064/89 which operates against the legal background of the prior competition law, and which was adopted in December 1989 in order to respond to the omission from the original Treaty of Rome of any provision regarding the legal control of mergers, applies to concentrations which have a Community dimension.

Before examining in depth the above-mentioned rules it is necessary to focus on some general features common to all EC competition rules, namely their federal nature, their extra-territorial application and the common definition they set out for 'undertakings'.

Articles 81 and 82 EC can be applied jointly. In addition, they share a concept of 'effect on trade between Member States'.

20.1 Federal nature of EC competition law

EC competition law does not replace the competition law of the Member States. Undertakings are required to comply with both national and Community competition rules subject to the principle of supremacy of Community law which requires that, in the case of a conflict between them, Community law prevails. The relationship between EC competition law and national law was examined in *Walt Wilhelm* v *Bundeskartellamt* Case 14/68 [1969] ECR 15. In this case, which related to the Dyestuffs cartel (*ICI* v *Commission* Case 48/69

---

[3] The IX Annual Report.

[1972] ECR 619), the Commission and the German cartel authority (Bundeskartellamt) conducted parallel investigations concerning one of the undertakings participating in the Dyestuffs cartel, Walt Wilhelm, which argued that the German authorities should stop their investigations. The Kammergericht Bundeskartellamt, within the preliminary ruling procedure, referred to the ECJ two questions: first, whether the German cartel authority could continue their investigations and, second, whether they should suspend investigations pending completion of the investigations carried out by the Commission. The ECJ emphasised the different objectives of national and Community competition law. Nevertheless, the ECJ held that parallel investigations regarding the same agreement are allowed, subject to the condition that the application of Community law does not prejudice 'the full and uniform application of Community law or the effects of measures taken or to be taken to implement it'. This is the only answer consistent with the supremacy of Community law. The implication of having two sets of proceedings is that an undertaking may face sanctions imposed by national authorities and the Community. In this respect the ECJ stated that a double sanction is not excluded under Community law provided the requirements of natural justice are satisfied. Thus, any previous sanction should be taken into account in determining any sanction which is to be imposed.

The principle of supremacy also implies that when an agreement is considered to be in breach of Community law it must also be regarded as unlawful by virtue of national law since it affects the intra-Community pattern of trade and thus cannot be partially lawful within the territory of a Member State. In respect of agreements which have obtained negative clearance the situation is different. They may not have appreciable effect on intra-Community trade but may produce important anti-competitive 'effects on competition within a single Member State. In *Giry and Guérlin* Cases 253/78 and 3/79 [1980] ECR 2327, in the context of an agreement falling within the de minimus rule, the ECJ held that Community law does not prevent national authorities from assessing the agreement in the light of national competition law. However, national authorities cannot impose their assessment of an agreement on the Commission on the ground of similarity between EC competition law and national law: *CICCE* Case 298/83 [1985] ECR 1105. A question which has not yet been answered is what happens if an agreement is exempted by the Commission under art 81(3) but is unlawful under national competition law. It is submitted that the requirement of uniformity in the interpretation and application of Community law as stated in *Walt Wilhelm* requires that such an agreement should be enforced under national law. The same approach should be applied to agreements which qualify for exemption under block exemption regulations.

20.2 Extra-territorial application of competition law

Extra-territorial jurisdiction was developed to respond to the internationalisation of criminal activities at the end of nineteenth century. It has also found its application in anti-trust cases, especially in the US anti-trust laws and EC competition rules. In the context of the common market the ECJ endorsed the extra-territorial application of EC competition law in the *Wood Pulp* cases. In this respect, the ECJ has delivered two judgments, one dealing solely with jurisdictional issues[4] and the other with the substance of the claim.[5]

In *Ahlström and Others v Commission (Re Wood Pulp Cartel)* Joined Cases 89, 104, 114, 116–117 and 125–129/85 [1988] ECR 5193; [1988] 4 CMLR 901 the Commission found more than 40 suppliers of wood pulp in violation of Community competition law, despite the fact that 40 out of 42 undertakings were not resident within the European Community (there were 11 undertakings from the USA, 6 from Canada, 11 from Sweden, 11 from Finland, one from Norway, one from Spain and one from Portugal). Non-EC undertakings were making sales into the Community in a variety of ways, including via agents, branches and subsidiaries located there. Fines were imposed on 36 of these undertakings for violation of art 81(1) EC. A number of them appealed to the ECJ against the decision. One of their arguments was that EC competition law was not capable of having extra-territorial effect and therefore the fines were unlawful.

The ECJ confirmed the extra-territorial application of EC competition law. The applicants argued that the Commission's decision was incompatible with public international law taking into account that the application of EC competition rules was founded exclusively on the economic repercussions within the common market of conduct restricting competition which was carried out outside the Community. The ECJ replied that:

'It should be observed that an infringement of art [81 EC], such as the conclusion of an agreement which has had the effect of restricting competition within the Common Market, consists of conduct made up of two elements: the formation of the agreement, decision or concerted practice and the implementation thereof. If the applicability of prohibitions laid down under competition law were made to depend on the place where the agreement, decision or concerted practice was formed, the result would obviously be to give undertakings an easy means of evading these prohibitions. The decisive factor is therefore the place where it is implemented.'

Merger Regulation 4064/89 is applied to undertakings from outside the EC if the following conditions are met: that the intended concentration will have both immediate and substantial effect in the Community, and that these effects must be foreseeable.[6]

The extra-territorial application of any national law as well as EC competition law creates many problems. The investigation of alleged breaches outside the territory of the Union often necessitates co-operation of competent authorities of a third State. Even more challenging is the actual enforcement outside Community territory of decisions of the Community competition authorities because a third State, where the offending undertaking is located, has no obligation to co-operate, to assist foreign authorities or to recognise and enforce their decisions. In this respect it is often left to the offending undertakings to plead guilty and pay the fine. This means that the undertaking concerned will co-operate in investigations only when forced to do so and that only powerful countries or blocks of countries will successfully enforce their decisions against an offending undertaking and

---

[4] *Ahlström and Others v Commission (Re Wood Pulp Cartel)* Joined Cases 89, 104, 114, 116, 117 and 125–129/85 [1988] ECR 5193: [1988] 4 CMLR 901.

[5] *Ahlström and Others v Commission* Joined Cases 89, 104, 114, 116, 117 and 125–129/85 [1993] 4 CMLR 407.

[6] See *Gencor Ltd v Commission* Case T–102/96 [1999] All ER (EC) 289. This case is examined in detail in Chapter 23 on mergers.

consequently obtain compensation, although in the context of a global economy the anti-competitive conduct of an undertaking may affects millions of consumers living all over the world. In this respect, the proceedings of the US anti-trust authorities against Hoffman-La Roche and other pharmaceutical giants participating in a conspiracy to eliminate competition in the pharmaceutical sector worldwide is very instructive. Hoffman-La Roche, a Swiss-based pharmaceutical multinational, was the leader of a worldwide conspiracy to fix, raise and maintain prices for the most commonly used vitamins A, B2, B5, C, E and Beta Carotene, to allocate market shares of such vitamins worldwide and to 'allot' contracts to supply vitamin pre-mixes to customers in the USA by rigging the bids for those contracts. The conspiracy lasted from January 1990 to February 1999. As Joel I Klein, Assistant Attorney-General in charge of the US Department of Justice Anti-trust Division emphasised, 'During the life of the conspiracy, virtually every American consumer paid artificially inflated prices for vitamins and vitamin-enriched foods in order to feed the greed of those defendants and their co-conspirators who reaped hundreds of million of dollars in additional revenues.'[7] During the investigation Hoffman-La Roche and other participating undertakings lied to the US anti-trust authorities in attempts to cover up the conspiracy. Only when faced with evidence provided by Rhone-Poulenc SA, a French pharmaceutical company which also participated in the conspiracy (but decided to co-operate with the US anti-competition authorities in order to qualify for protection from criminal proceedings under the US Corporate Leniency Program), did Hoffman-La Roche plead guilty, agree to pay the highest criminal fine ever imposed of $500 million and agree to co-operate with the investigation. The company director of Worldwide Marketing, Dr Sommer, a Swiss citizen, also agreed to submit to the jurisdiction of the US courts and pleaded quilty to charges which resulted in his serving a four-month prison term and paying a $100,000 fine. Money received from the fines was deposited into the Crime Victims Fund in the USA. This is designated to provide financial compensation to US victims of crime and other benefits in the USA. However, millions of consumers outside the USA, also victims of the conspiracy, will never be compensated, directly or indirectly.

Extra-territorial application of Community competition law is contrary to international comity and fairness and encourages confrontation between countries rather than co-operation in resolving competition issues. This is even more obvious in the context of the global economy, taking into account that anti-competitive conduct of undertakings may have a worldwide impact.[8]

The best solution is to establish a progressive and global approach towards the unification of substantive competition law at international level. So far this approach has not been very successful, although this question has attracted attention of the World Trade Organisation (WTO). Within the framework of the WTO a working group in charge of this

---

[7] See US Department of Justice press release of 20 May 1999: http://www.usdoj.gov/atr/public/press_release/1999/2450.htm.

[8] See, for example, the merger between two EC undertakings Guinness plc and Grand Metropolitan plc, cleared by the Commission on 16 October 1997, by the US FTC on 15 December 1997 and envisaged as subject to investigation by the Australian Competition and Consumer Commission (ACCC) which, after consultation which New Zealand and Canadian competition authorities, decided to abandon its action: ACCC Media Release, 20 January 1998. In general the merger required clearance in over 100 countries.

question has been established. From preparatory work carried out by the working group two approaches have emerged, one supported by the USA and based on bilateral co-operation agreements in competition matters and the other submitted by the EC and based on the adoption of an international agreement regarding co-operation in competition matters between regional competition authorities parallel to the adoption, in two stages, of an international framework of competition rules. During the first stage all members of the WTO will enact domestic competition laws, while in the second stage a gradual convergence of domestic competition laws will be undertaken under the auspices of WTO leading to certain common principles of competition law and procedure. Consequently, at the end of that stage it would be possible for the WTO to decide whether or not unification of substantive rules was feasible.

In the meantime the Community has decided to enter into bilateral competition co-operation agreements. They increase the effectiveness of enforcement of competition law and reduce the risk of conflicting or incompatible decisions being reached by two competition authorities in individual cases. So far the EC has concluded agreements with the USA and Canada.[9] It is expected that the third agreement will be signed with Japan.

20.3 Definition of an undertaking

Competition law applies only to undertakings. For that reason it is necessary to define this concept. Neither the Treaties nor secondary legislation provide a definition of undertakings. The Commission considers that any natural or legal person engaged in any economic or commercial activity should be regarded as an undertaking.[10] The definition based on economic activity means that EC competition law applies irrespective of:

1. The legal personality of the body in question. It can include individuals,[11] or a Committee organising the World Cup,[12] or members of a professional body.[13]
2. The legal form of the body in question, whether private individuals engaged in any form of business, commerce or profession, partnership, co-operatives, etc.
3. The economic purpose of the body in question. The making of profit is not important. For that reason a non-profit-making organisation which is carrying out some economic activity is within the scope of EC competition law.[14]
4. The change of legal form or name. In *CRAM* Joined Cases 29 and 30/83 [1984] ECR 1679 the ECJ held that the successor to an undertaking being investigated may be considered to be the same undertaking for competition law purposes.

However, in order to be regarded as an undertaking an entity must enjoy some autonomy in

---

[9] Council Decision 1999/445/EC ECSC: OJ L175 (1999).
[10] Answer 2290/84: OJ C203 (1985).
[11] *RAI/United*: OJ L157 (1978).
[12] OJ L326 (1992).
[13] OJ L203 (1993).
[14] See *Van Landewyck* Joined Cases 209–15 and 218/78 [1980] ECR 3125; *Fédération Française des Sociétés d'Assurance* Case 244/94 [1995] ECR I–4013.

determining its course of action on the market irrespective of whether or not it has a separate legal personality. This can be considered as follow:

1. A corporate body. A subsidiary will be regarded as a separate undertaking if both the parent undertaking and its subsidiary 'form a single economic unit within which the subsidiary has no real freedom to determine its course of action on the market': *Beguelin Import v GL Import Export* Case 22/71 [1971] ECR 949. This means that if a parent and its subsidiary, which is not capable of independent policy-making, enter into an agreement prohibited under art 81 EC there will not be a breach of that provision since that agreement (or a concerted practice) will reflect the allocation of functions within the corporate body. This is known under EC competition law as the 'group economic unit' doctrine: *Viho Europe* Case 73/95P [1996] ECR I–5457. On the basis of this doctrine, when a subsidiary established within the Community abuses its dominant position its behaviour is imputable to the parent company, irrespective of whether or not the parent company is established within the Community: *Centrafarm v Sterling Drug Inc* Case 15/74 [1974] ECR 1147.

2. A commercial agent. The Commission in its 1962 Notice stated that the true commercial agent who acts on behalf of a principal is not considered as an undertaking within the meaning of EC competition rules. However, the situation is different if he acts not as an auxiliary but enjoys a degree of independence permitting him to enter into agreements prohibited under art 81 EC. In *Suiker Unie* Case 40/73 [1975] ECR 1663 undertakings concerned acted as agents for each other and as principals on their own account in the sugar market. The ECJ held that taking into consideration the ambiguous relationships between them, they should be regarded as independent undertakings. It seems that in each case the Commission will assess the economic functions carried out by the agent in order to decide to what degree he acts as a genuine agent: *ASBL* Case 311/85 [1987] ECR 987.

3. An undertaking will be exempt from liability on the ground of lack of autonomy if its anti-competitive conduct was imposed upon it unilaterally by the national authorities: *Asia Motor France* Case T–387/94 [1996] ECR II–961.

Articles 81 and 82 EC also apply to public bodies provided they exercise commercial or economic activities (*Italy v Commission* Case 118/85 [1987] ECR 1987) and do not act in their capacity as public authorities.

Articles 81 and 82 do not apply to entities that carry out activities in the public interest. In *Eurocontrol* Case C–364/92 [1994] ECR I–43, an international organisation supervising and controlling air traffic over a large part of Europe was collecting route charges from airlines in order to finance its activities. A German airline refused to pay and argued that the charges were imposed in breach of art 81 EC. The ECJ held that Eurocontrol was not an undertaking within the meaning of EC competition law as it performed its function in the public interest, that is, for the safety of the passengers and thus its legal status and the way it was financed were irrelevant. Eurocontrol's collection of charges could not be separated from its main activities which were similar to public authorities. Also, a private company acting in the capacity of public authorities could not be regarded as an undertaking: *Diego Cali v SEPG* Case C–343/95 [1997] ECR I–1547. Public bodies entrusted with the operation of services of general economic interest, or having the character of a revenue-producing monopoly, are subject to EC competition rules 'in so far as the application of such rules does not obstruct the performance in law or in fact of the particular tasks assigned to them' (art 86(2) EC), unless their activities affect intra-Community trade to such an extent as would be contrary to the interest of the Community.

20.4 The concept of activity which 'may affect trade between Member States'

In order to breach arts 81 and 82 EC, agreements, decisions, concerted practices or abuses of a dominant position must have effect on intra-Community trade. In *Société Technique Minière* v *Maschinenbau Ulm* Case 56/65 [1966] ECR 235 the ECJ held that

> 'For this requirement to be fulfilled, it must be possible to foresee with a sufficient degree of probability on the basis of a set of objective factors of law or fact that the agreement in question may have an influence, direct or indirect, actual or potential, on the pattern of trade between Member States.'

This definition shows that the ECJ has taken the same approach to EC competition law as to art 28 EC, that is, it applies the *Dassonville* formula in the context of competition law.

The taking into account of potential effect means that even if an undertaking concerned does not in fact carry out a prohibited agreement or a decision it will, nevertheless, fall under the prohibition of Community law as being capable of constituting a threat to freedom of trade between Member States. In *Parker Pen* Case T–77/92 [1994] ECR II–549 a clause prohibiting export was ignored by a distributor but despite this the potential effect on the pattern of trade was considered as sufficient to condemn the agreement. Furthermore, it is irrelevant whether or not such a clause will affect intra-Community trade favourably or not favourably as this will be assessed later in order to determine the possible exemption under art 81(3) EC. Consequently, the argument that an agreement encourages an increase in the volume of trade between Member States is not sufficient to exclude the possibility that it may affect intra-Community trade: *Consten* v *Grundig* Cases 56 and 58/64 [1966] ECR 299.

The notion of 'trade' has been broadly interpreted by the Community institutions. It covers all economic activities, including the provision of commercial services such as banking (*Züchner* Case 172/80 [1981] ECR 2021), insurance (*Verband der Sachversicherer* Case 45/85 [1987] ECR 405) and financial services.[15] It encompasses also other activities of a commercial nature, such as the provision of exhibition and trade fairs[16] and the granting of aid to exporters by a professional body in order to finance promotion of their products abroad.[17] It includes not only import and export between Member States but also between Member States and a non-Member State as in the case of an agreement limiting export of Japanese cars to the United Kingdom: *BEUC and National Consumer Council* Case T–37/92 [1994] ECR II–285.

---

[15] *LSFM*: OJ L369 (1985).
[16] *UNIDI*: OJ L228 (1975).
[17] *Milchförderungsfonds*: OJ L35 (1985).

It should be noted that an agreement between undertakings in a single Member State may affect intra-Community trade if it creates or reinforces partitioning of the common market in accord with national borders (*Vereeninging van Cementhandelaren* Case 8/72 [1972] ECR 977; *Belasco* Case 246/86 [1989] ECR 2117) or limits the capacity of production in a Member State by, for example, fixing prices to be charged in that Member State[18] or by creating a common subsidiary responsible for production and commercialisation of their products.[19]

In the context of the requirement that to be in breach of art 81(1) EC conduct of undertakings must affect trade between Member States, it is important to emphasise that the agreement as a whole must be taken into consideration, not just every clause restricting competition: *Windsurfing International* Case 193/83 [1986] ECR 611. Also, if there is a network of agreements the actual circumstances, both economic and legal, in which each agreement was made must be taken into consideration: *Brasserie de Haecht* v *Wilkin-Janssens (No 1)* Case 23/67 [1967] ECR 407. Similarly, in the case of abuse of a dominant position, it is necessary to take into account the entirety of the commercial activities of an undertaking, including those outside the common market: *Commercial Solvents Corporation* v *Commission* Cases 6 and 7/73 [1974] ECR 223 and *Greenwich Film* Case 22/79 [1979] ECR 3275. Even if an abusive practice is principally directed towards imports from a non-Member State, art 82 EC still applies.[20]

The requirement that agreements, decisions, concerted practices and abuses of a dominant position must affect the pattern of trade between Member States is subject to a very important limitation, the so-called *de minimus* rule which was established in *Völk* v *Vervaecke* Case 5/69 [1969] ECR 295. Völk, a small undertaking manufacturing washing-machines, concluded an exclusive distribution agreement with Vervaecke, a Dutch distributor. Völk's share of the market in washing-machines was less than 1 per cent. When a dispute arose between the parties, a Dutch court referred to the ECJ a question whether art 81(1) EC should apply in view of the small share of the market held by Völk. The ECJ held that the exclusive distributorship agreement ensuring absolute territorial protection was outside the scope of art 81(1) EC as the effects produced on trade between Member States were not appreciable.

Under the *de minimis rule* some agreements *prima facie* in breach of art 81(1) EC are outside its scope of application where the market share of the parties is so minimal that their agreement has no effect on intra-Community trade. In this case the manufacture's share of the market (0.6 per cent) was considered by the ECJ as insignificant and the agreement itself concerned only 600 units. The *de minimus* rule applies also in the context of art 82 EC: *Hugin* Case 22/78 [1979] ECR 1869.

In order to help businesses to assess whether the *de minimis* rule applies to their agreement the Commission has published a Notice on Agreements of Minor Importance, which was revised in 1997.[21] The Notice is not binding but very useful for undertakings since if their agreement falls below the fixed thresholds they can implement it and do not have to

---

[18] *Verre Plat*: OJ L33 (1989).
[19] *Fiat-Itachi*: OJ L20 (1993).
[20] *Solvay*: OJ L152 (1991).
[21] OJ C373 (1997).

notify the Commission. The Commission states in its Notice that no infringement proceedings will be commenced in respect of any such agreement and if the parties mistakenly, but in good faith, fail to notify their agreement believing that it is within the scope of the Notice, the Commission will not impose fines on them. If the parties are uncertain whether or not their agreement is excluded from art 81(1) EC they should notify it to the Commission in the usual way. Horizontal agreements which are within the scope of the *de minimus* rule but have as their object price-fixing, restriction of production or sales or market sharing being *per se* contrary to art 81(1) EC, are excluded from the scope of the Notice. Although the Commission in general will not commence proceedings in respect of such agreements unless the interests of the Community require it, they should be notified to the Commission. Similar treatment is applied to vertical agreements which fix resale prices and confer territorial protection upon the participating undertakings or third undertakings, and therefore are in breach of art 81(1) EC.

The Notice distinguishes between three types of agreement:

1. Horizontal agreements. In the case of undertakings operating at the same level of production or marketing a threshold is fixed at 5 per cent, ie the aggregate market share held by participating undertakings in any of the relevant market must not exceed 5 per cent.
2. Vertical agreements. Agreements between undertakings operating at different economic levels in the distribution process are within the scope of the Notice if the aggregate market share of participating undertakings does not exceed in any of the relevant markets a threshold of 10 per cent.
3. Mixed agreements. A mixed horizontal/vertical agreement (or in the event that the classification of an agreement is difficult) for which a threshold of 5 per cent is applicable.

The Commission will consider agreements, whether horizontal, vertical or mixed, as protected by the Notice if they exceed the fixed threshold by no more that one-tenth in relation to the market share over two successive financial years.

The Community institutions have gradually broadened the scope of the concept of the effect on trade between Member States. As D G Goyder stated:

> 'In practice, the Commission will now assume that trade between Member States is affected by virtually any practice which brings about a noticeable effect on market conditions or structures and involves undertakings of a size above the level affected by the current Notice. The onus of proof will then effectively shift to the parties to prove the negative, in most cases a difficult task.'[22]

---

[22] In D G Goyder, *EC Competition Law*, 3rd ed, Oxford: Oxford University Press, 1998, p116.

21 Article 81 EC

21.1 Vertical and horizontal agreements

21.2 Agreements, decisions and concerted practices

21.3 'Which have as their object or effect'

21.4 Prevention, restriction or distortion of competition

21.5 Attenuation of the effect of the art 81(1) EC prohibition

21.6 Exemptions

21.7 Civil consequences of breaches of art 81(1) EC

Article 81 EC provides:

'(1) The following shall be prohibited as incompatible with the common market: all agreements between undertakings, decisions by associations of undertakings, and concerted practices which may affect trade between Member States and which have as their object or effect the prevention, restriction or distortion of competition within the common market, and in particular those which:
(a) directly or indirectly fix purchase or selling prices or any other trading conditions;
(b) limit or control production, markets, technical development, or investment;
(c) share markets or sources of supply;
(d) apply dissimilar conditions to equivalent transactions with other trading parties, thereby placing them at a competitive disadvantage;
(e) make the conclusion of contracts subject to acceptance by the other parties of supplementary obligations which, by their nature or according to commercial usage, have no connection with the subject of such contracts.
(2) Any agreements or decisions prohibited pursuant to this Article shall be automatically void.
(3) The provisions of paragraph 1 may, however, be declared inapplicable in the case of:
– any agreement or category of agreements between undertakings;
– any decision or category of decisions by associations of undertakings;
– any concerted practice or category of concerted practices,
which contributes to improving the production or distribution of goods or to promoting technical or economic progress, while allowing consumers a fair share of the resulting benefit, and which does not:
(a) impose on the undertakings concerned restrictions which are not indispensable to the attainment of these objectives;
(b) afford such undertakings the possibility of eliminating competition in respect of a substantial part of the products in question.'

For the application of art 81 EC it is necessary to make a distinction between horizontal and vertical agreements.

In order to breach art 81(1) EC a number of conditions must be met: the entity in question must be identified as an undertaking; its behaviour must be capable of affecting the pattern of trade between Member States; and it must enter into an unlawful arrangement which must have as its object or effect the prevention, restriction or distortion of competition within the common market.

However, in the circumstances enumerated in art 81(3) EC, arrangements which are *prima facie* in breach of art 81(1) EC may fall outside the art 81(1) EC prohibition. Agreements and decisions which infringe art 81(1) EC and which are not eligible for exemption under art 81(3) EC are, under art 81(2) EC, void from their inception and as such unenforceable in civil courts of the Member States.

All of the above-mentioned elements will be examined in succession.

21.1 Vertical and horizontal agreements

Article 81 EC applies to both vertical and horizontal agreements. A horizontal agreement is an agreement entered into by undertakings that compete with each at the same level of the production/distribution chain. For example, agreements between producers, or between manufacturers or between retailers are horizontal agreements

When undertakings which operate at different levels of the production/distribution chain enter into an agreement, that agreement is considered as a vertical agreement. The undertakings involved do not compete with each other because they operate at different levels of the market. Among vertical agreements the most popular are franchising and distribution agreements.

There were some doubts as to whether or not art 81 applies to vertical agreements, taking into consideration the fact that parties to such agreements are not on a footing of equality. This question was examined by the ECJ in *Consten Sarl and Grundig Gmbh* v *Commission* Cases 56 and 58/64 [1966] ECR 299; [1966] CMLR 418. Grundig, a large German manufacturer of electrical equipment, entered into an agreement with a French distributor, Consten, according to which Consten was appointed as Grundig's exclusive distributor in France, Corsica and the Saar region. The distribution agreement contained terms which, *inter alia*, allowed Consten to employ the Grundig trade mark ('GINT') and emblem in its promotions. On the basis of this authority, Consten registered the Grundig trade mark in France. Subsequently, a French competitor imported a number of Grundig products from Germany and attempted to sell these in the French market. Consten raised an action for trade-mark infringement against this rival, relying on the earlier registration of the trade-mark. The Commission objected to these proceedings and commenced an investigation into the functioning of the exclusive distribution agreement. The Commission found that the agreement was contrary to art 81(1) EC, being an agreement which had the object of distorting competition within the Community by restricting trade. Consten brought an action in the ECJ contesting these findings.

The ECJ confirmed that vertical agreements are within the scope of art 81 EC. In this respect the ECJ held that:

'Article 85 [art 81 EC] refers in a general way to all agreements which distort competition within the common market and does not lay down any distinction between those agreements based on whether they are made between competitors operating at the same level in the economic process or between non-competing persons operating at different level. In principle, no distinction can be made where the Treaty does not make any distinction.'

Although the level in the economy at which the parties operate is important, taking into account that horizontal agreements traditionally represent a more dangerous form of anti-competitive practices, vertical agreements may also distort competition by preventing or limiting the competition of third parties in respect of the products, and thus take an unjustified advantage at the expense of the consumer or user, contrary to the general aims of art 81 EC. The ECJ held that in this context it is irrelevant that parties to such an agreement are not equal as regards their position and function in the economy. The ECJ restrictively interpreted art 81 EC. It held that the agreement intended to isolate the French market for Grundig products and therefore partition the common market along national lines which in itself distorted competition in the common market. For that reason, without examining other factors such as economic data, the correctness of criteria which the Commission had applied in order to compare the French market with the German market, etc, the ECJ held that the agreement was in breach of art 81(1) EC and upheld the Commission's position in this matter

In relation to the trade mark, the ECJ held that the trade-mark owner, Grundig, could not grant a licence to Consten resulting in absolute territorial protection for the licensee. For that reason, Consten could not rely on its trade mark to prevent parallel import of Grundig products from other Member States. The use of the mark 'GINT' was for the purpose of partitioning the common market alongside the national market and as such in breach of art 81(1) EC.

21.2 Agreements, decisions and concerted practices

Article 81(1) EC prohibits all arrangements between undertakings capable of distorting competition within the common market, including cartels. It enumerates three types of arrangements: agreements between undertakings, decisions by associations of undertakings and concerted practices. Such practices are conceptually distinct from the other two types of arrangement, although their identification is not so obvious because, on the one hand, they are often interrelated and, on the other hand, it is not necessary for the purposes of art 81(1) EC to draw a clear dividing line between them. In this respect in *Enichem Anic* v *Commission* Case C–49/92P [1999] ECR I–4125 Anic argued that the Court of First Instance (CFI) committed an error in law in holding that Anic was responsible for all aspects of the conduct attributable to the relevant cartel, even if it was impossible to attribute to it individual infringements. The ECJ held that although art 81 distinguishes between 'concerted practices' 'agreements between undertakings' and 'decisions by associations of undertakings', its objective is to catch different forms of co-ordination and collusion between undertakings. As a result, the CFI was correct in considering that 'patterns of conduct by several undertakings were a manifestation of a single infringement, corresponding partly to an agreement and partly to a concerted practice.' Therefore, the two notions are not incompatible and certain conduct may be qualified as being in the first place a concerted practice and in the second place an agreement.

Agreements between undertakings

The concept of agreement refers to contracts concluded between undertakings. This is particularly evident in the context of vertical agreements.[1] However, in respect of horizontal agreements, it is very unlikely that undertakings concerned would enter into a formal contract. For that reason Community institutions apply a pragmatic approach in the identification of an agreement within the meaning of art 81(1) EC. Agreements have been defined as consensual arrangements between undertakings irrespective of whether or not they are formally binding contracts, and as involving the acceptance of an obligation irrespective of whether the obligation is legally binding. Consequently, an agreement will fall within the scope of art 81(1) EC, irrespective of whether or not it is:

1. verbal, oral or tacit (*Dunlop Slazenger International* Case T–43/92 [1994] ECR II–441);
2. signed or not by an undertaking;[2]
3. legally binding.

Consequently, an informal agreement such as a 'gentlemen's agreement' will be in breach of art 81(1) EC. In the Quinine Cartel cases (*ACF Chemiefarma* Case 41/69 [1970] ECR 661) the ECJ held that it suffices that an agreement 'amounted to the faithful expression of the joint intention of the parties to the agreement with regard to their conduct in the common market'. In this case a formal contract, signed and made public, fixing prices and quotas for quinine expressly excluded its application to the common market. However, it was supplemented by a gentlemen's agreement in writing extending its application to the EC, and containing a clause providing that the breach of its provisions would be considered a breach of the written agreement and enforceable by arbitration. This contract was unsigned and secret. Both contracts and others implementing oral and written agreements amounted to 'agreements' within the meaning of art 81(1) EC.

Even if a contract is contrary to the economic interests of one of the parties[3] or was legally terminated but still produces its unlawful effects (*EMI Records* Cases 51, 86 and 96/75 [1976] ECR 811) it is regarded as an agreement within the meaning of art 81(1) EC. Furthermore, the legal nature of an agreement is determined by the Community institutions in the light of factual considerations and not by the parties to it.[4]

Also, a unilateral act of an undertaking which forms part of the general framework of commercial relationships between the undertakings involved may be considered as an agreement within the meaning of art 81(1) EC. Circumstances such as these were at issue in *AEG Telefunken* Case 107/82 [1983] ECR 3151 concerning a refusal of AEG, a German producer of electronic goods, to supply some of its existing distributors who did not comply

---

[1] *Société Technique Minère v Maschinenbau Ulm GmbH* Case 56/65 [1966] ECR 235 and *Consten and Grundig* Cases 56 and 58/64 [1966] CMLR 418 are the first cases relating to vertical agreements.
[2] *BP-Kemi-DDSF* [1979] 3 CMLR 684. In this case the agreement was implemented by the parties although not formally signed by them.
[3] *Johnson and Johnson*: OJ L377 (1980); [1981] 2 CMLR 287.
[4] *Auditel and AGB Italia SpA*: OJ L306 (1993).

with resale prices recommended by AEG even though they were otherwise qualified to offer the services required under the distributorship agreements. The ECJ emphasised that the unilateral conduct of AEG

> '... forms part of the contractual relations between the undertaking and resellers. Indeed, in the case of the admission of a distributor, approval is based on the acceptance, tacit or express, by the contracting parties of the policy pursued by AEG which requires, *inter alia*, the exclusion from the network of all distributors who are qualified for admission but are not prepared to adhere to that policy.'

Another example was provided by *Sandoz* Case 277/87 [1990] ECR I–45 in which Sandoz, a pharmaceutical company, put on its invoices for the supply of pharmaceuticals the words 'export prohibited' in order to prevent parallel imports of its products to Italy, where prices were controlled by Sandoz and as a result much higher than in other Member States. The ECJ held that the unilateral act of Sandoz was part of the distribution agreement between Sandoz and its customers, irrespective of the actual adherence to it by Sandoz's distributors. The same applies to a circular issued by an undertaking. In *BMW Belgium SA* v *Commission* Cases 32 and 36–82/78 [1980] ECR 2435 a circular was issued by the Belgian subsidiary of BMW, without knowledge of the parent company but with approval of the BMW Belgium dealers' trade association, requiring dealers not to export BMWs from Belgium to Germany where prices were higher. A number of dealers acknowledged the circular in writing. They were fined for entering into an agreement prohibited by art 81(1) EC. The ECJ held that the circular in question was a part of the whole contractual framework between the parties involved.

Decisions by associations of undertakings

This concept refers to decisions of trade associations and any economic interest grouping of undertakings as defined in *Groupement des Cartes Bancaires CB and Europay International* Cases T–39 and 40/92 [1994] ECR II–49 irrespective of their legal form. Although the concept of 'associations' under art 81(1) EC is mainly concerned with trade associations of undertakings, the ECJ has given it a broad interpretation. As a result, it encompasses professional associations,[5] international organisations such as the International Railways Union (*UIC* Case T–14/93 [1995] ECR II–1503), groupings such as the European Broadcasting Union[6] which co-ordinates the Eurovision system, and even a maritime conference: *Compagnie Maritime Belge Transport* Case 300/93 [1996] ECR II–1910.

The distortion of competition may result from either a written constitution of an association which imposes certain rules of conduct on its members,[7] or subsequent decisions of its managing bodies which are binding and thus must be complied with by all its members. The question whether or not binding decisions are within in the scope of art

---

[5] *COAPI*: OJ L122 (1995).
[6] *Métropole Télévision SA and Reti Televisive Italiane SpA and Gestevisión Telecinco SA and Antena 3 de Televisión* v *Commision* Joined Cases T–528, 542, 543 and 546/93 [1996] ECR II–649.
[7] *National Sulphuric Acid Association*: OJ L260 (1980); [1980] 3 CMLR 429.

81(1) EC was answered by the ECJ in *Vereeniging van Cementhandelaren* Case 8/72 [1972] ECR 977. In this case a Dutch trade association, of which most Dutch cement dealers were members, recommended the prices at which cement should be sold in The Netherlands. The ECJ held that a non-binding recommendation would amount to a decision in so far as its acceptance by undertakings actually influenced their conduct on the market. In this case the trade association actually controlled the Dutch cement industry, taking into account detailed trading rules it imposed on its members (that is, the obligation to notify any change in management), the strict supervision of its members' accounts, the requirement that they had to sell to each other and thus eliminate the possibility of building up of stocks of cement by third parties, the expulsion of its members for non-compliance with these rules, etc. In this context its decision recommending target prices had a great impact on the level of prices: first, its members were actually complying with the recommendation and, second, it removed to a great extent the uncertainty as to prices as almost all dealers were charging the same as each other.

A decision of an association of undertakings which is subsequently extended to all undertakings by virtue of a legislative act is still within the prohibition of art 81(1) EC. In *BNIC v Clair* Case 123/83 [1985] ECR 391 a private trade association which was established at the request of the minister, who also appointed its chairman, recommended prices for cognac and the eaux de vie from which it is distilled. This decision which was in breach art 81(1) was subsequently extended to the entire industry and made binding under ministerial order. The ECJ held that decision unlawful and rejected the interference of public authorities as providing an excuse for the infringement of art 81(1) EC. If a government merely encourages trade associations to impose anti-competitive restrictions this will not constitute a defence for the assosiation concerned: *Fedetab* Case 209/78 [1980] ECR 3125. However, if a trade association is forced by the government through a mandatory act, whether legislative or administrative, to regulate industry in a manner contrary to art 81(1) EC, the association will not be in breach of art 81(1).[8]

A decision adopted by a federal-type association, that is its members are themselves associations, is also within the art 81(1) EC prohibition.[9]

Concerted practices

It derives from the very nature of a concerted practice that it does not have all the elements of contract but constitutes a form of informal co-ordination between undertakings. Concerted practices are most difficult to evidence taking into account that, first, they are implicit, secret arrangements which the participating undertakings will try to hide from the public view at all costs and, second, parallel behaviour of undertakings may be justified by other factors such as a high degree of market transparency or the oligopolistic tendencies of the market, in which situation the market is dominated by a small number of large undertakings. In this context it is extremely difficult to establish collusive practices as it is expected that when one producer changes its prices others will follow.

---

[8] *BNIC*: OJ L379 (1982).
[9] *Milchförderungsfonds*: OJ L35 (1985).

The ECJ provided some clarifications of the concept of concerted practices in *Imperial Chemical Industries Ltd* v *Commission (Dyestuffs)* Case 48/69 [1972] ECR 619. ICI was one of several undertakings which manufactured aniline dyestuffs. The leading producers of aniline dyestuffs increased their prices almost simultaneously on three occasion: in 1964 (10 per cent), 1965 (10–15 per cent) and 1967 (8 per cent). The Commission decided that these three general and uniform increases in prices indicated that there had been a concerted practice between the undertakings concerned contrary to art 81(1) EC and imposed fines on them. The undertakings challenged the Commission's decision on the grounds that the price increase merely reflected parallel behaviour in an oligopolistic market and did not result from concerted practices.

The ECJ confirmed the Commission's decision. It held that a concerted practice refers to a form of co-operation between undertakings which, without having been taken to the stage where an agreement properly so-called has been concluded, knowingly substitutes for the risk of competition practical co-operation between them. Therefore, co-ordination and co-operation between undertakings constituted an essential feature in determining whether or not they had been engaged in a concerted practice. In respect of parallel behaviour the ECJ stated that it may not by itself be identified with a concerted practice, although it provides strong evidence of such a practice in so far as it leads to conditions of competition which do not correspond to the normal conditions of the market, taking into account the nature of the products, the size and number of the undertakings, etc.

The ECJ emphasised that

'… it is contrary to the rules on competition contained in the Treaty for a producer to co-operate with his competitors, in any way whatsoever, in order to determine a co-ordinated course of action resulting in a price increase and to ensure its success by prior elimination of all uncertainty as to each other's conduct regarding the essential elements of that action, such as the amount, subject-matter, date and place of the increase.'

However the key element in the determination of whether or not the particular conduct of undertakings amounts to a concerted practice was provided in *Suiker Unie* Cases 40, 50, 54–56, 111, 113 and 114/73 [1976] 1 CMLR 295. In these cases the ECJ held that

'… the criteria of co-ordination and co-operation must be understood in the light of the concept inherent in the provision of the Treaty relating to competition that each economic operator must determine independently the policy which he intends to adopt on the Common Market.'

The ECJ emphasised that the autonomy of an undertaking must not be altered. This autonomy is called into question when competing undertakings intentionally exchange information, directly or indirectly, in order to influence the conduct of actual or potential competitors or to disclose to a competitor the adopted or envisaged course of conduct. There must be an intention to communicate information to the other party and the latter must be aware that it is receiving such, not accidentally but on purpose. The exchange of information must go beyond mutual awareness of what the other party is doing based on normal sources of information, such as the terms and conditions quoted to the customers which are easy to obtain and which will influence prices and policies adopted by competitors. Therefore, under art 81(1) EC intelligent conduct of an undertaking based on current and anticipated conduct of its competitors is not prohibited.

As already mentioned parallel behaviour may be explained by the nature and the structure of the market. This was considered in *Ahlström and Others v Commission (Re Wood Pulp Cartel)* Joined Cases 89, 104, 114, 116, 117 and 125–129/85 [1993] 4 CMLR 407. In the *Wood Pulp* cases the Commission found more than 40 suppliers of wood pulp in violation of Community competition law despite the fact that none of these companies was resident within the European Community. Fines were imposed on 36 of these companies for violation of art 81(1) EC. A number of the companies appealed against the decision to the ECJ. They challenged the Commission's finding that they breached art 81(1) EC through concertation of prices for their products by means of a system of quarterly price announcements.

The ECJ annulled the decision of the Commission that the undertakings concerned infringed art 81(1) through concertation of prices for their products on the grounds that the Commission had not provided a firm, precise and consistent body of evidence in this respect.

The Commission based its Decision on the economic analysis of the wood pulp market as it was not able to find physical evidence of concertation. The factors that the Commission took into account, *inter alia*, were the system of early announcements of prices which made prices transparent, the uniform fluctuation of prices, and the uniform approach to prices which could be explained in a narrow oligopolistic situation where undertakings had to follow a market leader, but in the present situation there were more than 50 producers of wood pulp and therefore the market was not oligopolistic. The Commission concluded that such uniform market behaviour could be explained only by a concerted practice of the undertakings concerned. The ECJ decided otherwise. The ECJ held that parallel conduct could not be regarded as furnishing proof of concertation unless concertation constituted the only plausible explanation. The ECJ appointed its own experts to analyse the market. Their findings convinced the ECJ that there may be explanations of parallel behaviour other than concertation, such as the natural structure of the market. In the present case the market was cyclical. In respect of transparency of prices, the early announcements were requested by customers (in view of the cyclical nature of the market), since they wanted to know as soon as possible the price for wood pulp. The ECJ held that

'... it must be stated that, in this case, concertation is not the only plausible explanation for the parallel conduct. To begin with, the system of price announcements may be regarded as constituting a rational response to the fact that the pulp market constituted a long-term market and to the need felt by both buyers and sellers to limit commercial risks. Further, the similarity in the dates of price announcements may be regarded as a direct result of the high degree of market transparency, which does not have to be described as artificial. Finally, the parallelism of prices and the price trends may be satisfactorily explained by the oligopolistic tendencies of the market and by the specific circumstances prevailing in certain periods. Accordingly, the parallel conduct established by the Commission does not constitute evidence of concentration.'

The conditions regarding the participation of an undertaking in a concerted practice were examined by the CFI in the so-called 'cartonboard' cases. Under the decision of the Commission of 13 July 1994 in 'cartonboard' 19 suppliers of cartonboard were found in breach of art 81(1) EC as they operated a price-fixing and market-sharing cartel. The decision was challenged by 17 of them, including Sarrio: *Sarrio SA v Commission* Cases

T–339 and 342/94 [1998] ECR II–1727; [1998] 5 CMLR 195. The Commission had found that the undertakings concerned fixed prices for cartonboard through committees set up under the auspices of the Product Group Paperboard (PGP), their trade association. In this respect a number of structures were set up comprising the President's Working Group (PWG) that took general decisions concerning the timing and level of price increases by producers and which submitted reports to the President's Conference (PC), the latter bringing together managing directors and managers of the undertakings twice a year. In 1987 the undertakings set up the Joint Marketing Committee (JMC) which essentially defined the mode of price policy decided by PWG, country-by-country and for the major customers, in order to achieve a system of equivalent prices in Europe. The Commission also discovered that there was a systematic exchange of information between the cartonboard suppliers operated by a secretarial company (Fides) registered in Switzerland which collated all reports on orders, production, sales and capacity utilisations by the undertakings concerned and sent back to them aggregated data. On appeal the undertakings submitted similar arguments, *inter alia*, concerning the proof of their participation in an agreement prohibited under art 81(1) EC. In this respect Sarrio argued that it had not participated in any agreement either to set prices (as it charged different prices for each transaction) or to fix the market shares and outputs of the participants, and that the Commission was wrong in considering that there was one overall infringement and that Sarrio was responsible for it as a whole.

The CFI confirmed the Commission decision. It stated that the cartel had been successful in co-ordinating prices and that, even though there were variations in prices, all prices were based on announced prices and that market shares had been regulated although not absolutely frozen. The CFI rejected the argument that although Sarrio had participated in an agreement which co-ordinated price changes it applied its own prices to each individual transaction. The CFI held that the agreement had impact on transaction prices as it provided the basis for price negotiation in each transaction and that Sarrio infringed art 81(1) EC solely by participating in the agreement. The CFI followed the same line of reasoning, while rejecting Sarrio's argument concerning no implementation of the agreement. The CFI stated that a serious anti-competitive intent is contrary to art 81(1) whether or not the agreement was in fact implemented.

As to the conditions under which an undertaking may be held responsible for an overall cartel, Sarrio argued that it had participated only in some, not all, aspects of the agreement. The CFI held that it was possible for a member of a cartel to be held liable for the overall cartel once it has become aware of the overall plan of the cartel, although its limited participation may constitute a mitigating factor in relation to the fine imposed by the Commission.

The question of collective responsibility attributed to individual undertakings for breach of art 81(1) EC was further explained by the ECJ in *Enichem Anic v Commission* CaseC–49/92P [1999] ECR I–4125. In this case the ECJ emphasised that responsibility for infringements of art 81 EC is personal, taking into account the nature and degree of the ensuing penalties. However, art 81 EC requires that the anti-competitive conduct results from collaboration by several undertakings and therefore each undertaking is a co-perpetrator of the infringement, although it participates in it in different forms depending upon a number of factors, such as its position in the market, the characteristics of the market itself, the objectives pursued and the means of implementation of anti-competitive practices chosen or envisaged by it. Consequently, the ECJ held that

> 'The mere fact that each undertaking takes part in the infringement in ways particular to it does not suffice to exclude its responsibility for the entire infringement, including conduct put into effect by other participating undertakings but sharing the same anti-competitive object or effect.'

The ECJ added that the infringement of art 81 EC may result not only from an isolated act but also from a series of acts or from continuous conduct. In the present case there was continuous conduct on the part of the undertakings concerned and therefore taking into account that the conduct of the undertaking involved was characterised by a single purpose, it would be artificial to notionally separate such continuous conduct into a series of acts which were in themselves in breach of art 81 EC. As a result, there was one infringement which 'progressively manifested itself in both agreements and concerted practices'. For an undertaking to be held liable for the whole infringement, even though it has participated only in some of its aspects, it is necessary to establish that it was aware of the offending conduct of the other participating undertakings or that it could reasonably have foreseen it and that it was ready to take the risk. However, the degree of participation in the infringement should be taken into consideration in the determination of the fine.

In respect of the burden of proof, the ECJ in *Hüls* Case C–199/92P [1999] ECR I–4287 (one of the *PVC Cartel* cases) held that it was the task of the Commission to establish that Hüls participated in the meetings at which price initiatives were decided, organised and monitored, that is that their purpose was contrary to art 81 EC. However, it was incumbent on Hüls to prove that it had not subscribed to those initiatives. Consequently, there was no reversal of the burden of proof. The concept of a concerted practice within the meaning of art 81 EC implies, apart from undertakings' concerting together, conduct on the market pursuant to those collusive practices, and a relationship of cause and effect between the two. This was established by the Commission in the present case. The ECJ held that there is a presumption that 'the undertakings participating in concerting arrangements and remaining active on the market take account of the information exchanged with their competitors when determining their conduct on that market, particularly when they concert together on a regular basis over a long period, as was the case here'. Consequently, it is for the undertaking concerned to prove the contrary. The ECJ emphasised that the principle of the presumption of innocence constitutes one of the fundamental principles of the Community legal order and as such applies to competition procedures. However, in the present case the Commission was not in breach of that principle.

21.3 'Which have as their object or effect'

Article 81 intends to catch all anti-competitive agreements between undertakings that have as their object or effect the prevention, restriction or distortion of competition. There is a very close connection between agreements whose objects or effects are the prevention, restriction or distortion of competititon and their effect on the intra-Community pattern of trade. If an agreement restricts, prevents or distorts competition its effect on intra-Community trade is obvious.

In *Société Technique Minière v Maschinenbau Ulm GmbH* Case 56/65 [1966] ECR 235 the ECJ stated that the terms 'object' and 'effect' are to be read disjointly. As a result, the Commission should, in the first place, establish whether or not an agreement has as its object the restriction of competition. If it has it is in breach of art 81 EC whether or not it produces any anti-competitive effect. Therefore, if the object of an agreement was to impose a ban on exports which *prima facie* restricts competition, it is not required that the Commission establishes that the agreement also has a restrictive effect on competition.[10] If an agreement does not intend to restrict competition, for example a standard distribution agreement, the Commission must assess its effect. However, an economic analysis is only necessary if an agreement has appreciable or potentially appreciable effects on intra-Community competition (see the *de minimus* rule).

There are a number of factors which should be taken into consideration in order to assess the effect of an agreement on the particular market:

1. The parties' combined share of the relevant market.[11] The combined market share may be assessed in percentage terms[12] or on a quantitative basis.[13] However, in *Miller* Case 19/77 [1978] ECR 131 the ECJ considered that an agreement in which the parties' combined share of the relevant market was only an 5 per cent had appreciable effect on intra-Community trade.
2. The type of agreement. Some agreements are capable of having appreciable effect even where the combined market share in not significant. These are mainly agreements which directly or indirectly fix prices, share markets, impose bans on export, or are one of a network of similar agreement which have a cumulative effect on the relevant market.
3. The position and the size of the parties concerned.
4. The nature and the quantity of the products concerned.
5. The number of undertakings competing within the relevant geographical and product market.
6. The general economic and legal context of the agreement.

21.4 Prevention, restriction or distortion of competition

Prevention of competition takes place when competition is partially or wholly precluded. Restriction occurs when existing competition is diminished and distortion occurs in either situation, if competition is restrained, intensified or increased. As Lasok put it:

'All three key words imply a manipulation of the market in a manner which is improper or

---

[10] *Arthur Bell*: OJ L235 (1978).
[11] See the Notices of the Commission on the determination of the relevant product market and geographical market in Chapter 22.
[12] In *Vimpoltu* 90 per cent (OJ L200 (1983)), in *Continental Michelin* 70 per cent: OJ L305 (1989).
[13] *Kawasaki*: OJ L16 (1979).

unlawful. It seems however, that all three could have been adequately represented by one, ie "restraint" on competition ... without adverse effect on the sharpness of the law.'

Indeed, agreements in breach of art 81(1) EC will normally restrict competition. For that reason the three terms in the context of EC competition law refer to the situation in which competition is restricted.

Article 81(1) provides a non-exhaustive list of agreements which will generally fall within the prohibition subject to the *de minimus* rule, subject to exemption and provided they affect intra-Community trade. There will be other agreements not listed which are prohibited because of their particular conditions or restrictions. The list sets out the most common types of anti-competitive agreement.

These are as follows:

Agreements which directly or indirectly fix purchase or selling prices or other trading conditions: art 81(1)(a) EC

Both vertical and horizontal agreements fall within this prohibition.

Price competition is one of the most efficient ways of eliminating competition in a particular product market. Normally, market forces determine the price for a particular product. However, in some circumstances undertakings may decide to interfere with market forces. Agreements which fix purchase or selling prices may do so directly, that is an agreement expressly and directly fixes prices, or indirectly, by providing for discounts, by granting allowances, and by providing for favourable credit terms or the terms of guarantees.

An agreement which intends to fix prices may have as its objective:

Uniformity of prices

Uniformity may be achieved ina number of ways. First, undertakings may decide to fix a common price for their products and revise that price periodically. In *Zinc Cartel* [1985] 2 CMLR 108 producers of zinc decided to fix a common 'producer price' for zinc in order to avoid price fluctuations of zinc on the London Metal Exchange. The members of the cartel sometimes charged different prices and provided for discounts. The Commission decided that this made no difference since the stability of the market price was ensured by the agreement.

Second, art 81(1)(a) EC prohibits the setting of indicative or recommended prices. In *Vereenining van Cementhandelaren* Case 8/72 [1972] ECR 977 the ECJ held that indicative prices set by an association of cement dealers in The Netherlands and applied uniformly to domestic and imported cement were in breach of art 81(1) EC, taking into account that any price fixing, even if the price is only indicative, affects competition by the fact that it permits all participating undertakings to foresee with a reasonable degree of certitude the price policy adopted by their competitors. However, in the context of vertical agreements a recommended price must be binding in order to be in breach of the prohibition of art 81(1) EC. In *Pronuptia* Case 161/84 [1986] ECR 353 the ECJ held that recommended prices within the framework of a distribution franchise agreement would not be unlawful if such recommendations were not binding on the franchisees. Thus, if the franchisee is free to fix his own price despite the franchiser's recommendation, the recommended price would not breach art 81(1) EC.

Third, the exchange of price information may lead to price harmonisation.[14] The Commission considers that the exchange of price information between undertakings is in breach of art 81(1) EC if the information exchanged concerns individual data of an undertaking relating directly to the prices charged or to the elements of a pricing policy, including discounts, costs, terms of trade, rates and dates of change. In *Sarrio* Cases T–339 and 342/92 [1998] ECR II–1727 the CFI provided some clarification of the law relating to the exchange of information between undertakings. The CFI held that the exchange of statistical data is not in itself an infringement of art 81(1). The mere fact that a system for the exchange of statistical information might be used for anti-competitive purposes does not make it contrary to art 81(1) EC, since in such circumstances it is necessary to establish its actual anti-competitive effect. It results from the case law of the ECJ that any scheme for the exchange of general information is permitted if it is carried out in such a manner as to exclude any information from which the behaviour of individual producers can be identified.

Prices may also be fixed indirectly. In *Re IFTRA Rules for Producers of Virgin Aluminium* [1975] 2 CMLR D20 a trade association of European manufacturers of virgin aluminium had adopted a standard contract containing fair trade rules (the IFTRA rules) which were to protect them 'against unfair competition'. Under these rules manufacturers agreed not to sell below their published price and to exchange information on the prices they charged their customers. The Commission considered the rules as an agreement in breach of art 81(1) EC. Even though the prices agreed were never applied, as the excess supply which was at the origin of their adoption had been reduced by an increase in demand, the Commission decided that their existence was sufficient since they were still in force, likely to be used if necessary and constituted a sufficient deterrent to any member of the association to act in a manner contrary to their letter and spirit.

Crystallisation of prices

This refers to the situation where prices are frozen and it occurs when undertakings involved establish the amount or percentage by which prices are to be increased. In *Assurance Incendie*[15] a minimum price was set below which prices were not to be reduced.. In *Hennessy/Henkell* [1981] 1 CMLR 601 the Commission decided that setting minimum and maximum prices was in breach of art 81(1) EC. In this case Hennessy, a French cognac producer, entered into a distributionship agreement with Henkell, a German distributor, under which Henessy controlled the resale price of its cognac in Germany in the following manner. Henkell was obliged to ask for Henessy's consent if it wanted to fix a resale price for cognac above cost plus 17 per cent or below cost plus 12 per cent. In exchange Henessy promised to fix its price giving Henkell a margin of 25 per cent. Henessy's justification based on the protection of the brand image of the product was rejected since in fact the Henessy pricing system was designed to protect its cognac against parallel imports.

---

[14] *Hasselblad*: OJ L161 (1982).
[15] OJ L35 (1985).

Discrimination by price

Price policy may be used by undertakings to maintain price disparities between Member States. This is prima facie in breach of art 81(1) EC and will never be exempted.

In *Pittsbourg Corning Europe* [1973] CMLR D2 a Belgian subsidiary of a US undertaking, which manufactured cellular glass and distributed it in Germany, Belgium and Holland, charged 40 per cent more for its product in Germany than in Belgium and Holland. In order to prevent parallel imports, the manufacturer required that its Belgian and Dutch distributors specify in their order the country of destination of the goods. When this system failed, as the Belgian and Dutch distributors were still selling to Germany, the prices for Belgium and The Netherlands were increased but subject to reduction if it could be demonstrated that the country of final destination was Belgium or The Netherlands.

Other trading conditions

The expression 'other trading conditions' refer to agreements which *per se* restrict access to the market, in particular exclusive and selective distribution and franchising agreements. These agreements are not prohibited under art 81(1) EC, although certain requirements imposed by them on the part of persons supplied are considered as being in breach of art 81(1)(a): see section 21.5.

Restrictions on trading conditions which are prohibited include export/import bans,[16] whether or not applied in practice (*Parker Pen* Case 77/92 [1994] ECR II–549), and other export/import deterrents and inducements. The Commission will always impose heavy penalties on an undertaking which imposes an export ban. *Miller International* v *Commission* Case 19/77 [1978] ECR 131 concerned Milller, a German subsidiary of an American undertaking, which produced cheap records and tapes and specialised in 'bargain offers'. This subsidiary imposed an export ban on its French distributors in order to prevent parallel imports to Germany where prices were higher. Miller was heavily fined, notwithstanding the fact that it had only 2.5 per cent of the total German record market, the ECJ taking into account the potential effect on intra-Community trade and the fact that if the effect had not been appreciable the imposition of a ban on its distributors would not have been necessary.

In general export bans are not capable of exemption, although in a case relating to intellectual property rights even an agreement ensuring absolute territorial protection was considered by the ECJ as not infringing art 81(1) EC: *Erauw-Jacquéry* v *La Hesbignonne* Case 27/87 [1988] 4 CMLR 576.

A prohibition imposed on distributors from one Member State against selling their products in another Member State without manufacturer/supplier consent has been condemned by the Community institutions.[17] Similarly, a prohibition imposed on distributors against selling to customers likely to engage in parallel import[18] was regarded as breaching art 81(1) EC.

---

[16] There are many examples: *Tepea* Case 28/77 [1978] ECR 1391; *Van Megen Sports Group* Case 49/95 [1996] ECR II–1799; *Adalat*: OJ L201 (1996).

[17] *Gerofabrick*: OJ L16 (1977); *Windsurfing International*: OJ L229 (1983); *Vico-Toshiba*: OJ L287 (1991); *Eco System*: OJ L66 (1992).

[18] *Tipp-Ex*: OJ L222 (1987).

Export deterrents and export boosters are both in breach of the art 81(1) prohibitions. In *Cimbel* [1973] CMLR D167 Belgian cement producers decided to collectively subsidise export by equalising receipts from domestic sales and from exports. The Commission decided that this arrangement artificially reinforced the competitive position of the participating undertakings in export markets, taking into account that undertakings in other Member States had to compete with all the members of Cimbel and not with each Belgian undertaking separately.

Agreements which control production, markets, technical developments or investments: art 81(1)(b) EC

These are normally horizontal agreements which will breach art 81(1)(b) EC. However, in some circumstances they may qualify for exemption.

Agreements which control production

This prohibition concerns agreements which are designed to reduce actual and potential production. Any agreement that intends to control production is anti-competitive, largely because such an agreement would lead to the elimination of small and medium-sized undertakings and the monopolisation of a particular market to the detriment of consumers. When there is a considerable over-capacity in an industry undertakings are tempted to enter into agreements limiting their production. The economic and social consequences of major recession in demand in certain industries have changed the approach of the Community institutions to agreements between undertakings aimed at limiting their production. In the Twelfth Annual Report the Commission provided its view on the reconstruction of industries in crisis. In certain circumstances the Commission is prepared to accept such agreements if it is shown that a structural over-capacity has affected all the undertakings concerned over a prolonged period of time and resulted in a significant reduction in their rate of capacity utilisation leading to a drop in output accompanied by substantial operating losses, and that there is no expectation of lasting improvement in the medium term. The Commission will grant exemption for such agreements provided that the reduction in over-capacity is permanent and irreversible and of an amount which will enable the existing undertakings in the industry to compete at the lower level of capacity. The reduction must facilitate specialisation by the undertaking concerned, and the timetable for the reduction in capacity must minimise the social consequences of that reduction, for example, the resulting unemployment.[19]

Agreements which control technical developments or investments

These agreements may qualify for exemption provided that the restrictions which they impose are ancillary to some desirable pro-competitive objectives which they intend to achieve. Such agreements are encouraged by the Commission when made between small and medium-sized undertakings.

---

[19] See *Synthetic Fibres* [1985] 1 CMLR 787.

The topic of agreements that control markets overlaps with the topic next examined and is therefore dealt with below.

Agreements to share markets or sources of supply: art 81(1)(c) EC

The main objective of this prohibition is to avoid the partition of the common market along the lines of national territories. It concerns both horizontal and vertical agreements.

One of the best examples of an agreement designed to share the market and the sources of supply was provided in the quinine cartel: *Boehringer Mannheim v Commission* Case 45/69 [1970] ECR 769. Quinine is mainly used for making medicines to treat malaria but is also used in synthetic quinidine, which is an ingredient in other pharmaceuticals. In 1958 undertakings from France, Germany and The Netherlands selling quinine decided to form a cartel in order to stabilise the quinine market which (due to the sale of surpluses of quinine by the government of the US and to new sources of supply established in Congo and Indonesia) was falling dramatically. Undertakings involved fixed prices for the bark, from which both quinine and synthetic quinidine are made, allocated purchases of the stock which was disposed of by the US government, allocated national markets to individual members of the cartel, allocated export markets outside the EC to the undertakings involved and decided in which markets its undertakings were allowed to compete whilst allocating to them quotas in relation to these markets. The agreement was concluded for a period of five years. In order to supervise its implementation, each party had to notify others of its quarterly sales and prices. Also compensatory sales were organised for undertakings unable to reach their export sales quotas. This agreement was completed by other 'gentlemen's agreements', some of them in writing, some oral. With the entry into force of the Treaty of Rome, the participating undertakings decided not to notify their agreements to the Commission. When investigated by the German Bundeskartellamt the undertakings concerned concluded a new agreement which fixed prices, allocated quotas and markets outside the EC. However, it was completed by a gentleman's agreement extending it to the EC countries. The Commission imposed fines upon the participating undertakings and the ECJ confirmed the Commission's decision but reduced the fines.

In respect of vertical agreements the most obvious example of agreements contravening art 81(1)(c) are exclusive distributorship agreements and exclusive purchasing agreements. In *Consten and Grundig* Cases 56 and 58/64 [1966] ECR 299; [1966] CMLR 418 the ECJ held that an exclusive distributorship agreement intended to isolate the French market for Grundig products and therefore partition the common market along national lines which in itself distorted competition in the common market.

However, as the ECJ decided in *Société Technique Minière v Maschinenbau* Case 56/65 [1971] ECR 235, not all exclusive distribution agreements are within the scope of art 81(1). In this case Société Technique Minière (STM), a French undertaking suppling equipment for public works, and Maschinenbau, a German producer of heavy grading machinery, entered into an exclusive distribution agreement under which Maschinenbau agreed not to supply to any other distributor in France and not to sell there itself any large earth levellers of the type dealt in by STM. STM agreed to buy a large number of them over a period of two years but could not then find a sufficient number of purchasers for them. When

Maschinenbau did not receive payment it sued SMT in France. SMT argued that the agreement, or at least some clauses in it was in breach of art 81(1) EC.

The ECJ held that exclusivity was essential to the setting up of a distribution system in the context of the high commercial risks taken by SMT when entering into the agreement as the product was highly specialised and expensive. The ECJ laid down a number of factors which should be taken into consideration in assessing whether or not an exclusive distribution agreement is within the scope of art 81(1) EC. They are:

1. the nature of the product and its volume, that is whether the supply was limited or unlimited in amount;
2. the importance of both the supplier and the distributor in the relevant market;
3. whether the agreement was one, or a part of a network of agreements, covering at least a substantial area or region of a Member State;
4. the degree of territorial protection afforded by the agreement, in particular whether it provides for absolute territorial protection and whether it allows parallel imports.

Provided the above factors are satisfied and an agreement neither affects intra-Community trade nor has as its object and effect the restriction of competition, it will fall outside the art 81(1) prohibition.

As to exclusive purchasing agreements, these in many ways closely resemble exclusive distribution agreements. Under exclusive distribution agreements the distributor is normally required to purchase goods from the manufacturer. Both parties potentially benefit from that arrangement. The manufacturer is able to calculate the demand for his product for the duration of the agreement, and adjust his production accordingly, and the distributor, in exchange for his commitment, receives more advantageous prices, technical assistance, preference in supply, etc. In dealing with exclusive purchasing agreements the Commission takes into consideration whether or not the purchaser is given an exclusive territory (see art 1 of Regulation 1984/83). If so, the agreement will fall within the scope of art 81(1) EC. In *Brasserie de Haecht* v *Wilkin-Janssens (No 1)* Case 23/67 [1967] ECR 407 the proprietors of a café in Esneux, Belgium, promised in exchange for a loan made by a brewery in Belgium to buy all their requirements for beer, lemonade and other drinks from the brewery for the duration of the loan and two further years. When the proprietors were sued by the brewery for breach of the contract they argued that the agreement infringed art 81(1) EC as it restricted trade between Member States by limiting the outlets in Belgium for breweries from other Member States. The ECJ held that the agreement should be assessed in its economic and legal context, in particular whether there was only one agreement or whether the agreement was a part of a network of similar agreements. If it was a separate agreement its effect on intra-Community trade was insignificant. However, if it formed part of a network of agreements its overall impact might result in making it difficult or even impossible for new undertakings to enter the market through the opening of new outlets. Therefore, exclusive purchasing agreements will not fall within the scope of art 81(1) if the dealer is not given an exclusive territory and provided they do not have a 'blocking' effect on potential new competitors: *Delimitis* v *Henninger Bräu* Case C–234/89 [1992] 5 CMLR 210.

Agreements which apply dissimilar conditions to equivalent transactions with other trading parties, thereby placing them at a competitive disadvantage: art 81(1)(d) EC

Article 81(1)(d) imposes an obligation on a manufacturer/producer to treat all his customers equally, that is to apply the same conditions to equivalent transactions. The principle of non-discrimination is at the centre of this provision. However, the prohibition of discrimination is neither absolute nor general. Some agreements in breach of the principle of non-discrimination may be capable of exemption if the difference in treatment is objectively justified: *Metro* Case 26/76 [1977] ECR 1875. For example 'quantity' discounts (discounts for bulk purchase) are allowed if they represent a genuine cost saving but not if they are 'fidelity' discounts and therefore based on the volume of transactions.

In this respect, the Commission applied art 81(1)(d) EC for the first time in the *German Ceramic Tiles Case* [1971] CMLR D6 in which a large number of German producers of ceramic tiles agreed through their trade association to grant buyers quantity discounts calculated on the basis of the total quantities purchased during the year from all German producers. This clause in itself was not unlawful but it was accompanied by two additional clauses which were in breach of art 81(1) EC. The first provided that only German undertakings were allowed to belong to the trade associations. The second provided that the rate of discount depended upon the quantity bought. As a result the clause encouraged German undertakings to buy more from German producers in order to obtain a better rate of discount. Furthermore, the buyers did not, for the duration of the year, know whether or not they had bought enough to qualify for a better discount rate and were thus deterred from buying in other Member States. In *JAZ International Belgium* Case 96/82 [1983] ECR 3369 the requirements imposed by a Belgian trade association that only washing-machines and dryers which had a certificate of conformity with Belgian standards could be installed in Belgium was found to be discriminatory since, first, membership of the association was restricted to manufacturers of such machines and sole importers of foreign manufactured machines (thereby excluding parallel importers) and, second, it was easy for its members to obtain certificates of conformity while non-members had to ask for an individual certificate of conformity for each machine concerned. In addition only the trade association was entitled to deliver certificates of conformity!

Agreements which make conclusion of contracts subject to acceptance by other parties of supplementary obligations which, by their nature and/or according to commercial usage, have no connection with the subject-matter of such contracts: art 81(1)(e) EC

This prohibition concerns tying agreements whereby the acceptance of an obligation not relating to the substance of the agreement is a pre-condition to its conclusion. This situation arises most often in the context of undertakings in a dominant position (art 82 EC), although it also occurs in the context of art 81(1) EC. For example, in *IFTRA Rules of European Manufacturers of Glass Containers* [1974] 2 CMLR D50 the members of a trade association of glass container manufacturers were obliged by the rules of the association, *inter alia*, to supply glass containers on a delivered basis and thus their customers could not save costs by organising their own transport.

In *Vaessen/Morris* [1979] 1 CMLR 511 the Commission condemned a clause which required a licensee to buy from the patentee not only a patented device for packing sausage meat into a casting to create *saucissons de Boulogne* but also the casting itself. Such clauses will always be in breach of art 81(1) EC and will require individual exemption under art 81(3) EC.

21.5 Attenuation of the effect of the art 81(1) EC prohibition

For any system to work properly it is necessary to distinguish what might be preferable in an ideal setting and what is possible in real life. Indeed, the literal interpretation of art 81(1) EC would result in extending its scope of application to such a point that almost all transactions with a European dimension will be unlawful. Thus, in order to take account of the complexity of the market arrangements the EC mechanism for correcting market distortions provides for exceptions which may be made to a general prohibition laid down in art 81(1) EC. These are of three kinds: permissible forms of co-operation between undertakings; the 'rule of reason'; and the system of exemption provided for in art 81(3) EC.

However, the approach to art 81(3) EC should by viewed in the light of the proposed reform of competition policy.[20] In May 1999 the Commission published a White Paper which proposes a profound reform of the rules implementing arts 81 and 82 EC. The Commission explains that there in a need for the modernisation of EC Competition law taking into account the globalisation of the economy, the enlargement of the European Union and the existence of a single market and single currency. Also, the Commission notes that some economic operators may take a protectionist attitude to mitigate the effects of price transparency and compensate for their lack of competitiveness.

The major change concerns the greater involvement of national authorities and courts in the enforcement of competition law. The Commission believes that EC competition law and policy has now been well established and thus the burden of enforcement may be shared with the national authorities and courts. The redistribution of resources between them will permit the Commission to concentrate on the most serious infringements of EC law. The main features of the proposed reform are:

1. The abolition of the current system of notification and authorisation. Undertakings would be able to obtain immediate enforcement of their agreements by national courts which, on the basis of the existing case law, would determine whether or not these agreements are in conformity with EC competition rules. As a result national courts and competition authorities would be entitled to grant individual exemption under art 81(3) and thus the entirety of art 81 would be directly applicable in national courts. Also national authorities may be allowed to withdraw the benefit of a block exemption in their territory if that territory, or part of it, constitutes a separate market. Undertakings

---

[20] Modernisation of the Rules Implementing arts 85 and 86 of the Treaty of Rome (arts 81 and 82 EC) (OJ C132 (1999)): the Commission's White Paper on the reform of the EC competition rules. The target date for the implementation of the reform in 2002.

may no longer be able to obtain immunity from fines through notification since the latter would be abolished. However, fines could be imposed for failure to comply with procedural requirements and also for proven infringements.

2. The extension *rationae materiae* of the scope of block exemption regulations so that the compatibility or otherwise of the vast majority of agreements with EC law would be easy to assess. In relation to art 81(1) and (3) EC the Commission would issue guidelines and notices as to their scope of application.

3. The presumption that a restrictive agreement is contrary to art 81(1) would be removed.

4. Small and medium-sized undertakings would largely be excluded from the scope of art 81(1).

5. New mechanisms would be set up to increase co-operation between the Commission and national authorities and national courts.

6. The Commission would supervise the system and would intervene whenever necessary to ensure that EC competition law is applied consistently and uniformly in the Member States. It would also initiate legislation in this area as well as draw up more notices and guidelines to assist national authorities in the application of EC competition rules and policies. The Commission's investigatory powers would be increased, especially to obtain information from undertakings under investigation.

Some elements of the reform, such as new competition rules for the distribution sector, have already been implemented (see below).

Permissible forms of co-operation

In order to reduce the administrative burden imposed on the Commission in dealing with applications for individual exemption the Commission has decided that certain categories of agreements should, in principle, be considered as being outside the scope of art 81(1) EC. The Commission has issued a number of notices, each providing a list of agreements deemed to fall outside the prohibition in art 81(1)EC. Although Commission notices have no binding force they provide an interesting insight into its approach to art 81(1) EC.

The first Communication adopted on 24 December 1962 concerned exclusive agency agreements.[21] According to the Commission, in a genuine exclusive agency agreement the agent is merely an auxiliary organ and as such forms an integral part of the principal's undertaking. However, the Commission will not rely on the legal classification made by the parties to the agreement. The Commission will determine the true relationship between the parties in the light of the factual situation. The key element in determining the true relationship between the parties is whether an agent accepts personal financial risks when acting for his principal. If so, he acts as an independent undertaking and his agreement is within the scope of art 81(1) EC.

The second Communication from the Commission adopted on 29 July 1968 concerned agreements, decisions and concerted practices in the field of co-operation agreements between undertakings.[22] The main objective of the notice is to exclude from the scope of art

---

[21] OJ C139 (1962).
[22] OJ C75 (1968), rect OJ C84 (1968).

81(1) EC co-operation agreements between small and medium-sized undertakings. In the framework of this book it is impossible to examine the Commission notices in details. So far the Commission has issued notices, *inter alia*, on agreements of minor importance, on sub-contracting agreements, on co-operative joint-ventures, etc.

The rule of reason

United States' anti-trust law and EC competition law have a lot in common. According to Morton, apart from the different objectives underlying competition policies in the USA and the EC the substantive provisions are very similar. For example, the approach to anti-competitive agreements under art 81 EC is parallel to that of s1 of the Sherman Act; art 82 EC is similar to s2 of the Sherman Act; and EC Merger Regulation 4064/89 is similar to the Hart-Scott-Rodino Act. Furthermore, EC competition law has endorsed, more or less, the American 'effect doctrine' while the US anti-trust system has become more sensitive to social policy and environmental issues. Whatever the difference between the two systems they are inspired by liberal considerations and aim at preventing undertakings from monopolising the market by entering into agreements that restrict or distort competition or from abusing their dominant position in the relevant market, or from forming mergers which substantially restrain competition.[23]

Therefore, it is not surprising that the 'rule of reason' which applies in the context of s1 of the Sherman Act has found its uses in the context of art 81 EC, albeit, as any mutation, it has developed its own features. Indeed, the US rule of reason is very different from its European counterpart. Under s1 of the Sherman Act there is no possibility of exemption – all agreements, combinations and conspiracies in restraint of trade are prohibited. This excessive rigidity had to be attenuated. The rule of reason has become the main tool for adjusting s1 of the Sherman Act to changing economic conditions. Its content has evolved according to economic reality. Under the rule of reason US courts are required to consider the overall impact of the agreement on competition within the relevant market. In order to do so, they have to identify and weigh the anti-competitive and pro-competitive effects it produces. If pro-competitive effects prevail the agreement is regarded not to be restrictive of competition. As a result, economic analysis is required in each case. As Goyder stated the US rule of reason is more relevant to art 81(3) than to art 81(1) and thus the difference between the two systems is profound since:

> 'The United States Courts may take into account all the positive and negative features of the restraint, as well as the context in which it is applied, remaining as free from statutory restriction as the courts of common law in assessing the local validity of contractual restraints between vendor and purchaser or employer and employee. By comparison, the Commission must operate within a rigid conceptual framework which allows less freedom of manoeuvre and requires the restriction to pass, not one single balancing test, but a cumulative series of four separate tests' (see art 81(3) EC).[24]

Taking into account the differences between the US rule of reason and the EC approach,

[23] For comparison between EC competition law and US anti-trust law: see S Morton, *Competitive Strategy*, http://www. antitrust.org/law/foreign.htlm, pp1–5.
[24] D G Goyder, *EC Competition Law*, 3rd ed, Oxford: Oxford University Press, 1998, p145.

some authors deny the rule's existence under EC competition law, whilst others find numerous examples of its application. Whatever the answer one thing is certain – the Community institutions have decided to limit the scope of application of art 81(1) EC. This was their response, especially that of the ECJ, to the argument that art 81 EC was too strictly interpreted and as result many agreements when assessed in the strict context of art 81(1) EC would be found to be ant-competitive whilst their assessment on the basis of an economic analysis would show that they did not have any serious restrictive effect on competition. In *Société Technique Minière* v *Machnenbau* Case 56/65 [1966] ECR 235 the ECJ relaxed its rigorous interpretation of art 81(1) EC and applied a more flexible approach, taking into account the economic context of the agreement at issue. In this respect the ECJ held that:

> 'The competition in question must be understood within the actual context in which it would occur in the absence of the agreement in dispute. In particular it may be doubted whether there is an interference with competition if the said agreement seems really necessary for the penetration of a new area by an undertaking.'

Thus, even an agreement which provides for absolute territorial protection is exempted from the scope of art 81(1) EC if such a clause is necessary from an economic point of view. This was confirmed in *Nungesser* v *Commission* Case 262/81 [1982] ECR 2105 in which it was held that an 'open', exclusive licensing agreement (that is, it does not affect the position of third parties such as parallel importers or licensees for other territories) for the exploitation of plant breeders' rights did not infringe art 81(1) EC as the clause granting absolute territorial protection was necessary in view of the considerable financial risk which the licensee was taking in cultivating and marketing a new product.

In contrast, in *Consten and Grundig* Cases 56 and 58/64 [1966] ECR 299; [1966] CMLR 418, the clause ensuring absolute territorial protection for Consten was aimed at isolating the French market. For that reason, without examining other factors (ie economic data, the correctness of criteria which the Commission had applied in order to compare the French market with the German market, etc) the ECJ held that the agreement was in breach of art 81(1) EC and upheld the Commission's position.

The case law indicates that the ECJ has applied the theory of ancillary restraint which is akin to the US rule of reason. It distinguishes between 'naked' and 'ancillary' restraint. Naked restraints are always unlawful, that is, fixing prices by means of a cartel (although prices may not be unreasonable) but ancillary restraint may be justified. In *US* v *Addyston Pipe and Steel*[25] Judge Taft described ancillary restraint as necessary to some transactions in order to make them viable. Ancillary restraints which would be unlawful if standing alone become acceptable if used to support pro-competitive transactions. The example given by Judge Taft concerned non-competition clauses normally contained in a business sale agreement and in particular an agreement in respect of partners who retired.[26] The ECJ adopted very similar reasoning in relation to horizontal agreements.

---

[25] See V Korah, *EEC Competition Law and Practice*, 4th ed, Oxford: OUP, 1990, pp119–120.

[26] 'Permitting sales of goodwill may be pro-competitive. It encourages the proprietor of the business to build up goodwill to sell later, and enables him to move on or retire and a younger man to take over. No one would pay for goodwill if next day the former proprietor could legally canvass his former customers': V Korah, *EEC Competition Law*, 4th ed, Oxford, 1990, p120. A similar approach was applied by the ECJ in *Remia BV* v *Commission* Case 42/84 [1985] ECR 2545.

Vertical agreements often impose certain requirements on distributors concerning the suitability of premises, the establishment of pre-sales advice services, after-sales services, the promotion of the product, adequacy of staff, financial stability, etc. The question whether these requirements are justified under art 81(1) EC was examined by the ECJ in *Metro v Saba (No 1)* Case 26/76 [1977] ECR 1875. Saba, a producer of electric and electronic equipment, refused access to its selective distribution network in Germany to Metro. Outside Germany the products were sold directly to a sole distributor dealing exclusively with approved specialist dealers who were serving the public. The German selective distribution system was open to wholesalers who were reselling goods purchased from Saba to approved specialist dealers, whose turnover had to be obtained from the sale of electric and electronic products. Metro, as a cash-and-carry self-service wholesaler established in Germany served retailers and the public. This was the main reason for Saba's refusal, although Metro did not fulfil other Saba requirements in that neither its trading premises nor its turnover nor the technical qualifications of its staff were appropriate to handle highly sophisticated electronic goods. Metro complained to the Commission which decided that in general the Saba system of selective distribution did not breach art 81(1) EC. Saba was entitled to prohibit direct supplies by wholesalers or sole distributors to consumers, although particular clauses – for example, prohibiting its wholesalers, sole distributors and specialised dealers from exporting to other EC countries or prohibiting 'cross-supplies' (wholesaler to wholesaler or retailer to retailer) – were condemned. Metro sought to annul the decision. The ECJ stated that a selective distribution system such as put in place by Saba is justified in so far as resellers are selected 'on the basis of objective criteria of a qualitative nature relating to the technical qualifications of the reseller and his staff and the suitability of his trading premises and that such conditions are laid down uniformly for all potential resellers and are not applied in a discriminatory fashion.' Therefore the reduction of price competition in favour of competition relating to factors other than price is allowed, provided: the supplier does not enjoy a dominant position in the relevant product market, that is, distributors are able to obtain supplies from other sources; the supplier's selective distribution system is not discriminatory, ie it is open to all undertakings; conditions are laid down uniformly for all potential dealers; and the distribution system intends to achieve a legitimate objective of improving competition in relation to factors other than price: *AEG Telefunken* Case 107/82 [1983] ECR 3151.

However, in the above case the ECJ disagreed with the Commission as to a number of the restrictions (for example, relating to the obligation on wholesalers to supply only appointed resellers). The ECJ found that they were legitimate requirements inherent to exclusive distribution agreements. The ECJ made it clear that 'qualitative criteria' should not go beyond what is necessary to maintain the quality of the goods or to ensure they are sold under proper conditions. What is necessary depends on the nature of the product. In *Vichy* Case T–19/91 [1992] ECR II–415 the requirement that in respect of all EC countries but France its cosmetics should be sold in retail pharmacies in which a qualified pharmacist was present was considered as being disproportionate, taking into account that the objectives which Vichy wanted to achieve outside France, that is, improving the quality both of its product and the service, as well as enhanced competition with other cosmetic manufacturers, could be achieved by less restrictive measures. Similarly, in *Re Ideal-*

Standard Agreement [1988] 4 CMLR 627 the requirements imposed on wholesalers that they specialised in the sale of plumbing fittings and sanitary wear, and have a specialised department for their sale, was considered as unjustified on the ground of the nature of the product, that is, plumbing fittings devices were not sufficiently technically advanced. In *L'Oréal* Case 31/80 [1980] ECR 3775 the requirement that the distributor should guarantee a minimum turnover was considered to be excessive.

In the context of franchise agreements the assessment of 'quantitative criteria' was examined by the ECJ in *Pronuptia* Case 161/84 [1986] ECR 353. Pronuptia de Paris, specialising in selling wedding dresses and other wedding accessories, entered into a franchise agreement with Mrs Schillgalis. In exchange for the exclusive right to use the trade mark 'Pronuptia de Paris' in three areas in Germany – Hamburg, Oldenburg and Hanover – Mrs Schillgalis was required to purchase 80 per cent of dresses intended to be sold by her directly from Pronuptia and a certain percentage of other dresses from the franchisor or from suppliers approved by the franchisor, to make the sale of wedding dresses her main business activity, to advertise in a manner approved by the franchisor, to sell in shops decorated and equipped according to the franchisor's requirements, to fix prices according to recommendations of the franchisor (although Mrs Schillgalis was free to fix her own prices), to pay 'entry' fees of DM 15,000 for the know-how and thereafter a royalty of 10 per cent on the initial sales of Pronuptia products, to refrain from transferring her shop to another location without the approval of the franchisor, and to refrain both during the agreement and for one year afterwards from competing in whatever way with Pronuptia outside her own territory. In return Pronuptia promised to refrain from opening any other Pronuptia shop in the territory covered by the agreement and to offer its assistance in all aspects of business from staff training to marketing.

When Pronuptia sued Mrs Schillgalis for non-payment of royalties, she argued that the agreement was void as contrary to art 81(1) EC. The German Supreme Court referred to the ECJ a preliminary question concerning the application of art 81 EC to franchise agreements.

The ECJ held that restrictions imposed by the franchisor are outside the scope of art 81(1) EC in two circumstances. First, it stated that the legitimate interests of the franchisor should be protected under Community law. The reason for this being that the franchisor should be protected from a risk that its know-how and assistance provided by it to the franchisees would be used to benefit its competitors. As a result, a clause preventing the franchisee, during and after termination of the agreement, from opening a shop in another territory selling the same or similar items and the requirement for franchisor approval of a proposed transfer of the shop to another party were not in breach of art 81(1) EC. Second, the Court said the franchisor is entitled to protect the reputation and the identity of its network and therefore to retain some measure of control in this respect. In particular, the requirements concerning the location of the shop, the lay out and decoration of the shop, the percentage and sources of supplies were legitimate. In respect of the price recommendations they were not in breach of art 81(1) EC if the franchisee was able to fix her own prices and thus there was not a concerted practice between the parties on prices. However, the clause restricting the franchisee from opening a second shop within her exclusive territory without the consent of the franchisor was in breach of art 81(1) EC, taking into account that it might lead to the division of a Member State's territory into a number of closed territories. In addition, this restriction would prevent the franchisee from benefiting from her investment, considering that

> '... a prospective franchisee would not take the risk of becoming part of the chain, investing its own money, paying a relatively high entry fee and undertaking to pay a substantial annual royalty, unless he could hope, thanks to a degree of protection against competition on the part of the franchisor and other franchisees, that his business would be profitable.'

Consequently, such a clause should be considered on an individual application for exemption under art 81(3) EC. In the case of Pronuptia this was granted by the Commission.

The Community institutions have taken a liberal approach to restrictions imposed by franchise distribution agreements considering their overall beneficial effect on trade and the advantages they offer to both the franchiser and the franchisee. Even a clause condemned in *Consten and Grunding* ensuring absolute territorial protection may fall outside the art 81(1) EC prohibition if it is considered as necessary to induce the franchisee to enter into the agreement.[27] The ECJ emphasised that for the purposes of art 81(1) EC a particular clause must be assessed in the light of the overall agreement and its economic context.

The Commission and Community judicature has limited the scope of art 81(1) EC in the context of vertical agreements, that is, distribution agreements,[28] franchising agreements[29] and exclusive purchasing agreements: *Delimitis* v *Henninger Bräu* Case C–234/89 [1992] 5 CMLR 210. The obvious explanation is that the limits of art 81(1) EC change according to the objectives of EC competition policy. The restrictive approach was necessary in the first stage of development of the EC. With time, the objective of the creation of the common market dictated a different approach which was more liberal but nevertheless ensured the integration of national economies of Member States into one common market. Now, the common market has achieved a certain degree of maturity and thus further relaxation of competition rules is advisable. This consideration can be seen in the Commission's *Green Paper on Vertical Restraints in Competition Policy*.[30] The Commission considers that agreements between producers and distributors can be used pro-competitively and anti-competitively and for that reason the scope of block exemptions should be increased while the current system should be maintained. The Green Paper emphasises that 'absolute territorial protection ... which may affect trade between Member States will not only continue to fall *per se* within art 85(1) [art 81(1)] but [is] unlikely to be exempted.' Furthermore, the Commission has drafted a proposal concerning the treatment of common ancillary restraints. In respect of purchase and supply agreements the Commission states that it will favour agreements for fixed quantities over agreements where there are no quantitative limitations in so far as there is no provision for exclusivity. In the latter case the duration must be strictly limited. Agreements for supply which favour the vendor will still require careful justification by the parties. In the context of intermediate products,

---

[27] See the Commission decision in *Computerland Europe SA* [1989] 4 CMLR 259.

[28] The principle of *Metro* v *Saba* has been applied to technically complex products: *Kodak* (OJ L147 (1970)); *IBM Personal Computers* (OJ L118 (1984)); product where the brand image is important: *Villeroy Boch* (OJ L376 (1985)), *MURAT* (OJ L348 (1983)).

[29] *Computerland* (see note 27); *Charles Jourdan*: OJ L35 (1989).

[30] COM(96)721 final, 22 January 1997.

supply arrangements for three years will generally be acceptable. Five years will have to be justified by specific market conditions, for example, limited sources of supply. Other arrangements, such as outsourcing or distribution agreements will be treated similarly.

21.6 Exemptions

Exemptions to the prohibition of art 81(1) EC may be granted under the conditions laid down in art 81(3). This article imposes four criteria which must be satisfied before exemption can be granted. Any agreement, decision or concerted practice may qualify for exemption provided the benefits from it outweigh the disadvantages resulting from the restriction that it imposes on competition,[31] and provided it fulfils two positive and two negative criteria.

The positive criteria are:

1. it must contribute to improving the production or distribution of goods or the promotion of technical or economic progress; and
2. it must allow consumers a fair share of the resulting benefit.

The negative criteria are:

1. it must not impose on the undertakings concerned restrictions which are not indispensable to the attainment of these objectives; and
2. it must not afford such undertakings the possibility of eliminating competition in respect of a substantial proportion of the products in question.

However, art 81 EC does not specify the body which is empowered to grant or refuse exemption. This task has been assigned to the Commission under art 9 of Council Regulation 17/62.[32] It was decided that the exclusive competence of the Commission to grant individual exemptions would ensure uniformity in the application and interpretation of art 81 EC. Soon after Regulation 17/62 was adopted the Commission received about 30,000 notifications of exclusive distribution agreements alone. In order to ease its workload the Council, under Regulation 19/65, empowered the Commission to adopt regulations exempting classes of agreements, namely exclusive distribution and purchasing agreements and agreements licensing intellectual property rights, so long as they conform with the exemption regulations. The first regulation adopted by the Commission under the said powers concerned exclusive distribution agreements and was embodied in Regulation 67/67. Therefore, the first stage for undertakings seeking to clarify whether their agreement may qualify for exemption is to determine whether it escapes the application of art 81(1) EC by virtue of block exemption. If this is not the case, or if there is any doubt as to its exemption, an undertaking is advised to notify its agreement to the Commission which will by applying the criteria laid down in art 81(3) EC, on an individual basis, decide whether to grant or to deny exemption.

---

[31] *Consten and Grundig* Cases 56 and 58/64 [1966] ECR 299; [1966] CMLR 418.
[32] OJ (1962).

As can be seen, exemptions from the application of art 81(1) by virtue of art 81(3) may be either on an individual basis or by block exemption.

Block exemptions

Each block exemption is contained in a regulation and EC regulations in competition matters are no different from those covering other areas of EC law. They are legally binding. The regulation containing a block exemption sets out restrictions both those which are permitted in the area under consideration, the 'whitelist', and those which are prohibited, the 'blacklist'. Sometimes, a regulation may contain a provision for opposition. This means that when a type of restriction is contained neither in the blacklist nor in the whitelist (that is, it is on the so-called 'greylist') the parties to an agreement must notify it to the Commission which has six months in which to oppose the clause. If there is no response from the Commission the clause is deemed lawful; if opposition is raised, the agreement will be treated as if application had been submitted for an individual exemption.

If an agreement strictly complies with every condition and term of the block exemption it enjoys the same protection as is afforded to an agreement exempted on an individual basis. When parties to an agreement decide to tailor it in terms similar to those of the relevant block exemption it is not necessary for them to quote it verbatim but they must ensure that the envisaged agreement does not contain any restriction not permitted by the block exemption, otherwise they have to notify it to the Commission. The ECJ has restrictively interpreted block exemptions.[33] Any doubt as to the legality of any additional restriction will be decided to the detriment of the parties.

Apart from easing the workload of the Commission, block exemptions offer an important benefit to undertakings. There is no need to notify to the Commission an agreement conforming to the terms of a block exemption regulation. Thus, parties avoid the delays and uncertainty of the procedure for individual exemption.

The number of regulations adopted either by the Council, or by the Commission under delegated authority from the Council, providing for block exemptions has considerably increased over the years. Also, as already mentioned the approach to block exemptions has undergone profound changes. Following the Commission *Green Paper on Vertical Restraints in Competition Policy*[34] the first piece of legislation reforming EC competition law materialised in the new block exemption on vertical agreements which entered into force on 1 June 2000. This replaced the former regulation on the block exemptions for exclusive distribution, exclusive purchasing and franchise agreements. The replacement regulation contains only a blacklist as opposed to the previous regulation which sets out a whitelist of permitted restrictions and a blacklist of prohibited restrictions. Under the new regulation the blacklisted restrictions are as follows:

1. Resale price maintenance, except maximum resale prices or recommended resale prices provided that they do not, in practice, amount to fixed, or minimum, resale prices.

---

[33] See *Delimitis* Case C–234/89 [1992] 5 CMLR 210, in which a single clause which was not set out in the whitelist, although it was not on the blacklist, was held by the ECJ as depriving the agreement of the benefit of the block exemption.

[34] COM(96)721 final, 22 January 1997.

2. Restrictions on resales apart from:

   a) active resales into an exclusive territory which are allocated by the supplier to another buyer;
   b) resales to unauthorised distributors by members of a selective distribution scheme; and
   c) resales of goods or services which are supplied for the purpose of incorporation into other products.

3. The prevention or restriction of active or passive sales to users by members of a selective distribution scheme.

4. The prevention or restriction of cross-supplies between distributors within a selective distribution scheme.

5. Restrictions, agreed between the supplier of spare parts and a buyer who incorporates and resells them, on sales of spare parts to independent repairers and service providers.

6. Any direct or indirect obligation imposed on members of a selective distribution scheme to sell or not to sell 'specified brands' of competing suppliers.

7. A non-competition obligation on the buyer exceeding five years in duration, unless the goods to which the agreement relates are resold by the buyer from premises owned or leased by the supplier, provided that the duration of the non-competition obligation does not exceed the period of occupancy of the premises by the buyer.

8. Non-competition obligations that extend beyond the duration of an agreement.

The exemption will apply where the supplier under an agreement has a share in the relevant product market of less than 30 per cent. This rule is subject to an exception, namely, when a supplier agrees to supply exclusively to a certain buyer the exemption will only apply where the buyer has a market share of less than 30 per cent.

The Commission considers that, in principle, vertical agreements do not have an adverse effect on competition. However, the market share test is introduced to make sure that when one of the parties to a vertical agreement has market power the agreement would not produce anti-competitive effects. The regulation also extends the categories of agreements which will be automatically exempted from the prohibition laid down in art 81(1) EC and under certain circumstances the regulation applies to some non-exclusive and selective distribution agreements or agreements for the supply or marketing of services.

The Commission intends to take the same approach as it has taken with the above regulation to all industries in respect of vertical restraints. As the Commission explains 'the new policy will increase the freedom to contract, especially for small and medium-sized companies and generally for companies without market power. It will take away the strait-jacket imposed by the Block Exemption Regulations currently in force.'

It is submitted that the new approach is a mixed blessing. On the one hand, fewer agreements will require notification to the Commission for individual exemption; on the other hand, it may be difficult for undertakings to assess their share in the relevant product market in order to determine whether or not their agreement is in conformity with art 81 EC.

Individual exemptions

There is no obligation imposed on the parties to an agreement to notify it to the Commission. It is an option. The most important advantage deriving from notification is that a notified agreement is, in principle, exempt from sanctions, although the Commission may decide otherwise in the case of a flagrant breach of EC competition law. An application for an individual exemption under art 81(3) EC must satisfy formal and substantive requirements.

Formal requirements

An application for exemption must be made on form A/B obtainable from the Commission. If it is submitted in any other form, that is, a letter. it will not be regarded as an application for notification: *Distillers* Case 30/78 [1980] ECR 2229. However, the ECJ decided in *Dutch Book Association* v *Eldi Records* Case 106/79 [1980] ECR 1137 that the text of the agreement attached to form A/B which was partially completed amounted to notification. Form A/B is also used for applications for negative clearance, but it does not qualify as a request for exemption unless the parties expressly specify it. The application must state the facts and the reason why the applicant considers that the intended agreement does not breach art 81(1) EC and/or satisfies the exemption criteria laid down in art 81(3) EC. Parties to the agreement and any person who can claim a 'sufficient interest' are entitled to be heard before a decision is taken. Exemption for individual agreements is given by a decision which is subject to appeal to the Community judicature. The decision must be published in the Official Journal.

Taking into account the reform of competition policy which abolishes the notification procedure, it is appropriate to mention only briefly. The less formal ways of obtaining clearance for an agreement from the Commission comprise negative clearances and comfort letters. Neither have binding force.[35]

In negative clearance the Commission certifies that on the basis of the facts in its possession the agreement, decision or concerted practice is not in breach of arts 81(1) or 82 EC. Consequently, the Commission only expresses its opinion, which may be changed in view of new information as to the circumstances. Under art 19(3) of Regulation 17/62 the Commission must, when it intends to grant negative clearance, publish a summary of the application in the Official Journal and invite all interested parties to submit their observations within a specific time limit, but not less than one month. The final decision must also be published. Before a national court negative clearance has more persuasive authority than a comfort letter but it is still not binding.

A comfort letter is often sent by the Commission in response to an application for individual exemption. It states the opinion of the Commission that the agreement is not in breach of EC competition law and that the file is closed. Most notified agreements are disposed of by the Commission in this manner.

---

[35] In *Lancôme* v *ETOS* Case 99/79 [1980] ECR 2511 the ECJ held that comfort letters are 'merely administrative letters' and as such neither bind national courts nor are reviewable under art 234 EC.

Substantive requirements

There are a number principles which guide the Commission in deciding whether or not an agreement may qualify for exemption. First, no agreement, even if it seriously restricts competition within the EC, can be *a priori* excluded from the benefit of exemption. In *Matra Hachette* Case T–17/93 [1994] ECR II–595 the CFI held that as a matter of principle there is no anti-competitive practice which cannot qualify for exemption provided that the criteria laid down in art 81(3) EC are satisfied. Second, the Commission takes into consideration the economic context of the agreement. In *Ford*[36] the Commission refused to grant exemption on the ground that one of the parties to the exclusive distribution agreement was already taking measures contrary to art 28 EC regarding goods which were covered by the intended agreement, although the agreement itself satisfied the criteria for exemption. Third, all four criteria laid down in art 81 (3) must be satisfied. If one of them is not fulfilled the agreement will not be exempted: *Métropole* Cases T–528, 542, 543 and 546/93 [1996] ECR II–649.

Although the notification procedure is likely to disappear in the near future the substantive requirements for exemption will remain the same. For that reason it is important to examine the four criteria laid down in art 81(3) EC.

Economic benefit. The first positive criterion requires that agreements, decisions or concerted practices must contribute 'to improving the production or distribution of goods or to promote technical or economic progress'. The criterion does not require that all four possible conditions are present; it is sufficient if only one of them occurs. The Commission in applying the first criterion must objectively compare advantages flowing from the agreement with the disadvantages resulting from the restriction that it imposes on competition. Advantages must prevail over disadvantages. Benefits are objectively assessed and refer to the general interest and not to the benefit which the parties to the agreement may derive from it for themselves in the production or distribution: *Consten and Grundig* Cases 56 and 58/64 [1966] ECR 299; [1966] CMLR 418.

Production

Improvements in production exist if the agreement results in an increase of productivity and capacity of production, the possibility of making a wider range of products, or the reduction of prices. Specialisation and joint-venture agreements are most likely to contribute to improvements in production. In *Amersham Buchler*[37] the Commission granted exemption on the ground that without the agreement the participating undertakings would hardly be able to offer such a wide range of products as they would with it. Agreements which reduce overcapacity of production in an industry in crisis may qualify for exemption. In *Synthetic Fibres* [1985] 1 CMLR 787 an agreement concluded among ten major producers of synthetic fibres intended to reduce the over-capacity of production by 18 per cent was granted exemption as it eased the financial burden of keeping under-utilised capacity open, allowed specialisation in the development of products offered to customers, raised the profitability of participating undertakings and alleviated the social consequences of restructuring by making arrangements for retraining and redeployment of redundant workers.

---

[36] OJ L327 (1983).
[37] OJ L314 (1982).

In *Clima Chappé/Buderus* [1970] CMLR D7 under a specialisation agreement a French undertaking, Clima Chappé, supplying air-conditioning apparatus, and a German undertaking, Buderus, new to the air-conditioning market, agreed to allocate to each other a number of air-conditioning products. For non-allocated products, each was to give preference to the other when buying, provided the price and quality were equal. Buderus agreed not to sell in France apart from selling to Clima Chappé while the latter promised not to sell in Germany apart from Buderus. In other Member States there were no restrictions on sales. The Commission granted exemption to the agreement on the ground that it would eliminate unnecessary duplication of effort.

In *Prym/Beka*[38] under an agreement Prym, in return for shares, sold its plant manufacturing needles to Beka (who also manufactured needles) and agreed to buy all its requirement for needles in future from Beka. Although the agreement lacked reciprocity, the Commission granted exemption taking into account that it would bring reduction in the price of the needles.

In *Bayer Gist-Brocades* [1976] 1 CMLR D98 the Commission granted exemption to a long-term research and development project between a German and a Dutch undertaking regarding production of penicillin. Each undertaking agreed to give up part of its production in favour of the other, allowing one party to specialise in the production of one particular penicillin product and the other in a different penicillin product.

Distribution
Improvements in distribution may result from selective distribution agreements, exclusive dealership networks and the organisation of trade fairs and exhibitions.

Selective distribution agreements are generally eligible for exemption as they result in savings due to rationalisation of production and distribution, and ensure continuity of supply and after-sales service. The limits for exemption in selective distribution agreements were set out in *Metro* Case 26/76 [1977] ECR 1875. If a selective distribution agreement is mainly used to reduce the number of distributors, limit exchanges or increase the price it will not be exempted.[39] In assessing the agreement the Commission takes a number of factors into account. First, the necessity of ensuring that distributors will make sufficient profit to promote the product and to maintain a sufficiently wide variety of product in stock. Second, the Commission assesses the nature of the product, that is whether it is technically complex, whether its price is relatively high, and whether it requires after-sales services of a particular quality. To qualify for exemption it is necessary that one of the above-mentioned features requires close co-operation between a manufacturer/supplier and its distributors which a different distribution network would not satisfy. However, a selective distribution agreement is not justified solely because the product in question is luxurious. Other factors will be taken into consideration, such as the structure of the relevant product market within the EC, the number of competitions, the market share of each party, etc. However, a selective distribution agreement which results in a limitation of price competition will not qualify for exemption.[40]

---

[38] OJ L296 (1973).
[39] *AEG Telefunken*: OJ L117 (1982).
[40] *Ideal- Standard Agreement*: OJ L20 (1985); [1988] 4 CMLR 627.

Exclusive distribution agreements may qualify for exemption provided they do not give absolute territorial protection: *Europair International and Durodyne-Europair Corporation* [1975] 1 CMLR D62; *Junghans* [1977] 1 CMLR D82. However, the Commission will authorise certain territorial protection when there are technical reasons for allowing allocation of territories. In *Transocean Marine Paint Association* [1967] CMLR D9 a number of small and medium-sized undertakings manufacturing and distributing marine paint decided to collaborate in order to produce marine paint to identical standards and to market it all over the world. The paint was sold under a single trade mark, although undertakings were allowed to add their own name and mark. They divided up markets alongside national borders and agreed to sell in each other's territory only on payment of a commission. The objective of the undertakings was to compete with multinationals on the worldwide marine paint market. The Commission granted exemption, notwithstanding the territorial restrictions, on the ground that during the launching period it would avoid fragmentation of the market. The Commission stated that the scheme would improve distribution, provide a better service for consumers and increase specialisation of participating undertakings. The use of the trade mark was considered as lawful since it did not partition the common market but was used to identify the product. Also, according to the Commission, the restriction on competition within the common market was compensated for by its intensification on an international scale.

In respect of exclusive supply agreements, they are eligible for exemption because in general they allow small and medium-sized undertakings to penetrate new markets. However, the Commission will refuse exemption if the volume of supply covered by the agreement is too significant as compared with the total sales of all suppliers/manufacturers in the relevant product market. In *Spices* [1978] 2 CMLR 116 the exclusive purchasing agreement was concluded between three major Belgian supermarket chains and a spice producer Brooke Bond Liebig with 39 per cent of the Belgian spice market. Although there were many other reasons to condemn the agreement, one of them was that the agreement covered a too substantial part of the market in spices.

Agreements to organise fairs and exhibitions may qualify for exemption if they result in reduction of the costs of participation.[41]

Promotion of technical or economic progress

Technical or economic progress concerns the improvement of the quality of products or services, introduction of new technology, the development of new and safer products and making of a wider range of products. It also includes the protection of environment[42] or the protection of employment: *Metro* Case 26/76 [1977] ECR 1875. Specialisation agreements involving common research and development qualify for exemption. In *ACEC-Berliet* [1968] CMLR D35 an agreement between ACEC, a manufacturer of electrical transmission systems for commercial vehicles, and Berliet, a French manufacturer of buses, to produce a new prototype bus equipped with a new transmission system supplied by ACEC exclusively to Berliet in France and not more than one outlet in any other Member State in exchange for which Berliet obtained the most favoured treatment from ACEC, as well as an undertaking

---

[41] *Internationale Dentalschau*: OJ L293 (1987); *Vifka*: OJ L291 (1986).
[42] *BBC Brown Boveri*: OJ L301 (1988).

to keep all information provided by Berliet confidential, was exempted on the ground that it promoted technical progress. Also agreements to co-operate in order to establish a common standard which results in the standardisation of the product are eligible for exemption. In *X/Open Group*[43] exemption was granted to computer manufacturers co-operating in order to produce a standard which would enable users to connect hardware and software from different sources. In *Re ABI*[44] an agreement between Italian banks was exempted on the ground that although it restricted competition in respect of charges imposed for their services it simplified and standardised banking procedures.

Economic progress is rarely invoked as a ground for exemption. However, it was a main factor in granting exemption to an agreement concluded between Iveco and Ford concerning the establishment of a common undertaking for manufacturing and selling cars.[45]

Benefit to consumers. The second positive criterion requires that an agreement, decision or concerted practice must not only contribute to improving the production or distribution of goods or to promoting technical or economic progress, but must also allow consumers a fair share of the resulting benefit The term 'consumers' applies to final consumers and to retailers.[46] The Commission takes into consideration the interests of the majority of consumers. In *VBBB/VBVB*[47] the Commission refused to grant exemption to an agreement between associations of booksellers and publishers in The Netherlands and Belgium imposing collective prices on books in the Dutch language in Belgium and in The Netherlands. Under this agreement less popular books on specific subjects published in a limited number of copies were to be subsidised by more popular books. The Commission condemned the agreement on the ground that it would be unfair to the majority of consumers, taking into account that they prefer popular books rather than specialised books which have a limited number of readers.

As to the term 'benefit' it covers not only the obvious benefit concerning the reduction of purchase prices but also improvement in the quality of product, improvement of after-sales service, the possibility of a greater range of products, the increase in the number or quality of outlets from which the products may be purchased and quicker delivery.

No restrictions that are not indispensable. The first negative criterion requires that an agreement, decision or a concerted practice must not impose on the undertakings concerned restrictions which are not indispensable to the attainment of the objectives of the agreement. It requires that the agreement must not go beyond what is absolutely necessary to achieve the objectives regarded as beneficial. The applicant must prove that this is the case: *Frubo* Case 71/74 [1975] ECR 563; *Remia* Case 42/84 [1985] ECR 2545. In order to assess whether the restriction is indispensable the Commission will apply the principle of proportionality. In *Rennet* Case 61/80 [1981] ECR 851 a co-operative at Leeuwaden producing animal rennet

---

[43] OJ L35 (1987).
[44] OJ Ll43 (1988).
[45] *Iveco/Ford*: OJ L230 (1988).
[46] *Kabel und Metallwerke Neumeyer/Luchaire* [1975] 2 CMLR D40.
[47] OJ L54 (1982); [1982] 2 CMLR 344.

and colouring agents for cheese failed to satisfy the indispensability condition although it met the two positive criteria. The co-operative, which accounted for 100 per cent of the Dutch national output of rennet and 90 per cent of the output of colouring agents (of which 94 per cent of the rennet and 80 per cent of the colouring agents went to its members), imposed on its members the obligation to purchase all their requirements from the co-operative. If they refused or withdrew from the co-operative, the latter imposed heavy pecuniary sanctions on them. The Commission and the ECJ decided that the economic advantage consisting of greater efficiency in rennet production in The Netherlands was outweighed by the restrictions that the co-operative imposed on its members. The same result could have been achieved by less restrictive measures.

In *Matra Hachette* Case T–17/93 [1994] ECR II–595 the CFI held that an agreement between Ford and Volkswagen satisfied the first negative criterion taking into account that even if the undertakings concerned had had sufficient financial and technical means to penetrate the market for the multi-purpose vehicle separately, each would have lost a lot of money in view of the technical and economic difficulties they would have had to overcome.

In many cases the Commission will grant exemption only if the parties remove from their agreement certain clauses which do not comply with the third criterion.

No possibility of eliminating competition. The second negative criterion requires that an agreement, decision or a restrictive practice must not result in eliminating competition in respect of a substantial part of the relevant product market. This situation exists if the undertakings concerned do not have an important share of the relevant market. In order to apply this criterion the Commission must determine the relevant geographical and product market.[48] However, an agreement for joint-research may qualify for exemption even if the undertakings concerned have a substantial share of the relevant product market.[49]

In assessing the fourth criterion the Commission normally examines competition between similar competing products (inter-brand competition) rather than competition between rival distributors of the same brand of products (intra-brand). The major factor in deciding whether or not to exempt an agreement under the fourth criterion will be the retention of reasonable competition between the different brands and the absence of any restriction on parallel import of these brands.

21.7 Civil consequences of breaches of art 81(1) EC

Article 81(2) EC states that agreements and decisions in breach of art 81(1) EC which do not qualify for exemption under art 81(3) EC are automatically void from their inception. The term 'automatically' means that they are prohibited *per se* and no decision to that effect is required from Community institutions or national courts: *Beguelin* Case 22/71 [1971] ECR 949; art 1 of Regulation 17/62. Concerted practices are not included in art 81(2) EC since they are informal arrangements and as such cannot be rendered void. It is not necessary for

[48] *Lightweight Paper*: OJ L182 (1972); *Kali und Salz v Commission* Joined Cases 19 and 20/74 [1975] ECR 499.
[49] *Continental Michelin*: OJ L305 (1989).

the entire agreement or decision to be declared null and void if it is possible to severe offending clauses without destroying the substance of the agreement. Whether or not it is possible to do so is a matter for national courts to decide. Indeed, neither the Commission nor the Community judicature can declare an agreement or a decision as void. Sometimes, Community institutions assist national courts in this task. For example, in *Consten and Grundig* Cases 56 and 58/64 [1966] ECR 299; [1966] CMLR 418 the ECJ severed the offending clauses of the agreement which were the clauses giving absolute territorial protection.

In this context art 81(2) EC poses a difficult challenge to national courts of the Member States in two sets of circumstances. First, when they have to determine what clauses (or whether the entire agreement) are void, taking into account the consequences of voidness and including the matter of validity and enforceability of other contracts concluded on the basis of void clauses or agreement.

Second, national courts have jurisdiction to apply art 81(2) EC, although only the Commission is empowered to grant exemption under art 81(3) EC. It may happen that an agreement which is in breach of art 81(1) EC may qualify for exemption and thus escape nullity. This will cause delays and additional costs for the parties to the proceedings whilst an application is made to the Commission

The proposed modernisation of art 81 EC will remedy the above-mentioned difficulties and for this reason alone should be welcomed!

22 Article 82 EC

22.1 The concept of joint dominant position

22.2 Dominance

22.3 The relevant market

22.4 The concept of abuse

Article 82 provides:

> 'Any abuse by one or more undertakings of a dominant position within the common market or in a substantial part of it shall be prohibited as incompatible with the common market in so far as it may affect trade between Member States.
>
> Such abuse may, in particular, consist in:
>
> (a) directly or indirectly imposing unfair purchase or selling prices or other unfair trading conditions;
>
> (b) limiting production, markets or technical development to the prejudice of consumers;
>
> (c) applying dissimilar conditions to equivalent transactions with other trading parties, thereby placing them at a competitive disadvantage;
>
> (d) making the conclusion of contracts subject to acceptance by the other parties of supplementary obligations which, by their nature or according to commercial usage, have no connection with the subject of such contracts.'

Under art 82 EC an abuse of a dominant position can never qualify for exemption. In this respect it is very important to distinguish between individual exemption and negative clearance. An undertaking may ask for negative clearance under which the Commission certifies that, on the basis of the facts in its possession, there are no grounds under arts 81(1) or 82 EC for action on its part in respect of an agreement, decision or practice. In *Tetra Pak (No 1)* Case T–51/89 [1990] ECR II–309 the CFI held that an exemption granted under art 81(3) EC, whether obtained on an individual basis or by virtue of a block exemption, cannot amount to exemption from a prohibition laid down in art 82.

Under art 81 EC a dominant position is not prohibited. What is unlawful is the abuse of a dominant position. A breach of art 82 occurs where the following four elements all exist:

- one or more undertaking
- in a dominant position within the common market or in a substantial part of it
- abuses that dominant position which abuse
- affects intra-Community trade.

The EC Treaty does not define any of the above-mentioned terms. Their meanings have gradually been clarified by the Commission and the Community judicature. Each of the elements must be examined separately.

22.1 The concept of joint dominant position

The question whether in the oligopolistic market (that is when two or more undertakings independent from each other hold a dominant position) art 82 EC applies was examined by the Commission in *Re Italian Flat Glass*.[1] In this case three Italian producers of flat glass, who held between them a 79–95 per cent share of the Italian market in flat glass, agreed to share the market by allocating quotas to each other and to fix prices for flat glass. The Commission held that the undertakings concerned breached not only art 81(1) EC but also art 82 EC as they acted on the market as a single entity. Even though this decision was partially annulled (in *Società Italiana Vetro v Commission (Re Italian Flat Glass)* Cases T–68, 77 and 78/89 [1992] 5 CMLR 302) because the Commission did not provide sufficient evidence as to dominance, the issue of the cumulative application of arts 81 and 82 EC was not called into question. However, the CFI emphasised that the Commission should, when dealing with art 82 EC, not merely recycle the evidence used in respect of the infringement of art 81(1) EC, that is, it should not deduce from the fact that the undertakings concerned held a substantial part of the market and by virtue of that fact (and no other facts), combined with their unlawful behaviour, claim that they collectively abused their dominant position contrary to art 82 EC. The Commission must clearly distinguish between the scope of application of each provision and thus must carry out an independent assessment of the factual situation in the light of the requirements laid down in arts 81(1) and 82 EC. The Commission followed the CFI's advice and in *Compagnie Maritime Belge and Others v Commission* Cases T–24–26 and 28/93 [1997] 4 CMLR 273[2] addressed separately breaches of art 8(1) EC and infringements of art 82 EC. The CFI confirmed the cumulative application of arts 81(1) and 82 EC. The CFI held that a joint dominant position consists in a number of undertakings being able together, in particular because of factors giving rise to a connection between them, to adopt a common policy on the market and act to a considerable extent independently of their competitors, their customers and ultimately consumers.

The concept of joint dominance was further explained in *Irish Sugar plc* Case T–228/97 [2000] All ER (EC) 198. In this case, Irish Sugar, a company incorporated under Irish law in 1933 by the Irish government, was the sole processor of sugar beet in Ireland and Northern Ireland. On the accession of Ireland to the Community, Irish Sugar was allocated the entire sugar quota for Ireland. Heavy losses suffered by Irish Sugar in the first half of 1980s forced the Irish government to reform the industry. A rationalisation scheme was implemented which resulted in gradual improvement of Irish Sugar's profitability. In April 1991 Irish Sugar was privatised. The mechanism for reducing the State's holding in Irish Sugar included the incorporation of a new holding company, Greencore plc, which acquired Irish Sugar.

As a main supplier of sugar in Ireland Irish Sugar held more than 90 per cent of the market share between 1985 and 1995. Imports of sugar came mainly from France through ASI, an Irish company established in Ireland. The very high cost of transport prevented competitors from other Member States importing sugar to Ireland. From 1990 onwards the

---

[1] OJ L33 (1989).

[2] Confirmed by the ECJ in *Compagnie Maritime Belge Transport* Case C–395/96P Judgment of 16 March 2000 (nyr). See also *France and Others v Commission* Cases C–68 and 30/95 [1998] ECR I–1375.

only domestic competitor of Irish Sugar on the retail market was an organisation named Round Tower. In 1993 four Irish food packers, including Gem Pack and Burcom (both packers of Irish Sugar and sugar imported by ASI) and ASI (using imported French sugar), launched 1 kg white granulated sugar brands. In response to ASI launching its own brand of retail sugar, ASI distributor Allied Distribution Merchants (ADM) was approached by Sugar Limited (SDL) offering to buy ASI brand sugar. This was accepted by ADM. Furthermore, a chain of supermarkets selling the ASI brand were approached by SDL and a deal was struck to swap the ASI brand for the Irish Sugar brand. Irish Sugar was informed by SDL of the product swap. A year later all competition of Irish Sugar on the retail sugar market withdrew or ceased to trade. In 1994 Irish Sugar launched its own brand of 1 kg retail sugar, distribution of which in Ireland was carried out by Sugar Limited (SDL) and in Northern Ireland by SDL's distributor, McKinney. McKinney was set up in 1976, and 51 per cent was owned by SDL. In 1989 SDL increased its shareholding to 60 per cent. Until February 1990 Irish Sugar held 51 per cent of the equity of SDL's parent company, Sugar Distributors Holding (SDH). The managing director of Irish Sugar and a number of other Irish Sugar directors were on the boards of SDH and SDL. In February 1990 Irish Sugar acquired all the remaining shares in SDH and became the sole owner of SDL.

The Commission investigated the commercialisation of sugar in Ireland in the period from 1985 onwards. The Commission stated that Irish Sugar was in breach of art 82 EC as:

1. It took measures to restrict the opportunities for transportation available to its competitors, especially in respect of ASI sugar imported from France, by threatening the main shipping company with the taking away of all Irish Sugar business if they continued to carry French sugar. Irish Sugar was successful as the shipping company agreed not to carry French sugar.
2. It swapped its own sugar for ASI sugar.
3. It sought to eliminate competition from the EU. In respect of the UK Irish Sugar applied selective rebates, including border rebates, and in respect of other Member States it granted sugar export rebates according to the Member State to which export was made, but only to some customers.

The Commission decided that Irish Sugar and SDL jointly held a dominant position on the sugar market between 1985 and February 1990.

Irish Sugar contested the Commission's decision, arguing that the links with SDL guaranteed the independence of the board of SDH/SDL. Furthermore, it argued that the concept of joint dominance could not apply to vertical relationships (SDL was its distributor) but only to horizontal relationships, and that the novelty of the concept of abuse of a joint dominant position had the effect that it had not yet any practical implementation.

The CFI held that Irish Sugar and SDL held a joint dominant position on the sugar market in Ireland. The Court stated that the factors connecting both undertakings provided sufficient evidence that they had the power to adopt a common market policy. These factors were: Irish Sugar's shareholding in SDH, its representation on the boards of SDH and SDL, the policy-making structure of the undertakings, the direct economic ties constituted by SDL's commitment to obtain all its sugar requirements from Irish Sugar, the financing of all consumer promotions and related offers by SDL to its customers by Irish Sugar, constant communications between both undertakings regarding all aspects of SDL's activities and monthly meetings between their representatives.

The CFI confirmed that a joint dominant position can apply to vertical relationships. The Court emphasised that nothing in art 82 EC precludes its application to a vertical relationship. The undertakings concerned were not integrated to such an extent as to constitute one undertaking. The CFI also held that the relationship between the undertakings was not exclusively based on a vertical commercial relationship as SDL was a competitor in the same market.

In respect of the novelty of the concept, the CFI held, first, that although the prohibited conduct took place before the Commission decision in *Italian Flat Glass*, it had been well established that the novelty of a concept should be taken into account when fixing the amount of the fine: *AKZO Chemie BV v Commission* Case C–62/86 [1991] ECR I–3359. Second, that even if that concept was not yet fully clarified (as the Commission admitted in its Communication of 10 December 1996),[3] its decision in *Italian Flat Glass* was adopted in December 1988.[4] Third, that the purpose of the conduct which constituted abuse of the joint dominant position was the protection of market position and the prevention of sugar imports into Ireland. This type of conduct always constituted an infringement of art 82 EC: *Compagnie Maritime Belge Transport* Cases T–26 and 28/93 [1997] 4 CMLR 273. Finally, both Irish Sugar and SDL were aware of the closeness of their economic links and the possibility of co-ordinating their conduct on the sugar market. As a result, the Commission was right in not taking into account the alleged novelty of the concept as a mitigating circumstance when fixing the fine.

The cumulative application of arts 81(1) and 82 will assist the Commission to tackle the problem of oligopolistic markets in which undertakings, without entering into prohibited agreements or concerted practices, adjust their conduct with their competitors in a manner advantageous to both parties. Such conduct may fall into the scope of art 82 EC.

It is important to note that art 82 refers to an abuse of a dominant position by one or more undertakings, not to a dominant position held by more than one undertaking.

22.2 Dominance

The ECJ defined the concept of dominance in *United Brands v Commission* Case 27/76 [1978] ECR 207 as being

> '... a position of economic strength enjoyed by an undertaking which enables it to prevent effective competition being maintained on the relevant market by giving it the power to behave to an appreciable extent independently of its competitors, customers, and ultimately of its consumers.'

This definition was further explained in *Hoffmann-La Roche* Case 85/76 [1979] ECR 461 in which the ECJ re-stated the above-mentioned definition and added that:

---

[3] Com(96)649 final.
[4] OJ L33 (1989).

'... such a position does not preclude some competition which it does where there is a monopoly or quasi-monopoly but enables the undertakings which profits by it, if not to determine, at least to have an appreciable influence on the conditions under which that competition will develop, and in any case to act largely in disregard of it so long as such conduct does not operate to its detriment.'

An undertaking is in a dominant position when it can act independently from its competitors and consumers and thus is not subject to normal competitive forces. The ECJ specified that in order to determine whether a dominant position exists, the market power of an undertaking must be assessed on the basis of a series of factors, one of the most important of which is the existence of a very large market share.

For the Commission the share of the market has always been an important factor in determining dominance. The CFI held in *Hilti v Commission* Case T–30/89 [1992] 4 CMLR 16 that very large shares are in themselves evidence of a dominant position. In this case it was established that Hilti had a share of between 70 per cent and 80 per cent in the relevant market. According to the CFI, this constituted in itself a clear indication of the existence of a dominant position. In *United Brands* Case 27/76 [1978] ECR 207 the ECJ held that market shares between 40 per cent and 45 per cent did not automatically indicate that an undertaking held a dominant position. In the 10th Report on Competition Policy, the Commission stated that in the context of a highly fragmented market a share of between 20 per cent and 40 per cent could be sufficient to establish the existence of dominance. However, there is no dominance if an undertaking has a share of less than 10 per cent of the market: *Metro-SB-Großmärkte GmbH & Co KG v Commission (No 2)* Case 75/80 [1986] ECR 3021. Also, in determining whether there is dominance the Community institutions take into account the market shares held by competitors. In *Michelin* Case 322/81 [1983] ECR 3461 the ECJ indicated that if the difference between the market share held by an undertaking allegedly holding a dominant position and the market share held by its competitors is considerable this may constitute evidence of the existence of dominance. However, the market share is not the only factor to be taken into consideration, especially if the market share held by an undertaking is below 50 per cent. In this respect in *United Brands* the Commission emphasised the importance of structural advantages enjoyed by an undertaking, in particular know-how, financial and technical resources, access to raw materials and outlets, trade-mark ownership, etc. In general, to determine whether a dominant position exists, all facts tending to prove or disprove the market power of the enterprise must be taken into account. Factors which have been taken into consideration are as follows:

1. In *Hoffmann-La Roche* – a big disparity between Roche's market share and that of its next largest competitor, Roche's very extensive and highly specialised sales network, its technological lead over its competitors and the absence of any potential competition.
2. In *United Brands* – a high degree of vertical integration of an undertaking (it owned plantations of bananas, fleets of refrigerated vessels, and warehouses in all important ports in Europe), technological lead, advertisement strategy based on the trade mark 'Chiquita', the existence of control at every stage of distribution, virtually unlimited supplies that would satisfy any demand.

3. In *Solvay*[5] – the capacity of production, high barriers to entry for potential competitors, protection against producers from non-member States by virtue of anti-dumping legislation.
4. In *Tetra Pak (No 1)* – technical lead over competitors.
5. In *Michelin* – technical and commercial lead and a considerable dispersion of competition.

The duration of 'power' in the market constitutes an important factor in assessing dominance. In *Hoffmann-La Roche* the ECJ held that market power held 'for some time' pointed to a position of dominance on a market. Therefore, even if an undertaking had a large market it would be difficult to argue that it was dominant on that market if the share was held for only a short period of time.

Apart from the situation where an undertaking enjoys a monopoly, either *de facto* or by the operation of law, there is no decisive factor. It is the task of Community institutions to consider all the appropriate factors in order to assess the real position of an undertaking in the relevant market. Indeed, only in the context of the relevant market can dominance or otherwise be ascertained. The relevant market may be considered as having three aspects: the product market, the geographical market and the temporal market. The overall relevant market and its aspects are examined below.

22.3 The relevant market

In respect of the relevant product market it is very important to examine the Notice on the Definition of the Relevant Market for the Purposes of Community Competition Law[6] issued by the Commission in 1997. In the Notice the Commission provides guidance for undertakings as to the manner in which it determines the concept of relevant product and geographical market, which are by their very nature impossible to define. Those concepts are vital for the application of arts 81 and 82 EC, Merger Regulation 4064/89 and also in relation to other areas such as transport or coal and steel.

The Notice sets out the means of assessing the relevant product and geographical market which are based on the existing practices of both the Commission and the ECJ. The Commission identifies three main factors of competitive constraint to which undertakings are subject and which identify the relevant market: demand substitutability, supply substitutability and potential competition. In relation to demand and supply substitutability the Notice provides examples in order to illustrate the reasoning of the Commission. Thus, to assess the demand substitutability a hypothetical situation is examined in which a small (up to 10 per cent) and permanent price increase is applied. If the existence of other products within a geographical market would make the price rise unprofitable due to loss of sales, those products are part of the market since in those circumstances the consumer would substitute one product for another.

The supply substitutability is determined by reference to the ability of competitors to

---

[5] OJ L152 (1991).
[6] OJ C37 (1997).

switch their resources, without significant increase in cost and risk, to manufacture a product which has been subject to a small and permanent price rise. If switching the production involves major investment or risks then there is no supply substitutability for the product in question. The Notice suggests that the third constraint, the impact of potential competition, is not applied when determining markets but at a later stage when the relevant market has been defined.

According to the Notice a product market 'comprises all those products and/or services which are regarded as interchangeable or substitutable by the consumer by reason of the products' characteristics, their prices and their intended use.' In order to establish whether there are possible relevant markets the Commission will take into consideration the following evidence:

1. evidence of substitution in the recent past, such as price changes and introduction of new products to the market;
2. views of customers and competitors in relation to the effect on the product market of a small and permanent price increase;
3. consumer preference which may be assessed by conducting surveys among consumers and retailers (also information gathered by the undertaking concerned may be useful);
4. costs and obstacles involved in switching demand to potential substitutes;
5. the category of consumers and price discrimination which is important where there is a clearly defined group of consumers.

In relation to a geographical market the Notice states that it 'comprises the area in which the undertakings concerned are involved in the supply and demand of products or services, in which the conditions of competition are sufficiently homogenous and which can be distinguished from neighbouring areas because the conditions of competition are appreciably different in those areas.' In order to identify a geographical market very similar criteria will be applied to those regarding a relevant product market, although not all of them will be relevant in any one case. The heads of evidence are:

1. past evidence of diversion of orders to other areas;
2. basic demand characteristics, that is whether there are local preferences based on brand, language, culture and the need for a local presence;
3. views of customers and retailers;
4. current geographical patterns of purchase;
5. trade flow patterns of shipment when ascertaining actual geographical patterns in the context of a large number of customers;
6. barriers and cost associated with switching orders to companies situated in other areas.

However, the Commission states that the heads of evidence taken into account may vary depending upon the nature of the anti-competitive conduct under investigation. This means that, for example, a geographical market for the same product will vary in the case of a concentration since it involves prospective analysis and in the case of restrictive practices which focuses on the past conduct of the undertaking.

The Notice provides useful comments on the range of evidence which it examines in each case for market definition purposes. It includes information forwarded by the undertakings under inquiry, by competitors, by customers and by trade associations. Visits and inspections are also part of the evidence-gathering procedure. Furthermore, the Notice specifies that in the determination of market share both volume sales and value sales are to be taken into consideration.

In the light of the above Notice it is interesting to examine the case law regarding the determination of the relevant product, geographical and temporal market.

The relevant product market

In the determination of the relevant product market the divergencies between the Commission and the undertaking under investigation usually follow a pattern, bearing in mind that undertakings always seek a broad interpretation and the Commission always seeks the opposite. The narrower the definition of a product market the greater the market share of any one undertaking. As mentioned above in the Commission Notice, in order to identify the relevant product market three main factors of competitive constraints are taken into consideration: demand substitutability, supply substitutability and potential competition.

In respect of demand substitutability (the demand-side substitutability) the question is whether consumers would switch to substitutes if prices were raised by a small but significant amount above competitive levels. If so, the relevant product market should be extended in order to include the substitutes. It would be unrealistic to require that all or even the majority of customers would switch. The decisive factor is whether a sufficiently large number of consumers would be likely to switch to prevent an undertaking in a dominant position from charging prices above competitive levels. In this context the question arises: what prices should be considered as competitive prices? Indeed, if an undertaking is in a dominant position the currently charged prices may already be above competitive prices. In such a situation it would be unprofitable for that undertaking to further raise prices since its product would be replaced by its closest substitutes as there is a limit to what consumers are likely to pay. Therefore, if the price currently charged already exceeds the competitive level, the relevant product market should not include its closest substitutes as the prices could not be raised above the current levels. This problem is known as the cellophane fallacy after a US case involving cellophane products.[7] It is for the Community institutions to decide whether the currently charged price is above the competitive levels, taking into account such factors as excessive profit made by an undertaking, past price fluctuations, etc. Furthermore, the question of demand substitutability must take into consideration the time factor. The question is how long an undertaking will be able to maintain prices above competitive levels. The product will be included in the same market if the delay before substitution takes place is so short that it would never be economically viable to raise prices in the first place. If substitution takes a long time, which depends on the nature of product but in general this is limited to one year, the product will not be included in the same market. In determining the relevant product market an economic analysis based on a factual situation is needed. As the Commission

---

[7] *US v El Du Pont de Nemours & Co* (1956) 351 US 377.

indicates in its Notice a number of factors will be taken into consideration in order to determine demand-side substitution.

In *United Brands v Commission* Case 27/76 [1978] ECR 207 it was necessary to determine whether the relevant product market was restricted to bananas or whether it encompassed other fruits such as oranges and apples. United Brands argued that bananas were interchangeable with other fruits such as apples and oranges and thus it did not enjoy a dominant position as it was not free from competitive pressures, taking into account the fact that any producers of other fruits were able to challenge its performance. The Commission and the ECJ decided otherwise. Bananas were considered as not substitutable by other fruits because a 'banana has certain characteristics, appearance, taste, softness, seedlessness, easy handling, and a constant level of production which enable it to satisfy the constant needs of an important section of the population consisting of the very young, the old and the sick.' In addition, the arrival on the market of seasonal fruits such as apples did not have any impact on the consumption of bananas and there was almost no fluctuation of prices for bananas. Therefore, there was no substitutability as the consumers of bananas were not likely to switch to other fruits in order to satisfy their needs, even if the increase in price was substantial.

Hilti v Commission Case T–30/89 [1992] 4 CMLR 16 constitutes another example of the manner in which the Commission determines demand substitutability. Hilti manufactured nail guns and the nails and cartridge strips for such equipment. After an investigation by the Commission, Hilti was found to have abused its dominant position within the EC market for each of these products, namely the market in nail guns, the market in cartridge strips and the market in nails. The Commission stated that Hilti abused its position, *inter alia*, by pursuing a policy of supplying cartridge strips to certain end users or distributors only when such cartridge strips were purchased with the necessary complement of nails (the 'tying' of cartridge strips and nails), by blocking the sale of competitors' nails by a policy of reducing discounts for orders of cartridges without nails (the reduction of discounts was based essentially on the fact that the customer was purchasing nails from Hilti's competitors), by exercising pressure on independent distributors (mainly in The Netherlands), by not fulfilling certain export orders (notably to the UK), by refusing to supply cartridges to independent nail manufacturers (mainly to the undertakings that complained to the Commission), etc.

Hilti challenged the Commission's definition of the relevant product market. Hilti argued that the alleged three markets for these products must be regarded as constituting a single indivisible market because none of the products could be used by consumers without the others.

The CFI upheld the decision of the Commission. The CFI stated that the Commission was correct in identifying three separate product markets because all the products could be manufactured separately and could be purchased by consumers without them having to buy the other products. The relevant product market was therefore the three distinct product markets.

The third criterion which should be taken into consideration is the assessment of potential competition. This is a very difficult criterion to apply. In *Irish Sugar plc* Case T–228/97 [2000] All ER (EC) 198 the applicant argued that the Commission did not properly assess potential competition on the industrial sugar market in Ireland. It stressed that, for the purpose of establishing the existence of potential competition, account must be taken of any unused manufacturing capacity capable of creating potential competition between manufacturers established on the market.

The supply substitutability (the supply-side substitution) refers to the situation when substitution takes place by suppliers. Will other undertakings which do not currently supply a product be able to supply it if prices are increased in the short run? If so, any supply-side substitutes should be included in the market. The important factor in assessing supply-substitutability is time. If supply-side substitution takes place within a short time (usually one year but it depends on the product) it refers to the supply-side substitution itself; if it takes longer than one year, it refers to the third criterion, the potential competition, that is, barriers to entry into the market. Supply-substitutability was defined by the Commission in *Torras/Sarrio*[8] which concerned the supply of paper for use in publishing. The coating used for paper determines the paper grade. Therefore, it is very simple to switch the production from one grade to another as it involves the same raw materials and can be done by the same plant. For consumers different grades are not substitutes. Therefore, if an undertaking increases prices for one grade of paper above competitive levels other undertakings may easily and quickly change their production in order to produce that grade. The Commission held that supply-side substitution undermined any potential market power in a particular grade. Therefore, the relevant product market was in publishing paper and not in a particular grade of paper. In assessing demand-side substitutability the most important factors are whether substitution will take place easily and quickly. If an important investment is needed or undertakings have no spare capacity or there are important costs involving the advertisement or distribution of a new product those undertakings would not normally be included in the market. In *Continental Can v Commission* Case 6/72 [1972] CMLR D11 the ECJ annulled the Commission decision on the ground that the Commission did not assess supply-side substitutability. In this case the Commission held that a takeover of Thomassen & Drijver-Verblifa NV (TDV), a large Dutch packaging undertaking, by Europemballage Corporation, a US undertaking held and controlled by another US undertaking Continental Can Co Inc (a powerful multinational with considerable technology relating to the making of metal cans and the machines with which cans are closed after filling), was in breach of art 82 EC. The facts were that Continental Can acquired 86 per cent of the shares in Schmalbach-Lubeca-Werke AG (SLW), a maker of cans and closing machines in West Germany. Continental Can wanted to transfer its shares in SLW to Europemballage and thus indirectly control large market shares. The Commission claimed that Continental Can, through its shares in SLW, was in a dominant position in three product markets:

1. for light containers for canned meat products;
2. for light containers for canned seafood;
3. for metal closures for glass containers

The ECJ disagreed. It held that in order to ascertain the relevant product market the products in question must be individualised

---

[8] OJ C58 (1992).

'... not only by the mere fact that they are used for packing certain products, but by particular characteristics of production which make them specially suitable for this purpose. Consequently, a dominant position in the market for light metal containers for meat and fish cannot be decisive, as long as it has not been provided that competitors from other sectors of the market for light metal containers are not in position to enter this market, by a simple adoption, with sufficient strength to create a serious counterweight.'

Indeed, supply-side substitution will restrict the undertaking from exploiting its market power.

However, if substitution cannot take place easily and quickly it is necessary to examine whether there are barriers to potential entry into the market, that is, to ascertain whether an undertaking concerned would have significant advantages over new entrants. These advantages may be divided into three categories:

1. Absolute advantages which refer to the situation in which a new undertaking does not have equal access to important assets (eg raw materials or intellectual property rights).
2. Strategic advantages which refer to the situation in which a new entrant will have to incur 'sunk costs', that is those which are necessary to enter the market but cannot be recovered on exit. If a new entrant expects to recover the entry costs it will be tempted to enter a new market. However, if an undertaking already active in a market would fiercely compete with a new entrant sunk costs may be prohibitive for a new entrant.
3. Exclusionary behaviour which refers not only to the reputation of an undertaking already active in a market (which undertaking may be known as being predatory) but also the extent to which that undertaking is tying up its distributors or retailers.

Another important consideration in assessing barriers to entry is the rate of innovation within the market. If that rate is very high it will be relatively easy for an undertaking to enter into a new market. The question of barriers to entry into a market was examined in *Hoffmann-La Roche v Commission* Case 85/76 [1979] ECR 461. That company had no potential competitors. Barriers to entry to the vitamins market, which is determined according to the anticipated growth over a long period of time, were very high because of the considerable amount of capital investment necessary. In addition, any unused manufacturing capacity capable of creating potential competition between manufacturers established in that market should be taken into consideration. In *Hoffman-La Roche* this factor reinforced the conclusion of the Commission as to its dominant position. La Roche admitted that during the period covered by the contested decision, its manufacturing capacity was sufficient to meet world demand without this surplus capacity placing the company in a difficult economic or financial situation. In *Eridania/ISI*[9] the Commission took into consideration the potential competition when deciding that the merger between Italian undertakings operating on the industrial sugar market did not create a risk of these undertakings occupying a dominant position on the market. It took into account the threat of imports of sugar at a lower price from neighbouring areas and the low cost of transport. In contrast, in *Irish Sugar plc v Commission* Case T–228/97 [2000] All ER (EC) 198, Irish Sugar argued that the Commission failed to take into account potential competition on the

---

[9] OJ C204 (1991).

industrial sugar market in Ireland. It claimed that due to the overproduction of sugar in the Community market there were many potential competitors that could supply the Irish market many times over without suffering any economic or financial difficulties. The CFI rejected this argument. The CFI held that the Commission had identified the applicant's residual and potential competitors on the industrial sugar market. The Commission determined that residual competition was very weak as only one undertaking had actually tried to import industrial sugar to Ireland (ASI) and had demonstrated that potential competition was unlikely to develop taking into account the impact of the cost of transport on imports of industrial sugar to Ireland 'particularly in the absence of a load travelling in the opposite direction'.

However, the determination of the relevant product market may also be inferred from the conduct of an undertaking. In *AKZO Chemie BV v Commission* Case C–62/86 [1991] ECR I–3359; [1993] 5 CMLR 197 the ECJ defined the relevant product market not by reference to demand and supply substitutability but by focusing on AKZO's behaviour.

In this case Engineering and Chemical Supplies (ECS), an English undertaking producing benzoyl peroxide (a chemical than can be used both for bleaching flour and as a catalyst in plastic manufacture), which had mainly operated in the flour additive sector, decided to expand its sales into the larger plastics sector in the United Kingdom and Ireland. The plastics sector was dominated by AKZO, a producer of organic peroxides including benzoyl peroxide (one of the main organic peroxides) which was also present in the flour additive sector. When one of the largest customers of AKZO in the plastics sector became a customer of ECS, AKZO threatened to reduce prices in the UK flour sector. ECS complained to the Commission. The Commission ordered interim measures under which AKZO's branch in the UK was to stay within the profit levels established prior to ECS's expansion to the plastics sector. The Commission found a memo prepared by one of the AKZO's directors stating that ECS's managing director was informed that 'aggressive commercial action would be taken on the milling side unless he refrained from selling his products to the plastics industry'.

The Commission found that AKZO had abused its dominant position in the market for organic peroxides by engaging in predatory pricing in order to eliminate ECS. AKZO challenged the methodology employed by the Commission in assessing the existence of a dominant position, in particular in the determination of the relevant product market and the geographical market, and claimed that its prices were not abusive as they always included an element of profit. The allegations of AKZO were rejected. The ECJ upheld the Commission's assessment of the relevant product market and relevant geographical market. In respect of identification of the relevant product market, the ECJ stated that AKZO applied price reductions in a sector of flour additives which was vital to ECS but only of limited importance to itself. Furthermore, AKZO was able to set off any losses that it incurred in the flour additives sector against profits from its activity in the plastics sector, a possibility not available to ECS. In respect of the flour market, the practices of AKZO in that market which were allegedly abusive would not be financially viable if AKZO was not in a dominant position. Therefore, by its action AKZO defined the relevant product market.

An undertaking can fall foul of art 82 EC without being a powerful multinational and without the relevant product market being very large. In *British Brass Band Instruments* v

Boosey & Hawkes [1988] 4 CMLR 67 the relevant product market was defined very narrowly as it concerned instruments for British style brass bands in which Boosey & Hawkes held a 90 per cent share. In this case the Commission emphasised that the important factor was whether the market, or in this case the sub-market, 'was sufficiently distinct in commercial reality'.

It is still uncertain whether the concept of the relevant product market includes supplies of spare parts for a product manufactured by an undertaking. In *Hugin Kassaregister AB* v *Commission* Case 22/78 [1979] ECR 1869 Hugin, a Swedish manufacturer of cash machines, supplied machines to Liptons Cash Registers and Business Equipment Ltd in the UK through its British subsidiary. Hugin supplied only 12 per cent of the cash registers in the common market but was held to be in a dominant position in respect of spare parts as they were not interchangeable with those of other cash registers. When Hugin refused to supply spare parts to Liptons, a British undertaking specialised in reconditioning and repairing used Hugin cash registers, the ECJ held that Hugin was technically in breach of art 82 EC, but found that there was insufficient effect on trade between Member States – taking into account that Lipton only provided services within a 50-mile radius of London and was not involved in export of any kind. Accordingly, Hugin was saved by the ECJ's rare application of the *de minimus* rule in the context of art 82 EC. Nevertheless, the Court had in effect confirmed the existence of a relevant product market in spare parts. However, this solution has not been followed in subsequent cases: *Volvo* v *Veng* Case 238/87 [1989] 4 CMLR 122; *Renault* Case 53/87 [1990] 4 CMLR 265.

Insignificant activities of an undertaking may also be caught by art 82 EC as can be seen in *General Motors Continental (GMC)* Case 26/75 [1975] ECR 1367, in which under Belgian law GMC was the only undertaking allowed to provide test certificates for second-hand imports of Opel cars. It was held to be in a dominant position in relation to issuing such certificates even though it delivered a mere five of them in 1973!

The relevant geographic market

In order to establish dominance it is necessary to determine the relevant geographic market, taking into account that the dominant position referred to in art 82 EC must be held 'within the common market or in a substantial part of it'. Geographic markets are defined using the same criteria as that used to define the product market. Therefore, the demand side and the supply side are the main factors in determining the relevant geographic market.

In *United Brands* Case 27/76 [1978] ECR 207 the ECJ held that the geographic market is an area in which 'the conditions of competition are sufficiently homogeneous for the effect of the economic power of the undertakings to be able to be evaluated'. The relevant geographic market may be the Community as a whole. A major factor in determining the geographic market is that within that market the cost and feasibility of transporting products are similar for all traders. This was taken into consideration in *Hilti* Case T–30/89 [1992] 4 CMLR 16. In this case the CFI upheld the Commission's conclusion that the relevant geographic market was the entire Community for two reasons: first, there were large price differences for Hilti products between the Member States and, second, transport costs for nails were low. The CFI held that:

'Those two factors make parallel trading highly likely between the national markets of the Community. It must therefore be concluded that the Commission was right in taking the view that the relevant geographic market in this case is the Community as a whole.'

In *United Brands* the ECJ held that the relevant geographic market encompassed all Member States except France, Italy and the UK. Indeed, in all Member States except these three the conditions of competition were sufficiently homogeneous, taking into account that in those markets there was free competition in respect of banana imports while the UK, France and Italy preferred bananas coming from their former colonies.

In respect of the substantive part of the common market the emphasis is put not on the geographic area but on the economic importance of the market located there. In Joined *Suiker Unie and Others* v *Commission* Cases 40–48, 50, 54–56, 111, 113 and 114/73 [1975] ECR 1663 the ECJ held that:

'For the purpose of determining whether a specific territory is large enough to amount to "a substantial part of the common market" within the meaning of art 86 of the Treaty [art 82 EC] the pattern of volume of the production and consumption of the said product as well as the habits and economic opportunities of vendors and purchasers must be considered.'

Therefore, if the common market in the relevant product is small, markets which are, in absolute terms, very small may, nevertheless, be within the scope of art 82 EC.

In *Michelin* Case 322/81 [1983] ECR 3461; [1985] 1 CMLR 282 the relevant market was confined to the territory of The Netherlands, but in *B & I Line* v *Sealink Harbours* [1992] 5 CMLR 255 the Commission decided that the port of Holyhead was a substantial part of the common market as it was an important corridor for ferry services between Ireland and the United Kingdom.

Therefore in order to determine whether or not a relevant geographic market constitutes a substantial part of the common market, every case will be assessed on the basis of the facts. Furthermore, the 1997 Commission Notice will be very useful. In this Notice the Commission provided the following definition of the relevant geographic market:

'… the area in which the undertakings concerned are involved in the supply and demand of products or services, in which the conditions of competition are sufficiently homogeneous and which can be distinguished from neighbouring areas because the conditions of competition are appreciably different in those areas.'

The relevant temporal market

The third dimension of the relevant market refers to time. The existence of a temporal market changes the position of an undertaking on the market because in order to enjoy a dominant position an undertaking must be capable of sustaining it for a considerable time. Temporal markets may refer to seasonal variations, such as summer months and winter months. United Brands argued that the banana market was seasonal as it was affected by the availability of fresh fruits in the summer. Both the Commission and the ECJ disagreed. The risk of customers changing their preferences according to seasons or the time of the day, for example in relation to peak and off-peak services (different rates applied for electricity or water or gas or telephone services during the day) must be taken into consideration.

The temporal market should be assessed from the point of view of consumers (for example, they may not consider bananas and apples as substitutes) and from the point of view of suppliers' capacity (for example, they may not be able to supply fresh strawberries in winter).

22.4 The concept of abuse

The concept of abuse is an objective concept. In *Hoffmann-La Roche* Case 85/76 [1979] ECR 461 the ECJ emphasised that this concept refers to the conduct of an undertaking in a dominant position

> '... which is such as to influence the structure of a market where, as the result of the very presence of the undertaking in question, the degree of competition is weakened and which, through recourse to methods different from those which condition normal competition in products or services on the basis of the transactions of commercial operators, has the effect of hindering the maintenance of the degree of competition still existing in the market or the growth of that competition.'

This definition is constantly applied by the Community institutions. It stresses the prejudicial effect on the common market of given conduct, irrespective of whether or not the undertaking concerned has the intention of distorting competition.

An undertaking in a dominant position is prohibited from eliminating its existing or potential competitors and thereby reinforcing its position by methods which are incompatible with competition on the merits. Consequently, as the ECJ emphasised, an undertaking in a dominant position, irrespective of the causes of its position 'has a special responsibility not to allow its conduct to impair genuine undistorted competition on the common market'. This means that the very presence of an undertaking in a dominant position weakens the degree of competition in a particular product or service market and thus such an undertaking should be very careful in its business conduct not to abuse its dominant position. Even a small reduction in competition may infringe art 82 EC. In *Hoffman-La Roche* the reduction of 5 per cent was regarded as sufficient to hold the undertaking responsible for breach of art 82 EC. On the one hand, an undertaking in a dominant position is allowed to take reasonable and appropriate steps to protect its commercial interests when they are attacked, but, on the other hand, such behaviour is prohibited if its purpose is to strengthen that dominant position and thereby abuse it.[10]

Article 82 EC sets out a non-exhaustive list of abuses: art 82(a)–(d). It is clear from the list that art 82 EC intends to catch both exploitative abuses, which occur when an undertaking is using its economic power to obtain benefits or to impose burdens, which are not obtainable or imposable within normal competition on the merits, at the expense of customers or consumers, and anti-competitive abuses which eliminate or limit competition from existing competitors or prevent new undertakings entering the market. In almost all cases investigated by the Commission undertakings enjoying a dominant position were

---

[10] *United Brands* Case 27/76 [1978] ECR 207; *Compagnie Maritime Belge Transport* Cases T–24–26 and 28/93 [1997] 4 CMLR 273.

guilty of both anti-competitive and exploitative abuses. Reprisal abuses form a third category of abuses.

Exploitative abuses

Examples of exploitative abuses are:

Excessively high prices

The definition of excessive high prices was provided by the ECJ in *General Motors Continental NV* v *Commission* Case 26/75 [1975] ECR 1367. The ECJ held that 'charging a price which is excessive because it has no reasonable relation to the economic value of the product supplied is ... an abuse.' This definition was applied in *United Brands* although the Commission finding of excessive price was rejected by the ECJ. Nevertheless, the ECJ emphasised that 'adequate evidence of excessive prices could be obtained objectively by means of an analysis of the cost structure, ascertaining the amount of the profit margin by comparison of the selling price of the product in question and the cost of producing it.'

Prices may be considered as excessive if they allow an undertaking to sustain profits higher than it could expect to earn in a competitive market. However, in some circumstances prices may, at first glance, seem excessive but in fact may be justified by objective considerations, such as a temporary increase of demand, greater efficiency of an undertaking than of its competitors in the relevant market, the introduction of an innovation where the profits earned are necessary in order to provide a fair return on the cost of the innovation and a fair reward for the risks taken by an undertaking in developing and introducing the innovation to the market. For these reasons, in many instances it is not easy to assess whether high prices are excessive and thus amount to an abuse.

Discriminatory prices

Discriminatory prices were examined in a number of cases. In *United Brands* Case 27/76 [1978] ECR 207 different prices were charged by United Brands for bananas in different Member States without any objective justification. The ECJ held that United Brands' prices were discriminatory because 'bananas unloaded in two Community ports on practically identical terms as regards costs, quality and quantity were sold to the customers at prices which differed considerably – by between 30 and 50 per cent – from one Member State to another, although the services offered were identical in each case.' United Brands explained that it fixed the prices taking into account what the market in a particular Member State would bear. The ECJ rejected this explanation and stated that the difference in prices can only be justified on the basis of objective criteria such as differences in transport costs, taxation, customs duties, labour wages, etc.

Price discrimination may take two forms: first, an undertaking may charge different customers different prices for the same product without any objective justification; and, second, an undertaking may charge different customers the same price even though the costs of supplying the product are very different taking into account objective criteria such as different transport costs. Therefore, price differentiation based on objective criteria is not in breach of art 82 EC, whilst price discrimination will be considered as an abuse. The circumstances of each case should be examined in order to decide whether or not an undertaking abuses its dominant position by charging different prices to different sets of customers.[11]

Other terms or conditions

Other terms or conditions refer to discrimination on terms rather than price. In *United Brands* the ban on the resale of unripened bananas was considered as an abuse because it confined the ripeners to the role of suppliers of the local market, limited sales outlets to the prejudice of consumers and isolated national markets.

Anti-competitive abuses

Examples of anti-competitive abuses are:

Tying-in

In tying-in arrangements an undertaking seeks to oblige or induce the buyer of goods or services to buy other goods or services from it. In *Tetra Pak Rausing SA v Commission (No 2)* Case C–333/94 [1996] ECR I–5951 the ECJ held that tie-in sales, when an undertaking in a dominant position makes the purchase of one product (the tying product) conditional on the purchase of a second product (the tied product), may amount to an abuse, even though tie-in sales are in conformity with commercial usages and even though the two products are closely associated, unless the 'natural link' between them can be objectively justified. Tetra Pak argued that both products – the filling machinery and the requisite cartons for aseptic milk products – constituted an 'integrated service'. The ECJ rejected this argument. It held that it would be justified in considering the manufacturing equipment and the cartons as forming a natural link and thus being treated as an integrated service only if there was no other independent manufacturers specialising in the production of non-aseptic cartons or if it was impossible for other manufacturers to start producing non-aseptic cartons for reasons relating to intellectual property rights. In *Hilti AG v Commission* Case T–30/89 [1992] 4 CMLR 16[12] the CFI held that Hilti abused its dominant position by requiring the end users or distributors of its patented cartridge strips to buy nails and 'tying-in' cartridges strips and nails. The argument submitted by Hilti that its tying-in arrangement was necessary for the protection of users against injury was rejected by the CFI as not sufficient to objectively justify the tie between both products. In many tying-in arrangements the owner of the 'tying' product refuses to supply a customer who wishes to buy the tying product but not the 'tied' product.

Also the imposition of an exclusive dealing requirement by a dominant undertaking could be an abuse. In *Hoffmann-La Roche* Case 85/76 [1979] ECR 461 under an exclusive purchase agreement 22 of its largest buyers of vitamins agreed to acquire all or most of their vitamin requirements from Hoffman-La Roche. The ECJ held that:

'... an undertaking which is in a dominant position on a market and ties purchasers – even if

---

[11] See *Hilti* and *AKZO*.
[12] This was confirmed by the ECJ in *Hilti AG v Commission* Case C–53/92P [1995] ECR I–667.

it does so at their request – by an obligation or promise on their part to obtain all or most of their requirements exclusively from the said undertaking abuses its dominant position within the meaning of art 86 of the Treaty [82 EC], whether the obligation in question is stipulated without further qualification or whether it is undertaken in consideration of the grant of a rebate.'

Indeed, exclusive purchasing or dealing agreements may lead to the foreclosure of a market if purchasers are tied to an undertaking which enjoys a dominant position. In such circumstances the ability of new competitors to enter the market is restricted as is the ability of the existing competitors to expand their market share.'

Discounts

Discounts granted by an undertaking in a dominant position are not in themselves in breach of art 82 EC. They constitute a form of price competition and as such encourage a customer to do business with a supplier on a long-term basis. They are in breach of art 82 EC only if they are anti-competitive, that is if they tend to remove or restrict the buyer's freedom to choose his sources of supply, to bar competitors from access to the market, to apply dissimilar conditions to equivalent transactions with other trading partners or to strengthen the dominant position by distorting competition.

There are many kinds of discount which may be granted to undertakings. In the light of art 82 EC the grant of the discount must be based on economic considerations and not tend to prevent the customers of an undertaking in a dominant position from obtaining supplies from competitors: *Michelin* v *Commission* Case 322/81 [1983] ECR 3461.

Export rebates. In *Irish Sugar* Case T–228/97 [2000] All ER (EC) 198 Irish Sugar granted rebates on sugar exported to other Member States but not to domestic customers. In addition, the rebate varied not according to the volume exported but to the customer and the Member State to which it was exported and thus constituted a two-fold discrimination in respect of domestic customers who, even though they did not export Irish sugar, were in growing competition from traders from other Member States. Irish Sugar did not challenge the findings of the Commission but defended its policy on the ground that it granted export rebates in conformity with the wish of the Irish government. The CFI emphasised that even though the Irish government encouraged the subsidised export of sugar its interference was not such as to deprive Irish Sugar of all independent choice in its commercial policy. As a result, the CFI rejected the defence.

Selective rebates. Irish Sugar granted rebates only to sugar packers who were not competing with it on the industrial sugar market but were doing so on the retail sugar market. According to the decision of the ECJ in *Hoffmann-La Roche*, if an undertaking in a dominant position requires two buyers of the same quantity of the same product to pay a different price according to whether or not they are competitors of their supplier in another market this constitutes an abuse within the meaning of art 82 EC.

Border rebates. Irish Sugar granted special rebates to certain retailers established in the area of the border between Ireland and Northern Ireland in order to restrict imports of cheaper retail sugar from Northern Ireland. This was discriminatory towards its distributors established in other areas of Ireland, was not based on objective economic criteria as it was not related to the quantity purchased, transport costs, etc, but was intended to eliminate competitors and divide markets. Irish Sugar argued that border rebates were lawful as it had to respond to attacks it had been subjected to by foreign competitors, particularly from the UK. The CFI rejected the defence.

Fidelity rebates. A fidelity rebate is a rebate that is conditional on the customer's purchasing all or a large part of its requirements from a particular undertaking. Fidelity rebates granted by an undertaking in a dominant position are in breach of art 82 EC if their purpose is to prevent customers from obtaining their supplies from competing producers. In *Hoffmann-La Roche* the 22 undertakings that agreed to purchase all or a large part of their vitamin requirements were granted fidelity rebates.[13]

Irish Sugar granted fidelity rebates only to potential customers of a competitor, and only to those who agreed to buy all or a large proportion of their retail sugar requirements from Irish Sugar. The aim of fidelity rebates was to tie a customer to the dominant supplier.

Discounts set at a predatory level. In Irish Sugar the Commission failed to provide sufficient evidence that Irish Sugar set discounts at predatory levels in order to eliminate its competitor which imported sugar from France. Indeed, discounts set at predatory level do constitute an abuse within the meaning of art 82 EC as they result in foreclosing a market.

Product swaps

Irish Sugar agreed with one wholesaler and one retailer to arrange the swapping of competing ASI retail sugar. The Commission stated that this product-swapping was an abuse pursuant to art 82 EC since it had as its object or effect the restriction or elimination of competition, in particular, by preventing new undertakings from entering the market. Irish Sugar argued that the ASI brand was not successful as it sold badly despite the price advantage, and that the volume swapped had no impact on trade between Member States. The CFI rejected these arguments. First, swapping took place at a very early stage of the launching of a new brand by ASI; second, the small amount swapped was taken into account by the Commission when fixing the fine; and, third, art 82 EC applies not only to practices which are capable of harming consumers directly but also those which harm them indirectly by undermining effective competition.[14]

Predatory prices

There is neither a Community definition of predatory pricing nor a recognised test under EC law for determining in what circumstances prices should be considered as such. In *AKZO Chemie BV v Commission* Case C–62/86 [1991] ECR I–3359 the ECJ held that predatory prices are:

---

[13] See also *Michelin* Case 322/81 [1983] ECR 3461; *British Plasterboard (BPB) Industries and British Gypsum Ltd. v Commission* Case C–310/93 [1995] ECR I–865.

[14] See also *Hoffmann-La Roche* Case 85/76 [1979] ECR 461.

'... prices below average total costs, that is to say, fixed costs plus variable costs, but above average variable costs must be regarded as abusive if they are determined as part of a plan for eliminating a competitor. Such prices can drive from the market undertakings which are perhaps as efficient as the dominant undertaking but which, because of their smaller resources, are incapable of withstanding the competition waged against them.'

Therefore, the Commission has to prove that the undertaking holding a dominant position intends to eliminate its competitors. In *AKZO* the conclusions of the Commission were based on an internal memorandum and the desire of AKZO to eliminate the expansion of its competition to the plastics market. In *Tetra Pak Rausing SA v Commission (No 2)* Case C–333/94P [1997] 4 CMLR 662 the ECJ stated that prices which are considerably lower than average variable cost are *per se* predatory and in such a case no proof of intention to eliminate competitors is necessary. However, if there is over-capacity or over-supply in the relevant product market, or if there is a restructuring of the market, an undertaking applying such prices would be able to escape the prohibition contained in art 82 EC.

Refusal to supply

In *Commercial Solvents Corporation v Commission* Cases 6 and 7/73 [1974] ECR 223 the refusal of Commercial Solvents, the world's only large-scale producer of raw materials from which the drug ethambutol could be made (and as such holding a dominant position in that sector), to supply raw materials to Zoja, one of the three makers of ethambutol in the EC, was considered as contrary to art 86(d) EC Treaty (art 82(d) EC). In *CBEN v CLT & IPB (Re Telemarketing)* Case 311/84 [1985] ECR 3261 an undertaking registered in Luxembourg and dominant over the transmission of advertisements to Belgium refused to transmit telemarketing spots unless its own answering services were used and was condemned by the ECJ for abusing its dominant position.[15]

The refusal of an undertaking dominant in a particular sector to supply or to give access to its facilities is considered as an abuse of that position on the market. In this context it is necessary to determine what facilities should be considered as essential. This is done on a case-by-case basis. In this respect Advocate-General Jacobs in his opinion in *Oscar Bronner Gmbh & Co KG v Mediaprint Zeitungs-und Eitschriftenverlag GmbH & Co KG* Case C–7/97 [1998] ECR I–779 stated that a facility is considered as essential if access to it is indispensable in order to compete in a related market, and duplication of which is impossible or extremely difficult owing to physical, geographic or legal constraints or is highly undesirable for reasons of public policy. Examples of essential facilities are ports,[16] bus stations and intellectual property rights. It should be noted that in *Oscar Bronner* the ECJ relaxed its strict approach to the refusal of an undertaking enjoying a dominant position to supply or to give access to its facilities.

In this case the Austrian Regional Court in Vienna referred to the ECJ for a preliminary ruling two questions on the interpretation of art 82 EC which had been raised in proceedings between two Austrian undertakings. The undertakings were Oscar Bronner, editor, publisher, manufacturer and distributor of the daily newspaper *Der Standard*, which

---

[15] See also *Independent Television Publications Limited v EC Commission* Case T–76/89 [1991] 4 CMLR 745.
[16] For example, the port of Holyhead in *B & I Line v Sealink Harbours* [1992] 5 CMLR 255.

in 1994 held 3.6 per cent of circulation and 6 per cent of advertising share of the Austrian daily newspaper market, and Mediaprint Zeitungs, publisher of two daily newspapers, which in 1994 held 46.8 per cent of the Austrian daily newspaper market in terms of circulation and 42 per cent in terms of advertising revenues. Mediaprint Zeitungs' two newspapers reached 53.3 per cent of the population above the age of 14 in private households and 71 per cent of all newspaper readers. Mediaprint set up a nation-wide delivery system consisting of delivering the newspapers directly to subscribers in the early hours of the morning. Oscar Bronner (for financial reasons) was not able to set up a similar system of delivery on its own and had to use a postal service for delivery of its newspaper which took place late in the mornings. Brunner sought an order requiring Mediaprint to cease abusing their alleged dominant position in the market by including Bronner's newspaper, *Der Standard*, in its home-delivery service against payment of reasonable remuneration. Mediaprint refused to do so.

The ECJ held that the refusal by a press undertaking, which held a very large share of the daily newspaper market in a Member State and operated the only nation-wide newspaper home-delivery scheme in that Member State, to allow the publisher of a rival newspaper, which by reason of its small circulation was unable either alone or in co-operation with other publishers to set up and operate its own home-delivery scheme in economically reasonable conditions, to have access to that scheme for appropriate remuneration did not constitute abuse of a dominant position within the meaning of art 82 EC.

In the above case the ECJ held that the essential facilities doctrine should apply only in exceptional circumstances. The ECJ specified three conditions under which the refusal of the dominant undertaking cannot be justified:

1. if the refusal to participate in the service comprising home delivery would be likely to eliminate all competition in the daily newspaper market;
2. if such a refusal is incapable of being objectively justified; and
3. if there is no actual or potential substitute in existence for that home-delivery scheme.

These three conditions were not satisfied in the present case and therefore the ECJ held that there was no abuse of a dominant position on the part of Mediaprint. The ECJ stated that other methods of distributing daily newspapers, such as by post and through sale in shops and at kiosks, even though they may be less advantageous for the distribution of certain newspapers, existed and might be used by the publishers of those daily newspapers. The ECJ added that there were no technical, legal or even economic obstacles making it impossible, or even unreasonably difficult, for any other publisher of daily newspapers to establish, alone or in co-operation with other publishers, its own nationwide home-delivery scheme and use it to distribute its own daily newspapers. The ECJ rejected the argument of Oscar Bronner that it was not economically viable, by reason of the small circulation of the daily newspaper to be distributed, to set up its own nationwide home-delivery system. The Court stated that in order to demonstrate that the creation of such a system is not a realistic potential alternative, and that access to the existing system is therefore indispensable, it was necessary to show objectively that the establishment of such a system was not economically viable for any of Mediaprint's actual or potential competitors in the daily newspaper market.

The ECJ in this case defined the scope of the doctrine of essential facilities. It held that undertakings are free to decide who is to have access to their facilities and assets. Only in exceptional cases can an undertaking claiming to be an alleged victim of the refusal of access rely on EC competition law to gain such access. The burden of proof lies with the alleged victim.

Actions in related markets

The ECJ in *Tetra Pak Rausing SA v Commission (No 2)* Case C–333/94P [1996] ECR I–5951 set out a very important principle. It stated that an undertaking that has a dominant position in one product market which expands its activity, without objective need, in a different but closely associated market in which it does not enjoy a dominant position, at the risk of eliminating all competition on that market, may be held liable under art 82 EC for abuses in that auxiliary market. In *Tetra Pak (No 2)* the ECJ held that Tetra Pak's activities in relation to the markets in non-aseptic machines and cartons constituted an abuse of its dominant position in the distinct, but closely associated, markets for aseptic machines and cartons used for the packaging of liquid foods. This principle has its origin in the judgment of the ECJ in *Commercial Solvents Corporation v Commission* Cases 6 and 7/73 [1974] ECR 223.

Reprisal abuses

Reprisal abuses occur when the conduct of un undertaking in a dominant position is directed at injuring another undertaking and thus it goes further than necessary. The best example is provided in *United Brands* Case 27/76 [1978] ECR 207 in which United Brands decided to punish its Danish distributor Olesen, who promoted a competitive brand of banana, by refusing to supply him with its 'Chiquita' banana. The ECJ held that the punitive action of United Brands was out of proportion to the alleged 'disloyal' conduct of Olesen and decided that un undertaking in a dominant position was not allowed to refuse to supply a long-standing distributor, so long as its orders placed on the supplier had remained within the normal range.

23 Merger Control

23.1   The scope of application of Merger Regulation 4064/89, as amended

23.2   The concept of collective dominance

23.3   The procedure under the Merger Regulation

23.4   Future reform of merger control

Unlike art 66 CS, which contains an explicit provision in respect of mergers between undertakings operating in the coal and steel sectors, the Treaty of Rome was totally silent on the topic of mergers. This lacuna had serious consequences for competition conditions within the EC. Undertakings were able to circumvent the application of arts 81(1) and 82 EC. Instead of entering into agreements prohibited by virtue of art 81(1) EC they could achieve the same objectives by merging with other undertakings. In respect of art 82 EC an undertaking in a dominant position, the existence of which, per se, weakened competition within the relevant market, could lawfully increase its market power by acquiring or merging with its competitors and thus even more reduce the competition to the detriment of its customers and ultimately consumers. The Commission was powerless to prevent such mergers between and acquisitions by undertakings with substantial market power.

The first attempt to bring mergers within the realm of EC competition law was made by the Commission in *Continental Can v Commission* Case 6/72 [1973] ECR 215. Although, the Commission failed to prove that Continental Can held a dominant position in the German market[1] the ECJ recognised that art 82 EC was, in principle, applicable to mergers. The ECJ interpreted art 82 EC teleologically and concluded that in the light of art 3(g) EC (which sets out the objective of EC competition policy) and art 2 EC (which emphasises the importance of harmonious development of economic activities) it would be contradictory to prohibit certain agreements and practices by virtue of art 81(1), whilst allowing an undertaking in a dominant position in the relevant market to merge and thus strengthen its position to the possible extent of eliminating any competition in that market. Allowing such a course would call into question the proper functioning of the common market. Shortly after the decision in Continental Can the Commission prepared its first draft Merger Regulation but the Council did not choose to endorse it. Accordingly, it took many years before the reluctance of the Member States to deal with mergers at Community level was overcome. The breakthrough was forced by the ECJ judgment in *BAT and RJ Reynolds v Commission and Philip Morris* Cases 142 and 156/84 [1987] ECR 4487.[1] In April 1981 two leading cigarette manufacturers, Rembrandt and Philip Morris entered into an agreement under which Philip Morris acquired 50 per cent equity interest in, and joint management of,

---

[1] The Commission failed to assess the supply-substitutability of the relevant product market.

Rothmans Holdings, until then a subsidiary of Rembrandt. BAT and other undertakings complained to the Commission. As a result, a new arrangement was made under which Philip Morris acquired 30 per cent equity interest in Rothmans and 24.9 per cent voting rights in Rothmans International, a subsidiary of Rothmans Holdings.

The second agreement together which other complementary arrangements, made sure that Philip Morris would neither be represented on the Rothmans International board nor have any managerial influence upon it. This agreement was exempted by the Commission. BAT and others challenged the Commission decision under art 230 EC. The ECJ upheld the Commission's decision on the grounds that the limited voting rights and the lack of managerial representation would prevent Philip Morris from restricting competition. The ECJ made an important statement in this case, first, confirming the application of art 81 EC to mergers and, second, it held that although the acquisition by one undertaking of an equity interest in its competitor does not in itself restrict competition, such an acquisition may restrict or distort competition on the relevant market. The ECJ emphasised that

> '... this will be true, in particular, where by the acquisition of a shareholding or through subsidiary clauses in the agreement, the investing company obtains legal or *de facto* control of the commercial conduct of the other company or where the agreement provides for commercial co-operation between the companies or creates a structure likely to be used for such co-operation. This may also be the case where the agreement gives the investing company the possibility of reinforcing its position at a later stage and taking effective control of the other company.'

The decision showed, first, that art 81 EC was not an appropriate tool to deal with mergers, taking into account the nullity sanction under art 81(2), the possibility of the revocability of exemption under art 81(3) and the lack of thresholds triggering its application to mergers. Second, that the ECJ by interpreting art 81 EC broadly extended the scope of the Treaty and thus judicially revised it. Third, that in order to avoid further judicial developments by the ECJ on the control of mergers, and the uncertainty of whether or not the Commission would exercise its discretion, the best option for the Member States was to adopt Community legislation on merger control, especially in the light of the then forthcoming completion of the common market. In March 1988 a new draft regulation was submitted to the Council which, after a number of amendments, was adopted on 21 December 1989 as Merger Regulation 4064/89 and came into force on 21 September 1990. It was updated on 26 June 1997 by Regulation 1310/97/EC which entered into force on 1 March 1998. The Merger Regulation is supplemented by a number of implementing and interpretative instruments such as: Regulation 447/98 on the notification, time limits and hearing which entered into force on 2 March 1998,[2] the Commission Notice Regarding Restrictions Ancillary to Concentrations, the Commission Notice on the Concept of Full Function Joint Ventures under the Merger Regulation, the Commission Notice on the Concept of Concentration under the Merger Regulation, the Commission Notice on the Concept of Undertakings Concerned under the Merger Regulation and the Commission Notice on Calculation of Turnover under the Merger Regulation.

The main changes introduced by Merger Regulation 1310/97/EC (the 1997 Regulation)

---

[2] OJ L61 (1998) and corrigendum: OJ L66 (1998).

concern the thresholds triggering application of Merger Regulation 4064/89 and the abolition of any distinction between 'co-operative' and 'concentrative' ventures.

23.1 The scope of application of Merger Regulation 4064/89, as amended

The Merger Regulation 4064/89 (MR) does not prohibit concentrations. Unlike arts 81 and 82 EC the repressive element is absent in the MR as the emphasis is not on the anti-competitive conduct of an undertaking but on the structure of the relevant market. Many concentrations are necessary in order to reinforce the competitiveness of EC undertakings. Only a concentration which is incompatible with the common market, that is that which creates or strengthens a dominant position, as a result of which effective competition would be significantly impeded in the EU or in a substantial part of it, would not be allowed to take place.

The MR applies to all sectors of the economy, apart from the coal and steel sectors which are covered by the Treaty of Paris (CS). At its expiry in 2001, the MR will apply to the above-mentioned sectors. The MR applies both to public and private undertakings, to undertakings which are established within and without the EU. Concentrations are within the scope of the MR if they satisfy two conditions, that is, they are regarded as 'concentrations' and have 'a Community dimension' within the meaning of the MR.

The concept of concentration

Article 23 of the MR states that the MR applies only to concentrations which permanently modify the structure of the undertakings concerned. The concept of concentration is defined in art 3 of the Regulation and covers two situations

1. the case where two or more previously independent undertakings merge; and
2. the case where one or more persons already controlling at least one or more undertakings, acquire, whether by purchase of securities or assets, by contract or by any other means, direct or indirect control of the whole or parts of one or more other undertakings.

The first type of concentration is not very complex and constitutes the classical illustration of mergers. There is no definition of a 'merger'. However, in the context of the MR it implies that where two or more undertakings cease to be distinct and independent from each other and form a single undertaking based on a voluntary act of both or all undertakings concerned a merger situation arises.

The second type of concentration refers to acquisitions, by whatever means, of control over the whole or part of other undertakings. Acquisition of control is more complex than mergers.

The Community dimension

The MR applies to all concentrations having a Community dimension. This in the following circumstances:

1. The basic rule is set out in art 1(2) of the MR, that is, a concentration has a 'Community dimension' where the combined aggregate worldwide turnover of all participating undertakings is over EUR 5 billion and the aggregate Community-wide turnover of each of at least two of the undertakings concerned is more than EUR 250 million, unless each of the undertakings concerned achieves more than two-thirds of its aggregate Community-wide turnover within one and the same Member State.
2. The 1997 Regulation modified the MR. It provides that concentrations are considered as having a Community dimension, even if they do not reach the above-mentioned thresholds, when:

   a) they have an EUR 2.5 billion aggregate world-wide turnover and an aggregate Community-wide turnover of EUR 100 million or more spread between not fewer than three Member States;
   b) each of at least two of the undertakings concerned must generate at least EUR 25 million turnover in not fewer than three Member States; and;
   c) the aggregate Community turnover of each of at least two of the undertakings concerned is more than EUR 100 million

   unless each of the undertakings concerned achieves more than two-thirds of its aggregate Community-wide turnover within a single Member State.

The 1997 Regulation provides for a 'one-stop shop' EU notification procedure for cross-border merger agreements involving at least three Member States and meeting a slightly lower turnover criteria than previously required. The lowering of the thresholds in order to bring more concentrations within the scope of the Merger Regulation offers a substantial advantage to undertakings involved in merger agreements stretching across at least three Member States and falling short of having a Community dimension. These undertakings, instead of being required to notify their deal to the competent authorities in the three or more Member States concerned and being subject to investigations in all those Member States (which imposed considerable hardship on them and was very time-consuming), will, under amended rules, obtain a decision from the Commission within the time limit specified in the Regulation.

The MR has an extra-territorial scope of application. The Commission enjoys a large measure of discretion in relation to the enforcement of arts 81 and 82 EC and has used it to avoid international disputes. This is not the case in relation to merger control under Regulation 4064/89. It seems that once the envisaged merger satisfies the threshold requirements, the Commission must act, or at least assess the proposed merger from the point of view of Community interests. The Community judicature, in order to justify the extra-territorial application of the MR, relies on the effects doctrine. Thus, its jurisdiction is justified 'when it is foreseeable that a proposed concentration will have an immediate and substantial effect in the Community'. This was held by the CFI in *Gencor Ltd v Commission of the European Communities* Case T–102/96 [1999] All ER (EC) 289.

Gencor Ltd, a company incorporated under South African law operating mainly in mineral resources and metals industries, held 46.5 per cent of Implats, also a company registered in South Africa, which brought together Gencor's activities in the platinum group metal (PGM) sector. Lonrho, an English company operating in various sectors such as mining, metals, hotels, agriculture and general trade, held 73 per cent of Eastern Platinum Ltd and Western Platinum Ltd (LPD), both incorporated under South African law which brought together Lonrho's activities in the PGM sector. The remaining 27 per cent of LPD was held by Gencor.

Gencor and Lonrho proposed to acquire joint control of Implats in order to control LPD. As a result of that transaction Implats was to be held as to 32 per cent by Gencor, 32 per cent by Lonrho and 36 per cent by the public. In practical terms, the concentration would eliminate competition between Gencor and Lonrho not only in the PGM sector in South Africa but also in the marketing of PGMs in the Community where Implats and LPD were important suppliers in this sector, which instead of being supplied by three South African companies would have only two suppliers, Implats/LPD and Amplats (the leading worldwide suppliers in the PGM sector). The proposed concentration was approved on 22 August 1995 by the South African Competition Board. On 17 November 1995 Gencor and Lonrho jointly notified the Commission of the above agreements. The Commission declared that the concentration was incompatible with the common market and the functioning of the EEA Agreement, because it would have led to the creation of a dominant duopoly position between Amplats and Implats/LPD in the world platinum and rhodium market as a result of which effective competition would have been significantly impeded in the common market.

On 28 June 1996 the applicant brought an action for the annulment of the contested decision on the grounds that the Commission had no jurisdiction under the MR since the transaction was carried out outside the Community and, in the alternative, if the MR did apply, it was unlawful and therefore inapplicable pursuant to art 241 EC. The CFI upheld the Commission's decision.

Prohibited concentrations under the MR

Provided that an intended concentration has a Community dimension within the meaning of the MR the Commission will have to assess whether it is compatible with the common market. A concentration which creates or strengthens a dominant position as a result of which effective competition will be significantly impeded in the common market or a substantial part of it, is incompatible with the common market. Under art 2 of the MR, in making the assessment, the Commission should take into consideration:

1. The necessity to maintain and develop effective competition within the common market in the light, *inter alia*, of the structure of all the markets concerned and the actual or potential competition from undertakings established either within or without the Community.
2. The market position of the undertakings concerned and their economic and financial power based on the following factors:

    a) the alternative available to suppliers and users and their access to supplies and markets;
    b) any legal barriers to entry;
    c) supply and demand trends for the relevant product market;
    d) the interests of the intermediate and ultimate consumers;

e) the development of technical and economic progress which must bring advantages to consumers and not constitute an obstacle to competition.

The Commission will assess a concentration with respect to the relevant product market and the relevant geographic market. The market share of the merged entity is a very important factor in assessing the compatibility of a concentration with the common market.

The economic assessment of mergers is carried out by a 'Merger Task Force' which operates within Directorate-General IV but has its own staff and procedures.

Joint-ventures

The Commission has often emphasised that it supports pro-competitive joint-ventures as they improve the competitiveness of the Community and reduce divisions in the markets. The 1997 Regulation abolishes the distinction between 'co-operative' and 'concentrative' ventures and establishes only one category for all of them – 'full-function' joint-ventures.

Article 3(2) of the MR defines a joint-venture which falls within its scope of application. It provides that 'The creation of a joint venture performing on a lasting basis all the functions of an autonomous economic entity shall constitute a concentration.' Under art 2(4) of the MR if a joint venture falls within that definition but has as its object or effect the co-ordination of the competitive behaviour of undertakings that remain independent, such co-ordination is assessed in the light of art 81(1) EC. The 1997 Regulation excludes ventures between a parent and its subsidiary when the former uses the latter in order to co-ordinate their business practices to the detriment of fair competition in the particular market. These kinds of situation are within the realm of arts 81 and 82 EC. A joint-venture between existing undertakings escapes the application of the amended rules unless it 'brings about a lasting change in the structure of the undertakings concerned' and has 'its own management and access to sufficient resources including finance, staff and assets ... in order to conduct on a lasting basis its business activities through its own management.'

23.2 The concept of collective dominance

Not only are concentrations which give the merged entity a dominant position on the relevant product and geographic markets prohibited but also concentrations which create or strengthen an oligopolistic market structure even though the merged entity on its own does not occupy a dominant position.[3]

In *Gencor Ltd v Commission of the European Communities* Case T–102/96 [1999] All ER (EC) 289, the concept of collective dominance was clarified. In this respect the CFI held that:

'The reference in the fifteenth recital in the preamble to the Regulation to a 25 per cent threshold for market share cannot justify a restrictive interpretation of the Regulation. Since oligopolistic markets in which one of the jointly dominant undertakings has a market share of

---

[3] *Kali und Salz v Commission* Joined Cases 19 and 20/74 [1975] ECR 499.

less than 25 per cent are relatively rare, that reference cannot remove cases of joint dominance from the scope of the Regulation. It is more common to find oligopolistic markets in which the dominant undertakings hold market shares of more than 25 per cent. Thus, of the market structures which encourage oligopolistic conduct most are those in which two, three or four suppliers each hold approximately the same market share.'

In *France* v *Commission* Cases C–68/94 and 30/95 [1998] ECR I–1375 the ECJ recognised the above concept but stated that there must be commercial or economic links between the undertakings so they are able to act as a single entity. The uncertainty whether there may be collective dominance without these links was answered in *Gencor*.

The ECJ stated that although not only economic and commercial links but also those of ownership or agreement and oligopolistic inter-dependence might be relevant, no links are actually necessary to establish joint dominance. In *Airtours/First Choice*[4] the Commission confirmed this approach. In April 1999 Airtours announced a hostile bid for First Choice which, if successful, would have resulted in 80 per cent of the package tour market in the UK being controlled by three undertakings, that is, the newly merged entity, Thomson and Thomas Cook. In *Gencor* the intended merger would have led to a duopolistic market whilst in Airtours/First Choice the collective dominance would have involved three undertakings.

These two decisions mark an important victory for the Commission in respect of its control of mergers in highly concentrated markets. First in Gencor/Lonhro and then Airtours/First Choice the Commission blocked a merger on the grounds of preventing an increase in the oligopolistic structure of the market. It seems that the Commission is very concerned that a small number of undertakings in an oligopolistic market are likely to collude.

23.3 The procedure under the Merger Regulation

The basic rule is that any concentration satisfying the criteria laid down by the MR should be notified to the Commission not more than one week after the conclusion of the agreement, announcement of the public bid, or the acquisition of a controlling interest. A concentration cannot be implemented either before its notification or until it has been cleared by the Commission as compatible with the Common Market, otherwise the Commission may declare it invalid. In practice, this is unlikely to occur, taking into account the adverse consequences which may derive from such a situation for the undertakings concerned.

The Commission takes an initial decision on the notification within one month, that is whether or not the Commission has serious doubts as to the compatibility of the concentration with EC law. This period may be extended to six weeks if a Member State informs the Commission that a concentration has an undesirable impact on competition within that Member State. If the Commission agrees with a Member State it may still carry out its investigation but has to take the interest of that Member State into account or it may refer the matter to the national authorities. The 1997 Regulation removes the discretion of

---

[4] Commission Press Release, 22 September 1999.

the Commission in relation to referral to the national competition authorities. The Commission is obliged to refer a concentration to the competent national authorities if a Member State or Member States concerned demonstrate that there is a distinct market which does not have a Community dimension.

If the Commission considers that the intended merger raises serious concern it has to open investigations which must be concluded within four months and which involve consultation with third parties. The time limit may be suspended by the Commission if it has obtained insufficient information from the undertaking concerned. Commitments, that is adjustments to the concentration, may be made by the undertakings concerned during the four-month period in order to satisfy the Commission's reservations on competition grounds. The Commission may declare the intended concentration as compatible with the common market but attach conditions to it. The MR alone applies to mergers which satisfy its criteria (not Regulation 17/62). The procedure is therefore different from that initiated under Regulation 17/62. The Form CO, which is a standard form for notification of concentration and is annexed to Regulation 447/98, has been amended. The 1997 Regulation requires that the undertakings concerned must summarise confidential information in a 'non-confidential form' which can be forwarded to interested parties, and impose on them the obligation to provide information on 'neighbouring markets' and not only the main market affected by the deal. There are also new provisions for oral hearings and for informal and confidential discussion of proposals. The undertakings concerned are permitted to comment on any objections by the Commission to the proposals. The position of the Hearing Officer has been formalised

There is one procedure for all joint-ventures and the same time limit as that for mergers, that is a maximum five months (one month for the initial examination followed, if necessary, by a four-month inquiry). As a result, full function joint-ventures will obtain a decision from the Commission in a very short period of time as compared with the old rules.

The Commission clears a very large proportion of applications relating to concentrations but usually makes its authorisation subject to conditions.

Under the MR the Commission is empowered to impose fines and pecuniary sanctions in the event of failure to notify or co-operate. Also the Commission may impose fines if the undertakings concerned fail to supply relevant information or incorrect information.

The Commission's first fine for failure to notify was EUR 33,000 imposed on the South Korean group, Samsung, for failure to notify its merger with a Californian firm, AST Research.

On 10 June 1997 the Commission authorised Samsung to take control of AST Research. However, when the EU Merger Task Force investigated the merger it discovered that the takeover had already taken place in January 1997, several months before the official notification was lodged with the EU authorities. Both companies were situated outside the territory of the European Union but the fact that they had significant business within the EU forced Samsung to notify the merger. The Commission decided to impose a relatively low fine for the following reasons:

1. although business activities of both undertakings in the EU were significant, their merger had no damaging effect on competition within the EU;
2. their failure to notify the Commission was not intentional;

3. although there was a delay they nevertheless filed the official notification with the competent authorities.

Samsung acknowledged its breach of the Merger Regulation and fully co-operated with the Commission in its investigation.[5]

In *Sanofi/Synthélabo* the Commission imposed a fine of EUR 50,000 on each of two undertakings for being grossly negligent and supplying incorrect information when notifying their intended merger.[6]

23.4 Future reform of merger control

In August 1999 the Commission published three draft notices proposing important changes to EU merger control practices and procedures. They concern:

The introduction of simplified procedures

In order to ease the workload of the Commission (from January 1999 to August 1999 the Commission issued 163 reasoned decisions, as compared with a total of 226 in 1998 and 134 in 1997) some concentrations would be eligible for the simplified procedure under which they would be deemed approved on the expiry of a one-month period from notification without the Commission having to adopt a formal reasoned opinion. On receipt of notification the Commission would publish a notice in the Official Journal that the concentration is eligible for the simplified procedure. After the expiry of the one-month deadline the Commission would publish a notice that the concentration is deemed to have been approved. Concentrations likely to be eligible for the simplified procedure are:

1. Joint-ventures which have no, or negligible, actual or foreseeable activities within the EEA, that is where the turnover of the joint-venture or the turnover of the activities contributing to the joint venture is less than EUR 100 million in the EEA and the total value of assets transferred to the joint venture is less than EUR 100 million in the EEA.
2. Mergers and acquisitions where none of the undertakings is involved in business activities in the same product and/or geographical market, or in any markets which are upstream or downstream of a product market in which any other party is engaged.
3. Mergers and concentrations where two or more undertakings are involved in a horizontal relationship (in the same product and geographical market) provided that their combined market share is less than 15 per cent, or mergers and concentrations where two or more undertakings are involved in a vertical relationship (in markets upstream or downstream of a product market) provided their combined market share is less than 25 per cent.

However, in some circumstances, even when the above-mentioned criteria are satisfied the Commission may decide not to apply the simplified procedure, namely:

---

[5] 2293 ER, February 1998, Business Brief, p3.
[6] OJ L95 (2000).

1. The intended concentration has conglomerate aspects, especially where one or more undertakings holds a market share of 25 per cent or more in any product market (especially where there is no horizontal or vertical relationship).
2. Where the assessment of the market share poses difficult problems, for example the market in new or not developed.
3. Where the market is characterised by high entry barriers, a high degree of concentration or poses other serious competition problems.
4. Where a full function joint venture risks the co-ordination of competitive behaviour within the meaning of art 2(4) of the MR.
5. A Member State or a third party has objected, within the prescribed time limit, to the notified concentration.

The codification of the Commission practices regarding the assessment, acceptance and implementation of commitments in Phases I and II of merger investigations

This concerns both substantive and procedural requirements. The Commission is very clear that promises not to abuse dominance are not sufficient. The Commission will accept commitments which will ensure a specific, lasting and appropriate solution to the problem created by the envisaged concentration. The implementation of commitments must occur within a short period of time and be speedy and effective.

The notice sets out deadlines for the submission of commitments in Phase I (three weeks from the submission of the notification) and in Phase II (no more than three months from the date of notification).

The clarification of the Commission's approach to ancillary restraints

This draft notice updates the Commission notice on ancillary restraints issued in 1990. Ancillary restraints are part of the merger and therefore they are not separately assessed in the context of art 81 EC. In the draft notice the term 'ancillary' is abandoned in favour of restraints 'directly related', meaning subordinate in importance to the main object of concentration, and 'necessary', meaning that in the absence of such restraints the proposed concentration could not be implemented or could only be implemented under more uncertain conditions, for example at higher cost.

The undertakings concerned must provide reasons why they wish restraints to be regarded as ancillary. If they fail to do so, restraints will not be covered by the final decision. However, the Commission may decide that certain restraints are not ancillary and examine them under art 81 EC.

24 Enforcement of Competition Law

24.1 Measures which may be adopted under Regulation 17/62

24.2 Complaints to the Commission in respect of infringements of EC competition law

24.3 The Commission's powers of investigation

24.4 Hearings

24.5 Access to documents

24.6 Fines

24.7 Judicial review of decisions adopted by the Commission in competition matters

24.8 Enforcement of EC competition law before national courts

Under art 83 EC the Council in empowered to adopt any appropriate measure in order to give effect to arts 81 and 82 EC. The first and the most important implementing measure is Council Regulation 17/62,[1] adopted by the Council in 1962, which provides detailed rules for the application of arts 81 and 82 EC. It charges the Commission with the task of enforcing EC competition law and ensuring that it is uniformly applied and interpreted throughout the Community. The exclusive competence of the Commission is subject to one exception. In respect of arts 81 and 82 EC, Regulation 17/62 provides that the Commission shares its enforcement powers with national authorities. So long as the Commission has not initiated proceedings under arts 81 and 82 national authorities are entitled to conduct investigations in respect of alleged infringements of EC competition law: art 9(3) of Regulation 17/62. The Commission has exclusive power to grant or to refuse to grant exemptions under art 81(3) EC. In this respect it is interesting to note that the Commission has issued a Notice on Co-operation between itself and the national competition authorities.[2]

24.1 Measures which may be adopted under Regulation 17/62

Under Regulation 17/62 the Commission is empowered to adopt the following measures:

1. *Negative clearance.* An undertaking may apply to the Commission for negative clearance in order to ascertain whether or not its agreement is within the scope of arts 81 or 82 EC. The Commission may issue its opinion that there are no grounds under either

---

[1] OJ Sp Ed 1959–62 p87.
[2] OJ C313 (1997).

provision for action on its part in respect of an agreement, decision or practice. Negative clearance is a statement of opinion of the Commission based on the facts in its possession. When circumstances change, or new facts emerge, the Commission may withdraw the negative clearance. Negative clearance is different from exemption as it has no binding force.

2. *Exemptions.* Exemption is necessary if an agreement is within the scope of application of art 81(1) EC. An exemption states that although an agreement, decision or practice is in breach of art 81(1) EC this provision is not, by virtue of art 81(3) EC, applicable. In order to obtain exemption the undertakings concerned must notify their agreement. Only the Commission may grant individual exemption. Agreements requiring exemption may be divided into three categories:

a) old agreements, which refers to agreements concluded between undertakings located in the original six Member States before the entry into force of Regulation 17/62 (they were to be notified before 1 November 1962);

b) accession agreements are those entered into between undertakings before their State of establishment became a Member State of the Community, and the Commission fixes the time limit for their notification after each accession;

c) new agreements, which comprises all other agreements which are in breach of arts 81(1) or 82 EC.

There are some agreements which need not be notified taking into account that they are generally considered as not being anti-competitive. Article 4(2) of Regulation 17/62 distinguishes three types of these agreements:

a) agreements entered into by undertakings established in one Member States which do not concern exports or imports between Member States;

b) agreements which only restrict 'the freedom of the party to the contract in determining the prices or conditions of business upon which the goods which he has obtained from the other party to the contract may be resold, or impose restrictions on the exercise of the rights of the assignee or user of industrial property rights – in particular patents, utility models, designs or trade marks – or of the persons entitled under a contract to the assignment, or grant, of such right to use a method of manufacture or knowledge relating to the use and to the application of industrial process';

c) agreements which have as their sole object standardisation, joint research and development, and specialisation in the manufacture of products.

There is no duty to notify an agreement to the Commission. However, the opportunity to obtain exemption or a comfort letter as well as immunity from fines in respect of acts taking place after notification, provided they are within the limits of the activity described in the notification, constitutes a strong incentive for the undertaking concerned to ask the Commission for individual exemption. A decision granting exemption is binding on national courts. The main disadvantage of notification is that the procedure is time-consuming and may require the undertakings concerned to modify their initial agreement. Furthermore, the Commission may start infringement proceedings on the ground of information provided in accordance with Form A/B which must be used in applications for negative clearance and in notifications for individual exemption.

3. *Comfort letters*. Taking into account the workload of the Commission, it often sends a comfort letter in response to an application for an individual exemption! A comfort letter states that the Commission has no reason to take further action in respect of the agreement and thus it is closing the file. The comfort letter is sent to the applicant if the Commission decides either that on the basis of the facts in its possession the agreement does not appear to be in breach of art 81(1), or that the agreement falls within the scope of a group exemption. A comfort letter is often referred to as a 'discomfort letter', taking into account its non-binding nature.

4. *A decision*. This is addressed to the undertaking concerned to terminate the infringement. Under art 3 of Regulation 17/62 the Commission may before taking a final decision order the undertaking concerned to terminate a breach of arts 81(1) or 82 EC or make a recommendation for termination of the infringement.

5. *Interim measures*. The Commission is empowered to order interim measures. In *Camera Care Ltd* v *Commission* Case 792/79R [1980] ECR 119 the ECJ held that the Commission may grant interim relief in urgent cases where there is immediate danger of irreparable damage to the complainant, or where there is a situation which is intolerable for the public interest.

6. *Pecuniary sanctions*. This subject will be dealt with in section 24.6 (below).

24.2 Complaints to the Commission in respect of infringements of EC competition law

The Commission may become aware of the infringement of EC competition law through an application for negative clearance or notification for individual exemption, or through any other sources ie press, TV, etc. The Commission may act *ex officio* or upon an application from a Member State or 'any natural or legal person who claims a legitimate interest' (art 3(2)(b) of Regulation 17/62). The form of complaint is not important; a complainant may send a simple letter, provided it is signed and the address and name of the complaining person are included, or it may be a formal letter of complaint written on the official form (Form C).

The Commission is under a duty to reply: *Demo-Studio Schmidt* Case 210/81 [1983] ECR 3045. Its failure to provide a reply, may result in an action for failure to act under art 232 EC.

In *Automec (No 2)* Case T–24/90 [1992] 5 CMLR 431 the CFI stated that the procedure before the Commission could be divided into three stages:

1. First stage: the submission of the complaint which is followed by the gathering of information by the Commission and involves informal contacts with the parties.

2. Second stage: the notification by the Commission of its intention not to pursue the complaint specifying the reasons for the Commission's decision and inviting the person who had lodged the complaint to submit his observations within a fixed time limit.

3. Third stage: following receipt of the observations from the complainant the Commission has a duty[3] either to initiate a procedure against the subject of the complaint or to adopt a definitive decision rejecting the complaint, against which decision proceedings for annulment may be brought before the Community judicature.

In *Guérin* Case C–282/95P [1997] ECR I–1503 the ECJ specified that at the end of the third stage the Commission is required to take a definitive position, ie start proceedings or issue a definitive decision within a reasonable time. The meaning of a reasonable time was clarified in *UPS Europe SA v Commission of the European Communities* Case T–127/98 [2000] 4 CMLR 94. This case involved a complaint from United Parcels Service Group (UPS) which distributes parcels throughout the world. On 7 July 1994 UPS sent a letter to the Commission complaining about the conduct and status of Deutsche Post AG, the German post office. UPS claimed that Deutsche Post was in breach of arts 82, 86, 87 and 88 EC. The Commission replied by letter on 21 March 1995 indicating that it would examine the complaint only in the light of art 82 EC. A number of letters were exchanged between the applicant and the Commission between July 1995 and November 1996. On 25 August 1997 the Commission informed the applicant that it was suspending its proceedings under art 82 EC and was proceeding instead under art 87 EC. On 22 October 1997 the applicant called upon the Commission to 'define its position' within the meaning of art 232 EC in respect of its complaint lodged on 7 July 1994 and to re-examine its position as to the suspension of proceedings under art 82 EC. On 19 December 1997 the Commission informed the applicant that whilst it would open the procedure provided for in art 87(2) EC at the beginning of 1998, there were no grounds to proceed under art 82 EC. In this letter the Commission invited the applicant to submit its observations, which the applicant did by a letter of 2 February 1998 objecting to the Commission's intention to stop proceedings under art 82 EC. On 2 June 1998 the applicant sent the Commission a formal letter of request referring to art 232 EC and asking the Commission to define its position in relation to its complaint. On 7 August 1998 the applicant commenced proceedings against the Commission for failure to act in relation to the complaint lodged on 7 July 1994, arguing that six months had elapsed since the applicant submitted, on 2 February 1998, its observations in respect of the Commission's letter of 19 December 1997.

Following from the above it was for the CFI to decide whether the period of four months, that is from the submission of the observations by the applicant on 2 February 1998 to the sending of the letter of formal request on 2 June 1998, during which time the Commission had failed to act, should be considered as a reasonable time. The Commission argued that a relatively short period of time had elapsed after its receipt of observations in February 1998, that the subject-matter of the complaint was very complex and that it did not waste time as the complaint had been examined in the light of arts 82 and 87 EC and at the end the Commission decided that proceedings under art 87 EC, that is regarding State aid, were the most appropriate to deal with the matter. The CFI held that none of the arguments put forward by the Commission could justify its failure to act. The CFI held that:

'The Commission had received the complaint alleging infringement of art 86 of the Treaty [82 EC] 47 months earlier and had already undertaken investigation of the case. Consequently, in

---

[3] See *Guérin* Case C–282/95P [1997] ECR I–1503.

considering whether the period between the lodgment of the applicant's observations following the notification under art 6 of Regulation No 99/63 and the sending of the formal request to the Commission is acceptable, it is appropriate to take account of the years already spent on the investigation, the present state of the investigation of the case and the attitudes of the parties considered as a whole.'

Taking into account these factors the Commission was perfectly able to 'define its position' much earlier. Consequently, the CFI held that the Commission failed to act as it had neither initiated a procedure against the person who was the subject of the complaint lodged by the applicant on 7 July 1994 nor had it adopted a definitive decision rejecting that complaint following the observation of 2 February 1998 submitted by the applicant.

If the Commission adopts a final decision on rejection or acceptance of the complaint the complainant has *locus standi* to seek judicial review of that decision under art 230 EC: *Metro (No I)* Case 26/76 [1977] ECR 1875.

24.3 The Commission's powers of investigation

Regulation 17/62 confers wide powers of investigation on the Commission, and the exercise of these powers is subject to conditions serving to ensure that the rights of the undertakings concerned are respected.

Obtaining information

Under art 11 the Commission has power to compel undertakings to provide 'all necessary information'. In *Orkem* Case 374/87 [1989] ECR 3283 the ECJ held that it is up to the Commission to decide what information is 'necessary'. The CFI held that 'necessary information' relates to anything which is connected to or has some relationship between the information requested and the infringement under investigation. In *Samenwerkende Elektriciteits Produktiebedrijven (SEP) NV v Commission* Case C–36/92P [1994] ECR I–1911 the ECJ further explained that information should be regarded as necessary if it has some connection with the alleged infringement, if it assists detection of or confirmation of the alleged infringement or if it confirms evidence already gathered by the Commission. The request for information may take two forms:

1. A simple request. The Commission may ask the competent authorities of the Member States, their officials and other servants, undertakings and associations of undertakings for information. In the request for information the Commission must specify the legal basis and the reason for its demand, as well as inform its addressee of the sanctions applicable if he refuses to provide requested information or provides inexact or misleading information.

2. A formal decision requiring the information to be provided. If an addressee of a simple request for information fails to provide it within a fixed time limit, or supplies incomplete or inexact information, the Commission may adopt a formal decision requiring the supply of information. If the undertaking further refuses to comply the Commission may adopt a decision imposing penalties. However, an undertaking is not

obliged to supply information which would incriminate it. In *Solvay* Case 27/88 [1989] ECR 3355 the ECJ held that it is the task of the Commission to prove the infringement of arts 81(1) or 82 EC and that the imposition of such an obligation on an undertaking would undermine its rights to defence.

In *Samenwerkende Elektriciteits Produktiebedrijven (SEP) NV v Commission* the ECJ examined the refusal of an undertaking to provide requested information. In this case the Commission opened an investigation into the commercial relationship between a Dutch electricity production company and its state-controlled gas supplier (Gasunie). This relationship was governed by a code of conduct. During the investigation, the Commission requested the electricity company to provide a copy of a contract with a Norwegian gas company (Statoil). The contract with the Norwegian supplier, which was not specifically the subject of the investigation, infringed the rights of the Dutch gas supplier which had a state-sponsored monopoly on the supply of gas in The Netherlands. The electricity company refused to provide a copy of the agreement to the Commission on two grounds. First, the production of the agreement was not necessary for the investigation. Second, the national authorities might obtain a copy and thereafter commence proceedings for infringing the national monopoly in the supply of gas.

The Commission issued an order compelling the disclosure of the contract and the applicant appealed against this decision. The CFI held that the Commission was entitled to have sight of the contract in order to assess the legality of related agreements under investigation. In this particular situation, the contract between the Dutch company and the Norwegian supplier was required by the Commission to identify a pattern of business conduct being pursued by the Dutch company. Referring to the applicant's claim that the disclosure of the contract might result in it falling into the hands of the national authorities, the Court held that the business activities of the company were adequately protected by the duty of confidentiality imposed by art 20 of Regulation 17/62. The applicant appealed to the ECJ.

As to the second justification provided by SEP, under art 11(2) of Regulation 17/62 the Commission is obliged to send to the competent national authorities of the Member State in which the undertaking concerned has its seat, a copy of any request for information and copies of the most important documents submitted to the Commission within the framework of competition proceedings. In this case the CFI stated that the Commission may, in particular when the undertaking concerned has raised the question of the document confidentiality before the Commission, exercise its discretion whether or not to send the contested document to the national authorities. The question whether or not national authorities may base national proceedings on such documents was answered in the negative by the ECJ in *Dirección General de Defensa de la Competenza v Asociación Española de Banca Privada* Case C–67/91 [1992] ECR I–4785. The ECJ held that art 20(2) of Regulation 17/62 prevented national authorities from using information received from the Commission for purposes other than those for which it was obtained, although such may be used in order to assess whether to institute national proceedings.

The ECJ did not share the CFI's opinion that art 20 of Regulation 17/62 adequately protected the applicant against action by the national authorities who had legitimately consulted the contract. They cannot be required to disregard it, in particular if it fell to them to determine the commercial policy of the competing undertaking supervised by them. In these circumstances it is for the Commission to decide whether or not a particular document contains business secrets. If so, the Commission must issue a reasoned decision informing the applicant that it intends to transmit a document to the national authorities notwithstanding the claim that the document is of a confidential nature with respect to those authorities. Before implementing this decision, the Commission must give the applicant an opportunity to bring an action before the Court with a view to having the decision made reviewed by it and to prevent the contested disclosure.

As a result, an action for annulment brought under art 230 EC, and not an action against the decision under art 11 of Regulation 17/62 ordering the document to be produced to the Commission, protects business secrets of the applicant since the obligation to produce the document does not necessarily mean that it can be transmitted to the competent national authorities.

Sectoral enquiries

Under art 12 of Regulation 17/62 the Commission is empowered to conduct general enquiries into any economic sector if there is a suspicion that competition conditions in that sector are restricted or distorted. The Commission is entitled to request information from undertakings in the sector under investigation. It seems that this provision has rarely been applied.

Inspections

Article 14 of regulation 17/62 defines the Commission's powers of investigation. Article 14(1) authorises the Commission to undertake all necessary investigations into undertakings and associations of undertakings including:

1. examination of books and other business records;
2. taking copies of or extracts from the books and business records;
3. asking for oral explanations on the spot;
4. entering any premises, land and means of transport of undertakings.

Investigations may be carried out under a 'simple' written authorisation given by the Commission or under a formal decision adopted by the Commission, with or without prior notification to the undertaking concerned.

The Court held in *National Panasonic* v *Commission* Case 136/79 [1980] ECR 2033 that the Commission may choose between the two above-mentioned possibilities in the light of the special features of each case. Both the written authorisation and the decision must specify the subject matter and purpose of the investigation. An undertaking is not obliged to submit to investigation under the 'simple authorisation'. Due notice of its refusal is, however, taken by the inspectors. In such a situation the Commission may adopt a decision. Also when the Commission fears that vital evidence may be destroyed, it adopts a decision. An undertaking is obliged to submit to an investigation ordered by way of a decision. Refusal to do so was examined in *Hoechst AG* v *Commission* Cases 46/87 and 227/88 [1989] ECR 2859; [1988] 4 CMLR 430.

In this case the Commission adopted a decision authorising search and seizure operations at the headquarters and premises of the plaintiff under art 14 of Regulation 17/62, which concerns procedure for conducting investigations into infringements of Community competition policy. The decision was adopted after the plaintiff had refused to accede to the Commission's request to hand over certain confidential documentation. In response to the refusal to disclose information, the Commission also imposed fines against the plaintiff.

The plaintiff objected to the conduct of the search on the ground that it infringed general principles of Community law. The plaintiff submitted a number of grounds in support of his contentions, the majority of which concerned the need to respect due process of law, particularly as enshrined in the European Convention on Human Rights. Regulation 17/62 was silent on a number of important issues concerning the rights of the suspects in such investigations. The Commission was required to derive applicable rules from the general principles of Community law.

The ECJ held that Regulation 17/62 must be interpreted so as to protect the rights of individuals against abuses of legal process, particularly as regards the principles contained in the European Convention on Human Rights. Such rights, including the protection of lawyer-client confidentiality, provided they are related to the subject-matter of the proceedings and a lawyer concerned is not an in-house lawyer,[4] must be respected as from the preliminary inquiry stage. In contrast, although particular regard must be had to the rights of the defence (*Michelin* v *Commission* Case 322/81 [1983] ECR 3461) they should be overridden during the investigations stage, taking into account that inspections may be decisive in providing evidence of the unlawful nature of conduct engaged in by undertakings for which they may be liable. The rights to defence regain their importance in the contentious proceedings which follow the delivery of the statement of objections. The Court recognised that it was a general principle of Community law that individuals should be protected from arbitrary and disproportionate intervention by public authorities in the sphere of private activities. It is the task of the ECJ to determine whether measures of investigation taken by the Commission are excessive: *San Michele and Others* v *Commission* Joined Cases 5–11/62 [1962] ECR 449.

The Commission officials may decide to carry out a so-called 'dawn raid' – that is arrive at the undertaking's premises without warning. In such event, the undertaking under investigation is legally obliged under art 14(3) of the Regulation to submit to an investigation ordered by the Commission decision. Under EC law alone, the Commission's officials are not entitled to enter the premises of the undertaking under investigation. They have to respect the relevant procedural guarantees laid down in the national law of the undertaking under investigation. It follows from art 14(6) that it is for each Member State to determine the conditions under which the national authorities will afford assistance to the Commission's officials. In that regard, the Member States are required to ensure that the Commission's action is effective, while respecting the general principles set out above. It follows that, within those limits, the appropriate procedural rules designed to ensure respect for the rights of undertakings are those laid down by national law.

By art 14(5), the Commission's officials may be assisted in carrying out their duties by

---

[4] *John Deere* [1985] 2 CMLR 554.

officials of the competent authority of the Member State in whose territory the investigation is to be made. Such assistance may be provided either at the request of that authority or of the Commission.

Finally, by virtue of art 14(6), where the carrying out of the investigation is opposed by an undertaking national authorities are required to assist if necessary. For that reason, art 14(6) of Regulation 17/62 provides that when an undertaking refuses to submit to investigations national authorities are required to provide necessary assistance to enable the Commission to make investigations. In the UK the Crown must obtain an injunction (for example a search and seizure order) from the Commercial Court to assist the Commission. National authorities are not entitled to call into question the need for the investigations since only the ECJ can review the acts of the Commission, but it is for them to decide upon the appropriate procedure to be applied in the investigations. The *Hoechst* case clarifies the rights of an undertaking in such investigations. The Commission is not permitted to carry out 'fishing expeditions'. The subject of the investigations must be specified in the authorisation or decision, that is, the suspicion which the Commission is seeking to verify must be clearly indicated, but, as the ECJ held in *Hoechst*, the Commission is not obliged to provide the addressee with all information at its disposal in relation to the alleged infringement.

24.4 Hearings

Under art 19 of Regulation 17/62 and art 9(2) of Regulation 99/63 the Commission is required to give the undertaking concerned the opportunity to be heard. The Commission may also hear applications from any natural or legal person who can 'show a sufficient interest'.

The first step of the contentious procedure starts when the Commission sends a written letter to the undertaking concerned specifying the objection raised against it. The 'statement of objection' must set forth clearly all the essential facts upon which the Commission relies against the undertaking. In the final decision the Commission must state only objections raised in the statement of objections in order to protect the responding undertaking's rights to be heard: *Ahlström Osakeyhtiö* Case 89/85 [1993] ECR I–1307. The Commission specifies a time limit for a written submission which an undertaking concerned may submit in response to the 'statement of objections'. An undertaking is not obliged to reply (*Hilti* Case T–30/89 [1991] ECR II–1439) although this is necessary if the undertaking wishes to have an opportunity to submit its arguments orally at an oral hearing where a sufficient interest is shown or where the Commission proposes to impose pecuniary sanctions.

In general the Commission will invite the parties concerned to an oral hearing. In order to ensure that the rights of the parties concerned are observed, hearings are conducted by persons appointed by the Commission and referred to as the 'Hearing Officer'. This post was created in 1982.[5] The Hearing Officer is familiar with the file, he ensures that the hearing is

---

[5] OJ C251/2 (1982) and the Commission Decision 94/810: OJ L330/67 (1994).

properly conducted, and he may, before the formal hearing, organise meetings with the parties concerned. He is entitled to get in touch with the Member of the Commission in charge of the case and he submits a report to the Director-General for Competition relating to the formal hearing and his conclusions. The persons summoned to attend the hearing must appear either in person or be represented by their legal or duly authorised representatives. They may be assisted by lawyers or any person who is entitled to plead before the ECJ (for example, law lecturers). At hearings lawyers can only assist the party and not represent him. The reason is that only factual matters are discussed at hearings and not legal arguments. Hearings are conducted in private and often last only one day.

24.5 Access to documents

Access to documents relevant to the case is of vital importance to the parties concerned. The extent to which a party can have access to documents was specified in a number of cases decided by the Community judicature and further explained by the Commission in its Notice on the Internal Rules of Procedure for Processing Requests for Access to the File in Competition Matters.[6] The principle that the interested parties should have access to all files held by the Commission is subject to three exceptions: *Hercules* Case T–7/89 [1991] ECR II–1711:

1. *Documents which relate to business secrets.* In *AKZO* Case 53/85 [1987] 1 CMLR 231 the ECJ emphasised that undertakings have legitimate interest in protecting their business secrets, taking into account the extremely serious damage which could result from improper communication of documents to a competitor. In *AKZO* the ECJ held that it is for the Commission to judge whether or not a particular document contains business secrets. If there is a request from a third party to consult a particular document the Commission must inform the undertaking from which this document was taken. If the undertaking concerned identifies that this document is of a confidential nature, the Commission has two options: first, it may agree with the undertaking concerned and thus this documents will not be communicated to a third party; and, second, the Commission may disagree, in which case it must give the undertaking an opportunity to state its views. If the Commission still disagrees, it is required to adopt a decision in that connection which contains an adequate statement of the reasons on which it is based and which must be notified to the undertaking concerned. The Commission must, before implementing its decision, give the undertaking an opportunity to bring an action before the ECJ with a view to having the decision made reviewed by it and to prevent disclosure of the document in question.
2. *Documents which do not form part of the investigation.* These are internal documents of the Commission (draft notices, projects, etc). These documents are not binding but their disclosure may prejudice the confidentiality of the Commission's deliberations in respect of the case in hand. Access to them is not permitted. In order to make them truly inaccessible they are not placed in the main file, although in *NMH Stahlwerke* Cases

---

[6] OJ C25/3 (1997).

T–134, 136–138, 141, 145, 147, 148, 151, 156 and 157/94R [1996] ECR II–537 the CFI held that a list of those documents, together with a short description of their content, should be attached to the main file in order to allow the parties to decide whether those documents were of any relevance to them and, if so, to apply for their disclosure.

3. *Confidential documents.* The Commission will refuse access to documents which it considers to be confidential. Reasons may be to protect the identity of an informer, that documents were supplied to the Commission subject to non-disclosure, and that documents relate to military secrets.

In relation to the above-mentioned exceptions the Commission tries to reconcile the opposing obligations of safeguarding the right of the defence and protecting confidential information.

If the Commission refuses access to documents in its possession without sufficient reasons its final decision may be annulled by the Community judicature: *Cimenteries CBR* Cases T–10–12 and 15/92 [1992] ECR II–2667. In *Hercules* Case C–51/92P [1999] ECR I–4235 the appellant, an undertaking which had participated in a cartel, challenged the Commission's refusal to have access to the replies of the other undertakings to the statement of objections. The ECJ held that a refusal to grant access would have led to annulment of the contested decision (Polypropylene Decision) only if the relevant documents were capable of having some influence on the procedural or substantive outcome of the case, that is, only if the rights of defence of the undertaking concerned had been infringed. This was not the case taking into account that although Hercules was granted access at a later stage, following joinder of the case, it did not draw from replies from other undertakings involved in the cartel any exonerating evidence and therefore there was no infringement of its rights of defence.

The matter of access to documents relating to ECJ proceedings was examined in *Baustahlgewebe GmbH* v *Commission of the European Communities* Case C–185/95P [1999] 4 CMLR 1203. On appeal from the CFI the appellant argued that he was entitled to consult such documents. The ECJ held that although the right of access to documents constitutes a fundamental principle of Community law 'contrary to the appellant's assertion, the general principles of Community law governing the right of access to the Commission's file do not apply, as such, to court proceedings, the latter being governed by the EC Statute of the Court of Justice and by the Rules of Procedure of the Court of First Instance.' However, the appellant was entitled to ask the CFI to order the Commission to produce certain documents in its possession. For the CFI to determine whether it was necessary to order the production of certain documents, the party requesting production must identify the documents which it wished to consult and provide the CFI with at least minimum information indicating the utility of those documents for the purposes of the proceedings. In the present case, the appellant did not sufficiently identify the documents in the file of which it sought production and therefore the CFI was right to reject its request for the production of documents.

24.6 Fines

In order to enforce EC competition law the Commission is empowered to impose pecuniary sanctions on undertakings. Financial penalties can be imposed for infringements that have already ceased (subject to the limitation period) as well as for ongoing infringements. They are of three kinds

1. *Procedural fines.* These may be imposed on an undertaking which refuses to supply information or when it provides incorrect or misleading information intentionally or negligently:

   a) in respect of applications for negative clearance or notifications;
   b) if requested by the Commission under art 11(3) or (5) of Regulation 17/62;
   c) in respect of a general inquiry into a sector of the economy by virtue of art 12 of Regulation 17/62;
   d) during investigations under arts 13 and 14 of the Regulation 17/62.

   These fines may also be imposed if an undertaking refuses to submit to investigations ordered by the Commission by the way of a decision adopted under art 14(3) of the Regulation. Procedural fines may range from EUR 100 to EUR 5,000. However, they are not of a criminal nature.

2. *Periodic penalty payments.* The Commission may impose these on an undertaking which refuses to terminate an infringement of arts 81 or 82 EC following the Commission's decision adopted under art 3 of Regulation 17/62, or to force an undertaking to refrain from any act prohibited by art 8(3) of the Regulation (abuse of exemption, supply of information, etc). They may also be applied if an undertaking refuses to supply information or supplies incorrect, incomplete or misleading information under art 11(5) or if an undertaking refuses to submit to investigations ordered by the Commission by virtue of a formal decision adopted under art 14(3) of Regulation 17/62. The payments may range from EUR 50 to 1,000 per day from the date specified by the Commission decision.

3. *'Substantive' fines.* Under art 15(2) of Regulation 17/62 the Commission is empowered to impose fines for intentional or negligent infringement of arts 81 and 82 EC, or the commission of a breach of any obligation imposed under a decision granting exemption. To find intention or negligence it is not necessary that the partners, or principal managers of an undertaking, have acted improperly or even been aware of an infringement. It suffices that the prohibited action was taken by a person authorised to act on behalf of the undertaking: *Musique Diffusion SA v Commission* Cases 100–103/80 [1983] 3 CMLR 221. Intentional infringement was defined by the ECJ as an act deliberately committed with the intention of achieving some object prohibited by the Treaty: *Gerard Züchner v Bayerische Vereinsbank AG* Case 172/80 [1981] ECR 2021. A negligent infringement occurs when an undertaking knew or ought to have known that its action would result in infringement of the prohibition: *United Brands* Case 27/76 [1977] ECR 207. An undertaking may be regarded as having acted intentionally or negligently even though it participated in an infringement under pressure.[7] This factor

---

[7] See *Tipp-Ex*: OJ L222 (1987).

will be considered when fixing the fine. The amount of fine is from EUR 1,000 upwards. The maximum fine that can be imposed is 10 per cent of an undertaking's turnover (which includes all group turnover) in the preceding financial year. In *Baustahlgewebe GmbH* v *Commission of the European Communities* Case C–185/95P [1999] 4 CMLR 1203 the ECJ implicitly confirmed that pecuniary sanctions imposed on legal persons for breach of EC Competition law are within the scope of criminal matters in the sense of art 6 of the European Convention on Human Rights. Also, in this case the ECJ held that the CFI has unlimited jurisdiction to determine the amount of fines.

It is interesting to note that in 1998 the Commission published a Notice regarding its fining policy under arts 81 and 82 EC with a view to ensuring the transparency and impartiality of its decisions.[8]

The Notice is not binding. The Commission enjoys a wide discretion in the determination of the amount of fine in each case. In practice, the Commission in determining the amount of fine takes into consideration two criteria: the gravity of the infringement and the duration of the infringement. The guidelines provide that the Commission's first task in assessing the amount of fine is to determine the basic amount by applying both criteria. The next step consists of adjusting the basic amount in the light of two sets of circumstances: it is increased by reference to aggravating circumstances or reduced by reference to attenuating circumstances.

The Commission identifies five sets of aggravating circumstances, but its list is not exhaustive. They are:

1. repeated infringements of the same type by the same undertaking;
2. refusal of the undertaking to co-operate with the Commission during its investigation or the obstruction of the investigation by an undertaking;
3. being the leader, or an instigator, of any infringement;
4. if an undertaking has made a substantial profit due to its anti-competitive conduct, the Commission would tend to increase the fine in order to encompass the profit;
5. if an undertaking has applied retaliatory measures against any other undertaking in order to enforce its anti-competitive conduct.

The list of attenuating circumstances (also not exhaustive) is:

1. the passive role of an undertaking consisting of the following of other undertakings in their infringement;
2. non-implementation in practice of an anti-competitive agreement or practice
3. termination of the infringement as soon as the Commission notifies it to an undertaking;
4. existence of reasonable doubt on the part of an undertaking as to its anti-competitive conduct;
5. unintentional or negligent infringement;
6. in the case of a cartel, effective co-operation with the Commission of an undertaking which was a party to the cartel.

---

[8] OJ C9 (1998); [1998] 3 CMLR 472.

The Commission will take into consideration the economic context of the infringement and the ability of un undertaking to actually pay the fine. The Commission states that in the context of trade associations it will, if possible, impose fines on individual members of the association rather than the trade association itself. A symbolic fine of EUR 1,000 may be imposed if the infringement is technical or relatively trivial.

The fining policy of the Commission has changed over the years. At first, the Commission imposed relatively small fines. The Commission in *Pioneer Hi-Fi Equipment*[9] indicated a change of policy. It stated that fines should be a real deterrent and should be increased in amount in cases of serious infringements. On appeal (*Musique Diffusion SA* v *Commission* Cases 100–103/80) the ECJ confirmed that the Commission was entitled to change its approach and to impose heavier fines than previously. The ECJ held that 'the proper application of the Community competition rules requires that the Commission may at any time adjust the levels of fines to the needs of that policy.' As a result the Commission has increased fines by a considerable amount.

On 28 January 1998 the Commission imposed the biggest ever fine on a single undertaking of EUR 102 million on the German car manufacturer, Volkswagen AG (VW).[10] The fine represented 10 per cent of VW's net profit for the year preceding the commencement of proceedings. The circumstances were that Volkswagen AG and its subsidiaries Audi AG and Autogerma SpA were in persistent breach of arts 81 and 82 EC by preventing franchised dealers in Italy from selling VW models to German and Austrian nationals who wished to purchase them in Italy where prices were lower than in Germany and Austria. The Commission stated that Volkswagen AG was in breach of the principle of the prohibition of discrimination on the grounds of nationality as embodied in art 12 EC.

24.7 Judicial review of decisions adopted by the Commission in competition matters

Any decision adopted by the Commission may be subject to judicial review under art 230 EC within a reasonable time. In this respect, it is interesting to examine *Baustahlgewebe GmbH* v *Commission of the European Communities* Case C–185/95P [1999] 4 CMLR 1203 in which, for the first time, the ECJ held that a Community court was in breach of the principle that the proceedings must be disposed of within a reasonable time.

On 20 October 1989 Baustahlgewebe brought action for annulment of a Commission Decision 89/515/EEC which imposed fines on 14 producers of welded steel mesh for infringement of art 85(1) EC Treaty (art 81(1) EC). After five years and six months the CFI delivered its decision, reducing the fine from ECU 4.4 million to ECU 3 million and partially annulling the Commission decision. The applicant claimed, *inter alia*, that the CFI was in

---

[9] OJ L60 (1980).

[10] See *Volkswagen AG and Others*, Decision 98/273/EC of 28 January 1998 ([1998] 5 CMLR 33). On appeal the CFI confirmed the existence and gravity of the infringement committed by Volkswagen (VW) but reduced the fine from EUR 102,000,000 to EUR 90,000,000, on the ground that the infringement had lasted for only three years (from 1993 to 1996), as the Commission did not properly prove that the infringement continued after that period: *Volkswagen* v *Commission* Case T–62/98 Judgment of 6 July 2000 (nyr).

breach of the principle that proceedings must be disposed of within a reasonable time as enshrined in art 6 of the European Convention on Human Rights, that the CFI infringed its rights of defence by refusing access to the file, and that a disproportionate fine was imposed upon it.

In order to determine whether or not the duration of the proceedings before the CFI had been excessive the ECJ made reference to art 6 of the European Convention on Human Rights and Fundamental Freedoms and the case law of the European Court of Human Rights in this area. Subsequently, the ECJ assessed the reasonableness of the period of five years and six months in the light of the circumstances of this case, in particular four criteria were taken into account: the importance of the case for the person concerned, its complexity, the conduct of the applicant and the conduct of the competent authorities. The ECJ concluded: that the case was of considerable importance, not only to the applicant but also to the third parties in view of the large number of persons concerned and the amount of the fine; that the case was complex; and that the applicant did not contribute to the protraction of the proceedings. The ECJ also held that the proceedings before the CFI were excessively protracted. For that reason the ECJ partially annulled the decision of the CFI. The ECJ stated that the excessive duration of proceedings before the CFI had no impact on the outcome of the case and decided that ECU 50,000 constituted fair satisfaction for a procedural irregularity of that kind. Accordingly, it reduced the amount of the fine imposed on the applicants to this amount. In this case the ECJ held, for the first time, that it was entitled to award 'reasonable satisfaction' within the meaning of art 50 of the ECHR for the excessive duration of the proceedings.

The question of the effect of an ECJ judgment annulling a Commission decision was examined in *Commission of the European Communities* v *Assidomän Kraft Products AB and Others* Case C–310/97P [1999] 5 CMLR 1253. In *Ahlström and Others* v *Commission (Re Wood Pulp Cartel)* Joined Cases 89, 104, 114, 116, 117 and 125–129/85 [1993] 4 CMLR 407 the Commission found more than 40 suppliers of wood pulp in violation of Community competition law despite the fact that none of these companies was resident within the European Community. Fines were imposed on 36 of these undertakings for violation of art 81(1) EC. Among those fined were nine Swedish undertakings, who paid their fines. Subsequently, 26 of the undertakings appealed to the ECJ against the decision. They challenged the Commission's finding that they had breached art 81(1) EC through concertation of prices for their products by means of a system of quarterly price announcements. However, the nine Swedish undertakings that had already paid fines, including AssiDomän, decided not to participate in the annulment proceedings.

The Court annulled the decision of the Commission that the undertakings concerned infringed art 81(1) EC through concertation of prices for their products on the grounds that the Commission had not provided a firm, precise and consistent body of evidence in this respect. As a result the ECJ annulled most of the fines entirely and reduced to EUR 20,000 the other fines imposed on the undertakings which had instituted proceedings.

AssiDomän Kraft Products and other undertakings which did not join in the annulment proceedings asked the Commission to reconsider their legal position in the light of the ECJ's judgment and to refund to each of them the fines which they paid to the extent that they exceeded the sum of EUR 20,000. However, the undertakings in question were not the addressees of the judgment. The Commission refused to refund them on the grounds that it had already complied with the ECJ order by reducing the fines in respect of the undertakings participating in the proceedings and that the decision of the ECJ had no necessary impact on the fines imposed upon the Swedish undertakings. The latter responded by challenging that decision before the Court of First Instance.

The Court of First Instance held that although the Commission issued one decision in the *Wood Pulp* case that decision, in fact, consisted of a bundle of 43 separate decisions, each of which was independent of the others. Consequently, the annulment or modification of 26 fines left the remaining fines unaffected. However, the CFI upheld the appeal of the Swedish undertakings on the ground of art 233 EC which provides that when an act adopted by an EC institution has been declared void that institution should take the necessary measures to comply with the judgment of the ECJ. The CFI decided that this obligation could extend to persons who were not party to any appeal before the ECJ and thus the Commission should re-examine the legality of the unchallenged decision in the light of the grounds of the annulling judgment and determine whether, following such re-examination, the fines paid must be refunded. The CFI annulled the Commission's decision refusing to refund the fines already paid by Swedish undertakings. At that stage, the Commission challenged the decision of the CFI which challenge was the subject of the current appeal.

The ECJ reversed the decision of the CFI. The ECJ held that the Swedish undertakings were not entitled to have the fines reduced. The ECJ justified its judgment on two grounds. First, the Community judicature cannot rule *ultra petita*, that is the scope of the annulment which it pronounces may not go further than that sought by the applicant and thus unchallenged aspects concerning other addressees did not form part of the matter to be tried by the Community judicature. Second, although the authority *erga omnes* exerted by an annulling judgment attaches to both the operative part and the *ratio decidendi* of the judgment, it cannot entail annulment of an act not challenged before the Community judicature but alleged to be vitiated by the same illegality. Consequently, art 233 EC cannot be interpreted as requiring the institution concerned to re-examine identical or similar decisions allegedly affected by the same irregularity addressed to addressees other than the applicant. The ECJ also added that the judgment of the CFI was contrary to art 230 EC since it sidestepped the time limit for bringing legal proceedings against acts adopted by EC institutions and thus undermined the principle of legal certainty. Furthermore, this principle also precluded the re-examination of unchallenged decisions.

The judgment of the ECJ is fully justified in so far as the Commission's decision is regarded as a bundle of individual decisions against each participating undertaking and not as a single decision addressed to all of them. This solution has been confirmed in *Limburgse Vinyl Maatschappij NV and Others v Commission (Re PVC Cartel (No 2))* [1999] 5 CMLR 303 in which a number of undertakings successfully challenged the Commission's decision on the ground that it had not been signed by the appropriate persons. The ECJ held that the challenged decision was binding on those undertakings who had not appealed.

Although the solution, which consisted of considering the Commission's decision as a bundle of separate decisions addressed to each participating undertaking, penalises undertakings which decide not to appeal it is, at the same time, fair. Undertakings may not challenge a Commission decision in competition matters for a number of reasons, the most important being that the appeal procedure involves considerable investment in terms of time and money. Hindsight is very useful but the fact is that if an undertaking has chosen to economise by not spending time and money on an appeal, and the judgment of the court in similar matters arrives after the limitation period has expired, it will be too late to jump on the bandwagon. Conversely, if the outcome is against the appellant the decision not to participate will be well justified.

24.8 Enforcement of EC competition law before national courts

The ECJ held in *BRT v SABAM* Case 127/73 [1974] ECR 51 that arts 81(1) and 82 EC are directly effective. They are both horizontally and vertically directly effective. As a result, an individual may rely on those provisions in proceedings before a national court against either a Member State or other individuals. The principle of effective protection of rights conferred by Community law on individuals (*Rewe-Zentralfinanz eG v Landwirtschaftskammer für das Saarland* Case 33/76 [1976] ECR 1989) requires that national procedural rules should not be applied in such a manner as to make the enforcement of Community rights more difficult than the enforcement of analogous national rights, and that the national procedural rules should not have the effect of making the enforcement of Community rights impossible in practice (*Comet* Case 45/76 [1976] ECR 2043), or even excessively difficult: *Amministrazione delle Finanze dello Stato v San Giorgio* Case 199/82 [1983] ECR 3595. For claimants, remedies available for breaches of arts 81(1) and 82 EC should be equivalent to those available for breaches of national law of a similar nature. In the light of the case law of the Community judicature, in particular relating to a Member State's liability in tort, there are no doubts that an individual has the right to claim damages before an English court. However, the basis for such action is still subject to controversy in England as it is not covered by any existing cause of action. This question was discussed by the House of Lords in 1983 in *Garden Cottage Foods Ltd v Milk Marketing Board* [1983] 3 CMLR 43, although it did not form part of the *ratio* of the case. The majority of the House of Lords was in favour of granting damages for a breach of art 86 as a breach of statutory duty, the statute being the 1972 European Communities Act.[11]

The proposed reform of EC Competition law will bring important changes to the enforcement of arts 81 and 82 EC through the national courts. In 1998 the Commission issued its Notice on Co-operation between the National Competition Authorities and the Commission in the Application of arts 81 and 82 EC.[12]

Many considerations have prompted the Commission to confer a greater role on national competition authorities within the framework of Community Competition law:

1. the application of the principle of subsidiarity;
2. the expansion of the EU to 15 Member States, and then up to 20 and more;
3. limited resources available to the Commission;

---

[11] Goyder examines the possible solutions and their implications in *EC Competition Law*, 3rd ed, Oxford: Oxford University Press, 1998, pp516–518.
[12] OJ C313 (1997).

4. the need for a coherent application of competition rules at national and Community level which requires that parallel proceedings before the Commission and national authorities should be avoided.

The Notice specifies that co-operation with national competition authorities will 'boost the effectiveness of arts 81 and 82 ... and will bolster the application of Community competition rules throughout the Community. Being closer to the activities and businesses that require monitoring, national authorities are often in a better position than the Commission to protect competition.'

The main features of the Notice are:

1. Reallotment of tasks between the Commission and national authorities in the application of Community competition law. The Notice suggests that in order to determine whether national authorities should deal with competition cases (whether on their own initiative or at the Commission's request) two criteria are to be taken into consideration: the effect of the infringement in respect of the relevant geographical market and the nature of the infringement, that is, whether, upon a preliminary examination, the case is likely to qualify for exemption under art 81(3) EC. If the relevant geographical market and the effect of infringement are limited to the territory of one Member State and the case is unlikely to obtain exemption national authorities should deal with it. Even though the criteria are satisfied, the Commission reserves to itself the right to act if the case presents 'a particular Community interest' from a legal perspective, ie when the matter may give rise to a new point of law or from an economic standpoint, in particular where access by undertakings from other Member States is significantly impeded and in the case of anti-competitive conduct of State monopolies of commercial character.

2. Co-operation between national authorities and the Commission. The Notice establishes guidelines as to first and subsequent seizure of the case. If the Commission is first seised three situations must be distinguished: if the Commission is seised *d'office*, or by means of a notification, it has exclusive competence to act; if, however, there is a complaint lodged by individuals or undertakings, the Commission will, if possible, redirect it by Directorate-General IV to national authorities. The Notice sets out detailed rules concerning the procedure and the conditions for the rejection of the complaint.

   If national authorities are first seised, irrespective of the procedural origin (be it on the own initiative of the national authorities, a notification submitted by the undertaking concerned to the national competition authorities, or a complaint from interested parties), they have to inform the Commission of any proceedings commenced by them in order that information can be passed to the authorities in other Member States. This will also facilitate the Commission to identify notifications 'made for dilatory purposes', that is in order to delay the imposition of an appropriate sanction by national authorities. The Commission is committed to discourage delaying tactics and such will be held against the undertaking concerned. The Notice provides also for a provisional opinion by the Commission to national authorities.

The impact of the Notice on undertakings should be assessed in the light of the exclusive competence of the Commission to grant exemption under art 81(3) EC. As a result, whenever an exemption is required, an undertaking must apply to the Commission. Second, the competence of national authorities to apply arts 81(1) and 82 EC is often restricted by national law. Legislation of several Member States does not provide competition authorities with the procedural means of applying arts 81(1) and 82 EC. In the Notice the Commission calls upon the Member States which have not yet enacted appropriate legislation to do so as soon as possible. At the time of writing, so far only eight of the 15 Member States have introduced enabling legislation: France, Germany, Spain, Greece, The Netherlands, Portugal, Italy and Belgium.

In practice, an undertaking should take into consideration many factors when choosing between national authorities or the Commission to bring an art 81- or art 82-based case: the factors include the inability of the Commission to award damages to an aggrieved party or to provide the remedy of restitution, the powers of the Commission to investigate the alleged infringement which are more extensive than those of national authorities, the cost of proceedings before national courts, the possibility for the Commission to impose substantial fines, the time factor, etc.[13]

---

[13] On this subject see: D Trapp and M Truman, 'Cherry Picking or Double Jeopardy' (1998) European Council, March, pp38–43.

25 Intellectual Property Rights

25.1 Intellectual property rights and the free movement of goods

25.2 Parallel imports from outside the EC and EEA

25.3 Intellectual property rights and arts 81 and 82 EC

25.4 Harmonisation of intellectual property rights

The essence of intellectual property rights is that they create a form of monopoly for the holder in order to either reward his creativity and investment in terms of time and money or to protect his commercial reputation and goodwill. Intellectual property rights include patents, trade marks, copyrights, registered designs, etc. Under national law the holder of intellectual property rights is protected against others copying or taking unfair advantage of his work or reputation. The period of protection varies depending on the national law of the Member State and the type of intellectual property. In the UK in respect of patents the patentee or holder enjoys exclusive rights for a period of 20 years. For trade marks the protection is indefinite, that is, it lasts as long as goods and services are supplied under that trade mark. For copyright the author of a work (literary work, artistic work, musical work, sound recordings, films and broadcasts) is protected either for 70 years after his death or 50 years after the creation of the protected work, depending on the type of work.

EC law recognises the importance of national protection of intellectual property rights in art 295 EC, which provides:

'... the Treaty shall in no way prejudice the rules in Member States governing the system of property ownership.'

However, the relationship between intellectual property rights and EC law is not easy. The fundamental objectives of EC law are in conflict with the very nature of intellectual property rights. Their exercise might affect, in particular, two areas of EC law: the free movement of goods and the provisions of the EC Treaty regarding competition law, especially arts 81 and 82 EC.

In respect of the free movement of goods art 28 EC prohibits the imposition of any quantitative restrictions and measures having equivalent effect. This provision clashes with the territorial protection granted to a holder of intellectual property rights who may use national law to partition the internal market along national lines in a number of ways. For example, he may charge different prices for the protected product in different Member States; he may restrict imports from one Member State to another; he may totally prevent any imports, since without his consent the protected product cannot be sold in another Member State. Thus, the exercise of his rights may seriously hinder the free movement of goods. Article 30 EC recognises that intellectual property rights may constitute measures equivalent to quantitative restrictions. It provides a derogation from art 28 EC, subject to a very important limitation which is that it must not constitute a means of arbitrary discrimination or a disguised restriction on trade between Member States.

In relation to EC competition law, the exclusive rights conferred on the holder of intellectual property rights are by their very nature anti-competitive, taking into account that they protect him from others copying or taking advantage of his work or reputation. Thus, he controls the market in respect of the protected products and he may be tempted to abuse his position to the detriment of competitors and consumers. How EC competition law deals with this will be further analysed in this chapter.

The obvious solution to the conflict between the exercise of intellectual property rights provided for under national laws of Member States and Community rules on freedom of movement of goods and competition is to harmonise these rights at Community level. The establishment of a unitary Community system in this area is not easy since there are considerable divergences between the laws of the Member States. However, much has been accomplished in this area: see section 25.4 below.

EC law both restricts the exercise of intellectual property rights and extends the rights enjoyed by holders of those rights. The principle of non-discrimination on grounds of nationality as embodied in art 12 EC applies to the exercise of intellectual property rights. It requires that nationals of one Member State are placed on an equal footing with nationals of other Member States in situations covered by Community law. This was recognised by the ECJ in *Phil Collins* v *Imtrat Handelsgesellschaft mbH; Patricia Im-und Export Verwaltungsgesellschaft mbH and Leif E Kraul* v *EMI Electrola GmbH* Joined Cases C–92 and 326/92 [1993] ECR I–5145. The performer Phil Collins, a British citizen, and EMI Electrola. the holder in Germany of the exclusive right to exploit the recordings of Cliff Richard's shows given in the UK, brought proceedings before a German court to stop the distribution in Germany of pirated tapes and of illegal records taken at Phil Collins' concerts in the USA and Cliff Richard's concerts in the UK. Under the German Copyright Act relief against unauthorised recording of concerts and the unauthorised distribution of such recordings was only available to German nationals. Phil Collins and EMI Electrola, argued that the German Copyright Act was in breach of art 12 EC. The German court referred this question to the ECJ under the preliminary ruling procedure.The ECJ held that although intellectual property rights including copyrights are governed by national laws they are subject to the requirements of the EC Treaty. Consequently, art 12 EC applied to the exercise of such rights. Taking into account that art 12 EC is directly effective, both performers were entitled to rely on it to challenge the discriminatory provisions of the German Copyright Act. The ECJ held that:

> '... art [12 EC] must be interpreted as meaning that it prevents the law of a Member State from refusing, under certain circumstances, authors and performing artists of other member States and their successors in title the right which is granted by the same law to nationals, to prohibit the marketing in national territory of a phonogram made without their consent, if the performance in question was given outside national territory.'

Also on the basis of the principle of non-discrimination the ECJ held that national law which requires a patent to be exploited only on the territory where the patent was granted, and which prohibits or restricts its development elsewhere and prevents patented goods manufactured elsewhere being imported into the State which grants the patent, was incompatible with EC law: *Commission* v *Italy* Case C–235/89 [1993] FSR 1 and *Commission* v *United Kingdom* Case C–30/90 [1992] ECR I–829. The Court confirmed that intellectual property rights are within the scope of application of the EC Treaty. Also, art 295 EC is subject to EC law. Therefore, a Member State is not allowed to enact national legislation relating to intellectual property rights which is contrary to the principles of EC law. In *Spain* v *Council* Case C–350/92 [1995] ECR I–1995 the ECJ held that Spain could not adopt national measures relating to intellectual property rights which would adversely affect the free movement of goods.

25.1 Intellectual property rights and the free movement of goods

A derogation to the free movement of goods embodied in art 30 EC applies to industrial and commercial property rights. However, in *Deutsche Grammophon GmbH* v *Metro-SB-Grössmarkte GmbH* Case 78/70 [1971] ECR 487 the ECJ extended its scope of application to copyrights and neighbouring rights.

Patents

In order to ensure, on the one hand, economic integration within the internal market and, on the other hand, exclusive territorial protection of intellectual property rights, the ECJ made a distinction between the existence of intellectual property rights and their exercise. Article 239 EC refers to the existence of such rights while arts 28, 29 and 30 EC relate to their exercise. Under art 239 EC Community law must not interfere with the existence of intellectual property rights but may restrict their exercise by virtue of arts 28–30 EC. This means that the granting of intellectual property rights, and the content of these rights is governed by national law, while Community law supervises their exercise. The extent of protection granted by national laws which EC law is prepared to tolerate was defined by the ECJ in *Centrafarm* v *Sterling Drug* Case 15/74 [1974] ECR 1147. In this case Sterling Drug Inc, a holder of the UK and Dutch patents for a drug called Negram, had marketed that drug itself or via its licensees in both countries. Centrafarm, a Dutch company, bought Negram in the UK and Germany, it being less expensive there, and resold it in The Netherlands. Sterling Drug Inc brought proceedings against Centrafarm before a Dutch court to prevent Centrafarm from marketing Negram in The Netherlands. The ECJ held that art 30 EC justifies a derogation from the free movement of goods only 'for the purposes of safeguarding rights which constitute the specific subject-matter of this property' and the specific subject-matter of the intellectual property in respect of patents is:

> '... the guarantee that the patentee, to reward the creative effort of the inventor, has the exclusive right to use an invention with a view to manufacturing industrial products and putting them into circulation for the first time, either directly or by grant of licences to third parties, as well as the right to oppose infringements.'

The specific subject-matter of intellectual property rights constitutes the essence of the property and is linked to the essential function of the rights claimed. The specific subject matter is protected under EC law.

In respect of other kinds of intellectual property rights, the specific subject matter was defined in similar terms. In *Centrafarm v Winthrop* Case 16/74 [1974] ECR 1183, in relation to trade-mark rights, the ECJ held that the specific subject-matter is 'the guarantee that the owner of the trade mark has the exclusive right to use that trade mark, for the purpose of putting products protected by the trade mark into circulation for the first time', either directly, or by the grant of licences to third parties. However, once the owner exercises this possibility his exclusive right is lost and consequently he cannot prevent the import of protected goods from that State into his own Member State. He has exhausted his right.

From the judgment of the ECJ in *Centrafarm v Sterling Drug* a distinction must be made between three situations:

1. A product protected by a patent is imported from a Member State where it is not patentable and where it has been manufactured by third parties without the consent of the patentee. The patentee is entitled to prevent its importation into any Member State where it is protected by a patent.
2. A product is protected under a number of patents in different Member States, their original proprietors are legally and economically independent. Each patentee is entitled to prevent its importation into his own Member State.
3. A product protected by a patent 'has been put onto the market in a legal manner, by the patentee himself or with his consent, in the Member State from which it has been imported.' The patentee cannot prevent its importation into his own Member State. His right is exhausted.

The first two situations concern the existence of intellectual property rights. Consequently, the obstacle to the free movement of goods which arises from the existence of national legislation concerning intellectual property rights is justified under EC law. However, the third situation concerns the exercise of intellectual property rights. EC law will not tolerate any obstacle to the free flow of goods between Member States in the third situation.

The concept of the 'exhaustion of rights' has been used in the area of intellectual property in order to achieve a compromise in an apparently irreconcilable conflict between article 28 EC, which provides for the free movement of goods and thus condemns all trading rules which are capable of hindering directly and indirectly, actually and potentially, intra-Community trade,[1] and art 30 EC which, amongst exceptions to arts 28–29 EC, includes the protection of industrial and commercial property. At the centre of the concept of the exhaustion of rights is the consent of the owner of intellectual property rights. Consent is assumed when the protected product is put onto the market by its owner, or through his subsidiary or when the owner and the undertaking that has first put the protected product into circulation are under common control. The concept of exhaustion of rights does not apply in two situations:

1. If the protected product has been put into circulation under compulsory licence. This was established in *Pharmon BV v Hoechst AG* Case 19/84 [1985] ECR 2281. In this case,

---

[1] The so-called *Dassonville* formula: Case 8/74 [1974] ECR 837.

Hoechst held a patent for the process to manufacture a drug called Frusimide in Germany, The Netherlands and the UK. In the UK Frusemide was manufactured under a compulsory licence by an undertaking named DDSA. Under UK law the consent of the holder of the patent is not required under a compulsory licence although royalties on sales are paid to him. Pharmon, a Dutch undertaking bought Frusimide in the UK and resold it in The Netherlands where Frusimide was more expensive. Hoechst brought proceedings against Pharmon to prevent the latter from marketing Frusimide in The Netherlands. The ECJ held that Hoechst was entitled to rely on its patent to prevent Pharmon from marketing Frusimide. The ECJ emphasised that under a compulsory licence the patentee could not be deemed to have consented to the marketing of its product by a third party and thereby be deprived of its rights to determine freely the conditions under which its product is marketed.

2. If the patent is not exploited in the territory of a Member State where it was granted but patented goods are manufactured in another country and then imported into the patent-granting Member State: *Commission v Italy* Case C–235/89 [1993] FSR 1; *Commission v United Kingdom* Case C–30/90 [1992] ECR I–829.

However, the doctrine of the exhaustion of rights applies even though the protected products have been put into circulation in the Member State where the invention is not patentable by the patentee or with his consent. In *Merck and Co Inc v Stephar BV* Case 187/80 [1981] ECR 2063 Merck held a Dutch patent relating to a drug used mainly in the treatment of high blood pressure. Merck was selling his drug in Italy. Under Italian law drugs were not patentable. Stephar bought the drug in Italy and imported it into The Netherlands where its price was much higher than in Italy. Merck brought proceedings against Stephar to prevent the latter from marketing the drug in The Netherlands. Merck argued that the impossibility of patenting its product in Italy deprived its creative effort from being rewarded. The ECJ disagreed and held that the right to obtain the reward for the patent holder was not guaranteed in all circumstances. It is for the holder of the patent to decide under what circumstances he will market his product, including the possibility of marketing it in a Member State in which his product is not patentable. If the proprietor of the patent decides to market the product in a Member State where his product is not patentable he must accept the consequences of his choice in the light of the principle of the free movement of goods. In such circumstances his consent is presumed and he cannot rely on his patent to prevent free movement of his products. However, in *Merck and Beecham* Joined Cases C–267 and 268/95 [1996] ECR I–6285 the ECJ qualified this principle. The ECJ held that the consent is presumed unless the proprietor of the patent proves that he is subject to a real and actual duty to market his product in a Member State in which his product is not patentable.

There is another possibility for the holder of intellectual propriety rights to avoid the application of the doctrine of the exhaustion of rights. In *EMI Electrola Gmbh v Patricia Im-und Export Verwaltungsgesellschaft mbH* Case 341/87 [1989] ECR 79 the ECJ held that a copyright owner may rely on his exclusive rights to prevent the sale, in the Member State in which he holds these rights, of copies of his work made lawfully in another Member State, without his consent. In this case copies of Cliff Richard records made in Denmark where his copyright had expired (for that reason they were made lawfully) were imported to Germany where he still held his exclusive copyright. EMI wanted to stop parallel import of his recordings. EMI applied to a German court for an order to stop these imports. The ECJ held that the lawful circulation of Cliff Richard's recordings in Denmark did not amount to consent. As a result EMI was allowed to stop imports from Denmark.

The rules examined above in respect of patents apply to other types of intellectual property rights, although some peculiarities attaching to them require further examination.

Trade-marks rights

Directive 89/104/EEC, the First Council Directive of 21 December 1988 to approximate the laws of the Member States relating to trade marks, which was implemented in the United Kingdom in the Trade Marks Act 1994, has brought important changes and clarification to the previous EC law in the trade-mark area.

The exhaustion of rights

In *Perfumes Christian Dior SA and Perfumes Christian Dior BV v Evora BV* Case C–337/95 [1997] ECR I–6013 the ECJ explained the meaning of the 'exhaustion of rights' in the context of art 5 and 7 of Directive 89/104 and provided indications as to the interpretation of arts 28 and 30 EC in relation to trade marks and copyrights and in particular specified when the owner of a trade mark or a holder of copyright may oppose the use of the protected goods by a reseller who habitually markets goods of the same kind but not always of the same quality.

The French company, Perfumes Christian Dior SA (Dior France), and the Dutch company, Perfumes Christian Dior BV (Dior Netherlands), brought an action against the Dutch company Evora which operates a chain of chemists' shops under the name of its subsidiary (Kruidvat), for infringement of Dior trade marks and copyrights, and for an order to stop Evora from advertising Dior products in a manner which damaged the luxurious image of Dior products. In a Christmas promotion in 1993 Kruidvat advertised some Dior products. Advertising leaflets of Evora depicted the packaging and bottles of some Dior products which, according to the judgment of the referring court, related clearly and directly to the goods offered for sale. The advertisement itself was carried out in a manner customary to retailers in this market sector. Kruidvat was neither a distributor of Dior France nor of Dior Netherlands. Dior products sold by the Kruidvat shops were supplied by Evora which obtained them by means of parallel imports.

The 'specific subject-matter' of intellectual property rights was defined by the ECJ in *Centrafarm v Winthrop* Case 16/74 [1974] ECR 1183 as 'the guarantee that the owner of the trade mark has the exclusive right to use that trade mark, for the purpose of putting products protected by the trade mark into circulation for the first time', either directly, or by the grant of licences to third parties. However, once the owner exercises this possibility his exclusive right is lost and consequently he cannot prevent import of protected goods from that State into other Member States. He has exhausted his right. For that reason Perfumes Dior did not challenge the legality of retailing the protected goods.

The ECJ starting point was arts 5–7 of the First Directive 89/104 of 21 December 1988 concerning the approximation of the laws of the Member States relating to trade marks. The

ECJ held that a proper interpretation of arts 5–7 requires that when trade-marked goods have been put on the Community market, by or with the consent of the owner of the trade mark, a reseller is entitled not only to resell those goods but also to make use of the trade mark to bring to the public's attention their further commercialisation. In the other words, an owner of a trade mark cannot prevent a reseller from advertising the protected goods since the purpose of the concept of 'exhaustion of rights' is to protect the internal market from being artificially partitioned by the owner of trade marks and especially it is aimed at abolishing price differences between Member States for the protected goods. Although the rights to make use of a trade mark by the reseller in order to attract attention to the further commercialisation of protected goods are not exhausted in the same way as the right to their resale, the latter would be more difficult if further commercialisation of those goods is not covered by the concept of the 'exhaustion of rights'. Indeed, this concept would be seriously undermined.

However, the ECJ held that in some circumstances the owner of a trade mark may stop a reseller from advertising the further commercialisation of goods. The legitimate interests of the trade-mark owner must be protected, especially when a reseller is using his trade marks for advertising in a manner which could damage the reputation of the trade marks. In this respect the ECJ emphasised that by virtue of art 7(2) of Directive 89/104 the trade-mark owner may prevent a reseller from damaging the reputation of his trade mark. This solution was previously applied in the context of trade marks.[2] However, the ECJ has not generalised the conditions in which the trade-mark owner may control a non-authorised reseller advertising the further commercialisation of protected goods under Community law. The ECJ based its conclusions on art 7(2) of Directive 89/104 and limited its reasoning to this particular case. According to the ECJ in order to strike a balance between the legitimate interests of the trade-mark owner regarding the image of luxury which he has succeeded in creating around his trade mark, and the right of a reseller to commercialise the protected goods by using advertising methods which are customary in his sector of trade, the reseller must 'endeavour to prevent his advertising from affecting the value of the trade mark by detracting from the allure and prestigious image of the goods in question and from their aura of luxury'. This requirement is particularly difficult to satisfy, taking into account the fact that the reseller is not an authorised distributor of Dior products. Under Community law the reseller has to advertise the protected goods using methods which are customary to his sector of trade, in a manner which would not damage the reputation of the trade mark in question, especially by avoiding association of the luxury products with other products he sells. This may lead to surprising results under national law. In many Member States, a non authorised distributor is obliged not to followed too closely the methods of sale and advertisement put in place by the trade-mark owner in relation to his network of exclusive distributors.[3] Furthermore, this solution is particularly troublesome for manufacturers and exclusive distributors of luxury perfumes as it places them in a precarious situation. Community competition law has gradually determined the legal framework for agreements between manufacturers and exclusive distributors of perfumes: *Yves Saint-Laurent et*

---

[2] See, for example, *Bristol* Cases C–427, 429 and 436/93 [1996] ECR I–3457.
[3] For example, in France see: C Vilmart and L de Montblanc, 'Le droit des marques contre les importations parallèles', *Les Echos*, 24 Novembre 1977.

Givenchy Cases T–19 and 88/92 [1996] ECR II–1851. However, under the principle of the free movement of goods (as interpreted in the *Perfumes Christian Dior* case), the ECJ has introduced insecurity since it permits non-authorised distributors to advertise and to further commercialise the protected goods. The obvious consequence for the authorised distributors is that they may lose their customers.

The ECJ held that in the context of the free movement of goods, that is under arts 28 and 30 EC, the owner of the trade mark or holder of copyright is precluded in relation to the bottles and packaging from preventing the reseller from advertising the further commercialisation of those goods in a manner customary to the reseller sector of trade, unless it is established in the light of the specific circumstances of the case that the use of those goods for that purpose damages their reputation. The ECJ held that the restriction of the owner of trade mark or copyright imposed upon a reseller regarding the advertisement of protected goods may constitute a quantitative restriction contrary to art 28 EC since it would render their commercialisation, and consequently access to the market for those goods, more difficult. As a result, art 28 EC and art 7 of Directive 89/104 should be interpreted in the same way.

The ECJ transposes its solution in respect of trade marks to copyright. The only difference is that the ECJ emphasises that 'the protection conferred by copyright as regards the reproduction of protected works in a reseller's advertising may not, in any event, be broader than that which is conferred on a trade-mark owner in the same circumstances.' The ECJ stated that in the context of the free movement of goods the owner of a trade mark or holder of copyright cannot prevent a reseller, who habitually markets articles of the same kind, but not necessarily of the same quality, as the protected goods, in ways customary in the reseller's sector of trade, from using a trade mark or a copyright for the purpose of advertisement of protected goods unless it is established, taking into account the circumstances of a particular case, that the use of the trade mark or copyright for that purpose seriously damages their reputation.

Further clarification of the concept of exhaustion of trade-mark rights was provided in *Bayerische Motorenwerke AG (BMW) and BMW Netherlands BV v Ronald Karel Deenik* Case C–63/97 [1999] 1 CMLR 1099 concerning unauthorised use of the BMW trade mark in advertisements for a garage business in the light of arts 5–7 of Directive 89/104. In this case a German car manufacturer, BMW, and its Dutch branch, BMW Netherlands, brought an action against Mr Deenik, an independent owner of a garage specialising in the sale of second-hand BMW cars and repair and maintenance of BMW cars, for using the BMW mark in advertisements of his business. The Hoge Raad (the Supreme Court of The Netherlands) considered that some of the advertisements might be unlawful in suggesting that Mr Deenik's business was affiliated to the trade-mark proprietor's distribution network, whilst other uses of the trade mark – such as 'repairs and maintenance of BMW', 'BMW specialist' – did not constitute infringement of that mark. The Hoge Raad referred five questions to the ECJ concerning the interpretation of arts 5–7 of Directive 89/104/EEC for a preliminary ruling.

In relation to art 5 of Directive 89/104/EEC the ECJ held that both the sale of second-hand BMW cars and services such as repair and maintenance of BMW cars were within the scope of art 5 of the Directive. In order to determine whether the use of a trade mark is lawful for advertisement purposes, the Court distinguished between the sale of goods covered by that trade mark and their repair and maintenance. In the first case, the ECJ confirmed its decision in *Perfumes Christian Dior* (see above), that is that a reseller is entitled to make use of the trade mark, to bring to the public's attention their further commercialisation, although the owner of a trade mark may stop a reseller from using his trade mark if the advertisement damages the reputation of the trade mark. If a reseller advertises the goods covered by a trade mark in a manner customary to the reseller's sector of trade, the owner of a trade mark may invoke art 7(2) of Directive 89/104/EEC to prohibit the use of its mark by a reseller in special circumstances. It occurs when a reseller advertises in such a manner as to induce the public to believe that there is a commercial connection between the two undertakings. This kind of advertisement is dishonest, unfair and harms the legitimate interests of the trade-mark owner. However, if there is no risk that the public will have the impression that there is a commercial connection between the two undertakings the reseller may derive advantage from using the trade mark in the advertisement, in particular to enhance the quality of his business.

In respect of the advertisement for repair and maintenance of BMW cars, the rule of the 'exhaustion of rights' does not apply as there is no further commercialisation of goods. In this context art 6(1)(c) of the Directive lays down the conditions for using a trade mark. A third party is entitled to use the trade mark to indicate the intended purpose of products or services, in particular as accessories or spare parts, provided that the use is necessary to indicate that purpose. In this context, the use of a trade mark is lawful provided there is no risk that the public will be induced to believe that there is a commercial link between the two undertakings.

The concept of confusion

Very often the proprietor of a trade mark tries to prevent the import of goods similar to his from another Member State where they are protected under a trade mark registered in that Member State which is so similar to his trade mark that it may confuse consumers in the Member State of importation.

The concept of confusion has caused many controversies mostly because of different approaches of national law of the Member States to the rights conferred by a trade mark. According to Mark Wing under the traditional approach favoured, *inter alia*, by the United Kingdom the main role of a trade mark is the 'identificatory function', that is, it indicates the origin of ownership of the goods. However, under the modern approach the trade mark is much more than the rational, physical indicator of origin since it 'is a messenger sending out messages of information which guarantee the product quality and provide valuable information for the consumer concerning the product, the company and the people behind that company.'[4] The holder of the trade mark should be protected from actual or potential, direct and indirect confusion regarding the origin of his products, including the possible conscious or subconscious association of the protected products by the consumers with a third party's sign or mark. Consequently, the trade mark should be protected against dilution, that is against the whittling away of its distinctive character. It implies that even though a consumer does not confuse the two trade marks, nevertheless when he is choosing

---

[4] M Wing and M Elsmore, '*Sabel* v *Puma* – Confusion is King' (1998) Journal of Business Law 485–494.

between two similar products having look-alike trade marks he automatically makes a conceptual association between them.

In *Terrapin (Overseas) Ltd* v *Terranova Industrie CA Kapferer and Co* Case 119/75 [1976] ECR 1039 a German undertaking, which was the proprietor of the trade mark Terrapin, sought to prevent an English company from registering its trade name Terranova in Germany, on the grounds that both undertakings dealt in building materials and the similarity of their name would lead to consumers to confusion. The ECJ held the German undertaking could rely on that art 28 EC to prevent the import of goods marketed under a trade mark giving rise to confusion provided that these rights were acquired by different proprietors under different national laws. However, the usual proviso of art 30 EC applied, ie, that the prevention of imports must not constitute arbitrary discrimination or a disguised restriction on intra-Community trade. The restriction on imports based on the confusion of consumers was invoked in a number of cases. In *Deutsche Renault AG* v *Audi AG* Case C–317/91 [1993] ECR I–6227 the ECJ held that Audi could rely on its German trade mark 'Quattro' to prevent the use of the trade mark 'Espace Quadra' in Germany by a Renault subsidiary established in Germany for a four-wheel drive vehicle marketed under this name in France and other countries if the use of that trade mark confused German consumers. It was the task of the German court to determine whether that was the case on the basis of German law. There was no Community meaning of the concept of confusion. Under the Directive this concept was examined by the ECJ in *Sabel BV* v *Puma AG, Rudolf Dassler Sport* Case C–151/95 [1998] 1 CMLR 445.

In this case Puma AG, a German company, brought proceedings against a Dutch company, Sabel BV, opposing the registration of a trade mark of SABEL in Germany under the international registration system of the Madrid Arrangement, on the basis that ideas conveyed by the pictorial elements of the mark consisting of the name of SABEL and the representation of a running leopard conflicted with its trade mark of a running puma. Both companies sold similar goods, that is leather and imitation leather products. The German Supreme Court (the Bundesgerichtshof) referred to the ECJ for a preliminary ruling a question on the interpretation of art 4(1)(b) of First Council Directive 89/104. This sets out the additional grounds on which registration of a trade mark may be refused or a registered mark declared invalid if, due to similarity or identity of an earlier registered trade mark with the trade mark to be registered (or already registered but later than the first trade mark), there is a likelihood of confusion of both trade marks on the part of the public, which includes the likelihood of association between the two marks. The German court asked the ECJ to clarify the meaning of the criterion 'likelihood of confusion ... which includes the likelihood of association with the earlier trade mark'.

The question asked by the German court was whether the simple likelihood of association between the two trade marks on the part of the public, excluding any likelihood of confusion, constitutes a sufficient reason to refuse the registration of the second trade mark. The Belgian, Luxembourg and Dutch governments insisted that the concept of 'likelihood of association' which was introduced, at their request, in art 4(1)(b) should have the same meaning as art 13a of the Uniform Benelux Law on Trade Marks, its predecessor, taking into account that the Benelux Court of Justice have already determined its meaning in a number of cases. According to them the concept of 'likelihood of association' covers three different notions: first, the likelihood of direct confusion where the public confuses the sign and marks in question; second, the likelihood of indirect confusion or association where the public makes connection between the holders of the sign and those of the mark and confuses them; and, finally, in the case of likelihood of association *stricto sensu*, where for the public the sign is similar to the mark and perception of the sign calls to mind the memory of the mark but there is no confusion between them. As a result, the ECJ was asked to determine whether the provision in question applies to the third situation, that is where there is a likelihood of association *sensu stricto*. In other words, the interpretation of art 4(1)(b) suggested by the Benelux countries protects the holder of a trade mark against the dilution of the distinctiveness of the trade mark. The United Kingdom and the Commission disagreed with the interpretation suggested by the Benelux countries. They argued that the likelihood of association and the likelihood of confusion are not two different concepts but the latter determines the scope of the former. Therefore, where there is no likelihood of confusion on the part of the public there cannot be the likelihood of association.

The ECJ referred to the preamble of the Directive which provides that the likelihood of confusion should be assessed on the basis of a number of factors, such as the recognition of the trade mark on the market, the association which can be made with the used or registered sign, etc. As a result, in order to decide whether, in a particular case, there is a likelihood of confusion all relevant factors should be taken into account, that is an overall impression given by the marks would indicate whether there is visual, aural or conceptual similarity between them. Consequently, the likelihood of confusion between the two marks depends upon the distinctiveness of the earlier mark either *per se* or because of the reputation its enjoys with the public. The ECJ emphasised that in this case because the earlier mark was not especially well known to the public and the idea conveyed by the pictorial element of the two trade marks was of little imaginative content, there was little risk that the public would confuse the two marks although it may associate them in the sense that one would simply bring the other to mind without a likelihood of confusion about the origin of the goods. As a result, the ECJ held that the criterion of 'likelihood of confusion which includes the likelihood of association with an earlier mark' means that the mere association which the consumers might make between two trade marks with analogous semantic content does not constitute in itself a sufficient ground for concluding that there is a likelihood of confusion.

The decision of the ECJ is in line with the traditional approach to trade marks. In this respect, it is interesting to note that the Advocate-General in *Sabel* v *Puma* mentioned with approval, on several occasions, *Wagamama Ltd* v *City Centre Restaurants* [1995] FSR 713. Advocate-General Jacobs emphasised that the restrictive interpretation of the concept of 'likelihood of association' would be in conformity with the objective of the Directive adopted under art 95 EC. Indeed, the extended scope of protection of trade marks would constitute an important obstacle to the free movement of goods as well as make the registration of many trade marks extremely difficult at Community level.

The change in attitude of the ECJ can be explained by the requirements of both the internal and the international market. In the context of the internal market the monopolistic tendencies of non-origin association is contrary to the free movement of goods and free competition. As to the international aspect this was discussed by Advocate-General

Jacobs who placed Directive 89/104, and particularly the concept of confusion, against the background of the Paris Convention[5] and the GATT TRIPS Agreement under which this concept is considered as the foundation for trade-mark protection.

The change of attitude of the ECJ acquires a new dimension if one compares the *Puma* case with *CNL Sucal v Hag (No 2)* Case C–10/89 [1990] ECR I–3711 in which the likelihood of confusion between both products was an essential factor in deciding the case. In *Hag (No 2)* the ECJ held that:

> 'To determine the exact effect of this exclusive right which is granted to the owner of the mark, it is necessary to take account of the essential function of the mark, which is to give the consumer or final user a guarantee of the identity of the origin of the marked product by enabling him to distinguish, without any possible confusion, that product from others of a different provenance.'

Article 5(1)(b) of Directive 89/104 concerning the risk of confusion was further examined by the ECJ in *Lloyd Schufabrik Meyer & Co Gmbh v Klijsen Handel BV* Case C–342/97 [1999] 2 CMLR 1343 in which the ECJ indicated the criteria which a referring court should take into consideration in order to assess the likelihood of confusion. Lloyd Schufabrik Meyer, a German manufacturer of shoes distributed under the trade mark 'Lloyd', sought an order restraining Klijsen Handel BV, a Dutch manufacturer of shoes distributed under the name 'Loint's', from using the trade mark 'Loint's' in Germany on the ground that 'Loint's' was likely to be confused with 'Lloyd' because of the aural similarity between them. Lloyd emphasised that its trade mark had a particularly distinctive character arising from the absence of descriptive elements, was well recognised on the market and had been used consistently and extensively since 1927. The referring court, the Landgericht Munchen I (Munich I Regional Court), doubted the likelihood of confusion on the part of the public on the ground that there was only aural similarity between trade marks.

The ECJ left it to the referring court to decide whether or not there was a likelihood of confusion between the trade marks, but indicated the criteria which the referring court should take into consideration in order to assess the likelihood of confusion. In this respect the ECJ repeated that the likelihood of confusion must be assessed globally, taking into account all factors relevant to the circumstances of the case, that is, does the overall impression given by the trade marks indicate whether there is visual, aural or conceptual similarity between them. Consequently, the likelihood of confusion between the two trade marks depends upon the distinctiveness of the earlier mark either *per se* or because of the reputation it enjoys with the public.[6] Thus, the more similar the goods or services covered by the trade marks and the greater the distinctiveness of the earlier mark, the greater would be the likelihood of confusion. In determining the distinctiveness of a trade mark it is necessary to take into consideration the greater or lesser capacity of the mark to identify the goods and services for which it had been registered as coming from a particular undertaking. In this respect, important factors are: the inherent characteristic of a mark,

---

[5] Paris Convention for the Protection of Industrial Property of 20 March 1983 as revised. However, both agreements allow the extension of the concept of confusion and thus Directive 89/104 as well as the Benelux law are in conformity with those international instruments. See M Wing, ibid note 4.

[6] See *Sabel* Case C–151/95 and *Canon* Case C–39/97 [1998] ECR I–5507.

including that it does or does not contain an element descriptive of the goods and services for which it has been registered; the consistent and extensive use of a trade mark over a very long period; its geographic market, etc. However, it is not possible to state in general terms, for example by referring to given percentages relating to the degree of recognition attained by the mark within the relevant section of the public, when a mark has a strong distinctive character.

The ECJ held in *Lloyd Schufabrik Meyer* that, taking into consideration all the above factors, it was possible that mere aural similarity between trade marks could create a likelihood of confusion in the light of art 5(1)(b) of Directive 89/104.

The doctrine of common origin of a trade mark

It may occur that, for various reasons, the right to use the original trade mark has been split. As a result, undertakings independent from each other and operating in different countries are lawfully using the same trade mark. There is an issue as to whether or not under EC law undertakings using a trade mark of common origin may rely on their trade-mark rights to prevent each other from importing protected goods into each other's territory. In *Van Zuylen Frères v Hag AG (No 1)* Case 192/73 [1974] ECR 731 a German undertaking was a proprietor of the 'Kaffee Hag' trade mark in Germany, Belgium, and Luxembourg. After World War II its rights to the mark in Belgium and Luxembourg were sequestrated and assigned to Van Zuylen. When a German undertaking imported its 'Kaffee Hag' coffee to Belgium, Van Zuylen sought to rely on its trade-mark rights to prevent the importation. The ECJ held that Van Zuylen was not entitled to rely on its trade mark to prevent the marketing in one Member State of a product lawfully made in another Member State under an identical mark. This decision was much criticised, in particular because the German undertaking had never consented to marketing its product in Belgium and therefore the principle of exhaustion of rights was not applicable. The ECJ reversed this decision in *CNL Sucal v Hag (No 2)* Case C–10/89 [1990] ECR I–3711, in which the then owner of the trade mark 'Kaffee Hag' in Belgium sought to sell its product in Germany and the German proprietor of 'Kaffee Hag' tried to prevent the importation. The ECJ allowed the German holder to rely on his trade mark to exclude products made by a third party, but bearing a trade mark with a common origin to his, in a manner that would partition the common market. The likelihood of confusion between both products was an essential factor in deciding the case.

This approach was confirmed and intensified in *IHT Internationale Heiztechnik GmbH v Ideal Standard Gmbh* Case C–9/93 [1994] ECR I–2789. The facts of this case were that the trade mark 'Ideal Standard' for sanitary fittings and heating equipment was held by two subsidiaries of an American company, one in France and another in Germany. The trade mark having belonged to the parent company, it had (in the hands of the subsidiaries) a common origin. The French subsidiary assigned the trade mark for France to an undertaking named SGT, which has an independent undertaking. When a German undertaking (IHT) sought to import from France to Germany heating equipment made by SGT and bearing the trade mark 'Ideal Standard', the German subsidiary successfully relied on its German trade mark to prevent the import of the offending products to Germany. The ECJ held that the principle in *Hag (No 2)* applied irrespective of whether the splitting of the original trade mark was due to an act of a public authority or a contractual assignment.

Rebranding and repackaging of the protected product

Repackaging of trade-marked products takes place when the original packaging is removed and the original trade mark is displayed on the new packaging. Rebranding involves the replacement of the original packaging and trade mark. A new trade mark appears on the new packaging. Repackaging and rebranding is often used by manufacturers of pharmaceutical products in order to sell them at different prices in different Member States. Very often a third party takes advantage of the price difference by buying such products in a Member State where they are cheaper, repackaging and/or rebranding them and then reselling them in a Member State where they are more expensive. The extent to which the owner of the trade mark can prevent a third party from doing this was the subject of a number of cases. In *Hoffmann-La Roche v Centrafarm* Case 102/77 [1978] ECR 1139, Centrafarm purchased valium in England for resale in Germany. Centrafarm repacked the pills in different quantities and both the original mark of Hoffman-La Roche and Centrafarm's mark were placed on the packaging. The ECJ held that such rebranding can only be opposed by the trade-mark owner to the extent justified by the 'subject-matter' of the trade-mark rights, namely to protect him against competitors who would abuse the reputation protected by the trade mark. The essential function of the trade mark is to guarantee to consumers or to final users the original identity of the protected product so as to avoid confusion. Furthermore, the trade-marked goods should not be tampered with without the trade-mark owner's consent. However, the ECJ emphasised that for the application of art 30 EC it was necessary that the prevention of rebranding/repackaging did not constitute a disguised restriction on trade between Member States. As a result the owner of a trade mark cannot use his trade mark to artificially partition the internal market. Whether or not this is the case should be determined on the basis of an objective test.

In *Centrafarm v American Home Products* Case 3/78 [1978] ECR 1823 the ECJ added a subjective test to the objective test set out in *Hoffman-La Roche* by stating that the prevention of rebranding would not be accepted if the owner of the trade mark, by adopting a particular marketing system for the protected products, intentionally contributed to the artificial partitioning of the internal market. In *Bristol-Myers Squibb v Paranova* Case C–427/93 [1996] ECR I–3514 the ECJ provided some clarification as to repackaging by parallel importers of protected products. Repackaging is allowed if:

1. it does not adversely affect the original condition of the product;
2. the new packaging clearly states the name of the manufacturer and the person who has repackaged the product;
3. the repackaging is not such as to damage the trade mark's reputation;
4. the parallel importer gives notice of its intention to the trade-mark owner and supplies samples if requested.

The above conditions are based on an objective test. The ECJ did not refer to a subjective test. This matter became a central issue in *Pharmacia and Upjohn SA v Paranova* Case C–379/97 [2000] 1 CMLR 51. Upjohn was selling an antibiotic under the name Dalacine in France, Dalacin C in Greece and Dalacin in Denmark. Paranova bought Dalacine in France and Dalacin C in Greece and resold it in Denmark where prices were higher. Paranova repackaged and rebranded the original products and sold them in Denmark as Dalacin. Paranova considered that because different trade marks were covering the same product

Upjohn was using them to partition the internal market. Upjohn sought an injunction preventing Paranova from selling its product in Denmark. Upjohn argued that a distinction should be made between repackaging and rebranding and that Paranova should provide evidence as to the subjective intention of Upjohn to partition the internal market. The ECJ held that the objective test was sufficient, leaving it to the national courts to decide whether it was 'objectively necessary' to replace the original trade mark. If the trade-mark owner uses the trade mark to hinder effective access to the market of the Member State of import, then the rebranding and repackaging is justified. The criterion of objective necessity would also be justified if the laws of the Member State of import prevent the use of the trade mark used in the Member State of export. However, if the reason for the rebranding is to secure a commercial advantage for the parallel import, the rebranding would not be objectively necessary and the owner of the trade mark would be entitled to prevent the repackaging and rebranding.

The decision of the ECJ has important consequences for both parallel importers and consumers. For parallel importers it will no longer be necessary to prove the subjective intention of the trade mark owner to partition the market, which is extremely difficult or even impossible to evidence. Now, they can rely on the objective test in order to prove that it is objectively necessary to repackage/rebrand the product for effective access to the market of the Member State of import. Consumers will also benefit from this solution. Parallel importers will cause the equalisation of prices for the same product within the internal market and thus consumers in some Member States will not be charged excessive prices.

Copyright

Under Community law trade marks and copyrights are treated differently in the context of the 'exhaustion of right'. In respect of trade marks under Community law no restrictions are imposed on the concept of the 'exhaustion of right'. In relation to copyright Community law has always made distinction between those rights which by their nature may be 'exhausted', for instance the right to prevent parallel imports once literary and artistic works have been put into circulation in a Member State (*Musik-Vertrieb v GEMA* Case 78/70 [1971] ECR 147), and those which cannot be 'exhausted' such as the right to hire video cassettes: *EMI Electrola, Warner Brothers Inc v Christiansen* Case 158/86 [1988] ECR 2605; *Coditel SA v Ciné Vog Films* Case 62/79 [1980] ECR 881.

25.2 Parallel imports from outside the EC and EEA

The principle of the exhaustion of intellectual property rights does not apply to imports from outside the EC and the European Economic Area: *EMI Records Ltd v CBS United Kingdom Ltd* Case 51/75 [1976] ECR 811; *Generics UK Ltd v Smith, Kline and French* Case C–191/90 [1993] 1 CMLR 89. The holder of intellectual property rights is entitled to prevent parallel import of protected products coming from non-Member States to a Member State. This solution was confirmed by the ECJ in *Silhouette International Schmied GmbH & Co Kg v Hartlauer Handelsgesellschaft mbH* Case C–355/96 [1998] ECR I–4799.

Silhouette, a well known manufacturer of top-quality spectacles, uses its trade mark 'Silhouette' registered in Austria and most countries in the world to sell its product. In October 1995 Silhouette sold 21,000 out-of-fashion spectacles frames to a Bulgarian company. Silhouette instructed its representative to inform the purchaser that the frames were to be resold only in Bulgaria and the states of the former Soviet Union and not in the territory of the EU. However, this restriction was not inserted into the contract and it was not clear whether in fact the purchaser was aware of such a restriction. In December 1995 the frames were resold to Hartlauer, a retailer in Austria that sells spectacles and frames for low prices. Hartlauer offered frames bearing Silhouette's trade mark for sale in Austria. Hartlauer was not supplied by Silhouette because that company considered that distribution of its products by Hartlauer would be harmful to its image as a manufacturer of top-quality fashion spectacles. Silhouette brought an action for interim relief before the Landesgericht Steyr, seeking an injunction restraining Hartlauer from offering spectacles or spectacle frames for sale in Austria under its trade mark, as the sale of cut-price and outmoded spectacles frames would damage its brand reputation within the EU. Silhouette argued that its trade-mark rights were not exhausted, within the meaning of Directive 89/104/EEC, as they are exhausted only when the goods have been put on the market in the EEA by the proprietor or with his consent. Hautlauer's answer was that Silhouette had not sold the frames subject to any prohibition of, or restriction on, reimportation and that the Austrian law implementing the Directive did not grant a right to seek prohibitory injunctions. Silhouette's action was dismissed by the Landesgericht Steyr and, on appeal, by the Oberlandesgericht Linz. Silhouette appealed to the Oberster Gerichtshof on a point of law.

The Austrian Oberster Gerichtshof (Supreme Court) referred to ECJ for a preliminary ruling under art 234 EC two questions concerning the interpretation of art 7(1) of Directive 89/104. In particular, the Austrian court asked whether the holder of a trade mark who has consented to market the protected products in the Community and in the EEA can prevent a third party from using his trade mark outside the EEA or whether he has exhausted his rights when the goods have been put in circulation, by or with his consent, in the Community and in the EEA.

At the time of the dispute Austria was only a member of the EEA. Its national law prior to the implementation of the Directive recognised the principle of international exhaustion according to which once goods had been marketed anywhere by or with the consent of the owner his rights were exhausted and therefore he had no control over the goods. Austrian rules implementing the Directive restricted the exhaustion principle to first marketing within the EEA. For that reason Hautlauder argued that the Directive applied only to the EEA and the question of international exhaustion was left to the national law of Member States. The ECJ rejected this argument. The Court considered that art 7 of the Directive had comprehensively resolved the question of exhaustion in the sense that it harmonised law in this area in all Member States. This solution ensures uniformity and is in conformity with the objectives of the Directive. The ECJ emphasised that if some Member States recognise the principle of international exhaustion, while others do not, the result may be barriers to the free movement of goods and services within the EEA.

The decision of the ECJ in the present case reinforces the protection conferred upon the proprietor of a trade mark under Community law. He is entitled to stop parallel imports. As a result, there is nothing to prevent him from setting up whatever differing commercial arrangements he likes inside and outside the EEA. However, this solution yields surprising results in the context of competition law, in particular in relation to elimination of obstacles to parallel imports. In *Javico* Case C–306/96 [1998] ECR I–1983 the ECJ held that a clause prohibiting parallel export to the EU of products put into circulation in third countries was *prima facie* in breach of art 81(1) EC. Therefore, an undertaking such as Silhouette can on the basis of article 7 of the Directive alone prevent parallel imports, while an undertaking such as Yves Saint-Laurent Perfumes (see *Javico*) which has concluded a commercial agreement with an undertaking situated in a third country will not only be stopped from doing this but in addition will face proceedings under art 81(1) EC!

Furthermore, the decision of the ECJ in *Silhouette* means that consumers in the EEA are no longer able to buy branded goods imported from outside the EEA and obtained from unauthorised sources at a low price.

In *Sebago Inc v GB-Unic SA* Case C–173/98 [1999] 2 CMLR 1317 the ECJ clarified the concept of consent in respect of art 7(1) of Directive 89/104. The ECJ held that the concept of consent must relate to each individual item of the product in respect of which exhaustion is pleaded. Sebago Inc, a company incorporated in the USA, the proprietor of two trade marks in the name of 'Docksides' and three trade marks in the name of 'Sebago' all registered in the Benelux countries for shoes, and Ancienne Maison Dubois et Fils SA, an exclusive distributor in the Benelux countries of shoes bearing Sebago's trade marks, brought joint proceedings against GB-Unic SA for infringement of Sebago's trade-mark rights by the marketing of shoes in the Community without Sebago's consent. GB-Unic SA, advertised and sold in its Maxi-GB hypermarkets in Belgium 2,561 pairs of 'Docksides' Sebago shoes manufactured in El Salvador, which it purchased from a Belgian company specialising in parallel importation. Sebago did not contest the fact that the shoes so sold were genuine Sebago shoes.

The ECJ restrictively interpreted the conditions under which the trade-mark owner's consent is deemed to have been given for the purposes of the exhaustion of his trade mark rights. Such consent must relate to each individual item of the product in respect of which exhaustion is pleaded. Therefore, the consent of Sebago to the marketing in the EEA of one batch of shoes bearing the mark does not exhaust its trade-mark rights in relation to the marketing of other batches of identical or similar shoes bearing the same mark, the marketing of which in the EEA Sebago has not consented to. This means that a particular product sold by or with consent of the trade-mark proprietor within the EEA could be resold freely within the territory of the EEA under the exhaustion principle, although a particular product sold by or with the consent of the trade-mark proprietor outside the EEA could not then be similarly resold freely within the EEA even if the trade mark proprietor authorises sale within the EEA of identical products.

The decision of the ECJ applies to parallel imports both from outside the EEA and between EEA countries. The decision of the ECJ is in line with its previous case law, in particular *Perfumes Christian Dior* Case C–337/95 [1997] ECR I–6013 and *Bayerische Motorenwerke AG (BMW) and BMW Netherlands BV v Ronald Karel Deenik* Case C–63/97 [1999] 1 CMLR 1099.

25.3 Intellectual property rights and arts 81 and 82 EC

The exercise of intellectual property rights may infringe EC competition law. It may breach both arts 81 and 82 EC.

Intellectual property rights and art 81 EC

By virtue of art 81 EC only agreements between undertakings are within its scope of application. Consequently, unilateral conduct of a holder of intellectual property rights, such as a refusal to grant a licence,[7] is excluded from the ambit of art 81 EC although it may be caught by art 82 EC. From a practical point of view it is very important to determine whether or not agreements relating to intellectual property rights can be exempted under block regulations. If so, anti-competitive clauses, being easy to identify, should be avoided in relevant agreements. In respect of patent licences, Regulation 240/96,[8] on the application of art 85(3) of the Treaty [art 81(3) EC] to certain categories of technology transfer agreements, covers patent, know-how and mixed (patent and known-how) licences.

Regulation 2349/84[9] adopted in 1984 was the first Regulation providing a group exemption for patent licences. Its current version is contained in Regulation 240/96. Article 3 of the Regulation is very helpful in assessing clauses which will be considered as anti-competitive in the context of art 81 EC as it contains the so-called 'blacklist'. The following clauses are prohibited by virtue of art 3:

1. imposing restrictions in the determination of prices, components of prices or discounts for the licensed products;
2. imposing requirements on one or both parties, without any objective justified reason, to refuse to meet orders from users or resellers in their respective territories who would market products in other territories within the common market or placing other barriers hindering resellers;
3. imposing an obligation on the licensee to assign in whole or in part to the licensor rights to improvements to or new applications of the licensed technology.

Articles 1 and 2(1) of Regulation 240/96 contain the so-called 'whitelist', a list of clauses which the parties are allowed to incorporate into their patent licence agreement. The 'whitelisted' clauses refer to the existence of intellectual property rights or to the 'specific subject-matter' of the patent

Clauses which concern the 'specific subject-matter' of the patent allow the licensor to impose certain obligations on the licensee, for example, not to grant sublicences or assign the licence,[10] to pay a minimum royalty[11] or to limit the production of the licensed product to the quantities the licensee requires in manufacturing his own products, to sell the

---

[7] See *Tiercé Ladbroke* Case T–505/93 [1997] ECR II–927.

[8] OJ L31 (1996). It entered into force on 1 April 1996 and will apply until 31 March 2006.

[9] OJ L219 (1984).

[10] Article 2(1) of Regulation 240/96: see *Nungesser v Commission* Case 258/78 [1982] ECR 45.

[11] Article 2(1) of Regulation 240/96: *Kaï Ottung* Case 320/87 [1989] ECR 1177. In this case the licensee undertook to pay royalties for an unlimited period. He stopped when the patent expired, but did not give six months' notice as required under the licence agreement. The ECJ held that when a licensee could freely terminate the agreement within a reasonable time, an obligation to pay royalties was not in breach of art 81(1) EC.

licensed product only as an integral part of or a replacement for his own products or otherwise in connection with the sale of his own products provided that such quantities are freely determined by the licensee, and not to divulge the know how, even after the termination of the agreement, as long as the know how remains secret or the patent is in force.

The Regulation determines the degree of territorial protection which a licensor is allowed to grant to a licensee. In this respect the licensee may be prohibited not only from pursuing an active sales policy outside the assigned territory, but also from responding to unsolicited orders coming from outside that territory. This is the recognition of absolute territorial protection. The licensor may also give absolute territorial protection to a licensee against licensees from other territories for a maximum of five years from the date when the protected product was first marketed in the EC. It is presumed that after that period a licensee would be sufficiently established on the market to compete with others and that he would have exploited the patent sufficiently to justify his initial investment.

In this context it is important to note that a licensee is free to sell within his assigned territory to both users and resellers. The latter are likely to resell for export. Neither the licensor in respect of his licensee nor the licensee are allowed to impose an export ban on those to whom the licensee sells the licensed products within the assigned territory. A ban on export from the EC to a third country was not considered by the Commission as in breach of art 81(1) EC, in particular the Commission in *Re Agreement between Kabel-und Metallwerke Neumeyer AG and Etablissement Luchaine SA* [1975] 2 CMLR D40 took into account the fact that there was little possibility that the product would be reimported. However the Commission in *Re Agreements between Gebruder Junghans GmbH* [1977] 1 CMLR D82 decided that such a ban in respect of a country with which the EC has close and preferential economic links could be in breach of art 81(1) EC.

Both vertical and horizontal agreements may breach art 81 EC. In respect of vertical agreements two types are potentially of an anti-competitive nature: cross-licensing involving reciprocal patent licences and agreements to pool intellectual property rights. Both types of agreement are outside the scope Regulation 240/96. Therefore, undertakings intending to enter into such agreements should apply to the Commission for an individual exemption.[12]

If an agreement apparently within the scope of art 81(1) EC does not qualify for a block exemption under a relevant regulation, or though being within a category covered by a block exemption regulation does not satisfy the criteria laid down in the relevant regulation for exemption, it should be notified to the Commission.

It emerges from the case law of the ECJ in respect of agreements relating to intellectual property rights that all clauses which concern the specific 'subject-matter' of the right in question are allowed. However, clauses related to the exercise of intellectual property rights (rather than to the 'subject-matter' of the right) are subject to the usual prohibitions of art 81(1) EC.

Intellectual property rights and art 82 EC

Technical superiority based on the possession of intellectual property rights constitute a

---

[12] See decision of the Commission in *Alcatel Espace and ANT Nachrichtentechnik* [1991] 4 CMLR 208.

factor which the Commission and the Community judicature will take into consideration in establishing dominance. In *Hoffmann-La Roche Co AG v Commission* Case 85/76 [1979] ECR 461[13] the ECJ held that 'Roche's technical lead over its competitors due to the fact that it is the proprietor of several patents relating to vitamin A, even after the expiration of these patents, is a further indication that it occupies a dominant position.' However, dominance is not prohibited under art 82 EC, what is in breach of that provision is the abuse of a dominant position.

In principle a refusal to grant a licence by an undertaking in a dominant position which is a proprietor of intellectual property rights does not constitute an abuse.[14] In *Volvo* Case 238/87 [1989] 4 CMLR 122 Volvo had a registered design and did not want to grant a licence. The ECJ ruled that the right to restrain third parties from exploiting the design was covered by the very subject-matter of its exclusive right. Consequently, a refusal to licence was not an abuse of the right. The ECJ added that certain conduct, when intellectual property rights conferred on their proprietor a dominant position, may in certain circumstances infringe art 82 EC. In the context of the above case he ECJ stated that such conduct occurs when any manufacturer (who is the proprietor of the relevant intellectual property rights) arbitrarily refuses to supply spare parts to independent repairers, fixes prices for spare parts at unfair levels or decides to stop production of spare parts knowing that many cars still in circulation would need them.

However, in the context of the doctrine of essential facilities the situation is different. In the absence of similar or substitutable products a refusal may constitute an abuse. In *Magill v Radio Telefis Eireann (RTE)* Case 241/91 [1995] ECR I–797 under Irish law RTE had a monopoly over the compilation of programme schedules for radio and television. The monopoly was reinforced by a copyright. RTE refused to licence the weekly programme details to Magill, an undertaking publishing weekly magazines that wanted to include programme schedules in its publication. The ECJ held that RTE was in breach of art 82 EC. Three matters were, in particular, taken into account by the ECJ: first, that the information was not available elsewhere, although there was 'specific, constant and regular' consumer demand for it; second, that RTE by refusing the licence was reserving to itself the secondary market of publishing weekly radio and television programmes; and, third, that there was no justification for the refusal 'either in the activity of television broadcasting or in that of publishing television magazines'. The ECJ recognised that the granting of a compulsory licence was an appropriate remedy to terminate the breach of art 82 EC! This case has a limited application. As Goyder pointed out 'the Commission treats the *Magill* judgment as having limited application, not requiring widespread compulsory licensing. Owners of intellectual property rights are normally entitled to decide whether to license or not. Merely to reach a negative decision is not to commit a breach of art [82 EC]'.[15]

The situation is different if an undertaking in a dominant position acquires intellectual property rights in order to reinforce a barrier to entry into the relevant product market by third parties. In *Tertra Pak (No 1)* Case T–51/89 [1990] ECR II–309 Tetra Pak had some 90 per cent market in the EU and thus enjoyed a dominant position in both machinery for

---

[13] See also: *Tetra Pak (No 1)* 88/501: OJ L272 (1988).
[14] *Chiron Corp v Organon Teknika (No 2)* [1968] FSR 393.
[15] *EC Competition Law*, 3rd ed, Oxford: Oxford University Press, 1998, p359.

manufacturing brick-shaped cartons and the aseptic cartons in which UHT milk was sold. Consumers preferred 'gable-shaped' cartons in which only fresh milk could be sold. For that reason, for many years Liquipak, an American company, was developing a gable-shaped carton for milk and necessary filling machinery. The only rival of Tetra Pak on the market, Elopak also tried to develop gable-shaped cartons. When Elopak was ready to launch its product, Tetra Pak acquired Liquipak, together with the exclusive licence for developing the gable-shaped, aseptic milk cartons and necessary filling machinery. Elopak complained to the Commission. The Commission, and subsequently the CFI, decided that Tetra Pak by acquiring an undertaking possessing an exclusive licence for rival technology abused its dominant position. The CFI ruled that the acquisition by an undertaking in a dominant position of an exclusive licence did not constitute in itself an abuse. However, in the circumstances of this case, in particular taking into account the very high barrier to entry to the relevant product market, the acquisition of the exclusivity of the licence not only strengthened the dominant position of Tetra Pak but also reinforced the barrier to entry of new competitors into the market. This was confirmed on appeal by the ECJ in *Tetra Pak (No 2)* Case C–333/94P [1997] 4 CMLR 662 in which the Court ruled that Tetrapak was trying to eliminate its competitors and a fine of EUR 75 million was imposed.

Article 82(d) EC prohibits the making of a contract subject to acceptance by the other parties of supplementary obligations unconnected with that contract, and is often breached by the proprietor of intellectual property rights by the tying of the product to another product which is available elsewhere at a better price. Obviously, undertakings which refuse to be tied are refused supplies of the 'tying' product. This occurred in *Hilti v Commission* Case T–30/89 [1991] ECR II–1439. Hilti manufactured nail guns and the nails and cartridge strips for such equipment. It had patents for nail guns and the cartridge strips. The Commission stated that Hilti abused its position, *inter alia*, by pursuing a policy of supplying cartridge strips to certain end users or distributors only when such cartridge strips were purchased with the necessary complement of nails ('tying' of cartridge strips and nails). During the investigation the Commission found that with respect to nails, since 1960 there had been independent producers, including the interveners, making nails for use in nail guns. Some of those producers were specialised and produce only nails, and indeed some made only nails designed for Hilti tools. Hilti was fined EUR 6 million. The ECJ upheld the decision of the Commission.

Article 82 EC has also been applied to collecting societies which often have a dominant position in the relevant market in the Member State of their establishment. Collecting societies may abuse their dominant position in two ways. First, in respect of their members when they impose discriminatory terms on nationals of other Member States[16] or in respect of the rights which they require their members to assign to them.[17] Second, in respect of those who seek a licence to exploit rights in work controlled by collecting societies, mainly by imposing unfair and unreasonable terms on users of copyright works.[18]

---

[16] Decision 71/224: *GEMA* [1971] CMLR D35.

[17] *Belgische Radio en Télévisie (BRT) v SV SABAM* Case 127/73 [1974] ECR 313. SABAM required the assignment of the author's copyrights for all categories of work and manners of exploitation and for the whole world. This was considered as an abuse under art 82 EC.

[18] In *GEMA*, the requirement that royalties should be paid for works unprotected by copyright was considered as abusive.

25.4 Harmonisation of intellectual property rights

The EC has been very active in harmonising the national laws of Member States on intellectual property rights.

Patent

At the time of writing there is no European system of patents. The national law of each Member State retains its importance in this area. The European Patent Convention is of limited importance, taking into account that it does not create a uniform protection right. The Community Patent Convention signed in Luxembourg in 1975, and revised in 1989, has never entered into force.

The Commission has recognised the necessity and desirability of the harmonisation of the substantive rules on patents at Community level. The Commission published a Green Paper on the Community Patent and the Patent System in Europe in June 1997. The follow-up to the Green Paper was published in February 1999.[19]

The European Patent Convention
The European Patent Convention was signed in October 1973 and entered into force in 1978. The Convention applies in all Member States and Switzerland, Liechtenstein, Monaco, and Cyprus. The Convention is not very ambitious and does not harmonise substantive rules on patent. It establishes a system under which a number of national patents can be granted at once instead of a number of separate procedures being commenced in each contracting State. The European Patent Convention provides for the grant by the European Patent Office (EPO) of European patents. The EPO has its headquarters in Munich and operates in parallel with the national patent offices. Applications for the grant of patents must be submitted in one of the official languages of the European Patent Office which are English, French and German. Under the Convention the applicant may chose to hold a patent in all contracting States, in some of them or in one of them. From the date of publication of the mention of its grant, a European patent confers on the proprietor, in each of the States for which it is granted, the same rights as would be conferred by the grant of a national patent. Under art 65 of the Convention a contracting State is permitted to prescribe that a European patent should be deemed *void ab initio* in that State if, where the text of the patent was not drawn up in that State's official language, the proprietor did not file a translation in that language. Some countries, *inter alia*, Germany have exercised that power.This provision was challenged as contrary to art 28 EC in *BASF AG* v *Präsident Des Deutschen Patentamts* Case C–44/99 (1999) The Times 12 October.

In this case the proprietor of a European patent for automotive paint sealer composition transferred that patent to BASF AG. The former proprietor of that patent had originally submitted a patent application drafted in English to the German Patent Office with effect, *inter alia*, in Germany. Mention of the grant had been published on 24 July 1996 in the European Patent Bulletin in conformity with German law. However, by order of 5 May 1997, the German Patent Office declared the patent *void ab initio* as no German translation had

---

[19] COM(99)42 final.

been filed by the former proprietor within the prescribed time limit, that is within three months of the mention of the grant of the European patent in the European Patent Bulletin.

BASF AG brought proceedings for annulment of the German Patent Office's decision. BASF AG argued that the German legislation was contrary to the free movement of goods as it constituted a measure having an equivalent effect to a quantitative restriction on imports. In this respect, BASF AG emphasised that in the light of the very high costs of translating patent specifications, proprietors of European patents were forced to select translation only in some Member States which resulted in the division of the internal market into 'protected zone' and 'free zone' and therefore constituted an obstacle to the free movement of goods.

The ECJ held that art 28 EC does not preclude a Member State from requiring patent holders to file a translation of the specifications of their patents in the official language of that Member State. The decision of the ECJ can be justified on two grounds.

First, under art 65 of the European Convention on the Grant of European Patents a Contracting State is permitted to prescribe that a European patent should be deemed *void ab initio* in that State if, where the text of the patent was not drawn up in that State's official language, the proprietor did not file a translation in that language. As already mentioned the Convention applies to four States outside the territory of the Community. It is an international treaty par excellence. In this context, it is difficult to envisage that, by a decision of the ECJ, a reservation to an international convention could be declared unlawful. Non-members, but contracting States to the Convention, are not bound by the decision of the ECJ.

Second, the ECJ emphasised that even supposing that the Convention creates a division in the internal market into 'protected zone' and 'free zone' the choice facing an inventor when deciding whether to apply for a patent limited to a single Member State or covering several Member States is the same irrespective of whether he applies for a European patent or a national patent. His choice will be made after an overall assessment of advantages and disadvantages of each option, which includes complex evaluations of the commercial interests of having protection in the various States compared to the costs (including translation costs entailed in obtaining the grant of a patent in those States).

Whilst it must be accepted that there will be differences in movements of goods depending on whether inventions are protected in all States or only some of them, the repercussions on intra-Community trade of any competition in the 'free zone' markets would depend on the actual, unforeseeable, decisions taken by all the operators concerned on the basis of economic conditions in the various markets. Those repercussions are too uncertain and indirect to be regarded as an obstacle to the free movement of goods within the meaning of art 28 EC.

The main drawback of the European Patent Convention is its lack of ambition. An applicant instead of obtaining a unitary European patent receives a group of equivalent national patents. As indicated by the above case the cost of 'translating' European patents into the appropriate languages for use as national patents is very high. The ECJ has no jurisdiction under the European Patent Convention. Consequently, there is no uniformity in its interpretation and application.

Creation of the Community patent

A communication of the Commission pursuant to a Green Paper emphasised three features of the future Community Patent. First, it must have a unitary character and once granted it would be effective throughout the Community. Second, it should be affordable for applicants. It should cost no more than a European patent covering a number of countries. The renewal fees, which under the European Patent Convention are paid in respect of each country covered by the patent, should be substantially lower and would cover all Member States. Third, the objective of the Community Patent would be to ensure as much legal certainty to the applicant as possible. Proceedings for infringement and relating to the validity of the patent should be uniform. Injunctions should be valid across the entire EU.

The Commission considers that the EPO should be responsible for issuing the Community Patent.

Trade marks

Regulation 40/94 of 20 December 1993 on Community trade marks provides for a single standard of registrability for a trade mark and grants protection to its proprietor throughout the Community. It was implemented in the United Kingdom by the Trade Marks Act 1994.

The Office for Harmonisation in the Internal Market (Trade Marks and Designs) was established in Alicante and started to accept applications on 1 January 1996. *Procter & Gamble Company* v *Office for Harmonisation in the Internal Market (Trade Marks and Designs)* Case T–163/98 [1999] 2 CMLR 1442 provides an interesting illustration of the application of Regulation 40/94. In this case the CFI delivered its first ever decision in respect of the Regulation. In this case Procter & Gamble Co, a US company, lodged an application for a Community trade mark with the Office for Harmonisation in the Internal Market (Trade Marks and Design) for the registration of the term 'Baby-Dry' for babies' diapers. The examiner rejected the application on the ground that the purpose of goods cannot be registered. Indeed, art 7(1)(c) of Regulation 40/94 excludes registration of trade marks consisting exclusively of signs or indications which may serve, in trade, to designate the intended purpose of the goods. The applicants appealed to the Board of Appeal of the Office against that decision. The Board of Appeal dismissed the applicant's appeal and also rejected an argument regarding art 7(3) of Regulation 40/94, which overrides art 7(1)(c) and provides that if the trade mark becomes distinctive in relation to the goods as a result of the use which has been made of it art 7(1)(c) does not apply, on the ground that this argument had not been raised before the examiner. The applicant challenged both grounds of refusal and sought further that it be permitted to adduce before the Court of First Instance evidence that the term 'Baby-Dry' had become distinctive as a result of the use made of it.

The CFI annulled the decision of the Board of Appeal of the Office for Harmonisation in the Internal Market (Trade Marks and Design). Under Regulation 40/94 the procedure is as follows: an applicant wishing to contest the examiner's decision has to file an appeal (art 59 of the Regulation), the appeal is submitted to the examiner for 'interlocutory revision' (art 60(1) of the Regulation), and if the decision is not rectified within a month, it is automatically remitted to the Board of Appeal: art 60(2) of Regulation 40/94. The CFI confirmed the decision of the Board of Appeal of the Office as to the substance. Under art

7(1)(c) of Regulation 40/94 the term 'Baby-Dry' is not capable of constituting a Community trade mark since it is composed exclusively of words which serve in trade to designate the intended purpose of the goods.

However, two interesting points were raised concerning the appeal procedures, both before the Board of Appeal of the Office and before the Court of First Instance. In respect of the Board of Appeal the CFI held that under art 62(1) the Board has to determine the appeal either by exercising any power within its competence with regard to the department which was responsible for the contested decision or by remitting the case to that department for further action. It results from that provision and from the scheme of Regulation 40/94 that the Board of Appeal has the same powers in deciding an appeal as the examiner and therefore should have examined the argument submitted in the alternative based on art 7(3) of the Regulation which the applicant expressly invoked. Indeed, the applicant wanted to submit evidence of acquired distinctiveness based on the fact that its products, 'Baby-Dry' diapers, had been on sale throughout Europe since 1993 and had been heavily advertised. The CFI held that the refusal cannot be solely based on the ground that the applicant invokes a new argument which was not raised before the examiner. The CFI held that the Board of Appeal should have either decided on the substance of that issue or remitted the matter to the examiner. For that reason, the CFI annulled the decision of the Board of Appeal.

With respect to the CFI's jurisdiction in appeals against the decisions of the Board of Appeal of the Office, the CFI stated that its jurisdiction to annul or alter the contested decision should be assessed in the light of art 63(3) of Regulation 40/94 which provides that an appeal may be brought before it on grounds of lack of competence, infringement of an essential procedural requirement, infringement of the Treaty, or misuse of power. As a result, the CFI had no jurisdiction to examine evidence of acquired distinctiveness of 'Baby-Dry' diapers based on art 7(3) of Regulation 40/94, as requested by the applicant, taking into account that the merits of the claim had not been considered by the Office.

Copyright

Copyright has been harmonised in the EC through EC directives. So far there are five directives on copyright and a number of proposals concerning artists' re-sale rights and copyright in the information societies. All five directives have been implemented in the UK.

Design right

Design rights have not yet been harmonised but a draft regulation introducing Community unitary design rights for both unregistered and registered design is, at the time of writing, in the process of being adopted. Also Directive 98/71[20] has been adopted in respect of registered designs. The Directive defines the terms 'design', sets out the criteria for registration and provides for a five-year period of protection for the design commencing from filing of the application. The Directive does not affect national or Community law

---

[20] OJ L298 (1998). The Directive must be implemented by 28 October 2001.

relating to unregistered design, trade marks or other distinctive signs. The Directive allows Member States to apply national rules protecting copyright to registered design. Also national procedural rules are applicable to design registration.

26 The State and the Common Market

26.1 State aid

26.2 Aid compatible with the common market

26.3 Discretionary exemptions: aid which the Commission may consider to be compatible with the common market

26.4 Institutional supervision under art 88 EC

26.5 State monopolies and public undertakings

The provisions of the EC Treaty apply not only to undertakings but also to Member States whose intervention in the market economy may distort competition within the common market. Those who drafted the EC Treaty were realistic. They knew that it would be impossible to prohibit a Member State from interfering with market forces, especially in times of recession. The EC Treaty aims to keep State aid under control in order to ensure the proper functioning of the common market, in particular to prevent undertakings from gaining an unfair competitive advantage over competitors as a result of assistance from a Member State. It also provides for supervision by the Community of public undertakings through which a Member State is directly engaged in commercial activities. Furthermore, the EC Treaty imposes an obligation on Member States to adjust State monopolies in order to satisfy the requirements of the common market, namely not to hinder the free flow of goods from one Member State to another.

26.1 State Aid

The Commission's seventh survey on State aid in the EU published in 1999[1] showed that total aid expenditure in the EU was running at approximately EUR 95 billion annually, of which about 40 per cent was granted to manufacturing industries, 35 per cent to transport and 13 per cent to agriculture. The survey highlighted that there had been a decrease in expenditure in all sectors apart from financial services. The decrease is, however, mainly due to reductions in the level of aid given to the former East Germany, and it does not reflect a downward trend across the EU. Some Member States such as Germany, Italy and France give the largest share of aid in absolute terms. The survey identified aids and subsidies as one of the few remaining distortions to competition in the common market. The survey concluded that there is continuing need for the vigilant monitoring and control of State aid. In this respect the EU has decided to modernise and streamline its policy in order to take a

---

[1] See http://europa.eu.int/comm/dg04/aid/other.htm.

stricter approach with regard to the monitoring and investigating of State aid. The new initiatives will be examined in this chapter.

The legal regime on State aid is governed by arts 87–89 EC. Article 87 EC establishes general substantive principles in respect of the assessment of the compatibility of aid granted by a Member State with the objectives of the common market. Article 88 EC lays down procedures for the Commission to control existing and new aid and art 89 EC confers on the Council the power to adopt implementing measures for the application of arts 88 and 89 EC.

Article 87 EC is at the centre of the legal regime on State aid. It provides:

'(1) Save as otherwise provided in this Treaty, any aid granted by a Member State or through State resources in any form whatsoever which distorts or threatens to distort competition by favouring certain undertakings or the production of certain goods shall, insofar as it affects trade between Member States, be incompatible with the common market.

(2) The following should be compatible with the common market:

(a) aid having a social character, granted to individual consumers, provided that such aid is granted without discrimination related to the origin of the products concerned;

(b) aid to make good the damage caused by natural disasters or exceptional occurrences;

(c) aid granted to the economy of certain areas of the Federal Republic of Germany affected by the division of Germany, insofar as such aid is required in order to compensate for the economic disadvantages caused by that division.

(3) The following may be considered to be compatible with the common market:

(a) aid to promote the economic development of areas where the standard of living is abnormally low or where there is serious underemployment;

(b) aid to promote the execution of an important project of common European interest or to remedy a serious disturbance in the economy of a Member State;

(c) aid to facilitate the development of certain economic activities or of certain economic areas, where such aid does not adversely affect trading conditions to an extent contrary to the common interest;

(d) aid to promote culture and heritage conservation where such aid does not affect trading conditions and competition in the Community to an extent that is contrary to the common interest;

(e) such other categories of aid as may be specified by decision of the Council acting by a qualified majority on a proposal from the Commission.'

Article 87 EC (*Capalongo v Maya* Case 77/72 [1973] ECR 611) is not directly effective.

In the application of art 87(1) aid is presumed to be incompatible with the common market if the following conditions are fulfilled:

1. it is granted 'by a Member State or through State resources';
2. it 'distorts or threatens to distort competition';
3. it 'favours certain undertakings or the production of certain goods';
4. it 'affects trade between Member States';
5. it is not covered by exemption/derogations provided by the EC Treaty.

However, before examining the above-mentioned conditions it is necessary to define the concept of State aid itself.

The concept of State aid

There is no definition of State aid in the EC Treaty. The case law of the Community judicature indicates that the concept of State aid has been interpreted broadly. The ECJ emphasised that the effect of the aid, not its form or its objective, is relevant in the context of art 87 EC.[2]

Forms of State aid

A non-exhaustive list of forms of aid was provided by the Commission in its reply to a Written Question in 1963.[3] It includes: direct subsidies, tax exemption, preferential interest rates, guarantees of loans on especially favourable terms, acquisition of land or buildings either gratuitously or on favourable terms, provision of goods and services on preferential terms, indemnities against operating losses and other measures of equivalent effect. This list was further extended in Doc.20.502/IV/68 to encompass: reimbursement of costs in the event of success; State guarantees, whether direct or indirect, to credit operations; preferential rediscount rates; dividend guarantees; preferential public ordering and deferred collection of fiscal or social contributions.

A broad definition of State aid was first provided in one of the earliest cases decided by the ECJ under the CS Treaty. In *De Gezamenlijke Steenkolenmijnen in Limburg* v *High Authority* Case 30/59 [1961] ECR 1 the ECJ defined State aid as 'any advantage conferred on a firm by the public authorities, without payment, or against a payment which corresponds only to a minimal extent to the figure at which the advantage can be valued.' Subsequently, State aid was described in *Amministrazione delle Finanze dello Stato* v *Denkavit Italiana* Case 61/79 [1980] ECR 1205, where the ECJ held that art 87(1) referred to:

> '... the decisions of Member States by which the latter, in pursuit of their own economic and social objectives, give, by unilateral and autonomous decisions, undertakings or other persons resources or procure for them advantages intended to encourage the attainment of the economic or social objective sought.'

The concept of State aid is larger than the concept of subsidies since it encompasses not only direct payments to a beneficiary but also includes measures, whatever their form, which alleviate charges which a beneficiary would otherwise have to bear, and thus without being subsidies in the strict sense are of the same nature and produce similar effects to subsidies.

Consequently, the concept includes a State intervention designed to mitigate charges which are normally included in the budget of an undertaking: *SFEI* Case C–39/94 [1996] ECR I–3547; *France* v *Commission* Case C–241/94 [1996] ECR I–4551. In *Syndicat Français de l'Express International* v *La Poste* Case C–39/94 [1996] ECR I–3547 the ECJ held that such measures as logistical and commercial assistance provided by a public undertaking, the French Post Office, to SFMI, its subsidiary set up under private law and designed to be an autonomous undertaking, constituted State aid. The logistical assistance consisted of making available to SFMI the use of postal infrastructure, such as buildings, staff and railway carriages, in return for an abnormally low consideration.

---

[2] For example, see *Commission* v *Italy* Case 173/73 [1974] ECR 709; *Deufil* Case 310/85 [1987] ECR 901.

[3] OJ Sp Ed (1963).

For a State aid to be incompatible with art 87(1) EC it is not necessary that such aid represents a cost to public finances. In *Commission v France* Case 290/83 [1985] ECR 439 the Commission alleged that France was in breach of art 87(1) as it encouraged a public body, Caisse Nationale de Crédit Agricole, to pay French farmers who were in difficulty a grant from funds made up from the operating surplus which certain private funds had accumulated over the years. The French government argued this was not a State aid because funds had been generated by the management of private funds. Although the ECJ dismissed the case on procedural grounds, it held that 'any State measure, in so far as it has the effect of according aid in any form whatsoever' may be considered as State aid and that it does not need to be financed from State resources. However, funds which are generated exclusively from voluntary contributions by private undertakings do not constitute aid but may be in breach of art 82 EC.[4] Nevertheless, if the use of such funds is subject to State approval, it will be within the scope of art 87.[5] Even the granting of a reduction of a social charge by a State to a private undertaking or financial incentives to privatisation[6] may constitute State aid. In *Italy v Commission (Re Italian Textiles)* Case 173/73 [1974] ECR 709 Italian legislation reduced from 15 per cent to 10 per cent, for the period of three years, the contribution of employers in the textile sector towards the family allowance within the general security system. The Italian government argued that the reduction should be considered as being of a social nature and that it was part of the Italian internal taxation system which was within the exclusive competence of a Member State. It also submitted that the high percentage of women employed in the textile sector put undertakings in this sector at a disadvantage as compared to other sectors. For that reason the reduction in social charges granted to employers was aimed at equalising their competitiveness. The ECJ disagreed. The Court decided that the measure was an aid on the grounds that the purpose or objective of the reduction was irrelevant in the context of art 87(1) and that in other sectors such as the electronics industry there was a high proportion of female workers but no similar tax reduction and therefore there was no objective justification for the reduction within the general social security system. It is submitted that the main reason for classifying the tax reduction as a State aid was its selective application to the textiles industry only. Consequently, selective exemption from internal taxation, irrespective of whether it is income tax, corporate tax or any other form of tax, will constitute State aid in so far as such exemption places its beneficiary in a more advantageous position as compared to other undertakings: *Banco Exterior de España* Case C–387/92 [1994] ECR I–877; *FFSA* Case T–106/95 [1997] ECR –II 229. Tax advantages should also be examined in the context of art 90 EC which prohibits discriminatory internal taxation.

However, the ECJ imposes an important limitation on the concept of State aid. In *Sloman Neptun* Cases C–72–73/91 [1993] RCT I–887 German merchant shipping legislation permitted German shipowners to employ nationals of third countries at rates of pay lower than those of German nationals and under less favourable social security conditions, thus allowing considerably reduced social security contributions. This was not regarded as a

---

[4] *Milchförderungsfonds*: OJ L35 (1985).
[5] In *Commission v France* Case 290/83 [1985] ECR 439 the ECJ held that the fund was financed by a public body and its distribution was subject to State approval.
[6] *British Aerospace/VSEL* [1995] 4 CMLR 323.

breach of art 87(1). The ECJ held that the system created under the legislation in question was not intended to grant an advantage to shipowners by imposing an additional burden for the State. Its consequence, the potential loss of tax revenue for a State, was 'inherent in the system'. Similarly, in *Petra Kirsammer-Hack* Case C–189/91,[7] an exemption granted to small businesses from a national system of protection of workers against unfair dismissal which entitled small businesses not to pay compensation to their employees in the event of unfair dismissal was not considered as State aid. The ECJ held that there was no direct or indirect transfer of financial resources from State funds and the legislation in question was intended to encourage the development of such business by reducing financial burdens imposed on them. The system created by the legislation in question did not create an advantage which would constitute an additional burden for the State.

Also, national legislation imposing minimum prices on certain products is outside the scope of art 87 EC, as the benefit it creates for national distributors of such products is not granted directly or indirectly from the State's resources: *Van Tiggele* Case 82/77 [1978] ECR 25.

The 'private investor' principle

In order to assess whether a measure granted by a State is within the scope of art 87 EC, the test of 'private investor' has been applied by the Community institutions. In *Belgium v Commission (Re Boch)* Case C–234/84 [1986] ECR 2263 the ECJ laid down the test in the following terms:

> 'An appropriate way of establishing whether such a measure is a State aid is to apply the criterion ... of determining to what extent the undertaking would be able to obtain the sums in question on the private capital markets. In the case of an undertaking whose capital is almost entirely held by the public authorities this test is, in particular, whether in similar circumstances a private shareholder, having regard to the foreseeability of obtaining a return and leaving aside all social, regional-policy and sectorial considerations, would have subscribed the capital in question.'

Consequently, in applying the test, Community institutions will assess whether in similar circumstances, a prudent private investor, would have made the same investment.

The hypothetical private investor is not necessarily looking for a short-term or speculative profit (*Italy v Commission (Re Alfa Romeo)* Case C–305/89 [1991] ECR I–1603) and may be motivated by other considerations such as the temporary survival of a company which has every chance to become profitable again: *Belgium v Commission* Case 234/84 [1986] ECR 2263.

Aid granted by a State or through State resources

Aid granted by a Member State

The ECJ has interpreted the concept of State broadly. It includes regional (*Commission v Italy* Case 169/82 [1984] ECR 1603) and local government bodies: *Germany v Commission* Case 248/84 [1987] ECR 4013. The definition of a public entity which should be treated as

---

[7] OJ C001 (1994).

an emanation of the State was provided by the ECJ in *Foster v British Gas* Case C–188/89 [1990] ECR I–3313. Three criteria must be satisfied by such an entity:

1. it has been made responsible by the State for providing a public service;
2. it provides that service under the control of the State;
3. it has special powers to provide that service, beyond those normally applicable in relations between individuals. In proceedings against such an entity an individual may rely on vertical direct effect of EC law.

Also included within the definition are public and private bodies authorised by the State to administer aid: *Steinike und Weinlig* Case 78/76 [1977] ECR 595.

Aid granted through State resources

The degree of control that a Member State exercises in respect of a private undertaking will indicate whether or not aid is granted through State resources. In *Van der Kooy v Commission* Case 67/85 [1986] ECR 219 in which Gasunie charged a preferential tariff to glasshouse growers for natural gas in The Netherlands, the ECJ held that Gasunie, although a private company, was nevertheless the 'state' within the meaning of art 87 EC on the basis of the following factors: the Dutch government held 50 per cent of its shares, it appointed half of the members of the board of directors, and, even though it did not use it in practice, had the power to veto the tariff adopted by the company. The ECJ emphasised that 'Gasunie in no way enjoys full autonomy in the fixing of gas tariffs but acts under the control and on the instructions of the public authorities. It is thus clear that Gasunie could not fix the tariff without taking account of the requirements of the public authorities.' Consequently aid incorporated into the tariff was granted by a Member State.

In *Commission v France* Case 290/83 [1985] ECR 439 the French National Agricultural Credit Fund through which aid was granted to French farmers constituted the 'State' within the meaning of art 87. Similarly, in *ENI-Lanerossi* Case C–303/88 [1991] ECR I–1433 a public corporation set up by Italian legislation, under which it was required to operate as an independent economic entity dependent on private capital for funds, was considered as a 'State' due to a number of factors, namely members of the board of directors and management board were appointed by the Italian Prime Minister, the corporation operated within directives issued by a ministerial committee and the repayment of loans was guaranteed by the Italian government.

Aid which distorts or threatens to distort competition

Only aid which distort or threaten to distort competition is unlawful. This requirement is expressly stated in arts 81 and 82 EC. Indeed, a State aid affects the competitors of the beneficiary as it artificially strengthens the beneficiary's position in the relevant product market.

If aid granted by a Member State affects only the domestic market or markets outside the EU,[8] such aid is outside the scope of art 87. However, the economic affairs of the various

---

[8] However, if an undertaking which has received a State aid, sells its product on international markets, including the common market, such aid will be within the scope of art 87 EC: see *Phillip Morris* Case 730/79 [1980] ECR 2671; *Maribel* (OJ L95 (1997)).

Member States are so interwoven that almost any aid granted by a Member State distorts or threatens to distort competition within the common market.[9] In *Italy v Commission* Case 173/73 [1974] ECR 709 the ECJ stated that in order to assess whether there is distortion of competition because of the granting of aid 'the point of departure must necessarily be the competitive position existing within the common market before the adoption of the measure in issue'.

In *Philip Morris* Case 730/79 [1980] ECR 2671 the ECJ took into consideration the following factors: the share of the Dutch market after the investment (50 per cent), the percentage of its expected exports to other Member States (80 per cent), and the proportion of the aid in the company's investment capital (3.8 per cent). In this case the Commission did not analyse the relevant product market from the economic perspective. In subsequent cases the ECJ was more demanding. In *Leeuwarder Papierwarenfabriek BV* Case 318/82 [1985] ECR 3727 the ECJ dismissed the case on the grounds that the Commission failed to submit any economic analyses of the relevant product market and therefore did not establish that the aid affected or could affect competition and the pattern of trade between Member States.

Aid which favours certain undertakings or the production of certain goods

General measures of economic policy are outside the scope of art 87 EC. In principle they have effect on all undertakings in a Member State. Among general measures of economic policy are: the reduction of interest rates, the devaluation of national currencies, the reduction of the level of taxation on industry as a whole, etc. Such measures are, however, subject to the requirements of arts 98 and 99 EC. State assistance for vocational training[10] or for job creation in the field of social security and social infrastructure, or the provision by public authorities of infrastructure which is normally provided by the State (but not if carried out specifically in the interest of one or more undertakings) are considered as general measures of economic policy. In this respect the Commission decided that the UK contribution to the construction of the Channel tunnel link was not State aid as it constituted one of 14 priority Trans-European network projects and provided an important international connection for persons and goods.[11] Only a measure which favours certain undertakings or the production of certain goods, and results in creating an advantage for the recipient undertaking as compared with its competitors, is unlawful.

Aid which affects the common market

The requirement that aid granted to an undertaking must affect intra-Community trade is encompassed in arts 81 and 82 EC Treaty. Therefore, it has the same meaning under art 87(1) EC. The case law of the Community judicature shows that this requirement has been interpreted widely. It includes the situation where an undertaking beneficiary of a State aid

---

[9] For example: see *France v Commission* Case 102/87 [1988] ECR 4067; *Het Vlaamse Gewet v Commission* Case T–214/95 [1998] ECR II–717.

[10] See *Saint-Gobain* (OJ L215 (1991)); *Ford/Volkswagen* (OJ C257 (1991)).

[11] (1996)10 EU Focus 3.

did not export its products. In *France v Commission* Case 102/87 [1988] ECR 4067 the ECJ held that when an undertaking is in competition with undertakings from other Member States, even if it does not itself export its products, the fact that it is State-aided may affect intra-Community trade. In particular this may occur if there is over-capacity in the relevant sector, taking into account that when domestic production is increased as a result of aid granted to an undertaking, undertakings from other Member States have less chance to sell their products in the market in that Member State. Therefore, the potential effect on intra-Community trade is taken into consideration.

The question whether the *de minimus* rule applies in the context of art 87(1) EC was the subject of many controversies. However, its introduction was only a question of time taking into account the resources of the Commission and the reform of the common market legislation with the aim of simplifying it. In 1992 the Community adopted its guidelines on State aid for small and medium-sized enterprises (SMEs), in which the application of the *de minimus* rule was recognised.[12] The guidelines were amended in 1996 in the Commission's Notice on the *de minimus* rule for State aid.[13] It applies to all undertakings, although it is of particular importance to SMEs since it covers aid of less than EUR 100,000 per undertaking over a period of three years with the exception of export aid. Under Regulation 994/98 of 7 May 1998 on the application of arts 87 and 88 to certain categories of horizontal aid, the *de minimus* rule was formally acknowledged.[14]

26.2 Aid compatible with the common market

Article 87(2) EC enumerates three types of aid compatible *de jure* with the common market. In addition, under Regulation 994/98 certain categories of horizontal aid are exempt from the notification requirements. The Commission often emphasises that derogations under this article must be construed restrictively.[15]

Article 87(2)(a) EC refers to all aid having social character granted to individual consumers without discrimination related to the origin of the products concerned

The recipient of such aid must be an individual consumer not un undertaking. In *Benedeti v Munari* Case 52/76 [1977] ECR 163 a reduction of the price of bread for consumers was incompatible with this provision because aid was granted to the milling undertakings and not directly to consumers. However, a tax relief granted to consumers buying cars fitted with pollution reduction devices was compatible with the common market.[16]

---

[12] OJ C213 (1992).
[13] OJ C68 (1996).
[14] This question is dealt with later in section 26.2.
[15] *Seadler*: OJ L295 (1987).
[16] Agence Europe, 31 March 1990, no 5234 (new series) 8; see also *Maribel* (OJ L95 (1997)) in respect of aid for the Fonds national pour l'emploi.

Article 87(2)(b) refers to aid to make good damage caused by natural disasters or exceptional occurrences

Such aid in designed to re-establish pre-existing competition conditions for undertakings affected by natural disasters or other exceptional circumstances such as earthquakes,[17] floods, droughts, volcanic eruptions, etc.

Article 87(2)(c) relates to aid to certain areas of the Federal Republic of Germany

This provision was introduced to the original Treaty by the former West Germany in order to provide assistance to areas affected by World War II and the subsequent division of Germany. Since the reunification of Germany on 3 October 1990 the Commission considers that there is no justification for special treatment of these regions. The provisions of the EC Treaty on State aid apply to the reunited Germany as a whole, although the Commission has recognised that the five new German Länder may benefit from the derogations provided for in art 87(3)(c) which require individual authorisation of the Commission. In this respect the Commission approved the aid package submitted by the German government for the acquisition and reconstruction of plants previously owned by the former Democratic German Republic at Mosel and Chemnitz[18] under which important financial assistance was granted for the Volkswagen group investing in these regions.

The application of art 87(2)(c) EC to the former East Germany is a matter of controversy between the Commission and the German government. The Commission considers that this provision should be interpreted strictly, especially in the light of the fact that in 1997 more than 1,300 applications for aid intended to assist the former East Germany were submitted to the Commission in overall terms representing in excess of 30 per cent of the total actual aid for the whole Community. If art 87(2)(c) applies to the former East Germany the Commission will have no control over financial assistance granted by the German government as this would qualify for automatic exemption. It is submitted that the approach of the Commission is in conformity with the objectives of the EC Treaty, in particular the need to ensure the proper functioning of the common market. However, it would be for the ECJ to resolve the controversy and the German government has certainly one good argument: the very existence of art 87(2)(c) which should have been deleted by the Treaty of Amsterdam if it does not apply any more.

Exemption under Regulation 994/98 of 7 May 1998 on the application of arts 87 and 88 to certain categories of horizontal aid[19]

Under this Regulation the Commission is empowered to exempt certain categories of aid from the notification requirements of art 87(3) EC. The regulation specifies two categories of aid which will be covered by secondary legislation:

---

[17] *Mezzogiorno* (OJ L86 (1991)); *Italy* v *Commission* Case C–364/90 [1993] ECR I–2097.
[18] OJ L385 (1994).
[19] OJ L142 (1998). The Regulation entered into force on 15 May 1998.

1. aid for small and medium-sized enterprises, research and development, environmental protection and training;
2. aid that complies with the map approved by the Commission for each Member State for the grant of regional aid.

A regulation adopted on the basis of Regulation 994/98 must satisfy a number of conditions in respect of the purpose of the aid, the categories of recipients, thresholds, monitoring conditions, etc, as well as conditions imposed on Member States to ensure transparency and proper monitoring of the aid.

26.3 Discretionary exemptions: aid which the Commission may consider to be compatible with the common market

Article 87(3) sets out categories of aid which are compatible with the common market. The first four categories are subject to supervision by the Commission and involve the exercise of the Commission's discretion. The Commission has established general rules under which it exercises its wide discretion in respect of art 87(3) EC. These rules are known as the theory of compensatory justification under which 'if the Commission has to use its discretionary power not to raise objection to an aid proposal, it must contain a compensatory justification which takes the form of a contribution by the beneficiary of aid over and above the effects of normal play of market forces to the achievement of Community objectives as contained in derogations of art [87(3) EC]'.[20] Subsequently, the Commission refined and developed the theory. The Commission will take into consideration three factors in exercising its discretion:

1. whether the aid promotes a development in the interests of the entire Community;
2. whether the aid is necessary (this incorporated the theory of compensatory justification);
3. whether the degree to which it distorts competition may be justified by the objective of the aid.[21]

Article 87(3)(a): aid to promote economic development in severely depressed areas

The important factor in assessing whether or not a particular regional aid should be granted is that the Commission must make its socio-economic assessment in the Community context rather than from the national perspective of a particular Member State. This requirement was established in *Philip Morris* Case 730/79 [1980] ECR 2671. In this case the government of The Netherlands wanted to grant aid in the form of subsidy to a subsidiary of Philip Morris, the second largest group of tobacco manufacturers in the world. The subsidy was designed to help the company to reorganise. The company planned to close two factories but to extend one and thus create new jobs. The factory to be enlarged was situated in the region of Bergen-op-Zoom of The Netherlands. In this region unemployment was

---

[20] 10th Report on Competition Policy (1980), point 213.
[21] 12th Report on Competition Policy (1982), point 160.

higher than the national average in The Netherlands. The ECJ held that the determination of whether or not a particular region is severely depressed should be made in the Community context.

In 1988 the Commission issued Guidelines for National Regional Aid[22] which restate and clarify the principles and practices of the Commission in respect of regional aid. The guidelines will be reviewed in 2003 and are intended to be applied until the year 2006. The main policy change they introduce concerns a reduction in the volume of regional aid. The guidelines emphasise that aid should be granted to the poorest regions of the EU with a view to combating unemployment. In respect of art 87(3)(a), in assessing the level of development of a region in relation to the Community average, its classification under the Nomenclature of Statistical Territorial Units (NUTS) will still apply. NUTS classifies all 69 regions within the EU at three levels. NUTS level 3 regions, in which GDP per capita measured in purchasing power standard (PPS) is less than 75 per cent of the EU average, will be eligible for exemption under art 87(3)(a). The aid intensity ceilings are lower than previously. The highest permissible aid intensity is set at 65 per cent of initial investment for 'outmost' regions, 50 per cent for regions where GDP is less than 60 per cent of the Community average and 40 per cent for regions where GDP is between 60 and 75 per cent of the Community average.

Article 87(3)(b): aid for important projects of common European interest or to remedy a serious disturbance in the economy of a Member State

This provision refers to two situations: first, aid designed to promote a project of European dimensions and, second, remedial measures designed to assist the entire economy of a Member State. In respect of the first category of aid in *Exécutif Régional Wallon* v *Commission (Re Glaverbel)* Cases 62 and 72/87 [1988] ECR 1573 the ECJ ruled that it is not sufficient for a research and development project to introduce new technology, it must in addition involve common European interest. The ECJ emphasised that a research and development project will qualify for aid under art 87(3)(b) if it 'forms part of a transnational European programme supported jointly by a number of Governments of the Member States, or arises from concerted action by a number of Member States to combat a common threat'. In this case the common threat was related to environmental pollution.

There are many examples of aid which was granted to promote the execution of projects of common European interests such as: the airbus project,[23] the project to develop a common standard for high-definition colour television,[24] the project to create an earth radio digital system, the Eprom projects (semi-conductors) and a software factory project.[25]

In the above context it is important to note the EU's financial contribution to research and development. From a modest beginning initiated with the creation of the Joint Research Centre in 1959 under the EA Treaty, research and development has become one of the priorities of the Community.

---

[22] OJ C74 (1998).
[23] EC Bull 4/74, point 2112.
[24] 19th Report on Competition Policy (1989), point 151.
[25] 12th Report on Competition Policy (1982), point 144.

The Treaty of Maastricht introduced Title XV on Research and Technological Development, although the Community competences in this area were previously recognised in art 130f of the SEA. The Community action in research and technological development is based on a multi-annual framework programme which is implemented through specific programmes developed within each activity. The Council unanimously adopts such multi-annual programmes according to the procedure laid down in art 251 EC.

The Fifth Framework programme (1998–2002)[26] was launched on 26 February 1999. As compared to other framework programmes it simplifies procedures, reduces payment times, improves information and assistance for small and medium-sized undertakings, etc. Thirty-one countries, including all candidate countries, the EEA countries, Switzerland and Israel, are associated with the programme.

The main purpose of these programmes is to encourage high quality co-operation among undertakings, research centres and universities in their research and technical development activities. In practice, the Community contributes financially to research and technical development projects although it may also set up joint undertakings or other structures necessary for the efficient execution of the programmes.[27] Among such programmes Eureka, founded by M Thatcher and F Mitterand to support transnational co-operation on research projects, is one of the most successful. There are hundreds of projects running under the scheme and the Commission celebrated its tenth anniversary by offering an additional EUR 2.7 billion available in grants for 150 new projects.[28]

Aid to remedy a serious disturbance in the economy of a Member State was approved following the energy crisis of 1974. The disturbance must be serious and affect the entire economy of a Member State.

Article 87(3)(c): aid to facilitate the development of certain economic activities or areas

This provision covers sectorial or regional aid. The 1998 Guidelines on National Regional Aid specify the Community policy in respect of regions eligible for aid under art 87(3)(c). This provision applies to regions which are less developed as compared with other regions of a Member State and the Community as a whole. The Commission identifies those regions by using two criteria: income per capita and structural unemployment assessed in the context of a Member State. Measures granted by a Member State must secure productive investment and job creation linked to the investment.

It is very difficult for rich Member States to justify the granting of aid to any of its poorer regions under art 87(3) EC. The better the Member State's economic position as compared to the Community average, the more drastic must be the disparity between a poor region in question as compared to other regions of that Member State. Unlike art 87(3)(a) which applies to rural areas, the so-called 'outmost'regions, traditionally poor as compared to the rest of the EU, art 87(3)(c) applies to developed areas having general economic problems

---

[26] Decisions 182/1999/EC and 1999/64/EA: OJ 26 (1998).
[27] Article 171 EC.
[28] P Matthews, 'Eureka Comes of Age with New Initiatives', The European, 23–29 January 1997, p26.

often relating to a decline of traditional industries: *Germany v Commission* Case 248/84 [1987] ECR 4013.

In respect of sectoral aid the Commission's policy in a number of sectors in based on the provisions of the three founding Treaties. The CS Treaty applies to steel[29] and coal[30] industries and under the EC Treaty the Community is responsible for the development of common policies in the following sectors: agriculture, fisheries and transport.

The Commission is very reluctant to authorise aid to industries in decline or in crisis, in particular to preserve the existing *status quo* without substantially restructuring the sector in question. Although the Commission assesses sectoral aid on a case-by-case basis, there are some general principles applicable to sectoral aid. First, aid must not serve to save a bankrupt or non-viable industry or delay its inevitable decline,[31] although the Commission recognises that in certain circumstances aid may be granted to facilitate the necessary restructuring of an industry taking into account the economic and social implication of its disappearance.[32] Second, aid must be granted either for a short period of time or for a longer period subject to a clearly fixed timetable of progressively reducing payments. Third, aid must be strictly necessary and proportionate to the objective sought.

In respect of industries such as shipbuilding, car manufacture, synthetic fibres and clothing which are subject to strong international competition, the Community has set up sectoral aid schemes.

Article 87(3)(d): aid to promote culture and heritage conservation

For the first time, the Treaty of Maastricht included culture within the competences of the EC, albeit in a limited manner. Title XII, devoted to culture, emphasises in art 151(1) EC that the EC shall contribute to:

> '... the flowering of the cultures of the Member States, while respecting their national and regional diversity and at the same time bringing the common cultural heritage to the fore.'

The Treaty of Amsterdam made no changes to art 151 EC. Culture is within the exclusive competence of the Member States. Article 151(5) EC expressly denies the EC any power to harmonise national laws and regulations in this area. As a result, the Council by a unanimous vote may adopt solely non-binding incentive measures. Therefore, cultural matters are subject to Council resolutions. Additionally, the EC-sponsored programmes which support and complement actions adopted by the Member States. They are the Raphael programme in the field of cultural heritage which was established in October 1997,[33] Kaleidoscope for the performing arts and Ariane for literature, including translation. The five-years framework programme (2000–04) creating a single financing and programming framework covers the three above-mentioned programmes.

In this context State aid granted with a view to promoting and developing national culture will be favourably assessed by the Commission. In this respect the Commission

---

[29] Decision 2496/96/ECSC laid down rules for State aid to the steel industry: OJ L338 (1996).
[30] Decision 3632/93 laid down rules for State aid in the coal industry: OJ L329 (1993).
[31] For example, *Bremer-Vulkan Werft*: OJ L250 (1997).
[32] For example, *Aer Lingus*: OJ L54 (1994).
[33] Decision 2228/97/EC: OJ L305 (1997).

approved a German scheme designed to assist the film industry by imposing a levy on pre-recorded video cassettes[34] and a French scheme extending the levy imposed on cinema admissions and television station revenue[35] to sales of pre-recorded video cassettes in order to finance film production and high-quality television programmes.

Article 87(3)(e): aid which the Council may consider compatible with the common market

Under this provision the Council is empowered to exempt other categories of aid in two situations: first, acting by QMV on a proposal submitted by the Commission, and, second, acting by unanimity on the application of a Member State. These possibilities may be used only in exceptional circumstances.[36]

26.4 Institutional supervision under art 88 EC

Article 88 EC lays down the procedure for the Commissions's supervision of existing aid and of new aid, both of which must be notified to the Commission.

In 1998 the Commission received 812 notifications of either new aid or the amending of existing aid, and registered 159 cases of unnotified aid. In 563 cases the Commission raised no objections. In 91 cases the Commission decided to initiate proceedings under art 88(2), of which 48 ended with final negative decisions and three with conditional final decisions. In the remaining the Commission issued positive final decisions. In nine cases measures under art 88(1) EC were proposed by the Commission.[37]

The substantial number of cases, the budgetary discipline imposed on the Member States participating in the third stage of EMU and the requirements of the common market prompted the Commission to reform its State aid policy and practices. The adoption of Regulation 659/1999, which lays down detailed rules for the application of art 88 EC,[38] constitutes one of the most significant developments. This procedural Regulation consolidated and brought together the Commission's practices and the case law of the ECJ. The regulation applies in respect of both 'existing' and 'new' aid.

'Existing aid'

The term 'existing aid' refers to aid which was already in existence before the adoption of the Treaty of Rome creating the EC, or in respect of Member States which subsequently joined the Community, before their accession to the Communities. Existing aid also encompasses aid which has already been approved by the Commission. In *Namur-Les Assurance du Crédit SA v Office National du Ducroire* Case C–44/93 [1994] ECR I–3829 the ECJ ruled that any

---

[34] 22nd Competition Report (1992), point 442.
[35] Commission Competition Policy Report (1993), para 544.
[36] 17th Report on Competition Policy (1987), point 274.
[37] General Report (1999), point 202.
[38] OJ L83 (1999).

measure to grant or to alter the 'existing aid' or initial plans to grant aid notified to the Commission must be considered as 'new'aid.

'Existing aid' is under constant review. The Commission must ensure its compatibility with the development and functioning of the Common market. Under Regulation 659/1999 if the Commission decides that 'existing aid' is no longer compatible with the common market, it may issue recommendations to the Member States concerned. The recommendation may propose, in particular: substantive amendment of the aid scheme, introduction of procedural requirements or abolition of the 'existing aid'. Furthermore, the Regulation requires that Member States submit annual reports on all existing aid, including aid schemes on which no specific reporting obligations have been imposed by a Commission decision.

'New aid'

New aid concerns 'plans to grant or alter aid'. New aid must be notified to the Commission in sufficient time by the Member State concerned, which is required to provide all necessary information, to allow the Commission to assess whether the aid is compatible or not with the common market. Therefore, any new aid is subject to the Commission's preventative control. A Member State must not grant new aid before the Commission has taken a decision or is deemed to have taken a decision authorising it ('standstill clause'). Within two months of receiving the notification the Commission must take a decision whether to clear the aid, to decide that the notified measure does not involve State aid or initiate a more detailed enquiry under art 88(2) EC. During that period the Commission is entitled to ask for more information from a Member State concerned. Under Regulation 659/1999, if a Member State fails to provide the information, the notification is deemed to be withdrawn, unless it can be shown that the information is not available. If the period of two months elapses and the Commission has failed to take a decision, the aid is deemed to be authorised, provided the Member State concerned gives prior notice of intention to implement the aid. Whatever decision is taken by the Commission it must be published in the Official Journal.

If the Commission decides to clear the aid, any interested parties may challenge that decision before the CFI. If the Commission decides to start an in-depth inquiry under art 88(2) EC, the notice published in the Official Journal will invite Member States, beneficiaries of the intended aid, and third parties, such as competitors or trade associations, to submit their comments, usually within 30 days, although the Regulation does not specify the time-limit. There is no formal time limit for investigations. The Commission's objective is to conclude investigations within six months, a more realistic deadline seems to be 18 months. This procedure applies only to notified aid. If the Member State fails to comply with a conditional or negative decision, the Commission may refer the matter directly to the ECJ. The procedure under art 88(2) is ended by a final decision which may clear the aid, prohibit the aid or clear the aid subject to conditions laid down by the Commission. For unnotified aid the Commission is not bound by the deadlines provided in the Regulation.

Failure to notify

If a Member State fails to notify new aid in breach of art 88(3) EC which imposes a clear, precise and unconditional obligation on a Member State concerned, or notifies new aid but implements it without waiting for the Commission's decision, the compatibility of the new aid with the requirements of the common market must be assessed by the Commission. In *France v Commission (Re Boussac)* Case 301/87 [1990] ECR 307 the ECJ refused to endorse the Commission's view that failure to notify amounts to a sufficiently serious breach of EC law by the Member State concerned to render the aid unlawful.

However, individuals are protected against a Member State's failure to notify new aid. The ECJ held in *Lorenz v Germany* Case 120/73 [1973] ECR 1471 that the stand-still clause in art 88(3) EC is directly effective. In *Salmon* Case C–354/90 [1991] ECR I–5505 the ECJ held that a decision of the Commission declaring compatible aid granted in breach of procedural requirements of art 88(3) EC can never have the effect of retroactively regularising such aid. It is still illegal within the national legal order and consequently it may be challenged before national courts by aggravated parties. The ECJ emphasised than any other interpretation of art 88(2) would encourage Member States to disregard that provision and thus render it useless in practice. Also a national court is empowered to order repayment of aid under the stand-still provision unless there are exceptional circumstances under which it would be inappropriate to order repayment of the aid: *Syndicat Français de l'Express International v La Poste* Case C–39/94 [1996] ECR I– 3547.

Investigation procedure under art 88(2) EC

If, after the preliminary examination, the Commission has serious doubts as to the compatibility of the measure with the common market, it may commence the investigation procedure provided for in art 88(2) EC. The procedure applies to notified, unnotified, and existing aid.

The Commission must notify all interested parties that it intends to open the art 88(2) procedure and invite them to submit their comments. No specific form of notification is required. Usually, the Commission publishes a communication in the Official Journal. In *Intermills* Case 323/82 [1984] ECR 3809 the ECJ held that such a publication was sufficient to notify all interested parties. In the same case the ECJ defined 'all interested parties' as the beneficiary of aid, the Member State concerned and any person, firm or association which might be injured by the grant of aid, in particular, the beneficiary's competitors and any trade association concerned. Such persons being individually and directly concerned are entitled to bring proceedings against the Commission if the latter fails to open the investigation procedure envisaged in art 88(2) EC. In *Cook* Case C–198/91 [1993] ECR I–2487 the ECJ specified the circumstances under which the Commission is obliged to open the investigation procedure. If the Commission has serious difficulties in determining the compatibility of aid with the common market it must open the investigation procedure. In this case the Commission did not raise objections to the granting of aid to a Spanish steel casting undertaking which considerably increased its production capacity. The ECJ considered that the Commission based its decision on the absence of over-capacity in the sector concerned without taking into account the relevant statistics and other information.

Therefore, the Commission had no objective basis on which to reach the decision that there was no over-capacity in the sector in question. In these circumstances the Commission had serious doubts about the compatibility of the measure with the common market and should have opened an investigation.[39]

The second situation in which the Commission must open an investigation as prescribed in art 88(2) EC is when it considers that the aid can only be authorised under certain conditions which were not mentioned in the notification and are not generally applicable. This restriction may concern the amount of the aid, its duration, etc.

The third situation in which the Commission is required to open an investigation is when it finds that authorised aid is being misused. The best example in provided in *British Aerospace and Rover Group* v *Commission* Case C–294/90 [1992] ECR I–493 in which the UK government had granted additional aid not covered by the initial decision. The additional £44.4 million aid constituted illegal aid and the UK authorities were required to recover it from the beneficiaries.

Under art 10 of Regulation 659/1999 any complaints to the Commission must be examined without delay. If the Commission suspects that unlawful aid has been granted it may request further information from a Member State concerned. If no response is given to the request the Commission may take its decision on the basis of the information in its possession, for example, the information provided by the complainant.

Under Regulation 659/1999 the Commission may issue injunctions requiring the Member State to suspend any aid until the Commission has taken a decision on its compatibility or to recover the aid provisionally (with interest) pending the outcome of the investigations. In the second situation three conditions must be satisfied:

1. the measure must be, without any doubt, a State aid;
2. there must urgency;
3. there must be a serious risk of substantial and irreparable damage to a competitor.

The above-mentioned conditions emphasise the exceptional character of interim injunctions.

The decision of the Commission

At the end of an investigation the Commission must adopt a reasoned decision,[40] either recognising that the measure does not involve aid under art 91(1) or is eligible for exemption under arts 92(2) or (3), or approving the measure subject to conditions, or declaring the measure incompatible with the common market. All decisions must be published in the Official Journal.

Under art 22 of Regulation 659/1999 the Commission has additional powers to monitor compliance with its decisions. The Commission is empowered to undertake on-site monitoring visits, in particular Commission officials may enter premises of the undertaking

---

[39] See also *SIDE* Case T–49/93 [1995] ECR II–2501.

[40] In the absence of sufficient reasoning a negative decision may be annulled by the ECJ: *Italy* v *Commission* Case 360/90 [1993] ECR I–2097; *Pleuger Worthington* Joined Cases 324 and 342/90 [1994] ECR I–1173; *Sytraval and Brink's France* Case T–95/94 [1995] ECR II–2651.

concerned, may require oral explanations and may examine the undertaking's books and business records and take copies. These powers, and their limitations, are similar to those granted to the Commission under Regulation 17/62 in competition matters. Also the Commission may request assistance from the relevant authorities of the Member State where the undertaking is located to enable the Commission to carry out the monitoring visits.

Recovery of unnotified and unlawful aid

The EC Treaty is silent on the matter of recovery of unlawful aid. However, it has long been established that the Commission is entitled to recover unlawful aid (*Commission v Germany* Case 70/72 [1973] ECR 813). The ECJ ruled in *Belgium v Commission* Case C–142/87 [1990] ECR I–959 that the objective of the recovery of State aid is to re-establish the conditions of competition existing before the granting of such aid. However, only aid which is both unlawful and incompatible with the common market can be recovered.[41] Not only aid which was unnotified but also aid granted in accordance with a Commission decision may be recovered if such a decision was later annulled by the ECJ: *CIRFS v Commission* Case C–313/90 [1993] ECR I–2557.

Regulation 659/1999 confirms the right of the Commission to recover unlawful aid, together with interest at a commercial rate running from the time the aid was granted.[42] A Member State is required to take all necessary steps without delay to recover the aid in accordance with national procedures. Normally the Commission identifies the entity which is required to repay the aid. However, if the beneficiary of unlawful aid has subsequently been sold or transferred, the rule on the transfer of liability applies. In *Italy v Commission* Case C–305/89 [1991] ECR I–1645 the recipient of the State aid, Alfa Romeo, sold some of its assets to Fiat. However, Fiat accepted only some of the Alfa Romeo liabilities, all other liabilities were transferred to the former Alfa Romeo holding company, Finmeccanica. It was the latter that was required to repay the unlawful aid.

It is only in exceptional cases, where recovery would breach EC legal principles, that recovery is not required. In this respect, the case law of the ECJ shows that the beneficiary of unlawful aid has a duty to ensure that aid has been granted lawfully before receiving such aid.[43] Consequently, he can not rely on the principle of legitimate expectations. The ECJ held in *Commission v Germany* Case C–5/89 [1990] ECR I–3437 that:

'… in view of the mandatory nature of the supervision of State aid by the Commission under art [88 EC], undertakings to which an aid has been granted may not, in principle, entertain a legitimate expectation that the aid is lawful unless it has been granted in compliance with the procedure laid down in that article. A diligent businessman should normally be able to determine whether that procedure has been followed.'

---

[41] See *Fédération Nationale du Commerce Extérieur des Produits Alimentaires and Syndicat National des Négociants et Transformeurs de Saumon v French Republic* Case C–354/90 [1991] ECR I–5505.
[42] In *British Aerospace v Commission* CaseC–294/90 [1992] ECR I–493 in addition to the granted aid of £44.4 million, £13.2 million in interest was recovered.
[43] See *BUG-Alutechnik* Case C–5/89 [1990] ECR I–3437; *Ferriere Acciaierie Sarde v Commission* Case C–102/92 [1993] ECR I–801.

The principle of legitimate expectation can only be invoked in exceptional circumstances, for example when because of unreasonable delay on the part of the Commission in taking a decision the beneficiary was led to believe that the aid in question was granted lawfully. In *RSV v Commission* Case 223/85 [1987] ECR 4617 the ECJ ruled that delay of 26 months by the Commission in adopting a decision was unjustified and therefore no refund was required.

It may happen that the recovery of unlawful aid is impossible. The ECJ has established strict conditions on the impossibility of recovery. The rule is that a Member State is not allowed to rely on provisions, practices, or circumstances existing in its internal legal system in order to escape the obligation to recover unlawful aid. Neither the passing of a national limitation period for the revocation of an administrative act (*Commission v Germany* Case C–5/89 [1990] ECR I–3437), nor the fact that the beneficiary would face difficult financial circumstances, including bankruptcy (*Commission v Belgium* Case 52/84 [1986] ECR 89), amount to absolute impossibility. Further, a Member State is precluded from granting aid to compensate an undertaking for refunding unlawful aid.[44]

The role of national courts in the enforcement of the EC Treaty provisions on State aid

Article 87 EC is not directly effective. The interested parties can neither rely solely on it in proceedings in the national courts, nor challenge the validity of the aid, nor ask a national court to decide whether or not the aid in question is compatible with the provisions of the EC Treaty: *Steinike and Weinlig* Case 78/76 [1977] ECR 595; *Lornoy* Case C–17/91 [1992] ECR I–6523. The Commission has exclusive jurisdiction to investigate and to deal with notified State aid. However, unnotified aid or notified aid which was implemented without being cleared by the Commission is within the competence of national courts. This is based on the direct effect of art 88(3) EC. In this situation a national court is entitled to order the refund of unlawful aid.

In addition, a national court has jurisdiction to deal with actions brought in respect of a Member State's refusal to comply with a Commission decision within the time limit specified in the decision, whether the decision modifies or abolishes the existing aid[45] or denies authorisation of new aid. Interested parties may challenge indirectly before a national court a decision of the Commission to authorise aid or its failure to institute an investigation under art 93(2) EC. They may also challenge both decisions of national authorities to grant aid and national implementing measures. In the field of State aid, as in any other area covered by the EC Treaty, aggravated parties may sue a Member State for damages for breach of the State-aid rules.

The Commission is in favour of extending co-operation in the area of State aid between national courts and itself and thus decentralising enforcement of the rules relating to State aid. The Commission issued a Notice in this respect.[46] In practice, national courts are still insufficiently involved in the enforcement of EC rules on State aid. The report prepared by

---

[44] Decision of the Commission in respect of Italian legislation, the so called 'Law Prodi': EU Bull 12–1994, point 63.
[45] For example, *Capolongo* Case 77/72 [1973] ECR 611.
[46] OJ C312 (1995).

the Associations Européenne d'Avocats[47] at the request of the Commission on the application of arts 87 and 88 EC by national courts showed that there were only 115 cases in national courts in this area, and only three of the complaining competitors of State-aided beneficiaries were successful. Most cases were decided in the context of discriminatory taxation.[48] Whilst the report recommended further clarification of the EC provisions on State aid and education of national lawyers and judges, it indicated that there was no need to harmonise national procedural or substantive rules on State aid. This is a contradictory statement bearing in mind, as pointed out in the report, that injunctions are not available in some jurisdiction.

It is interesting to note that the Commission has adopted a number of guidelines, notices, frameworks and codes aimed at clarifying the EC provisions on State aid such as the multi-sectoral framework for regional aid for large investment projects,[49] a Notice on the application of the state aid rules to direct taxation measures,[50] a Notice laying down a framework for assessing the compatibility with the common market of training aid falling within the scope of art 87(1) EC,[51] Guidelines on State aid for rescuing and restructuring firms in difficulty, etc.[52]

Implementing legislation for the application of arts 87 and 88 EC

Apart from legislation adopted by the Council in respect of common policies under the EC Treaty in respect of agriculture, fisheries and transport, and exceptionally in shipbuilding, and under the CS Treaty in respect of coal and steel, the Council, until recently, did not use art 89 EC to enact legislation for the control of State aid. This has changed with the adoption of the Treaty of Amsterdam. Since then the Council has adopted two important regulations:

1. Council Regulation 659/1999 laying down detailed rules for the application of art 88 adopted on 22 March 1999. This procedural Regulation has already been examined in this chapter. It certainly constitutes a step forward as it increases transparency and legal certainty in the field of State aid.
2. Council Regulation 994/98 of 7 May 1998 on the application of arts 87 and 88 to certain categories of horizontal State aid under which the Commission is empowered to adopt block exemptions in respect of certain categories of horizontal State aid. This Regulation has also been examined in this chapter. Under the Regulation certain categories of aid, which are unlikely to have an important impact on competition in the common market, will be exempted from the notification. It also formally recognises the *de minimus* rule.

---

[47] C Mehta, *Hoping for Plain Sailing* (1999), European Council, October, p53.
[48] One successful case was *R v Customs & Excise, ex parte Lunn Poly* [1998] 2 CMLR 560.
[49] OJ C107 (1998).
[50] OJ C184 (1998).
[51] OJ C343 (1988).
[52] EU Bull 7/8–1999, point 1.3.43.

26.5 State monopolies and public undertakings

State monopolies

Article 31 EC states that:

> 'Member States shall adjust any monopolies of commercial character so as to ensure that no discrimination regarding the conditions under which goods are procured and marketed exists between nationals of Member States.
>
> This provision of this article shall apply to any body through which a Member State, in law or in fact, either directly or indirectly supervises, determines or appreciably influences imports or exports between member States. This provisions shall likewise apply to monopolies delegated by the State to others.'

A monopoly of commercial character may constitute an obstacle to the free movement of goods insofar as it is the only seller of imported products on the national market and therefore occupies a dominant position on the relevant product market. In addition, a State monopoly enjoys exclusive rights, or privileges, to produce or market goods. The ECJ emphasised that the very existence of exclusive import rights constitutes a barrier to the free movement of goods since it withholds from economic operators in other Member States the opportunity to offer their products to consumers in the Member State concerned and, at the same time, takes away from consumers in that Member State the right to choose: *Pubblico Ministero* v *Manghera* Case 59/75 [1976] ECR 91; *Commission* v *Greece* Case C–347/88 [1990] ECR I–4747.

Article 31 EC applies only to monopolies of a commercial character run by the State directly, or by bodies supervised by the State or monopolies 'delegated' by the State to private bodies[53] but still under State control. State monopolies are often created to produce revenue for a Member State (eg a State monopoly in the supply of alcohol, tobacco, matches, etc).

State monopolies are not prohibited under EC law in so far as they do not operate in a discriminatory manner and thus create an obstacle to the free movement of goods and distort competition within the common market. Article 31(1) EC requires the progressive adjustment of State monopolies of Member States in order to eliminate discrimination between nationals of Member States in respect of conditions under which goods are procured and marketed, whilst art 31(2) prohibits the introduction of any new measures contrary to paragraph 1.

In *Hansen* v *Hauptzollamt Flensburg* Case 91/78 [1979] ECR 935 the ECJ held that art 31 EC applies only to intra-Community trade in goods. Consequently, goods imported from third countries are excluded from its scope of application since they are covered by the common commercial policy.

Article 31 EC, being limited to the free movent of goods, does not apply to services (*Gervais* Case C–17/94 [1995] ECR I–4353), although a monopoly in provision of a service

---

[53] For example, in *Rewe-Zentral AG* Case 120/78 [1979] ECR 649 a monopoly to sell alcohol in Germany was delegated to Bundesmonopolverwaltung.

may be caught by the provisions of the EC Treaty relating to the free movement of services.[54] Monopoly rights conferred on some professions (pharmacists, opticians, etc) are excluded from the scope of art 31 EC. However, if such monopolies discriminate against imported products they may be in breach of arts 28 and 29 EC

Both paragraphs (1) and (2) of art 31 EC are directly effective.[55]

After numerous enforcement actions brought by the Commission under art 31 EC Member States, in general, have adjusted State monopolies to avoid discriminating against imported products. Under art 86 EC State monopolies are subject to the rules of the EC Treaty 'insofar as the application of such rules does not obstruct the performance, in law or in fact, of the particular tasks assigned to them'. Article 86 applies not only to state monopolies but also to any public undertaking to which Member States grant special or exclusive rights.

Public undertakings

The definition of both types of undertaking was specified in *France, Italy and the United Kingdom v Commission* Cases 188–190/80 [1982] ECR 2545 as meaning

'... any undertaking over which the public authorities may exercise directly or indirectly a dominant influence ... such influence is to be presumed when the public authorities directly or indirectly hold the major part of the undertaking's subscribed capital, control the majority of the votes, or can appoint more than half of the members of its administrative, managerial or supervisory body.'

Public undertakings and State monopolies and the rules of competition

Article 86 EC consists of three paragraphs. Under art 86(1) EC public undertakings or undertakings to which a Member State has conferred special or exclusive rights are subject to the provisions of the EC Treaty, especially the rules on competition.

Under art 86(2) EC public undertakings and State monopolies escape not only from the application of the EC provisions regarding the free movement of goods but Community law as such if the performance of the particular tasks assigned to them can only be achieved through the grant of such rights and provided that the development of trade is not affected to such an extent as would be contrary to the interests of the Community. The ECJ held that, taking into account the scope of application of paragraphs 1 and 2 of art 86 and their combined effect, 'paragraph 2 may be relied upon to justify the grant by a Member State, to an undertaking entrusted with the operation of services of general economic interest, of exclusive rights which are contrary to, in particular, art [31 EC]': *Commission v The Netherlands* Case C–157/94 [1997] ECR I–5699. The conditions of application of art 86(2) are the following:

---

[54] *Sacchi* Case 155/73 [1974] ECR 409, unless such a monopoly has effect on the free movement of goods: *Société Coopérative d'Amélioration de l'Elevage et d'Insémination Artificielle du Béarn v Mialocq* Case 271/81 [1983] ECR 2057.

[55] In respect of art 31(1): *Costa v ENEL* Case 6/64 [1964] ECR 1143; in respect of art 31(2): *Rewe-Zentrale* Case 45/75 [1976] ECR 181.

1. the holder of the exclusive rights must be entrusted with the operation of services of general economic interest,
2. it would be impossible for the holder of such exclusive rights to perform the particular task assigned to him if the rules of the EC Treaty were applied to him; and
3. the derogation from the application of EC Treaty granted to the holder of the exclusive rights must not affect intra-Community trade to such an extent that the interests of the Community are damaged.

The ECJ in Joined Cases C–157/94 [1997] ECR I–5699, C–158/94 [1997] ECR I–5789, C–159/94 [1997] ECR I–5815 and C–160/94 [1997] ECR I–5851 (*Commission of the European Communities, supported by the United Kingdom of Great Britain and Northern Ireland v Kingdom of The Netherlands, Italian Republic, French Republic and Kingdom of Spain*) provided interesting clarification in relation to the conditions of applicability of art 86(2) EC.

In these cases the Commission brought proceedings under art 226 EC against The Netherlands, Italy, France and Spain for failure to fulfil their obligations under arts 28, 29 and 31 EC. The alleged failure consisted of establishing and maintaining, as part of a national monopoly of a commercial character, exclusive import and export rights in the electricity and gas industry. The Commission argued that those rights constituted measures equivalent to quantitative restrictions as they prevented producers in other Member States from selling their products in the Member States in question and deprived potential customers from freely choosing their sources of supply.

The main reason for the Commission bringing proceedings was that the completion of the internal market in gas and electricity was extremely difficult to accomplish by way of Community legislation. The Commission expected that the ECJ would contribute to the creation of common rules permitting deregulation of national markets in electricity and gas and thus fill the gap created by the absence of Community legislation in those sectors. The strategy employed by the Commission brought the desired result by an indirect route. The situation was that the Member States were reluctant to allow the Commission and the ECJ to create the internal market in electricity based on the case law of the ECJ especially in the light of its previous decisions in this area.[56] This and the Opinion of Advocate-General Cosmas delivered on 26 November 1996 in which he condemned Italy for maintaining exclusive rights to export electricity and France for maintaining exclusive rights to export electricity and natural gas as contrary to the free movement of goods and to art 31 EC prompted the Member States to act. The Council decided to adopt Directive 96/92 on common rules for the internal market in electricity on 19 December 1996. This was the main reason for the dismissal of the Commission's application. In this context the ECJ acted diplomatically and dismissed the Commission's application whilst providing important indications as to the scope of application of art 86(2) EC, in particular in respect of three matters.

First, on the link between the obligations imposed on an undertaking entrusted with the operation of services of general economic interest and the subject-matter of such services.

---

[56] For example, *Amelo* Case C–393/92 [1994] ECR I–1477 in which the ECJ interpreted extensively the competences of the Commission in relation to art 86(3) EC.

Only those obligations which are designed to make direct contribution to satisfying that interest can be considered as falling within the particular tasks entrusted to an undertaking.

On this basis the ECJ rejected the argument of the French government that the French EFD (electricity company) had a specific task within the meaning of art 86(2) EC in relation to the protection of the environment and town and country planning since those tasks are not specific to this undertaking and to its business but apply more or less generally to all economic operators. However, the ECJ emphasised that 'such obligations or constraints may be taken into consideration for the purpose of considering to what extent derogations from the Treaty rules which it is sought to justify are necessary in order to enable the undertaking in question to perform the task of general interest entrusted to it.'

Second, the ECJ applied a liberal approach in assessing the necessity for an undertaking entrusted with the operation of services of general interest to exercise exclusive import and export rights. In this respect, until the decision of the ECJ in *Corbeau* Case C–320/91 [1993] ECR I–2562 it was necessary to demonstrate incompatibility between the requirements imposed by the EC Treaty and the performance of the tasks of general economic interest entrusted to an undertaking in order to fulfil the conditions for the application of art 86(2) EC. In *Corbeau* the ECJ ruled that the conditions for the application of art 86(2) EC are fulfilled if the maintenance of exclusive rights is necessary to enable the undertaking concerned to perform tasks of general economic interest under economically acceptable conditions. In the joined cases under consideration the Commission argued that the requirements of art 86(2) EC are satisfied only if the economic viability of the undertaking entrusted with the operation of a service of general economic interest is threatened. The ECJ rejected this strict approach and stated that in order for the conditions for the application of art 86(2) EC to be fulfilled 'it is sufficient that, in the absence of the rights at issue, it would not be possible for the undertaking to perform the particular tasks entrusted to it, defined by reference to its public-service obligations'. The ECJ emphasised that the intrinsic characteristics of electricity and gas in terms of their production, transmission, transportation and distribution imply that the opening up of the national market would involve considerable changes in the way those industries run, especially with respect to performance of the obligations of supply, continuity of supply and equal treatment as between customers or consumers. Although the Commission suggested alternative means which would replace the existing exclusive import and export rights conferred on the undertakings concerned such as grants or equalisation of the costs linked with public-service obligations, it did not demonstrate their relevance in respect of the particular features of the French system for the supply of electricity and gas. For that reason the ECJ held that 'it is not in a position, in these proceedings, to consider whether, by maintaining exclusive import and export rights for EDF and DF (French electricity companies), the French Republic has in fact gone further than was necessary to enable those establishments to perform, under economically acceptable conditions, the tasks of general economic interests assigned to them'.

Third, the ECJ stated that the Commission had failed to demonstrate that the maintenance of exclusive rights affected the development of trade to such an extent as would be contrary to the interests of the Community, mainly because the Commission did not define the Community interest in relation to which the development of trade must be assessed. In this respect the Advocate-General stated that

'... the actual wording of that sentence (particularly the use of the phase "development of trade" and the verb "be affected") is ... conducive to the conclusion that the draftsmen of the Treaty intended using that provision to exclude the application of the derogation provided for in art 86(2) in relation to measures which, in addition to *potentially* restricting trade in the Community, have *in practice* done so, the restrictive effects being so great that intra-Community trade in the sector in question is practically non-existent.'

He concluded that taking into account the data provided by the Member States the intra-Community trade in electricity and gas had significantly increased in the then recent years and that there was no evidence that the maintenance of exclusive rights affects the development of trade to such an extent as would be contrary to the interests of the Community.

Under art 86(3) EC the Commission must ensure that art 86 is complied with. For that purpose the Commission is empowered to issue directives and decisions. Directive 80/723 on the transparency of financial relations between Member States and public undertakings was the first directive adopted by the Commission on the basis of art 86(3) EC. The Directive requires Member States to keep accounts of such relations for five years and make information available to the Commission on request.[57] The Commission has been particularly active in the telecommunications sector.[58] The first decision adopted by the Commission under art 86(3) concerned Greek legislation, requiring all public property in Greece to be insured by Greek insurance companies in the public sector.[59]

---

[57] The Directive was unsuccessfully challenged in *France, Italy and the United Kingdom v Commission* Joined Cases 188–190/80 [1982] ECR 2545. Almost all directives adopted by the Commission on the basis of art 86(3) have been challenged.

[58] Directive 88/301 on competition in the markets in telecommunications terminal equipment (OJ L131(1988)); Directive 90/388 on competition in the markets for telecommunications services (OJ L192 (1990)); Directive 95/51 amending Directive 90/388 by extending its application to cable television networks (OJ L256 (1995)).

[59] Greece refused to comply with the decision. As a result, the Commission brought proceedings under art 226 EC. The ECJ in *Commission v Greece* Case 226/87 [1988] ECR 3611 upheld the Commission's decision.

Index

Please note that references to footnotes have an 'n' following the page number.

Abuse concept, competition law, 518–525
  anti-competitive abuses, 520–525
    discounts, 521–522
    predatory prices, 522–523
    product swaps, 522
    rebates, 521–522
    refusal to supply, 523–525
    tying-in, 520–521
  exploitative abuses
    discriminatory prices, 519–520
    excessively high prices, 519
  reprisal abuses, 525
Access to legal process principle, 185
Accession, Acts of *see* Acts of Accession
ACE (economics programme), 44
ACPC (Advisory Committee on Procurements
  and Contracts), 291
Acquired rights principle, 184
Acquis communautare, 34–35, 207
Acte clair, 311, 316, 317, 318
Actio popularis, 271
Actions against Community institutions,
  annulment
    art 230 EC, applicants under, 264–273
    conditions for challenging acts,
      258–264
    effect of, 275–277
    grounds for, 273–275
  art 288(2) EC,
    autonomous nature of actions,
      285–286
    conditions for Community liability,
      289–291
    parties to proceedings under, 286
  damages, non-contractual liability,
    285–299
    art 288(2) EC, 285–286, 289–291
    causation, 298–299
    Community and Member States, liability
      distinguished, 287–289
    Community and servants, liability
      distinguished, 287
    damage suffered, 295–298
    joint liability, Community and Member
      State, 288–289
    legislative acts, 292–295
    national authorities, liability of, 288
    'Schöppenstedt formula', 292–293,
      295

Actions against Community institutions,
  damages, non-contractual liability *(contd.)*
    time limit, 287
    unlawful acts, application or
      implementation, 288
    unlawful conduct, 289–291
    wrongful or negligent implementation or
      application of lawful Acts, 288
  direct action,
    annulment, 257–277
    failure to act, 281–285
  failure to act, direct action, 281–285
    administrative procedure, 283–284
    applicants, 282–283
    defaulting institution, 282
    judicial procedure, 284–285
    procedure, 283–285
  illegality plea, art 241 EC, 278–281
    applicants, 279–280
    exclusive jurisdiction of courts, 280
    requirements, 279
    successful action, effect of, 280–281
  legislative acts, liability for, 292–295
    breach of superior rule of law, 293
    protection of individual, superior rule for,
      293–294
    sufficiently serious breach, 294–295
Acts of Accession,
  'acquis communautare', 34
  admission procedure, 35, 36
  European Commission, competences of,
    124
  Greece, 39
  primary sources of Community law, 165
  United Kingdom, 37, 45–46
Addonnino Committee (1984), 58
Adenauer, Konrad, 21
Advisory Committee on Procurements and
  Contracts (ACPC), 291
Agency for Health and Safety, 109
Agenda 2000, 41
Airbus Industries programme, 53
Amsterdam Summit (1997), 65, 66, 82, 85,
  89–90
Amsterdam Treaty *see* Treaty of Amsterdam
Ancillary restraint theory, 490, 535
Angelli, Giovanni, 9
Annulment, direct actions for,
  art 230 EC, applicants under, 264–273

Annulment, direct actions for, art 230 EC,
  applicants under (*contd.*)
    non-privileged, *266–273*
    privileged, *264–265*
    semi-privileged, *265–266*
  Community acts, conditions for challenging,
    258–264
  effect of, *275–277*
  grounds for, *273–275*
    competence, lack of, *274*
    infringement, *274–275*
    misuse of powers, *275*
  infringement
    essential procedural requirement, *274*
    Treaty or rule of law relating to
      application, *274–275*
Anti-dumping cases, *270*
Arbeloa, Victor, *73*
Ariane programme, *593*
Article 18 (free movement, right of), *395–399*
Article 30 EC, *386–392*
  health and life, protection of, *390–391*
  national treasures, protection of, *392*
  public morality, *388–389*
  public policy, *389–390*
  public security, *389–390*
Article 81 EC (anti-competitive practices,
  prohibition of), *469–503*
  agreements,
    acceptance of obligations not relating to
      substance of, *486–487*
    equivalent transactions, dissimilar
      conditions, *486*
    exclusive, *484, 485*
    franchise, *492–493*
    generally, *471–473*
    horizontal, *468, 470–471*
    investments, controlling, *483*
    market sharing, *484–485*
    object or effect, having as, *478–479*
    production, controlling, *483*
    supply sources, sharing, *484–485*
    technical developments, controlling,
      483
    trade conditions, fixing, *480–483*
    undertakings, between, *472–473,
      478–479*
    vertical, *468, 470–471, 484, 491*
  attenuation of effect of prohibition,
    487–488
  breaches, civil consequences, *502–503*
  co-operation, permissible forms, *488–489*
  competition – prevention, restriction or
    distortion of, *479–487*

Article 81 EC (anti-competitive practices,
  prohibition of), competition – prevention,
  restriction or distortion of (*contd.*)
    acceptance of obligations not relating to
      substance of agreement, *486–487*
    equivalent transactions, dissimilar
      conditions, *486*
    investments, agreements controlling,
      483
    markets, sharing, *484–485*
    production, agreements controlling,
      483
    supply sources, sharing, *484–485*
    technical developments, agreements
      controlling, *483*
    trading conditions, agreements fixing,
      480–483
  concerted practices, *471–472, 474–478*
  decisions, *471–472*
    undertakings, associations of, *473–474*
  exemptions, *494–502*
    benefit to consumers, *501*
    block, *495–496*
    distribution improvements, *499–500*
    economic benefit, *498*
    formal requirements, *497*
    individual, *497–502*
    no possibility of eliminating competition,
      502
    no restrictions not indispensable,
      501–502
    production improvements, *498–499*
    progress, technical or economic,
      promotion of, *500–501*
    substantive requirements, *498*
  general provisions, *469–470*
  horizontal agreements, *470–471*
  intellectual property rights, and, *572–573*
  rule of reason, *489–494*
  Sherman Act, *489*
  trading conditions, agreements fixing,
    480–483
    crystallisation of prices, *481*
    discrimination by price, *482*
    uniformity of prices, *480–481*
  undertakings,
    agreements between, *472–473,
      478–479*
    decisions by associations of, *473–474*
  vertical agreements, *468, 470–471, 484,
    491*
Article 82 EC (dominant position), *504–525*
  abuse concept, *518–525*

Article 82 EC (dominant position), abuse concept
(*contd.*)
    anti-competitive abuses,   *520–525*
    border rebates,   *521–522*
    discounts,   *521–522*
    discriminatory prices,   *519–520*
    excessively high prices,   *519*
    exploitative abuses,   *519–520*
    export rebates,   *521*
    fidelity rebates,   *522*
    predatory prices,   *522*
    product swaps,   *522*
    refusal to supply,   *523–525*
    related markets,   *525*
    reprisal abuses,   *525*
    selective rebates,   *521*
    tying-in,   *520–521*
    dominance,   *507–509*
    intellectual property rights, and,   *573–575*
    joint dominant position concept,   *505–507*
    relevant geographic market,   *516–517*
    relevant market,   *509–511*
    relevant product market,   *511–516*
    relevant temporal market,   *517–518*
    share of market,   *508–509*
    substitutability of products,   *509–514*
Article 87 EC (State aid),
    application of, implementing legislation for,
        600
    compatible with common market,   *594*
    culture, promotion of,   *593–594*
    disturbance in Member State economy,
        remedying,   *591–592*
    economic activities or areas, facilitating,
        592–593
    heritage conservation,   *593–594*
    horizontal aid application, exemption under
        Regulation 994/98,   *589–590*
    projects of common European interest,
        591–592
    severely depressed areas, promotion of
        economic development,   *590–591*
Article 88 EC (State aid),
    Commission decisions,   *597–598*
    existing,   *594–595*
    failure to notify,   *596*
    horizontal aid application, exemption under
        Regulation 994/98,   *589–590*
    institutional supervision under,   *594–600*
    investigation procedure under,   *596–597*
    legislation for application of, implementing,
        600
    national courts, role in enforcement of EC
        Treaty provisions,   *599–600*

Article 88 EC (State aid) (*contd.*)
    new,   *595*
    'standstill clause',   *595*
    unlawful, recovery of,   *598–599*
    unnotified, recovery of,   *598–599*
Article 226 EC, action under,
    defences,   *241–249*
        force majeure,   *243–244*
        successful,   *241–244*
        uncertainties as to exact meaning of
            obligation,   *243–244*
        unlawful obligation,   *242–243*
        unsuccessful,   *244–249*
    determination of obligation likely to give rise
        to action,   *233–235*
    failure to comply with ruling under,   *253*
    failure to fulfil obligations,   *232–233*
    procedure,   *235–241*
        administrative stage,   *237–238*
        informal phase,   *235–237*
        judicial proceedings,   *238–241*
        letter of formal notice,   *237*
        reasoned opinion,   *237–238*
Article 227 EC, action under,   *249–251*
Article 228 EC, pecuniary sanctions under,
    253–255
Article 230 EC, applicants under,   *264–273*
    non-privileged,   *266–273*
        direct concern,   *272–273*
        individual concern,   *267–272*
        reviewable acts,   *266–267*
    privileged,   *264–265*
    semi-privileged,   *265–266*
Article 232 EC, failure to act, direct action for,
    281–285
    applicants,   *282–283*
    defaulting institution,   *282*
    procedure,   *283–285*
Article 234 EC, preliminary rulings,   *300–328*
    ECJ, referral to
        arbitration, private,   *305–306*
        CILFIT case,   *316–318*
        Community law capable of being referred,
            302–303
        courts referring,   *303–305*
        Da Costa principle,   *316, 321*
        discretion to refer,   *310–314*
        discretionary and compulsory reference,
            distinguished,   *309*
        effect,   *321–322*
        general jurisdiction,   *301–307*
        interlocutory proceedings, references in,
            307

Article 234 EC, preliminary rulings, ECJ, referral
to (*contd.*)
  interpretation of Community law,
    307–322
    mandatory,   *314–319*
    procedure,   *319–321*
    territorial jurisdiction,   *306–307*
    tribunals referring,   *303–305*
  purpose of rulings,   *301*
  validity of Community law,   *322–328*
    effect of ruling on validity,   *324–325*
    interim relief,   *325–328*
    requirements in referrals,   *322–323*
Article 241 EC, illegality plea,   *278–281*
  applicants,   *279–280*
  effect of a successful action under,
    280–281
  exclusive jurisdiction of Community courts,
    280
  requirements imposed,   *279*
Article 288 EC,
  action against Community institutions
    autonomous nature,   *285–286*
    conditions for Community liability,
      289–291
    parties to proceedings under,   *286*
Assembly of the European Communities,   *129.*
    See also European Parliament (EP)
Assent procedure,   *36, 155*
Association, right to,   *188*
Asylum seekers,   *83–85*
Atlantic Charter,   *14, 23*
Attlee, Clement,   *24*
Auditors, Court of,   *148*
Austria,   *39–40, 60*

Badinter Report (1991),   *94*
Bangemann, Martin,   *121*
Bankruptcy convention,   *179*
Bans,   *360–361, 482*
Basle/Nyborg Agreement (1987),   *53*
Belgium,   *92*
Benelux Court,   *306n*
Benelux Union,   *19–20*
'Beschlusse' (decisions),   *176*
Beveridge, William,   *8*
Bevin, Ernest,   *16, 24*
Blair, Tony,   *65n*
'Blue Streak' missile,   *26, 27*
Border rebates,   *521–522*
Bosnia,   *94*
Bremen Summit (1978),   *52*
Bretherton, Russell,   *24*

Bretton Woods Conference (1944),   *13, 51n*
Briand, Aristide,   *9*
BRITE (Basic Research in Industrial
    Technologies for Europe),   *53*
Brussels Convention on Jurisdiction and the
    Enforcement of Judgments in Civil and
    Commercial Matters (1968),   *34, 179,*
    303
Brussels Summit (1978),   *52*
Brussels Summit (1985),   *58*
Brussels Summit (1988),   *56*
Brussels Treaty (1948),   *18*
Budgetary Treaties,   *55, 134*
Butler, Rab,   *25*

Cabiati, Attillo,   *9*
CAP *see* Common Agricultural Policy
Capabilities Commitment Conference (2000),
    101
Causation, Community liability, action for
    damages,   *298–299*
CCT (Common Customs Tariff),   *333, 334*
CE (Compulsory Expenditure),   *134*
CELAD (Comité Europénne de Lutte Anti-
    Drogues),   *102*
Central and Eastern Europe,   *44–45*
Certain Institutions Common to the European
    Communities, (1957 Convention),   *50,*
    137
CFI (Court of First Instance),   *141, 142,*
    146–148, 182
CFSP (Common, Foreign and Security Policy),
    93–101
  assessment,   *101*
  common defence policy,   *99–101*
  Community institutions, role under,   *98*
  High Representative, post of,   *97*
  institutions,   *96–97*
  management,   *98–99*
  Member States, commitments under,   *98*
  objectives,   *95–96*
Children, rights of,   *411–412*
Churchill, Sir Winston,   *8, 14, 17, 23, 24, 27*
CIREA (Centre for Information, Discussion and
    Exchange on Asylum),   *84*
CIREFI (Centre for Information, Discussion and
    Exchange on the Crossing of Borders and
    Immigration),   *84*
Clinton, Bill,   *91*
CN (Combined Nomenclature),   *333*
Co-decision procedure,   *135, 153–155*
Cockfield, Lord,   *58*
Cold War,   *15, 18, 22*

Collective dominance concept,   *531–532*
Collegiality principle,   *122, 123*
Colonna Report (1970),   *53*
COMECON (Council for Mutual Economic
    Assistance),   *40*
Comfort letters,   *538*
Comitology system,   *126, 159*
Commission, the *see* European Commission
Committee of European Economic Co-operation,
    16
Committee of Permanent Representatives
    (COREPER),   *97, 112, 115, 151*
Committee of the Regions,   *149–150*
Committee of Transport,   *150*
Common Agricultural Policy,
    Agenda 2000,   *41–42*
    European unity, history,   *27–28*
    financing,   *56*
    Luxembourg Accord,   *49*
    reform,   *59–60*
    UK, not benefiting from,   *38*
Common Commercial Policy,   *207, 333*
Common Customs Tariff (CCT),   *333, 334*
Common, Foreign and Security Policy *see* CFSP
    (Common, Foreign and Security Policy)
Common market,
    internal market, and,   *329*
    State aid
        affecting,   *587–588*
        compatible with,   *588–594*
    taxation, harmonisation of,   *354*
Common origin doctrine,   *567*
Communism, European unity, history of,
    9–10
Communist Manifesto,   *9*
Community acts, conditions for challenging,
    258–264
    reviewable,   *260–264*
        author of act,   *260–262*
        nature of act,   *262–264*
    time limits,   *258–259*
Community Customs Code,   *333–334*
Community law,
    direct applicability,   *191, 192–198*
        decisions,   *195–198*
        directives,   *195–198*
        dualist theory,   *192*
        'effet utile',   *197*
        founding treaties, of,   *193–194*
        monist theory,   *192–193*
        regulations,   *194–195*
    direct effect,   *191, 198–217*
        'as far as possible' caveat,   *212*

Community law, direct effect (*contd.*)
        criteria,   *200*
        decisions,   *215–216*
        directives,   *204–207*
        horizontal,   *201–217*
        international agreements,   *216–217*
        Marleasing case,   *210, 211, 214–214*
        national law, interpretation,   *208–214*
        regulations,   *203–204*
        State, concept of,   *207–208*
        Van Gend en Loos case,   *198–199*
        vertical,   *201–217*
        Von Colson case,   *209*
    enforcement,   *230–256*
        art 95(9) EC,   *255*
        art 226 EC,   *231–249, 253*
        art 227 EC,   *249–251*
        art 228(2) EC, pecuniary sanctions under,
            253–255
        art 298 EC,   *256*
        direct actions, annulment,   *257–277*
        failure to act, direct action for,
            281–285
        indirect actions, illegality plea (art 241
            EC),   *278–281*
        ruling confirming failure to fulfil
            obligations under EC Treaty,
            251–255
        simplified procedures,   *255–256*
    fundamental principles,   *191–229*
        direct applicability,   *192–198*
        direct effect,   *198–217*
        State liability,   *222–229*
        supremacy,   *217–222*
        tort, Member States' liability,   *222–229*
    interpretation by ECJ (art 234 EC),
        307–322
        determination of factual and legal context
            of dispute,   *313–314*
        discretion of national courts and
            tribunals to refer,   *310–314*
        discretionary and compulsory reference
            by national courts, distinguished,
            309
        genuine disputes, existence of,
            311–313
        mandatory referral of national courts of
            last resort,   *314–319*
        preliminary rulings, effect of,   *321–322*
        procedure before ECJ,   *319–321*
        relevance of referred questions to main
            dispute,   *313*
        see also Article 234 EC, preliminary
            rulings

Community law (*contd.*)
  preliminary rulings (art 234 EC),
    ECJ,
      general jurisdiction,   *301–307*
      interpretation of law,   *307–322*
    validity of law,   *322–328*
  sources,   *161–190*
    complementary,   *178–181*
    ECJ, case law,   *182–183*
    external, derived from international
      commitments of Communities,
      177–178
    general principles,   *183–190*
    primary,   *162–167*
    secondary,   *167–176*
  supremacy of,   *217–222*
    UK, in,   *222*
Community Patent Agreement (1989),   *179*
Community Patent Convention (1975),   *179,*
  576
Company taxation,   *355–356*
Competences,
  Council of Ministers,   *118–119*
  European Commission (EC),   *123–129*
  European Parliament (EP),   *132–137*
  subsidiarity principle,   *68–69*
Competition law,   *459–468*
  abuse concept,
    anti-competitive abuses,   *520–525*
    exploitative abuses,   *519–520*
    reprisal abuses,   *525*
  activities affecting trade between States,
    466–468
  Annual Reports,   *459, 483*
  art 81 EC (anti-competitive practices),
    469–503
    agreements,   *470–473, 478–479,*
      480–487
    attenuation of effect of prohibition,
      487–494
    civil consequences,   *502–503*
    concerted practices,   *471–472, 474–478*
    decisions,   *471–472, 473–474*
    distortion of competition,   *479–487*
    exemptions,   *494–502*
    horizontal agreements,   *470–471*
    prevention of competition,   *479–487*
    restriction of competition,   *479–487*
    vertical agreements,   *468, 470–471,*
      484, 491
  art 82 EC (dominant position),   *504–525*
    abuse concept,   *518–525*
    dominance,   *507–509*

Competition law, art 82 EC (dominant position)
  (*contd.*)
    joint dominant position,   *505–507*
    relevant geographic market,   *516–517*
    relevant market,   *509–511*
    relevant product market,   *511–516*
    relevant temporal market,   *517–518*
    share of market,   *508–509*
    substitutability of products,   *509–514*
  concerted practices,   *471–472, 474–478*
  economic efficiency,   *459–460*
  enforcement by Commission,   *536–554*
    documents, access to,   *545–546*
    fines,   *547–549*
    hearings,   *544–545*
    infringements, complaints in respect of,
      538–540
    judicial review of decisions,   *549–552*
    national courts, before,   *552–554*
    periodic penalty payments,   *547*
    powers of investigation,   *540–544*
    Regulation 17/62, measures which may
      be adopted under,   *536–538*
  European Commission, powers of
    investigation,
    inspections,   *542–544*
    obtaining information,   *540–542*
    sectoral enquiries,   *542*
  extra-territorial application,   *461–464*
  federal nature of,   *460–461*
  merger control,   *526–535*
    collective dominance concept,
      531–532
    future reform,   *534–535*
    Regulation 4064/89 (MR),   *527–531,*
      532–534
  monopolies, and,   *601–605*
  objective, principal,   *459*
  prices,
    crystallisation,   *481*
    discrimination,   *482, 519–520*
    excessively high,   *519*
    predatory,   *522–523*
    uniformity,   *480–481*
  Regulation 17/62, enforcement under,
    comfort letters,   *538*
    decisions,   *538*
    exemptions,   *537–538*
    interim measures,   *538*
    negative clearance,   *536–537*
    pecuniary sanctions,   *538*
  State aid, distorting or threatening to distort
    competition,   *586–587*

Competition law (*contd.*)
  substitutability of products,   *509–514*
  undertakings, and,   *602–605*
Concentration camps,   *10, 12*
Concentration concept, merger control,
  528–531
  Community dimension,   *528–530*
  joint-ventures,   *531*
  prohibited concentrations,   *530–531*
Concerted practices,   *471–472, 474–478*
  'cartonboard' cases,   *476–477*
Concordat of Worms,   *5*
Confidentiality principle,   *185*
Confusion concept,   *563–567*
Congress of Europe,   *17*
Consultation procedure,   *151–153*
Contra legem,   *211, 212, 214*
Convention, European *see* ECHR (European
    Convention for the Protection of Human
    Rights and Fundamental Freedoms)
Convention on Mutual Recognition of Companies
    and Legal Persons (1968),   *179, 303*
Copenhagen Summit (1973),   *51*
Copenhagen Summit (1993),   *41*
Copyright,   *562, 569, 579*
COREPER (Committee of Permanent
    Representatives),   *97, 112, 115, 151*
COREU European correspondence system,
    157
Corfu Summit (1994),   *41*
Corpus Juris Canonici (Corpus of Canon Law),
    6
Corpus Juris Civilis,   *3*
COSINE (infrastructure programme),   *44*
Coudenhove-Kalergi, Count Richard,   *8–9*
Council of Europe,
    Convention on Participation of Foreigners in
        Public Life (1992),   *399*
    European Defence Community,   *22*
    integration, Western European,   *17–18*
Council of the European Union,   *113–119*
    competences,   *118–119*
    composition,   *113–114*
    COREPER,   *115, 151*
    Presidency,   *114*
    sessions,   *115–116*
    subsidiarity principle,   *71*
    voting,   *116–118*
Council of Ministers *see* Council of the European
    Union
Court of Auditors,   *148*
Court of First Instance (CFI),   *141, 142,
    146–148, 182*

Croatia,   *94*
Crockett, Andrew,   *79*
Crocodile Club,   *58*
CS (European Coal and Steel Community),
    admission to,   *30*
    consolidation of European Communities,
        46–47
    establishment,   *21*
    founding treaty,   *46–47, 137, 162, 164,
        173, 258. See also* Founding treaties
    Messina Conference,   *22–23*
Customs Code Committee,   *159, 334*
Customs Convention (1944),   *19–20*
Customs duties, prohibition,   *336–343*
    art 23,   *336-338*
    art 25,   *336-338*
    exceptions,   *339–343*
        charge must be proportionate to cost of
            service,   *342*
        mandatory service,   *342–343*
        service must be of genuine benefit to
            trader,   *340–341*
        service must provide specific benefit to
            trader,   *341*
    see also Equivalent effect
Customs union,   *332–335*
    external aspects,   *333–334*
    internal aspect,   *335*
Cyber Crime, Draft Convention on,   *105*
Cyprus,   *32, 35, 43*

Damnum emergens (actual loss),   *295*
Dassonville formula,   *361–367, 378, 379–380,
    384, 466*
    domestic products, and,   *363, 367–377*
    imported products, and,   *364, 365*
    licences, imported goods,   *365*
    national measures encouraging
        discrimination,   *362–363*
    phyto-sanitary inspections,   *365–367*
    price of goods, restrictions relating to,
        363–364
    technical standards,   *364–365*
Davignon Report (1970),   *51*
De Gaulle, General Charles André Joseph Marie,
    26, 27, 28, 49
De minimis rule,   *248, 467–468, 480, 588, 600*
Death Penalty, Declaration on Abolition of,   *89*
Declaration of Anglo-French Union (1940),   *8*
Declaration on European Identity (1973),   *32*
Decretals (papal laws and decisions),   *6*
Definitions,
    abuse concept,   *518*

Definitions (*contd.*)
    collective dominance concept,   *531–532*
    concentration concept,   *528*
    dominance,   *507–509*
    employment in public service,   *450–451*
    horizontal direct effect,   *201*
    intellectual property rights,   *555*
    joint dominant position,   *505–507*
    joint-ventures,   *531*
    Locus standi,   *265n*
    mergers,   *528*
    official authority, exercise of,   *450–451*
    quantitative restrictions,   *360–361*
    State,   *207–208*
    trade,   *466–468*
    undertakings,   *464–466, 602*
    vertical direct effect,   *201*
    workers,   *407–409*
Delors I package,   *56–57, 59–60*
Delors, Jacques,   *58, 60, 61*
Denmark,   *36, 37, 58–59*
Design right,   *579–580*
Direct applicability principle,   *191, 192–198*
    decisions,   *195–198*
    directives,   *195–198*
    dualist theory,   *192*
    founding treaties,   *193–194*
    monist theory,   *192–193*
    regulations,   *194–195*
Direct effect principle,   *191, 198–217*
    'as far as possible' caveat,   *212*
    criteria,   *200*
    decisions,   *215–216*
    directives,   *204–207*
    horizontal effect,   *201–207*
    international agreements,   *216–217*
    Marleasing case,   *210, 211, 214–215*
    national law, interpretation,   *208–214*
    regulations,   *203–204*
    State, concept of,   *207–208*
    Van Gend en Loos case,   *198–199*
    vertical effect,   *201–207*
    Von Colson case,   *209*
Discounts,   *521–522*
Discrimination,
    Dassonville formula, national measures,   *362–363*
    direct,   *345–346*
    and establishment, right of,   *432–435*
    indirect,   *347–348, 415*
    and prices,   *482, 519–520*
    reverse,   *346–347, 429–430*
    services,   *freedom to supply, 442–443*

Discrimination (*contd.*)
    taxation, internal,   *345–348*
    Treaty of Amsterdam,   *89*
    workers, free movement of,   *414–422*
      derogations from national rules,   *421–422*
      education,   *419–420*
      eligibility for employment,   *417–418*
      equality in employment,   *418–419*
      housing issues, equal treatment,   *421*
      Trade Union rights,   *421*
    see also Non-discrimination principle
Domestic goods, equivalent effect,
    customs' duties, prohibition of
      imported goods, and,   *338–339*
      solely applicable charges,   *339*
    Dassonville formula
      national measures applicable,   *367–377*
      preferences,   *363*
    national measures
      domestic market,   *377–379*
      export, for,   *377–379*
      selling arrangements,   *379–385*
Dominant position *see* Article 82 EC (dominant position)
Dooge, James,   *58*
Drug addiction legislation,   *103*
Dublin Convention (1990),   *85–86*
Dublin Summit (1975),   *45*
Dublin Summit (1990),   *40, 61*
Dublin Summit (1996),   *76–77*
Dumbarton Oaks Conference (1944),   *14*
Dura lex, sed lex,   *3*

EA (European Atomic Energy Community),
    admission to,   *30*
    consolidation of Communities,   *48–49*
    establishment,   *23*
    founding treaty,   *137, 162, 164, 168, 258, 302. See also* Founding treaties
EBRD (European Bank for Reconstruction and Development),   *44*
EC (European Economic Community),
    company law, harmonisation of,   *431–432*
    competition law, federal nature of,   *460–461*
    consolidation of European Communities,   *48–49*
    establishment, exercise of right by legal persons,   *431–432*
    founding treaty,   *137, 162, 164–165, 168, 258, 302, 394. See also specific articles;* Founding treaties

EC (European Economic Community) (*contd.*)
  parallel imports from outside the,
    569–571
ECB (European Central Bank) *see* European
  Central Bank (ECB)
ECHR (European Convention for the Protection
  of Human Rights and Fundamental
  Freedoms),
    Council of Europe,   18
    EU, legal requirements for admission,   33
    workers, families of,   411
ECJ *see* European Court of Justice (ECJ)
Ecofin,   113
Economic integration,
  Middle Ages
    commercial communities, medieval,
      6–7
    Hanseatic League,   7–8
    lex mercatoria,   6–7
  relaunch,   57–58
  western Europe
    Benelux Union,   19–20
    Schuman Plan,   20–21
Economic and Monetary Union (EMU) *see* EMU
  (Economic and Monetary Union)
Economic and professional activities, right to
  exercise,   188
Economic and Social Committee,   148–149
ECU (European Currency Unit),   52
Eden, Anthony,   22, 24, 25, 26
Edinburgh Summit (1992),   70, 115
Education rights,   419–420
EEA *see* European Economic Area (EEA)
EEC (European Economic Community),
    22–23, 63
EEIG (European Economic Interest Grouping),
    431–432
Effet utile principle,   197, 204, 205, 207, 216
EFTA (European Free Trade Association),   25
EIS (European Information System),   86
Elections, participation in,   399–401
EMCDA (European Monitoring Centre for Drugs
  and Addiction),   103
Emergency Travel Documents,   402
EMI (European Monetary Institute),   76
Employment rights,
  non-discrimination principle
    eligibility,   417–418
    equality,   418–419
    Member State territory, right to remain
      following employment,   422–423
    public service,   450–451
    Treaty of Amsterdam,   91

'Empty chair' crisis,   49
EMS (European Monetary System),   52, 53, 76,
    112
EMU (Economic and Monetary Union),   74–79
  assessment,   79
  consolidation of European unity,   51–53
  'coronation' theory,   74–75
  economic union,   74–75
  monetary union,   75–78
  Stage I,   76
  Stage II,   76–77
  Stage III ,   77–78
  taxation, harmonisation of,   354
  UK, reluctance to participate,   38
Enforcement of Community law,   230–256
  art 226 EC, action under,   231–249
    defences,   241–249
    determination of obligation likely to give
      rise to,   233–235
    failure to fulfil obligation under Treaty,
      232–233
    procedure,   235–241
  art 227 EC, action under,   249–251
  ruling confirming failure to fulfil obligations,
    251–255
    art 226 EC,   253
    art 228(2) EC,   253–255
  simplified procedures,
    art 95(9) EC,   255
    art 298 EC,   256
  see also Competition law: enforcement by
    Commission
Entscheidunsen (decisions),   176
Environmental Agency, European,   109
EP *see* European Parliament (EP)
EPC (European Political Co-operation),   51,
    93–94
EPO (European Patent Office),   576
Equal treatment principle,   188, 368, 421
Equality in respect of economic regulation
  principle,   185
Equity principle,   3
Equivalent effect,
  Cassis de Dijon,   367–377, 379, 381, 384
    service provision,   428
  customs duties, prohibition,
    art 23,   336–338
    art 25,   336–338
    domestic goods only,   339
    domestic and imported goods,
      338–339
    imported goods only,   338
  Dassonville formula,   361–367, 378,
    379–380, 384, 466

Equivalent effect, *Dassonville* formula (*contd.*)
    domestic products, and,   *363, 367–377*
    imported products, and,   *364, 365*
    licences, imported goods,   *365*
    national measures encouraging
      discrimination,   *362–363*
    phyto-sanitary inspections,   *365–367*
    price of goods, restrictions relating to,
      363–364
    technical standards, restrictions relating
      to,   *364–365*
  defined,   *360–361*
  domestic goods,
    Cassis de Dijon,   *367–377*
    customs duties, prohibition of,
      338–339
    domestic market,   *377–379*
    export, for,   *377–379*
  exports, measures applicable to (art 29 EC),
    377–379
  imported goods,
    customs duties, prohibition of,
      338–339
    Dassonville formula,   *364, 365*
    licences,   *365*
    national measures applicable to,
      367–377
  Keck principle,
    legal consequences,   *381–385*
    scope of application,   *380–381*
    selling arrangements, national measures,
      379
    services provision, and,   *428*
  national measures,
    advertising,   *374–375*
    Cassis de Dijon,   *367–377, 379, 381*
    domestic products,   *377–379*
    environment, protection of,   *371*
    fraud prevention,   *372*
    generic names, use of,   *372*
    imported goods,   *367–377*
    language,   *373–374*
    presentation of products,   *372*
    press diversity, maintenance of,   *372*
    proportionality principle,   *372*
    selling arrangements, domestic and
      imported goods,   *379–385*
    socio-cultural identity of Member State,
      protection of,   *371*
    working conditions, improvement of,
      371
  see also Quantitative restrictions
ERDF (European Regional Development Fund),
  54, 126

Erga omnes,   *172, 551*
ERM (European Exchange Rate Mechanism),
  52
ESCB (European System of Central Banks),
  77, 78, 148
ESPRIT (European Strategic Programme for
  Research and Development),   *53*
Establishment, right of,   *431–441*
  abolition of restrictions, general programme
    for,   *426–429*
  diplomas, recognition of,   *436–440*
  lawyers,   *440–441*
  legal persons,   *425, 431–435*
    'Delaware' effect,   *435*
    EC, harmonisation of company law
      within,   *431–432*
    non-discrimination principle,
      428–429, 432–435
  limitations,   *431*
  natural persons,   *424–425*
  professional bodies, rules established by,
    441
  qualifications, recognition of,   *436–440*
  reverse discrimination,   *429–430*
  Reyners case,   *426–427, 428*
  self-employed persons,   *435–436*
  see also Services, right to supply and receive
EU (European Union),
  admission to,   *30–36*
    economic and political requirements,
      33–35
    legal requirements,   *31–33*
    procedure for,   *35–36*
  citizenship of,   *393–405*
    assessment of,   *405*
    consular protection,   *401–403*
    diplomatic protection,   *401–403*
    elections, municipal, participation in,
      399–401
    European Parliament, and,   *401,*
      403–404
    free movement, right of,   *395–399*
    Ombudsman, right to apply to,
      404–405
    residence, right of,   *395–399*
  expulsion from,   *45–46*
  internal market, as,   *330*
  tax, harmonisation within,   *354–356*
    company,   *355–356*
    excise duty,   *355*
    VAT,   *354–355*
Taxation, Communication on,   *354*
Treaty on *see* Maastricht Treaty (1992); TEU
  (Treaty on European Union)

EU (European Union) (*contd.*)
   withdrawal from,   *45–46*
   see also Council of the European Union
Eureka programme,   *592*
Euro, the,   *76, 78*
Euronet-DIANE programme,   *53*
European Agency for Evaluation of Medical
   Products,   *109*
European Agricultural Guidance and Guarantee
   Fund,   *126*
European Atomic Energy Community (EA),
   48–49
European Bank for Reconstruction and
   Development (EBRD),   *44*
European Central Bank (ECB),
   annulment, direct actions for,   *257*
   failure to act, direct action for,   *282*
   institutions of Communities,   *109, 148*
   monetary union,   *78*
   secondary sources of Community law,   *168*
European Coal and Steel Community (CS) *see* CS
   (European Coal and Steel Community)
European Commission,   *119–129*
   Code of Conduct,   *121*
   collegiality principle,   *122, 123*
   Communication on Immigration and Asylum
     Policy (1994),   *85–86*
   competences,   *123–129*
     comitology system,   *126, 159*
     executive powers,   *126–128*
     'guardian of the Treaty',   *123–125*
     international functions,   *129*
     legislative measures, initiator of,
       125–126
   competition law, enforcement of
     documents, access to,   *545–546*
     fines,   *547–549*
     hearings,   *544–545*
     infringements, complaints in respect of,
       538–540
     judicial review of decisions,   *549–552*
     national courts,   *552–554*
     Notice on Co-operation between the
       National Competition Authorities,
       552–554
     Notice on the Internal Rules of Procedure
       for Processing Requests for Access to
       File,   *545*
     periodic penalty payments,   *547*
     powers of investigation,   *540–544*
     Regulation 17/62, measures adopted
       under,   *536–538*
   composition,   *119–120*

European Commission (*contd.*)
   EU enlargement
     Agenda 2000,   *41–42*
     East Germany,   *40*
     Turkey,   *42–43*
     Europe and the Challenge of Enlargement
       report,   *32–33*
   executive powers,   *126–128*
   functioning,   *122–123*
   Guidelines for National Regional Aid,   *591,*
     592
   international functions,   *129*
   legislative measures, initiator of,   *125–126*
   Luxembourg Accord,   *49*
   merger control,   *526, 535*
   patents, Green Paper on,   *576*
   Reform Strategy Programme,   *121n*
   Relevant Market, Notice on Definition of,
     509–511
   Rules of Procedure,   *121n, 122*
   Social Action Programme (1998-2000),
     90–91
   State aid, art 88 EC
     decisions,   *597–598*
     existing aid,   *594–595*
     failure to notify,   *596*
     investigation procedure,   *596–597*
     new aid,   *595*
     unnotified and unlawful aid, recovery of,
       598–599
   subsidiarity principle,   *71*
   Taxation, Communication on,   *354*
   term of office,   *120–122*
European Communities,
   consolidation,   *46–64*
     budgetary matters,   *55–56*
     development aid,   *54*
     Economic and Military Union (EMU),
       51–53
     European Atomic Energy Community
       (EA),   *48–49*
     European Coal and Steel Community
       (CS),   *46–48*
     European Council, recognition of,   *56*
     European Economic Community (EC),
       48–49
     European integration, relaunch of,
       57–58
     European Parliament (EP),   *55*
     Hague Summit (1969),   *50–51*
     Luxembourg Accord,   *49–50*
     Merger Treaty (1965),   *50, 302n*
     political co-operation, establishment,
       51

European Communities, consolidation (*contd.*)
    Single European Act (SEA),   *58–59*
    social policy,   *54*
    stagnation years (1970-85),   *55–57*
    technical co-operation,   *53*
    Treaty on European Union (TEU),
        62–64
  evolution of,   *29–64*
    consolidation,   *46–64*
    EU membership,   *30–36*
    territorial expansion,   *36–46*
  institutions
    actions against,   *257–299*
    advisory committees,   *150*
    Committee of the Regions,   *149–150*
    Council of Ministers,   *113–119*
    Court of Auditors,   *148*
    Court of First Instance (CFI),   *146–148*
    Economic and Social Committee,
        148–149
    European Commission,   *71, 119–129*
    European Council,   *56, 111–112*
    European Court of Justice (ECJ),
        72–74, 137–146
    European Parliament (EP),   *55, 72,*
        91–92, 129–137
    funding programmes,   *150*
    legislative procedures,   *150–155*
    transparency principle,   *92, 155–160*
  legislative procedures
    assent,   *155*
    co-decision,   *153–155*
    consultation,   *151–153*
  territorial expansion,   *36–46*
    first enlargement,   *36–38*
    second enlargement,   *38–39*
    third enlargement,   *39*
    fourth enlargement,   *39–40*
    and Cyprus,   *43*
    de facto enlargement,   *40*
    and German Democratic Republic,   *40*
    and Malta,   *43*
    and Turkey,   *42–43*
    withdrawal and expulsion from EU,
        45–46
European Convention *see* ECHR (European
    Convention for the Protection of Human
    Rights and Fundamental Freedoms)
European Council,
  consolidation of European Communities,
      56
  functioning,   *112*
  tasks,   *111–112*

European Court of Justice (ECJ),   *137–146*
  acquis, judicial,   *34, 207*
  Advocates-General, function of,   *138, 139,*
      140
  art 234 EC
    arbitration, private,   *305–306*
    CILFIT case,   *316–318*
    Community law capable of being referred,
        302–303
    Courts referring,   *303–305, 309–319*
    Da Costa principle,   *316, 321*
    discretion to refer,   *310–314*
    discretionary and compulsory reference
        by national courts, distinction
        between,   *309*
    interpretation of Community law,
        307–322
    interlocutory proceedings, references in,
        307
    jurisdiction,   *301–307*
    mandatory referral,   *314–319*
    preliminary rulings, effect concerning
        interpretation of Community law,
        321–322
    procedure,   *319–321*
    territorial jurisdiction,   *306–307*
    tribunals referring,   *303–305, 309–319*
    validity of Community law,   *322–328*
  case law,   *182–183*
  composition,   *138*
  discretion to refer to (art 234 EC,
      preliminary rulings),   *310–314*
    determination of factual and legal context
        of dispute,   *313–314*
    existence of genuine dispute,   *311–313*
    relevance of referred question to main
        dispute,   *313*
  EU, legal requirements for admission,   *31,*
      32
  functioning,   *140*
  judges,   *139, 140*
  judgments, revision and interpretation,
      144
  jurisdiction,   *145–146*
    consultative,   *146*
    contentious proceedings,   *145*
    non-contentious proceedings,   *146*
  Official Journal,   *144*
  organisation,   *139–140*
  procedure
    amendments introduced July 2000
        141–142
    costs,   *143–144*

European Court of Justice (ECJ), procedure (*contd.*)
    language,   *143*
    parties to proceedings,   *143*
    reforms, long-term,   *142*
    third party intervention,   *144*
    traditional,   *140–141*
   Rules of Procedure,   *110, 137n, 141, 143, 310, 319, 320, 321*
   subsidiarity principle,   *72–74*
   term of office,   *139*
European Currency Unit (ECU),   *52*
European Defence Community,   *22*
European Development Fund,   *126*
European Economic Area (EEA),
   EU, territorial expansion,   *40*
   parallel imports from outside the,   *569–571*
European Economic Community (EC),
   consolidation of European Communities,   *48–49*
European Economic Community (EEC),   *22–23, 63*
European Economic Interest Grouping (EEIG),   *431–432*
European Environmental Agency,   *109, 150*
European Exchange Rate Mechanism (ERM),   *52*
European Free Trade Association (EFTA),   *25*
European Information System (EIS),   *86*
European Investment Bank,   *91, 107n*
European Monetary Institute (EMI),   *76, 148*
European Monetary System (EMS),   *52, 53, 76, 112*
European Monitoring Centre for Drugs and Drug Addiction,   *109*
European Parliament (EP),   *129–137*
   Amsterdam Treaty,   *72, 91–92*
   assent procedure, EU admission,   *36*
   challenging of Community Acts,   *257*
   competences,   *132–137*
     budgetary powers,   *134–135*
     external relations, role in,   *136–137*
     legislative powers,   *135*
     political control,   *132–134, 169*
   composition,   *129–131*
   consolidation of European Communities,   *55*
   elections to, participation in,   *401*
   Enlarged Bureau,   *131*
   functioning,   *131–132*
   Luxembourg Accord,   *49*
   MEPs,   *130, 131–132, 133*

European Parliament (EP) (*contd.*)
   Official Journal,   *132*
   petition, right to,   *403–404*
   powers, extension of,   *91–92*
   question-time,   *132–133*
   Rules of Procedure,   *131, 404*
   sessions,   *132*
   stagnation years (1970-85),   *55*
   subsidiarity principle,   *72*
European Patent Convention,   *576–578*
European Patent Office (EPO),   *576*
European Political Co-operation (EPC),   *51, 93–94*
European Recovery Programme 1948-51 (Marshall Plan),   *16–17*
European Regional Development Fund (ERDF),   *54, 126*
European Social Fund,   *54, 126, 150*
European Space Agency programme,   *53*
European System of Central Banks (ESCB),   *77, 78, 148*
European Training Foundation,   *150*
European Union *see* EU (European Union)
European unity, history of,   *1–28*
   Communism,   *9–10*
   Middle Ages
     commercial communities, medieval,   *6–7*
     fairs in,   *7*
     Hanseatic League,   *7–8*
     integration, economic,   *6–8*
     lex mercatoria,   *6–7*
     Roman Catholic Church,   *4–6*
   Nazism,   *11–12*
   Roman Empire,   *2–4*
   twentieth century,   *8–9*
   United Kingdom
     European integration, and,   *23–26*
     French refusal of British accession,   *26–28*
   United States
     Marshall Plan,   *16–17*
     reconstruction,   *15–16*
     vision of post-war world,   *12–15*
   western European integration,   *17–23*
     Council of Europe,   *17–18*
     Defence Community,   *22*
     economic,   *19–21*
     Messina Conference (1955),   *22–23*
     military,   *18–19*
     UK, and,   *23–26*
Europol,   *103*
'Eurosclerosis',   *55*

Evolution of European Communities *see*
    European Communities: evolution of
Exceptio inadempleti contractus, 244
Exception prejudicielle, 316
Excise duties, 355
Exhaustion of rights doctrine, 558–563
Export rebates, 521

Fairness principle, 3
Falcons Programme (1998-2002), 103
FAO (Food and Agriculture Organisation), 370
Faute de service, 289
Faute personnelle, 289
Federal Republic of Germany (FRG), 40, 60
Fidelity rebates, 522
Fifth Framework programme (1998-2002),
    592
Finland, 39, 40
First Instance, Court of, 146–148
First Social Action Programme (1974), 54
First World War, 12
Fontainebleu Summit (1984), 39, 56, 58, 111
Food and Agriculture Organisation (FAO), 370
Force majeure, 243–244, 259
Founding treaties, 162–165
    Commission, 119–120
    direct applicability, 193–194
    direct effect, 201–202
        not applicable, 203
    modifications and amendments
        common assent of Member States,
            166–167
        'decisions' of Council, 167
        implied powers doctrine, 167
        simplified procedures provided for,
            167
    protocols, declarations and conventions
        annexed to, 165
    supremacy of Community law, no mention
        in, 217
    see also CS (European Coal and Steel
        Community): founding treaty; EA
        (European Atomic Energy Community):
        founding treaty; EC (European
        Economic Community): founding treaty
Four Freedoms, 14
Fourteen Point Plan, 12
France,
    Amsterdam Treaty, 92
    British accession, refusal of, 26–28
    Conseil d'Etat, 138, 140
    free movement of goods, restrictions,
        358–359

France (*contd.*)
    Schuman Plan, 20–21, 24
    taxation, discriminatory, 347
    Vichy regime, 23
Francital, 20
Free movement of goods,
    intellectual property rights
        copyright, 569, 579
        patents, 557–560
        trade marks, 560–569
    internal market, creation, 329–331
    see also Competition law; Equivalent effect;
        Qualitative restrictions; Taxation,
        internal (discriminatory nature)
Free movement of persons,
    EU citizens, 395–399
    exceptions
        criminal convictions, previous,
            455–456
        economic considerations, 456
        personal conduct, 453–455
        procedural safeguards, 456–458
        public health, 453, 456
        public policy and security, 452–456
        public service, employment in,
            450–451
    'Playboy Directive', 395
    Treaty of Amsterdam, 81
    workers, 406–423
Free speech, right to, 188
FRG (Federal Republic of Germany), 40, 60
Fyfe, Maxwell, 22

GAFI (Groupe d'Action Finacière Internationale),
    102
GAM'92 (Groupe d'Assistance Mutuelle), 103
GATT (General Agreement on Tariffs and Trade),
    13, 14
GDR (German Democratic Republic), 40, 61
General Affairs Council, 113
General Agreement on Tariffs and Trade (GATT),
    13, 14
Germany,
    competition law, 460–461
    EU competences, opposition to expansion,
        65
    European Communities, expansion of, 40
    hegemony within Community, 60–61
    Legal Implications of the Return of the Sarre
        to the Federal Republic Convention,
        1957, 166
    Schuman Plan, 21
    state aid, 589

Germany (*contd.*)
  subsidiarity principle, *67–68*
  see also Nazism
Good faith, in (*Bone fides* principle), *3, 6, 184*
Gorbachev, Michail, *10*
Goring, Herman, *12*
Greece,
  EU admission, *32, 33, 35, 38–39*
  Integrated Mediterranean Programmes,
    39
  SEA, *58–59*
Greenland, *46*
Gulf Crisis (1990-91), *94, 99*

Hague meeting (1948), *17*
Hague Summit (1969), *50–51, 53, 56, 93*
Hallsten, Walter, *49, 230*
Hanover Summit (1988), *60*
Hanseatic League, *7–8*
HDG (Horizontal Drugs Group), *103*
Health and life, protection of,
  art 30 EC, *390–391*
  free movement of persons, exceptions,
    453, 456
Health and Safety at Work, Agency for, *109*
Heath, Sir Edward, *28*
Hellenic Republic, *38–39*
Helsinki European Council, *42, 100*
Helsinki European Summit (1999), *354*
Hierarchy of legal measures principle, *185*
Hiroshima bomb, *23*
History of European unity *see* European unity,
  history of
Hitler, Adolf, *9, 11–12*
Horizontal agreements, *468, 470–471*
Horizontal direct effect, *201–202*
Housing rights, *421*
Human rights, fundamental, *187–189*
Humanism principle, *3*
Hungary, *60*
Hybrid regulations, *266*

IEFTA (Industrial European Free Trade
  Association), *25*
IGCs (Inter-governmental Conferences), *42,*
  58, 61, 62
Illegality plea *see* Article 241 EC, illegality plea
Immigration rights, Treaty of Amsterdam,
  83–85
Implied powers doctrine, *167*
Imported goods, equivalent effect,
  customs' duties, prohibition of
    domestic goods, and, *338–339*

Imported goods, equivalent effect, customs'
  duties, prohibition of (*contd.*)
    soley applicable, *338*
  Dassonville formula
    licences, *365*
    marketing restrictions, *364*
  national measures
    Cassis de Dijon, *367–377, 379, 381*
    Keck, *379, 380–385*
    selling arrangements, *379–385*
  see also Intellectual property rights: parallel
    imports, outside EC and EEA
Industrial European Free Trade Association
  (IEFTA), *25*
Insolvency Convention (1995), *179*
Institutions, European Communities,
  106–160
  actions against
    damages, non-contractual liability of
      Community, *285–299*
    direct, *257–277, 281–285*
    indirect, *278–281*
  advisory committees, *150*
  co-decision procedure, *135, 153–155*
  Committee of the Regions, *149–150*
  consultation procedure, *151–153*
  Council of Ministers, *113–119*
  Court of Auditors, *148*
  Court of First Instance (CFI), *146–148*
  Economic and Social Committee,
    148–149
  Edinburgh Council Decision, Brussels
    meeting (1993), *108–109*
  European Commission, *71, 119–129*
  European Council, *56, 111–112*
  European Court of Justice (ECJ), *72–74,*
    137–146
  European Parliament (EP), *55, 72, 91–92,*
    129–137
  funding programmes, *150*
  languages, *110*
  legislative procedures, *150–155*
  privileges, *110*
  transparency principle, *92, 155–160*
Integration,
  Middle Ages
    commercial communities, medieval,
      6–7
    Hanseatic League, *7–8*
    lex mercatoria, *6–7*
    monist system, compatible with, *193*
  western Europe
    Council of Europe, *17–18*

Integration, western Europe (*contd.*)
    Defence Community,   *22*
    economic,   *19–21*
    Messina Conference (1955),   *22–23*
    military,   *18–19*
    UK, and,   *23–26*
Intellectual property rights,   *555–580*
    art 81 EC,   *572–573*
    art 82 EC,   *573–575*
    'blacklisted' clauses,   *572*
    copyright,   *562, 569, 579*
    defined,   *555*
    essential facilities doctrine,   *574*
    exhaustion of rights,   *558–563*
    free movement of goods
        copyright,   *569, 579*
        patents,   *557–560*
        trade-mark rights,   *560–569*
    harmonisation
        copyright,   *579*
        design right,   *579–580*
        patents,   *576–578*
        trade marks,   *578–579*
    parallel imports, outside EC and EEA,
        569–571
    patents,   *557–560, 576–578*
    protections,   *555*
    'specific subject-matter',   *560, 572, 573*
    trade marks
        common origin doctrine,   *567*
        confusion concept,   *563–567*
        exhaustion of rights,   *560–563*
        'identificatory function',   *563*
        rebranding and repackaging of product,
        568–569
        Uniform Benelux Law on,   *564*
    'whitelisted' clauses,   *572*
Inter-governmental Conferences (IGCs),
    Dublin Summit (1990),   *61*
    Institutional Reform,   *42, 116, 142*
    integration, relaunch of,   *58*
Interlocutory proceedings,   *307. See also*
    Preliminary rulings
Internal Market Council,   *113*
Internal market, creation,   *329–331*
Internal Market Programme,   *58*
International Bank for Reconstruction and
    Development (World Bank),   *13*
International Convention on the Harmonised
    Commodity Description and Coding
    System,   *333*
International Monetary Fund,   *13, 51*
International Trade Organisation,   *13*

Investiture Controversy,   *5*
Ioannina Compromise (1994),   *40, 117*
Irish Republic,
    EU accession,   *36, 37*
    joint dominant position case law,   *505–507*
    Mark Licensing Scheme of the Institute for
        Industrial Research and Standards,
        362
    Ministry of Industry,   *362–363*
Italy,   *58, 194–195*

Jenkins, Roy,   *52*
JHA (justice and home affairs),   *63*
Joint dominant position concept,   *505–507*
Joint-ventures,   *531*
Judicial review, competition law,   *549–552*
Justice and Home Affairs Council,   *103, 105*

Kaleidoscope programme,   *593*
Kalina, Robert,   *76*
Karamanlis, Konstantinos,   *33*
Kennedy, John Fitzgerald,   *27*
Kings Henry III and King Henry IV,   *5*
Kings Otto I and III,   *4–5*
Kohl, Helmut,   *38, 60, 61, 65*
Korean Peninsula Energy Development
    Organisation,   *96*
Kristallnacht (Night of Broken Glass, 1938),
    11

Labour and Social Affairs Council,   *91*
Lawlessness (*Summum ius summa inuria*),   *3*
Lawrie-Blum, Deborah,   *407*
Lawyers, right of establishment,   *440–441*
League of Nations,   *9, 13, 14*
Lebensraum,   *11*
Legal persons, right of establishment and to
    supply services,   *425, 431–435*
Legislative procedures, European Communities,
    assent,   *155*
    co-decision,   *153–155*
    consultation,   *151–153*
Legitimate expectations doctrine,   *184,*
    598–599
Lenin (Vladimir Ilich Ulyanov),   *9*
Lex mercatoria,   *6–7*
Lisbon Summit (1992),   *70, 94*
Lisbon Summit (2000),   *331*
Locus standi,
    annulment, direct actions for,   *257*
    competition law, enforcement of,   *540*
    defined,   *265n*
    failure to act,   *282*

Locus standi (*contd.*)
  illegality plea, *278, 279*
  non-privileged applicants, *266, 271, 272, 283*
  Pillar 3 , *104*
  preliminary rulings, *326*
  privileged applicants, *242*
  semi-privileged applicants, *265*
London School of Economics, *79*
Lucrum cessans, *295*
'Luns/Westerterp' procedure, *136*
Luxembourg Accord (1966), *49–50, 117*

Maastricht Treaty (1992),
  Commission, composition, *120*
  competences, division of, *88*
  culture promotion, *593*
  European Parliament, *130–131, 135*
  founding treaties, revision of, *166*
  institutions of European Communities, role in development, *108, 148*
  Research and Technological Development, *592*
  subsidiarity principle, *69–70*
  and WEU, and, *18*
  see also TEU (Treaty on European Union)
Macmillan, Harold, *24, 26, 27, 28*
Madrid Summit (1989), *60, 83*
Madrid Summit (1995), *75*
Malta, *35, 43*
Mann, Thomas, *60*
Markets, relevant, *509–511*
  geographic, *516–517*
  product, *511–516*
  temporal, *517–518*
Marshall Plan (European Recovery Programme 1948-51), *16–17*
Marx, Karl, *9*
Massigli, Réné, *21n*
ME (European Mutual Society), *432*
Medical Products, European Agency for Evaluation of, *109*
Medical secrecy, right to, *188*
Merger control, *526–535*
  collective dominance concept, *531–532*
  Continental Can case, *526–527*
  future reform, *534–535*
    ancillary restraints, clarification of approach to, *535*
    codification of Commission practices, *535*
    simplified procedures, introduction of, *534–535*

Merger control (*contd.*)
  Regulation 4064/89 (MR) *see* MR (Merger Regulation 4064/89)
Merger Treaty (1965), *50, 110, 164, 166, 302n*
Messina Conference (1955), *22–23*
Milan Summit (1985), *58*
Military integration, Western Europe, *18–19*
Mitterand, François, *57, 60n, 61, 592*
Molotov-Ribbentrop Non-aggression Pact (1939), *10*
Monnet, Jean, *21, 22, 24, 30n*
Monopolies, *601–605*
Morality, public, *388–389*
MR (Merger Regulation 4064/89),
  application, *462*
  competition law, principal objective, *459*
  establishment, *527*
  procedure under, *532–534*
  relevant market, *509*
  scope of application
    Community dimension, *528–530*
    concentration concept, *528*
    cross-border agreements, *529*
    joint ventures, *531*
    prohibited concentrations, *530–531*
  see also Merger control
Mutual recognition principle, *445*
  Convention (1968), *303*

Nagy, Imre, *10*
NAP (National Action Plan), *91*
Naples Convention on Mutual Assistance between Customs Administrations (1967), *179*
National Socialist German Worker's Party, *11–12*
NATO (North Atlantic Treaty Organisation),
  France, independence of, *27*
  military integration, *18–19*
Natural persons, *424–425*
Nazism, *9, 11–12*
NCE (Non-Compulsory Expenditure), *134, 135*
Negative clearance, *536–537*
New Europe Consulting Ltd (NEC), *296, 297*
Nice European Council, *101*
NKVD (military police), *10*
Nomenclature of Statistical Territorial Units (NUTS), *591*
Non-discrimination principle, *414–422*
  derogations from national rules, *421–422*
  education, *419–420*
  employment
    eligibility for, *417–418*

Non-discrimination principle, employment (*contd.*)
    equality in, *418–419*
    equal treatment, *421*
    establishment, right of, *428–429, 432–435*
    housing, *421*
    intellectual property rights, *556*
    services provision, *428–429, 442–443*
    trade union rights, *420*
    see also Discrimination
Non-retroactivity of administrative acts principle, *184*
North Atlantic Treaty Organisation *see* NATO (North Atlantic Treaty Organisation)
North-East Atlantic Fisheries Convention, *250*
Norway, *40*
Noyau dur, *162*
Nulla poena sine lege principle, *188*
Nuremberg Laws (1935), *11*
NUTS (Nomenclature of Statistical Territorial Units), *591*

OEEC (Organisation for European Economic Co-operation), *17, 25*
Office for Harmonisation in the Internal Market (Trade Markets and Designs), *109, 578*
Office for Veterinary and Plant Health Inspection and Control, *109, 150*
Official authority, exercise of, *450–451*
Official Journal of European Communities (OJ), *132, 144, 170, 258*
Ombudsman, right to apply to, *404–405*
OPEC (Organisation of Petroleum Exporting Countries), *55*
Organisation for Security and Co-operation in Europe (formerly CSCE), *99*

'Palma Document', *83*
Pan-European Movement, *8–9*
Papadopoulos, Colonel G, *33*
Paris Treaty (1951), *30*
Patents,
    free movement of goods, *557–560*
    harmonisation of rights, *576–578*
Patere legem principle, *184*
Pax Romana, *1–2*
Permanent Court of International Justice (PCIJ), *198*
Persons, free movement of *see* Free movement of persons
Petersberg Declaration (1992), *99, 100*
Petitions, Committee on, *403*

Phare (Aid and Assistance for the Reconstruction of the Economy in Central and Eastern Europe) Programme, *44, 150, 296, 297*
Pharmaceutical Society of Great Britain, *358*
Pilsudski, Marshall Josef, *9–10*
'Plan G', *25*
Plenitudo potestas, *5*
Plevin, Réné, *22*
Poland, partition of, *10*
Pompidou, George, *50*
Pope Gregory VII, *5*
Pope John XXII, *67*
Pope Leon IX, *5*
Pope Pius XI, *67*
Portugal, *39*
PPS (purchasing power standard), *591*
Praetor peregrinus, *3*
Pre-emption doctrine, *375*
Preliminary rulings *see* Article 234 EC, preliminary rulings
Prices,
    crystallisation, *481*
    discrimination, *482, 519–520*
    excessively high, *519*
    predatory, *522–523*
    uniformity, *480–481*
Primus inter pares, *122*
Principles of Community law,
    direct applicability, *192–198*
        decisions, *198*
        directives, *195–198*
        founding treaties, *193–194*
        regulations, *194–195*
    direct effect, *198–217*
        criteria, *200*
        vertical and horizontal, *201–217*
    State liability, *222–229*
    supremacy, *217–222*
    tort, States' liability, *222–229*
'Private investor' principle, *585*
Prodi, Romano, *121*
Product swaps, *522*
Professional bodies, rules established by, *441*
Property, right to, *188*
Proportionality principle, *73, 372, 387*
Protection of business secrets principle, *185*
Public policy,
    art 30 EC, *389–390*
    free movement of persons, exceptions, *452–456*
Public security,
    art 30 EC, *389–390*
    free movement of persons, exceptions, *452–456*

Purchasing power standard (PPS), *591*
PWGOT (Police Working Group on Terrorism), *102*

Qualified majority voting (QMV), *50, 116, 117*
Quantitative restrictions,
    defined, *360–361*
    import licences, *365*
    imported goods, marketing of, *364*
    Member States, measures taken by,
        358–360
    phyto-sanitary inspections, *365–367*
    price of goods, *363–364*
    professional bodies, *358*
    public bodies, *358*
    technical standards, *364–365*
    see also Equivalent effect
Quotas, *360–361*

RACE (Research into Advanced Communications
    in Europe), *53*
Raphael programme, *593*
Ratio decidendi, *551*
Ratione loci, *287*
Ratione materiae, *162, 307, 396, 404, 488*
Ratione personae, *287*
Ratione temporis, *287*
Rauf Denktash movement, *32*
Rebates, *521–522*
Red Army, *9, 10*
Regions, Committee of, *149–150*
REITOX (European Information Network on
    Drugs and Drug Addiction), *103*
Religious freedom, right to, *188*
Residence rights, territories of Member States,
    395–399
    permits, *414*
Riga Treaty (1920), *10*
Robbins, Lionel, *8*
Roman Empire, *2–4*
Rome Convention on the Law Applicable to
    Contractual Obligations (1980), *179, 303*
Rome Summit (1990), *94*
Rome, Treaties of (1957), *26, 27, 118, 131, 526*
Roosevelt, Franklin, *14*
Round Table Movement, *8*
Rule of reason, *368–369, 384, 386, 489–494*
Russia *see* Soviet Union, Former

Sakharow, Andrey, *33*
San Francisco Conference (1945), *14*
Santa Maria Da Feira European Council, *101*
Santer, Jacques, *65, 121*

Scandinavia, EU entry, *39–40*
SCE (European Co-operative Society), *432*
Schengen I, *81*
Schengen II, *81–83*
Schmidt, Helmut, *52*
'Schöppenstedt formula', *292–293, 295*
Schuman Plan, *20–21, 24, 46*
Schuman, Robert, *20–21, 22*
SE (*Societas Europea*), *432*
SEA *see* Single European Act (SEA)
Seattle conference (1999), *14*
Second World War, *12, 23*
Selective rebates, *521*
Self-employment, establishment, right of,
    435–436
Sensu stricto, *565*
Serbia, *94*
Services, provision of, *441–449*
    abolition of restrictions, general programme
        for, *426–429*
    freedom to receive, *447–449*
    legal persons, *425*
    limitations, *431*
    mutual recognition principle, *445*
    national restrictions, justification for,
        445–447
    non-discrimination principle, *442–443*
    prohibition of indistinctly applicable
        measures liable to prohibit or impede,
        443–445
    reverse discrimination, *429–430*
    Van Binsbergen case, *427–428*
    see also Establishment, right of
SIGMA (government and management
    programme), *44*
Single European Act (SEA),
    CFSP, *93*
    co-operation procedure, abandonment of,
        150
    comitology system, recognition of, *126*
    consolidation of European Communities,
        58–59
    EPC, *51*
    founding treaties, revision of, *166*
    free market of goods, *329*
    qualified majority voting, *50*
    subsidiarity principle, *69*
SIRENE system (Supplementary Information
    Request at the National Entries), *82*
'Skybolt' missile, *27*
SMEs (small and medium-sized enterprises),
    588
Smithsonian Agreement (1971), *51*

'Snake in the tunnel',   51–52
Social Charter (Community Charter of
    Fundamental Social Rights of Workers),
    89–91
Social Fund, European,   54, 126, 150
Solemn Declaration on European Union (1983),
    51
Solidarity principle,   186
Sources of Community law,   161–190
    complementary
        assessment,   181
        conventions concluded between Member
            States,   178–179
        Council meetings, decisions and
            agreements,   179–180
        declarations, resolutions and common
            positions adopted by common accord,
            180
    ECJ, case law,   182–183
    external, derived from international
        commitments,   177–178
    founding treaties,   162–165
        modifications and amendments,
            166–167
        protocols, declarations and conventions
            annexed to,   165
    general principles,   183–190
        common to laws of Member States,
            184–185
        fundamental human rights,   187–189
        inferred from nature of Communities,
            185–187
    primary,   162–167
        Acts of Accession,   165
        founding treaties,   162–165, 166–167
    secondary,   167–176
        art 249 EC, acts not mentioned in,   176
        decisions,   175
        directives,   173–175, 176
        non-binding acts,   176
        opinions,   176
        recommendations,   176
        regulations,   172, 176
Soviet Union, Former,
    Communism,   9–10
    United States, relationship with,   22
    Warsaw, battle of,   9–10
Spaak, Paul-Henri,   22, 25
Spain,   39, 92
Spinelli, Altiero,   58
Spouses, rights of,   410–411
'Stability and Growth Pact',   77, 96, 101
Stalin, Joseph,   10, 14, 15

State aid,   581–600
    art 87 EC
        application of aid, implementation of
            legislation,   600
        compatible with common market,   594
        culture, promotion of,   593–594
        disturbance in Member State economy,
            remedying,   591–592
        economic activities or areas, facilitating,
            592–593
        heritage conservation,   593–594
        horizontal aid application, exemption
            under Regulation 994/98,   589–590
        projects of common European interest,
            591–592
        severely depressed areas, promotion of
            economic development,   590–591
    art 88 EC
        Commission decisions,   597–598
        existing aid,   594–595
        failure to notify,   596
        institutional supervision under,
            594–600
        investigation procedure,   596–597
        legislation for application, implementing,
            600
        national courts, role in enforcement of
            EC Treaty provisions,   599–600
        new aid,   595
        'standstill clause',   595
        unlawful aid, recovery of,   598–599
        unnotified aid, recovery of,   598–599
    common market
        affecting,   587–588
        compatible with,   588–594
    competition, distorting or threatening to
        distort,   586–587
    concept of,   583–585
    culture, promoting,   593–594
    discretionary exemptions (art 87 EC)
        common market, compatible with,   594
        culture, promoting,   593–594
        development of certain economic
            activities or areas,   592–593
        heritage conservation,   593–594
        projects of common European interest,
            591–592
        remedying of disturbance in Member
            State economy,   591–592
        severely depressed areas, promotion of
            economic development,   590–591
    disturbances in Member State economy,
        remedying,   591–592

State aid (*contd.*)
    economic activities or areas, facilitating,
        592–593
    exceptional occurrences, making good
        damage caused by,   *589*
    Federal Republic of Germany, certain areas,
        589
    forms of,   *583–585*
    Guidelines for National Regional Aid,   *591,*
        592
    heritage conservation,   *593–594*
    individual consumers, granted to,   *588*
    Member State, granted by,   *585–586*
    natural disasters, making good damage
        caused by,   *589*
    'private investor' principle,   *585*
    production of certain goods, favouring,
        587
    projects of common European interest,
        591–592
    Regulation 994/98, exemption under,
        589–590
    resources, granted through,   *586*
    severely depressed areas, promotion of
        economic development (Art 87 EC),
        590–591
    social character,   *588*
    undertakings, favouring,   *587*
State, concept of,   *207–208*
State liability principle,   *222–229*
State monopolies,   *601–602*
Status quo ante,   *245*
Steiner, Josephine,   *241*
Stralsund Treaty (1370),   *8*
Streseman, Gustav,   *9*
Stricto sensu,   *565*
Stuttgard Summit (1983),   *51*
Subsidiarity principle,   *67–74*
    assessment of,   *74*
    competences, allocation of,   *68–69*
    European Commission,   *71*
    European Court of Justice,   *72–74*
    European Parliament,   *72*
    implementation,   *70*
    Maastricht Treaty,   *69–70. See also* TEU
        (Treaty on European Union)
    origin,   *67*
    proportionality,   *73*
    Treaty of Amsterdam, under,   *70–71*
Substitutability principle,
    demand,   *511–513*
    supply,   *509–510, 513*
Suez crisis (1956),   *26*

Supremacy principle,   *217–222, 461*
Sweden,   *39, 40*

TACIS (Technical Assistance to the CIS and
    Georgia),   *150*
Tampere European Council,   *86n*
Tapie, Bernard,   *130*
TARIC (Community tariff),   *333*
Taxation, internal (discriminatory nature),
    344–356
    art 90 EC,
        art 25, and,   *351–353*
        art 28, and,   *353*
        art 87, and,   *353*
    assessment of,   *348–349*
    company tax,   *355–356*
    direct discrimination,   *345–346*
    excise duty,   *355*
    harmonisation within EU,   *354–356*
        company tax,   *355–356*
        excise duty,   *355*
        VAT,   *354–355*
    indirect discrimination,   *347–348*
    objective justification,   *349*
    products in competition (art 90(2) EC),
        350–351
    reverse discrimination,   *346–347*
    similar products (art 90(1) EC),   *350*
    spirit cases,   *350–351*
    VAT,   *354–355*
Taxation Policy Group (TPG),   *354*
Teheran conference (1943),   *14*
Telefónica,   *121*
Tempus (Trans-European Mobility Programme
    for University Students),   *44*
TEU (Treaty on European Union),
    'acquis communautare',   *34*
    admission procedure,   *31*
    contents,   *62*
    EEC, renaming of,   *63*
    EMU,   *74, 75*
    European Commission
        EP, accountable to,   *132*
        extension of term of office,   *120*
    European Communities, fourth enlargement,
        40
    main objective,   *63*
    ratification,   *61, 62*
    revision of,   *65*
    'Temple' structure,   *62–63. See also* Treaty
        of Amsterdam
    TREVI groups,   *102, 103*
    see also Maastricht Treaty (1992)

Thatcher, Margaret, *38, 60n, 94, 133, 592*
Third Reich, *11–12*
'Three Wise Men' Report (1979), *57*
Tindemans, Leo (Belgian Prime Minister), *29, 57*
Tort, Member States, liability of, *222–229*
TPG (Taxation Policy Group), *354*
Trade, defined, *466–468*
Trade marks,
    common origin doctrine, *567*
    confusion concept, *563–567*
    exhaustion of rights, *560–563*
    harmonisation of rights, *578–579*
    'identificatory function', *563*
    rebranding and repackaging of protected
        product, *568–569*
    Uniform Benelux Law, *564*
Trade union rights, *421*
Transfer Pricing Arbitration Convention (1990), *179*
Transparency principle, *92, 155–160*
Transport Committee, *150*
Treasures, national, protection of, *392*
Treaties of Rome (1957), *26, 27, 118, 131, 526*
Treaty of Accession (EU entry), *35, 36, 37, 39, 40, 45–46*
Treaty of Amsterdam, *65–105*
    co-decision procedure, *135, 153–155*
    Common, Foreign and Security Policy (Pillar 2), *63, 93–101*
    assessment, *101*
    common defence policy, *99–101*
    Community institutions, role under, *98*
    institutions, *96–97*
    main objectives, *95–96*
    management of, *98–99*
    Member States, commitments under, *98*
    common market, *334*
    criminal matters, police and judicial co-operation in
    assessment, *104–105*
    organisational structure, *103–104*
    Pillar 1, *88*
    Pillar 3, *101–105, 63*
    culture promotion, *593*
    draft, *65–66*
    employment, *91*
    European Commission, competences, *125*
    European Community (Pillar 1), *62–63, 66–93*
        asylum, *83–85*

Treaty of Amsterdam, European Community (Pillar 1) (*contd.*)
    civil matters, judicial co-operation, *86–88*
    criminal matters, police and judicial co-operation, *88*
    draft Convention, crossing of external borders, *86*
    Dublin Convention (1990), *85–86*
    Economic and Monetary Union (EMU), *74–79*
    employment, *91*
    European Parliament, extension of powers, *91–92*
    free movement of persons, *81*
    immigration, *83–85*
    non-discrimination principle, extension of scope, *89*
    progressive creation of area of freedom, security and justice, *80–89*
    Schengen II, *81–83*
    Social Charter, incorporation into EC Treaty, *89–91*
    subsidiarity principle, *67–74*
    Title IV, assessment of, *88–89*
    Transparency Principle, establishment of, *92, 155–160*
    violation of freedoms, suspension of rights, *79–80*
    founding treaties, revision of, *166*
    human rights, protection of, *189*
    legislative procedures, simplification of, *150*
    Pillar 1 (European Community), *66–93*
    Pillar 2 (Common, Foreign and Security Policy), *93–101*
    Pillar 3 (Police co-operation in criminal matters), *63, 101–105*
    preliminary rulings, *302*
    qualified majority voting, *116*
    WEU, and, *18*
Treaty of the Benelux Economic Union (1958), *20*
Treaty of Brussels (1948), *18*
Treaty of Paris (1951), *30, 162*
Treaty of Riga (1920), *10*
Treaty of Stralsund (1370), *8*
TREVI group (Terrorism, Radicalism, Extremism and Political Violence), *102, 103*
Trotsky, Leon, *9*
Truman, Harry, *15*
Turkey, *32, 42–43*
Twelve Tables, *2–3*

Tying-in arrangements, *520–521*

Ultra petita, *277, 551*
Ultra vires, *274*
Ulyanov, Vladimir Ilich (Lenin), *9*
Undertakings,
 agreements between, *472–473*
  object or effect, having as, *478–479*
 decisions by associations of, *473–474*
 defined, *464–466, 602*
 monopolies, and, *602–605*
 sanctions against, *547–548*
 State aid favouring, *587*
 see also Competition law
Union of Law, *230*
United Kingdom,
 Acts of Accession, *37, 45–46*
 EU enlargement, *36–38*
 French refusal of British accession, *26–28*
 integration, and, *23–26*
 Pharmaceutical Society of Great Britain, *358*
 supremacy of Community law, *222*
United Nations,
 Charter, *14, 19*
 constitution, *15*
 Declaration of (1942), *14*
 purposes, main, *14n*
 Relief and Rehabilitation Administration (1943), *13*
United States,
 competition law, *463–464*
 Crime Victims Fund, *463*
 'effect doctrine', *489*
 Marshall Plan, *16–17*
 NATO, contribution to, *19*
 post-war world, vision of, *12–15*
 reconstruction, European, *15–16*
 Soviet Union, relationship with, *22*
 UK, and, *23*
Unjust enrichment principle, *185*
Uruguary Round, *13, 14n*

Value Added Tax (VAT), *354–355*
Vertical agreements, *468, 470–471, 484, 491*
Vertical direct effect, *201–202*
Vested rights principle, *184*
Vienna Action Plan (1998), *87*

Vienna Convention on the Law of Treaties (1969), *45, 162, 165, 182, 244*
'Visegrad' countries, *44*
Volksgemeinschaft, *11*
Von Hindenburg, Field Marshal Paul, *11*

Washington Summit (1999), *100*
Werner Report, *51*
Western European Union *see* WEU (Western European Union)
WEU (Western European Union),
 common defence policy, *100*
 Gulf Crisis, and, *99*
 military integration, *18*
Weygard, General Maxime, *10*
WHO (World Health Organisation), *72, 370, 456*
Wilson, Harold, *24, 28*
Wilson, Woodrow, *12, 13*
Workers, free movement of, *406–423*
 definitions, *407–409*
 employment
  eligibility for, *417–418*
  equality in, *418–419*
  Member State territory, right to remain following, *422–423*
 entry, right of, *412–413*
 families of, *409–412*
  children, *411–412*
  spouses, *410–411*
 Member State territory, right to remain after employment, *422–423*
 non-discrimination principle, *414–422*
  education, *419–420*
  employment, *417–419*
  equal treatment, housing, *421*
  national rules, derogations from, *421–422*
  trade union rights, *421*
 residence permits, *414*
 secondary legislation, *406*
World Bank (International Bank for Reconstruction and Development), *13*
WTO (World Trade Organisation), *13, 14, 331, 463–464*

Yalta Conference (1945), *14, 27*
Yugoslavia, crisis in, *94–95*

Law Update 2000

Law Update 2001 edition – due February 2001

An annual review of the most recent developments in specific legal subject areas, useful for law students at degree and professional levels, others with law elements in their courses and also practitioners seeking a quick update.

Published around February every year, the Law Update summarises the major legal developments during the course of the previous year. In conjunction with Old Bailey Press textbooks it gives the student a significant advantage when revising for examinations.

Contents

Administrative Law • Civil and Criminal Procedure • Commercial Law • Company Law • Conflict of Laws • Constitutional Law • Contract Law • Conveyancing • Criminal Law • Criminology • English Legal System • Equity and Trusts • European Union Law • Evidence • Family Law • Jurisprudence • Land Law • Law of International Trade • Public International Law • Revenue Law • Succession • Tort

For further information on contents or to place an order, please contact:

Mail Order
Old Bailey Press
200 Greyhound Road
London
W14 9RY

Telephone No: 020 7385 3377
Fax No: 020 7381 3377

ISBN 1 85836 347 0
Soft cover 246 x 175 mm
392 pages   £9.95
Published February 2000

Old Bailey Press

The Old Bailey Press integrated student law library is tailor-made to help you at every stage of your studies from the preliminaries of each subject through to the final examination. The series of Textbooks, Revision WorkBooks, 150 Leading Cases/Casebooks and Cracknell's Statutes are interrelated to provide you with a comprehensive set of study materials.

You can buy Old Bailey Press books from your University Bookshop, your local Bookshop, direct using this form, or you can order a free catalogue of our titles from the address shown overleaf.

The following subjects each have a Textbook, 150 Leading Cases/Casebook, Revision WorkBook and Cracknell's Statutes unless otherwise stated.

Administrative Law
Commercial Law
Company Law
Conflict of Laws
Constitutional Law
Conveyancing (Textbook and Casebook)
Criminal Law
Criminology (Textbook and Sourcebook)
English and European Legal Systems
Equity and Trusts
Evidence
Family Law
Jurisprudence: The Philosophy of Law (Textbook, Sourcebook and
    Revision WorkBook)
Land: The Law of Real Property
Law of International Trade
Law of the European Union
Legal Skills and System
Obligations: Contract Law
Obligations: The Law of Tort
Public International Law
Revenue Law (Textbook,
    Sourcebook and Revision
    WorkBook)
Succession

Mail order prices:	
Textbook	£11.95
150 Leading Cases/Casebook	£9.95
Revision WorkBook	£7.95
Cracknell's Statutes	£9.95
Suggested Solutions 1998–1999	£6.95
Law Update 2000	£9.95
The Practitioner's Handbook 2000	£54.95

To complete your order, please fill in the form below:

Module	Books required	Quantity	Price	Cost
		Postage		
		TOTAL		

For Europe, add 15% postage and packing (£20 maximum).
For the rest of the world, add 40% for airmail.

ORDERING

By telephone to Mail Order at 020 7385 3377, with your credit card to hand.

By fax to 020 7381 3377 (giving your credit card details).

By post to:

Mail Order, Old Bailey Press, 200 Greyhound Road, London W14 9RY.

When ordering by post, please enclose full payment by cheque or banker's draft, or complete the credit card details below. You may also order a free catalogue of our complete range of titles from this address.

We aim to despatch your books within 3 working days of receiving your order.

Name

Address

Postcode   Telephone

Total value of order, including postage: £

I enclose a cheque/banker's draft for the above sum, or

charge my   ☐ Access/Mastercard   ☐ Visa   ☐ American Express
Card number

☐☐ ☐☐☐☐ ☐☐☐☐ ☐☐☐☐

☐☐☐☐

....Date: ....